Maine Fishing Depth Maps

Lakes & Ponds by County

I0810974

No portion of this book may be photocopied, electronically stored, or reproduced in any manner without written permission from the publisher.

Important Notices

Garmin has made reasonable efforts to provide you with accurate maps and related information, but we cannot exclude the possibility of errors or omissions in sources or of changes in actual conditions. GARMIN MAKES NO WARRANTIES OF ANY KIND, EITHER EXPRESS OR IMPLIED, INCLUDING THE WARRANTIES OF MECHANTABILITY AND FITNESS FOR A PARTICULAR PURPOSE. GARMIN SHALL NOT BE LIABLE TO ANY PERSON UNDER ANY LEGAL OR EQUITABLE THEORY FOR DAMAGES ARISING OUT OF THE USE OF THIS PUBLICATION, INCLUDING, WITHOUT LIMITATION, FOR DIRECT, CONSEQUENTIAL, OR INCIDENTAL DAMAGES.

Nothing in this publication implies any fishing regulations or the right to use private property. You should respect all landowner restrictions.

Safety Information

Do not use this publication for marine navigation, as hazards have not been marked, depth soundings are only approximate, and other information necessary to performing this function safely has not been depicted.

California Prop 65 Warning

⚠ **WARNING:** Cancer and Reproductive Harm - www.p65warnings.ca.gov

Copyright © 2022 Garmin Ltd. or its Affiliates. All rights reserved.

2 DeLorme Dr. Suite 200, Yarmouth, Maine 04096
www.garmin.com/DeLormeAtlas
Printed in Canada.

Table of Contents

Androscoggin County

Allen Pond, Greene ... 15
Androscoggin Lake, Leeds ... 15
Auburn Lake, Auburn ... 15
Bartlett Pond, Livermore ... 15
Beals Pond, Turner, *see Crystal Pond*
Bear and Little Bear Ponds, Turner ... 15
Berry Pond, Greene ... 16
Black Pond, Turner ... 16
Blacksnake Pond, Turner, *see Black Pond*
Brettuns Pond, Livermore ... 16
Crystal Pond, Turner ... 16
Island Pond, Leeds ... 16
Lake Auburn, Auburn, *see Auburn Lake*
Lard Pond, Turner ... 16
Little Bear Pond, Turner, *see Bear and Little Bear Ponds*
Little Sabattus Pond, Greene ... 16
Little Wilson Pond, Turner ... 16
Long Pond, Livermore ... 17
Loon Pond, Sabattus ... 17
Lower Range Pond, Poland ... 17
Middle Range Pond, Poland ... 17
Moose Hill Pond, Livermore Falls ... 17
Mud Pond, Mechanic Falls, *see Oxford County*
Nelson Pond, Livermore ... 17
No Name Pond, Lewiston ... 17
Pleasant Pond, Turner ... 17
Round Pond, Livermore ... 18
Round Pond, Turner ... 18
Runaround Pond, Durham ... 18
Sabattus Pond, Greene, Sabattus, Wales ... 18
Sandy Bottom Pond, Turner ... 18
School House Pond, Livermore Falls ... 18
Spear Pond, Sabattus, *see Loon Pond*
Sutherland Pond, Sabattus ... 19
Taylor Pond, Auburn ... 19
Thompson Lake, Poland, *see Oxford County*
Tripp Pond, Poland ... 19
Upper Range Pond, Poland ... 19
Worthley Pond, Poland ... 19

Aroostook County

Alder Brook Lake, Chapman ... 19
Arnold Brook Lake, Presque Isle ... 19
B Lake, Smyrna, Hammond ... 20
Barker Lake, New Limerick, *see Bradbury Lake*
Basil Pond, Fort Kent ... 20
Beau Lake T19 R11 WELS, Big Twenty Twp ... 20
Beaver Tail Pond, T14 R9 WELS, T14 R10 WELS ... 20
Ben Lake, Wallagrass Plt ... 20
Bennett Lake, Easton ... 20
Big Machias Lake, T12 R8 WELS ... 20
Billings Pond, T11 R9 WELS ... 20
Black Lake, Fort Kent ... 20
Black Lake, T15 R9 WELS, *see Black Pond*
Black Pond T15 R9 WELS ... 20
Black Pond St. John Plt ... 21
Blake Lake, T16 R6 WELS ... 21
Bourgoin Lake, St. Agatha, Frenchville ... 21
Brackett Lake, Weston ... 21
Bradbury Lake, New Limerick ... 21
Bradford Pond, Moro Plt ... 21
Bran Lake, St. Francis ... 21
Butterfield Lake, Caswell Plt ... 21
California Pond, New Canada ... 21
Caribou Lake, Washburn ... 21
Caribou Pond, T11 R9 WELS, T11 RlO WELS ... 22
Carlisle Pond, T8 R3 WELS ... 22
Carr Pond, T13 R8 WELS ... 22
Carry Lake, Littleton ... 22
Carry Pond, T16 R4 WELS ... 22
Center Pond, T10 R8 WELS ... 22
Chandler Lake, T9 R8 WELS, *see Chandler Pond*
Chandler Pond, T9 R8 WELS ... 22
Clayton Lake, T11 R14 WELS ... 22
Clayton Lake, T12 R8 WELS ... 22
Cochrane Lake, Smyrna, New Limerick ... 22
Conroy Lake, Monticello ... 23
County Road Lake, New Limerick ... 23
Crater Pond, T15 R9 WELS ... 23
Cross Lake, T16 R5 WELS, T17 R5 WELS ... 23
Crystal Lake, Hersey ... 23
Cunliffe Lake, T12 R13 WELS ... 23
Daigle Pond, New Canada ... 23
Deboullie Pond, T15 R9 WELS ... 23
Deep Lake, Littleton ... 23
Deer Pond, St. John Plt ... 24
Deering Lake, Weston, Orient ... 24
Denny Pond, T15 R9 WELS ... 24
Depot Lake, T13 R16 WELS ... 24
Dickey Pond, T17 R5 WELS ... 24
Dickwood Lake, Eagle Lake ... 24
Dimock Pond, New Canada ... 24
Drews Lake, New Limerick, Oakfield, Linneus, *see Meduxnekeag Lake*
Eagle Lake, Wallagrass Plt, Eagle Lake, T16 R5 WELS, T16 R6 WELS ... 24
East Grand Lake, Weston, Orient, Danforth ... 24
Easton Pond, Easton ... 25
Echo Lake, Presque Isle ... 25
Falls Brook Lake, T18 R10 WELS, *see Falls Pond*
Falls Pond, T18 R10 WELS, Allagash Plt ... 25
Farrar Pond, T11 R10 WELS ... 25
Faulkner Lake, Weston ... 25
Ferguson Pond, T14 R8 WELS ... 25
Fifth Pelletier Brook Lake, T15 R9 WELS ... 25
First Chase Pond, T14 R9 WELS ... 25
First Musquacook Lake, T11 R11 WELS, T11 R12 WELS ... 25
First Pelletier Brook Lake, T16 R9 WELS ... 25
First Sly Brook Lake, New Canada ... 25
First and Second Wallagrass Lakes, T16 R8 WELS, St John Plt, Wallagrass Plt, Eagle Lake ... 26
Fischer Lake, Fort Fairfield ... 26
Fish Lake, T13 WELS, T14 R8 WELS, *see Fish River Lake*
Fish River Lake, T13 R8 WELS, T14 R8 WELS ... 26
Flinn Pond, T1 R5 WELS, Benedicta ... 26
Fourth Musquacook Lake, T10 R11 WELS, T11 R11 WELS ... 26
Fourth Pelletier Brook Lake, T16 R9 WELS ... 26
Fox Pond, T17 R12 WELS ... 26
Galilee Pond, T15 R9 WELS ... 26
Gardner Lake, T15 R9 WELS, *see Gardner Pond*
Gardner Pond, T15 R9 WELS ... 27
Gerard Pond, Caswell Plt ... 27
Germain Lake, Madawaska ... 27
Gilbert Pond, St. John Plt ... 27
Gilman Pond, Moro Plt ... 27
Glancy Lake, New Limerick ... 27
Glazier Lake, T18 R10 WELS ... 27
Gould Pond, New Limerick ... 28
Grand Lake, Weston, Orient, Danforth, *see East Grand Lake*
Grass Pond, Moro Plt ... 28
Green Pond, Moro Plt ... 28
Green Pond, New Limerick ... 28
Greenlaw Pond, T12 R7 WELS, T12 R8 WELS ... 28
Grey Pond, T12 R13 WELS ... 28
Hafey Pond, T18 R11 WELS ... 28
Hale Pond, Moro Plt ... 28
Hanson Lake, Mapleton ... 28
Harvey Pond, T12 R13 WELS, *see Long Lake and Harvey Pond*
Haywire Pond, T1 R5 WELS ... 28
Horseshoe Pond, T11 R10 WELS ... 28
Hourglass Pond, T14 R9 WELS, *see First Chase Pond*
Hunnewell Lake, St. John Plt ... 29
Hunter Pond, Linneus ... 29
Isie Lake, Eagle Lake ... 29
Island Pond, T14 R8 WELS ... 29
Island Pond, T15 R9 WELS ... 29
Jalbert Pond, St. John Plt, *see Gilbert Pond*
Jones Pond, Big Twenty Twp ... 29
Ketchum Lake, TD R2 WELS ... 29
Lambert Pond, New Limerick ... 29
Lindsay Lake, Easton ... 29
Little Black Brook Lake, Caswell Plt ... 29
Little East Lake, T17 R14 WELS ... 29
Little Falls Brook Lake, Allagash Plt, *see Little Falls Pond*
Little Falls Pond, Allagash Plt ... 29
Little Gilbert Pond, St. John Plt ... 30
Little Jalbert Pond, St. John Plt, *see Little Gilbert Pond*
Little Machias Lake, Nashville Plt ... 30
Logan Lake, Littleton, Houlton ... 30
Longfellow Lake, Weston, Orient, *see Deering Lake*
Long Lake, Littleton ... 30
Long Lake, Oakfield ... 30
Long Lake, T17 R3 WELS, T17 R4 WELS, St. Agatha ... 30
Long Lake and Harvey Pond, T11 R13 WELS, T12 R13 WELS ... 30
Long Pond, T11 R10 WELS, T11 R11 WELS ... 31
Lower Hot Brook Lake, Bancroft, *see Washington County*
Lower Mattawamkeag Lake, T4 R3 WELS, Island Falls, *see Mattawamkeag Lakes*
Lucifee Pond, T14 R8 WELS ... 31
Macwahoc Lake, T3 R4 WELS, Sherman, *see Upper Macwachoc Lake*
Madawaska Lake, T16 R4 WELS, Westmanland ... 31
Mattaseunk Lake, Molunkus Twp ... 31
Mattawamkeag Lakes, T4 R3 WELS, Island Falls ... 31
McClusky Lake, T14 R5 WELS, T15 R5 WELS ... 32

McGowan Pond, T11 R8 WELS, T12 R8 WELS 32
McKeen Lake, T14 R10 WELS 32
McLean Lake, St. Francis 32
Meduxnekeag Lake, New Limerick, Oakfield, Linneus 32
Mink Marsh Pond, T11 R10 WELS, T10 R10 WELS 32
Moccasin Pond, T14 R8 WELS 32
Molunkus Lake, Molunkus Twp, Macwahoc Plt, T1 R5 WELS 32
Monson Pond, Fort Fairfield 32
Mosquito Brook Pond, T14 R7 WELS 32
Mud Lake, T6 R6 WELS, Moro Plt, *see Pleasant and Mud Lakes, Penobscot County*
Mud Lake, Stockholm 33
Mud Lake, T17 R4 WELS, T17 R5 WELS 33
Mud Pond, Linneus 33
Mud Pond, T15 R9 WELS 33
Munson Pond, Fort Fairfield, *see Monson Pond*
Negro Brook Lakes, T15 R9 WELS, T16 R9 WELS, *see First, Second, Third, Fourth, Fifth and Sixth Pelletier Brook Lakes*
Nickerson Lake, New Limerick, Linneus 33
North Little Black Pond, T15 R9 WELS 33
North Pond, T8 R3 WELS, Dudley Twp 33
North Pond, T14 R9 WELS 33
Number Nine Lake, T9 R3 WELS 33
Pennington Pond, T15 R6 WELS 33
Perch Pond, T15 R9 WELS 34
Petes Pond, T13 R10 WELS 34
Pickett Mountain Pond, T6 R6 WELS, Moro Plt 34
Pleasant Lake, Island Falls, T4 R3 WELS 34
Pleasant Pond, Island Falls, T4 R3 WELS, *see Pleasant Lake*
Plunkett Pond, Benedicta, Silver Ridge Twp 34
Portage Lake, Portage Lake 34
Portland Lake, Bridgewater 34
Pratt Lake, T11 R9 WELS 35
Presley Lake, T12 R17 WELS 35
Presque Isle Lake, T9 R3 WELS 35
Pushineer Pond, T15 R9 WELS 35
Read Lake, Merrill 35
Reed Pond, Macwahoc Plt 35
Rideout Pond, T19 R12 WELS 35
Ritter Lake, Bridgewater 35
Robbins Brook Pond, T12 R11 WELS 35
Rockabema Lake, Moro Plt 35
Ross Lake, Littleton, Monticello 35
Round Mountain Pond, T11 R8 WELS 35
Round Pond, T13 R12 WELS 36
Round Pond, T14 R8 WELS 36
Rowe Lake, T11 R8 WELS 36
St. Croix Lake, St. Croix Twp, Webbertown Twp 36
St. Froid Lake, Winterville Plt, T14 R7 WELS 36
Salmon Brook Lake, Perham 36
Second Chase Pond, T14 R9 WELS 36
Second Musquacook Lake, T11 R11 WELS 36
Second Pelletier Brook Lake, T16 R9 WELS 37
Second Sly Brook Lake, New Canada 37
Second Wallagrass Lake, T16 R8 WELS *see First and Second Wallagrass Lakes*
Secret Pond, Moro Plt 37
Silver Lake, T15 R5 WELS 37
Sixth Pelletier Brook Lake, T15 R9 WELS 37
Skitacook Lake, T4 R3 WELS, Oakfield 37
Soldier Pond, Wallagrass Plt 37
South Little Black Pond, T15 R9 WELS 37
Spaulding Pond, Oakfield 37
Spectacle Pond, T10 R8 WELS 37
Squapan Lake, Masardis, Squapan Twp, Ashland, T11 R4 WELS 38
Square Lake, T16 R5 WELS, T15 R5 WELS 38
Squirrel Pond, T11 R10 WELS 38
Sterling Pond, T13 R7 WELS 38
Stink Pond, T15 R9 WELS 38
Sucker Lake, Weston, *see Washington County*
Third Chase Pond, T14 R9 WELS 38
Third Musquacook Lake, T11 R11 WELS 38
Third Pelletier Brook Lake, T16 R9 WELS 38
Third Sly Brook Lake, New Canada 39
Third Wallagrass Lake, St. John Plt 39
Timoney Lake, Oakfield, Smyrna 39
Togue Pond, T15 R9 WELS 39
Tote Road Pond, Moro Plt 39
Trafton Lake, Limestone 39
Two Mile Pond, T16 R14 WELS, T16 R13 WELS 39
Ugh Lake, T12 R14 WELS 39
Umcolcus Lake, T7 R5 WELS, T7 R6 WELS 39
Umsaskis Lake, T11 R13 WELS 40
Upper Hudson Pond, T11 R10 WELS 40
Upper Macwahoc Lake, T3 R4 WELS, Sherman 40
Upper Mattawamkeag Lake, Island Falls, *see Mattawamkeag Lakes*
Upper McNally Pond, T11 R10 WELS 40
Upper Pond, T15 R9 WELS 40
Weeks Pond, T11 R8 WELS 40
Wheelock Lake, St. John Plt 40
Whitehead Lake, Bridgewater 41
Wytopitlock Lake, T2 R4 WELS, Glenwood 41

Cumberland County

Adams Pond, Bridgton 41
Aldens Pond, Gorham 41
Anonymous Pond, Harrison, *see Crystal Lake*
Barker Pond, Sebago, Hiram 41
Bay of Naples, Naples, *see Brandy Pond*
Beaver Pond, Bridgton 41
Bonny Eagle Lake, Standish, Buxton 41
Bonny Pond, Standish, Buxton, *see Bonny Eagle Lake*
Brandy Pond, Naples 42
Coffee Pond, Casco 42
Coffin Pond, Brunswick 42
Cold Rain Pond, Naples 42
Collins Pond, Windham 42
Crescent Lake, Casco, Raymond 42
Crystal Lake, Harrison 43
Crystal Lake, Gray 43
Duck Lake, Falmouth, Windham, *see Highland Lake*
Dumpling Pond, Casco 43
Dundee Pond, Gorham, Windham 43
Forest Lake, Gray, Windham, Cumberland 43
Fosters Pond, Bridgton, *see Ingalls Pond*
Great Pond, Cape Elizabeth 43
Hancock Pond, Sebago, Denmark 44
Highland Lake, Bridgton 44
Highland Lake, Falmouth, Windham 44
Holt Pond, Bridgton 44
Ingalls Pond, Baldwin 44
Ingalls Pond, Bridgton 45
Island Pond, Harrison 45
Lily Pond, New Gloucester 45
Little Duck Pond, Windham 45
Little Sebago Lake, Gray, Windham 45
Little Watchic Pond, Standish 46
Long Lake, Bridgton, Naples 46
Lower Mud Pond, Windham 46
Mild Pond, Falmouth 46
Moose Pond, Bridgton, Denmark, Sweden 46
North Gorham Pond, Windham, Gorham 47
Notched Pond, Raymond, Gray 47
Nubble Pond, Raymond 47
Otter Pond, Bridgton 47
Otter Ponds, Standish 47
Owl Pond, Casco 48
Panther Pond, Raymond 48
Parker Pond, Casco 48
Peabody Pond, Sebago, Bridgton 48
Perley Pond, Sebago 49
Pettingill Pond, Windham 49
Pleasant Lake, Casco, Otisfield 49
Rattlesnake Pond, Casco, Raymond, *see Cresent Lake*
Raymond Pond, Raymond 49
Rich Mill Pond, Standish 49
Richville Mill Pond, Standish, *see Rich Mill Pond*
Robson Pond, Bridgton, *see Wood Pond*
Sabbathday Lake, New Gloucester 49
Sabbathday Pond, New Gloucester, *see Sabathday Lake*
Sand Pond, Baldwin 50
Sebago Lake, Naples, Casco, Standish, Windham, Raymond, Sebago 50
Southeast Pond, Baldwin, Sebago 50
Thomas Pond, Casco, Raymond 51
Trickey Pond, Naples 51
Upper Mud Pond, Windham 51
Watchic Pond, Standish 51
Wood Pond, Bridgton 51

Franklin County

Arnold Pond, Coburn Gore 52
Bag Pond, Chain of Ponds Twp, *see Chain of Ponds*
Ballard Pond, Farmington, Temple 52
Barnard Pond, Eustis 52
Beal Pond, Madrid 52
Beattie Pond, Beattie Twp, Lowelltown Twp 52
Beaver Mountain Lake, Sandy River Plt 52
Beaver Pond, Township D 52
Beaver Pond, Seven Ponds Twp 52
Big Indian Pond, Lowelltown Twp *see Indian Pond*
Big Island Pond, Chain of Ponds Twp, Seven Ponds Twp 52
Blanchard Pond Alder Stream Twp 52
Bugeye Pond, Kibby Twp, Chain of Ponds Twp 52
Caribou Bog, Chain of Ponds Twp 52
Chain of Ponds, Chain of Ponds Twp 53

Clearwater Pond, Industry, Farmington 53
Cloutman Pond, Rangeley 53
Cow Pond, Lang Twp 53
Crowell Pond, New Sharon, Chesterville, Vienna 53
Cupsuptic Lake, Rangeley, Adamstwon Twp, *see Mooselookmeguntic and Cupsuptic Lakes*
Dead River Flowage, Eustis, *see Flagstaff Lake*
Dodge Pond, Rangeley 53
Drury Pond, Temple 53
Dutton Pond, Kingfield 53
Eddy Pond, Sandy River Plt 53
Egypt Pond, Chesterville, Vienna 53
Flagstaff Lake, Eustis, Dead River Twp, Flagstaff Twp, Bigelow Twp, Carrying Place Twp 54
Flatiron Pond, Davis Twp 54
Gammon Pond, Freeman Twp, New Portland, *see Somerset County*
Grants Pond, Massachusetts Gore 54
Greely Pond, Dallas Plt 54
Greenbush Pond, Jim Pond Twp 54
Grindstone Pond, Kingfield 54
Gull Pond, Dallas Plt 54
Haley Pond, Rangeley, Dallas Plt 55
Harvey Pond, Madrid 55
Hills Pond, Perkins Twp 55
Horseshoe Pond, Chesterville 55
Horseshoe Pond, Coburn Gore, Chain of Ponds Twp 55
Indian Pond, Lowelltown Twp 55
Jim Pond, Jim Pond Twp 55
Johns Pond, Davis Twp 55
Kamankeag Pond, Davis Twp 55
Kennebago Lake, Davis Twp, Stetsontown Twp 55
Kimball Pond, New Sharon, *see Kennebec County*
Ledge Pond, Sandy River Plt 56
Little Greely Pond, Dallas Plt 56
Little Island Pond Seven Ponds Twp 56
Little Jim Pond, Jim Pond Twp, King and Bartlett Twp 56
Little Kennebago Lake, Stetsontown Twp 56
Little Northwest Pond, Massachusetts Gore 56
Little Swift River Pond, Township E 56
Long Cove Pond, Phillips 56
Long Pond, Chain of Ponds Twp, *see Chain of Ponds*
Long Pond, Sandy River Plt, *see Beaver Mountain Lake*
Long Pond, Township D, Township E 56
Long Pond, Seven Ponds Twp 56
Loon Lake, Rangeley, Dallas Plt 57
Lower Pond, Chain of Ponds Twp, *see Chain of Ponds*
L Pond, Seven Ponds Twp 57
Lufkin Pond, Phillips 57
Massachusetts Bog, Massachusetts Gore 57
McIntire Pond, New Sharon 57
Midway Pond, Sandy River Plt 57
Mirror Lake, Jay, *see Parker Pond*
Mooselookmeguntic and Cupsuptic Lakes, Rangeley, Rangeley Plt, Adamstown Twp, Richardsontown Twp 57
Mountain Pond, Rangeley Plt 58
Mount Blue Pond, Avon 58
Moxie Pond, Township D 58
Mud Pond, Twp 6 North of Weld 58
Mud Pond, Jim Pond Twp 58
Natanis Pond, Chain of Ponds Twp, *see Chain of Ponds*
Norcross Pond, Chesterville 58
North Pond, Chesterville 58
Northwest Pond, Massachusetts Gore 58
Otter Pond, Chain of Ponds Twp 58
Parker Pond, Jay 58
Parkis Pond, Jay, *see Parker Pond*
Pease Pond, Wilton 58
Perry Pond, Sandy River Plt 59
Pine Tree Pond, Sandy River Plt, *see South Pond*
Pinnacle Pond, Kingfield 59
Podunk Pond, Carthage 59
Porter Lake, Strong, New Vineyard 59
Quimby Pond, Rangeley 59
Rangeley Lake, Rangeley, Sandy River Plt, Rangeley Plt 59
Redington Pond, Carrabasset Valley 60
Redington Pond, Redington Twp 60
Rock Pond, Chain of Ponds Twp 60
Rock Pond, Sandy River Plt 60
Ross Pond, Rangeley 60
Round Pond, Chain of Ponds Twp, *see Chain of Ponds*
Round Pond, Chesterville 60
Round Pond, Township E 60
Round Pond, Rangeley 60
Sabbath Day Pond, Township E 60
Saddleback Lake, Dallas Plt 60
Saddleback Pond, Sandy River Plt 60
Sand Pond, Chesterville 61
Sandy River Ponds, Sandy River Plt 61
Schoolhouse Pond, Avon 61
Secret Pond, Seven Ponds Twp 61
Shiloh Pond, Kingfield, *see Dutton Pond*
South Boundary Pond, Massachusetts Gore 61
South Pond, Sandy River Plt 61
Spencer Pond, Township D 61
Staples Pond, Temple 61
Stetson Pond, Phillips 61
Stratton Brook Pond Wyman 61
Tea Pond, Jim Pond Twp 61
Tim Pond, Tim Pond Twp 62
Toothaker Pond, Phillips 62
Trout Pond, Madrid, *see Beal Pond*
Tufts Pond, Kingfield 62
Tumbledown Pond, Twp 6 North of Weld 62
Twin Island Pond, Lowelltown Twp 62
Varnum Pond, Wilton, Temple 62
Weathering Pond, Eustis, *see Welhem Pond*
Webb Lake, Weld, Carthage 62
Welhern Pond, Eustis 62
Wilson Pond, Wilton 62

Hancock County

Abrams Pond, Eastbrook, Franklin 63
Alamoosook Lake, Orland 63
Allen Pond, T35 MD 63
Alligator Lake, T34 MD, T28 MD 63
Aunt Betty Pond, Bar Harbor 63
Beech Hill Pond, Otis 63
Billings Pond, Blue Hill, *see First Pond*
Bracey Pond, T34 MD 63
Branch Lake, Ellsworth 63
Brandy Pond, T39 MD 64
Brewer Lake, Bucksport, *see Penobscot County*
Bubble Pond, Bar Harbor 64
Burnt Land Pond, T35 MD 64
Burnt Pond, Otis 64
Burnt Pond, Otis, Dedham 64
Chicken Mill Pond, Gouldsboro 64
Craig Pond, Orland 64
Crystal Pond, T40 MD 64
Debec Pond, Amherst 64
Deer Lake, T34 MD 64
Donnell Pond Franklin, T9 SD 64
Douglas Pond, Rlue H81, *see Second Pond*
Duck Lake, Oqiton Twp 65
Duck Pond, Franklin 65
Dutton Pond, Amherst 65
Eagle Lake, Bar Harbor 65
Eagle Lake, T34 MD 65
Echo Lake, Mt. Desert 65
First Pond, Blue Hill 65
Flanders Pond, Sullivan 65
Floods Pond, Otis 66
Forbes Pond, Gouldsboro 66
Fourth Pond, Blue Hill 66
Fox Pond, T10 SD 66
Frost Pond, Sedgwick 66
Gassabias Lake, T41 MD 66
Georges Pond, Franklin 66
Giles Pond, Aurora 66
Goose Pond, Dedham 66
Goose Pond, Swans Island 66
Graham Lake, T8 SD, Ellsworth, Mariaville, Waltham 67
Grassy Pond, Otis, Clitton, *see Lower Springy Pond*
Great Pond, Franklin 67
Great Pond, Great Pond 67
Great Pond, Mt. Desert, Southwest Harbor, *see Long Pond*
Green Lake, Dedham, Ellsworth 67
Green Lake, T35 MD 67
Green Lake, T35 MD 67
Halfmile Pond, Amherst 67
Halfmile Pond, Aurora 67
Halfmoon Pond, Bar Harbor 68
Hancock Pond Bucksport 68
Harriman Pond, Dedham 68
Hatcase Pond, Dedham 68
Heart Pond, Orland 68
Hodgdon Pond, Tremont, Mt. Desert 68
Hopkins Pond, Marlaville, Clifton 68
Horseshoe Lake, T35 MD 68
Hurd Pond, Dedham 68
Jacob Buck Pond, Bucksport 68
Jellison Hill Pond, Amherst 68
Jones Pond, Gouldsboro 68
Jordan Pond, Mt. Desert 69
Killman Pond, Oqiton Twp 69
King Pond, Great Pond 69
Lake Wood, Bar Harbor 69
Leonard Lake, Ellsworth 69
Lily Pond, Deer Isle 69
Little Long Pond, T10 SD 69
Little Pond, Great Pond 69
Little Round Pond, Mt. Desert 69
Little Tunk Pond, Sullivan 69
Little Webb Pond, Waltham 69
Long Pond, Bucksport 69
Long Pond, Great Pond, Aurora 69

Long Pond, Mt. Desert....69
Long Pond, Mt. Desert, Southwest Harbor....70
Long Pond, Sullivan....70
Long Pond, T10 SD....70
Loon Pond, T40 MD....70
Lovejoy Pond, T34 MD....70
Lower and Middle Lead Mountain Ponds, T28 MD....70
Lower Breakneck Pond, Bar Harbor....70
Lower Hadlock Pond, Mt. Desert....70
Lower Middle Branch Pond, Aurora....70
Lower Patten Pond, Ellsworth, Surry....70
Lower Pistol Lake, T3 ND....71
Lower Sabao Lake, T35 MD....71
Lower Springy Pond, Otis, Clifton....71
Lower Unknown Lake, T4 ND, *see Middle and Lower Unknown Lakes*
Middle and Lower Unknown Lakes, T4 ND....71
Middle Chain Lake, T4 ND....71
Middle Lead Mountain Pond, T28 MD, *see Lower and Middle Lead Mountain Ponds*
Middle Oxhead Pond, T40 MD....71
Middle Pistol Lake, T4 ND....71
Molasses Pond, Eastbrook....71
Morancy Pond, T7 SD....71
Moulton Pond, Dedham, Bucksport....72
Mountainy Pond, Dedham....72
Myrick Pond, T10 SD....72
Narraguagus Lake, T16 MD, T10 SD, T9 SD....72
Nicatous Lake, T3 ND, T40 MD, T41 MD....72
Norris Pond, Blue Hill, *see Noyes Pond*
Noyes Pond, Blue Hill....72
Partridge Pond, Amherst....73
Phillips Lake, Dedham....73
Pickerel Pond, T32 MD....73
Pierce Pond, Penobscot....73
Porter Pond, T3 ND....73
Pughole Pond, T41 MD....73
Ritt Pond, Great Pond....73
Rocky Pond, Orland....73
Rocky Pond, Otis....73
Rocky Pond, T22 MD....74
Round Pond, Mt. Desert....74
Round Pond, T7 SD, T10 SD, Steuben, *see Washington County*
Salmon Pond, T10 SD....74
Seal Cove Pond, Tremont....74
Second Pond, Dedham....74
Side Pistol Lake, T3 ND, T4 ND....74
Silver Lake, Bucksport....74
Simmons Pond, Hancock....74
Somes Pond Mt. Desert....74
Spectacle Pond, Osborn....74
Spring Lake, T3 ND....75
Spring River Lake, T10 SD....75
Stiles Lake, T35 MD....75
The Tarn, Bar Harbor....75
Third Pond, Blue Hill....75
Thurston Pond, Bucksport....75
Tilden Pond, T10 SD....75
Titcomb Pond, T32 MD....75
Toddy Pond, Orland, Surry, Penobscot, Blue Hill....75
Torrey Pond, Deer Isle....75
Trout Pond, T40 MD....76
Tunk Lake, T10 SD, T7 SD, Sullivan....76
Upper Breakneck Pond, Bar Harbor....76
Upper Chain Lake, T4 ND....76
Upper Hadlock Pond, Mt. Desert....76
Upper Lead Mountain Pond, T28 MD, T22 MD....76
Upper Middle Branch Pond, Aurora....76
Upper Oxhead Pond, T40 MD....77
Upper Patten Pond, Ellsworth, Surry, Orland....77
Upper Pistol Lake, T4 ND....77
Upper Sabao Lake, T41 MD....77
Upper Unknown Lake, T4 ND....77
Walker Pond, Brooksville....77
Webb Pond, Eastbrook, Waltham....77
West Bay Pond, T7 SD, Gouldsboro....77
West Lake T3 ND, T40 MD....77
Wight Pond, Penobscot....77
Williams Pond, Bucksport....78
Williams Pond, T28 MD....78
Witchhole Pond, Bar Harbor....78
Woods Pond, Blue Hill, *see Third Pond*
Youngs Pond, Otis....78

Kennebec County

Anderson Pond, Augusta....78
Androscoggin Lake, Wayne, Leeds....78
Annabessacook Lake, Monmouth, Winthrop....78
Basin Pond, Fayette....78
Belgrade Lakes, Belgrade, Oakland, Rome, Smithfield, *see East Pond, Great Pond, and North Pond*
Berry and Dexter Ponds, Wayne, Winthrop....78
Black Pond, Vienna....78
Brainard Pond, Readfield....78
Branch Pond, China, Palermo....78
Buker Pond, Litchfield....79
Burgess Pond, Fayette....79
Chamberlain Pond, Belgrade....79
China Lake, China, Vassalboro....79
Cobbossee Lake, Winthrop, Manchester, Monmouth, West Gardiner, Litchfield, *see Cobbosseecontee Lake*
Cobbosseecontee Lake, Winthrop, Manchester, Monmouth, West Gardiner, Litchfield....79
Cochnewagan Pond, Monmouth....79
Crotched Pond, Mt. Vernon, Fayette, Readfield, *see Echo Lake*
Crowell Pond, Vienna, *see Franklin County*
Dam Pond, Augusta....80
David Pond, Fayette....80
Desert Pond, Mt. Vernon....80
Dexter Pond, Wayne, Winthrop, *see Berry and Dexter Ponds*
Dutton Pond, China, Albion....80
East Lake, Oakland, Smithfield, *see East Pond*
East Pond, Oakland, Smithfield....80
Echo Lake, Mt. Vernon, Fayette, Readfield....80
Egypt Pond, Chesterville, Vienna, *see Franklin County*
Ellis Pond, Oakland, Belgrade, *see Salmon Lake*
Evans Pond, China....81
Fairbanks Pond, Manchester....81
Figure Eight Pond, Sidney, Manchester....81
Flying Pond, Vienna....81
Gould and Wellman Ponds, Sidney, Belgrade....81
Great Lake, Belgrade, Rome, *see Great Pond*
Great Pond, Belgrade, Rome....81
Greeley Pond, Augusta....81
Greeley Pond, Readfield, Mt. Vernon, *see Torsey Pond*
Hales Pond, Fayette....81
Hamilton Pond, Belgrade....81
Hopkins Pond, Mt. Vernon....82
Hudson Pond, Farmingdale, Manchester, *see Hutchinson Pond*
Hutchinson Pond, Farmingdale, Manchester....82
Ingham Pond, Mt. Vernon....82
Jamies Pond, Manchester, Farmingdale....82
Jimmie Pond, Manchester, Farmingdale, *see Jamies Pond*
Jimmy Pond, Litchfield....82
Joe Pond, Sidney, Belgrade....82
Joice Pond, Pittston....82
Joy Pond, Pittston, *see Joice Pond*
Kezar Pond, Winthrop....82
Kidder Pond, Vienna....82
Kimball Pond, Vienna, New Sharon....82
Lake Annabessacook, Monmouth, Winthrop, *see Annabessacook Lake*
Lily Pond, Sidney....82
Little Cobbosseecontee Lake, Winthrop....83
Little Purgatory Pond, Litchfield....83
Little Togus Pond, Augusta....83
Long Pond, Belgrade, Mt. Vernon, Rome....83
Long Pond, Windsor, Somerville....83
Loon Pond, Litchfield....83
Lovejoy Pond, Albion....83
Lovejoy Pond, Fayette, Readfield, Wayne....84
Lower Narrows Pond, Winthrop....84
Maranacook Lake, Readfield, Winthrop....84
McGrath Pond, Oakland, Belgrade, *see Salmon Lake and McGrath Pond*
Messalonskee Lake, Belgrade, Sidney, Oakland....84
Mill Pond, Readfield....84
Minnehonk Lake, Mt. Vernon....84
Moody Pond, Windsor....85
Moose Pond, Mt. Vernon....85
Mosher Pond, Fayette....85
Mud Pond, Windsor....85
Mud Pond, Winslow, China....85
Nehumkeag Pond, Pittston....85
North and Little Ponds, Rome, Mercer, Smithfield....85
Parker Pond, Mt. Vernon, Vienna....85
Pattee Pond, Winslow....86
Penney Pond, Belgrade, Sidney....86
Pleasant Pond, Litchfield, Gardiner, West Gardiner....86
Pocasset Lake, Wayne....86
Purgatory Pond, Litchfield, Monmouth, *see Woodbury Pond*
Salmon Lake and McGrath Pond, Oakland, Belgrade....86
Sanborn Pond, Farmingdale, Manchester, *see Hutchinson Pond*
Sand and Woodbury Ponds, Litchfield, Monmouth....86
Savade Pond, Windsor....87
Schoolhouse Pond, Fayette....87
Shed Pond, Manchester, Readfield....87
Silver Lake, Sidney, Manchester, *see Figure Eight Pond*

Spectacle Pond, Vassalboro, Augusta 87
Tacoma Lakes, Litchfield, Monmouth, *see Sand and Woodbury Ponds*
Taylor Pond, Mt. Vernon 87
Threecornered Pond, Augusta 87
Threemile Pond, China, Vassalboro, Windsor 87
Tilton Pond, Fayette 87
Tinkham Pond, Chelsea 87
Togus Pond, Augusta 88
Tolman Pond, Augusta 88
Torsey Lake, Readfield, Mt. Vernon 88
Upper Narrows Pond, Winthrop 88
Ward Pond, Sidney 88
Watson Pond, Rome 88
Webber Pond, Vassalboro 88
Wellman Pond, Belgrade, Sidney, *see Gould and Wellman Ponds*
Whittier Pond, Rome 89
Whittier Pond, Vienna 89
Wilson Pond, Monmouth, Wayne 89
Woodbury Pond, Litchfield, Monmouth, *see Sand and Woodbury Ponds*

Knox County

Alford Lake, Hope 89
Chickawaukie Pond, Rockport, Rockland 89
Crawford Pond, Union, Warren 89
Crystal Pond, Washington 90
Fish Pond, Hope, *see Hobbs and Fish Ponds*
Forest Lake, Friendship 90
Forest Pond, Friendship, *see Forest Lake*
Fresh Pond, North Haven 90
Grassy Pond, Rockport 90
Havener Pond, Warren, *see Lincoln County*
Hobbs and Fish Ponds, Hope 90
Hosmer Pond, Camden 90
Iron Pond, Washington 90
Lermond Pond, Hope, Union 91
Lilly Pond, Rockport 91
Lily Pond, Hope 91
Long Pond, Isle au Haut 91
Maces Pond, Rockport 91
Mansfield Pond, Hope 91
Megunticook Lake, Camden, Lincolnville, Hope 91
Mill Pond, Appleton, *see Sherman's Mill Pond*
Muddy Pond, Washington, *see Spring Pond*
North Pond, Warren 92
Rocky Pond, Rockport 92
Round Pond, Union 92
Round Pond, Vinalhaven 92
Sennebec Pond, Union, Appleton 92
Seven Tree Pond, Union, Warren 92
Sherman's Mill Pond, Appleton 92
South Pond, Warren 93
Spring Pond, Washington 93
Turner's Lake, Isle au Haut, *see Long Pond*
Washington Pond, Washington 93

Lincoln County

Adams Pond, Boothbay 93
Biscay Pond, Bremen, Bristol, Damariscotta 93
Boyd Pond, Bristol 93
Clark Cove Pond, Bristol 93
Clary Lake, Jefferson, Whitefield, *see Pleasant Pond*
Cooks Pond, Nobleboro 93
Damariscotta Lake, Jefferson 94
Deer Meadow Pond, Jefferson 94
Duckpuddle Pond, Nobleboro, Waldoboro 94
Dyer Long Pond, Jefferson 94
Gardiner Pond, Wiscasset 94
Givens Pond, Whitefield 94
Gross Pond, Waldoboro, *see Peters Pond*
Hastings Pond, Bristol 95
Havener Pond, Warren, Waldoboro 95
Ice Pond, Bristol 95
James Pond, Somerville 95
Kalers Pond, Waldoboro 95
Knickerbocker Lakes, Boothbay 95
Knickerbocker Pond, Boothbay, *see Knickerbocker Lakes*
Lily Pond, Edgecomb 95
Little Dyer Pond, Jefferson 95
Little Medomak Pond, Waldoboro 96
Long Pond, Somerville, Jefferson 96
McCurdy Pond, Bremen 96
Medomak Pond, Waldoboro 96
Muddy Pond, Damariscotta 96
Musquash Pond, Jefferson 96
Paradise Pond, Damariscotta, *see Muddy Pond*
Pemaquid Pond, Damariscotta 97
Peters Pond, Bremen, *see Webber Pond*
Peters Pond, Waldoboro 97
Pinkham Pond, Alna 97
Pleasant Pond, Jefferson, Whitefield 97
Ross Pond, Bristol 97
Sherman Lake, Newcastle 97
Sidensparker Pond, Waldoboro 97
Storer Pond, Waldoboro, *see Little Medomak Pond*
Three Corner Pond, Jefferson 97
Travel Pond, Jefferson 98
Turner Pond, Somerville, Palermo 98
Weary Pond, Whitefield 98
Webber Pond, Bremen 98
West Harbor Pond, Boothbay Harbor 98
Wiley Pond, Boothbay 98

Oxford County

Abbie Pond, Bowmantown Twp 98
Abbotts Pond, Sumner 98
Anasagunticook Lake, Canton, Hartford 98
Aziscohos Lake, Parkertown Twp, Lincoln Plt, Lynchtown Twp 99
Aziscohos Pond, Magalloway Plt 99
Aziscoo Lake, Parkertown Twp, Lincoln Plt, Lynchtown Twp, *see Aziscohos Lake*
B Pond, Upton 99
Back Pond, Stoneham, Lovell 99
Barker Pond, Hiram, *see Cumberland County*
Bear Pond, Waterford 99
Beaver Pond, Denmark 99
Beaver Pond, Magalloway Plt 99
Bickford Pond, Porter 99
Big Concord Pond, Woodstock 99
Big Ellis Pond, Roxbury, Byron, *see Ellis Pond*
Bird Pond, Norway 99
Black Pond, Porter 100
Bradley Pond, Lovell 100
Broken Bridge Pond, Albany Twp 100
Bryant Pond, Woodstock, Greenwood 100
Bunganock Pond, Hartford 100
Burnt Meadow Pond, Brownfield 100
C Pond, C Surplus 100
Canton Lake, Canton, Hartford, *see Anasagunticook Lake*
Chapman Pond, Porter 100
Christopher Lake, Woodstock, Greenwood, *see Bryant Pond*
Clays Pond, Fryeburg 100
Clemons and Little Clemons Ponds, Hiram 100
Colcord Pond, Porter 100
Concord Pond Woodstock, *see Big Concord Pond*
Crocker Pond, Albany Twp 100
Cupsuptic Lake, Adamstown Twp, Rangeley, *see Mooselookmeguntic and Cupsuptic Lakes*
Cupsuptic Pond, Oxbow Twp 101
Cushman Pond, Lovell 101
Cushman Pond, Sumner 101
East Richardson Ponds, Adamstown Twp 101
Ellis Pond, Roxbury, Byron 101
Farrington Pond, Lovell 101
Five Kezar Ponds, Lowell, Waterford, Stoneham, *see Back, Jewett, Middle, Mud, and Weymouth Ponds*
Forest Pond, Canton 101
Garland Pond, Byron, *see Little Ellis Pond*
Granger Pond, Denmark 101
Green Pond, Oxford 101
Halfmoon Pond, Mexico, Carthage 101
Hall Pond, Paris 101
Hancock Pond, Denmark, *see Cumberland County*
Hicks Pond, Greenwood 102
Hobbs Pond, Norway, *see Little Pennesseewassee Pond*
Hogan Pond, Oxford 102
Horseshoe Pond, Lovell, Stoneham 102
Howard Pond, Hanover 102
Hunt Pond, Fryeburg 102
Hutchinson Pond, Albany Twp 102
Indian Pond, Greenwood 102
Island Pond, Waterford, Harrison, *see Cumberland County*
Jaybird Pond, Hiram, Porter 102
Jewett Pond, Waterford 102
Joes Pond, Rumford 102
Keewaydin Lake, Stoneham 102
Keoka Lake, Waterford 102
Keys Pond, Sweden 103
Kezar Lake, Lovell 103
Kezar Pond, Fryeburg 103
Labrador Pond, Sumner 103
Lake Anasagunticook, Canton, Hartford, *see Anasagunticook Lake*
Lincoln Pond, Parkertown Twp 103
Little Bear Pond, Hartford, *see Androscoggin County*
Little Beaver Pond, Magalloway Plt 103
Little Clemons Pond, Hiram, *see Clemons and Little Clemons Ponds*
Little Concord Pond, Woodstock 103
Little Ellis Pond Byron 103
Little Labrador Pond, Sumner 103
Little Moose Pond, Waterford 103
Little Pennesseewassee Pond, Norway 104
Little Pond, Denmark 104

Long Pond, Denmark....104
Long Pond, Waterford....104
Lovewell Pond, Fryeburg....104
Lower Black Pond, Oxbow Twp....104
Lower East Richardson Pond, Adamstown Twp, *see East Richardson Ponds*
Lower Kimball Pond, Fryeburg....104
Lower Richardson Lake, Township C, Magalloway Plt, Richardstown Twp, *see Richardson Lakes*
Lower Spectacle Pond, Porter, *see Spectacle Ponds*
Marshall Pond, Oxford, Hebron....104
McWain Pond, Waterford, *see Long Pond*
Middle Pond Lovell, Waterford....104
Mine Pond, Porter....104
Molechunkamunk Lake, Richardsontown Twp, Magalloway Plt, *see Upper Richardson Lake*
Mollidgewock Pond, Upton....104
Mooselookmeguntic and Cupsuptic Lakes, Rangeley, Adamstown Twp, Richardsontown Twp, Rangeley Plt....104
Moose Pond, Otisfield....105
Moose Pond, West Paris....105
Moose Pond, Waterford, *see Little Moose Pond*
Mud Pond, Greenwood....105
Mud Pond, Lower Cupsuptic Twp....105
Mud Pond, Oxford....105
Mud Pond, Waterford, Lovell....105
Nelson Pond, Livermore, *see Androscoggin County*
North Pond, Norway....105
North Pond, Sumner....105
North Pond, Woodstock, Greenwood....105
Otter Pond, Parmachenee Twp....105
Oversett Pond, Greenwood....105
Papoose Pond, Waterford....106
Parmachenee Lake, Lynchtown Twp, Parmachenee Twp....106
Pennesseewassee Lake, Norway....106
Pequawket Lake, Brownfield....106
Pequawket Pond, Brownfield, *see Pequawket Lake*
Perley Pond, Denmark....106
Pickerel Pond, Denmark....106
Plain Pond, Porter....106
Pleasant Pond, Brownfield, Fryeburg, Denmark....106
Pleasant Pond, Sumner....106
Pond in the River, Township C, C Surplus, Upton....107
Proctor Pond, Albany Twp....107
Rattlesnake Pond, Brownfield, *see Pequawket Lake*
Richardson Lakes, Richardsontown Twp, Township C, Magalloway Plt....107
Richardson Pond, Adamstown Twp, Lincoln Plt, *see West Richardson Pond*
Round Pond, Fryeburg....107
Round Pond, Greenwood, *see South and Round Ponds*
Roxbury Pond, Roxbury, Byron, *see Ellis Pond*
Sand Pond, Denmark, *see Walden Pond*
Sand Pond, Norway....107
Saturday Pond Otisfield....107
Sawyer Lake, Parkertown Twp, Lincoln Plt, Lynchtown Twp, *see Aziscohos Lake*
Shagg Pond, Woodstock....107
Silver Lake, Roxbury, Byron, *see Ellis Pond*
Songo Pond, Albany Twp....107
South Pond, Buckfield....107
South and Round Ponds, Greenwood....107
Speck Pond, Grafton Twp....108
Spectacle Ponds, Porter....108
Stanley Pond, Hiram, Porter....108
Stearns Pond, Sweden....108
Sturtevant Pond, Magalloway Plt....108
Sunday Pond, Magalloway Plt....108
Swan Pond, Hartford....108
Thompson Lake, Oxford, Otisfield, Poland, Casco....108
Trafton Pond, Hiram, Porter....108
Trout Pond, Stoneham....108
Twitchell Pond, Greenwood....108
Umbagog Lake, Magalloway Plt....109
Upper East Richardson Pond, Adamstown Twp, *see East Richardson Ponds*
Upper Richardson Lake, Richardsontown Twp, *see Richardson Lakes*
Upper Spectacle Pond, Porter, *see Spectacle Ponds*
Virginia Lake, Stoneham....109
Walden Pond, Denmark....109
Washburn Pond, Sumner, Woodstock....109
Webber Pond, Sweden....109
Wellekennebacook Lake, Township C, Magalloway Plt, Richardsontown Twp, *see Lower Richardson Lake*
Wells Pond, Parmachenee Twp....109
West Richardson Pond, Adamstown Twp, Lincoln Plt....109
Weymouth Pond, Stoneham....109
Whitney Pond, Oxford....109
Whitney Pond, Stoneham....109
Worthley Pond, Peru....109

Penobscot County

Ambajejus Lake, T1 R9 WELS, *see Pemadumcook Chain of Lakes*
Ben Annis Pond, Hermon....110
Billfish Pond, T6 R8 WELS, Trout Brook Twp, *see Piscataquis County*
Black Cat Pond, T8 R6 WELS....110
Bottle Lake, Lakeville....110
Bowlin Pond, T5 R8 WELS....110
Brewer Lake, Orrington, Holden, Bucksport....110
Brooks Pond, Corinna....110
Cambolasse Pond, Lincoln....110
Caribou, Long, and Egg Ponds, Lincoln....110
Cedar Lake, Long A Twp, T3 R9 NWP....111
Center Pond, Lincoln....111
Center Pond, Dixmont....111
Chemo Pond, Bradley, Eddington, Clifton....111
Cold Stream Pond, Enfield, Lincoln, Lowell...111
Crooked Pond, Lincoln....111
Cut Lake, T7 R6 WELS, T8 R6 WELS....111
Davis Pond, Eddington, Holden....112
Davis Pond, T5 R7 WELS, *see Wapiti Pond*
Duck Lake, Lakeville....112
Egg Pond, Lincoln, *see Caribou, Long, and Egg Ponds*
Elbow Lake, T3 Indian Purchase, *see Pemadumcook Chain of Lakes*
Endless Lake, T3 R9 NWP....112
Escutasis Lake, Lowell, Burlington, *see Eskutassis Lake*
Eskutassis Lake, Lowell, Burlington....112
Etna Pond, Carmel, Etna, Stetson....112
Fields Pond, Orrington....112
First and Second Matagamon Lakes, T6 R8 WELS, Trout Brook Twp, *see Matagamon Lake*
Fitts Pond, Clifton....112
Flatiron Pond, T3 R9 NWP....112
Folsom Pond, Lincoln....112
Garland Pond, Garland....113
George Pond, Hermon....113
Gould Pond, Dexter....113
Grand Lake, T6 R8 WELS, Trout Brook Twp, *see Matagamon Lake*
Grand Lake Seboeis, T8 R7 WELS, T7 R7 WELS, *see Seboeis Grand Lake*
Green Mountain Pond, T6 R6 WELS....113
Green Pond Lee, T3 R1 NBPP....113
Hammond Pond, Hampden....113
Hay Lake, T6 R8 WELS....113
Hay Pond, T6 R8 WELS....113
Hermon Pond, Hermon....113
Holbrook Pond, Holden....113
Hopkins Pond, Clifton, Mariaville....113
Horseshoe Lake, Lakeville, T5 R1 NBPP, T5 ND BPP....113
Hot Pond, T6 R6 WELS, T6 R7 WELS....114
House Pond Lee....114
Ireland Pond, T7 R8 WELS....114
Jerry Pond, Millinocket, TA R7 WELS....114
Jerry Pond, T5 R7 WELS....114
Jones Pond, T7 R8 WELS, T8 R8 WELS....114
Junior Lake, Lakeville, Pukakon Twp....114
Katahdin Lake, T3 R8 WELS....114
Keg Lake, Lakeville....114
Kimball Pond, T5 R8 WELS....115
LaPomkeag Lake, T8 R7 WELS, T8 R6 WELS, *see Upper LaPomkeag Lake*
Lawton Pond, Mount Chase....115
Little Hathorn Pond, T4 R8 WELS....115
Little Madasgascal Pond, Burlington, T3 R1 NBPP, *see Madagascal and Little Madagascal Ponds*
Little Mattamiscontis Lake, T3 R9 NWP....115
Little Pushaw Pond, Hudson....115
Little Round Pond, Lincoln....115
Little Salmon Stream Lake, T1 R6 WELS....115
Lombard Lake, Lakeville....115
Long Pond, Lincoln, *see Caribou, Long, and Egg Ponds*
Lost Pond, T7 R7 WELS....115
Lowell Lake, Caroll Plt, Springfield....115
Lower Jo-Mary Lake, T4 Indian Purchase, *see Piscataquis County*
Lower LaPomkeag Lake, T8 R7 WELS....115
Lower Pug Lake, Lakeville....116
Lower Shin Pond, Mount Chase, T5 R7 WELS....116
Lower Springy Pond, Otis, Clifton, *see Hancock County*
Lunksoos Lake, T4 R7 WELS....116
Madagascal and Little Madagascal Ponds, Burlington, T3 R1 NBPP....116
Matagamon Lake, T6 R8 WELS, Trout Brook Twp....116
Mattakeunk Lake, Lee....116

Mattamiscontis Lake, T2 R9 NWP, T3 R9 NWP 117
Mattanawcook Pond, Lincoln 117
Medunkeunk Lake, T2 R9 NWP 117
Messer Pond, T5 R8 WELS 117
Middle Jo-Mary and Turkeytail Lakes, T4 Indian Purchase, TA R10 WELS 117
Millimagassett Lake, T7 R8 WELS 117
Millnocket Lake, T1 R8 WELS, T1 R9 WELS, T2 R9 WELS 118
Mill Privilege Lake, T5 R1 NBPP, Carroll Plt 118
Mountain Catcher Pond, T6 R8 WELS, Trout Brook Twp 118
Mower Pond, Corinna 118
Mud Lake, T6 R6 WELS, Moro Plt, *see Pleasant and Mud Lakes*
Mud Pond, Old Town 118
Nokomis Pond, Newport, *see Somerset County*
Nollesemic Lake, Hopkins Academy Grant, Long A Twp, T3 R9 NWP 118
North Twin Lake, T4 Indian Purchase, *see Pemadumcook Chain of Lakes*
Number Three Pond, Lee, T3 R1 NBPP 118
Parks Pond, Clifton 118
Patten Pond, Hampden 119
Peaked Mountain Pond, T4 R7 WELS 119
Pemadumcook Chain of Lakes, T3 Indian Purchase, T4 Indian Purchase, T1 R9 WELS, T1 R10 WELS 119
Pickett Mountain Pond, T6 R6 WELS, Moro Plt 119
Pickerel Pond, Alton 119
Pleasant and Mud Lakes, T6 R6 WELS, Moro Plt 119
Pleasant Lake, Stetson 119
Plymouth Pond, Plymouth 120
Puffers Pond, Dexter 120
Pug Pond, Alton 120
Pushaw Lake, Old Town, Hudson, Glenburn, Orono 120
Round Pond, Plymouth 120
Round Pond, Soldlertown Twp 120
Round Pond, T3 R1 NBPP, Lee 120
Rush Pond, Herseytown Twp 120
Salmon Stream Lake, T1 R6 WELS 120
Saponac Pond, Burlington, Grand Falls Twp 121
Sawtelle Deadwater, T6 R7 WELS 121
Scraggly Lake, T5 R1 NBPP, T6 R1 NBPP 121
Scraggly Lake, T7 R8 WELS 121
Sebasticook Lake, Newport 121
Seboeis Grand Lake, T8 R7 WELS, T7 R7 WELS 122
Shaw Lake, T5 R1 NBPP, T6 R1 NBPP 122
Smith Pond, T3 Indian Purchase 122
Snag Pond, Lincoln 122
Snowshoe Lake, T7 R7 WELS 122
South Branch Lake, Seboeis Plt, T2 R8 NWP 122
South Twin Lake, T4 Indian Purchase, *see Pemadumcook Chain of Lakes*
Stump Pond, Lincoln, *see Snag Pond*
Sweets Pond, Orrington 122
Swetts Pond, Orrington, *see Sweets Pond*
Sysladobsis Lake, Lakeville, T5 ND BPP 123
Tracy Pond Hermon 123
Trout Pond, Grand Falls Twp 123
Trout Pond, Lowell 123
Trout Pond, Soldiertown Twp 123
Turkeytail Lake, T4 Indian Purchase, *see Middle Jo-Mary and Turkeytail Lakes*
Umcolcus Lake, T7 R6 WELS, T8 R6 WELS, T7 R5 WELS, T8 R5 WELS 123
Upper Cold Stream Pond, Lincoln 123
Upper Jo-Mary Lake, Veazie Gore, *see Piscataquis County*
Upper LaPomkeag Lake, T8 R6 WELS, T8 R7 WELS 123
Upper Pond, Lincoln 124
Upper Pug Lake, Lakeville 124
Upper Shin Pond, T6 R6 WELS, Mount Chase 124
Upper Sysladobsis Lake, Lakeville 124
Wadleigh Pond, T4 Indian Purchase 124
Wapiti Pond, T5 R7 WELS 124
Wassookeag Lake, Dexter 124
Weir Pond, Lee, T3 R1 NBPP 124
West Garland Pond, Garland 124
West Grand Lake, T6 ND BPP, *see Washington County*
Weymouth Pond, Corinna, St. Albans 124
White Horse Lake, T7 R7 WELS 125
Wiley Pond, Patten 125

Piscataquis County

Abbee Pond, Brownville 125
Abol Pond, T2 R9 WELS 125
Allagash Lake, T8 R14 WELS, T7 R14 WELS 125
Alligator Pond, TA R10 WELS 125
Ambejejus Lake, T1 R9 WELS, *see Pemadumcook Chain of Lakes*
Aroostook Pond, T7 R9 WELS, *see Big Beaver Pond and Little Beaver Pond*
B Pond, TB R11 WELS 125
Badger Pond, Willimantic 125
Bartlett Pond, T10 R9 WELS 125
Basin Ponds, Mt. Katahdin Twp 125
Bear Pond, Bowerbank 125
Bear Pond, Rainbow Twp 126
Bear Pond, T2 R13 WELS 126
Beaver Pond, Shawtown Twp 126
Bell Pond, Monson 126
Bennett Pond, Parkman 126
Benson Pond, Willimantic, Bowerbank, *see Big Benson Pond*
Big Beaver Pond, Rainbow Twp 126
Big Beaver Pond, T7 R9 WELS 126
Big Bennett Pond, Guilford 126
Big Benson Pond, Willimantic, Bowerbank 126
Big Boardman Pond, TA R11 WELS, *see Big Boardway Pond*
Big Boardway Pond, TA R11 WELS 126
Big Bunker Pond, Shirley, Monson 126
Big Caribou Pond, T7 R10 WELS 127
Big Duck Pond, East Middlesex Canal Grant 127
Big Eagle Lake, Eagle Lake Twp, T7 R12 WELS, Soper Mountain Twp, T9 R13 WELS, *see Eagle Lake*
Big Fisher Pond, T2 R12 WELS 127
Big Greenwood Pond, Elliotsville Twp, Willimantic 127
Big Hurd Pond, T6 R15 WELS 127
Big Indian Pond, Moosehead Junction Twp 127
Big Lyford Pond, Shawtown Twp 127
Big Minister Pond, T2 R10 WELS 127
Big Murphy Pond, Rainbow Twp, *see Murphy Ponds*
Big Notch Pond, Moosehead Junction Twp, *see Notch Ponds*
Big Pine Pond, T3 R13 WELS 127
Big Pleasant Lake, T9 R11 WELS, T10 R11 WELS 127
Big Moose Pond, Moosehead Junction Twp 128
Big Pleasant Pond, TA R11 WELS 128
Big Reed Pond, T8 R10 WELS 128
Billfish Pond, Trout Brook Twp, T6 R8 WELS 128
Birch Ridge Ponds, TA R11 WELS 128
Blood Pond, T2 R13 WELS 128
Bluff Pond, Frenchtown Twp 128
Bluffer Pond, T8 R11 WELS 128
Boardway Pond, TA R11 WELS, *see Big Boardway Pond*
Boyd Lake, Orneville Twp 128
Branns Mill Pond, Dover-Foxcroft 128
Brown Pond, Bowdoin College Grant West 128
Brown Pond, T8 R9 WELS 128
Brown Pond, T9 R9 WELS 129
Buck Pond, Rainbow Twp 129
Buckley Pond, T8 R10 WELS 129
Burden Pond, Bowerbank 129
Burnham Pond, Big Moose Twp 129
Bunker Pond, Shirley, Monson, *see Big Bunker Pond*
Caribou Lake, T2 R12 WELS, T3 R12 WELS, T3 R13 WELS, *see Chesuncook Lake*
Carpenter Pond, T7 R11 WELS 129
Carry Pond, T3 R11 WELS 129
Caucomgomoc Lake, T7 R15 WELS, T7 R14 WELS, T6 R15 WELS, T6 R14 WELS 129
Cedar Pond, TB R10 WELS 129
Celia Pond, T3 R10 WELS 129
Center Pond, Sangerville 130
Chamberlain Lake, Eagle Lake Twp, T7 R13 WELS, T7 R12 WELS, T6 R12 WELS, T6 R11 WELS 130
Chandler Pond, T8 R10 WELS, T7 R10 WELS 130
Chase Lake, T9 R10 WELS 130
Chase Pond, T9 R10 WELS, T10 R10 WELS, *see Island Pond*
Chemquasabamticook Lake, T10 R15 WELS, T9 R15 WELS, T9 R14 WELS 130
Chesuncook Lake, T3 R11 WELS, T3 R12 WELS, T4 R12 WELS, T5 R12 WELS, T3 R13 WELS, T4 R13 WELS, Chesuncook Twp 130
Chesuncook Pond, T3 R11 WELS, Rainbow Twp 131
Church Pond, TA R10 WELS 131
Churchill and Heron Lakes, T9 R12 WELS, T9 R13 WELS, T10 R12 WELS 131
Clear Lake, T10 R11 WELS 131
Cliff and Twin Lakes, T9 R12 WELS, Soper Mountain Twp 131
Clifford Pond, Rainbow Twp 131
Coffeelos Pond, T6 R11 WELS 131
Cooper Pond, TA R10 WELS 131
Crawford Pond, TA R11 WELS 132
Crescent Pond, T9 R15 WELS 132
Crockett Pond, Blanchard Plt 132

Cuxabexis Lake, T5 R12 WELS,
T6 R12 WELS........132
Daggett Pond, T7 R14 WELS........132
Daicey Pond, T3 R10 WELS........132
Daisey Pond, T2 R10 WELS........132
Deep Pond, T4 R9 WELS........132
Deer Pond, T3 R13 WELS........132
Doe Pond, Monson........132
Doughnut Pond, Rainbow Twp........132
Doughty Ponds, Monson........132
Dow Pond, Sebec........133
Draper Pond, T3 R10 WELS........133
Duck Pond, T2 R13 WELS, *see Blood Pond*
Duck Pond, T4 R11 WELS........133
Dunham Pond, Guilford........133
Dwelley Pond, Nesourdnahunk Twp........133
Eagle Lake, Eagle Lake Twp, T7 R12 WELS,
Soper Mountain Twp, T9 R13 WELS........133
East Branch Pond, T7 R11 WELS........133
East Chairback Pond, T7 R9 NWP........133
East Pond, T5 R9 NWP, Brownville,
see Ebeemee Lake
Ebeemee Lake, T5 R9 NWP, Brownville........133
Echo Lake, T9 R11 WELS........133
Elbow Lake, T3 Indian Purchase,
see Pemadumcook Chain of Lakes
Elbow Pond, T3 R10 WELS........134
Female Pond, T1 R12 WELS........134
Fifth Debsconeag Lake, Rainbow Twp,
T1 R11 WELS........134
Fifth Musquacook Lake, T10 R11 WELS........134
First Buttermilk Pond, Bowerbank........134
First Currier Pond, T9 R11 WELS........134
First Davis Pond, Guilford........134
First Debsconeag Lake, T2 R10 WELS........134
First Little Lyford Pond,
Bowdoin College Grant East........134
First West Branch Pond, Shawtown Twp........134
Fitzgerald Pond, Big Moose Twp........134
Fogg Pond, Bowdoin College Grant West........135
Foss Pond, Kingsbury Plt........135
Foss and Knowlton Pond, T3 R10 WELS........135
Fourth Debsconeag Lake, T1 R11 WELS,
T1 R10 WELS........135
Fourth Lake, T7 R11 WELS........135
Fourth Musquacook Lake, T10 R11 WELS,
T11 R11 WELS........135
Fowler Pond, T3 R11 WELS........135
Frost Pond, T3 R11 WELS,
T3 R12 WELS........135
Frost Pond, Trout Brook Twp........135
Garland Pond, Sebec, Dover-Foxcroft........135
Gauntlet Pond, TB R10 WELS........136
Grassy Pond, T2 R12 WELS........136
Greenleaf Pond, Abbot........136
Greenwood Pond, TB R11 WELS,
Bowdoin College Grant East........136
Grenell Pond, Greenville........136
Grindstone Pond, Willimantic........136
Hale Pond, T2 R10 WELS........136
Harlow Pond, Parkman, *see Manhanock and Harlow Ponds*
Harrington Lake, T4 R11 WELS,
T3 R11 WELS........136
Harrow Lake, T10 R12 WELS,
T10 R11 WELS........136
Hay Pond, T7 R11 WELS........136
Haymock Lake, T8 R11 WELS,
T7 R11 WELS........137
Hebron Lake, Monson........137
Hedgehog Pond,
Bowdoin College Grant West........137
Henderson Pond, TA R11 WELS........137
Heron Lake, T9 R12 WELS, T10 R12 WELS,
see Churchill and Heron Lakes
High Pond, Trout Brook Twp........137
Holbrook Pond, Rainbow Twp,
T3 R11 WELS........137
Horserace Ponds, Rainbow Twp,
T3 R11 WELS........137
Horseshoe Pond,
Bowdoin College Grant West........137
Horseshoe Pond, T5 R9 NWP,
see Ebeemee Lake
Houston Pond, T7 R9 NWP,
Katahdin Iron Works Twp........137
Hudson Pond, T6 R10 WELS........137
Hurd Pond, T2 R10 WELS........138
Indian Pond, Bowdoin College Grant West........138
Indian Pond, T7 R12 WELS........138
Indian Pond, T7 R9 NWP........138
Island Pond, T9 R10 WELS,
T10 R10 WELS........138
Jackson Pond, T3 R11 WELS,
T3 R10 WELS........138
Jaquith Pond, Brownville........138
Jewett Pond, Spencer Bay Twp........138
Johnson Pond, T8 R14 WELS........138
Johnston Pond, TA R10 WELS........139
Jo-Mary Pond, TB R10 WELS........139
Juniper Knee Pond, Elliotsville Twp........139
Kelly Pond, T2 R12 WELS........139
Kidney Pond, T3 R10 WELS........139
Kingsbury and Mayfield Ponds, Kingbury Plt,
Mayfield Twp, Brighton Plt........139
Lake Hebron, Monson, *see Hebron Lake*
Lazy Tom Pond, T1 R13 WELS........139
Leadbetter Pond, T9 R11 WELS........139
Leavitt Pond, T1 R11 WELS........139
Leonard Pond, T10 R9 WELS........139
Lily Pad Pond, T3 R10 WELS........139
Little Beaver Pond, T7 R9 WELS........139
Little Benson Pond, Bowerbank........140
Little Bluffer Pond, T8 R11 WELS........140
Little Carpenter Pond, T7 R11 WELS........140
Little Churchill Pond, T10 R13 WELS........140
Little Frost Pond, T3 R12 WELS........140
Little Greenwood Pond, Elliotsville Twp........140
Little Houston Pond,
Katahdin Iron Works Twp........140
Little Hurd Pond, T2 R10 WELS........140
Little Indian Pond, T7 R12 WELS........140
Little Lobster Lake, Lobster Twp........140
Little Minister Pond, T2 R10 WELS........140
Little Moxie Pond, East Moxie Twp........140
Little Moose Pond,
Moosehead Junction Twp........141
Little Mud Pond, Greenville........141
Little Murphy Pond, Rainbow Twp,
see Murphy Ponds
Little Nesowadnehunk Lake, T5 R11 WELS,
see Little Sourdnahunk Lake
Little Notch Pond, Moosehead Junction Twp,
see Notch Ponds
Little Pillsbury Pond, T8 R11 WELS........141
Little Pleasant Pond, T10 R11 WELS........141
Little Reed Pond, T8 R10 WELS........141
Little Rocky Pond, TA R11 WELS........141
Little Rocky Pond, T3 R10 WELS........141
Little Sourdnahunk Lake, T5 R11 WELS........141
Little Spencer Pond,
East Middlesex Canal Grant........141
Little Wassataquoik Lake, T4 R10 WELS........141
Lobster Lake, Lobster Twp,
Northeast Carry Twp, TX R14 WELS,
East Middlesex Canal Grant........141
Long Bog, Shawtown Twp........142
Long Pond, TA R11 WELS, T1 R11 WELS........142
Long Pond, Bowdoin College Grant West,
T7 R9 NWP, Elliotsville Twp,
Bowdoin College Grant East........142
Long Pond, Trout Brook Twp........142
Longley Pond, T6 R13 WELS........142
Loon Lake, T6 R15 WELS........142
Lost Pond, T3 R10 WELS........142
Lower Basin Pond, Mt. Katahdin Twp,
see Basin Ponds
Lower Bean Pond, Rainbow Twp........142
Lower Doughty Pond, Monson,
see Doughty Ponds
Lower Ebeemee Lake, T5 R9 NWP,
see Ebeemee Lake
Lower Ellis Pond, T7 R14 WELS........142
Lower Fowler Pond, Trout Brook Twp........143
Lower Hudson Pond, T10 R10 WELS........143
Lower Jo-Mary Lake, T1 R10 WELS,
TA R10 WELS, T4 Indian Purchase........143
Lower South Branch Pond, T5 R9 WELS........143
Lower Togue Pond, T2 R9 WELS........143
Lower Twin Pond, T2 R9 WELS,
see Twin Ponds
Lower Wilson Pond, Greenville........143
Lower Yoke Pond, TA R11 WELS,
see Yoke Ponds
Lucky Pond, Spencer Bay Twp........143
Manhanock and Harlow Ponds, Sangerville,
Parkman........143
Marble Pond, Blanchard Plt........143
Mathews Pond, T8 R10 WELS........144
McPherson Pond, T10 R10 WELS........144
Middle Branch Pond, T5 R9 NWP........144
Middle Elbow Pond, T10 R10 WELS........144
Middle Fowler Pond, T5 R9 WELS........144
Millinocket Lake, T1 R9 WELS, T1 R8 WELS,
T2 R9 WELS, T2 R8 WELS........144
Millinocket Lake, T7 R9 WELS, T7 R10 WELS,
T8 R9 WELS........144
Mitchell Pond, T7 R9 WELS........144
Monkey Pond, TA R11 WELS........144
Monson Pond, Monson........144
Moose Pond, Chesuncook Twp,
T5 R12 WELS, *see Chesuncook Lake*
Moose Pond, T1 R9 WELS........145
Moosehead Lake, Greenville, Beaver Cove Plt,
Lily Bay Twp, Spencer Bay Twp,
Days Academy Grant, Kineo Twp,
Northeast Carry Twp, Seboomook Twp,
Big W Twp, Little W Twp, West Middlesex
Canal Grant, Tomhegan Twp, Rockwood Strip,
Taunton and Raynham Academy Grant,
Sandbar Tract, Misery Gore, Sapling Twp, Big
Moose Twp, Moosehead Junction Twp,
Harfords Point Twp, Cove Point Twp........145
Mooseleuk Lake, T10 R9 WELS........145
Mountain Brook Pond,
Bowdoin College Grant West........145

Mountain Pond, Beaver Cove, Bowdoin College Grant West 145
Mountain Pond, T10 R10 WELS 145
Mountain View Pond, Big Moose Twp, *see Fitzgerald Pond*
Mountain View Pond, TA R11 WELS 145
Mud Pond, T6 R12 WELS 145
Mud Greenwood Pond, Willimantic 146
Munsungan Lake, T8 R10 WELS, T8 R9 WELS, T9 R10 WELS 146
Murphy Ponds, Rainbow Twp 146
Nahmakanta Lake, T1 R11 WELS, Rainbow Twp 146
Narrow Pond, T8 R14 WELS 146
Nesowadnehunk Lake, T4 R10 WELS, Nesourdnahunk Twp, T5 R11 WELS, T4 R11 WELS, *see Sourdnahunk Lake*
North Pond, Elliotsville 146
North Twin Lake, T4 Indian Purchase, *see Pemadumcook Chain of Lakes*
Norton Pond, Brownville 146
Notch Pond, Bowdoin College Grant West 146
Notch Ponds, Moosehead Junction Twp 146
Onawa Lake, Elliotsville Twp, Willimantic 146
Ordway Pond, Shirley 147
Otter Pond, T3 R13 WELS 147
Otter Pond, T8 R14 WELS 147
Passamagamet Lake, T1 R9 WELS, T1 R10 WELS 147
Peaked Mountain Pond, T10 R10 WELS, T10 R11 WELS 147
Pearl Pond, T5 R9 NWP, *see Ebeemee Lake*
Pemadumcook Chain of Lakes, T1 R10 WELS, T1 R9 WELS, T4 Indian Purchase, T3 Indian Purchase 147
Penobscot Pond, T1 R12 WELS, T1 R11 WELS 147
Peters Pond, Brownville, *see Norton Pond*
Pillsbury Pond, T8 R11 WELS 148
Pingree Pond, Parkman 148
Piper Pond, Abbot 148
Pleasant Lake, T9 R11 WELS, T10 R11 WELS, *see Big Pleasant Lake*
Poland Pond, T7 R15 WELS, T7 R14 WELS 148
Pollywog Pond, Rainbow Twp, T1 R11 WELS 148
Prentiss Pond, T1 R11 WELS 148
Pretty Pond, T8 R11 WELS 148
Priestly Lake, T10 R13 WELS 148
Prong Pond, Greenville, Beaver Cove Plt 148
Punchbowl Pond, Blanchard Plt 148
Rabbit Pond, Elliotsville Twp 149
Ragged Lake, T2 R13 WELS, T3 R13 WELS 149
Ragged Pond, T9 R10 WELS 149
Rainbow Deadwaters, Rainbow Twp 149
Rainbow Lake, Rainbow Twp 149
Ripogenus Lake, T3 R11 WELS, T3 R12 WELS, *see Chesuncook Lake*
Roach Ponds
- First Roach Pond, Frenchtown Twp 149
- Second Roach Pond, T1 R12 WELS, Shawtown Twp 149
- Third Roach Pond, Shawtown Twp 150
- Fourth Roach Pond, Shawtown Twp 150
- Fifth Roach Pond, Shawtown Twp, *see Beaver Pond*
- Sixth Roach Pond, Shawtown Twp 150
- Seventh Roach Pond, TA R11 WELS 150

Rocky Pond, T3 R10 WELS 150
Rocky Pond, TA R11 WELS 150
Ross Lake, T10 R15 WELS, T9 R15 WELS, T9 R14 WELS, *see Chemquasabamticook Lake*
Round Pond, T2 R9 WELS 150
Round Pond, T6 R11 WELS, *see Telos Lake and Round Pond*
Round Pond, T7 R14 WELS 150
Rum Pond, Greenville, Bowdoin College Grant West 150
Russell Pond, T4 R9 WELS 150
Saddle Pond, T7 R9 WELS 150
Salmon Pond, Greenville 150
Sandy Stream Pond, Mt. Katahdin Twp 151
Sawyer Pond, Greenville 151
Schoodic Lake, Lake View Plt, Brownville 151
Sebec Lake, Willimantic, Bowerbank, Dover-Foxcroft, Sebec 151
Seboeis Lake, T4 R9 NWP, Lakeview Plt 151
Second Buttermilk Pond, Bowerbank 151
Second Currier Pond, T9 R11 WELS 151
Second Davis Pond, Guilford, Willimantic 151
Second Debsconeag Lake, T2 R10 WELS 151
Second Little Lyford Pond, Bowdoin College Grant East, Bowdoin College Grant West 152
Second and Third West Branch Ponds, Shawtown Twp 152
Secret Pond, Elliotsville Twp 152
Secret Pond, Greenville 152
Shadow Pond, Cove Point Twp, Greenville, Moosehead Junction Twp 152
Shirley Pond, Shirley 152
Silver Lake, Katahdin Iron Works Twp 152
Sing Sing Pond, T1 R11 WELS 152
Six Ponds, T4 R9 WELS 152
Sixth Debsconeag Pond, Rainbow Twp, T1 R11 WELS 152
Slaughter Pond, T3 R11 WELS 152
Smith Pond, Elliotsville Twp 152
Snake Bog, T7 R11 WELS, *see Stink Pond and Snake Bog*
Snake Pond, T7 R11 WELS 153
Snows Pond, Dover-Foxcroft 153
Soper Pond, Soper Mountain Twp 153
Sourdnahunk Lake, T4 R10 WELS, Nesourdnahunk Twp, T5 R11 WELS, T4 R11 WELS 153
South Twin Lake, T4 Indian Purchase, *see Pemadumcook Chain of Lakes*
Spectacle Pond, Blanchard Plt 153
Spectacle Ponds, Monson 153
Spencer Pond, Spencer Bay Twp, East Middlesex Canal Grant 153
Spider Lake, T9 R11 WELS, T9 R12 WELS ..153
Spring Pond, T7 R10 WELS 153
Spruce Mountain Pond, TB R11 WELS 153
Stink Pond and Snake Bog, T7 R11 WELS ...154
Telos Lake and Round Pond, T6 R11 WELS 154
Ten-Forty Pond, T2 R12 WELS, *see Unnamed Pond*
Thanksgiving Pond, Blanchard Plt 154
Third Buttermilk Pond, Bowerbank, *see Burden Pond*
Third Debsconeag Lake, T2 R10 WELS, T1 R10 WELS 154
Third Lake, T7 R10 WELS 154
Third Matagamon Lake, T7 R10 WELS, *see Third Lake*
Third West Branch Pond, Shawtown Twp, *see Second and Third West Branch Ponds*
Thissell Pond, T5 R11 WELS 154
Tom Young Pond, East Middlesex Canal Grant 154
Tracy Pond, T3 R10 WELS 154
Trout Pond, Bowdoin College Grant West 154
Trout Pond, Moosehead Junction Twp 154
Trout Pond, Shawtown Twp 154
Trout Ponds, T2 R9 WELS, *see Twin Ponds*
Turtle Pond, Lake View Plt 155
Twin Lake, T9 R12 WELS, *see Cliff and Twin Lakes*
Twin Ponds, T2 R9 WELS 155
Umbazooksus Lake, T6 R13 WELS 155
Unnamed Pond, T2 R12 WELS 155
Upper Basin Pond, Mt. Katahdin Twp, *see Basin Ponds*
Upper Bluffer Pond, T8 R11 WELS 155
Upper Doughty Pond, Monson, *see Doughty Ponds*
Upper Ebeemee Lake, T4 R9 NWP, TB R10 WELS 155
Upper Elbow Pond, T10 R10 WELS, T10 R11 WELS 155
Upper Island Pond, T10 R10 WELS 155
Upper Jo-Mary Lake, TB R10 WELS, TA R10 WELS, Veazie Gore 155
Upper Portage Pond, T9 R11 WELS 156
Upper Russell Pond, T9 R14 WELS 156
Upper Soper Pond, T8 R11 WELS 156
Upper South Branch Pond, T5 R9 WELS 156
Upper Togue Pond, T2 R9 WELS 156
Upper Twin Pond, T2 R9 WELS, *see Twin Ponds*
Upper Wilson Pond, Bowdoin College Grant West, Greenville....156
Upper Yoke Pond, TA R11 WELS, *see Yoke Ponds*
Wadleigh Pond, T1 R11 WELS 156
Wadleigh Pond, T8 R15 WELS 156
Wassataquoik Lake, T4 R9 WELS, T4 R10 WELS 156
Webster Lake, T6 R10 WELS, T6 R11 WELS 156
West Chairback Pond, T7 R9 NWP 157
West Pond, T5 R9 NWP, *see Ebeemee Lake*
Whetstone Pond, Blanchard Plt, Kingsbury Plt 157
Whidden Ponds, Mt. Katahdin Twp 157
Woodman Pond, Rainbow Twp 157
Yoke Ponds, TA R11 WELS 157

Sagadahoc County

Center Pond, Phippsburg 157
Lily Pond, Bath, West Bath 157
Mud Pond, Richmond, *see Pleasant Pond*
Nequasset Lake, Woolwich 157
Pleasant Pond, Richmond 157
Sewall Pond, Arrowsic 158
Sprague Pond, Phippsburg 158
Wat-tuh Lake, Phippsburg 158
Winnegance Creek, Phippsburg, West Bath 158
Winnegance Pond, Phippsburg, West Bath, *see Winnegance Creek*

Somerset County

Alder Pond, Alder Brook Twp ... 158
Attean Pond, Attean Twp ... 158
Austin Pond, Bald Mountain Twp ... 158
Baker Lake, T7 R17 WELS ... 158
Baker Pond, Caratunk ... 159
Baker Pond, Solon ... 159
Baker Pond, T5 R6 BKP WKR ... 159
Baker Pond, Tomhegan Twp ... 159
Bald Mountain Pond, Bald Mountain Twp ... 159
Barker Pond, Cornville ... 159
Barrett Pond, Holeb Twp ... 159
Basin Pond, Pierce Pond Twp ... 159
Bean Pond, Pleasant Ridge Plt, *see Beans Pond*
Beans Pond, Pleasant Ridge Plt ... 160
Beck Pond, T3 R5 BKP WKR ... 160
Big Bartley Pond, Holeb Twp ... 160
Big Dimmick Pond, Caratunk ... 160
Big Fish Pond, Holeb Twp, *see Fish Pond*
Big Grenier Pond, T4 R5 NBKP ... 160
Big Indian Pond, St. Albans ... 160
Big Wood Pond, Attean Twp, Jackman, Dennistown Plt, *see Wood Pond*
Bill Morris Pond, T3 R5 BKP WKR ... 160
Black Brook Pond, Moxie Gore ... 161
Black Hill Pond, Embden ... 161
Blakeslee Lake, T5 R6 BKP WKR ... 161
Brassua Lake, Brassua Twp, Taunton and Raynham Academy Grant, Rockwood Strip T1 R1, Rockwood Strip T2 R1, Sandwich Academy Grant, Tomhegan Twp ... 161
Butler Pond, King and Bartlett Twp ... 161
Butler Pond, Lexington Twp, Kingfield ... 162
Cambridge Pond, Cambridge ... 162
Canada Falls Lake, Alder Brook Twp, Pittson Academy Grant, Soldiertown Twp ... 162
Carlton Bog, Troy, *see Waldo County*
Center Pond, Soldiertown Twp ... 162
Chase Pond, Moscow ... 162
Chase Pond, Solon ... 162
Chase Stream Pond, Misery Twp, Chase Stream Twp ... 162
Cheney Pond, Hammond Twp, Prentiss Twp ... 162
Chub Pond, Hobbstown Twp ... 162
Clear Pond, Pleasant Ridge Plt ... 162
Clearwater Pond, Attean Twp ... 163
Clish Pond, T5 R20 WELS ... 163
Coldstream Pond, Misery Twp, Parlin Pond Twp, Johnson Mountain Twp ... 163
Crocker Pond, Dennistown Plt ... 163
Daymond Pond, Moose River ... 163
Dead River Flowage, Dead River Twp, Flagstaff Twp, Bigelow Twp, Carrying Place Town Twp, *see Flagstaff Lake*
Deadstream Pond, West Forks Plt, Chase Stream Plt ... 163
Deer Pond, King and Bartlett Twp ... 163
Demo Pond, Rockwood Strip T2 R1 ... 163
Desolation Pond, T8 R16 WELS ... 163
Dingley Pond, T4 R5 NBKP ... 163
Dixon Pond, Pierce Pond Twp ... 163
Dole Pond, Dole Brook Twp ... 163
Dority Pond, Hammond Twp, Prentiss Twp ... 164
Duncan Pond, Prentiss Twp ... 164
Durgin Pond, Johnson Mountain Twp ... 164
East Carry Pond, Carrying Place Town Twp ... 164
East Pond, Smithfield ... 164
Ellis Pond, Chase Stream Twp ... 164
Embden Pond, Embden ... 164
Enchanted Pond, Upper Enchanted Twp ... 164
Everett Pond, King and Bartlett Twp ... 165
Fahi Pond, Embden ... 165
Felker Pond, King and Bartlett Twp ... 165
Fifth St. John Pond, T5 R17 WELS, T6 R17 WELS ... 165
First St. John Pond, T4 R17 WELS, *see Upper and Lower First St. John Ponds*
Fish Pond, Moxie Gore ... 165
Fish Pond, Holeb Twp ... 165
Fish Pond, Thorndike Twp ... 165
Fisher Pond, T4 R5 NBKP ... 165
Flagstaff Lake, Dead River Twp, Flagstaff Twp, Bigelow Twp, Carrying Place Town Twp ... 165
Fogg Pond, Long Pond Twp ... 166
Foley Pond, Comstock Twp ... 166
Fourth St. John Pond, T5 R17 WELS ... 166
Frost Pond, T4 R5 NBKP ... 166
Frypan Pond, Squaretown Twp ... 166
Gammon Pond, New Portland, Freeman Twp ... 166
Grace Pond, Upper Enchanted Twp ... 166
Grass Pond, Pierce Pond Twp ... 166
Great Moose Lake, Hartland, Harmony, *see Moose Pond*
Halfmoon Pond, St. Albans ... 166
Hall Pond, Prentiss Twp ... 166
Hancock Pond, Embden, Lexington Twp ... 166
Hayden Lake, Madison, *see Wesserunsett Lake*
Heald Pond, Moose River ... 167
Heald Pond, Caratunk, *see Heald Ponds*
Heald Ponds, Caratunk ... 167
Holeb Pond, Holeb Twp, Attean Twp ... 167
Horseshoe Pond, Chase Stream Twp ... 167
Horseshoe Pond, T3 R5 BKP WKR ... 167
Hurricane Pond, T5 R20 WELS ... 167
Indian Pond, Indian Stream Twp, Chase Stream Twp, Sapling Twp ... 167
Indian Pond, Lexington Twp ... 167
Indian Pond, St. Albans, *see Big Indian Pond*
Iron Pond, T5 R6 BKP WKR, Hobbstown Twp ... 168
Ironbound Pond, Alder Brook Twp ... 168
Ironbound Pond, Solon, Athens, *see Wentworth Pond*
Island Pond, Chase Stream Twp ... 168
Jackson Pond, Concord Twp ... 168
Jewett Pond, Pleasant Ridge Plt ... 168
Jones Pond, Bald Mountain Twp ... 168
Kilgore Pond, Pierce Pond Twp, Bowtown Twp ... 168
King and Bartlett Lake, King and Bartlett Twp ... 168
King Pond, Bowtown Twp ... 168
Kingsbury and Mayfield Ponds, Mayfield Twp, Kingsbury Plt, Brighton Plt ... 168
Knights Pond, Moxie Gore ... 169
Lake George, Skowhegan, Canaan ... 169
Lane Pond, Comstock Twp ... 169
Lang and Little Lang Ponds, Parlin Pond Twp ... 169
Lily Pond, Concord Twp ... 169
Little Austin Pond, Bald Mountain Twp ... 169
Little Big Wood Pond, Dennistown Plt, Attean Twp ... 169
Little Chase Stream Pond, Misery Twp ... 169
Little Dimmick Pond, Caratunk ... 169
Little Dingley Pond, T4 R5 NBKP ... 170
Little Enchanted Pond, Upper Enchanted Twp ... 170
Little Fish Pond, Alder Brook Twp ... 170
Little Heald Pond, Caratunk, *see Heald Ponds*
Little Indian Pond, St. Albans ... 170
Little Jim Pond, King and Bartlett Twp, *see Franklin County*
Little King Lake, King and Bartlett Twp ... 170
Little Lane Pond, Hammond Twp ... 170
Little Lang Pond, Parlin Pond Twp, *see Lang and Little Lang Ponds*
Little Long Pond, Chase Stream Twp, *see Long Pond*
Little Otter Pond, Sandwich Academy Grant .. 170
Little Pond, Rome, *see North and Little Ponds*
Little Turner Pond, Forsyth Twp ... 170
Long Pond, Chase Stream Twp ... 170
Long Pond, Dole Brook Twp ... 170
Long Pond, Forsyth Twp, Holeb Twp ... 170
Long Pond, King and Bartlett Twp ... 171
Long Pond, Long Pond Twp, Jackman ... 171
Long Pond, Taunton and Raynham Academy Grant ... 171
Long Pond, The Forks Plt ... 171
Loon Pond, Attean Twp, Holeb Twp ... 171
Lost Pond, Pleasant Ridge Twp ... 171
Lost Pond, Russell Pond Twp ... 171
Lower First St. John Pond, T4, R17 WELS, *see Upper and Lower First St. John Ponds*
Lower Shaw Pond, T3 R4 BKP WKR, *see Shaw and Lower Shaw Ponds*
Lower Welman Pond, Prentiss Twp, *see Welman Ponds*
Luther Pond, Thorndike Twp ... 171
MacDougall Pond, Caratunk ... 172
Martin Pond The Forks Plt, *see Long Pond*
Mary Petuche Pond, Prentiss Twp ... 172
Mayfield Pond, Mayfield Twp, Brighton Twp, *see Kingsbury and Mayfield Ponds*
McKenney Pond, Holeb Twp ... 172
Merrill Pond, Concord Twp, *see Lily Pond*
Middle Carry Pond, Carrying Place Town Twp ... 172
Mill Pond, Pleasant Ridge Plt, *see Clear Pond*
Misery Pond, Misery Twp ... 172
Moore Pond, Bradstreet Twp ... 172
Moose Pond, Bowtown Twp ... 172
Moose Pond, Hartland, Harmony ... 172
Morrill Pond, Hartland ... 173
Mosquito Pond, The Forks Plt ... 173
Mountain Dimmick Pond, Caratunk ... 173
Moxie Pond, East Moxie Twp, The Forks Plt, Bald Mountain Twp ... 173
Nokomis Pond, Newport, Palmyra ... 173
North and Little Ponds, Smithfield, Mercer, Rome ... 173
North Otter Pond, Bowtown Twp ... 173
Oaks Pond, Skowhegan ... 173
Otter Pond, Bowtown Twp ... 173
Otter Pond, Sandwich Academy Grant ... 174
Palmer Pond, Mayfield Twp ... 174
Parker Pond, T3 R5 BKP WKR ... 174

Parlin Pond, Parlin Pond Twp, Johnson Mountain Twp.....174
Penobscot Lake, Dole Brook Twp, Hammond Twp, Prentiss Twp, T4 R5 NBKP.....174
Pickerel Pond, Pierce Pond Twp.....174
Pierce Pond, Pierce Pond Twp, Bowtown Twp.....174
Pleasant Pond, Caratunk, The Forks Plt.....175
Rancourt Pond, Dennistown Plt.....175
Ripley Pond, Ripley.....175
Robinson Pond, Caratunk.....175
Rock Pond, T5 R6 BKP WKR.....175
Roderique Pond, Rockwood Strip T2 R1.....175
Round Pond, Chase Stream Twp.....175
Round Pond, Squaretown Twp.....175
Rowe Pond, Pleasant Ridge Plt.....175
Russell Pond, Russell Pond Twp.....175
Sandy Pond, Embden.....175
Seboomook Lake, Pittston Academy Grant, Plymouth Twp, Seboomook Twp.....176
Second St. John Pond, T4 R17 WELS.....176
Shaw and Lower Shaw Ponds, T3 R4 BKP WKR.....176
Sibley Pond, Canaan, Pittsfield.....176
Smith Pond, Brighton Plt.....176
Smith Pond, Parlin Pond Twp, Misery Twp.....176
Spaulding Pond, Dole Brook Twp.....177
Spectacle Pond, King and Bartlett Twp.....177
Spencer Lake, Hobbstown Twp, T3 R5 BKP WKR.....177
Split Rock Pond, Pierce Pond Twp.....177
Spring Lake, T3 R4 BKP WKR.....177
Spruce Pond, Lexington Twp.....177
Stafford Pond, Hartland.....177
Starbird Pond, Hartland.....178
St. Francis Lake, T8 R16 WELS.....178
Sugar Berth Pond, Dennistown Plt.....178
Supply Pond, Jackman, Moose River.....178
Ten Thousand Acre Pond, Chase Stream Twp.....178
Third St. John Pond, T4 R17 WELS, T5 R17 WELS.....178
Tomhegan Pond, West Middlesex Canal Grant, Soldiertown Twp.....178
Trickey Pond, Alder Brook Twp.....178
Turner Pond, Forsyth Twp.....178
Turner Pond, T7 R16 WELS.....178
Upper and Lower First St. John Ponds, T4 R17 WELS.....178
Upper Dingley Pond, T4 R5 NBKP.....179
Upper Misery Pond, Misery Twp.....179
Upper Welman Pond, Prentiss Twp, *see Welman Ponds*
Weeks Pond, Brighton Plt, *see Smith Pond*
Welman Ponds, Prentiss Twp.....179
Wentworth Pond, Solon, Athens.....179
Wesserunsett Lake, Madison.....179
West Carry Pond, Carrying Place Town Twp.....179
Weymouth Pond, St. Albans, *see Penobscot County*
Whipple Pond, T5 R7 BKP WKR.....179
Whites Pond, Palmyra.....179
Wood Pond, Attean Twp, Jackman, Dennistown Plt.....180
Wyman Lake, Moscow, Pleasant Ridge Plt.....180
Wyman Pond, Brighton Plt.....180

Waldo County

Basin Pond, Monroe.....180
Beech Pond, Palermo.....180
Belden Pond, Palermo.....181
Bowler Pond, Palermo.....181
Branch Pond, Palermo, China.....181
Cain Pond, Searsport.....181
Cargill Pond, Liberty.....181
Carlton Bog, Troy, Detroit, *see Carlton Pond*
Carlton Pond, Troy, Detroit.....181
Chisholm Pond, Palermo.....182
Colby Pond, Liberty.....182
Coleman Pond, Lincolnville.....182
Cross Pond, Morrill.....182
Dave's Pond, Montville, *see Kingdom Bog*
Dolliff Pond, Morrill.....182
Dutton Pond, Knox.....182
Ellis Pond, Brooks.....182
Foster Pond, Palermo.....183
Freedom Pond, Freedom, *see Sandy Pond*
Halfmoon Pond, Brooks.....183
Halfmoon Pond, Searsport.....183
Hurds Pond, Swanville.....183
Jump Pond, Palermo.....183
Kingdom Bog, Montville.....183
Knight Pond, Northport.....183
Lake Passagassawaukeag, Brooks, *see Passagassawaukeag Lake*
Lake Saint George, Liberty, *see Saint George Lake*
Lawry Pond, Searsmont.....183
Ledge Pond, Montville.....184
Levenseller Pond, Searsmont, Lincolnville.....184
Lilly Pond, Montville, *see Kingdom Bog*
Lower Mason Pond, Belfast.....184
Mason Pond, Belfast, *see Lower Mason Pond*
Meadow Pond, Islesboro.....184
Megunticook Lake, Lincolnville, *see Knox County*
Mixer Pond, Knox, Morrill.....184
Moody Pond, Lincolnville.....184
Nichols Pond, Swanville.....184
Norton Pond, Lincolnville.....184
Passagassawaukeag Lake, Brooks.....184
Pitcher Pond, Lincolnville, Northport.....184
Quantabacook Lake, Searsmont, Morrill.....185
Randall Pond, Brooks, *see Passagassawaukeag Lake*
Saban Pond, Palermo.....185
Sanborn Pond, Brooks, Knox.....185
Sandy Pond, Freedom.....185
St. George Lake, Liberty.....185
Sheepscot Pond, Palermo.....186
Smiths Mill Pond, Morrill.....186
Stevens Pond, Liberty.....186
Swan Lake, Swanville, Searsport, Frankfort.....186
Thistle Pond, Monroe.....186
Tilden Pond, Belmont.....186
Toddy Pond, Swanville, Brooks.....187
Trues Pond, Montville, Liberty.....187
Turner Pond, Palermo, *see Lincoln County*
Unity Pond, Unity, Burnham, Troy.....187
Upper Mason Pond, Belfast.....187

Washington County

Bald Ledge Pond, Charlotte, *see Ledge Pond*
Barren Pond, T24 MD BPP.....188
Barrows Lake, Alexander.....188
Baskahegan Lake, Brookton Twp, Topsfield.....188
Beddington Lake, Beddington.....188
Big and Little Greenland Lakes, Danforth.....188
Big Lake, T27 ED BPP, Grand Lake Stream Plt, No. 21 Twp.....188
Bog Lake, Northfield.....189
Bonney Brook Lake, Grand Lake Stream Plt.....189
Bowles Lake, T189 MD BPP.....189
Boyden Lake, Perry, Robbinston.....189
Cathance Lake, No. 14 Plt, Cooper.....189
Chiputneticook Lakes Danforth, *see Grand Lake and Spednik Lake*
Clifford Lake, T26 ED BPP, T27 ED BPP.....189
Coleback Lake, Charlotte.....189
Crawford Lake, Crawford, No. 21 Twp.....190
Crooked Brook Flowage, Danforth.....190
Drake Lake, Forest Twp.....190
Eastern Lake, Robbinston.....190
East Grand Lake, Danforth, Weston, *see Grand Lake*
East Monroe Pond, T43 MD BPP.....190
East Musquash Lake, Topsfield.....190
East Pike Brook Pond, T18 MD BPP.....190
Farrow Lake, Topsfield.....191
Fifth Machias Lake, T36 MD BPP.....191
First Chain Lake, T26 ED BPP.....191
First Machias Lake, T37 MD BPP.....191
First Mopang Lake, T30 MD BPP.....191
Fourth Machias Lake, T5 ND BPP, T42 MD BPP.....191
Fulton Lake, Northfield.....191
Gardner Lake, East Machias, Marion Twp, Whiting.....191
Goulding Lake, Robbinston.....191
Grand Lake, Danforth, Weston.....192
Hadley Lake, East Machias.....192
Hobart Lake, Edmunds Twp.....192
Horseshoe Lake, Lakeville, T5 R1 NBPP, T5 ND BPP, *see Penobscot County*
Horseshoe Pond, T18 MD BPP.....192
Hosea Pug Lake, T26 ED BPP.....192
Howard Lake, Calais, Robbinston.....193
Indian Lake, Whiting.....193
Jackson Brook Lake, Brookton Twp, Forest Twp.....193
James Pond, Charlotte.....193
Keeley Lake, Marshfield.....193
Keenes Lake, Calais.....193
LaCoute Lake, Vanceboro.....193
Lake Cathance, No. 14 Plt, Cooper, *see Cathance Lake*
Lambert Lake, Lambert Lake Twp, T11 R3 NBPP.....193
Ledge Pond, Charlotte.....193
Lily Lake, Trescott Twp.....193
Lily Lake, T30 MD BPP.....194
Little Cathance Lake, No. 14 Plt.....194
Little Greenland Lake, Danforth, *see Big and Little Greenland Lakes*
Little Lily Lake, Marshfield, East Machias.....194
Little Pickerel Pond, Brookton Twp.....194
Little Tomah Lake, Topsfield, Codyville Plt.....194
Long Lake, Princeton, Indian Twp.....194
Long Lake, T18 ED BPP, T19 ED BPP, Wesley, Northfield.....194
Love Lake, T19 ED BPP, Crawford.....194
Lower Hot Brook Lake, Danforth, T8 R4 NBPP.....194

Lower Oxbrook Lake, T6 ND BPP, T6 R1 NBPP 194
Marks Lake, Marshfield 194
Meddybemps Lake, Meddybemps, Alexander, Baileyville, Baring Plt 195
Moneymaker Lake, Robbinston 195
Monroe Lake, T43 MD BPP 195
Montegail Pond, T19 MD BPP 195
Mopang First Lake, T30 MD BPP, *see First Mopang Lake*
Mopang Lake, Devereaux Twp 195
Mopang Second Lake, Devereaux Twp, T30 MD BPP, *see Second Mopang Lake*
Nash's Lake, Calais 195
North Beaverdam Lake, T26 ED BPP 195
North Myers Pond, Columbia 196
Orange Lake, Whiting 196
Orie Lake, T6 R1 NBPP, Kossuth Twp 196
Otter Lake, Wesley 196
Patrick Lake, Marion Twp, No. 14 Plt 196
Peaked Mountain Pond, T19 MD BPP, Northfield, Centerville 196
Peep Lake, T30 MD BPP 196
Pennamaquan Lake, Charlotte 196
Pickerel Pond, Topsfield 196
Pineo Pond, Deblois 196
Pleasant Lake, Alexander 196
Pleasant Lake, Kossuth Twp, T6 R1 NBPP 197
Pleasant River Lake, Beddington, Devereaux Twp 197
Pocomoonshine Lake, Princeton, Alexander 197
Pocumcus Lake, T5 ND BPP, T6 ND BPP 197
Possum Lake, T26 ED BPP 197
Pug Lake, T26 ED BPP 198
Rand Lake, Robbinston 198
Roaring Lake, Whiting 198
Rocky and Sunken Lakes, Whiting, Marion Twp, Edmunds Twp 198
Rocky Lake, T18 ED BPP 198
Round Lake, Charlotte 198
Round Lake, T18 ED BPP, T19 ED BPP 198
Round Pond, Steuben, T7 SD, T10 SD 198
Salmon Pond, T30 MD BPP 198
Sam Hill Lake, T199 MD BPP 199
Schoodic Lake, T18 MD BPP, Cherryfield, Columbia 199
Scraggly Lake, T5 R1 NBPP, T6 R1 NBPP, *see Penobscot County*
Second Lake, Marion Twp 199
Second and Third Lakes, T37 MD BPP 199
Second Chain Lake, T199 MD BPP, T37 MD BPP, T26 ED BPP 199
Second Machias Lake T37 MD BPP 199
Second Marks Lake, Marshfield 199
Second Mopang Lake, Devereaux Twp, T30 MD BPP 199
Shattuck Lake, Robbinston, Calais 200
Shaw Lake, T6 R1 NBPP, T5 R1 NBPP 200
Silver Pug Lake, T26 ED BPP, *see Pug Lake*
Six Mile Lake, Marshfield 200
South Beaverdam Lake, T26 ED BPP 200
Southwest Pond, Beddington 200
Spednik Lake, Forest Twp, T11 R3 NBPP, Vanceboro 200
Spruce Mountain Lake, Beddington 201
Sucker Lake Danforth, Weston 201
Sunken Lake, Whiting, *see Rocky and Sunken Lakes*
Third Chain Lake, T26 ED BPP 201
Third Lake, T37 MD BPP, *see Second and Third Lakes*
Third Machias Lake, T42 MD BPP, T43 MD BPP 201
Trout Lake, Kossuth Twp 201
Trout Lake, T31 MD BPP 201
Unnamed Pond, T31 MD BPP 201
Upper Hot Brook Lake, T8 R4 NBPP, Danforth 201
Upper Oxbrook Lake, T6 R1 NBPP, Talmadge 202
Vining Lake, Cooper, No. 14 Plt 202
Wabassus Lake, T5 ND BPP, T6 ND BPP, T43 MD BPP 202
Western Lake, Robbinston 202
West Grand Lake, T5 ND BPP, T6 R1 NBPP, T6 ND BPP, Grand Lake Stream Plt 202
West Monroe Pond, T43 MD BPP 202
West Musquash Lake, T6 R1 NBPP, Talmadge 203
West Pike Brook Pond, T18 MD BPP 203

York County

Adams Pond, Newfield 203
Alewife Pond, Kennebunk 203
Balch Pond, Newfield 203
Barker Pond, Lyman, *see Parker Pond*
Bartlett Pond, Waterboro, Lyman 203
Bauneg Beg Pond, Sanford, North Berwick 203
Beaver Dam Pond, Berwick 203
Blake's Mill Pond, Limington, *see Webster's Mill Pond*
Bonny Eagle Lake, Buxton, Standish 204
Bonny Pond, Buxton, Standish *see Bonny Eagle Lake*
Boyd Pond, Limington 204
Brimstone Pond, Arundel 204
Bunganut Pond, Lyman 204
Cox Pond, South Berwick 204
Deer Pond, Hollis 204
Deering Pond, Sanford 205
Doles Pond, Limington 205
Duck Pond, Buxton 205
Ell Pond, Sanford 205
Estes Lake, Sanford, Alfred 205
Granny Kent Pond, Shapleigh 205
Great East Lake, Acton 205
Hansen Pond, Acton, Shapleigh 206
Hatfield Pond, Berwick, *see Murdock Lake*
Hidden Lake, Newfield, *see Pinkham Pond*
Holland Pond, Limerick 206
Horn Pond, Acton 206
Horne Pond, Limington 206
Isinglass Pond, Limington, Waterboro 206
Kennebunk Pond, Lyman 206
Killick Pond, Hollis 207
Knights Pond, South Berwick 207
Lake Caroline, York, *see Passaconway Pond*
Lake Murdock, Berwick, *see Murdock Lake*
Leighs Mill Pond, South Berwick 207
Little Boyd Pond, Limington, *see Unnamed Pond*
Little Ossipee Pond, Waterboro, *see Little Ossipee Lake*
Little Ossipee River Flowage, Waterboro, Limerick 207
Little Ossipee Lake, Waterboro 207
Lone Pond, Waterboro 208
Long Pond, Parsonfield 208
Loon Pond, Acton 208
L Pond, Sanford, *see Ell Pond*
Middle Branch Pond, Waterford, Alfred 208
Milton Pond, Lebanon, *see Town House and Milton Ponds*
Mirror Lake, Newfield, *see Turner Pond*
Moody Pond, Waterboro 208
Moose Pond, Acton 208
Mousam Lake, Shapleigh, Acton 208
Mud Pond, Newfield 209
Murdock Lake, Berwick 209
Northeast Pond, Lebanon 209
North Shapleigh Pond, Shapleigh, Newfield 209
Northwest Pond, Waterboro 210
Parker Pond, Lyman 210
Passaconway Pond, York 210
Pequawket Lake, Limington, *see Horne Pond*
Pickerel Pond, Limerick 210
Pinkham Pond, Newfield 210
Poverty Pond, Newfield 210
Province Lake, Parsonfield 210
Roberts and Wadley Ponds, Lyman 211
Rock Haven Lake, Newfield, *see Adams Pond*
Round Pond, Lyman, Dayton 211
Round Pond, Newfield 211
Sand Pond, Limington 211
Scituate Pond, York 211
Shaker Pond, Alfred 211
Shapleigh Pond, Shapleigh, Newfield, *see North Shapleigh Pond*
Smarts Pond, Newfield 212
Sokokis Lake, Limerick, *see Holland Pond*
Spaulding Pond, Lebanon 212
Square Pond, Acton, Shapleigh 212
Swan Pond, Acton 212
Swan Pond, Lyman 212
Symmes Pond, Newfield 212
Town House and Milton Ponds, Lebanon 213
Turner Pond, Newfield 213
Unnamed Pond, Limington 213
Wadley Pond, Lyman, *see Roberts and Wadley Ponds*
Wards Pond, Limington 213
Warren Pond, South Berwick 213
Webster's Mill Pond, Limington 213
West Pond, Parsonfield 214
Wilcox Pond, Biddeford 214
Wilson Lake, Acton 214
York Pond, Eliot 214

List of Abbreviations

BrT	Brown Trout	LmB	Largemouth Bass
BkT	Brook Trout	SmB	Smallmouth Bass
RbT	Rainbow Trout	WhP	White Perch
Sal	Landlocked Salmon	Csk	Cusk
Tog	Togue (Lake Trout)	WhF	Whitefish
Smt	Smelt	Pic	Pickerel

Androscoggin County

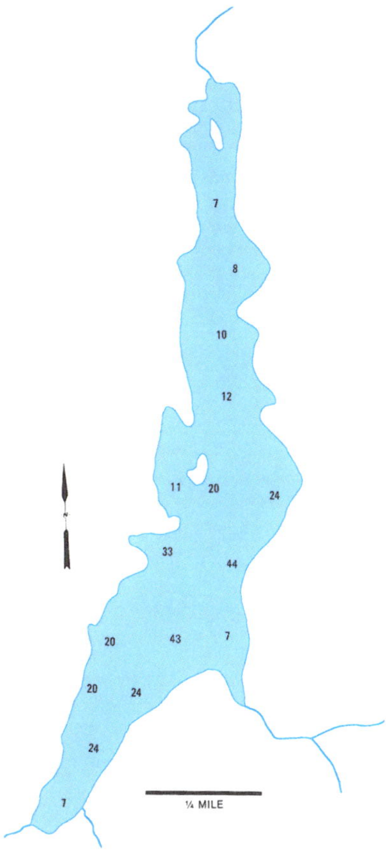

Allen Pond

Greene, Maine Atlas Map 12, D-1
Acres: 183, Max. Depth: 44 feet

BrT	BkT	RbT	Sal	Tog	Smt	LmB	SmB	WhP	Csk	WhF	Pic
✓	✓	✓				✓	✓	✓			✓

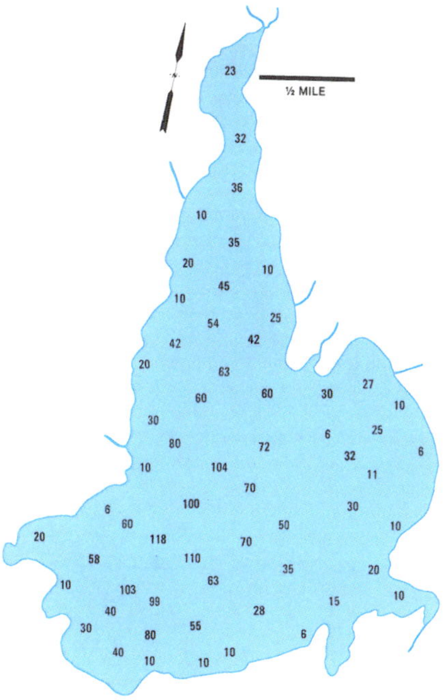

Auburn Lake

Auburn, Maine Atlas Map 11, E-4
Acres: 2,260, Max. Depth: 118 feet, Boat Launch

BrT	BkT	RbT	Sal	Tog	Smt	LmB	SmB	WhP	Csk	WhF	Pic
	✓		✓	✓	✓		✓	✓			✓

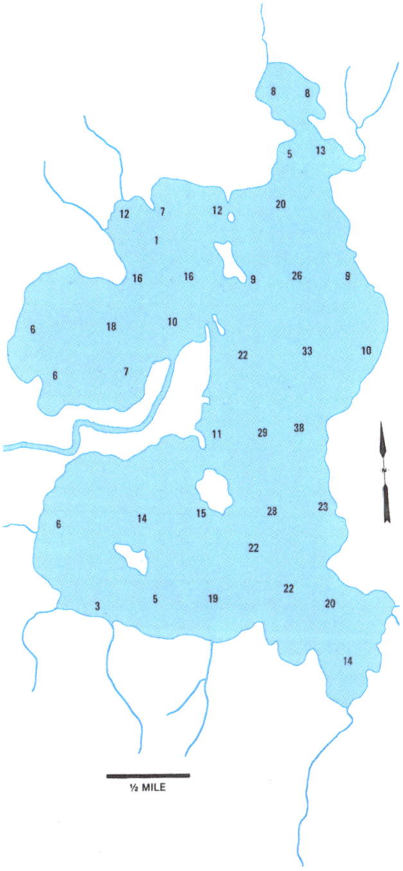

Androscoggin Lake

Leeds, Maine Atlas Map 12, C-1
Acres: 3,826, Max. Depth: 38 feet, Boat Launch

BrT	BkT	RbT	Sal	Tog	Smt	LmB	SmB	WhP	Csk	WhF	Pic
✓	✓				✓	✓	✓	✓	✓		✓

Bartlett Pond

Livermore
Maine Atlas
Map 11, B-5
Acres: 26
Max. Depth:
26 feet

BrT	LmB
BkT ✓	SmB
RbT	WhP
Sal	Csk
Tog	WhF
Smt	Pic

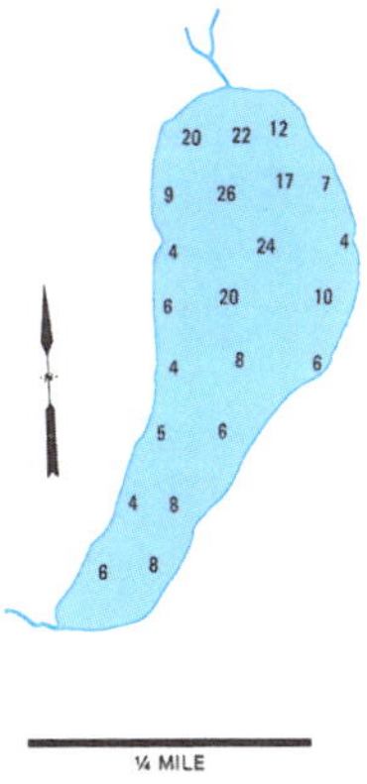

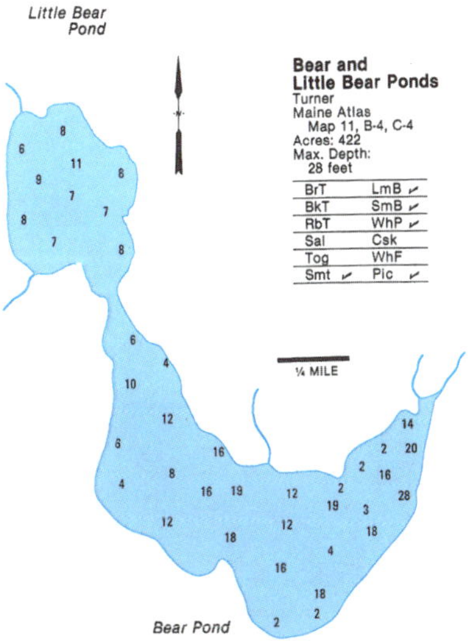

Bear and Little Bear Ponds

Turner
Maine Atlas
Map 11, B-4, C-4
Acres: 422
Max. Depth:
28 feet

BrT	LmB ✓
BkT	SmB ✓
RbT	WhP ✓
Sal	Csk
Tog	WhF
Smt ✓	Pic ✓

Androscoggin

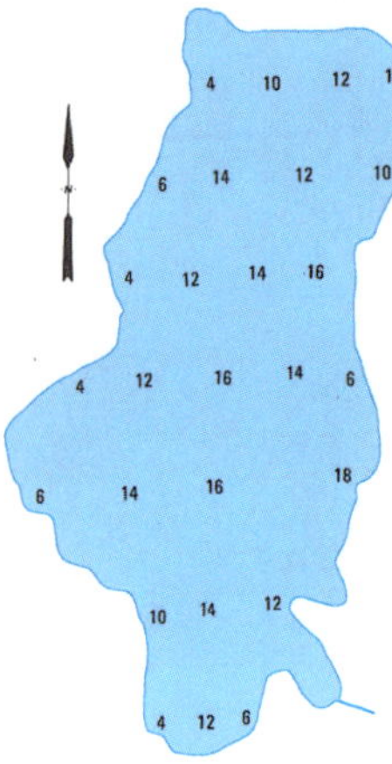

Berry Pond
Greene
Maine Atlas
Map 11, D-5
Acres: 31
Max. Depth:
16 feet

BrT	LmB
BkT	SmB ✓
RbT	WhP
Sal	Csk
Tog	WhF
Smt	Pic ✓

Island Pond
Leeds
Maine Atlas
Map 12, C-1
Acres: 18
Max. Depth:
30 feet

BrT	LmB
BkT	SmB ✓
RbT	WhP
Sal	Csk
Tog	WhF
Smt	Pic ✓

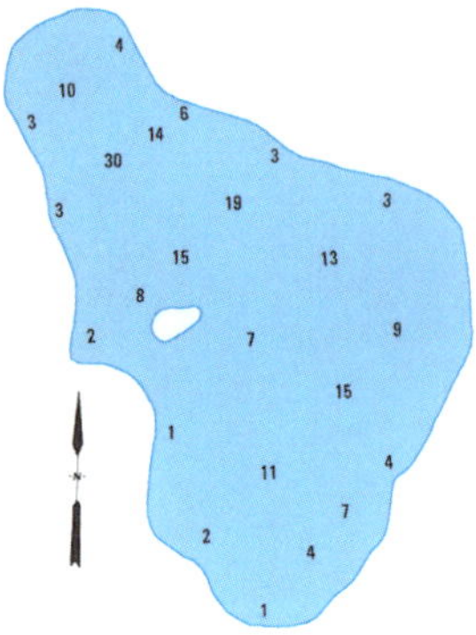

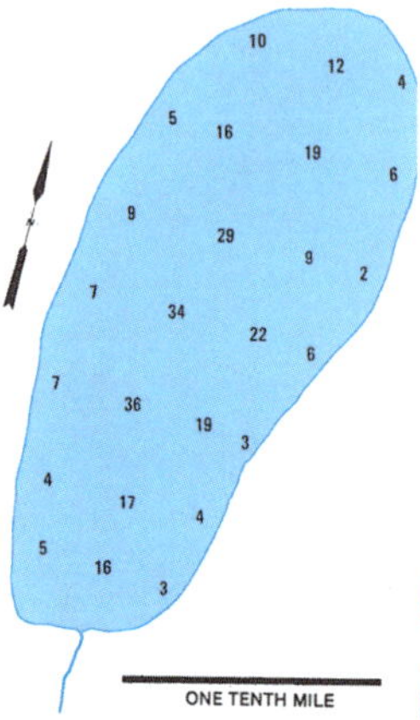

Black Pond
Turner
Maine Atlas
Map 11, D-4
Acres: 12
Max. Depth:
36 feet

BrT	LmB
BkT ✓	SmB
RbT	WhP
Sal	Csk
Tog	WhF
Smt	Pic

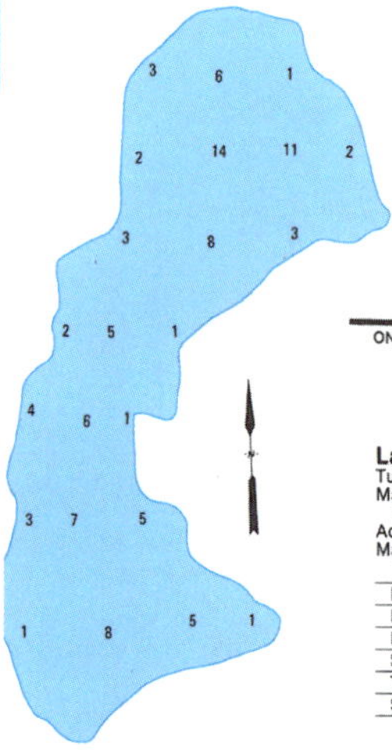

Lard Pond
Turner
Maine Atlas
Map 11, D-5
Acres: 14
Max. Depth:
14 feet

BrT	LmB ✓
BkT	SmB
RbT	WhP ✓
Sal	Csk
Tog	WhF
Smt	Pic ✓

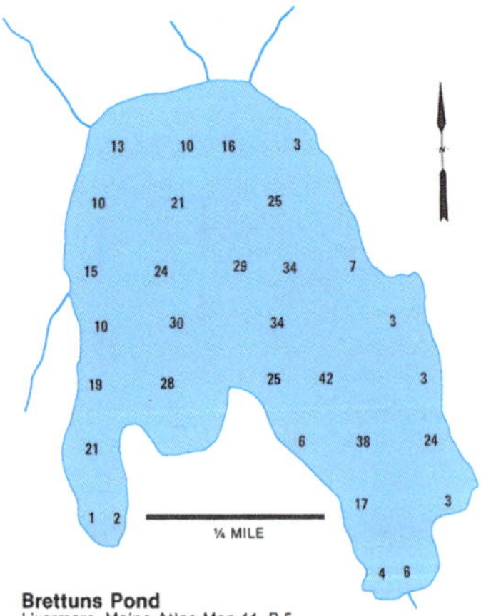

Brettuns Pond
Livermore, Maine Atlas Map 11, B-5
Acres: 154, Max. Depth: 42 feet, Boat Launch

BrT	BkT	RbT	Sal	Tog	Smt	LmB	SmB	WhP	Csk	WhF	Pic
✓	✓				✓		✓	✓			✓

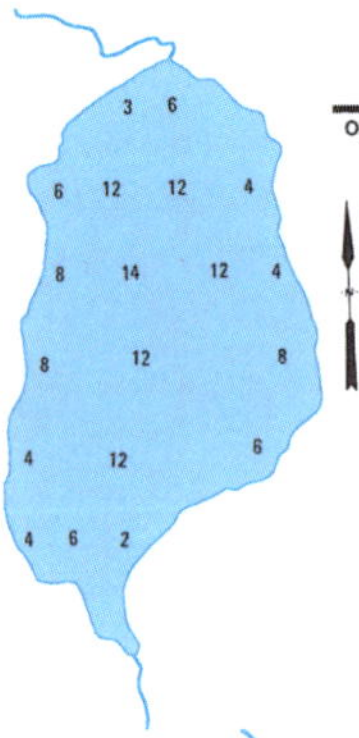

Little Sabattus Pond
Greene
Maine Atlas
Map 12, D-1
Acres: 25
Max. Depth:
14 feet
Boat Launch

BrT	LmB
BkT	SmB
RbT	WhP
Sal	Csk
Tog	WhF
Smt	Pic ✓

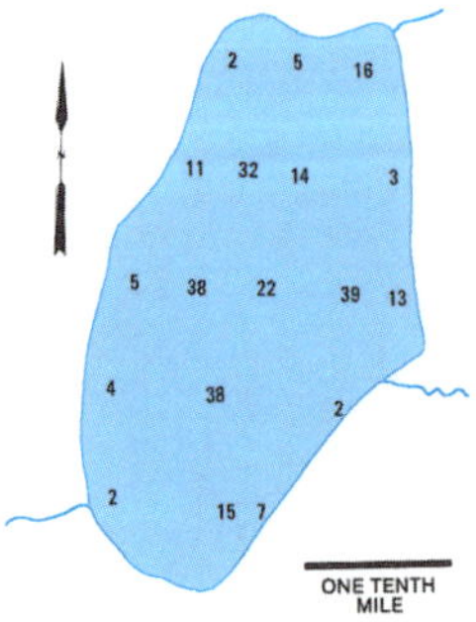

Crystal Pond
Turner
Maine Atlas
Map 11, C-4
Acres: 35
Max. Depth:
39 feet

BrT ✓	LmB ✓
BkT ✓	SmB ✓
RbT	WhP ✓
Sal	Csk
Tog	WhF
Smt ✓	Pic ✓

Little Wilson Pond
Turner
Maine Atlas
Map 11, D-4
Acres: 111
Max. Depth:
56 feet

BrT ✓	LmB ✓
BkT ✓	SmB
RbT	WhP
Sal	Csk
Tog	WhF
Smt ✓	Pic ✓

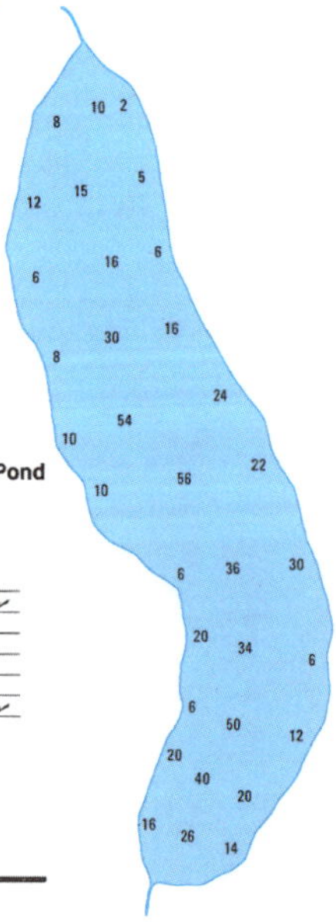

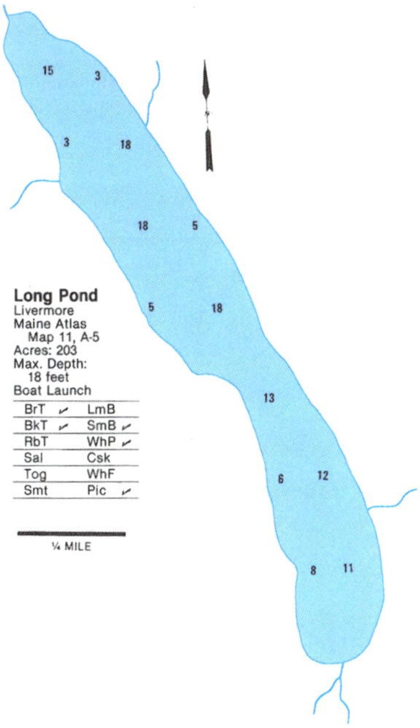

Long Pond
Livermore
Maine Atlas
Map 11, A-5
Acres: 203
Max. Depth:
18 feet
Boat Launch

BrT	✓	LmB	
BkT	✓	SmB	✓
RbT		WhP	✓
Sal		Csk	
Tog		WhF	
Smt		Pic	✓

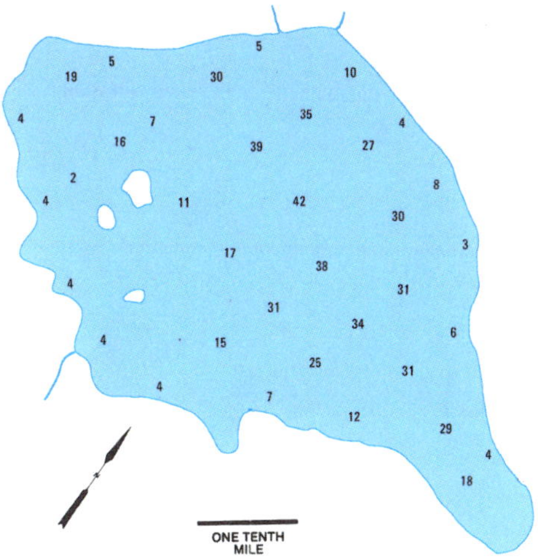

Moose Hill Pond
Livermore Falls, Maine Atlas Map 12, A-1
Acres: 99, Max. Depth: 42 feet.

BrT	BkT	RbT	Sal	Tog	Smt	LmB	SmB	WhP	Csk	WhF	Pic
							✓				✓

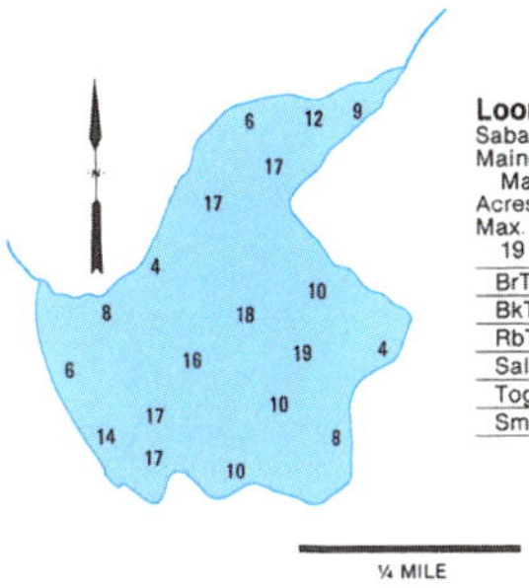

Loon Pond
Sabattus
Maine Atlas
Map 12, E-2
Acres: 70
Max. Depth:
19 feet

BrT		LmB	
BkT		SmB	✓
RbT		WhP	✓
Sal		Csk	
Tog		WhF	
Smt		Pic	✓

Nelson Pond
Livermore
Maine Atlas
Map 11, A-4, B-4
Acres: 11
Max. Depth:
16 feet

BrT		LmB	
BkT		SmB	✓
RbT		WhP	
Sal		Csk	
Tog		WhF	
Smt		Pic	✓

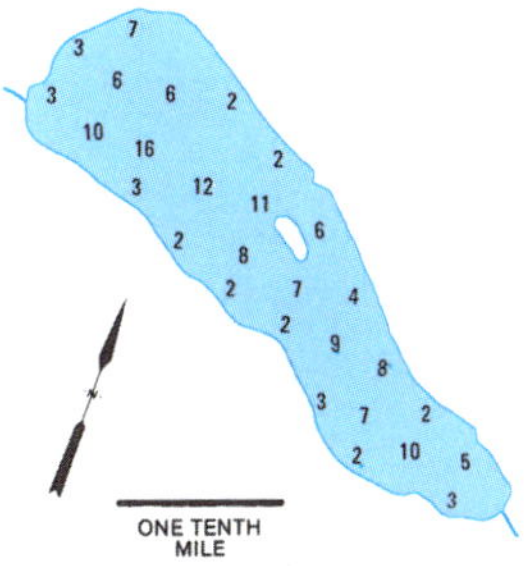

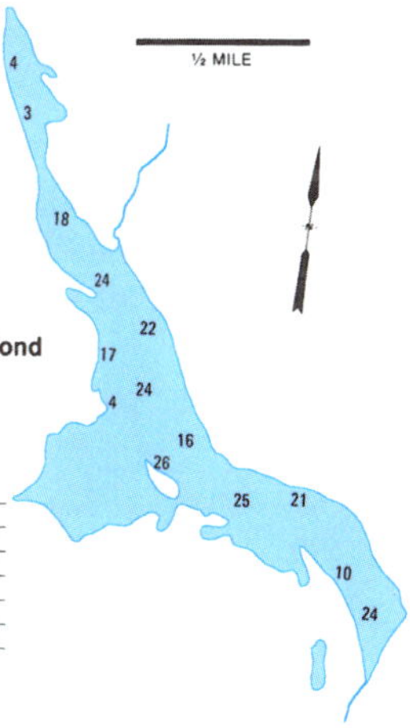

Lower Range Pond
Poland
Maine Atlas
Map 5, A-3
Acres: 290
Max. Depth:
41 feet
Boat Launch

BrT	✓	LmB	
BkT	✓	SmB	✓
RbT		WhP	✓
Sal		Csk	
Tog		WhF	
Smt		Pic	✓

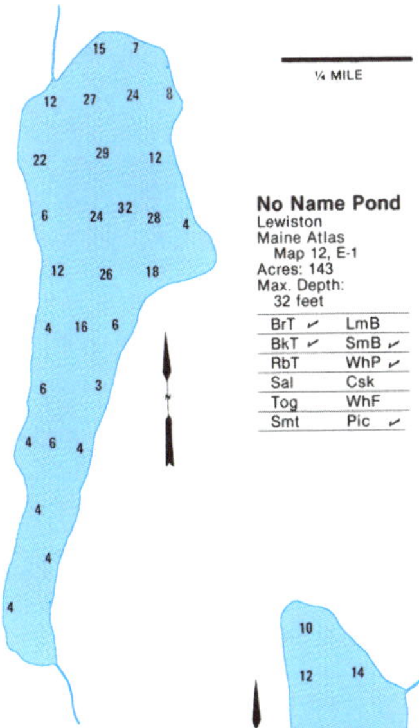

No Name Pond
Lewiston
Maine Atlas
Map 12, E-1
Acres: 143
Max. Depth:
32 feet

BrT	✓	LmB	
BkT	✓	SmB	✓
RbT		WhP	✓
Sal		Csk	
Tog		WhF	
Smt		Pic	✓

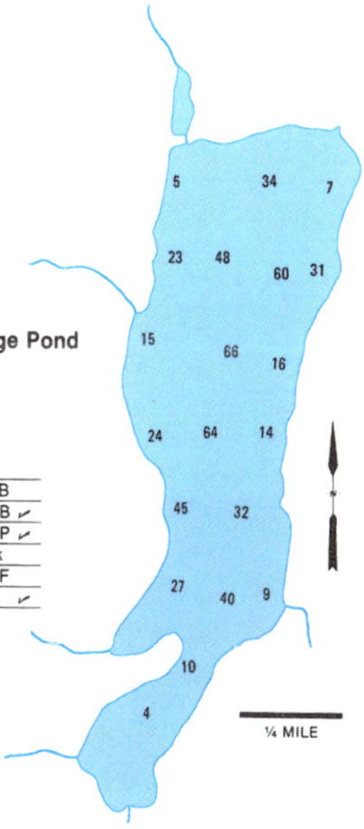

Middle Range Pond
Poland
Maine Atlas
Map 5, A-3
Acres: 366
Max. Depth:
66 feet
Boat Launch

BrT	✓	LmB	
BkT	✓	SmB	✓
RbT	✓	WhP	✓
Sal	✓	Csk	
Tog	✓	WhF	
Smt	✓	Pic	✓

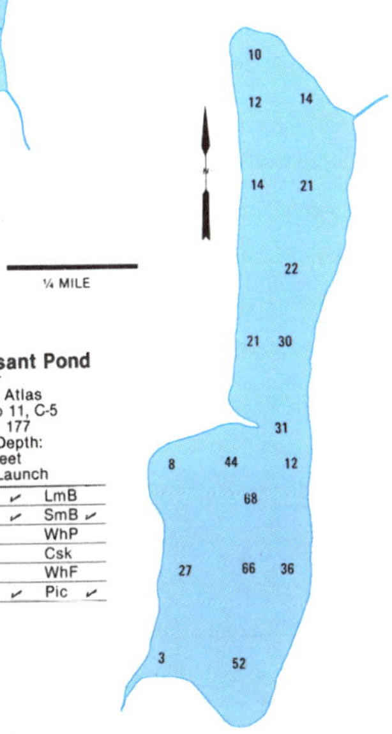

Pleasant Pond
Turner
Maine Atlas
Map 11, C-5
Acres: 177
Max. Depth:
68 feet
Boat Launch

BrT	✓	LmB	
BkT	✓	SmB	✓
RbT		WhP	
Sal		Csk	
Tog		WhF	
Smt	✓	Pic	✓

Androscoggin

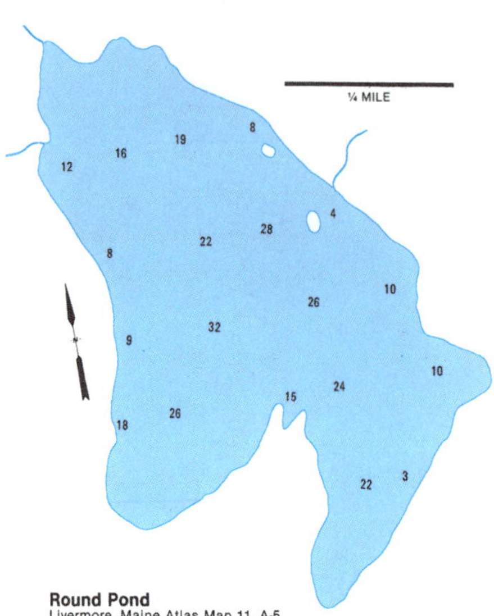

Round Pond
Livermore, Maine Atlas Map 11, A-5
Acres: 166, Max. Depth: 32 feet

BrT	BkT	RbT	Sal	Tog	Smt	LmB	SmB	WhP	Csk	WhF	Pic
✓	✓				✓		✓	✓			✓

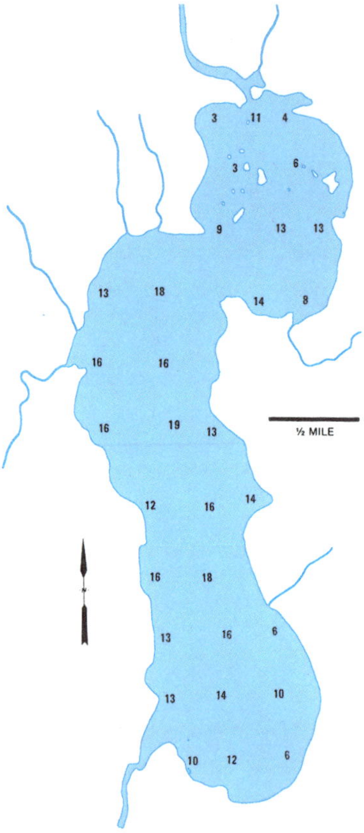

Sabattus Pond
Greene, Sabattus, Wales, Maine Atlas Map 12, E-1
Acres: 1,787, Max. Depth: 19 feet, Boat Launch

BrT	BkT	RbT	Sal	Tog	Smt	LmB	SmB	WhP	Csk	WhF	Pic
					✓	✓	✓	✓			✓

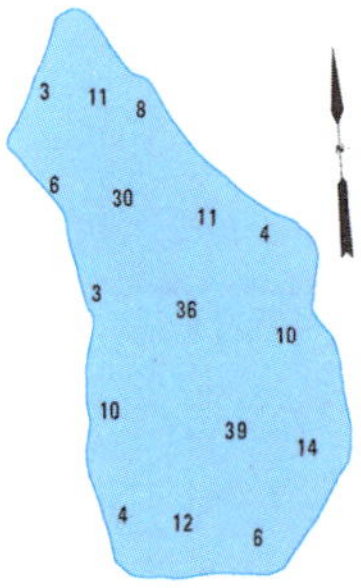

ONE TENTH MILE

Round Pond
Turner
Maine Atlas
Map 11, D-5
Acres: 12
Max. Depth:
39 feet

BrT	✓	LmB	
BkT		SmB	
RbT		WhP	
Sal		Csk	
Tog		WhF	
Smt		Pic	✓

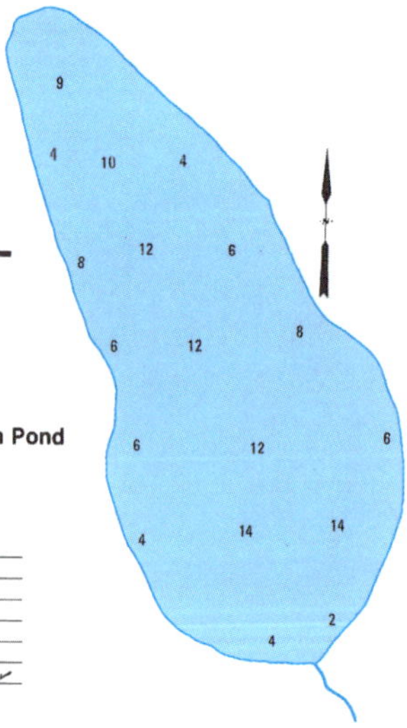

ONE TENTH MILE

Sandy Bottom Pond
Turner
Maine Atlas
Map 11, D-4
Acres: 25
Max. Depth:
14 feet

BrT		LmB	
BkT		SmB	
RbT		WhP	
Sal		Csk	
Tog		WhF	
Smt		Pic	✓

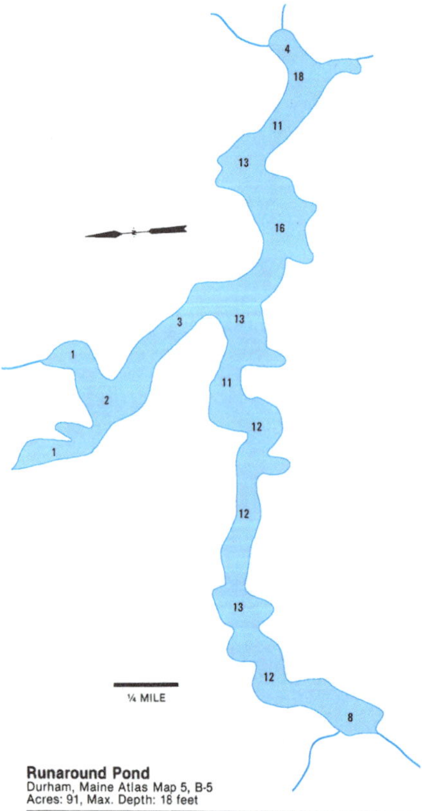

Runaround Pond
Durham, Maine Atlas Map 5, B-5
Acres: 91, Max. Depth: 18 feet

BrT	BkT	RbT	Sal	Tog	Smt	LmB	SmB	WhP	Csk	WhF	Pic
						✓					✓

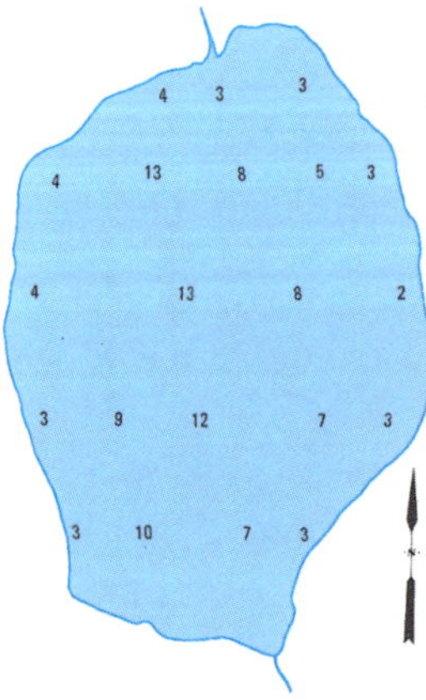

ONE TENTH MILE

School House Pond
Livermore Falls
Maine Atlas
Map 12, A-1
Acres: 19
Max. Depth:
13 feet

BrT		LmB	✓
BkT		SmB	
RbT		WhP	
Sal		Csk	
Tog		WhF	
Smt		Pic	✓

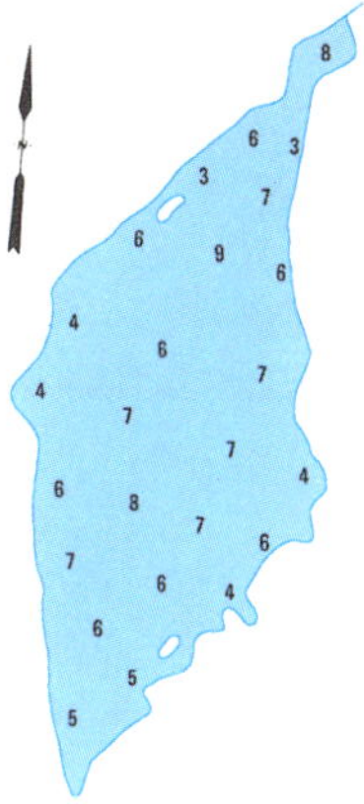

Sutherland Pond
Sabattus
Maine Atlas
Map 12, E-2
Acres: 53
Max. Depth:
9 feet

BrT		LmB	
BkT		SmB	
RbT		WhP	
Sal		Csk	
Tog		WhF	
Smt		Pic	✓

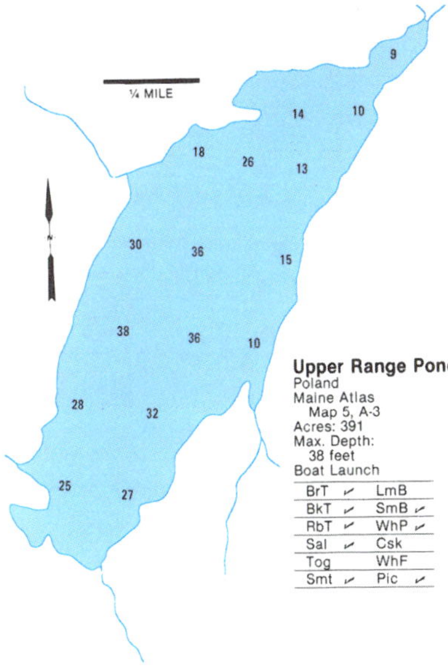

Upper Range Pond
Poland
Maine Atlas
Map 5, A-3
Acres: 391
Max. Depth:
38 feet
Boat Launch

BrT	✓	LmB	
BkT	✓	SmB	✓
RbT	✓	WhP	✓
Sal	✓	Csk	
Tog		WhF	
Smt	✓	Pic	✓

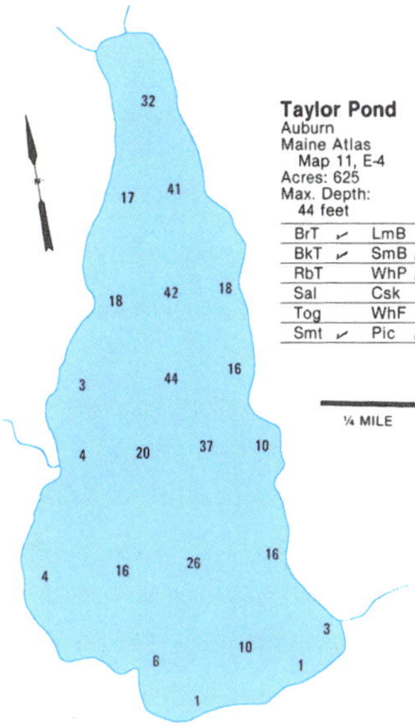

Taylor Pond
Auburn
Maine Atlas
Map 11, E-4
Acres: 625
Max. Depth:
44 feet

BrT	✓	LmB	
BkT	✓	SmB	✓
RbT		WhP	✓
Sal		Csk	
Tog		WhF	
Smt	✓	Pic	✓

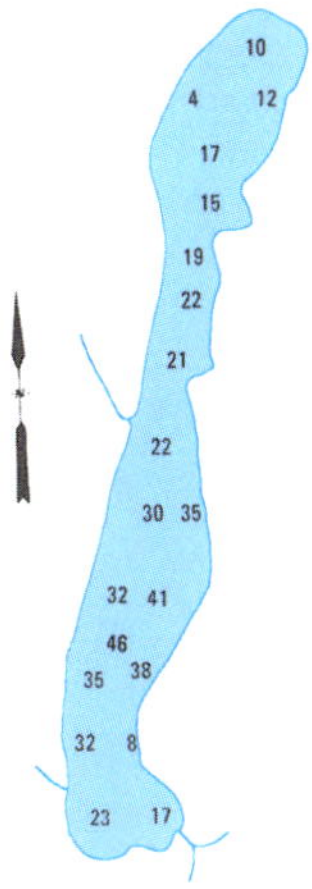

Worthley Pond
Poland
Maine Atlas
Map 5, A-3
Acres: 42
Max. Depth:
46 feet

BrT	✓	LmB	
BkT	✓	SmB	
RbT		WhP	
Sal		Csk	
Tog		WhF	
Smt		Pic	✓

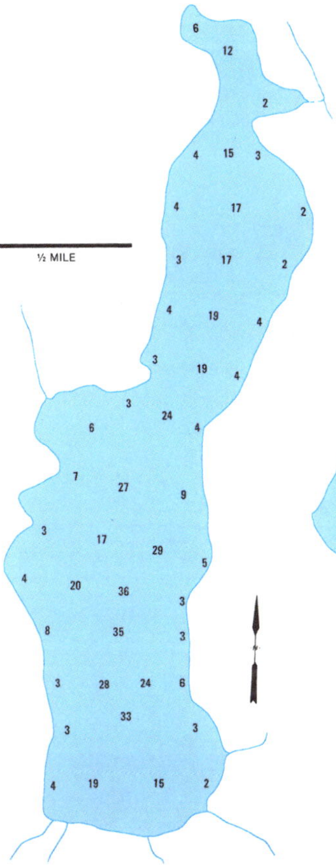

Tripp Pond
Poland, Maine Atlas Map 5, A-2
Acres: 768, Max. Depth: 36 feet.

BrT	BkT	RbT	Sal	Tog	Smt	LmB	SmB	WhP	Csk	WhF	Pic
✓	✓		✓		✓	✓	✓	✓	✓		✓

Aroostook County

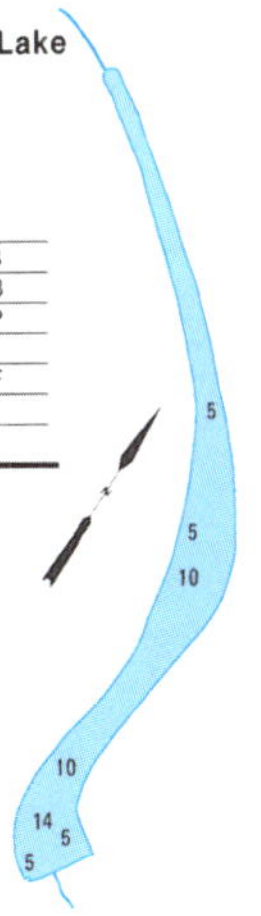

Alder Brook Lake
Chapman
Maine Atlas
Map 64, E-5
Acres: 16
Max. Depth:
14 feet
Boat Launch

BrT		LmB	
BkT	✓	SmB	
RbT		WhP	
Sal		Csk	
Tog		WhF	
Smt		Pic	

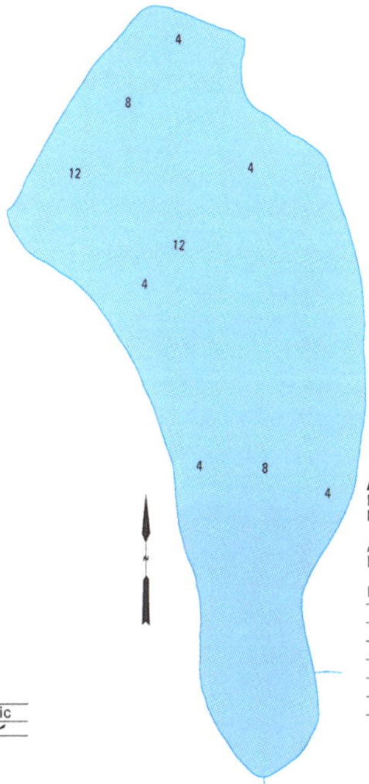

Arnold Brook Lake
Presque Isle
Maine Atlas
Map 65, E-1
Acres: 395
Max. Depth:
12 feet
Boat Launch

BrT		LmB	
BkT	✓	SmB	
RbT		WhP	
Sal		Csk	
Tog		WhF	
Smt		Pic	

Aroostook

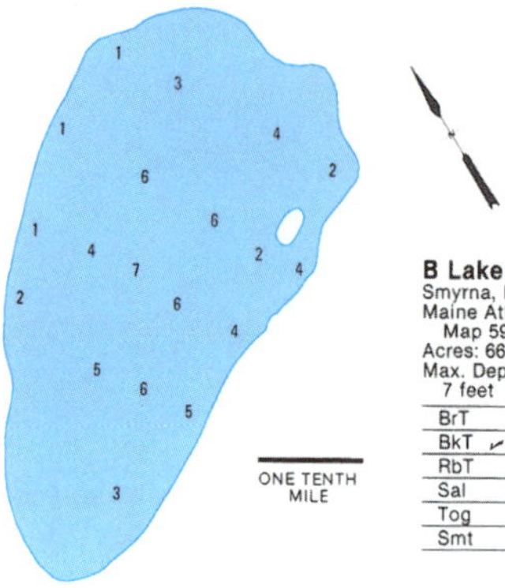

B Lake
Smyrna, Hammond
Maine Atlas
Map 59, E-1
Acres: 66
Max. Depth:
7 feet

BrT	LmB
BkT ✓	SmB
RbT	WhP
Sal	Csk
Tog	WhF
Smt	Pic

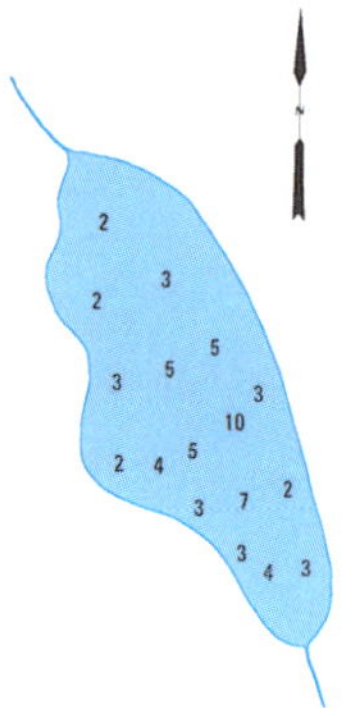

Bennett Lake
Easton
Maine Atlas
Map 65, E-3
Acres: 12
Max. Depth:
10 feet

BrT	LmB
BkT ✓	SmB
RbT	WhP
Sal	Csk
Tog	WhF
Smt	Pic

ONE TENTH MILE

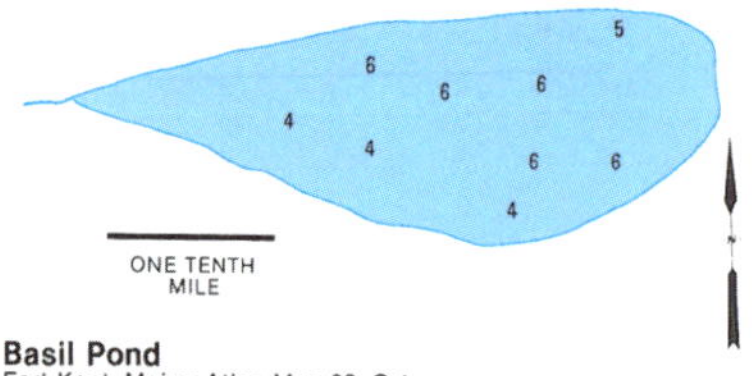

Basil Pond
Fort Kent, Maine Atlas Map 68, C-1
Acres: 19, Max. Depth: 6 feet, Boat Launch

BrT	BkT	RbT	Sal	Tog	Smt	LmB	SmB	WhP	Csk	WhF	Pic
	✓										

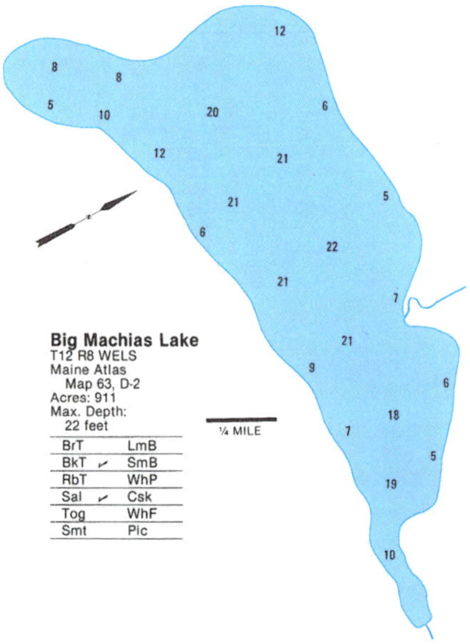

Big Machias Lake
T12 R8 WELS
Maine Atlas
Map 63, D-2
Acres: 911
Max. Depth:
22 feet

BrT	LmB
BkT ✓	SmB
RbT	WhP
Sal ✓	Csk
Tog	WhF
Smt	Pic

Beau Lake
T19 R11 WELS,
Big Twenty Twp
Maine Atlas
Map 66, A-4, B-4
Acres: 2,003
Max. Depth:
168 feet
Boat Launch

BrT	LmB
BkT ✓	SmB
RbT	WhP
Sal ✓	Csk ✓
Tog ✓	WhF ✓
Smt	Pic

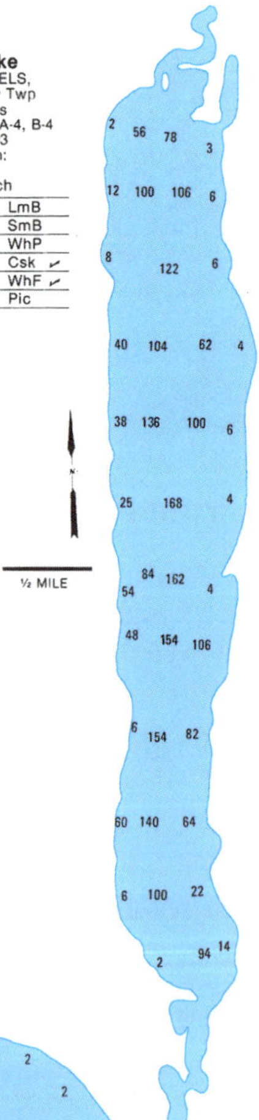

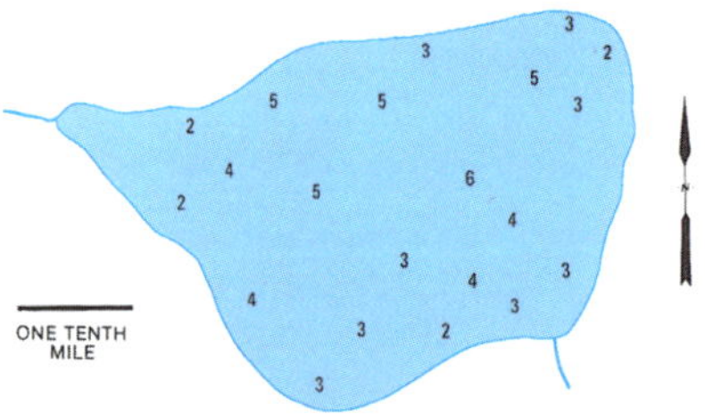

Billings Pond
T11 R9 WELS, Maine Atlas Map 63, E-1
Acres: 64, Max. Depth: 6 feet

BrT	BkT	RbT	Sal	Tog	Smt	LmB	SmB	WhP	Csk	WhF	Pic
	✓										

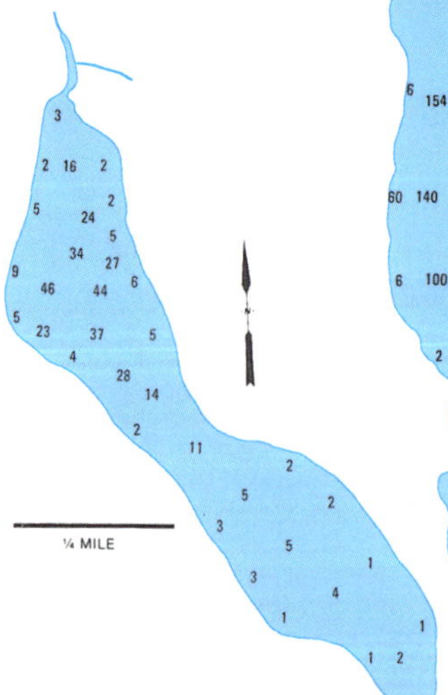

Beaver Tail Pond
T14 R9 WELS, T14 R10 WELS, Maine Atlas Map 62, B-5
Acres: 128, Max. Depth: 46 feet

BrT	BkT	RbT	Sal	Tog	Smt	LmB	SmB	WhP	Csk	WhF	Pic
	✓										

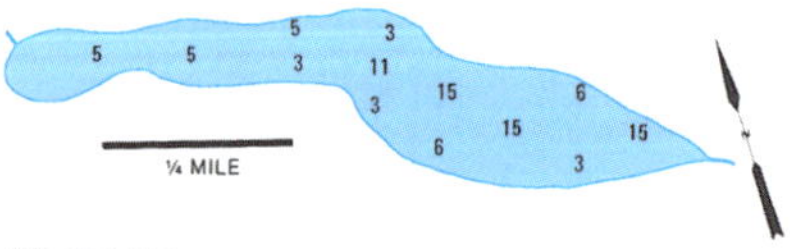

Black Lake
Fort Kent, Maine Atlas Map 68, C-1
Acres: 51, Max. Depth: 15 feet, Boat Launch

BrT	BkT	RbT	Sal	Tog	Smt	LmB	SmB	WhP	Csk	WhF	Pic
	✓										

Ben Lake
Wallagrass Plt
Maine Atlas
Map 67, D-4
Acres: 37
Max. Depth:
32 feet
Boat Launch

BrT	LmB
BkT ✓	SmB
RbT	WhP
Sal	Csk
Tog	WhF
Smt	Pic

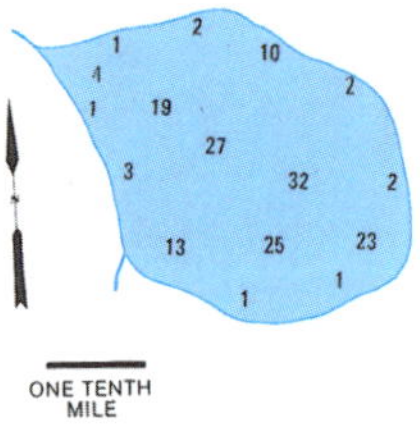

Black Pond
T15 R9 WELS
Maine Atlas
Map 63, A-1, A-2
Acres: 147
Max. Depth:
90 feet

BrT ✓	LmB
BkT ✓	SmB
RbT	WhP
Sal	Csk
Tog	WhF
Smt	Pic

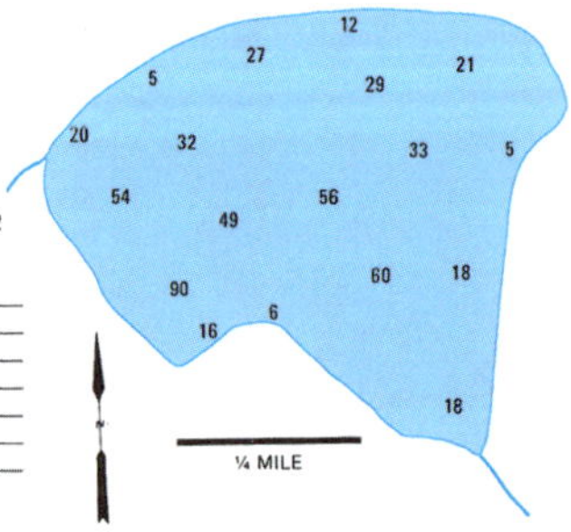

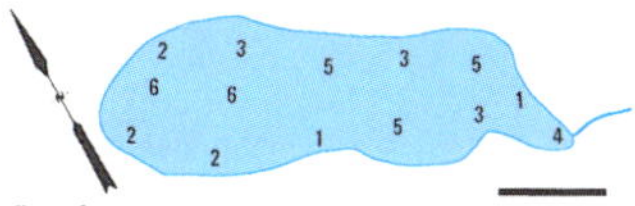

Black Pond

St. John Plt, Maine Atlas Map 67, C-3
Acres: 21, Max. Depth: 6 feet, Boat Launch

BrT	BkT	RbT	Sal	Tog	Smt	LmB	SmB	WhP	Csk	WhF	Pic
	✓										

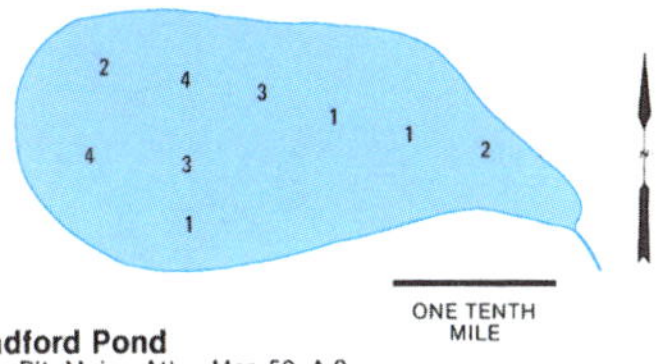

Bradford Pond

Moro Plt, Maine Atlas Map 52, A-2
Acres: 12, Max. Depth: 4 feet

BrT	BkT	RbT	Sal	Tog	Smt	LmB	SmB	WhP	Csk	WhF	Pic
	✓										

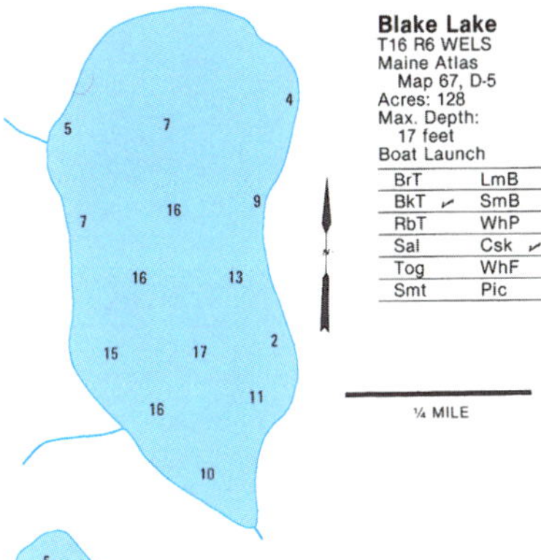

Blake Lake

T16 R6 WELS
Maine Atlas
Map 67, D-5
Acres: 128
Max. Depth:
17 feet
Boat Launch

BrT		LmB	
BkT	✓	SmB	
RbT		WhP	
Sal		Csk	✓
Tog		WhF	
Smt		Pic	

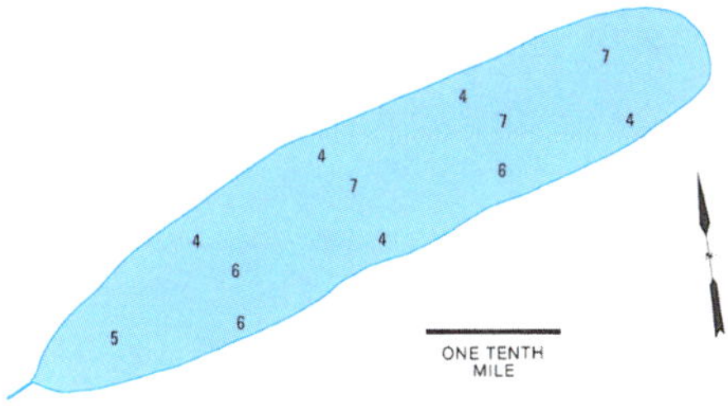

Bran Lake

St. Francis, Maine Atlas Map 67, D-1,
Acres: 32, Max. Depth: 7 feet, Boat Launch

BrT	BkT	RbT	Sal	Tog	Smt	LmB	SmB	WhP	Csk	WhF	Pic
	✓										

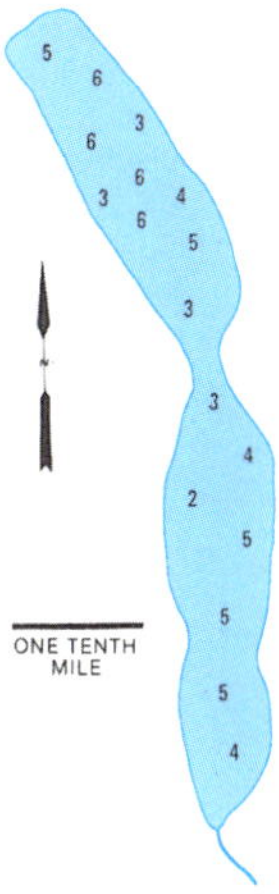

Bourgoin Lake

St. Agatha,
Frenchville
Maine Atlas
Map 68, B-2, C-2
Acres: 22
Max. Depth:
6 feet

BrT		LmB	
BkT	✓	SmB	
RbT		WhP	
Sal		Csk	
Tog		WhF	
Smt		Pic	

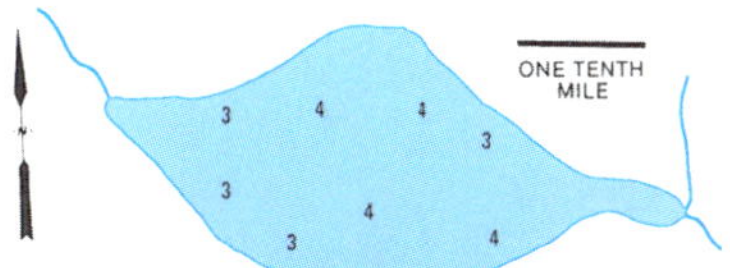

Butterfield Lake

Caswell Plt, Maine Atlas Map 65, A-3
Acres: 13, Max. Depth: 4 feet

BrT	BkT	RbT	Sal	Tog	Smt	LmB	SmB	WhP	Csk	WhF	Pic
	✓										

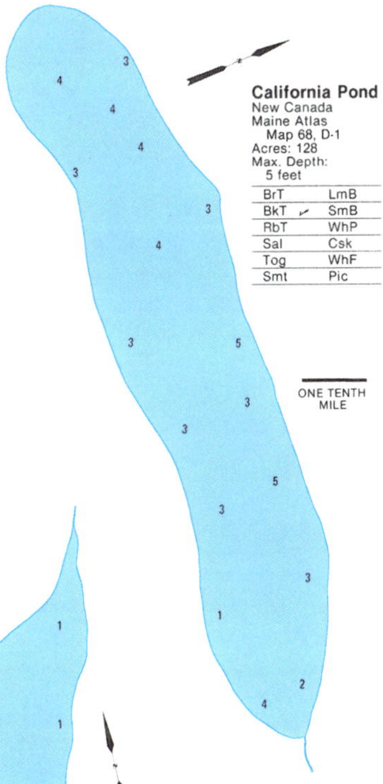

California Pond

New Canada
Maine Atlas
Map 68, D-1
Acres: 128
Max. Depth:
5 feet

BrT		LmB	
BkT	✓	SmB	
RbT		WhP	
Sal		Csk	
Tog		WhF	
Smt		Pic	

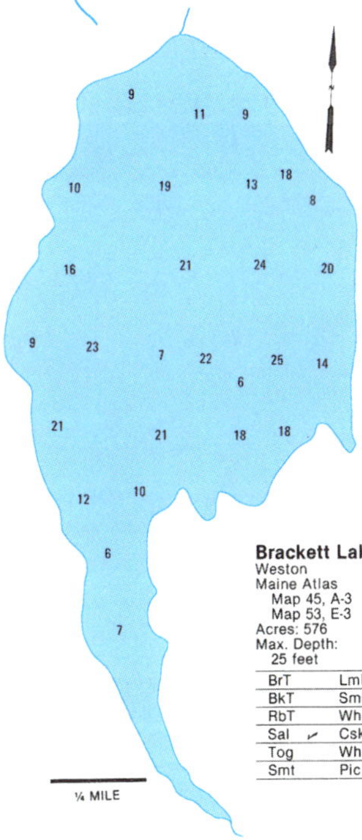

Brackett Lake

Weston
Maine Atlas
Map 45, A-3
Map 53, E-3
Acres: 576
Max. Depth:
25 feet

BrT		LmB	
BkT		SmB	✓
RbT		WhP	
Sal	✓	Csk	
Tog		WhF	
Smt		Pic	

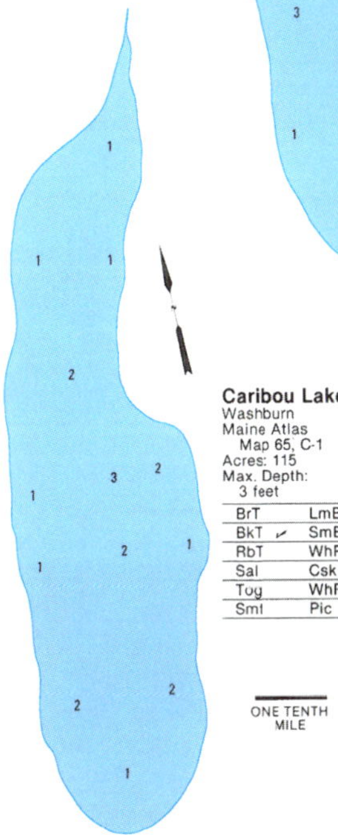

Caribou Lake

Washburn
Maine Atlas
Map 65, C-1
Acres: 115
Max. Depth:
3 feet

BrT		LmB	
BkT	✓	SmB	
RbT		WhP	
Sal		Csk	
Tog		WhF	
Smt		Pic	

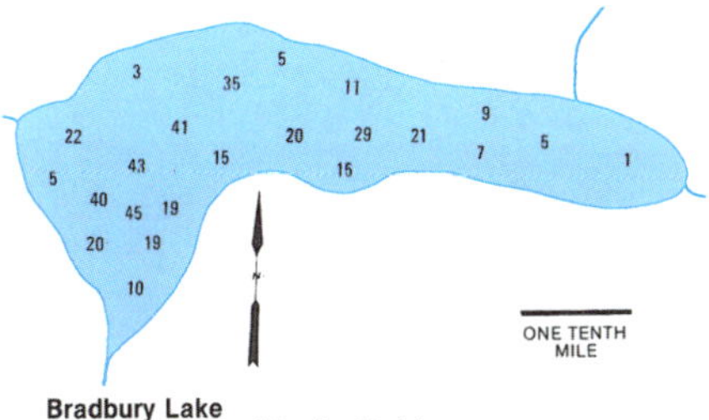

Bradbury Lake

New Limerick, Maine Atlas Map 53, A-1
Acres: 38, Max. Depth: 45 feet

BrT	BkT	RbT	Sal	Tog	Smt	LmB	SmB	WhP	Csk	WhF	Pic
	✓		✓								

Aroostook

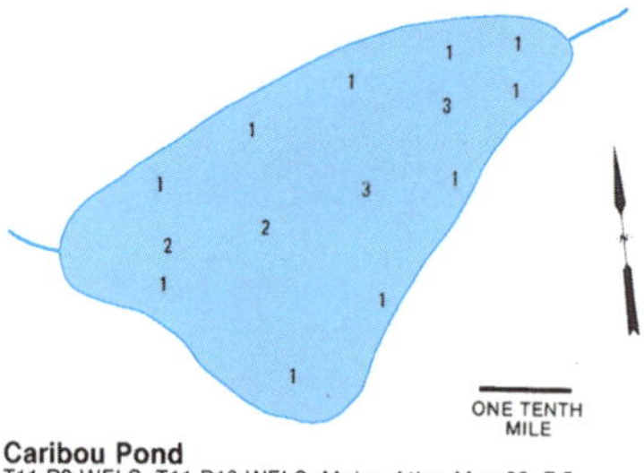

Caribou Pond

T11 R9 WELS, T11 R10 WELS, Maine Atlas Map 62, E-5
Acres: 12, Max. Depth: 3 feet

BrT	BkT	RbT	Sal	Tog	Smt	LmB	SmB	WhP	Csk	WhF	Pic
	✓										

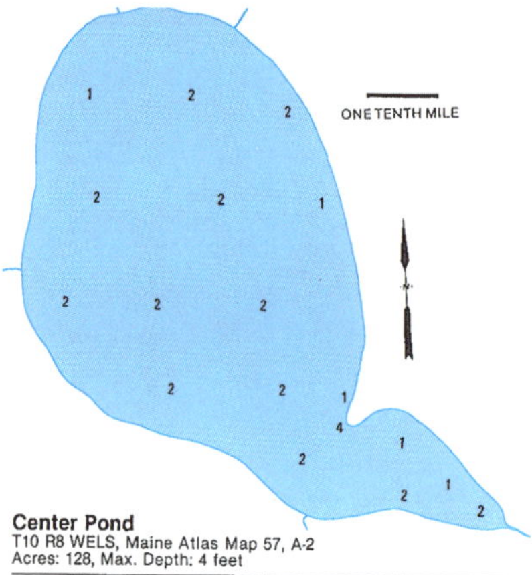

Center Pond

T10 R8 WELS, Maine Atlas Map 57, A-2
Acres: 128, Max. Depth: 4 feet

BrT	BkT	RbT	Sal	Tog	Smt	LmB	SmB	WhP	Csk	WhF	Pic
	✓										

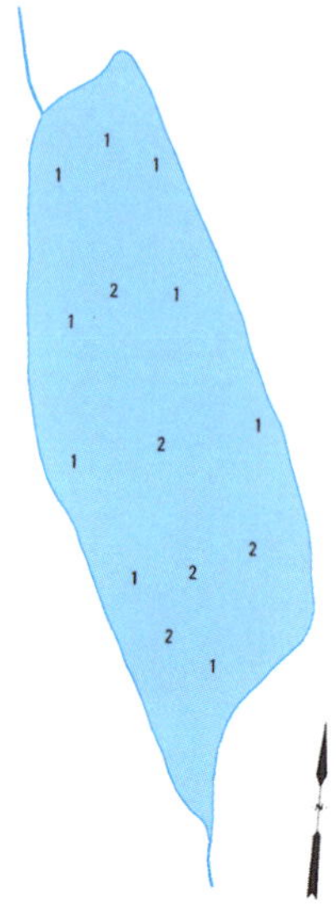

Carlisle Pond

T8 R3 WELS
Maine Atlas
Map 58, D-5
Acres: 21
Max. Depth:
2 feet

BrT		LmB	
BkT	✓	SmB	
RbT		WhP	
Sal		Csk	
Tog		WhF	
Smt		Pic	

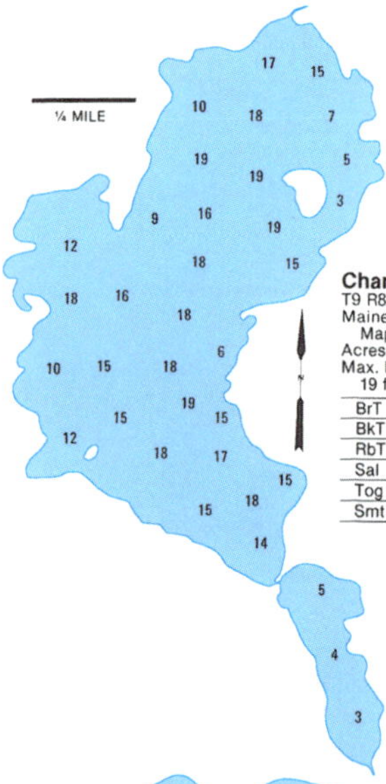

Chandler Pond

T9 R8 WELS
Maine Atlas
Map 57, B-3
Acres: 401
Max. Depth:
19 feet

BrT		LmB	
BkT	✓	SmB	
RbT		WhP	
Sal	✓	Csk	
Tog		WhF	
Smt	✓	Pic	

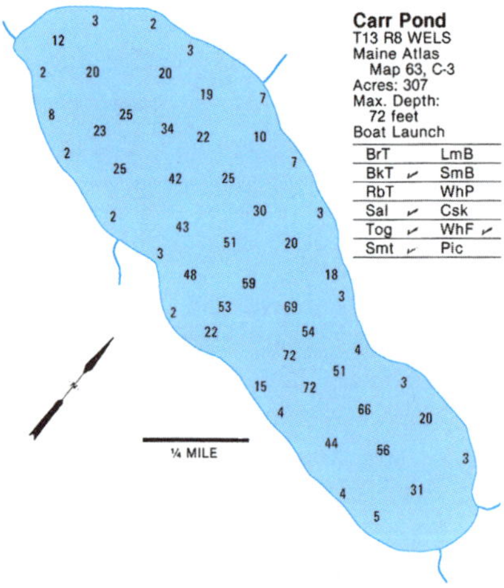

Carr Pond

T13 R8 WELS
Maine Atlas
Map 63, C-3
Acres: 307
Max. Depth:
72 feet
Boat Launch

BrT		LmB	
BkT	✓	SmB	
RbT		WhP	
Sal	✓	Csk	
Tog	✓	WhF	✓
Smt	✓	Pic	

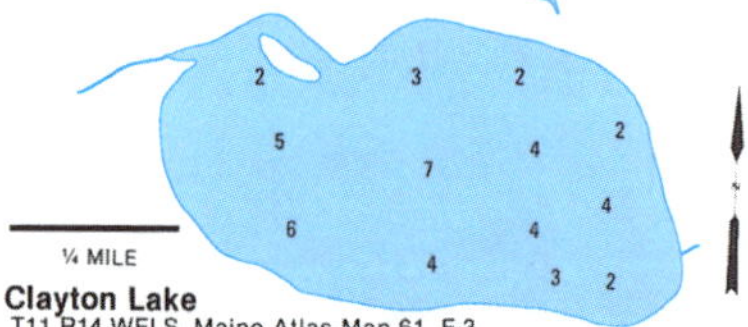

Clayton Lake

T11 R14 WELS, Maine Atlas Map 61, E-3
Acres: 166, Max. Depth: 7 feet

BrT	BkT	RbT	Sal	Tog	Smt	LmB	SmB	WhP	Csk	WhF	Pic
	✓										

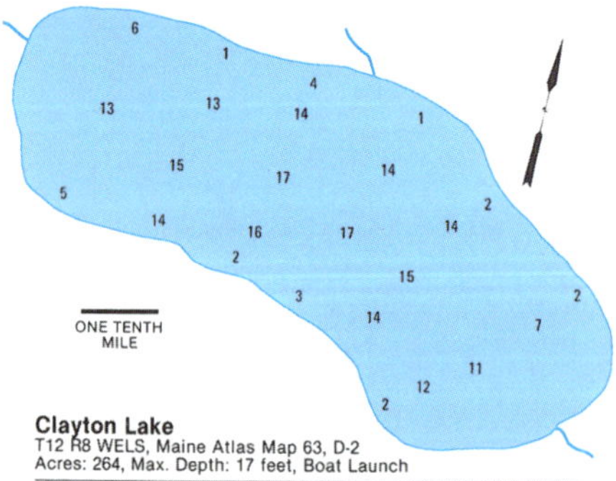

Clayton Lake

T12 R8 WELS, Maine Atlas Map 63, D-2
Acres: 264, Max. Depth: 17 feet, Boat Launch

BrT	BkT	RbT	Sal	Tog	Smt	LmB	SmB	WhP	Csk	WhF	Pic
	✓		✓							✓	

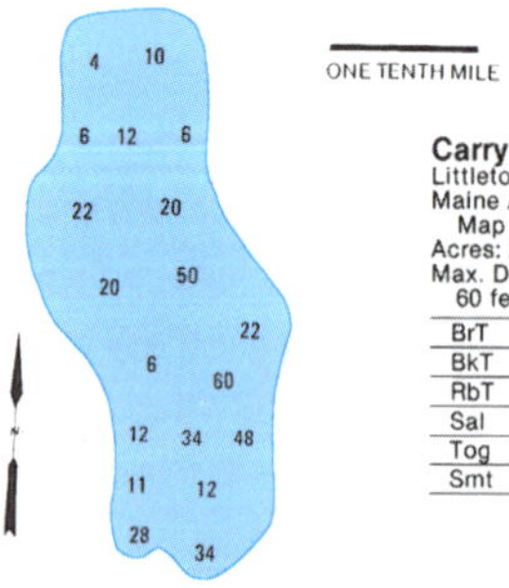

Carry Lake

Littleton
Maine Atlas
Map 59, E-3
Acres: 20
Max. Depth:
60 feet

BrT		LmB	
BkT	✓	SmB	
RbT		WhP	
Sal		Csk	
Tog		WhF	
Smt		Pic	

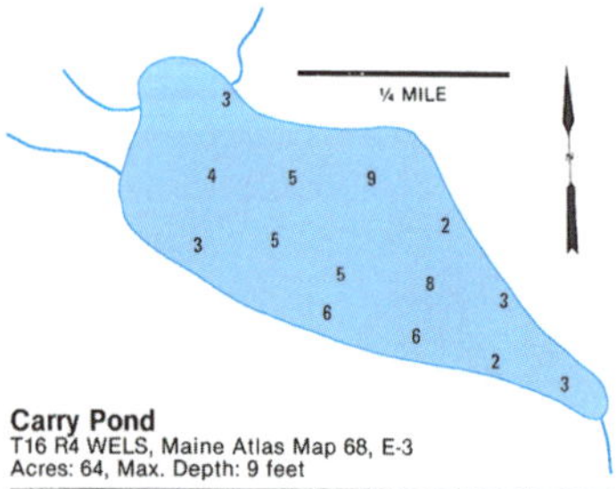

Carry Pond

T16 R4 WELS, Maine Atlas Map 68, E-3
Acres: 64, Max. Depth: 9 feet

BrT	BkT	RbT	Sal	Tog	Smt	LmB	SmB	WhP	Csk	WhF	Pic
	✓										

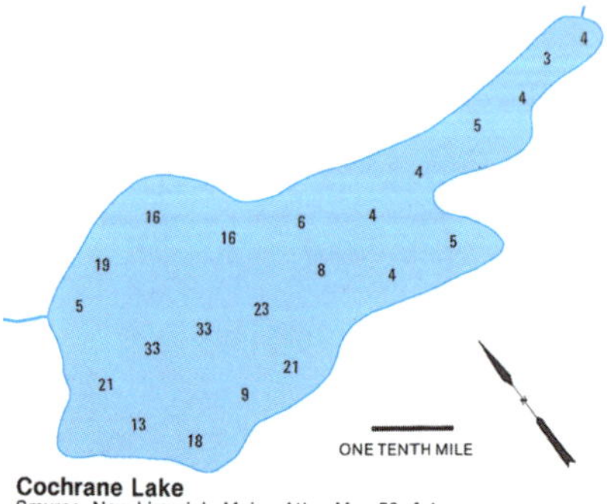

Cochrane Lake

Smyrna, New Limerick, Maine Atlas Map 53, A-1
Acres: 79, Max. Depth: 33 feet

BrT	BkT	RbT	Sal	Tog	Smt	LmB	SmB	WhP	Csk	WhF	Pic
✓	✓		✓					✓			✓

Comments: Splake.

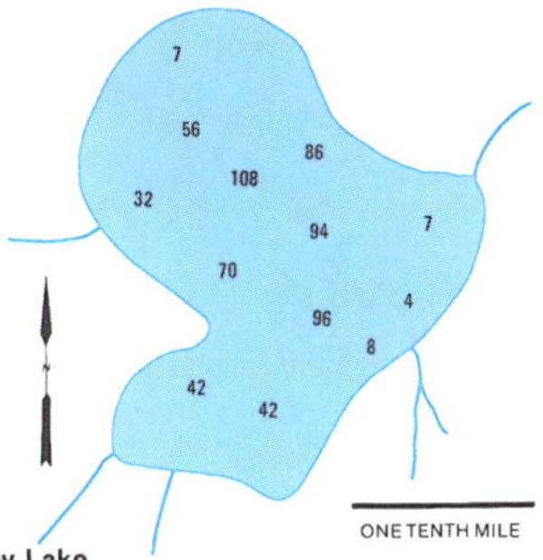

Conroy Lake
Monticello, Maine Atlas Map 59, D-3
Acres: 25, Max. Depth: 108 feet

BrT	BkT	RbT	Sal	Tog	Smt	LmB	SmB	WhP	Csk	WhF	Pic
	✓				✓						

Comments: Splake.

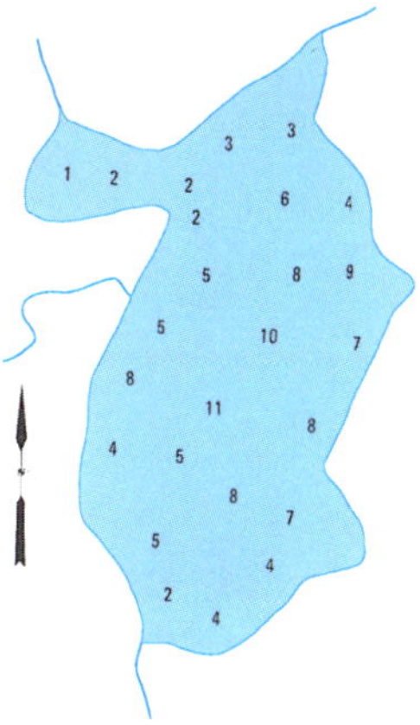

Crystal Lake
Hersey
Maine Atlas
Map 52, B-2
Acres: 137
Max. Depth:
11 feet

BrT	LmB
BkT ✓	SmB
RbT	WhP
Sal	Csk
Tog	WhF
Smt	Pic ✓

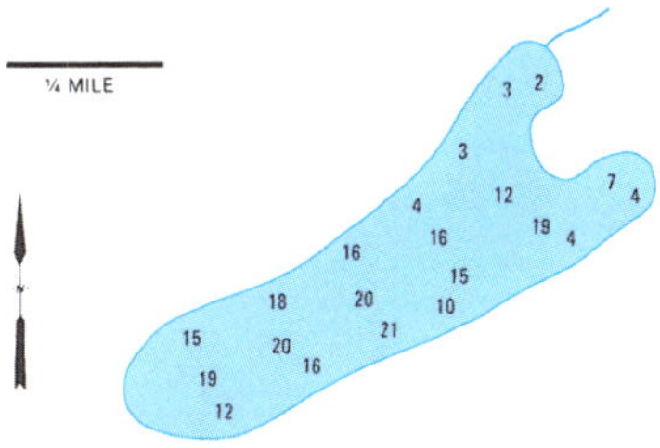

County Road Lake
New Limerick, Maine Atlas Map 53, A-1
Acres: 25, Max. Depth: 21 feet

BrT	BkT	RbT	Sal	Tog	Smt	LmB	SmB	WhP	Csk	WhF	Pic
											✓

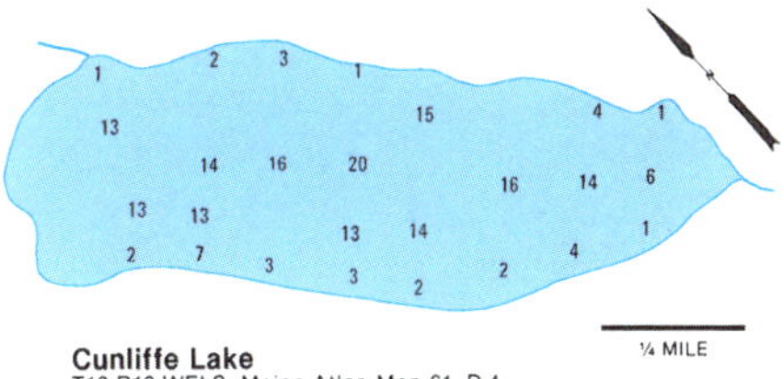

Cunliffe Lake
T12 R13 WELS, Maine Atlas Map 61, D-4
Acres: 134, Max. Depth: 20 feet

BrT	BkT	RbT	Sal	Tog	Smt	LmB	SmB	WhP	Csk	WhF	Pic
	✓								✓	✓	

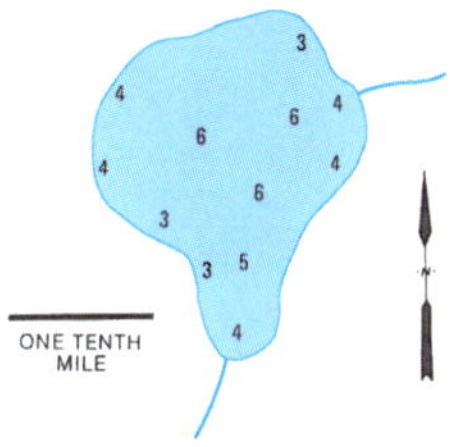

Crater Pond
T15 R9 WELS
Maine Atlas
Map 63, A-1
Acres: 12
Max. Depth:
6 feet
Boat Launch

BrT	LmB
BkT ✓	SmB
RbT	WhP
Sal	Csk
Tog	WhF
Smt	Pic

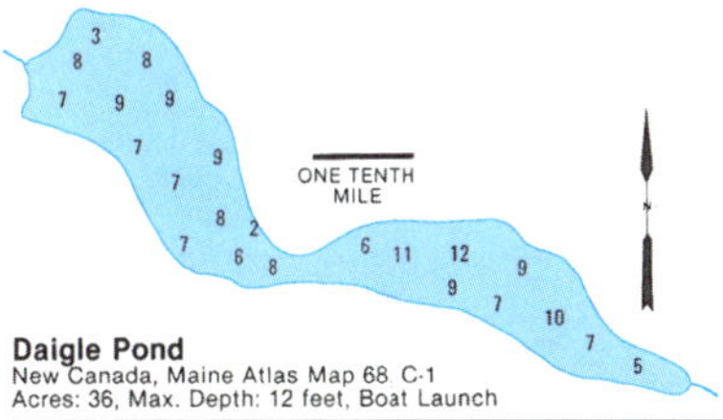

Daigle Pond
New Canada, Maine Atlas Map 68, C-1
Acres: 36, Max. Depth: 12 feet, Boat Launch

BrT	BkT	RbT	Sal	Tog	Smt	LmB	SmB	WhP	Csk	WhF	Pic
✓	✓										

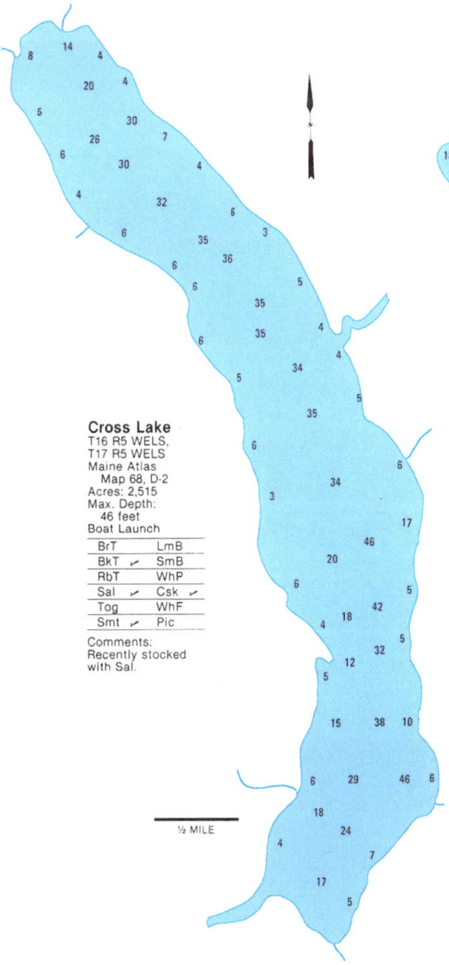

Cross Lake
T16 R5 WELS,
T17 R5 WELS
Maine Atlas
Map 68, D-2
Acres: 2,515
Max. Depth:
46 feet
Boat Launch

BrT	LmB
BkT ✓	SmB
RbT	WhP
Sal ✓	Csk ✓
Tog	WhF
Smt ✓	Pic

Comments:
Recently stocked
with Sal.

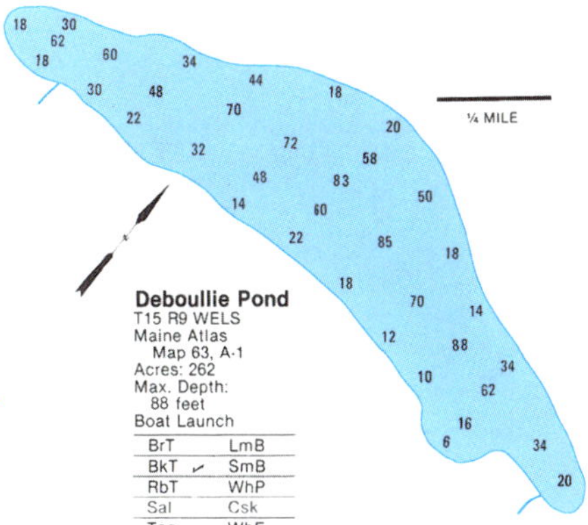

Deboullie Pond
T15 R9 WELS
Maine Atlas
Map 63, A-1
Acres: 262
Max. Depth:
88 feet
Boat Launch

BrT	LmB
BkT ✓	SmB
RbT	WhP
Sal	Csk
Tog	WhF
Smt	Pic

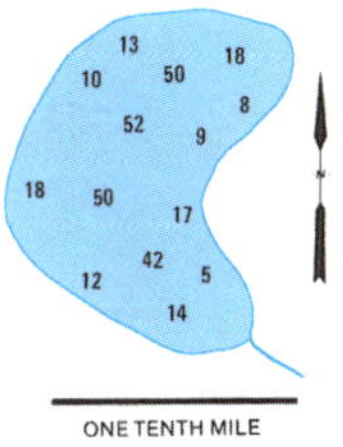

Deep Lake
Littleton
Maine Atlas
Map 59, E-3
Acres: 6
Max. Depth:
52 feet

BrT	LmB
BkT ✓	SmB
RbT	WhP
Sal	Csk
Tog	WhF
Smt	Pic

Aroostook

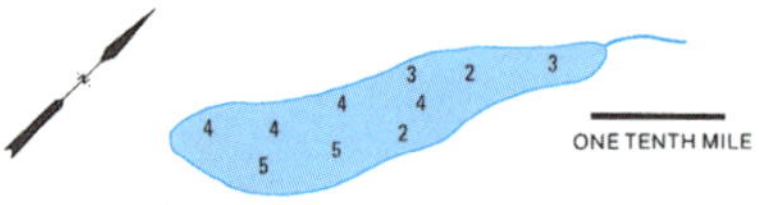

Deer Pond
St. John Plantation, Maine Atlas Map 67, D-3
Acres: 14, Max. Depth: 5 feet, Boat Launch

BrT	BkT	RbT	Sal	Tog	Smt	LmB	SmB	WhP	Csk	WhF	Pic
	✓										

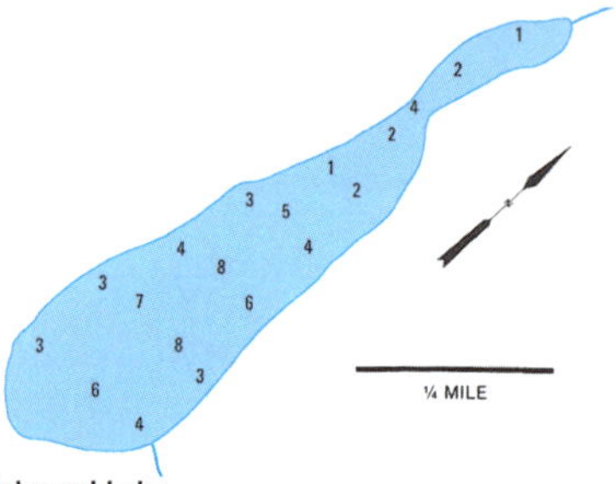

Dickwood Lake
Eagle Lake, Maine Atlas Map 67, D-3, E-3
Acres: 96, Max. Depth: 8 feet, Boat Launch

BrT	BkT	RbT	Sal	Tog	Smt	LmB	SmB	WhP	Csk	WhF	Pic
✓	✓										

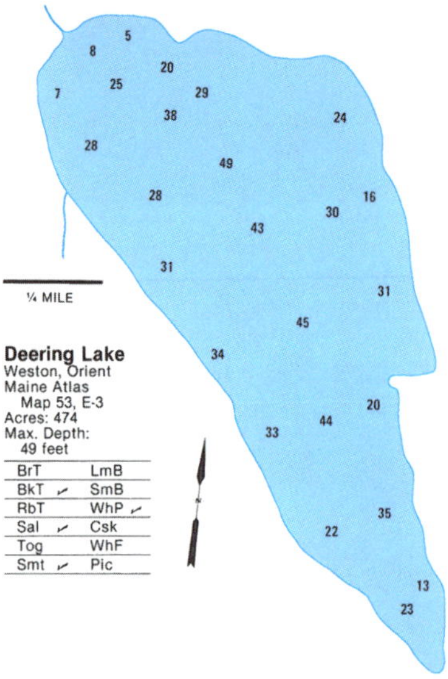

Deering Lake
Weston, Orient
Maine Atlas
Map 53, E-3
Acres: 474
Max. Depth:
49 feet

BrT		LmB	
BkT	✓	SmB	
RbT		WhP	✓
Sal	✓	Csk	
Tog		WhF	
Smt	✓	Pic	

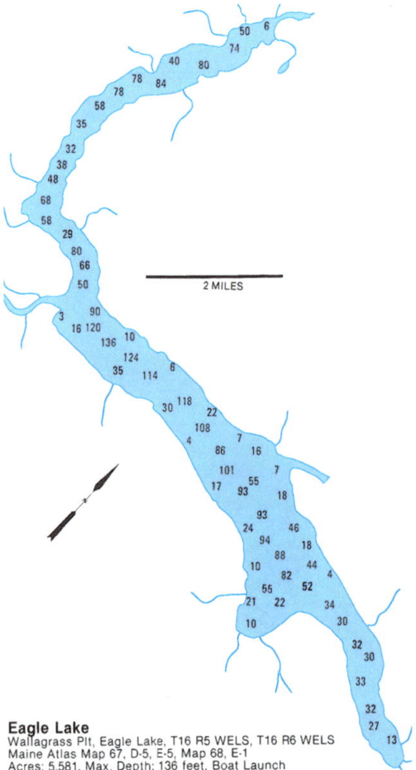

Eagle Lake
Wallagrass Plt, Eagle Lake, T16 R5 WELS, T16 R6 WELS
Maine Atlas Map 67, D-5, E-5, Map 68, E-1
Acres: 5,581, Max. Depth: 136 feet, Boat Launch

BrT	BkT	RbT	Sal	Tog	Smt	LmB	SmB	WhP	Csk	WhF	Pic
	✓		✓	✓	✓				✓		

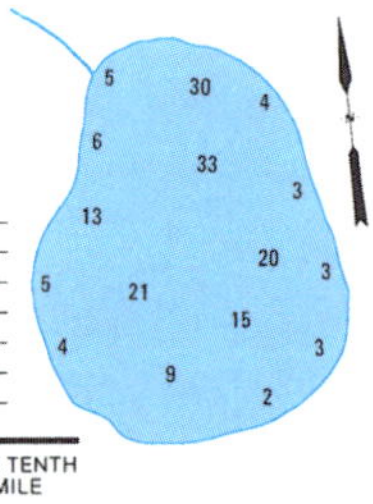

Denny Pond
T15 R9 WELS
Maine Atlas
Map 63, A-1
Acres: 25
Max. Depth:
33 feet
Boat Launch

BrT		LmB	
BkT	✓	SmB	
RbT		WhP	
Sal		Csk	
Tog		WhF	
Smt		Pic	

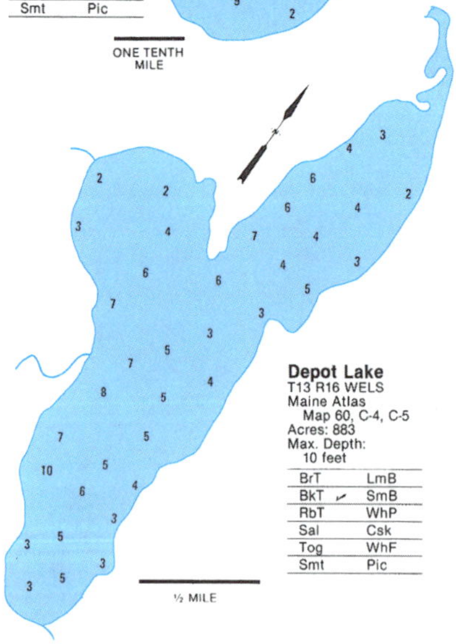

Depot Lake
T13 R16 WELS
Maine Atlas
Map 60, C-4, C-5
Acres: 883
Max. Depth:
10 feet

BrT		LmB	
BkT	✓	SmB	
RbT		WhP	
Sal		Csk	
Tog		WhF	
Smt		Pic	

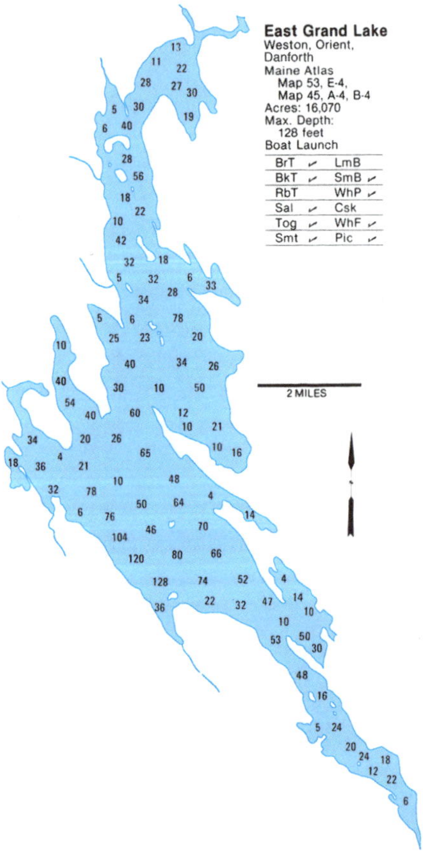

East Grand Lake
Weston, Orient,
Danforth
Maine Atlas
Map 53, E-4,
Map 45, A-4, B-4
Acres: 16,070
Max. Depth:
128 feet
Boat Launch

BrT	✓	LmB	
BkT	✓	SmB	✓
RbT		WhP	✓
Sal	✓	Csk	
Tog	✓	WhF	✓
Smt	✓	Pic	✓

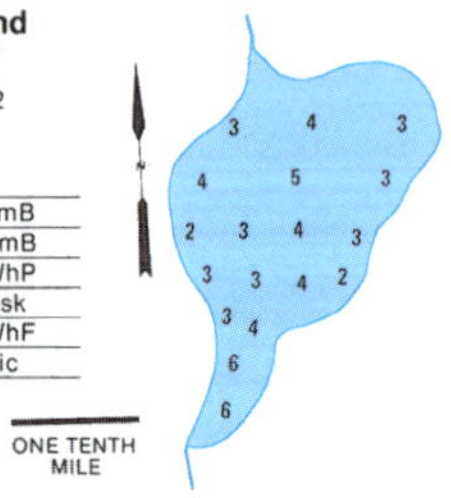

Dickey Pond
T17 R5 WELS
Maine Atlas
Map 68, C-2
Acres: 13
Max. Depth:
6 feet

BrT		LmB	
BkT	✓	SmB	
RbT		WhP	
Sal		Csk	
Tog		WhF	
Smt		Pic	

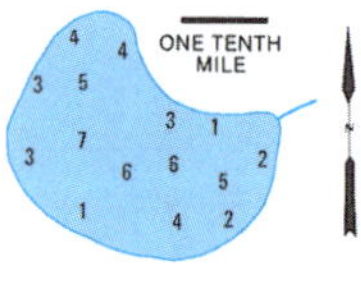

Dimock Pond
New Canada
Maine Atlas
Map 68, D-1
Acres: 4
Max. Depth:
7 feet

BrT		LmB	
BkT	✓	SmB	
RbT		WhP	
Sal		Csk	
Tog		WhF	
Smt		Pic	

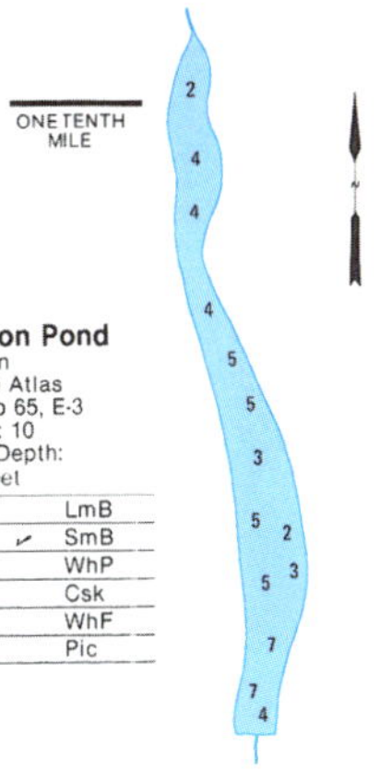

Easton Pond
Easton
Maine Atlas
Map 65, E-3
Acres: 10
Max. Depth:
7 feet

BrT		LmB	
BkT	✓	SmB	
RbT		WhP	
Sal		Csk	
Tog		WhF	
Smt		Pic	

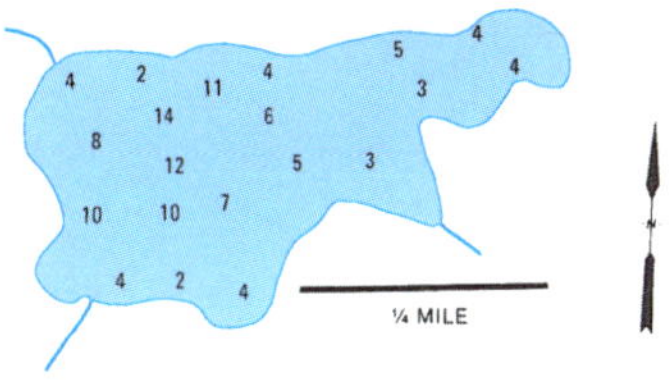

Ferguson Pond
T14 R8 WELS, Maine Atlas Map 63, B-3
Acres: 51, Max. Depth: 14 feet

BrT	BkT	RbT	Sal	Tog	Smt	LmB	SmB	WhP	Csk	WhF	Pic
	✓										

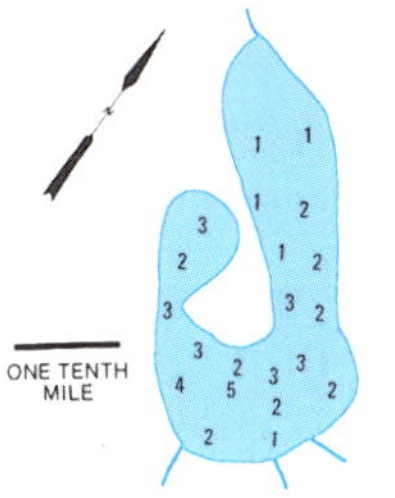

Fifth Pelletier Brook Lake
T15 R9 WELS
Maine Atlas
Map 63, A-1
Acres: 27
Max. Depth:
5 feet

BrT		LmB	
BkT	✓	SmB	
RbT		WhP	
Sal		Csk	
Tog		WhF	
Smt		Pic	

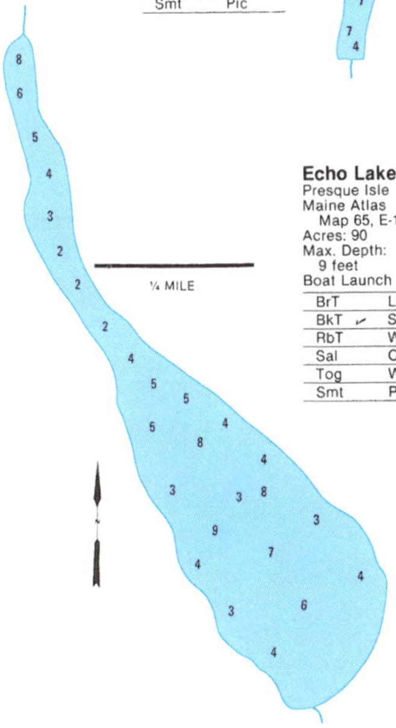

Echo Lake
Presque Isle
Maine Atlas
Map 65, E-1
Acres: 90
Max. Depth:
9 feet
Boat Launch

BrT		LmB	
BkT	✓	SmB	
RbT		WhP	
Sal		Csk	
Tog		WhF	
Smt		Pic	

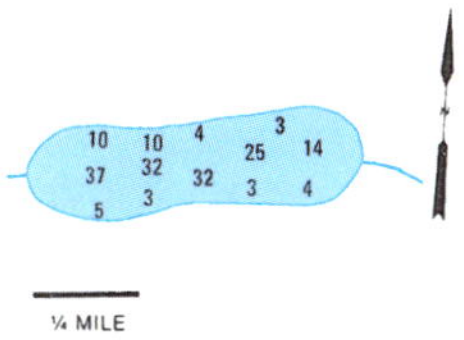

First Chase Pond
T14 R9 WELS
Maine Atlas
Map 63, B-1
Acres: 12
Max. Depth:
37 feet

BrT		LmB	
BkT	✓	SmB	
RbT		WhP	
Sal		Csk	
Tog	✓	WhF	
Smt		Pic	

First Musquacook Lake
T11 R11 WELS,
T11 R12 WELS
Maine Atlas
Map 62, D-2
Acres: 698
Max. Depth:
48 feet

BrT		LmB	
BkT	✓	SmB	
RbT		WhP	
Sal		Csk	✓
Tog	✓	WhF	✓
Smt	✓	Pic	

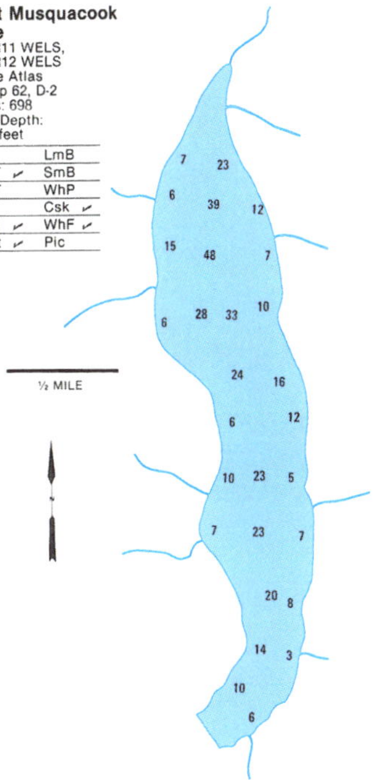

Falls Pond
T18 R10 WELS,
Allagash Plt
Maine Atlas
Map 66, D-4
Acres: 256
Max. Depth:
7 feet
Boat Launch

BrT		LmB	
BkT	✓	SmB	
RbT		WhP	
Sal		Csk	
Tog		WhF	
Smt		Pic	

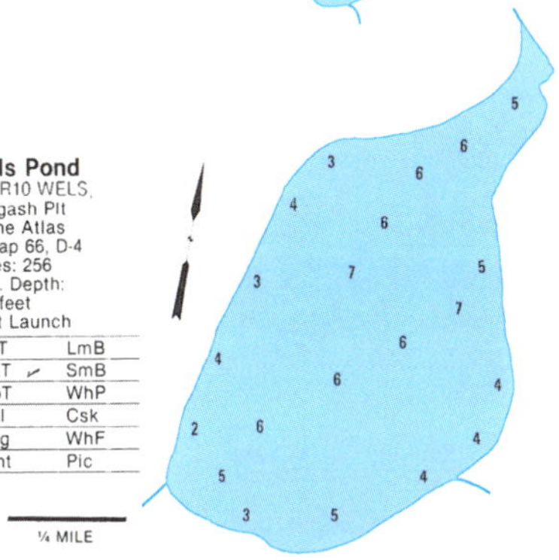

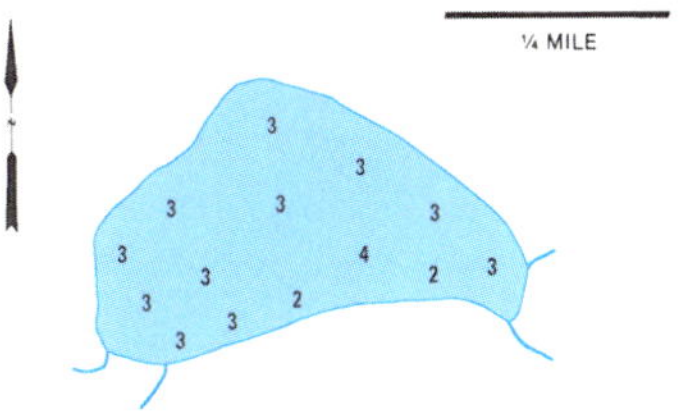

Farrar Pond
T11 R10 WELS, Maine Atlas Map 62, E-5
Acres: 51, Max. Depth: 4 feet

BrT	BkT	RbT	Sal	Tog	Smt	LmB	SmB	WhP	Csk	WhF	Pic
	✓										

First Pelletier Brook Lake
T16 R9 WELS
Maine Atlas
Map 67, E-1
Acres: 25
Max. Depth:
12 feet
Boat Launch

BrT		LmB	
BkT	✓	SmB	
RbT		WhP	
Sal		Csk	
Tog		WhF	
Smt		Pic	

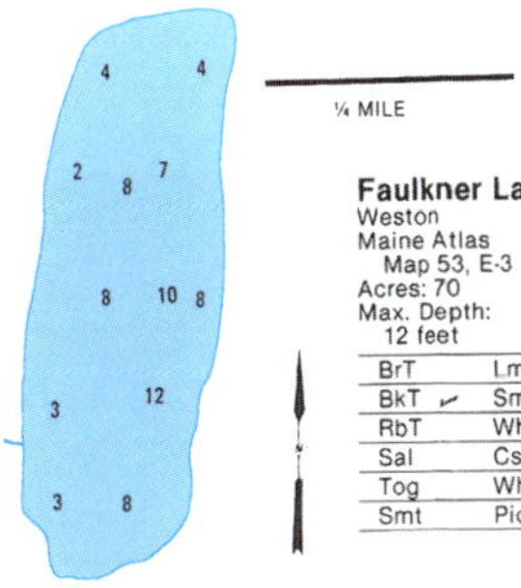

Faulkner Lake
Weston
Maine Atlas
Map 53, E-3
Acres: 70
Max. Depth:
12 feet

BrT		LmB	
BkT	✓	SmB	
RbT		WhP	
Sal		Csk	
Tog		WhF	
Smt		Pic	✓

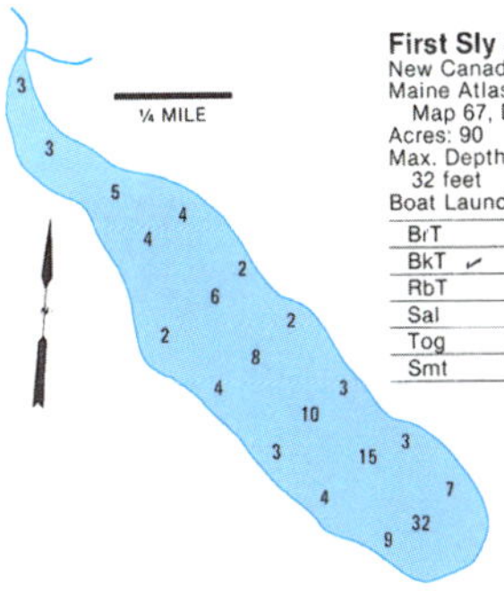

First Sly Brook Lake
New Canada
Maine Atlas
Map 67, D-5
Acres: 90
Max. Depth:
32 feet
Boat Launch

BrT		LmB	
BkT	✓	SmB	
RbT		WhP	
Sal		Csk	
Tog		WhF	
Smt		Pic	

Aroostook

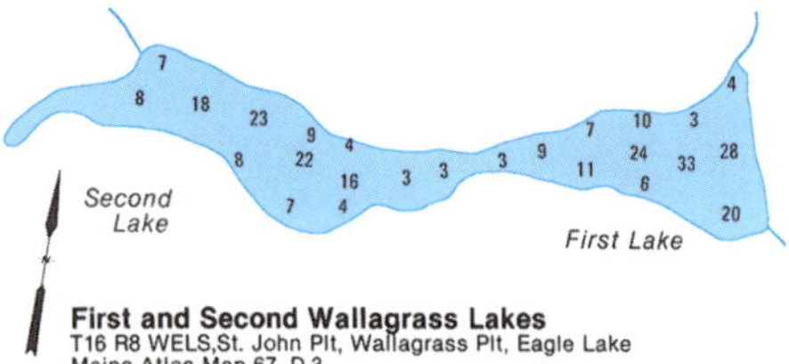

First and Second Wallagrass Lakes

T16 R8 WELS,St. John Plt, Wallagrass Plt, Eagle Lake
Maine Atlas Map 67, D-3
Acres: 281, Max. Depth: First-33 feet, Second-23 feet, Boat Launch

BrT	BkT	RbT	Sal	Tog	Smt	LmB	SmB	WhP	Csk	WhF	Pic
	✓		✓							✓	

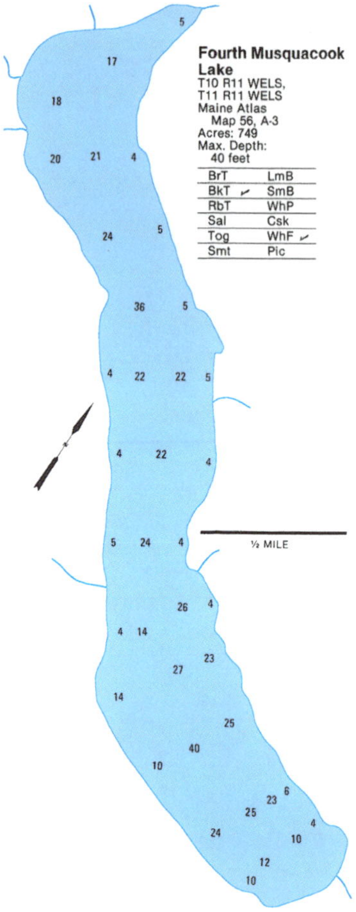

Fourth Musquacook Lake

T10 R11 WELS,
T11 R11 WELS
Maine Atlas
Map 56, A-3
Acres: 749
Max. Depth:
40 feet

BrT		LmB	
BkT	✓	SmB	
RbT		WhP	
Sal		Csk	
Tog		WhF	✓
Smt		Pic	

Fischer Lake

Fort Fairfield
Maine Atlas
Map 65, D-4
Acres: 10
Max. Depth:
6 feet

BrT		LmB	
BkT	✓	SmB	
RbT		WhP	
Sal		Csk	
Tog		WhF	
Smt		Pic	

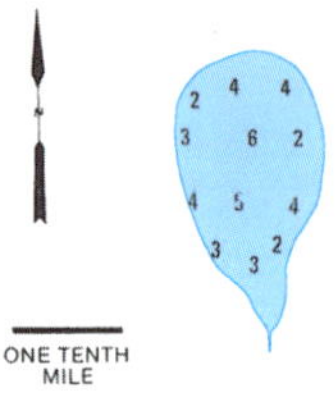

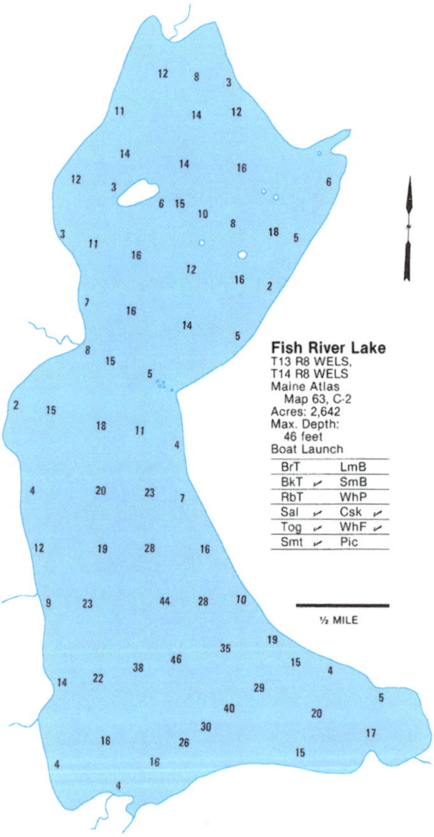

Fish River Lake

T13 R8 WELS,
T14 R8 WELS
Maine Atlas
Map 63, C-2
Acres: 2,642
Max. Depth:
46 feet
Boat Launch

BrT		LmB	
BkT	✓	SmB	
RbT		WhP	
Sal	✓	Csk	✓
Tog	✓	WhF	✓
Smt	✓	Pic	

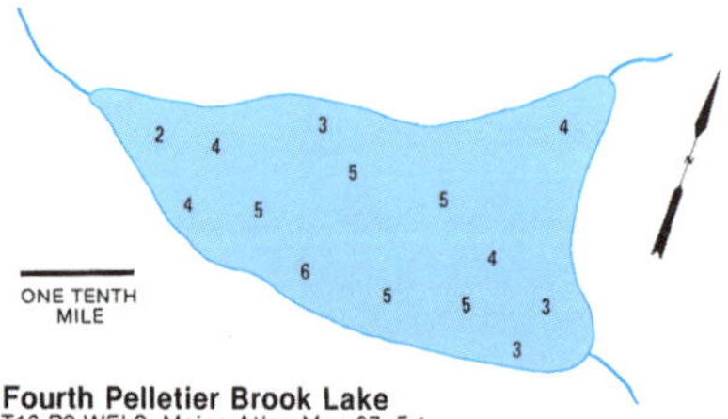

Fourth Pelletier Brook Lake

T16 R9 WELS, Maine Atlas Map 67, E-1
Acres: 49, Max. Depth: 6 feet.

BrT	BkT	RbT	Sal	Tog	Smt	LmB	SmB	WhP	Csk	WhF	Pic
	✓										

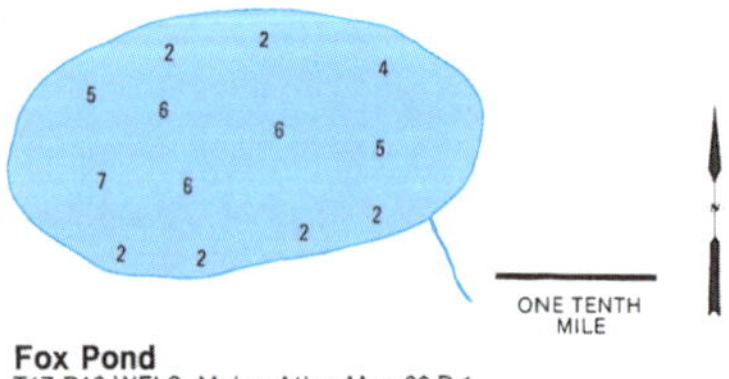

Fox Pond

T17 R12 WELS, Maine Atlas Map 66,D-1
Acres: 23, Max. Depth: 7 feet

BrT	BkT	RbT	Sal	Tog	Smt	LmB	SmB	WhP	Csk	WhF	Pic
	✓										

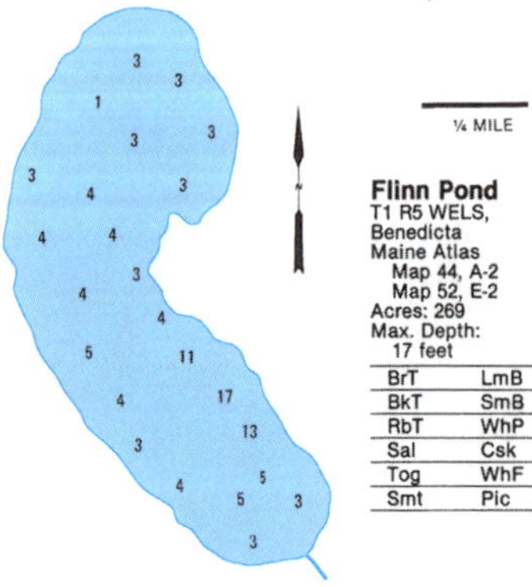

Flinn Pond

T1 R5 WELS,
Benedicta
Maine Atlas
Map 44, A-2
Map 52, E-2
Acres: 269
Max. Depth:
17 feet

BrT		LmB	
BkT		SmB	
RbT		WhP	
Sal		Csk	
Tog		WhF	
Smt		Pic	✓

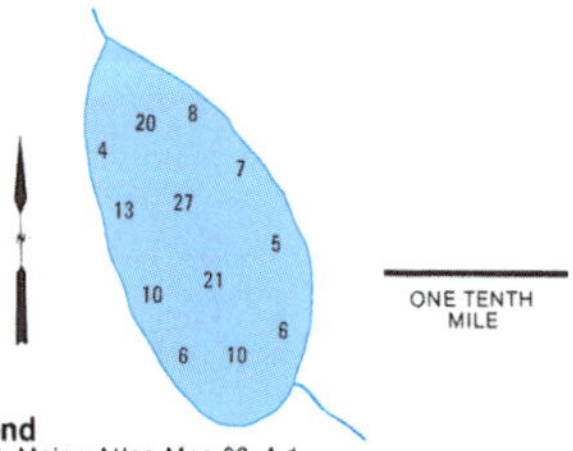

Galilee Pond

T15 R9 WELS, Maine Atlas Map 63, A-1
Acres: 9, Max. Depth: 27 feet

BrT	BkT	RbT	Sal	Tog	Smt	LmB	SmB	WhP	Csk	WhF	Pic
	✓										

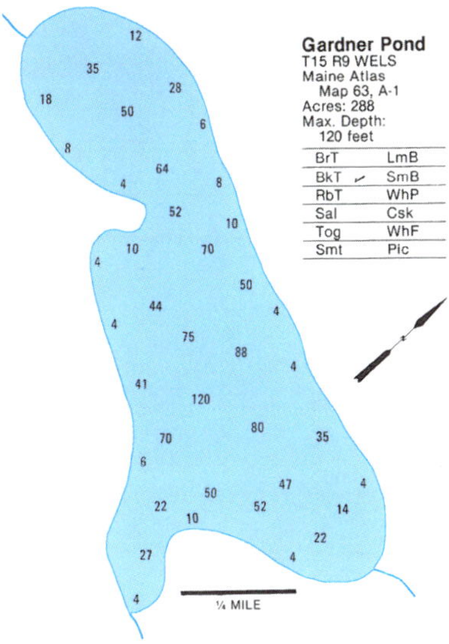

Gardner Pond

T15 R9 WELS
Maine Atlas
Map 63, A-1
Acres: 288
Max. Depth:
120 feet

BrT		LmB	
BkT	✓	SmB	
RbT		WhP	
Sal		Csk	
Tog		WhF	
Smt		Pic	

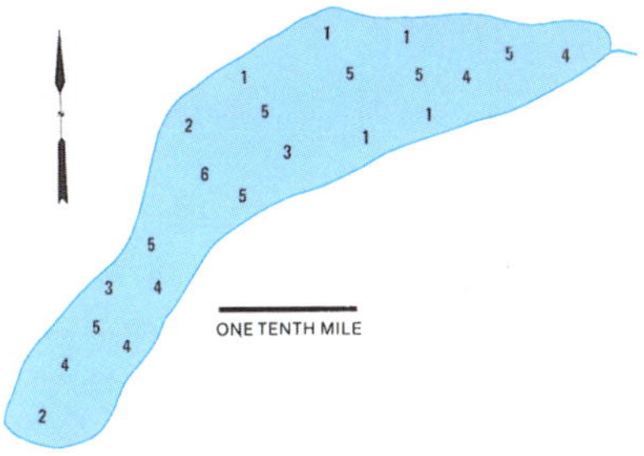

Gilman Pond

Moro Plt, Maine Atlas Map 58, E-1
Acres: 19, Max. Depth: 6 feet

BrT	BkT	RbT	Sal	Tog	Smt	LmB	SmB	WhP	Csk	WhF	Pic
	✓										

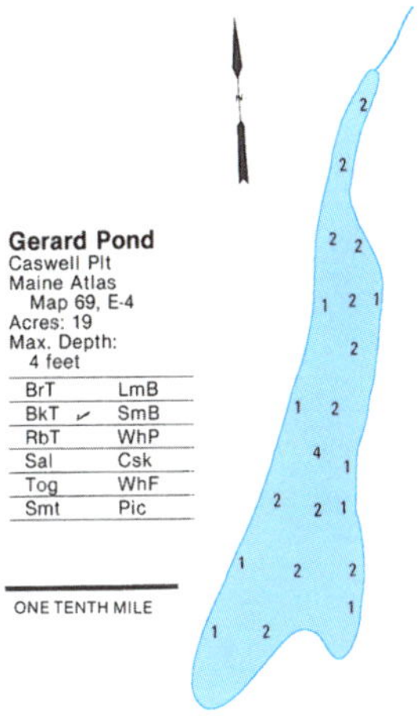

Gerard Pond

Caswell Plt
Maine Atlas
Map 69, E-4
Acres: 19
Max. Depth:
4 feet

BrT		LmB	
BkT	✓	SmB	
RbT		WhP	
Sal		Csk	
Tog		WhF	
Smt		Pic	

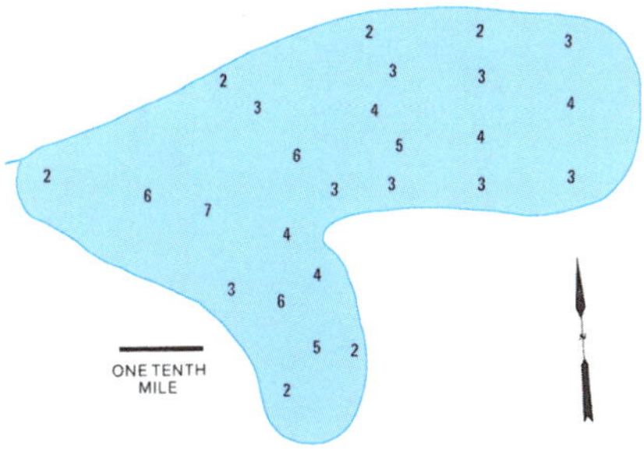

Glancy Lake

New Limerick, Maine Atlas Map 53, A-2
Acres: 22, Max. Depth: 7 feet

BrT	BkT	RbT	Sal	Tog	Smt	LmB	SmB	WhP	Csk	WhF	Pic
											✓

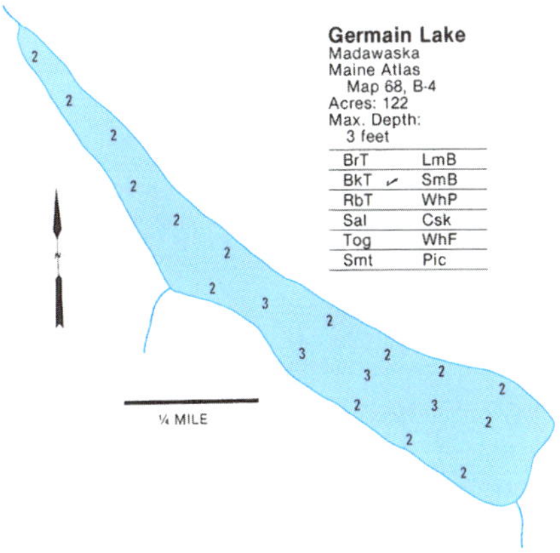

Germain Lake

Madawaska
Maine Atlas
Map 68, B-4
Acres: 122
Max. Depth:
3 feet

BrT		LmB	
BkT	✓	SmB	
RbT		WhP	
Sal		Csk	
Tog		WhF	
Smt		Pic	

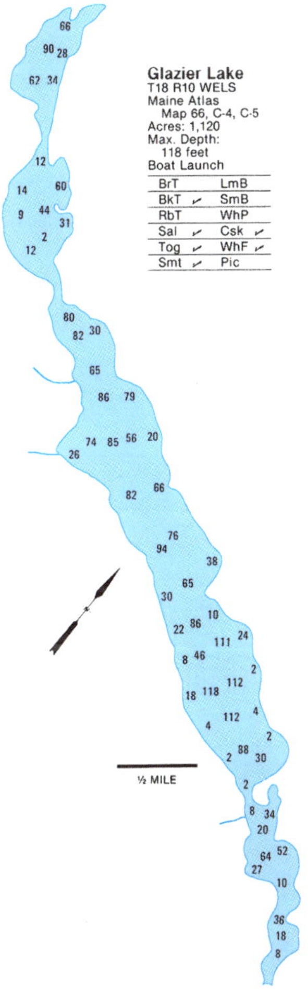

Glazier Lake

T18 R10 WELS
Maine Atlas
Map 66, C-4, C-5
Acres: 1,120
Max. Depth:
118 feet
Boat Launch

BrT		LmB	
BkT	✓	SmB	
RbT		WhP	
Sal	✓	Csk	✓
Tog	✓	WhF	✓
Smt	✓	Pic	

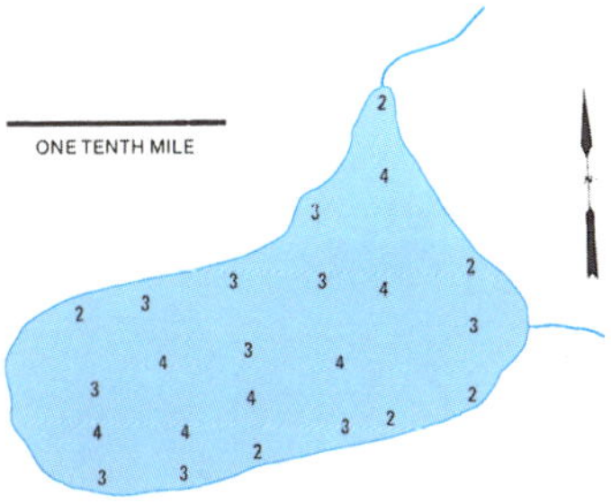

Gilbert Pond

St. John Plt, Maine Atlas Map 67, D-2
Acres: 12, Max. Depth: 4 feet

BrT	BkT	RbT	Sal	Tog	Smt	LmB	SmB	WhP	Csk	WhF	Pic
	✓										

Aroostook

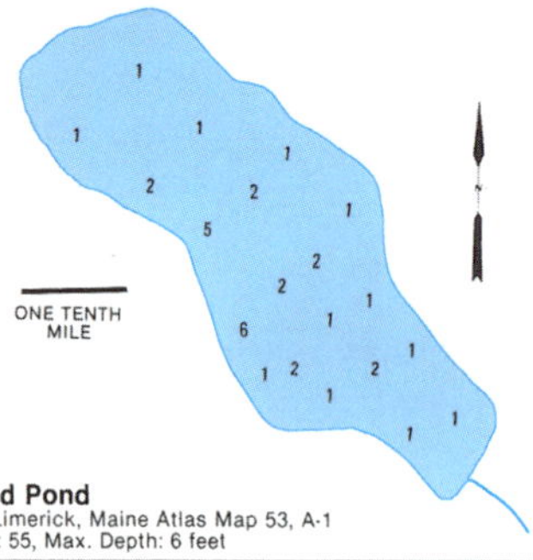

Gould Pond
New Limerick, Maine Atlas Map 53, A-1
Acres: 55, Max. Depth: 6 feet

BrT	BkT	RbT	Sal	Tog	Smt	LmB	SmB	WhP	Csk	WhF	Pic
	✓										

Hafey Pond
T18 R11 WELS
Maine Atlas
Map 66, B-3
Acres: 23
Max. Depth:
5 feet

BrT	LmB
BkT ✓	SmB
RbT	WhP
Sal	Csk
Tog	WhF
Smt	Pic

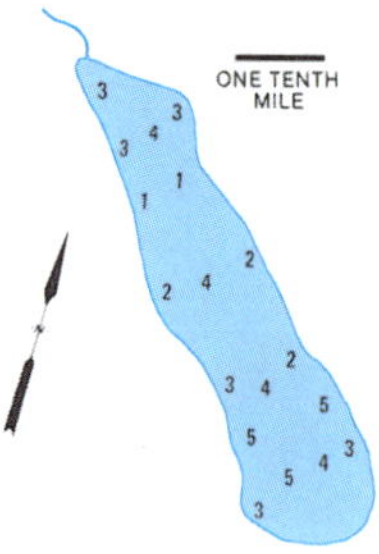

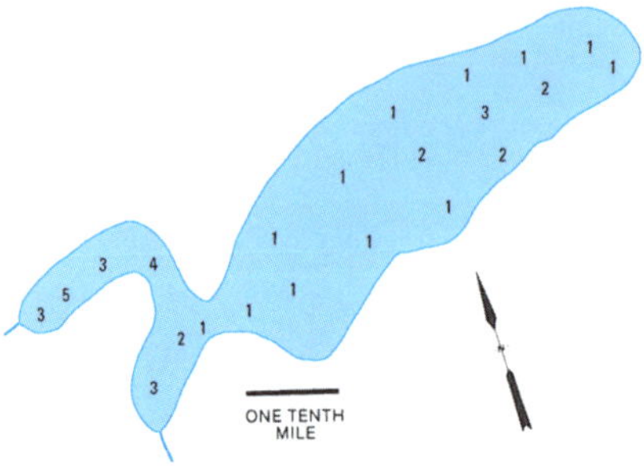

Grass Pond
Moro Plt, Maine Atlas Map 52, A-1
Acres: 55, Max. Depth: 5 feet

BrT	BkT	RbT	Sal	Tog	Smt	LmB	SmB	WhP	Csk	WhF	Pic
	✓										

Hale Pond
Moro Plt
Maine Atlas
Map 52, A-2
Acres: 38
Max. Depth:
39 feet

BrT	LmB
BkT ✓	SmB
RbT	WhP
Sal	Csk
Tog	WhF
Smt	Pic

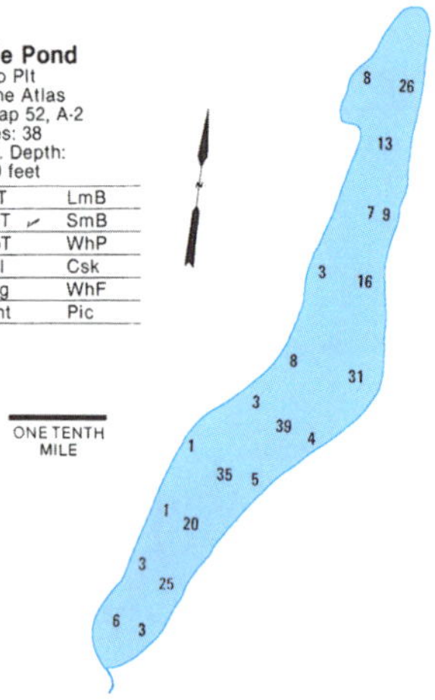

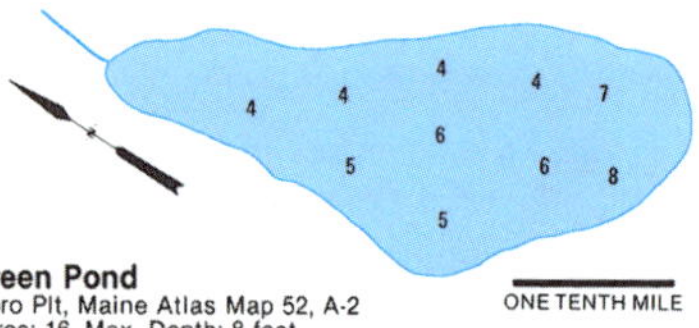

Green Pond
Moro Plt, Maine Atlas Map 52, A-2
Acres: 16, Max. Depth: 8 feet

BrT	BkT	RbT	Sal	Tog	Smt	LmB	SmB	WhP	Csk	WhF	Pic
	✓										

Hanson Lake
Mapleton
Maine Atlas
Map 65, D-1
Acres: 118
Max. Depth:
32 feet
Boat Launch

BrT	LmB
BkT ✓	SmB
RbT	WhP
Sal	Csk
Tog	WhF
Smt	Pic

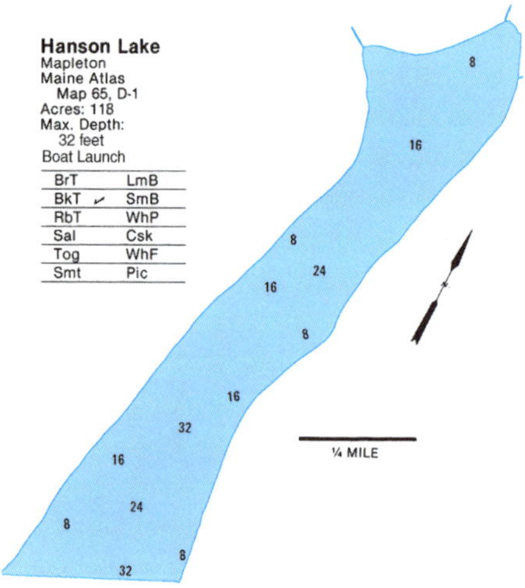

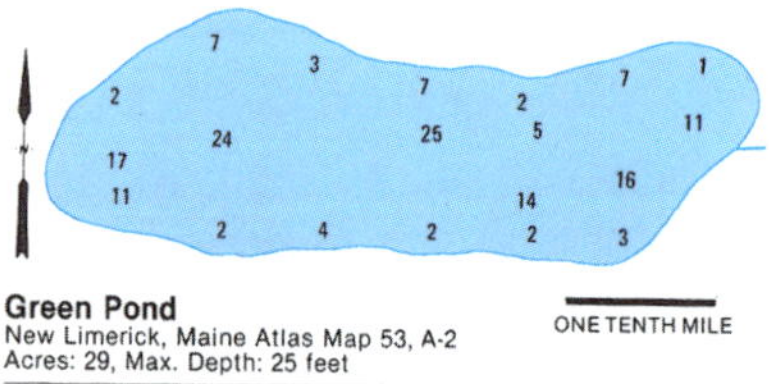

Green Pond
New Limerick, Maine Atlas Map 53, A-2
Acres: 29, Max. Depth: 25 feet

BrT	BkT	RbT	Sal	Tog	Smt	LmB	SmB	WhP	Csk	WhF	Pic
	✓										✓

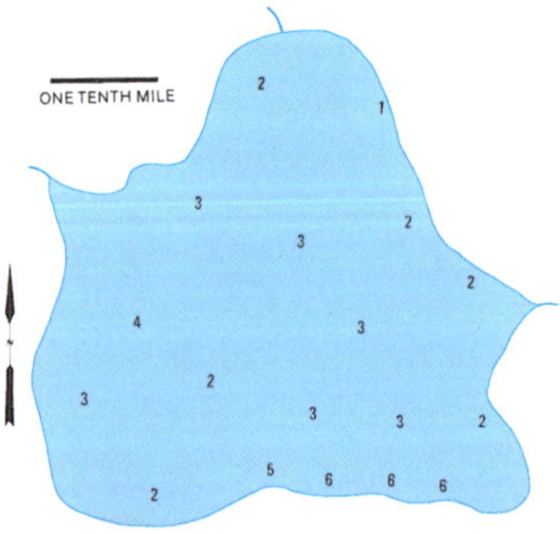

Greenlaw Pond
T12 R7 WELS, T12 R8 WELS, Maine Atlas Map 63, D-3
Acres: 109, Max. Depth: 6 feet

BrT	BkT	RbT	Sal	Tog	Smt	LmB	SmB	WhP	Csk	WhF	Pic
	✓										

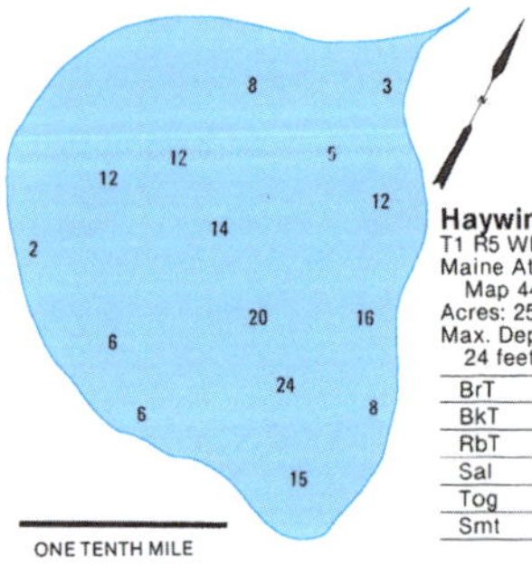

Haywire Pond
T1 R5 WELS
Maine Atlas
Map 44, A-3
Acres: 25
Max. Depth:
24 feet

BrT	LmB
BkT	SmB
RbT	WhP
Sal	Csk
Tog	WhF
Smt	Pic ✓

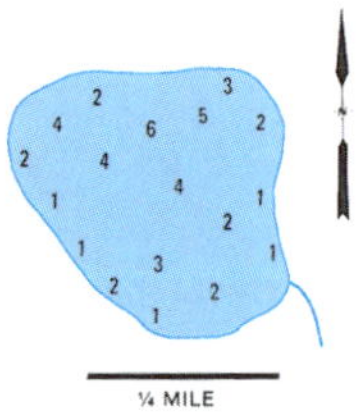

Grey Pond
T12 R13 WELS
Maine Atlas
Map 61, D-5
Acres: 28
Max. Depth:
6 feet

BrT	LmB
BkT ✓	SmB
RbT	WhP
Sal	Csk
Tog	WhF
Smt	Pic

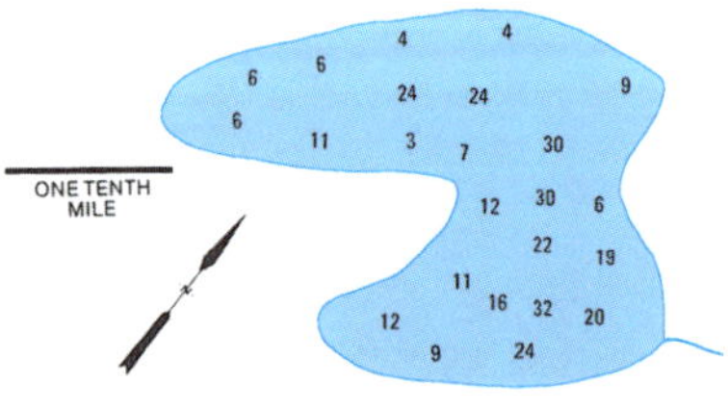

Horseshoe Pond
T11 R10 WELS, Maine Atlas Map 62, E-5
Acres: 23, Max. Depth: 32 feet, Boat Launch

BrT	BkT	RbT	Sal	Tog	Smt	LmB	SmB	WhP	Csk	WhF	Pic
	✓										

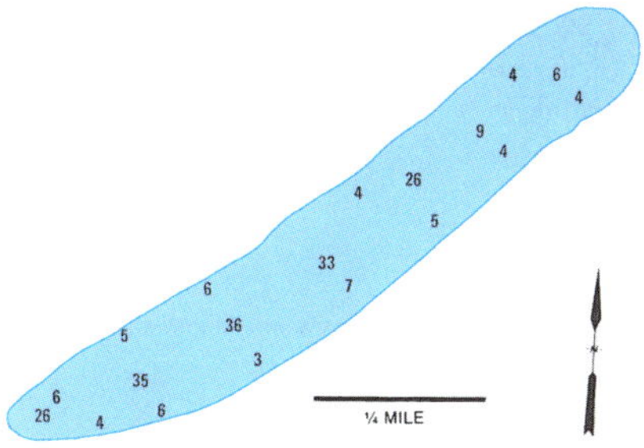

Hunnewell Lake
St. John Plt, Maine Atlas Map 67, C-2, D-2
Acres: 64, Max. Depth: 36 feet, Boat Launch

BrT	BkT	RbT	Sal	Tog	Smt	LmB	SmB	WhP	Csk	WhF	Pic
	✓										

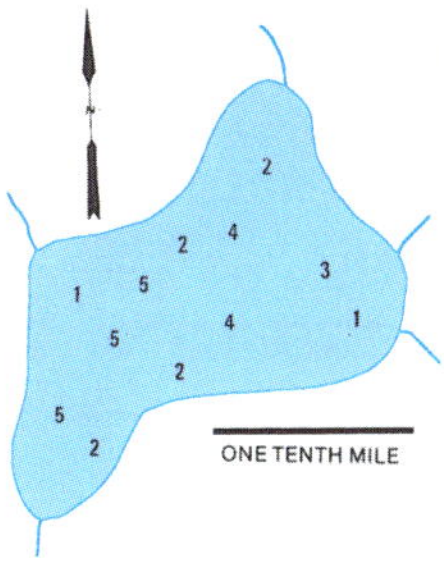

Ketchum Lake
TD R2 WELS
Maine Atlas
Map 59, B-2
Acres: 4
Max. Depth:
5 feet

BrT		LmB	
BkT	✓	SmB	
RbT		WhP	
Sal		Csk	
Tog		WhF	
Smt		Pic	

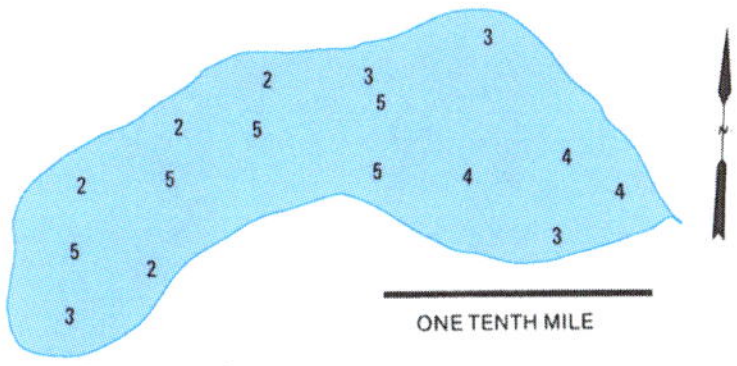

Lambert Pond
New Limerick, Maine Atlas Map 53, A-2
Acres: 6, Max. Depth: 5 feet

BrT	BkT	RbT	Sal	Tog	Smt	LmB	SmB	WhP	Csk	WhF	Pic
	✓										

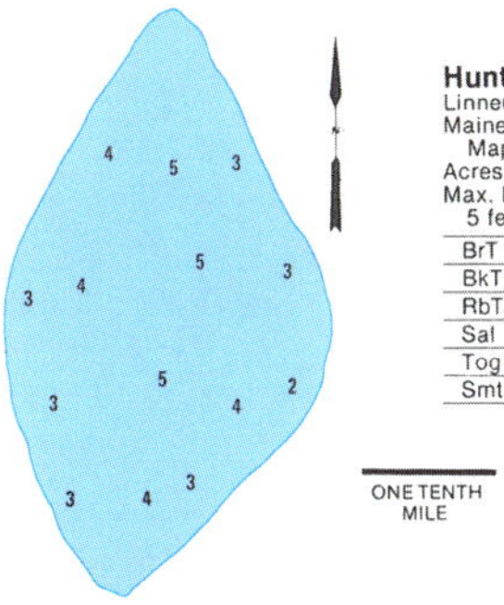

Hunter Pond
Linneus
Maine Atlas
Map 53, B-2
Acres: 12
Max. Depth:
5 feet

BrT		LmB	
BkT		SmB	
RbT		WhP	
Sal		Csk	
Tog		WhF	
Smt		Pic	✓

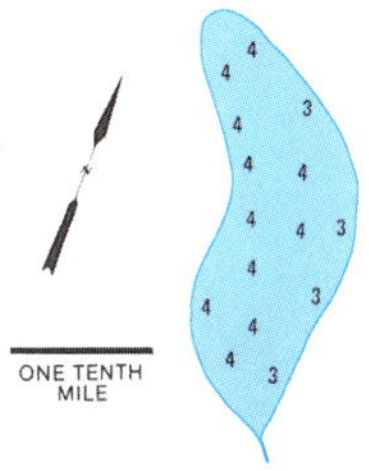

Lindsay Lake
Easton
Maine Atlas
Map 65, D-4
Acres: 6
Max. Depth:
4 feet

BrT		LmB	
BkT	✓	SmB	
RbT		WhP	
Sal		Csk	
Tog		WhF	
Smt		Pic	

Isie Lake
Eagle Lake
Maine Atlas
Map 67, E-4
Acres: 3
Max. Depth:
4 feet

BrT		LmB	
BkT	✓	SmB	
RbT		WhP	
Sal		Csk	
Tog		WhF	
Smt		Pic	

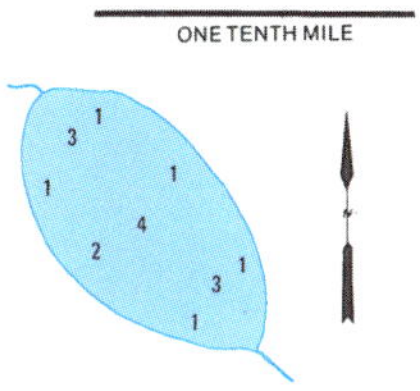

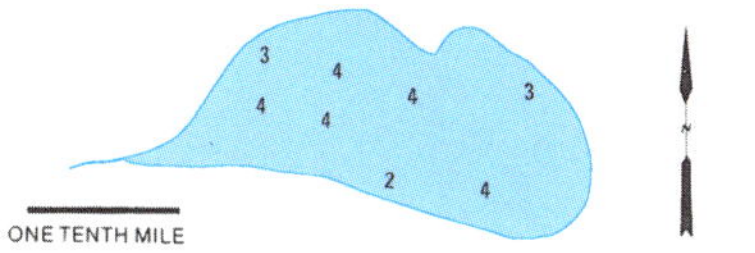

Little Black Brook Lake
Caswell Plt, Maine Atlas Map 69, E-3
Acres: 13, Max. Depth: 4 feet

BrT	BkT	RbT	Sal	Tog	Smt	LmB	SmB	WhP	Csk	WhF	Pic
	✓										

Island Pond
T14 R8 WELS
Maine Atlas
Map 63, B-3
Acres: 27
Max. Depth:
18 feet

BrT		LmB	
BkT	✓	SmB	
RbT		WhP	
Sal		Csk	✓
Tog		WhF	
Smt		Pic	

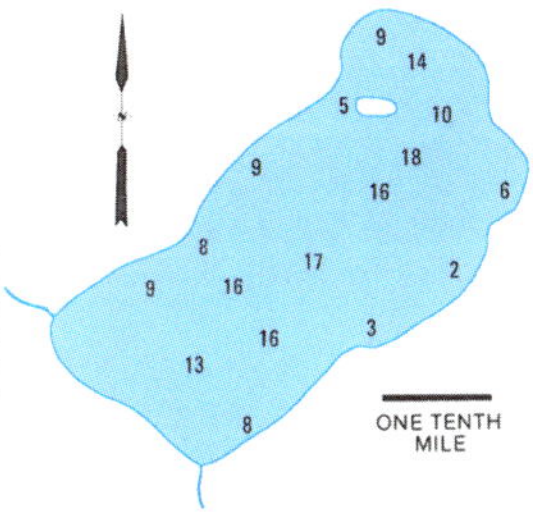

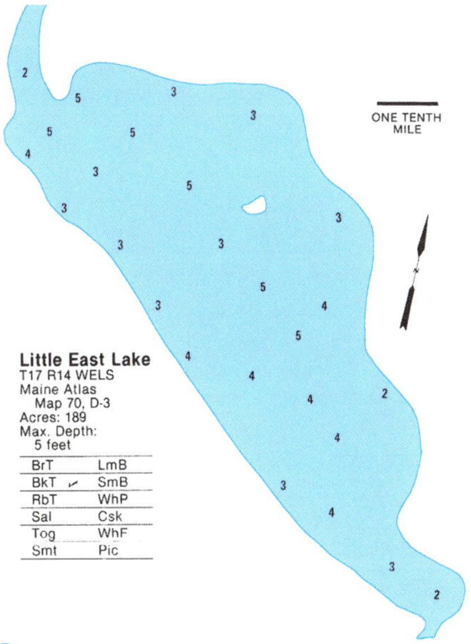

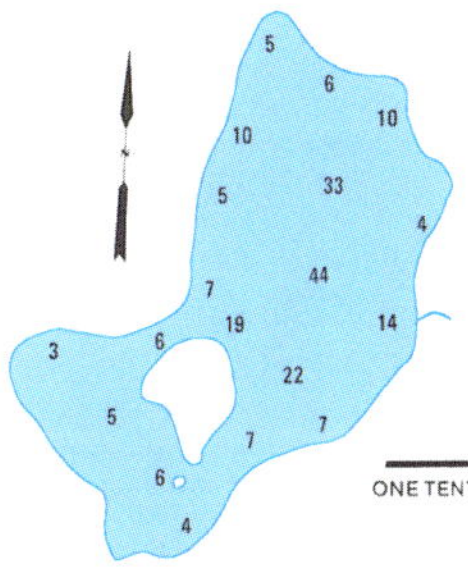

Island Pond
T15 R9 WELS
Maine Atlas
Map 63, A-1
Acres: 32
Max. Depth:
44 feet

BrT		LmB	
BkT	✓	SmB	
RbT		WhP	
Sal		Csk	
Tog		WhF	
Smt		Pic	

Little East Lake
T17 R14 WELS
Maine Atlas
Map 70, D-3
Acres: 189
Max. Depth:
5 feet

BrT		LmB	
BkT	✓	SmB	
RbT		WhP	
Sal		Csk	
Tog		WhF	
Smt		Pic	

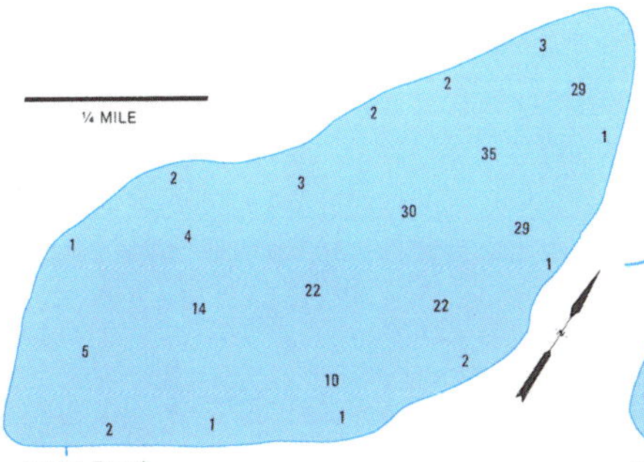

Jones Pond
Big Twenty Twp, Maine Atlas Map 66, A-3
Acres: 77, Max. Depth: 35 feet, Boat Launch

BrT	BkT	RbT	Sal	Tog	Smt	LmB	SmB	WhP	Csk	WhF	Pic
	✓										

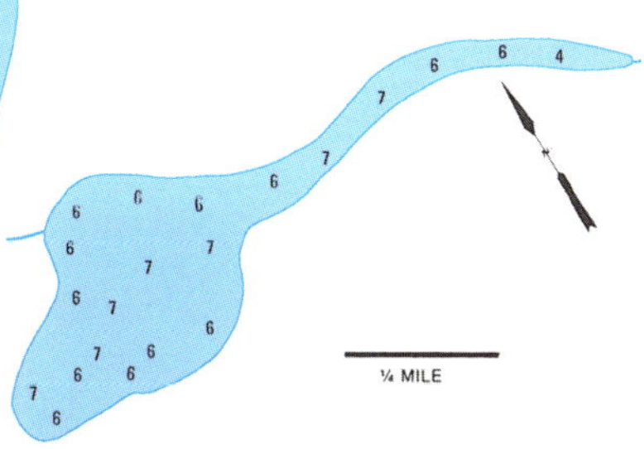

Little Falls Pond
Allagash Plt, Maine Atlas Map 66, C-3
Acres: 74, Max. Depth: 7 feet, Boat Launch

BrT	BkT	RbT	Sal	Tog	Smt	LmB	SmB	WhP	Csk	WhF	Pic
	✓										

Aroostook

Little Gilbert Pond

St. John Plt
Maine Atlas
Map 67, D-2
Acres: 6
Max. Depth:
4 feet

BrT		LmB	
BkT	✓	SmB	
RbT		WhP	
Sal		Csk	
Tog		WhF	
Smt		Pic	

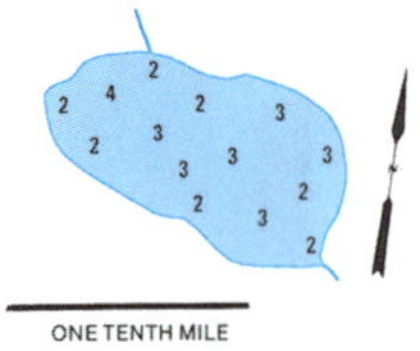

Long Lake

T17 R3 WELS,
T17 R4 WELS,
St. Agatha
Maine Atlas
Map 68, C-3
Acres: 6,000
Max. Depth:
163 feet
Boat Launch

BrT		LmB	
BkT	✓	SmB	
RbT		WhP	
Sal	✓	Csk	✓
Tog		WhF	
Smt	✓	Pic	

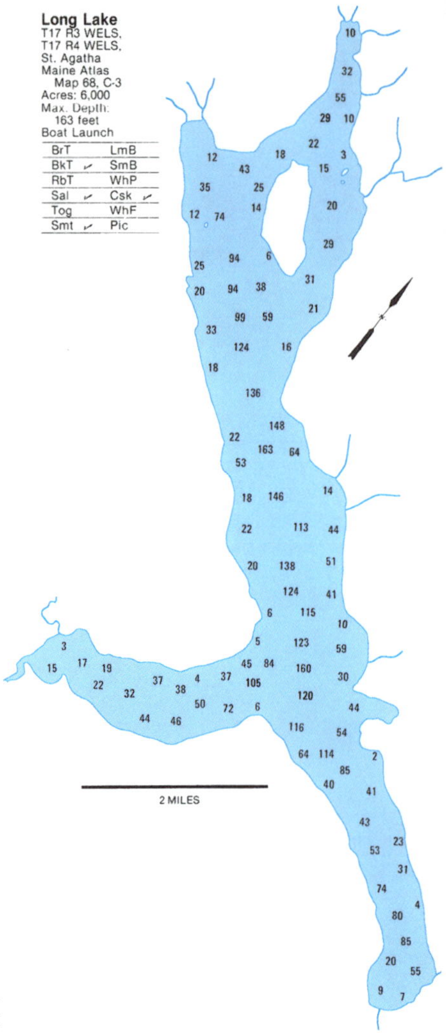

Little Machias Lake

Nashville Plt
Maine Atlas
Map 63, D-5
Acres: 275
Max. Depth:
18 feet
Boat Launch

BrT		LmB	
BkT	✓	SmB	
RbT		WhP	
Sal	✓	Csk	
Tog		WhF	
Smt	✓	Pic	

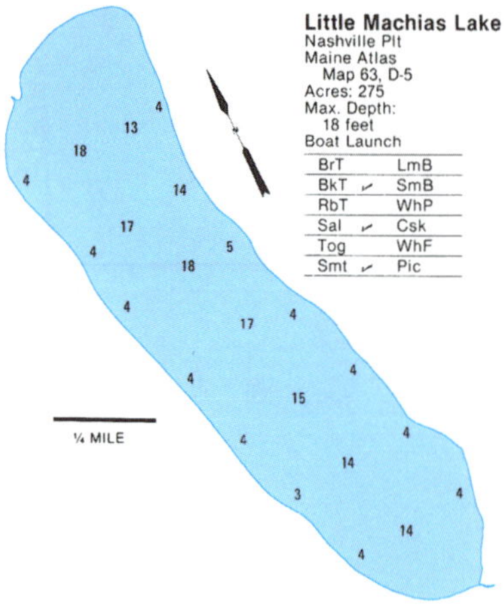

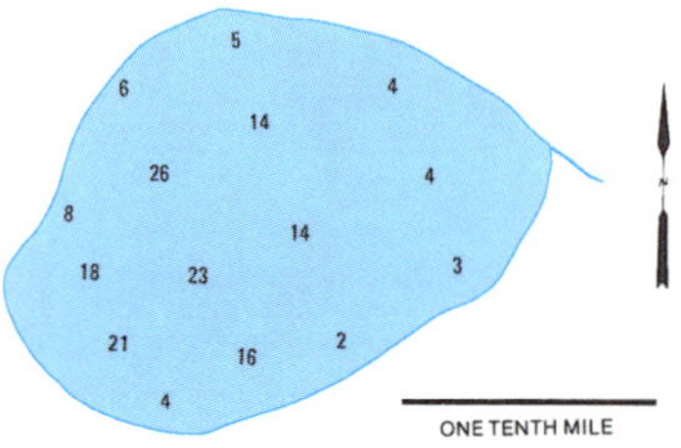

Logan Lake

Littleton, Houlton, Maine Atlas Map 59, E-3
Acres: 13, Max. Depth: 26 feet

BrT	BkT	RbT	Sal	Tog	Smt	LmB	SmB	WhP	Csk	WhF	Pic
	✓										

Long Lake

Littleton
Maine Atlas
Map 59, E-3
Acres: 19
Max. Depth:
32 feet

BrT		LmB	
BkT	✓	SmB	
RbT		WhP	
Sal		Csk	
Tog		WhF	
Smt		Pic	

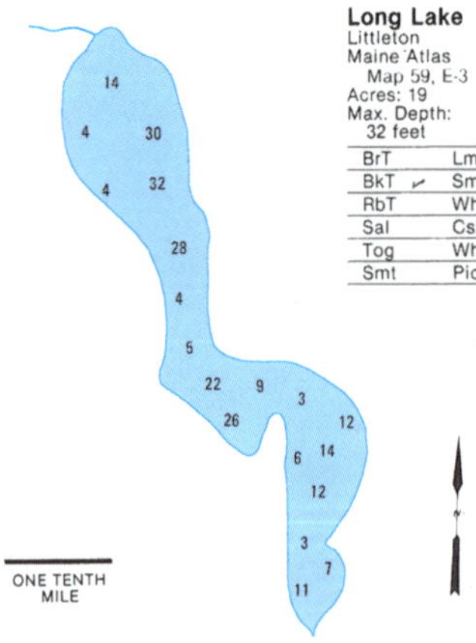

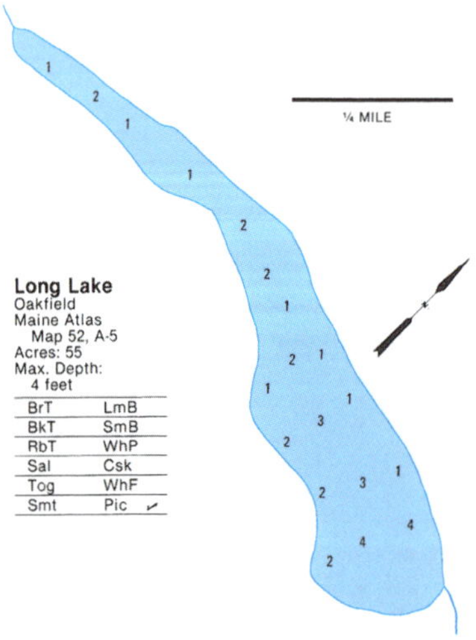

Long Lake

Oakfield
Maine Atlas
Map 52, A-5
Acres: 55
Max. Depth:
4 feet

BrT		LmB	
BkT		SmB	
RbT		WhP	
Sal		Csk	
Tog		WhF	
Smt		Pic	✓

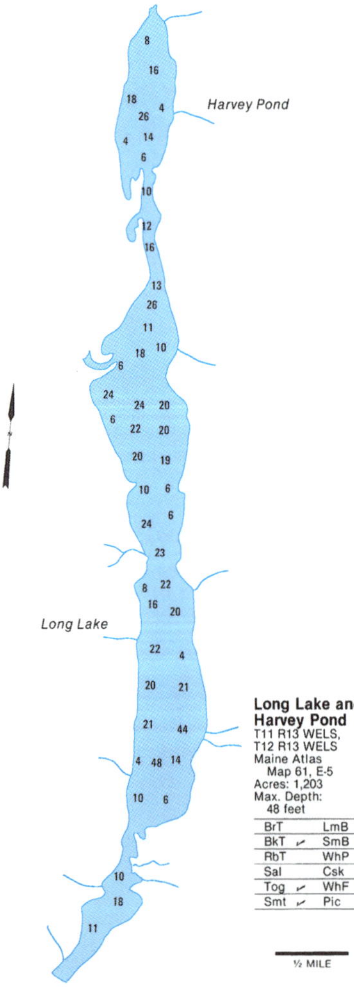

Long Lake and Harvey Pond

T11 R13 WELS,
T12 R13 WELS
Maine Atlas
Map 61, E-5
Acres: 1,203
Max. Depth:
48 feet

BrT		LmB	
BkT	✓	SmB	
RbT		WhP	
Sal		Csk	✓
Tog	✓	WhF	✓
Smt	✓	Pic	

Long Pond

T11 R10 WELS, T11 R11 WELS, Maine Atlas Map 62, E-3, E-4
Acres: 128, Max. Depth: 9 feet.

BrT	BkT	RbT	Sal	Tog	Smt	LmB	SmB	WhP	Csk	WhF	Pic
	✓								✓		

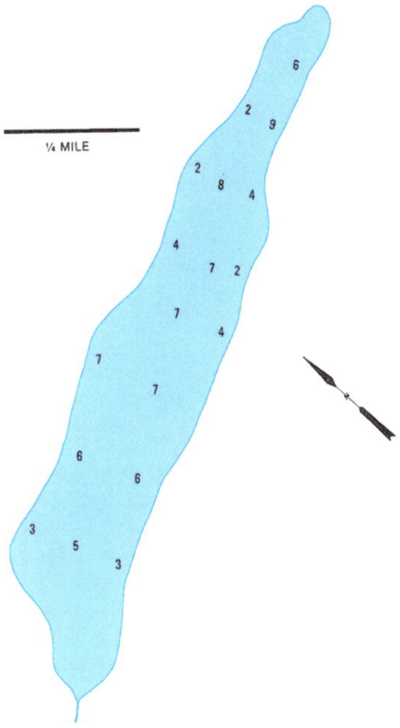

Mattaseunk Lake

Molunkus Twp
Maine Atlas
Map 44, B-2
Acres: 576
Max. Depth:
21 feet
Boat Launch

BrT	LmB
BkT	SmB
RbT	WhP ✓
Sal	Csk
Tog	WhF
Smt	Pic ✓

Lucifee Pond

T14 R8 WELS
Maine Atlas
Map 63, B-2, B-3
Acres: 13
Max. Depth:
5 feet

BrT ✓	LmB
BkT ✓	SmB
RbT	WhP
Sal	Csk
Tog	WhF
Smt	Pic

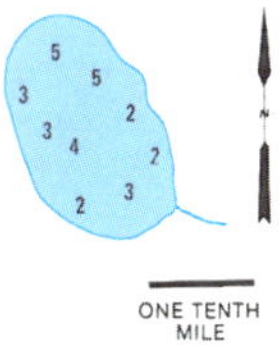

Mattawamkeag Lake

T4 R3 WELS,
Island Falls
Maine Atlas
Map 52, B-4, C-4
Acres: 3,330
Max. Depth:
47 feet
Boat Launch

BrT	LmB
BkT ✓	SmB ✓
RbT	WhP ✓
Sal ✓	Csk
Tog	WhF ✓
Smt ✓	Pic ✓

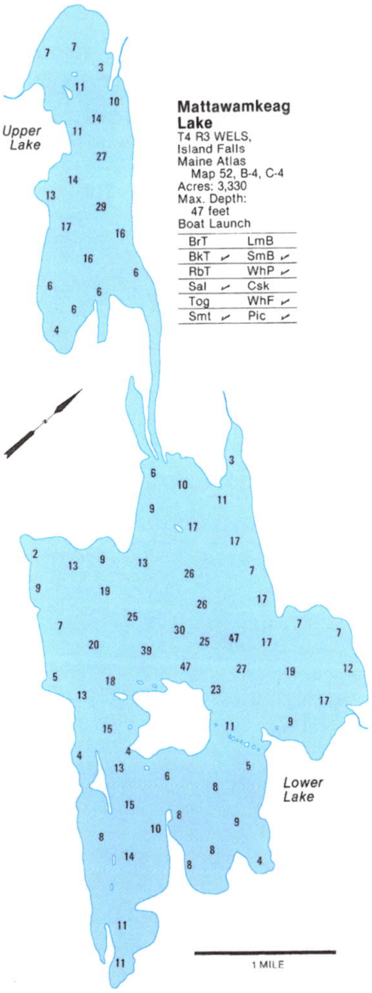

Madawaska Lake

T16 R4 WELS,
Westmanland
Maine Atlas
Map 68, E-4
Acres: 1,526
Max. Depth:
Upper-38 feet,
Lower-32 feet
Boat Launch

BrT	LmB
BkT ✓	SmB
RbT	WhP
Sal ✓	Csk ✓
Tog	WhF
Smt ✓	Pic

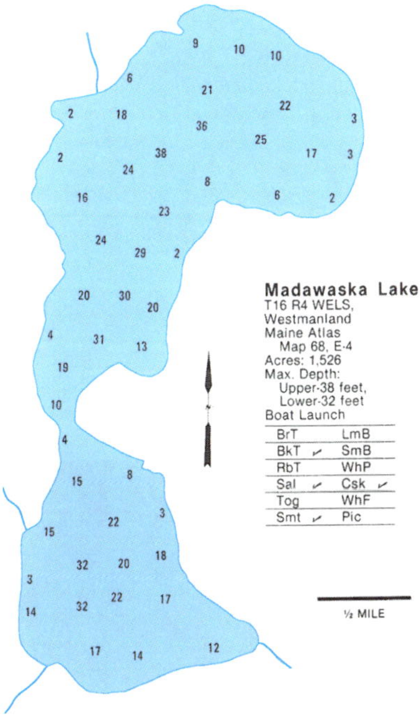

Aroostook

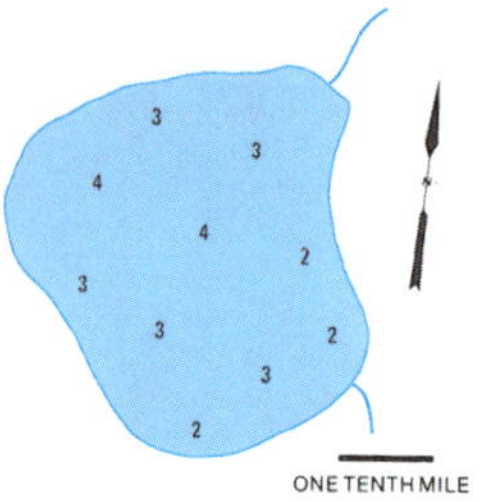

McClusky Lake

T14 R5 WELS,
T15 R5 WELS
Maine Atlas
Map 64, A-1
Acres: 49
Max. Depth:
4 feet

BrT		LmB	
BkT	✓	SmB	
RbT		WhP	
Sal		Csk	
Tog		WhF	
Smt		Pic	

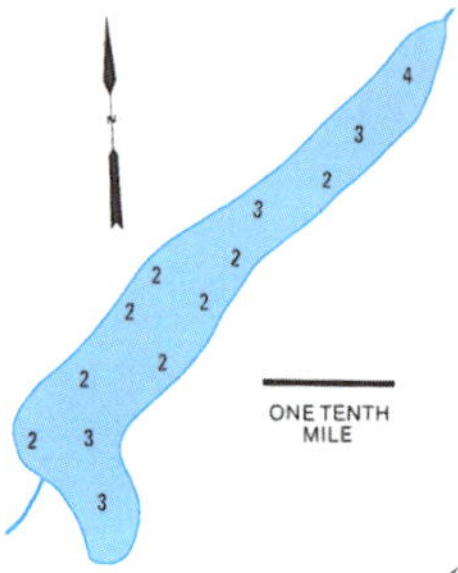

Mink Marsh Pond

T11 R10 WELS,
T10 R10 WELS
Maine Atlas
Map 56, A-5
Acres: 13
Max. Depth:
4 feet

BrT		LmB	
BkT	✓	SmB	
RbT		WhP	
Sal		Csk	
Tog		WhF	
Smt		Pic	

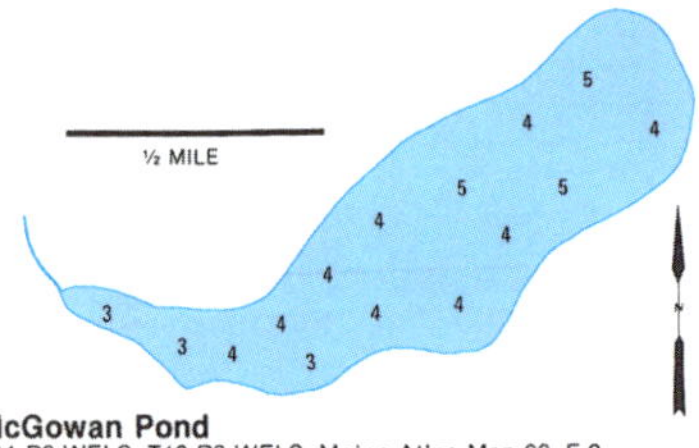

McGowan Pond

T11 R8 WELS, T12 R8 WELS, Maine Atlas Map 63, E-2
Acres: 160, Max. Depth: 5 feet

BrT	BkT	RbT	Sal	Tog	Smt	LmB	SmB	WhP	Csk	WhF	Pic
	✓										

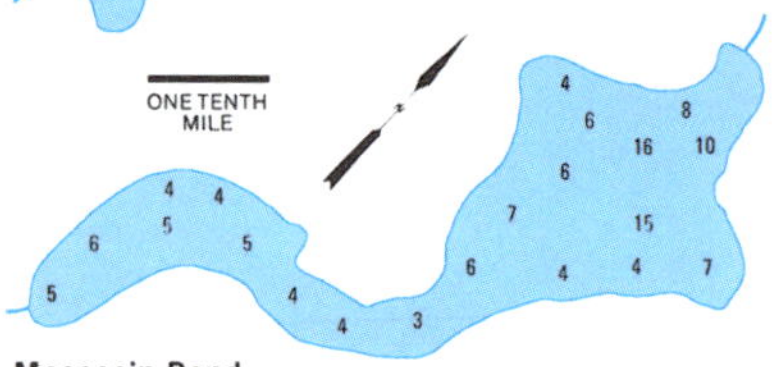

Moccasin Pond

T14 R8 WELS, Maine Atlas Map 63, B-3
Acres: 32, Max. Depth: 16 feet

BrT	BkT	RbT	Sal	Tog	Smt	LmB	SmB	WhP	Csk	WhF	Pic
	✓										

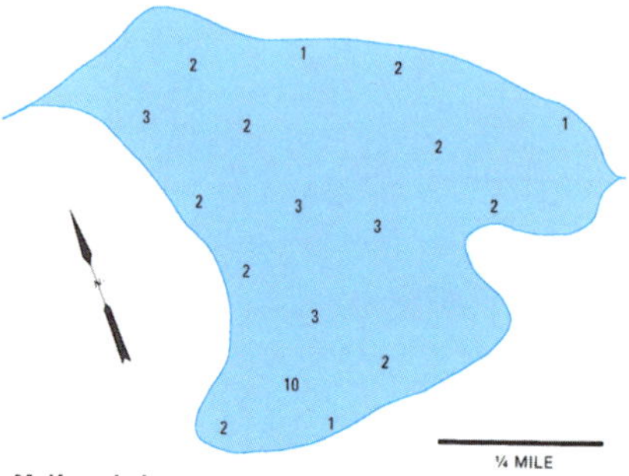

McKeen Lake

T14 R10 WELS, Maine Atlas Map 62, B-4
Acres: 147, Max. Depth: 10 feet

BrT	BkT	RbT	Sal	Tog	Smt	LmB	SmB	WhP	Csk	WhF	Pic
	✓										

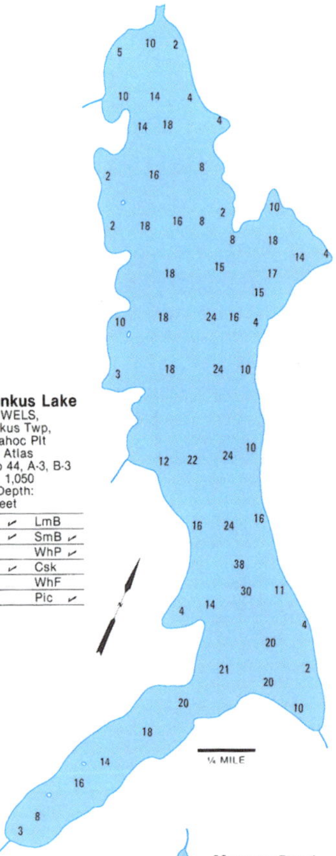

Molunkus Lake

T1 R5 WELS,
Molunkus Twp,
Macwahoc Plt
Maine Atlas
Map 44, A-3, B-3
Acres: 1,050
Max. Depth:
38 feet

BrT	✓	LmB	
BkT	✓	SmB	✓
RbT		WhP	✓
Sal	✓	Csk	
Tog		WhF	
Smt		Pic	✓

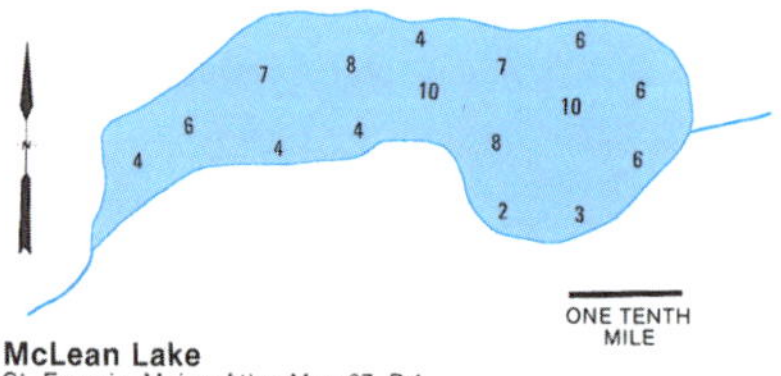

McLean Lake

St. Francis, Maine Atlas Map 67, D-1
Acres: 34, Max. Depth: 10 feet, Boat Launch

BrT	BkT	RbT	Sal	Tog	Smt	LmB	SmB	WhP	Csk	WhF	Pic
	✓										

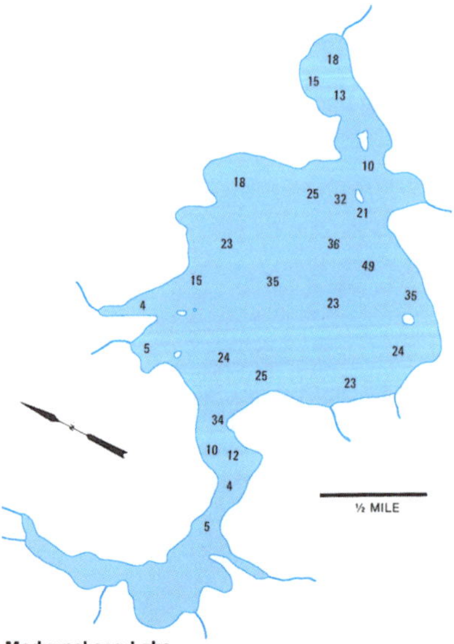

Meduxnekeag Lake

New Limerick, Oakfield, Linneus, Maine Atlas Map 53, A-1
Acres: 1,057, Max. Depth: 49 feet, Boat Launch

BrT	BkT	RbT	Sal	Tog	Smt	LmB	SmB	WhP	Csk	WhF	Pic
✓	✓		✓		✓			✓			

Comments: Splake.

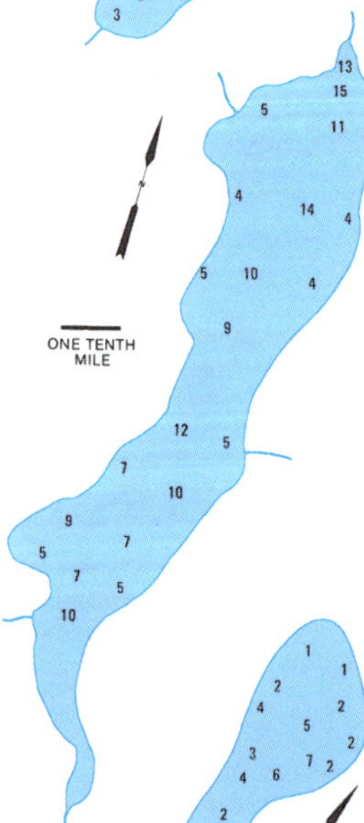

Monson Pond

Fort Fairfield
Maine Atlas
Map 65, D-4
Acres: 160
Max. Depth:
15 feet
Boat Launch

BrT		LmB	
BkT	✓	SmB	
RbT		WhP	
Sal		Csk	
Tog		WhF	
Smt		Pic	

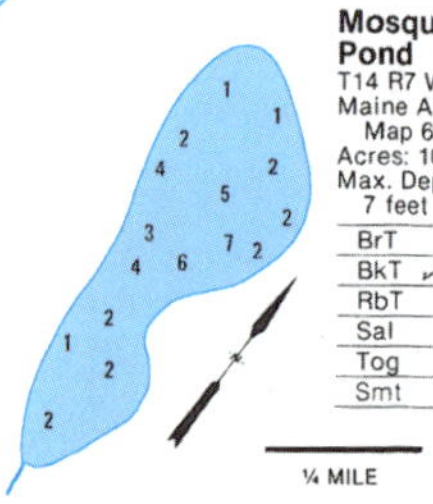

Mosquito Brook Pond

T14 R7 WELS
Maine Atlas
Map 63, B-5
Acres: 10
Max. Depth:
7 feet

BrT		LmB	
BkT	✓	SmB	
RbT		WhP	
Sal		Csk	
Tog		WhF	
Smt		Pic	

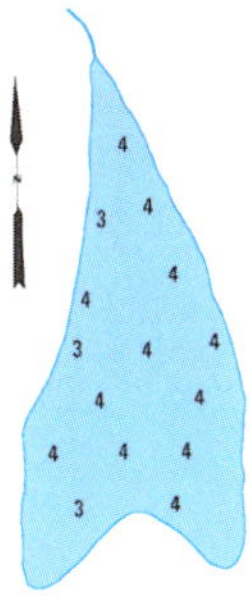

Mud Lake
Stockholm
Maine Atlas
Map 68, D-5, E-5
Acres: 45
Max. Depth:
4 feet

BrT		LmB	
BkT	✓	SmB	
RbT		WhP	
Sal		Csk	
Tog		WhF	
Smt		Pic	

¼ MILE

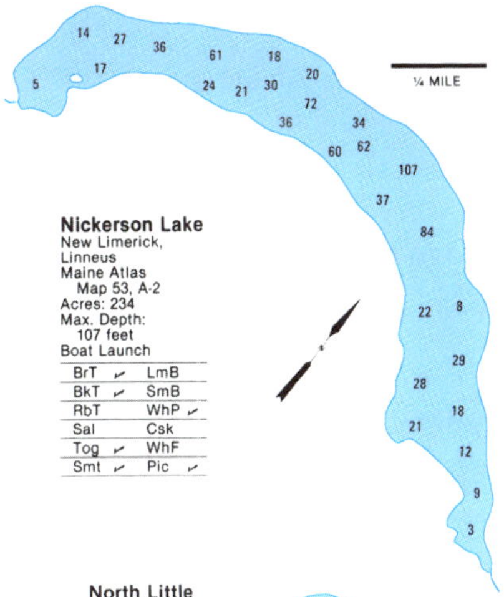

Nickerson Lake
New Limerick,
Linneus
Maine Atlas
Map 53, A-2
Acres: 234
Max. Depth:
107 feet
Boat Launch

BrT	✓	LmB	
BkT	✓	SmB	
RbT		WhP	✓
Sal		Csk	
Tog	✓	WhF	
Smt	✓	Pic	✓

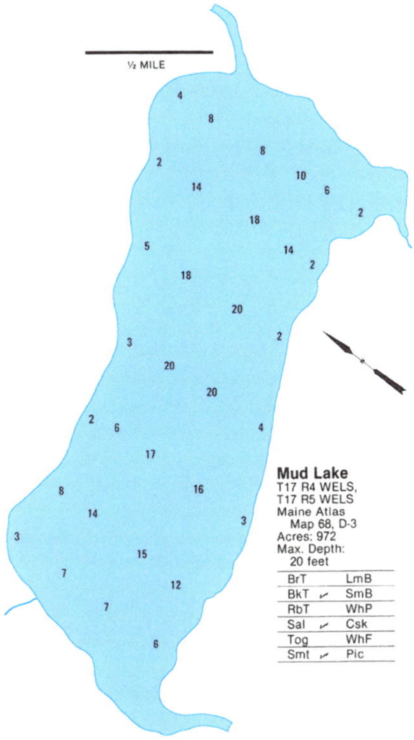

Mud Lake
T17 R4 WELS,
T17 R5 WELS
Maine Atlas
Map 68, D-3
Acres: 972
Max. Depth:
20 feet

BrT		LmB	
BkT	✓	SmB	
RbT		WhP	
Sal	✓	Csk	
Tog		WhF	
Smt	✓	Pic	

North Little Black Pond
T15 R9 WELS
Maine Atlas
Map 63, A-1
Acres: 6
Max. Depth:
12 feet

BrT		LmB	
BkT	✓	SmB	
RbT		WhP	
Sal		Csk	
Tog		WhF	
Smt		Pic	

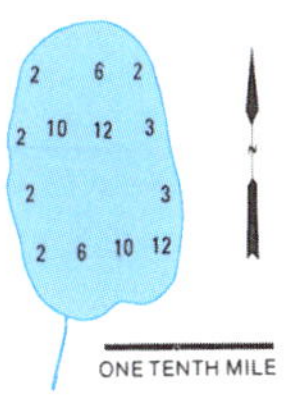

North Pond
T8 R3 WELS,
Dudley Twp
Maine Atlas
Map 58, D-5
Acres: 16
Max. Depth:
4 feet

BrT		LmB	
BkT	✓	SmB	
RbT		WhP	
Sal		Csk	
Tog		WhF	
Smt		Pic	

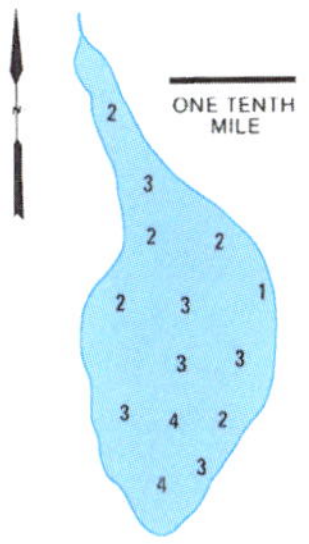

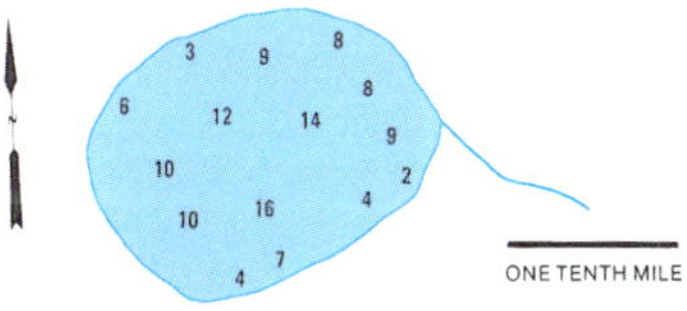

North Pond
T14 R9 WELS, Maine Atlas Map 63, A-1
Acres: 15, Max. Depth: 16 feet

BrT	BkT	RbT	Sal	Tog	Smt	LmB	SmB	WhP	Csk	WhF	Pic
	✓										

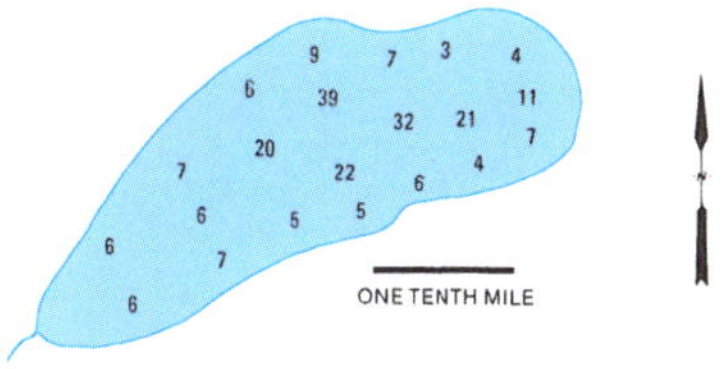

Mud Pond
Linneus, Maine Atlas Map 53, B-1
Acres: 19, Max. Depth: 39 feet

BrT	BkT	RbT	Sal	Tog	Smt	LmB	SmB	WhP	Csk	WhF	Pic
	✓										✓

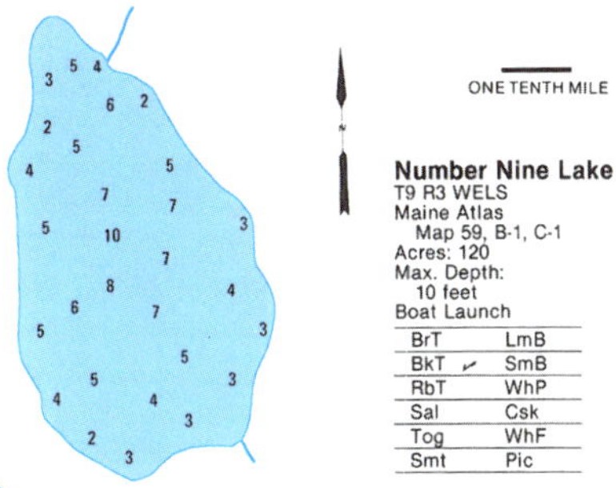

Number Nine Lake
T9 R3 WELS
Maine Atlas
Map 59, B-1, C-1
Acres: 120
Max. Depth:
10 feet
Boat Launch

BrT		LmB	
BkT	✓	SmB	
RbT		WhP	
Sal		Csk	
Tog		WhF	
Smt		Pic	

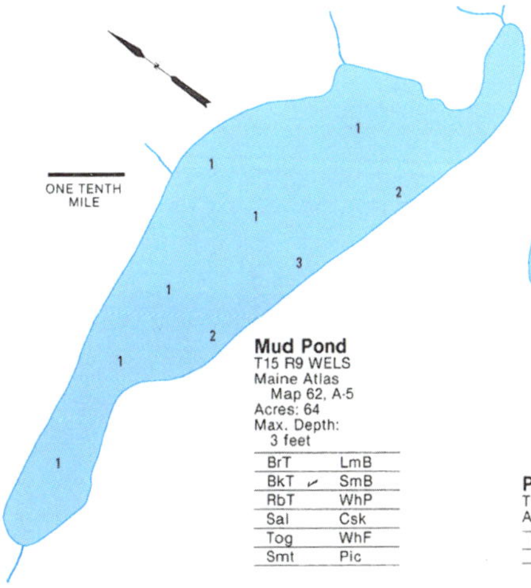

Mud Pond
T15 R9 WELS
Maine Atlas
Map 62, A-5
Acres: 64
Max. Depth:
3 feet

BrT		LmB	
BkT	✓	SmB	
RbT		WhP	
Sal		Csk	
Tog		WhF	
Smt		Pic	

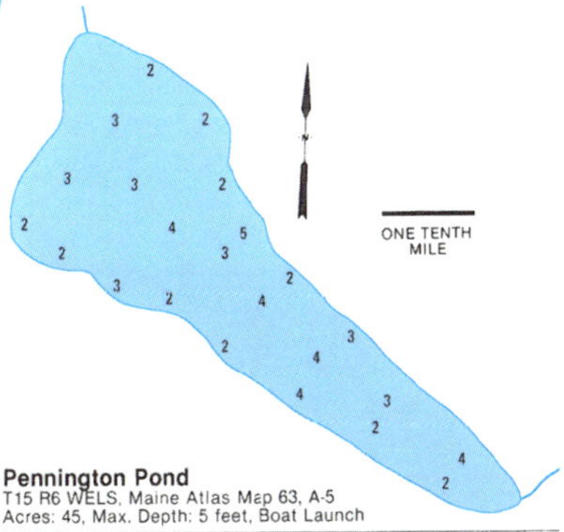

Pennington Pond
T15 R6 WELS, Maine Atlas Map 63, A-5
Acres: 45, Max. Depth: 5 feet, Boat Launch

BrT	BkT	RbT	Sal	Tog	Smt	LmB	SmB	WhP	Csk	WhF	Pic
	✓										

Aroostook

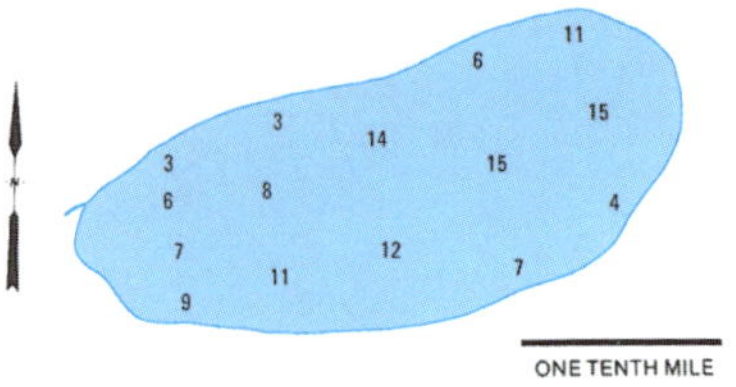

Perch Pond
T15 R9 WELS, Maine Atlas Map 63, A-1
Acres: 17, Max. Depth: 15 feet, Boat Launch

BrT	BkT	RbT	Sal	Tog	Smt	LmB	SmB	WhP	Csk	WhF	Pic
	✓										

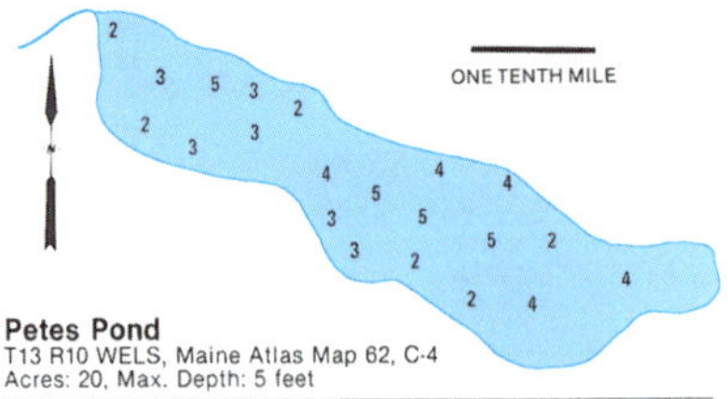

Petes Pond
T13 R10 WELS, Maine Atlas Map 62, C-4
Acres: 20, Max. Depth: 5 feet

BrT	BkT	RbT	Sal	Tog	Smt	LmB	SmB	WhP	Csk	WhF	Pic
	✓										

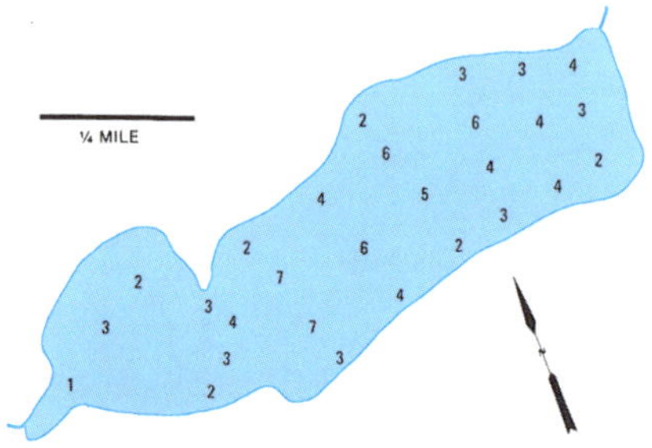

Pickett Mountain Pond
T6 R6 WELS, Moro Plt, Maine Atlas Map 52, A-1
Acres: 173, Max. Depth: 7 feet

BrT	BkT	RbT	Sal	Tog	Smt	LmB	SmB	WhP	Csk	WhF	Pic
✓	✓										

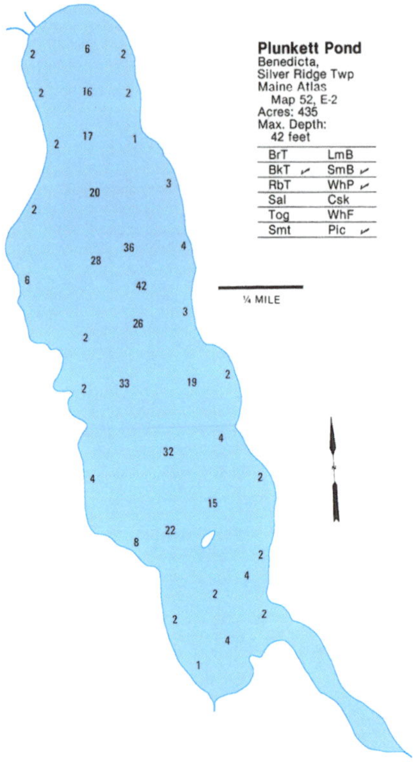

Plunkett Pond
Benedicta,
Silver Ridge Twp
Maine Atlas
Map 52, E-2
Acres: 435
Max. Depth:
42 feet

BrT		LmB	
BkT	✓	SmB	✓
RbT		WhP	✓
Sal		Csk	
Tog		WhF	
Smt		Pic	✓

Portage Lake
Portage Lake, Maine Atlas Map 63, C-5, Map 64, C-1
Acres: 2,474, Max. Depth: 25 feet, Boat Launch

BrT	BkT	RbT	Sal	Tog	Smt	LmB	SmB	WhP	Csk	WhF	Pic
	✓		✓		✓				✓		

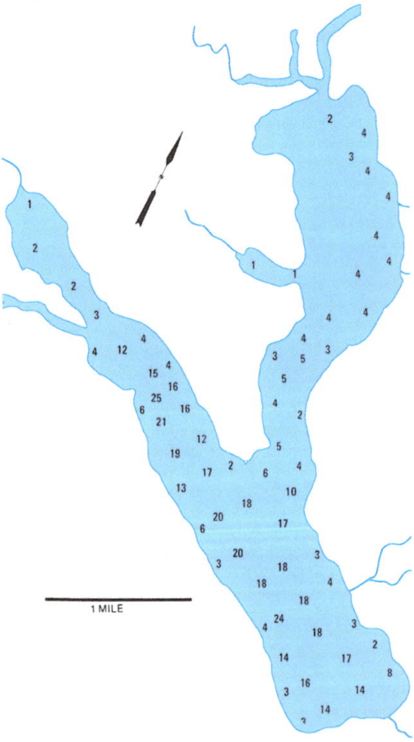

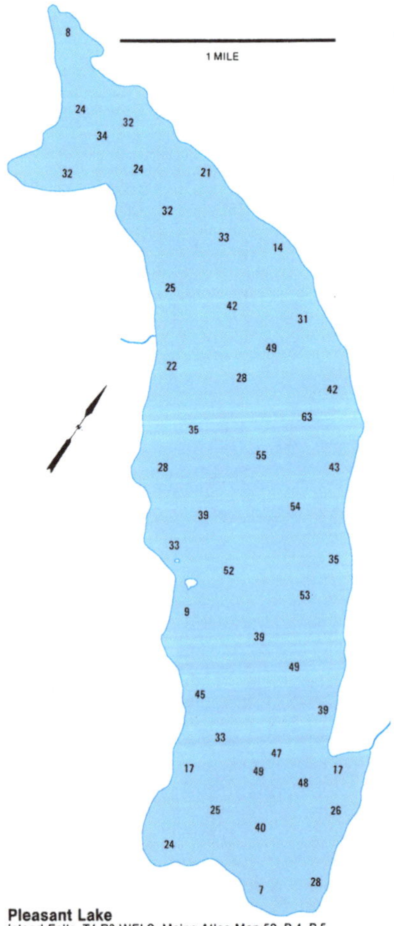

Pleasant Lake
Island Falls, T4 R3 WELS, Maine Atlas Map 52, B-4, B-5
Acres: 1,832, Max. Depth: 63 feet, Boat Launch

BrT	BkT	RbT	Sal	Tog	Smt	LmB	SmB	WhP	Csk	WhF	Pic
✓	✓		✓		✓		✓	✓	✓		✓

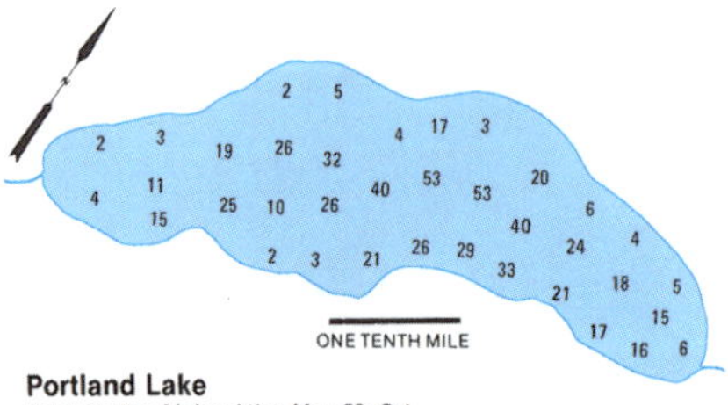

Portland Lake
Bridgewater, Maine Atlas Map 59, C-4
Acres: 41, Max. Depth: 53 feet

BrT	BkT	RbT	Sal	Tog	Smt	LmB	SmB	WhP	Csk	WhF	Pic
	✓		✓								

Pratt Lake

T11 R9 WELS, Maine Atlas Map 63, E-1
Acres: 96, Max. Depth: 11 feet, Boat Launch

BrT	BkT	RbT	Sal	Tog	Smt	LmB	SmB	WhP	Csk	WhF	Pic
	✓		✓								

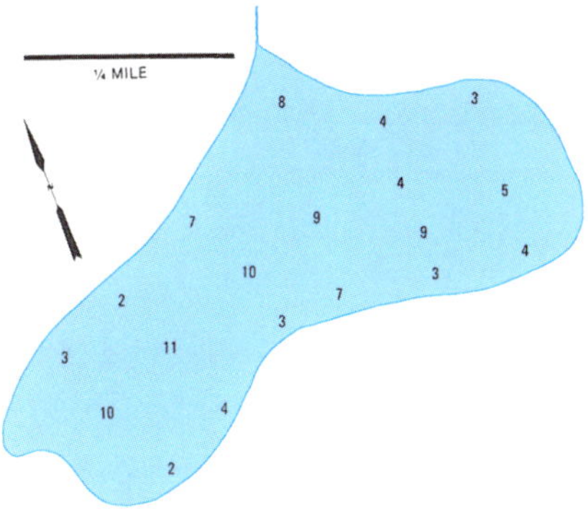

Rideout Pond

T19 R12 WELS, Maine Atlas Map 66, B-1
Acres: 1, Max. Depth: 69 feet

BrT	BkT	RbT	Sal	Tog	Smt	LmB	SmB	WhP	Csk	WhF	Pic
	✓										

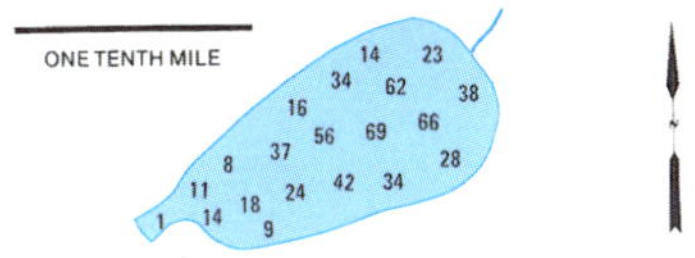

Ritter Lake

Bridgewater
Maine Atlas
Map 59, C-4
Acres: 5
Max. Depth:
12 feet

BrT		LmB	
BkT	✓	SmB	
RbT		WhP	
Sal		Csk	
Tog		WhF	
Smt		Pic	

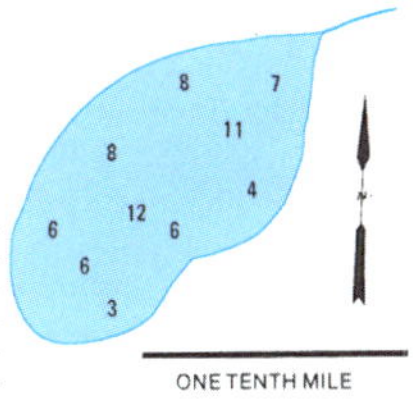

Presley Lake

T12 R17 WELS
Maine Atlas
Map 60, D-3, D-4
Acres: 202
Max. Depth:
5 feet

BrT		LmB	
BkT	✓	SmB	
RbT		WhP	
Sal		Csk	
Tog		WhF	
Smt		Pic	

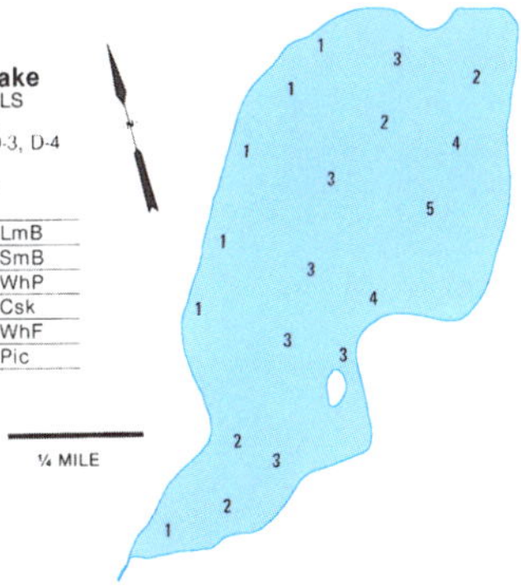

Robbins Brook Pond

T12 R11 WELS
Maine Atlas
Map 62, D-2, D-3
Acres: 27
Max. Depth:
14 feet

BrT		LmB	
BkT	✓	SmB	
RbT		WhP	
Sal		Csk	
Tog		WhF	
Smt		Pic	

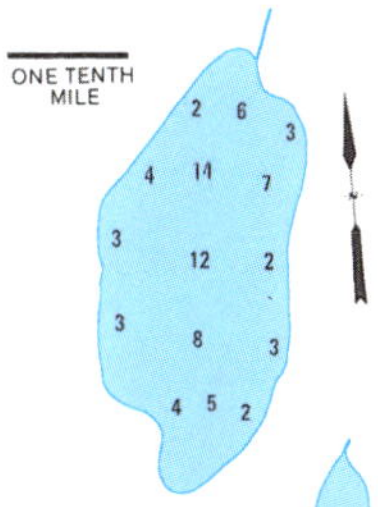

Presque Isle Lake

T9 R3 WELS, Maine Atlas Map 58, C-5
Acres: 38, Max. Depth: 3 feet

BrT	BkT	RbT	Sal	Tog	Smt	LmB	SmB	WhP	Csk	WhF	Pic
	✓										

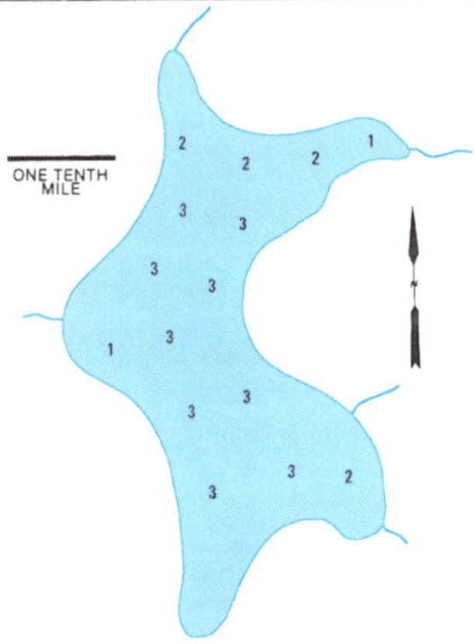

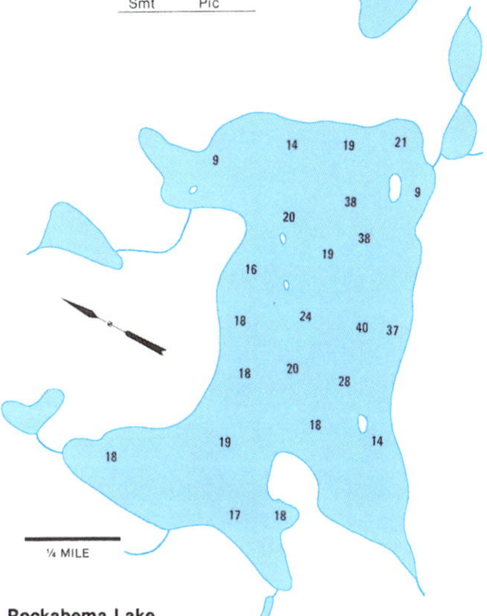

Rockabema Lake

Moro Plt, Maine Atlas Map 58, E-2
Acres: 339, Max. Depth: 40 feet, Boat Launch.

BrT	BkT	RbT	Sal	Tog	Smt	LmB	SmB	WhP	Csk	WhF	Pic
	✓		✓								

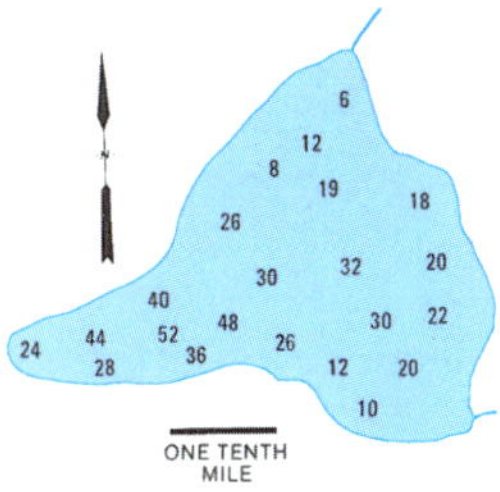

Pushineer Pond

T15 R9 WELS
Maine Atlas
Map 63, A-1
Acres: 55
Max. Depth:
52 feet
Boat Launch

BrT		LmB	
BkT	✓	SmB	
RbT		WhP	
Sal		Csk	
Tog		WhF	
Smt		Pic	

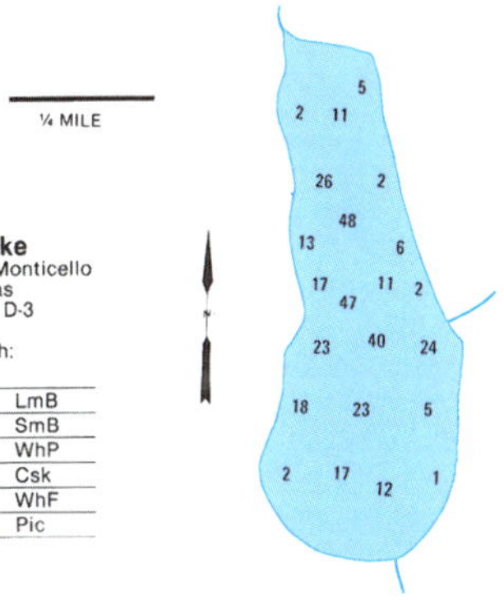

Ross Lake

Littleton, Monticello
Maine Atlas
Map 59, D-3
Acres: 32
Max. Depth:
48 feet

BrT		LmB	
BkT	✓	SmB	
RbT		WhP	
Sal		Csk	
Tog		WhF	
Smt		Pic	

Read Lake

Merrill
Maine Atlas
Map 58, E-4
Acres: 5
Max. Depth:
5 feet

BrT		LmB	
BkT	✓	SmB	
RbT		WhP	
Sal		Csk	
Tog		WhF	
Smt		Pic	

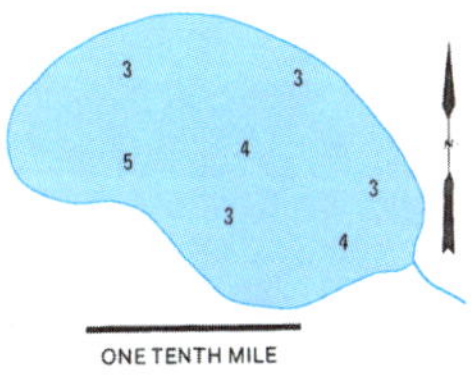

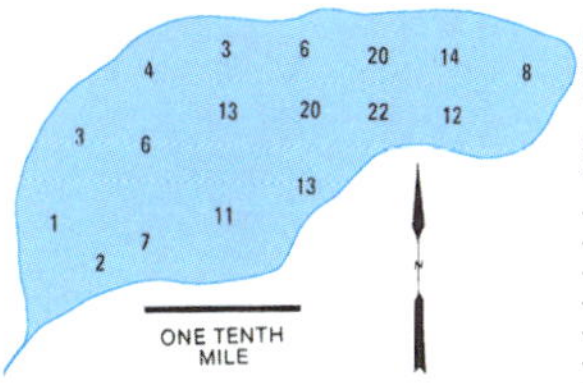

Reed Pond

Macwahoc Plt
Maine Atlas
Map 44, B-4
Acres: 35
Max. Depth:
22 feet

BrT		LmB	
BkT		SmB	
RbT		WhP	
Sal		Csk	
Tog		WhF	
Smt		Pic	✓

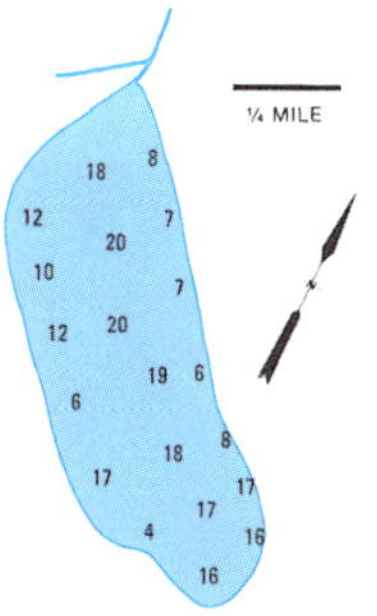

Round Mountain Pond

T11 R8 WELS
Maine Atlas
Map 63, E-2
Acres: 38
Max. Depth:
20 feet
Boat Launch

BrT		LmB	
BkT	✓	SmB	
RbT		WhP	
Sal		Csk	
Tog		WhF	
Smt		Pic	

Comments: Splake.

Aroostook

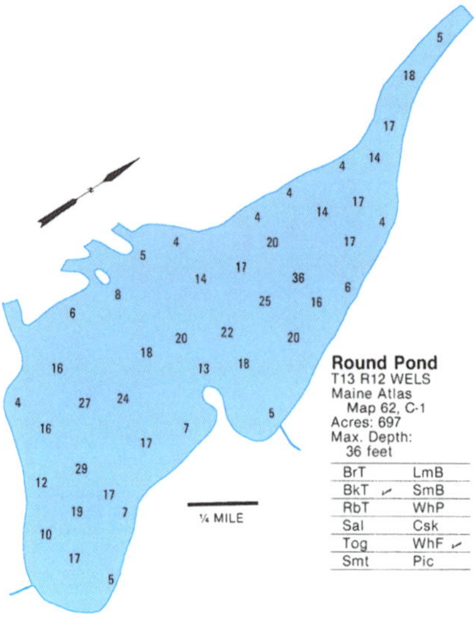

Round Pond

T13 R12 WELS
Maine Atlas
Map 62, C-1
Acres: 697
Max. Depth:
36 feet

BrT		LmB	
BkT	✓	SmB	
RbT		WhP	
Sal		Csk	
Tog		WhF	✓
Smt		Pic	

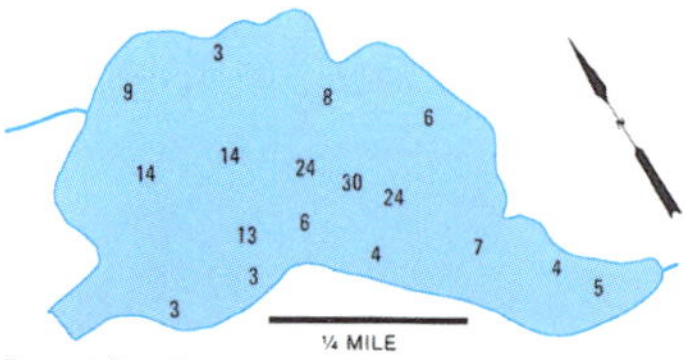

Round Pond

T14 R8 WELS, Maine Atlas Map 63, B-2, B-3
Acres: 90, Max. Depth: 30 feet

BrT	BkT	RbT	Sal	Tog	Smt	LmB	SmB	WhP	Csk	WhF	Pic
	✓		✓		✓						

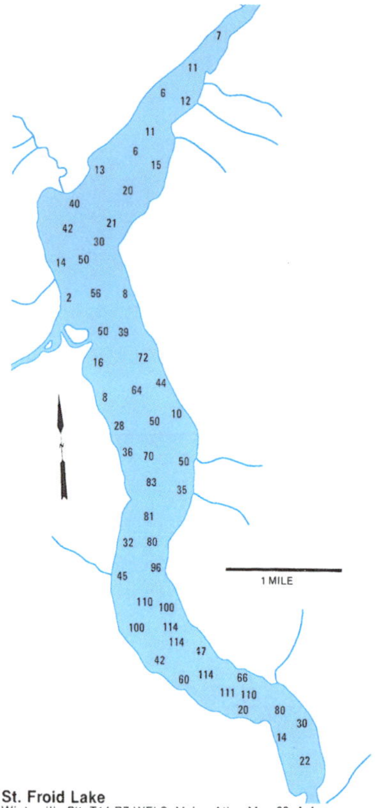

St. Froid Lake

Winterville Plt, T14 R7 WELS, Maine Atlas Map 63, A-4
Acres: 2,400, Max. Depth: 114 feet, Boat Launch

BrT	BkT	RbT	Sal	Tog	Smt	LmB	SmB	WhP	Csk	WhF	Pic
	✓		✓	✓	✓				✓	✓	

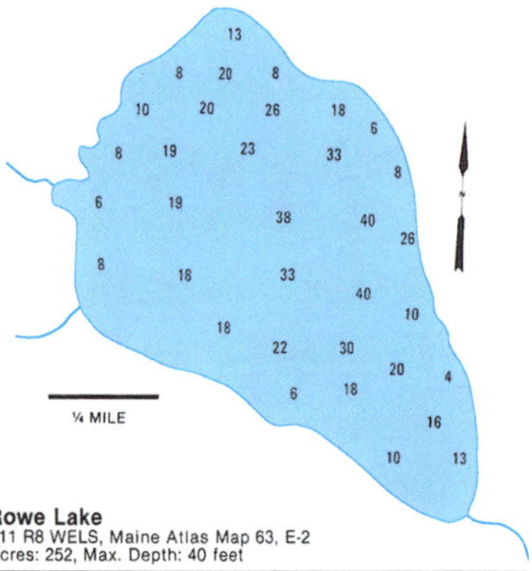

Rowe Lake

T11 R8 WELS, Maine Atlas Map 63, E-2
Acres: 252, Max. Depth: 40 feet

BrT	BkT	RbT	Sal	Tog	Smt	LmB	SmB	WhP	Csk	WhF	Pic
	✓		✓		✓						

Comments: Splake.

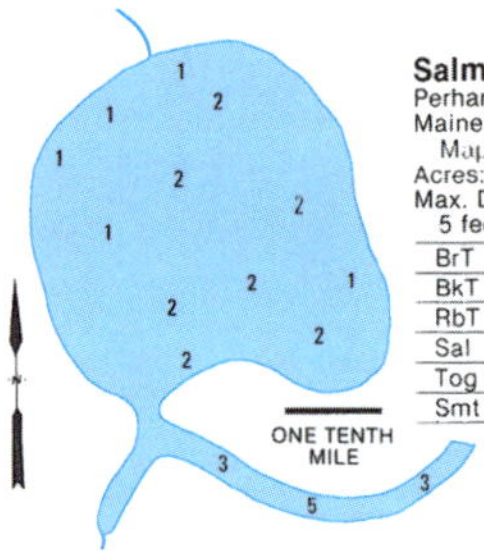

Salmon Brook Lake

Perham
Maine Atlas
Map 64, B-4
Acres: 51
Max. Depth:
5 feet

BrT		LmB	
BkT	✓	SmB	
RbT		WhP	
Sal		Csk	
Tog		WhF	
Smt		Pic	

Second Chase Pond

T14 R9 WELS, Maine Atlas Map 62, B-5, Map 63, B-1
Acres: 182, Max. Depth: 123 feet

BrT	BkT	RbT	Sal	Tog	Smt	LmB	SmB	WhP	Csk	WhF	Pic
	✓			✓							

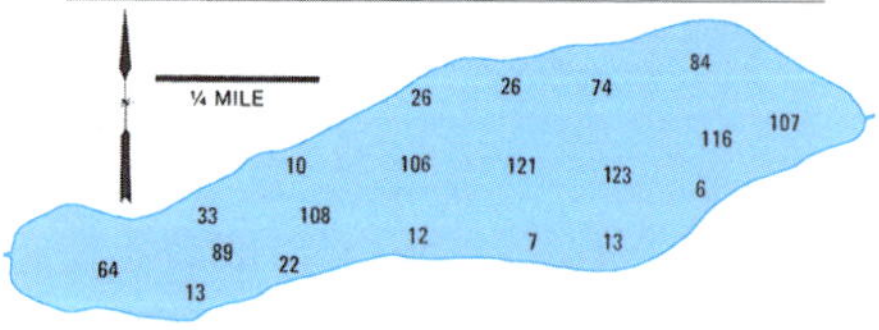

St. Croix Lake

St. Croix Twp,
Webbertown Twp
Maine Atlas
Map 58, D-4
Acres: 416
Max. Depth:
9 feet

BrT		LmB	
BkT	✓	SmB	
RbT		WhP	
Sal		Csk	
Tog		WhF	
Smt		Pic	

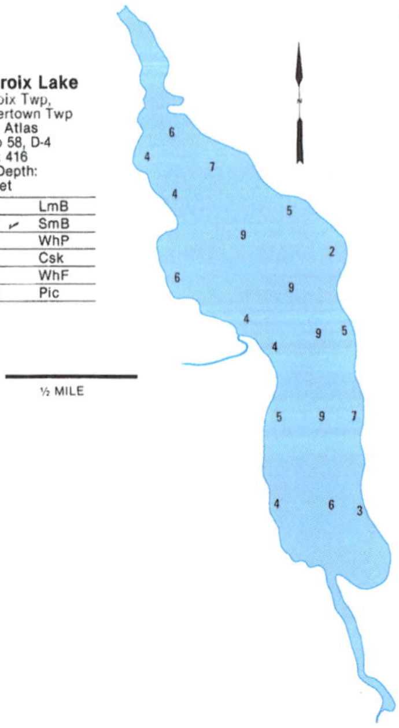

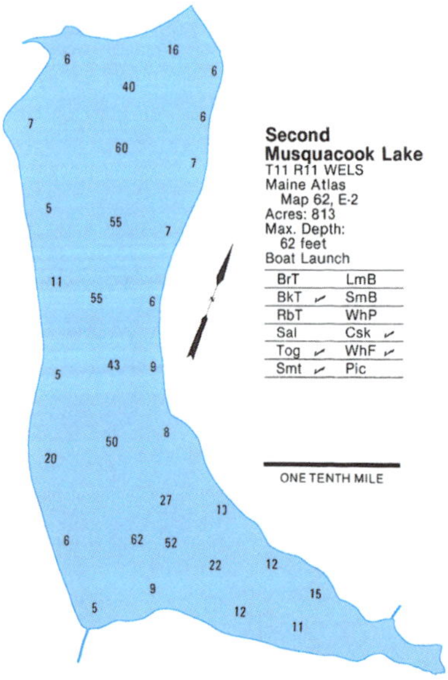

Second Musquacook Lake

T11 R11 WELS
Maine Atlas
Map 62, E-2
Acres: 813
Max. Depth:
62 feet
Boat Launch

BrT		LmB	
BkT	✓	SmB	
RbT		WhP	
Sal		Csk	✓
Tog	✓	WhF	✓
Smt	✓	Pic	

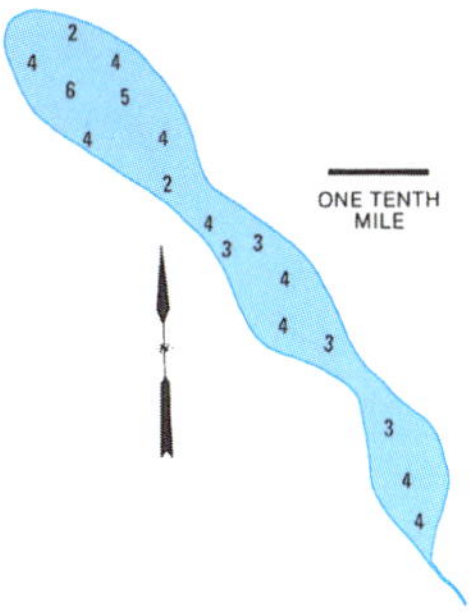

Second Pelletier Brook Lake

T16 R9 WELS
Maine Atlas
Map 67, E-1
Acres: 26
Max. Depth:
6 feet

BrT		LmB	
BkT	✓	SmB	
RbT		WhP	
Sal		Csk	
Tog		WhF	
Smt		Pic	

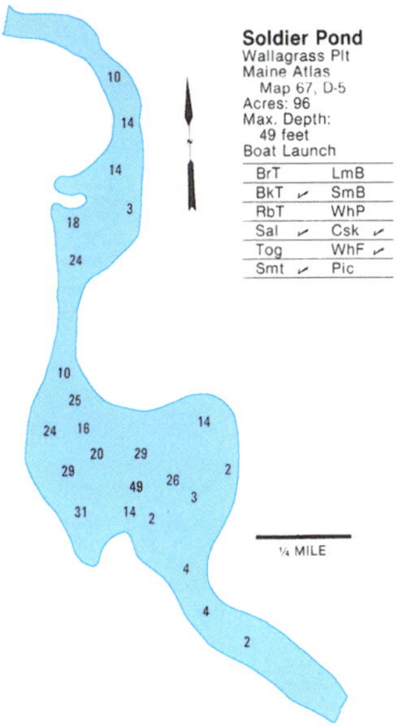

Soldier Pond

Wallagrass Plt
Maine Atlas
Map 67, D-5
Acres: 96
Max. Depth:
49 feet
Boat Launch

BrT		LmB	
BkT	✓	SmB	
RbT		WhP	
Sal	✓	Csk	✓
Tog		WhF	✓
Smt	✓	Pic	

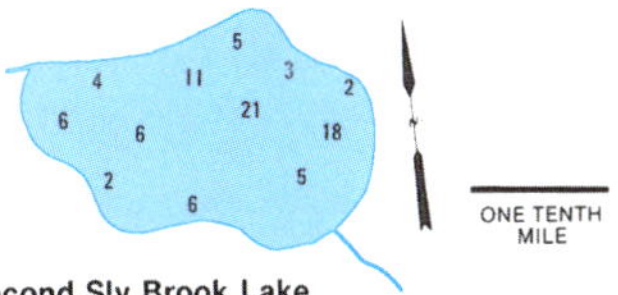

Second Sly Brook Lake

New Canada, Maine Atlas Map 67, D-5
Acres: 13, Max. Depth: 21 feet, Boat Launch

BrT	BkT	RbT	Sal	Tog	Smt	LmB	SmB	WhP	Csk	WhF	Pic
	✓										

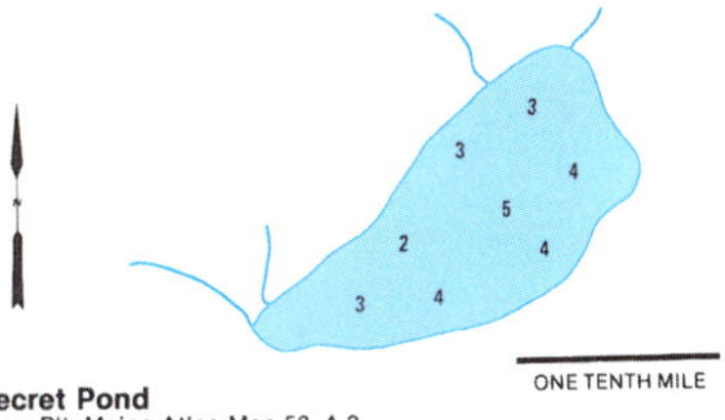

Secret Pond

Moro Plt, Maine Atlas Map 52, A-2
Acres: 6, Max. Depth: 5 feet

BrT	BkT	RbT	Sal	Tog	Smt	LmB	SmB	WhP	Csk	WhF	Pic
	✓										

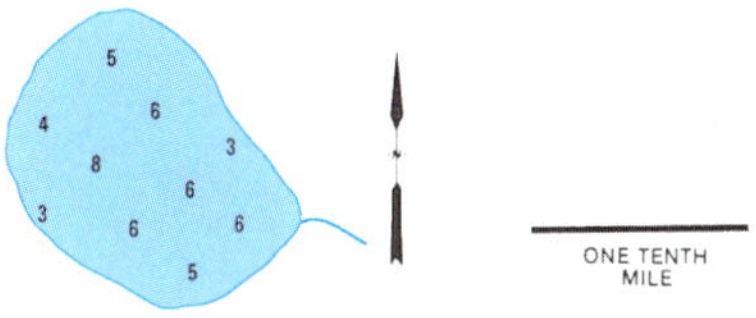

South Little Black Pond

T15 R9 WELS, Maine Atlas Map 63, A-1
Acres: 7, Max. Depth: 8 feet

BrT	BkT	RbT	Sal	Tog	Smt	LmB	SmB	WhP	Csk	WhF	Pic
	✓										

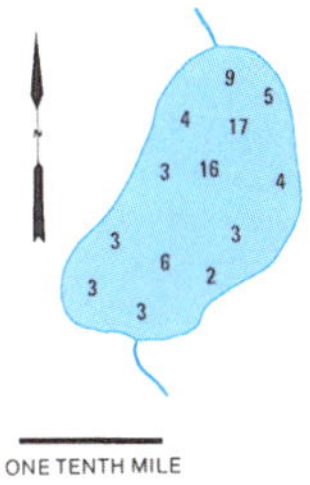

Silver Lake

T15 R5 WELS
Maine Atlas
Map 64, A-1
Acres: 13
Max. Depth:
17 feet

BrT		LmB	
BkT	✓	SmB	
RbT		WhP	
Sal		Csk	
Tog		WhF	
Smt		Pic	

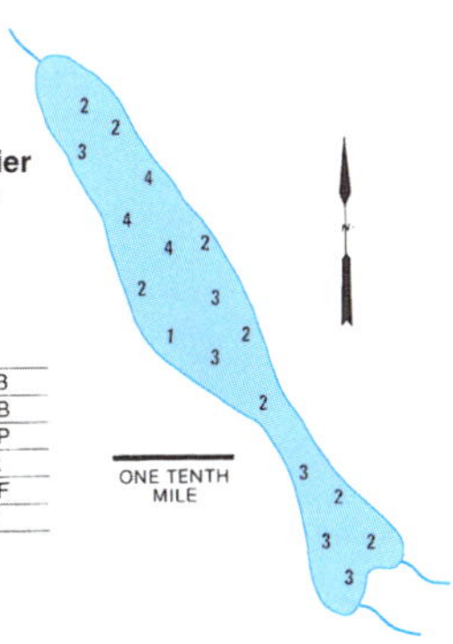

Sixth Pelletier Brook Lake

T15 R9 WELS
Maine Atlas
Map 62, A-5
Acres: 25
Max. Depth:
4 feet
Boat Launch

BrT		LmB	
BkT	✓	SmB	
RbT		WhP	
Sal		Csk	
Tog		WhF	
Smt		Pic	

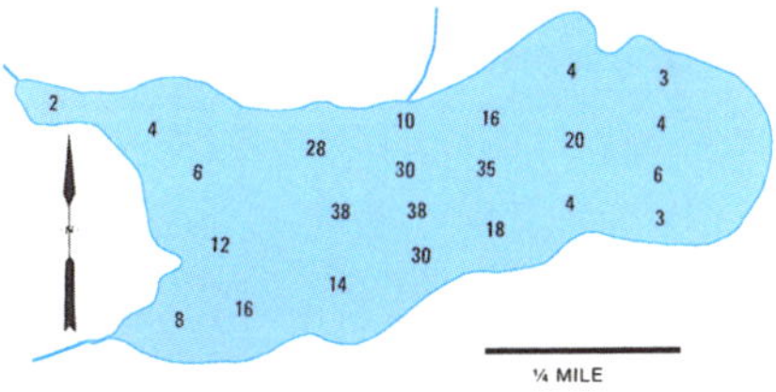

Spaulding Lake

Oakfield, Maine Atlas Map 52, A-5
Acres: 125, Max. Depth: 38 feet, Boat Launch

BrT	BkT	RbT	Sal	Tog	Smt	LmB	SmB	WhP	Csk	WhF	Pic
	✓		✓		✓			✓			✓

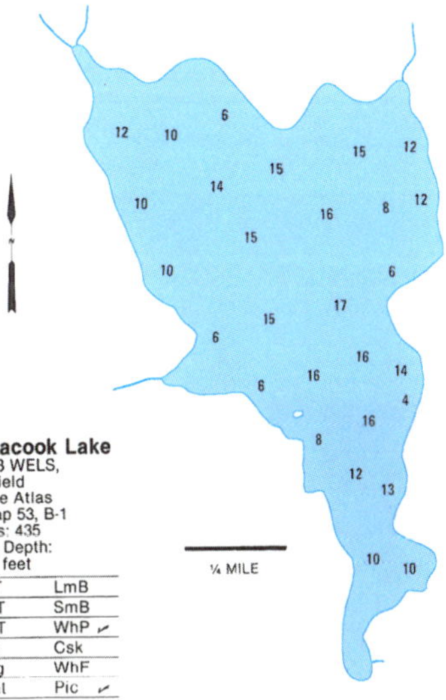

Skitacook Lake

T4 R3 WELS,
Oakfield
Maine Atlas
Map 53, B-1
Acres: 435
Max. Depth:
17 feet

BrT		LmB	
BkT		SmB	
RbT		WhP	✓
Sal		Csk	
Tog		WhF	
Smt		Pic	✓

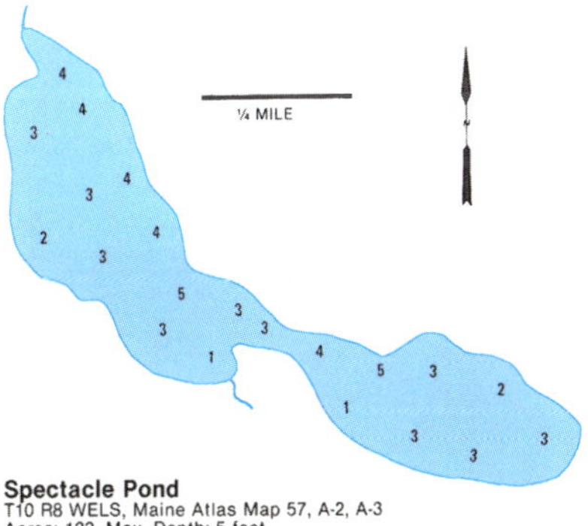

Spectacle Pond

T10 R8 WELS, Maine Atlas Map 57, A-2, A-3
Acres: 122, Max. Depth: 5 feet

BrT	BkT	RbT	Sal	Tog	Smt	LmB	SmB	WhP	Csk	WhF	Pic
	✓										

Aroostook

Squapan Lake

T11 R4 WELS, Masardis, Ashland, Squapan Twp
Maine Atlas Map 58, A-3, A-4, Map 64, E-4
Acres: 5,120
Max. Depth: 58 feet
Boat Launch

BrT		LmB	
BkT	✓	SmB	
RbT		WhP	
Sal	✓	Csk	✓
Tog		WhF	
Smt	✓	Pic	

Comments: Splake.

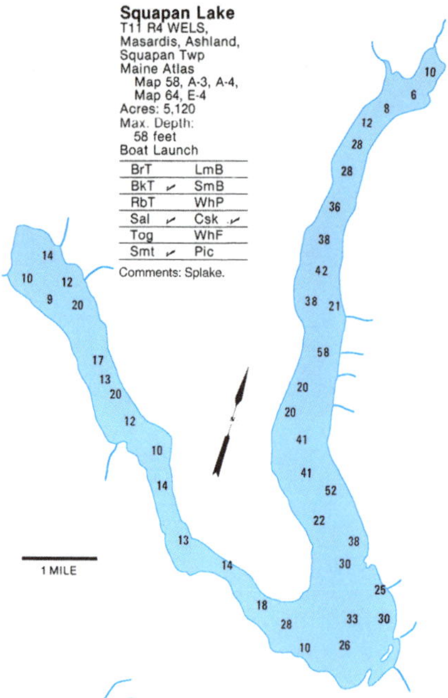

Sterling Pond

T13 R7 WELS
Maine Atlas Map 63, C-4 D-4
Acres: 38
Max. Depth: 4 feet

BrT		LmB	
BkT	✓	SmB	
RbT		WhP	
Sal		Csk	
Tog		WhF	
Smt		Pic	

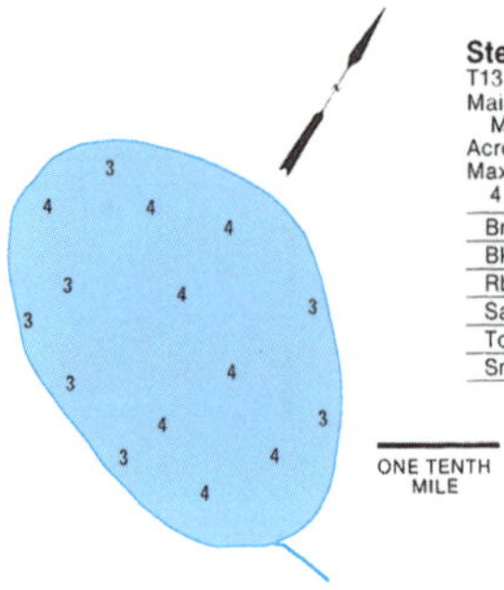

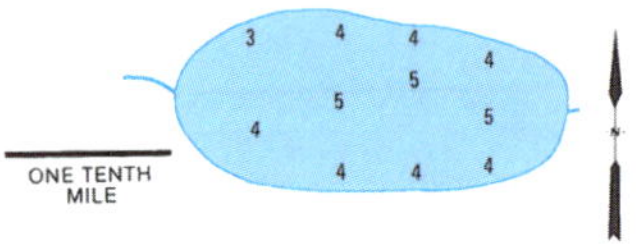

Stink Pond

T15 R9 WELS, Maine Atlas Map 63, A-2
Acres:16, Max. Depth: 5 feet

BrT	BkT	RbT	Sal	Tog	Smt	LmB	SmB	WhP	Csk	WhF	Pic
	✓										

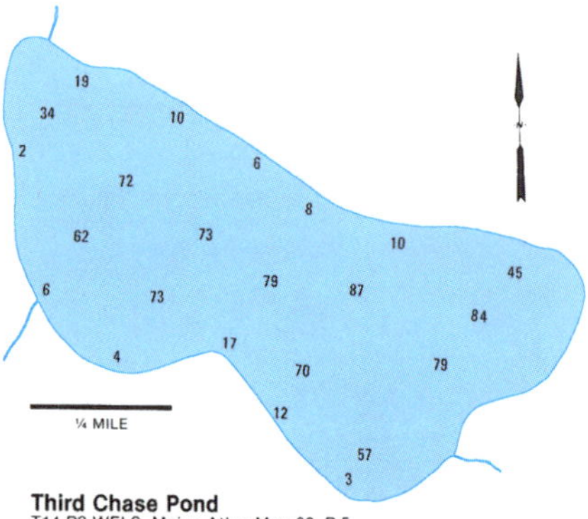

Third Chase Pond

T14 R9 WELS, Maine Atlas Map 62, B-5
Acres: 102, Max. Depth: 87 feet, Boat Launch

BrT	BkT	RbT	Sal	Tog	Smt	LmB	SmB	WhP	Csk	WhF	Pic
	✓			✓							

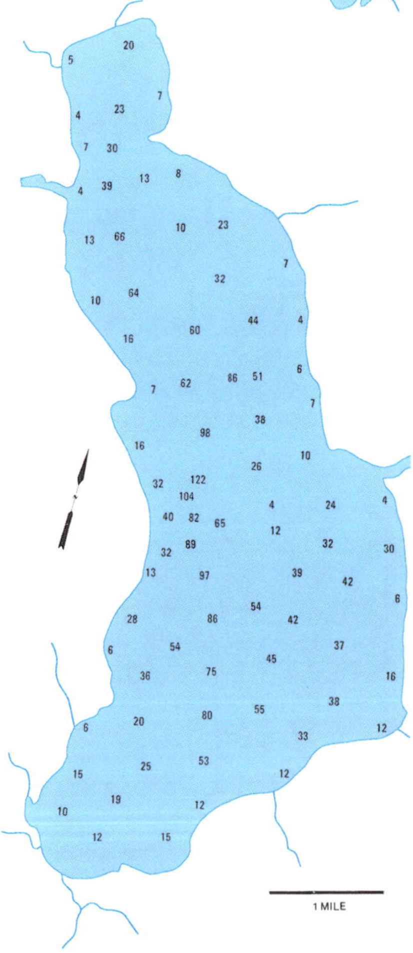

Square Lake

T16 R5 WELS, T15 R5 WELS, Maine Atlas Map 68, D-2, D-3, E-2, E-3
Acres: 8,150, Max. Depth: 122 feet

BrT	BkT	RbT	Sal	Tog	Smt	LmB	SmB	WhP	Csk	WhF	Pic
	✓		✓		✓				✓		

Comments: Recently stocked with Sal.

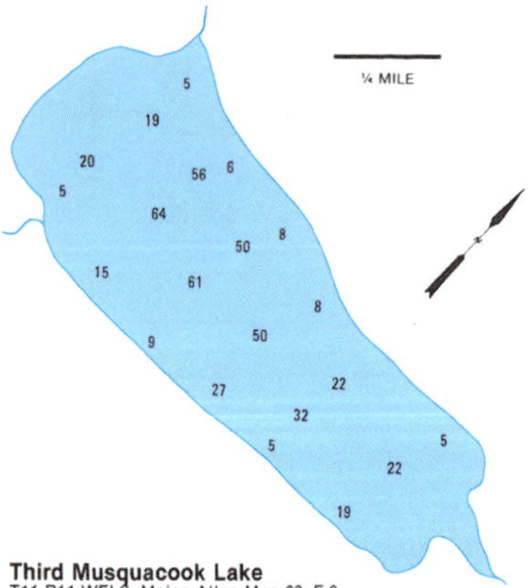

Third Musquacook Lake

T11 R11 WELS, Maine Atlas Map 62, E-3
Acres: 397, Max. Depth: 64 feet

BrT	BkT	RbT	Sal	Tog	Smt	LmB	SmB	WhP	Csk	WhF	Pic
	✓			✓	✓				✓	✓	

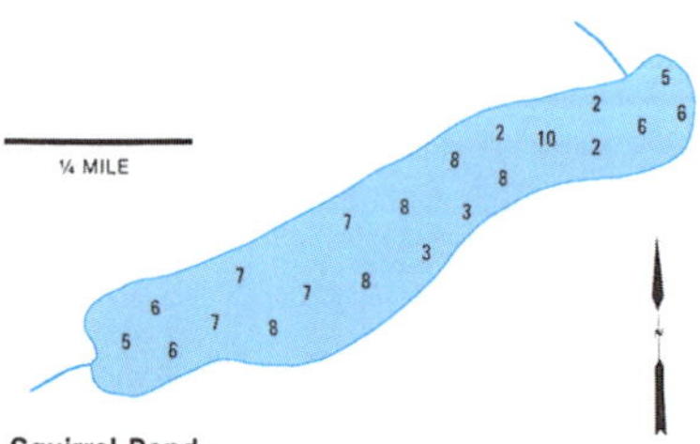

Squirrel Pond

T11 R10 WELS, Maine Atlas Map 62, E-4
Acres: 51, Max. Depth: 10 feet

BrT	BkT	RbT	Sal	Tog	Smt	LmB	SmB	WhP	Csk	WhF	Pic
	✓										

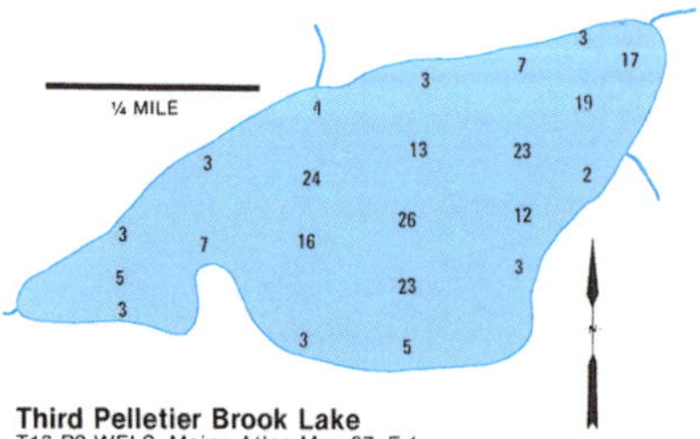

Third Pelletier Brook Lake

T16 R9 WELS, Maine Atlas Map 67, E-1
Acres: 83, Max. Depth: 26 feet, Boat Launch

BrT	BkT	RbT	Sal	Tog	Smt	LmB	SmB	WhP	Csk	WhF	Pic
	✓										

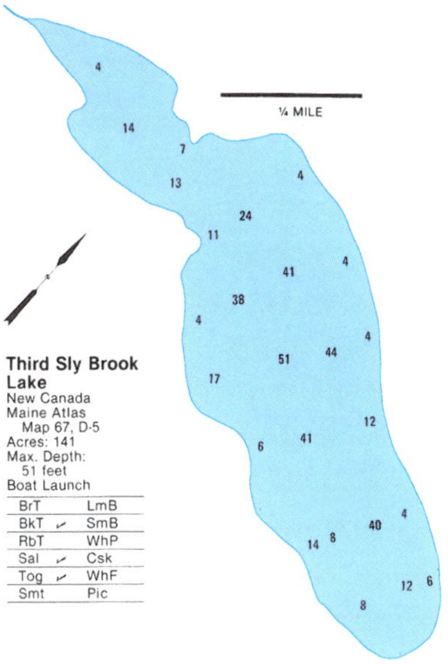

Third Sly Brook Lake
New Canada
Maine Atlas
Map 67, D-5
Acres: 141
Max. Depth:
51 feet
Boat Launch

BrT	LmB
BkT ✓	SmB
RbT	WhP
Sal ✓	Csk
Tog ✓	WhF
Smt	Pic

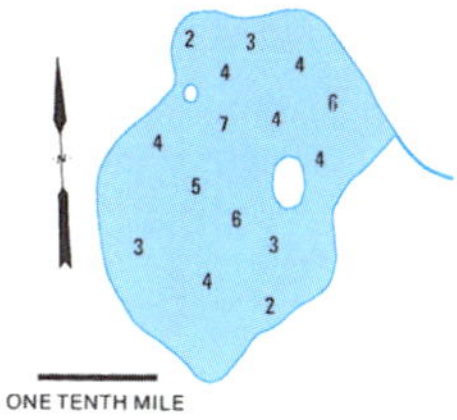

Tote Road Pond
Moro Plt
Maine Atlas
Map 52, A-2
Acres: 25
Max. Depth:
7 feet

BrT	LmB
BkT ✓	SmB
RbT	WhP
Sal	Csk
Tog	WhF
Smt	Pic

Trafton Lake
Limestone
Maine Atlas
Map 65, A-3
Acres: 85
Max. Depth:
50 feet
Boat Launch

BrT	LmB
BkT ✓	SmB
RbT	WhP
Sal	Csk
Tog	WhF
Smt	Pic

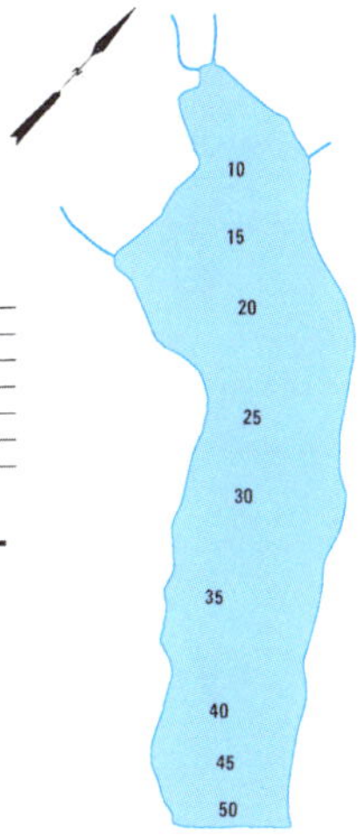

Third Wallagrass Lake
St. John Plt, Maine Atlas Map 67, D-2
Acres: 45, Max. Depth: 8 feet, Boat Launch

BrT	BkT	RbT	Sal	Tog	Smt	LmB	SmB	WhP	Csk	WhF	Pic
	✓										

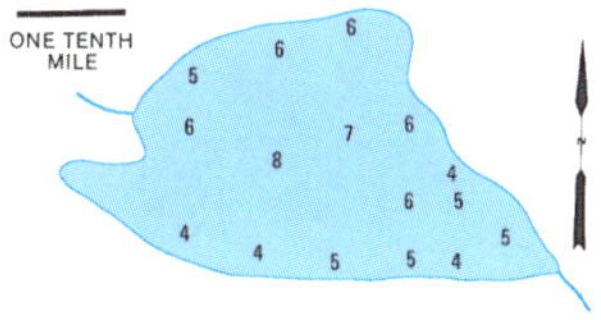

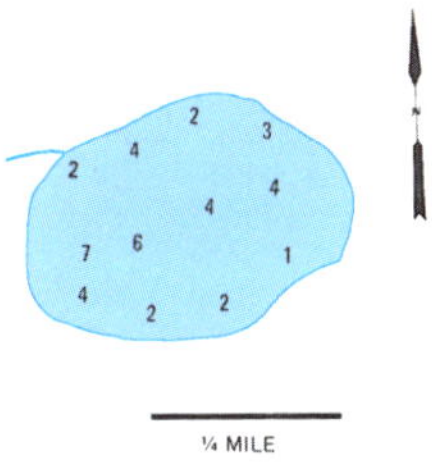

Two Mile Pond
T16 R14 WELS,
T16 R13 WELS
Maine Atlas
Map 70, E-4
Acres: 12
Max. Depth:
7 feet

BrT	LmB
BkT ✓	SmB
RbT	WhP
Sal	Csk
Tog	WhF
Smt	Pic

Timoney Lake
Oakfield, Smyrna
Maine Atlas
Map 52, A-5,
Map 53, A-1
Acres: 57
Max. Depth:
42 feet
Boat Launch

BrT	LmB
BkT ✓	SmB
RbT	WhP
Sal	Csk
Tog	WhF
Smt	Pic

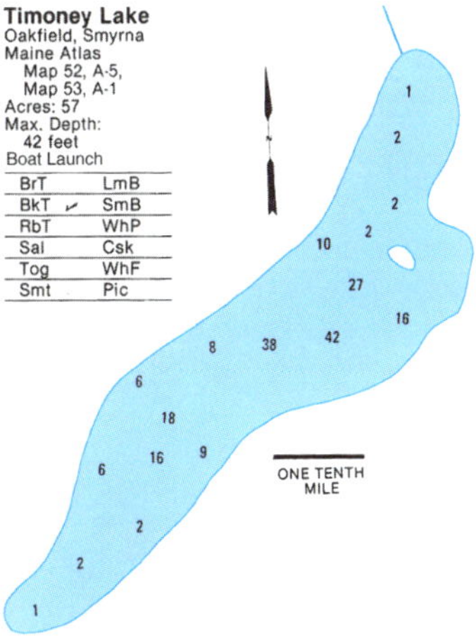

Ugh Lake
T12 R14 WELS
Maine Atlas
Map 61, D-3
Acres: 79
Max. Depth:
7 feet

BrT	LmB
BkT ✓	SmB
RbT	WhP
Sal	Csk
Tog	WhF
Smt	Pic

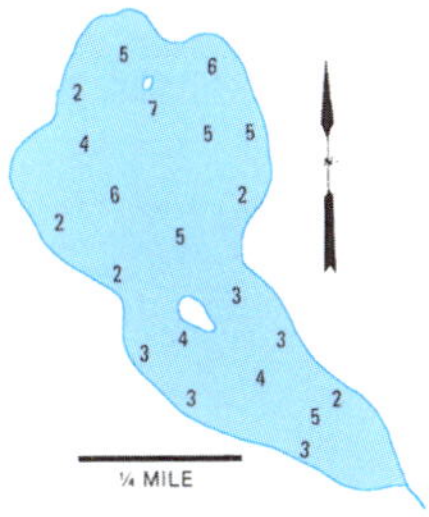

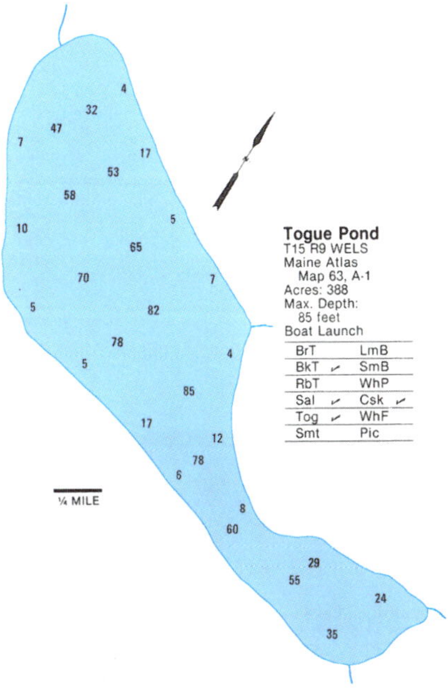

Togue Pond
T15 R9 WELS
Maine Atlas
Map 63, A-1
Acres: 388
Max. Depth:
85 feet
Boat Launch

BrT	LmB
BkT ✓	SmB
RbT	WhP
Sal ✓	Csk ✓
Tog ✓	WhF
Smt	Pic

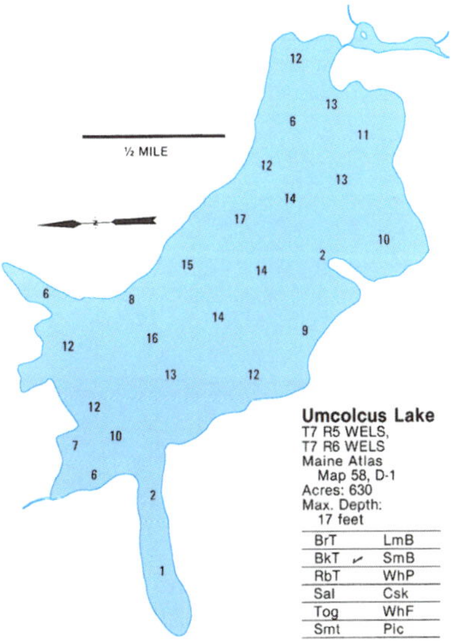

Umcolcus Lake
T7 R5 WELS,
T7 R6 WELS
Maine Atlas
Map 58, D-1
Acres: 630
Max. Depth:
17 feet

BrT	LmB
BkT ✓	SmB
RbT	WhP
Sal	Csk
Tog	WhF
Smt	Pic

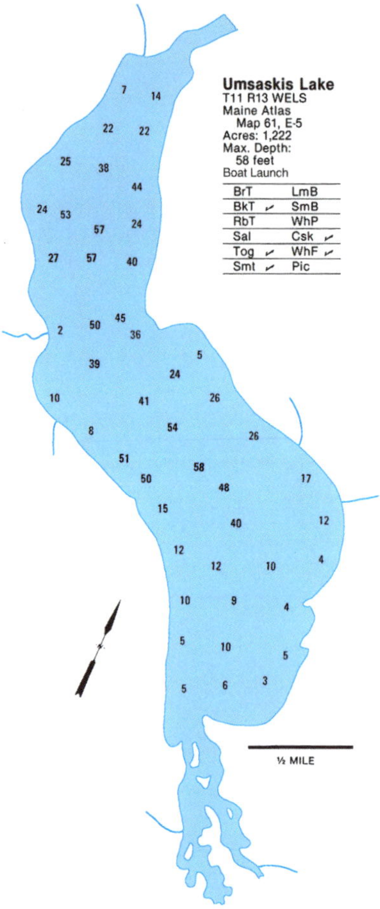

Umsaskis Lake

T11 R13 WELS
Maine Atlas
Map 61, E-5
Acres: 1,222
Max. Depth:
58 feet
Boat Launch

BrT		LmB	
BkT	✓	SmB	
RbT		WhP	
Sal		Csk	✓
Tog	✓	WhF	✓
Smt	✓	Pic	

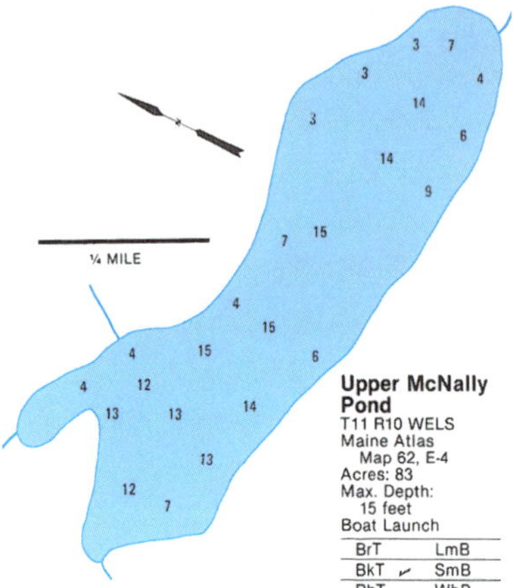

Upper McNally Pond

T11 R10 WELS
Maine Atlas
Map 62, E-4
Acres: 83
Max. Depth:
15 feet
Boat Launch

BrT		LmB	
BkT	✓	SmB	
RbT		WhP	
Sal		Csk	
Tog		WhF	

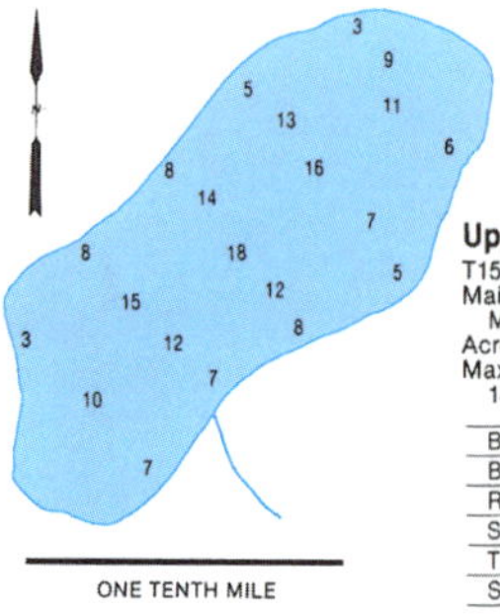

Upper Pond

T15 R9 WELS
Maine Atlas
Map 63, A-1
Acres: 17
Max. Depth:
18 feet

BrT		LmB	
BkT	✓	SmB	
RbT		WhP	
Sal		Csk	
Tog		WhF	
Smt		Pic	

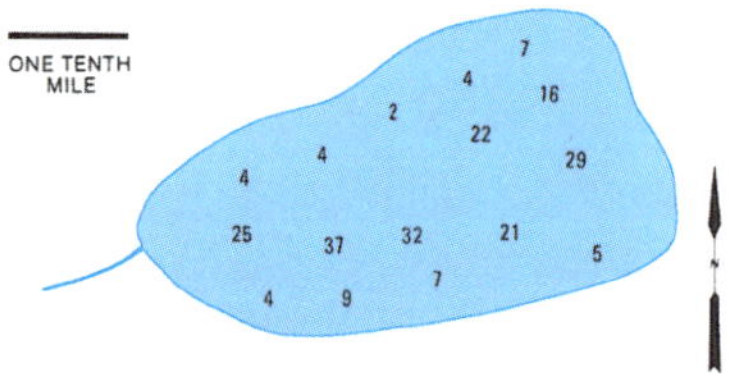

Upper Hudson Pond

T11 R10 WELS, Maine Atlas Map 56, A-4
Acres: 32, Max. Depth: 37 feet

BrT	BkT	RbT	Sal	Tog	Smt	LmB	SmB	WhP	Csk	WhF	Pic
	✓				✓						

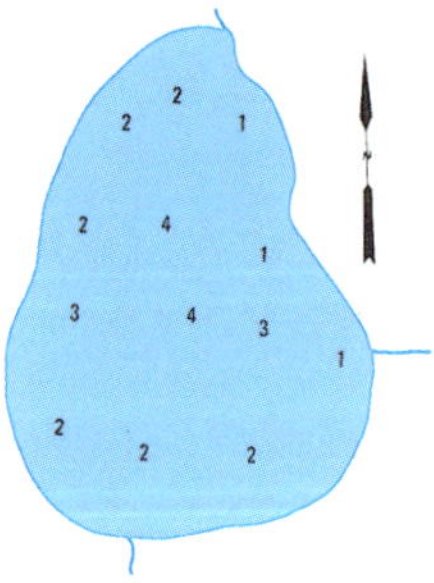

Weeks Pond

T11 R8 WELS
Maine Atlas
Map 57, A-2
Acres: 13
Max. Depth:
4 feet

BrT		LmB	
BkT	✓	SmB	
RbT		WhP	
Sal		Csk	
Tog		WhF	
Smt		Pic	

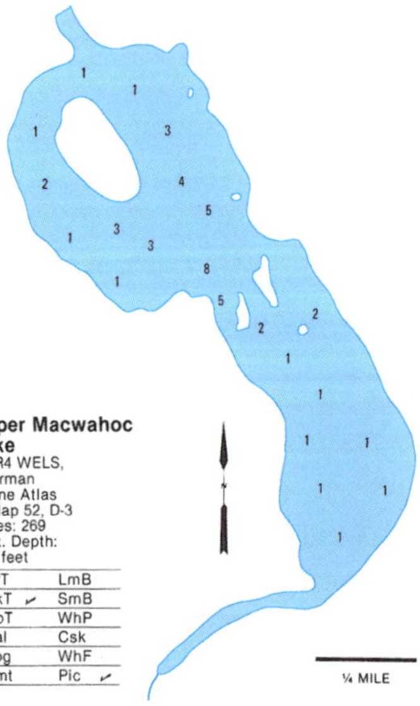

Upper Macwahoc Lake

T3 R4 WELS,
Sherman
Maine Atlas
Map 52, D-3
Acres: 269
Max. Depth:
8 feet

BrT		LmB	
BkT	✓	SmB	
RbT		WhP	
Sal		Csk	
Tog		WhF	
Smt		Pic	✓

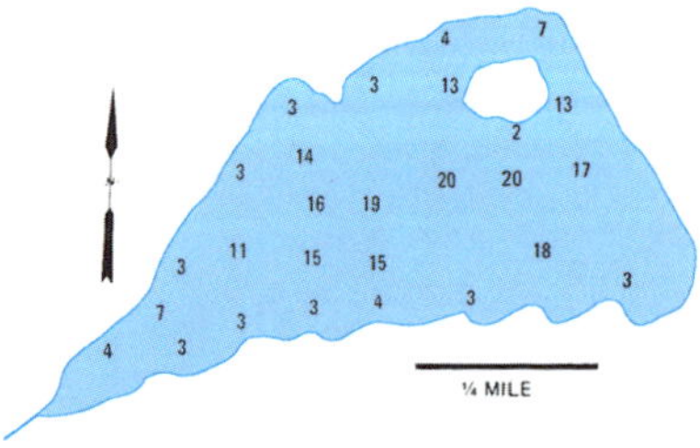

Wheelock Lake

St. John Plt, Maine Atlas Map 67, C-3
Acres: 160, Max. Depth: 20 feet

BrT	BkT	RbT	Sal	Tog	Smt	LmB	SmB	WhP	Csk	WhF	Pic
	✓										

Whitehead Lake
Bridgewater
Maine Atlas
Map 59, B-3
Acres: 21
Max. Depth:
14 feet

BrT	LmB
BkT ✓	SmB
RbT	WhP
Sal	Csk
Tog	WhF
Smt	Pic

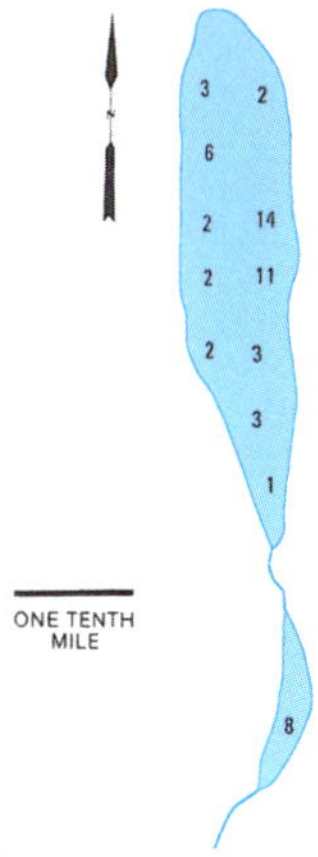

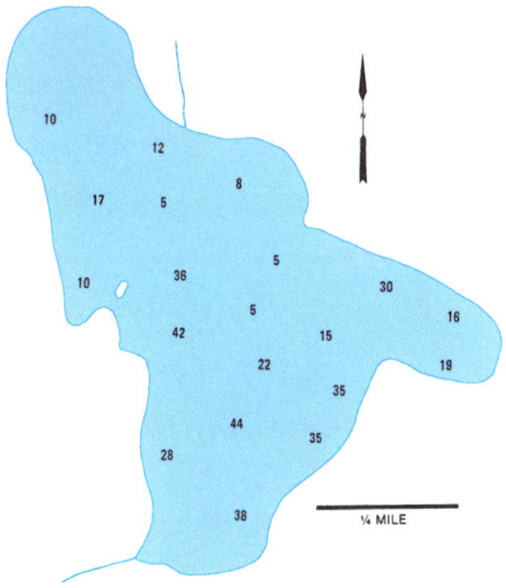

Barker Pond
Sebago, Hiram, Maine Atlas Map 4, C-3, C-4
Acres: 206, Max. Depth: 44 feet

BrT	BkT	RbT	Sal	Tog	Smt	LmB	SmB	WhP	Csk	WhF	Pic
						✓	✓				✓

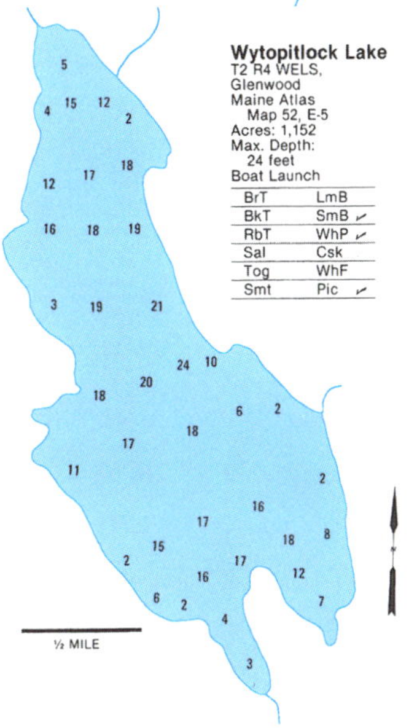

Wytopitlock Lake
T2 R4 WELS,
Glenwood
Maine Atlas
Map 52, E-5
Acres: 1,152
Max. Depth:
24 feet
Boat Launch

BrT	LmB
BkT	SmB ✓
RbT	WhP ✓
Sal	Csk
Tog	WhF
Smt	Pic ✓

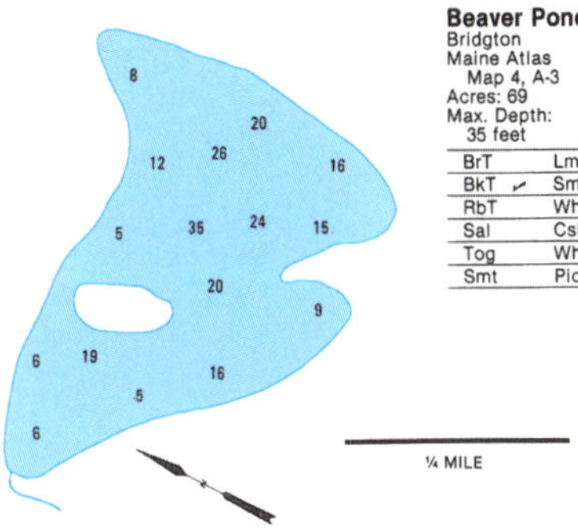

Beaver Pond
Bridgton
Maine Atlas
Map 4, A-3
Acres: 69
Max. Depth:
35 feet

BrT	LmB
BkT ✓	SmB
RbT	WhP
Sal	Csk
Tog	WhF
Smt	Pic ✓

Cumberland County

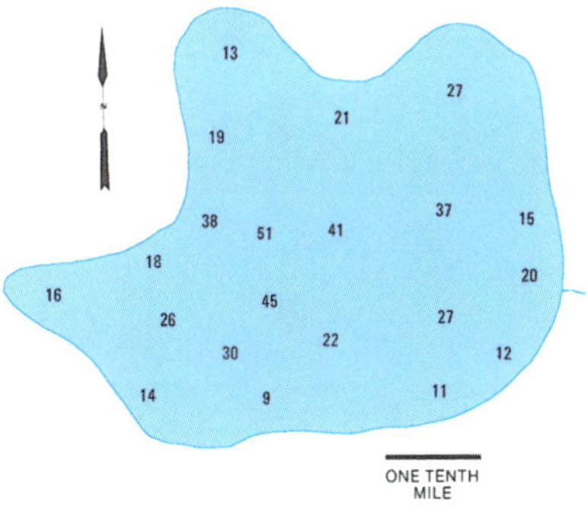

Adams Pond
Bridgton, Maine Atlas Map 4, B-4
Acres: 45, Max. Depth: 51 feet

BrT	BkT	RbT	Sal	Tog	Smt	LmB	SmB	WhP	Csk	WhF	Pic
	✓										

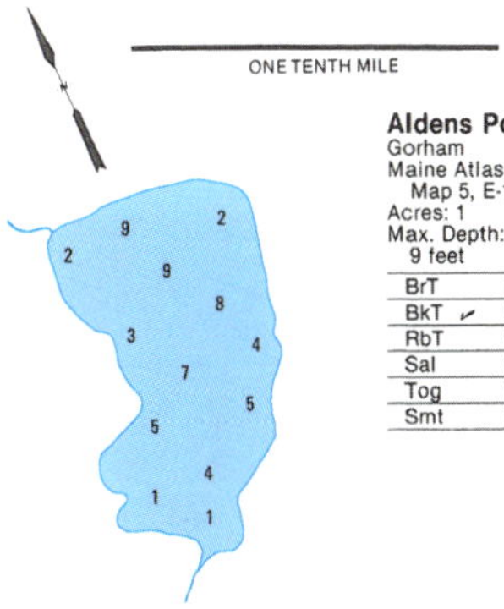

Aldens Pond
Gorham
Maine Atlas
Map 5, E-1, E-2
Acres: 1
Max. Depth:
9 feet

BrT	LmB
BkT ✓	SmB
RbT	WhP
Sal	Csk
Tog	WhF
Smt	Pic ✓

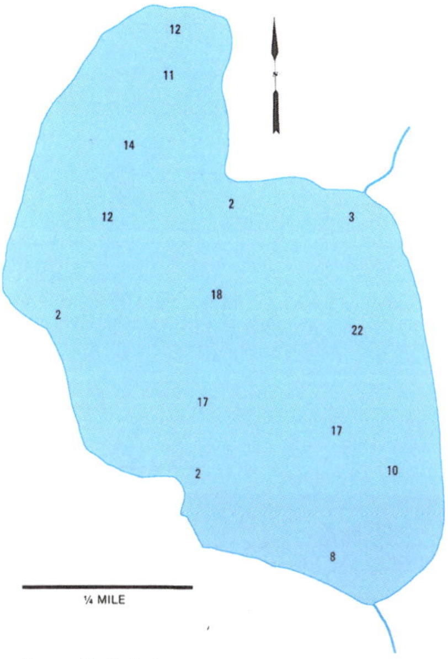

Bonny Eagle Lake
Standish, Buxton, Maine Atlas Map 4, E-5
Acres: 211, Max. Depth: 22 feet

BrT	BkT	RbT	Sal	Tog	Smt	LmB	SmB	WhP	Csk	WhF	Pic
✓						✓	✓				✓

Cumberland

Brandy Pond
Naples, Maine Atlas Map 4, B-5; Map 5, B-1
Acres: 762, Max. Depth: 44 feet

BrT	BkT	RbT	Sal	Tog	Smt	LmB	SmB	WhP	Csk	WhF	Pic
✓	✓		✓		✓	✓	✓	✓	✓		✓

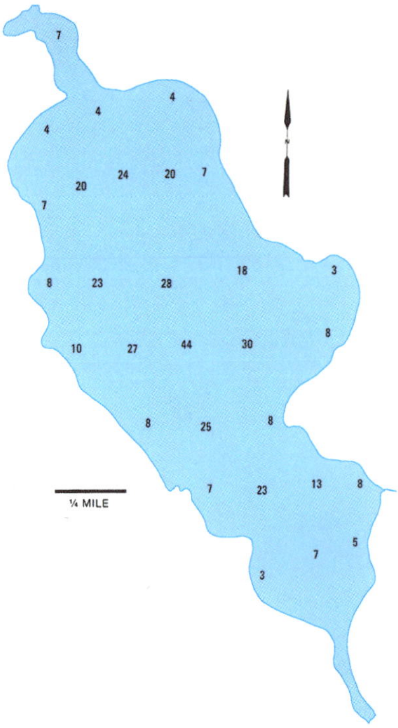

Cold Rain Pond
Naples
Maine Atlas
Map 4, B-4, B-5
Acres: 38
Max. Depth:
36 feet

BrT		LmB	
BkT	✓	SmB	
RbT		WhP	
Sal		Csk	
Tog		WhF	
Smt	✓	Pic	✓

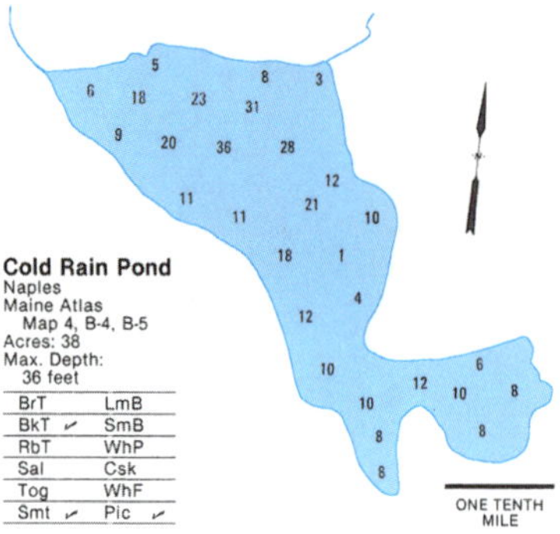

Collins Pond
Windham
Maine Atlas
Map 5, C-2, D-2
Acres: 45
Max. Depth:
18 feet

BrT	✓	LmB	✓
BkT		SmB	✓
RbT		WhP	✓
Sal		Csk	
Tog		WhF	
Smt		Pic	✓

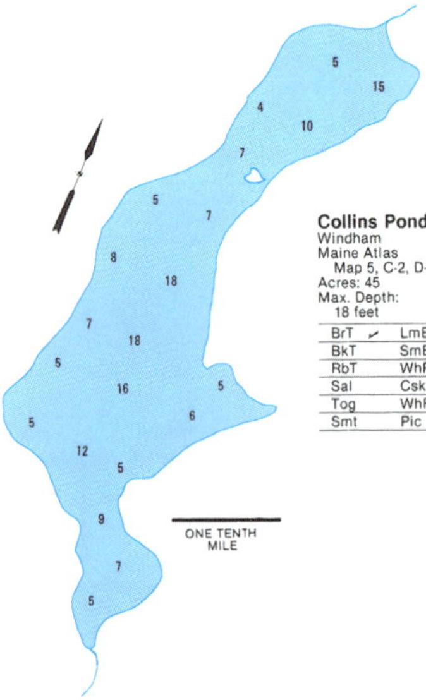

Coffee Pond
Casco
Maine Atlas
Map 5, B-1, B-2
Acres: 137
Max. Depth:
70 feet

BrT		LmB	
BkT	✓	SmB	✓
RbT		WhP	
Sal		Csk	
Tog		WhF	
Smt	✓	Pic	

Comments: Splake.

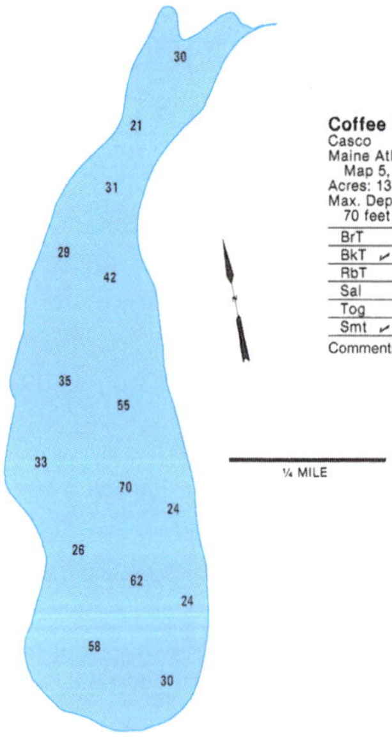

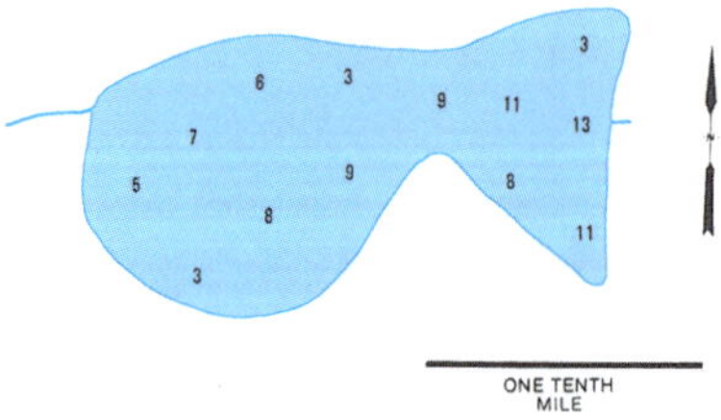

Coffin Pond
Brunswick, Maine Atlas Map 6, C-3, C-4
Acres: 5, Max. Depth: 13 feet

BrT	BkT	RbT	Sal	Tog	Smt	LmB	SmB	WhP	Csk	WhF	Pic
	✓						✓				

Crescent Lake
Casco, Raymond
Maine Atlas
Map 5, B-2
Acres: 716
Max. Depth:
54 feet
Boat Launch

BrT		LmB	✓
BkT		SmB	✓
RbT		WhP	✓
Sal	✓	Csk	
Tog		WhF	
Smt	✓	Pic	✓

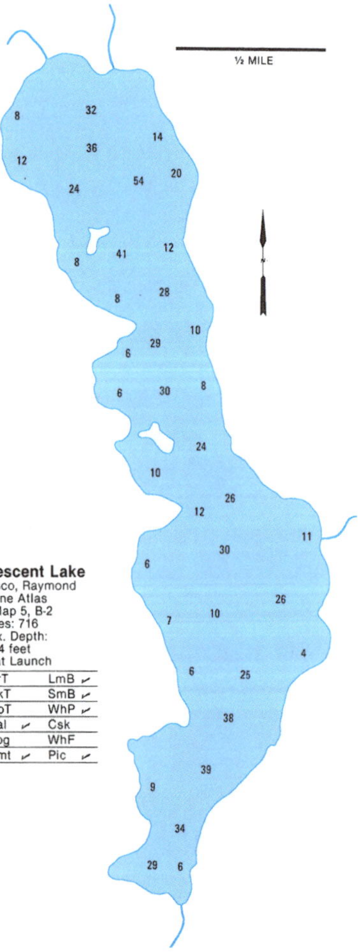

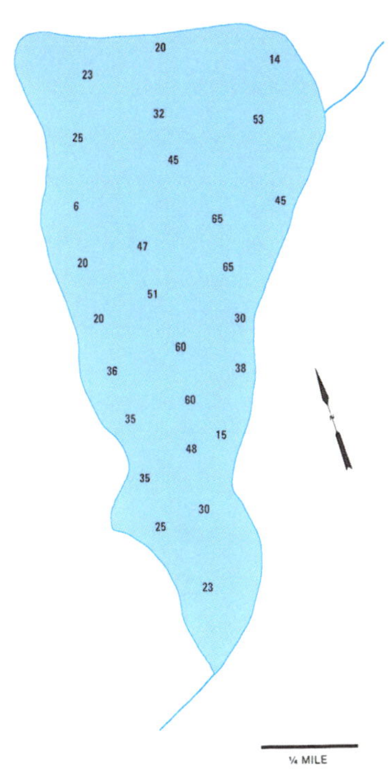

Crystal Lake

Harrison, Maine Atlas Map 10, E-4
Acres: 461, Max. Depth: 65 feet, Boat Launch

BrT	BkT	RbT	Sal	Tog	Smt	LmB	SmB	WhP	Csk	WhF	Pic
	✓		✓	✓	✓	✓	✓	✓			✓

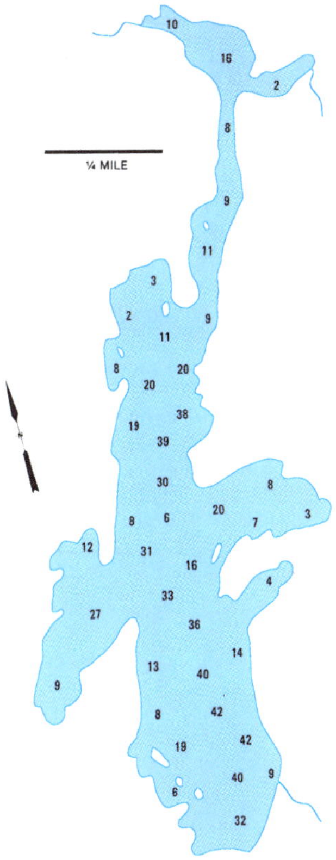

Dundee Pond

Gorham, Windham, Maine Atlas Map 5, D-2
Acres: 173, Max. Depth: 42 feet

BrT	BkT	RbT	Sal	Tog	Smt	LmB	SmB	WhP	Csk	WhF	Pic
✓	✓		✓			✓	✓	✓			✓

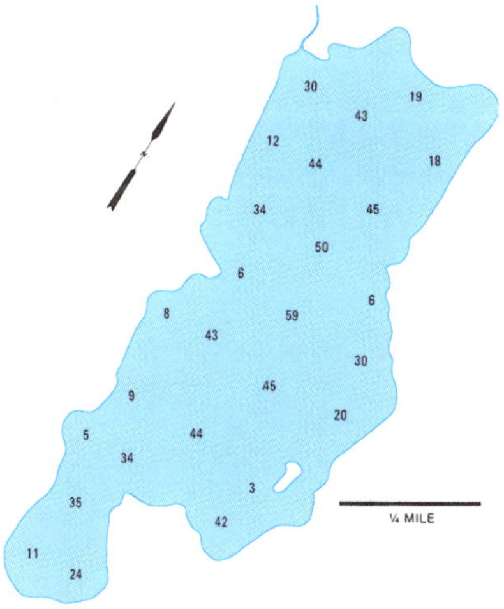

Crystal Lake

Gray, Maine Atlas Map 5, B-3
Acres: 189, Max. Depth: 59 feet, Boat Launch

BrT	BkT	RbT	Sal	Tog	Smt	LmB	SmB	WhP	Csk	WhF	Pic
✓	✓	✓					✓	✓			✓

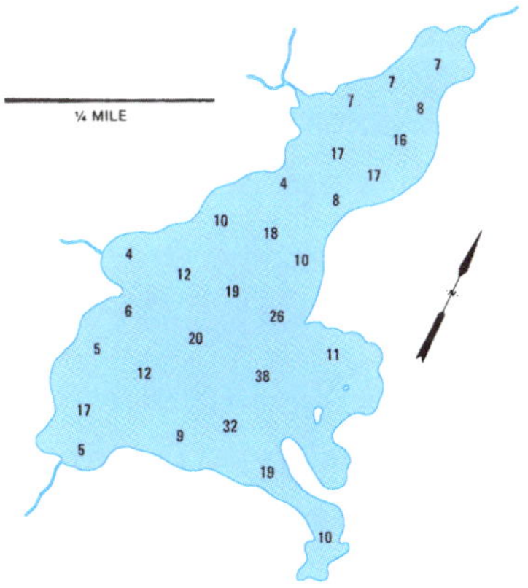

Forest Lake

Gray, Windham, Cumberland, Maine Atlas Map 5, D-3, D-4
Acres: 198, Max. Depth: 38 feet

BrT	BkT	RbT	Sal	Tog	Smt	LmB	SmB	WhP	Csk	WhF	Pic
✓							✓				✓

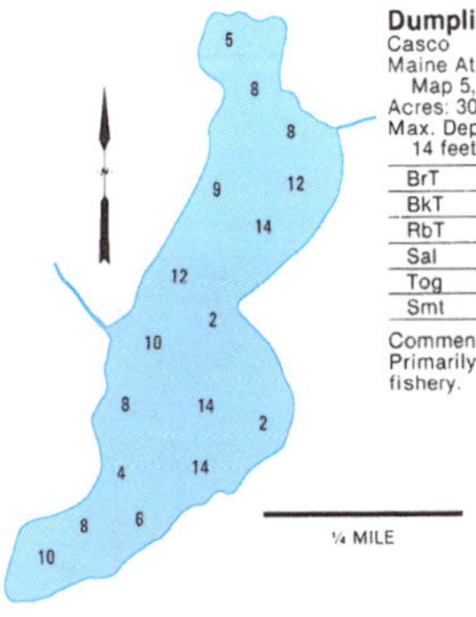

Dumpling Pond

Casco
Maine Atlas
Map 5, B-1, B-2
Acres: 30
Max. Depth:
14 feet

BrT		LmB	✓
BkT		SmB	✓
RbT		WhP	
Sal		Csk	
Tog		WhF	
Smt		Pic	✓

Comments:
Primarily warm water fishery.

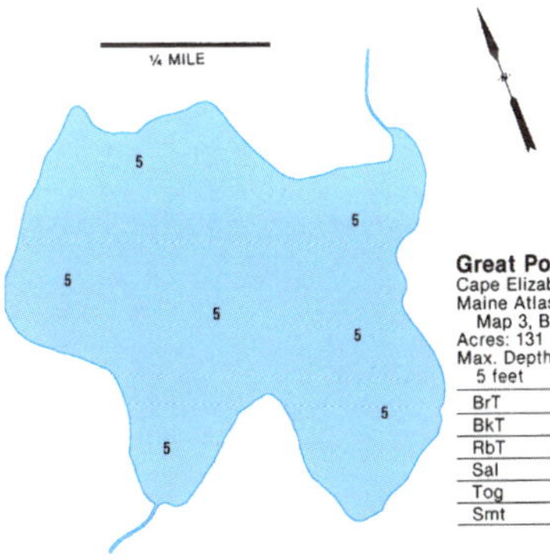

Great Pond

Cape Elizabeth
Maine Atlas
Map 3, B-5
Acres: 131
Max. Depth:
5 feet

BrT		LmB	
BkT		SmB	
RbT		WhP	
Sal		Csk	
Tog		WhF	
Smt		Pic	✓

Cumberland

Hancock Pond

Sebago, Denmark, Maine Atlas Map 4, B-3
Acres: 858, Max. Depth: 59 feet, Boat Launch

BrT	BkT	RbT	Sal	Tog	Smt	LmB	SmB	WhP	Csk	WhF	Pic
✓					✓	✓	✓	✓			✓

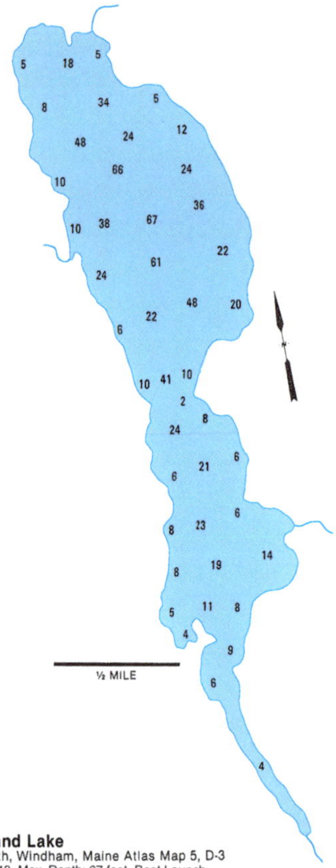

Highland Lake

Falmouth, Windham, Maine Atlas Map 5, D-3
Acres: 640, Max. Depth; 67 feet, Boat Launch

BrT	BkT	RbT	Sal	Tog	Smt	LmB	SmB	WhP	Csk	WhF	Pic
✓	✓	✓	✓		✓	✓	✓	✓			✓

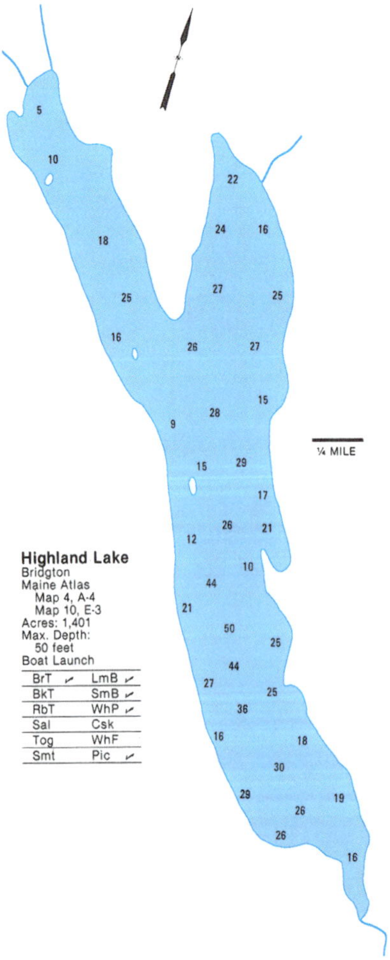

Highland Lake

Bridgton
Maine Atlas
Map 4, A-4
Map 10, E-3
Acres: 1,401
Max. Depth:
50 feet
Boat Launch

BrT	✓	LmB	✓
BkT		SmB	✓
RbT		WhP	✓
Sal		Csk	
Tog		WhF	
Smt		Pic	✓

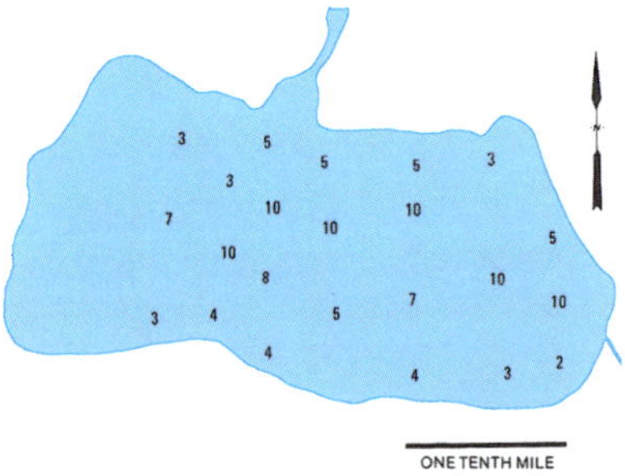

Holt Pond

Bridgton, Maine Atlas Map 4, B-4
Acres: 25, Max. Depth: 10 feet

BrT	BkT	RbT	Sal	Tog	Smt	LmB	SmB	WhP	Csk	WhF	Pic
						✓					✓

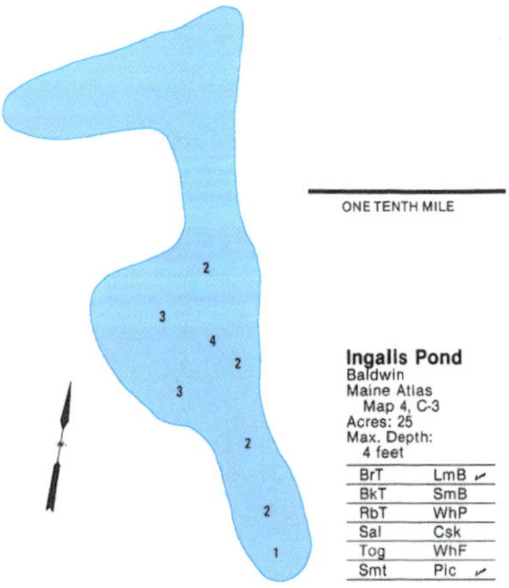

Ingalls Pond

Baldwin
Maine Atlas
Map 4, C-3
Acres: 25
Max. Depth:
4 feet

BrT		LmB	✓
BkT		SmB	
RbT		WhP	
Sal		Csk	
Tog		WhF	
Smt		Pic	✓

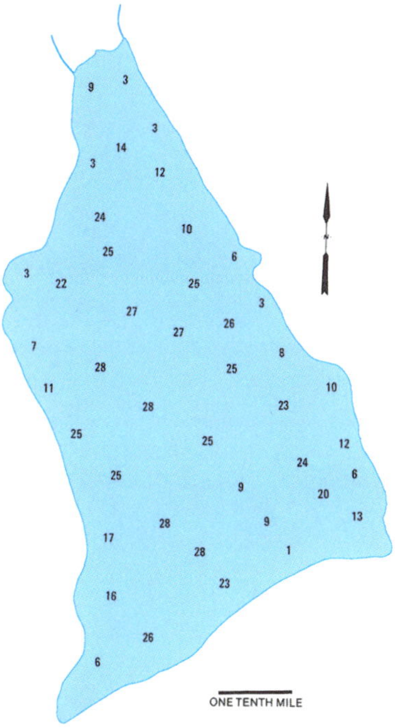

Ingalls Pond

Bridgton, Maine Atlas Map 4, B-4
Acres: 141, Max. Depth: 28 feet

BrT	BkT	RbT	Sal	Tog	Smt	LmB	SmB	WhP	Csk	WhF	Pic
	✓						✓				✓

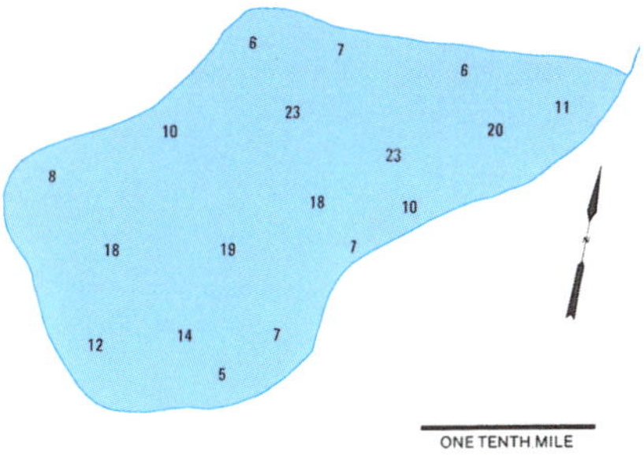

Lily Pond

New Gloucester, Maine Atlas Map 5, B-4
Acres: 38, Max. Depth: 23 feet

BrT	BkT	RbT	Sal	Tog	Smt	LmB	SmB	WhP	Csk	WhF	Pic
	✓	✓				✓					✓

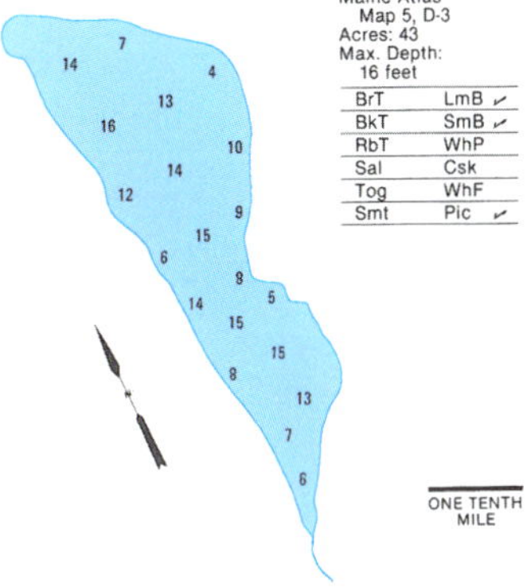

Little Duck Pond

Windham
Maine Atlas
Map 5, D-3
Acres: 43
Max. Depth:
16 feet

BrT	LmB ✓
BkT	SmB ✓
RbT	WhP
Sal	Csk
Tog	WhF
Smt	Pic ✓

Island Pond

Harrison, Maine Atlas Map 10, E-5
Acres: 166, Max. Depth: 48 feet

BrT	BkT	RbT	Sal	Tog	Smt	LmB	SmB	WhP	Csk	WhF	Pic
	✓						✓				✓

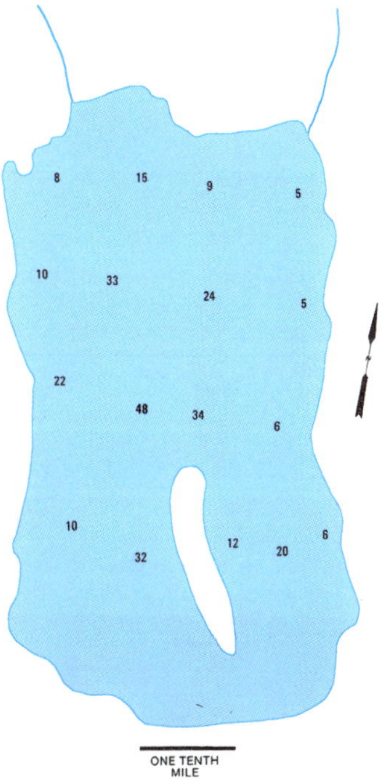

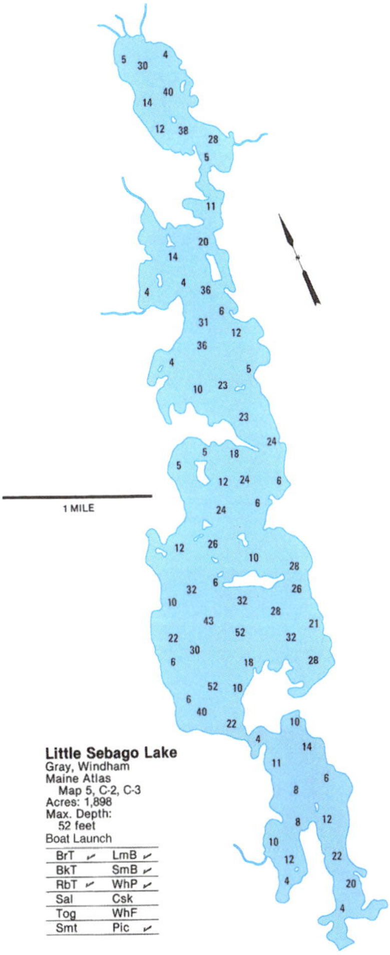

Little Sebago Lake

Gray, Windham
Maine Atlas
Map 5, C-2, C-3
Acres: 1,898
Max. Depth:
52 feet
Boat Launch

BrT ✓	LmB ✓
BkT	SmB ✓
RbT ✓	WhP ✓
Sal	Csk
Tog	WhF
Smt	Pic ✓

Cumberland

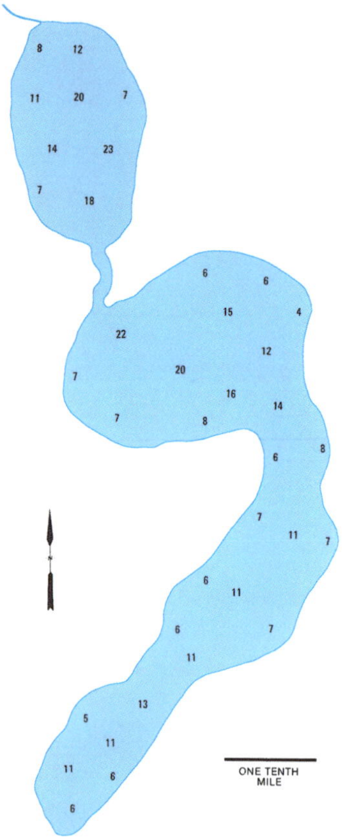

Little Watchic Pond
Standish, Maine Atlas Map 4, D-5
Acres: 55, Max. Depth: 22 feet

BrT	BkT	RbT	Sal	Tog	Smt	LmB	SmB	WhP	Csk	WhF	Pic
						✓					✓

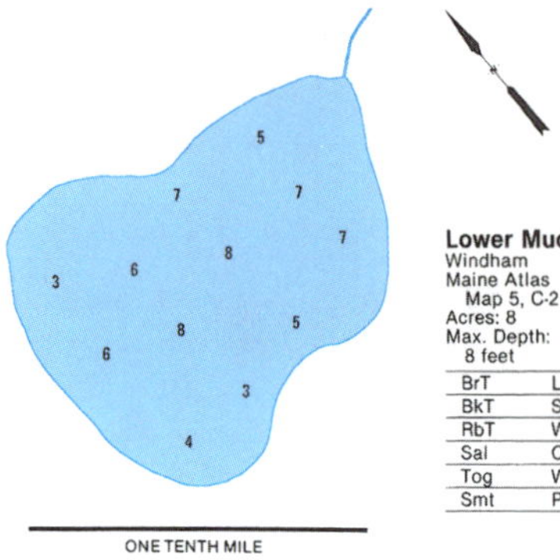

Lower Mud Pond
Windham
Maine Atlas
Map 5, C-2
Acres: 8
Max. Depth:
8 feet

BrT		LmB	✓
BkT		SmB	✓
RbT		WhP	
Sal		Csk	
Tog		WhF	
Smt		Pic	✓

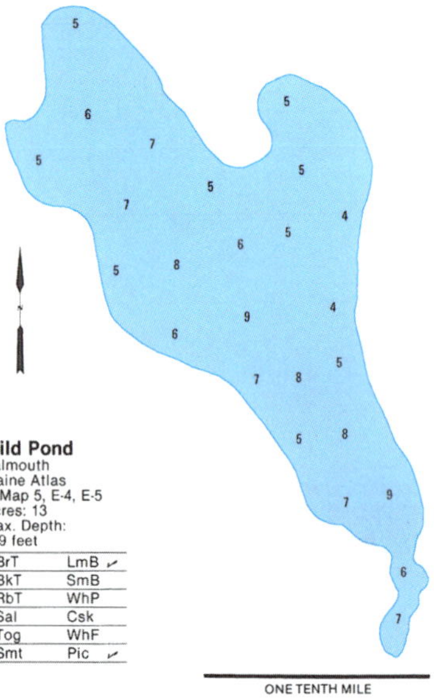

Mild Pond
Falmouth
Maine Atlas
Map 5, E-4, E-5
Acres: 13
Max. Depth:
9 feet

BrT		LmB	✓
BkT		SmB	
RbT		WhP	
Sal		Csk	
Tog		WhF	
Smt		Pic	✓

Long Lake
Bridgton, Naples
Maine Atlas
Map 4, A-5, B-5,
Map 10, E-4
Acres: 4,867
Max. Depth:
59 feet
Boat Launch

BrT	✓	LmB	✓
BkT		SmB	✓
RbT		WhP	✓
Sal	✓	Csk	✓
Tog	✓	WhF	
Smt	✓	Pic	✓

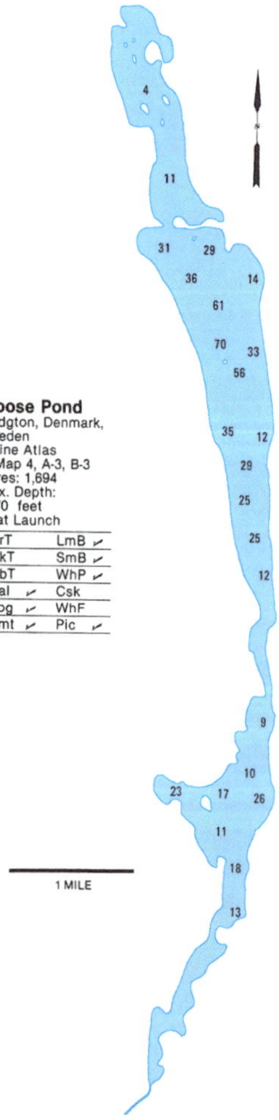

Moose Pond
Bridgton, Denmark,
Sweden
Maine Atlas
Map 4, A-3, B-3
Acres: 1,694
Max. Depth:
70 feet
Boat Launch

BrT		LmB	✓
BkT		SmB	✓
RbT		WhP	✓
Sal	✓	Csk	
Tog	✓	WhF	
Smt	✓	Pic	✓

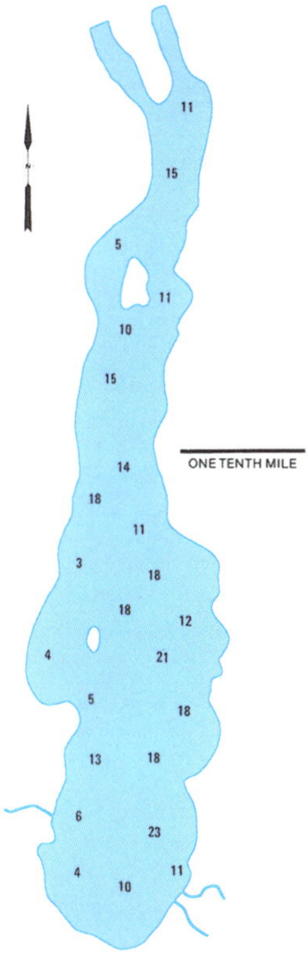

North Gorham Pond
Windham, Gorham, Maine Atlas Map 5, D-2
Acres: 128, Max. Depth: 23 feet

BrT	BkT	RbT	Sal	Tog	Smt	LmB	SmB	WhP	Csk	WhF	Pic
			✓				✓	✓			✓

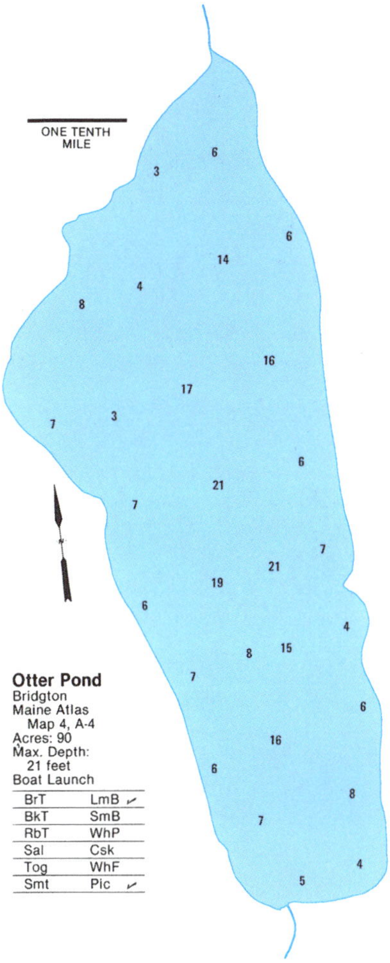

Otter Pond
Bridgton
Maine Atlas
Map 4, A-4
Acres: 90
Max. Depth:
21 feet
Boat Launch

BrT	LmB ✓
BkT	SmB
RbT	WhP
Sal	Csk
Tog	WhF
Smt	Pic ✓

Notched Pond
Raymond, Gray, Maine Atlas Map 5, B-3
Acres: 77, Max. Depth: 21 feet

BrT	BkT	RbT	Sal	Tog	Smt	LmB	SmB	WhP	Csk	WhF	Pic
						✓					✓

Otter Ponds
Standish
Maine Atlas
Map 5, D-1
Acres: First-6,
Second-12
Third-7, Fourth-6
Max. Depth:
First-32 feet
Second-39 feet
Third-26 feet
Fourth-21 feet

BrT	LmB ✓
BkT ✓	SmB ✓
RbT	WhP
Sal	Csk
Tog	WhF
Smt	Pic ✓

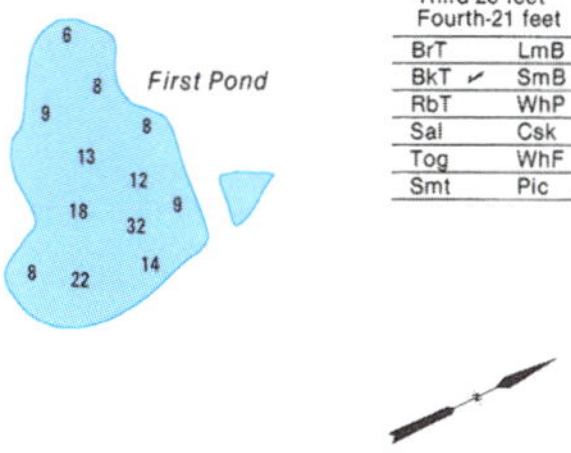

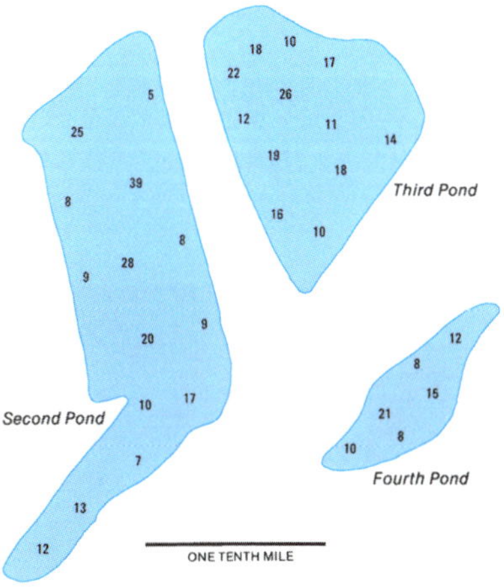

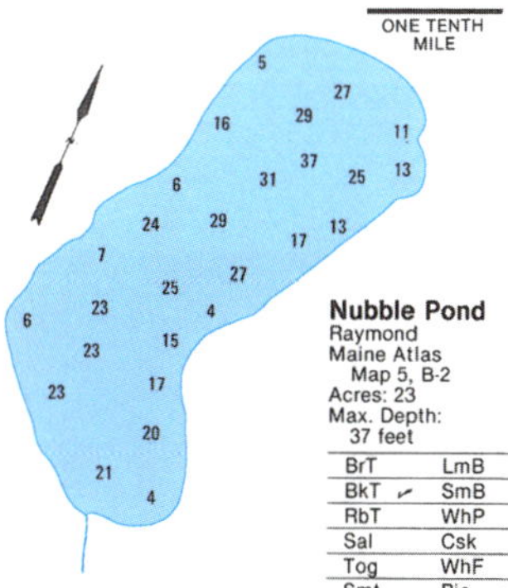

Nubble Pond
Raymond
Maine Atlas
Map 5, B-2
Acres: 23
Max. Depth:
37 feet

BrT	LmB
BkT ✓	SmB
RbT	WhP
Sal	Csk
Tog	WhF
Smt	Pic ✓

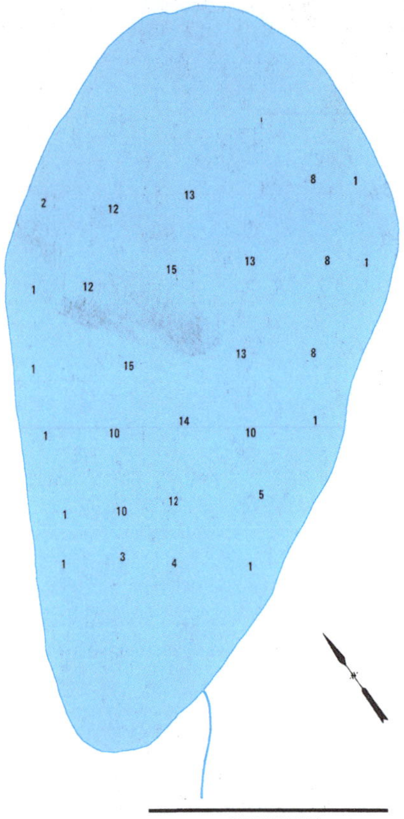

Owl Pond
Casco, Maine Atlas Map 5, A-1, B-1
Acres: 20, Max. Depth: 15 feet

BrT	BkT	RbT	Sal	Tog	Smt	LmB	SmB	WhP	Csk	WhF	Pic
						✓	✓				✓

Parker Pond
Casco, Maine Atlas Map 5, B-1
Acres: 166, Max. Depth: 19 feet

BrT	BkT	RbT	Sal	Tog	Smt	LmB	SmB	WhP	Csk	WhF	Pic
✓	✓						✓	✓			✓

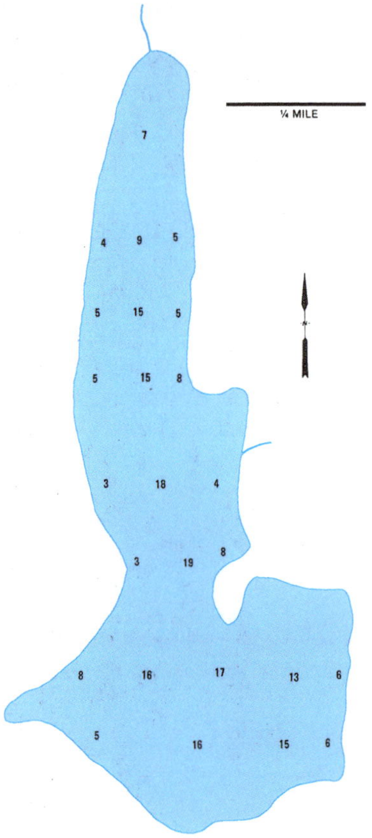

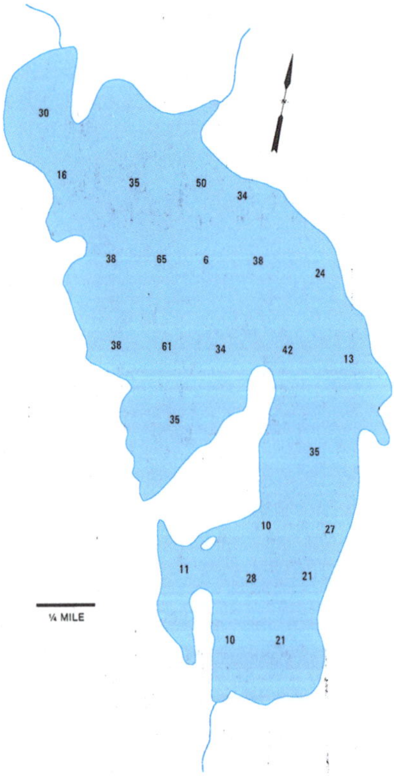

Panther Pond
Raymond, Maine Atlas Map 5, B-2, C-2
Acres: 1,439, Max. Depth: 65 feet, Boat Launch

BrT	BkT	RbT	Sal	Tog	Smt	LmB	SmB	WhP	Csk	WhF	Pic
	✓		✓	✓		✓	✓	✓	✓		✓

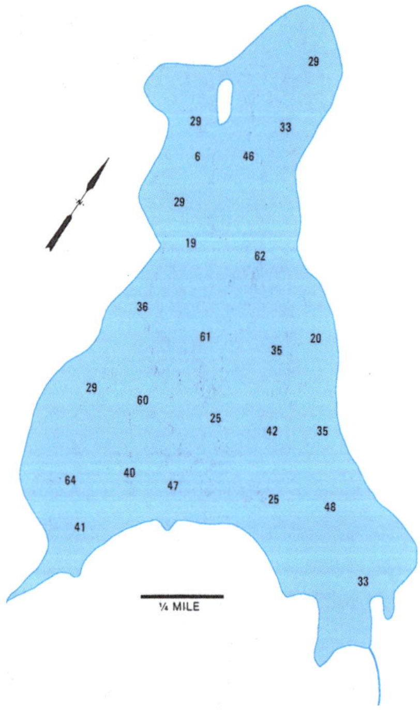

Peabody Pond
Sebago, Bridgton, Maine Atlas Map 4, B-4
Acres: 735, Max. Depth: 64 feet

BrT	BkT	RbT	Sal	Tog	Smt	LmB	SmB	WhP	Csk	WhF	Pic
	✓		✓	✓	✓		✓				✓

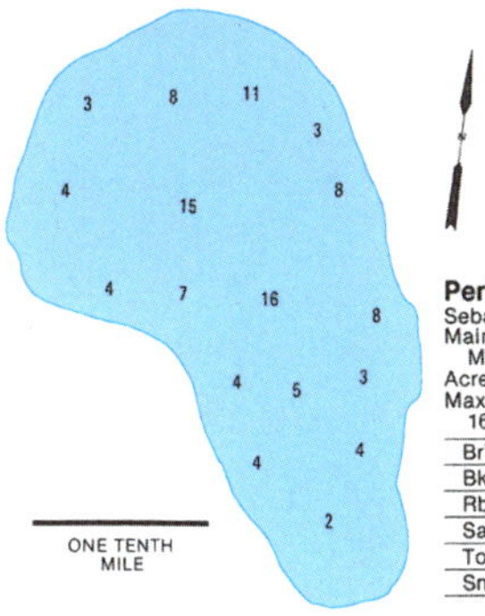

Perley Pond

Sebago
Maine Atlas
Map 4, C-4
Acres: 29
Max. Depth:
16 feet

BrT		LmB	✓
BkT		SmB	
RbT		WhP	
Sal		Csk	
Tog		WhF	
Smt		Pic	✓

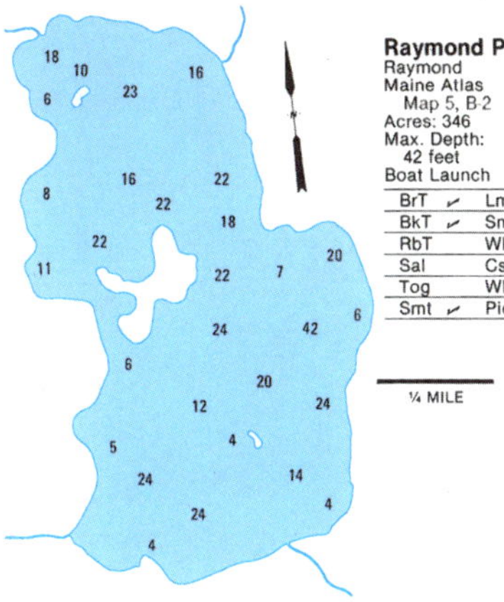

Raymond Pond

Raymond
Maine Atlas
Map 5, B-2
Acres: 346
Max. Depth:
42 feet
Boat Launch

BrT	✓	LmB	✓
BkT	✓	SmB	✓
RbT		WhP	✓
Sal		Csk	
Tog		WhF	
Smt	✓	Pic	✓

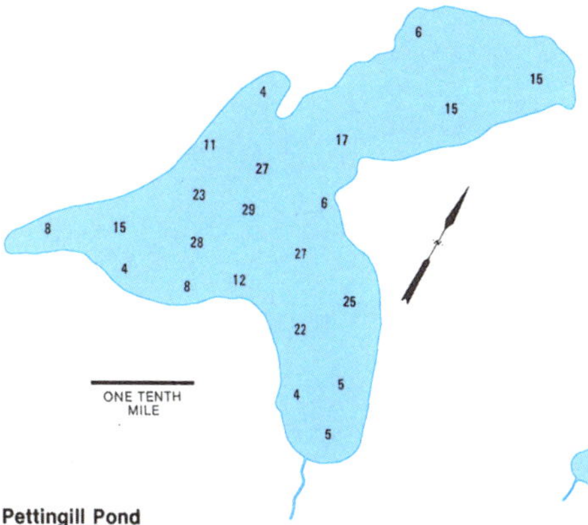

Pettingill Pond

Windham, Maine Atlas Map Map 5, C-2
Acres: 36, Max. Depth: 29 feet

BrT	BkT	RbT	Sal	Tog	Smt	LmB	SmB	WhP	Csk	WhF	Pic
✓							✓	✓			✓

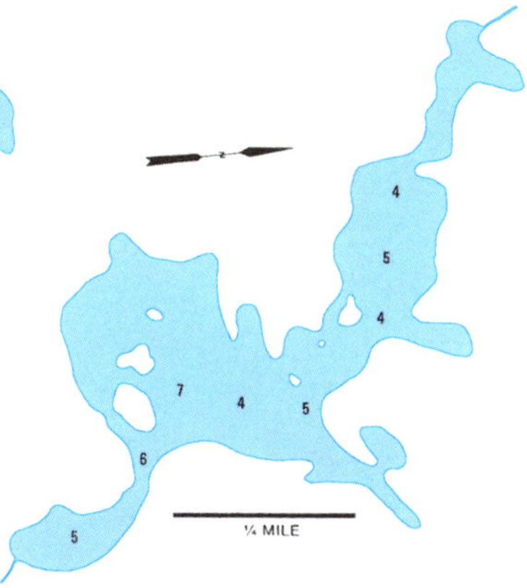

Rich Mill Pond

Standish, Maine Atlas Map 5, D-1
Acres: 77, Max. Depth: 7 feet

BrT	BkT	RbT	Sal	Tog	Smt	LmB	SmB	WhP	Csk	WhF	Pic
						✓	✓				✓

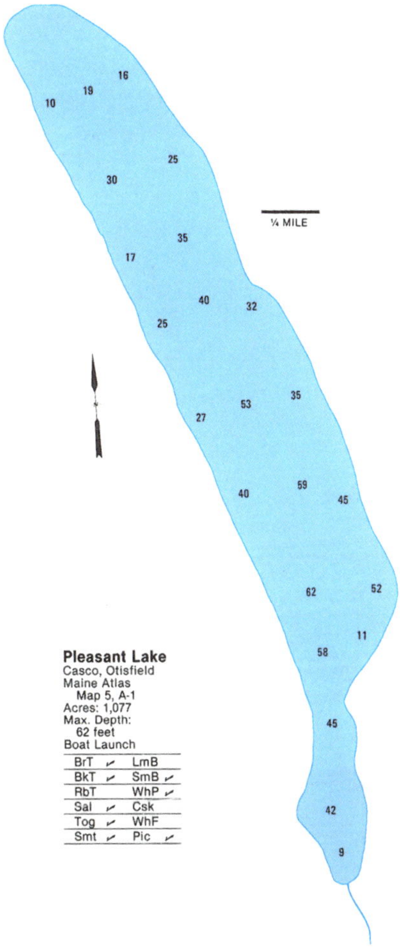

Pleasant Lake

Casco, Otisfield
Maine Atlas
Map 5, A-1
Acres: 1,077
Max. Depth:
62 feet
Boat Launch

BrT	✓	LmB	
BkT	✓	SmB	✓
RbT		WhP	✓
Sal	✓	Csk	
Tog	✓	WhF	
Smt	✓	Pic	✓

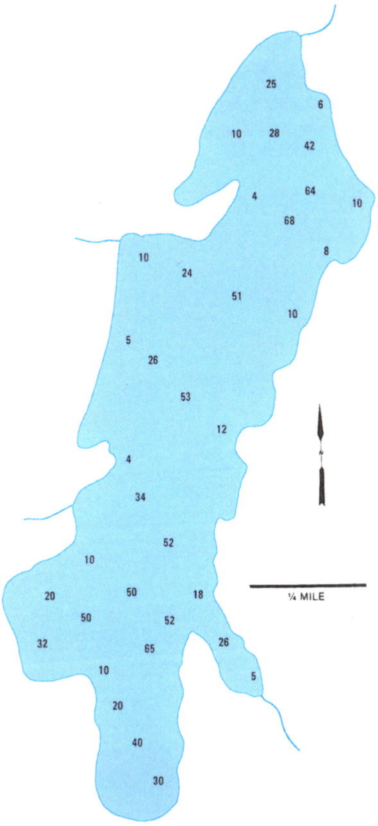

Sabbathday Lake

New Gloucester, Maine Atlas Map 5, B-3
Acres: 340, Max. Depth: 68 feet

BrT	BkT	RbT	Sal	Tog	Smt	LmB	SmB	WhP	Csk	WhF	Pic
✓	✓			✓	✓		✓				

Cumberland

Sand Pond
Baldwin
Maine Atlas
Map 4, D-4
Acres: 61
Max. Depth:
18 feet
Boat Launch

BrT ✓	LmB ✓
BkT ✓	SmB ✓
RbT	WhP
Sal	Csk
Tog	WhF
Smt	Pic

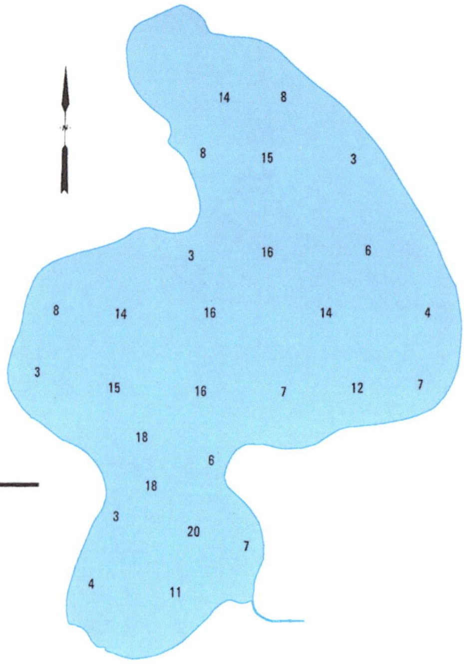

¼ MILE

Sebago Lake
Naples, Casco, Standish, Windham, Raymond, Sebago, Maine Atlas Map 4, C-5, Acres: 28,771, Max. Depth 316 feet, Boat Launch

BrT	BkT	RbT	Sal	Tog	Smt	LmB	SmB	WhP	Csk	WhF	Pic
✓	✓		✓	✓	✓	✓	✓	✓	✓		✓

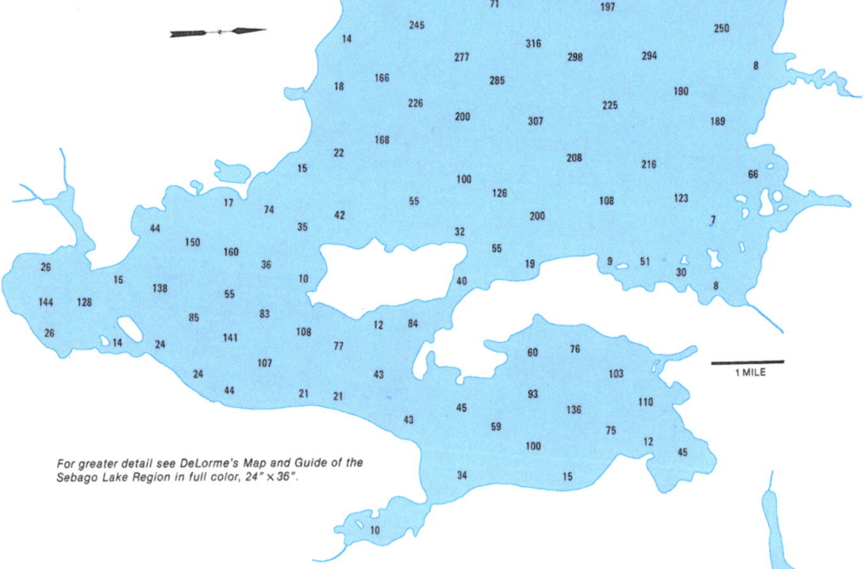

1 MILE

For greater detail see DeLorme's Map and Guide of the Sebago Lake Region in full color, 24" × 36".

Southeast Pond
Baldwin, Sebago, Maine Atlas Map 4, C-3
Acres: 173, Max. Depth: 30 feet

BrT	BkT	RbT	Sal	Tog	Smt	LmB	SmB	WhP	Csk	WhF	Pic
						✓	✓	✓			✓

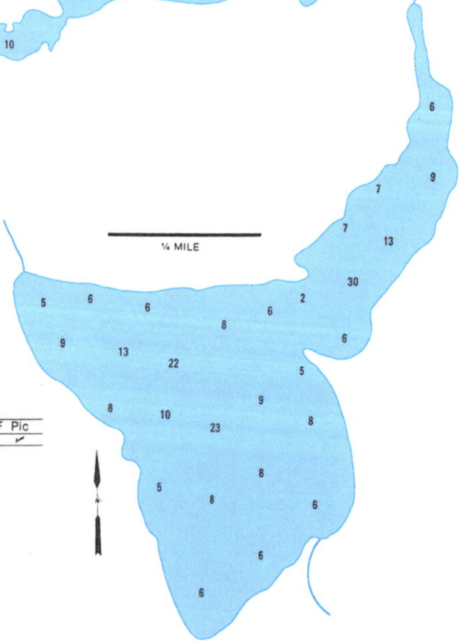

¼ MILE

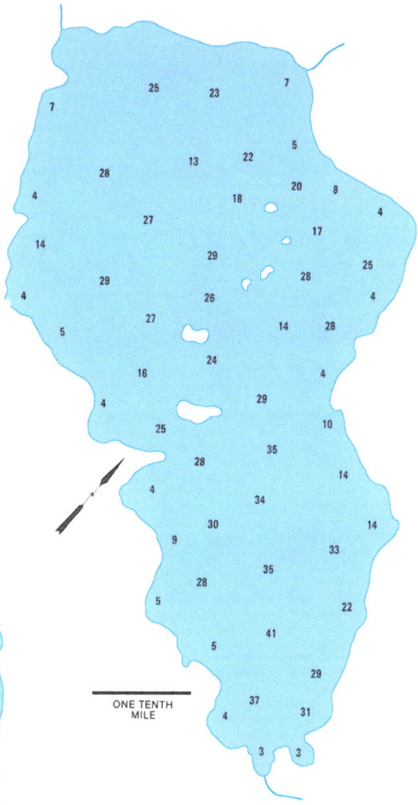

Thomas Pond
Casco, Raymond, Maine Atlas Map 5, B-1
Acres: 442, Max. Depth: 64 feet, Boat Launch

BrT	BkT	RbT	Sal	Tog	Smt	LmB	SmB	WhP	Csk	WhF	Pic
✓	✓		✓		✓	✓	✓	✓			✓

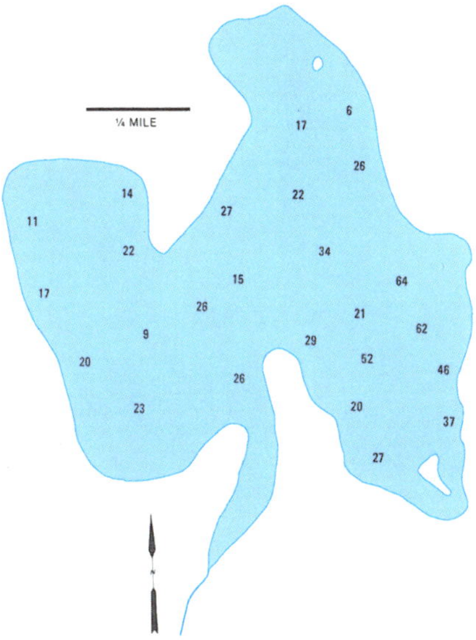

Watchic Pond
Standish, Maine Atlas Map 4, D-5
Acres: 448, Max. Depth: 41 feet

BrT	BkT	RbT	Sal	Tog	Smt	LmB	SmB	WhP	Csk	WhF	Pic
✓					✓	✓	✓	✓			✓

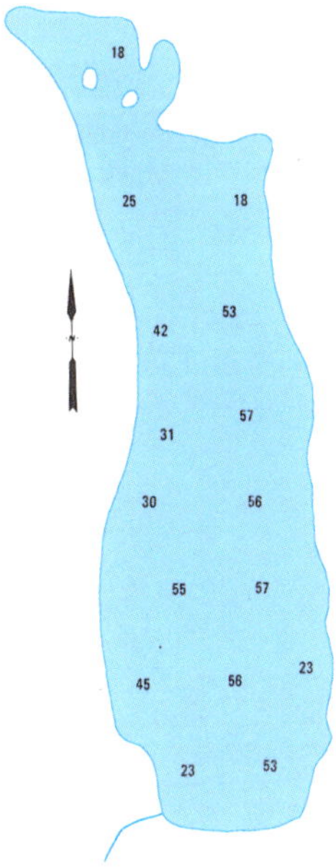

Trickey Pond
Naples
Maine Atlas
Map 4, B-5
Acres: 311
Max. Depth:
57 feet
Boat Launch

BrT		LmB	
BkT	✓	SmB	✓
RbT		WhP	
Sal	✓	Csk	
Tog	✓	WhF	
Smt	✓	Pic	✓

Comments: Splake.

¼ MILE

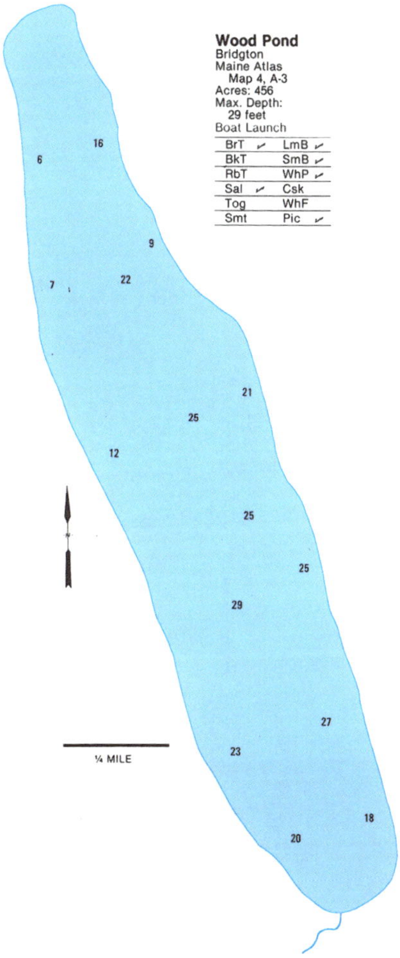

Wood Pond
Bridgton
Maine Atlas
Map 4, A-3
Acres: 456
Max. Depth:
29 feet
Boat Launch

BrT	✓	LmB	✓
BkT		SmB	✓
RbT		WhP	✓
Sal	✓	Csk	
Tog		WhF	
Smt		Pic	✓

¼ MILE

Upper Mud Pond
Windham
Maine Atlas
Map 5, C-2
Acres: 7
Max. Depth:
9 feet

BrT		LmB	✓
BkT		SmB	✓
RbT		WhP	
Sal		Csk	
Tog		WhF	
Smt		Pic	✓

ONE TENTH MILE

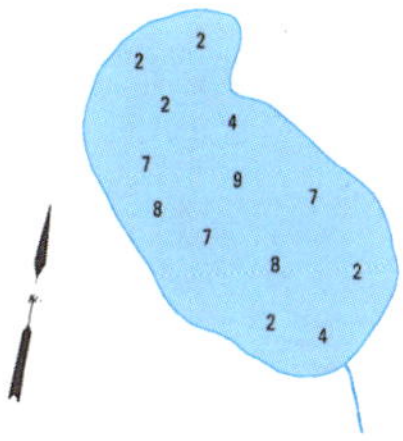

Franklin County

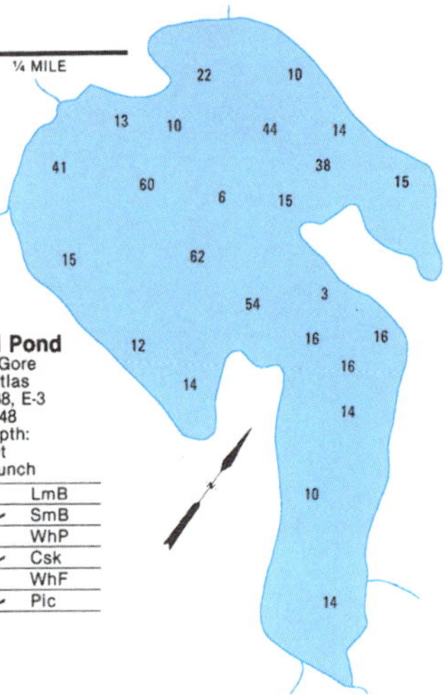

Arnold Pond
Coburn Gore
Maine Atlas
Map 38, E-3
Acres: 148
Max. Depth:
62 feet
Boat Launch

BrT		LmB	
BkT	✓	SmB	
RbT		WhP	
Sal	✓	Csk	
Tog		WhF	
Smt	✓	Pic	

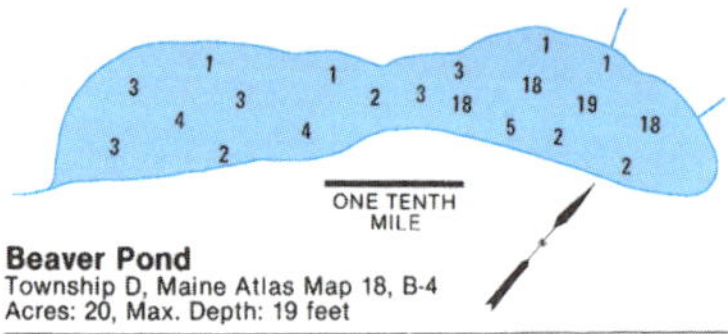

Beaver Pond
Township D, Maine Atlas Map 18, B-4
Acres: 20, Max. Depth: 19 feet

BrT	BkT	RbT	Sal	Tog	Smt	LmB	SmB	WhP	Csk	WhF	Pic
	✓										

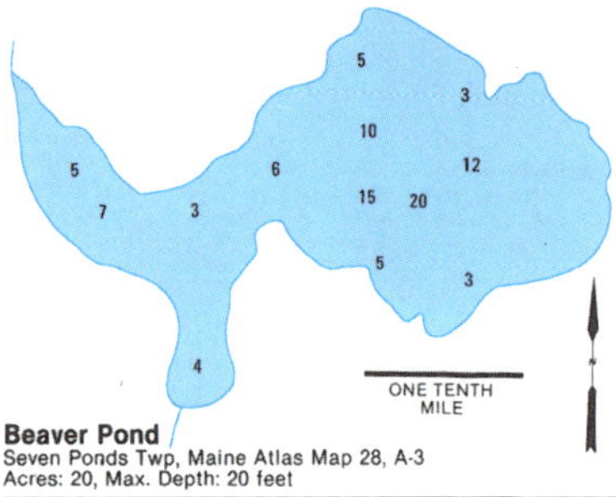

Beaver Pond
Seven Ponds Twp, Maine Atlas Map 28, A-3
Acres: 20, Max. Depth: 20 feet

BrT	BkT	RbT	Sal	Tog	Smt	LmB	SmB	WhP	Csk	WhF	Pic
	✓										

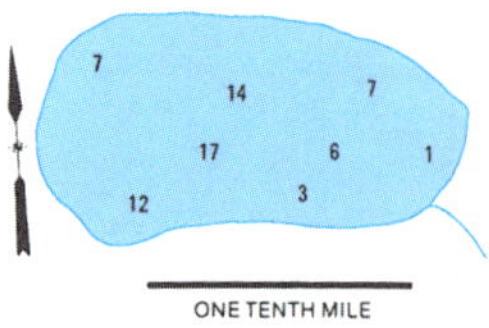

Ballard Pond
Farmington, Temple
Maine Atlas
Map 19, C-5
Acres: 3
Max. Depth:
17 feet

BrT		LmB	
BkT		SmB	
RbT		WhP	
Sal		Csk	
Tog		WhF	
Smt		Pic	✓

Barnard Pond
Eustis
Maine Atlas
Map 29, B-1
Acres: 17
Max. Depth:
27 feet

BrT		LmB	
BkT	✓	SmB	
RbT		WhP	
Sal		Csk	
Tog		WhF	
Smt		Pic	

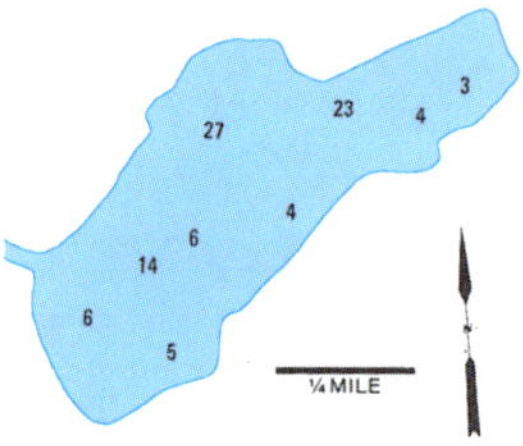

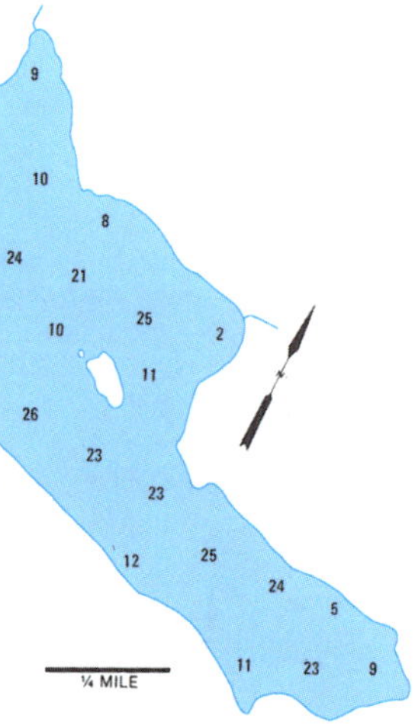

Big Island Pond
Chain of Ponds Twp,
Seven Ponds Twp
Maine Atlas
Map 28, A-3, A-4
Acres: 350
Max. Depth:
40 feet

BrT		LmB	
BkT	✓	SmB	
RbT		WhP	
Sal		Csk	
Tog		WhF	
Smt		Pic	

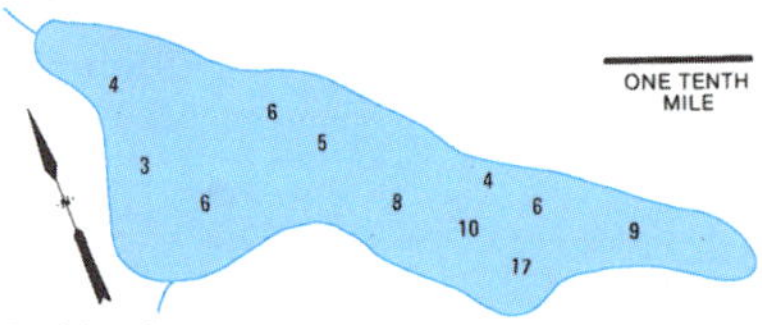

Beal Pond
Madrid, Maine Atlas Map 19, A-2, A-3
Acres: 32, Max. Depth: 17 feet

BrT	BkT	RbT	Sal	Tog	Smt	LmB	SmB	WhP	Csk	WhF	Pic
	✓				✓						

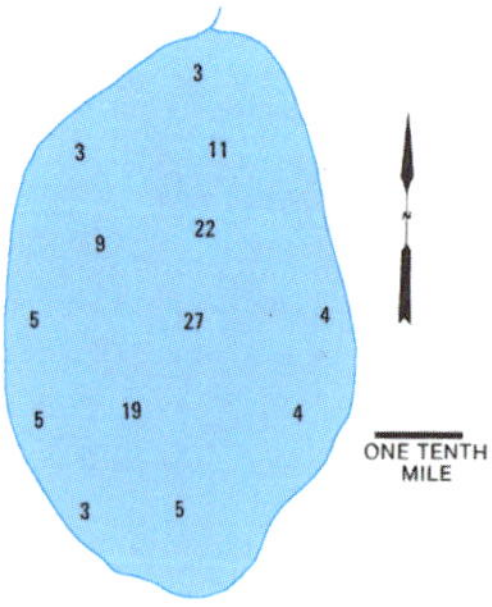

Blanchard Pond
Alder Stream Twp
Maine Atlas
Map 28, A-5
Acres: 9
Max. Depth:
27 feet

BrT		LmB	
BkT	✓	SmB	
RbT		WhP	
Sal		Csk	
Tog		WhF	
Smt		Pic	

Beattie Pond
Beattie Twp,
Lowelltown Twp
Maine Atlas
Map 38, C-5
Acres: 27
Max. Depth:
11 feet

BrT		LmB	
BkT	✓	SmB	
RbT		WhP	
Sal		Csk	
Tog		WhF	
Smt		Pic	

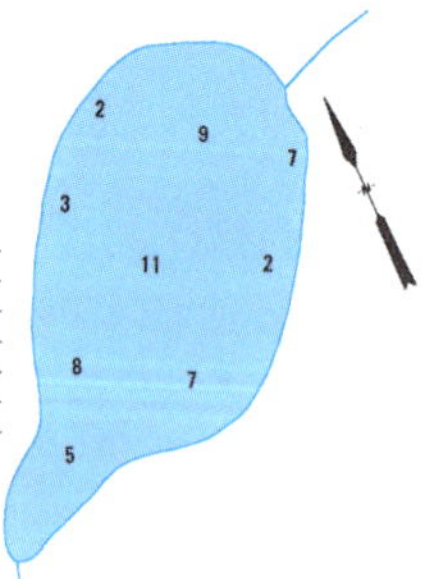

Bugeye Pond
Kibby Twp,
Chain of Ponds Twp
Maine Atlas
Map 28, A-5
Acres: 6
Max. Depth:
10 feet

BrT		LmB	
BkT	✓	SmB	
RbT		WhP	
Sal		Csk	
Tog		WhF	
Smt		Pic	

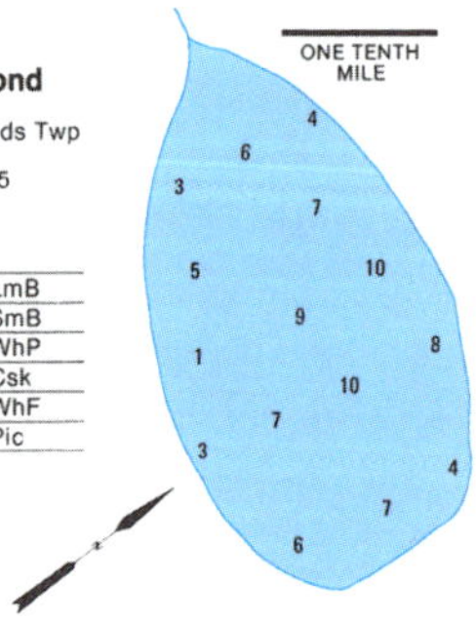

Beaver Mountain Lake
Sandy River Plt
Maine Atlas
Map 18, A-5
Acres: 543
Max. Depth:
52 feet
Boat Launch

BrT		LmB	
BkT	✓	SmB	
RbT		WhP	
Sal	✓	Csk	
Tog		WhF	
Smt	✓	Pic	

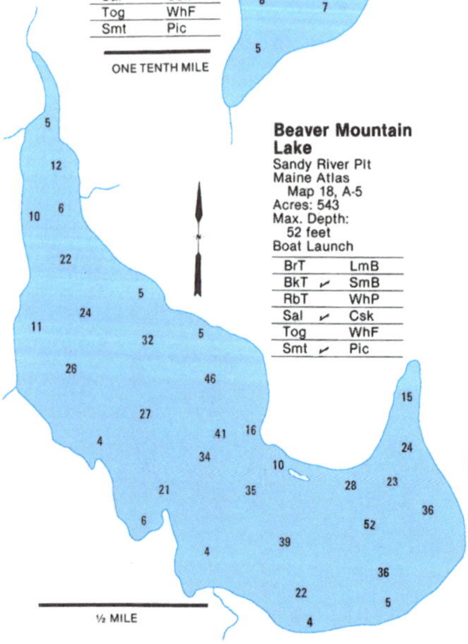

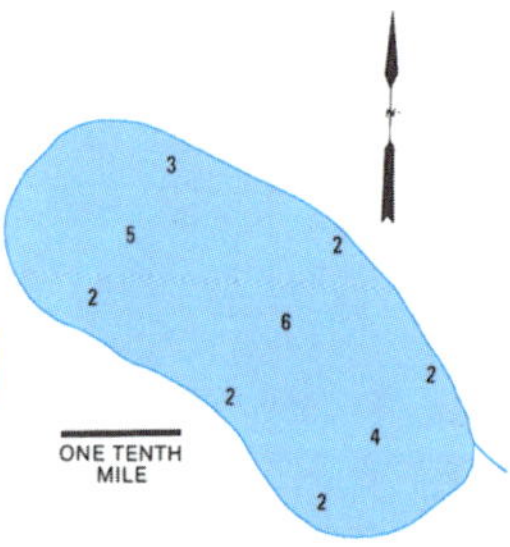

Caribou Bog
Chain of Ponds Twp
Maine Atlas
Map 38, E-3, E-4
Acres: 5
Max. Depth:
6 feet

BrT		LmB	
BkT	✓	SmB	
RbT		WhP	
Sal		Csk	
Tog		WhF	
Smt		Pic	

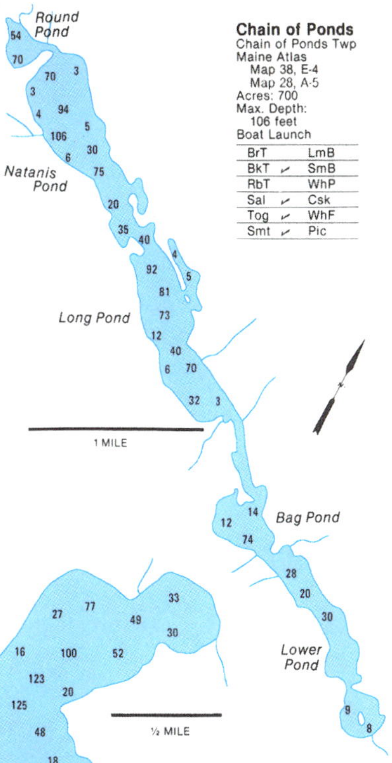

Chain of Ponds

Chain of Ponds Twp
Maine Atlas
Map 38, E-4
Map 28, A-5
Acres: 700
Max. Depth:
106 feet
Boat Launch

BrT	LmB
BkT ✓	SmB
RbT	WhP
Sal ✓	Csk
Tog ✓	WhF
Smt ✓	Pic

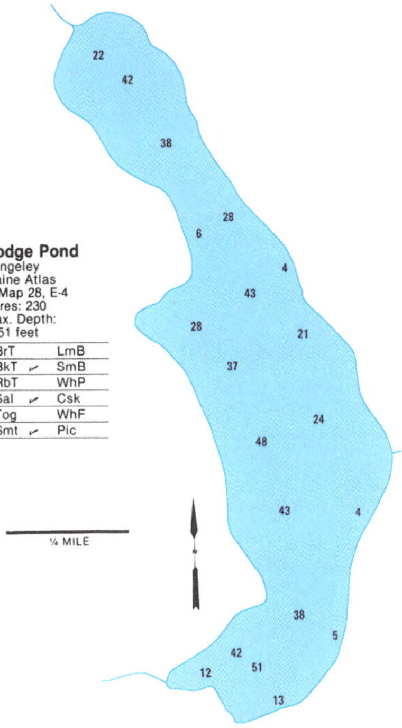

Dodge Pond

Rangeley
Maine Atlas
Map 28, E-4
Acres: 230
Max. Depth:
51 feet

BrT	LmB
BkT ✓	SmB
RbT	WhP
Sal ✓	Csk
Tog	WhF
Smt ✓	Pic

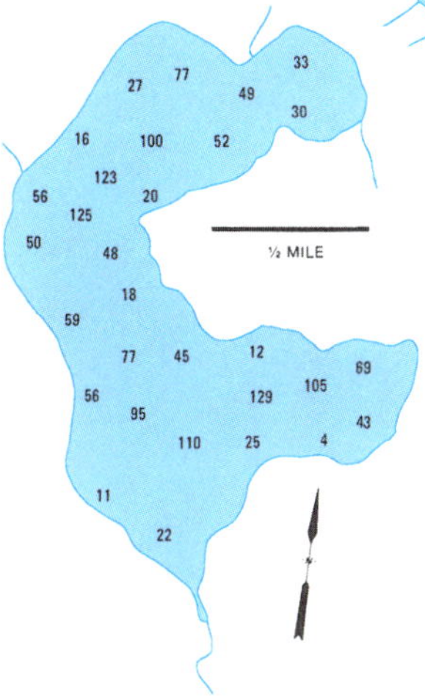

Clearwater Pond

Industry, Farmington
Maine Atlas
Map 20, C-1
Acres: 751
Max. Depth:
129 feet
Boat Launch

BrT	LmB
BkT ✓	SmB ✓
RbT	WhP ✓
Sal ✓	Csk ✓
Tog ✓	WhF ✓
Smt	Pic

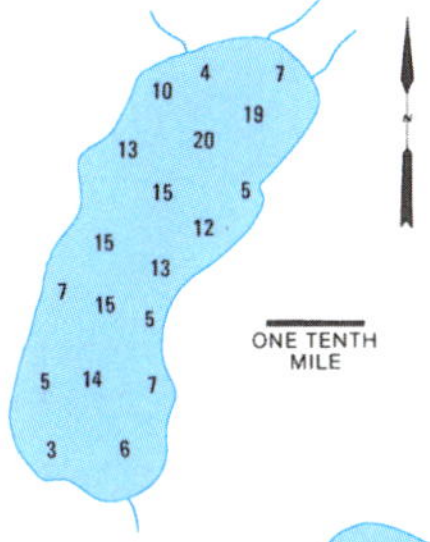

Drury Pond

Temple
Maine Atlas
Map 19, C-5
Acres: 34
Max. Depth:
20 feet

BrT	LmB
BkT ✓	SmB
RbT	WhP
Sal	Csk
Tog	WhF
Smt	Pic ✓

Dutton Pond

Kingfield
Maine Atlas
Map 29, D-5
Acres: 20
Max. Depth:
39 feet

BrT	LmB
BkT ✓	SmB
RbT	WhP
Sal	Csk
Tog	WhF
Smt	Pic

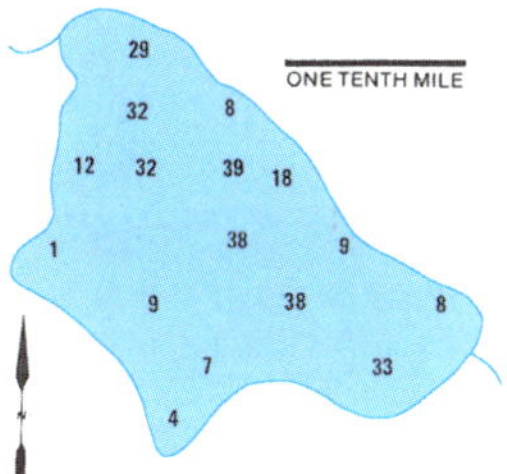

Cloutman Pond

Rangeley
Maine Atlas
Map 28, D-3
Acres: 20
Max. Depth:
5 feet

BrT	LmB
BkT ✓	SmB
RbT	WhP
Sal	Csk
Tog	WhF
Smt	Pic

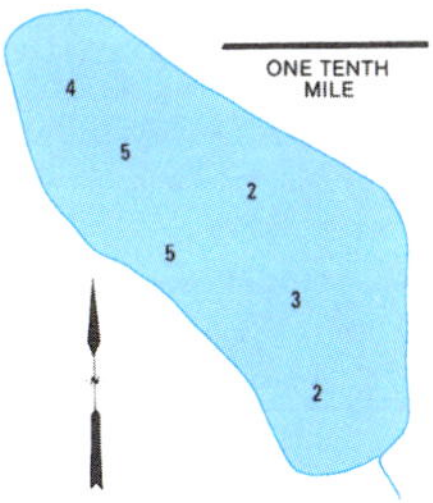

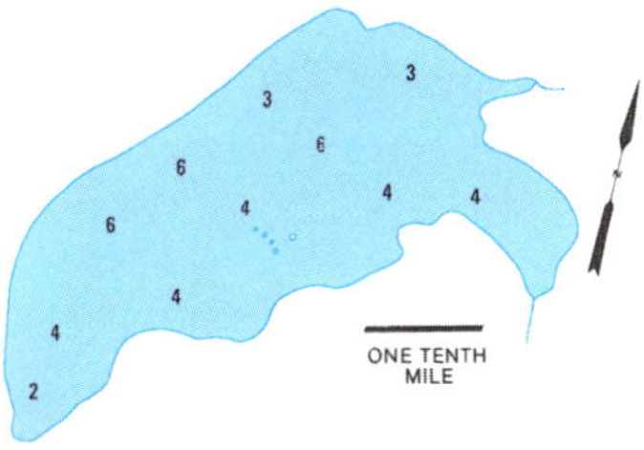

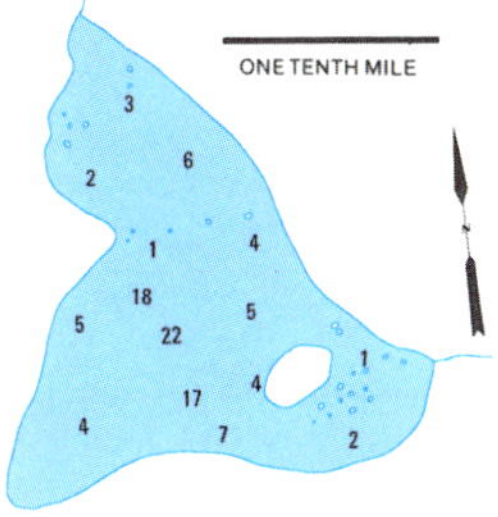

Eddy Pond

Sandy River Plt
Maine Atlas
Map 29, E-1
Acres: 9
Max. Depth:
22 feet

BrT	LmB
BkT ✓	SmB
RbT	WhP
Sal	Csk
Tog	WhF
Smt	Pic

Cow Pond

Lang Twp, Maine Atlas Map 28, D-5
Acres: 62, Max. Depth: 6 feet

BrT	BkT	RbT	Sal	Tog	Smt	LmB	SmB	WhP	Csk	WhF	Pic
	✓				✓						

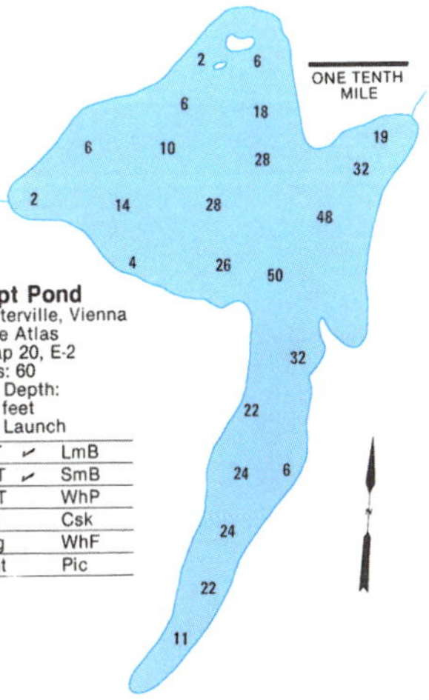

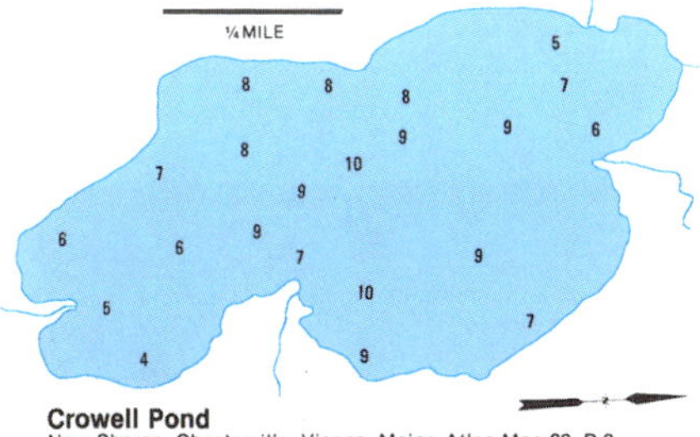

Egypt Pond

Chesterville, Vienna
Maine Atlas
Map 20, E-2
Acres: 60
Max. Depth:
50 feet
Boat Launch

BrT ✓	LmB
BkT ✓	SmB
RbT	WhP
Sal	Csk
Tog	WhF
Smt	Pic

Crowell Pond

New Sharon, Chesterville, Vienna, Maine Atlas Map 20, D-2
Acres: 211, Max. Depth: 10 feet

BrT	BkT	RbT	Sal	Tog	Smt	LmB	SmB	WhP	Csk	WhF	Pic
	✓					✓	✓	✓			✓

Franklin

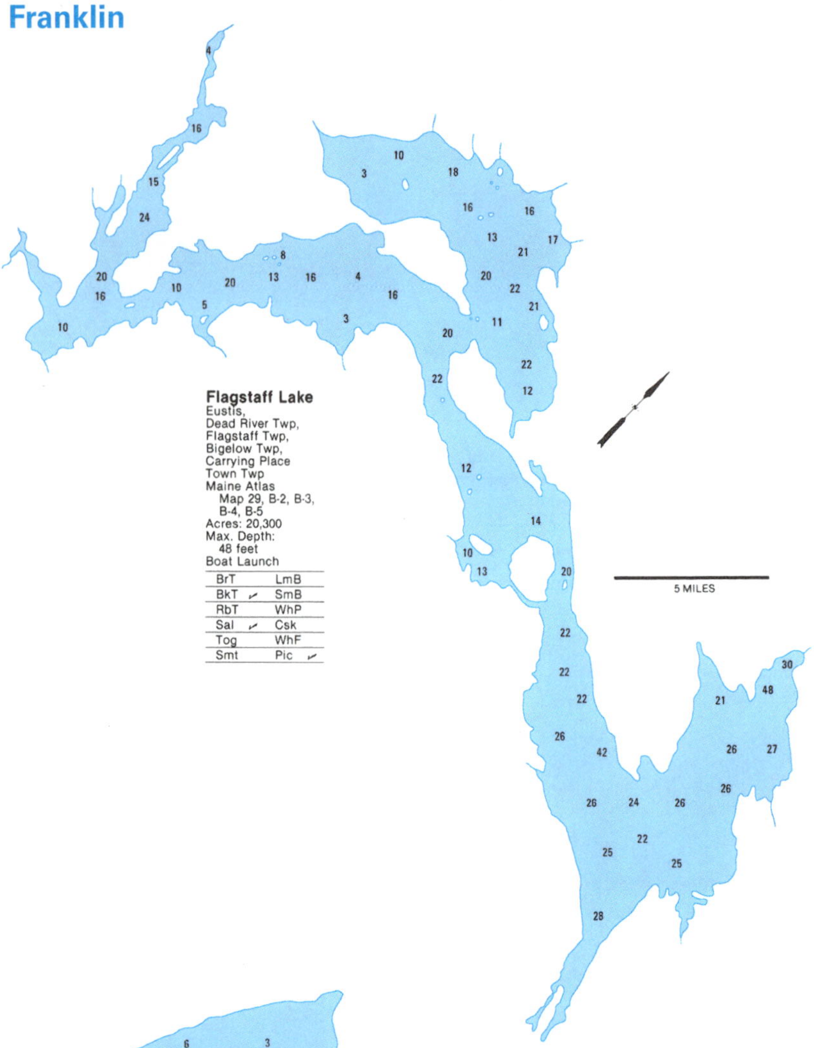

Flagstaff Lake
Eustis,
Dead River Twp,
Flagstaff Twp,
Bigelow Twp,
Carrying Place
Town Twp
Maine Atlas
Map 29, B-2, B-3,
B-4, B-5
Acres: 20,300
Max. Depth:
48 feet
Boat Launch

BrT		LmB	
BkT	✓	SmB	
RbT		WhP	
Sal	✓	Csk	
Tog		WhF	
Smt		Pic	✓

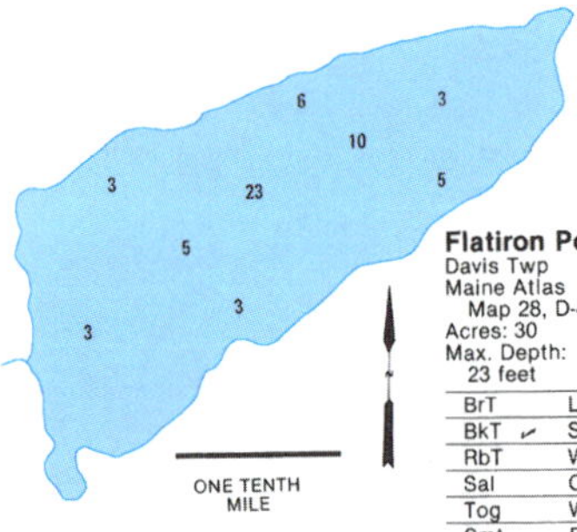

Flatiron Pond
Davis Twp
Maine Atlas
Map 28, D-4
Acres: 30
Max. Depth:
23 feet

BrT		LmB	
BkT	✓	SmB	
RbT		WhP	
Sal		Csk	
Tog		WhF	
Smt		Pic	

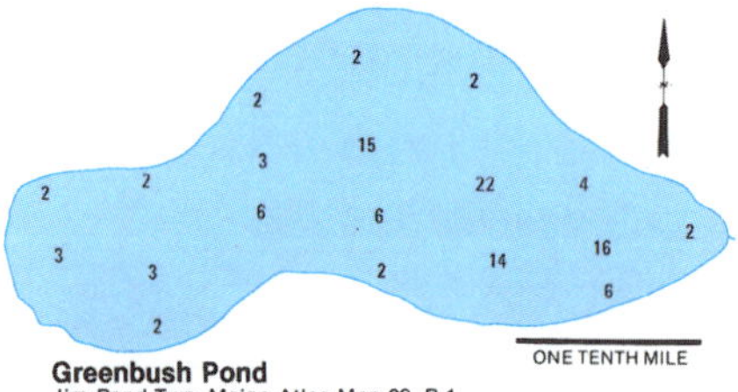

Greenbush Pond
Jim Pond Twp, Maine Atlas Map 29, B-1
Acres: 21, Max. Depth: 22 feet

BrT	BkT	RbT	Sal	Tog	Smt	LmB	SmB	WhP	Csk	WhF	Pic
	✓										

Grants Pond
Massachusetts Gore
Maine Atlas
Map 28, A-3
Acres: 20
Max. Depth:
6 feet

BrT		LmB	
BkT	✓	SmB	
RbT		WhP	
Sal		Csk	
Tog		WhF	
Smt		Pic	

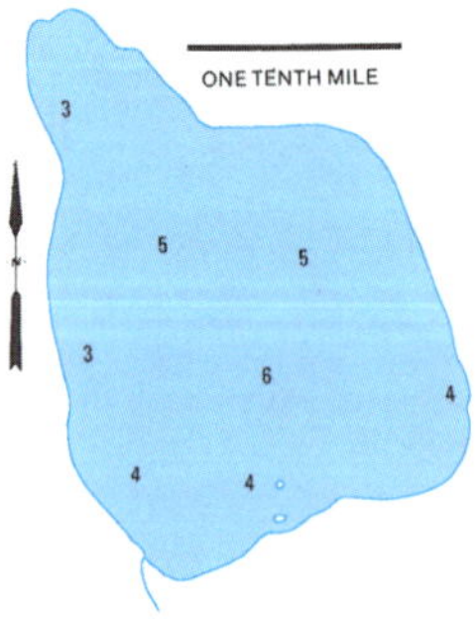

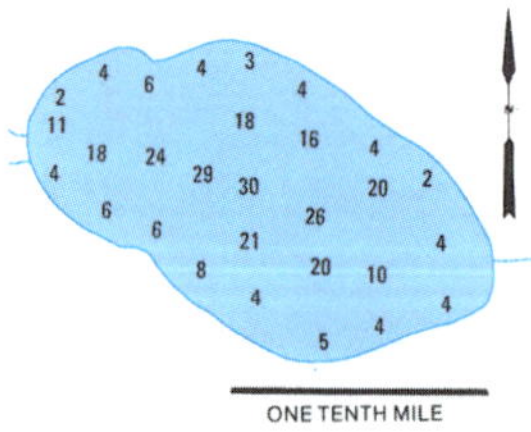

Grindstone Pond
Kingfield
Maine Atlas
Map 29, E-5
Acres: 6
Max. Depth:
30 feet

BrT	✓	LmB	
BkT	✓	SmB	
RbT		WhP	
Sal		Csk	
Tog		WhF	
Smt		Pic	

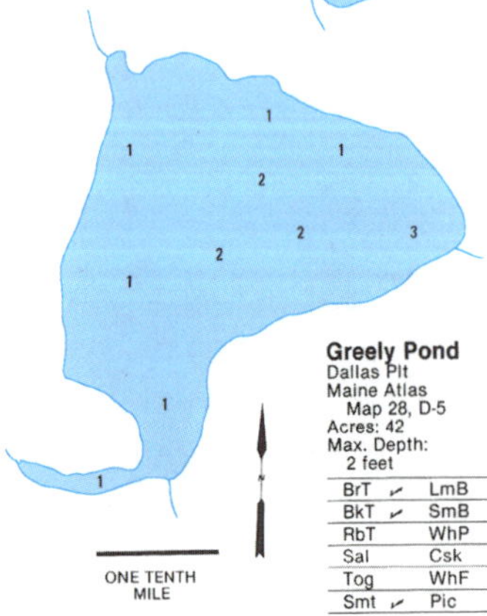

Greely Pond
Dallas Plt
Maine Atlas
Map 28, D-5
Acres: 42
Max. Depth:
2 feet

BrT	✓	LmB	
BkT	✓	SmB	
RbT		WhP	
Sal		Csk	
Tog		WhF	
Smt	✓	Pic	

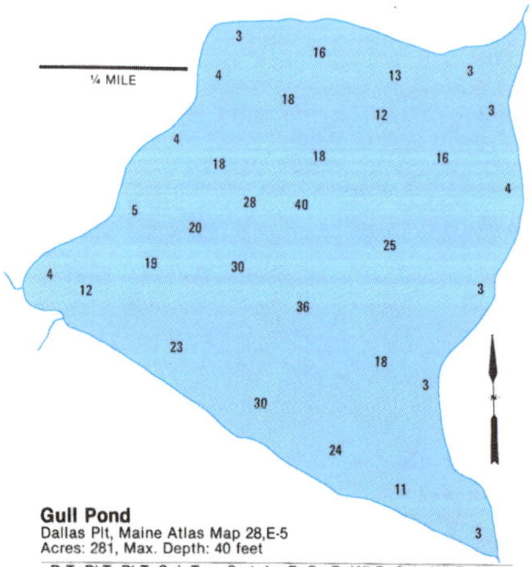

Gull Pond
Dallas Plt, Maine Atlas Map 28,E-5
Acres: 281, Max. Depth: 40 feet

BrT	BkT	RbT	Sal	Tog	Smt	LmB	SmB	WhP	Csk	WhF	Pic
	✓		✓								

Haley Pond
Rangeley, Dallas Plt
Maine Atlas
Map 28, E-5
Acres: 170
Max. Depth:
23 feet
Boat Launch

BrT		LmB	
BkT	✓	SmB	
RbT		WhP	
Sal	✓	Csk	
Tog		WhF	
Smt	✓	Pic	

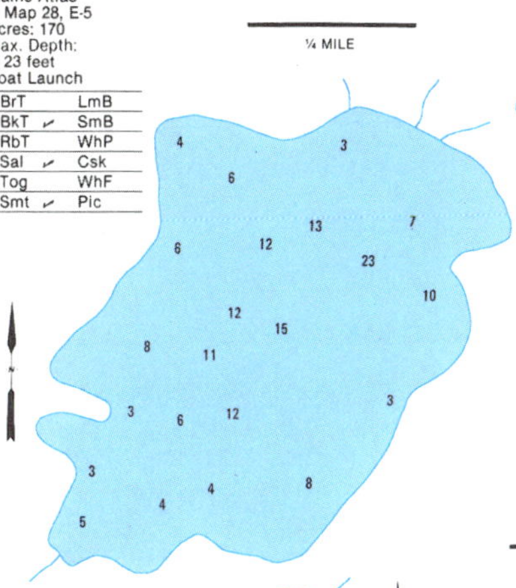

Jim Pond
Jim Pond Twp
Maine Atlas
Map 29, A-1
Acres: 320
Max. Depth:
125 feet
Boat Launch

BrT		LmB	
BkT	✓	SmB	
RbT		WhP	
Sal	✓	Csk	✓
Tog	✓	WhF	✓
Smt	✓	Pic	

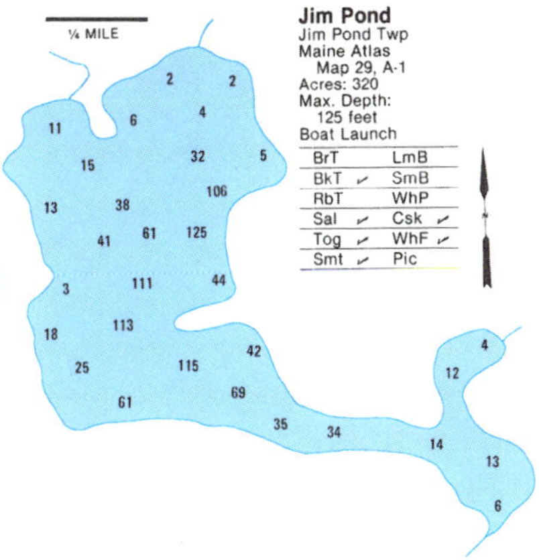

Harvey Pond
Madrid
Maine Atlas
Map 19, A-1
Acres: 10
Max. Depth:
8 feet

BrT		LmB	
BkT	✓	SmB	
RbT		WhP	
Sal		Csk	
Tog		WhF	
Smt		Pic	

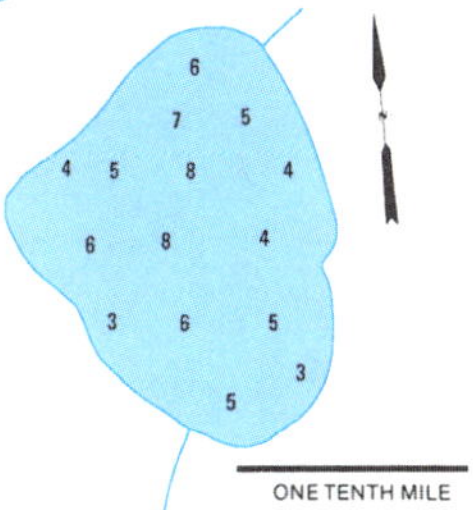

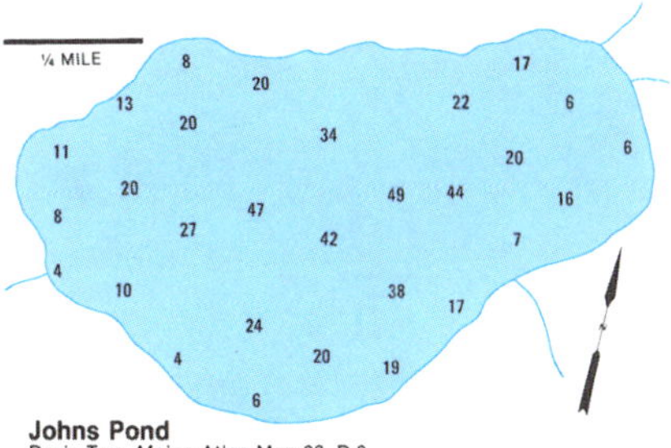

Johns Pond
Davis Twp, Maine Atlas Map 28, D-3
Acres: 267, Max. Depth: 49 feet

BrT	BkT	RbT	Sal	Tog	Smt	LmB	SmB	WhP	Csk	WhF	Pic
	✓		✓								

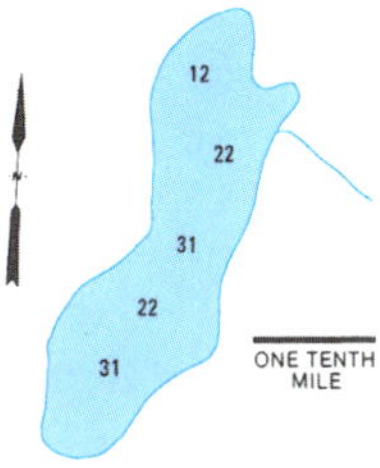

Hills Pond
Perkins Twp
Maine Atlas
Map 19, C-3
Acres: 19
Max. Depth:
31 feet

BrT		LmB	
BkT	✓	SmB	
RbT		WhP	
Sal		Csk	
Tog		WhF	
Smt		Pic	

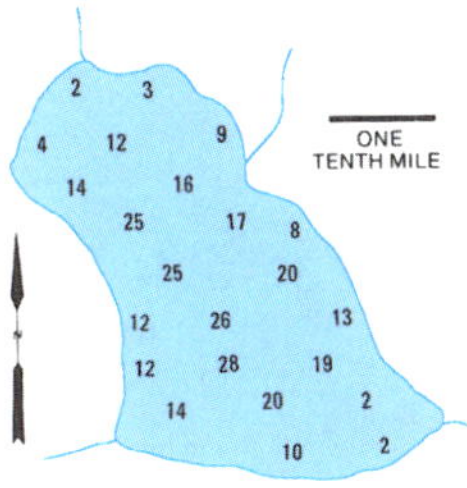

Kamankeag Pond
Davis Twp
Maine Atlas
Map 28, D-3
Acres: 40
Max. Depth:
28 feet

BrT		LmB	
BkT	✓	SmB	
RbT		WhP	
Sal		Csk	
Tog		WhF	
Smt		Pic	

Horseshoe Pond
Chesterville
Maine Atlas
Map 20, E-1
Acres: 58
Max. Depth:
12 feet

BrT		LmB	
BkT		SmB	✓
RbT		WhP	
Sal		Csk	
Tog		WhF	
Smt		Pic	✓

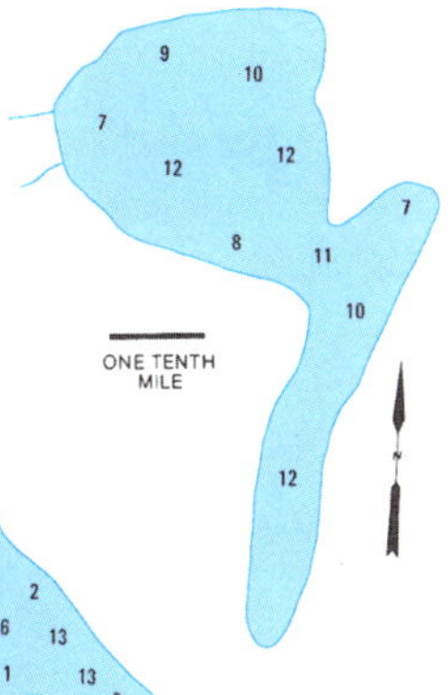

Horseshoe Pond
Coburn Gore, Chain of Ponds Twp, Maine Atlas Map 38, E-3
Acres: 37, Max. Depth: 13 feet

BrT	BkT	RbT	Sal	Tog	Smt	LmB	SmB	WhP	Csk	WhF	Pic
	✓		✓								

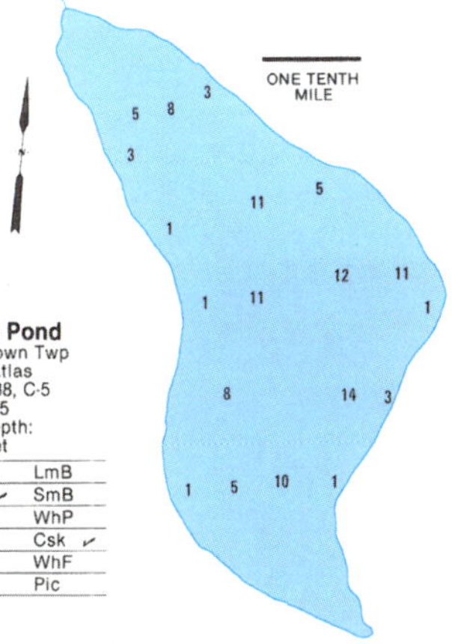

Indian Pond
Lowelltown Twp
Maine Atlas
Map 38, C-5
Acres: 75
Max. Depth:
14 feet

BrT		LmB	
BkT	✓	SmB	
RbT		WhP	
Sal		Csk	✓
Tog		WhF	
Smt		Pic	

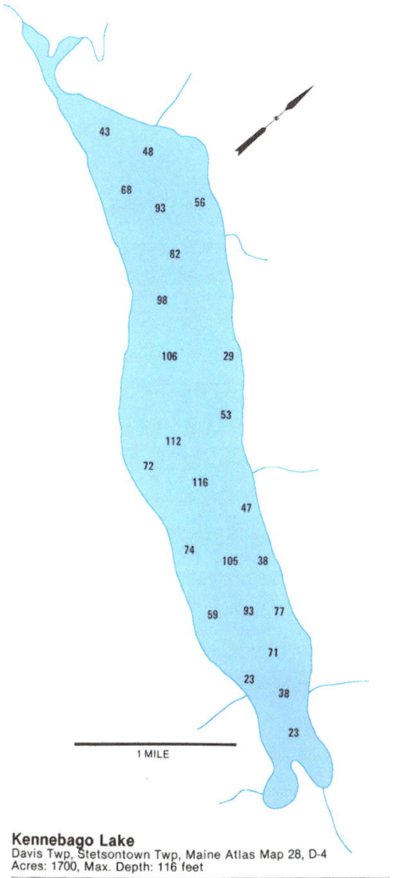

Kennebago Lake
Davis Twp, Stetsontown Twp, Maine Atlas Map 28, D-4
Acres: 1700, Max. Depth: 116 feet

BrT	BkT	RbT	Sal	Tog	Smt	LmB	SmB	WhP	Csk	WhF	Pic
✓	✓		✓		✓						

Franklin

Ledge Pond
Sandy River Plt
Maine Atlas
Map 19, A-1
Acres: 6
Max. Depth:
24 feet

BrT	LmB
BkT ✓	SmB
RbT	WhP
Sal	Csk
Tog	WhF
Smt	Pic

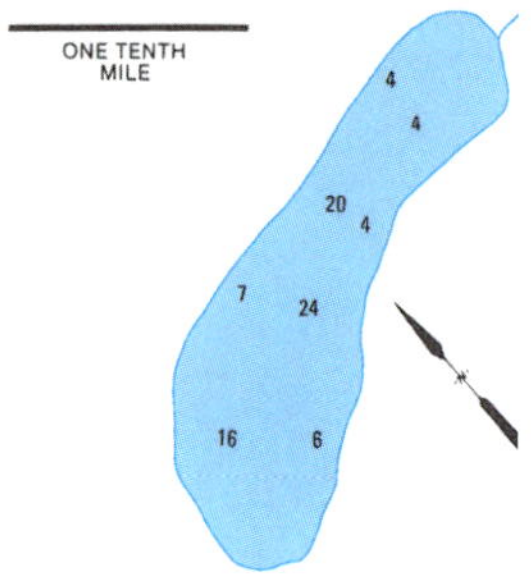

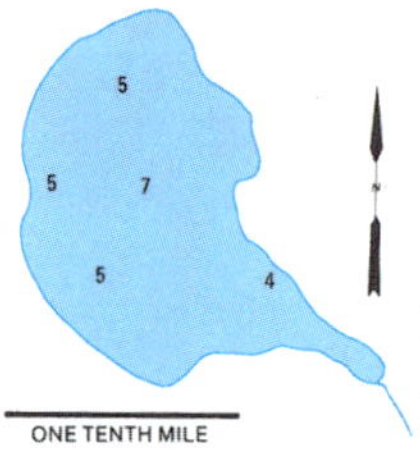

Little Northwest Pond
Massachusetts Gore
Maine Atlas
Map 28, A-3
Acres: 10
Max. Depth:
7 feet

BrT	LmB
BkT ✓	SmB
RbT	WhP
Sal	Csk
Tog	WhF
Smt	Pic

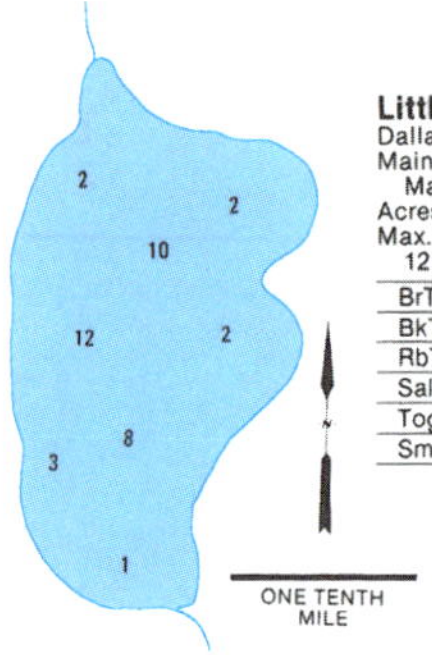

Little Greely Pond
Dallas Plt
Maine Atlas
Map 28, D-5
Acres: 15
Max. Depth:
12 feet

BrT	LmB
BkT ✓	SmB
RbT	WhP
Sal	Csk
Tog	WhF
Smt	Pic

Little Swift River Pond
Township E
Maine Atlas
Map 18, A-5
Acres: 15
Max. Depth:
22 feet

BrT	LmB
BkT ✓	SmB
RbT	WhP
Sal	Csk
Tog	WhF
Smt	Pic

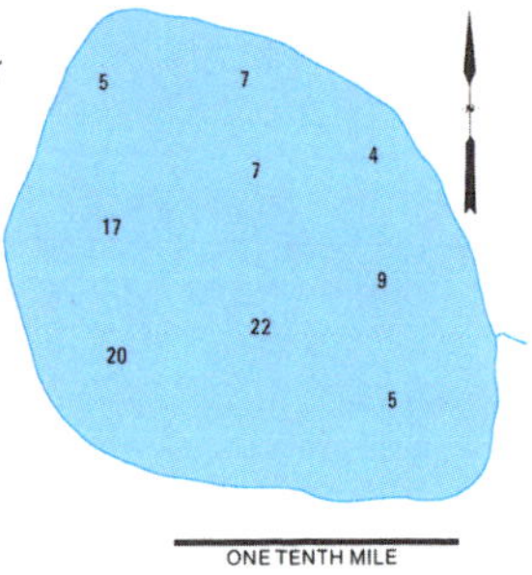

Little Island Pond
Seven Ponds Twp
Maine Atlas
Map 28, A-3
Acres: 50
Max. Depth:
38 feet

BrT	LmB
BkT ✓	SmB
RbT	WhP
Sal	Csk
Tog	WhF
Smt	Pic

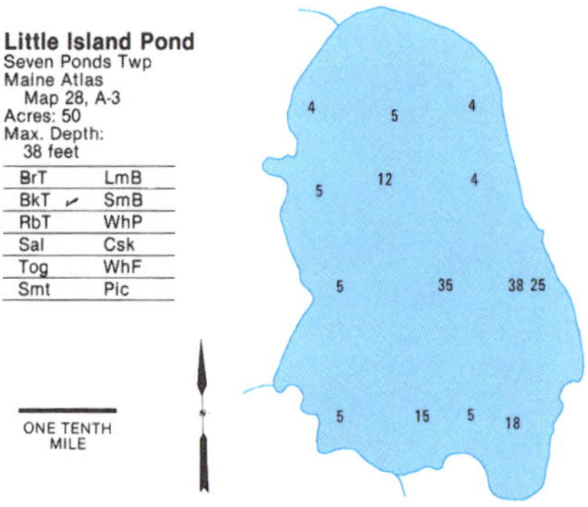

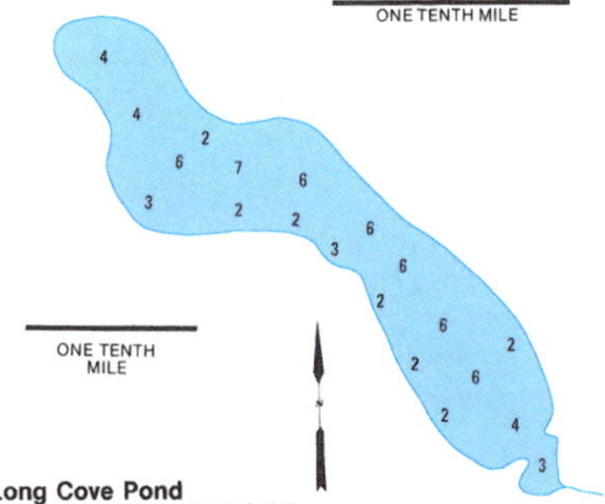

Long Cove Pond
Phillips, Maine Atlas Map 19, A-3
Acres: 12, Max. Depth: 7 feet

BrT	BkT	RbT	Sal	Tog	Smt	LmB	SmB	WhP	Csk	WhF	Pic
	✓										

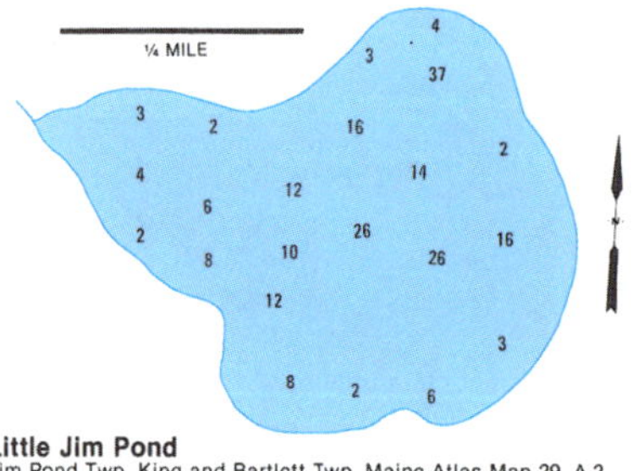

Little Jim Pond
Jim Pond Twp, King and Bartlett Twp, Maine Atlas Map 29, A-2
Acres: 64, Max. Depth: 37 feet

BrT	BkT	RbT	Sal	Tog	Smt	LmB	SmB	WhP	Csk	WhF	Pic
	✓			✓							

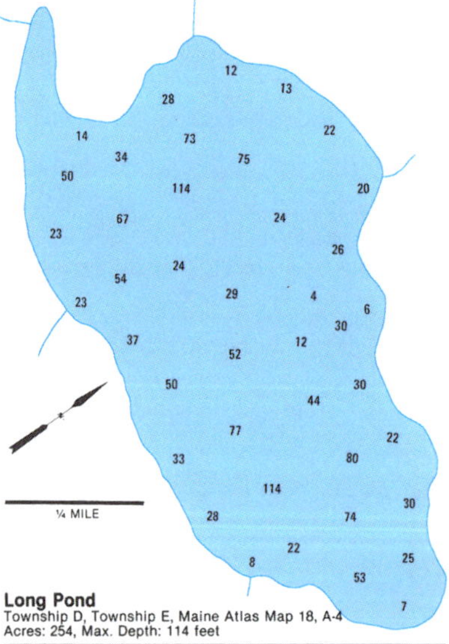

Long Pond
Township D, Township E, Maine Atlas Map 18, A-4
Acres: 254, Max. Depth: 114 feet

BrT	BkT	RbT	Sal	Tog	Smt	LmB	SmB	WhP	Csk	WhF	Pic
	✓				✓						

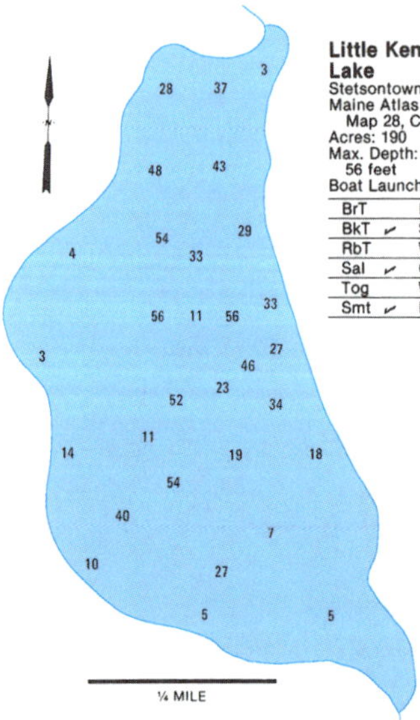

Little Kennebago Lake
Stetsontown Twp
Maine Atlas
Map 28, C-3
Acres: 190
Max. Depth:
56 feet
Boat Launch

BrT	LmB
BkT ✓	SmB
RbT	WhP
Sal ✓	Csk
Tog	WhF
Smt ✓	Pic

Long Pond
Seven Ponds Twp
Maine Atlas
Map 28, A-3, B-3
Acres: 50
Max. Depth:
15 feet

BrT	LmB
BkT ✓	SmB
RbT	WhP
Sal	Csk
Tog	WhF
Smt	Pic

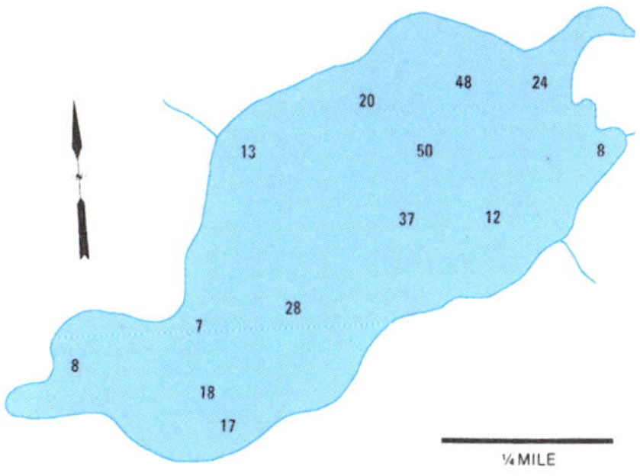

Loon Lake
Rangeley, Dallas Plt, Maine Atlas Map 28, D-5
Acres: 192, Max. Depth: 50 feet

BrT	BkT	RbT	Sal	Tog	Smt	LmB	SmB	WhP	Csk	WhF	Pic
	✓		✓		✓						

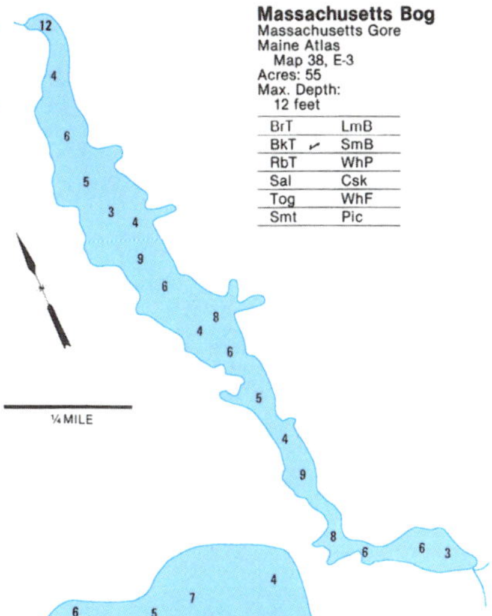

Massachusetts Bog
Massachusetts Gore
Maine Atlas
Map 38, E-3
Acres: 55
Max. Depth:
12 feet

BrT	LmB
BkT ✓	SmB
RbT	WhP
Sal	Csk
Tog	WhF
Smt	Pic

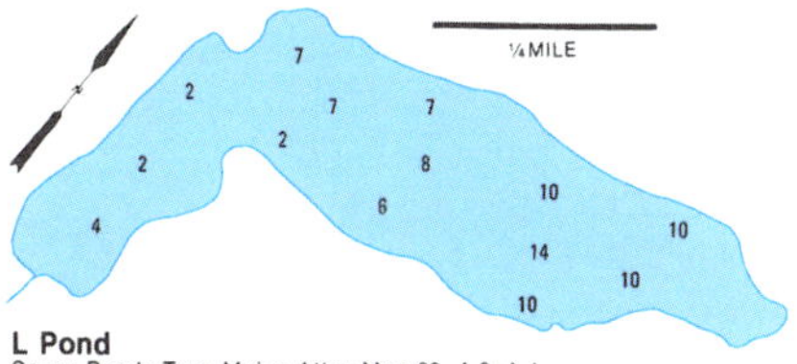

L Pond
Seven Ponds Twp, Maine Atlas Map 28, A-3, A-4
Acres: 100, Max. Depth: 14 feet

BrT	BkT	RbT	Sal	Tog	Smt	LmB	SmB	WhP	Csk	WhF	Pic
	✓										

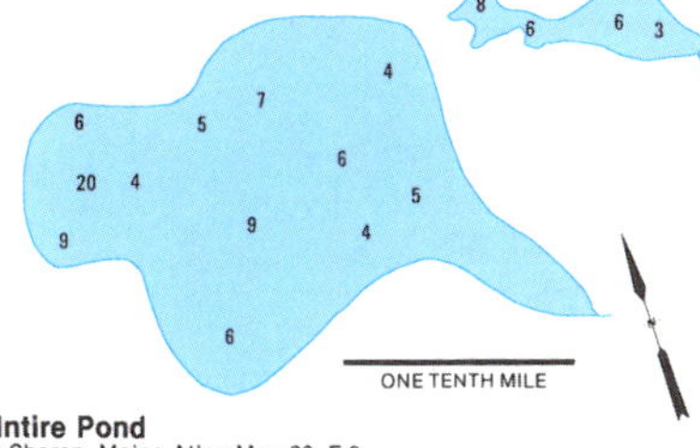

McIntire Pond
New Sharon, Maine Atlas Map 20, E-3
Acres: 20, Max. Depth: 20 feet

BrT	BkT	RbT	Sal	Tog	Smt	LmB	SmB	WhP	Csk	WhF	Pic
	✓										

Lufkin Pond
Phillips
Maine Atlas
Map 19, A-2
Acres: 47
Max. Depth:
28 feet

BrT ✓	LmB
BkT ✓	SmB ✓
RbT	WhP ✓
Sal	Csk
Tog	WhF
Smt	Pic

Comments: Splake.

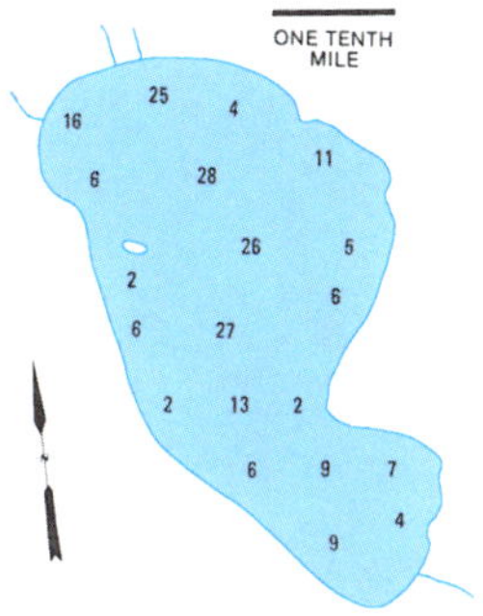

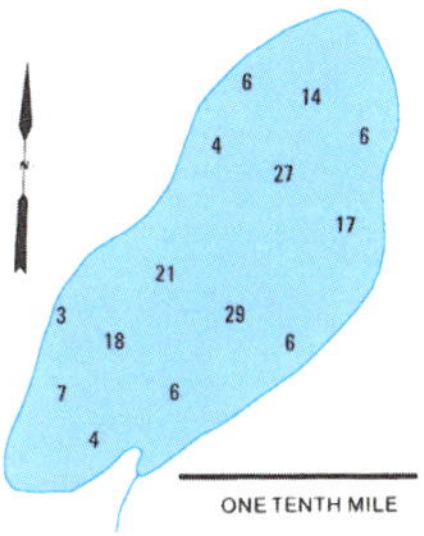

Midway Pond
Sandy River Plt
Maine Atlas
Map 29, E-1
Acres: 7
Max. Depth:
29 feet

BrT	LmB
BkT ✓	SmB
RbT	WhP
Sal	Csk
Tog	WhF
Smt	Pic

Mooselookmeguntic and Cupsuptic Lakes
Rangeley, Rangeley Plt, Adamstown Twp, Richardsontown Twp
Maine Atlas Map 28, E-2, E-3, Map 18, A-2, A-3
Acres: 16,300, Max. Depth: 123 feet, Boat Launch

BrT	BkT	RbT	Sal	Tog	Smt	LmB	SmB	WhP	Csk	WhF	Pic
	✓		✓		✓						

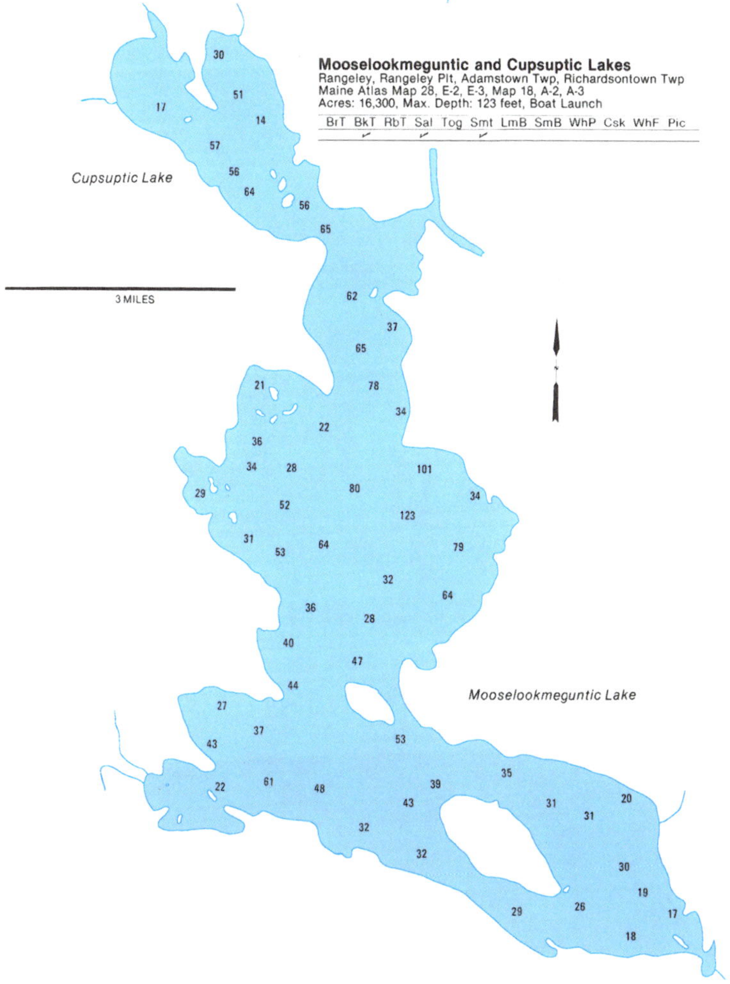

Franklin

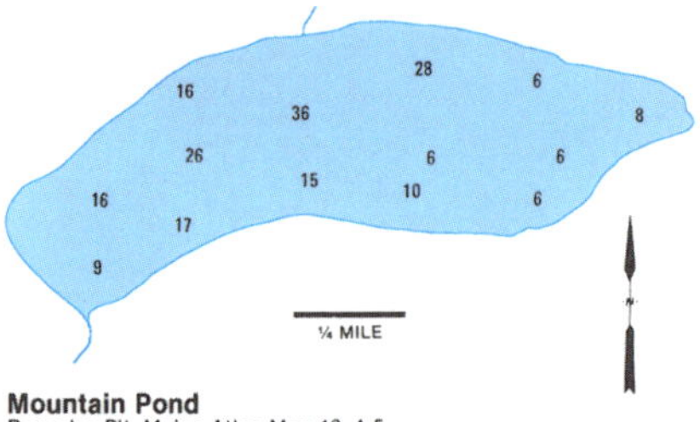

Mountain Pond
Rangeley Plt, Maine Atlas Map 18, A-5
Acres: 40, Max. Depth: 36 feet

BrT	BkT	RbT	Sal	Tog	Smt	LmB	SmB	WhP	Csk	WhF	Pic
	✓										

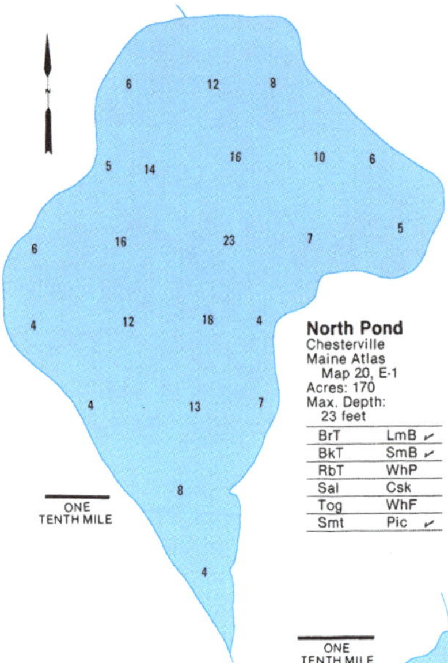

North Pond
Chesterville
Maine Atlas
Map 20, E-1
Acres: 170
Max. Depth:
23 feet

BrT		LmB	✓
BkT		SmB	✓
RbT		WhP	
Sal		Csk	
Tog		WhF	
Smt		Pic	✓

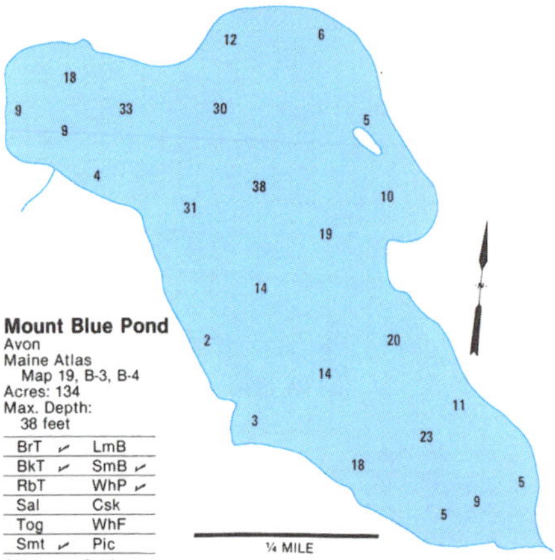

Mount Blue Pond
Avon
Maine Atlas
Map 19, B-3, B-4
Acres: 134
Max. Depth:
38 feet

BrT	✓	LmB	
BkT	✓	SmB	✓
RbT		WhP	✓
Sal		Csk	
Tog		WhF	
Smt	✓	Pic	

Comments: Splake.

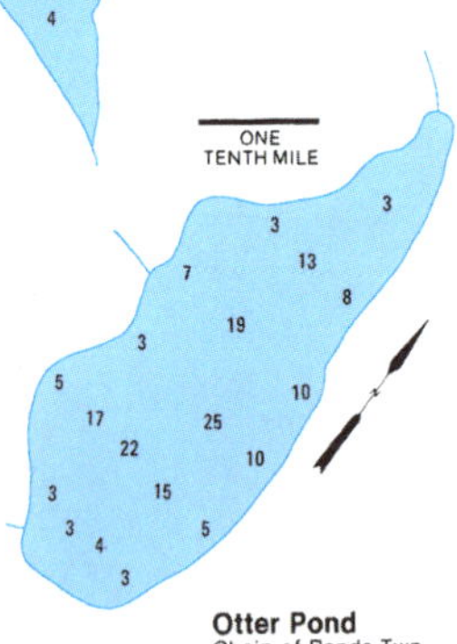

Northwest Pond
Massachusetts Gore
Maine Atlas
Map 28, A-3
Acres: 45
Max. Depth:
25 feet

BrT		LmB	
BkT	✓	SmB	
RbT		WhP	
Sal		Csk	
Tog		WhF	
Smt		Pic	

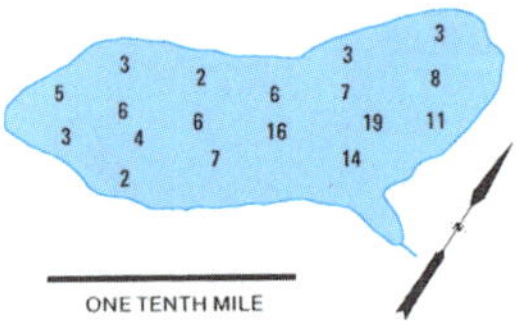

Moxie Pond
Township D
Maine Atlas
Map 18, A-4
Acres: 6
Max. Depth:
19 feet

BrT		LmB	
BkT	✓	SmB	
RbT		WhP	
Sal		Csk	
Tog		WhF	
Smt		Pic	

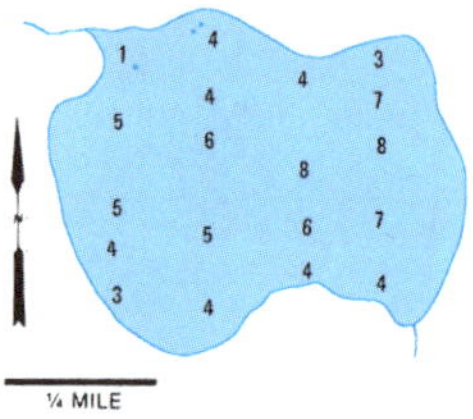

Otter Pond
Chain of Ponds Twp
Maine Atlas
Map 38, E-3
Acres: 30
Max. Depth:
8 feet

BrT		LmB	
BkT	✓	SmB	
RbT		WhP	
Sal		Csk	
Tog		WhF	
Smt		Pic	

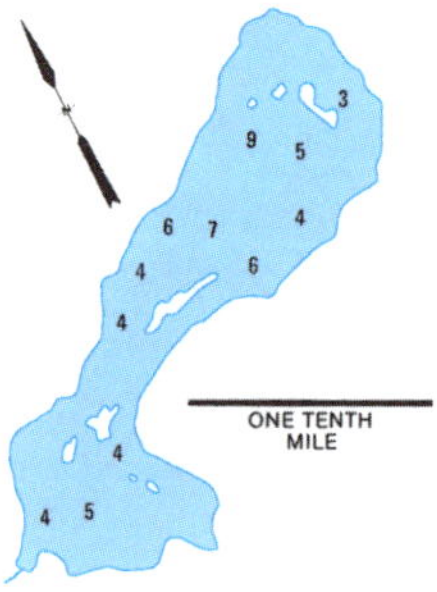

Mud Pond
Twp 6 North
of Weld
Maine Atlas
Map 19, A-1, A-2
Acres: 9
Max. Depth:
9 feet

BrT		LmB	
BkT	✓	SmB	
RbT		WhP	
Sal		Csk	
Tog		WhF	
Smt		Pic	

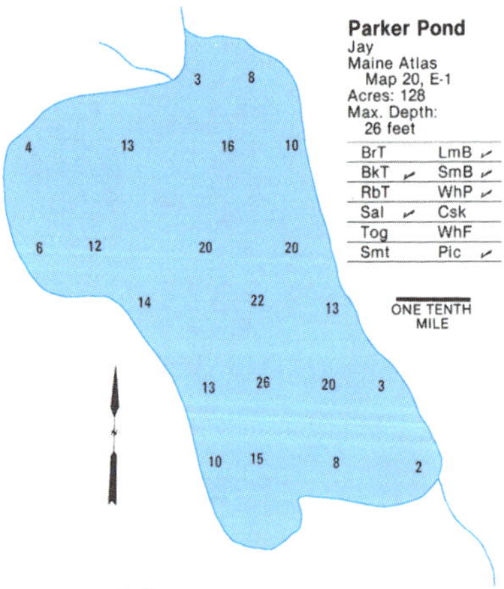

Parker Pond
Jay
Maine Atlas
Map 20, E-1
Acres: 128
Max. Depth:
26 feet

BrT		LmB	✓
BkT	✓	SmB	✓
RbT		WhP	✓
Sal	✓	Csk	
Tog		WhF	
Smt		Pic	✓

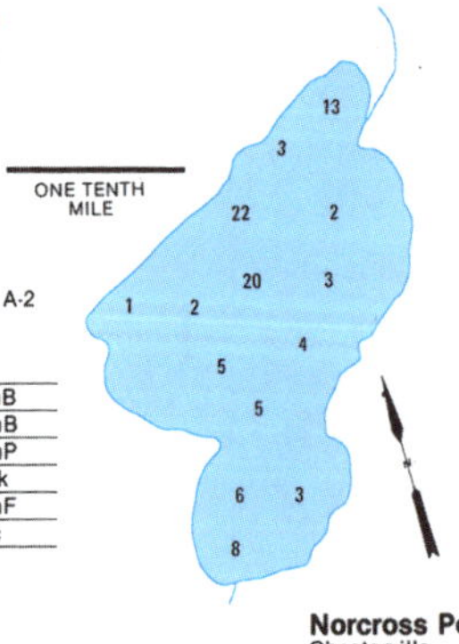

Mud Pond
Jim Pond Twp
Maine Atlas
Map 29, A-1, A-2
Acres: 14
Max. Depth:
22 feet

BrT		LmB	
BkT	✓	SmB	
RbT		WhP	
Sal		Csk	
Tog		WhF	
Smt		Pic	

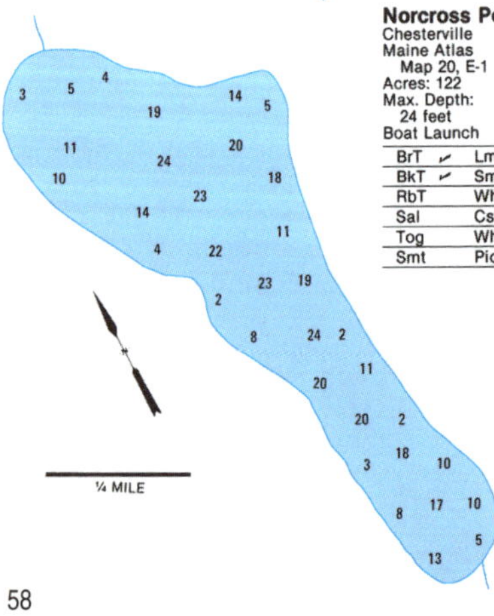

Norcross Pond
Chesterville
Maine Atlas
Map 20, E-1
Acres: 122
Max. Depth:
24 feet
Boat Launch

BrT	✓	LmB	✓
BkT	✓	SmB	
RbT		WhP	✓
Sal		Csk	
Tog		WhF	
Smt		Pic	✓

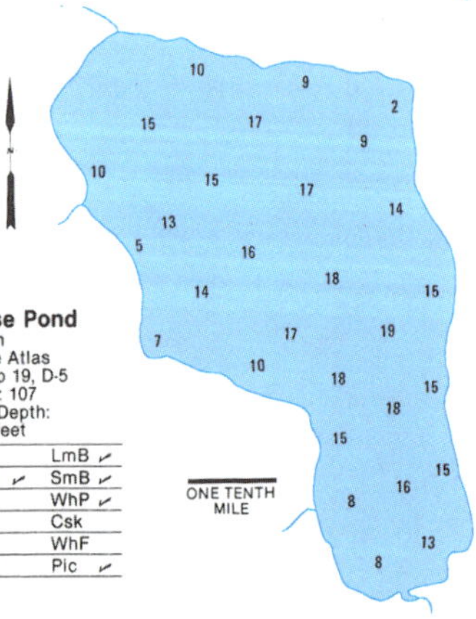

Pease Pond
Wilton
Maine Atlas
Map 19, D-5
Acres: 107
Max. Depth:
19 feet

BrT		LmB	✓
BkT	✓	SmB	✓
RbT		WhP	✓
Sal		Csk	
Tog		WhF	
Smt		Pic	✓

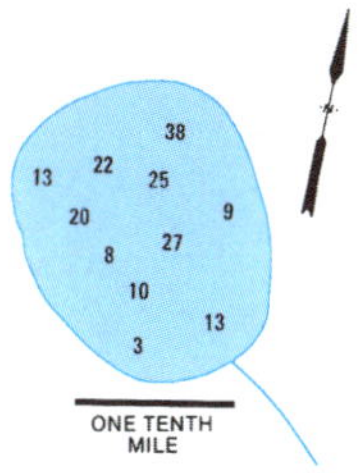

Perry Pond
Sandy River Plt
Maine Atlas
Map 19, A-1
Acres: 6
Max. Depth:
38 feet

BrT		LmB
BkT	✓	SmB
RbT		WhP
Sal		Csk
Tog		WhF
Smt		Pic

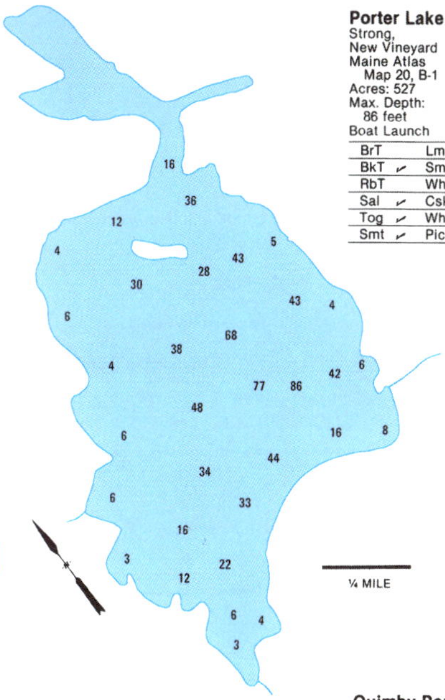

Porter Lake
Strong,
New Vineyard
Maine Atlas
Map 20, B-1
Acres: 527
Max. Depth:
86 feet
Boat Launch

BrT		LmB	
BkT	✓	SmB	
RbT		WhP	✓
Sal	✓	Csk	
Tog	✓	WhF	
Smt	✓	Pic	✓

ONE TENTH MILE

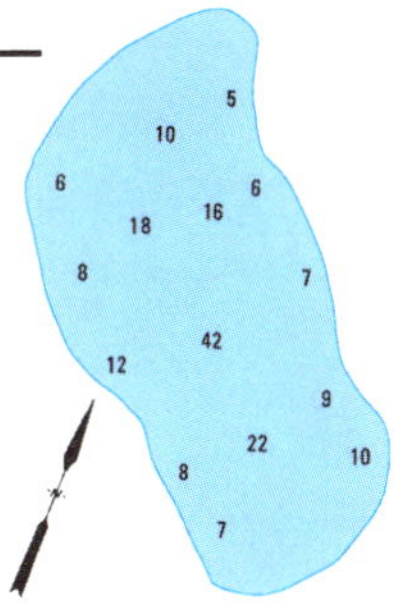

Pinnacle Pond
Kingfield
Maine Atlas
Map 29, E-5
Acres: 4
Max. Depth:
42 feet

BrT		LmB
BkT	✓	SmB
RbT		WhP
Sal		Csk
Tog		WhF
Smt		Pic

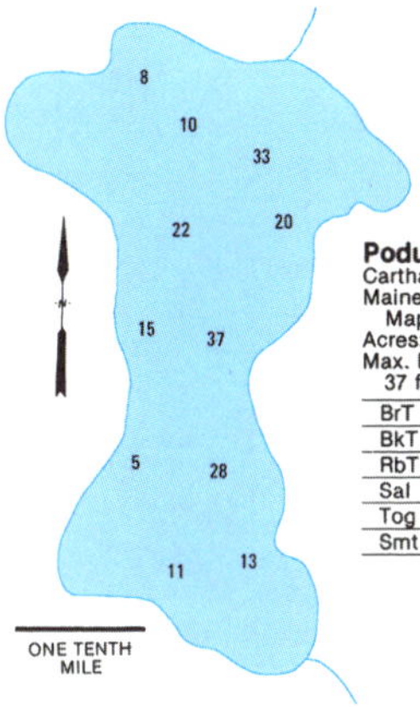

Podunk Pond
Carthage
Maine Atlas
Map 19, D-3
Acres: 51
Max. Depth:
37 feet

BrT		LmB
BkT	✓	SmB
RbT		WhP
Sal		Csk
Tog		WhF
Smt		Pic

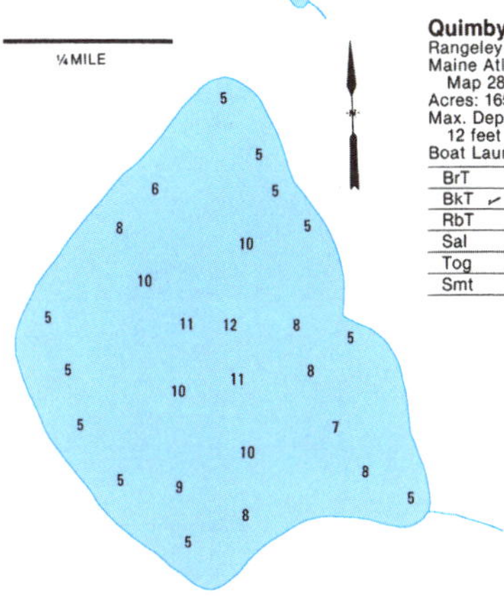

Quimby Pond
Rangeley
Maine Atlas
Map 28, E-3, E-4
Acres: 165
Max. Depth:
12 feet
Boat Launch

BrT		LmB
BkT	✓	SmB
RbT		WhP
Sal		Csk
Tog		WhF
Smt		Pic

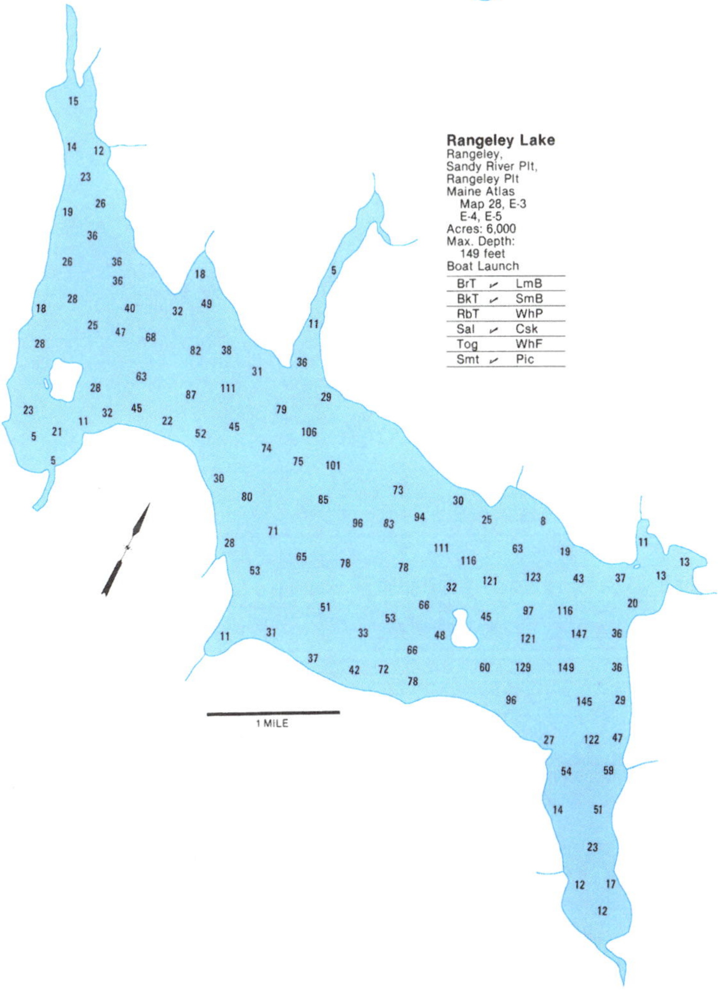

Rangeley Lake
Rangeley,
Sandy River Plt,
Rangeley Plt
Maine Atlas
Map 28, E-3
E-4, E-5
Acres: 6,000
Max. Depth:
149 feet
Boat Launch

BrT	✓	LmB
BkT	✓	SmB
RbT		WhP
Sal	✓	Csk
Tog		WhF
Smt	✓	Pic

Franklin

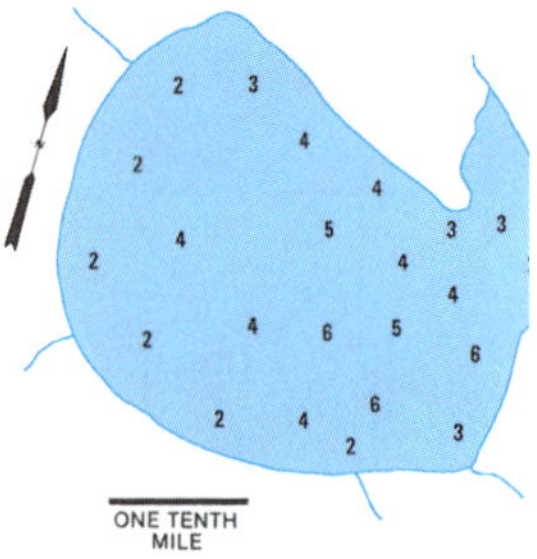

Redington Pond
Carrabasset Valley
Maine Atlas
Map 29, D-5
Acres: 64
Max. Depth:
6 feet

BrT		LmB
BkT	✓	SmB
RbT		WhP
Sal		Csk
Tog		WhF
Smt		Pic

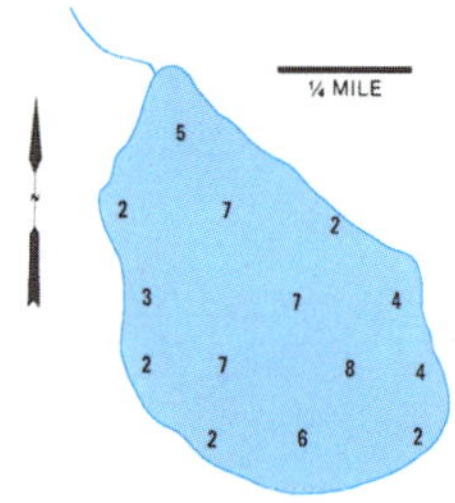

Round Pond
Township E
Maine Atlas
Map 18, A-4 A-5
Acres: 42
Max. Depth:
8 feet

BrT		LmB
BkT	✓	SmB
RbT		WhP
Sal		Csk
Tog		WhF
Smt		Pic

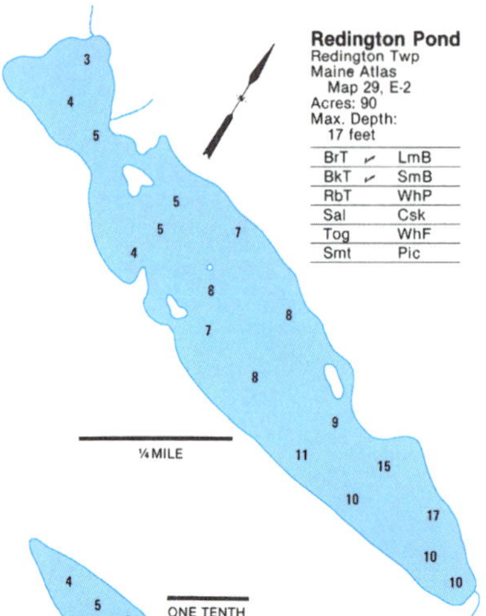

Redington Pond
Redington Twp
Maine Atlas
Map 29, E-2
Acres: 90
Max. Depth:
17 feet

BrT	✓	LmB
BkT	✓	SmB
RbT		WhP
Sal		Csk
Tog		WhF
Smt		Pic

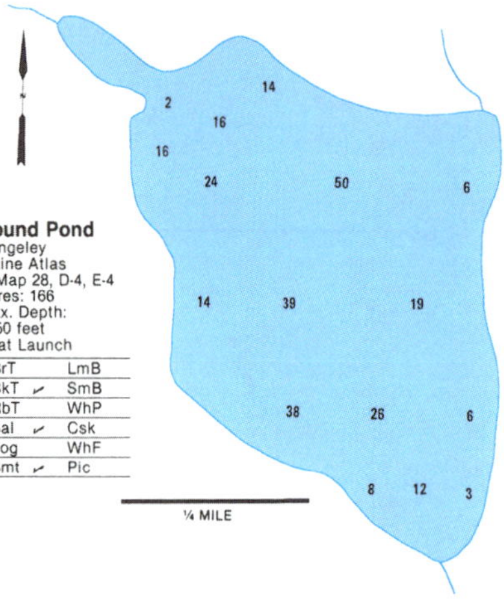

Round Pond
Rangeley
Maine Atlas
Map 28, D-4, E-4
Acres: 166
Max. Depth:
50 feet
Boat Launch

BrT		LmB
BkT	✓	SmB
RbT		WhP
Sal	✓	Csk
Tog		WhF
Smt	✓	Pic

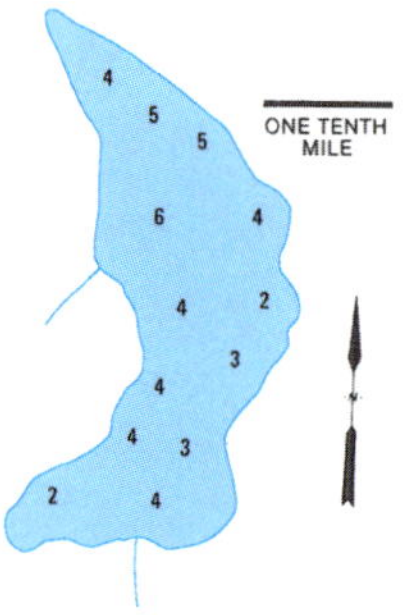

Rock Pond
Chain of Ponds Twp
Maine Atlas
Map 28, A-3
Acres: 26
Max. Depth:
6 feet

BrT		LmB
BkT	✓	SmB
RbT		WhP
Sal		Csk
Tog		WhF
Smt		Pic

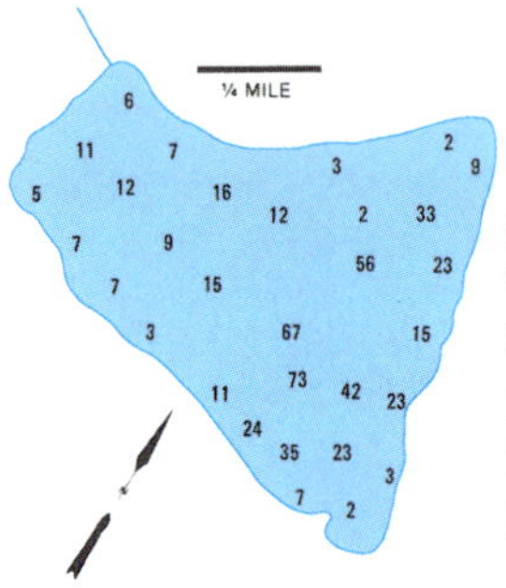

Sabbath Day Pond
Township E
Maine Atlas
Map 18, A-4, A-5
Acres: 57
Max. Depth:
73 feet

BrT		LmB
BkT	✓	SmB
RbT		WhP
Sal		Csk
Tog		WhF
Smt	✓	Pic

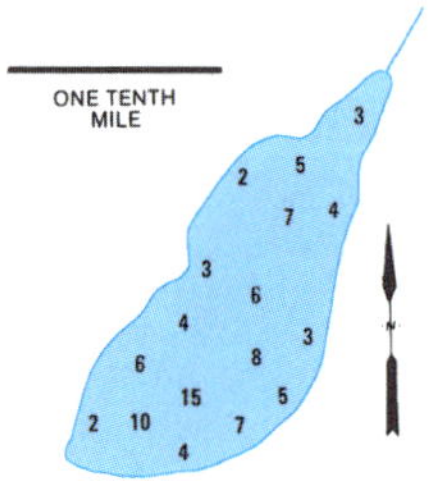

Rock Pond
Sandy River Plt
Maine Atlas
Map 29, E-1
Acres: 7
Max. Depth:
15 feet

BrT		LmB
BkT	✓	SmB
RbT		WhP
Sal		Csk
Tog		WhF
Smt		Pic

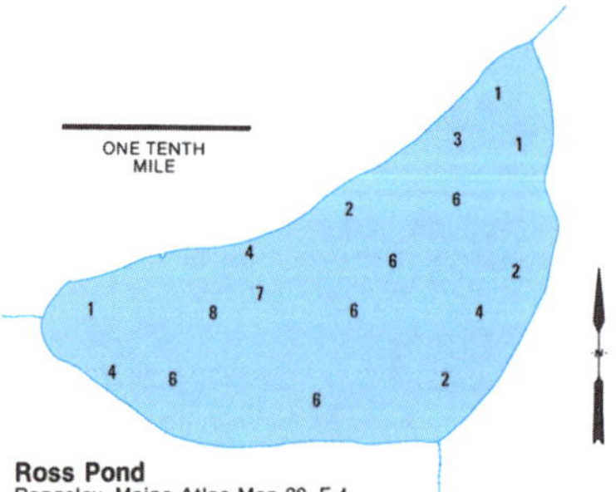

Ross Pond
Rangeley, Maine Atlas Map 28, E-4
Acres: 26, Max. Depth: 8 feet

BrT	BkT	RbT	Sal	Tog	Smt	LmB	SmB	WhP	Csk	WhF	Pic
	✓										

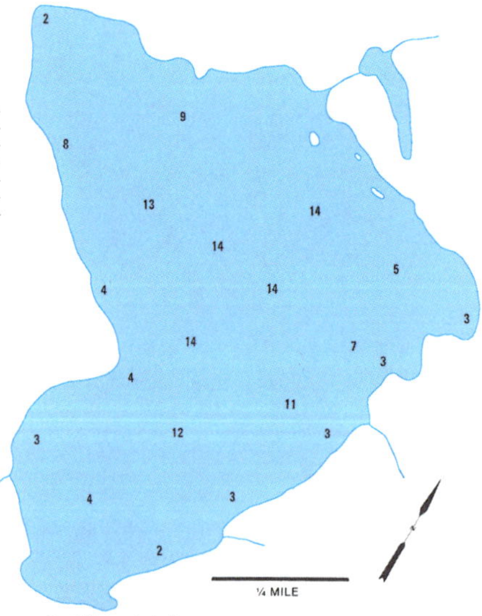

Saddleback Lake
Dallas Plt, Maine Atlas Map 29, E-1
Acres: 358, Max. Depth: 14 feet, Boat Launch

BrT	BkT	RbT	Sal	Tog	Smt	LmB	SmB	WhP	Csk	WhF	Pic
	✓										

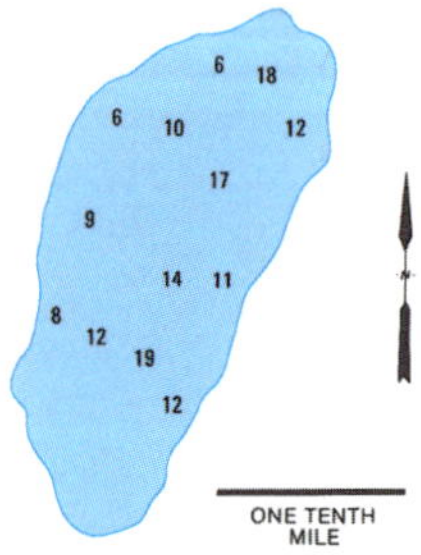

Round Pond
Chesterville
Maine Atlas
Map 20, E-1
Acres: 17
Max. Depth:
19 feet

BrT		LmB
BkT	✓	SmB
RbT		WhP
Sal		Csk
Tog		WhF
Smt		Pic

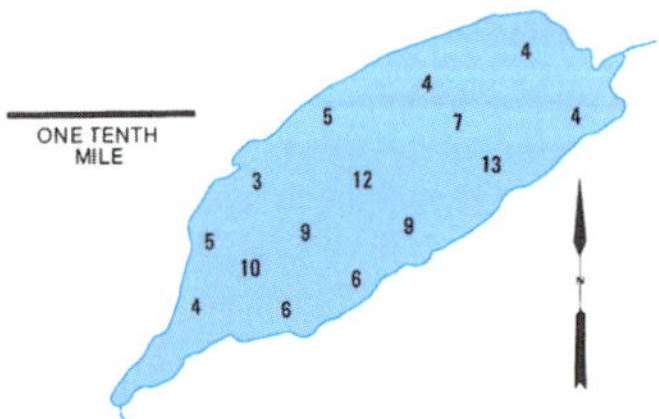

Saddleback Pond
Sandy River Plt, Maine Atlas Map 19, A-1, A-2
Acres: 13, Max. Depth: 13 feet

BrT	BkT	RbT	Sal	Tog	Smt	LmB	SmB	WhP	Csk	WhF	Pic
	✓										

Sand Pond
Chesterville
Maine Atlas
Map 20, E-1
Acres: 103
Max. Depth:
23 feet
Boat Launch

BrT		LmB	✓
BkT		SmB	
RbT		WhP	✓
Sal		Csk	
Tog		WhF	
Smt		Pic	✓

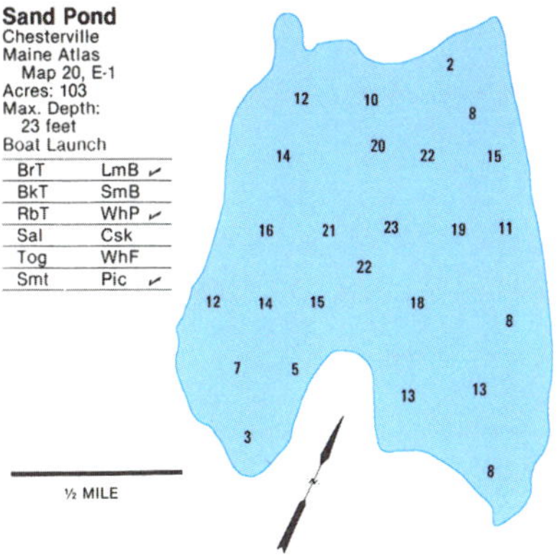

South Pond
Sandy River Plt
Maine Atlas
Map 19, A-1
Acres: 9
Max. Depth:
29 feet

BrT		LmB	
BkT	✓	SmB	
RbT		WhP	
Sal		Csk	
Tog		WhF	
Smt		Pic	

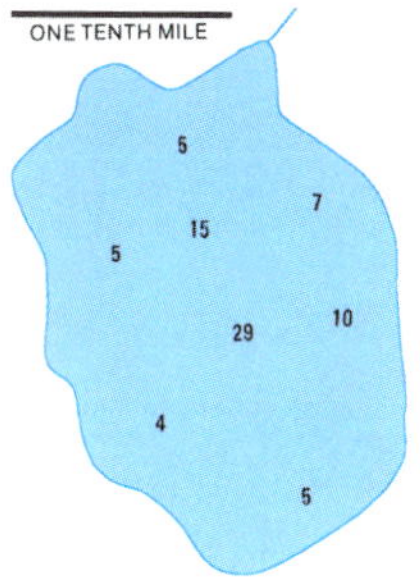

Spencer Pond
Township D
Maine Atlas
Map 18, B-4
Acres: 15
Max. Depth:
30 feet

BrT		LmB	
BkT	✓	SmB	
RbT		WhP	
Sal		Csk	
Tog		WhF	
Smt		Pic	

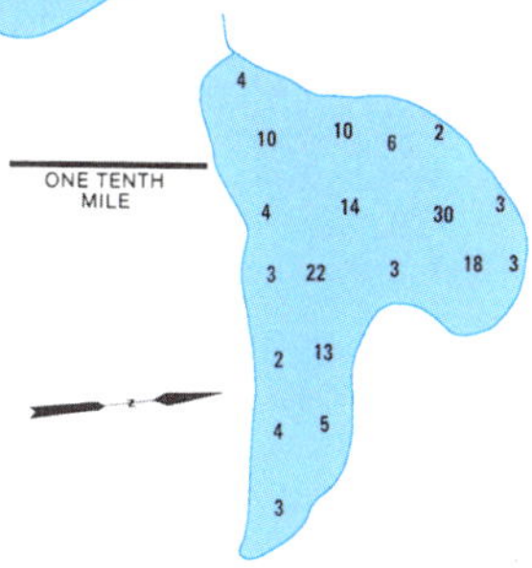

Sandy River Ponds
Sandy River Plt
Maine Atlas
Map 19, A-1
Acres: Upper-28
Middle-70
Lower-17
Max. Depth:
Upper-14 feet
Middle-58 feet
Lower-21 feet

BrT		LmB	
BkT	✓	SmB	
RbT		WhP	
Sal		Csk	
Tog		WhF	
Smt	✓	Pic	

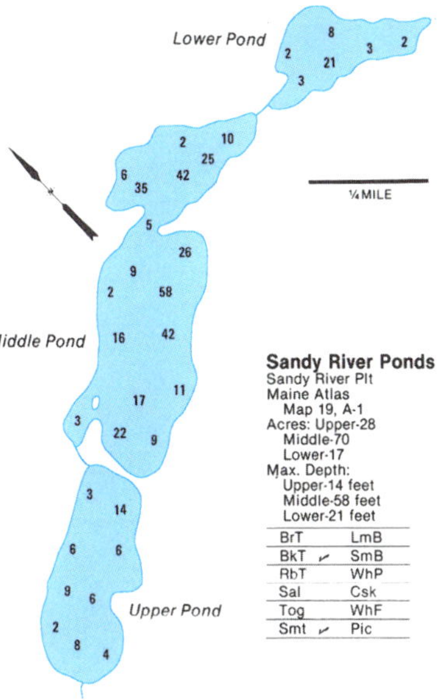

Staples Pond
Temple
Maine Atlas
Map 19, C-5
Acres: 64
Max. Depth:
44 feet

BrT	✓	LmB	
BkT		SmB	
RbT		WhP	
Sal		Csk	
Tog		WhF	
Smt	✓	Pic	✓

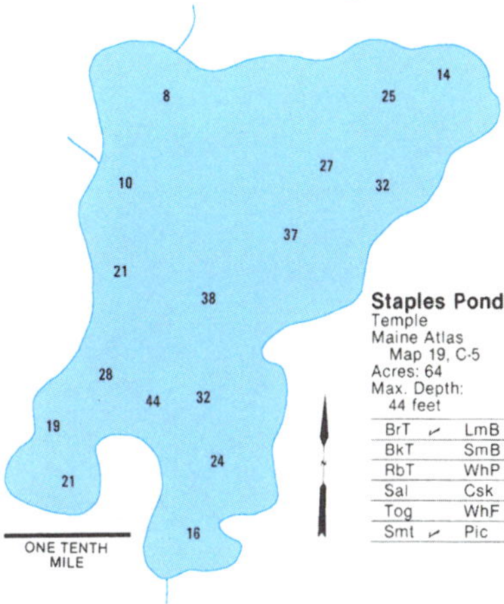

Schoolhouse Pond
Avon
Maine Atlas
Map 19, B-4
Acres: 3
Max. Depth:
20 feet

BrT		LmB	
BkT	✓	SmB	
RbT		WhP	
Sal		Csk	
Tog		WhF	
Smt		Pic	

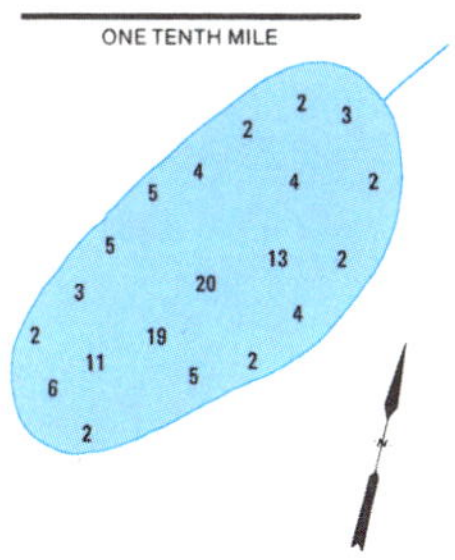

Stetson Pond
Phillips
Maine Atlas
Map 19, A-2
Acres: 11
Max. Depth:
36 feet

BrT		LmB	
BkT	✓	SmB	
RbT		WhP	
Sal		Csk	
Tog		WhF	
Smt		Pic	

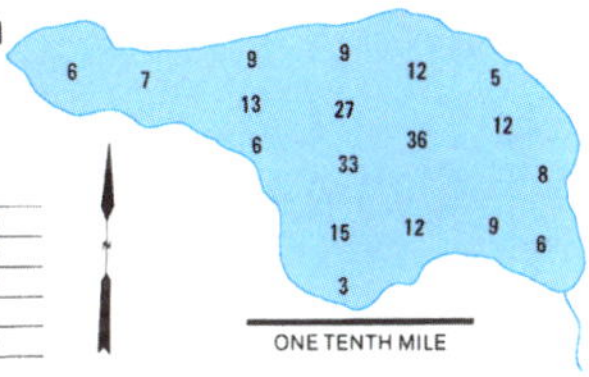

Stratton Brook Pond
Wyman Twp
Maine Atlas
Map 29, C-4
Acres: 26
Max. Depth:
6 feet

BrT		LmB	
BkT	✓	SmB	
RbT		WhP	
Sal		Csk	
Tog		WhF	
Smt		Pic	✓

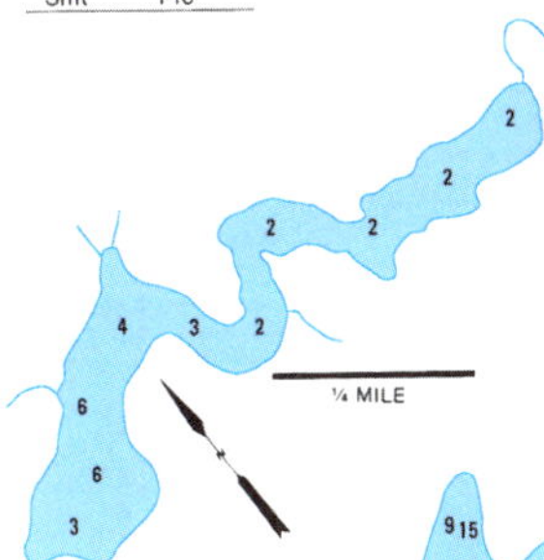

Secret Pond
Seven Ponds Twp
Maine Atlas
Map 28, A-3, B-3
Acres: 10
Max. Depth:
9 feet

BrT		LmB	
BkT	✓	SmB	
RbT		WhP	
Sal		Csk	
Tog		WhF	
Smt		Pic	

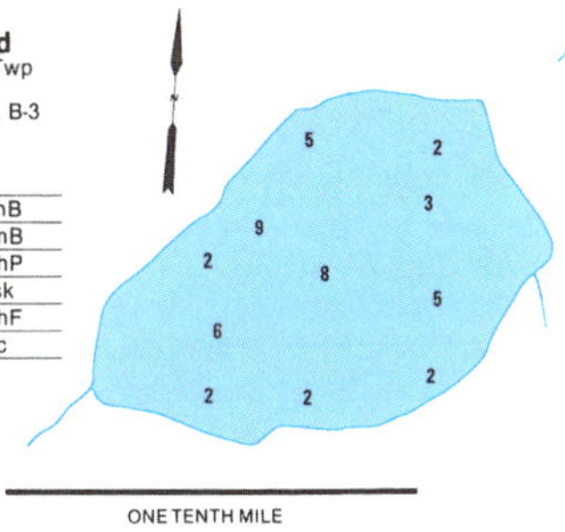

Tea Pond
Jim Pond Twp
Maine Atlas
Map 29, B-1
Acres: 90
Max. Depth:
115 feet

BrT		LmB	
BkT	✓	SmB	
RbT		WhP	
Sal	✓	Csk	
Tog	✓	WhF	✓
Smt	✓	Pic	

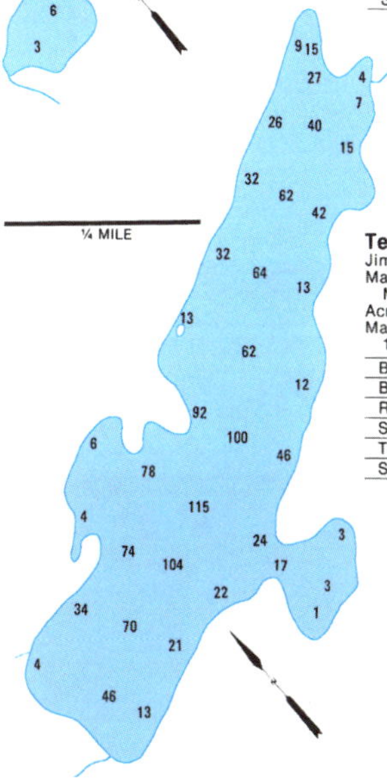

South Boundary Pond
Massachusetts Gore
Maine Atlas
Map 28, A-3
Acres: 10
Max. Depth:
5 feet

BrT		LmB	
BkT	✓	SmB	
RbT		WhP	
Sal		Csk	
Tog		WhF	
Smt		Pic	

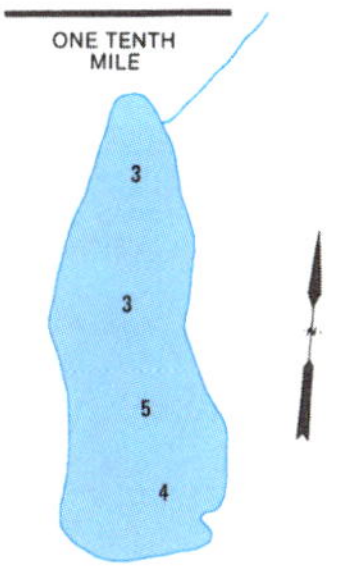

Franklin

Tufts Pond
Kingfield
Maine Atlas
Map 29, E-5
Acres: 53
Max. Depth:
43 feet

BrT	✓	LmB	
BkT	✓	SmB	
RbT		WhP	
Sal		Csk	
Tog		WhF	
Smt	✓	Pic	

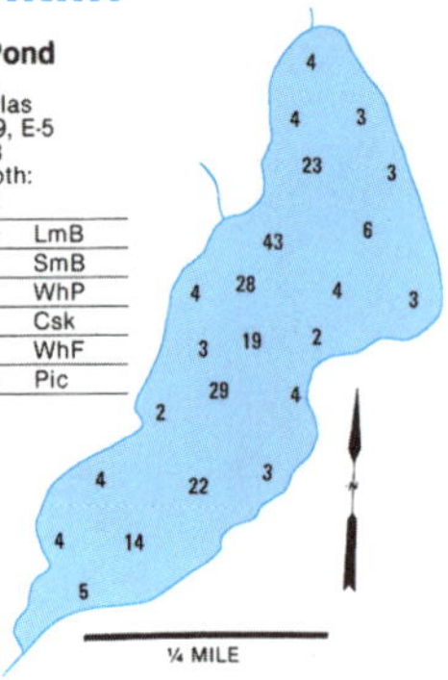

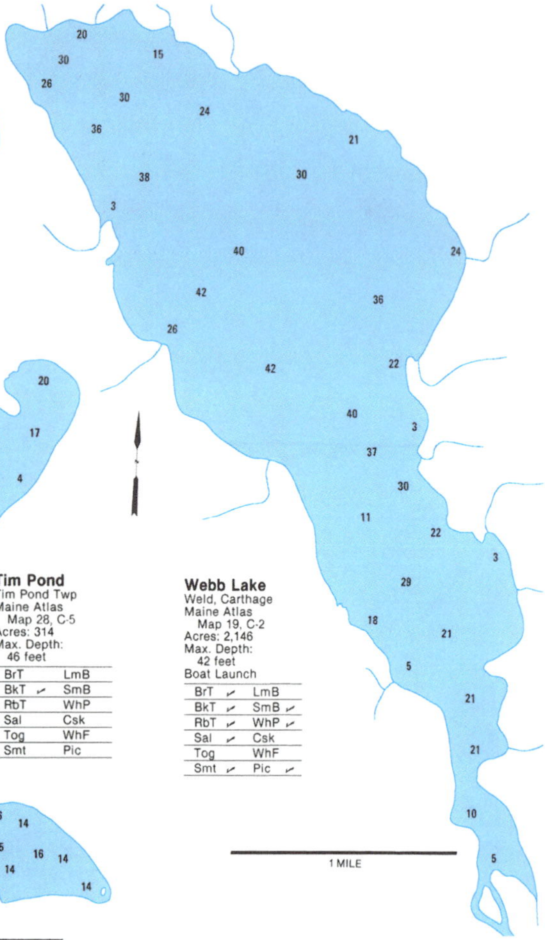

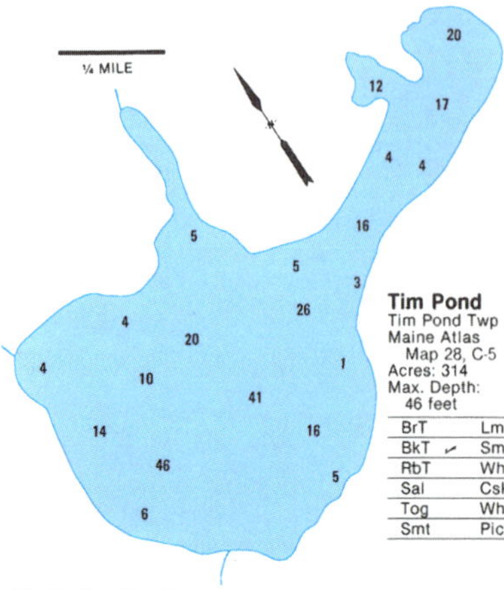

Tim Pond
Tim Pond Twp
Maine Atlas
Map 28, C-5
Acres: 314
Max. Depth:
46 feet

BrT		LmB	
BkT	✓	SmB	
RbT		WhP	
Sal		Csk	
Tog		WhF	
Smt		Pic	

Webb Lake
Weld, Carthage
Maine Atlas
Map 19, C-2
Acres: 2,146
Max. Depth:
42 feet
Boat Launch

BrT	✓	LmB	
BkT	✓	SmB	✓
RbT	✓	WhP	✓
Sal	✓	Csk	
Tog		WhF	
Smt	✓	Pic	✓

Toothaker Pond
Phillips
Maine Atlas
Map 19, A-3
Acres: 30
Max. Depth:
20 feet

BrT		LmB	
BkT	✓	SmB	
RbT		WhP	
Sal		Csk	
Tog		WhF	
Smt		Pic	

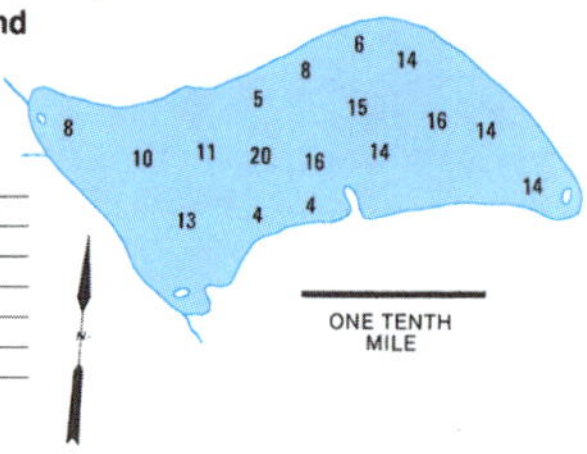

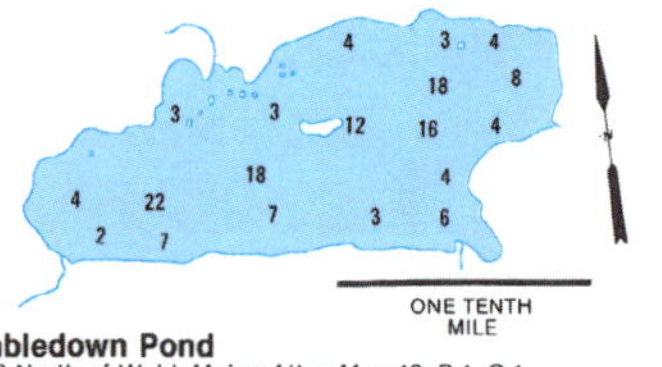

Tumbledown Pond
Twp 6 North of Weld, Maine Atlas Map 19, B-1, C-1
Acres: 9, Max. Depth: 22 feet

BrT	BkT	RbT	Sal	Tog	Smt	LmB	SmB	WhP	Csk	WhF	Pic
	✓										

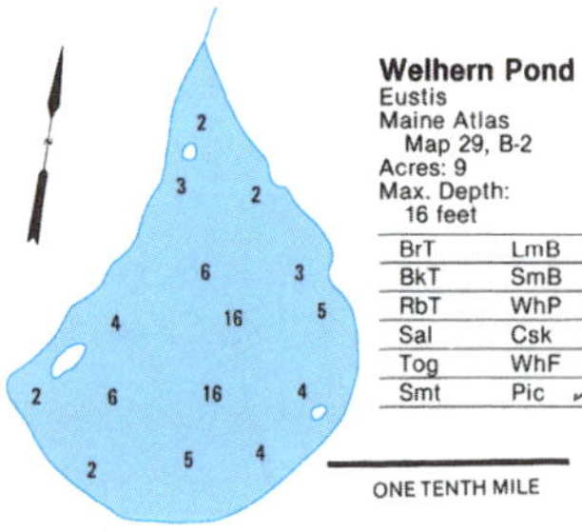

Welhern Pond
Eustis
Maine Atlas
Map 29, B-2
Acres: 9
Max. Depth:
16 feet

BrT		LmB	
BkT		SmB	
RbT		WhP	
Sal		Csk	
Tog		WhF	
Smt		Pic	✓

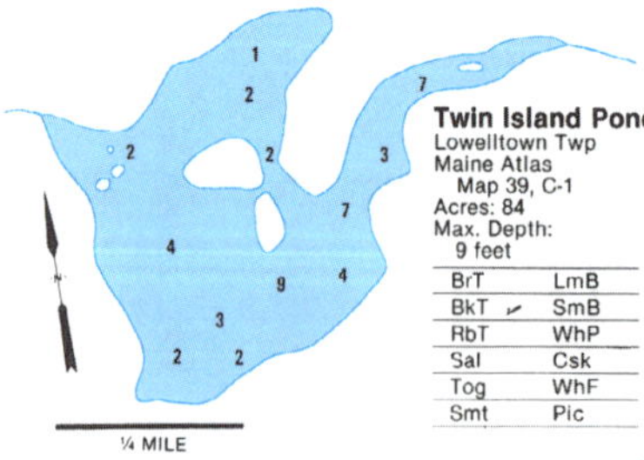

Twin Island Pond
Lowelltown Twp
Maine Atlas
Map 39, C-1
Acres: 84
Max. Depth:
9 feet

BrT		LmB	
BkT	✓	SmB	
RbT		WhP	
Sal		Csk	
Tog		WhF	
Smt		Pic	

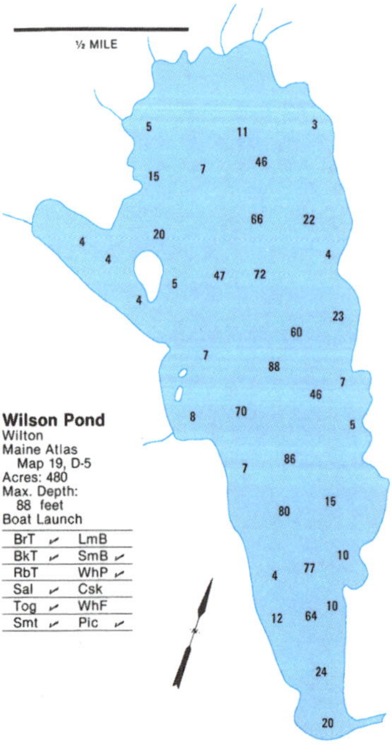

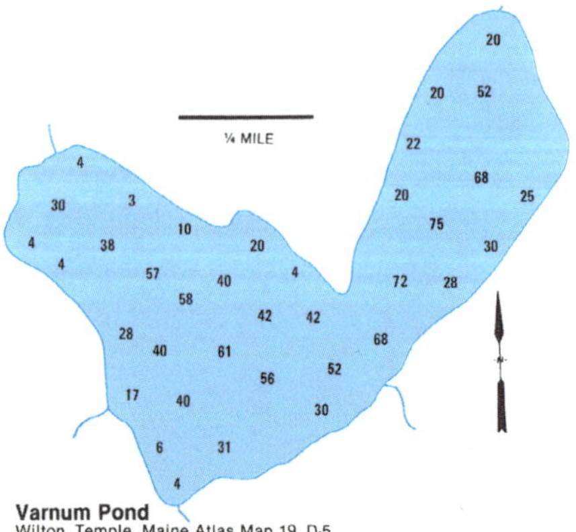

Wilson Pond
Wilton
Maine Atlas
Map 19, D-5
Acres: 480
Max. Depth:
88 feet
Boat Launch

BrT	✓	LmB	
BkT	✓	SmB	✓
RbT		WhP	✓
Sal	✓	Csk	
Tog	✓	WhF	
Smt	✓	Pic	✓

Varnum Pond
Wilton, Temple, Maine Atlas Map 19, D-5
Acres: 370, Max. Depth: 75 feet

BrT	BkT	RbT	Sal	Tog	Smt	LmB	SmB	WhP	Csk	WhF	Pic
	✓		✓	✓	✓						✓

Hancock County

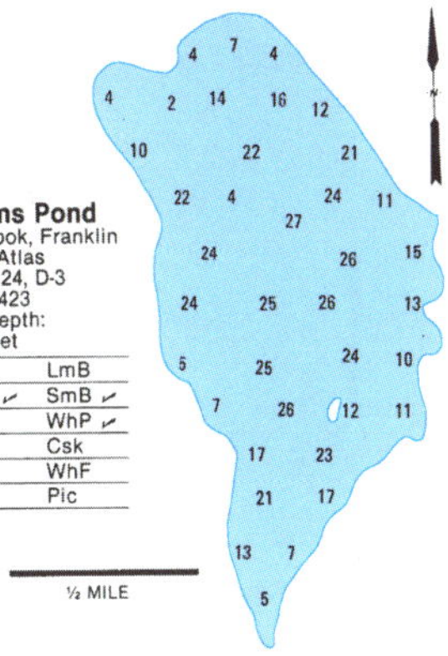

Abrams Pond
Eastbrook, Franklin
Maine Atlas
Map 24, D-3
Acres: 423
Max. Depth:
27 feet

BrT	LmB
BkT ✓	SmB ✓
RbT	WhP ✓
Sal	Csk
Tog	WhF
Smt	Pic

Aunt Betty Pond
Bar Harbor
Maine Atlas
Map 16, B-3
Acres: 34
Max. Depth:
7 feet

BrT	LmB
BkT ✓	SmB
RbT	WhP
Sal	Csk
Tog	WhF
Smt	Pic

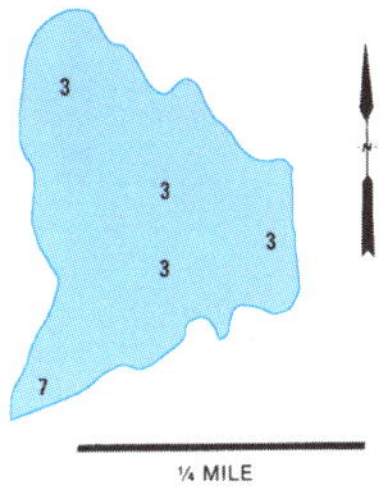

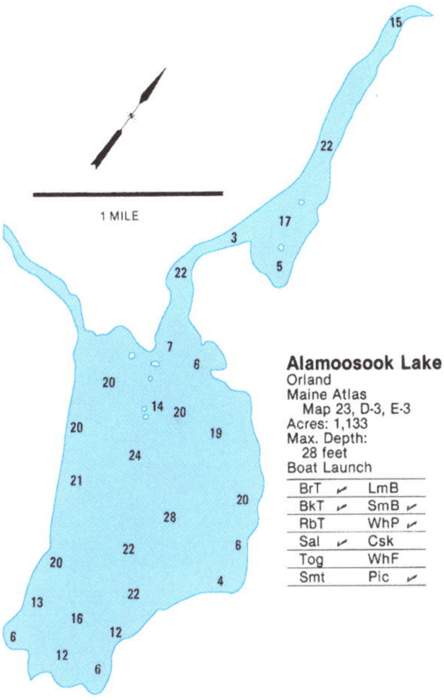

Alamoosook Lake
Orland
Maine Atlas
Map 23, D-3, E-3
Acres: 1,133
Max. Depth:
28 feet
Boat Launch

BrT ✓	LmB
BkT ✓	SmB ✓
RbT	WhP ✓
Sal ✓	Csk
Tog	WhF
Smt	Pic ✓

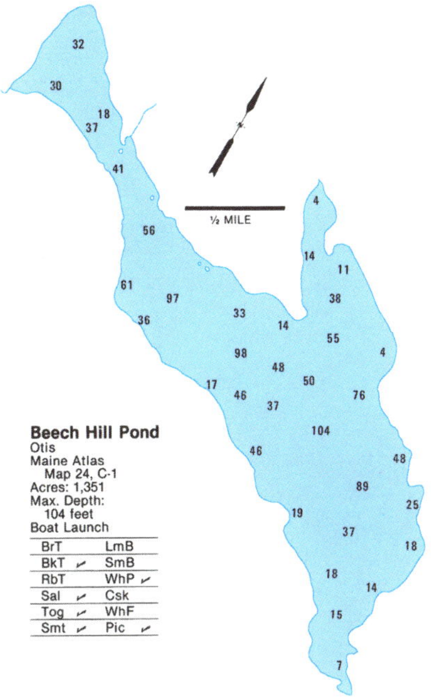

Beech Hill Pond
Otis
Maine Atlas
Map 24, C-1
Acres: 1,351
Max. Depth:
104 feet
Boat Launch

BrT	LmB
BkT ✓	SmB
RbT	WhP ✓
Sal ✓	Csk
Tog ✓	WhF
Smt ✓	Pic ✓

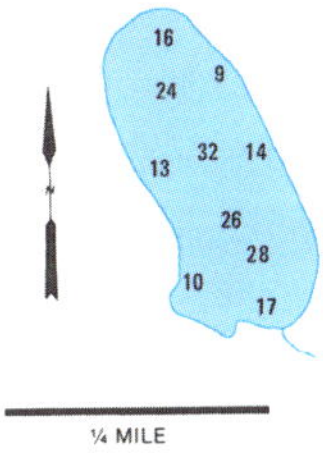

Bracey Pond
T34 MD
Maine Atlas
Map 34, E-5
Acres: 14
Max. Depth:
32 feet

BrT	LmB
BkT ✓	SmB
RbT	WhP
Sal	Csk
Tog	WhF
Smt	Pic ✓

Allen Pond
T35 MD, Maine Atlas Map 34, E-5
Acres: 83, Max. Depth: 27 feet

BrT	BkT	RbT	Sal	Tog	Smt	LmB	SmB	WhP	Csk	WhF	Pic
	✓										✓

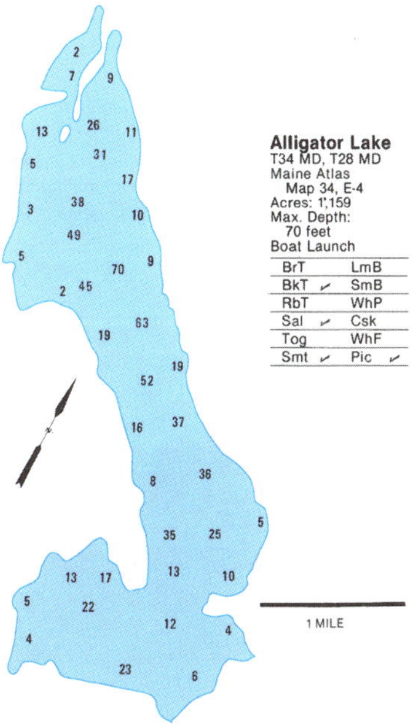

Alligator Lake
T34 MD, T28 MD
Maine Atlas
Map 34, E-4
Acres: 1,159
Max. Depth:
70 feet
Boat Launch

BrT	LmB
BkT ✓	SmB
RbT	WhP
Sal ✓	Csk
Tog	WhF
Smt ✓	Pic ✓

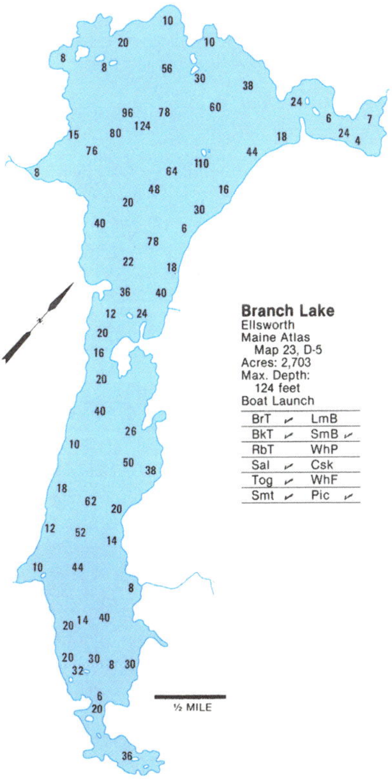

Branch Lake
Ellsworth
Maine Atlas
Map 23, D-5
Acres: 2,703
Max. Depth:
124 feet
Boat Launch

BrT ✓	LmB
BkT ✓	SmB ✓
RbT	WhP
Sal ✓	Csk
Tog ✓	WhF
Smt ✓	Pic ✓

Hancock

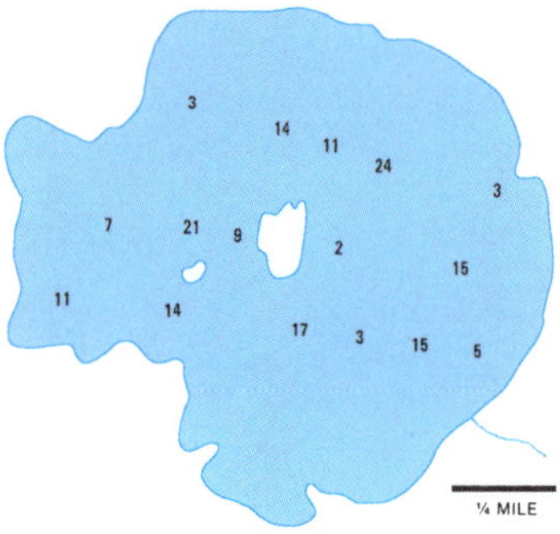

Brandy Pond

T39 MD, Maine Atlas Map 34,D-3
Acres: 723, Max. Depth: 24 feet

BrT	BkT	RbT	Sal	Tog	Smt	LmB	SmB	WhP	Csk	WhF	Pic
✓	✓										✓

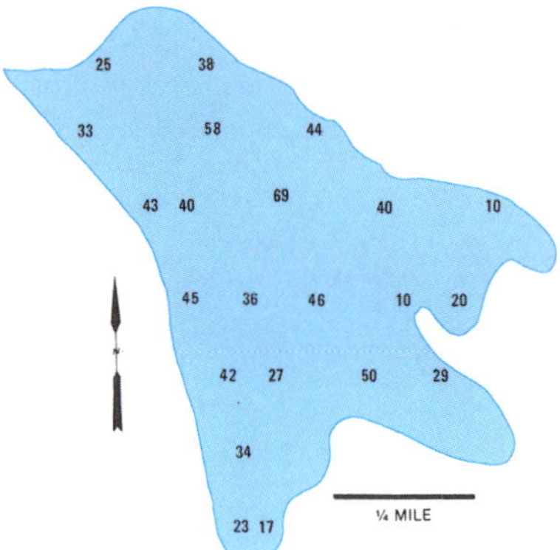

Craig Pond

Orland, Maine Atlas Map 23, D-3, D-4, E-3, E-4
Acres: 218, Max. Depth: 69 feet, Boat Launch

BrT	BkT	RbT	Sal	Tog	Smt	LmB	SmB	WhP	Csk	WhF	Pic
	✓		✓	✓	✓						

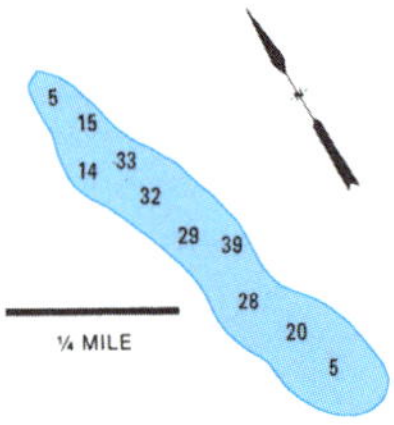

Bubble Pond

Bar Harbor
Maine Atlas
Map 16, B-4
Acres: 32
Max. Depth:
39 feet

BrT		LmB	
BkT	✓	SmB	
RbT		WhP	
Sal		Csk	
Tog		WhF	
Smt		Pic	

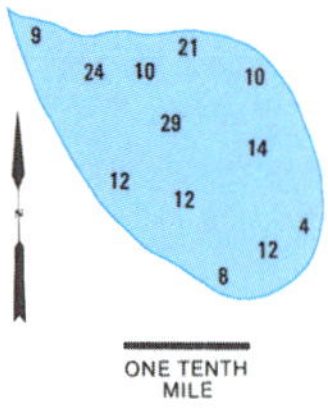

Crystal Pond

T40 MD
Maine Atlas
Map 34, D-4
Acres: 19
Max. Depth:
29 feet

BrT		LmB	
BkT	✓	SmB	
RbT		WhP	
Sal		Csk	
Tog		WhF	
Smt		Pic	

Burnt Land Pond

T35 MD
Maine Atlas
Map 35, D-1
Acres: 80
Max. Depth:
40 feet
Boat Launch

BrT		LmB	
BkT	✓	SmB	
RbT		WhP	✓
Sal		Csk	
Tog		WhF	
Smt		Pic	✓

Comments: Splake.

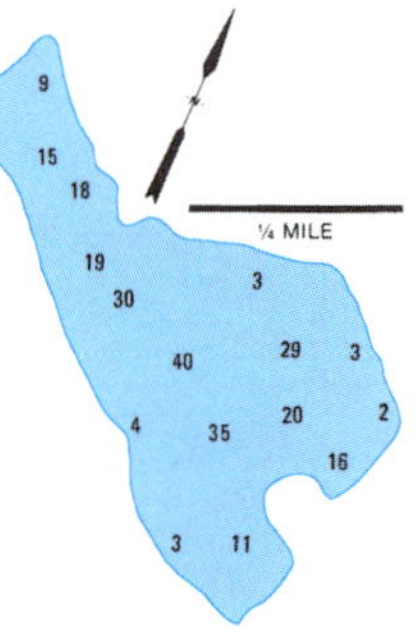

Debec Pond

Amherst
Maine Atlas
Map 24, B-1
Acres: 31
Max. Depth:
16 feet
Boat Launch

BrT		LmB	
BkT	✓	SmB	
RbT		WhP	
Sal		Csk	
Tog		WhF	
Smt		Pic	

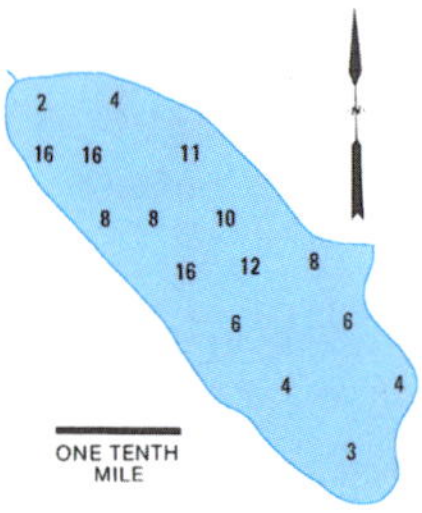

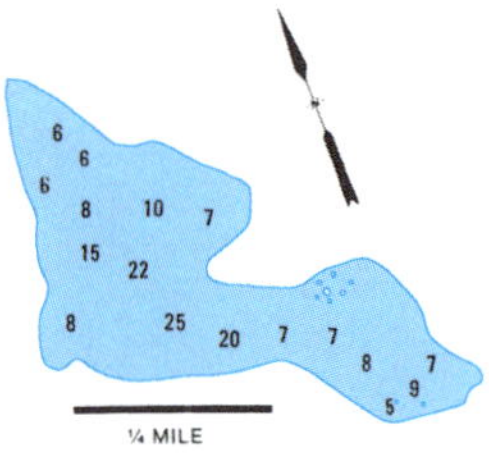

Burnt Pond

Otis
Maine Atlas
Map 24, C-1
Acres: 70
Max. Depth:
25 feet

BrT		LmB	
BkT		SmB	
RbT		WhP	
Sal		Csk	
Tog		WhF	
Smt		Pic	✓

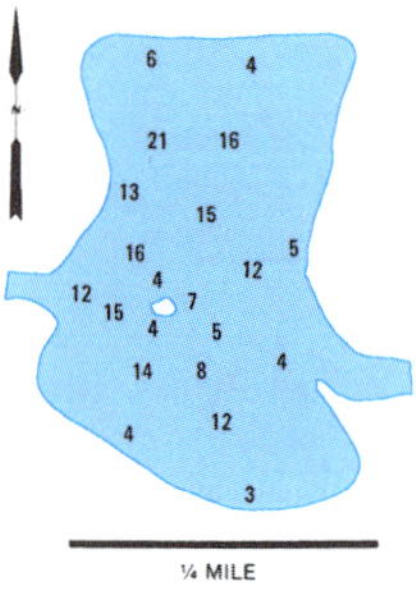

Deer Lake

T34 MD
Maine Atlas
Map 34, E-5
Acres: 38
Max. Depth:
21 feet

BrT		LmB	
BkT		SmB	
RbT		WhP	
Sal		Csk	
Tog		WhF	
Smt		Pic	✓

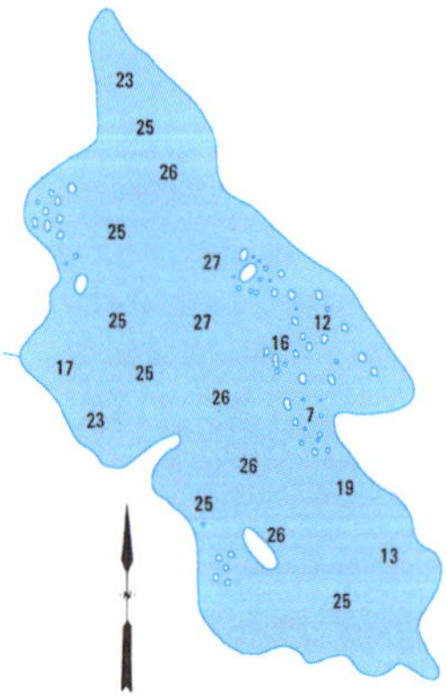

Burnt Pond

Otis, Dedham
Maine Atlas
Map 23, B-5
Acres: 316
Max. Depth:
27 feet

BrT		LmB	
BkT	✓	SmB	
RbT		WhP	
Sal		Csk	
Tog		WhF	
Smt		Pic	

¼ MILE

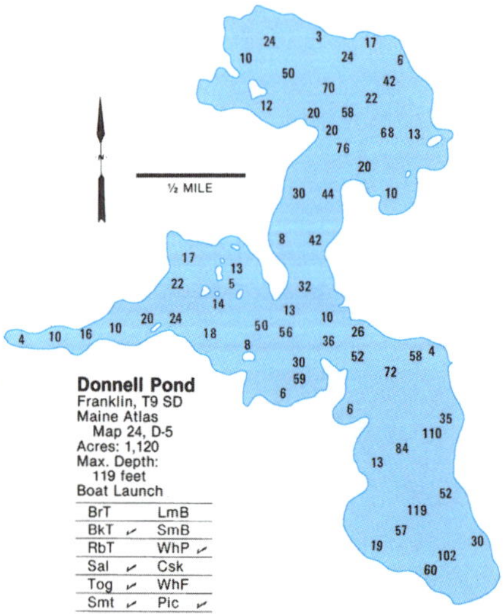

Chicken Mill Pond

Gouldsboro
Maine Atlas
Map 17, A-1
Acres: 27
Max. Depth:
7 feet

BrT		LmB	
BkT	✓	SmB	
RbT		WhP	
Sal		Csk	
Tog		WhF	
Smt		Pic	

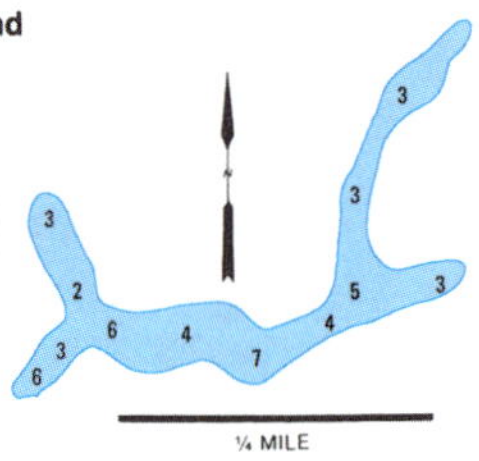

Donnell Pond

Franklin, T9 SD
Maine Atlas
Map 24, D-5
Acres: 1,120
Max. Depth:
119 feet
Boat Launch

BrT		LmB	
BkT	✓	SmB	
RbT		WhP	✓
Sal	✓	Csk	
Tog	✓	WhF	
Smt	✓	Pic	✓

Duck Lake

Oquton TWP, Maine Atlas Map 34, C-5
Acres: 1,222, Max. Depth: 88 feet, Boat Launch

BrT	BkT	RbT	Sal	Tog	Smt	LmB	SmB	WhP	Csk	WhF	Pic
	✓		✓	✓	✓					✓	

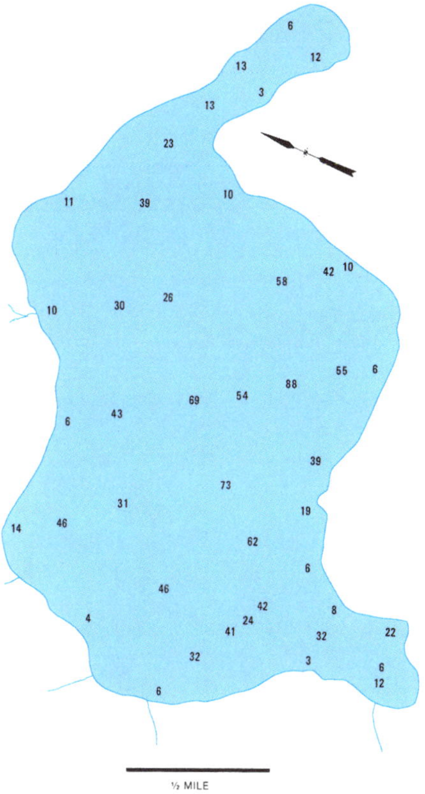

Eagle Lake

T34 MD
Maine Atlas
Map 34, D-4, D-5
Acres: 260
Max. Depth:
24 feet
Boat Launch

BrT	LmB
BkT	SmB
RbT	WhP
Sal	Csk
Tog	WhF
Smt	Pic ✓

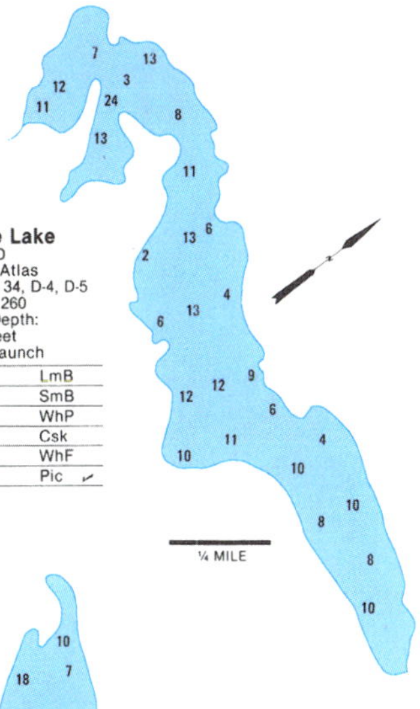

Echo Lake

Mt Desert
Maine Atlas
Map 16, B-2, C-2
Acres: 237
Max. Depth:
66 feet
Boat Launch

BrT	LmB
BkT ✓	SmB
RbT	WhP ✓
Sal ✓	Csk
Tog	WhF
Smt ✓	Pic

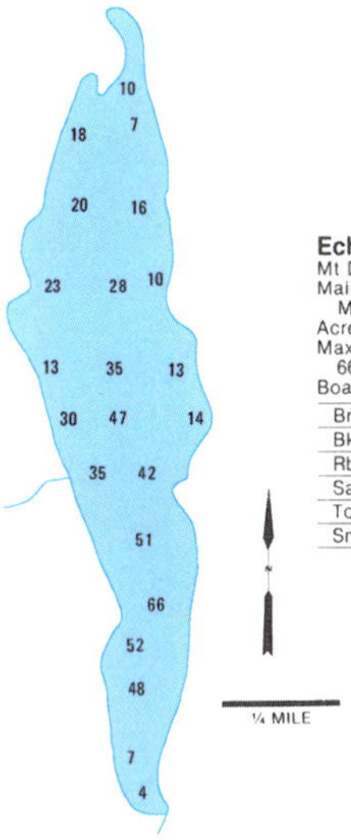

Duck Pond

Franklin
Maine Atlas
Map 24, D-4
Acres: 45
Max. Depth:
21 feet

BrT	LmB
BkT	SmB
RbT	WhP ✓
Sal	Csk
Tog	WhF
Smt	Pic ✓

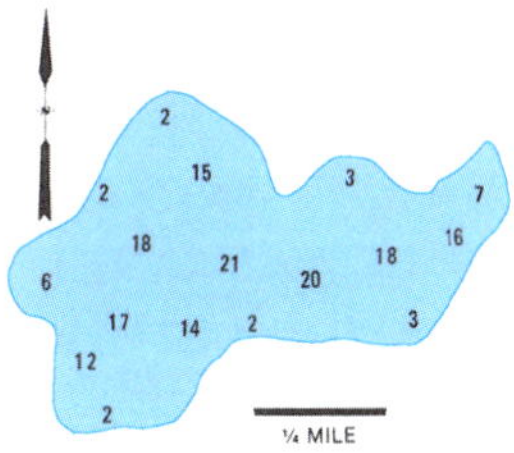

First Pond

Blue Hill
Maine Atlas
Map 15, B-4
Acres: 93
Max. Depth:
37 feet

BrT	LmB
BkT ✓	SmB
RbT	WhP ✓
Sal	Csk
Tog	WhF
Smt	Pic

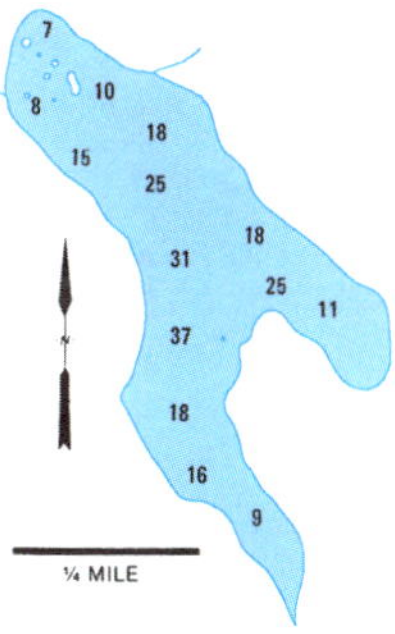

Dutton Pond

Amherst
Maine Atlas
Map 24, A-2
Acres: 17
Max. Depth:
35 feet
Boat Launch

BrT	LmB
BkT ✓	SmB
RbT	WhP
Sal	Csk
Tog	WhF
Smt	Pic

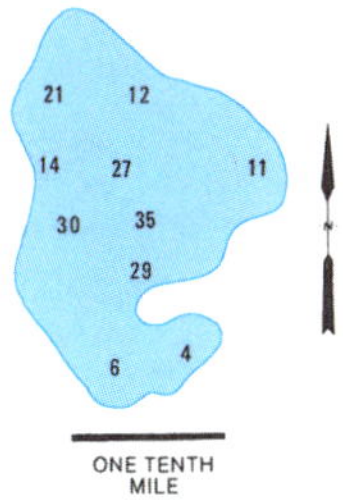

Eagle Lake

Bar Harbor
Maine Atlas
Map 16, B-3, B-4
Acres: 436
Max. Depth:
110 feet
Boat Launch

BrT	LmB
BkT ✓	SmB
RbT	WhP
Sal ✓	Csk
Tog ✓	WhF
Smt ✓	Pic

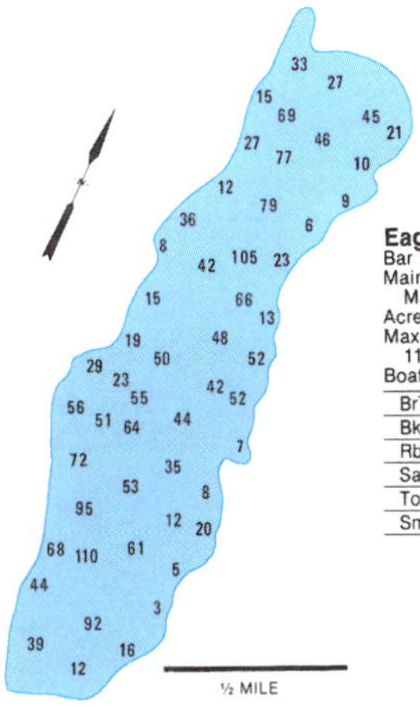

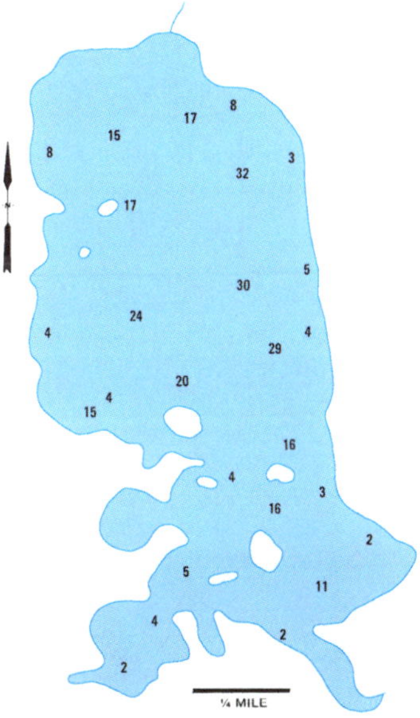

Flanders Pond

Sullivan, Maine Atlas Map 24, E-5
Acres: 537, Max. Depth: 32 feet

BrT	BkT	RbT	Sal	Tog	Smt	LmB	SmB	WhP	Csk	WhF	Pic
✓	✓						✓				

Hancock

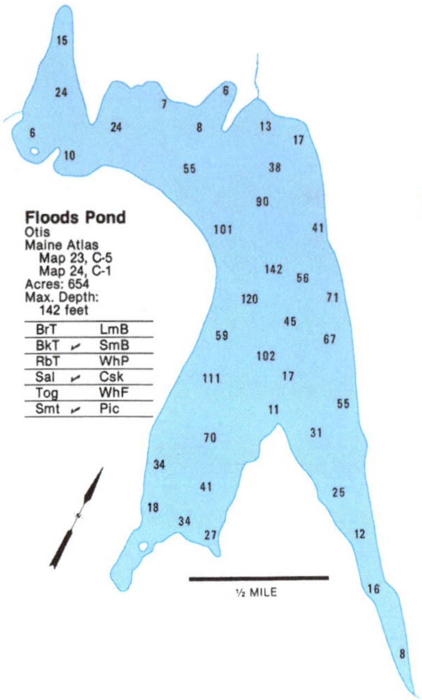

Floods Pond
Otis
Maine Atlas
Map 23, C-5
Map 24, C-1
Acres: 654
Max. Depth:
142 feet

BrT		LmB	
BkT	✓	SmB	
RbT		WhP	
Sal	✓	Csk	
Tog		WhF	
Smt	✓	Pic	

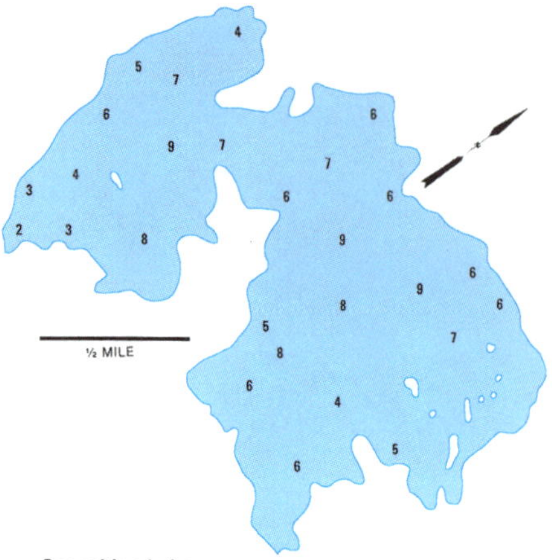

Gassabias Lake
T41 MD, Maine Atlas Map 35, C-1
Acres: 896, Max. Depth: 9 feet, Boat Launch

BrT	BkT	RbT	Sal	Tog	Smt	LmB	SmB	WhP	Csk	WhF	Pic
	✓						✓	✓			✓

Forbes Pond
Gouldsboro, Maine Atlas Map 17, A-1
Acres: 208, Max. Depth: 11 feet, Boat Launch

BrT	BkT	RbT	Sal	Tog	Smt	LmB	SmB	WhP	Csk	WhF	Pic
	✓					✓					

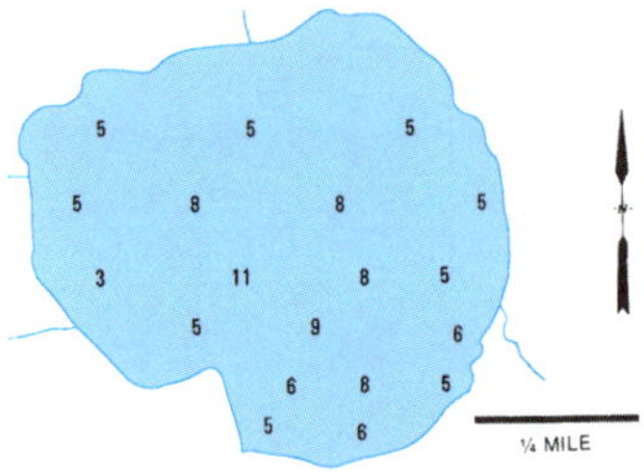

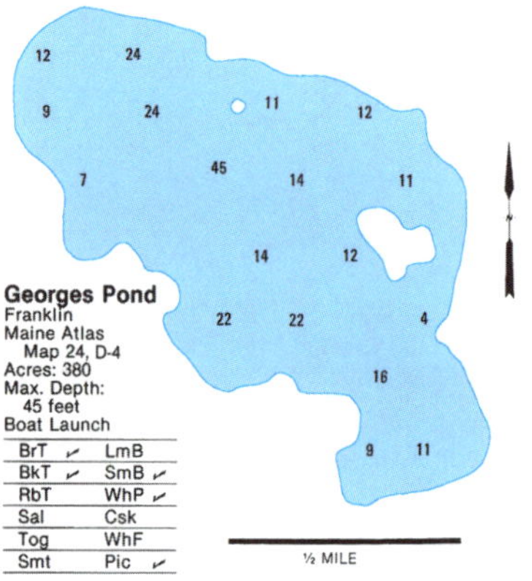

Georges Pond
Franklin
Maine Atlas
Map 24, D-4
Acres: 380
Max. Depth:
45 feet
Boat Launch

BrT	✓	LmB	
BkT	✓	SmB	✓
RbT		WhP	✓
Sal		Csk	
Tog		WhF	
Smt		Pic	✓

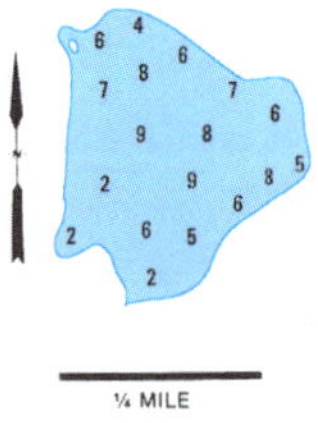

Fourth Pond
Blue Hill
Maine Atlas
Map 15, B-4
Acres: 50
Max. Depth:
9 feet

BrT		LmB	
BkT	✓	SmB	
RbT		WhP	
Sal		Csk	
Tog		WhF	
Smt		Pic	

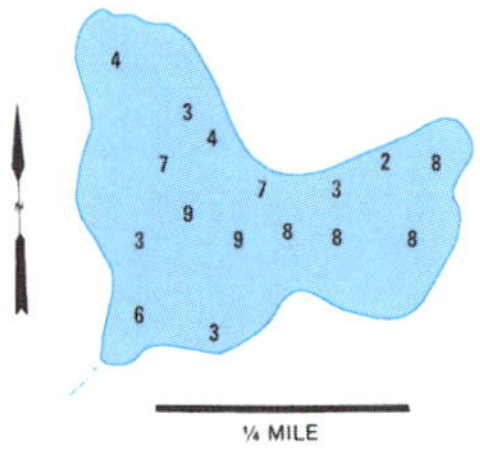

Giles Pond
Aurora
Maine Atlas
Map 24, A-3
Acres: 64
Max. Depth:
9 feet
Boat Launch

BrT	✓	LmB	
BkT	✓	SmB	
RbT		WhP	
Sal		Csk	
Tog		WhF	
Smt		Pic	

Fox Pond
T10 SD
Maine Atlas
Map 24, D-5
Acres: 77
Max. Depth:
29 feet

BrT	✓	LmB	
BkT	✓	SmB	
RbT		WhP	
Sal		Csk	
Tog		WhF	
Smt		Pic	

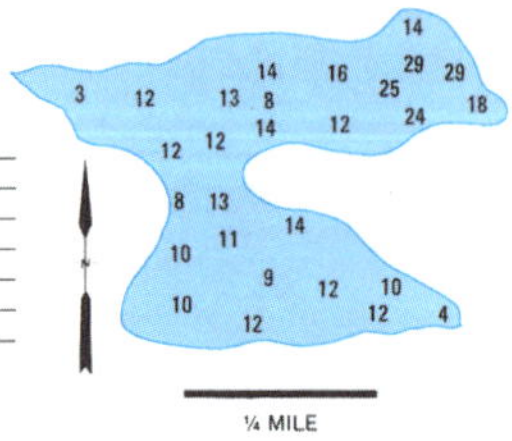

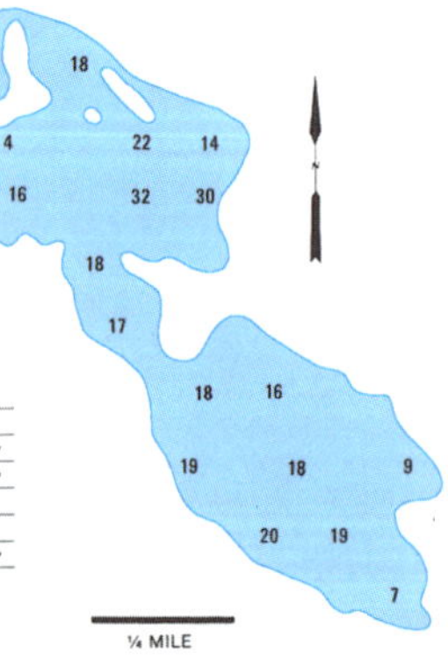

Goose Pond
Dedham
Maine Atlas
Map 23, C-4, D-4
C-5, D-5
Acres: 202
Max. Depth:
32 feet
Boat Launch

BrT		LmB	
BkT	✓	SmB	✓
RbT		WhP	✓
Sal	✓	Csk	
Tog		WhF	
Smt	✓	Pic	✓

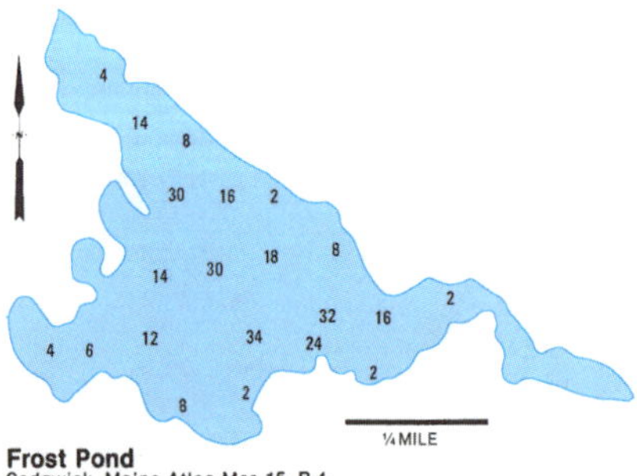

Frost Pond
Sedgwick, Maine Atlas Map 15, B-4
Acres: 154, Max. Depth: 34 feet

BrT	BkT	RbT	Sal	Tog	Smt	LmB	SmB	WhP	Csk	WhF	Pic
								✓			

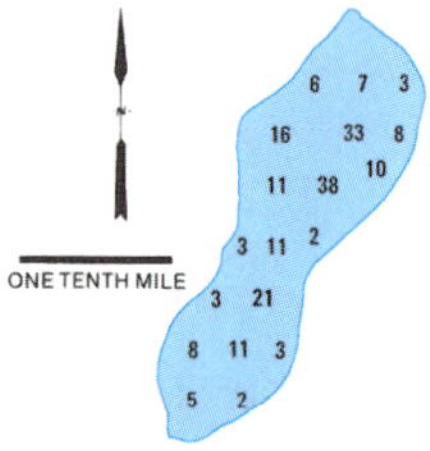

Goose Pond
Swans Island
Maine Atlas
Map 16, E-1, E-2
Acres: 38
Max. Depth:
38 feet

BrT		LmB	
BkT	✓	SmB	
RbT		WhP	
Sal		Csk	
Tog		WhF	
Smt		Pic	

Graham Lake

Ellsworth, Mariaville, Waltham, T8 SD, Maine Atlas Map 24, C-1, D-1
Acres: 7,865, Max. Depth: 47 feet, Boat Launch

BrT	BkT	RbT	Sal	Tog	Smt	LmB	SmB	WhP	Csk	WhF	Pic
✓	✓		✓		✓		✓	✓			✓

Green Lake

Dedham, Ellsworth
Maine Atlas
Map 23, C-5, D-5
Map 24, D-1
Acres: 2,989
Max. Depth:
170 feet
Boat Launch

BrT		LmB	
BkT	✓	SmB	✓
RbT		WhP	✓
Sal	✓	Csk	
Tog	✓	WhF	
Smt	✓	Pic	✓

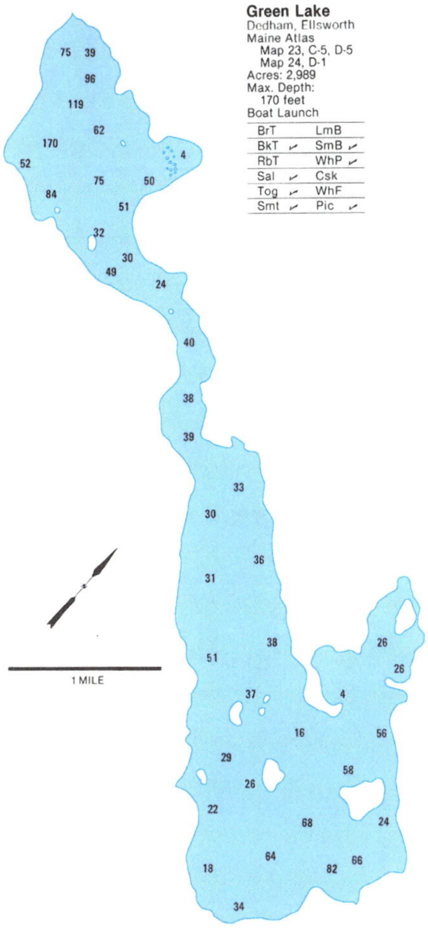

Green Lake

T35 MD
Maine Atlas
Map 35, E-1
Acres: 83
Max. Depth:
14 feet

BrT		LmB	
BkT		SmB	
RbT		WhP	✓
Sal		Csk	
Tog		WhF	
Smt		Pic	✓

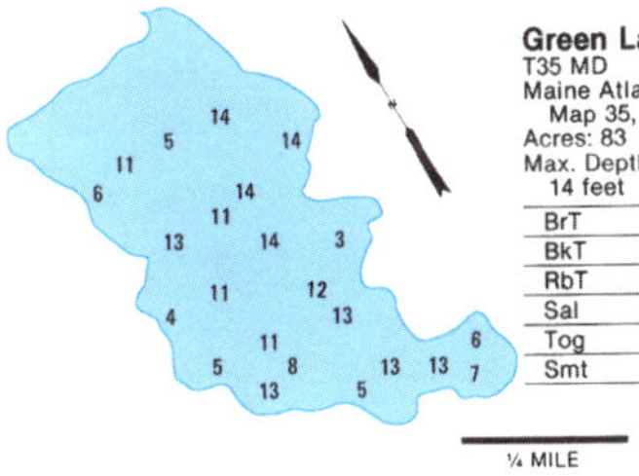

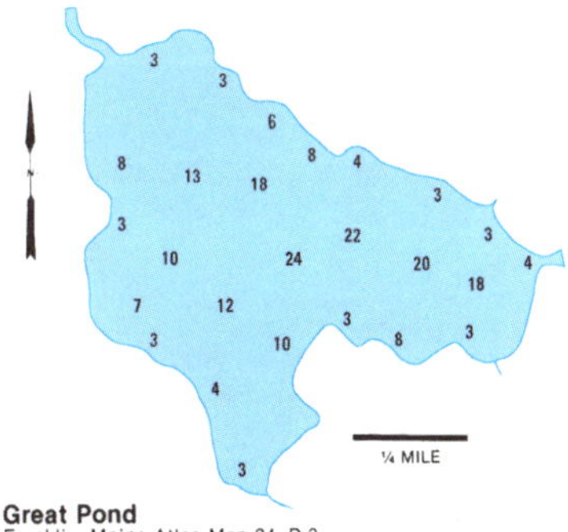

Great Pond

Franklin, Maine Atlas Map 24, D-3
Acres: 262, Max. Depth: 24 feet

BrT	BkT	RbT	Sal	Tog	Smt	LmB	SmB	WhP	Csk	WhF	Pic
	✓							✓			✓

Green Lake

T35 MD
Maine Atlas
Map 35, D-1
Acres: 64
Max. Depth:
12 feet
Boat Launch

BrT		LmB	
BkT	✓	SmB	
RbT		WhP	
Sal		Csk	
Tog		WhF	
Smt		Pic	

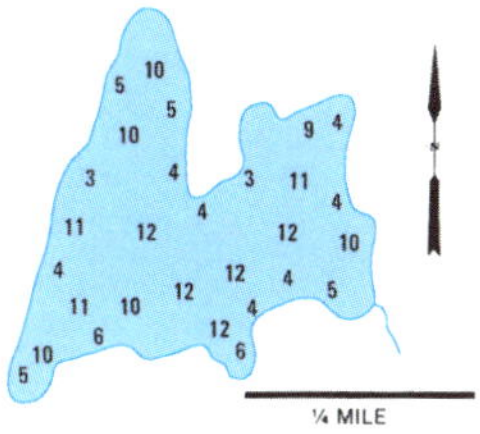

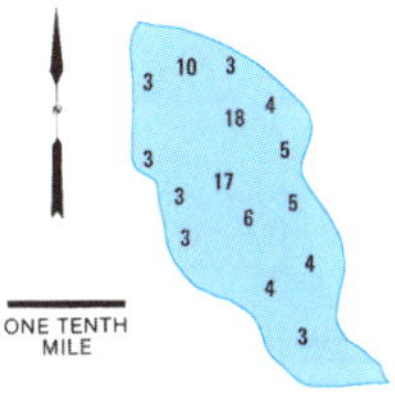

Halfmile Pond

Amherst
Maine Atlas
Map 24, A-1
Acres: 29
Max. Depth:
18 feet
Boat Launch

BrT		LmB	
BkT	✓	SmB	
RbT		WhP	
Sal		Csk	
Tog		WhF	
Smt		Pic	

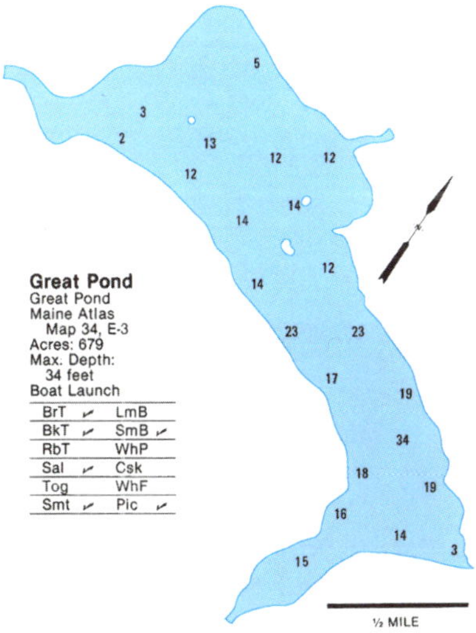

Great Pond

Great Pond
Maine Atlas
Map 34, E-3
Acres: 679
Max. Depth:
34 feet
Boat Launch

BrT	✓	LmB	
BkT	✓	SmB	✓
RbT		WhP	
Sal	✓	Csk	
Tog		WhF	
Smt	✓	Pic	✓

Halfmile Pond

Aurora
Maine Atlas
Map 24, A-3, A-4
Acres: 109
Max. Depth:
61 feet

BrT		LmB	
BkT	✓	SmB	
RbT		WhP	
Sal		Csk	
Tog	✓	WhF	
Smt	✓	Pic	

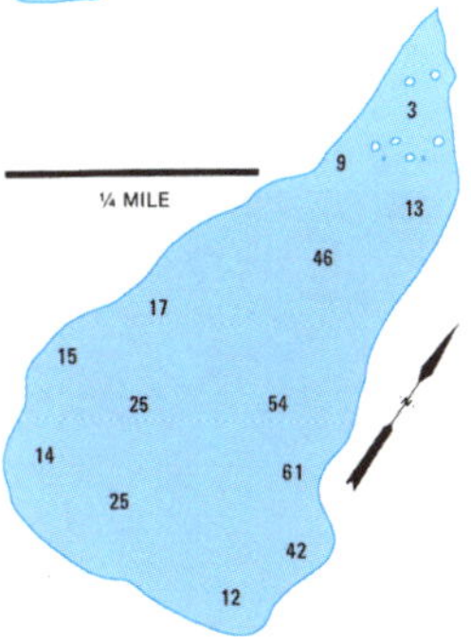

Hancock

Halfmoon Pond
Bar Harbor
Maine Atlas
Map 16, B-3, B-4
Acres: 3
Max. Depth:
20 feet

BrT	LmB
BkT ✓	SmB
RbT	WhP
Sal	Csk
Tog	WhF
Smt	Pic

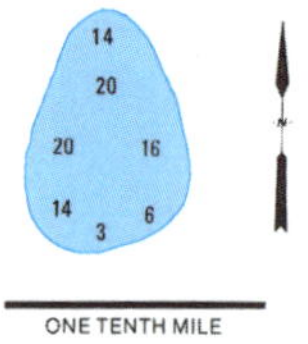

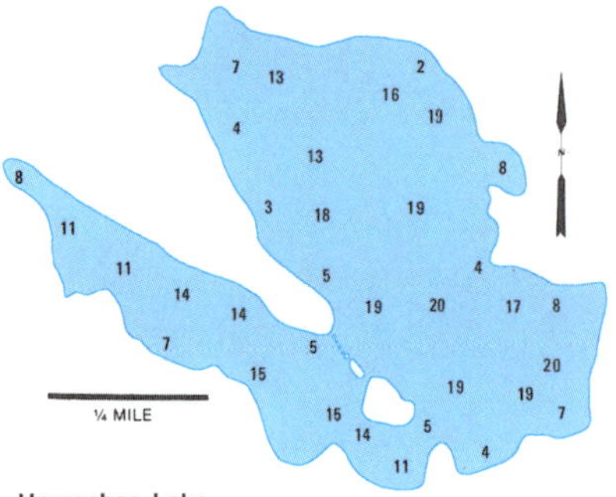

Horseshoe Lake
T35 MD, Maine Atlas Map 35, D-1
Acres: 202, Max. Depth: 20 feet, Boat Launch

BrT	BkT	RbT	Sal	Tog	Smt	LmB	SmB	WhP	Csk	WhF	Pic
								✓			✓

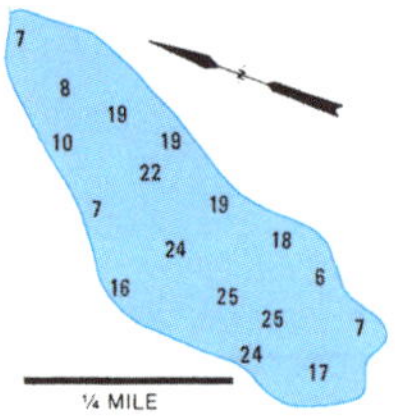

Hancock Pond
Bucksport
Maine Atlas
Map 23, D-3
Acres: 59
Max. Depth:
25 feet

BrT ✓	LmB
BkT ✓	SmB
RbT	WhP
Sal	Csk
Tog	WhF
Smt ✓	Pic ✓

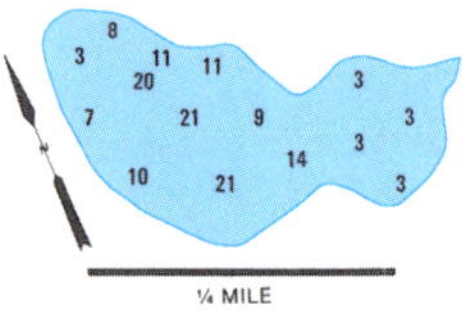

Hurd Pond
Dedham
Maine Atlas
Map 23, C-4
Acres: 38
Max. Depth:
21 feet

BrT	LmB
BkT ✓	SmB
RbT	WhP ✓
Sal	Csk
Tog	WhF
Smt	Pic

Harriman Pond
Dedham
Maine Atlas
Map 23, D-4
Acres: 45
Max. Depth:
75 feet
Boat Launch

BrT ✓	LmB
BkT ✓	SmB
RbT	WhP
Sal	Csk
Tog	WhF
Smt ✓	Pic

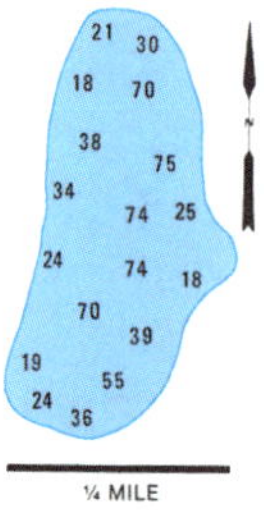

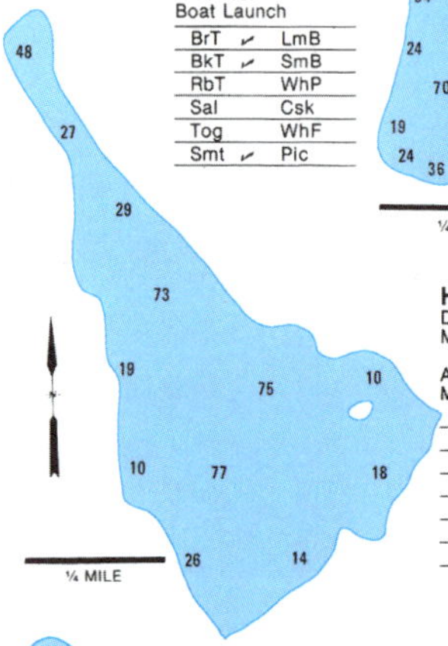

Hatcase Pond
Dedham
Maine Atlas
Map 23, C-5
Acres: 168
Max. Depth:
77 feet

BrT	LmB
BkT ✓	SmB ✓
RbT	WhP
Sal	Csk
Tog	WhF
Smt ✓	Pic ✓

Jacob Buck Pond
Bucksport
Maine Atlas
Map 23, D-2, D-3
Acres: 190
Max. Depth:
52 feet

BrT	LmB
BkT ✓	SmB
RbT	WhP ✓
Sal ✓	Csk
Tog	WhF
Smt ✓	Pic ✓

Comments: Splake.

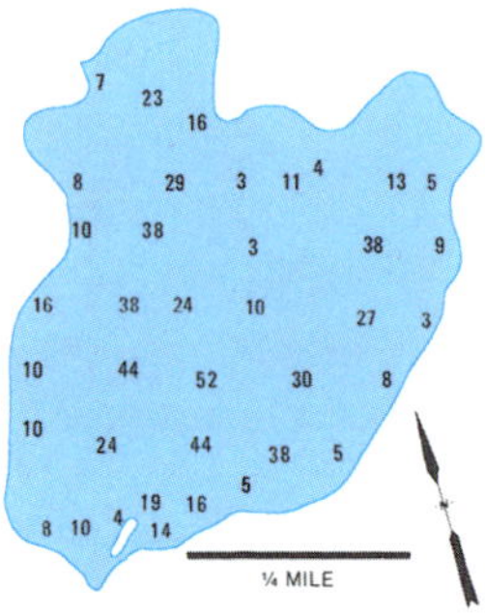

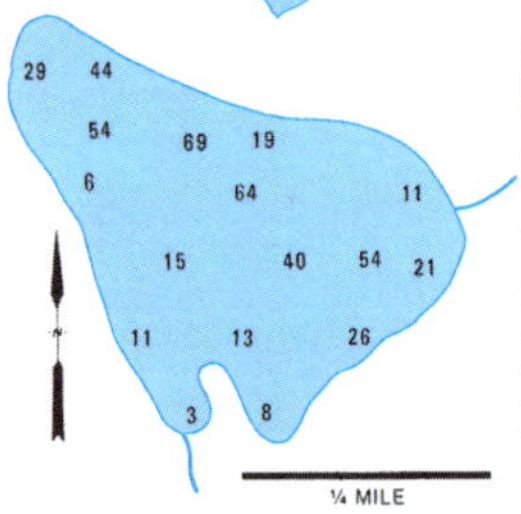

Heart Pond
Orland
Maine Atlas
Map 23, E-4
Acres: 73
Max. Depth:
69 feet
Boat Launch

BrT ✓	LmB
BkT ✓	SmB
RbT	WhP
Sal ✓	Csk
Tog ✓	WhF
Smt ✓	Pic

Comments: Splake.

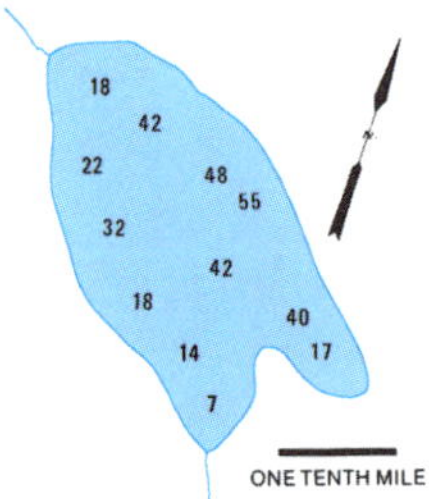

Jellison Hill Pond
Amherst
Maine Atlas
Map 24, B-1
Acres: 45
Max. Depth:
55 feet

BrT	LmB
BkT ✓	SmB
RbT	WhP
Sal	Csk
Tog	WhF
Smt	Pic

Hodgdon Pond
Tremont, Mt. Desert
Maine Atlas
Map 16, C-2
Acres: 35
Max. Depth:
22 feet

BrT	LmB
BkT	SmB ✓
RbT	WhP ✓
Sal	Csk
Tog	WhF
Smt	Pic

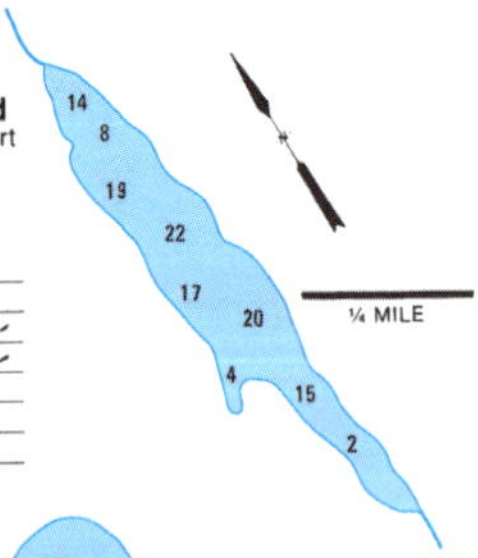

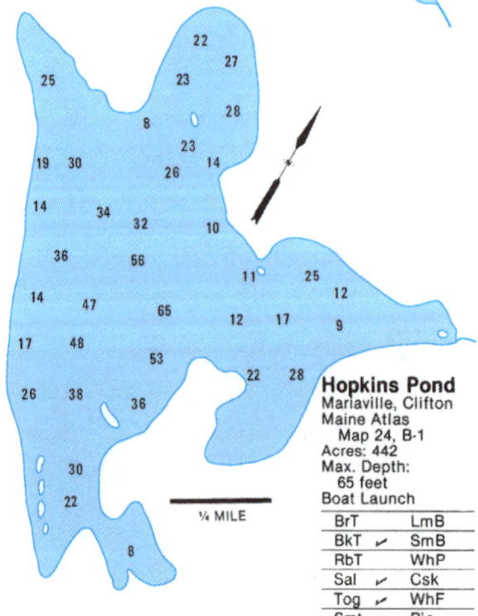

Hopkins Pond
Mariaville, Clifton
Maine Atlas
Map 24, B-1
Acres: 442
Max. Depth:
65 feet
Boat Launch

BrT	LmB
BkT ✓	SmB
RbT	WhP
Sal ✓	Csk
Tog ✓	WhF
Smt ✓	Pic

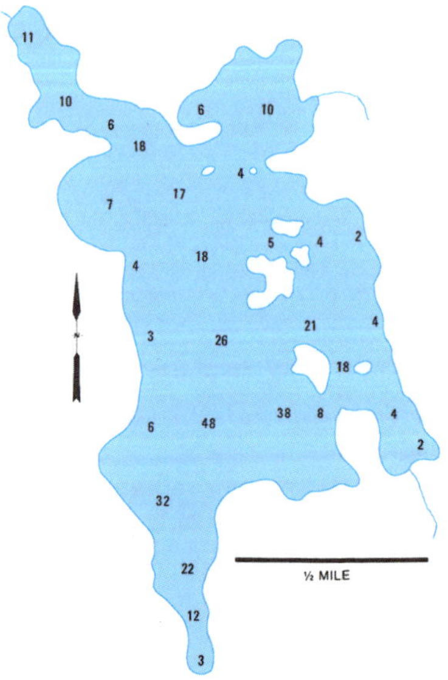

Jones Pond
Gouldsboro, Maine Atlas Map 17, A-1, Map 16, A-5
Acres: 467, Max. Depth: 48 feet, Boat Launch

BrT	BkT	RbT	Sal	Tog	Smt	LmB	SmB	WhP	Csk	WhF	Pic
✓	✓	✓	✓				✓				✓

Jordan Pond
Mt. Desert
Maine Atlas
Map 16, C-3, B-3
Acres: 187
Max. Depth:
150 feet
Boat Launch

BrT		LmB	
BkT	✓	SmB	
RbT		WhP	
Sal	✓	Csk	
Tog	✓	WhF	
Smt	✓	Pic	

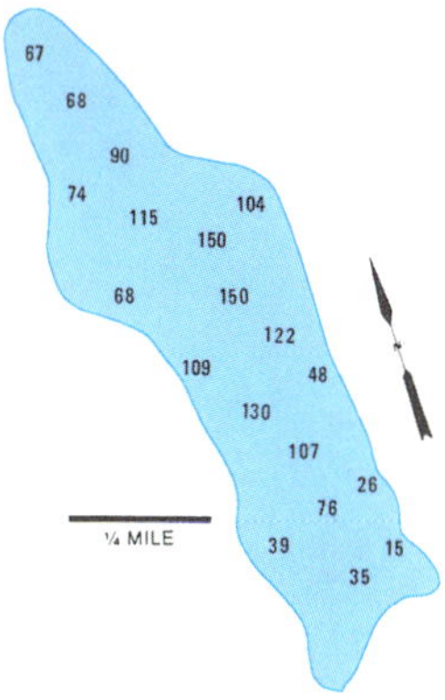

Little Pond
Great Pond
Maine Atlas
Map 34, E-3
Acres: 32
Max. Depth:
17 feet

BrT		LmB	
BkT		SmB	
RbT		WhP	
Sal		Csk	
Tog		WhF	
Smt		Pic	✓

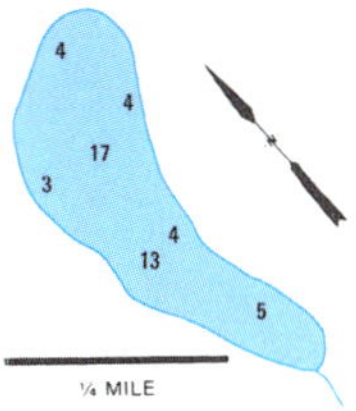

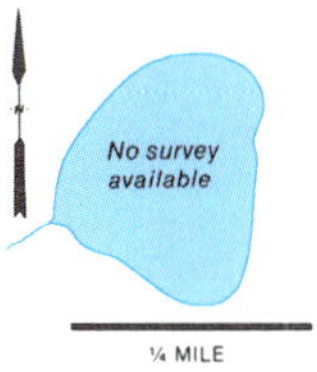

Little Round Pond
Mt. Desert
Maine Atlas
Map 16, B-2
Acres: 16
Max. Depth:
17 feet

BrT		LmB	
BkT	✓	SmB	
RbT		WhP	
Sal		Csk	
Tog		WhF	
Smt		Pic	✓

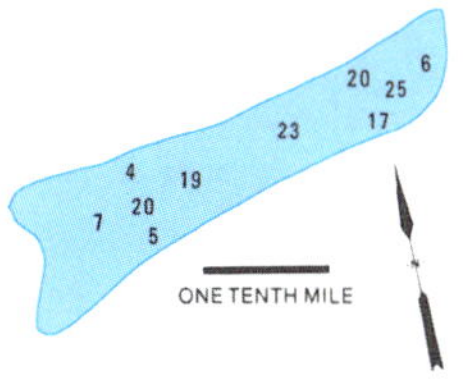

Killman Pond
Oqiton Twp
Maine Atlas
Map 35, B-1
Acres: 22
Max. Depth:
25 feet

BrT		LmB	
BkT	✓	SmB	
RbT		WhP	
Sal		Csk	
Tog		WhF	
Smt		Pic	

Little Tunk Pond
Sullivan
Maine Atlas
Map 24, E-5
Acres: 141
Max. Depth:
24 feet

BrT		LmB	
BkT	✓	SmB	
RbT		WhP	
Sal		Csk	
Tog		WhF	
Smt		Pic	

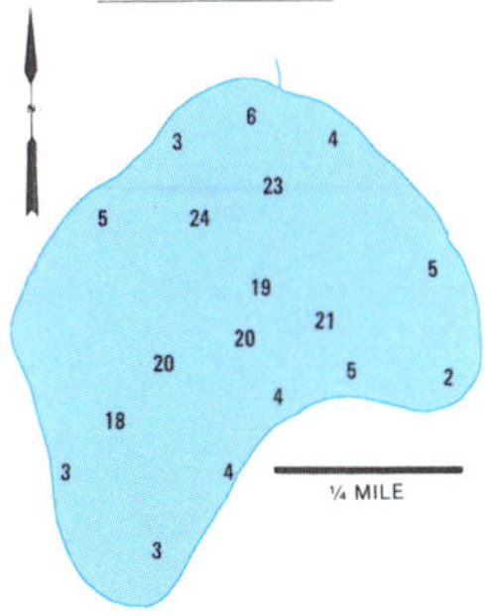

King Pond
Great Pond
Maine Atlas
Map 34, E-3
Acres: 148
Max. Depth:
22 feet
Boat Launch

BrT	✓	LmB	
BkT	✓	SmB	
RbT		WhP	
Sal		Csk	
Tog		WhF	
Smt		Pic	

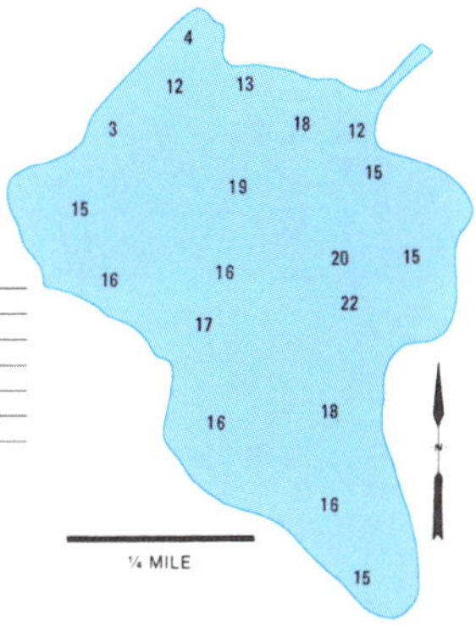

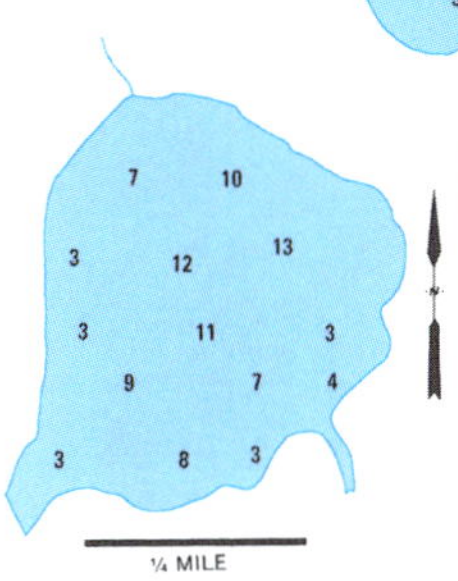

Little Webb Pond
Waltham
Maine Atlas
Map 24, C-3
Acres: 77
Max. Depth:
13 feet

BrT		LmB	
BkT		SmB	✓
RbT		WhP	✓
Sal		Csk	
Tog		WhF	
Smt		Pic	✓

Comments: Access through Webb Pond.

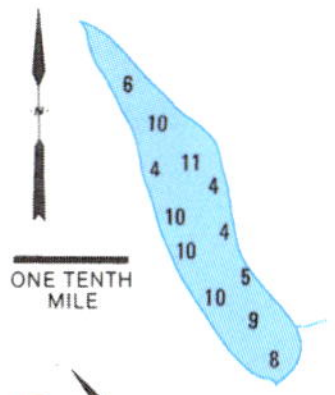

Lake Wood
Bar Harbor
Maine Atlas
Map 16, B-3
Acres: 16
Max. Depth:
11 feet

BrT		LmB	
BkT	✓	SmB	
RbT		WhP	
Sal		Csk	
Tog		WhF	
Smt	✓	Pic	

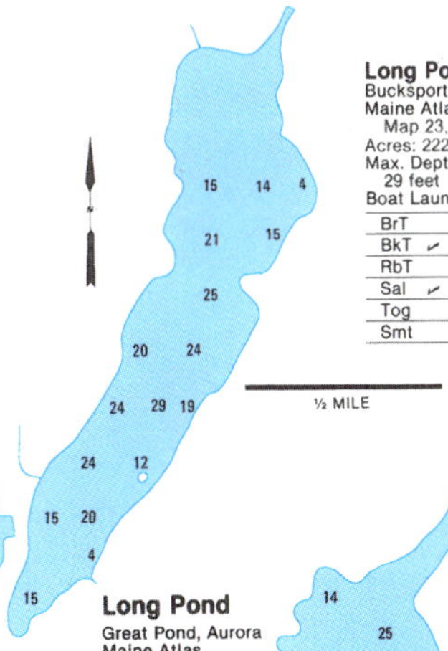

Long Pond
Bucksport
Maine Atlas
Map 23, C-3, D-3
Acres: 222
Max. Depth:
29 feet
Boat Launch

BrT		LmB	
BkT	✓	SmB	✓
RbT		WhP	✓
Sal	✓	Csk	
Tog		WhF	
Smt		Pic	✓

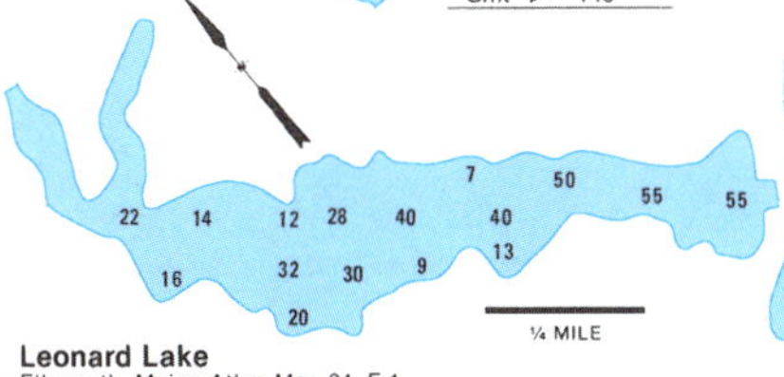

Leonard Lake
Ellsworth, Maine Atlas Map 24, E-1
Acres: 90, Max. Depth: 55 feet, Boat Launch

BrT	BkT	RbT	Sal	Tog	Smt	LmB	SmB	WhP	Csk	WhF	Pic
							✓	✓			✓

Long Pond
Great Pond, Aurora
Maine Atlas
Map 34, E-3,
Map 24, A-3
Acres: 271
Max. Depth:
36 feet
Boat Launch

BrT		LmB	
BkT	✓	SmB	
RbT		WhP	
Sal	✓	Csk	
Tog		WhF	
Smt	✓	Pic	

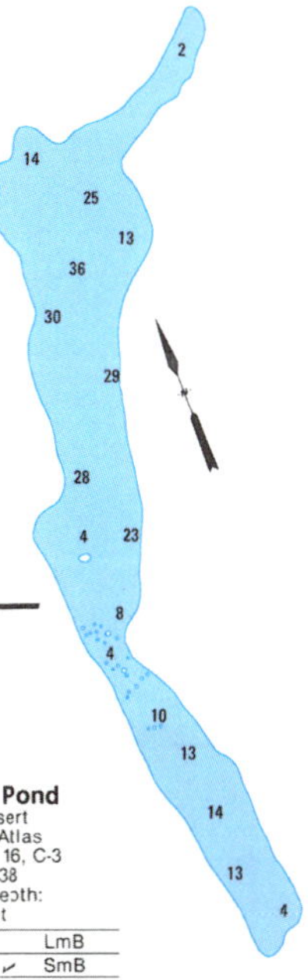

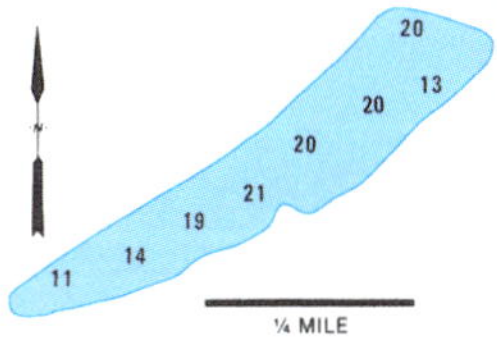

Lily Pond
Deer Isle
Maine Atlas
Map 15, D-3
Acres: 37
Max. Depth:
21 feet

BrT	✓	LmB	
BkT	✓	SmB	
RbT		WhP	
Sal		Csk	
Tog		WhF	
Smt	✓	Pic	

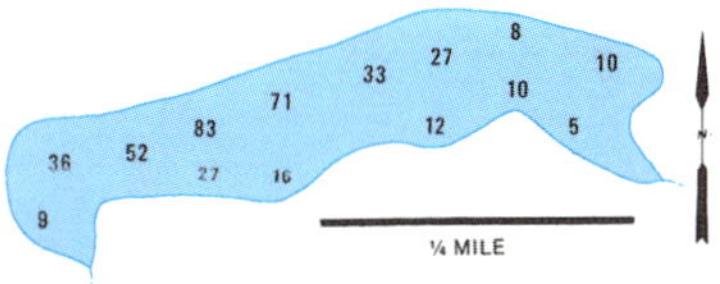

Little Long Pond
T10 SD, Maine Atlas Map 25, D-1
Acres: 55, Max. Depth: 83 feet

BrT	BkT	RbT	Sal	Tog	Smt	LmB	SmB	WhP	Csk	WhF	Pic
	✓				✓						

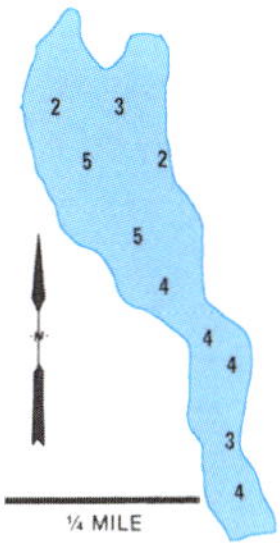

Long Pond
Mt. Desert
Maine Atlas
Map 16, C-3
Acres: 38
Max. Depth:
5 feet

BrT		LmB	
BkT	✓	SmB	
RbT		WhP	
Sal	✓	Csk	
Tog		WhF	
Smt		Pic	

Hancock

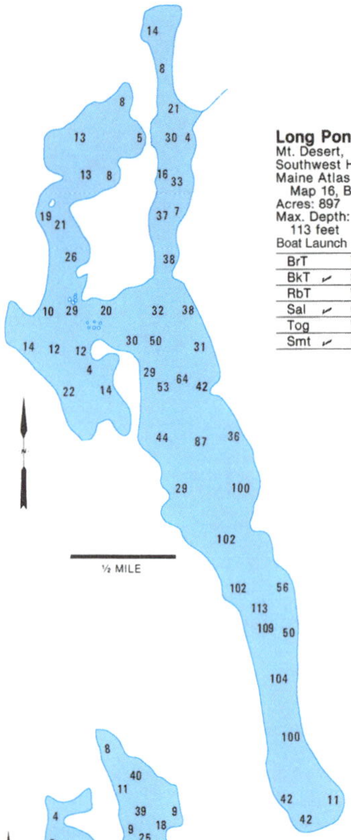

Long Pond
Mt. Desert, Southwest Harbor
Maine Atlas
Map 16, B-2, C-2
Acres: 897
Max. Depth:
113 feet
Boat Launch

BrT		LmB	
BkT	✓	SmB	✓
RbT		WhP	
Sal	✓	Csk	
Tog		WhF	
Smt	✓	Pic	✓

Lower and Middle Lead Mountain Ponds
T28 MD, Maine Atlas Map 24, A-4, A-5
Acres: 486, Max. Depth: 31 feet, Boat Launch

BrT	BkT	RbT	Sal	Tog	Smt	LmB	SmB	WhP	Csk	WhF	Pic
✓	✓				✓			✓			✓

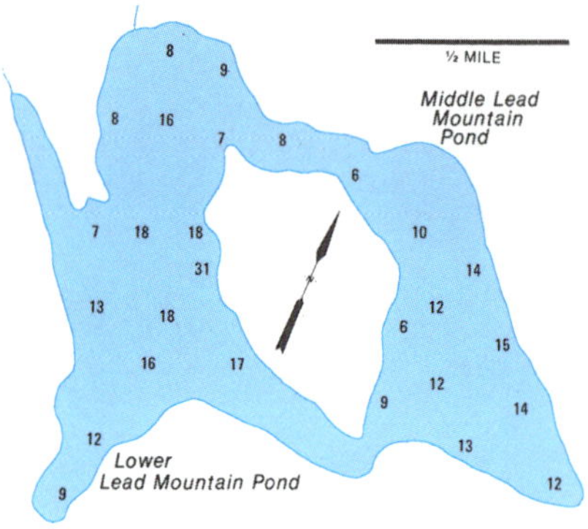

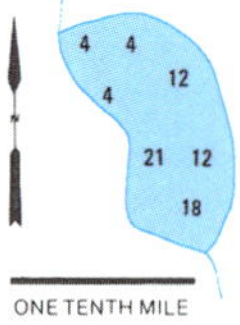

Lower Breakneck Pond
Bar Harbor
Maine Atlas
Map 16, B-3
Acres: 8
Max. Depth:
21 feet

BrT		LmB	
BkT	✓	SmB	
RbT		WhP	
Sal		Csk	
Tog		WhF	
Smt		Pic	

Long Pond
Sullivan
Maine Atlas
Map 24, E-4
Acres: 58
Max. Depth:
57 feet

BrT		LmB	
BkT	✓	SmB	
RbT		WhP	
Sal	✓	Csk	
Tog		WhF	
Smt	✓	Pic	

Lower Hadlock Pond
Mt. Desert
Maine Atlas
Map 16, C-3
Acres: 39
Max. Depth:
40 feet

BrT	✓	LmB	
BkT	✓	SmB	
RbT		WhP	✓
Sal		Csk	
Tog		WhF	
Smt		Pic	

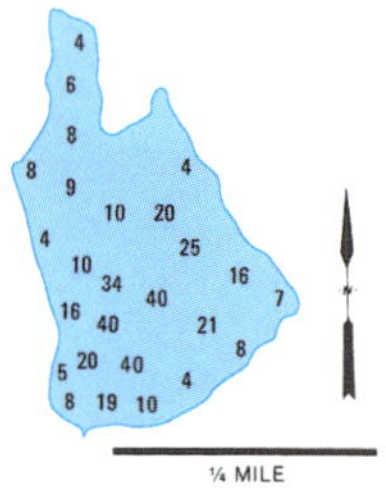

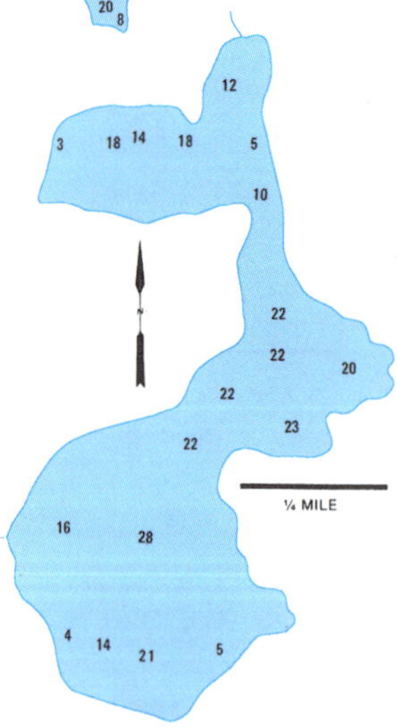

Long Pond
T10 SD
Maine Atlas
Map 25, D-1
Acres: 205
Max. Depth:
28 feet
Boat Launch

BrT	✓	LmB	
BkT	✓	SmB	
RbT		WhP	
Sal	✓	Csk	
Tog		WhF	
Smt	✓	Pic	

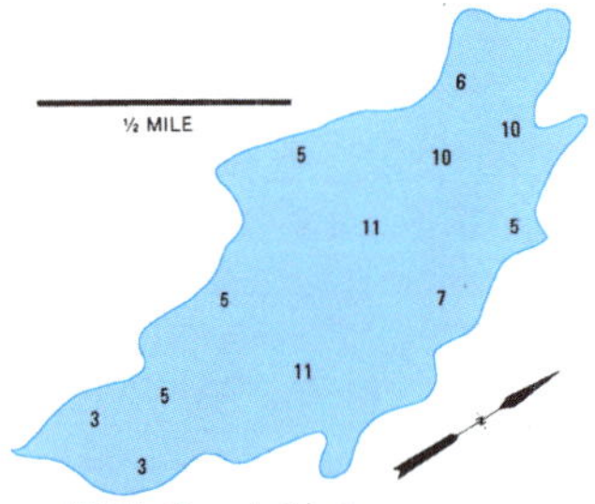

Lower Middle Branch Pond
Aurora, Maine Atlas Map 24, A-4
Acres: 310, Max. Depth: 11 feet

BrT	BkT	RbT	Sal	Tog	Smt	LmB	SmB	WhP	Csk	WhF	Pic
								✓			✓

Loon Pond
T40 MD
Maine Atlas
Map 34, D-4
Acres: 13
Max. Depth:
36 feet

BrT		LmB	
BkT	✓	SmB	
RbT		WhP	
Sal		Csk	
Tog		WhF	
Smt		Pic	

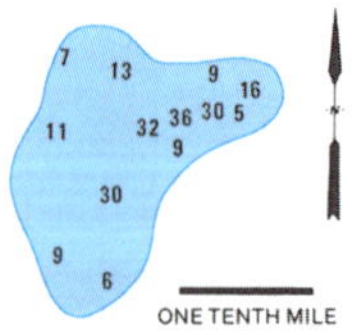

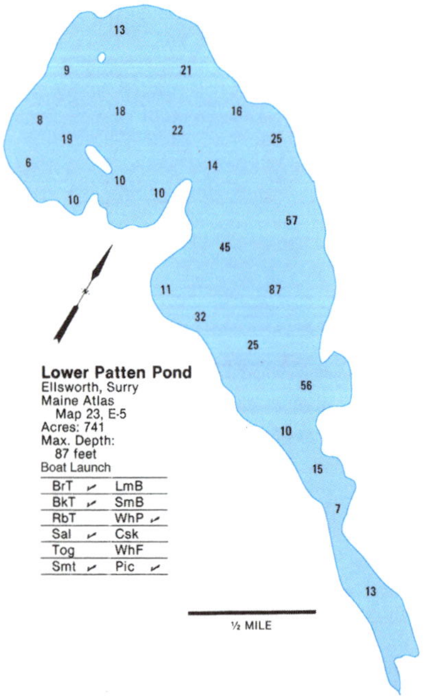

Lower Patten Pond
Ellsworth, Surry
Maine Atlas
Map 23, E-5
Acres: 741
Max. Depth:
87 feet
Boat Launch

BrT	✓	LmB	
BkT	✓	SmB	
RbT		WhP	✓
Sal	✓	Csk	
Tog		WhF	
Smt	✓	Pic	✓

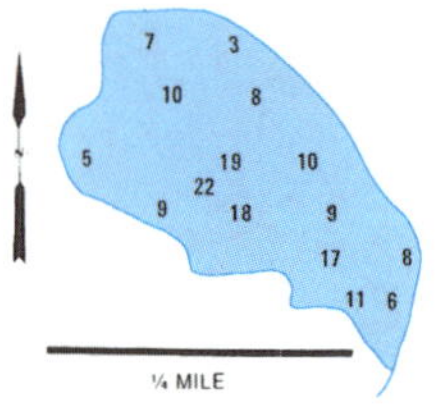

Lovejoy Pond
T34 MD
Maine Atlas
Map 34, E-5
Acres: 40
Max. Depth:
22 feet

BrT		LmB	
BkT	✓	SmB	
RbT		WhP	
Sal		Csk	
Tog		WhF	
Smt		Pic	

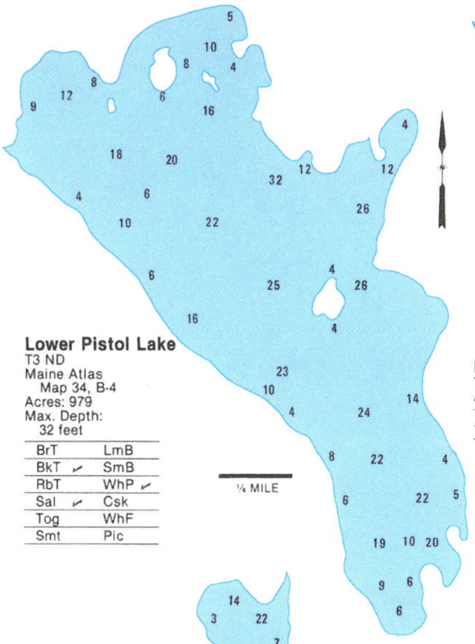

Lower Pistol Lake
T3 ND
Maine Atlas
Map 34, B-4
Acres: 979
Max. Depth:
32 feet

BrT		LmB	
BkT	✓	SmB	
RbT		WhP	✓
Sal	✓	Csk	
Tog		WhF	
Smt		Pic	

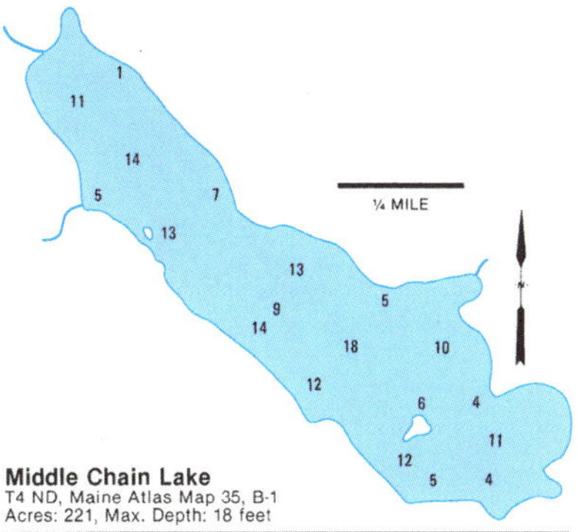

Middle Chain Lake
T4 ND, Maine Atlas Map 35, B-1
Acres: 221, Max. Depth: 18 feet

BrT	BkT	RbT	Sal	Tog	Smt	LmB	SmB	WhP	Csk	WhF	Pic
	✓						✓	✓			✓

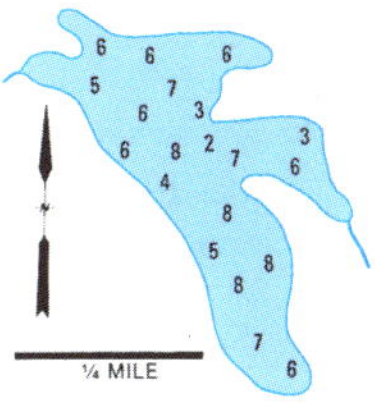

Middle Oxhead Pond
T40 MD
Maine Atlas
Map 34, C-4, D-4
Acres: 38
Max. Depth:
8 feet

BrT		LmB	
BkT	✓	SmB	
RbT		WhP	
Sal		Csk	
Tog		WhF	
Smt		Pic	✓

Lower Sabao Lake
T35 MD
Maine Atlas
Map 35, D-1, E-1
Acres: 755
Max. Depth:
34 feet
Boat Launch

BrT		LmB	
BkT	✓	SmB	
RbT		WhP	✓
Sal		Csk	
Tog		WhF	
Smt		Pic	✓

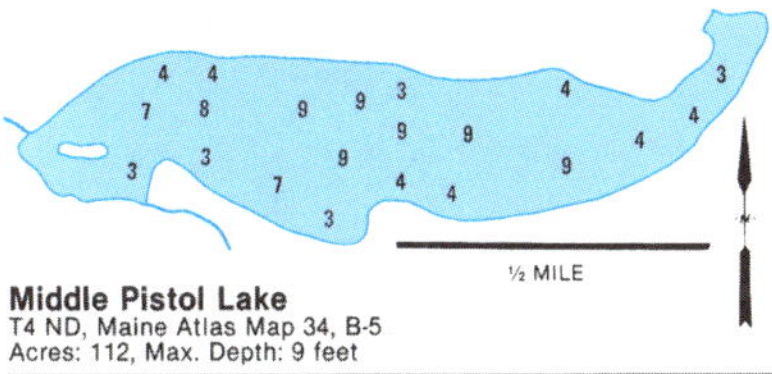

Middle Pistol Lake
T4 ND, Maine Atlas Map 34, B-5
Acres: 112, Max. Depth: 9 feet

BrT	BkT	RbT	Sal	Tog	Smt	LmB	SmB	WhP	Csk	WhF	Pic
	✓							✓			

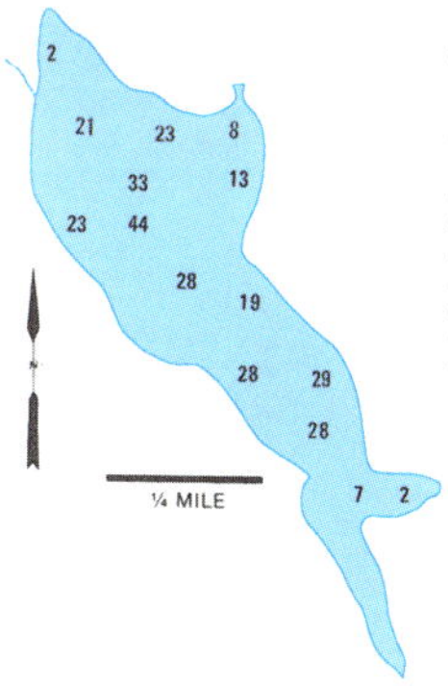

Lower Springy Pond
Otis, Clifton
Maine Atlas
Map 24, B-1
Acres: 114
Max. Depth:
44 feet

BrT		LmB	
BkT	✓	SmB	
RbT		WhP	✓
Sal	✓	Csk	
Tog		WhF	
Smt	✓	Pic	✓

Comments: Splake.

Molasses Pond
Eastbrook
Maine Atlas
Map 24, C-4, D-4
Acres: 1,252
Max. Depth:
47 feet
Boat Launch

BrT	✓	LmB	
BkT	✓	SmB	
RbT		WhP	✓
Sal	✓	Csk	
Tog		WhF	
Smt	✓	Pic	✓

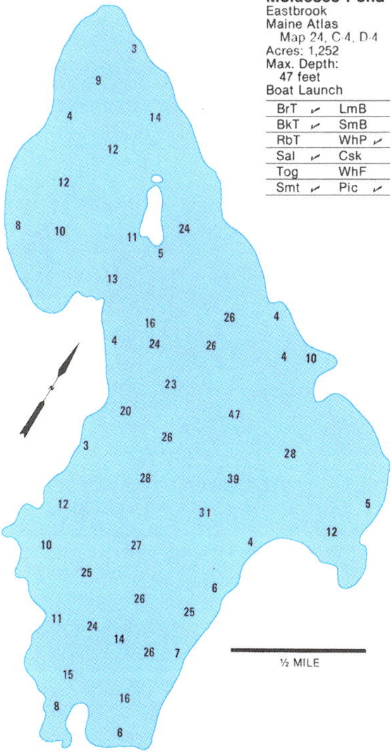

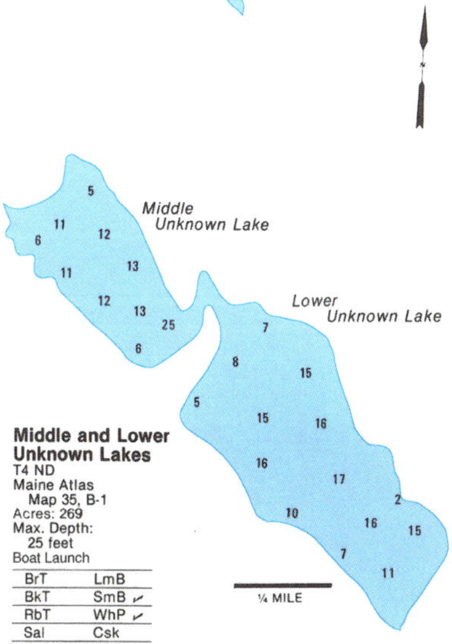

Middle and Lower Unknown Lakes
T4 ND
Maine Atlas
Map 35, B-1
Acres: 269
Max. Depth:
25 feet
Boat Launch

BrT		LmB	
BkT		SmB	✓
RbT		WhP	✓
Sal		Csk	
Tog		WhF	
Smt		Pic	✓

Morancy Pond
T7 SD, Sullivan, Maine Atlas Map 24, E-5
Acres: 64, Max. Depth: 14 feet

BrT	BkT	RbT	Sal	Tog	Smt	LmB	SmB	WhP	Csk	WhF	Pic
	✓										✓

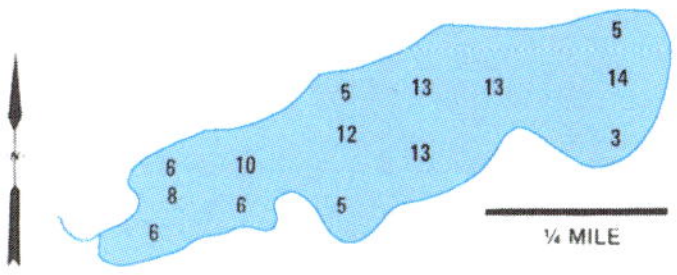

Hancock

Moulton Pond

Dedham, Bucksport
Maine Atlas
Map 23, C-4
Acres: 45
Max. Depth:
35 feet

BrT	✓	LmB	
BkT	✓	SmB	
RbT		WhP	✓
Sal		Csk	
Tog		WhF	
Smt	✓	Pic	✓

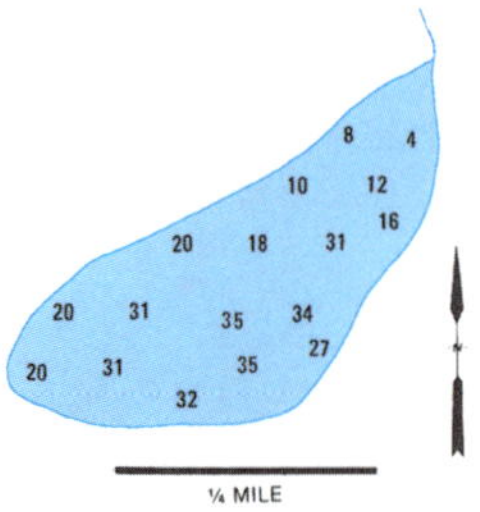

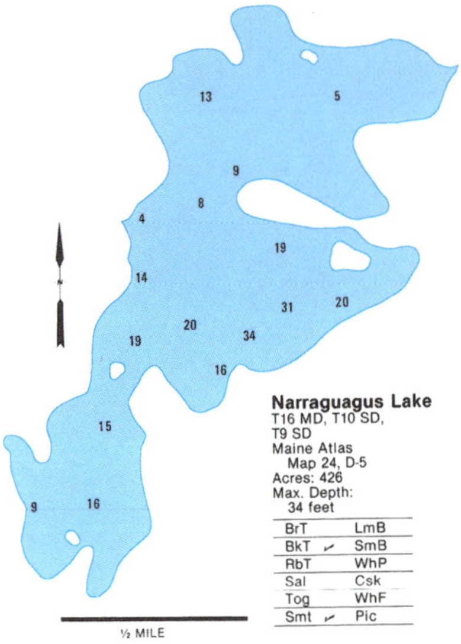

Narraguagus Lake

T16 MD, T10 SD,
T9 SD
Maine Atlas
Map 24, D-5
Acres: 426
Max. Depth:
34 feet

BrT		LmB	
BkT	✓	SmB	
RbT		WhP	
Sal		Csk	
Tog		WhF	
Smt	✓	Pic	

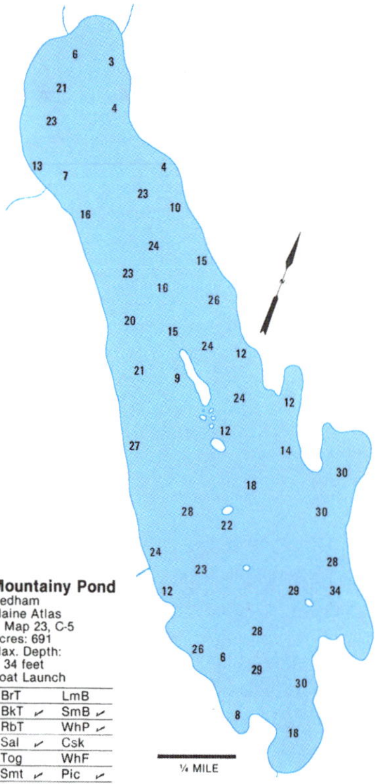

Mountainy Pond

Dedham
Maine Atlas
Map 23, C-5
Acres: 691
Max. Depth:
34 feet
Boat Launch

BrT		LmB	
BkT	✓	SmB	✓
RbT		WhP	✓
Sal	✓	Csk	
Tog		WhF	
Smt	✓	Pic	✓

Nicatous Lake

T3 ND, T40 MD,
T41 MD
Maine Atlas
Map 34, C-5, D-5
Acres: 5,165
Max. Depth:
56 feet
Boat Launch

BrT	✓	LmB	
BkT	✓	SmB	✓
RbT		WhP	✓
Sal	✓	Csk	
Tog		WhF	
Smt	✓	Pic	✓

Comments: Splake.

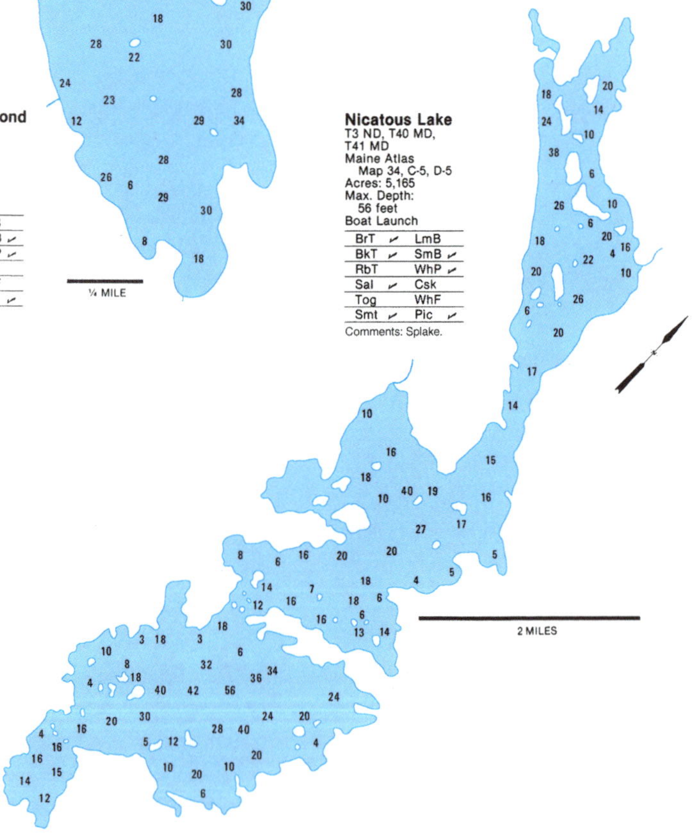

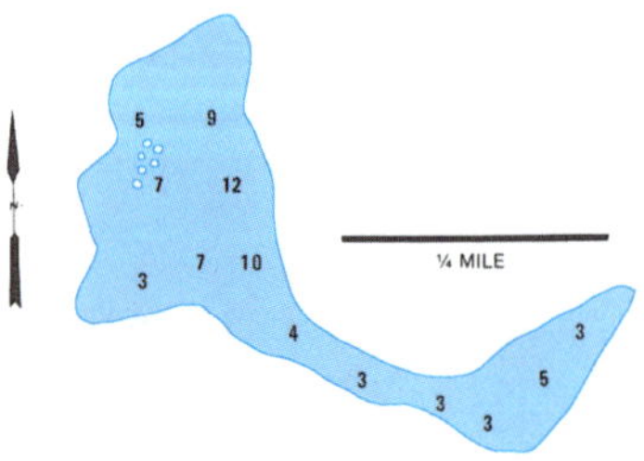

Myrick Pond

T10 SD, Maine Atlas Map 25, D-1
Acres: 45, Max. Depth: 12 feet

BrT	BkT	RbT	Sal	Tog	Smt	LmB	SmB	WhP	Csk	WhF	Pic
	✓										

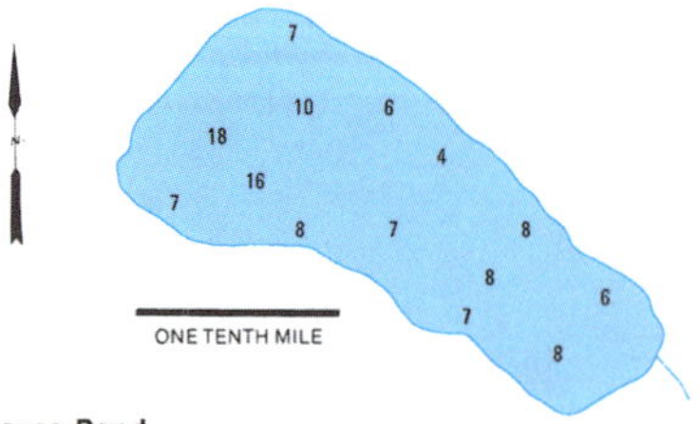

Noyes Pond

Blue Hill, Maine Atlas Map 15, A-5
Acres: 23, Max. Depth: 18 feet

BrT	BkT	RbT	Sal	Tog	Smt	LmB	SmB	WhP	Csk	WhF	Pic
	✓										

Partridge Pond
Amherst
Maine Atlas
Map 24, A-2
Acres: 28
Max. Depth:
22 feet

BrT		LmB	
BkT	✓	SmB	
RbT		WhP	
Sal		Csk	
Tog		WhF	
Smt		Pic	

Pughole Pond
T41 MD
Maine Atlas
Map 35, D-1
Acres: 70
Max. Depth:
18 feet

BrT		LmB	
BkT	✓	SmB	
RbT		WhP	✓
Sal		Csk	
Tog		WhF	
Smt		Pic	

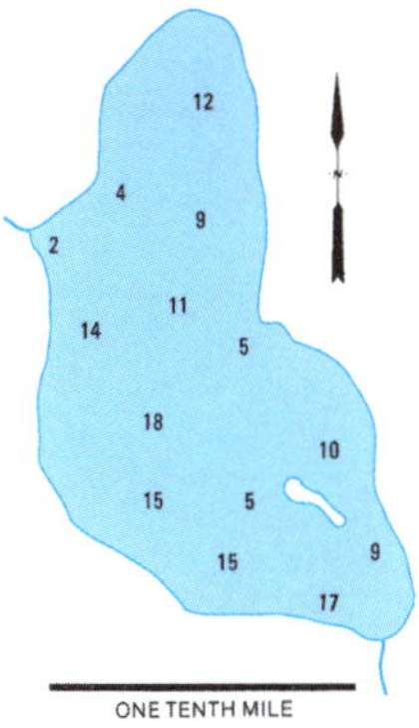

Phillips Lake
Dedham
Maine Atlas
Map 23, C-4
Acres: 828
Max. Depth:
98 feet
Boat Launch

BrT	✓	LmB	
BkT	✓	SmB	✓
RbT		WhP	✓
Sal	✓	Csk	
Tog	✓	WhF	
Smt	✓	Pic	✓

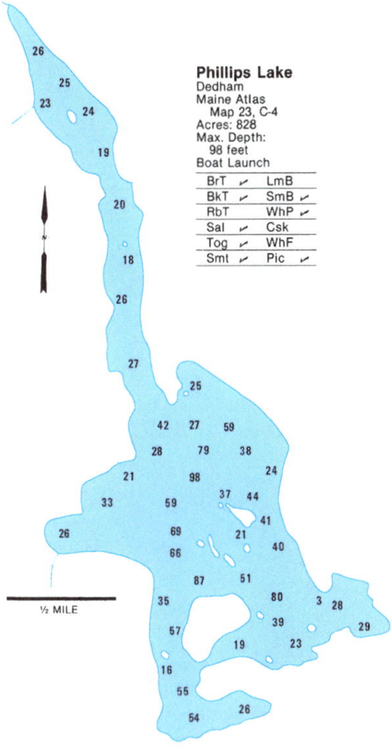

Rift Pond
Great Pond
Maine Atlas
Map 34, E-3
Acres: 126
Max. Depth:
34 feet

BrT		LmB	
BkT	✓	SmB	
RbT		WhP	
Sal		Csk	
Tog		WhF	
Smt	✓	Pic	

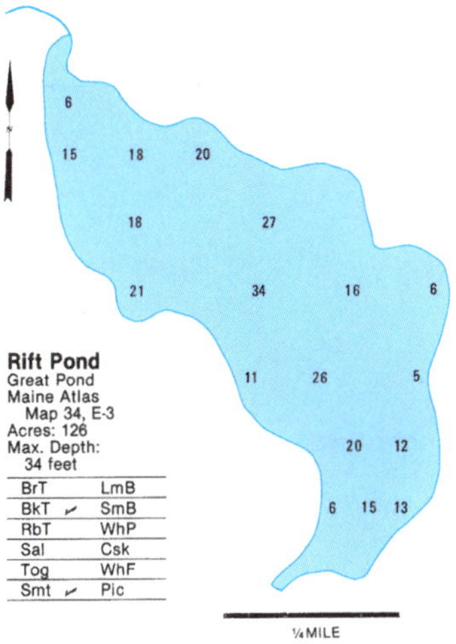

Pickerel Pond
T32 MD
Maine Atlas
Map 34, E-1
Acres: 11
Max. Depth:
24 feet
Boat Launch

BrT		LmB	
BkT	✓	SmB	
RbT		WhP	
Sal		Csk	
Tog		WhF	
Smt		Pic	✓

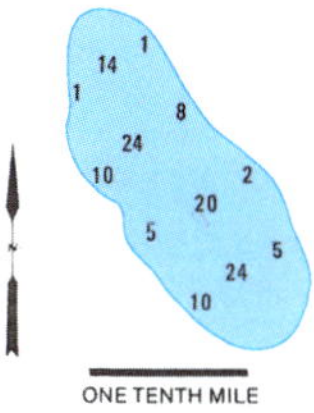

Rocky Pond
Orland, Maine Atlas Map 23, D-4
Acres: 153, Max. Depth: 14 feet

BrT	BkT	RbT	Sal	Tog	Smt	LmB	SmB	WhP	Csk	WhF	Pic
	✓						✓				

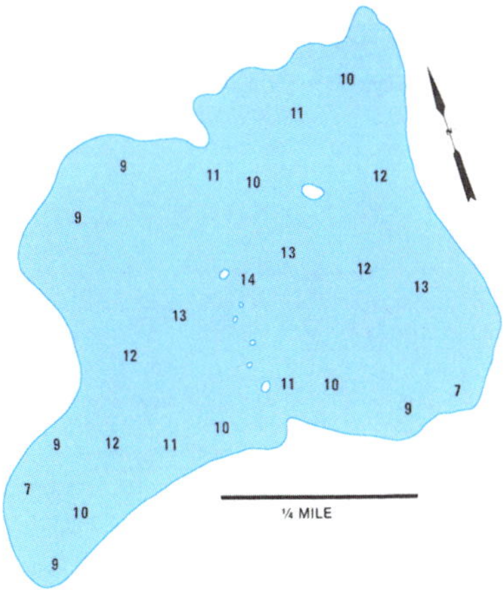

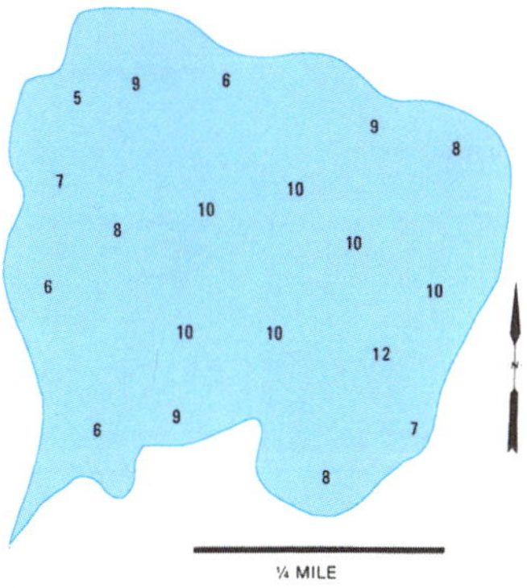

Pierce Pond
Penobscot, Maine Atlas Map 15, A-3
Acres: 118, Max. Depth: 12 feet, Boat Launch

BrT	BkT	RbT	Sal	Tog	Smt	LmB	SmB	WhP	Csk	WhF	Pic
						✓		✓			

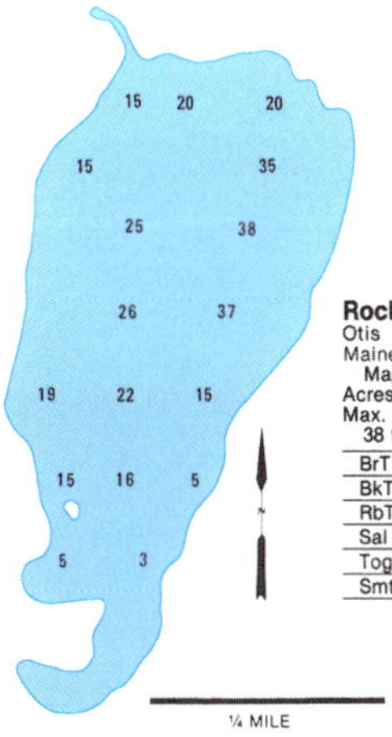

Rocky Pond
Otis
Maine Atlas
Map 24, C-1
Acres: 128
Max. Depth:
38 feet

BrT		LmB	
BkT	✓	SmB	✓
RbT		WhP	✓
Sal	✓	Csk	
Tog		WhF	
Smt		Pic	✓

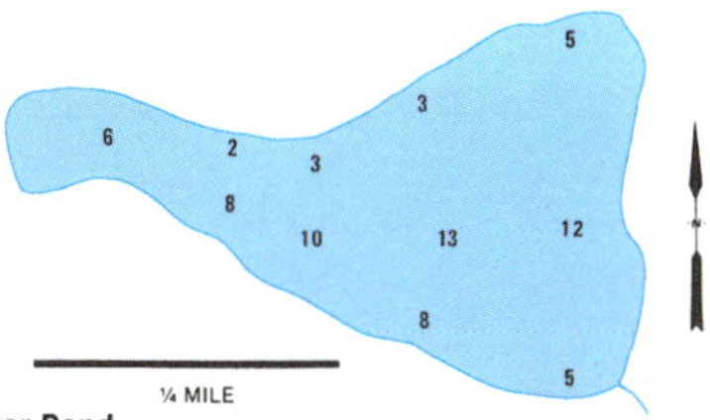

Porter Pond
T3 ND, Maine Atlas Map 34, C-4
Acres: 58, Max. Depth: 13 feet

BrT	BkT	RbT	Sal	Tog	Smt	LmB	SmB	WhP	Csk	WhF	Pic
	✓										

Hancock

Rocky Pond
T22 MD, Maine Atlas Map 24, B-5
Acres: 666, Max. Depth: 30 feet, Boat Launch

BrT	BkT	RbT	Sal	Tog	Smt	LmB	SmB	WhP	Csk	WhF	Pic
					✓			✓			✓

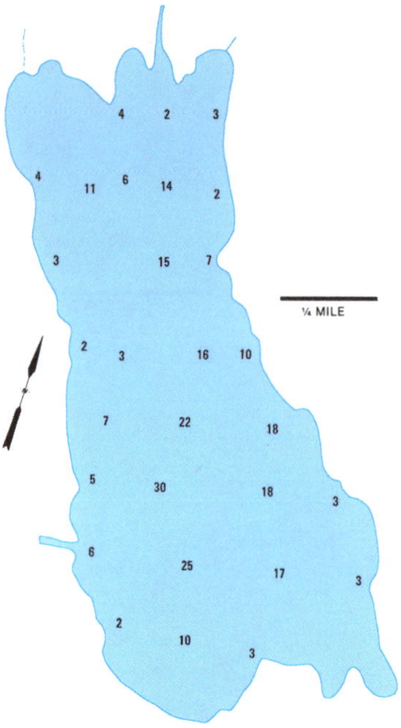

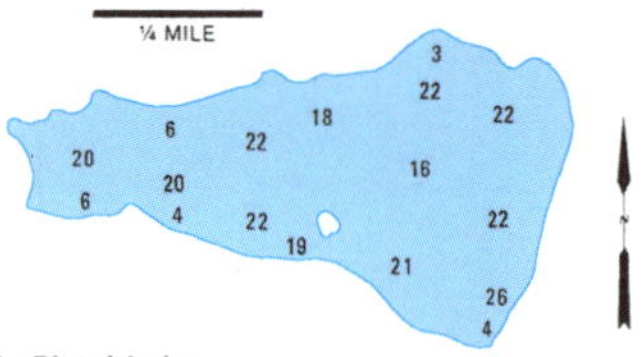

Side Pistol Lake
T3 ND, T4 ND, Maine Atlas Map 34, B-4, B-5
Acres: 147, Max. Depth: 26 feet

BrT	BkT	RbT	Sal	Tog	Smt	LmB	SmB	WhP	Csk	WhF	Pic
✓	✓							✓			

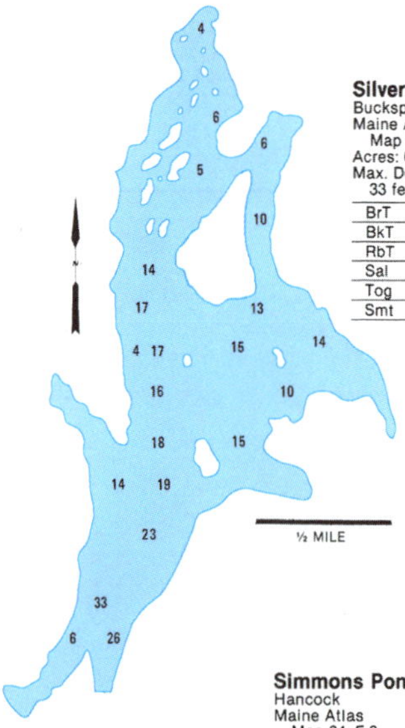

Silver Lake
Bucksport
Maine Atlas
Map 23, D-2
Acres: 630
Max. Depth:
33 feet

BrT		LmB	
BkT		SmB	✓
RbT		WhP	✓
Sal		Csk	
Tog		WhF	
Smt		Pic	✓

Round Pond
Mt. Desert
Maine Atlas
Map 16, B-2
Acres: 38
Max. Depth:
19 feet

BrT	✓	LmB	
BkT	✓	SmB	✓
RbT		WhP	
Sal		Csk	
Tog		WhF	
Smt		Pic	✓

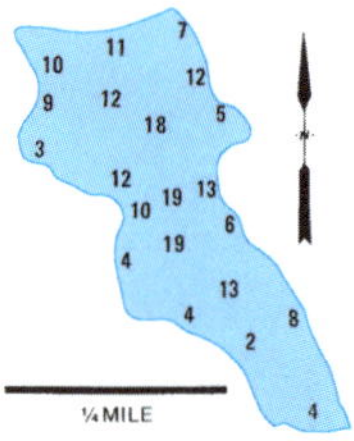

Simmons Pond
Hancock
Maine Atlas
Map 24, E-2
Acres: 7
Max. Depth:
27 feet

BrT		LmB	
BkT	✓	SmB	
RbT		WhP	
Sal		Csk	
Tog		WhF	
Smt		Pic	

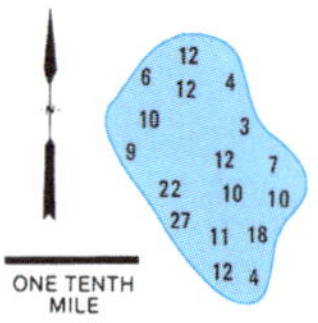

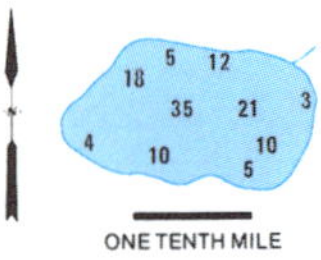

Salmon Pond
T10 SD
Maine Atlas
Map 24, D-5
Acres: 10
Max. Depth:
35 feet

BrT		LmB	
BkT	✓	SmB	
RbT		WhP	
Sal		Csk	
Tog		WhF	
Smt	✓	Pic	

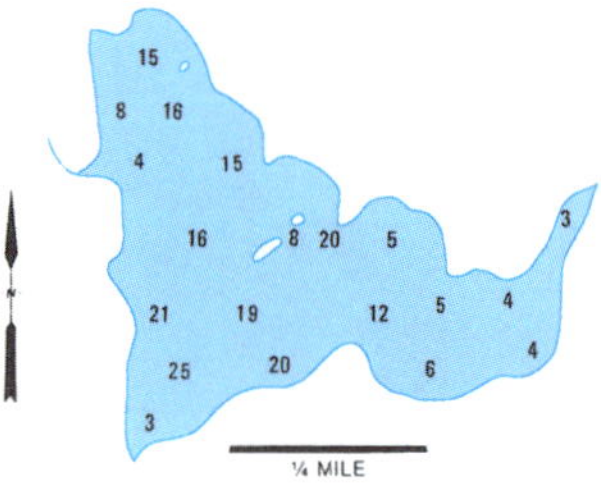

Somes Pond
Mt. Desert, Maine Atlas Map 16, B-2
Acres: 104, Max. Depth: 25 feet

BrT	BkT	RbT	Sal	Tog	Smt	LmB	SmB	WhP	Csk	WhF	Pic
	✓		✓		✓		✓				✓

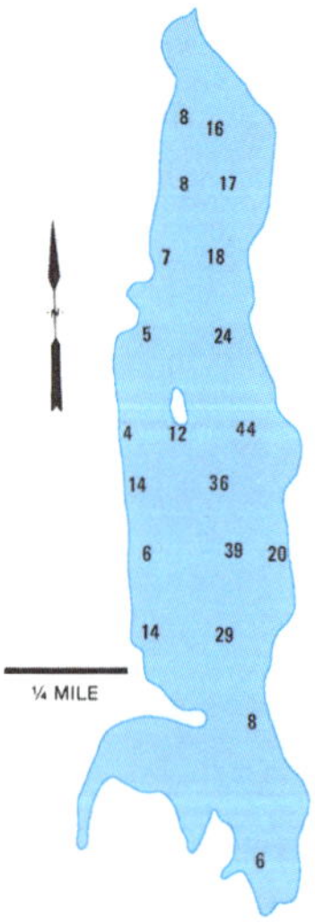

Seal Cove Pond
Tremont
Maine Atlas
Map 16, C-2
Acres: 283
Max. Depth:
44 feet

BrT	✓	LmB	
BkT	✓	SmB	✓
RbT		WhP	✓
Sal		Csk	
Tog		WhF	
Smt	✓	Pic	

Second Pond
Dedham
Maine Atlas
Map 23, C-4, C-5
Acres: 64
Max. Depth:
40 feet

BrT		LmB	
BkT	✓	SmB	
RbT		WhP	
Sal		Csk	
Tog		WhF	
Smt		Pic	✓

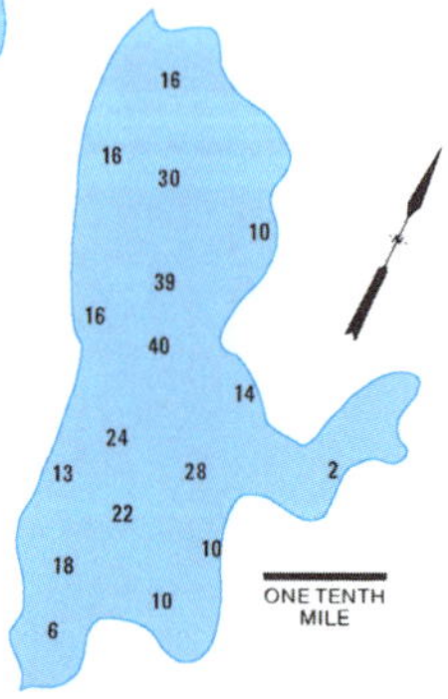

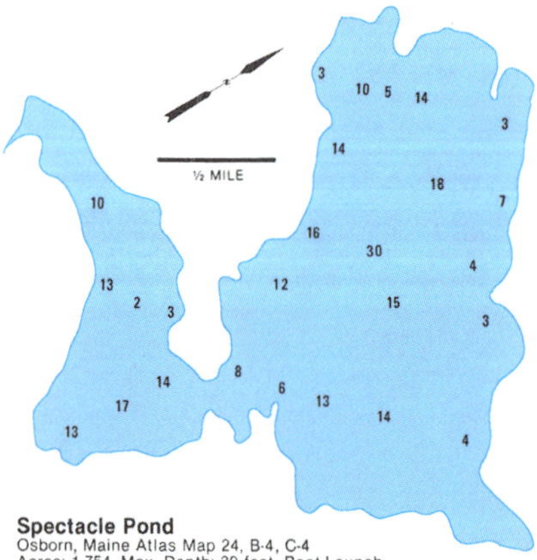

Spectacle Pond
Osborn, Maine Atlas Map 24, B-4, C-4
Acres: 1,754, Max. Depth: 30 feet, Boat Launch

BrT	BkT	RbT	Sal	Tog	Smt	LmB	SmB	WhP	Csk	WhF	Pic
✓	✓						✓	✓			✓

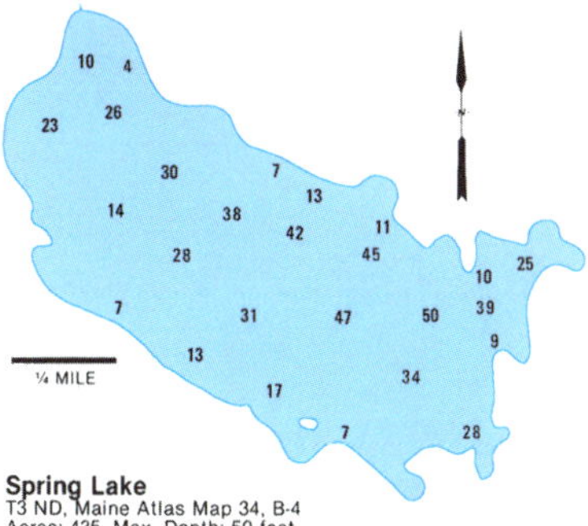

Spring Lake

T3 ND, Maine Atlas Map 34, B-4
Acres: 435, Max. Depth: 50 feet

BrT	BkT	RbT	Sal	Tog	Smt	LmB	SmB	WhP	Csk	WhF	Pic
	✓		✓		✓			✓			✓

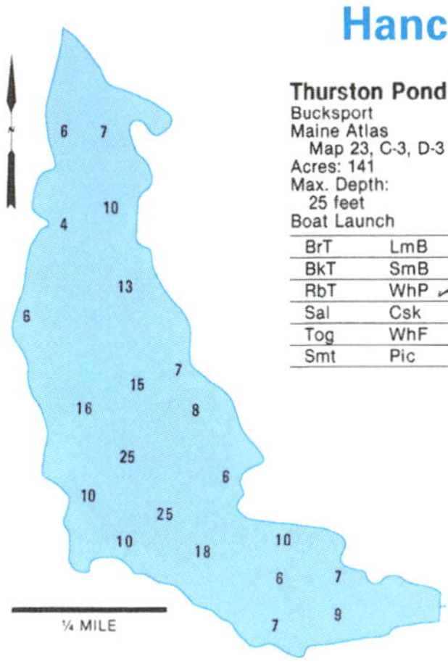

Thurston Pond

Bucksport
Maine Atlas
Map 23, C-3, D-3
Acres: 141
Max. Depth:
25 feet
Boat Launch

BrT		LmB	
BkT		SmB	
RbT		WhP	✓
Sal		Csk	
Tog		WhF	
Smt		Pic	

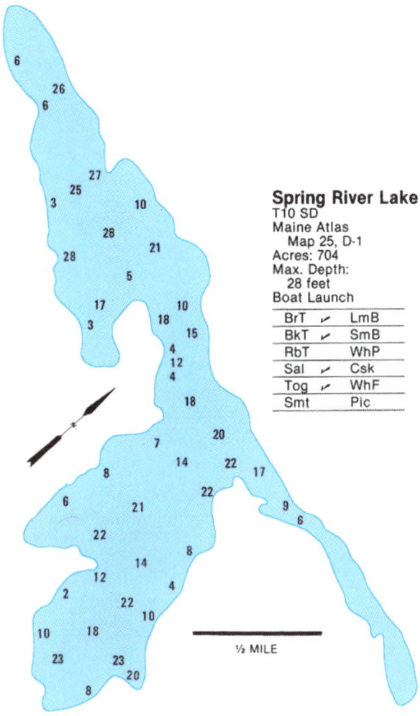

Spring River Lake

T10 SD
Maine Atlas
Map 25, D-1
Acres: 704
Max. Depth:
28 feet
Boat Launch

BrT	✓	LmB	
BkT	✓	SmB	
RbT		WhP	
Sal	✓	Csk	
Tog	✓	WhF	
Smt		Pic	

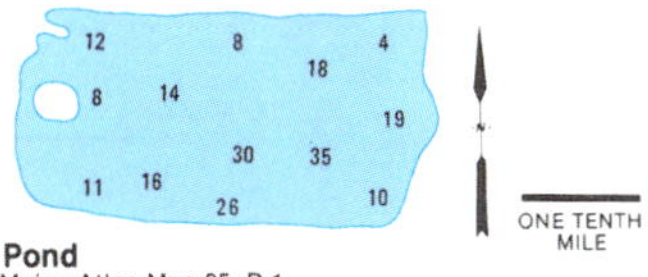

Tilden Pond

T10 SD, Maine Atlas Map 25, D-1
Acres: 36, Max. Depth: 35 feet

BrT	BkT	RbT	Sal	Tog	Smt	LmB	SmB	WhP	Csk	WhF	Pic
	✓				✓						

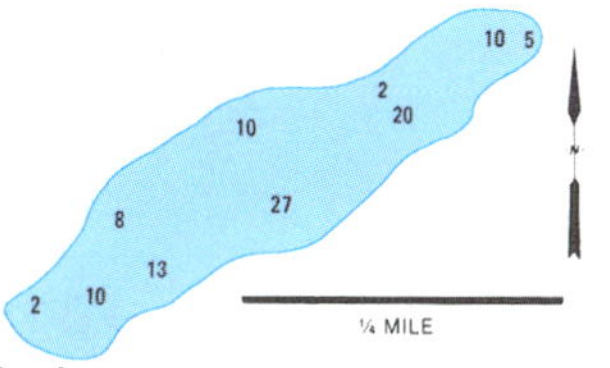

Titcomb Pond

T32 MD, Maine Atlas Map 34, E-1
Acres: 38, Max. Depth: 27 feet

BrT	BkT	RbT	Sal	Tog	Smt	LmB	SmB	WhP	Csk	WhF	Pic
	✓										

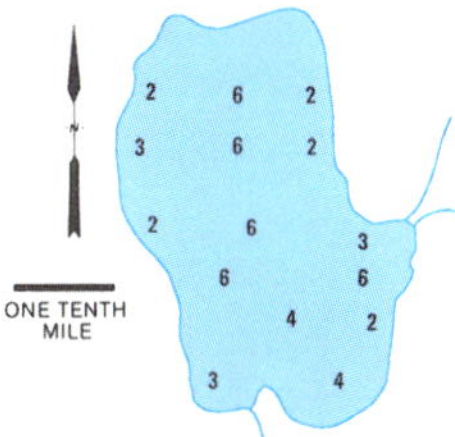

Stiles Lake

T35 MD
Maine Atlas
Map 35, E-1
Acres: 51
Max. Depth:
6 feet

BrT		LmB	
BkT		SmB	
RbT		WhP	
Sal		Csk	
Tog		WhF	
Smt		Pic	✓

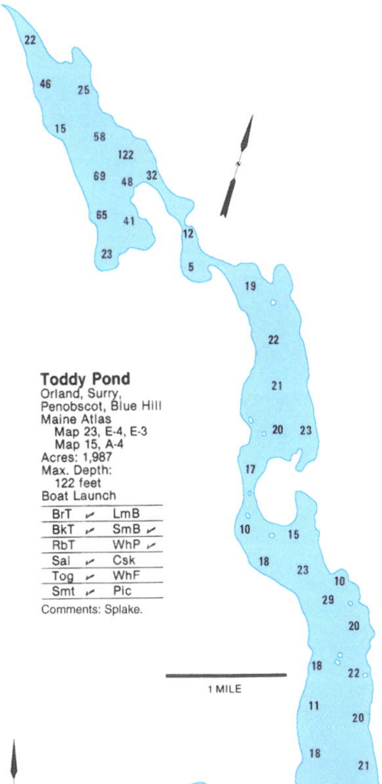

Toddy Pond

Orland, Surry,
Penobscot, Blue Hill
Maine Atlas
Map 23, E-4, E-3
Map 15, A-4
Acres: 1,987
Max. Depth:
122 feet
Boat Launch

BrT	✓	LmB	
BkT	✓	SmB	✓
RbT		WhP	✓
Sal	✓	Csk	
Tog	✓	WhF	
Smt	✓	Pic	

Comments: Splake.

The Tarn

Bar Harbor
Maine Atlas
Map 16, B-4
Acres: 8
Max. Depth:
4 feet

BrT		LmB	
BkT	✓	SmB	
RbT		WhP	
Sal		Csk	
Tog		WhF	
Smt		Pic	

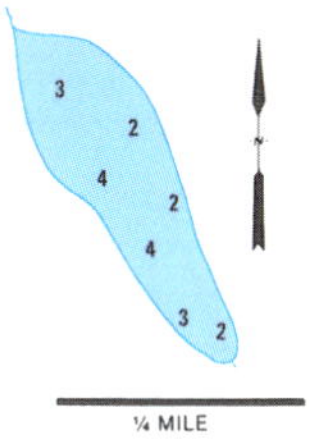

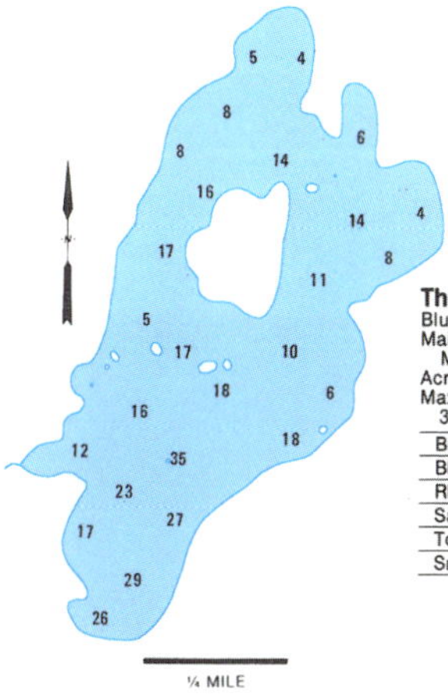

Third Pond

Blue Hill
Maine Atlas
Map 15, B-4
Acres: 206
Max. Depth:
35 feet

BrT		LmB	
BkT	✓	SmB	
RbT		WhP	✓
Sal		Csk	
Tog		WhF	
Smt		Pic	

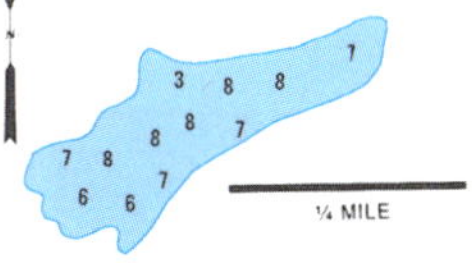

Torrey Pond

Deer Isle, Maine Atlas Map 15, D-4
Acres: 20, Max. Depth: 8 feet

BrT	BkT	RbT	Sal	Tog	Smt	LmB	SmB	WhP	Csk	WhF	Pic
						✓					

Hancock

Trout Pond

T40 MD
Maine Atlas
Map 34, D-4
Acres: 6
Max. Depth:
39 feet

BrT	LmB
BkT ✓	SmB
RbT	WhP
Sal	Csk
Tog	WhF
Smt	Pic

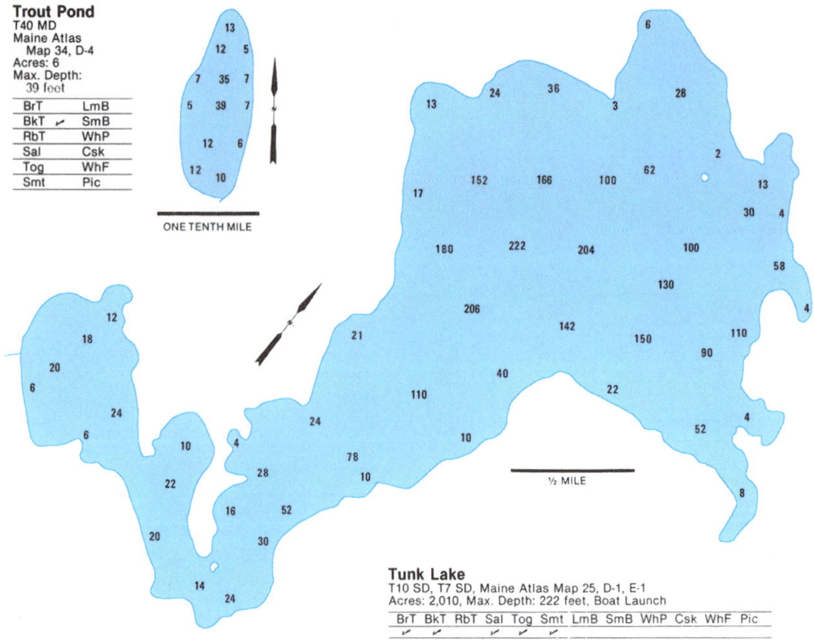

Tunk Lake

T10 SD, T7 SD, Maine Atlas Map 25, D-1, E-1
Acres: 2,010, Max. Depth: 222 feet, Boat Launch

BrT	BkT	RbT	Sal	Tog	Smt	LmB	SmB	WhP	Csk	WhF	Pic
✓	✓		✓	✓	✓						

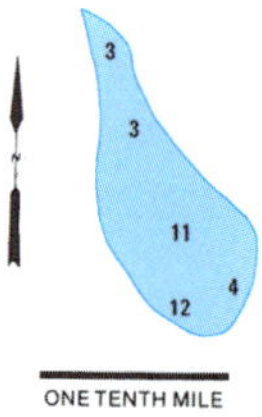

Upper Breakneck Pond

Bar Harbor
Maine Atlas
Map 16, B-3
Acres: 9
Max. Depth:
12 feet

BrT	LmB
BkT ✓	SmB
RbT	WhP
Sal	Csk
Tog	WhF
Smt	Pic

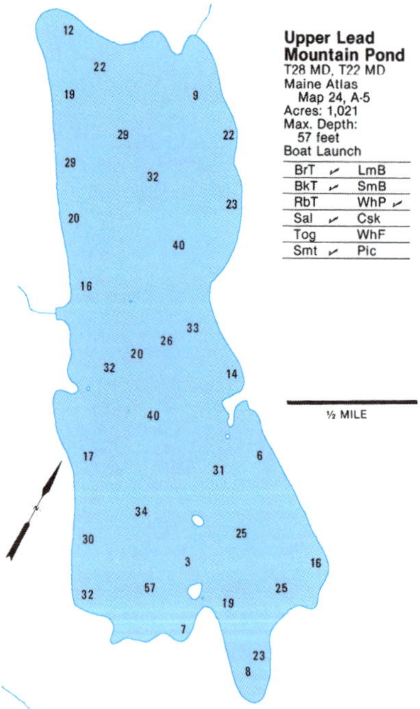

Upper Lead Mountain Pond

T28 MD, T22 MD
Maine Atlas
Map 24, A-5
Acres: 1,021
Max. Depth:
57 feet
Boat Launch

BrT ✓	LmB
BkT ✓	SmB
RbT	WhP ✓
Sal ✓	Csk
Tog	WhF
Smt ✓	Pic

Upper Chain Lake

T4 ND, Maine Atlas Map 34, B-5
Acres: 717, Max. Depth: 30 feet, Boat Launch

BrT	BkT	RbT	Sal	Tog	Smt	LmB	SmB	WhP	Csk	WhF	Pic
	✓						✓	✓			✓

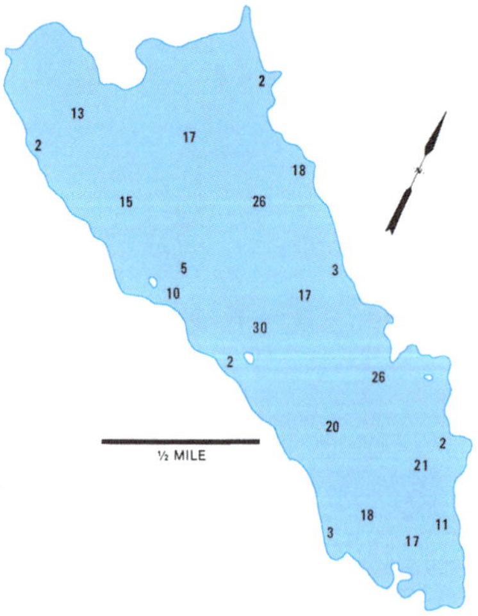

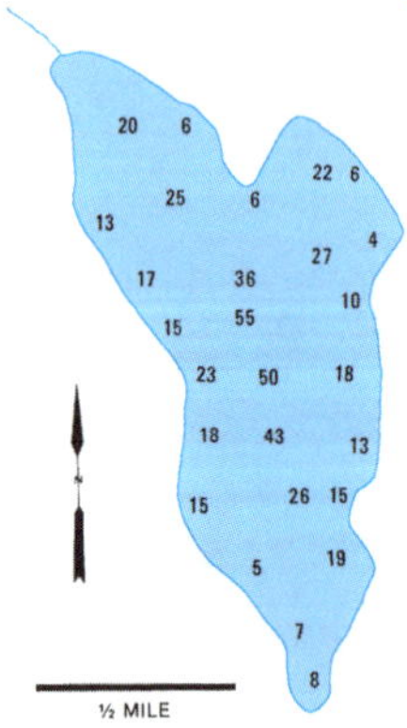

Upper Middle Branch Pond

Aurora
Maine Atlas
Map 24, A-4
Acres: 467
Max. Depth:
55 feet
Boat Launch

BrT	LmB
BkT ✓	SmB
RbT	WhP ✓
Sal ✓	Csk
Tog	WhF
Smt	Pic

Upper Hadlock Pond

Mt. Desert
Maine Atlas
Map 16, C-3
Acres: 35
Max. Depth:
37 feet

BrT ✓	LmB
BkT ✓	SmB
RbT	WhP
Sal	Csk
Tog	WhF
Smt ✓	Pic

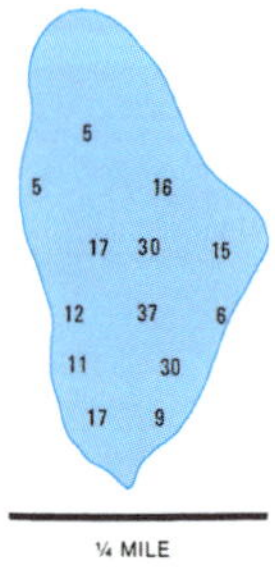

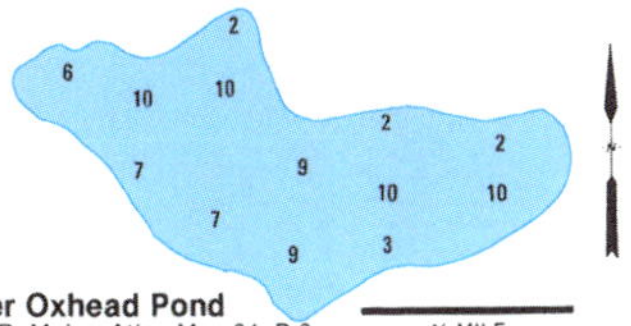

Upper Oxhead Pond
T40 MD, Maine Atlas Map 34, D-3
Acres: 87, Max. Depth: 10 feet

BrT	BkT	RbT	Sal	Tog	Smt	LmB	SmB	WhP	Csk	WhF	Pic
✓	✓										

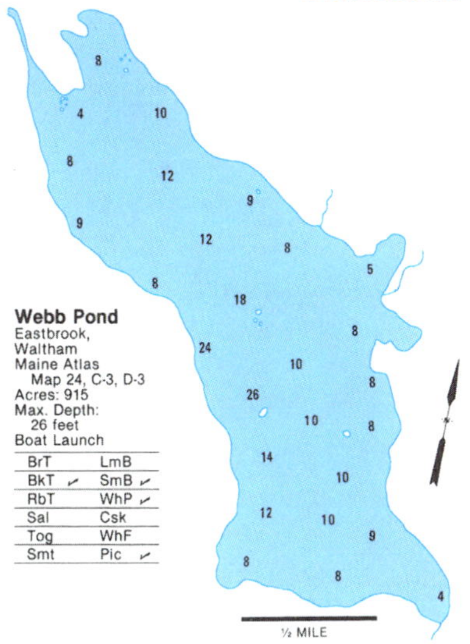

Webb Pond
Eastbrook,
Waltham
Maine Atlas
Map 24, C-3, D-3
Acres: 915
Max. Depth:
26 feet
Boat Launch

BrT		LmB	
BkT	✓	SmB	✓
RbT		WhP	✓
Sal		Csk	
Tog		WhF	
Smt		Pic	✓

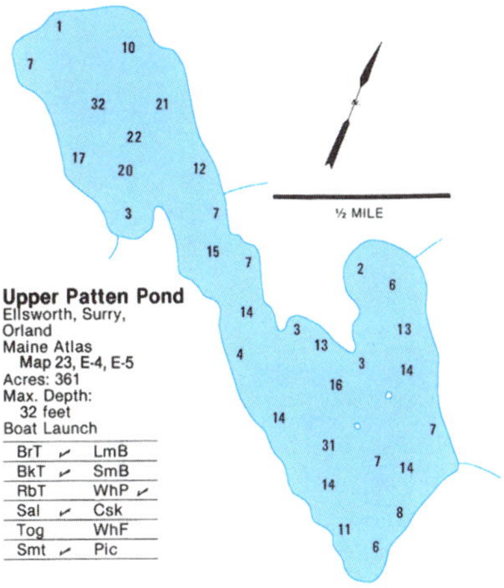

Upper Patten Pond
Ellsworth, Surry,
Orland
Maine Atlas
Map 23, E-4, E-5
Acres: 361
Max. Depth:
32 feet
Boat Launch

BrT	✓	LmB	
BkT	✓	SmB	
RbT		WhP	✓
Sal	✓	Csk	
Tog		WhF	
Smt	✓	Pic	

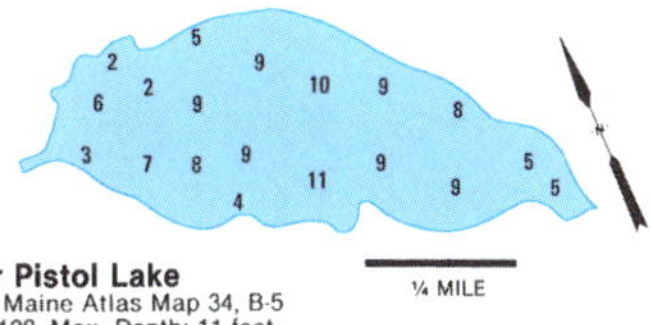

Upper Pistol Lake
T4 ND, Maine Atlas Map 34, B-5
Acres: 128, Max. Depth: 11 feet

BrT	BkT	RbT	Sal	Tog	Smt	LmB	SmB	WhP	Csk	WhF	Pic
	✓							✓			

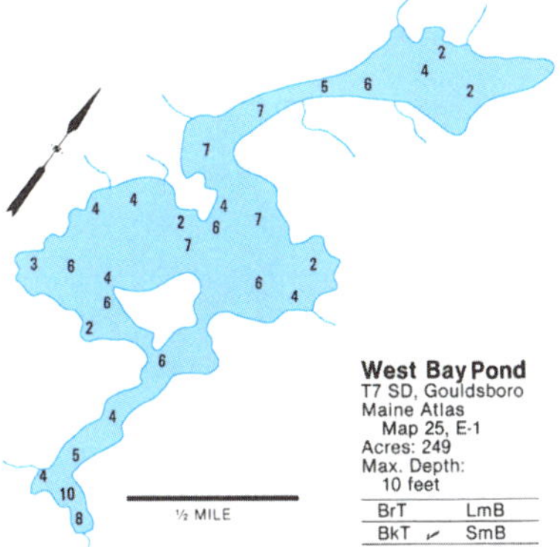

West Bay Pond
T7 SD, Gouldsboro
Maine Atlas
Map 25, E-1
Acres: 249
Max. Depth:
10 feet

BrT		LmB	
BkT	✓	SmB	
RbT		WhP	
Sal		Csk	
Tog		WhF	
Smt		Pic	

Upper Sabao Lake
T41 MD, Maine Atlas Map 35, D-1
Acres: 486, Max. Depth: 41 feet

BrT	BkT	RbT	Sal	Tog	Smt	LmB	SmB	WhP	Csk	WhF	Pic
	✓				✓			✓			

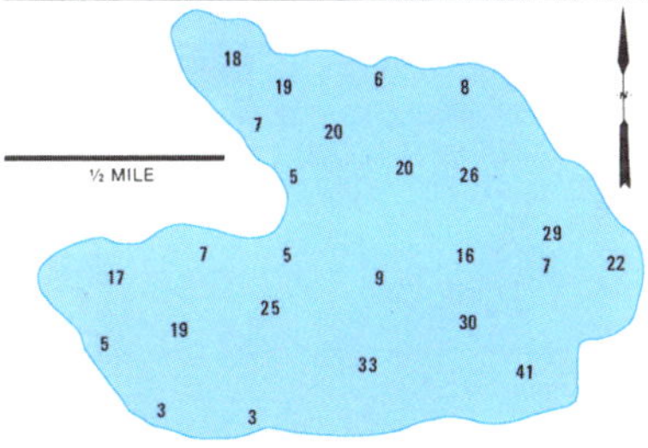

West Lake
T3 ND, T40 MD, Maine Atlas Map 34, C-4
Acres: 1,344, Max. Depth: 70 feet, Boat Launch

BrT	BkT	RbT	Sal	Tog	Smt	LmB	SmB	WhP	Csk	WhF	Pic
	✓		✓					✓			✓

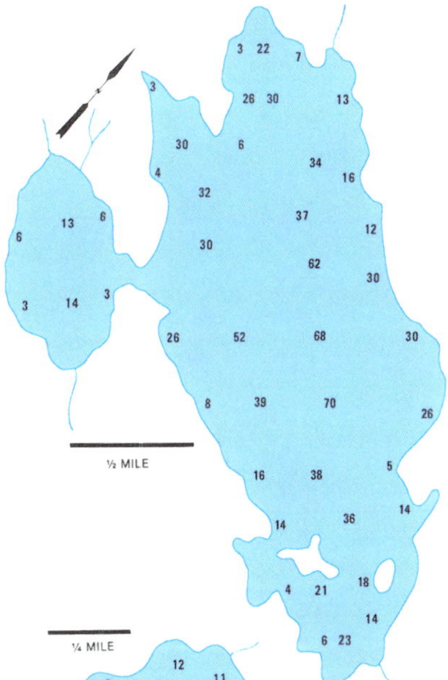

Upper Unknown Lake
T4 ND
Maine Atlas
Map 34, B-5
Map 35, B-1
Acres: 58
Max. Depth:
14 feet

BrT		LmB	
BkT		SmB	
RbT		WhP	
Sal		Csk	
Tog		WhF	
Smt		Pic	✓

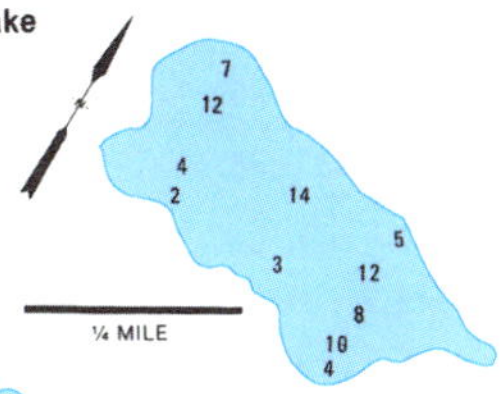

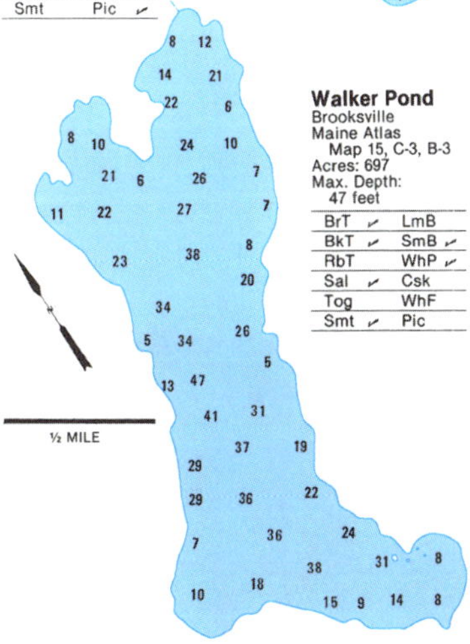

Walker Pond
Brooksville
Maine Atlas
Map 15, C-3, B-3
Acres: 697
Max. Depth:
47 feet

BrT	✓	LmB	
BkT	✓	SmB	✓
RbT		WhP	✓
Sal	✓	Csk	
Tog		WhF	
Smt	✓	Pic	

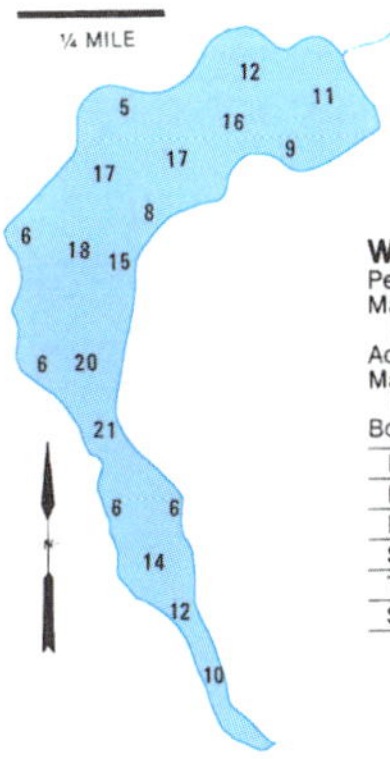

Wight Pond
Penobscot
Maine Atlas
Map 15, A-3
Acres: 135
Max. Depth:
21 feet
Boat Launch

BrT		LmB	✓
BkT		SmB	
RbT		WhP	✓
Sal		Csk	
Tog		WhF	
Smt		Pic	✓

Hancock

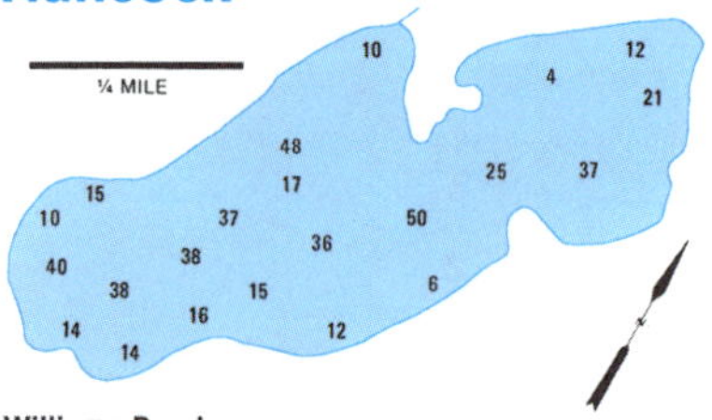

Williams Pond
Bucksport, Maine Atlas Map 23, D-2
Acres: 112, Max. Depth: 50 feet

BrT	BkT	RbT	Sal	Tog	Smt	LmB	SmB	WhP	Csk	WhF	Pic
	✓						✓	✓			✓

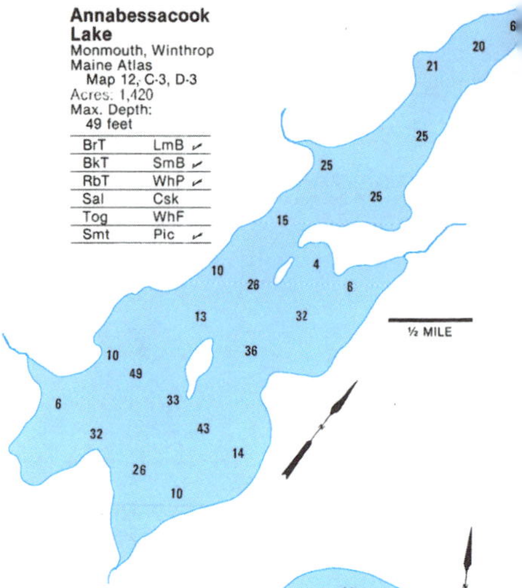

Annabessacook Lake
Monmouth, Winthrop
Maine Atlas
Map 12, C-3, D-3
Acres: 1,420
Max. Depth:
49 feet

BrT		LmB	✓
BkT		SmB	✓
RbT		WhP	✓
Sal		Csk	
Tog		WhF	
Smt		Pic	✓

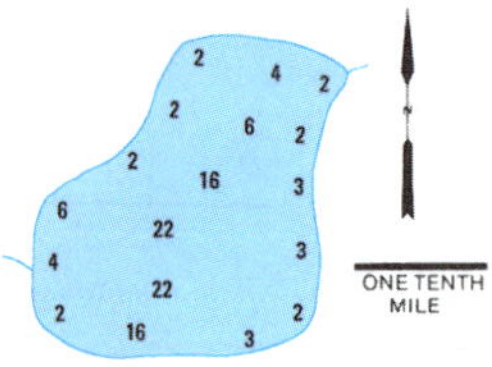

Williams Pond
T28 MD
Maine Atlas
Map 24, A-5
Acres: 19
Max. Depth:
22 feet

BrT		LmB	
BkT	✓	SmB	
RbT		WhP	
Sal		Csk	
Tog		WhF	
Smt		Pic	✓

Witchhole Pond
Bar Harbor
Maine Atlas
Map 16, B-4
Acres: 28
Max. Depth:
33 feet

BrT		LmB	
BkT	✓	SmB	
RbT		WhP	
Sal		Csk	
Tog		WhF	
Smt		Pic	

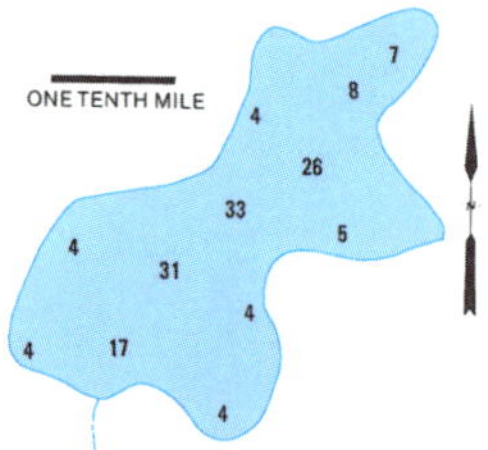

Basin Pond
Fayette
Maine Atlas
Map 12, A-2
Acres: 34
Max. Depth:
106 feet
Boat Launch

BrT		LmB	
BkT	✓	SmB	
RbT		WhP	
Sal		Csk	
Tog		WhF	
Smt	✓	Pic	

Comments: Splake.

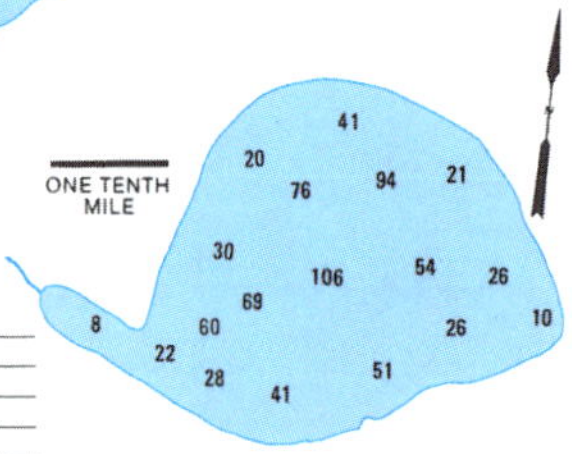

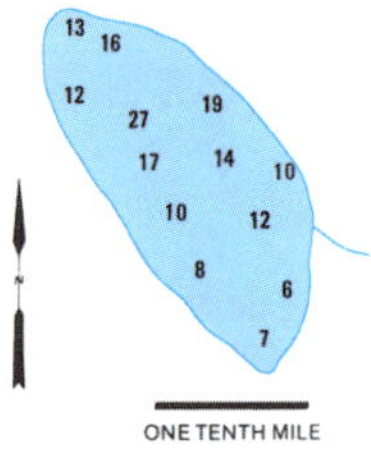

Youngs Pond
Otis
Maine Atlas
Map 24, C-1
Acres: 13
Max. Depth:
27 feet
Boat Launch

BrT		LmB	
BkT	✓	SmB	
RbT		WhP	
Sal		Csk	
Tog		WhF	
Smt		Pic	

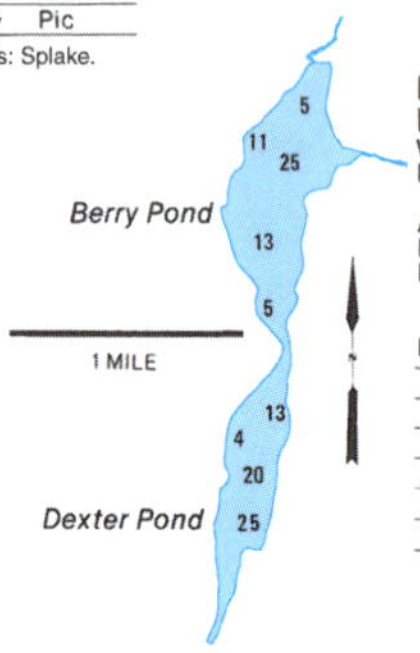

Berry and Dexter Ponds
Wayne, Winthrop
Maine Atlas
Map 12, B-2, C-2
Acres: Berry-170
Dexter-120
Max. Depth:
Berry-25 feet
Dexter-25 feet
Boat Launch

BrT		LmB	✓
BkT	✓	SmB	✓
RbT		WhP	✓
Sal		Csk	
Tog		WhF	
Smt		Pic	✓

Kennebec County

Anderson Pond
Augusta
Maine Atlas
Map 13, B-2
Acres: 12
Max. Depth:
33 feet

BrT		LmB	
BkT		SmB	
RbT		WhP	✓
Sal		Csk	
Tog		WhF	
Smt	✓	Pic	✓

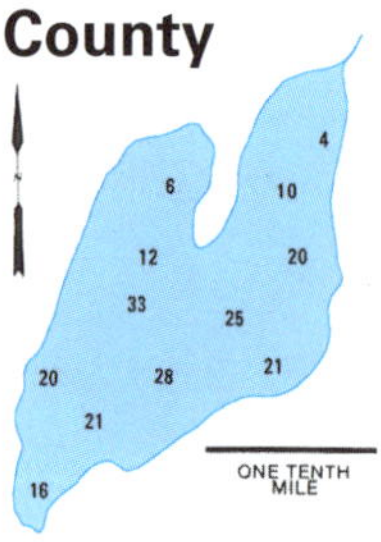

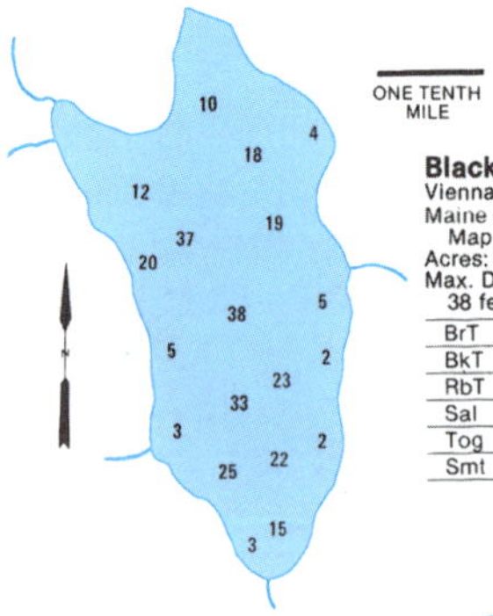

Black Pond
Vienna
Maine Atlas
Map 20, E-2
Acres: 37
Max. Depth:
38 feet

BrT		LmB	✓
BkT		SmB	
RbT		WhP	✓
Sal		Csk	
Tog		WhF	
Smt		Pic	✓

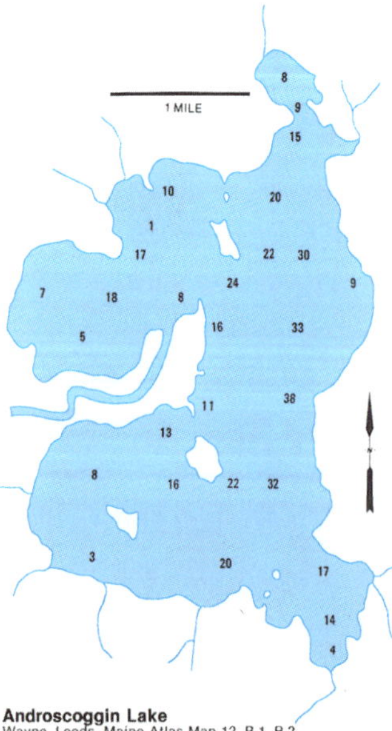

Androscoggin Lake
Wayne, Leeds, Maine Atlas Map 12, B-1, B-2
Acres: 3,826 Max. Depth: 38 feet, Boat Launch

BrT	BkT	RbT	Sal	Tog	Smt	LmB	SmB	WhP	Csk	WhF	Pic
✓	✓				✓	✓	✓	✓	✓		✓

Brainard Pond
Readfield
Maine Atlas
Map 12, B-3, B-4
Acres: 20
Max. Depth:
13 feet

BrT		LmB	✓
BkT		SmB	
RbT		WhP	
Sal		Csk	
Tog		WhF	
Smt		Pic	✓

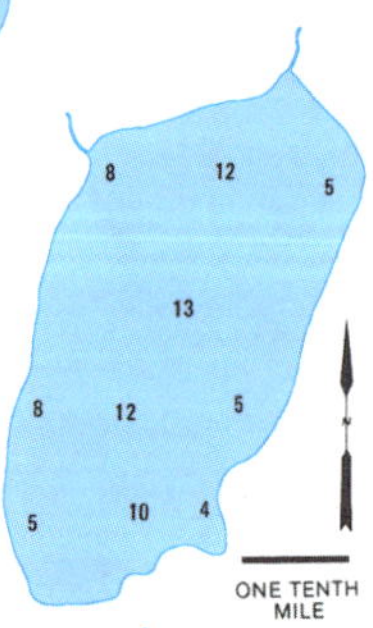

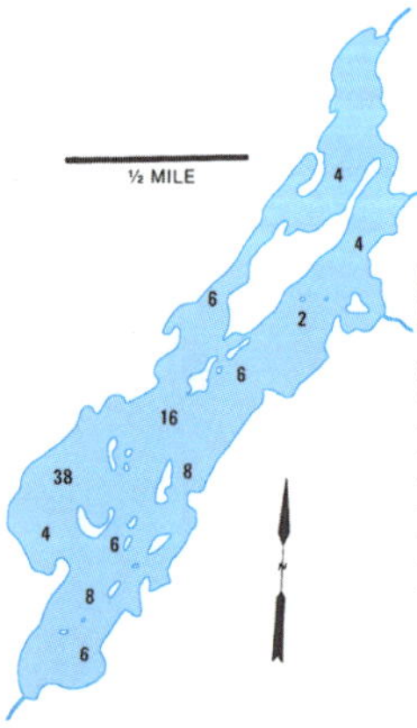

Branch Pond
China, Palermo
Maine Atlas
Map 13, A-4, B-4
Acres: 322
Max. Depth:
38 feet

BrT	✓	LmB	
BkT	✓	SmB	
RbT		WhP	✓
Sal		Csk	
Tog		WhF	
Smt		Pic	✓

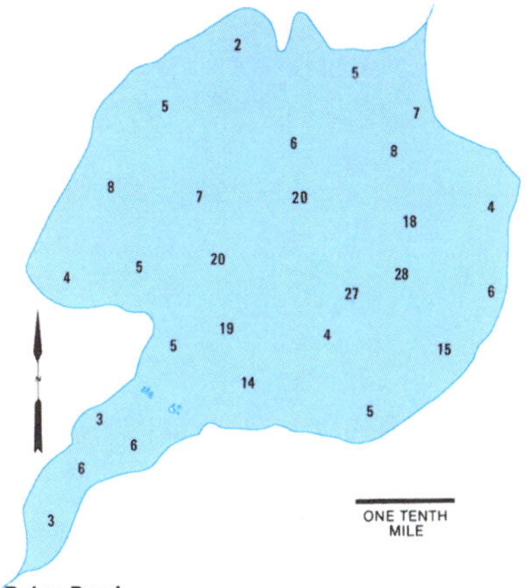

Buker Pond
Litchfield, Maine Atlas Map 12, D-3, E-3
Acres: 75, Max. Depth: 28 feet,

BrT	BkT	RbT	Sal	Tog	Smt	LmB	SmB	WhP	Csk	WhF	Pic
✓	✓					✓	✓	✓			✓

Cobbosseecontee Lake
Winthrop,
Manchester,
Monmouth,
West Gardiner,
Litchfield
Maine Atlas
Map 12, C-3
Acres: 5,543
Max. Depth:
100 feet
Boat Launch

BrT	✓	LmB	✓
BkT	✓	SmB	✓
RbT		WhP	✓
Sal	✓	Csk	
Tog		WhF	
Smt		Pic	✓

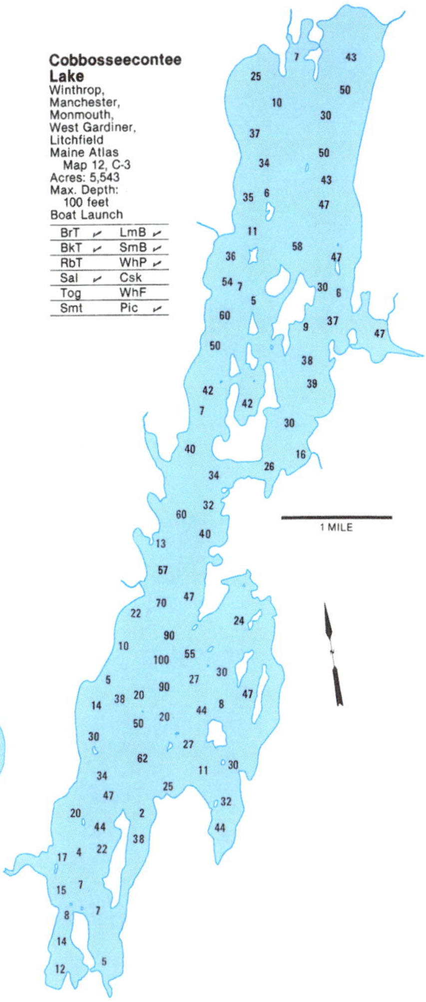

Burgess Pond
Fayette
Maine Atlas
Map 12, A-1
Acres: 24
Max. Depth:
26 feet

BrT		LmB	
BkT		SmB	
RbT		WhP	
Sal		Csk	
Tog		WhF	
Smt		Pic	✓

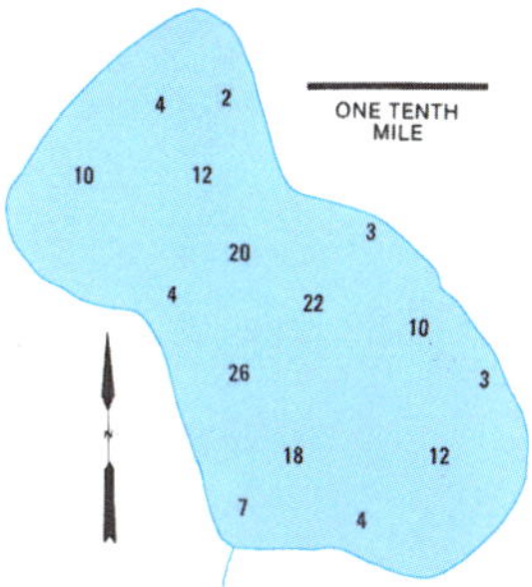

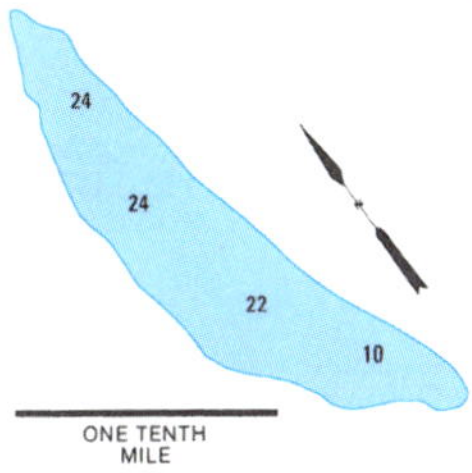

Chamberlain Pond
Belgrade
Maine Atlas
Map 12, B-4, B-5
Acres: 6
Max. Depth:
24 feet

BrT	✓	LmB	
BkT	✓	SmB	
RbT		WhP	
Sal		Csk	
Tog		WhF	
Smt		Pic	

China Lake
China, Vassalboro
Maine Atlas
Map 13, A-3
Acres: 3,922
Max. Depth:
85 feet
Boat Launch

BrT	✓	LmB	✓
BkT	✓	SmB	✓
RbT		WhP	✓
Sal	✓	Csk	
Tog	✓	WhF	
Smt	✓	Pic	✓

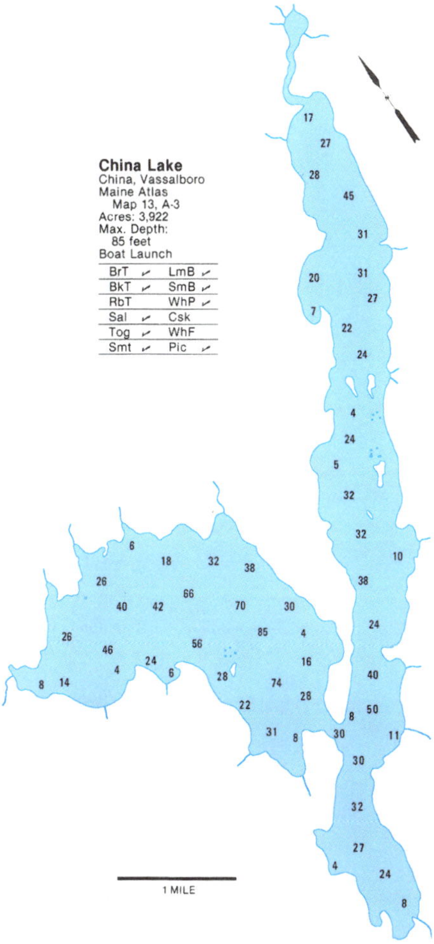

Cochnewagan Pond
Monmouth
Maine Atlas
Map 12, D-2
Acres: 385
Max. Depth:
28 feet
Boat Launch

BrT	✓	LmB	✓
BkT	✓	SmB	✓
RbT		WhP	✓
Sal		Csk	
Tog		WhF	
Smt		Pic	✓

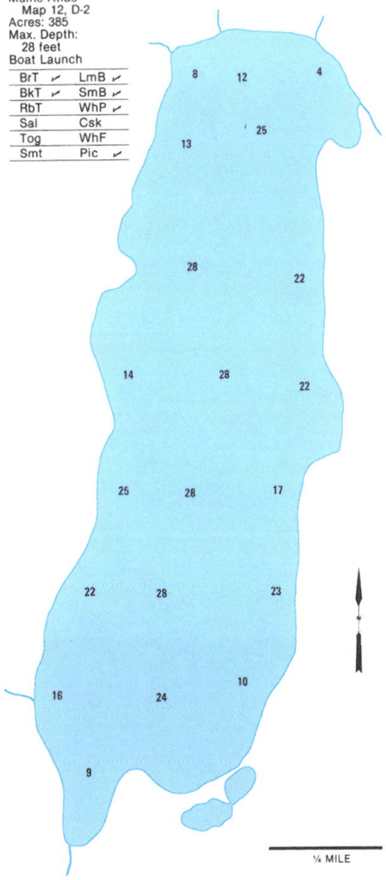

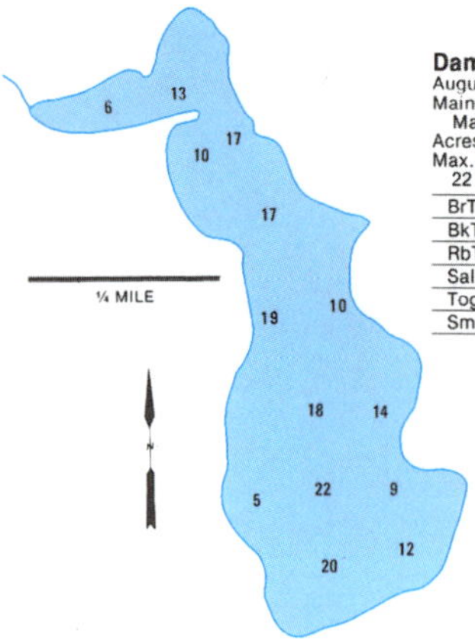

Dam Pond
Augusta
Maine Atlas
Map 13, B-1
Acres: 87
Max. Depth:
22 feet

BrT		LmB	✓
BkT		SmB	✓
RbT		WhP	✓
Sal		Csk	
Tog		WhF	
Smt		Pic	✓

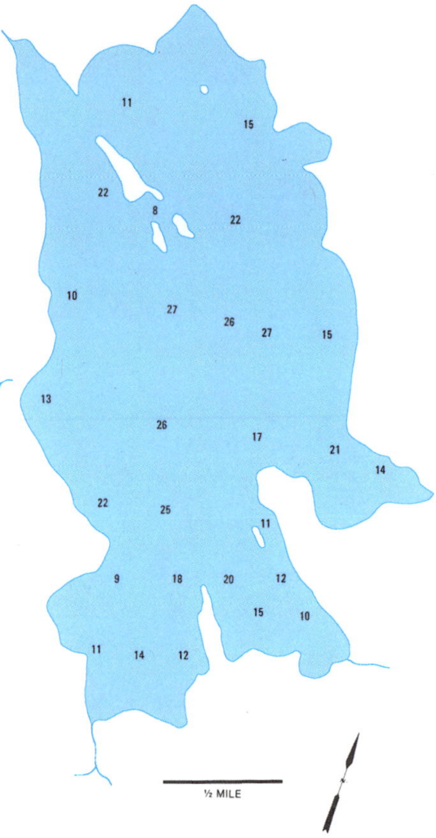

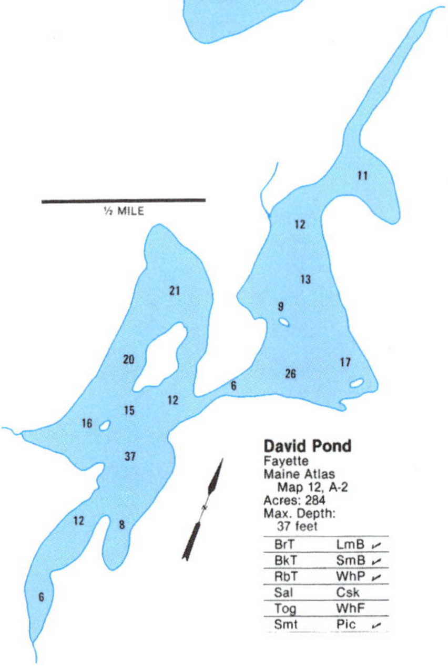

David Pond
Fayette
Maine Atlas
Map 12, A-2
Acres: 284
Max. Depth:
37 feet

BrT		LmB	✓
BkT		SmB	✓
RbT		WhP	✓
Sal		Csk	
Tog		WhF	
Smt		Pic	✓

East Pond
Oakland, Smithfield, Maine Atlas Map 20, D-5
Acres: 1,823, Max. Depth: 27 feet, Boat Launch

BrT	BkT	RbT	Sal	Tog	Smt	LmB	SmB	WhP	Csk	WhF	Pic
✓	✓				✓	✓	✓	✓			✓

Desert Pond
Mt. Vernon
Maine Atlas
Map 12, A-2, A-3
Acres: 23
Max. Depth:
36 feet
Boat Launch

BrT		LmB	
BkT	✓	SmB	
RbT		WhP	
Sal		Csk	
Tog		WhF	
Smt		Pic	

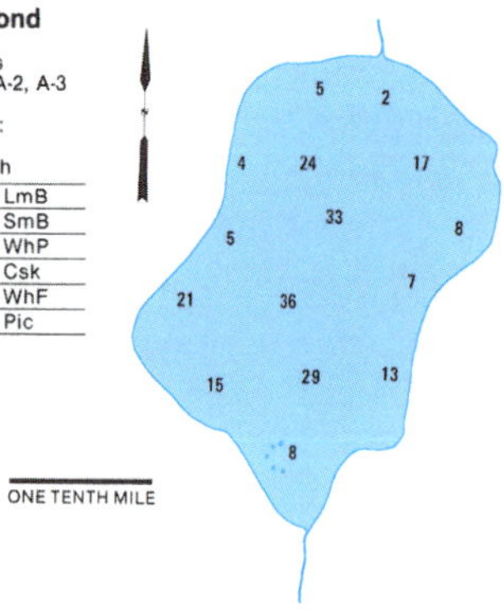

Echo Lake
Mt. Vernon,
Fayette,
Readfield
Maine Atlas
Map 12, A-2, B-2
Acres: 1,061
Max. Depth:
117 feet
Boat Launch

BrT		LmB	✓
BkT	✓	SmB	✓
RbT		WhP	✓
Sal	✓	Csk	✓
Tog	✓	WhF	
Smt	✓	Pic	✓

Comments: Splake.

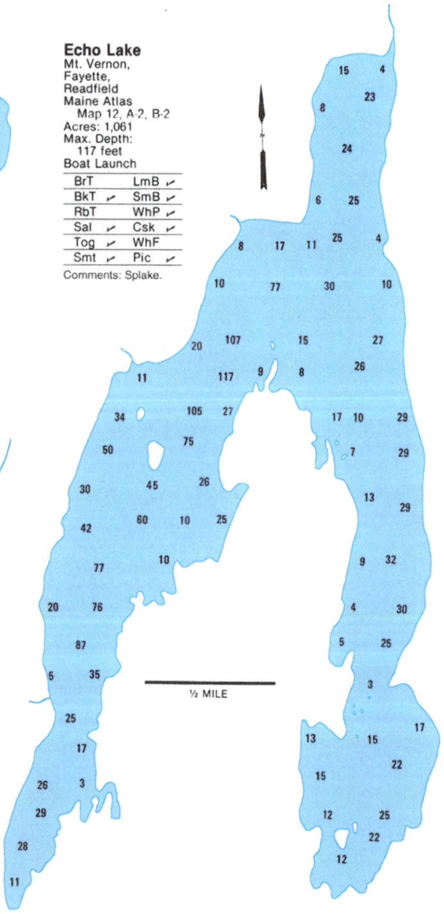

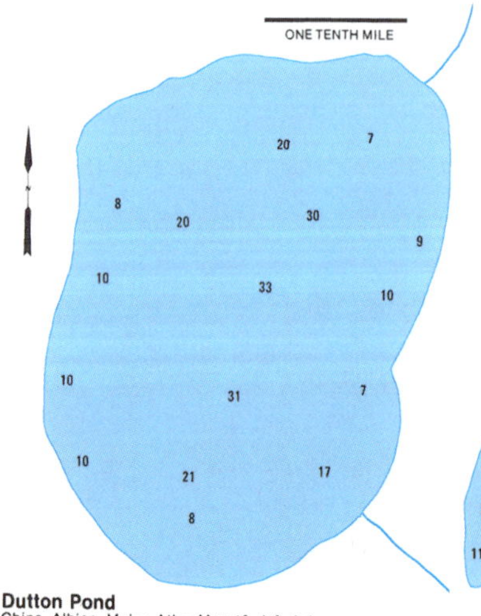

Dutton Pond
China, Albion, Maine Atlas Map 13, A-3, A-4
Acres: 56, Max. Depth: 33 feet

BrT	BkT	RbT	Sal	Tog	Smt	LmB	SmB	WhP	Csk	WhF	Pic
						✓	✓	✓			✓

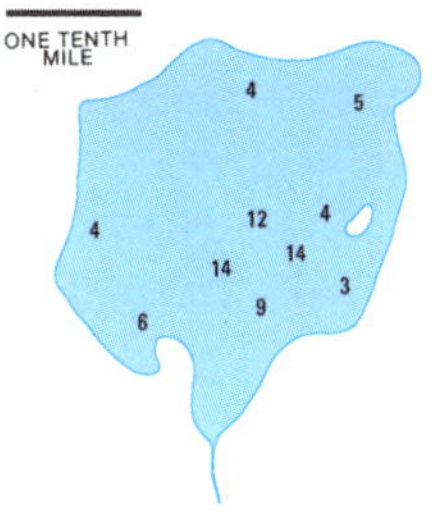

Evans Pond

China
Maine Atlas
Map 13, A-3
Acres: 19
Max. Depth:
14 feet

BrT		LmB	
BkT		SmB	
RbT		WhP	
Sal		Csk	
Tog		WhF	
Smt		Pic	✓

Great Pond

Belgrade, Rome, Maine Atlas Map 20, E-5, Map 12, A-4, A-5
Acres: 8,239, Max. Depth: 69 feet, Boat Launch

BrT	BkT	RbT	Sal	Tog	Smt	LmB	SmB	WhP	Csk	WhF	Pic
✓	✓		✓		✓	✓	✓	✓			✓

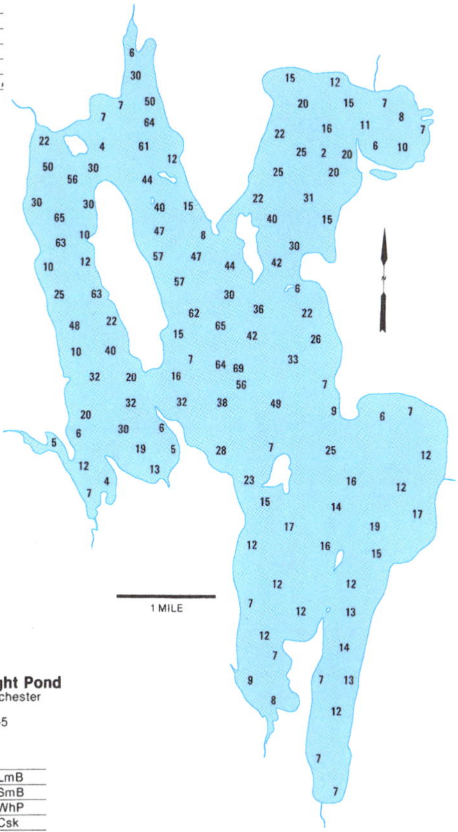

Fairbanks Pond

Manchester
Maine Atlas
Map 12, B-4 B-5
Acres: 14
Max. Depth:
35 feet

BrT	✓	LmB	
BkT	✓	SmB	
RbT		WhP	✓
Sal		Csk	
Tog		WhF	
Smt		Pic	✓

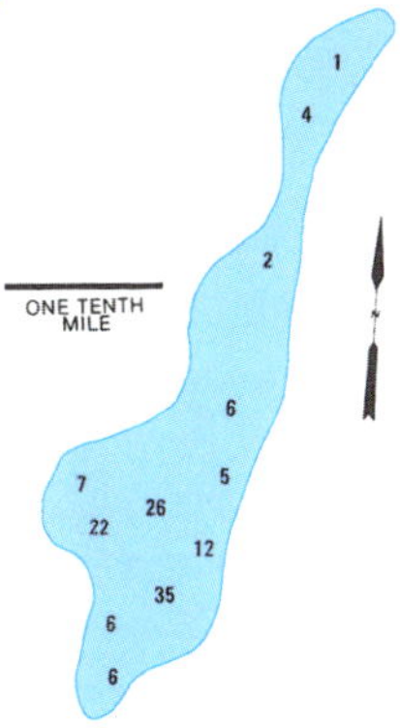

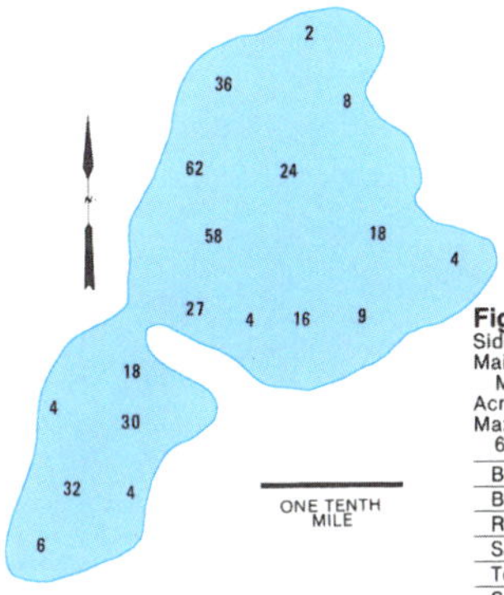

Figure Eight Pond

Sidney, Manchester
Maine Atlas
Map 12, B-5
Acres: 29
Max. Depth:
62 feet

BrT	✓	LmB	
BkT		SmB	
RbT		WhP	
Sal		Csk	
Tog		WhF	
Smt		Pic	

Flying Pond

Vienna
Maine Atlas
Map 20, E-3
Acres: 360
Max. Depth:
80 feet
Boat Launch

BrT	✓	LmB	✓
BkT	✓	SmB	✓
RbT		WhP	
Sal	✓	Csk	✓
Tog	✓	WhF	
Smt	✓	Pic	✓

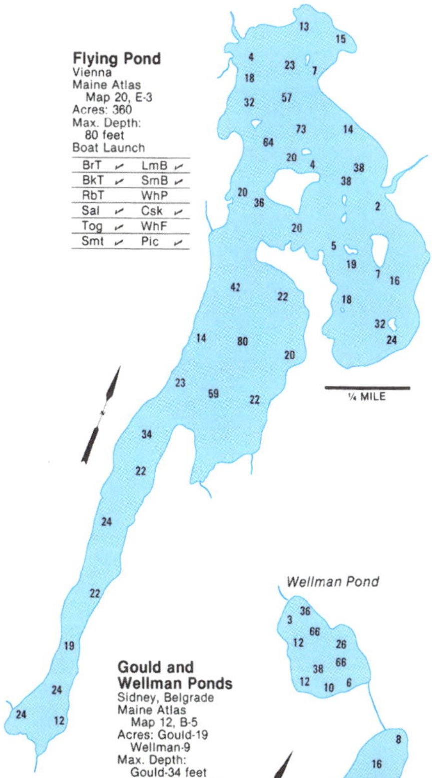

Greeley Pond

Augusta
Maine Atlas
Map 13, C-1
Acres: 51
Max. Depth:
15 feet

BrT		LmB	✓
BkT		SmB	✓
RbT		WhP	✓
Sal		Csk	
Tog		WhF	
Smt		Pic	✓

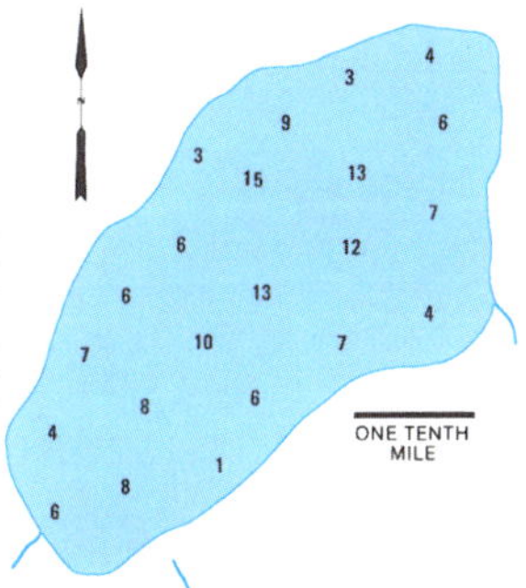

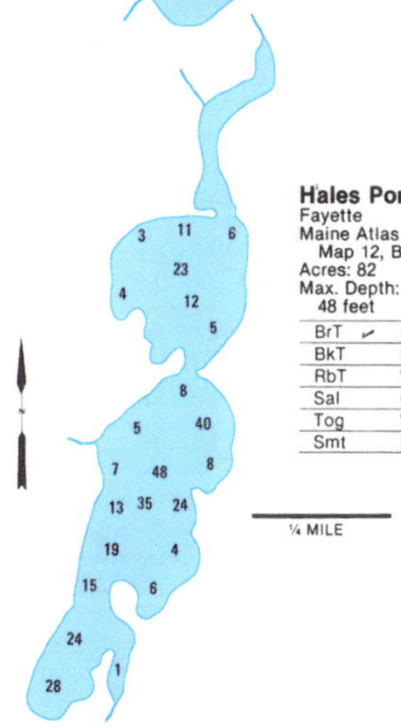

Hales Pond

Fayette
Maine Atlas
Map 12, B-2
Acres: 82
Max. Depth:
48 feet

BrT	✓	LmB	
BkT		SmB	✓
RbT		WhP	✓
Sal		Csk	
Tog		WhF	
Smt		Pic	✓

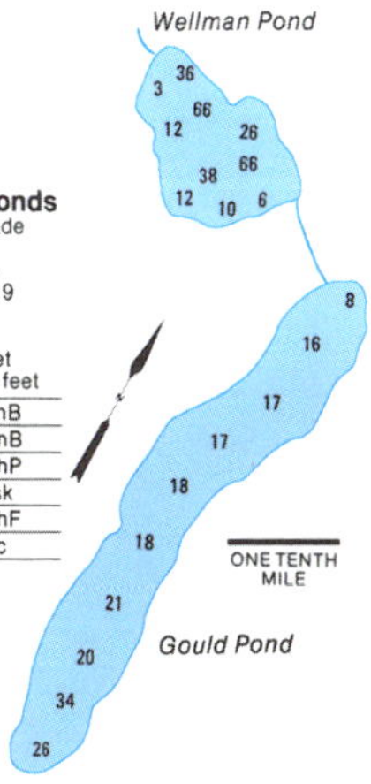

Gould and Wellman Ponds

Sidney, Belgrade
Maine Atlas
Map 12, B-5
Acres: Gould-19
Wellman-9
Max. Depth:
Gould-34 feet
Wellman-66 feet

BrT	✓	LmB	
BkT	✓	SmB	
RbT		WhP	
Sal		Csk	
Tog		WhF	
Smt		Pic	

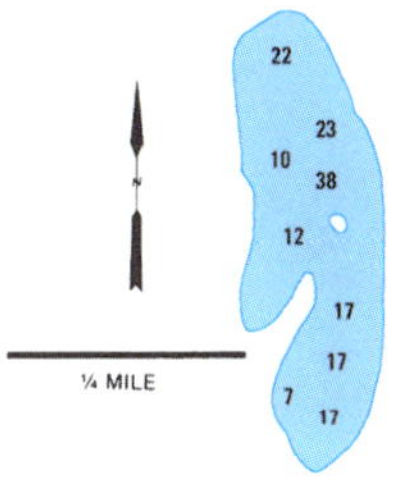

Hamilton Pond

Belgrade
Maine Atlas
Map 12, A-4, A-5
Acres: 19
Max. Depth:
38 feet

BrT	✓	LmB	
BkT		SmB	
RbT		WhP	
Sal		Csk	
Tog		WhF	
Smt		Pic	✓

Kennebec

Hopkins Pond

Mt. Vernon
Maine Atlas
Map 12, A-3
Acres: 25
Max. Depth:
22 feet

BrT		LmB	✓
BkT		SmB	✓
RbT		WhP	
Sal		Csk	
Tog		WhF	
Smt		Pic	✓

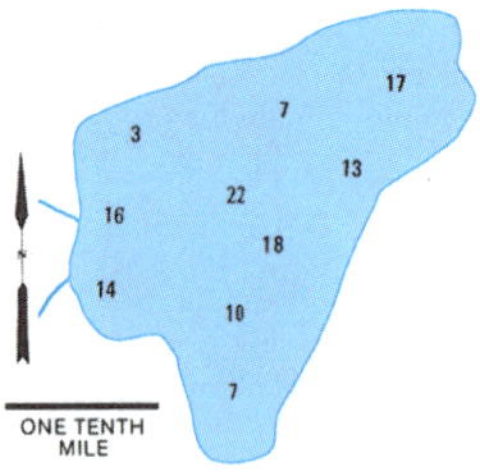

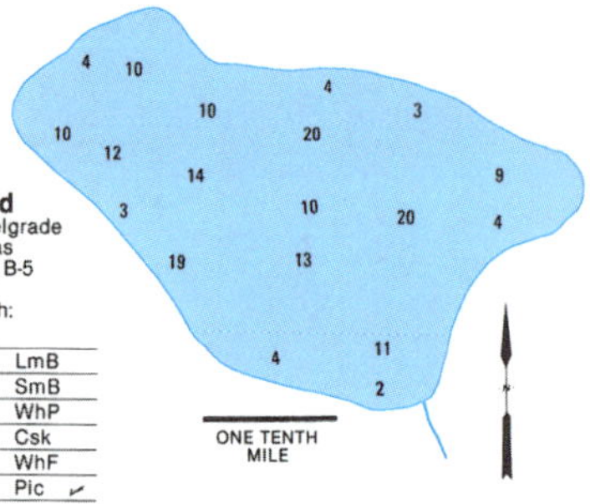

Joe Pond

Sidney, Belgrade
Maine Atlas
Map 12, B-5
Acres: 40
Max. Depth:
20 feet

BrT		LmB	
BkT		SmB	
RbT		WhP	
Sal		Csk	
Tog		WhF	
Smt		Pic	✓

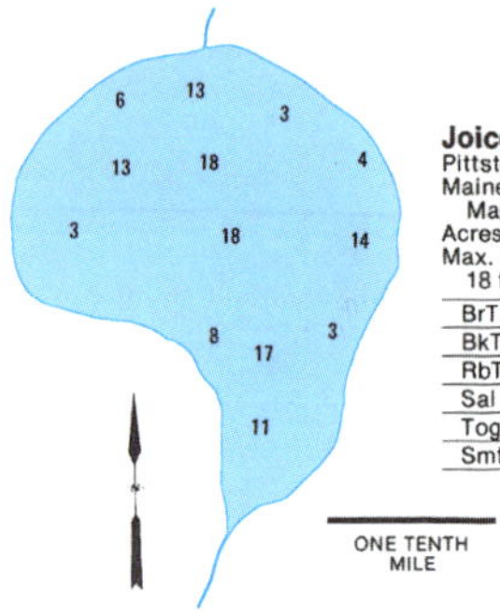

Hutchinson Pond

Farmingdale,
Manchester
Maine Atlas
Map 12, C-4, D-4
Acres: 100
Max. Depth:
24 feet

BrT		LmB	✓
BkT		SmB	✓
RbT		WhP	✓
Sal		Csk	
Tog		WhF	
Smt		Pic	✓

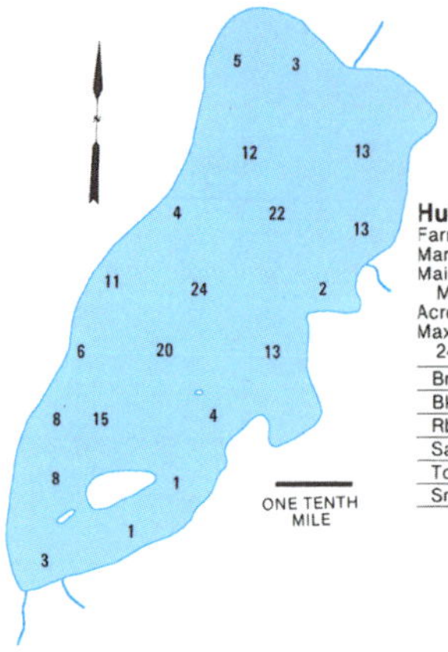

Joice Pond

Pittston
Maine Atlas
Map 13, D-1, D-2
Acres: 22
Max. Depth:
18 feet

BrT		LmB	
BkT		SmB	
RbT		WhP	✓
Sal		Csk	
Tog		WhF	
Smt		Pic	✓

Ingham Pond

Mt. Vernon
Maine Atlas
Map 12, A-3
Acres: 50
Max. Depth:
19 feet

BrT		LmB	✓
BkT		SmB	✓
RbT		WhP	✓
Sal	✓	Csk	
Tog		WhF	
Smt		Pic	✓

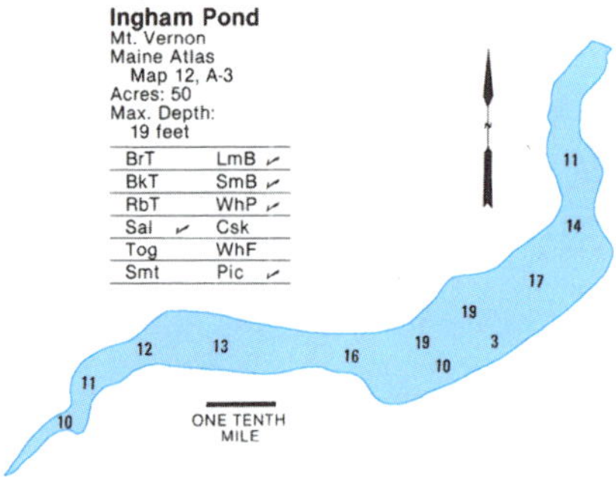

Kezar Pond

Winthrop
Maine Atlas
Map 12, C-3, C-4
Acres: 18
Max. Depth:
23 feet

BrT		LmB	✓
BkT		SmB	✓
RbT		WhP	✓
Sal		Csk	
Tog		WhF	
Smt		Pic	✓

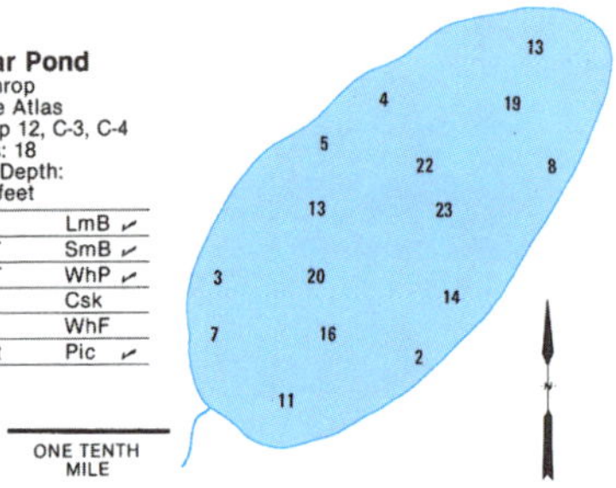

Jamies Pond

Manchester,
Farmingdale
Maine Atlas
Map 12, C-4
Acres: 107
Max. Depth:
75 feet
Boat Launch

BrT		LmB	✓
BkT	✓	SmB	✓
RbT		WhP	✓
Sal		Csk	
Tog		WhF	
Smt	✓	Pic	✓

Comments: Splake.

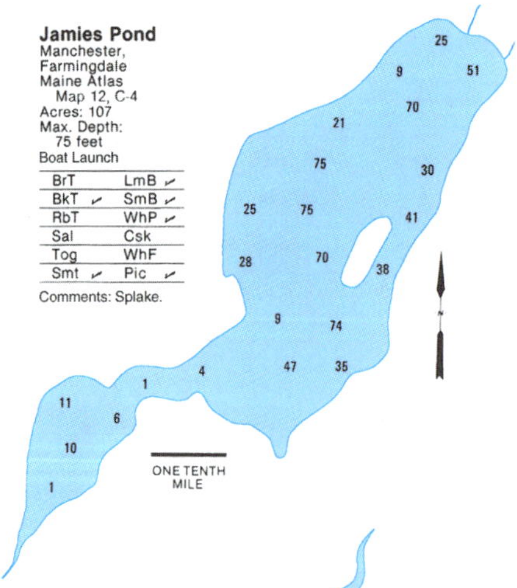

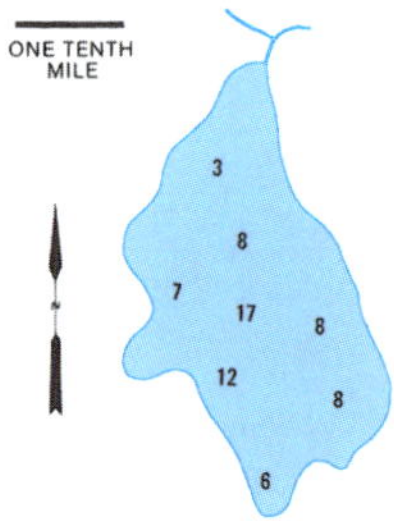

Kidder Pond

Vienna
Maine Atlas
Map 20, E-3
Acres: 19
Max. Depth:
17 feet

BrT		LmB	
BkT	✓	SmB	
RbT		WhP	
Sal		Csk	
Tog		WhF	
Smt		Pic	✓

Kimball Pond

Vienna, New Sharon
Maine Atlas
Map 20, E-3
Acres: 25
Max. Depth:
19 feet
Boat Launch

BrT		LmB	
BkT	✓	SmB	
RbT		WhP	
Sal		Csk	
Tog		WhF	
Smt		Pic	

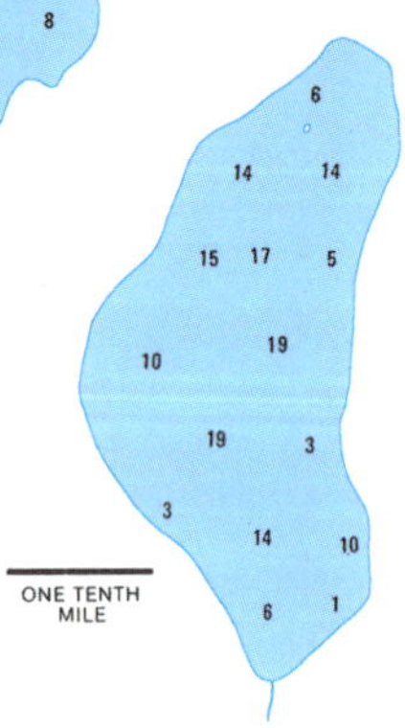

Jimmy Pond

Litchfield
Maine Atlas
Map 12, E-2, E-3
Acres: 44
Max. Depth:
32 feet

BrT	✓	LmB	✓
BkT	✓	SmB	✓
RbT		WhP	✓
Sal		Csk	
Tog		WhF	
Smt		Pic	

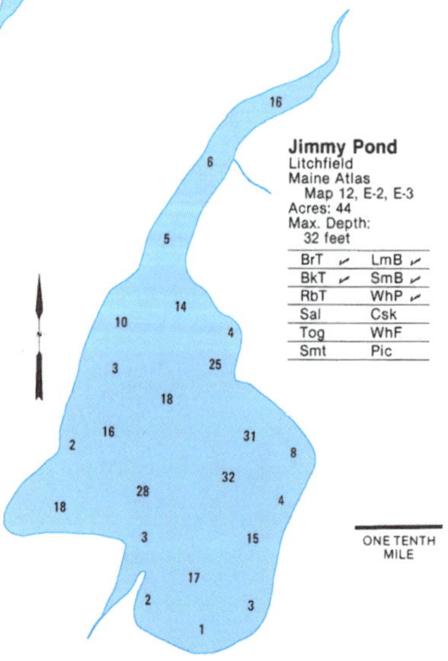

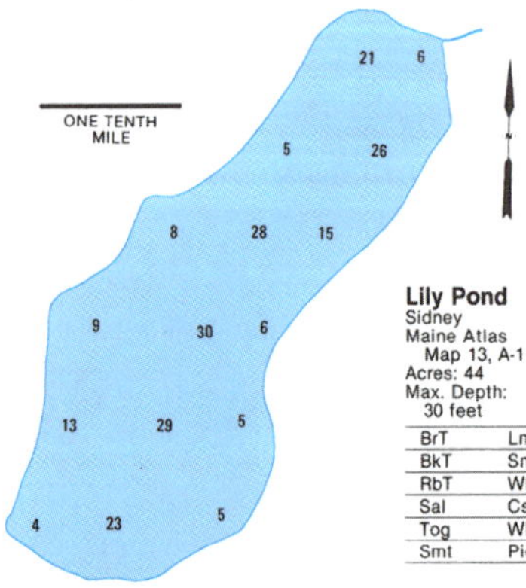

Lily Pond

Sidney
Maine Atlas
Map 13, A-1
Acres: 44
Max. Depth:
30 feet

BrT		LmB	✓
BkT		SmB	
RbT		WhP	✓
Sal		Csk	
Tog		WhF	
Smt		Pic	✓

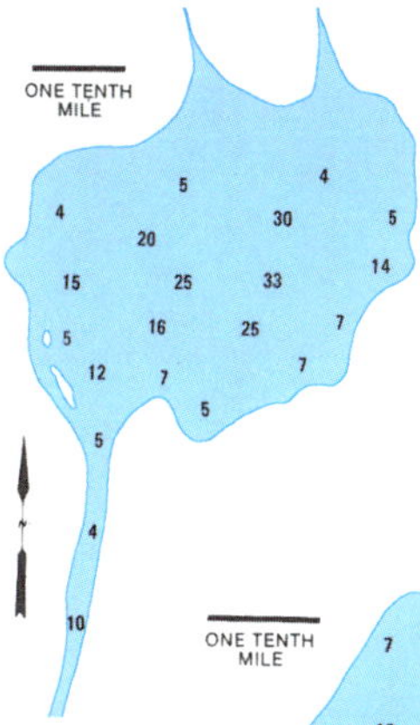

Little Cobbosseecontee Lake
Winthrop
Maine Atlas
Map 12, C-4
Acres: 74
Max. Depth:
33 feet

BrT		LmB	✓
BkT		SmB	✓
RbT		WhP	✓
Sal		Csk	
Tog		WhF	
Smt		Pic	✓

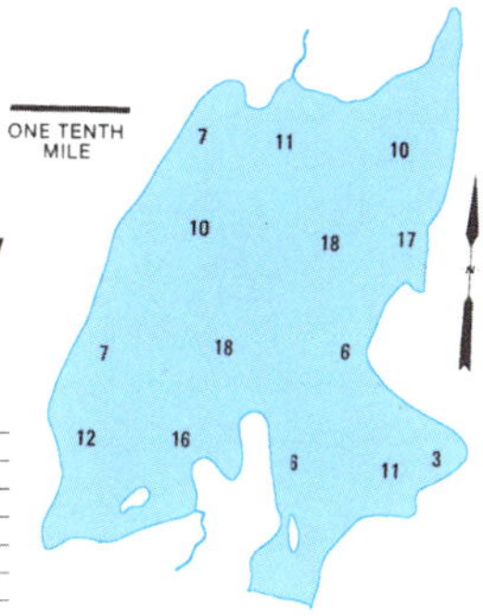

Little Purgatory Pond
Litchfield
Maine Atlas
Map 12, D-3
Acres: 44
Max. Depth:
18 feet

BrT	✓	LmB	✓
BkT		SmB	✓
RbT		WhP	✓
Sal		Csk	
Tog		WhF	
Smt		Pic	✓

Long Pond
Windsor, Somerville
Maine Atlas
Map 13, C-3
Acres: 747
Max. Depth:
16 feet

BrT		LmB	✓
BkT		SmB	✓
RbT		WhP	✓
Sal	✓	Csk	
Tog		WhF	
Smt		Pic	✓

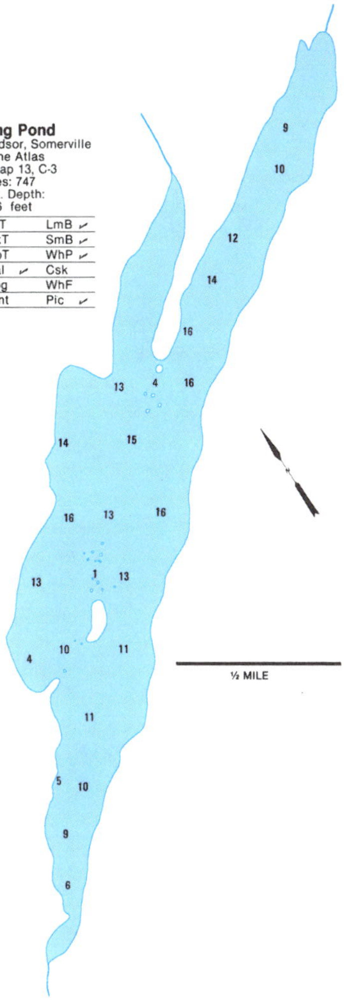

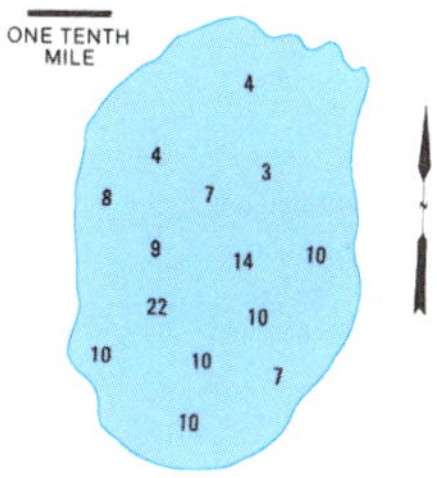

Little Togus Pond
Augusta
Maine Atlas
Map 13, C-2
Acres: 93
Max. Depth:
22 feet

BrT		LmB	✓
BkT		SmB	✓
RbT		WhP	✓
Sal		Csk	
Tog		WhF	
Smt		Pic	✓

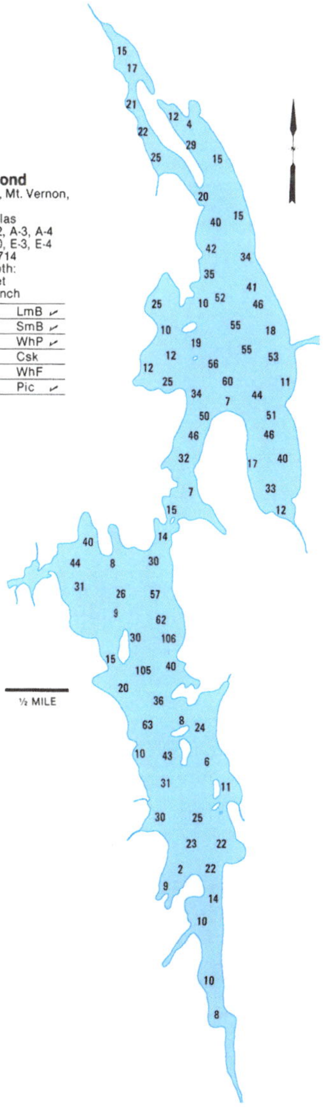

Long Pond
Belgrade, Mt. Vernon, Rome
Maine Atlas
Map 12, A-3, A-4
Map 20, E-3, E-4
Acres: 2,714
Max. Depth:
106 feet
Boat Launch

BrT		LmB	✓
BkT	✓	SmB	✓
RbT		WhP	✓
Sal	✓	Csk	
Tog		WhF	
Smt	✓	Pic	✓

Loon Pond
Litchfield
Maine Atlas
Map 12, E-3
Acres: 26
Max. Depth:
20 feet

BrT		LmB	
BkT		SmB	
RbT		WhP	✓
Sal		Csk	
Tog		WhF	
Smt		Pic	✓

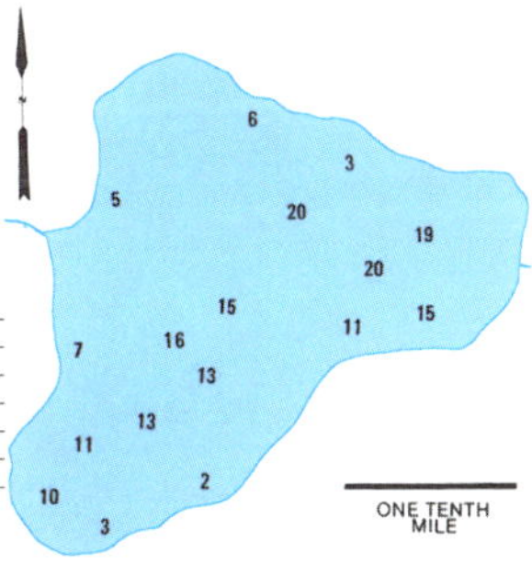

Lovejoy Pond
Albion
Maine Atlas
Map 21, E-4
Acres: 324
Max. Depth:
32 feet

BrT		LmB	✓
BkT		SmB	✓
RbT		WhP	✓
Sal		Csk	
Tog		WhF	
Smt		Pic	✓

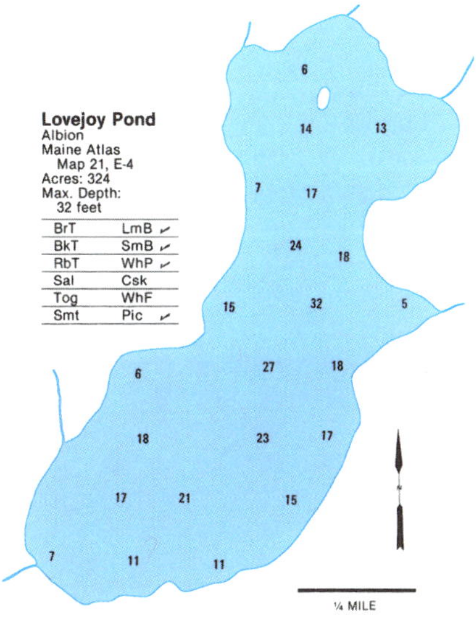

Kennebec

Lovejoy Pond
Fayette,
Readfield,
Wayne
Maine Atlas
Map 12, B-2
Acres: 366
Max. Depth:
22 feet

Species		Species	
BrT		LmB	✓
BkT	✓	SmB	✓
RbT		WhP	✓
Sal		Csk	
Tog		WhF	
Smt		Pic	✓

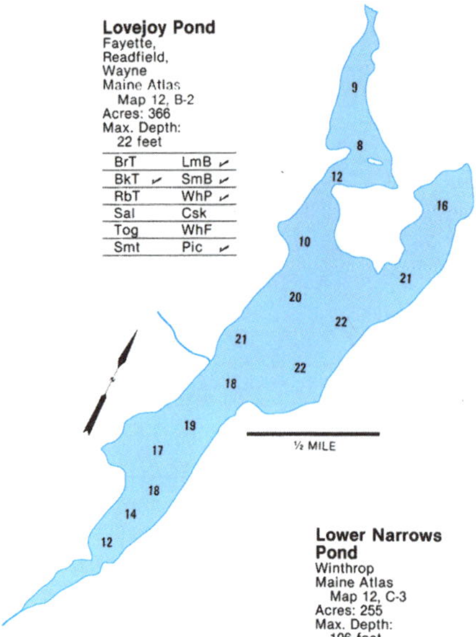

Messalonskee Lake
Belgrade, Sidney
Oakland
Maine Atlas
Map 12, A-5
Map 20, E-5
Map 21, E-1
Acres: 3,510
Max. Depth:
113 feet
Boat Launch

Species		Species	
BrT	✓	LmB	✓
BkT	✓	SmB	✓
RbT		WhP	✓
Sal	✓	Csk	
Tog	✓	WhF	
Smt	✓	Pic	✓

Comments: Splake.

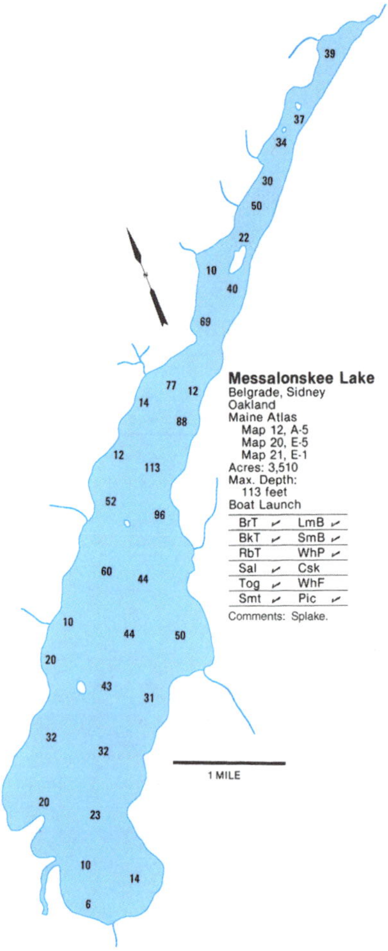

Lower Narrows Pond
Winthrop
Maine Atlas
Map 12, C-3
Acres: 255
Max. Depth:
106 feet

Species		Species	
BrT	✓	LmB	✓
BkT	✓	SmB	✓
RbT		WhP	✓
Sal	✓	Csk	
Tog	✓	WhF	
Smt	✓	Pic	✓

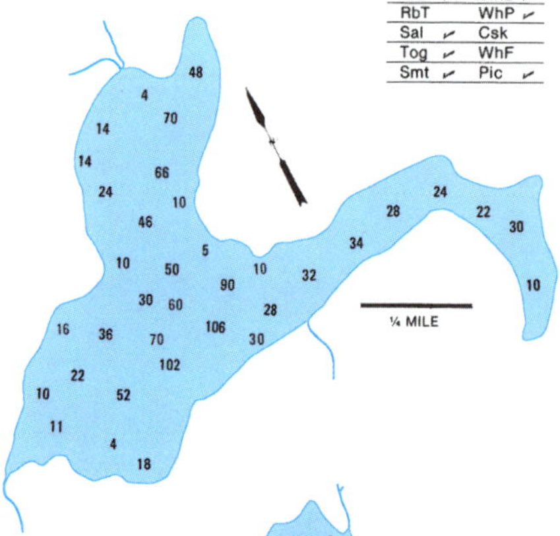

Mill Pond
Readfield
Maine Atlas
Map 12, B-3, B-4
Acres: 12
Max. Depth:
8 feet

Species		Species	
BrT		LmB	✓
BkT		SmB	
RbT		WhP	✓
Sal		Csk	
Tog		WhF	
Smt		Pic	✓

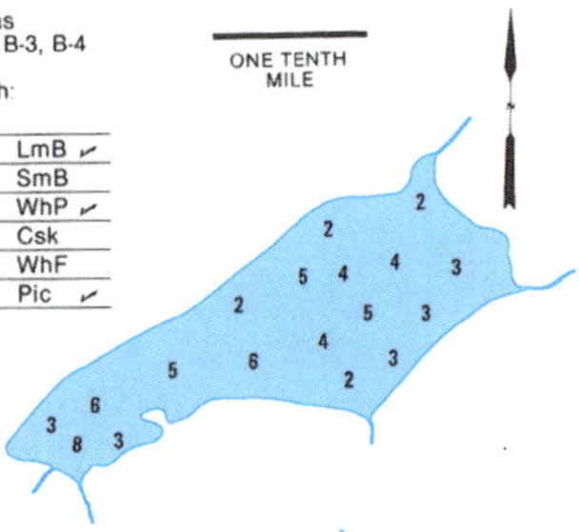

Maranacook Lake
Readfield, Winthrop
Maine Atlas
Map 12, B-3
Acres: 1,673
Max. Depth:
128 feet
Boat Launch

Species		Species	
BrT	✓	LmB	✓
BkT	✓	SmB	✓
RbT		WhP	✓
Sal	✓	Csk	
Tog	✓	WhF	
Smt	✓	Pic	✓

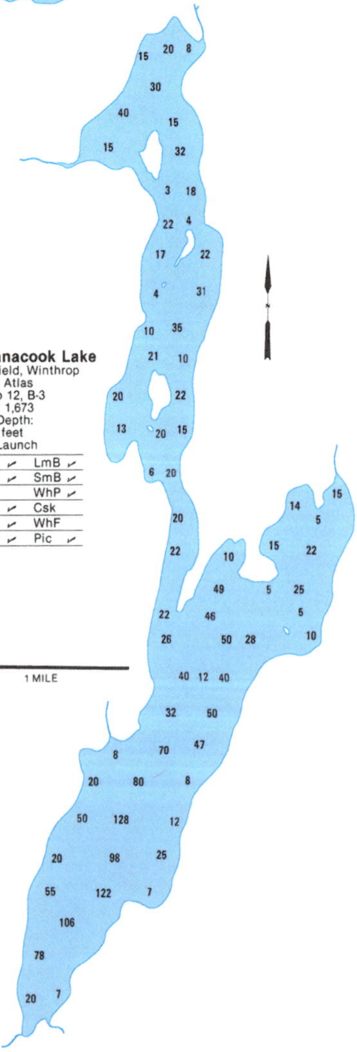

Minnehonk Lake
Mt. Vernon
Maine Atlas
Map 12, A-2
Acres: 99
Max. Depth:
73 feet

Species		Species	
BrT	✓	LmB	✓
BkT	✓	SmB	✓
RbT		WhP	
Sal	✓	Csk	✓
Tog	✓	WhF	
Smt	✓	Pic	✓

Coments: Splake.

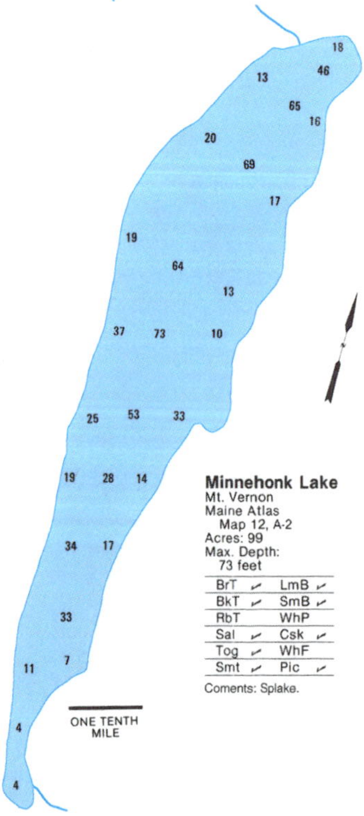

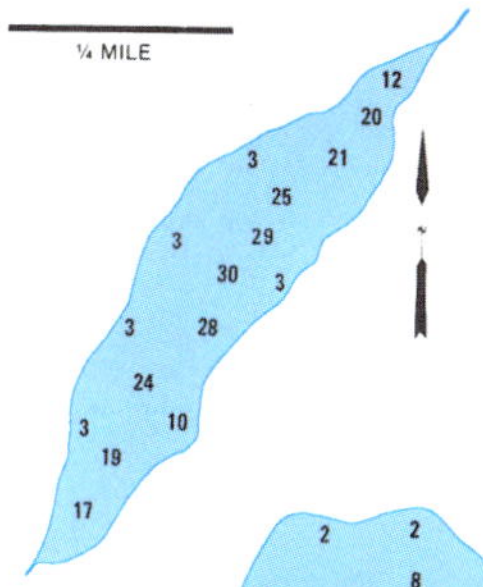

Moody Pond
Windsor
Maine Atlas
Map 13, C-2
Acres: 32
Max. Depth:
30 feet

BrT		LmB	
BkT		SmB	
RbT		WhP	
Sal		Csk	
Tog		WhF	
Smt	✓	Pic	✓

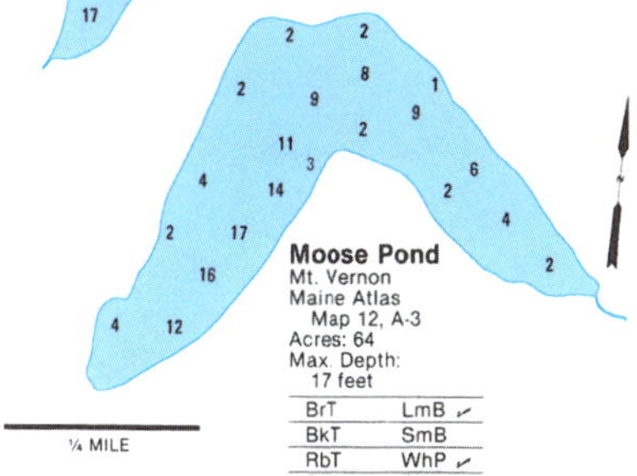

Moose Pond
Mt. Vernon
Maine Atlas
Map 12, A-3
Acres: 64
Max. Depth:
17 feet

BrT		LmB	✓
BkT		SmB	
RbT		WhP	✓
Sal		Csk	
Tog		WhF	
Smt		Pic	✓

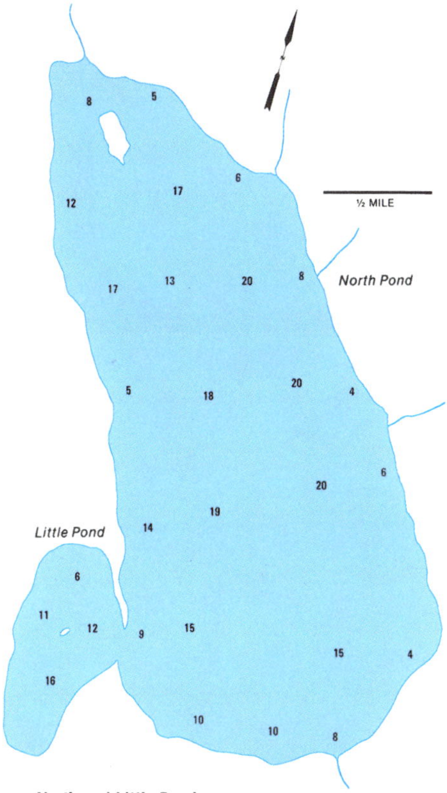

North and Little Ponds
Rome, Mercer, Smithfield, Maine Atlas Map 20, D-4
Acres: 2,115 Max. Depth: 20 feet, Boat Launch

BrT	BkT	RbT	Sal	Tog	Smt	LmB	SmB	WhP	Csk	WhF	Pic
✓						✓	✓	✓			✓

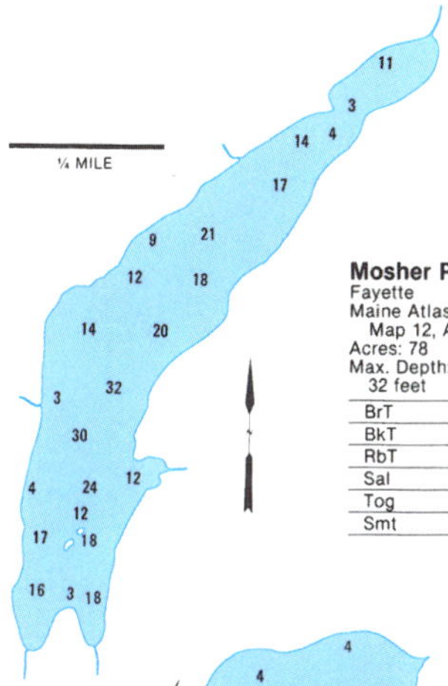

Mosher Pond
Fayette
Maine Atlas
Map 12, A-1
Acres: 78
Max. Depth:
32 feet

BrT		LmB	✓
BkT		SmB	✓
RbT		WhP	✓
Sal		Csk	
Tog		WhF	
Smt		Pic	✓

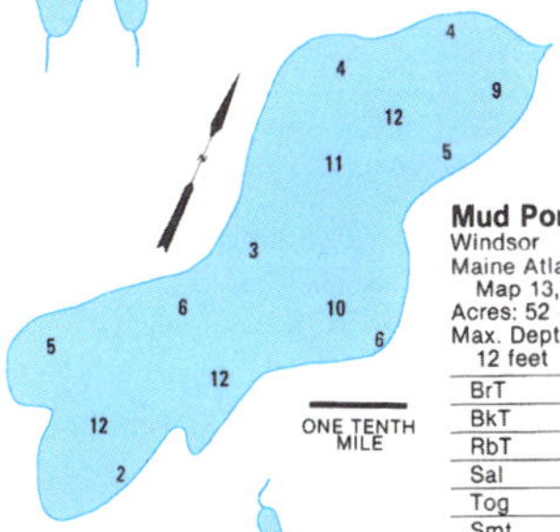

Mud Pond
Windsor
Maine Atlas
Map 13, C-2
Acres: 52
Max. Depth:
12 feet

BrT		LmB	✓
BkT		SmB	✓
RbT		WhP	✓
Sal		Csk	
Tog		WhF	
Smt		Pic	✓

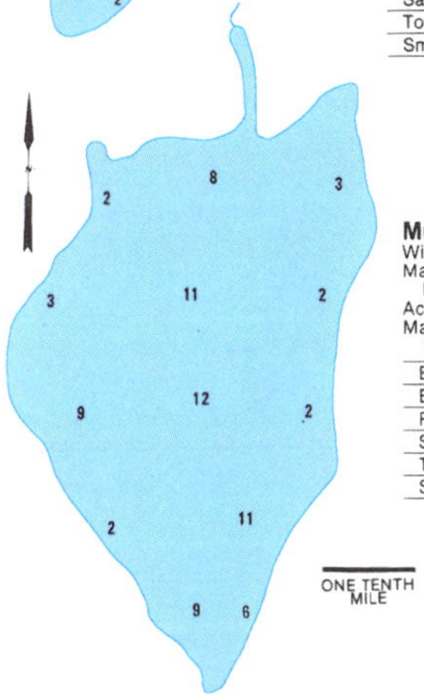

Mud Pond
Winslow, China
Maine Atlas
Map 13, A-3
Acres: 112
Max. Depth:
12 feet

BrT		LmB	✓
BkT		SmB	✓
RbT		WhP	✓
Sal		Csk	
Tog		WhF	
Smt		Pic	✓

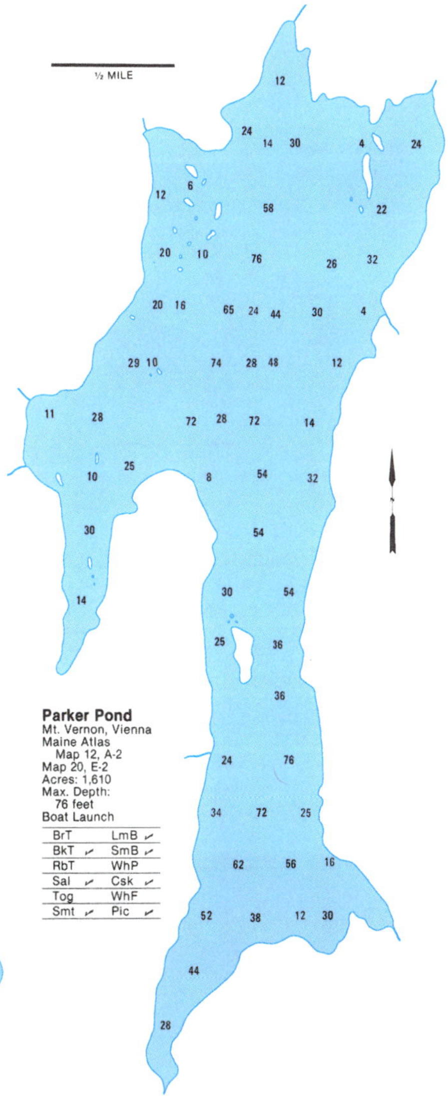

Parker Pond
Mt. Vernon, Vienna
Maine Atlas
Map 12, A-2
Map 20, E-2
Acres: 1,610
Max. Depth:
76 feet
Boat Launch

BrT		LmB	✓
BkT	✓	SmB	✓
RbT		WhP	
Sal	✓	Csk	✓
Tog		WhF	
Smt	✓	Pic	✓

Nehumkeag Pond
Pittston
Maine Atlas
Map 13, D-1
Acres: 173
Max. Depth:
15 feet

BrT		LmB	✓
BkT		SmB	
RbT		WhP	✓
Sal		Csk	
Tog		WhF	
Smt		Pic	✓

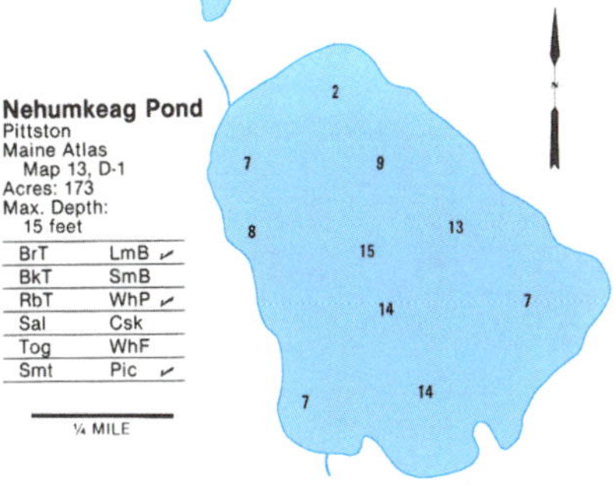

Kennebec

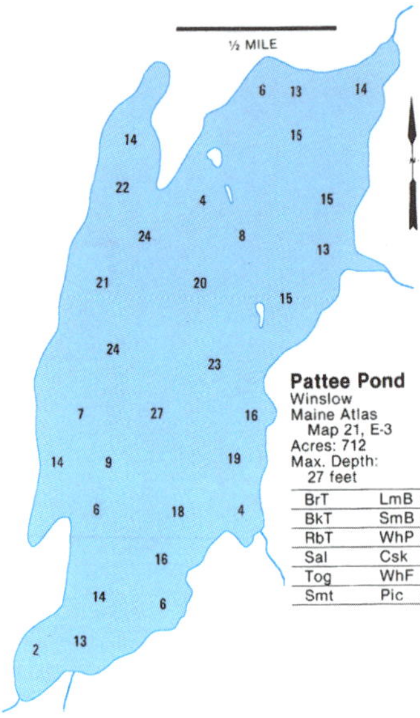

Pattee Pond
Winslow
Maine Atlas
Map 21, E-3
Acres: 712
Max. Depth:
27 feet

BrT		LmB	✓
BkT		SmB	✓
RbT		WhP	✓
Sal		Csk	
Tog		WhF	
Smt		Pic	✓

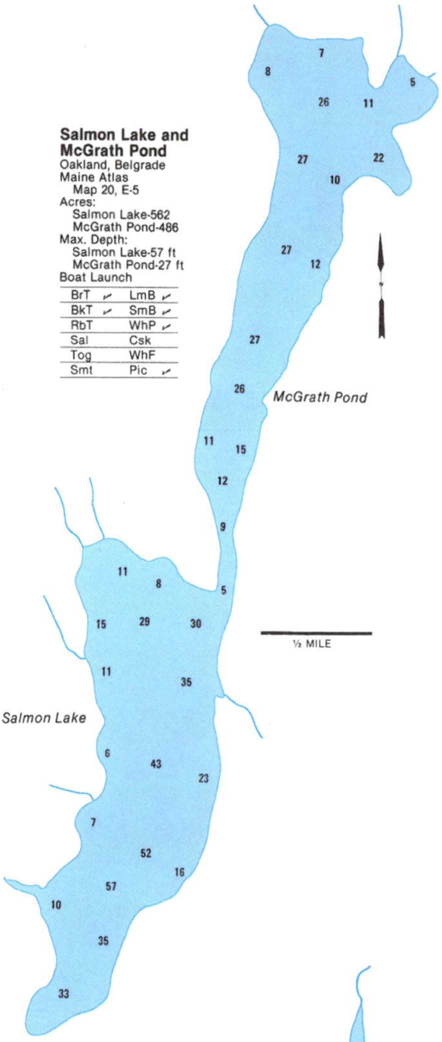

Salmon Lake and McGrath Pond
Oakland, Belgrade
Maine Atlas
Map 20, E-5
Acres:
Salmon Lake-562
McGrath Pond-486
Max. Depth:
Salmon Lake-57 ft
McGrath Pond-27 ft
Boat Launch

BrT	✓	LmB	✓
BkT	✓	SmB	✓
RbT		WhP	✓
Sal		Csk	
Tog		WhF	
Smt		Pic	✓

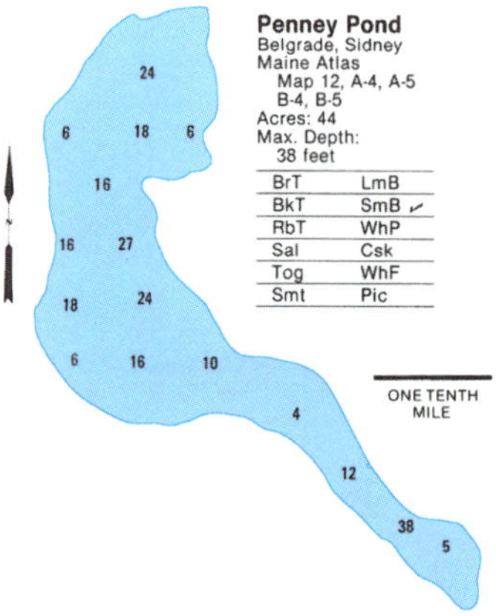

Penney Pond
Belgrade, Sidney
Maine Atlas
Map 12, A-4, A-5
B-4, B-5
Acres: 44
Max. Depth:
38 feet

BrT		LmB	
BkT		SmB	✓
RbT		WhP	
Sal		Csk	
Tog		WhF	
Smt		Pic	

Pleasant Pond
Litchfield,
Gardiner,
West Gardiner
Maine Atlas
Map 12, D-4
Acres: 746
Max. Depth:
26 feet
Boat Launch

BrT	✓	LmB	✓
BkT	✓	SmB	✓
RbT		WhP	✓
Sal		Csk	
Tog		WhF	
Smt		Pic	✓

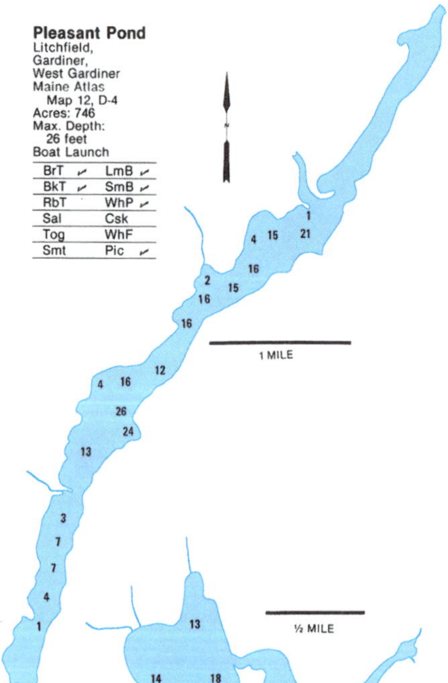

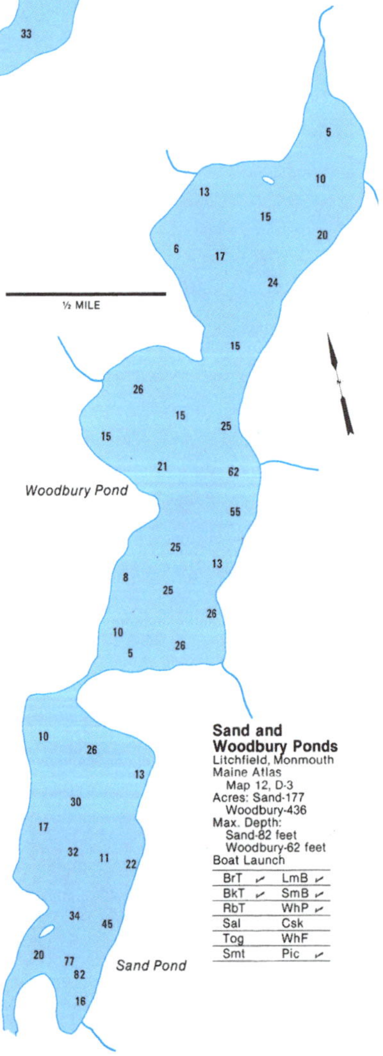

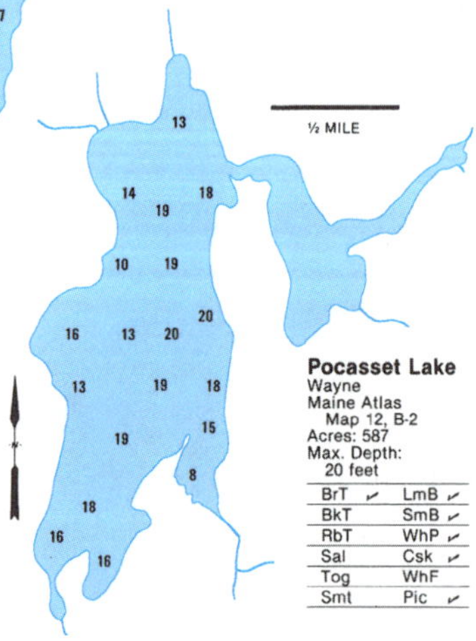

Pocasset Lake
Wayne
Maine Atlas
Map 12, B-2
Acres: 587
Max. Depth:
20 feet

BrT	✓	LmB	✓
BkT		SmB	✓
RbT		WhP	✓
Sal		Csk	✓
Tog		WhF	
Smt		Pic	✓

Sand and Woodbury Ponds
Litchfield, Monmouth
Maine Atlas
Map 12, D-3
Acres: Sand-177
Woodbury-436
Max. Depth:
Sand-82 feet
Woodbury-62 feet
Boat Launch

BrT	✓	LmB	✓
BkT	✓	SmB	✓
RbT		WhP	✓
Sal		Csk	
Tog		WhF	
Smt		Pic	✓

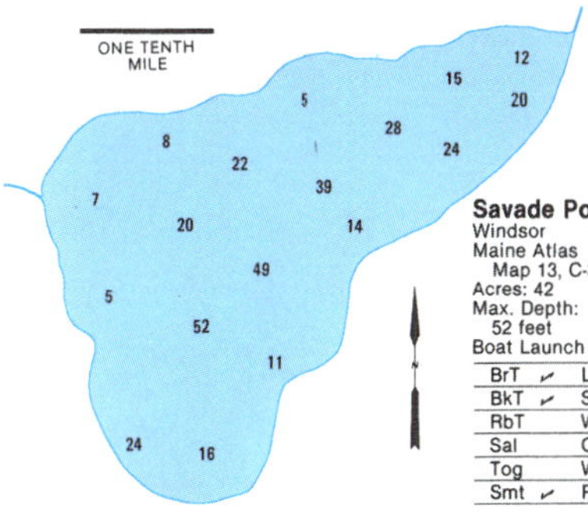

Savade Pond

Windsor
Maine Atlas
Map 13, C-3
Acres: 42
Max. Depth:
52 feet
Boat Launch

BrT	✓	LmB	
BkT	✓	SmB	
RbT		WhP	✓
Sal		Csk	
Tog		WhF	
Smt	✓	Pic	✓

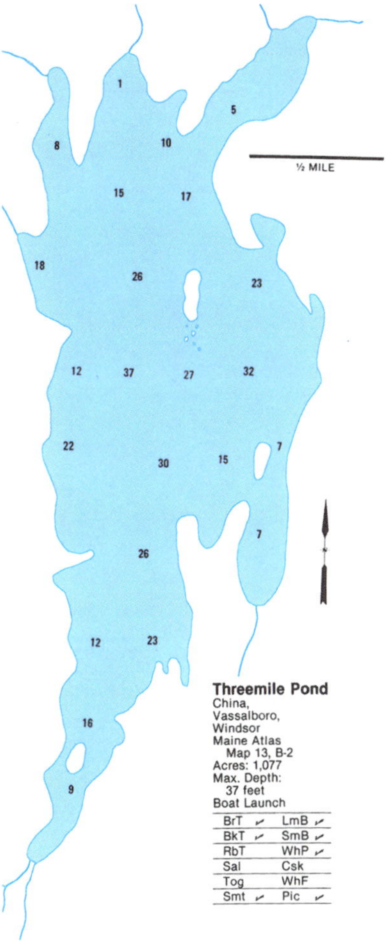

Threemile Pond

China,
Vassalboro,
Windsor
Maine Atlas
Map 13, B-2
Acres: 1,077
Max. Depth:
37 feet
Boat Launch

BrT	✓	LmB	✓
BkT	✓	SmB	✓
RbT		WhP	✓
Sal		Csk	
Tog		WhF	
Smt	✓	Pic	✓

Schoolhouse Pond

Fayette
Maine Atlas
Map 12, A-1
Acres: 19
Max. Depth:
13 feet

BrT		LmB	✓
BkT		SmB	
RbT		WhP	
Sal		Csk	
Tog		WhF	
Smt		Pic	✓

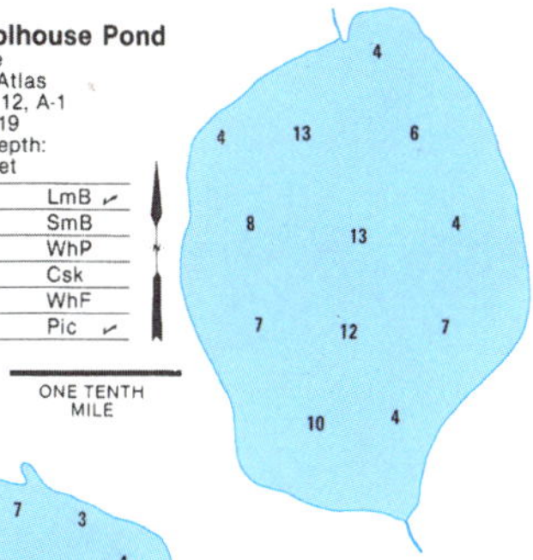

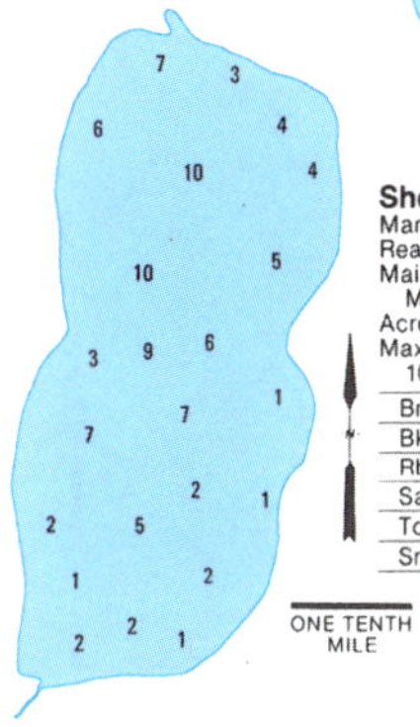

Shed Pond

Manchester,
Readfield
Maine Atlas
Map 12, B-4
Acres: 37
Max. Depth:
10 feet

BrT		LmB	
BkT		SmB	
RbT		WhP	
Sal		Csk	
Tog		WhF	
Smt		Pic	✓

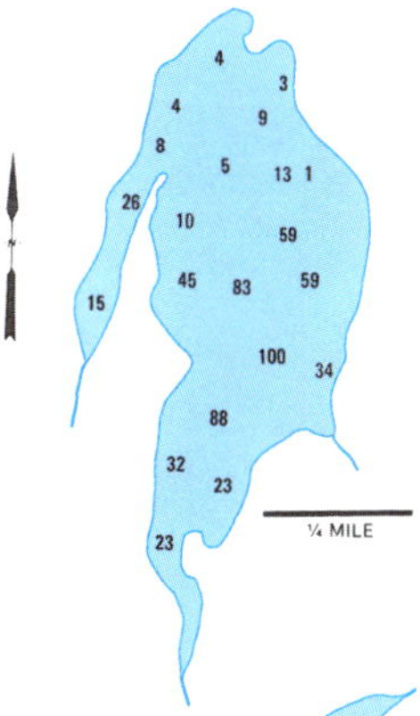

Spectacle Pond

Vassalboro,
Augusta
Maine Atlas
Map 13, B-1, B-2
Acres: 139
Max. Depth:
100 feet
Boat Launch

BrT	✓	LmB	✓
BkT	✓	SmB	✓
RbT		WhP	✓
Sal		Csk	
Tog		WhF	
Smt	✓	Pic	✓

Tilton Pond

Fayette
Maine Atlas
Map 12, A-2
Acres: 114
Max. Depth:
44 feet
Boat Launch

BrT	✓	LmB	✓
BkT		SmB	✓
RbT		WhP	✓
Sal		Csk	
Tog		WhF	
Smt		Pic	✓

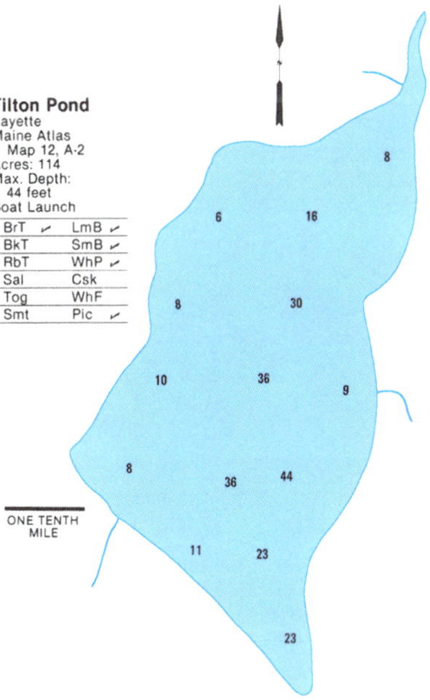

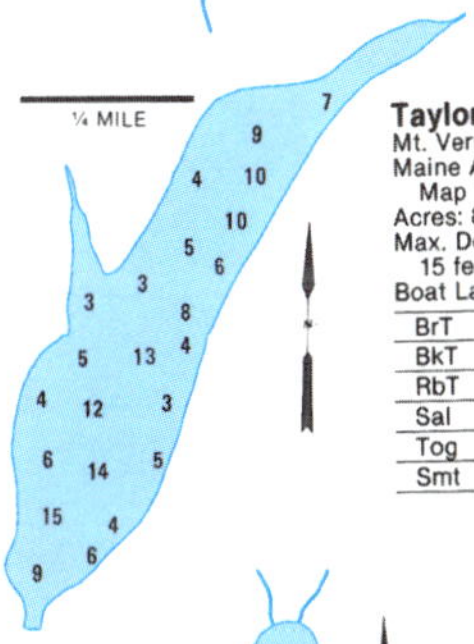

Taylor Pond

Mt. Vernon
Maine Atlas
Map 12, A-2
Acres: 83
Max. Depth:
15 feet
Boat Launch

BrT		LmB	✓
BkT	✓	SmB	✓
RbT		WhP	
Sal	✓	Csk	
Tog		WhF	
Smt		Pic	✓

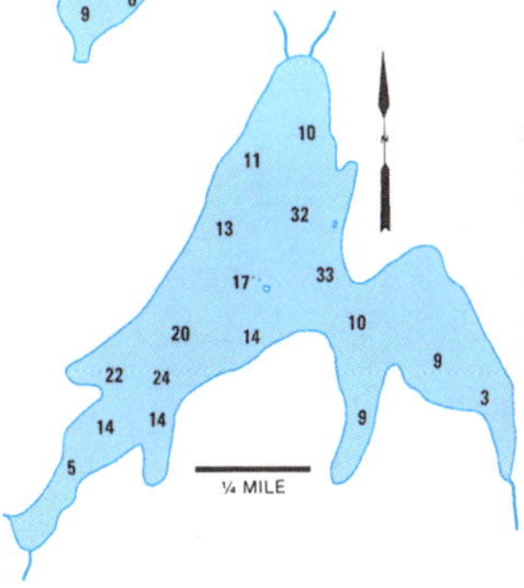

Threecornered Pond

Augusta
Maine Atlas
Map 13, B-2
Acres: 195
Max. Depth:
33 feet

BrT		LmB	✓
BkT		SmB	✓
RbT		WhP	✓
Sal		Csk	
Tog		WhF	
Smt		Pic	✓

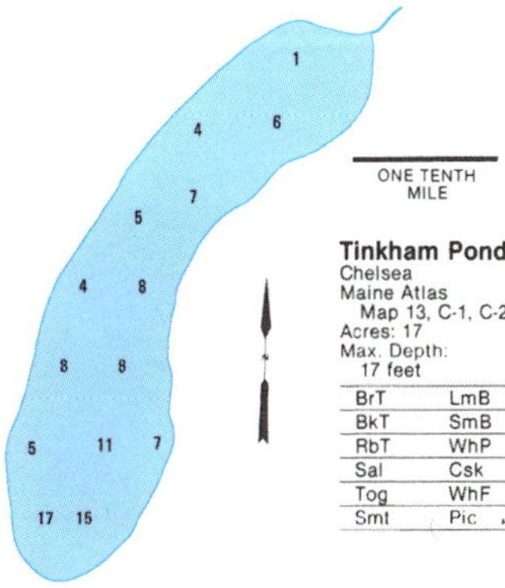

Tinkham Pond

Chelsea
Maine Atlas
Map 13, C-1, C-2
Acres: 17
Max. Depth:
17 feet

BrT		LmB	
BkT		SmB	
RbT		WhP	
Sal		Csk	
Tog		WhF	
Smt		Pic	✓

Kennebec

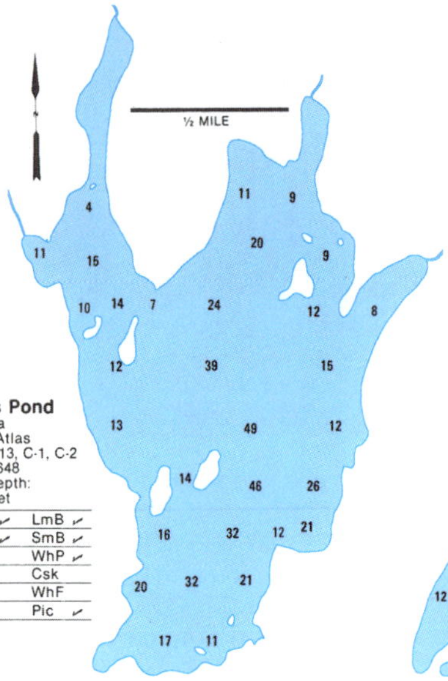

Togus Pond

Augusta
Maine Atlas
Map 13, C-1, C-2
Acres: 648
Max. Depth:
49 feet

BrT	✓	LmB	✓
BkT	✓	SmB	✓
RbT		WhP	✓
Sal		Csk	
Tog		WhF	
Smt		Pic	✓

Upper Narrows Pond

Winthrop
Maine Atlas
Map 12, C-3
Acres: 279
Max. Depth:
54 feet
Boat Launch

BrT		LmB	✓
BkT	✓	SmB	✓
RbT		WhP	✓
Sal	✓	Csk	
Tog	✓	WhF	
Smt	✓	Pic	✓

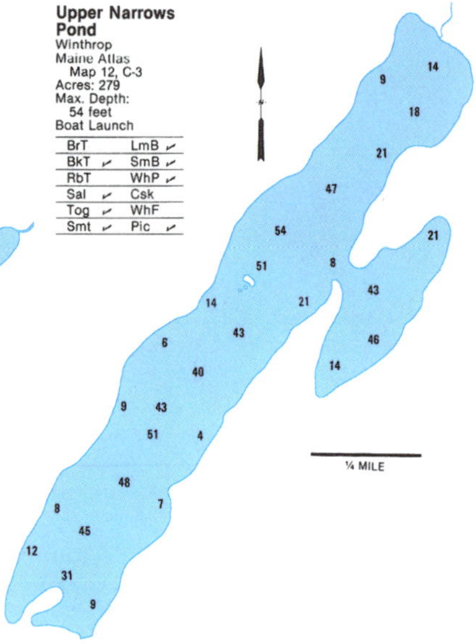

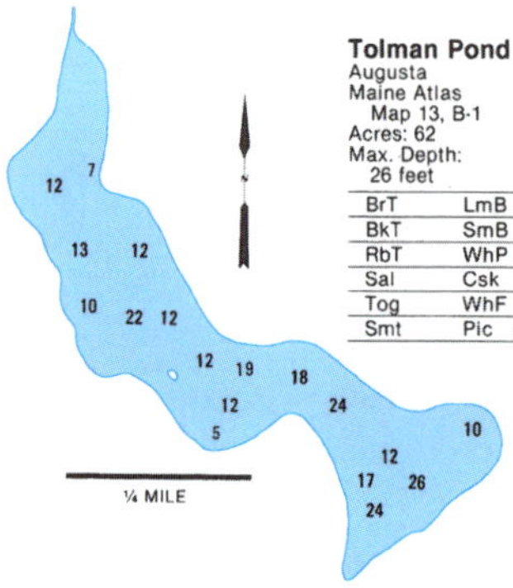

Tolman Pond

Augusta
Maine Atlas
Map 13, B-1
Acres: 62
Max. Depth:
26 feet

BrT		LmB	✓
BkT		SmB	✓
RbT		WhP	✓
Sal		Csk	
Tog		WhF	
Smt		Pic	✓

Ward Pond

Sidney
Maine Atlas
Map 12, A-5, B-5
Acres: 52
Max. Depth:
34 feet

BrT		LmB	✓
BkT		SmB	✓
RbT		WhP	✓
Sal		Csk	
Tog		WhF	
Smt		Pic	✓

ONE TENTH MILE

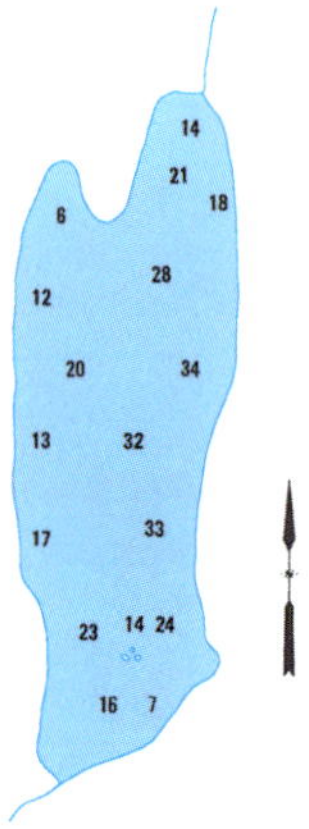

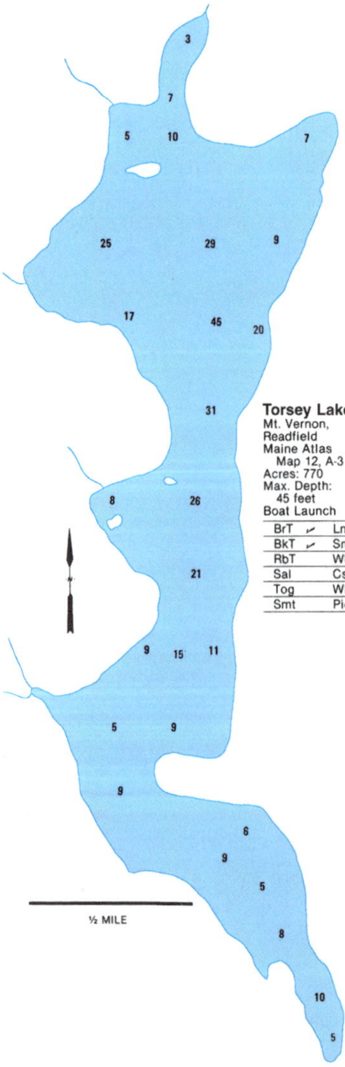

Watson Pond

Rome
Maine Atlas
Map 20, E-3
Acres: 66
Max. Depth:
24 feet

BrT		LmB	✓
BkT		SmB	
RbT		WhP	✓
Sal		Csk	
Tog	✓	WhF	
Smt		Pic	

¼ MILE

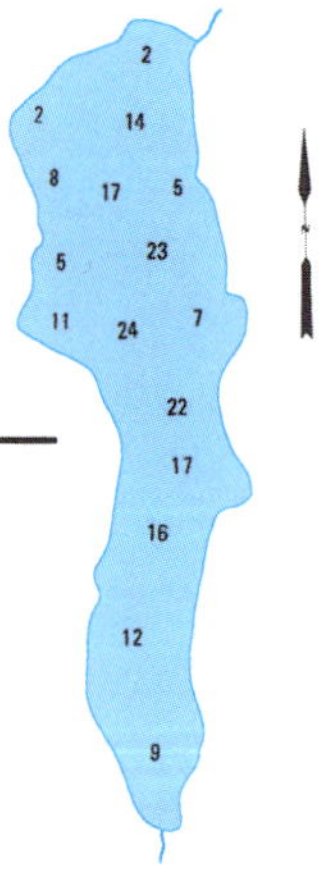

Torsey Lake

Mt. Vernon,
Readfield
Maine Atlas
Map 12, A-3
Acres: 770
Max. Depth:
45 feet
Boat Launch

BrT	✓	LmB	
BkT	✓	SmB	✓
RbT		WhP	✓
Sal		Csk	
Tog		WhF	
Smt		Pic	✓

Webber Pond

Vassalboro
Maine Atlas
Map 13, A-1, A-2,
B-1, B-2
Acres: 1,252
Max. Depth:
41 feet
Boat Launch

BrT	✓	LmB	✓
BkT	✓	SmB	✓
RbT		WhP	✓
Sal	✓	Csk	
Tog		WhF	
Smt	✓	Pic	✓

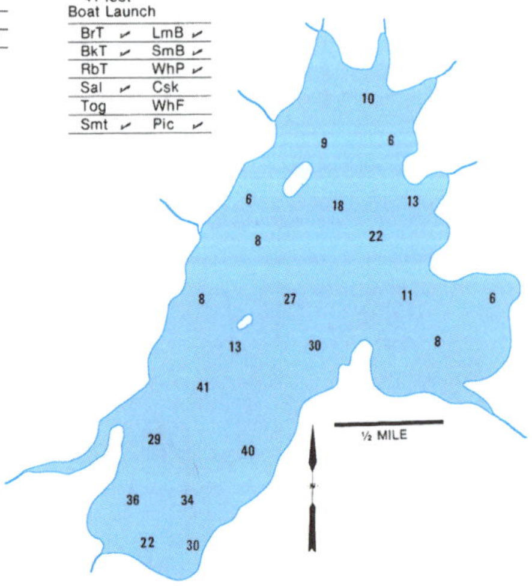

Knox County

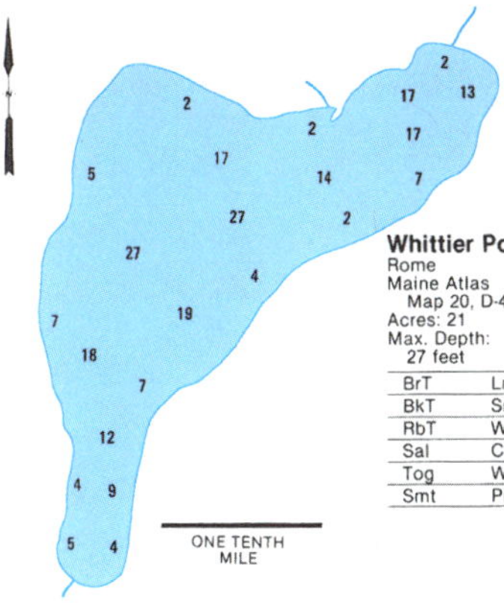

Whittier Pond

Rome
Maine Atlas
Map 20, D-4, E-4
Acres: 21
Max. Depth:
27 feet

BrT		LmB	
BkT		SmB	✓
RbT		WhP	
Sal		Csk	
Tog		WhF	
Smt		Pic	✓

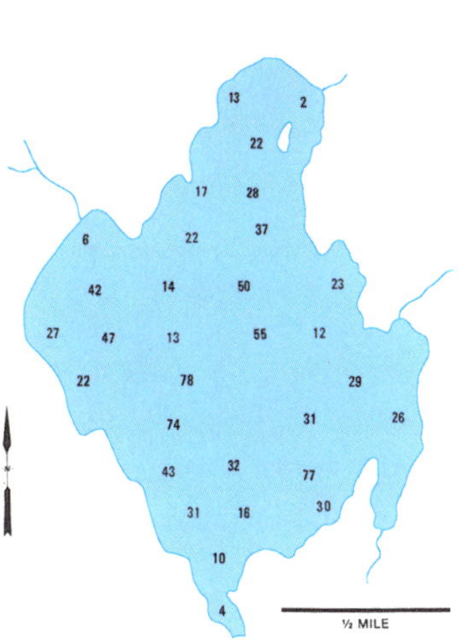

Alford Lake

Hope, Maine Atlas Map 14, C-2,D-2
Acres: 542, Max. Depth: 78 feet, Boat Launch

BrT	BkT	RbT	Sal	Tog	Smt	LmB	SmB	WhP	Csk	WhF	Pic
✓	✓	✓	✓		✓		✓	✓			✓

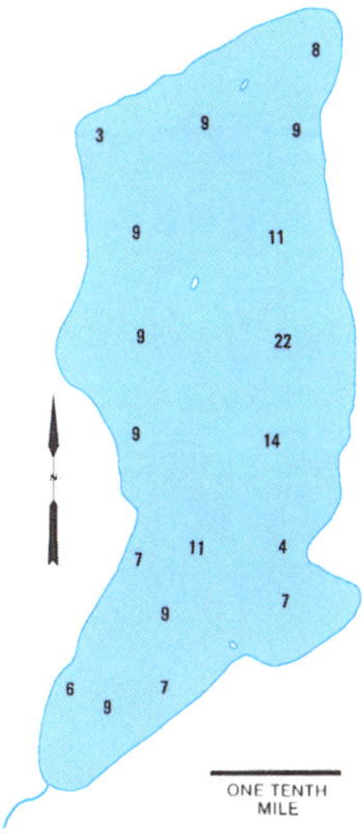

Whittier Pond

Vienna
Maine Atlas
Map 20, E-2
Acres: 44
Max. Depth:
22 feet

BrT		LmB	✓
BkT		SmB	✓
RbT		WhP	✓
Sal		Csk	
Tog		WhF	
Smt		Pic	✓

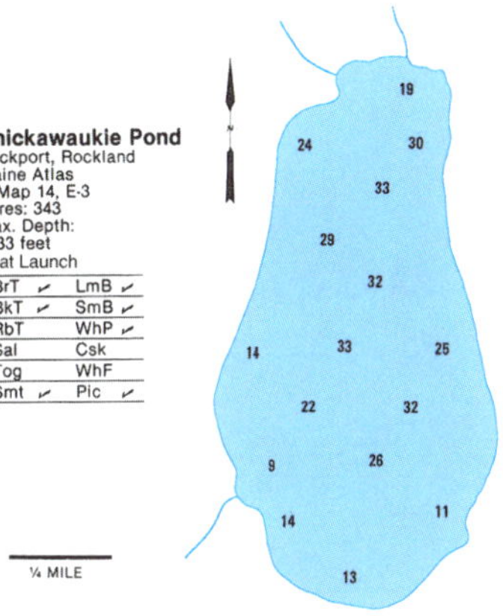

Chickawaukie Pond

Rockport, Rockland
Maine Atlas
Map 14, E-3
Acres: 343
Max. Depth:
33 feet
Boat Launch

BrT	✓	LmB	✓
BkT	✓	SmB	✓
RbT		WhP	✓
Sal		Csk	
Tog		WhF	
Smt	✓	Pic	✓

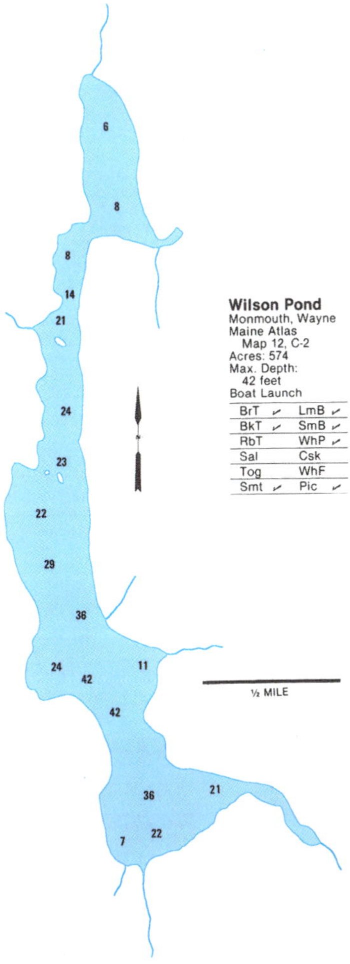

Wilson Pond

Monmouth, Wayne
Maine Atlas
Map 12, C-2
Acres: 574
Max. Depth:
42 feet
Boat Launch

BrT	✓	LmB	✓
BkT	✓	SmB	✓
RbT		WhP	✓
Sal		Csk	
Tog		WhF	
Smt	✓	Pic	✓

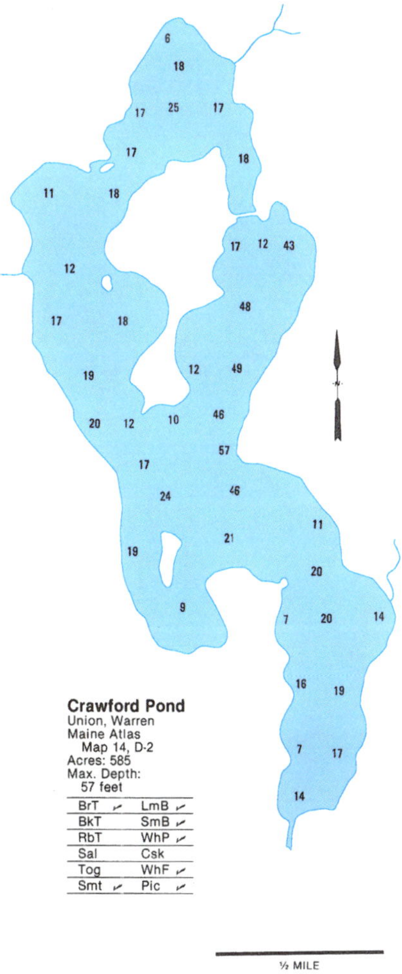

Crawford Pond

Union, Warren
Maine Atlas
Map 14, D-2
Acres: 585
Max. Depth:
57 feet

BrT	✓	LmB	✓
BkT		SmB	✓
RbT		WhP	✓
Sal		Csk	
Tog		WhF	✓
Smt	✓	Pic	✓

Knox

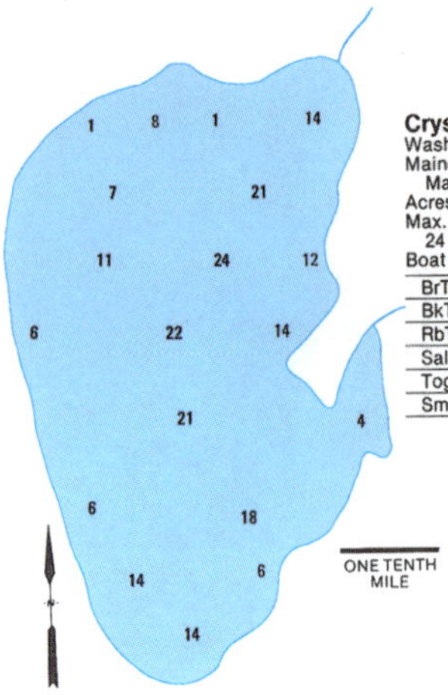

Crystal Pond

Washington
Maine Atlas
Map 13, C-5
Acres: 83
Max. Depth:
24 feet
Boat Launch

BrT	✓	LmB	
BkT	✓	SmB	✓
RbT		WhP	
Sal		Csk	
Tog		WhF	
Smt		Pic	✓

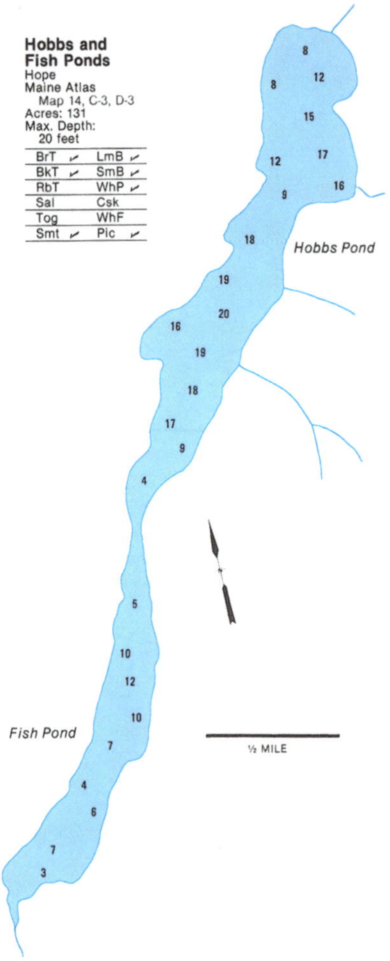

Hobbs and Fish Ponds

Hope
Maine Atlas
Map 14, C-3, D-3
Acres: 131
Max. Depth:
20 feet

BrT	✓	LmB	✓
BkT	✓	SmB	✓
RbT		WhP	✓
Sal		Csk	
Tog		WhF	
Smt	✓	Pic	✓

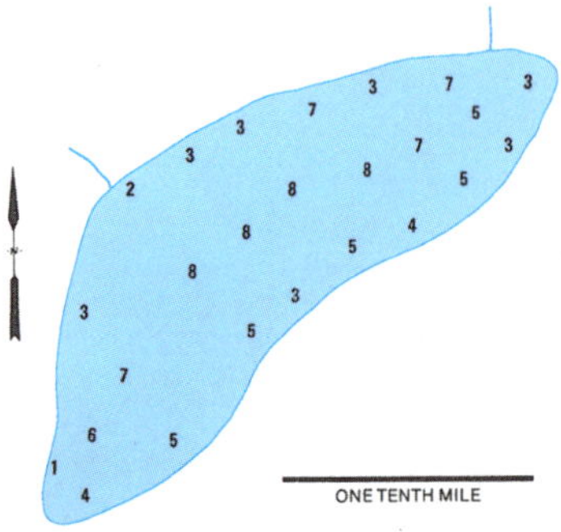

Forest Lake

Friendship, Maine Atlas Map 7, A-5, B-5
Acres: 6, Max. Depth: 8 feet

BrT	BkT	RbT	Sal	Tog	Smt	LmB	SmB	WhP	Csk	WhF	Pic
						✓					

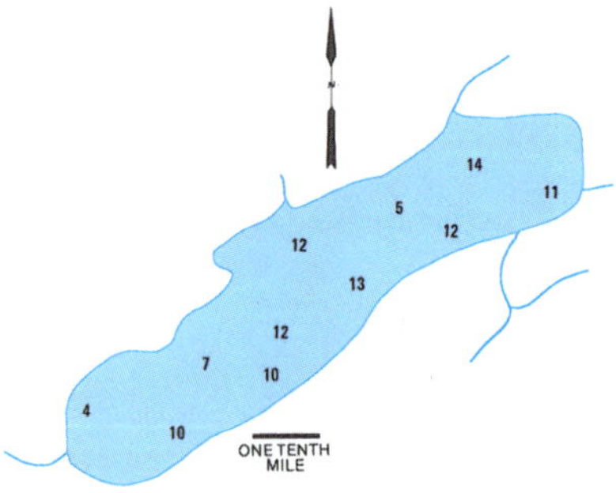

Fresh Pond

North Haven, Maine Atlas Map 15, E-1
Acres: 85, Max. Depth: 14 feet

BrT	BkT	RbT	Sal	Tog	Smt	LmB	SmB	WhP	Csk	WhF	Pic
						✓		✓			

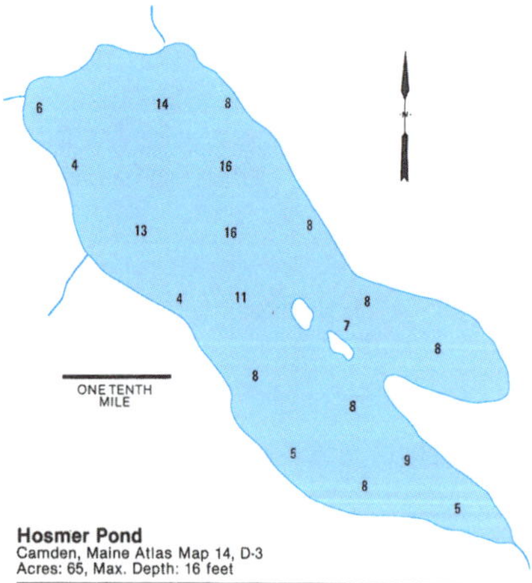

Hosmer Pond

Camden, Maine Atlas Map 14, D-3
Acres: 65, Max. Depth: 16 feet

BrT	BkT	RbT	Sal	Tog	Smt	LmB	SmB	WhP	Csk	WhF	Pic
✓	✓				✓			✓			✓

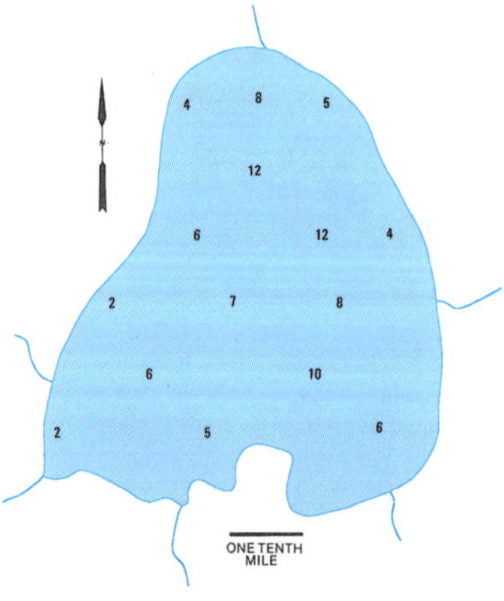

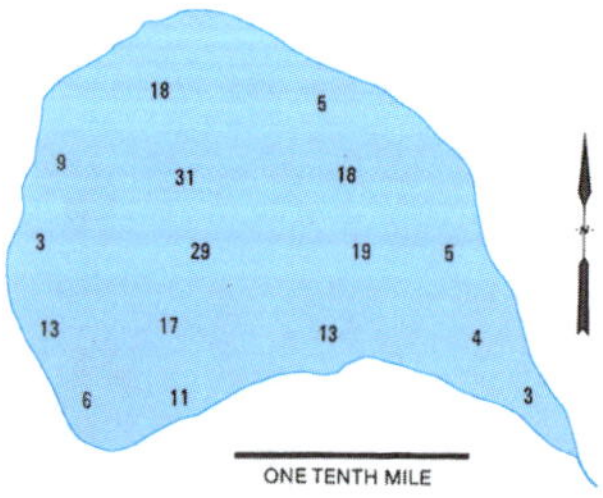

Iron Pond

Washington, Maine Atlas Map 13, D-5
Acres: 17, Max. Depth: 31 feet

BrT	BkT	RbT	Sal	Tog	Smt	LmB	SmB	WhP	Csk	WhF	Pic
✓	✓										

Grassy Pond

Rockport, Maine Atlas Map 14, D-2
Acres: 136, Max. Depth: 12 feet

BrT	BkT	RbT	Sal	Tog	Smt	LmB	SmB	WhP	Csk	WhF	Pic
						✓	✓				✓

Lermond Pond
Hope, Union
Maine Atlas
Map 14, D-2
Acres: 156
Max. Depth:
30 feet

BrT	✓	LmB	✓
BkT		SmB	✓
RbT		WhP	✓
Sal		Csk	
Tog		WhF	
Smt	✓	Pic	✓

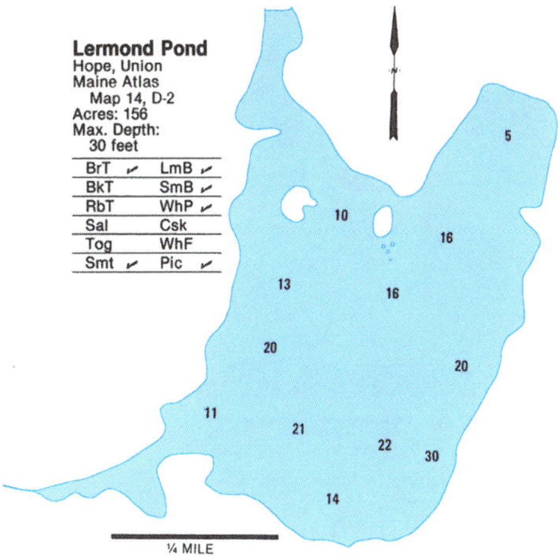

Maces Pond
Rockport
Maine Atlas
Map 14, D-3, E-3
Acres: 25
Max. Depth:
10 feet

BrT		LmB	✓
BkT		SmB	✓
RbT		WhP	✓
Sal		Csk	
Tog		WhF	
Smt		Pic	✓

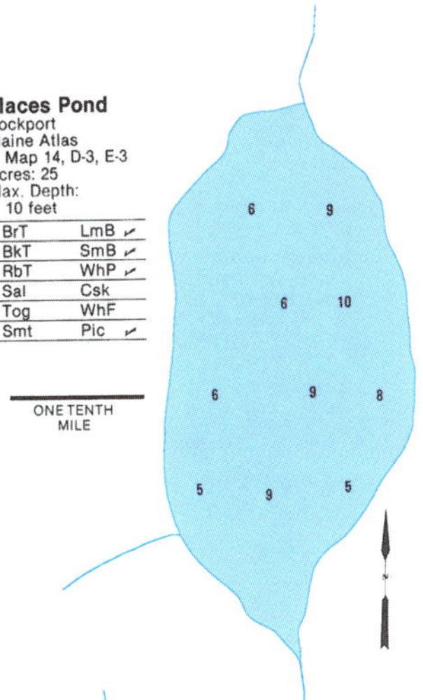

Lilly Pond
Rockport
Maine Atlas
Map 14, D-4
Acres: 30
Max. Depth:
24 feet

BrT		LmB	
BkT		SmB	✓
RbT		WhP	✓
Sal		Csk	
Tog		WhF	
Smt		Pic	✓

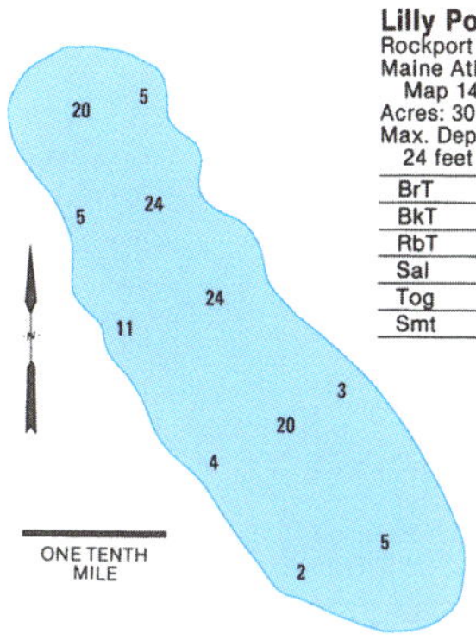

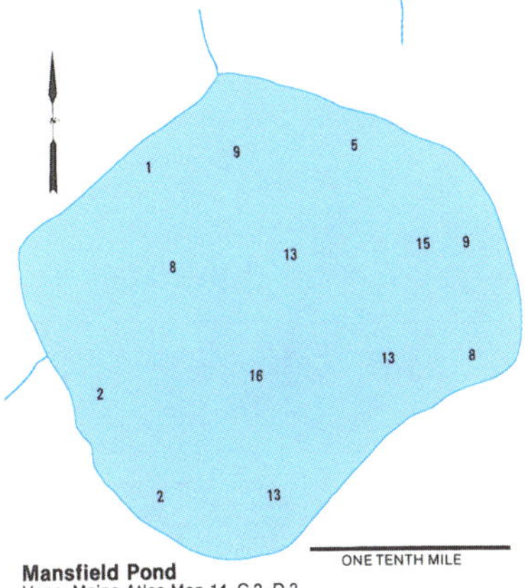

Mansfield Pond
Hope, Maine Atlas Map 14, C-2, D-2
Acres: 27, Max. Depth: 16 feet

BrT	BkT	RbT	Sal	Tog	Smt	LmB	SmB	WhP	Csk	WhF	Pic
✓	✓					✓	✓	✓			✓

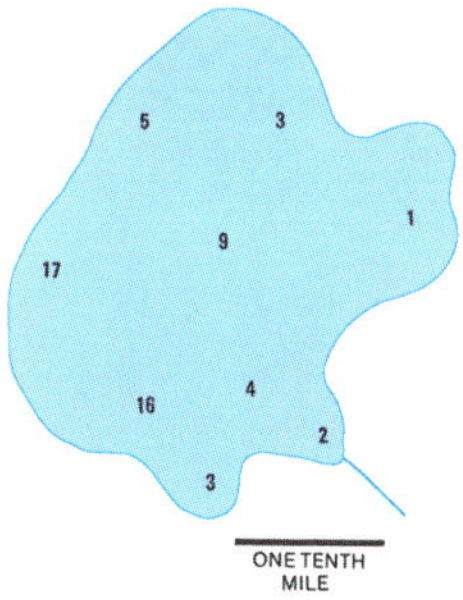

Lily Pond
Hope
Maine Atlas
Map 14, C-2, D-2
Acres: 32
Max. Depth:
17 feet

BrT		LmB	
BkT		SmB	
RbT		WhP	
Sal		Csk	
Tog		WhF	
Smt		Pic	✓

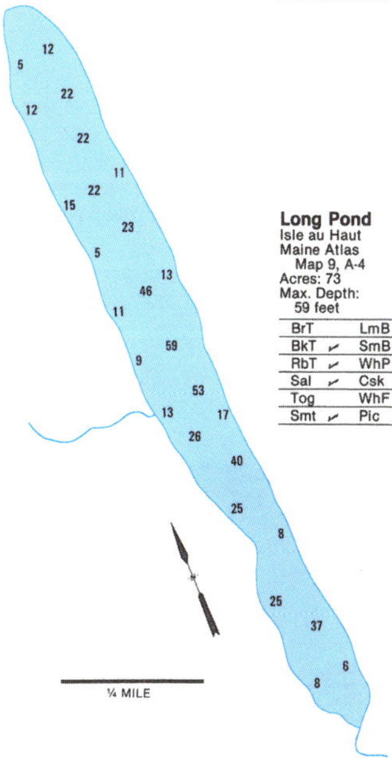

Long Pond
Isle au Haut
Maine Atlas
Map 9, A-4
Acres: 73
Max. Depth:
59 feet

BrT		LmB	
BkT	✓	SmB	
RbT	✓	WhP	
Sal	✓	Csk	
Tog		WhF	
Smt	✓	Pic	

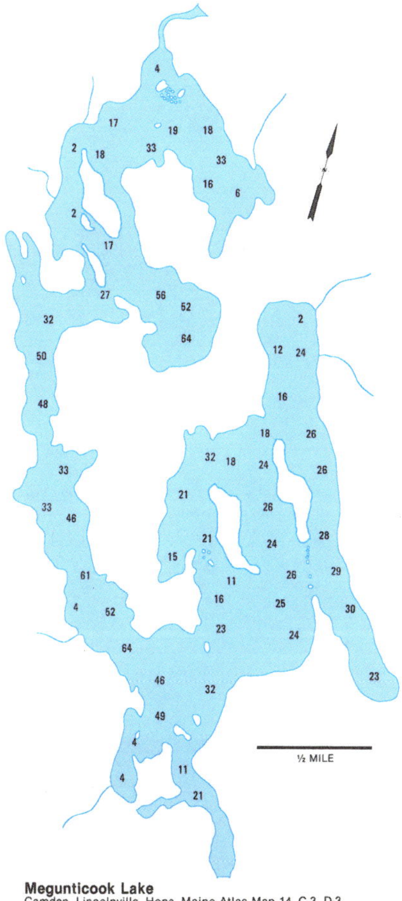

Megunticook Lake
Camden, Lincolnville, Hope, Maine Atlas Map 14, C-3, D-3
Acres: 1,220, Max. Depth: 64 feet

BrT	BkT	RbT	Sal	Tog	Smt	LmB	SmB	WhP	Csk	WhF	Pic
✓	✓	✓	✓		✓	✓	✓	✓			

Knox

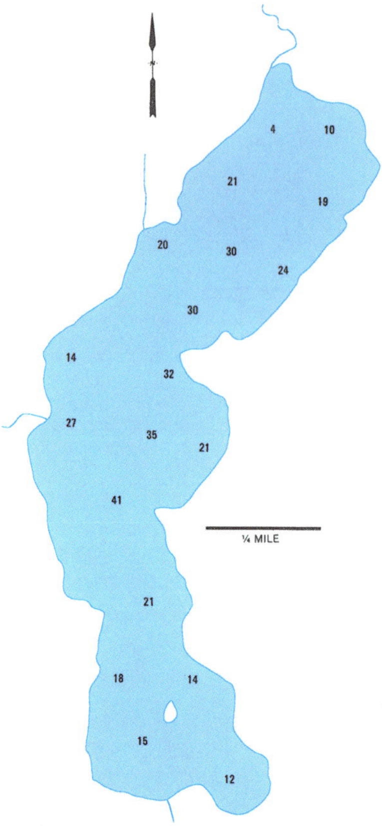

North Pond

Warren, Maine Atlas Map 14, E-1
Acres: 326, Max. Depth: 41 feet

BrT	BkT	RbT	Sal	Tog	Smt	LmB	SmB	WhP	Csk	WhF	Pic
✓						✓	✓	✓			✓

Round Pond

Vinalhaven
Maine Atlas
Map 9, A-1
Acres: 6
Max. Depth:
20 feet

BrT		LmB	
BkT		SmB	
RbT		WhP	✓
Sal		Csk	
Tog		WhF	
Smt		Pic	

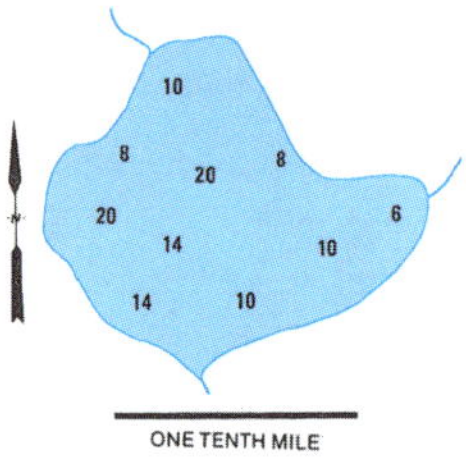

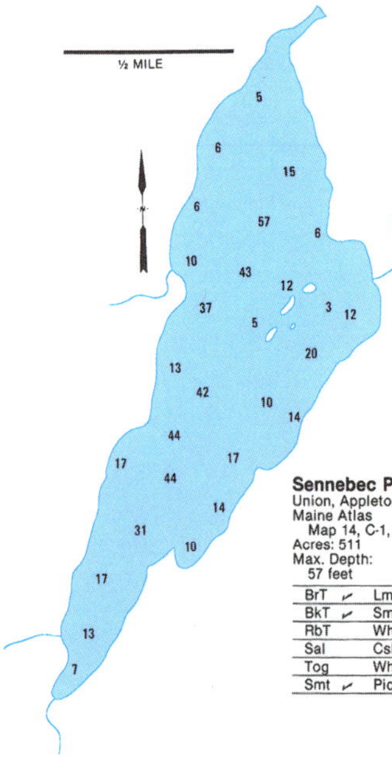

Sennebec Pond

Union, Appleton
Maine Atlas
Map 14, C-1, D-1
Acres: 511
Max. Depth:
57 feet

BrT	✓	LmB	✓
BkT	✓	SmB	✓
RbT		WhP	✓
Sal		Csk	
Tog		WhF	
Smt	✓	Pic	✓

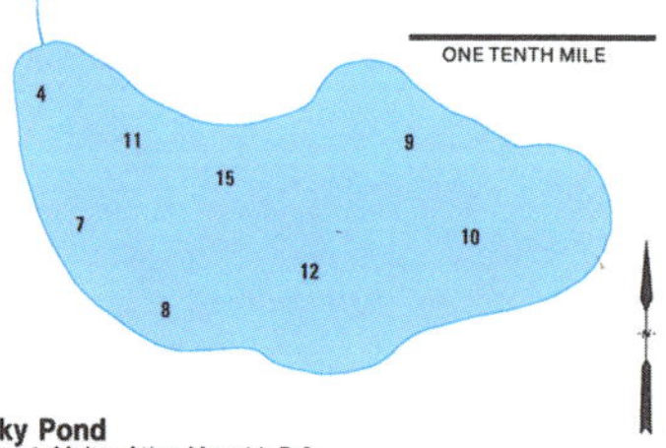

Rocky Pond

Rockport, Maine Atlas Map 14, D-3
Acres: 13, Max. Depth: 15 feet

BrT	BkT	RbT	Sal	Tog	Smt	LmB	SmB	WhP	Csk	WhF	Pic
							✓	✓			✓

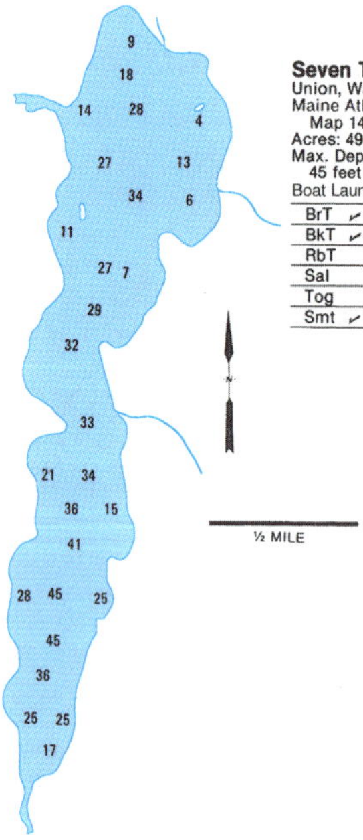

Seven Tree Pond

Union, Warren
Maine Atlas
Map 14, D-1
Acres: 490
Max. Depth:
45 feet
Boat Launch

BrT	✓	LmB	✓
BkT	✓	SmB	✓
RbT		WhP	✓
Sal		Csk	
Tog		WhF	
Smt	✓	Pic	✓

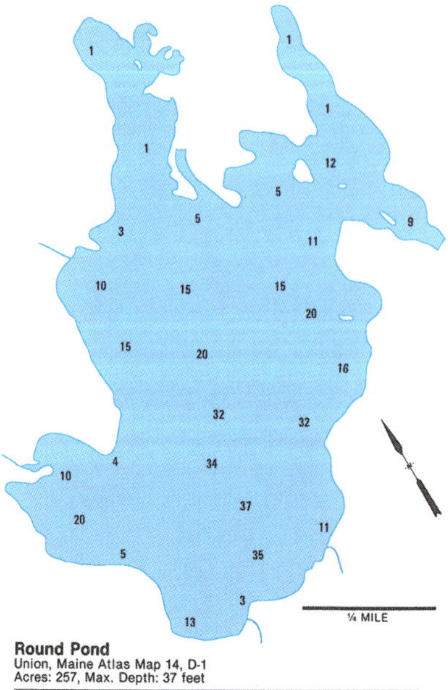

Round Pond

Union, Maine Atlas Map 14, D-1
Acres: 257, Max. Depth: 37 feet

BrT	BkT	RbT	Sal	Tog	Smt	LmB	SmB	WhP	Csk	WhF	Pic
✓					✓	✓	✓	✓			✓

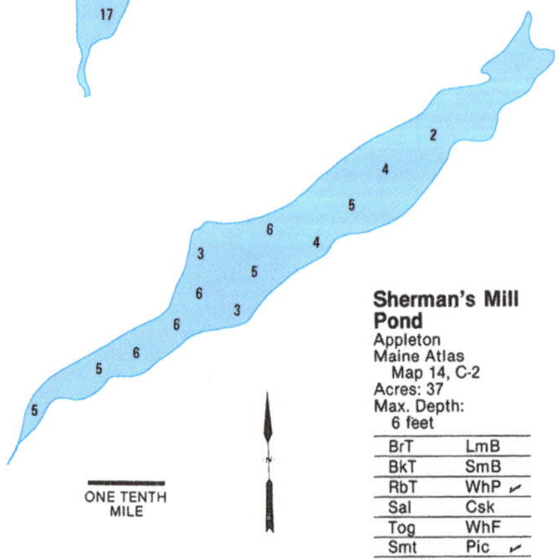

Sherman's Mill Pond

Appleton
Maine Atlas
Map 14, C-2
Acres: 37
Max. Depth:
6 feet

BrT		LmB	
BkT		SmB	
RbT		WhP	✓
Sal		Csk	
Tog		WhF	
Smt		Pic	✓

Lincoln County

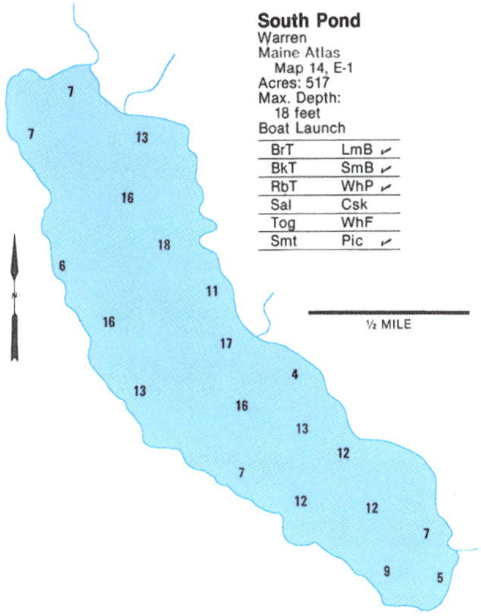

South Pond
Warren
Maine Atlas
Map 14, E-1
Acres: 517
Max. Depth:
18 feet
Boat Launch

BrT		LmB	✓
BkT		SmB	✓
RbT		WhP	✓
Sal		Csk	
Tog		WhF	
Smt		Pic	✓

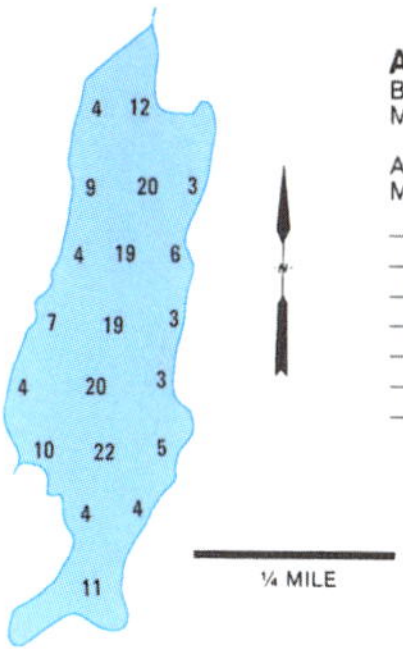

Adams Pond
Boothbay
Maine Atlas
Map 7, C-2
Acres: 73
Max. Depth:
22 feet

BrT	✓	LmB	✓
BkT	✓	SmB	
RbT		WhP	
Sal		Csk	
Tog		WhF	
Smt		Pic	

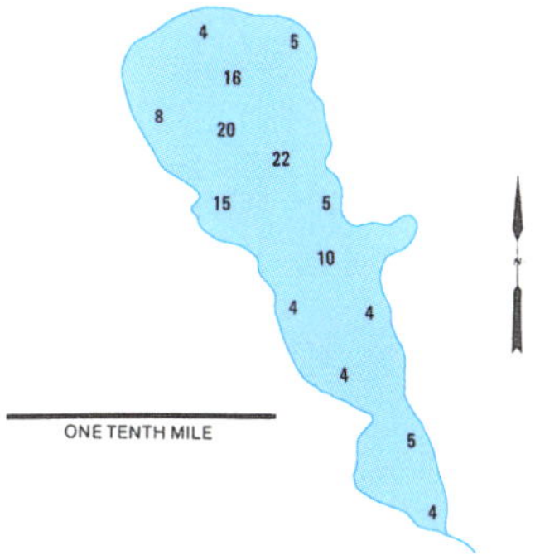

Spring Pond
Washington, Maine Atlas Map 13, C-4
Acres: 15, Max. Depth: 22 feet

BrT	BkT	RbT	Sal	Tog	Smt	LmB	SmB	WhP	Csk	WhF	Pic
											✓

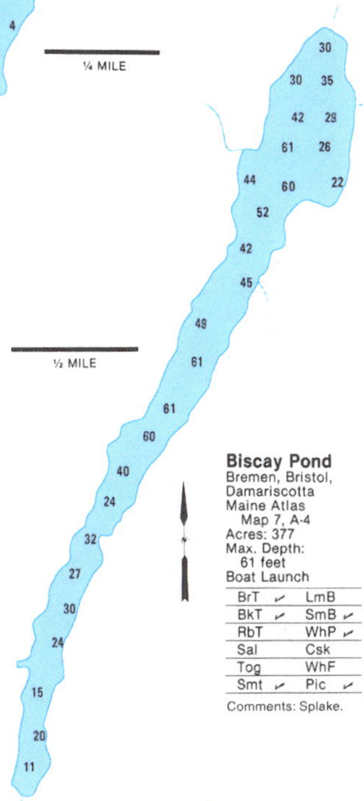

Biscay Pond
Bremen, Bristol,
Damariscotta
Maine Atlas
Map 7, A-4
Acres: 377
Max. Depth:
61 feet
Boat Launch

BrT	✓	LmB	
BkT	✓	SmB	✓
RbT		WhP	✓
Sal		Csk	
Tog		WhF	
Smt	✓	Pic	✓

Comments: Splake.

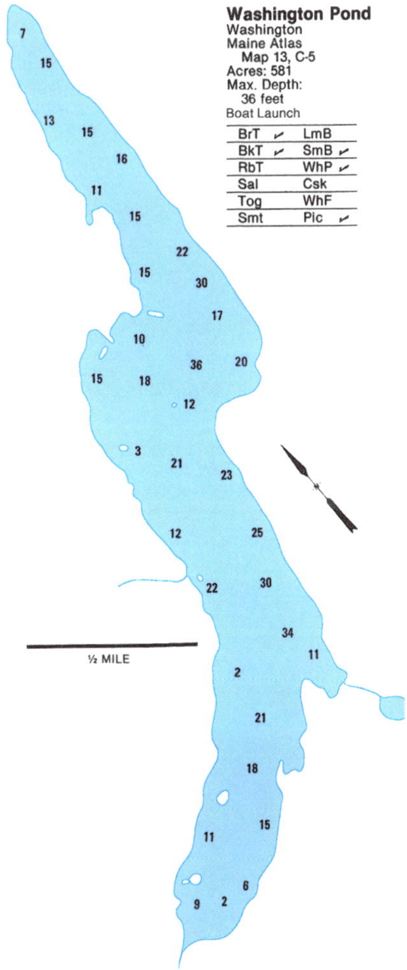

Washington Pond
Washington
Maine Atlas
Map 13, C-5
Acres: 581
Max. Depth:
36 feet
Boat Launch

BrT	✓	LmB	
BkT	✓	SmB	✓
RbT		WhP	✓
Sal		Csk	
Tog		WhF	
Smt		Pic	✓

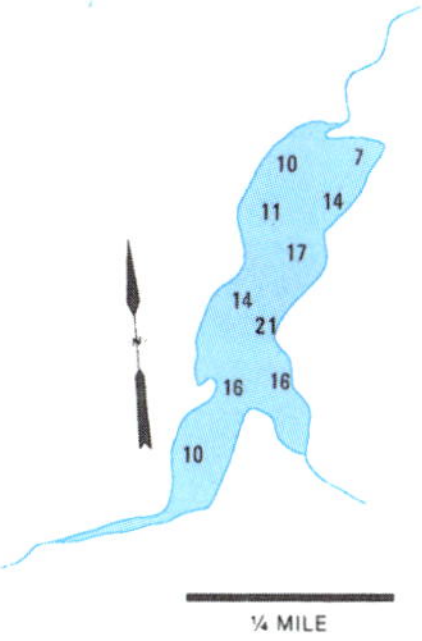

Boyd Pond
Bristol
Maine Atlas
Map 7, B-3, B-4
Acres: 50
Max. Depth:
21 feet

BrT	✓	LmB	
BkT	✓	SmB	✓
RbT		WhP	✓
Sal		Csk	
Tog		WhF	
Smt		Pic	✓

Clark Cove Pond
Bristol
Maine Atlas
Map 7, B-3
Acres: 31
Max. Depth:
11 feet

BrT	✓	LmB	
BkT	✓	SmB	
RbT	✓	WhP	
Sal		Csk	
Tog		WhF	
Smt		Pic	

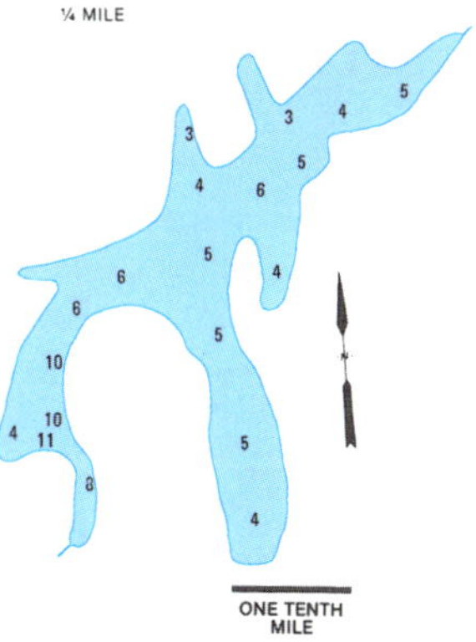

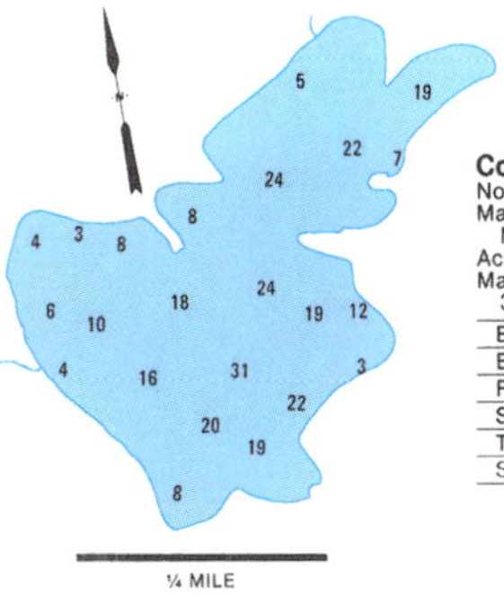

Cooks Pond
Nobleboro
Maine Atlas
Map 13, E-4
Acres: 60
Max. Depth:
31 feet

BrT		LmB	
BkT		SmB	✓
RbT		WhP	✓
Sal		Csk	
Tog		WhF	
Smt		Pic	✓

Lincoln

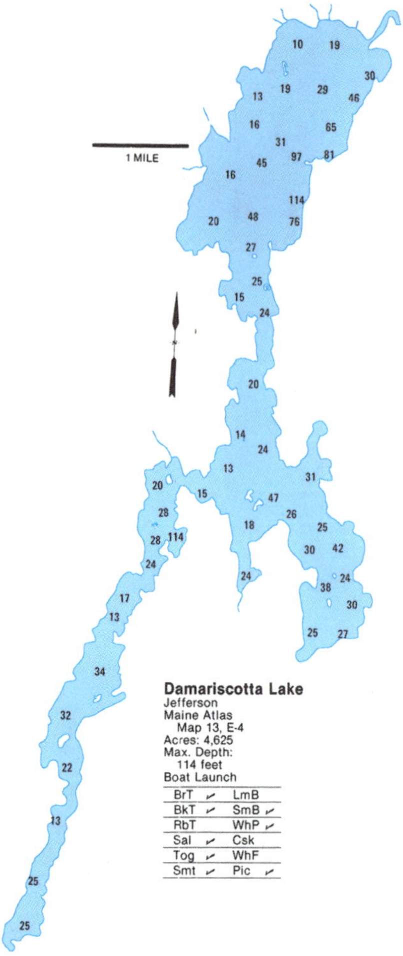

Damariscotta Lake

Jefferson
Maine Atlas
Map 13, E-4
Acres: 4,625
Max. Depth:
114 feet
Boat Launch

BrT	✓	LmB	
BkT	✓	SmB	✓
RbT		WhP	✓
Sal	✓	Csk	
Tog	✓	WhF	
Smt	✓	Pic	✓

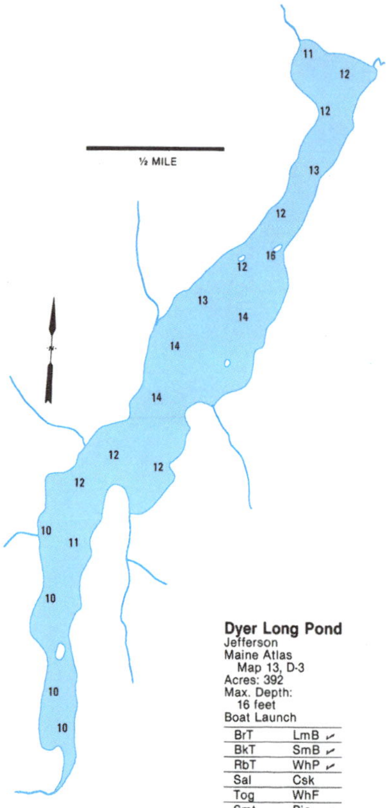

Dyer Long Pond

Jefferson
Maine Atlas
Map 13, D-3
Acres: 392
Max. Depth:
16 feet
Boat Launch

BrT		LmB	✓
BkT		SmB	✓
RbT		WhP	✓
Sal		Csk	
Tog		WhF	
Smt		Pic	✓

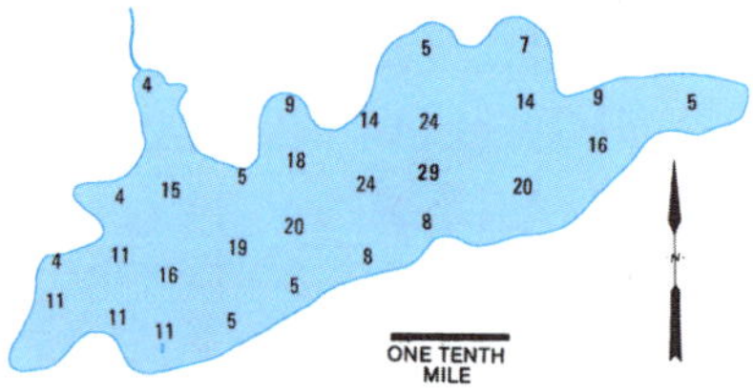

Deer Meadow Pond

Jefferson, Maine Atlas Map 13, E-3
Acres: 49, Max. Depth: 29 feet

BrT	BkT	RbT	Sal	Tog	Smt	LmB	SmB	WhP	Csk	WhF	Pic
	✓							✓			

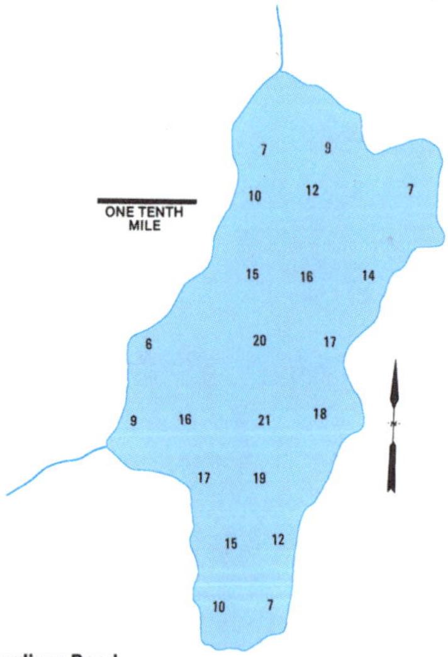

Gardiner Pond

Wiscasset, Maine Atlas Map 7, A-1
Acres: 58, Max. Depth: 21 feet,

BrT	BkT	RbT	Sal	Tog	Smt	LmB	SmB	WhP	Csk	WhF	Pic
							✓				✓

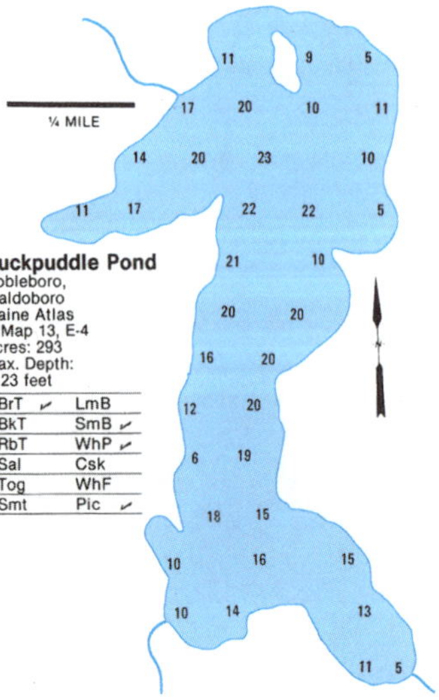

Duckpuddle Pond

Nobleboro,
Waldoboro
Maine Atlas
Map 13, E-4
Acres: 293
Max. Depth:
23 feet

BrT	✓	LmB	
BkT		SmB	✓
RbT		WhP	✓
Sal		Csk	
Tog		WhF	
Smt		Pic	✓

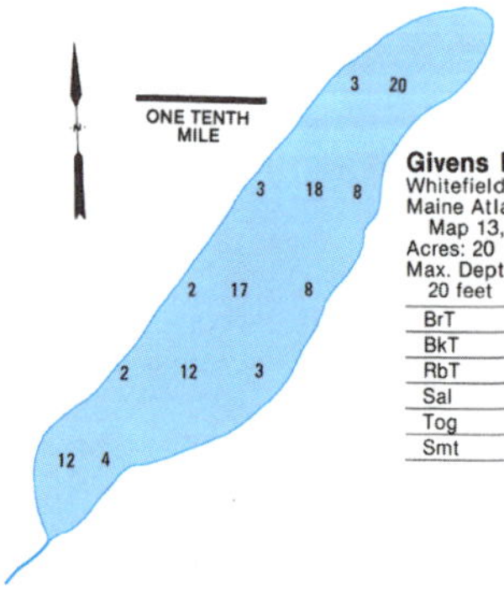

Givens Pond

Whitefield
Maine Atlas
Map 13, C-2
Acres: 20
Max. Depth:
20 feet

BrT		LmB	
BkT		SmB	
RbT		WhP	
Sal		Csk	
Tog		WhF	
Smt		Pic	✓

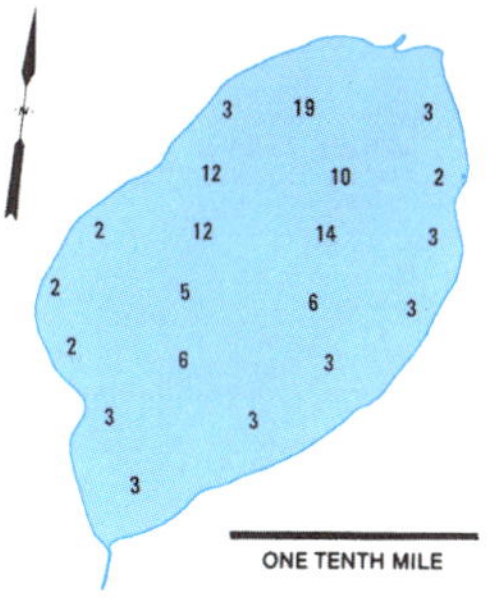

Hastings Pond

Bristol
Maine Atlas
Map 7, C-4
Acres: 11
Max. Depth:
19 feet
Boat Launch

BrT	LmB
BkT ✓	SmB
RbT	WhP
Sal	Csk
Tog	WhF
Smt	Pic

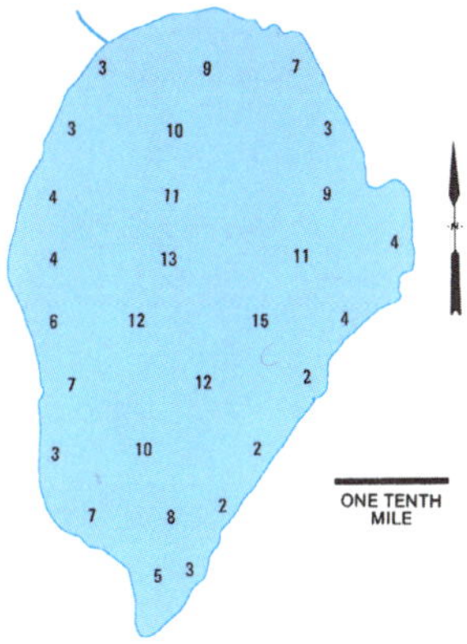

Kalers Pond

Waldoboro, Maine Atlas Map 13, E-4
Acres: 75, Max. Depth: 15 feet

BrT	BkT	RbT	Sal	Tog	Smt	LmB	SmB	WhP	Csk	WhF	Pic
✓											✓

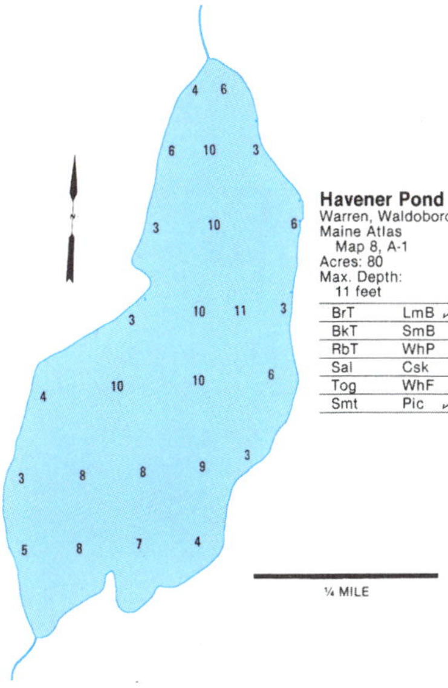

Havener Pond

Warren, Waldoboro
Maine Atlas
Map 8, A-1
Acres: 80
Max. Depth:
11 feet

BrT	LmB ✓
BkT	SmB
RbT	WhP
Sal	Csk
Tog	WhF
Smt	Pic ✓

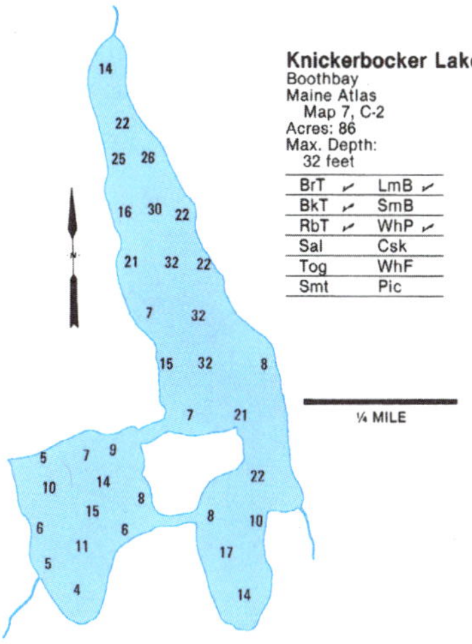

Knickerbocker Lakes

Boothbay
Maine Atlas
Map 7, C-2
Acres: 86
Max. Depth:
32 feet

BrT ✓	LmB ✓
BkT ✓	SmB
RbT ✓	WhP ✓
Sal	Csk
Tog	WhF
Smt	Pic

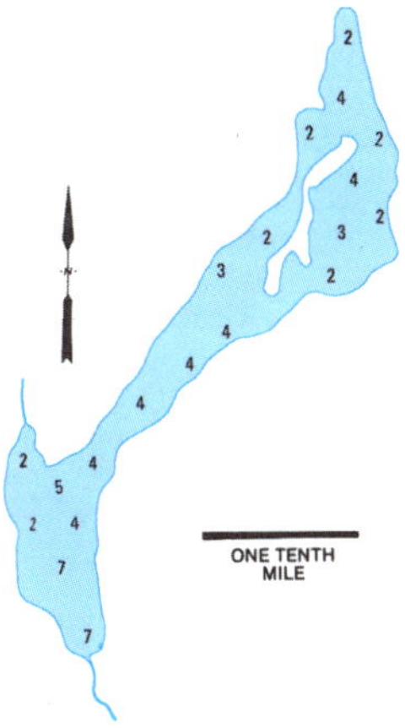

Ice Pond

Bristol
Maine Atlas
Map 7, C-4
Acres: 8
Max. Depth:
7 feet

BrT	LmB ✓
BkT ✓	SmB
RbT	WhP
Sal	Csk
Tog	WhF
Smt	Pic

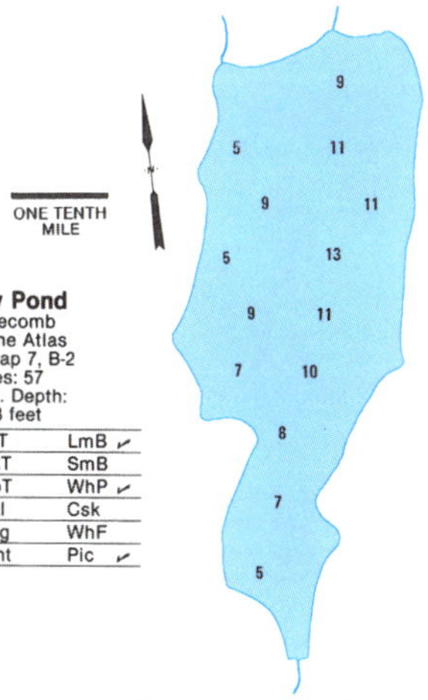

Lily Pond

Edgecomb
Maine Atlas
Map 7, B-2
Acres: 57
Max. Depth:
13 feet

BrT	LmB ✓
BkT	SmB
RbT	WhP ✓
Sal	Csk
Tog	WhF
Smt	Pic ✓

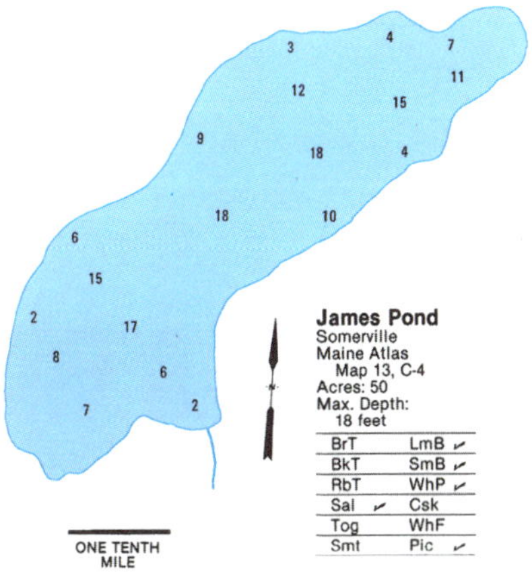

James Pond

Somerville
Maine Atlas
Map 13, C-4
Acres: 50
Max. Depth:
18 feet

BrT	LmB ✓
BkT	SmB ✓
RbT	WhP ✓
Sal ✓	Csk
Tog	WhF
Smt	Pic ✓

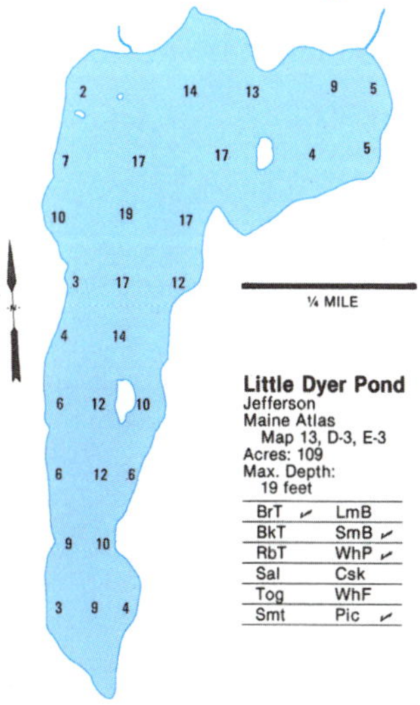

Little Dyer Pond

Jefferson
Maine Atlas
Map 13, D-3, E-3
Acres: 109
Max. Depth:
19 feet

BrT ✓	LmB
BkT	SmB ✓
RbT	WhP ✓
Sal	Csk
Tog	WhF
Smt	Pic ✓

Lincoln

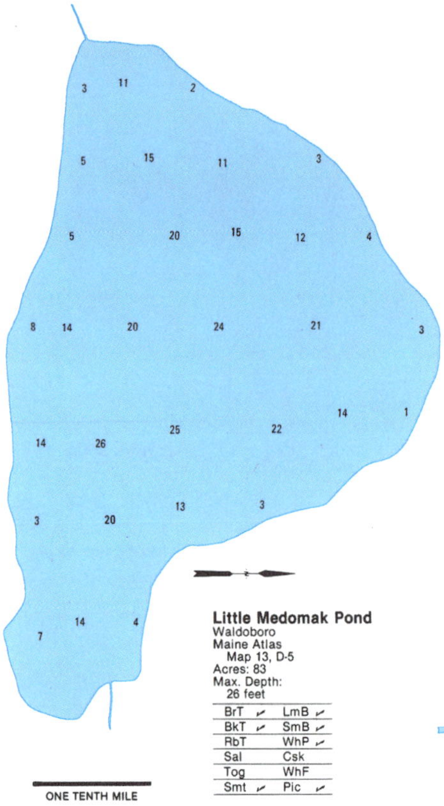

Little Medomak Pond
Waldoboro
Maine Atlas
Map 13, D-5
Acres: 83
Max. Depth:
26 feet

BrT	✓	LmB	✓
BkT	✓	SmB	✓
RbT		WhP	✓
Sal		Csk	
Tog		WhF	
Smt	✓	Pic	✓

McCurdy Pond
Bremen
Maine Atlas
Map 7, A-4
Acres: 207
Max. Depth:
41 feet

BrT	✓	LmB	
BkT		SmB	✓
RbT		WhP	✓
Sal		Csk	
Tog		WhF	
Smt	✓	Pic	✓

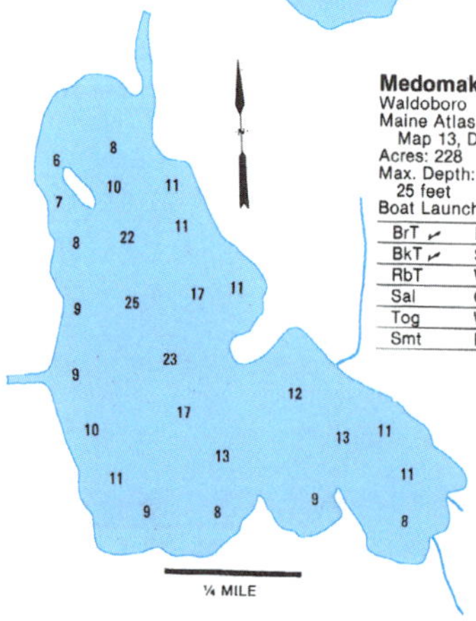

Medomak Pond
Waldoboro
Maine Atlas
Map 13, D-5
Acres: 228
Max. Depth:
25 feet
Boat Launch

BrT	✓	LmB	✓
BkT	✓	SmB	✓
RbT		WhP	✓
Sal		Csk	
Tog		WhF	
Smt		Pic	✓

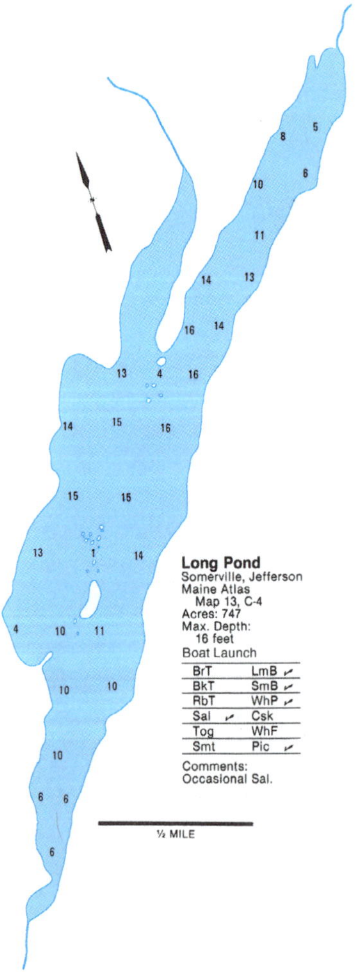

Long Pond
Somerville, Jefferson
Maine Atlas
Map 13, C-4
Acres: 747
Max. Depth:
16 feet
Boat Launch

BrT		LmB	✓
BkT		SmB	✓
RbT		WhP	✓
Sal	✓	Csk	
Tog		WhF	
Smt		Pic	✓

Comments:
Occasional Sal.

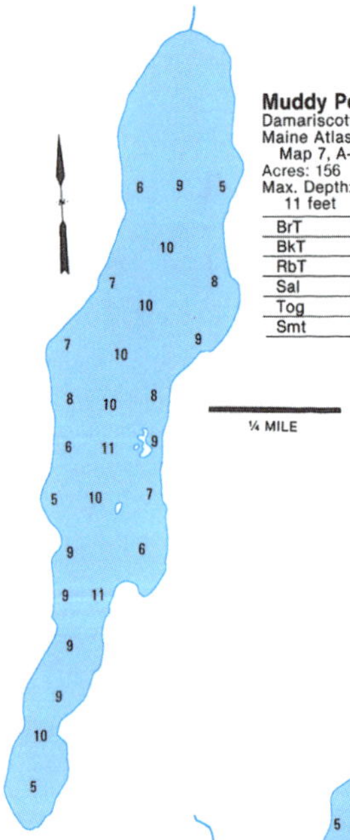

Muddy Pond
Damariscotta
Maine Atlas
Map 7, A-4
Acres: 156
Max. Depth:
11 feet

BrT		LmB	
BkT		SmB	✓
RbT		WhP	
Sal		Csk	
Tog		WhF	
Smt		Pic	✓

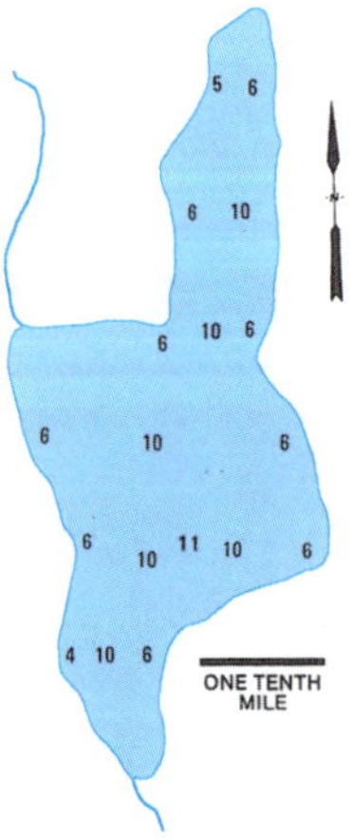

Musquash Pond
Jefferson
Maine Atlas
Map 13, E-3
Acres: 29
Max. Depth:
11 feet

BrT		LmB	
BkT		SmB	
RbT		WhP	✓
Sal		Csk	
Tog		WhF	
Smt		Pic	✓

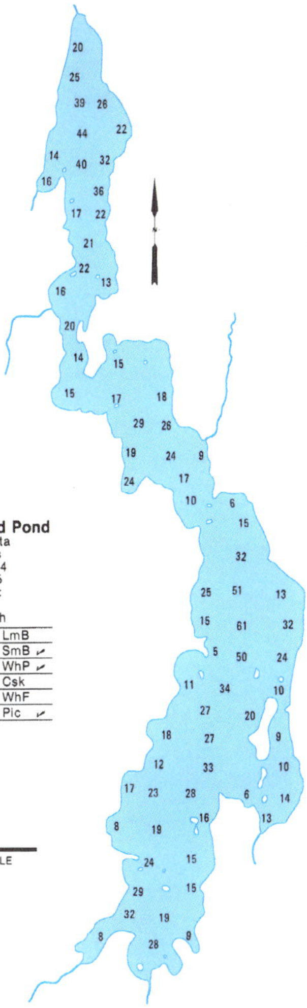

Pemaquid Pond

Damariscotta
Maine Atlas
Map 7, A-4
Acres: 1,515
Max. Depth:
61 feet
Boat Launch

BrT	✓	LmB	
BkT	✓	SmB	✓
RbT		WhP	✓
Sal		Csk	
Tog		WhF	
Smt		Pic	✓

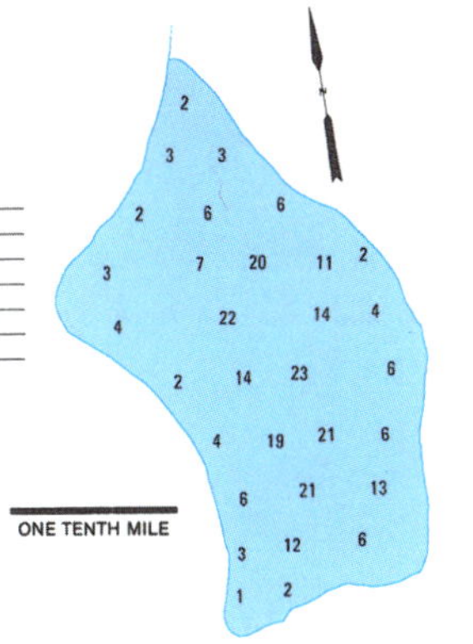

Ross Pond

Bristol
Maine Atlas
Map 7, B-4
Acres: 21
Max. Depth:
23 feet

BrT	✓	LmB	
BkT	✓	SmB	
RbT		WhP	
Sal		Csk	
Tog		WhF	
Smt		Pic	

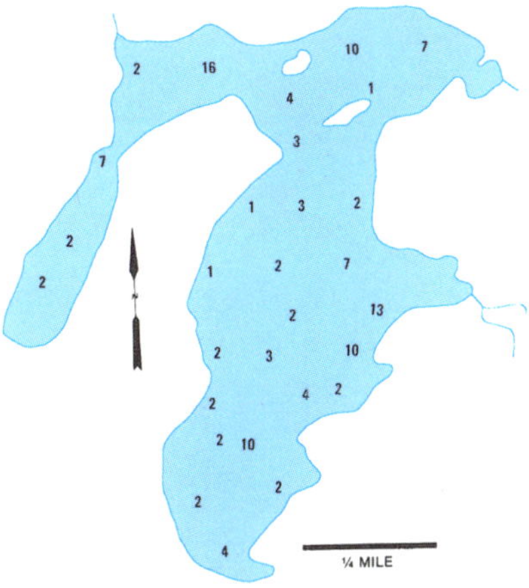

Sherman Lake

Newcastle, Maine Atlas Map 7, A-2, B-2
Acres: 237, Max. Depth: 16 feet, Boat Launch

BrT	BkT	RbT	Sal	Tog	Smt	LmB	SmB	WhP	Csk	WhF	Pic
						✓		✓			✓

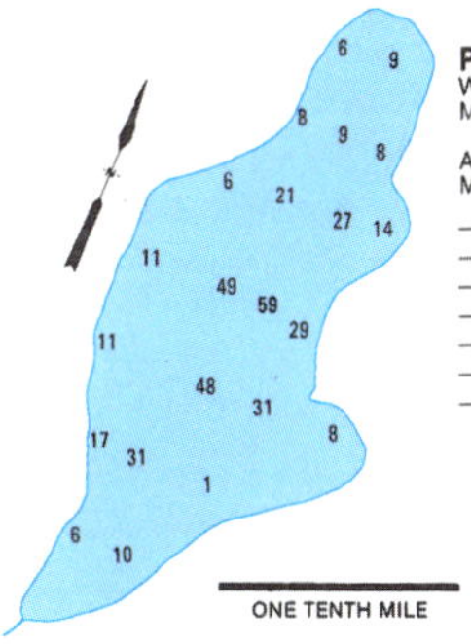

Peters Pond

Waldoboro
Maine Atlas
Map 7, A-5
Acres: 10
Max. Depth:
59 feet

BrT		LmB	
BkT	✓	SmB	
RbT		WhP	
Sal		Csk	
Tog		WhF	
Smt		Pic	

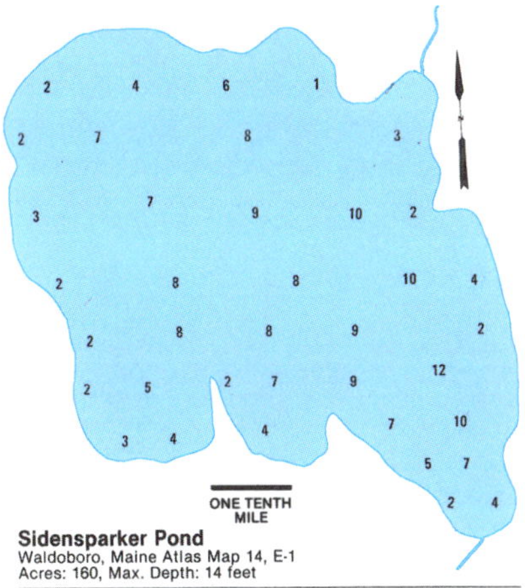

Sidensparker Pond

Waldoboro, Maine Atlas Map 14, E-1
Acres: 160, Max. Depth: 14 feet

BrT	BkT	RbT	Sal	Tog	Smt	LmB	SmB	WhP	Csk	WhF	Pic
						✓		✓			✓

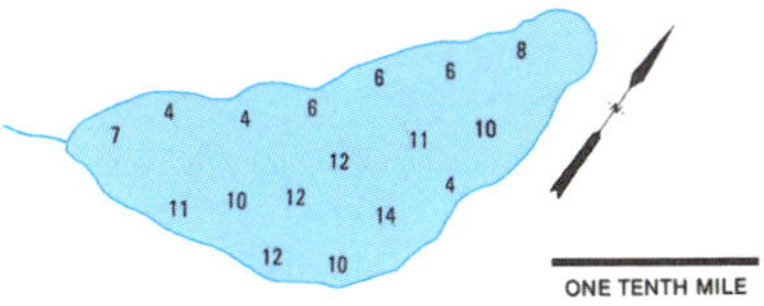

Pinkham Pond

Alna, Maine Atlas Map 13, E-2
Acres: 13, Max. Depth: 14 feet

BrT	BkT	RbT	Sal	Tog	Smt	LmB	SmB	WhP	Csk	WhF	Pic
✓	✓							✓			✓

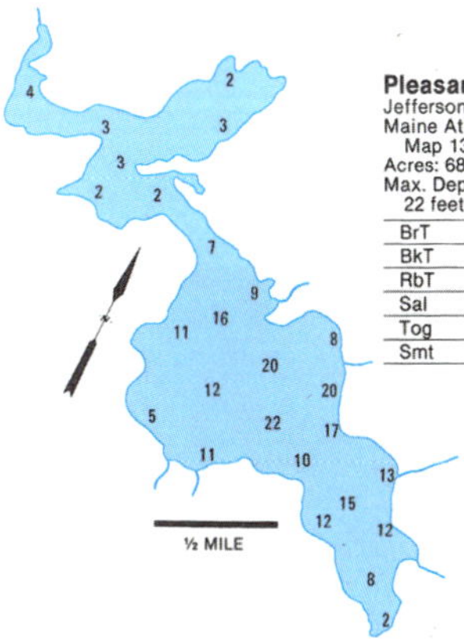

Pleasant Pond

Jefferson
Maine Atlas
Map 13, D-3
Acres: 682
Max. Depth:
22 feet

BrT		LmB	✓
BkT		SmB	✓
RbT		WhP	✓
Sal		Csk	
Tog		WhF	
Smt		Pic	✓

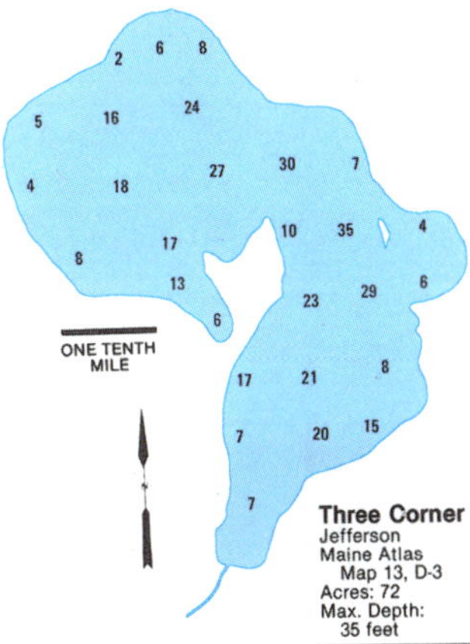

Three Corner Pond

Jefferson
Maine Atlas
Map 13, D-3
Acres: 72
Max. Depth:
35 feet

BrT		LmB	✓
BkT		SmB	
RbT		WhP	✓
Sal		Csk	
Tog		WhF	
Smt	✓	Pic	✓

Lincoln

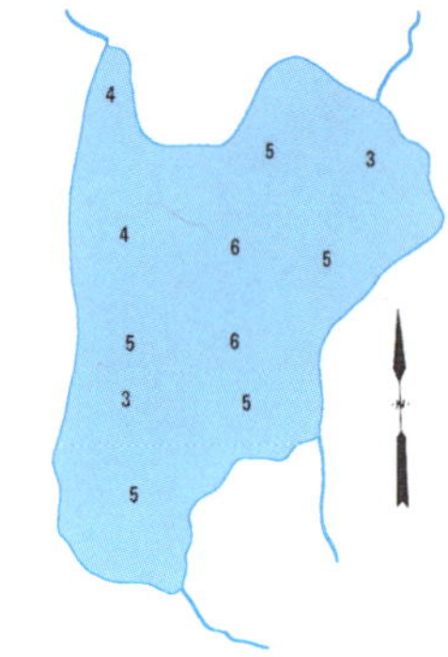

Travel Pond
Jefferson
Maine Atlas
Map 13, C-3, D-3
Acres: 102
Max. Depth:
6 feet

BrT	LmB
BkT	SmB
RbT	WhP ✓
Sal	Csk
Tog	WhF
Smt	Pic ✓

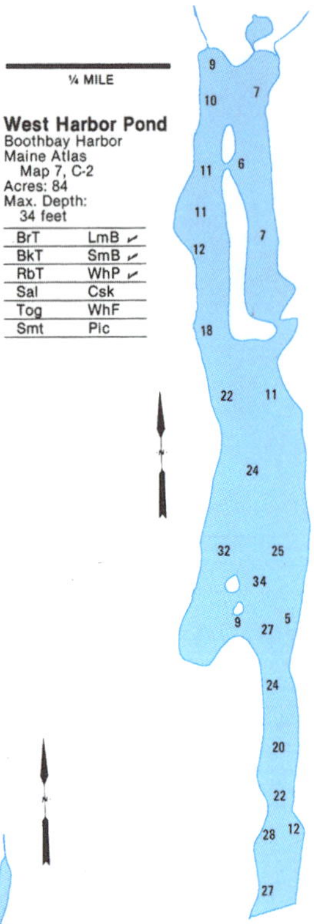

West Harbor Pond
Boothbay Harbor
Maine Atlas
Map 7, C-2
Acres: 84
Max. Depth:
34 feet

BrT	LmB ✓
BkT	SmB ✓
RbT	WhP ✓
Sal	Csk
Tog	WhF
Smt	Pic

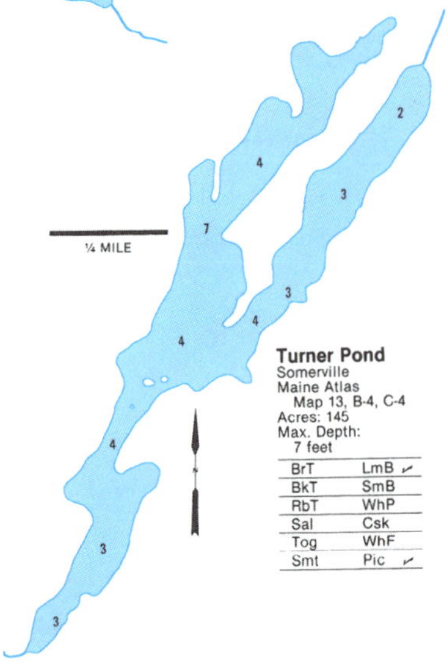

Turner Pond
Somerville
Maine Atlas
Map 13, B-4, C-4
Acres: 145
Max. Depth:
7 feet

BrT	LmB ✓
BkT	SmB
RbT	WhP
Sal	Csk
Tog	WhF
Smt	Pic ✓

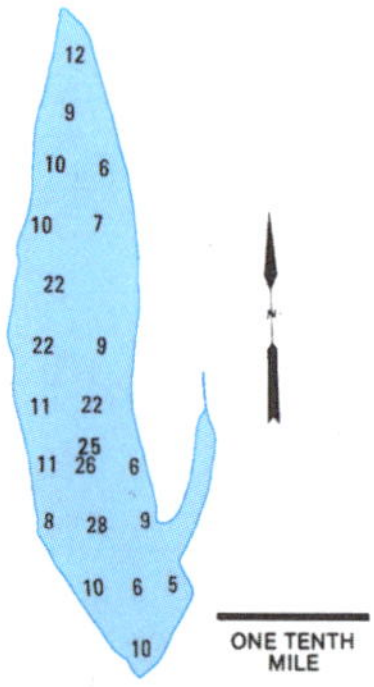

Wiley Pond
Boothbay, Maine Atlas Map 7, C-2
Acres: 18, Max. Depth: 25 feet, Boat Launch

BrT	BkT	RbT	Sal	Tog	Smt	LmB	SmB	WhP	Csk	WhF	Pic
	✓										

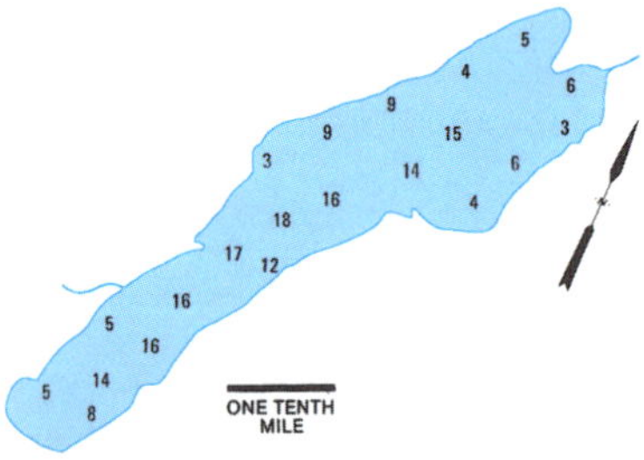

Weary Pond
Whitefield, Maine Atlas Map 13, D-2
Acres: 42, Max. Depth: 18 feet

BrT	BkT	RbT	Sal	Tog	Smt	LmB	SmB	WhP	Csk	WhF	Pic
							✓				

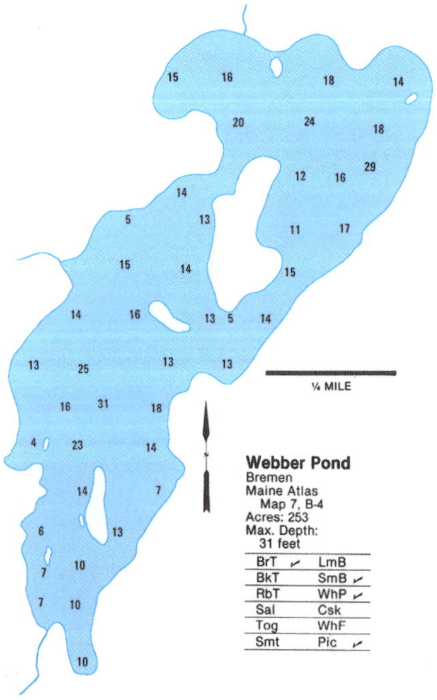

Webber Pond
Bremen
Maine Atlas
Map 7, B-4
Acres: 253
Max. Depth:
31 feet

BrT ✓	LmB
BkT	SmB ✓
RbT	WhP ✓
Sal	Csk
Tog	WhF
Smt	Pic ✓

Oxford County

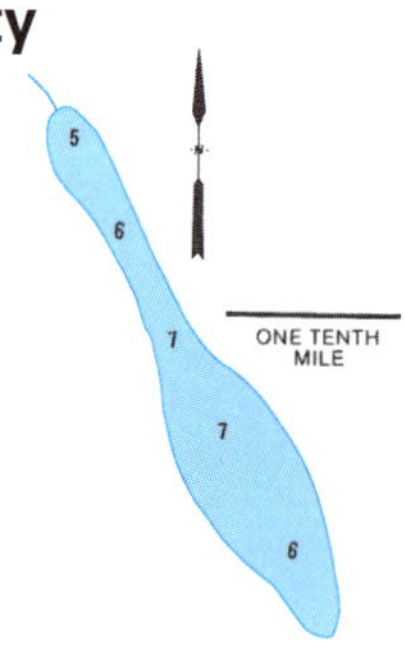

Abbie Pond
Bowmantown Twp
Maine Atlas
Map 28, A-1
Acres: 12
Max. Depth:
7 feet

BrT	LmB
BkT ✓	SmB
RbT	WhP
Sal	Csk
Tog	WhF
Smt	Pic

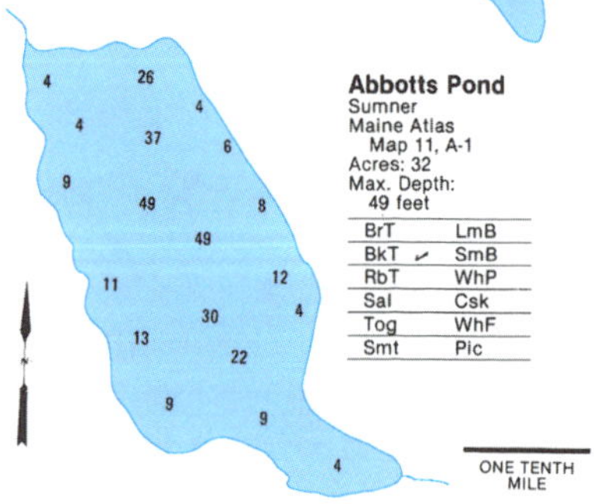

Abbotts Pond
Sumner
Maine Atlas
Map 11, A-1
Acres: 32
Max. Depth:
49 feet

BrT	LmB
BkT ✓	SmB
RbT	WhP
Sal	Csk
Tog	WhF
Smt	Pic

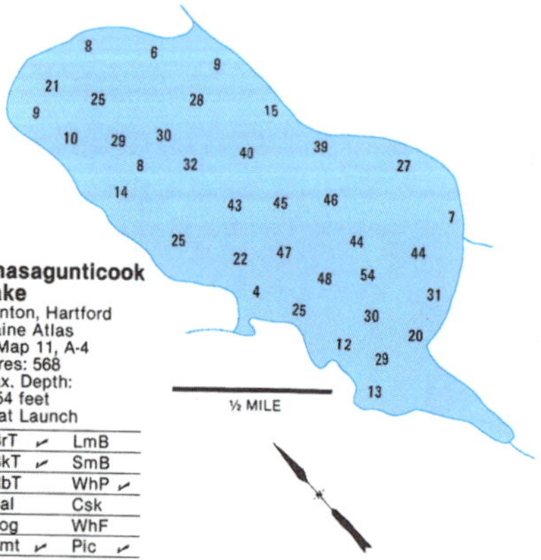

Anasagunticook Lake
Canton, Hartford
Maine Atlas
Map 11, A-4
Acres: 568
Max. Depth:
54 feet
Boat Launch

BrT ✓	LmB
BkT ✓	SmB
RbT	WhP ✓
Sal	Csk
Tog	WhF
Smt ✓	Pic ✓

Comments: Splake.

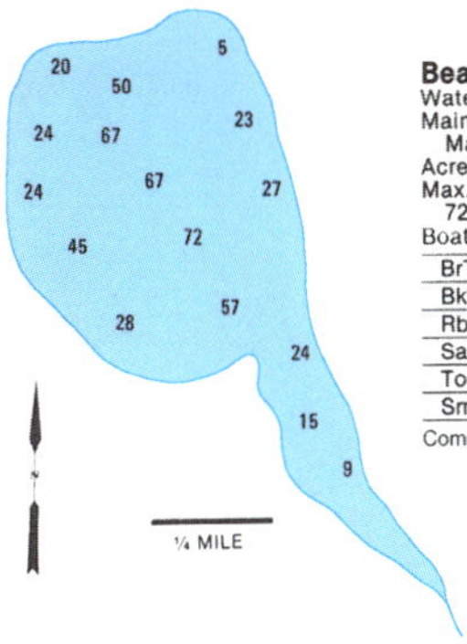

Bear Pond
Waterford
Maine Atlas
Map 10, E-4
Acres: 218
Max. Depth:
72 feet
Boat Launch

BrT		LmB	
BkT	✓	SmB	
RbT		WhP	✓
Sal	✓	Csk	
Tog	✓	WhF	
Smt	✓	Pic	✓

Comments: Splake.

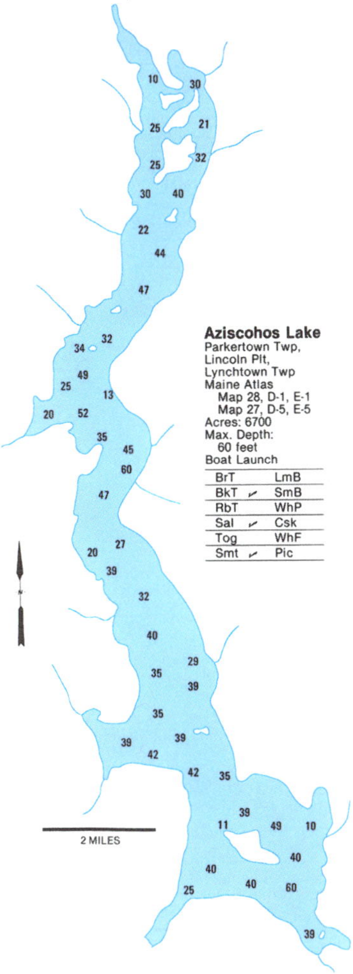

Aziscohos Lake
Parkertown Twp,
Lincoln Plt,
Lynchtown Twp
Maine Atlas
Map 28, D-1, E-1
Map 27, D-5, E-5
Acres: 6700
Max. Depth:
60 feet
Boat Launch

BrT		LmB	
BkT	✓	SmB	
RbT		WhP	
Sal	✓	Csk	
Tog		WhF	
Smt	✓	Pic	

Beaver Pond
Denmark
Maine Atlas
Map 4, A-2, A-3,
B-2, B-3
Acres: 128
Max. Depth:
8 feet

BrT		LmB	✓
BkT		SmB	
RbT		WhP	
Sal		Csk	
Tog		WhF	
Smt		Pic	✓

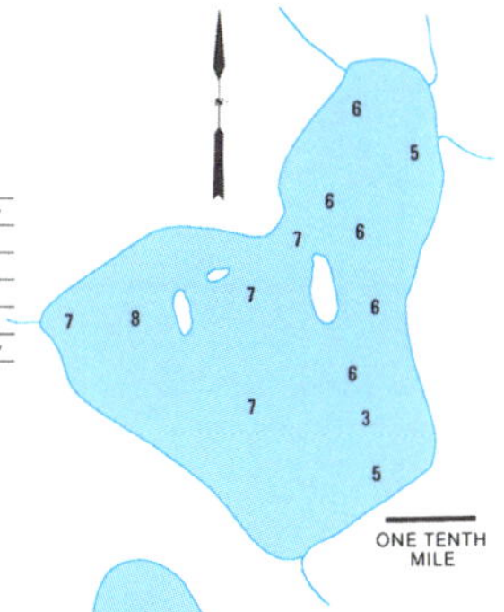

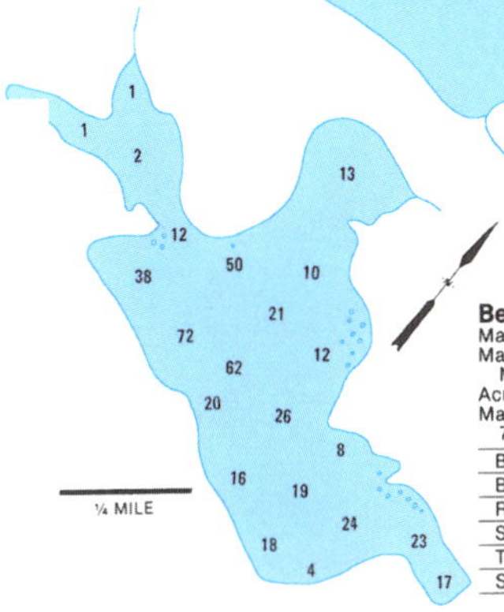

Beaver Pond
Magalloway Plt
Maine Atlas
Map 18, A-1
Acres: 179
Max. Depth:
72 feet

BrT		LmB	
BkT	✓	SmB	
RbT		WhP	
Sal		Csk	
Tog		WhF	
Smt	✓	Pic	

Aziscohos Pond
Magalloway Plt
Maine Atlas
Map 18, A-1
Acres: 12
Max. Depth:
32 feet

BrT		LmB	
BkT	✓	SmB	
RbT		WhP	
Sal		Csk	
Tog		WhF	
Smt		Pic	

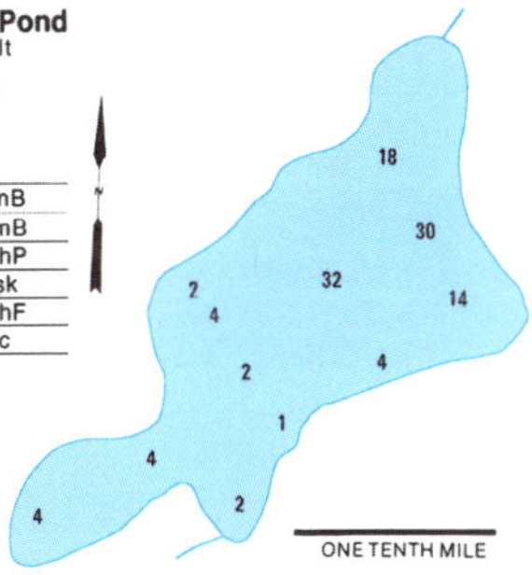

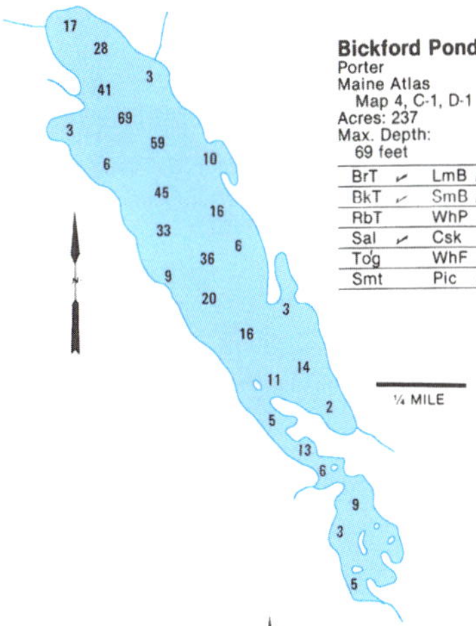

Bickford Pond
Porter
Maine Atlas
Map 4, C-1, D-1
Acres: 237
Max. Depth:
69 feet

BrT	✓	LmB	✓
BkT	✓	SmB	✓
RbT		WhP	
Sal	✓	Csk	
Tog		WhF	
Smt		Pic	✓

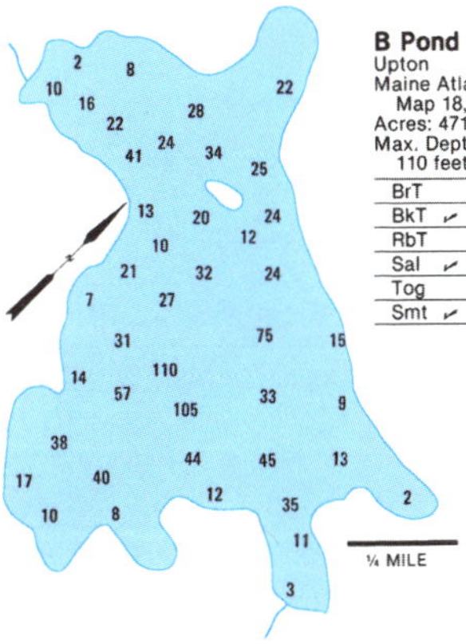

B Pond
Upton
Maine Atlas
Map 18, B-1, C-1
Acres: 471
Max. Depth:
110 feet

BrT		LmB	
BkT	✓	SmB	
RbT		WhP	
Sal	✓	Csk	
Tog		WhF	
Smt	✓	Pic	✓

Big Concord Pond
Woodstock
Maine Atlas
Map 11, A-1
Acres: 135
Max. Depth:
12 feet

BrT		LmB	
BkT		SmB	✓
RbT		WhP	✓
Sal		Csk	
Tog		WhF	
Smt		Pic	✓

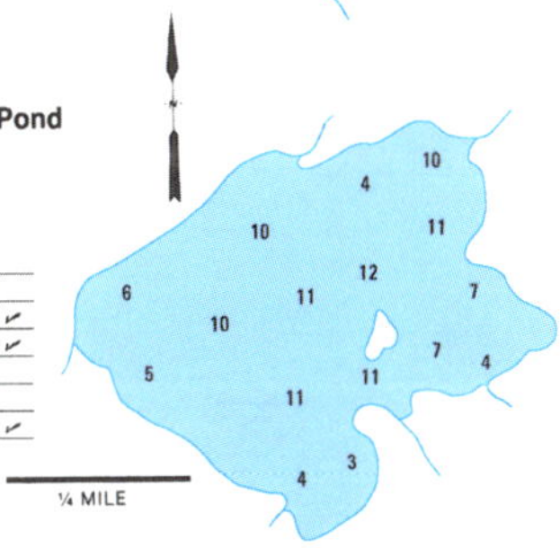

Back Pond
Stonehem, Lovell
Maine Atlas
Map 10, D-3
Acres: 62
Max. Depth:
32 feet

BrT		LmB	
BkT	✓	SmB	
RbT		WhP	
Sal		Csk	
Tog		WhF	
Smt		Pic	✓

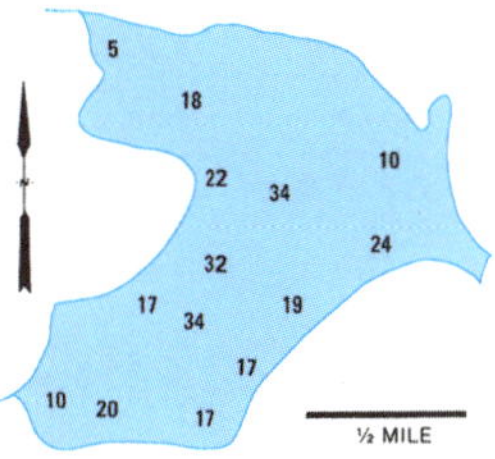

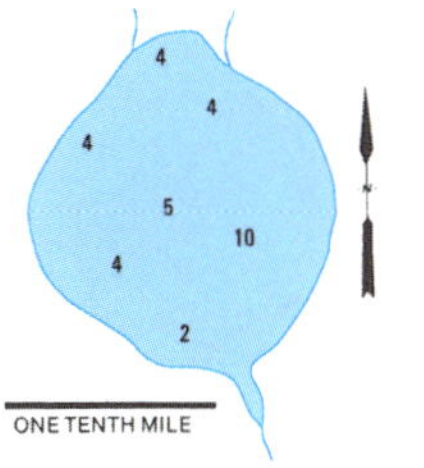

Bird Pond
Norway
Maine Atlas
Map 11, C-1, D-1
Acres: 4
Max. Depth:
10 feet

BrT		LmB	
BkT		SmB	
RbT		WhP	
Sal		Csk	
Tog		WhF	
Smt		Pic	✓

Oxford

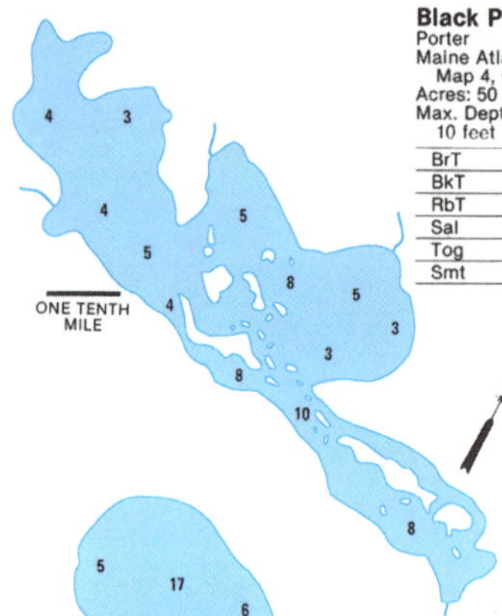

Black Pond
Porter
Maine Atlas
Map 4, C-2, D-2
Acres: 50
Max. Depth:
10 feet

BrT		LmB	✓
BkT		SmB	
RbT		WhP	
Sal		Csk	
Tog		WhF	
Smt		Pic	✓

C Pond
C Surplus, Maine Atlas Map 18, C-2
Acres: 173, Max. Depth: 36 feet

BrT	BkT	RbT	Sal	Tog	Smt	LmB	SmB	WhP	Csk	WhF	Pic
	✓				✓						

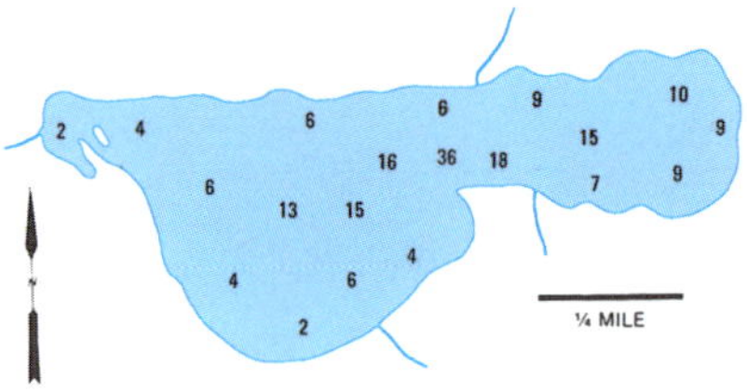

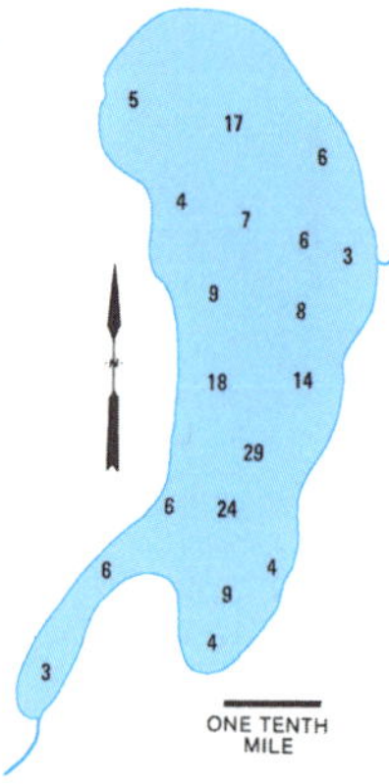

Bradley Pond
Lovell
Maine Atlas
Map 10, D-2
Acres: 34
Max. Depth:
29 feet

BrT	✓	LmB	✓
BkT	✓	SmB	✓
RbT		WhP	
Sal		Csk	
Tog		WhF	
Smt		Pic	✓

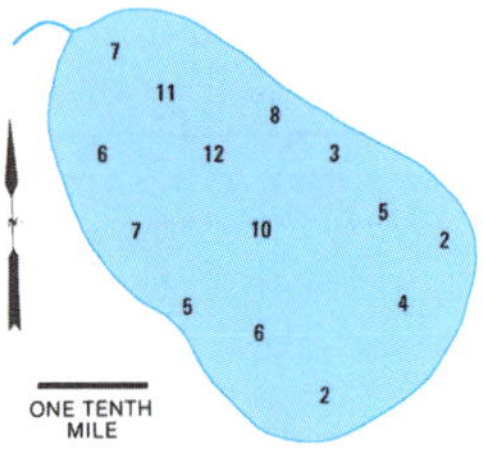

Chapman Pond
Porter
Maine Atlas
Map 4, C-2
Acres: 13
Max. Depth:
12 feet

BrT		LmB	
BkT	✓	SmB	
RbT		WhP	
Sal		Csk	
Tog		WhF	
Smt		Pic	✓

Clays Pond
Fryeburg
Maine Atlas
Map 4, B-1
Acres: 21
Max. Depth:
21 feet
Boat Launch

BrT	✓	LmB	
BkT	✓	SmB	
RbT		WhP	
Sal		Csk	
Tog		WhF	
Smt		Pic	✓

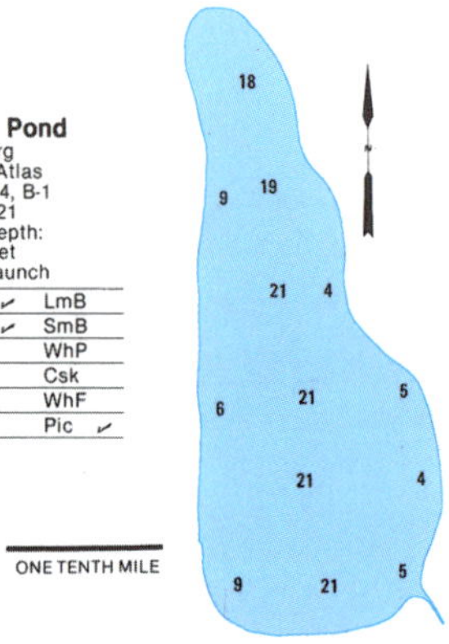

Broken Bridge Pond
Albany Twp
Maine Atlas
Map 10, C-3
Acres: 18
Max. Depth:
25 feet

BrT		LmB	
BkT	✓	SmB	
RbT		WhP	
Sal		Csk	
Tog		WhF	
Smt		Pic	

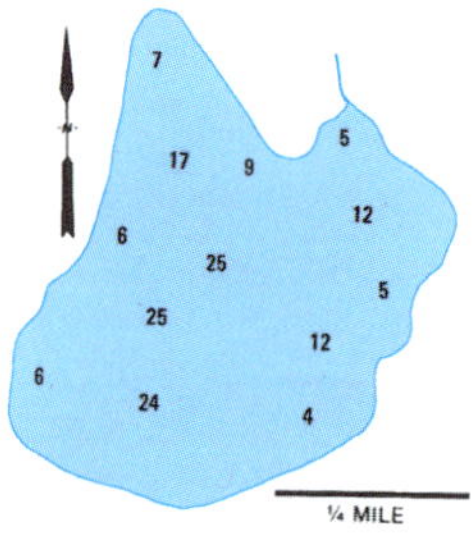

Bryant Pond
Woodstock,
Greenwood
Maine Atlas
Map 10, B-5
Acres: 278
Max. Depth:
63 feet
Boat Launch

BrT	✓	LmB	
BkT	✓	SmB	
RbT		WhP	
Sal	✓	Csk	
Tog		WhF	
Smt	✓	Pic	✓

Comments: Splake.

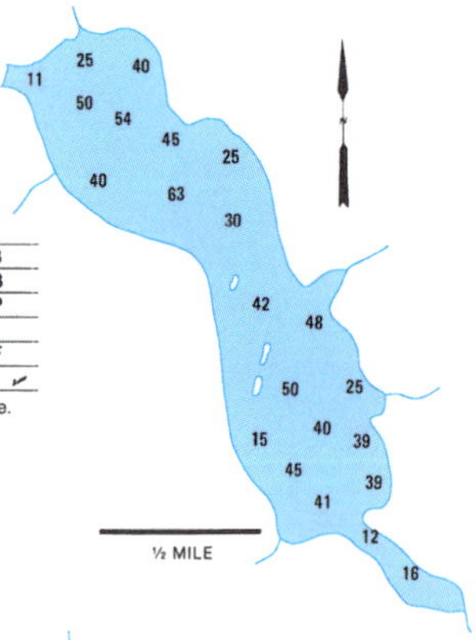

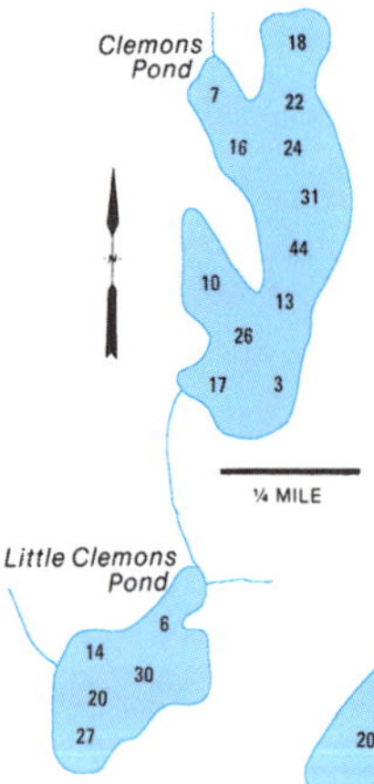

Clemons and Little Clemons Ponds
Hiram
Maine Atlas
Map 4, C-2
Acres: Clemons-64,
Little Clemons-25
Max. Depth:
Clemons-44 feet
Little Clemons-
30 feet
Boat Launch

BrT		LmB	✓
BkT	✓	SmB	✓
RbT		WhP	
Sal		Csk	
Tog		WhF	
Smt	✓	Pic	✓

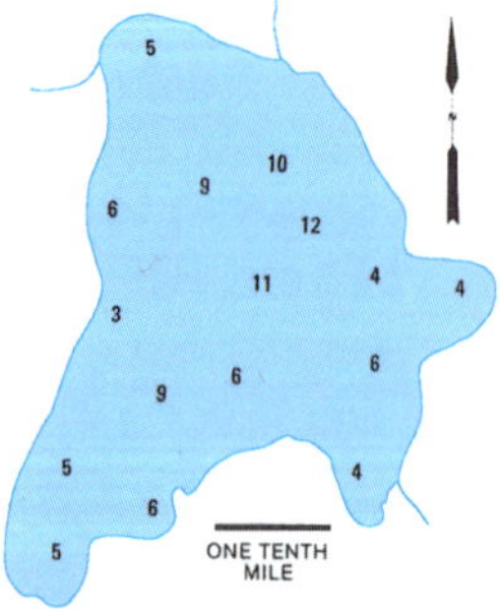

Bunganock Pond
Hartford
Maine Atlas
Map 11, B-3
Acres: 51
Max. Depth:
12 feet
Boat Launch

BrT	✓	LmB	
BkT		SmB	
RbT		WhP	
Sal		Csk	
Tog		WhF	
Smt		Pic	✓

Colcord Pond
Porter
Maine Atlas
Map 4, C-1
Acres: 304
Max. Depth:
105 feet

BrT		LmB	✓
BkT	✓	SmB	
RbT		WhP	
Sal	✓	Csk	
Tog	✓	WhF	
Smt		Pic	✓

Comments: Splake.

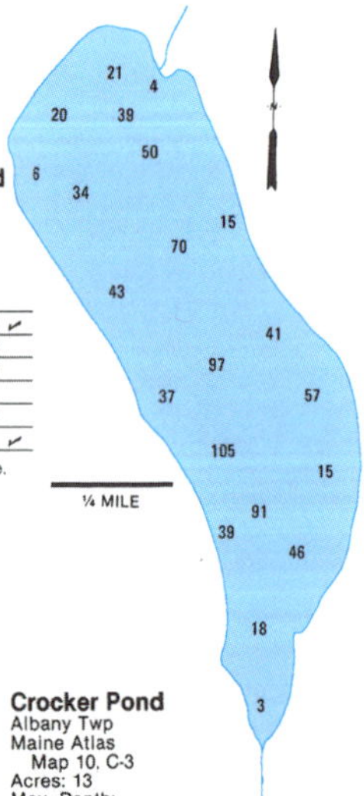

Burnt Meadow Pond
Brownfield
Maine Atlas
Map 4, B-2
Acres: 69
Max. Depth:
45 feet
Boat Launch

BrT	✓	LmB	
BkT	✓	SmB	
RbT		WhP	
Sal		Csk	
Tog		WhF	
Smt	✓	Pic	✓

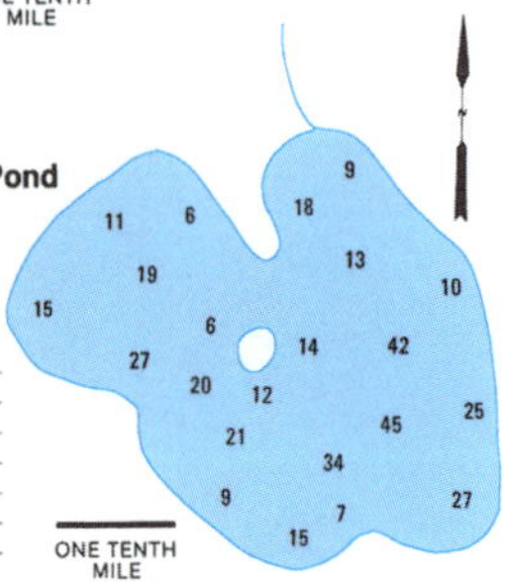

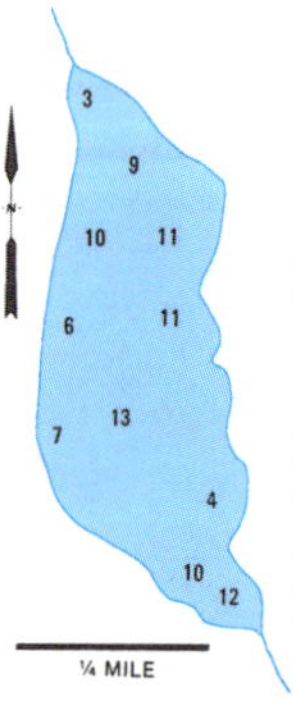

Crocker Pond
Albany Twp
Maine Atlas
Map 10, C-3
Acres: 13
Max. Depth:
13 feet

BrT		LmB	
BkT	✓	SmB	
RbT		WhP	
Sal		Csk	
Tog		WhF	
Smt		Pic	

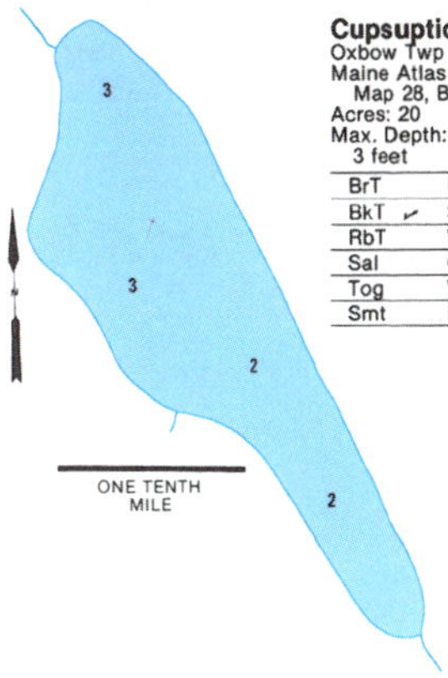

Cupsuptic Pond
Oxbow Twp
Maine Atlas
Map 28, B-2
Acres: 20
Max. Depth:
3 feet

BrT		LmB	
BkT	✓	SmB	
RbT		WhP	
Sal		Csk	
Tog		WhF	
Smt		Pic	

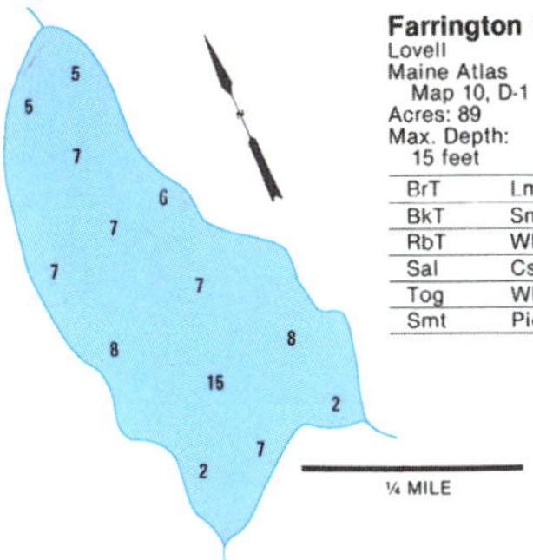

Farrington Pond
Lovell
Maine Atlas
Map 10, D-1
Acres: 89
Max. Depth:
15 feet

BrT		LmB	✓
BkT		SmB	✓
RbT		WhP	
Sal		Csk	
Tog		WhF	
Smt		Pic	✓

Forest Pond
Canton
Maine Atlas
Map 11, A-4
Acres: 51
Max. Depth:
23 feet

BrT		LmB	✓
BkT	✓	SmB	✓
RbT	✓	WhP	
Sal		Csk	
Tog		WhF	
Smt		Pic	✓

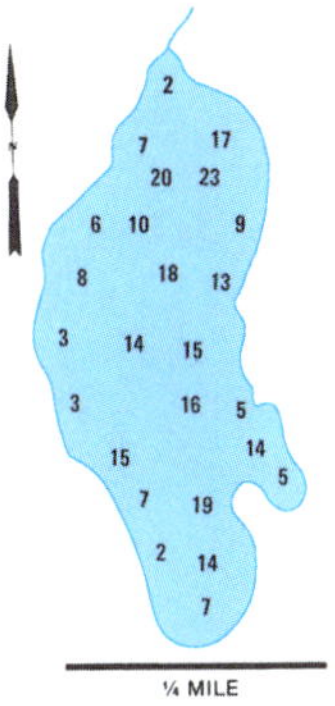

Cushman Pond
Lovell
Maine Atlas
Map 10, D-2, D-3
Acres: 32
Max. Depth:
21 feet

BrT		LmB	
BkT	✓	SmB	
RbT		WhP	
Sal		Csk	
Tog		WhF	
Smt		Pic	

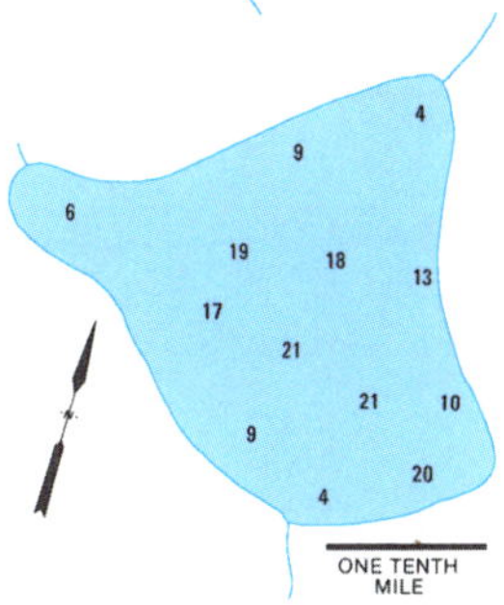

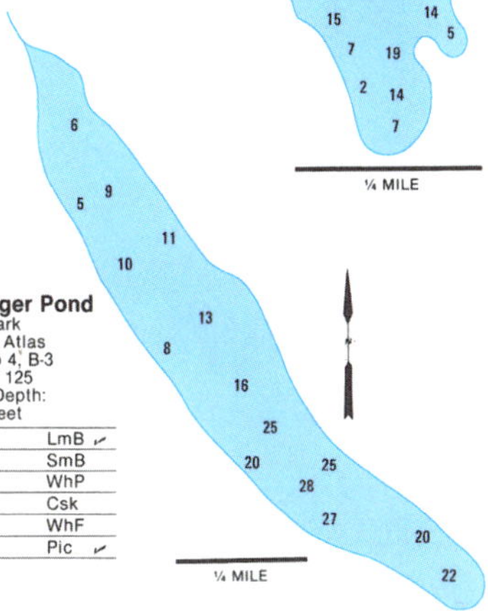

Granger Pond
Denmark
Maine Atlas
Map 4, B-3
Acres: 125
Max. Depth:
28 feet

BrT		LmB	✓
BkT		SmB	
RbT		WhP	
Sal		Csk	
Tog		WhF	
Smt		Pic	✓

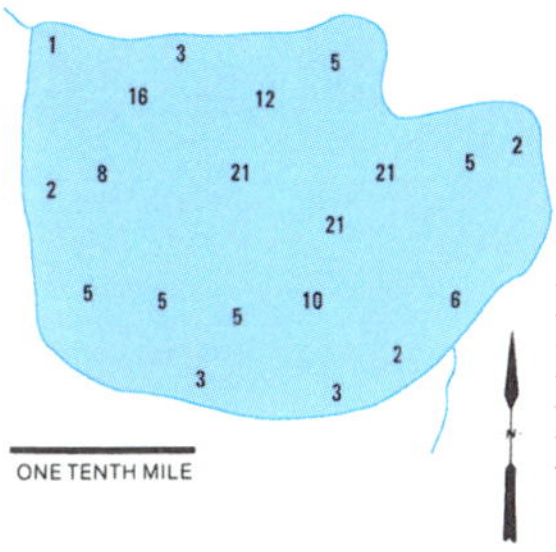

Cushman Pond
Sumner
Maine Atlas
Map 11, B-3
Acres: 15
Max. Depth:
21 feet

BrT		LmB	
BkT	✓	SmB	
RbT		WhP	
Sal		Csk	
Tog		WhF	
Smt		Pic	

East Richardson Ponds
Adamstown Twp
Maine Atlas
Map 28, E-2
Acres: Upper-85, Lower-54
Max. Depth:
Upper-20 feet,
Lower-15 feet

BrT		LmB	
BkT	✓	SmB	
RbT		WhP	
Sal		Csk	
Tog		WhF	
Smt	✓	Pic	

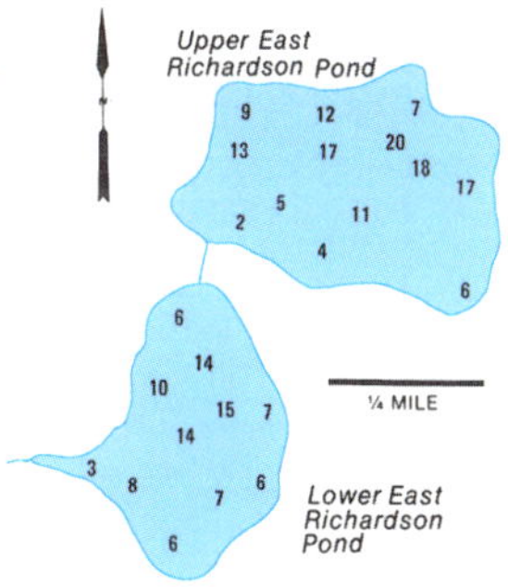

Green Pond
Oxford
Maine Atlas
Map 11, E-2
Acres: 38
Max. Depth:
28 feet

BrT		LmB	
BkT		SmB	
RbT		WhP	✓
Sal		Csk	
Tog		WhF	
Smt		Pic	

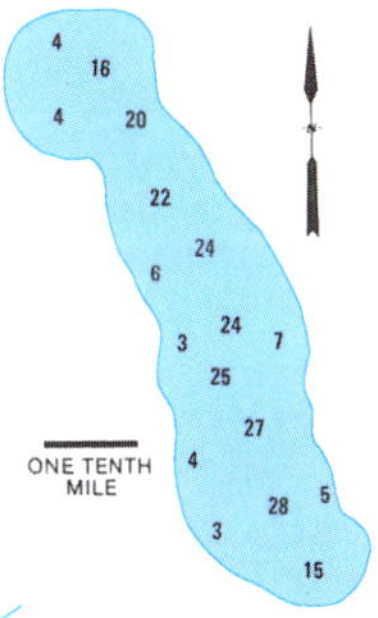

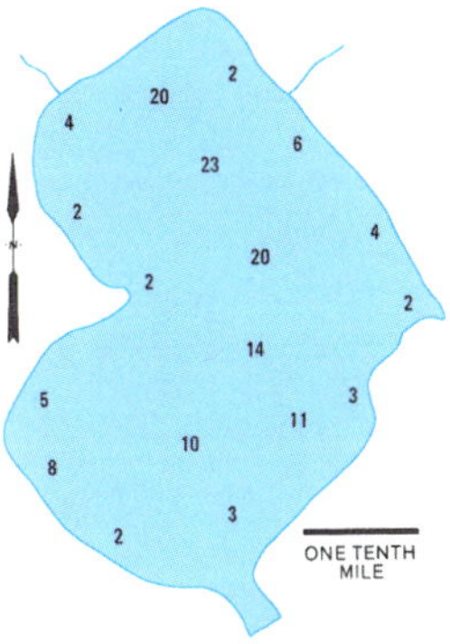

Halfmoon Pond
Mexico, Carthage
Maine Atlas
Map 19, D-1
Acres: 60
Max. Depth:
23 feet

BrT		LmB	
BkT	✓	SmB	
RbT		WhP	
Sal		Csk	
Tog		WhF	
Smt		Pic	✓

Comments:
Primarily pickerel fishery.

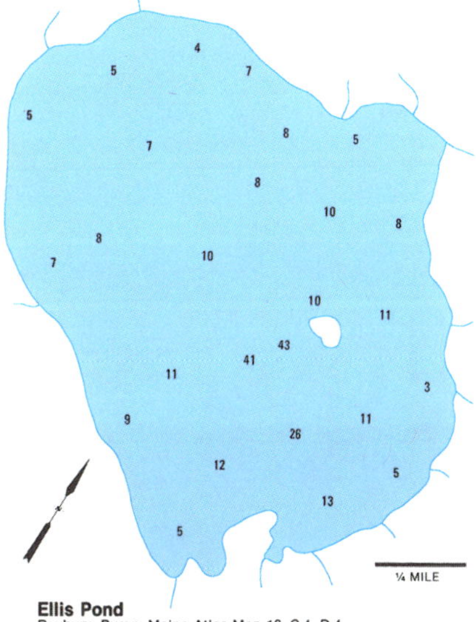

Ellis Pond
Roxbury, Byron, Maine Atlas Map 18, C-4, D-4
Acres: 896, Max. Depth: 43 feet, Boat Launch

BrT	BkT	RbT	Sal	Tog	Smt	LmB	SmB	WhP	Csk	WhF	Pic
	✓					✓	✓	✓			✓

Hall Pond
Paris
Maine Atlas
Map 11, D-2
Acres: 51
Max. Depth:
26 feet

BrT	✓	LmB	
BkT	✓	SmB	
RbT		WhP	
Sal		Csk	
Tog		WhF	
Smt		Pic	

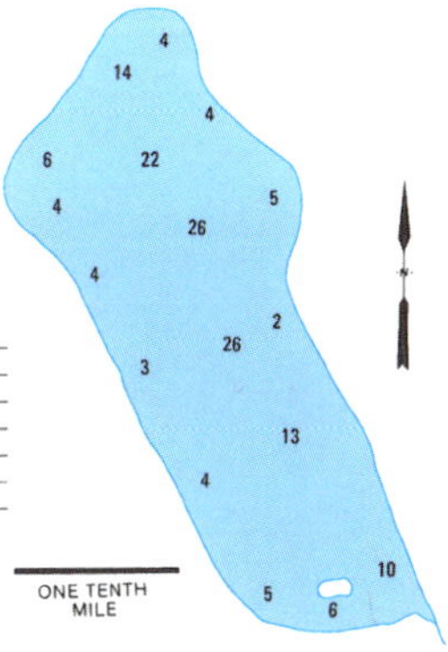

Oxford

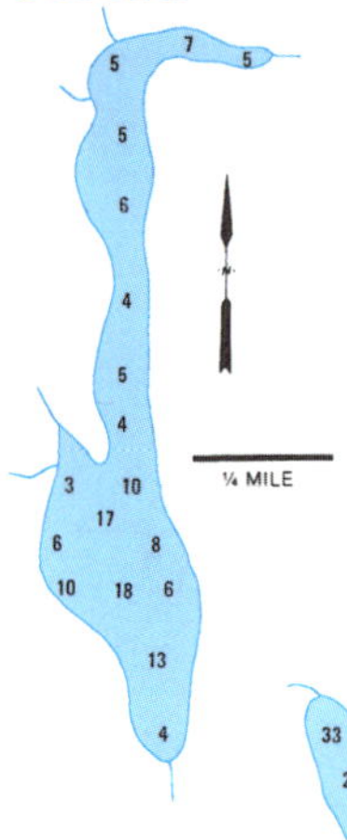

Hicks Pond
Greenwood
Maine Atlas
Map 10, C-5
Acres: 89
Max. Depth:
18 feet

BrT		LmB	✓
BkT		SmB	✓
RbT		WhP	
Sal		Csk	
Tog		WhF	
Smt		Pic	✓

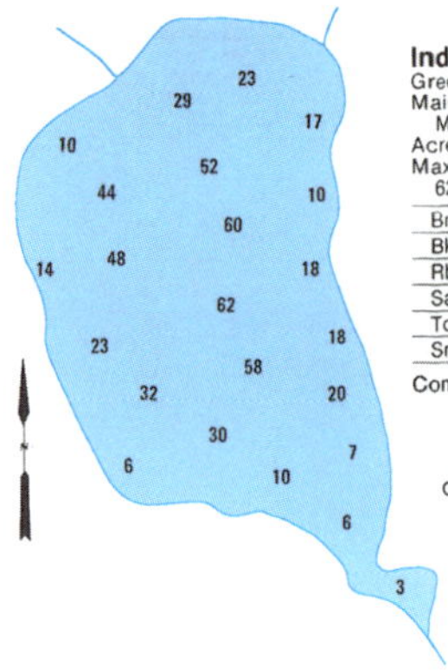

Indian Pond
Greenwood
Maine Atlas
Map 10, B-5
Acres: 68
Max. Depth:
62 feet

BrT		LmB	
BkT	✓	SmB	
RbT		WhP	
Sal		Csk	
Tog		WhF	
Smt	✓	Pic	✓

Comments: Splake.

Hogan Pond
Oxford
Maine Atlas
Map 11, E-2
Acres: 177
Max. Depth:
34 feet

BrT		LmB	✓
BkT		SmB	✓
RbT		WhP	✓
Sal		Csk	
Tog		WhF	
Smt		Pic	✓

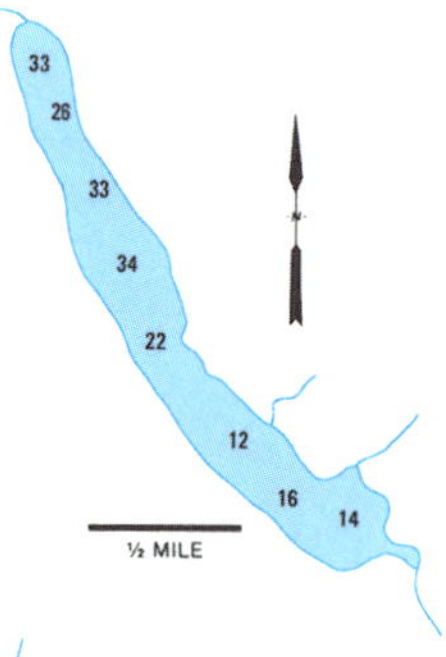

Jaybird Pond
Hiram, Porter
Maine Atlas
Map 4, C-2
Acres: 13
Max. Depth:
21 feet

BrT	✓	LmB	✓
BkT	✓	SmB	
RbT	✓	WhP	
Sal		Csk	
Tog		WhF	
Smt		Pic	

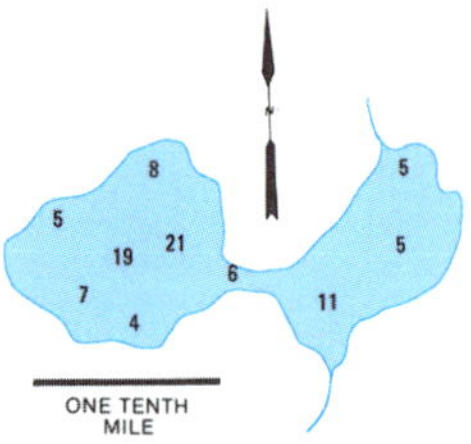

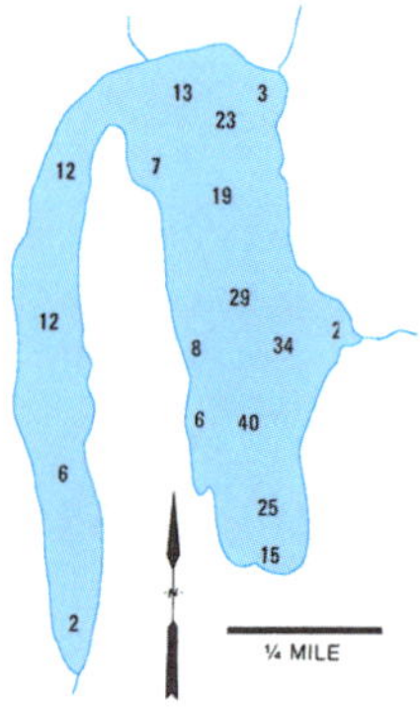

Horseshoe Pond
Lovell, Stoneham
Maine Atlas
Map 10, D-1
Acres: 132
Max. Depth:
40 feet
Boat Launch

BrT	✓	LmB	
BkT	✓	SmB	✓
RbT		WhP	
Sal		Csk	
Tog		WhF	
Smt	✓	Pic	✓

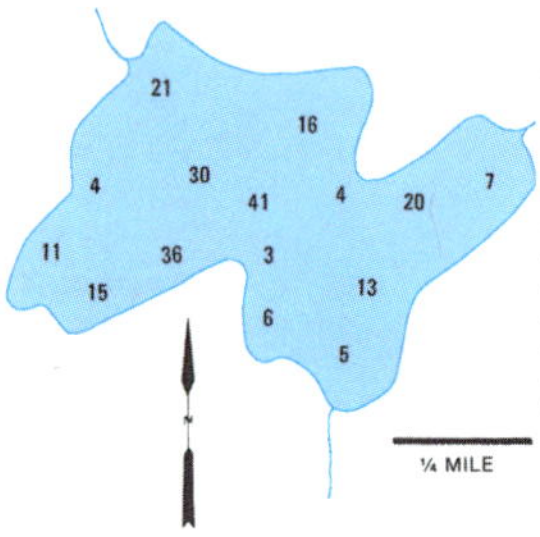

Jewett Pond
Waterford
Maine Atlas
Map 10, D-3
Acres: 32
Max. Depth:
41 feet

BrT		LmB	
BkT		SmB	✓
RbT		WhP	
Sal		Csk	
Tog		WhF	
Smt		Pic	✓

Howard Pond
Hanover
Maine Atlas
Map 18, E-4
Acres: 109
Max. Depth:
118 feet

BrT		LmB	
BkT	✓	SmB	
RbT		WhP	
Sal	✓	Csk	
Tog		WhF	
Smt	✓	Pic	

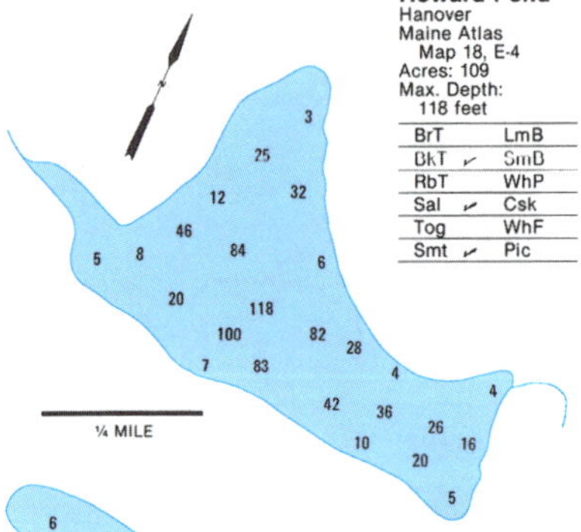

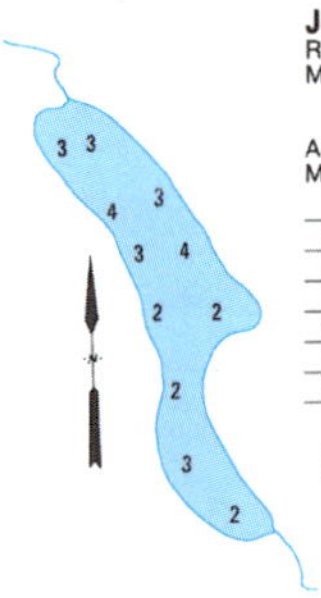

Joes Pond
Rumford
Maine Atlas
Map 18, E-5
Map 19, E-1
Acres: 15
Max. Depth:
4 feet

BrT		LmB	
BkT		SmB	
RbT		WhP	
Sal		Csk	
Tog		WhF	
Smt		Pic	✓

Keewaydin Lake
Stoneham
Maine Atlas
Map 10, C-2, C-3
Acres: 307
Max. Depth:
52 feet
Boat Launch

BrT		LmB	
BkT	✓	SmB	✓
RbT		WhP	✓
Sal	✓	Csk	
Tog	✓	WhF	
Smt	✓	Pic	✓

Comments: Splake.

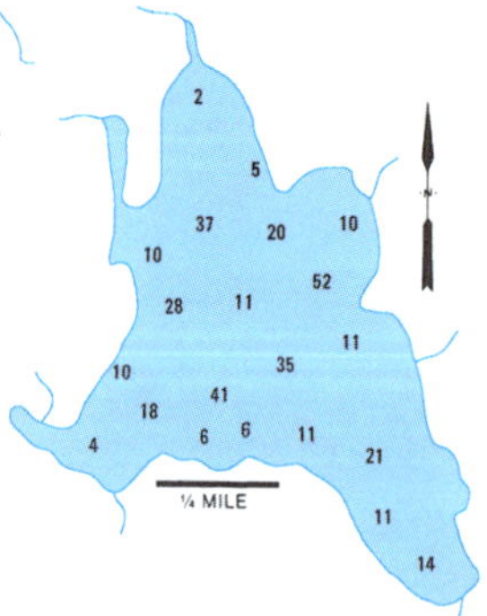

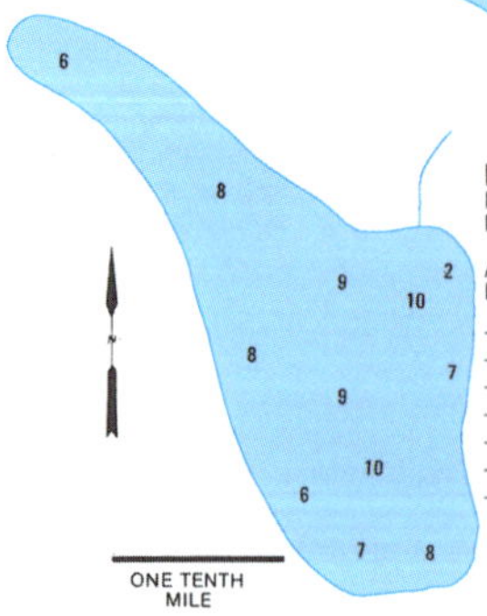

Hunt Pond
Fryeburg
Maine Atlas
Map 10, E-1
Acres: 25
Max. Depth:
10 feet

BrT		LmB	
BkT		SmB	
RbT		WhP	
Sal		Csk	
Tog		WhF	
Smt		Pic	✓

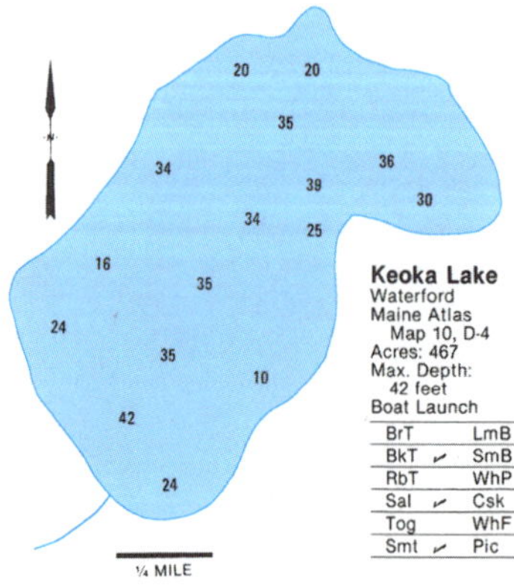

Keoka Lake
Waterford
Maine Atlas
Map 10, D-4
Acres: 467
Max. Depth:
42 feet
Boat Launch

BrT		LmB	
BkT	✓	SmB	✓
RbT		WhP	
Sal	✓	Csk	
Tog		WhF	
Smt	✓	Pic	✓

Hutchinson Pond
Albany Twp
Maine Atlas
Map 10, C-4
Acres: 93
Max. Depth:
38 feet
Boat Launch

BrT	✓	LmB	✓
BkT	✓	SmB	✓
RbT		WhP	
Sal		Csk	
Tog		WhF	
Smt	✓	Pic	✓

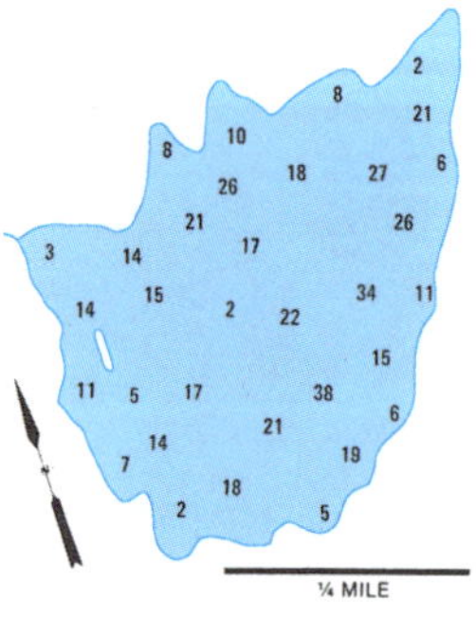

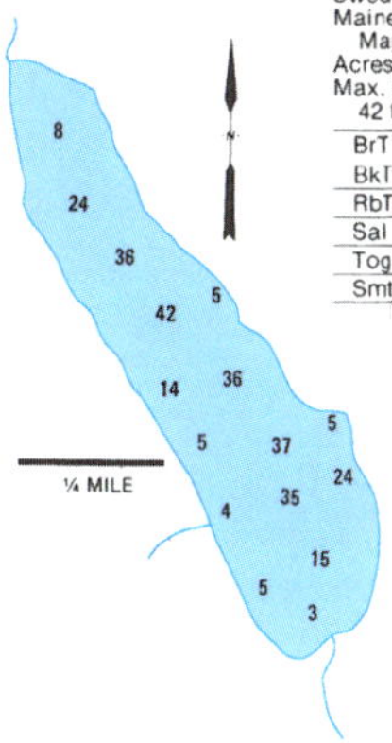

Keys Pond
Sweden
Maine Atlas
Map 10, E-3
Acres: 192
Max. Depth:
42 feet

BrT		LmB	
BkT	✓	SmB	
RbT		WhP	
Sal		Csk	
Tog		WhF	
Smt		Pic	✓

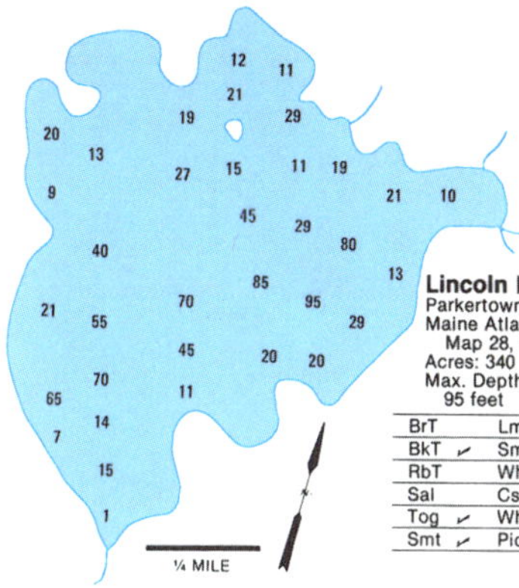

Lincoln Pond
Parkertown Twp
Maine Atlas
Map 28, D-1
Acres: 340
Max. Depth:
95 feet

BrT		LmB	
BkT	✓	SmB	
RbT		WhP	
Sal		Csk	
Tog	✓	WhF	
Smt	✓	Pic	

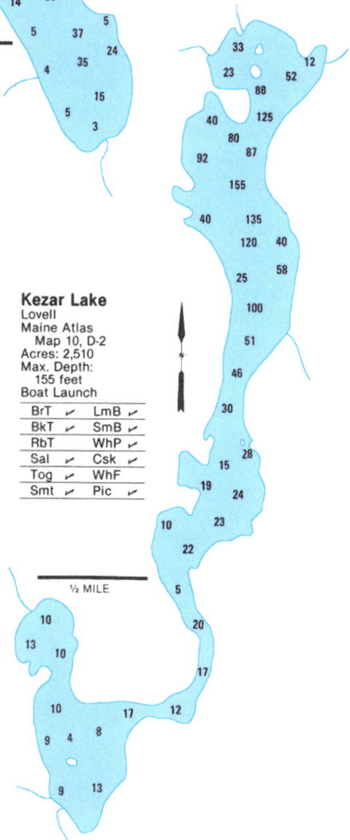

Kezar Lake
Lovell
Maine Atlas
Map 10, D-2
Acres: 2,510
Max. Depth:
155 feet
Boat Launch

BrT	✓	LmB	✓
BkT	✓	SmB	✓
RbT		WhP	✓
Sal	✓	Csk	✓
Tog	✓	WhF	
Smt	✓	Pic	✓

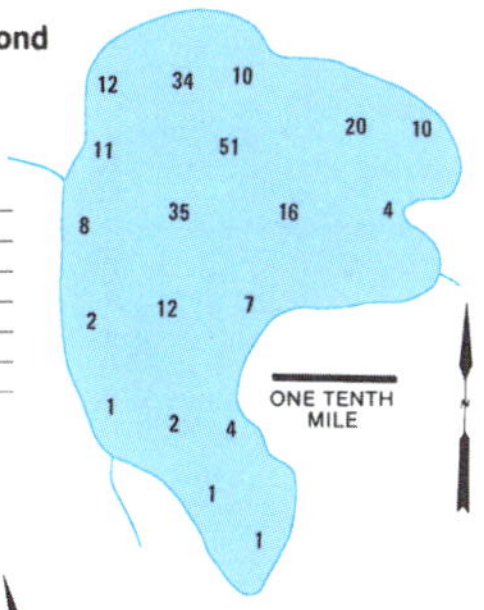

Little Beaver Pond
Magalloway Plt
Maine Atlas
Map 18, A-1
Acres: 50
Max. Depth:
51 feet

BrT		LmB	
BkT	✓	SmB	
RbT		WhP	
Sal		Csk	
Tog		WhF	
Smt	✓	Pic	

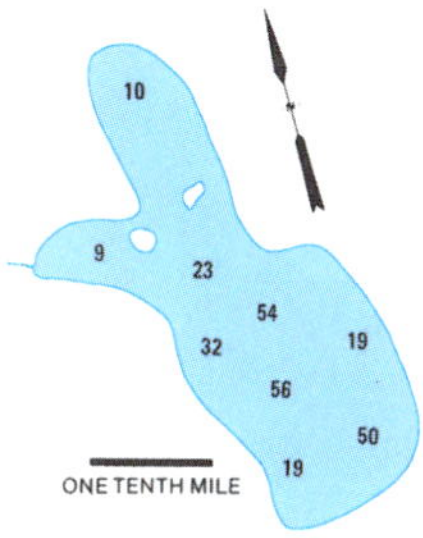

Little Concord Pond
Woodstock
Maine Atlas
Map 11, A-1
Acres: 26
Max. Depth:
56 feet

BrT		LmB	
BkT	✓	SmB	
RbT		WhP	
Sal		Csk	
Tog		WhF	
Smt	✓	Pic	✓

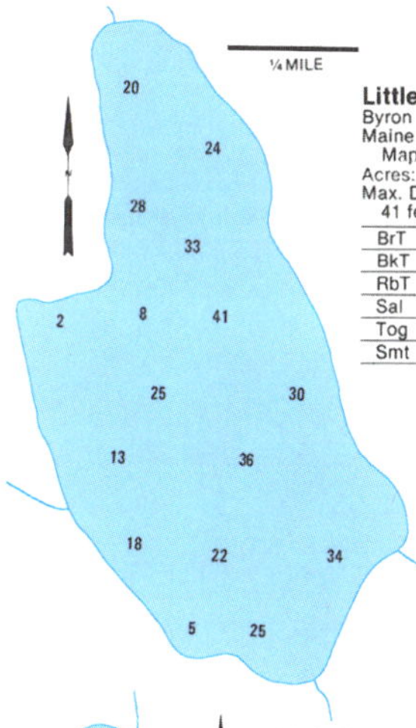

Little Ellis Pond
Byron
Maine Atlas
Map 18, C-4, C-5
Acres: 297
Max. Depth:
41 feet

BrT		LmB	
BkT	✓	SmB	
RbT		WhP	
Sal	✓	Csk	
Tog		WhF	
Smt	✓	Pic	

Kezar Pond
Fryeburg, Maine Atlas Map 4, A-2, Map 10, E-2
Acres: 1,447, Max. Depth: 12 feet

BrT	BkT	RbT	Sal	Tog	Smt	LmB	SmB	WhP	Csk	WhF	Pic
						✓	✓	✓			✓

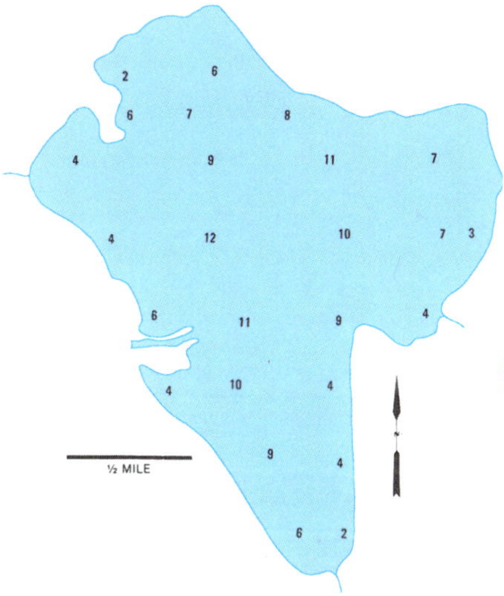

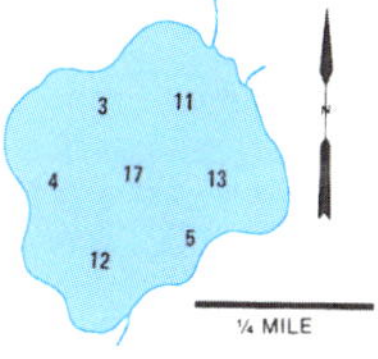

Little Labrador Pond
Sumner
Maine Atlas
Map 11, B-2, B-3
Acres: 13
Max. Depth:
17 feet

BrT		LmB	
BkT		SmB	
RbT		WhP	
Sal		Csk	
Tog		WhF	
Smt		Pic	✓

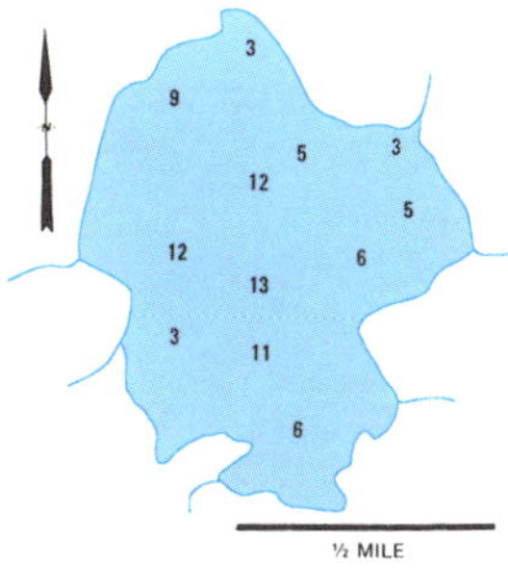

Labrador Pond
Sumner
Maine Atlas
Map 11, B-2
Acres: 115
Max. Depth:
13 feet

BrT		LmB	✓
BkT		SmB	
RbT		WhP	
Sal		Csk	
Tog		WhF	
Smt		Pic	✓

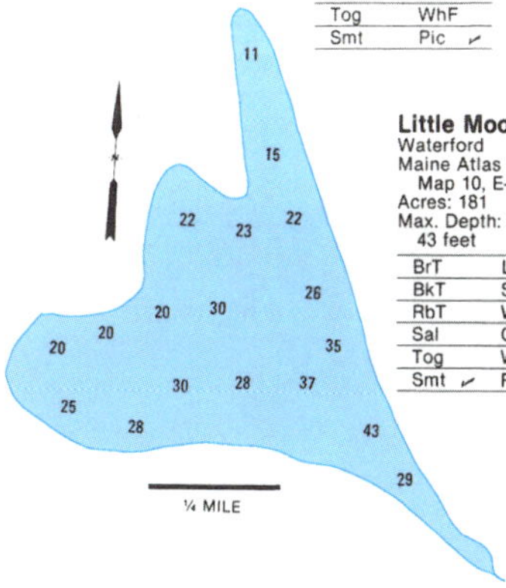

Little Moose Pond
Waterford
Maine Atlas
Map 10, E-3, E-4
Acres: 181
Max. Depth:
43 feet

BrT		LmB	
BkT		SmB	
RbT		WhP	✓
Sal		Csk	
Tog		WhF	
Smt	✓	Pic	✓

Oxford

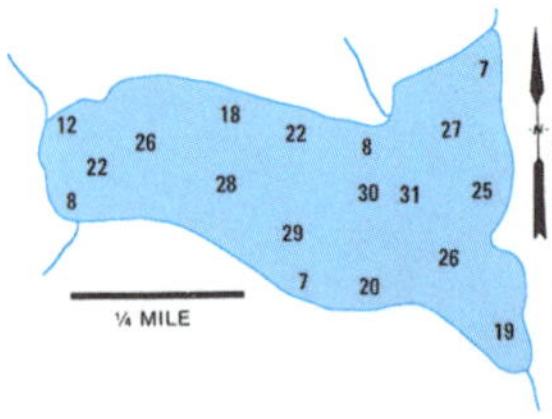

Little Pennesseewassee Pond

Norway
Maine Atlas
Map 10, D-5
Acres: 96
Max. Depth:
31 feet
Boat Launch

BrT	✓	LmB	
BkT	✓	SmB	✓
RbT		WhP	
Sal		Csk	
Tog		WhF	
Smt	✓	Pic	✓

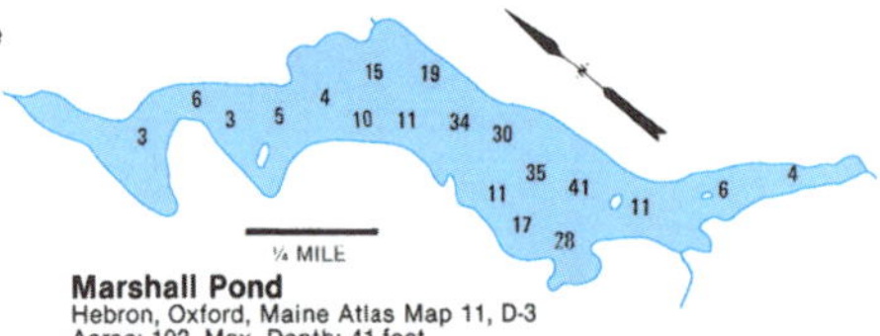

Marshall Pond

Hebron, Oxford, Maine Atlas Map 11, D-3
Acres: 102, Max. Depth: 41 feet

BrT	BkT	RbT	Sal	Tog	Smt	LmB	SmB	WhP	Csk	WhF	Pic
							✓				✓

Little Pond

Denmark
Maine Atlas
Map 4, B-3
Acres: 40
Max. Depth:
13 feet

BrT		LmB	✓
BkT		SmB	
RbT		WhP	
Sal		Csk	
Tog		WhF	
Smt		Pic	✓

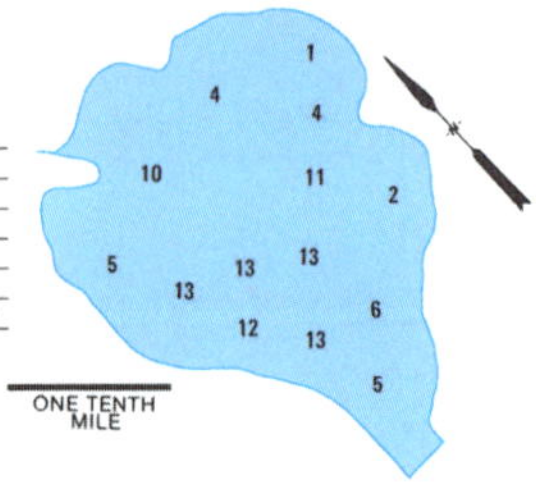

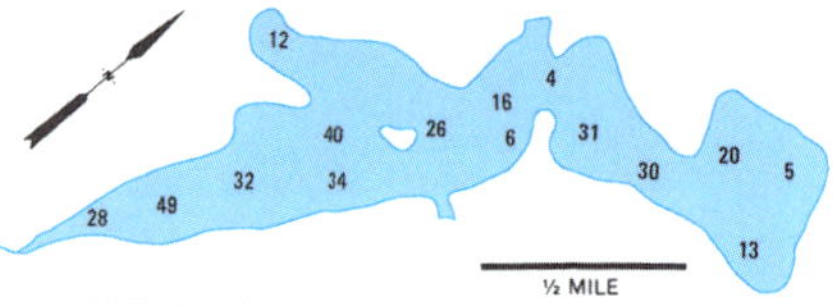

Middle Pond

Waterford, Lovell, Maine Atlas Map 10, D-3
Acres: 72, Max. Depth: 49 feet

BrT	BkT	RbT	Sal	Tog	Smt	LmB	SmB	WhP	Csk	WhF	Pic
							✓				✓

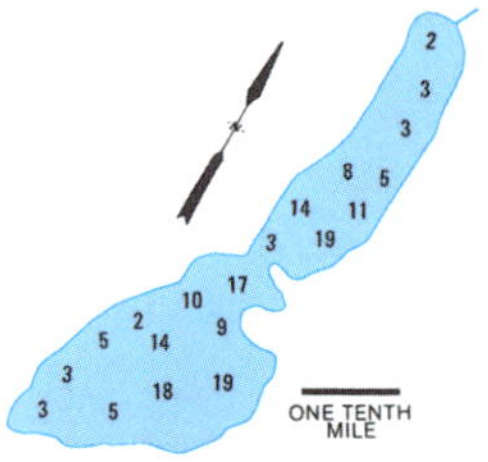

Long Pond

Denmark
Maine Atlas
Map 4, A-2, B-2
Acres: 55
Max. Depth:
19 feet

BrT		LmB	
BkT	✓	SmB	
RbT	✓	WhP	
Sal		Csk	
Tog		WhF	
Smt		Pic	

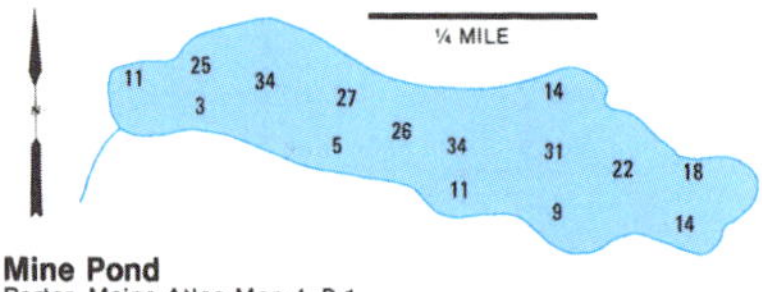

Mine Pond

Porter, Maine Atlas Map 4, D-1
Acres: 58, Max. Depth: 34 feet

BrT	BkT	RbT	Sal	Tog	Smt	LmB	SmB	WhP	Csk	WhF	Pic
✓	✓	✓									✓

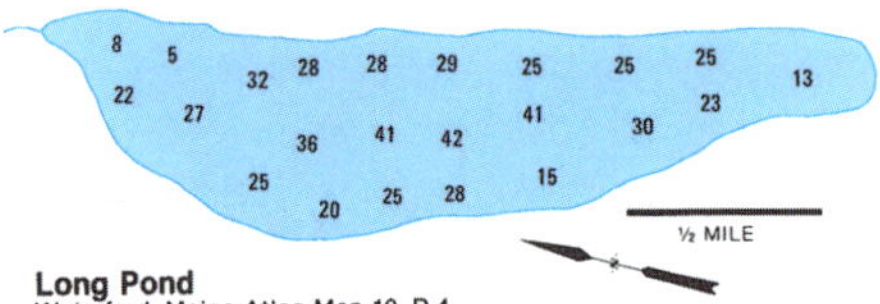

Long Pond

Waterford, Maine Atlas Map 10, D-4
Acres: 473, Max. Depth: 42 feet

BrT	BkT	RbT	Sal	Tog	Smt	LmB	SmB	WhP	Csk	WhF	Pic
					✓	✓	✓				✓

Mollidgewock Pond

Upton
Maine Atlas
Map 17, C-5
Acres: 24
Max. Depth:
8 feet

BrT	✓	LmB	
BkT	✓	SmB	
RbT		WhP	
Sal		Csk	
Tog		WhF	
Smt		Pic	✓

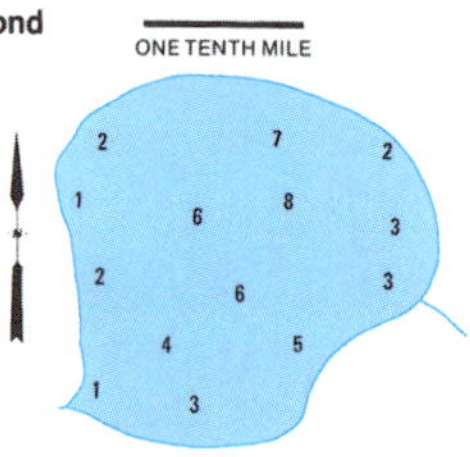

Lovewell Pond

Fryeburg, Maine Atlas Map 4, A-1, B-1
Acres: 1,065, Max. Depth: 45 feet, Boat Launch

BrT	BkT	RbT	Sal	Tog	Smt	LmB	SmB	WhP	Csk	WhF	Pic
✓							✓	✓			✓

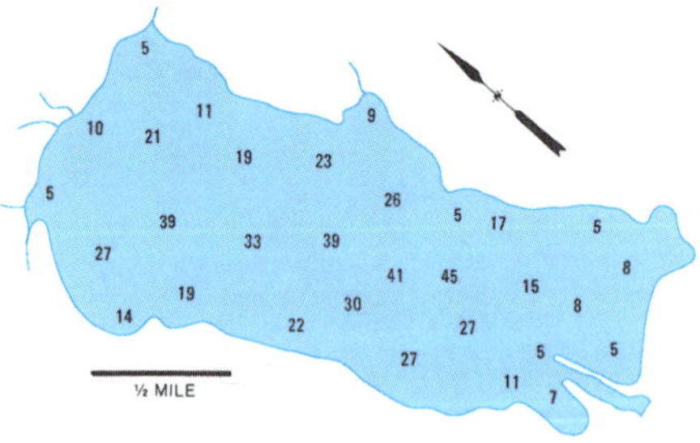

Lower Black Pond

Oxbow Twp
Maine Atlas
Map 28, A-1
Acres: 30
Max. Depth:
38 feet

BrT		LmB	
BkT	✓	SmB	
RbT		WhP	
Sal		Csk	
Tog		WhF	
Smt		Pic	

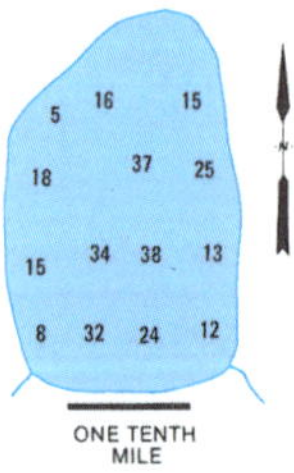

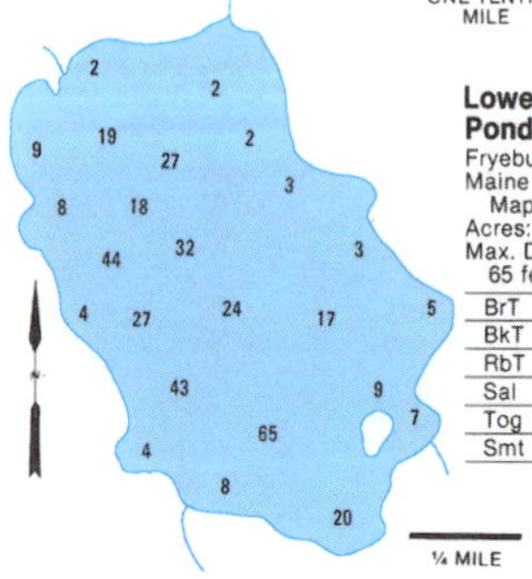

Lower Kimball Pond

Fryeburg
Maine Atlas
Map 10, E-1
Acres: 486
Max. Depth:
65 feet

BrT	✓	LmB	
BkT		SmB	✓
RbT		WhP	✓
Sal		Csk	
Tog		WhF	
Smt		Pic	✓

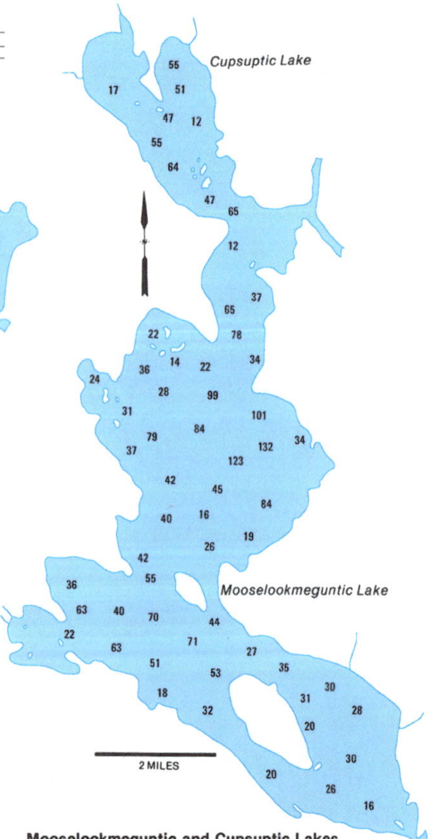

Mooselookmeguntic and Cupsuptic Lakes

Rangeley, Adamstown Twp, Richardsontown Twp, Rangeley Plt
Maine Atlas Map 18, A-2, A-3, Map 28, E-2, E-3
Acres: 16,300, Max. Depth: 132 feet, Boat Launch

BrT	BkT	RbT	Sal	Tog	Smt	LmB	SmB	WhP	Csk	WhF	Pic
✓	✓		✓		✓						

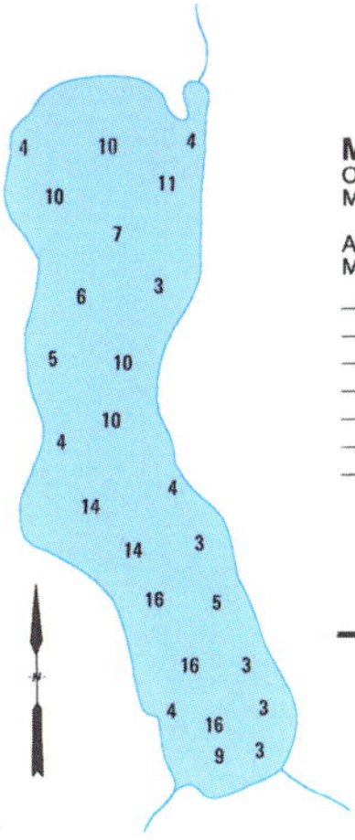

Moose Pond

Otisfield
Maine Atlas
Map 11, E-1
Acres: 160
Max. Depth:
16 feet

BrT		LmB	✓
BkT		SmB	
RbT		WhP	
Sal		Csk	
Tog		WhF	
Smt		Pic	

¼ MILE

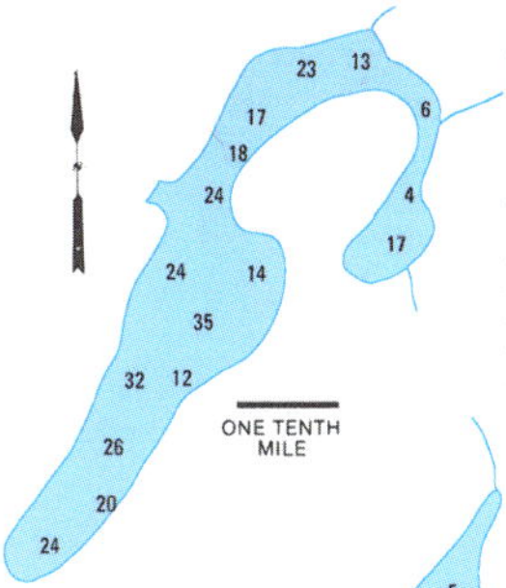

Mud Pond

Waterford, Lovell
Maine Atlas
Map 10, D-3
Acres: 45
Max. Depth:
35 feet

BrT		LmB	
BkT		SmB	✓
RbT		WhP	✓
Sal		Csk	
Tog		WhF	
Smt		Pic	✓

North Pond

Norway
Maine Atlas
Map 10, C-5
Map 11, C-1
Acres: 147
Max. Depth:
10 feet
Boat Launch

BrT		LmB	
BkT		SmB	
RbT		WhP	
Sal		Csk	
Tog		WhF	
Smt		Pic	✓

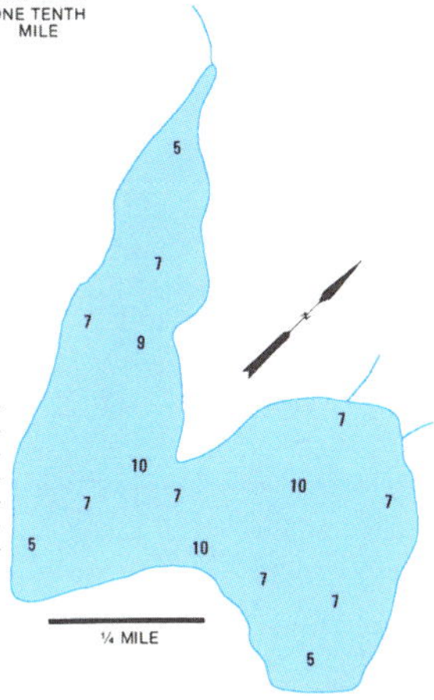

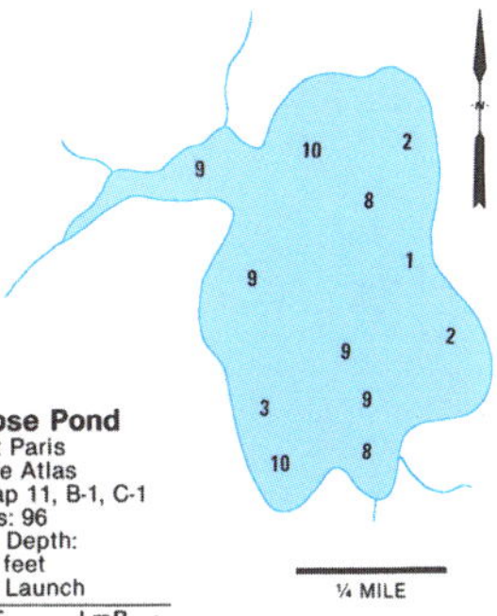

Moose Pond

West Paris
Maine Atlas
Map 11, B-1, C-1
Acres: 96
Max. Depth:
10 feet
Boat Launch

BrT		LmB	✓
BkT		SmB	
RbT		WhP	
Sal		Csk	
Tog		WhF	
Smt		Pic	✓

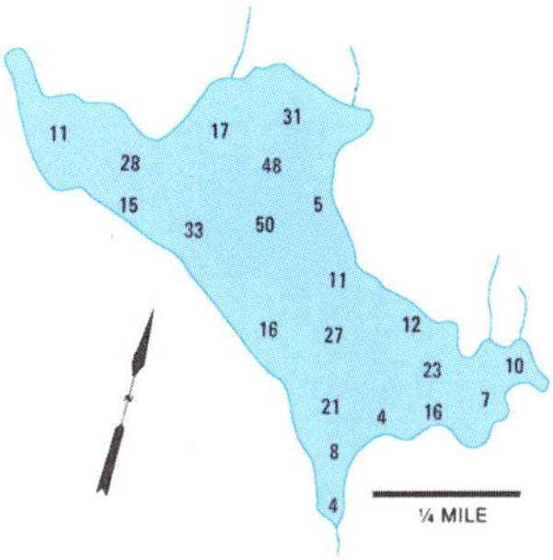

North Pond

Sumner
Maine Atlas
Map 11, C-3
Acres: 128
Max. Depth:
50 feet

BrT	✓	LmB	
BkT	✓	SmB	✓
RbT		WhP	
Sal		Csk	
Tog		WhF	
Smt	✓	Pic	✓

Comments: Splake.

Mud Pond

Greenwood
Maine Atlas
Map 10, C-5
Acres: 58
Max. Depth:
6 feet

BrT		LmB	✓
BkT		SmB	
RbT		WhP	
Sal		Csk	
Tog		WhF	
Smt		Pic	✓

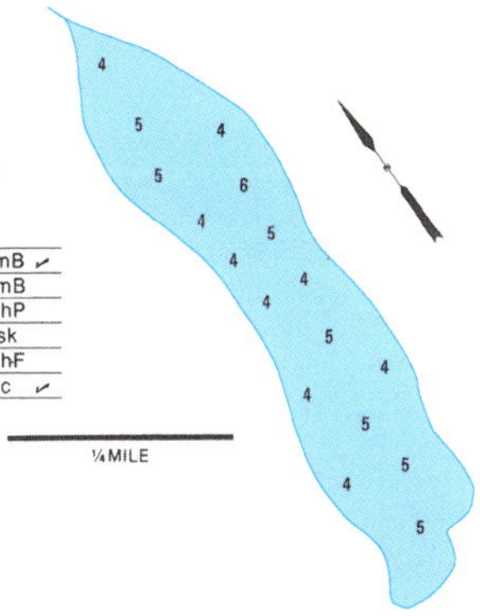

North Pond

Woodstock,
Greenwood
Maine Atlas
Map 10, B-4
Acres: 284
Max. Depth:
37 feet

BrT	✓	LmB	✓
BkT		SmB	✓
RbT		WhP	✓
Sal		Csk	
Tog		WhF	
Smt		Pic	✓

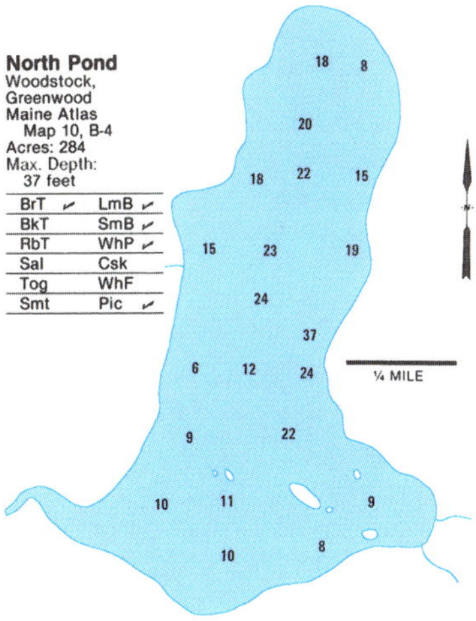

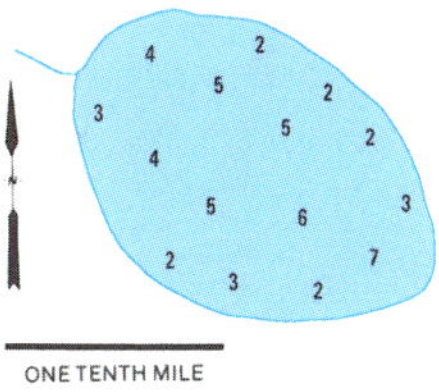

Mud Pond

Lower Cupsuptic Twp
Maine Atlas
Map 28, D-3
Acres: 6
Max. Depth:
7 feet

BrT		LmB	
BkT	✓	SmB	
RbT		WhP	
Sal		Csk	
Tog		WhF	
Smt		Pic	

Otter Pond

Parmachenee Twp
Maine Atlas
Map 28, B-1
Acres: 14
Max. Depth:
18 feet

BrT		LmB	
BkT	✓	SmB	
RbT		WhP	
Sal		Csk	
Tog		WhF	
Smt		Pic	

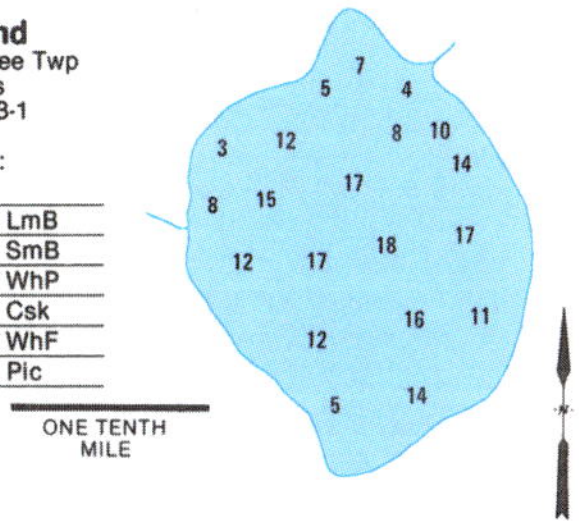

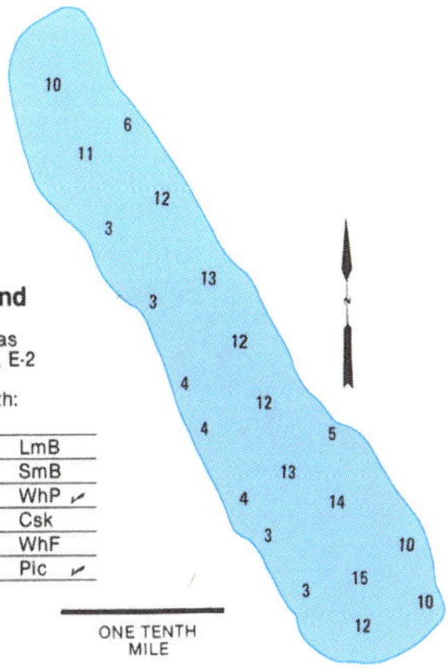

Mud Pond

Oxford
Maine Atlas
Map 11, E-2
Acres: 19
Max. Depth:
15 feet

BrT		LmB	
BkT		SmB	
RbT		WhP	✓
Sal		Csk	
Tog		WhF	
Smt		Pic	✓

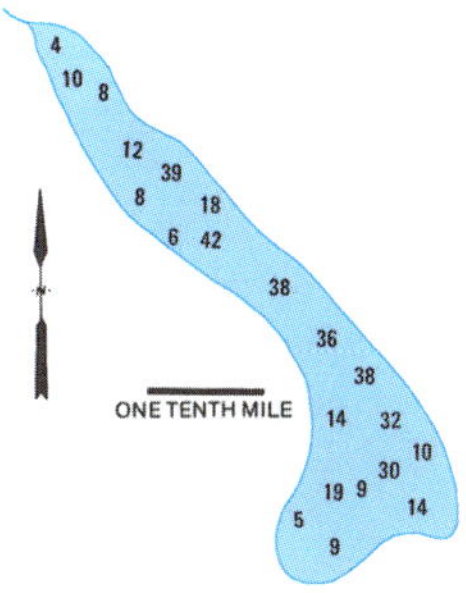

Oversett Pond

Greenwood
Maine Atlas
Map 10, C-4
Acres: 18
Max. Depth:
42 feet

BrT	✓	LmB	
BkT	✓	SmB	
RbT	✓	WhP	
Sal		Csk	
Tog		WhF	
Smt		Pic	

Oxford

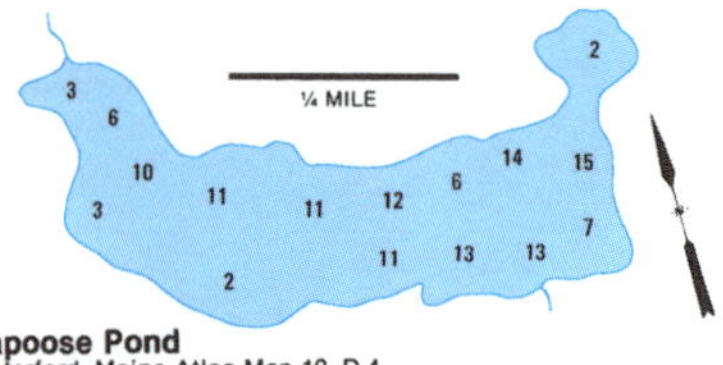

Papoose Pond
Waterford, Maine Atlas Map 10, D-4
Acres: 64, Max. Depth: 15 feet

BrT	BkT	RbT	Sal	Tog	Smt	LmB	SmB	WhP	Csk	WhF	Pic
			✓				✓	✓			✓

Pequawket Lake
Brownfield
Maine Atlas
Map 4, C-2
Acres: 87
Max. Depth:
20 feet

BrT		LmB	✓
BkT		SmB	✓
RbT		WhP	✓
Sal		Csk	
Tog		WhF	
Smt		Pic	✓

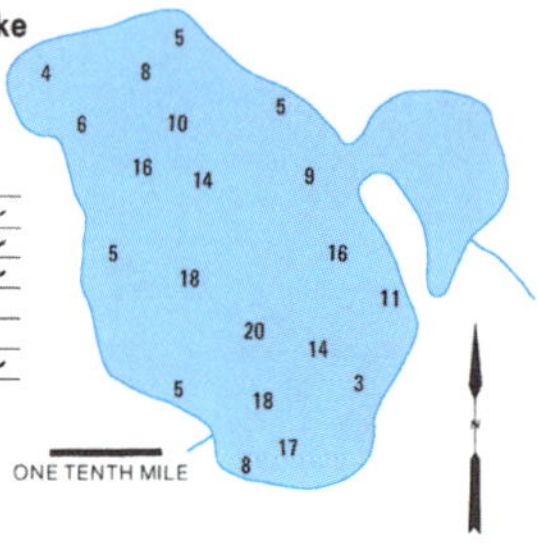

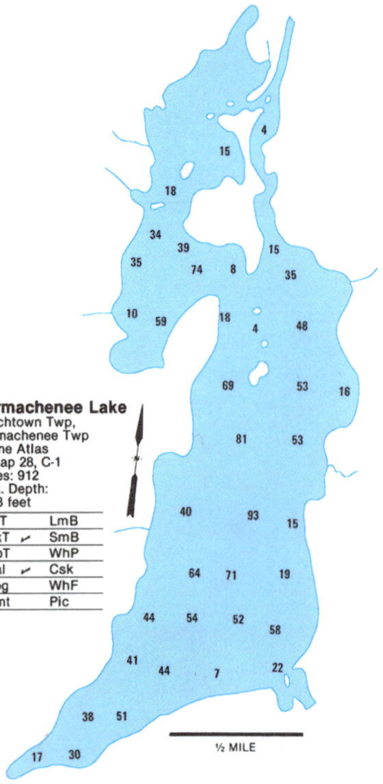

Parmachenee Lake
Lynchtown Twp,
Parmachenee Twp
Maine Atlas
Map 28, C-1
Acres: 912
Max. Depth:
93 feet

BrT		LmB	
BkT	✓	SmB	
RbT		WhP	
Sal	✓	Csk	
Tog		WhF	
Smt		Pic	

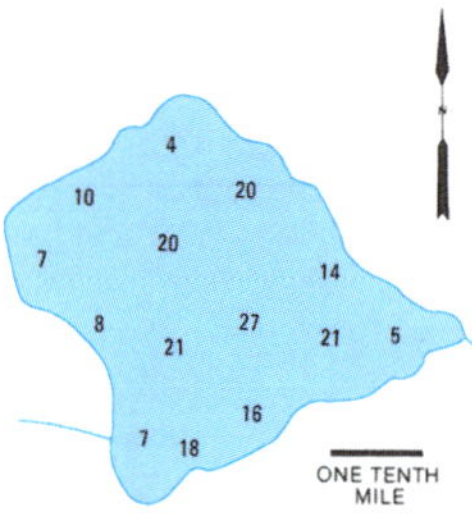

Perley Pond
Denmark
Maine Atlas
Map 4, B-4
Acres: 79
Max. Depth:
27 feet
Boat Launch

BrT		LmB	✓
BkT		SmB	
RbT		WhP	
Sal		Csk	
Tog		WhF	
Smt		Pic	✓

Pickerel Pond
Denmark
Maine Atlas
Map 4, B-4
Acres: 40
Max. Depth:
18 feet

BrT		LmB	✓
BkT		SmB	
RbT		WhP	
Sal		Csk	
Tog		WhF	
Smt		Pic	✓

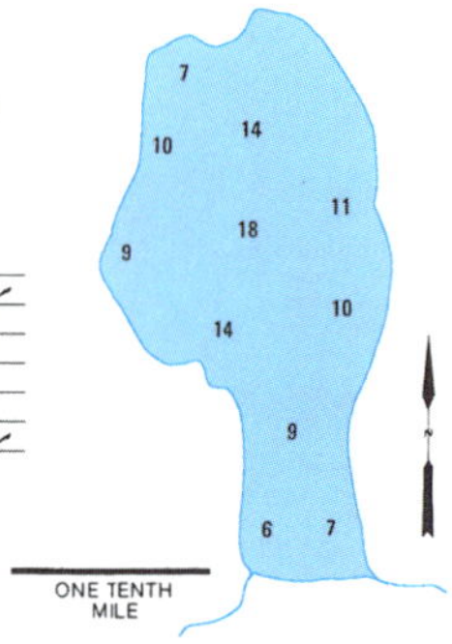

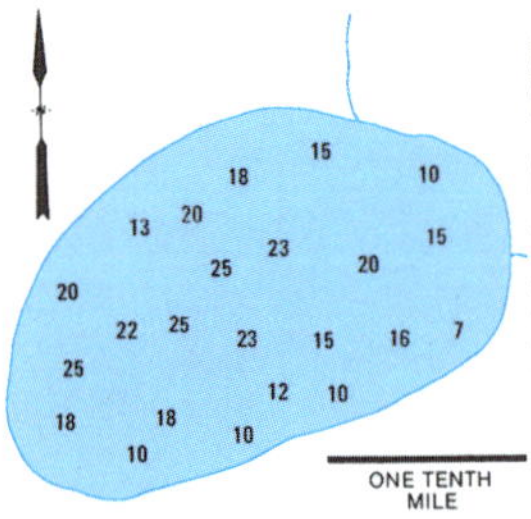

Plain Pond
Porter
Maine Atlas
Map 4, D-1
Acres: 16
Max. Depth:
25 feet

BrT		LmB	
BkT		SmB	
RbT		WhP	
Sal		Csk	
Tog		WhF	
Smt		Pic	✓

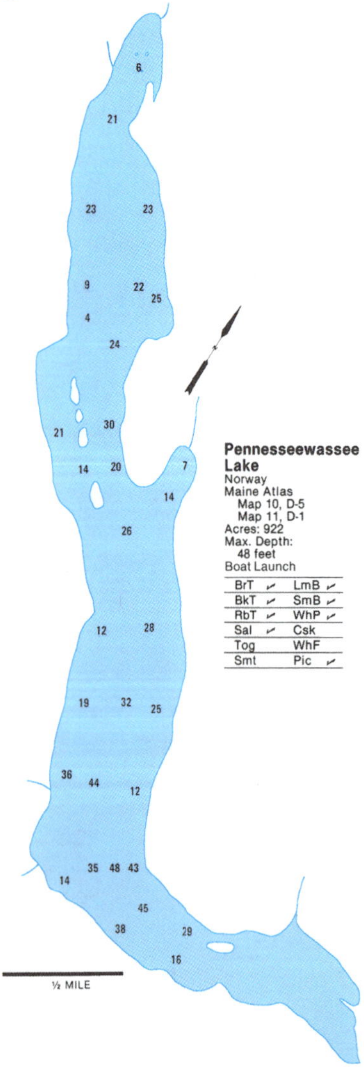

Pennesseewassee Lake
Norway
Maine Atlas
Map 10, D-5
Map 11, D-1
Acres: 922
Max. Depth:
48 feet
Boat Launch

BrT	✓	LmB	✓
BkT	✓	SmB	✓
RbT	✓	WhP	✓
Sal	✓	Csk	
Tog		WhF	
Smt		Pic	✓

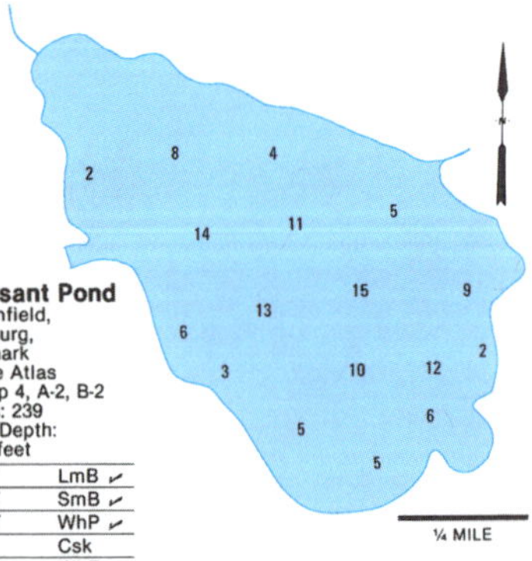

Pleasant Pond
Brownfield,
Fryeburg,
Denmark
Maine Atlas
Map 4, A-2, B-2
Acres: 239
Max. Depth:
15 feet

BrT		LmB	✓
BkT		SmB	✓
RbT		WhP	✓
Sal		Csk	
Tog		WhF	
Smt		Pic	✓

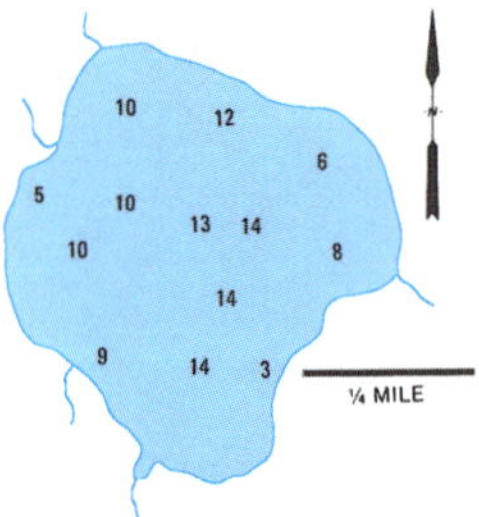

Pleasant Pond
Sumner
Maine Atlas
Map 11, B-2
Acres: 115
Max. Depth:
14 feet

BrT		LmB	✓
BkT		SmB	
RbT		WhP	
Sal		Csk	
Tog		WhF	
Smt		Pic	✓

Pond in the River
Township C,
C Surplus, Upton
Maine Atlas
Map 18, B-1
Acres: 512
Max. Depth:
40 feet

BrT	✓	LmB	
BkT	✓	SmB	
RbT		WhP	
Sal	✓	Csk	
Tog		WhF	
Smt	✓	Pic	✓

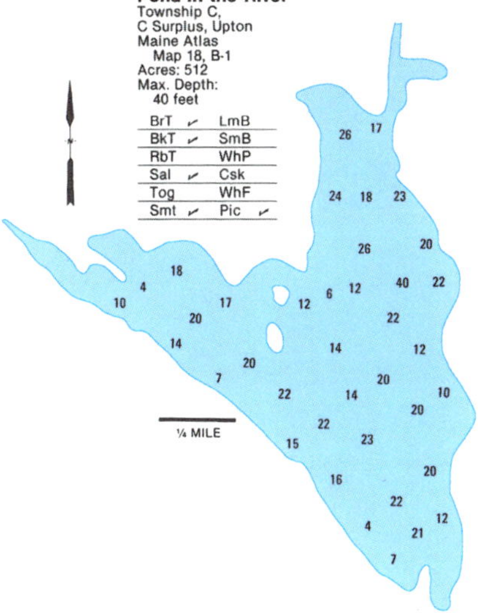

Round Pond
Fryeburg
Maine Atlas
Map 4, A-1, B-1
Acres: 6
Max. Depth:
14 feet

BrT		LmB	
BkT	✓	SmB	
RbT		WhP	
Sal		Csk	
Tog		WhF	
Smt		Pic	✓

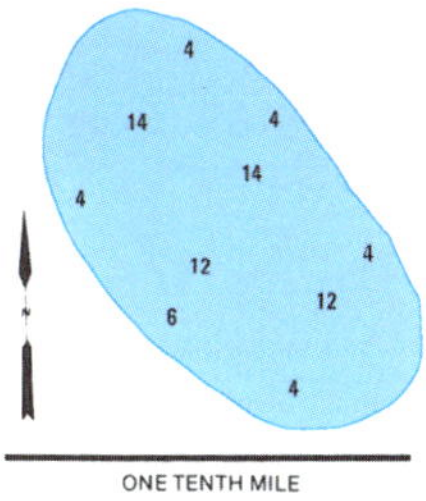

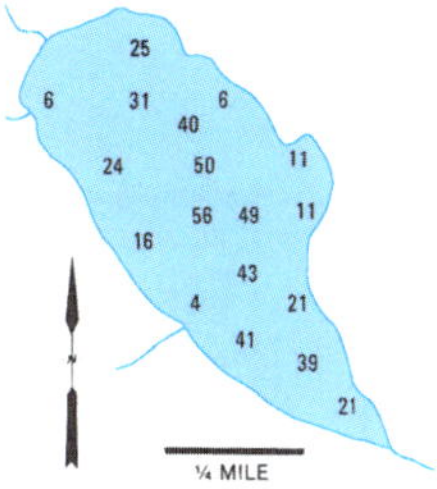

Sand Pond
Norway
Maine Atlas
Map 10, D-5
Acres: 141
Max. Depth:
56 feet

BrT	✓	LmB	
BkT		SmB	✓
RbT		WhP	
Sal		Csk	
Tog		WhF	
Smt		Pic	✓

Saturday Pond
Otisfield
Maine Atlas
Map 11, E-1
Acres: 179
Max. Depth:
25 feet

BrT		LmB	✓
BkT		SmB	✓
RbT		WhP	✓
Sal		Csk	
Tog		WhF	
Smt		Pic	

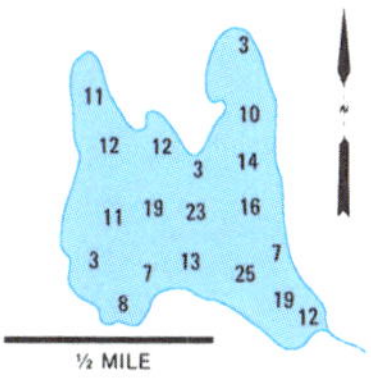

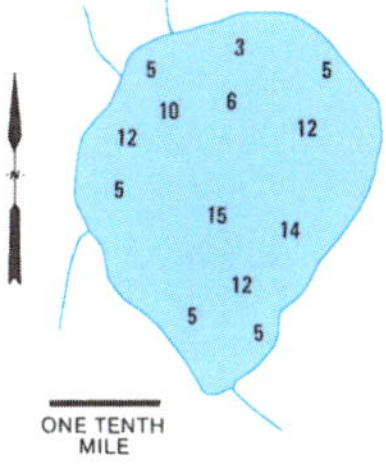

Proctor Pond
Albany Twp
Maine Atlas
Map 10, D-3
Acres: 45
Max. Depth:
15 feet

BrT		LmB	
BkT		SmB	✓
RbT		WhP	
Sal		Csk	
Tog		WhF	
Smt		Pic	✓

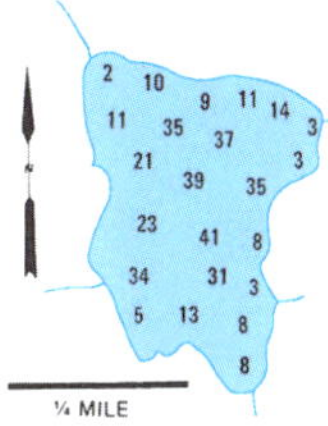

Shagg Pond
Woodstock
Maine Atlas
Map 11, A-1
Acres: 64
Max. Depth:
41 feet
Boat Launch

BrT		LmB	
BkT	✓	SmB	
RbT		WhP	
Sal		Csk	
Tog		WhF	
Smt	✓	Pic	

Comments: Splake.

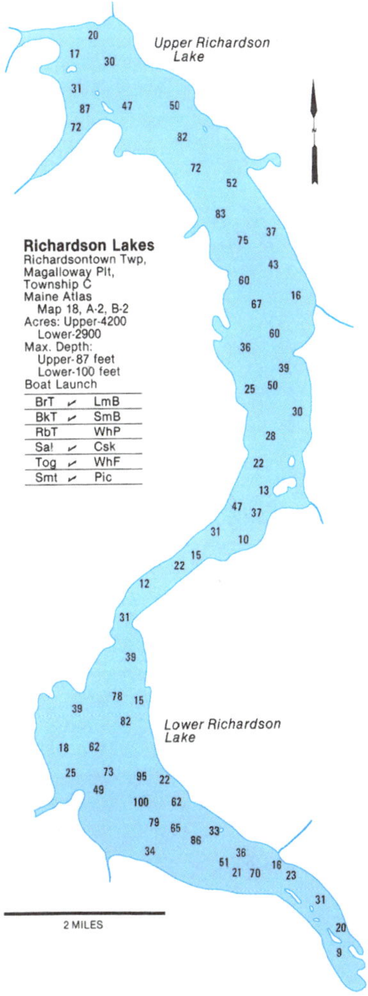

Richardson Lakes
Richardsontown Twp,
Magalloway Plt,
Township C
Maine Atlas
Map 18, A-2, B-2
Acres: Upper-4200
Lower-2900
Max. Depth:
Upper-87 feet
Lower-100 feet
Boat Launch

BrT	✓	LmB	
BkT	✓	SmB	
RbT		WhP	
Sal	✓	Csk	
Tog	✓	WhF	
Smt	✓	Pic	

Songo Pond
Albany Twp
Maine Atlas
Map 10, B-3
Acres: 224
Max. Depth:
25 feet

BrT		LmB	
BkT	✓	SmB	✓
RbT		WhP	✓
Sal	✓	Csk	
Tog		WhF	
Smt	✓	Pic	✓

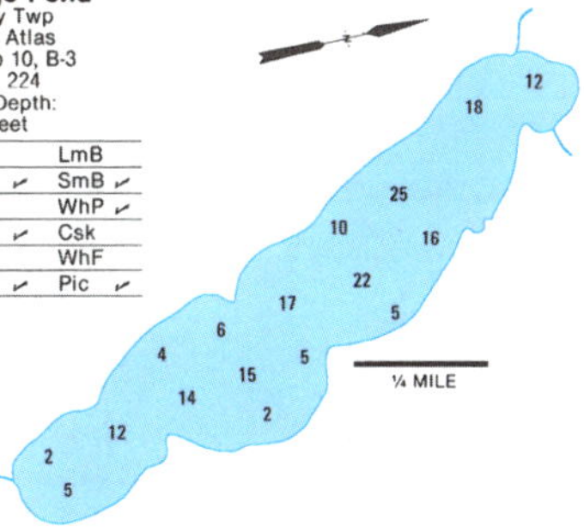

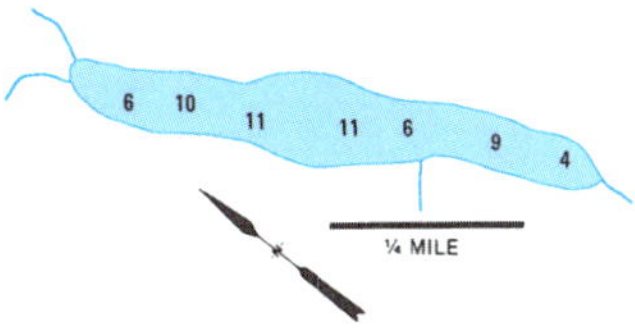

South Pond
Buckfield, Maine Atlas Map 11, C-3
Acres: 32, Max. Depth: 11 feet

BrT	BkT	RbT	Sal	Tog	Smt	LmB	SmB	WhP	Csk	WhF	Pic
											✓

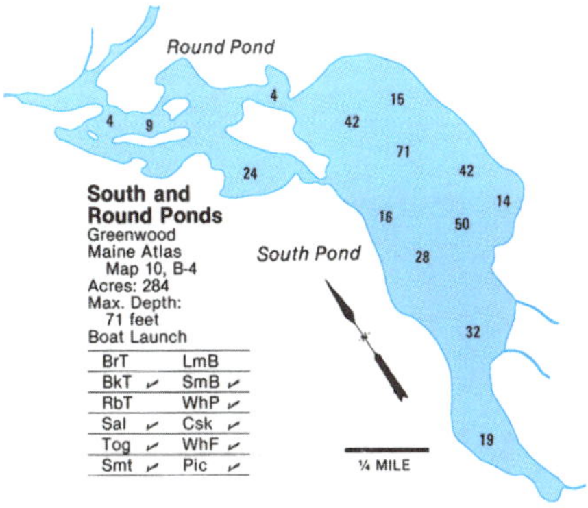

South and Round Ponds
Greenwood
Maine Atlas
Map 10, B-4
Acres: 284
Max. Depth:
71 feet
Boat Launch

BrT		LmB	
BkT	✓	SmB	✓
RbT		WhP	✓
Sal	✓	Csk	✓
Tog	✓	WhF	✓
Smt	✓	Pic	✓

Speck Pond

Grafton Twp
Maine Atlas
Map 18, E-1
Acres: 9
Max. Depth:
36 feet

BrT	LmB
BkT ✓	SmB
RbT	WhP
Sal	Csk
Tog	WhF
Smt	Pic

Comments:
Highest pond above sea level in state.

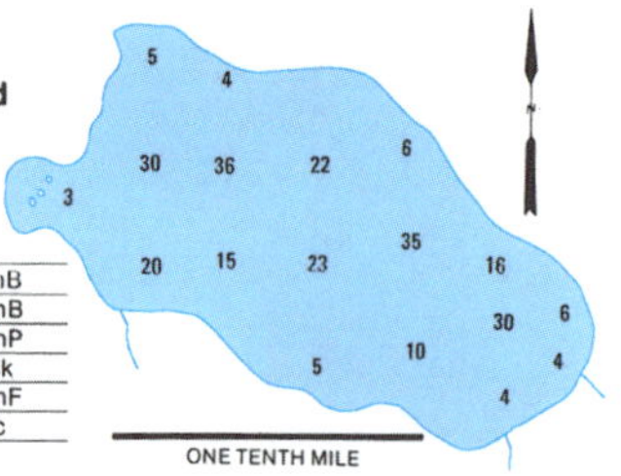

Swan Pond

Hartford
Maine Atlas
Map 11, C-3, C-4
Acres: 13
Max. Depth:
18 feet

BrT	LmB
BkT	SmB
RbT	WhP
Sal	Csk
Tog	WhF
Smt	Pic ✓

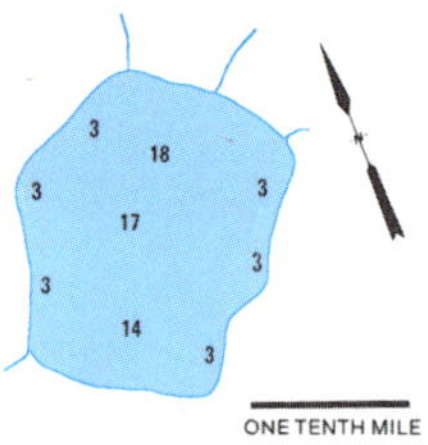

Spectacle Ponds

Porter
Maine Atlas
Map 4, D-2
Acres: First-57
Second-45
Max. Depth:
First-29 feet
Second-15 feet

BrT	LmB ✓
BkT ✓	SmB
RbT	WhP
Sal	Csk
Tog	WhF
Smt	Pic ✓

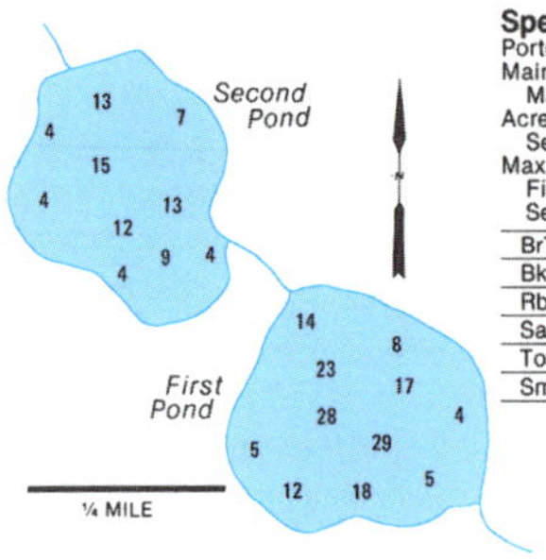

Thompson Lake

Oxford, Otisfield,
Poland, Casco
Maine Atlas
Map 5, A-1, A-2
Map 11, E-1
Acres: 4,426
Max. Depth:
121 feet
Boat Launch

BrT	LmB ✓
BkT	SmB ✓
RbT	WhP
Sal ✓	Csk ✓
Tog ✓	WhF
Smt ✓	Pic ✓

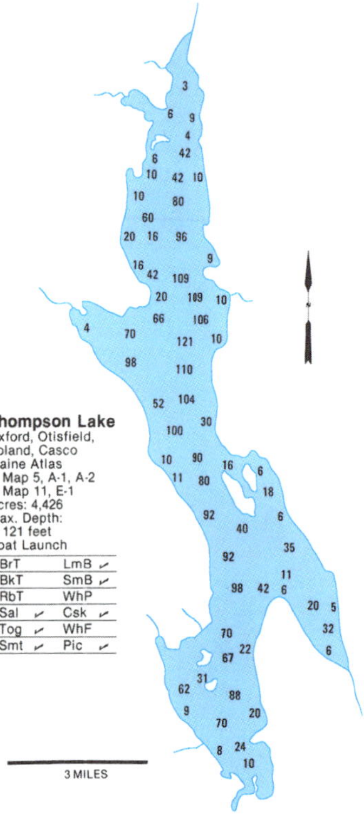

Stanley Pond

Hiram, Porter
Maine Atlas
Map 4, C-2, D-2
Acres: 137
Max. Depth:
75 feet
Boat Launch

BrT ✓	LmB ✓
BkT ✓	SmB ✓
RbT ✓	WhP
Sal ✓	Csk
Tog	WhF
Smt	Pic ✓

Comments: Splake.

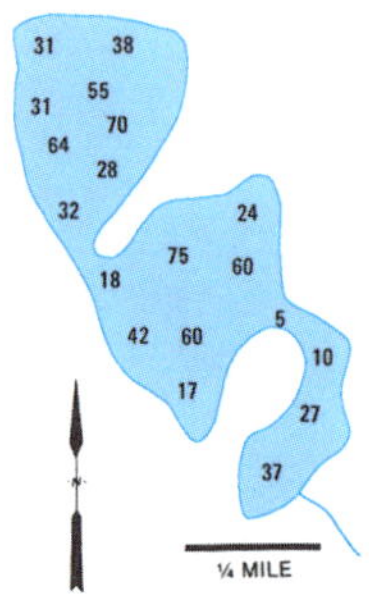

Stearns Pond

Sweden
Maine Atlas
Map 10, E-3
Acres: 255
Max. Depth:
47 feet
Boat Launch

BrT ✓	LmB ✓
BkT	SmB ✓
RbT	WhP ✓
Sal	Csk
Tog	WhF
Smt	Pic ✓

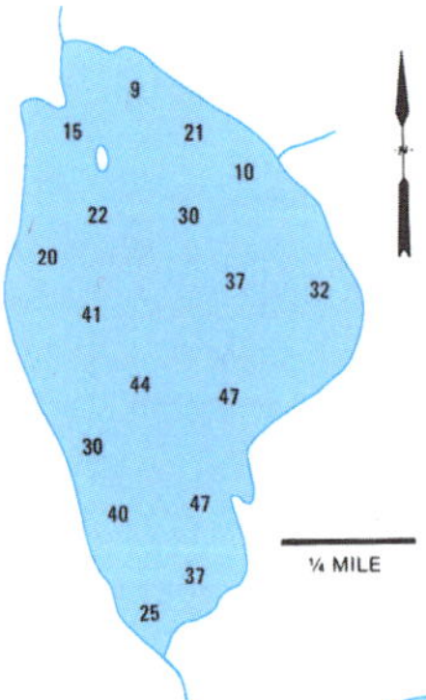

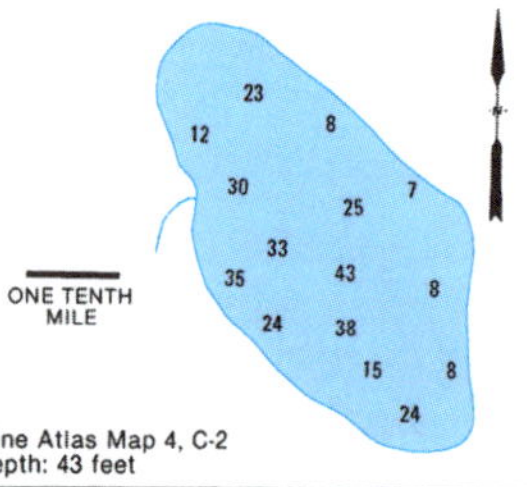

Trafton Pond

Hiram, Porter, Maine Atlas Map 4, C-2
Acres: 56, Max. Depth: 43 feet

BrT	BkT	RbT	Sal	Tog	Smt	LmB	SmB	WhP	Csk	WhF	Pic
	✓										✓

Comments: Recently stocked with BkT.

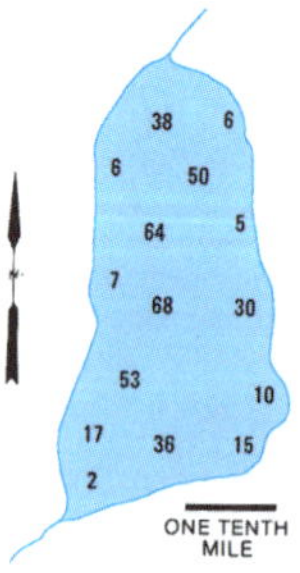

Trout Pond

Stoneham
Maine Atlas
Map 10, D-2, D-3
Acres: 64
Max. Depth:
68 feet

BrT	LmB
BkT ✓	SmB ✓
RbT	WhP
Sal	Csk
Tog	WhF
Smt ✓	Pic

Coments: Wild Brook Trout fishery

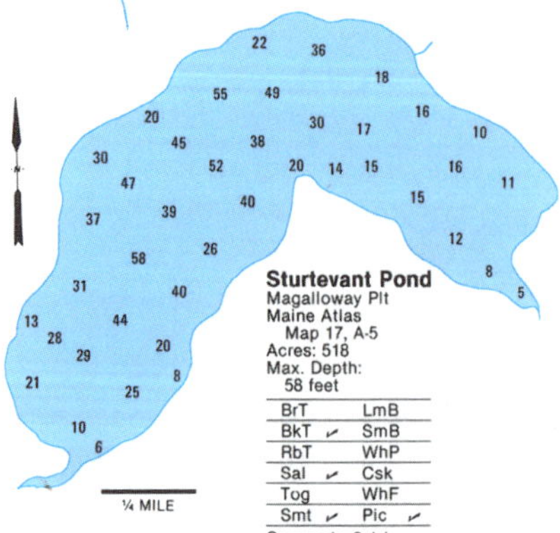

Sturtevant Pond

Magalloway Plt
Maine Atlas
Map 17, A-5
Acres: 518
Max. Depth:
58 feet

BrT	LmB
BkT ✓	SmB
RbT	WhP
Sal ✓	Csk
Tog	WhF
Smt ✓	Pic ✓

Comments: Splake.

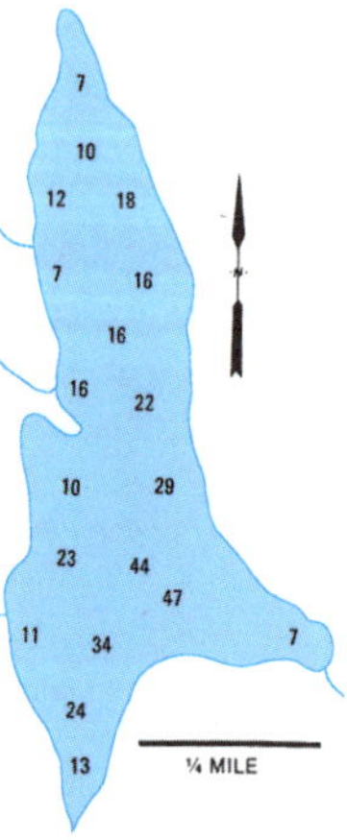

Twitchell Pond

Greenwood
Maine Atlas
Map 10, B-4
Acres: 158
Max. Depth:
47 feet
Boat Launch

BrT ✓	LmB
BkT ✓	SmB ✓
RbT	WhP ✓
Sal	Csk
Tog	WhF
Smt ✓	Pic ✓

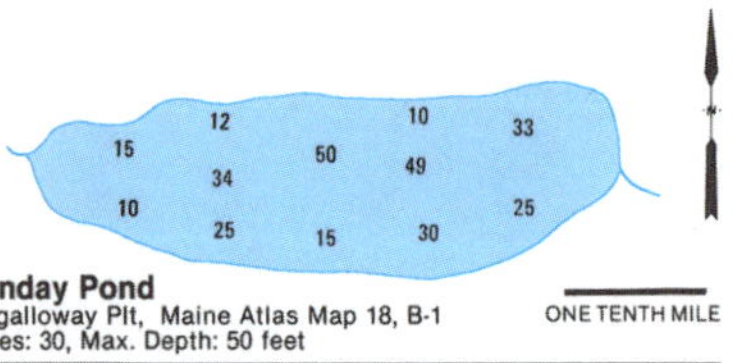

Sunday Pond

Magalloway Plt, Maine Atlas Map 18, B-1
Acres: 30, Max. Depth: 50 feet

BrT	BkT	RbT	Sal	Tog	Smt	LmB	SmB	WhP	Csk	WhF	Pic
	✓										

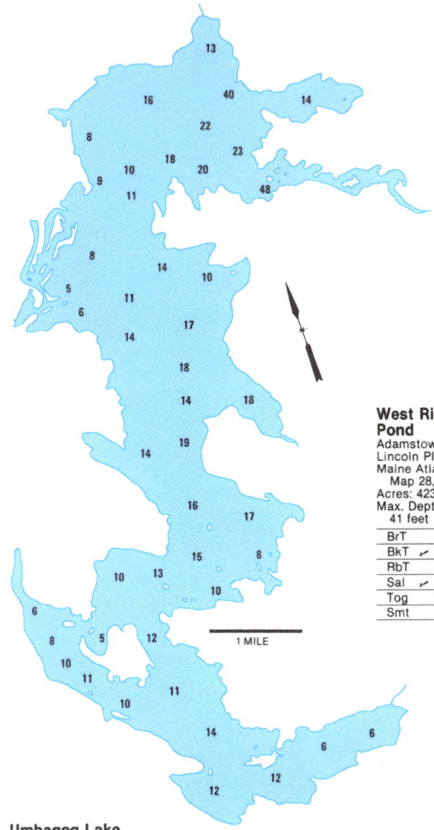

Umbagog Lake

Magalloway Plt, Upton, Maine Atlas Map 17, B-5
Acres: 7,850, Max. Depth: 48 feet

BrT	BkT	RbT	Sal	Tog	Smt	LmB	SmB	WhP	Csk	WhF	Pic
✓	✓		✓								✓

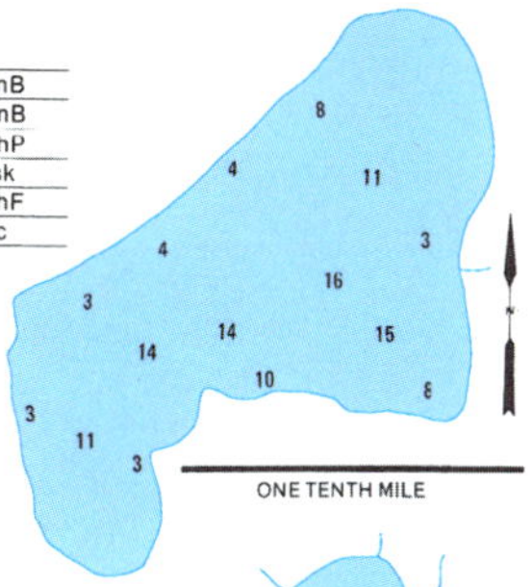

Wells Pond

Parmachenee Twp
Maine Atlas
Map 28, B-1
Acres: 7
Max. Depth:
16 feet

BrT		LmB
BkT	✓	SmB
RbT		WhP
Sal		Csk
Tog		WhF
Smt		Pic

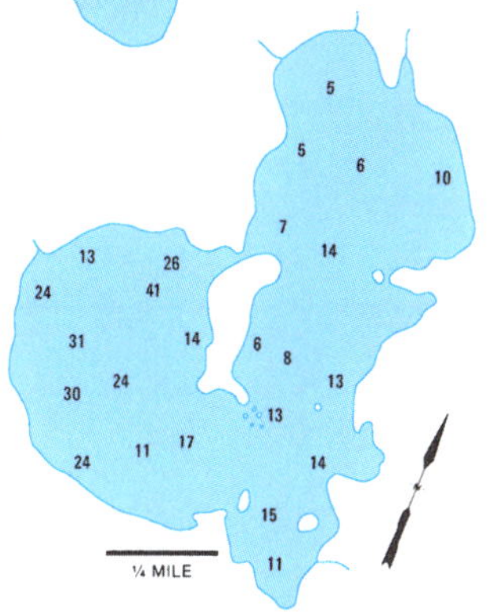

West Richardson Pond

Adamstown Twp,
Lincoln Plt
Maine Atlas
Map 28, E-1
Acres: 423
Max. Depth:
41 feet

BrT		LmB
BkT	✓	SmB
RbT		WhP
Sal	✓	Csk
Tog		WhF
Smt		Pic

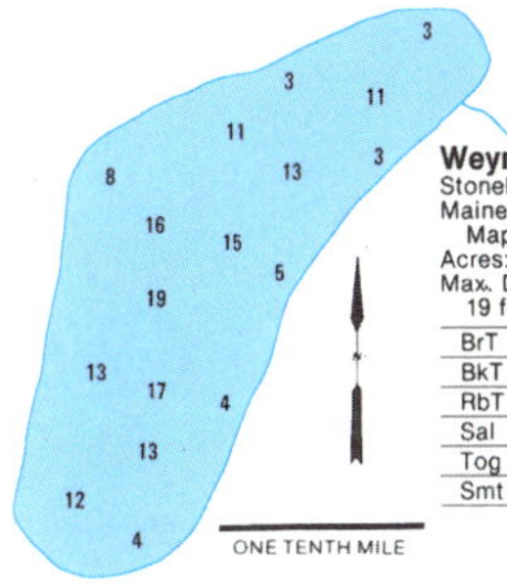

Weymouth Pond

Stoneham
Maine Atlas
Map 10, D-3
Acres: 16
Max. Depth:
19 feet

BrT		LmB	
BkT		SmB	
RbT		WhP	
Sal		Csk	
Tog		WhF	✓
Smt		Pic	

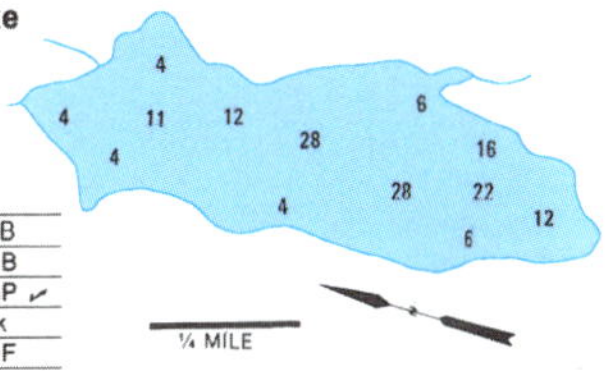

Virginia Lake

Stoneham
Maine Atlas
Map 10, C-2
Acres: 128
Max. Depth:
28 feet
Boat Launch

BrT		LmB	
BkT	✓	SmB	
RbT		WhP	✓
Sal		Csk	
Tog		WhF	
Smt		Pic	✓

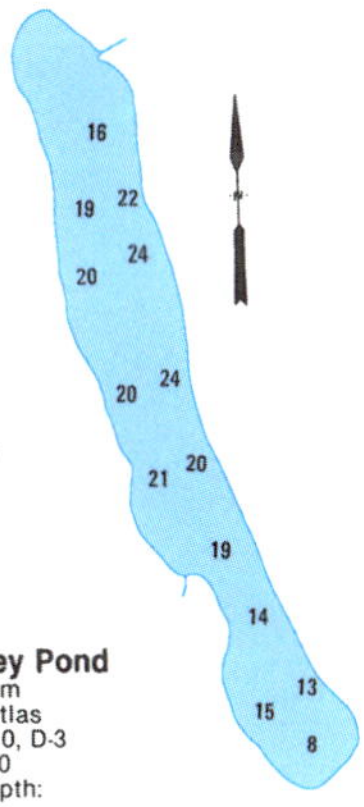

Whitney Pond

Oxford
Maine Atlas
Map 11, E-2
Acres: 170
Max. Depth:
24 feet

BrT		LmB	✓
BkT		SmB	✓
RbT		WhP	✓
Sal		Csk	
Tog		WhF	
Smt		Pic	✓

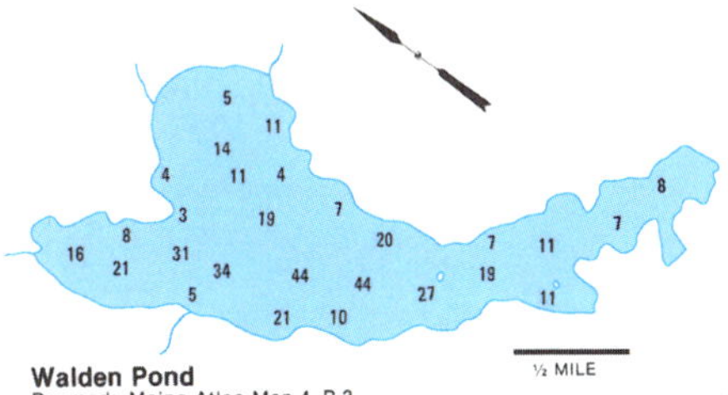

Walden Pond

Denmark, Maine Atlas Map 4, B-3
Acres: 256, Max. Depth: 44 feet

BrT	BkT	RbT	Sal	Tog	Smt	LmB	SmB	WhP	Csk	WhF	Pic
✓	✓				✓	✓	✓				✓

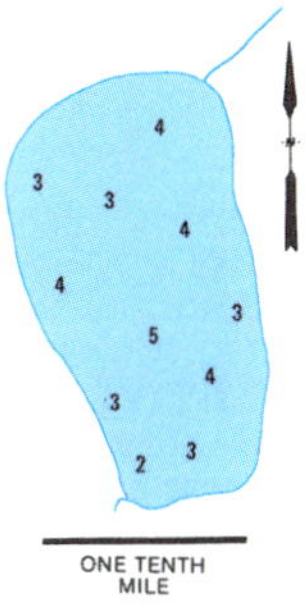

Whitney Pond

Stoneham
Maine Atlas
Map 10, D-3
Acres: 10
Max. Depth:
5 feet

BrT		LmB	
BkT		SmB	
RbT		WhP	
Sal		Csk	
Tog		WhF	
Smt		Pic	✓

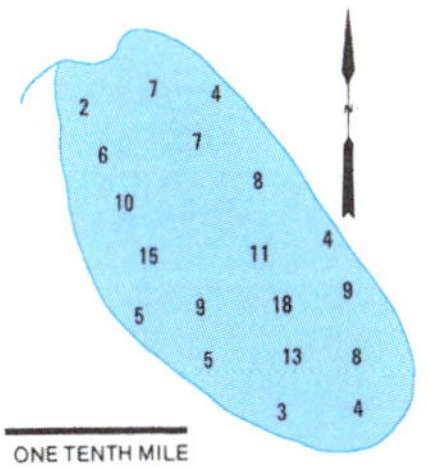

Washburn Pond

Sumner, Woodstock
Maine Atlas
Map 11, A-1, B-1
Acres: 12
Max. Depth:
18 feet

BrT		LmB
BkT	✓	SmB
RbT		WhP
Sal		Csk
Tog		WhF
Smt		Pic

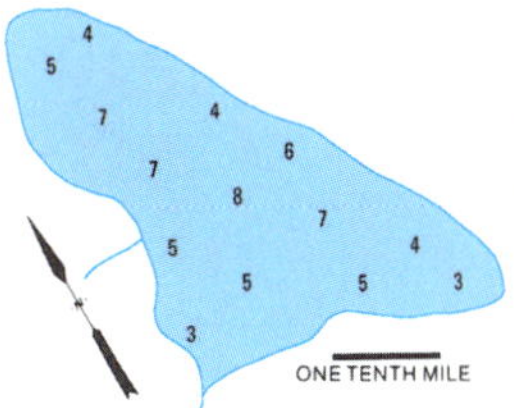

Webber Pond

Sweden
Maine Atlas
Map 10, E-3
Acres: 32
Max. Depth:
8 feet

BrT		LmB	
BkT		SmB	
RbT		WhP	
Sal		Csk	
Tog		WhF	
Smt		Pic	✓

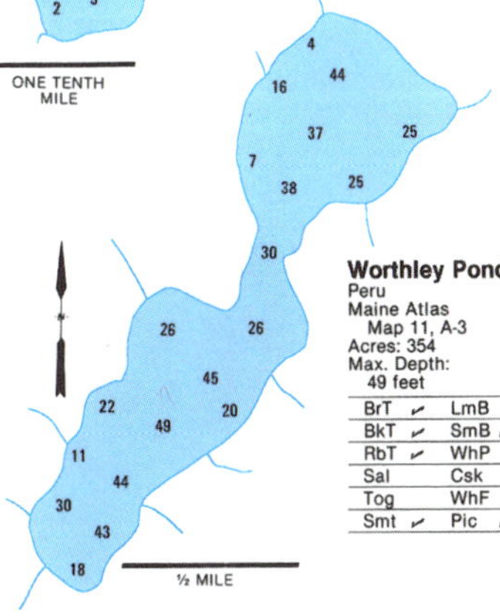

Worthley Pond

Peru
Maine Atlas
Map 11, A-3
Acres: 354
Max. Depth:
49 feet

BrT	✓	LmB	
BkT	✓	SmB	✓
RbT	✓	WhP	
Sal		Csk	
Tog		WhF	
Smt	✓	Pic	✓

Penobscot County

Ben Annis Pond
Hermon
Maine Atlas
Map 22, B-5
Acres: 25
Max. Depth:
9 feet

BrT	LmB
BkT	SmB ✓
RbT	WhP ✓
Sal	Csk
Tog	WhF
Smt	Pic ✓

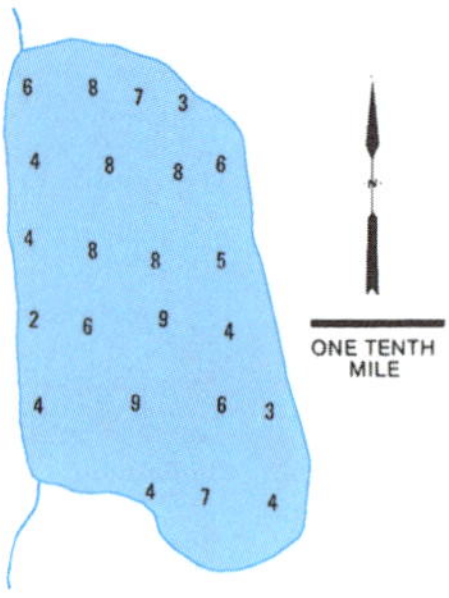

Brooks Pond
Corinna
Maine Atlas
Map 22, A-2
Acres: 31
Max. Depth:
11 feet
Boat Launch

BrT	LmB ✓
BkT	SmB ✓
RbT	WhP ✓
Sal	Csk
Tog	WhF
Smt	Pic ✓

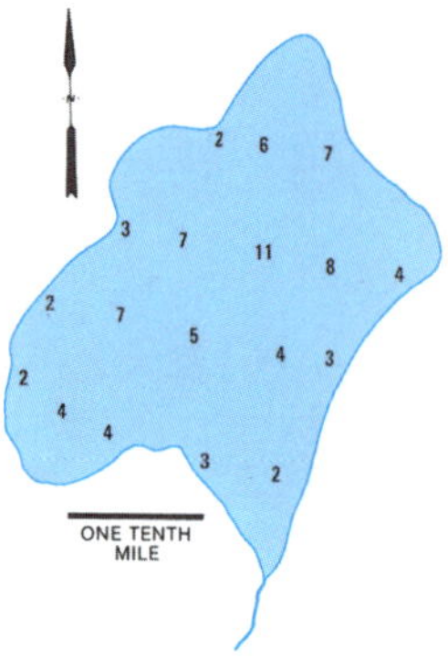

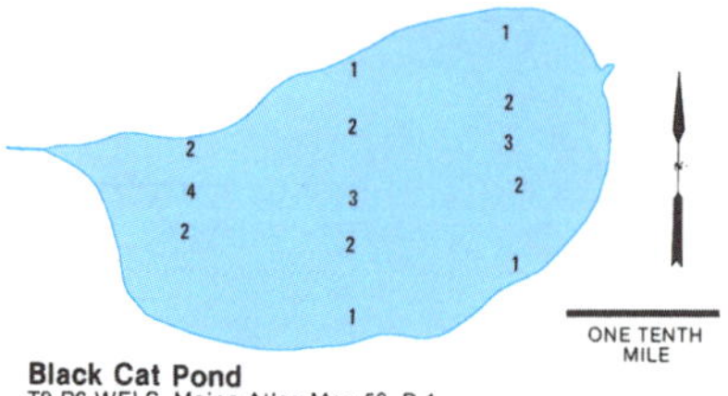

Black Cat Pond
T8 R6 WELS, Maine Atlas Map 58, D-1
Acres: 27, Max. Depth: 4 feet

BrT	BkT	RbT	Sal	Tog	Smt	LmB	SmB	WhP	Csk	WhF	Pic
	✓										

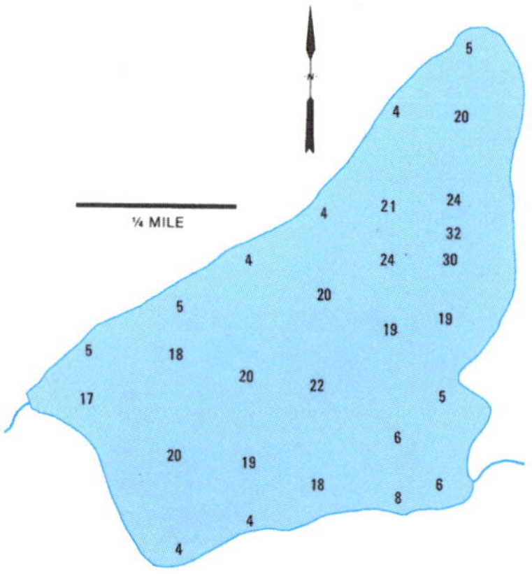

Cambolasse Pond
Lincoln, Maine Atlas Map 44, E-1
Acres: 211, Max. Depth: 32 feet

BrT	BkT	RbT	Sal	Tog	Smt	LmB	SmB	WhP	Csk	WhF	Pic
							✓	✓			✓

Bottle Lake
Lakeville
Maine Atlas
Map 35, A-1
Acres: 281
Max. Depth:
42 feet
Boat Launch

BrT	LmB
BkT ✓	SmB ✓
RbT	WhP ✓
Sal	Csk
Tog	WhF
Smt	Pic ✓

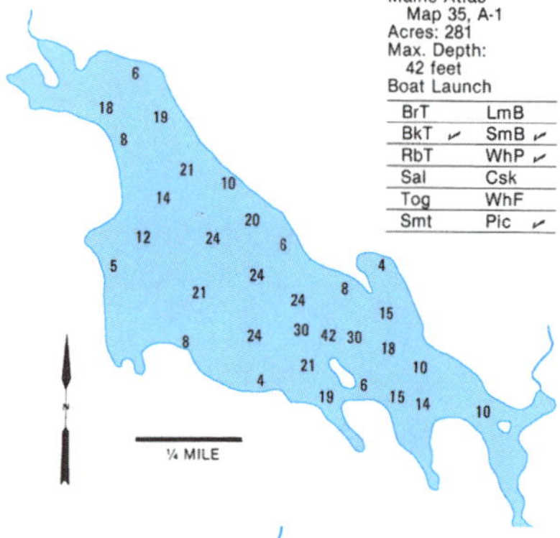

Bowlin Pond
T5 R8 WELS
Maine Atlas
Map 51, B-3
Acres: 115
Max. Depth:
12 feet

BrT	LmB
BkT ✓	SmB ✓
RbT	WhP
Sal	Csk
Tog	WhF
Smt	Pic

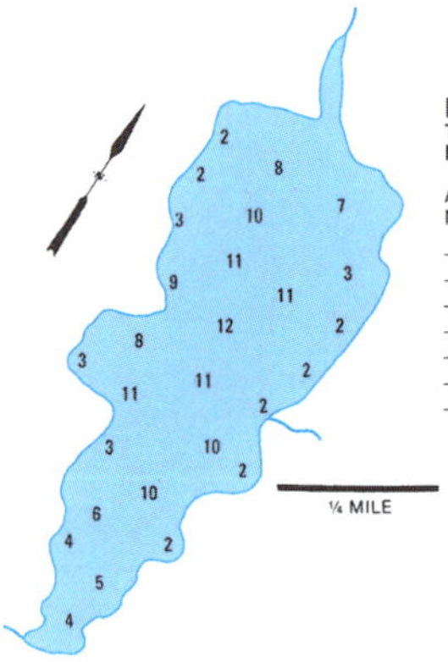

Caribou, Long, and Egg Ponds
Lincoln
Maine Atlas
Map 44, E-1, E-2
Acres: 825
Max. Depth:
46 feet
Boat Launch

BrT	LmB
BkT ✓	SmB ✓
RbT	WhP ✓
Sal	Csk
Tog	WhF
Smt	Pic ✓

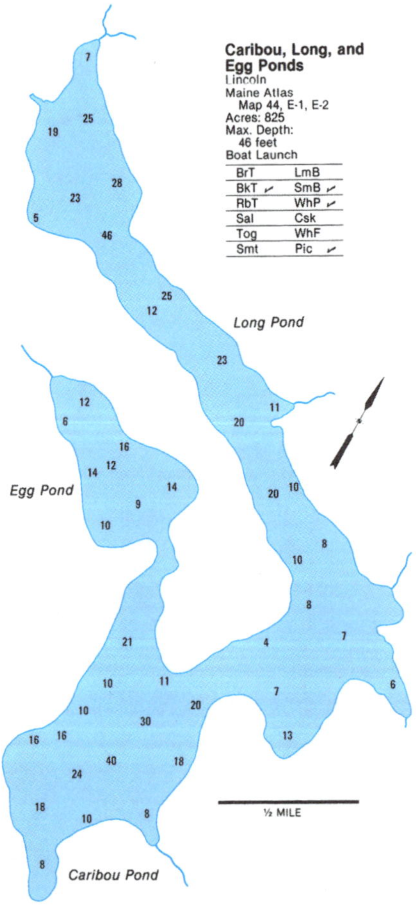

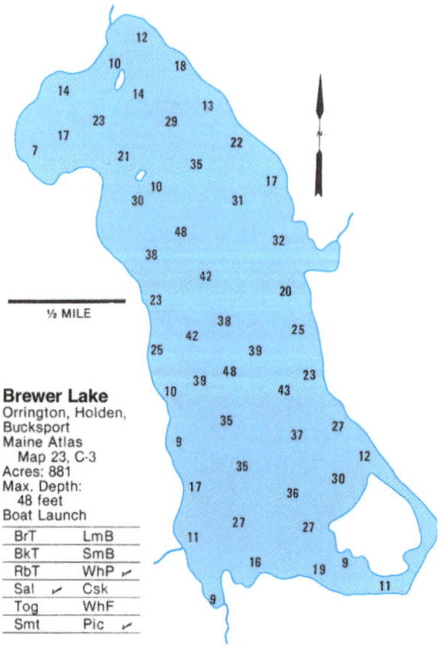

Brewer Lake
Orrington, Holden,
Bucksport
Maine Atlas
Map 23, C-3
Acres: 881
Max. Depth:
48 feet
Boat Launch

BrT	LmB
BkT	SmB
RbT	WhP ✓
Sal ✓	Csk
Tog	WhF
Smt	Pic ✓

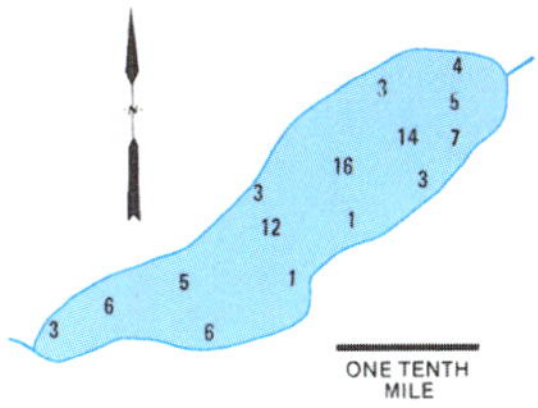

Center Pond

Dixmont
Maine Atlas
Map 22, C-3
Acres: 14
Max. Depth:
16 feet

BrT		LmB	
BkT	✓	SmB	
RbT		WhP	
Sal		Csk	
Tog		WhF	
Smt		Pic	✓

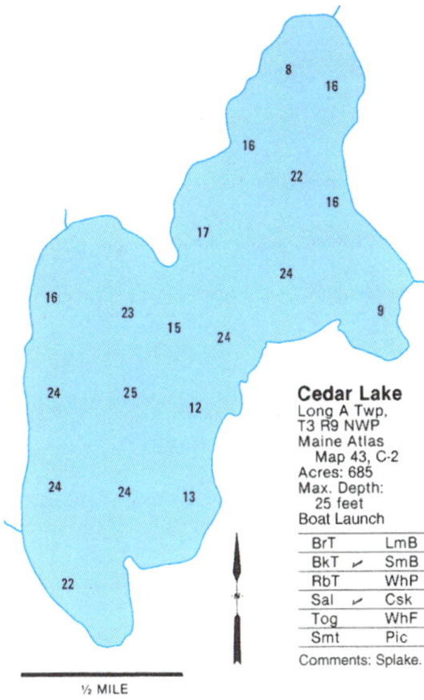

Cedar Lake

Long A Twp,
T3 R9 NWP
Maine Atlas
Map 43, C-2
Acres: 685
Max. Depth:
25 feet
Boat Launch

BrT		LmB	
BkT	✓	SmB	
RbT		WhP	✓
Sal	✓	Csk	
Tog		WhF	
Smt		Pic	

Comments: Splake.

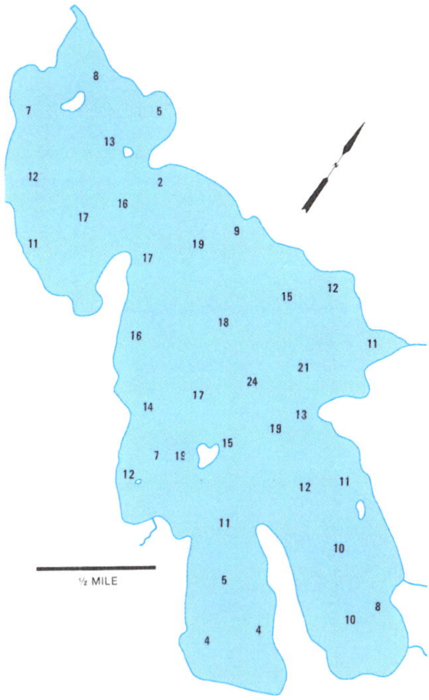

Chemo Pond

Bradley, Eddington, Clifton, Maine Atlas Map 23, B-4, B-5
Acres: 1,146, Max. Depth: 24 feet, Boat Launch

BrT	BkT	RbT	Sal	Tog	Smt	LmB	SmB	WhP	Csk	WhF	Pic
							✓	✓			✓

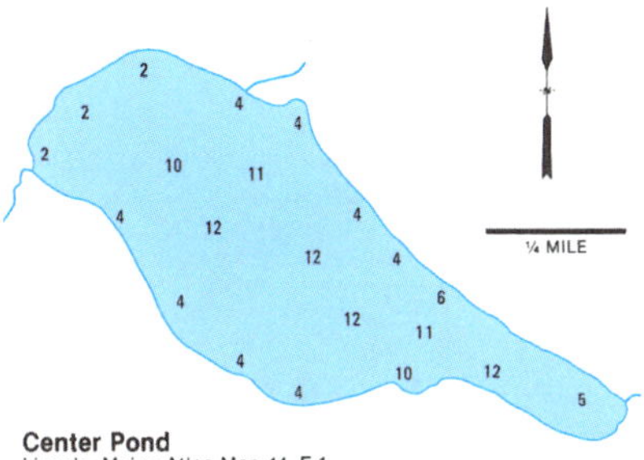

Center Pond

Lincoln, Maine Atlas Map 44, E-1
Acres: 192, Max. Depth: 12 feet

BrT	BkT	RbT	Sal	Tog	Smt	LmB	SmB	WhP	Csk	WhF	Pic
								✓			✓

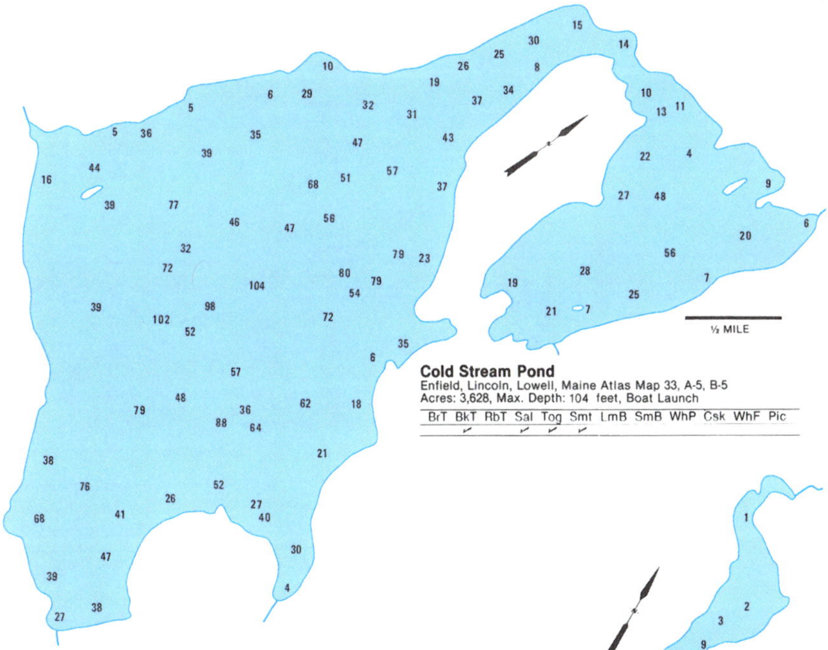

Cold Stream Pond

Enfield, Lincoln, Lowell, Maine Atlas Map 33, A-5, B-5
Acres: 3,628, Max. Depth: 104 feet, Boat Launch

BrT	BkT	RbT	Sal	Tog	Smt	LmB	SmB	WhP	Csk	WhF	Pic
	✓		✓	✓	✓						

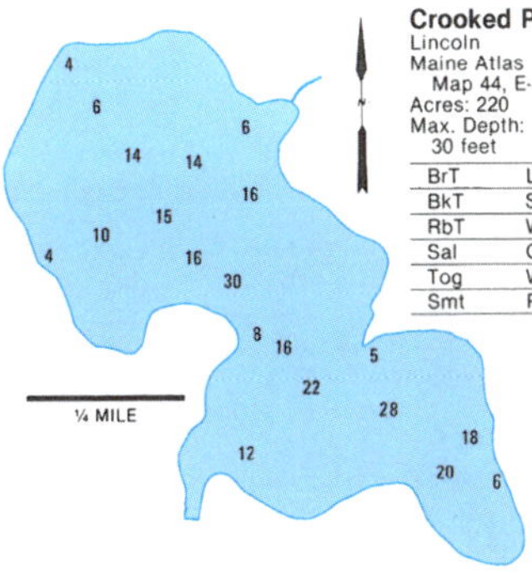

Crooked Pond

Lincoln
Maine Atlas
Map 44, E-1
Acres: 220
Max. Depth:
30 feet

BrT		LmB	
BkT		SmB	✓
RbT		WhP	✓
Sal		Csk	
Tog		WhF	
Smt		Pic	✓

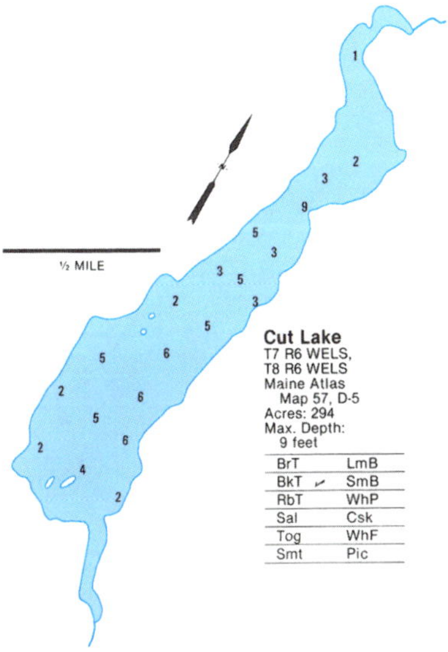

Cut Lake

T7 R6 WELS,
T8 R6 WELS
Maine Atlas
Map 57, D-5
Acres: 294
Max. Depth:
9 feet

BrT		LmB	
BkT	✓	SmB	
RbT		WhP	
Sal		Csk	
Tog		WhF	
Smt		Pic	

Penobscot

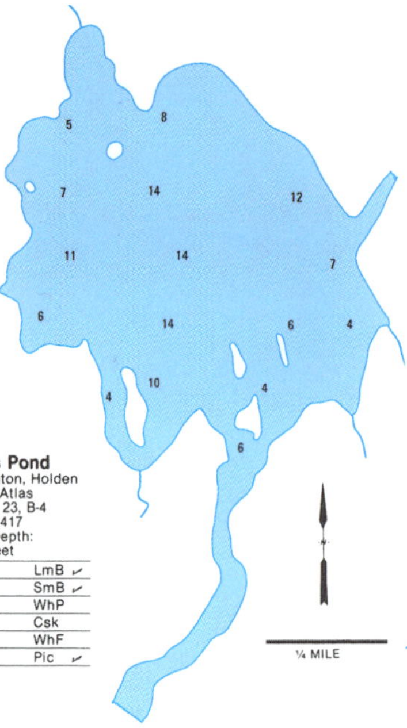

Davis Pond
Eddington, Holden
Maine Atlas
Map 23, B-4
Acres: 417
Max. Depth:
14 feet

BrT	LmB ✓
BkT	SmB ✓
RbT	WhP
Sal	Csk
Tog	WhF
Smt	Pic ✓

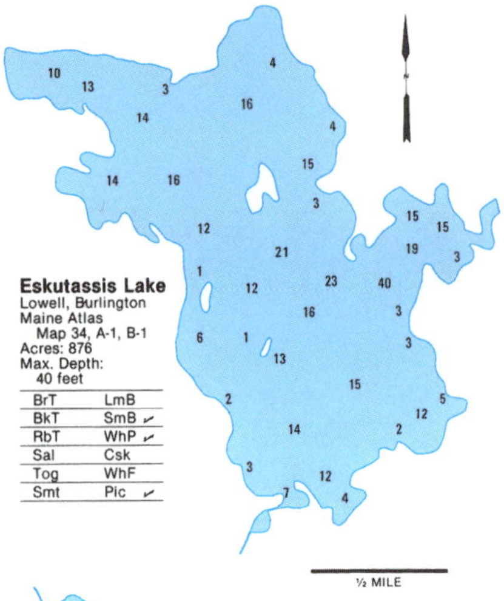

Eskutassis Lake
Lowell, Burlington
Maine Atlas
Map 34, A-1, B-1
Acres: 876
Max. Depth:
40 feet

BrT	LmB
BkT	SmB ✓
RbT	WhP ✓
Sal	Csk
Tog	WhF
Smt	Pic ✓

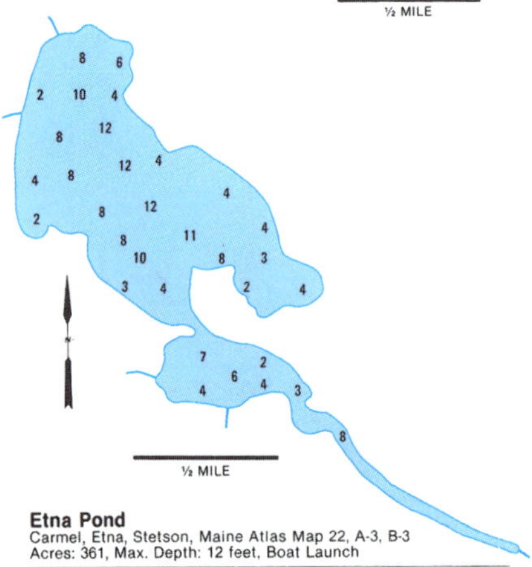

Etna Pond
Carmel, Etna, Stetson, Maine Atlas Map 22, A-3, B-3
Acres: 361, Max. Depth: 12 feet, Boat Launch

BrT	BkT	RbT	Sal	Tog	Smt	LmB	SmB	WhP	Csk	WhF	Pic
	✓						✓	✓			✓

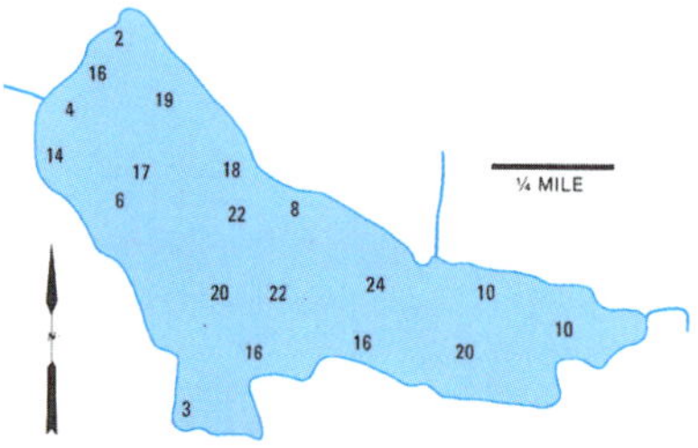

Duck Lake
Lakeville, Maine Atlas Map 45, E-1
Acres: 256, Max. Depth: 24 feet, Boat Launch

BrT	BkT	RbT	Sal	Tog	Smt	LmB	SmB	WhP	Csk	WhF	Pic
	✓		✓		✓		✓	✓			✓

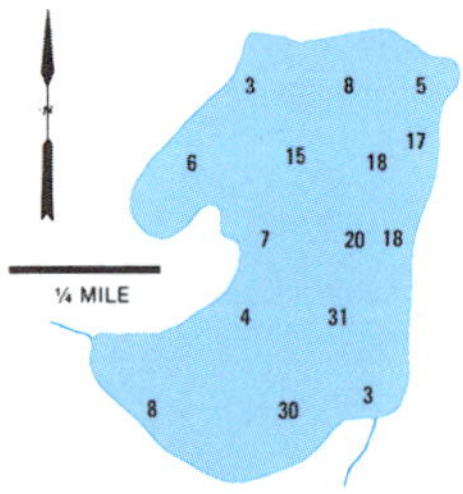

Fields Pond
Orrington
Maine Atlas
Map 23, C-3
Acres: 182
Max. Depth:
31 feet
Boat Launch

BrT	LmB
BkT ✓	SmB ✓
RbT	WhP ✓
Sal	Csk
Tog	WhF
Smt	Pic ✓

Fitts Pond
Clifton
Maine Atlas
Map 23, B-5
Acres: 106
Max. Depth:
64 feet

BrT	LmB
BkT ✓	SmB
RbT	WhP
Sal	Csk
Tog	WhF
Smt ✓	Pic ✓

Comments: Splake.

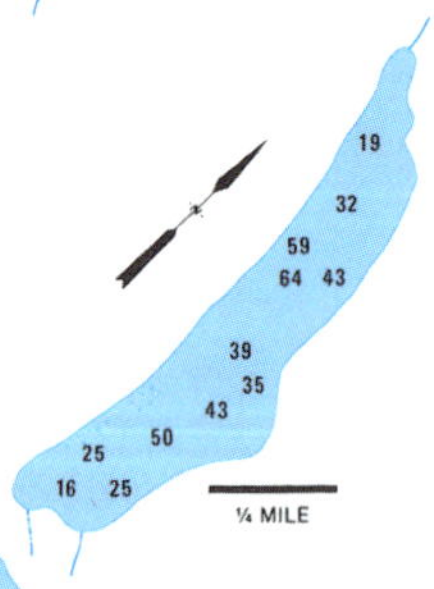

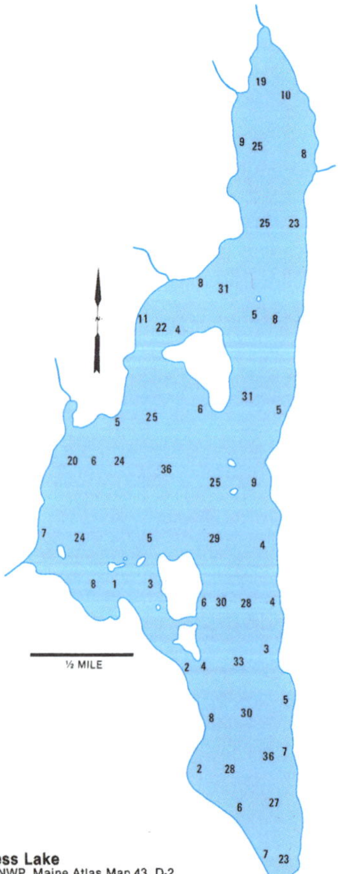

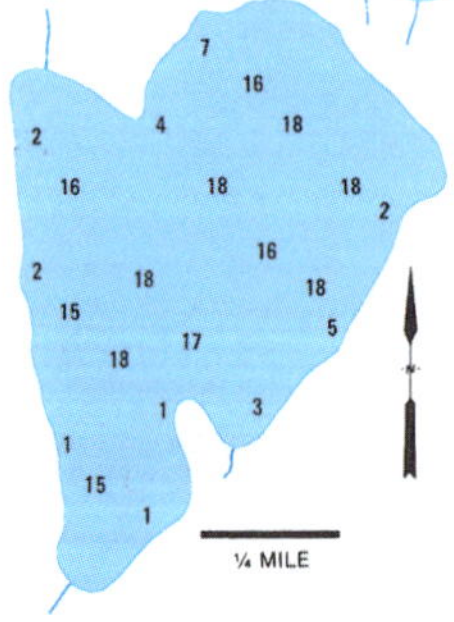

Flatiron Pond
T3 R9 NWP
Maine Atlas
Map 43, C-2
Acres: 284
Max. Depth:
18 feet

BrT	LmB
BkT	SmB
RbT	WhP ✓
Sal	Csk
Tog	WhF
Smt	Pic

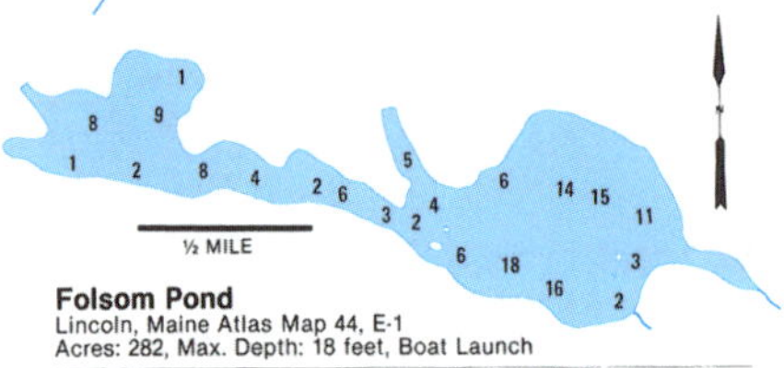

Endless Lake
T3 R9 NWP, Maine Atlas Map 43, D-2
Acres: 1,499, Max. Depth: 36 feet

BrT	BkT	RbT	Sal	Tog	Smt	LmB	SmB	WhP	Csk	WhF	Pic
	✓		✓				✓	✓			✓

Comments: Splake.

Folsom Pond
Lincoln, Maine Atlas Map 44, E-1
Acres: 282, Max. Depth: 18 feet, Boat Launch

BrT	BkT	RbT	Sal	Tog	Smt	LmB	SmB	WhP	Csk	WhF	Pic
							✓	✓			✓

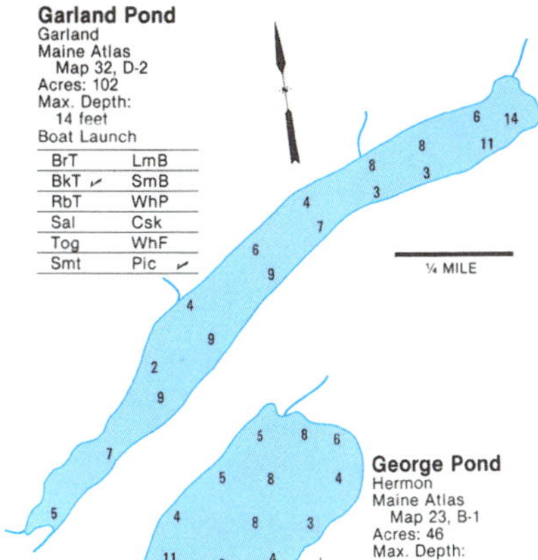

Garland Pond
Garland
Maine Atlas
Map 32, D-2
Acres: 102
Max. Depth:
14 feet
Boat Launch

BrT		LmB	
BkT	✓	SmB	
RbT		WhP	
Sal		Csk	
Tog		WhF	
Smt		Pic	✓

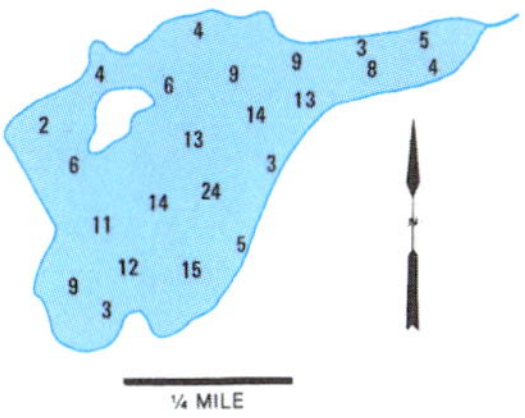

Hay Pond
T6 R8 WELS
Maine Atlas
Map 51, A-2
Map 57, E-2
Acres: 134
Max. Depth:
24 feet

BrT		LmB	
BkT	✓	SmB	
RbT		WhP	
Sal		Csk	
Tog		WhF	
Smt		Pic	

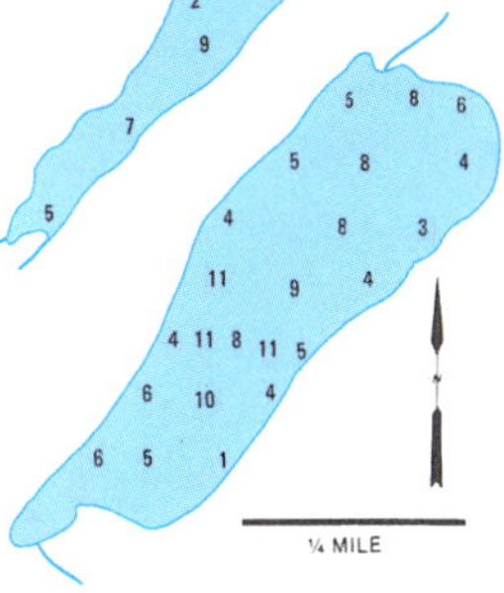

George Pond
Hermon
Maine Atlas
Map 23, B-1
Acres: 46
Max. Depth:
11 feet

BrT		LmB	
BkT		SmB	✓
RbT		WhP	✓
Sal		Csk	
Tog		WhF	
Smt		Pic	✓

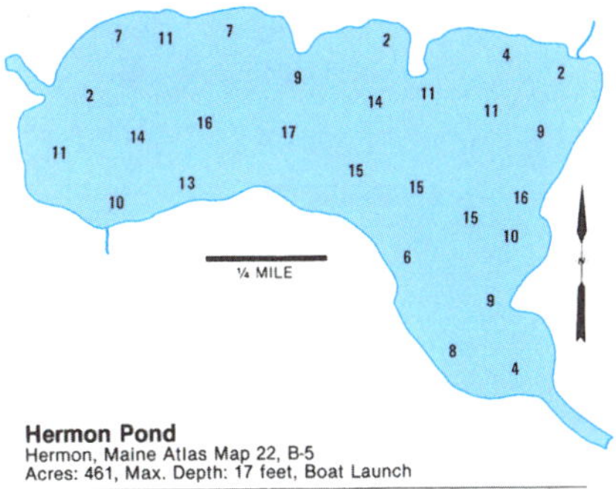

Hermon Pond
Hermon, Maine Atlas Map 22, B-5
Acres: 461, Max. Depth: 17 feet, Boat Launch

BrT	BkT	RbT	Sal	Tog	Smt	LmB	SmB	WhP	Csk	WhF	Pic
	✓				✓		✓	✓			✓

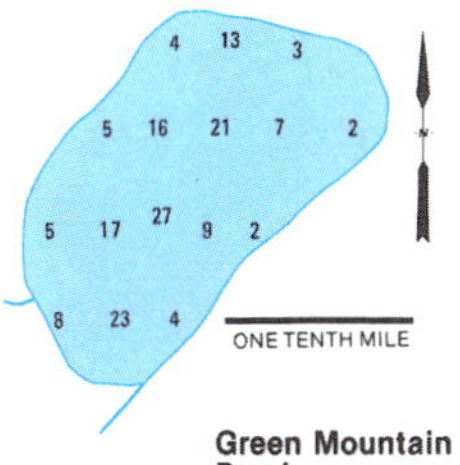

Gould Pond
Dexter
Maine Atlas
Map 32, E-1
Acres: 8
Max. Depth:
27 feet

BrT		LmB	
BkT		SmB	
RbT		WhP	
Sal		Csk	
Tog		WhF	
Smt		Pic	✓

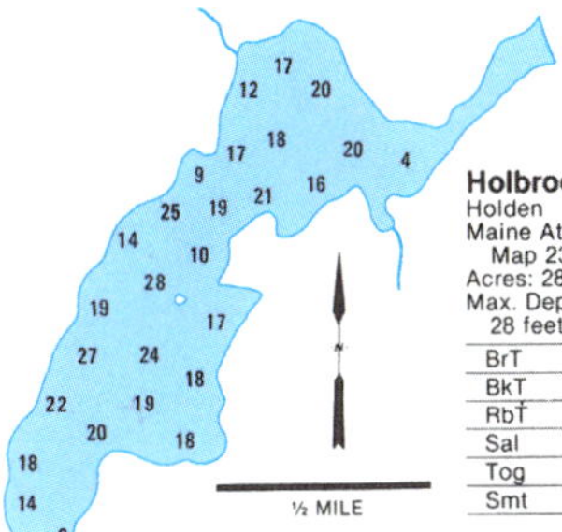

Holbrook Pond
Holden
Maine Atlas
Map 23, B-4, C-4
Acres: 280
Max. Depth:
28 feet

BrT		LmB	
BkT		SmB	✓
RbT		WhP	✓
Sal		Csk	
Tog		WhF	
Smt		Pic	✓

Green Mountain Pond
T6 R6 WELS
Maine Atlas
Map 58, E-1
Acres: 6
Max. Depth:
23 feet

BrT		LmB	
BkT	✓	SmB	
RbT		WhP	
Sal		Csk	
Tog		WhF	
Smt		Pic	

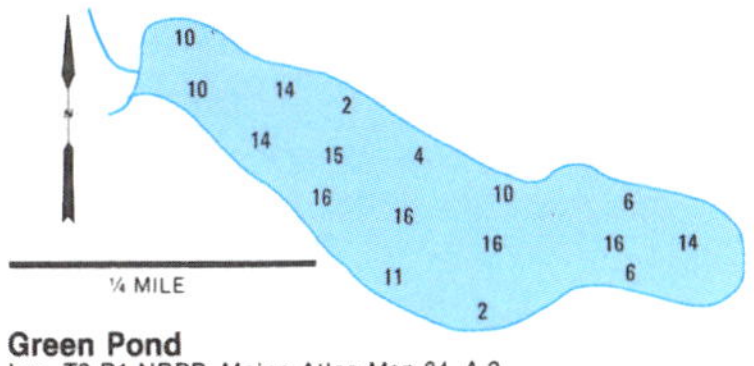

Green Pond
Lee, T3 R1 NBPP, Maine Atlas Map 34, A-3
Acres: 110, Max. Depth: 16 feet

BrT	BkT	RbT	Sal	Tog	Smt	LmB	SmB	WhP	Csk	WhF	Pic
	✓										✓

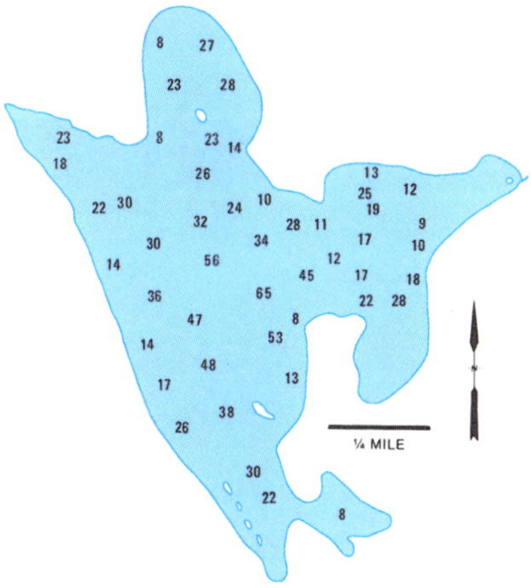

Hopkins Pond
Clifton, Mariaville, Maine Atlas Map 24, B-1
Acres: 442, Max. Depth: 65 feet,

BrT	BkT	RbT	Sal	Tog	Smt	LmB	SmB	WhP	Csk	WhF	Pic
	✓		✓	✓	✓						

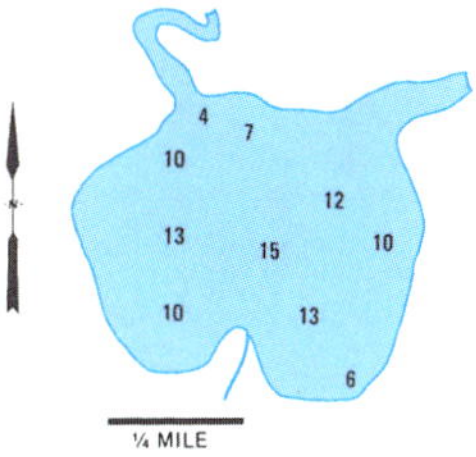

Hammond Pond
Hampden
Maine Atlas
Map 22, B-5
Acres: 83
Max. Depth:
15 feet

BrT		LmB	
BkT		SmB	✓
RbT		WhP	✓
Sal		Csk	
Tog		WhF	
Smt		Pic	✓

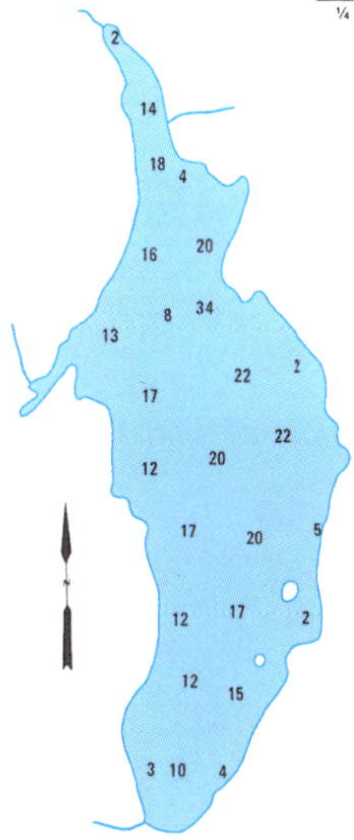

Hay Lake
T6 R8 WELS
Maine Atlas
Map 51, A-3
Acres: 588
Max. Depth:
34 feet
Boat Launch

BrT		LmB	
BkT	✓	SmB	
RbT		WhP	
Sal	✓	Csk	
Tog		WhF	
Smt		Pic	

½ MILE

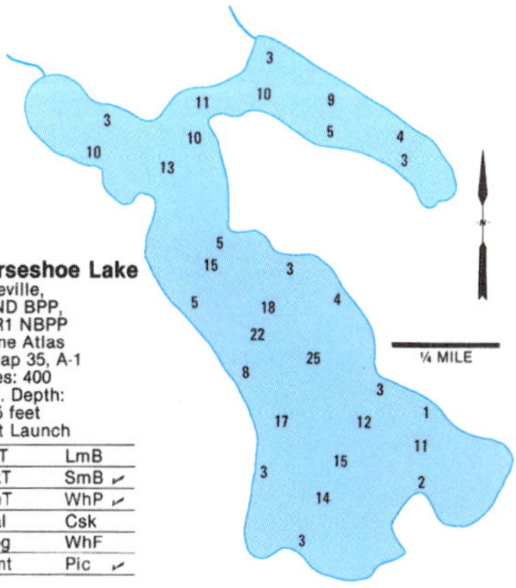

Horseshoe Lake
Lakeville,
T5 ND BPP,
T5 R1 NBPP
Maine Atlas
Map 35, A-1
Acres: 400
Max. Depth:
25 feet
Boat Launch

BrT		LmB	
BkT		SmB	✓
RbT		WhP	✓
Sal		Csk	
Tog		WhF	
Smt		Pic	✓

Penobscot

Hot Pond
T6 R6 WELS,
T6 R7 WELS
Maine Atlas
Map 51, A-5
Acres: 70
Max. Depth:
7 feet

BrT		LmB	
BkT		SmB	
RbT		WhP	
Sal		Csk	
Tog		WhF	
Smt		Pic	✓

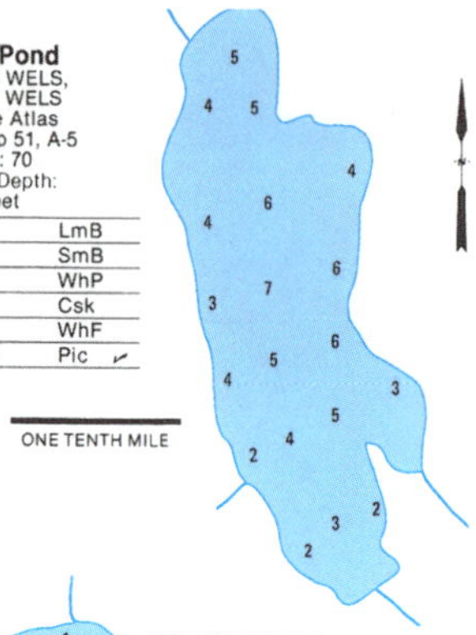

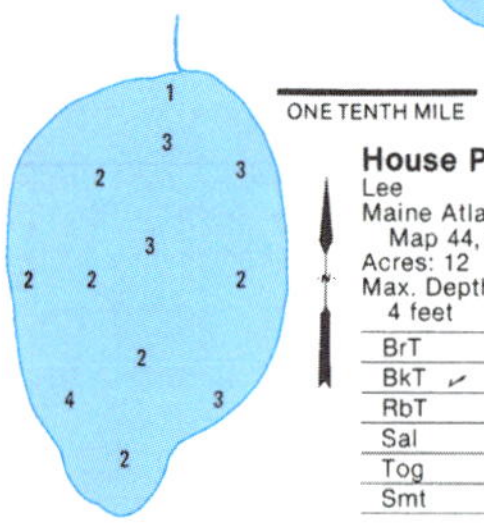

House Pond
Lee
Maine Atlas
Map 44, E-3
Acres: 12
Max. Depth:
4 feet

BrT		LmB	
BkT	✓	SmB	
RbT		WhP	
Sal		Csk	
Tog		WhF	
Smt		Pic	

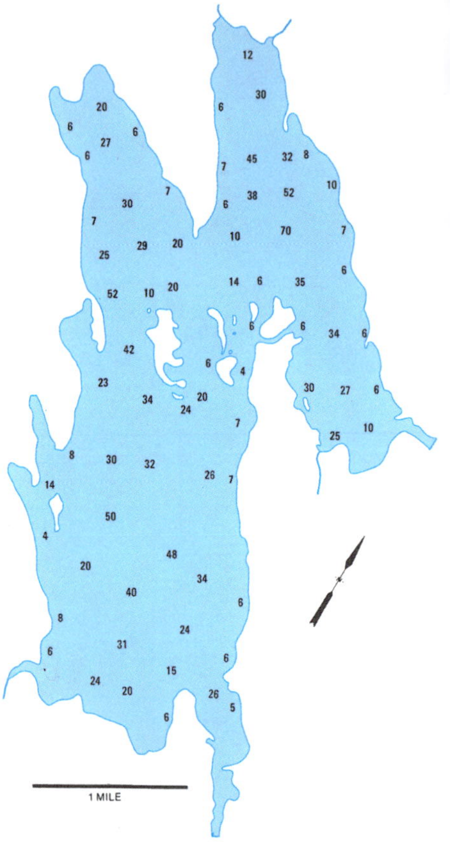

Ireland Pond
T7 R8 WELS
Maine Atlas
Map 57, D-2
Acres: 30
Max. Depth:
35 feet

BrT		LmB	
BkT	✓	SmB	
RbT		WhP	
Sal		Csk	
Tog		WhF	
Smt		Pic	

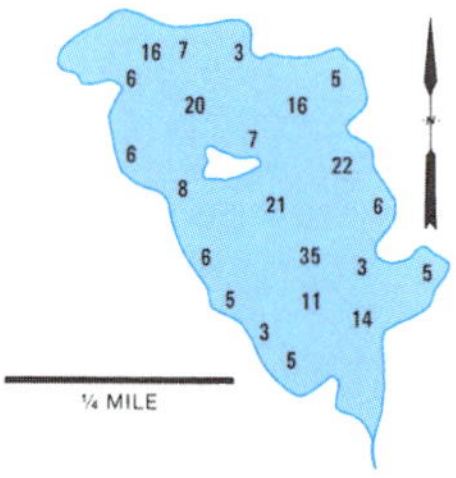

Junior Lake
Lakeville, Pukakon Twp, Maine Atlas Map 35, A-1, A-2
Acres: 3,866, Max. Depth: 70 feet

BrT	BkT	RbT	Sal	Tog	Smt	LmB	SmB	WhP	Csk	WhF	Pic
			✓	✓	✓		✓	✓			✓

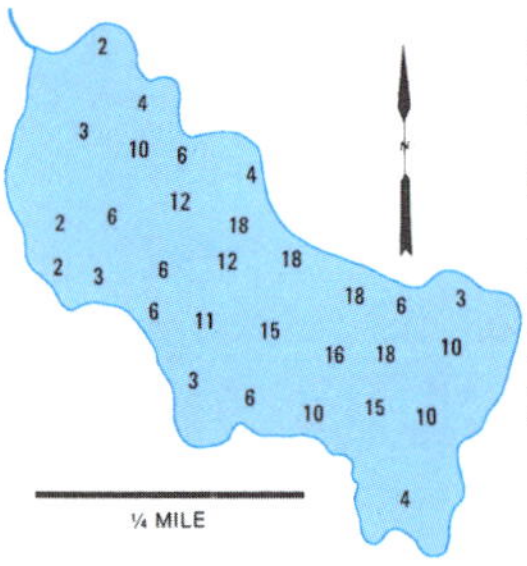

Jerry Pond
Millinocket,
TA R7 WELS
Maine Atlas
Map 43, A-3, B-3
Acres: 66
Max. Depth:
18 feet

BrT		LmB	
BkT	✓	SmB	
RbT		WhP	
Sal		Csk	
Tog		WhF	
Smt		Pic	

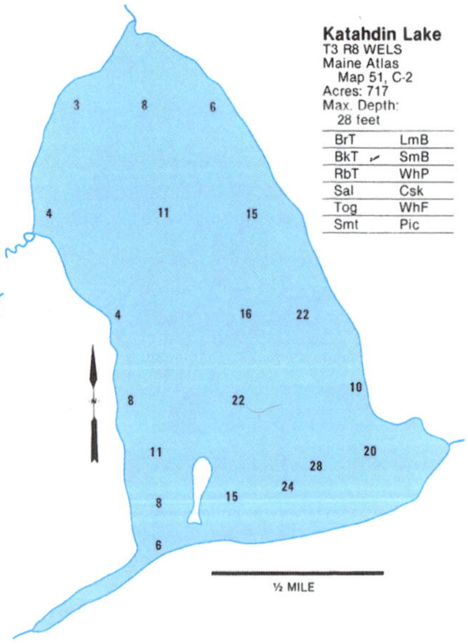

Katahdin Lake
T3 R8 WELS
Maine Atlas
Map 51, C-2
Acres: 717
Max. Depth:
28 feet

BrT		LmB	
BkT	✓	SmB	
RbT		WhP	
Sal		Csk	
Tog		WhF	
Smt		Pic	

Jerry Pond
T5 R7 WELS
Maine Atlas
Map 51, A-3
Acres: 272
Max. Depth:
13 feet

BrT		LmB	
BkT	✓	SmB	
RbT		WhP	
Sal		Csk	
Tog		WhF	
Smt		Pic	

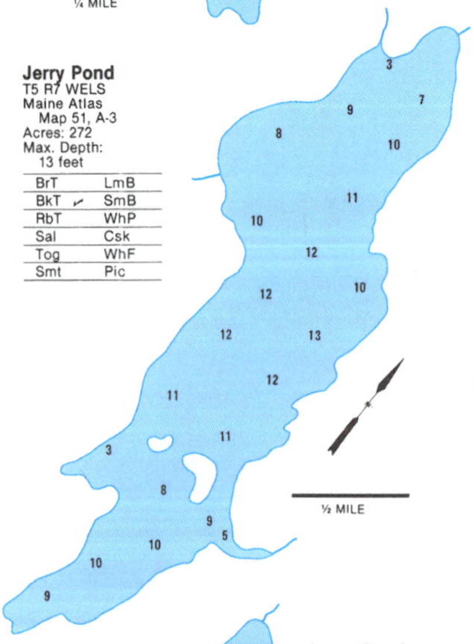

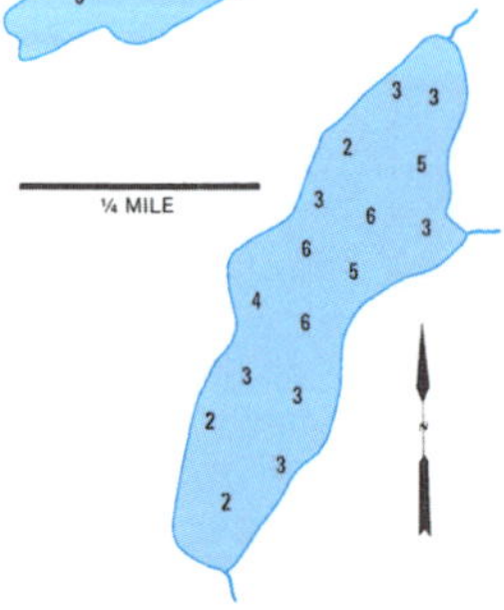

Jones Pond
T7 R8 WELS,
T8 R8 WELS
Maine Atlas
Map 57, D-3
Acres: 32
Max. Depth:
6 feet

BrT		LmB	
BkT	✓	SmB	
RbT		WhP	
Sal		Csk	
Tog		WhF	
Smt		Pic	

Keg Lake
Lakeville
Maine Atlas
Map 35, A-1
Acres: 378
Max. Depth:
40 feet

BrT		LmB	
BkT		SmB	✓
RbT		WhP	✓
Sal		Csk	
Tog		WhF	
Smt	✓	Pic	✓

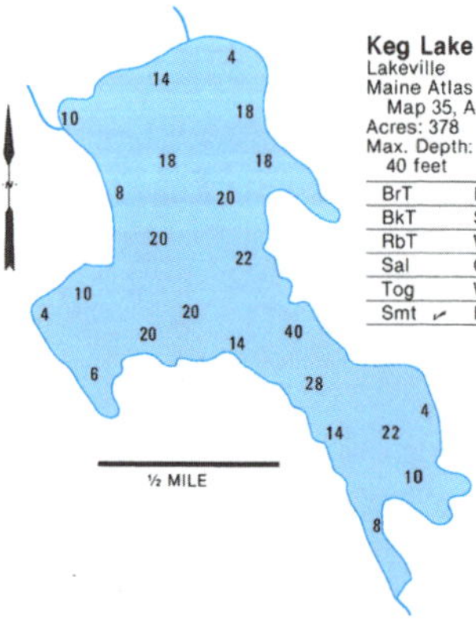

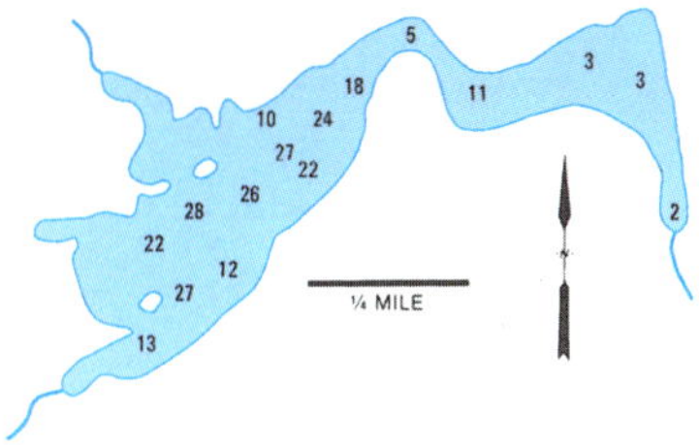

Kimball Pond
T5 R8 WELS, Maine Atlas Map 51, A-2, A-3
Acres: 64, Max. Depth: 28 feet

BrT	BkT	RbT	Sal	Tog	Smt	LmB	SmB	WhP	Csk	WhF	Pic
	✓										

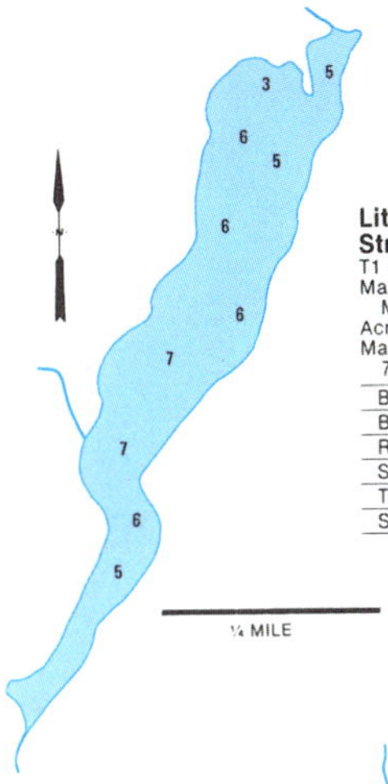

Little Salmon Stream Lake
T1 R6 WELS
Maine Atlas
Map 52, E-1
Acres: 218
Max. Depth:
7 feet

BrT		LmB	
BkT		SmB	✓
RbT		WhP	
Sal		Csk	
Tog		WhF	
Smt		Pic	✓

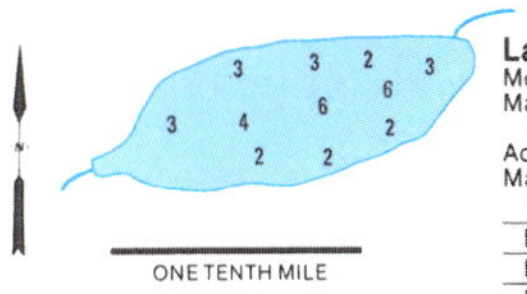

Lawton Pond
Mount Chase
Maine Atlas
Map 52, B-1
Acres: 4
Max. Depth:
6 feet

BrT		LmB	
BkT	✓	SmB	
RbT		WhP	
Sal		Csk	
Tog		WhF	
Smt		Pic	

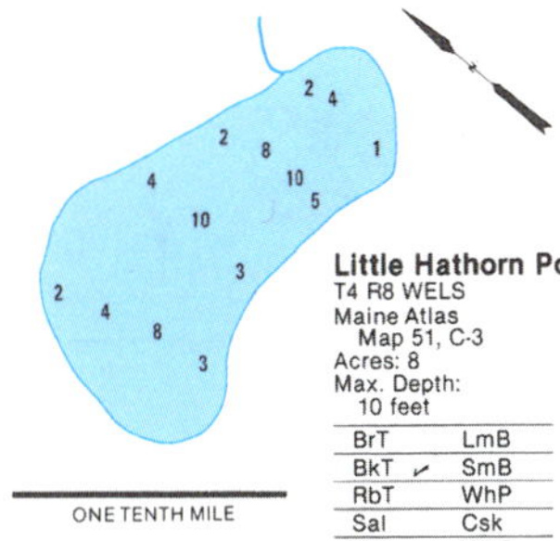

Little Hathorn Pond
T4 R8 WELS
Maine Atlas
Map 51, C-3
Acres: 8
Max. Depth:
10 feet

BrT		LmB	
BkT	✓	SmB	
RbT		WhP	
Sal		Csk	
Tog		WhF	
Smt		Pic	

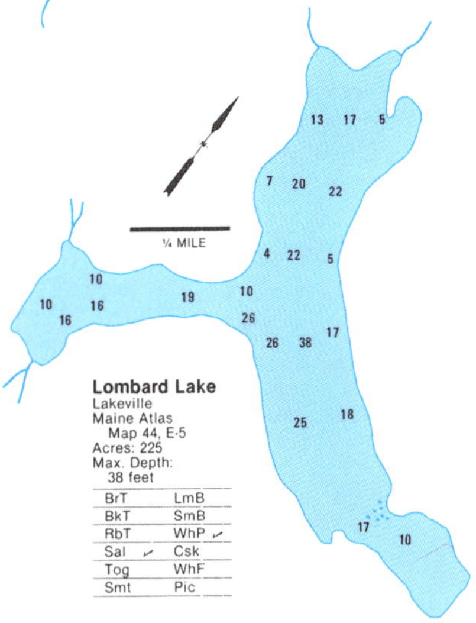

Lombard Lake
Lakeville
Maine Atlas
Map 44, E-5
Acres: 225
Max. Depth:
38 feet

BrT		LmB	
BkT		SmB	
RbT		WhP	✓
Sal	✓	Csk	
Tog		WhF	
Smt		Pic	

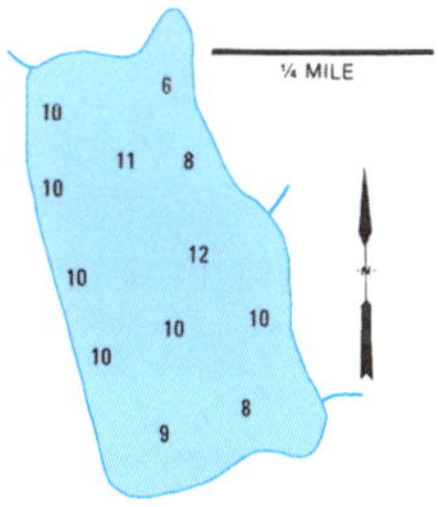

Little Mattamiscontis Lake
T3 R9 NWP
Maine Atlas
Map 43, D-3
Acres: 275
Max. Depth:
12 feet

BrT		LmB	
BkT		SmB	
RbT		WhP	✓
Sal		Csk	
Tog		WhF	
Smt		Pic	✓

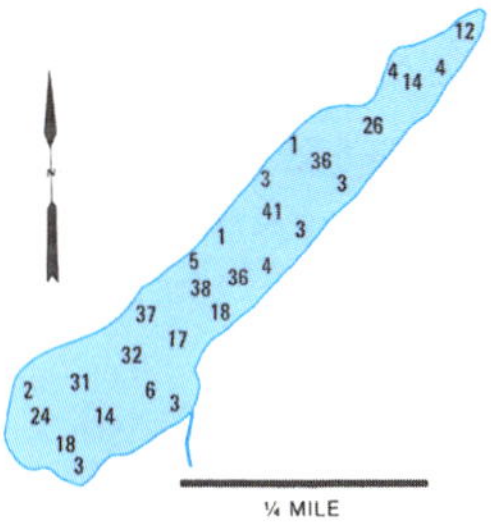

Lost Pond
T7 R7 WELS
Maine Atlas
Map 57, D-4
Acres: 38
Max. Depth:
41 feet

BrT		LmB	
BkT	✓	SmB	
RbT		WhP	
Sal		Csk	
Tog		WhF	
Smt		Pic	

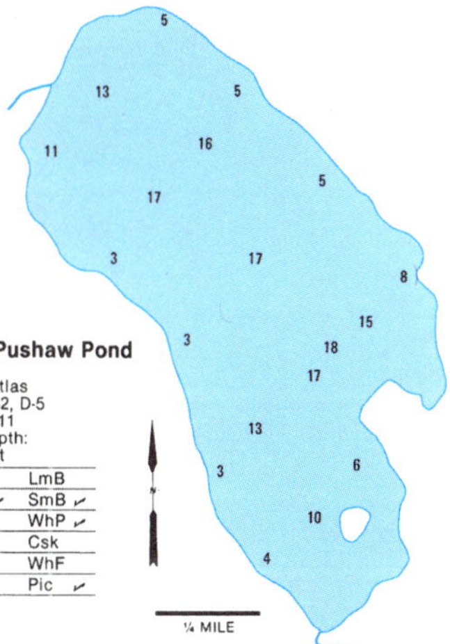

Little Pushaw Pond
Hudson
Maine Atlas
Map 32, D-5
Acres: 411
Max. Depth:
18 feet

BrT		LmB	
BkT	✓	SmB	✓
RbT		WhP	✓
Sal		Csk	
Tog		WhF	
Smt		Pic	✓

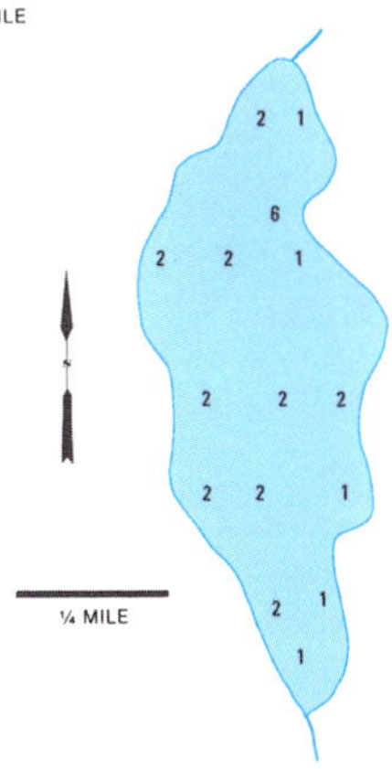

Lowell Lake
Carroll Plt,
Springfield
Maine Atlas
Map 44, E-5
Acres: 115
Max. Depth:
6 feet

BrT		LmB	
BkT		SmB	
RbT		WhP	
Sal		Csk	
Tog		WhF	
Smt		Pic	✓

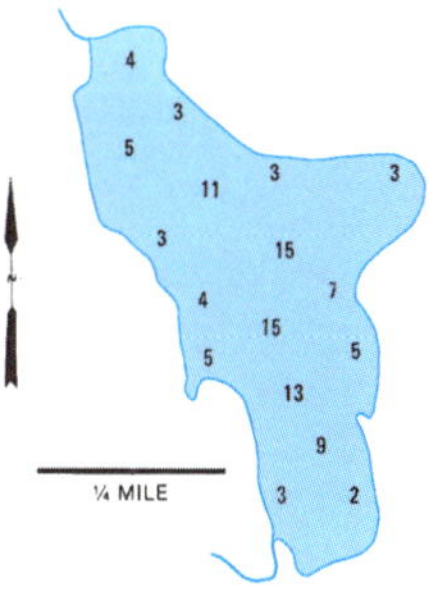

Little Round Pond
Lincoln
Maine Atlas
Map 34, A-1
Acres: 75
Max. Depth:
15 feet
Boat Launch

BrT		LmB	
BkT	✓	SmB	
RbT		WhP	
Sal		Csk	
Tog		WhF	
Smt		Pic	

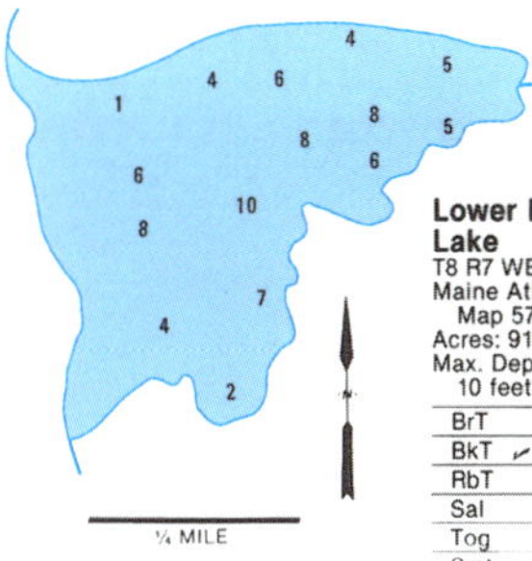

Lower LaPomkeag Lake
T8 R7 WELS
Maine Atlas
Map 57, C-4
Acres: 91
Max. Depth:
10 feet

BrT		LmB	
BkT	✓	SmB	
RbT		WhP	
Sal		Csk	
Tog		WhF	
Smt		Pic	

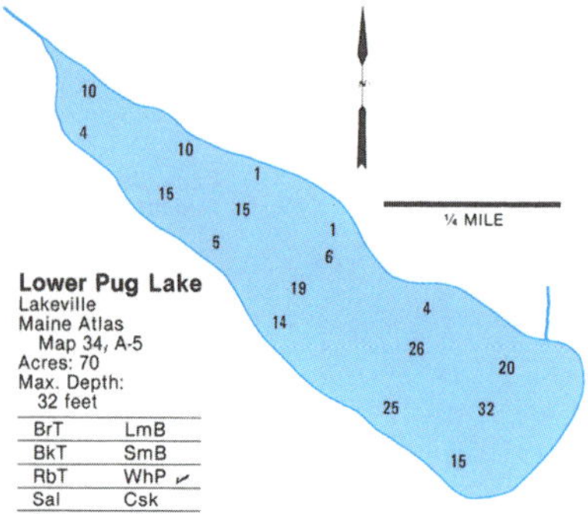

Lower Pug Lake
Lakeville
Maine Atlas
Map 34, A-5
Acres: 70
Max. Depth:
32 feet

BrT	LmB
BkT	SmB
RbT	WhP ✓
Sal	Csk
Tog	WhF
Smt	Pic ✓

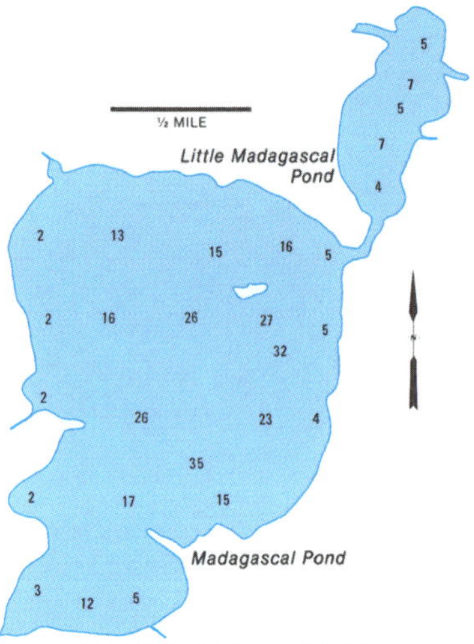

Madagascal and Little Madagascal Ponds
Burlington, T3 R1 NBPP, Maine Atlas Map 34, A-2, A-3
Acres: Madagascal-750, Little-40
Max. Depth: Madagascal-35 feet, Little-7 feet

BrT	BkT	RbT	Sal	Tog	Smt	LmB	SmB	WhP	Csk	WhF	Pic
	✓						✓				✓

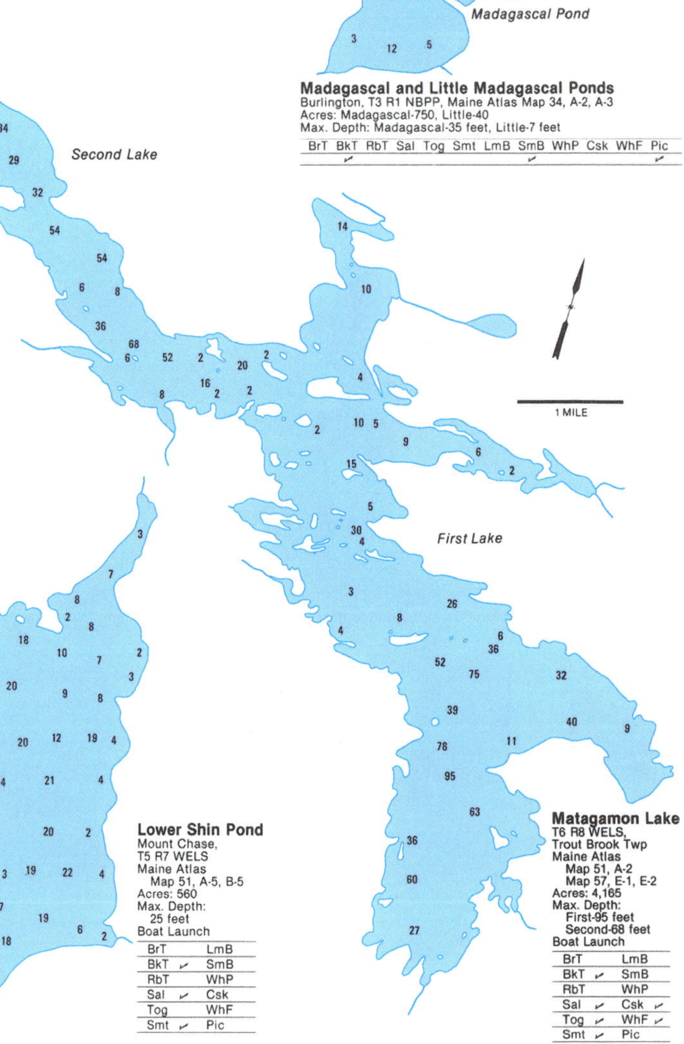

Matagamon Lake
T6 R8 WELS,
Trout Brook Twp
Maine Atlas
Map 51, A-2
Map 57, E-1, E-2
Acres: 4,165
Max. Depth:
First-95 feet
Second-68 feet
Boat Launch

BrT	LmB
BkT ✓	SmB
RbT	WhP
Sal ✓	Csk ✓
Tog ✓	WhF ✓
Smt ✓	Pic

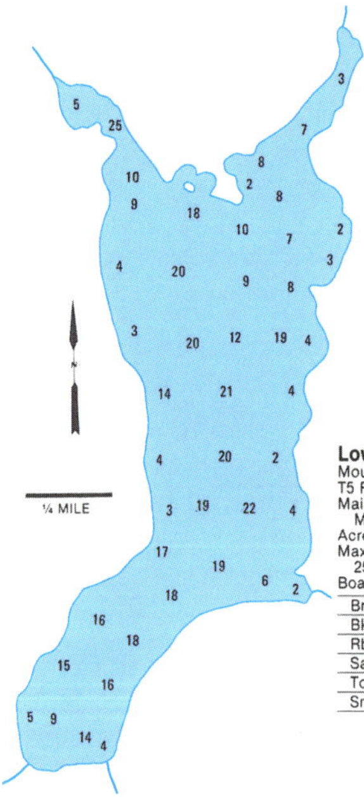

Lower Shin Pond
Mount Chase,
T5 R7 WELS
Maine Atlas
Map 51, A-5, B-5
Acres: 560
Max. Depth:
25 feet
Boat Launch

BrT	LmB
BkT ✓	SmB
RbT	WhP
Sal ✓	Csk
Tog	WhF
Smt ✓	Pic

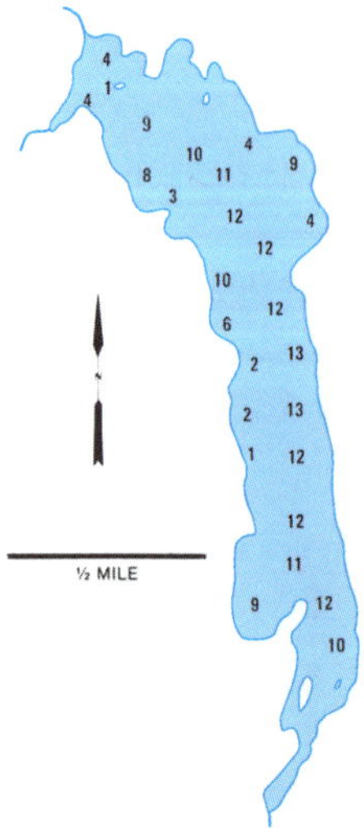

Lunksoos Lake
T4 R7 WELS
Maine Atlas
Map 51, B-3
Acres: 288
Max. Depth:
13 feet

BrT	LmB
BkT ✓	SmB
RbT	WhP
Sal	Csk
Tog	WhF
Smt	Pic

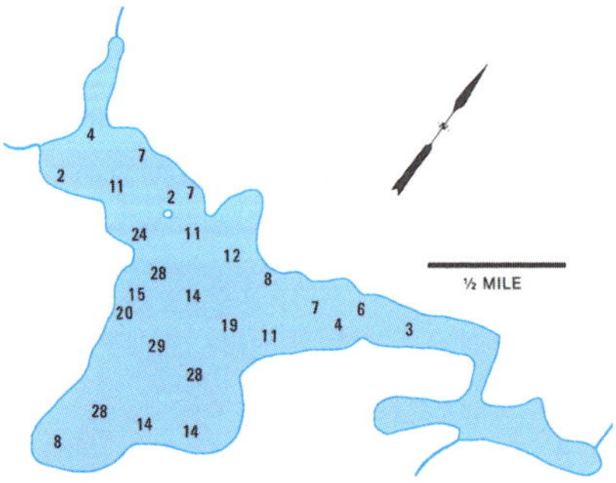

Mattakeunk Lake
Lee, Maine Atlas Map 44, E-3
Acres: 570, Max. Depth: 29 feet

BrT	BkT	RbT	Sal	Tog	Smt	LmB	SmB	WhP	Csk	WhF	Pic
	✓							✓			✓

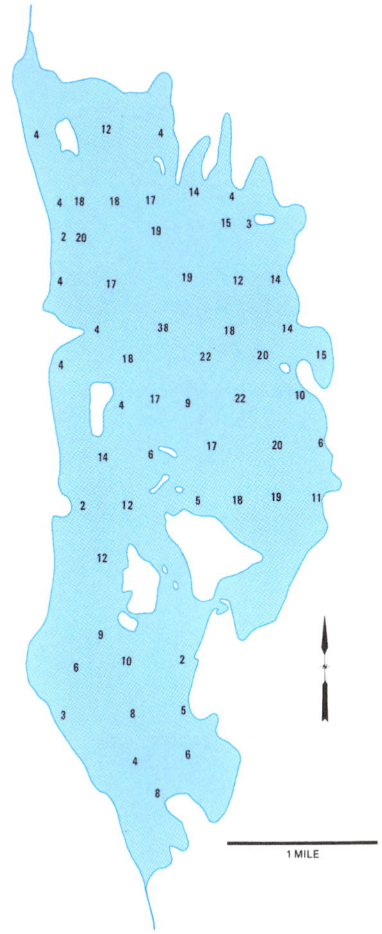

Mattamiscontis Lake

T2 R9 NWP, T3 R9 NWP, Maine Atlas Map 43, C-3, D-3
Acres: 1,025, Max. Depth: 38 feet

BrT	BkT	RbT	Sal	Tog	Smt	LmB	SmB	WhP	Csk	WhF	Pic
	✓							✓			✓

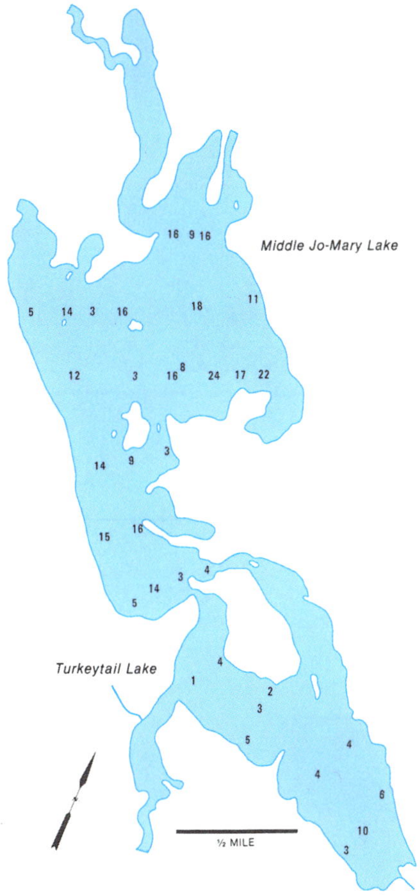

Middle Jo-Mary and Turkeytail Lakes

T4 Indian Purchase, TA R10 WELS, Maine Atlas Map 42, B-5
Acres: 1,152, Max. Depth: 24 feet

BrT	BkT	RbT	Sal	Tog	Smt	LmB	SmB	WhP	Csk	WhF	Pic
	✓		✓					✓			✓

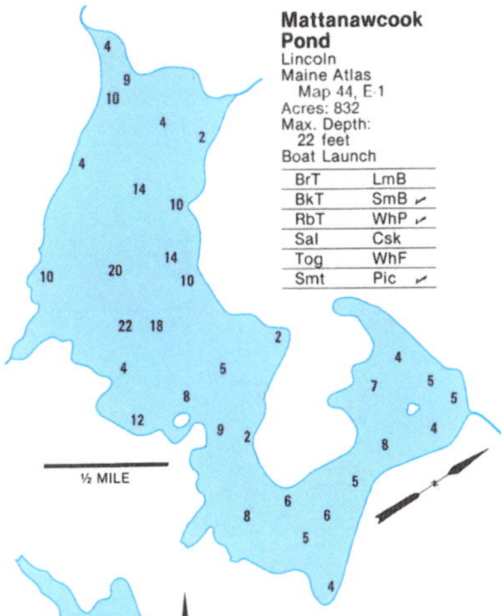

Mattanawcook Pond

Lincoln
Maine Atlas
Map 44, E-1
Acres: 832
Max. Depth:
22 feet
Boat Launch

BrT	LmB
BkT	SmB ✓
RbT	WhP ✓
Sal	Csk
Tog	WhF
Smt	Pic ✓

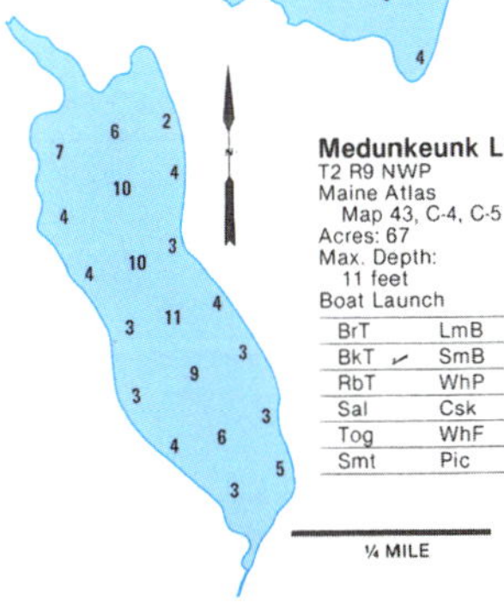

Medunkeunk Lake

T2 R9 NWP
Maine Atlas
Map 43, C-4, C-5
Acres: 67
Max. Depth:
11 feet
Boat Launch

BrT	LmB
BkT ✓	SmB
RbT	WhP
Sal	Csk
Tog	WhF
Smt	Pic

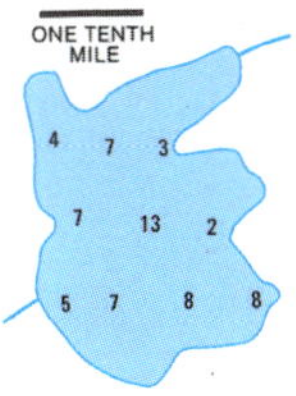

Messer Pond

T5 R8 WELS
Maine Atlas
Map 51, B-2
Acres: 27
Max. Depth:
13 feet

BrT	LmB
BkT ✓	SmB
RbT	WhP
Sal	Csk
Tog	WhF
Smt	Pic

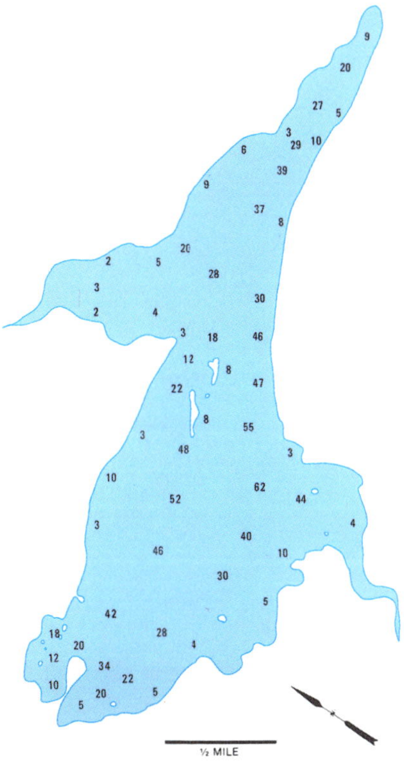

Millimagassett Lake

T7 R8 WELS, Maine Atlas Map 57, D-2
Acres: 1,410, Max. Depth: 62 feet

BrT	BkT	RbT	Sal	Tog	Smt	LmB	SmB	WhP	Csk	WhF	Pic
	✓		✓	✓	✓						

Penobscot

Millinocket Lake

T1 R8 WELS, T1 R9 WELS, T2 R8 WELS, T2 R9 WELS
Maine Atlas Map 51, E-2, Map 43, A-1, A-2
Acres: 8,960, Max. Depth: 86 feet, Boat Launch

BrT	BkT	RbT	Sal	Tog	Smt	LmB	SmB	WhP	Csk	WhF	Pic
	✓		✓	✓	✓			✓	✓	✓	✓

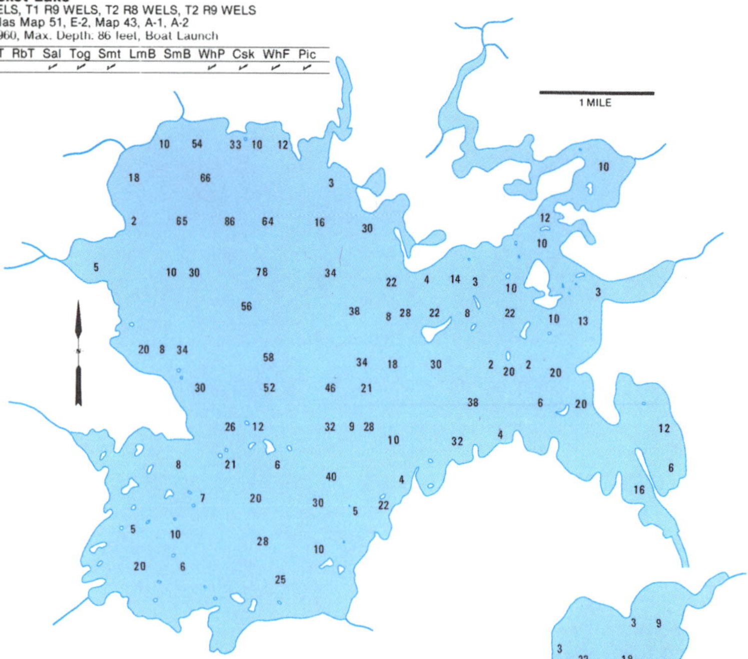

Mill Privilege Lake

T5 R1 NBPP,
Carroll Plt
Maine Atlas
Map 45, E-1
Acres: 109
Max. Depth:
28 feet
Boat Launch

BrT	LmB
BkT ✓	SmB ✓
RbT	WhP ✓
Sal	Csk
Tog	WhF
Smt	Pic

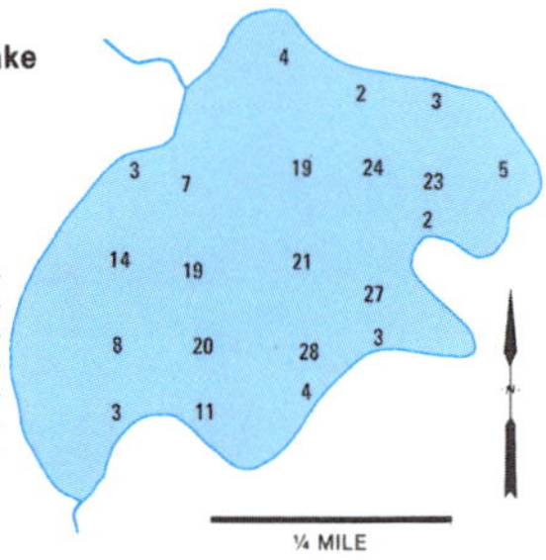

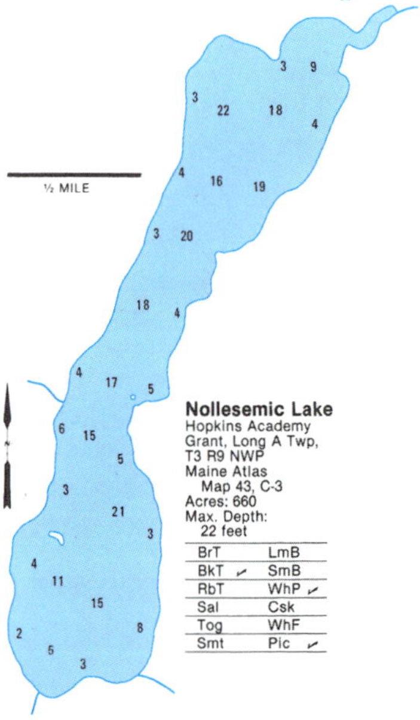

Nollesemic Lake

Hopkins Academy
Grant, Long A Twp,
T3 R9 NWP
Maine Atlas
Map 43, C-3
Acres: 660
Max. Depth:
22 feet

BrT	LmB
BkT ✓	SmB
RbT	WhP ✓
Sal	Csk
Tog	WhF
Smt	Pic ✓

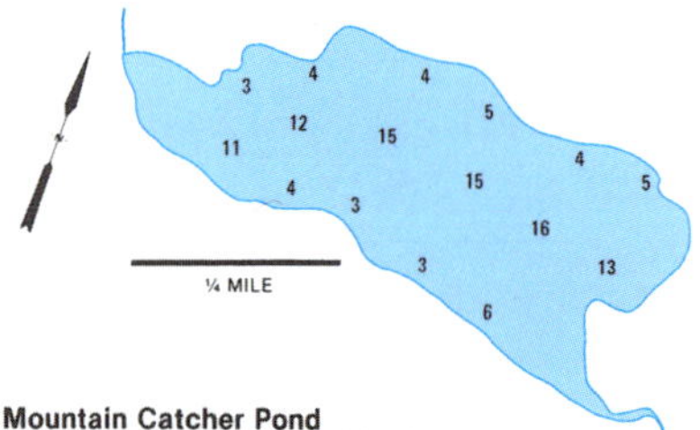

Mountain Catcher Pond

T6 R8 WELS, Trout Brook Twp, Maine Atlas Map 57, E-2
Acres: 90, Max. Depth: 16 feet

BrT	BkT	RbT	Sal	Tog	Smt	LmB	SmB	WhP	Csk	WhF	Pic
	✓										

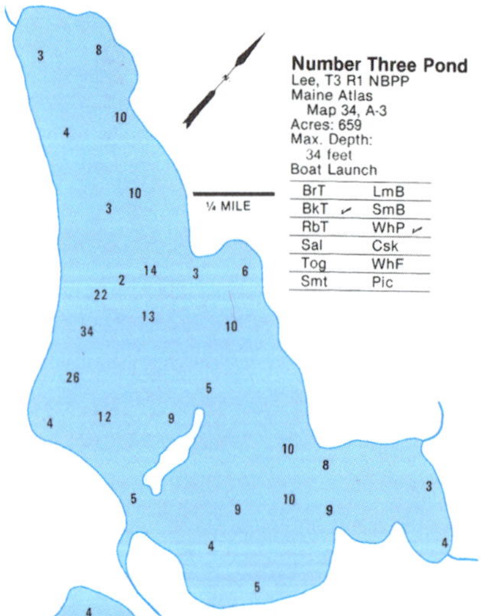

Number Three Pond

Lee, T3 R1 NBPP
Maine Atlas
Map 34, A-3
Acres: 659
Max. Depth:
34 feet
Boat Launch

BrT	LmB
BkT ✓	SmB
RbT	WhP ✓
Sal	Csk
Tog	WhF
Smt	Pic

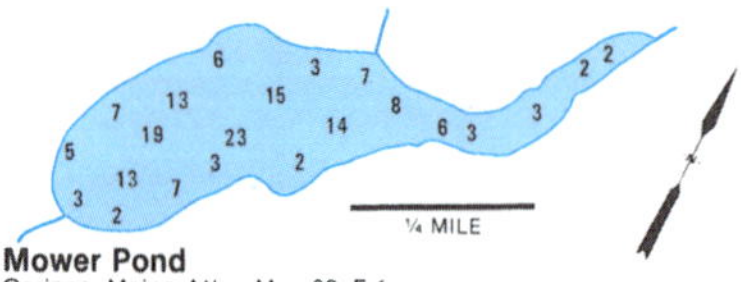

Mower Pond

Corinna, Maine Atlas Map 32, E-1
Acres: 75, Max. Depth: 23 feet, Boat Launch

BrT	BkT	RbT	Sal	Tog	Smt	LmB	SmB	WhP	Csk	WhF	Pic
							✓	✓			✓

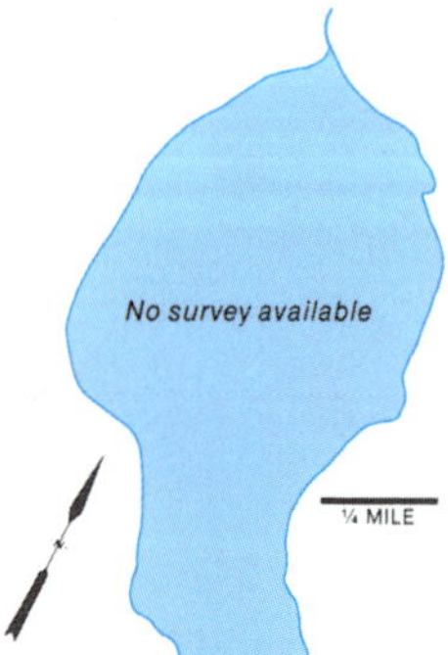

Mud Pond

Old Town
Maine Atlas
Map 33, E-2
Acres: 385
Max. Depth:
12 feet
Boat Launch

BrT	LmB
BkT ✓	SmB
RbT	WhP ✓
Sal	Csk
Tog	WhF
Smt	Pic ✓

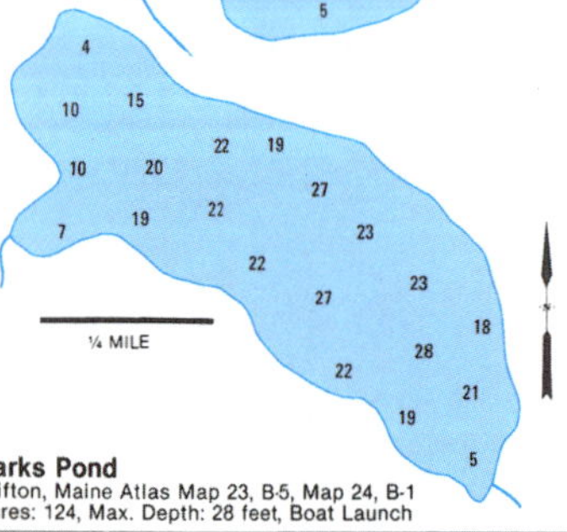

Parks Pond

Clifton, Maine Atlas Map 23, B-5, Map 24, B-1
Acres: 124, Max. Depth: 28 feet, Boat Launch

BrT	BkT	RbT	Sal	Tog	Smt	LmB	SmB	WhP	Csk	WhF	Pic
✓	✓						✓	✓			✓

Patten Pond

Hampden
Maine Atlas
Map 22, B-5
Acres: 46
Max. Depth:
12 feet

BrT	LmB
BkT	SmB ✓
RbT	WhP ✓
Sal	Csk
Tog	WhF
Smt	Pic ✓

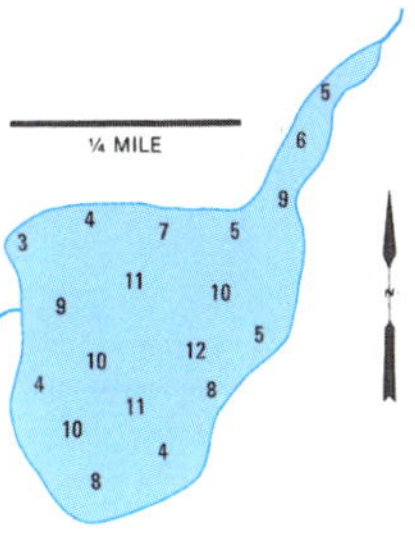

Pickerel Pond

Alton
Maine Atlas
Map 33, D-2
Acres: 77
Max. Depth:
5 feet

BrT	LmB
BkT	SmB
RbT	WhP
Sal	Csk
Tog	WhF
Smt	Pic ✓

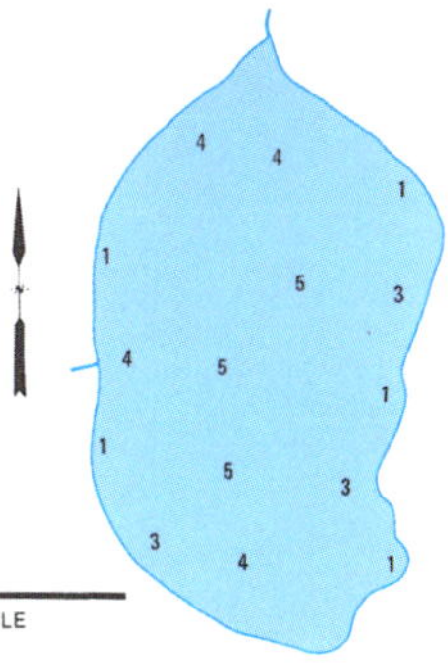

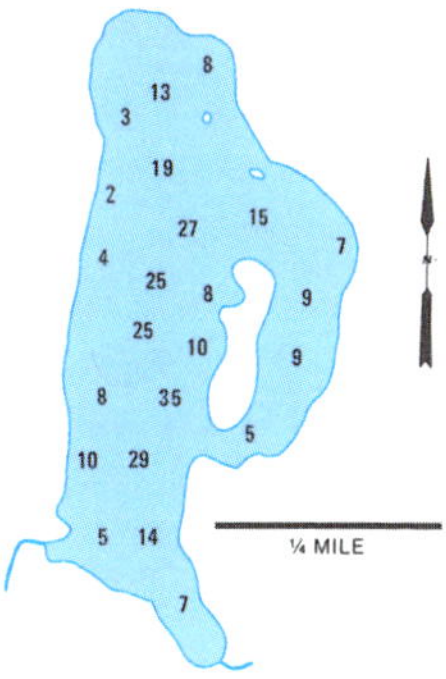

Peaked Mountain Pond

T4 R7 WELS
Maine Atlas
Map 51, B-4
Acres: 61
Max. Depth:
35 feet

BrT	LmB
BkT ✓	SmB
RbT	WhP
Sal	Csk
Tog	WhF
Smt	Pic

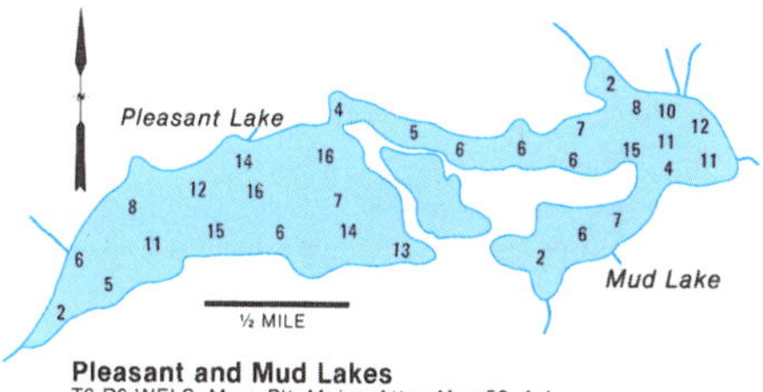

Pleasant and Mud Lakes

T6 R6 WELS, Moro Plt, Maine Atlas Map 52, A-1
Acres: Pleasant-170, Mud-155
Max. Depth: Pleasant-16 feet, Mud-15 feet, Boat Launch

BrT	BkT	RbT	Sal	Tog	Smt	LmB	SmB	WhP	Csk	WhF	Pic
	✓		✓								

Pemadumcook Chain of Lakes

T3 Indian Purchase, T4 Indian Purchase, T1 R10 WELS, T1 R9 WELS
Maine Atlas Map 42, A-5, Map 43, A-1, B-1
Acres: 18,300, Max. Depth: 101 feet, Boat Launch

BrT	BkT	RbT	Sal	Tog	Smt	LmB	SmB	WhP	Csk	WhF	Pic
	✓		✓	✓	✓			✓	✓	✓	✓

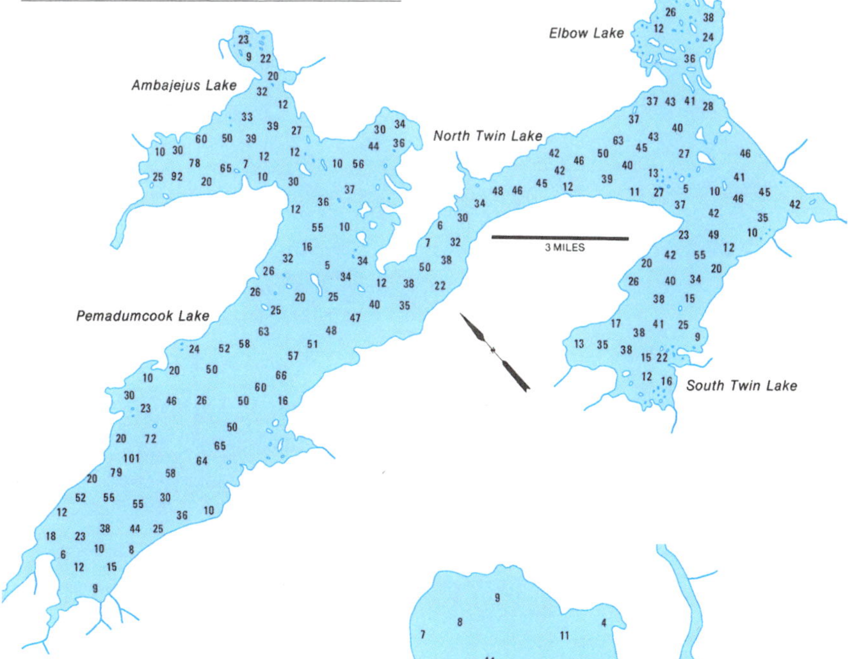

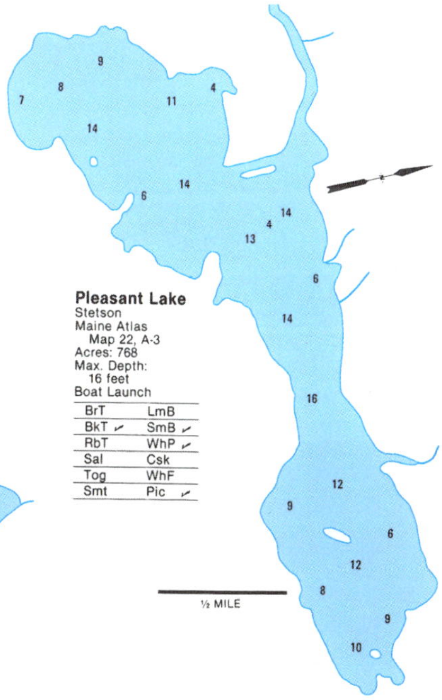

Pleasant Lake

Stetson
Maine Atlas
Map 22, A-3
Acres: 768
Max. Depth:
16 feet
Boat Launch

BrT	LmB
BkT ✓	SmB ✓
RbT	WhP ✓
Sal	Csk
Tog	WhF
Smt	Pic ✓

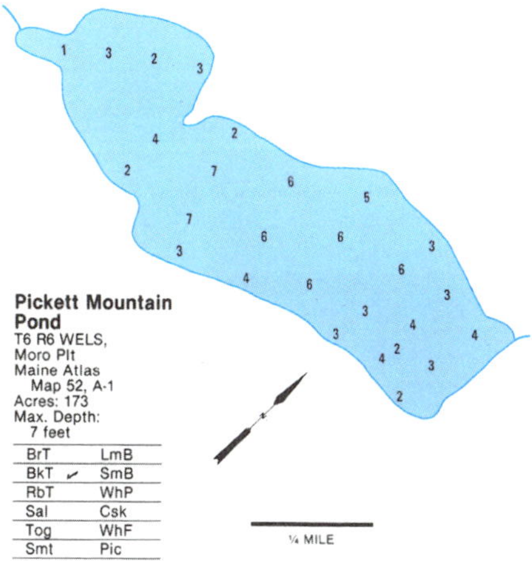

Pickett Mountain Pond

T6 R6 WELS,
Moro Plt
Maine Atlas
Map 52, A-1
Acres: 173
Max. Depth:
7 feet

BrT	LmB
BkT ✓	SmB
RbT	WhP
Sal	Csk
Tog	WhF
Smt	Pic

Penobscot

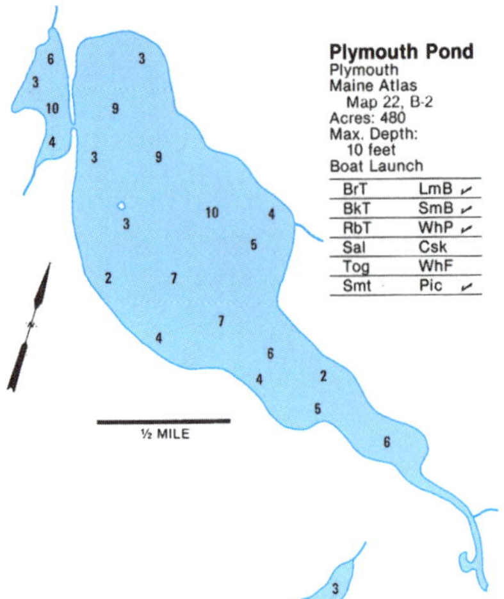

Plymouth Pond

Plymouth
Maine Atlas
Map 22, B-2
Acres: 480
Max. Depth:
10 feet
Boat Launch

BrT	LmB ✓
BkT	SmB ✓
RbT	WhP ✓
Sal	Csk
Tog	WhF
Smt	Pic ✓

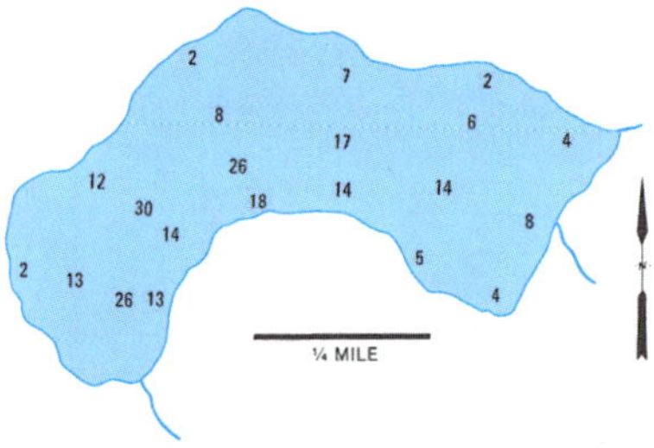

Round Pond

Plymouth, Maine Atlas Map 22, C-2
Acres: 134, Max. Depth: 30 feet

BrT	BkT	RbT	Sal	Tog	Smt	LmB	SmB	WhP	Csk	WhF	Pic
	✓					✓	✓	✓			✓

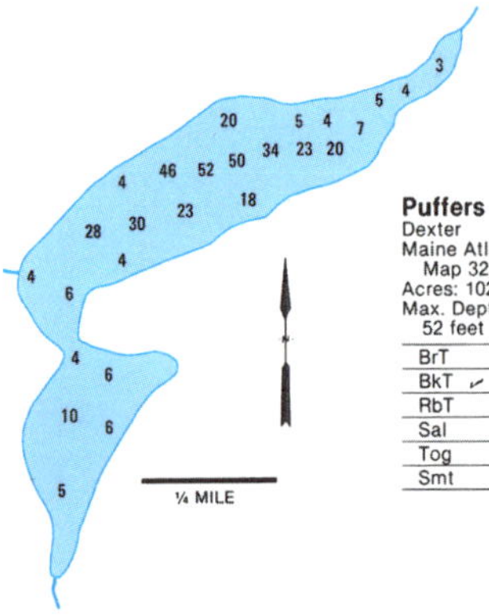

Puffers Pond

Dexter
Maine Atlas
Map 32, D-1
Acres: 102
Max. Depth:
52 feet

BrT	LmB
BkT ✓	SmB
RbT	WhP
Sal	Csk
Tog	WhF
Smt	Pic ✓

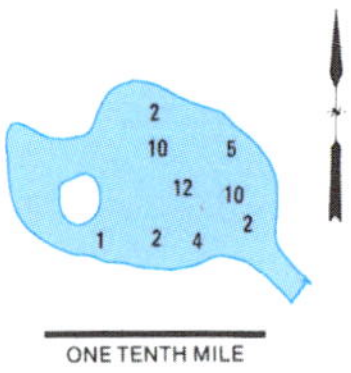

Round Pond

Soldiertown Twp
Maine Atlas
Map 51, E-4, E-5
Acres: 3
Max. Depth:
12 feet

BrT	LmB
BkT	SmB ✓
RbT	WhP
Sal	Csk
Tog	WhF
Smt	Pic ✓

Pug Pond

Alton
Maine Atlas
Map 33, D-2
Acres: 12
Max. Depth:
12 feet

BrT	LmB
BkT	SmB
RbT	WhP
Sal	Csk
Tog	WhF
Smt	Pic ✓

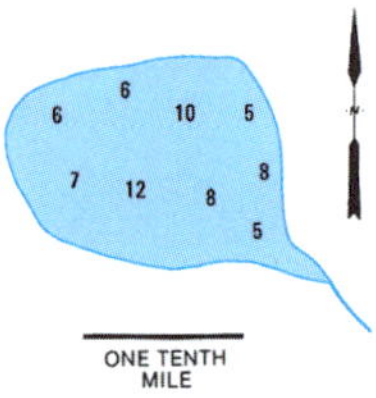

Round Pond

T3 R1 NBPP, Lee
Maine Atlas
Map 44, E-4
Acres: 10
Max. Depth:
29 feet

BrT	LmB
BkT ✓	SmB
RbT	WhP
Sal	Csk
Tog	WhF
Smt	Pic

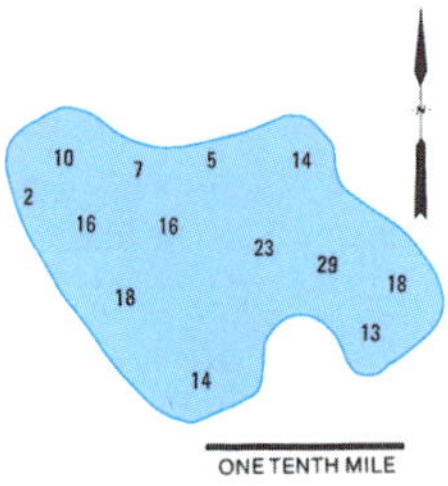

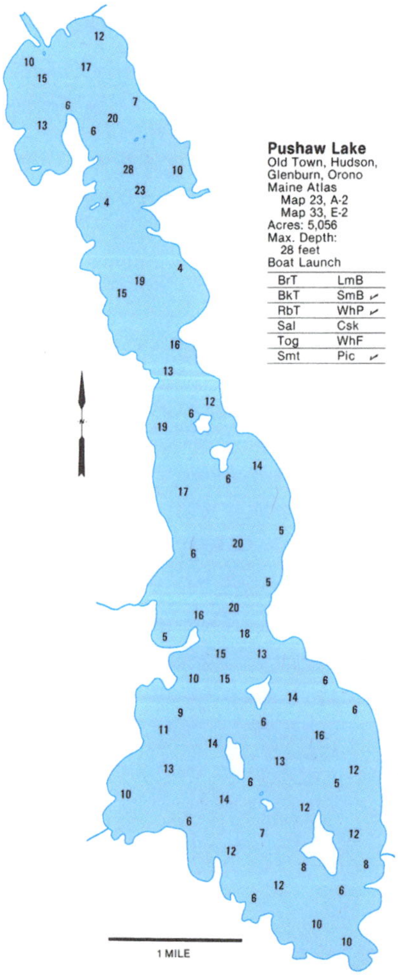

Pushaw Lake

Old Town, Hudson,
Glenburn, Orono
Maine Atlas
Map 23, A-2
Map 33, E-2
Acres: 5,056
Max. Depth:
28 feet
Boat Launch

BrT	LmB
BkT	SmB ✓
RbT	WhP ✓
Sal	Csk
Tog	WhF
Smt	Pic ✓

Rush Pond

Herseytown Twp
Maine Atlas
Map 52, E-1
Acres: 243
Max. Depth:
12 feet

BrT	LmB
BkT	SmB
RbT	WhP
Sal	Csk
Tog	WhF
Smt	Pic ✓

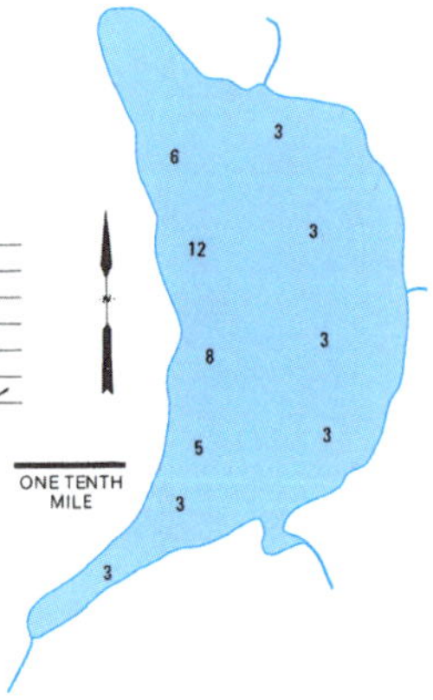

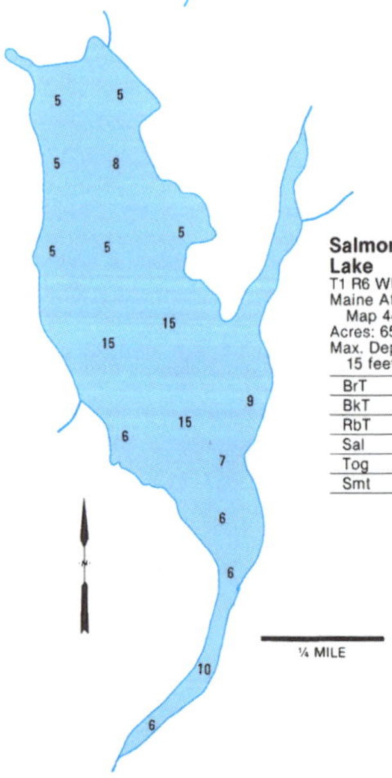

Salmon Stream Lake

T1 R6 WELS
Maine Atlas
Map 44, A-1
Acres: 659
Max. Depth:
15 feet

BrT	LmB
BkT	SmB ✓
RbT	WhP
Sal	Csk
Tog	WhF
Smt	Pic ✓

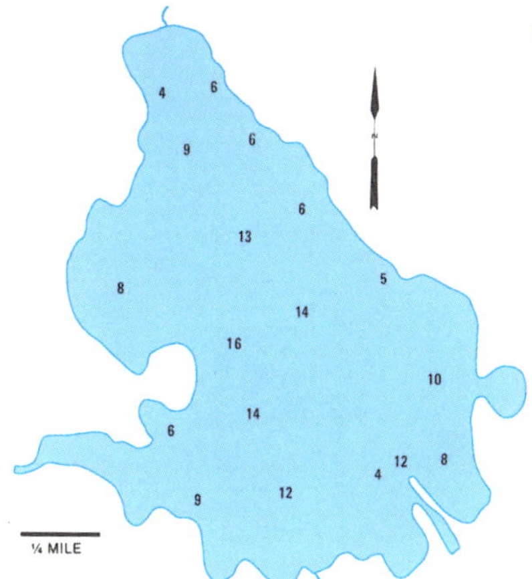

Saponac Pond

Burlington, Grand FallsTwp, Maine Atlas Map 34, B-2
Acres: 922, Max. Depth: 16 feet, Boat Launch

BrT	BkT	RbT	Sal	Tog	Smt	LmB	SmB	WhP	Csk	WhF	Pic
							✓	✓			✓

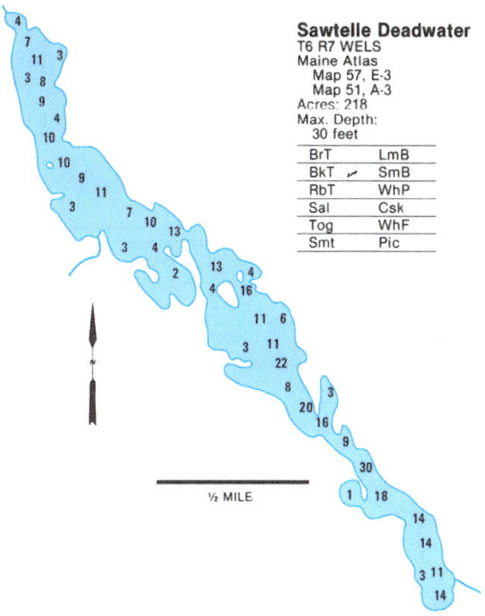

Sawtelle Deadwater

T6 R7 WELS
Maine Atlas
Map 57, E-3
Map 51, A-3
Acres: 218
Max. Depth:
30 feet

BrT		LmB	
BkT	✓	SmB	
RbT		WhP	
Sal		Csk	
Tog		WhF	
Smt		Pic	

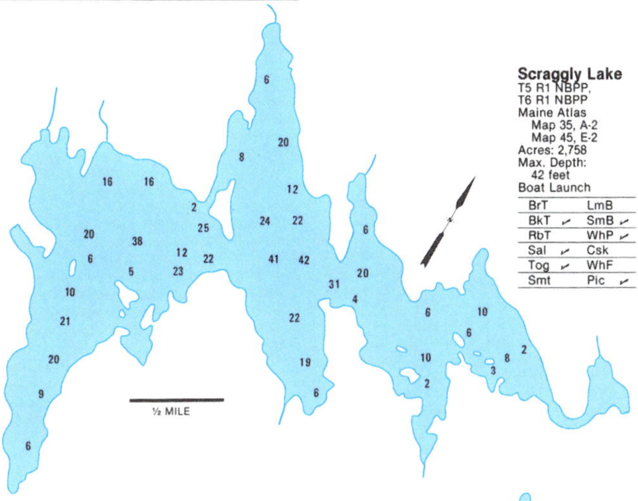

Scraggly Lake

T5 R1 NBPP,
T6 R1 NBPP
Maine Atlas
Map 35, A-2
Map 45, E-2
Acres: 2,758
Max. Depth:
42 feet
Boat Launch

BrT		LmB	
BkT	✓	SmB	✓
RbT		WhP	✓
Sal	✓	Csk	
Tog	✓	WhF	
Smt		Pic	✓

Scraggly Lake

T7 R8 WELS
Maine Atlas
Map 57, E-2, E-3
Acres: 842
Max. Depth:
70 feet
Boat Launch

BrT	✓	LmB	
BkT	✓	SmB	
RbT		WhP	
Sal	✓	Csk	
Tog	✓	WhF	
Smt	✓	Pic	

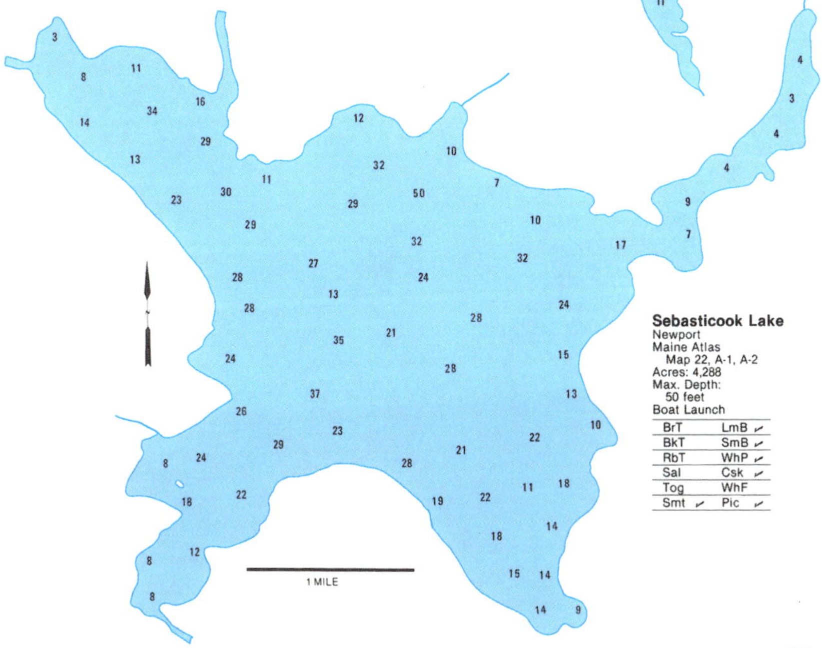

Sebasticook Lake

Newport
Maine Atlas
Map 22, A-1, A-2
Acres: 4,288
Max. Depth:
50 feet
Boat Launch

BrT		LmB	✓
BkT		SmB	✓
RbT		WhP	✓
Sal		Csk	✓
Tog		WhF	
Smt	✓	Pic	✓

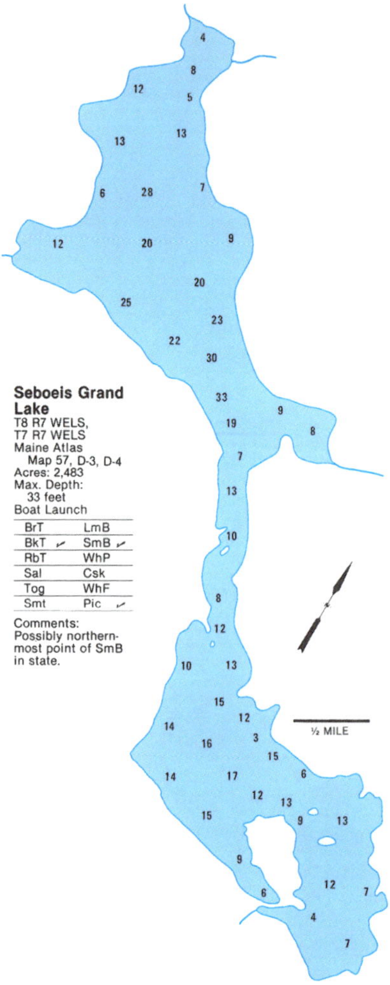

Seboeis Grand Lake

T8 R7 WELS,
T7 R7 WELS
Maine Atlas
Map 57, D-3, D-4
Acres: 2,483
Max. Depth:
33 feet
Boat Launch

BrT		LmB	
BkT	✓	SmB	✓
RbT		WhP	
Sal		Csk	
Tog		WhF	
Smt		Pic	✓

Comments:
Possibly northern-most point of SmB in state.

Snag Pond

Lincoln
Maine Atlas
Map 44, E-1
Acres: 160
Max. Depth:
13 feet

BrT		LmB	
BkT		SmB	✓
RbT		WhP	✓
Sal		Csk	
Tog		WhF	
Smt		Pic	✓

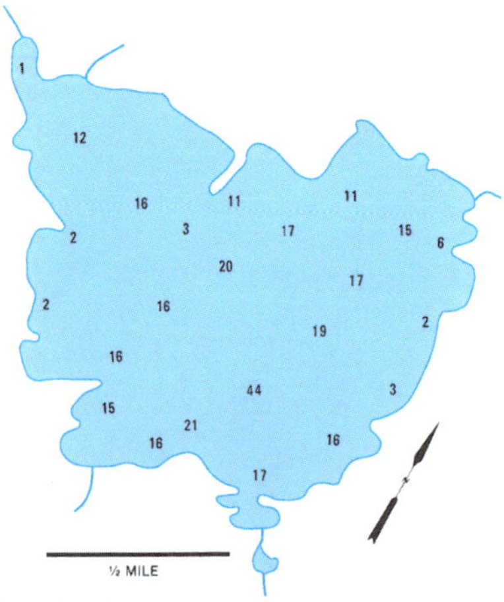

Snowshoe Lake

T7 R7 WELS, Maine Atlas Map 57, D-4, E-4
Acres: 638, Max. Depth: 44 feet, Boat Launch

BrT	BkT	RbT	Sal	Tog	Smt	LmB	SmB	WhP	Csk	WhF	Pic
							✓			✓	✓

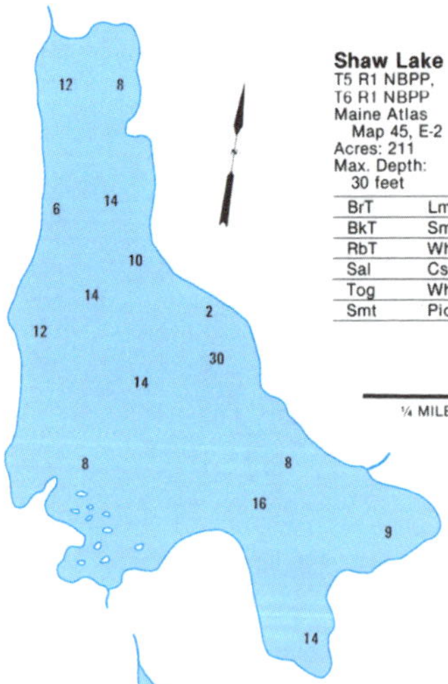

Shaw Lake

T5 R1 NBPP,
T6 R1 NBPP
Maine Atlas
Map 45, E-2
Acres: 211
Max. Depth:
30 feet

BrT		LmB	
BkT		SmB	✓
RbT		WhP	✓
Sal		Csk	
Tog		WhF	
Smt		Pic	✓

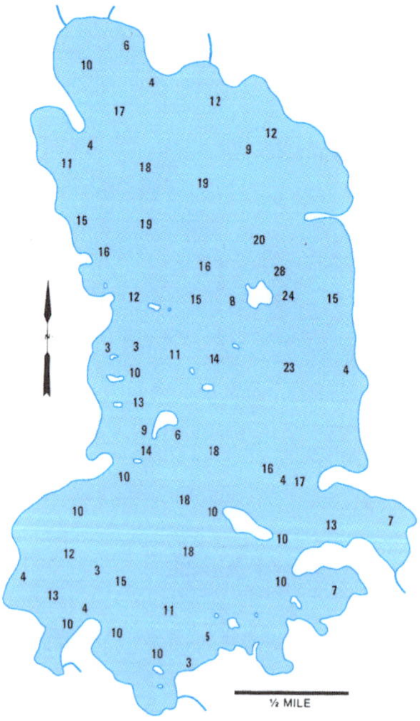

South Branch Lake

Seboeis Plt, T2 R8 NWP, Maine Atlas Map 43, E-3
Acres: 2,035, Max. Depth: 28 feet, Boat Launch

BrT	BkT	RbT	Sal	Tog	Smt	LmB	SmB	WhP	Csk	WhF	Pic
							✓	✓			✓

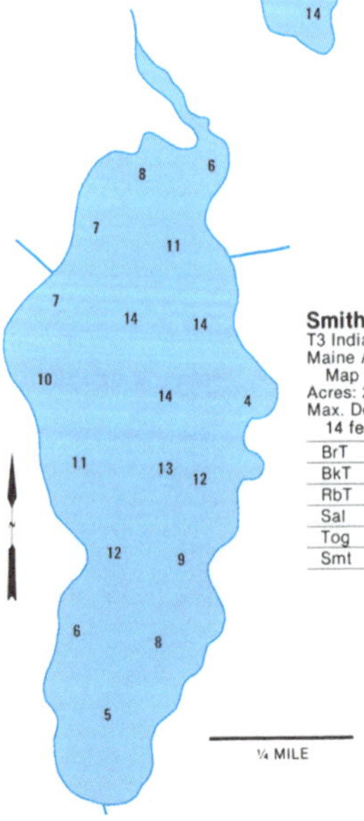

Smith Pond

T3 Indian Purchase
Maine Atlas
Map 43, A-2
Acres: 208
Max. Depth:
14 feet

BrT		LmB	
BkT	✓	SmB	
RbT		WhP	
Sal		Csk	
Tog		WhF	
Smt		Pic	

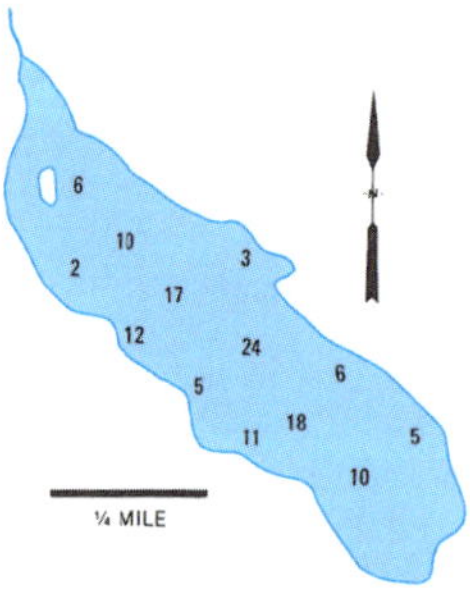

Sweets Pond

Orrington
Maine Atlas
Map 23, C-2
Acres: 125
Max. Depth:
24 feet
Boat Launch

BrT		LmB	
BkT		SmB	✓
RbT		WhP	✓
Sal		Csk	
Tog		WhF	
Smt		Pic	✓

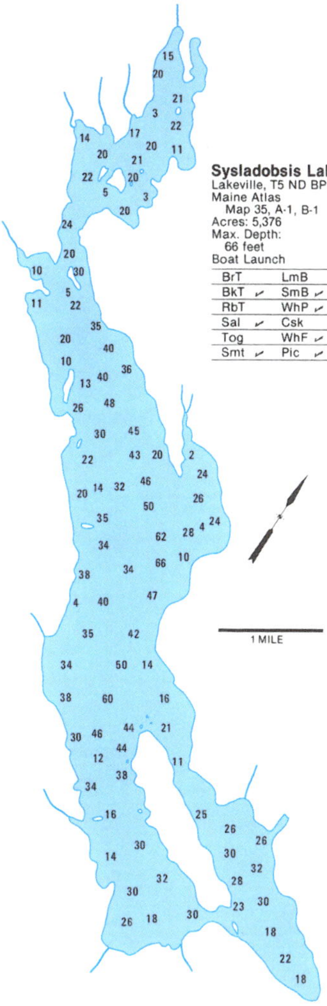

Sysladobsis Lake
Lakeville, T5 ND BPP
Maine Atlas
Map 35, A-1, B-1
Acres: 5,376
Max. Depth:
66 feet
Boat Launch

BrT		LmB	
BkT	✓	SmB	✓
RbT		WhP	✓
Sal	✓	Csk	
Tog		WhF	✓
Smt	✓	Pic	✓

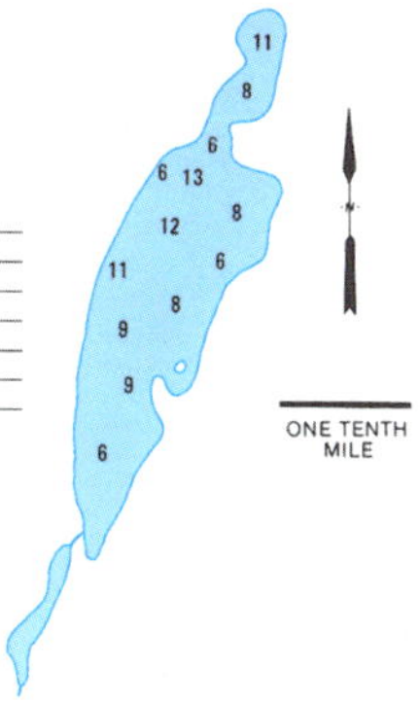

Trout Pond
Soldiertown Twp
Maine Atlas
Map 51, D-3
Acres: 19
Max. Depth:
13 feet

BrT		LmB	
BkT	✓	SmB	
RbT		WhP	
Sal		Csk	
Tog		WhF	
Smt		Pic	

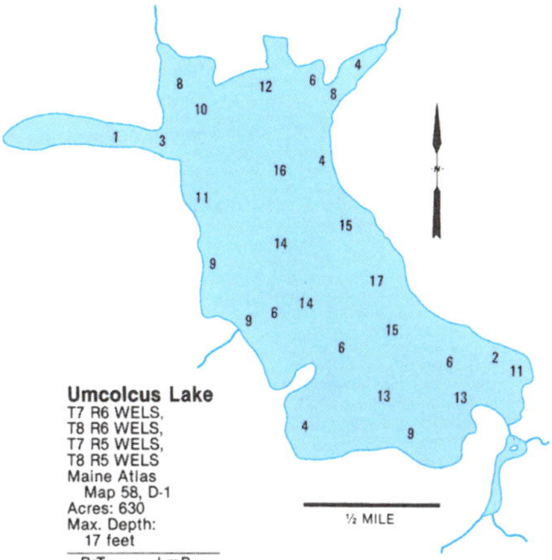

Umcolcus Lake
T7 R6 WELS,
T8 R6 WELS,
T7 R5 WELS,
T8 R5 WELS
Maine Atlas
Map 58, D-1
Acres: 630
Max. Depth:
17 feet

BrT		LmB	
BkT	✓	SmB	
RbT		WhP	
Sal	✓	Csk	
Tog		WhF	
Smt	✓	Pic	

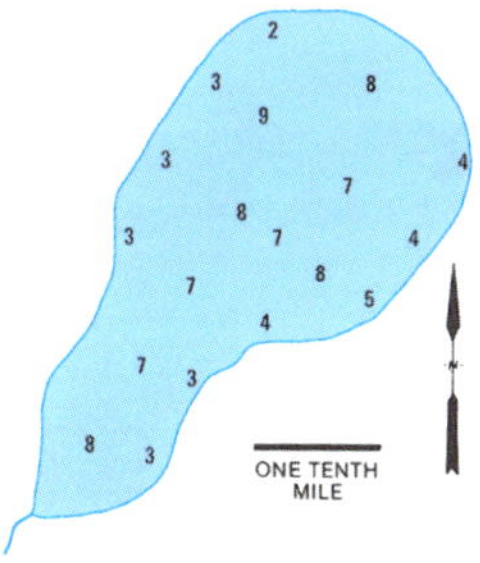

Tracy Pond
Hermon
Maine Atlas
Map 22, B-5
Acres: 52
Max. Depth:
9 feet

BrT		LmB	
BkT		SmB	✓
RbT		WhP	✓
Sal		Csk	
Tog		WhF	
Smt		Pic	✓

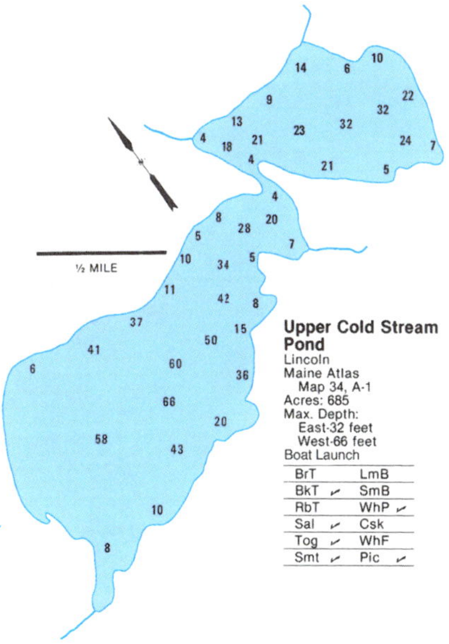

Upper Cold Stream Pond
Lincoln
Maine Atlas
Map 34, A-1
Acres: 685
Max. Depth:
East-32 feet
West-66 feet
Boat Launch

BrT		LmB	
BkT	✓	SmB	
RbT		WhP	✓
Sal	✓	Csk	
Tog	✓	WhF	
Smt	✓	Pic	✓

Trout Pond
Grand Falls Twp
Maine Atlas
Map 34, C-2
Acres: 15
Max. Depth:
8 feet

BrT		LmB	
BkT	✓	SmB	
RbT		WhP	
Sal		Csk	
Tog		WhF	
Smt		Pic	

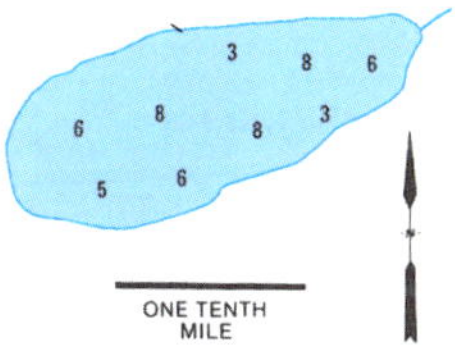

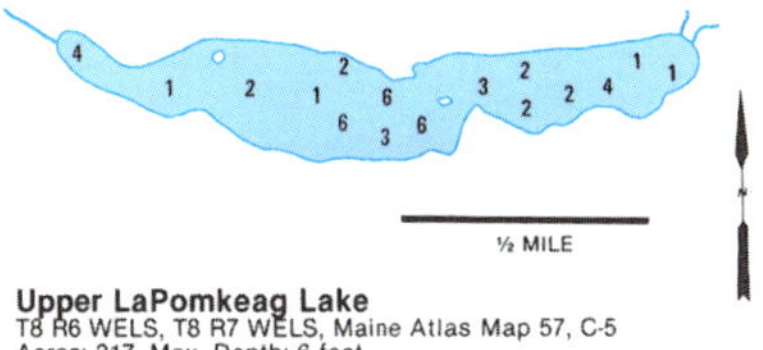

Upper LaPomkeag Lake
T8 R6 WELS, T8 R7 WELS, Maine Atlas Map 57, C-5
Acres: 217, Max. Depth: 6 feet

BrT	BkT	RbT	Sal	Tog	Smt	LmB	SmB	WhP	Csk	WhF	Pic
	✓										

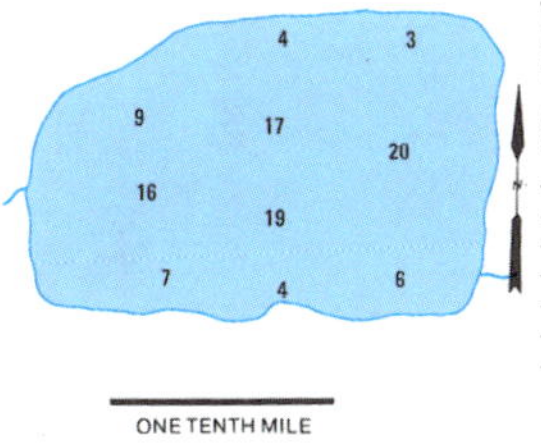

Trout Pond
Lowell
Maine Atlas
Map 34, B-1
Acres: 20
Max. Depth:
20 feet

BrT		LmB	
BkT	✓	SmB	
RbT		WhP	
Sal		Csk	
Tog		WhF	
Smt		Pic	

Penobscot

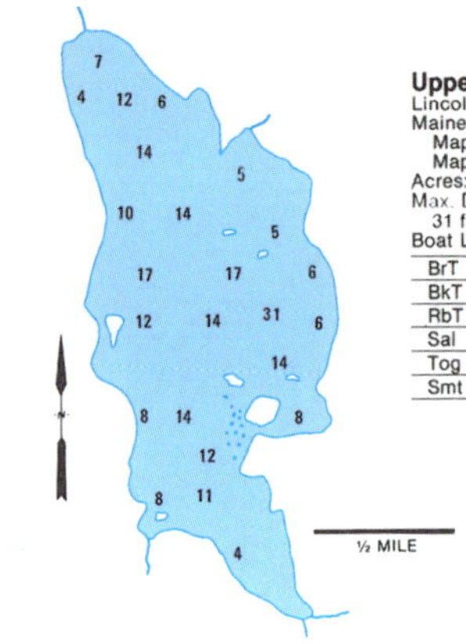

Upper Pond
Lincoln
Maine Atlas
Map 34, A-1
Map 44, E-1
Acres: 506
Max. Depth:
31 feet
Boat Launch

BrT		LmB	
BkT	✓	SmB	
RbT		WhP	✓
Sal		Csk	
Tog		WhF	
Smt		Pic	

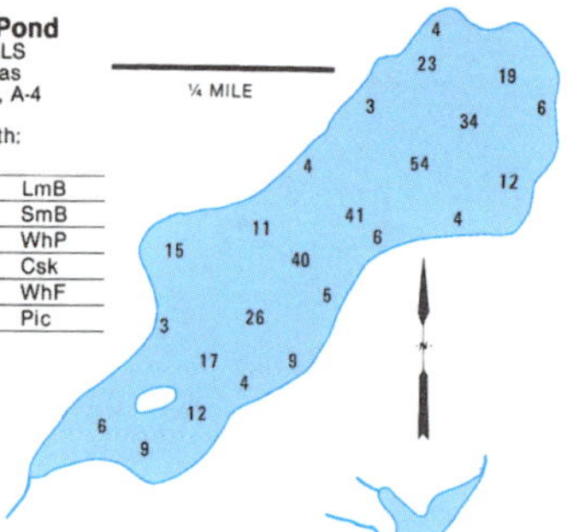

Wapiti Pond
T5 R7 WELS
Maine Atlas
Map 51, A-4
Acres: 58
Max. Depth:
54 feet

BrT		LmB	
BkT	✓	SmB	
RbT		WhP	
Sal		Csk	
Tog		WhF	
Smt		Pic	

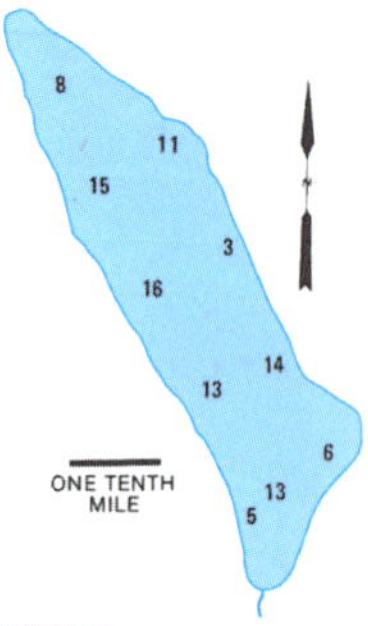

Upper Pug Lake
Lakeville
Maine Atlas
Map 34, A-5
Acres: 50
Max. Depth:
16 feet

BrT		LmB	
BkT		SmB	
RbT		WhP	✓
Sal		Csk	
Tog		WhF	
Smt		Pic	✓

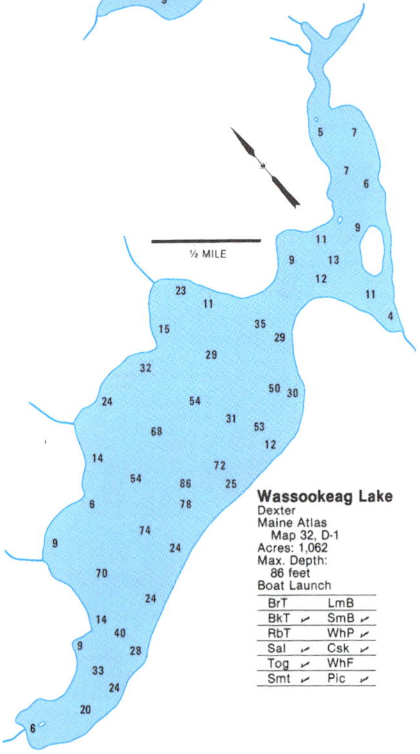

Wassookeag Lake
Dexter
Maine Atlas
Map 32, D-1
Acres: 1,062
Max. Depth:
86 feet
Boat Launch

BrT		LmB	
BkT	✓	SmB	✓
RbT		WhP	✓
Sal	✓	Csk	✓
Tog	✓	WhF	
Smt	✓	Pic	✓

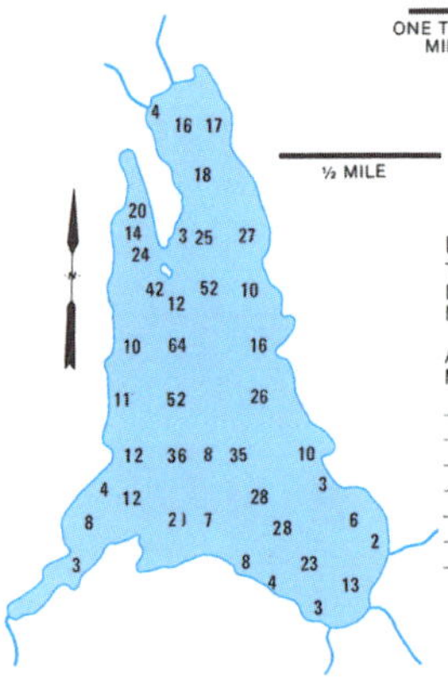

Upper Shin Pond
T6 R6 WELS,
Mount Chase
Maine Atlas
Map 51, A-5
Acres: 544
Max. Depth:
64 feet

BrT		LmB	
BkT	✓	SmB	
RbT		WhP	
Sal	✓	Csk	
Tog		WhF	
Smt	✓	Pic	

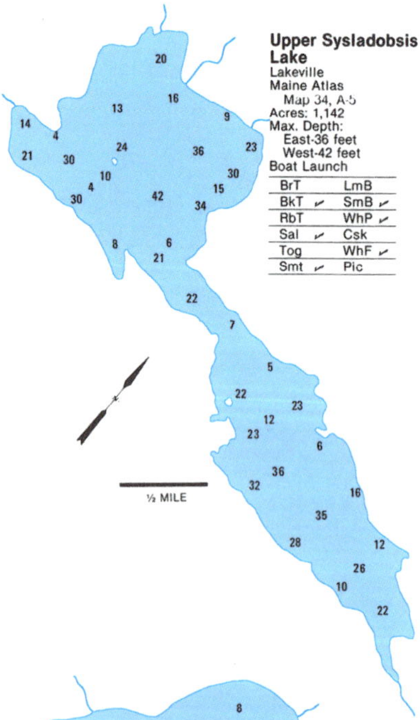

Upper Sysladobsis Lake
Lakeville
Maine Atlas
Map 34, A-5
Acres: 1,142
Max. Depth:
East-36 feet
West-42 feet
Boat Launch

BrT		LmB	
BkT	✓	SmB	✓
RbT		WhP	✓
Sal	✓	Csk	
Tog		WhF	✓
Smt	✓	Pic	

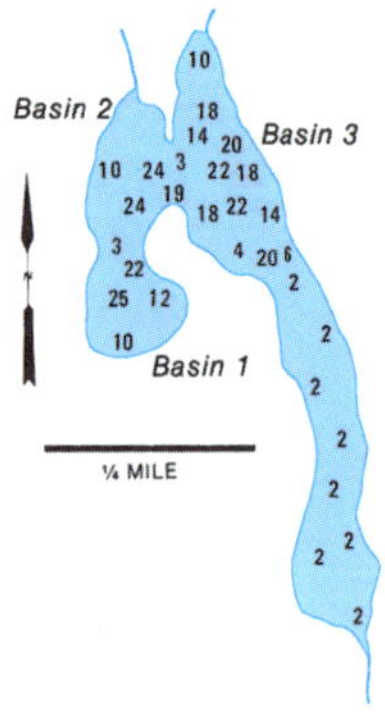

Weir Pond
Lee, T3 R1 NBPP
Maine Atlas
Map 44, E-4
Acres: 45
Max. Depth:
Basin #1-25 feet
Basin #2-24 feet
Basin #3-22 feet

BrT		LmB	
BkT	✓	SmB	
RbT		WhP	
Sal		Csk	
Tog		WhF	
Smt		Pic	✓

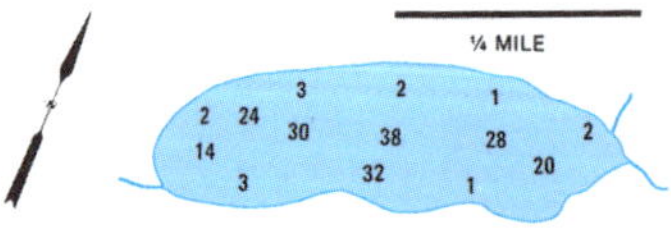

West Garland Pond
Garland, Maine Atlas Map 32, D-2
Acres: 32, Max. Depth: 38 feet, Boat Launch

BrT	BkT	RbT	Sal	Tog	Smt	LmB	SmB	WhP	Csk	WhF	Pic
	✓										✓

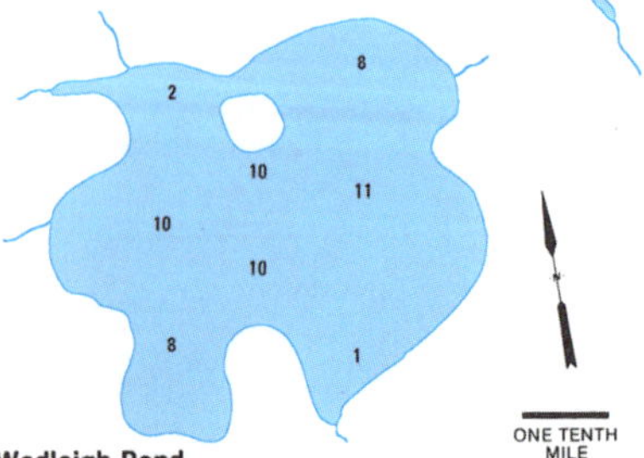

Wadleigh Pond
T4 Indian Purchase, Maine Atlas Map 43, A-1
Acres: 97, Max. Depth: 11 feet

BrT	BkT	RbT	Sal	Tog	Smt	LmB	SmB	WhP	Csk	WhF	Pic
											✓

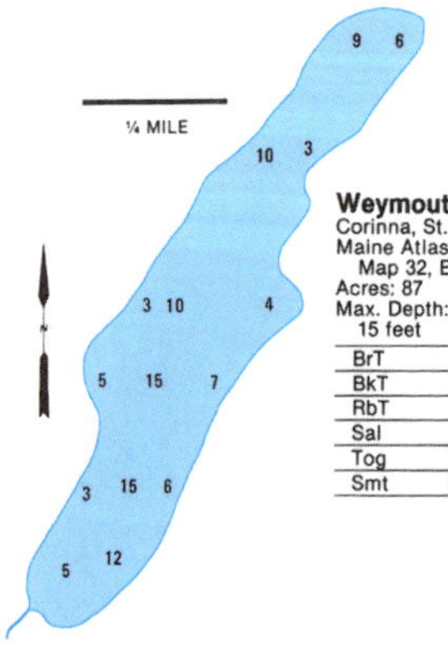

Weymouth Pond
Corinna, St. Albans
Maine Atlas
Map 32, E-1
Acres: 87
Max. Depth:
15 feet

BrT		LmB	
BkT		SmB	✓
RbT		WhP	✓
Sal		Csk	
Tog		WhF	
Smt		Pic	✓

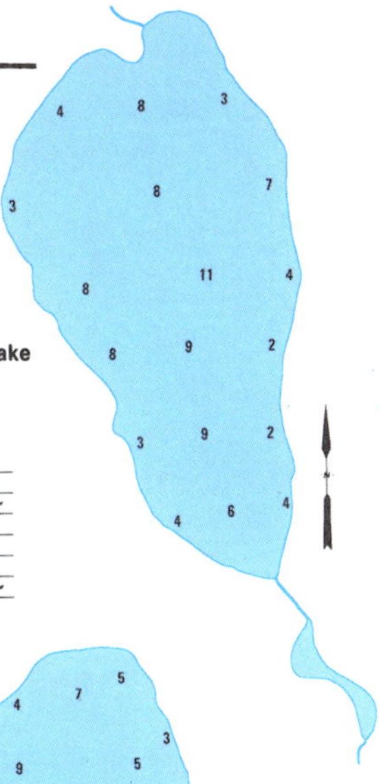

White Horse Lake
T7 R7 WELS
Maine Atlas
Map 57, E-4
Acres: 218
Max. Depth:
11 feet

BrT	LmB
BkT	SmB ✓
RbT	WhP
Sal	Csk
Tog	WhF
Smt	Pic ✓

Alligator Pond
TA R11 WELS
Maine Atlas
Map 42, B-2
Acres: 47
Max. Depth:
26 feet

BrT	LmB
BkT ✓	SmB
RbT	WhP
Sal	Csk
Tog	WhF
Smt	Pic

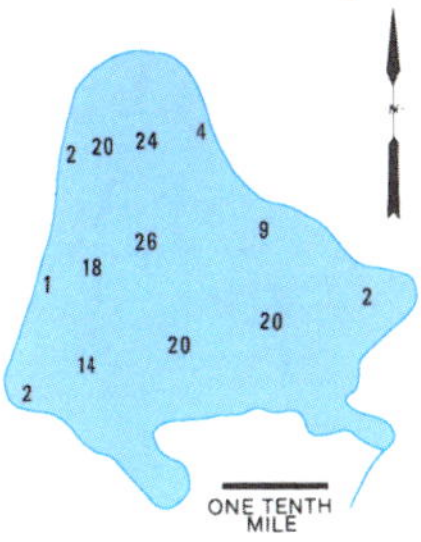

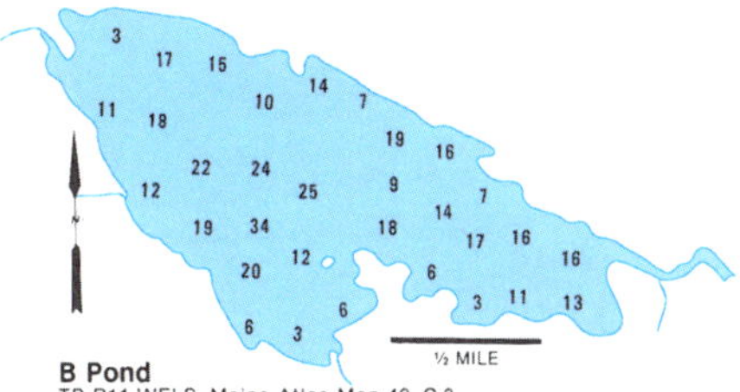

B Pond
TB R11 WELS, Maine Atlas Map 42, C-3
Acres: 644, Max. Depth: 34 feet

BrT	BkT	RbT	Sal	Tog	Smt	LmB	SmB	WhP	Csk	WhF	Pic
	✓										

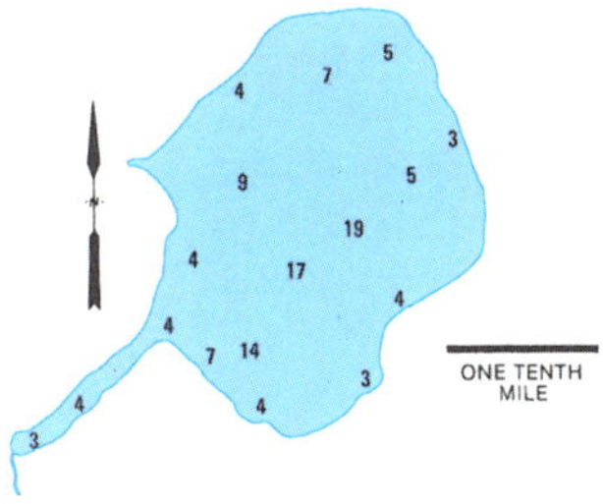

Wiley Pond
Patten, Maine Atlas Map 51, B-5, C-5
Acres: 32, Max. Depth: 19 feet

BrT	BkT	RbT	Sal	Tog	Smt	LmB	SmB	WhP	Csk	WhF	Pic
	✓										

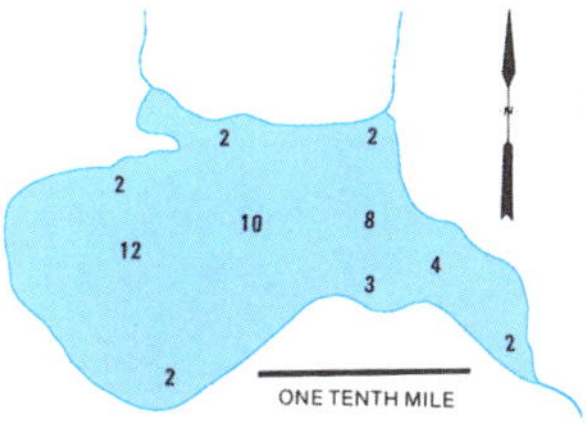

Badger Pond
Willimantic
Maine Atlas
Map 31, A-4
Acres: 15
Max. Depth:
12 feet

BrT	LmB
BkT	SmB
RbT	WhP
Sal	Csk
Tog	WhF
Smt	Pic ✓

Piscataquis County

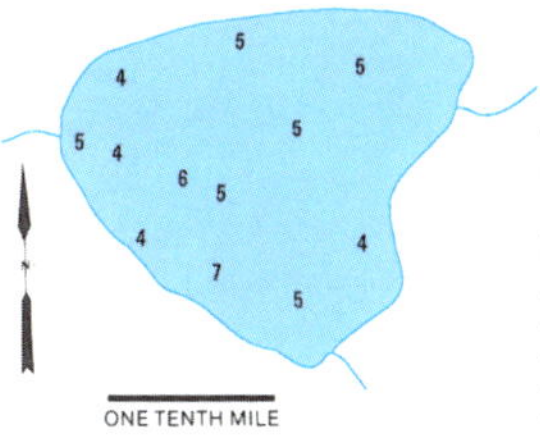

Abbee Pond
Brownville
Maine Atlas
Map 32, A-4
Acres: 26
Max. Depth:
7 feet

BrT	LmB
BkT	SmB
RbT	WhP
Sal	Csk
Tog	WhF
Smt	Pic ✓

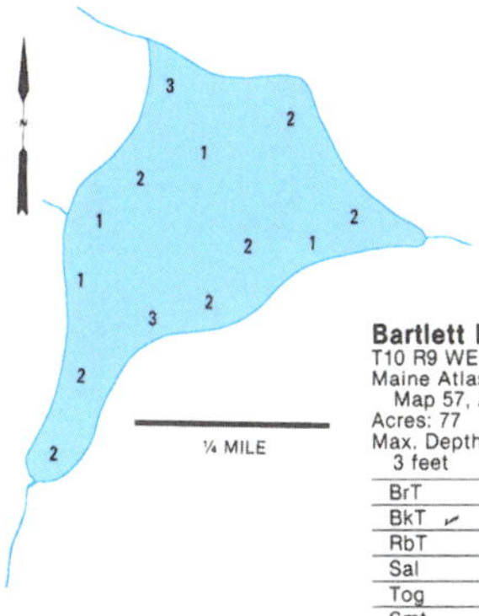

Bartlett Pond
T10 R9 WELS
Maine Atlas
Map 57, A-1
Acres: 77
Max. Depth:
3 feet

BrT	LmB
BkT ✓	SmB
RbT	WhP
Sal	Csk
Tog	WhF
Smt	Pic

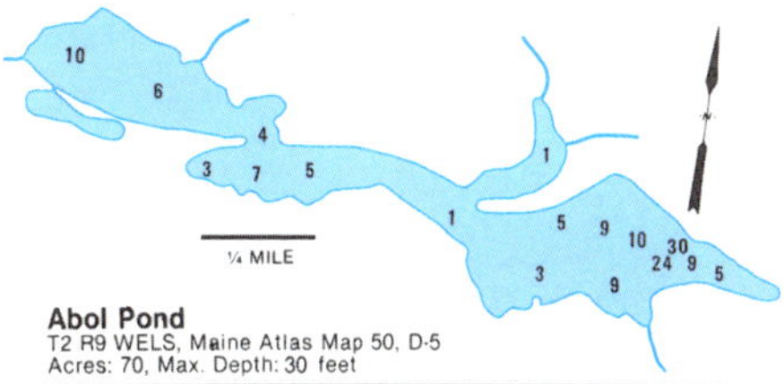

Abol Pond
T2 R9 WELS, Maine Atlas Map 50, D-5
Acres: 70, Max. Depth: 30 feet

BrT	BkT	RbT	Sal	Tog	Smt	LmB	SmB	WhP	Csk	WhF	Pic
	✓										

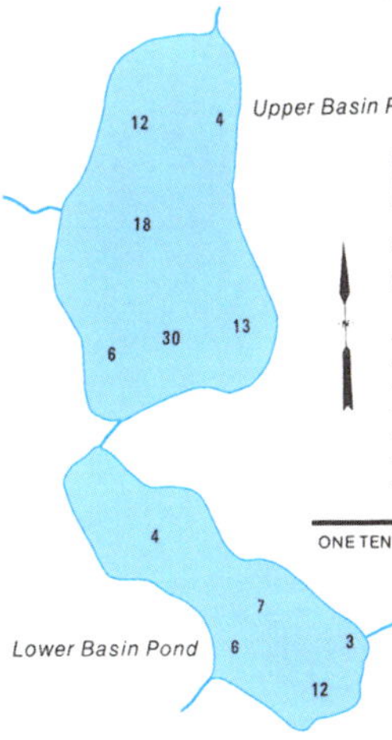

Basin Ponds
Mt Katahdin Twp
Maine Atlas
Map 51, C-1
Acres: Upper-20,
Lower-15
Max. Depth:
Upper-30 feet,
Lower-12 feet

BrT	LmB
BkT ✓	SmB
RbT	WhP
Sal	Csk
Tog	WhF
Smt	Pic

ONE TENTH MILE

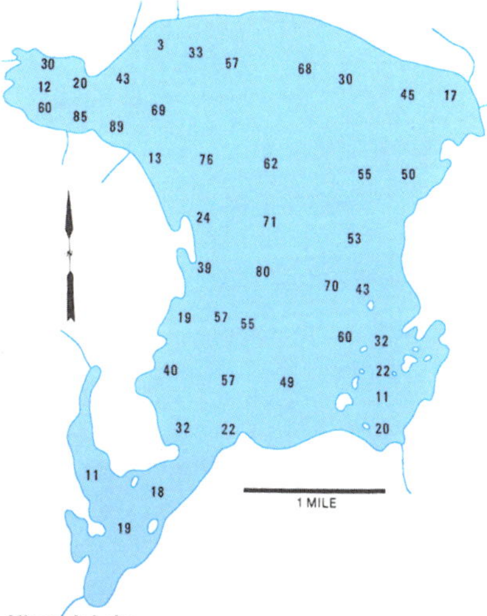

Allagash Lake
T8 R14 WELS, T7 R14 WELS, Maine Atlas Map 55, C-3, D-3
Acres: 4260, Max. Depth: 89 feet

BrT	BkT	RbT	Sal	Tog	Smt	LmB	SmB	WhP	Csk	WhF	Pic
	✓			✓	✓				✓	✓	

Bear Pond
Bowerbank
Maine Atlas
Map 32, A-1
Acres: 42
Max. Depth:
48 feet

BrT	LmB
BkT ✓	SmB ✓
RbT	WhP ✓
Sal	Csk
Tog	WhF
Smt	Pic

Comments: Splake.

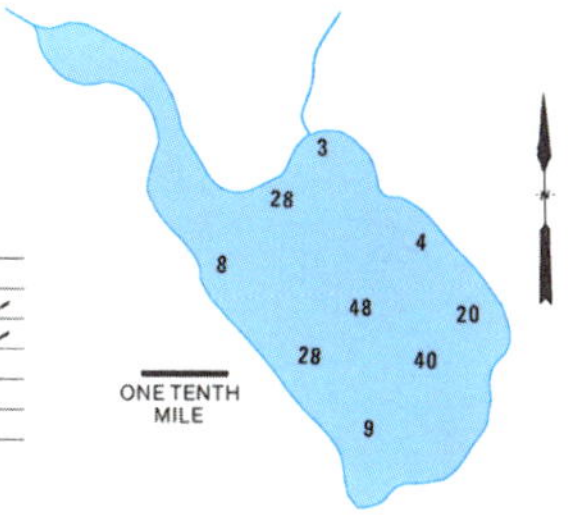

Piscataquis

Bear Pond
Rainbow Twp
Maine Atlas
Map 50, E-2
Acres: 30
Max. Depth:
94 feet

BrT	LmB
BkT ✓	SmB
RbT	WhP
Sal	Csk
Tog	WhF
Smt	Pic

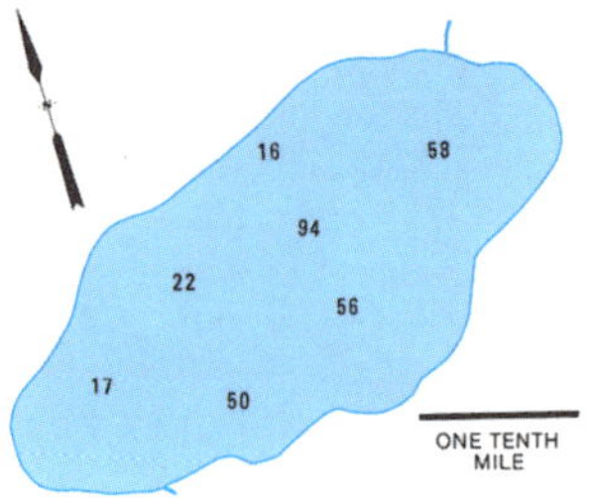

Big Beaver Pond
T7 R9 WELS
Maine Atlas
Map 57, D-1
Acres: 329
Max. Depth:
24 feet

BrT	LmB
BkT ✓	SmB
RbT	WhP
Sal	Csk
Tog	WhF
Smt	Pic

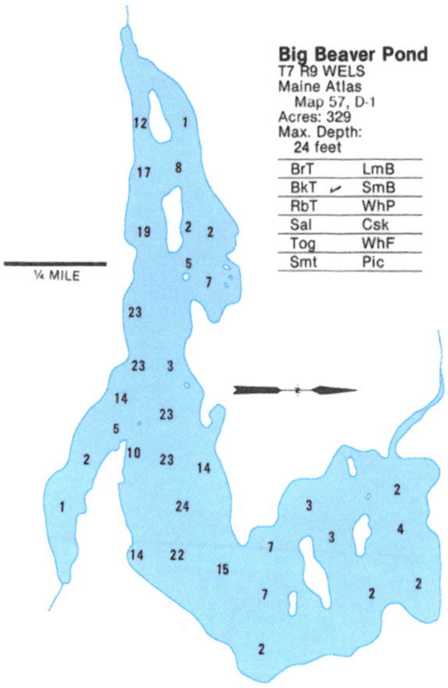

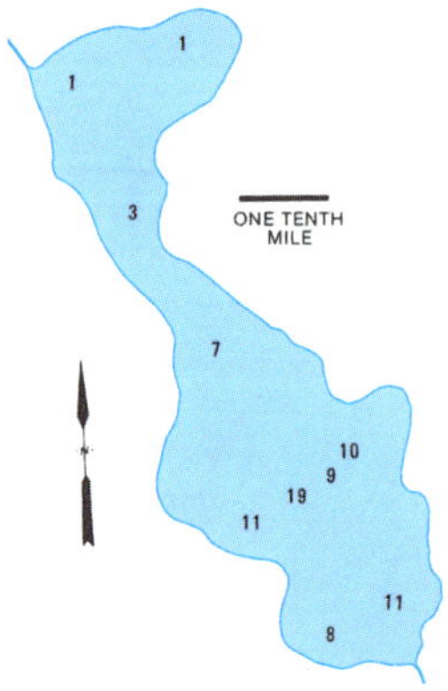

Bear Pond
T2 R13 WELS
Maine Atlas
Map 50, E-1
Acres: 81
Max. Depth:
19 feet

BrT	LmB
BkT ✓	SmB
RbT	WhP
Sal	Csk
Tog	WhF
Smt	Pic

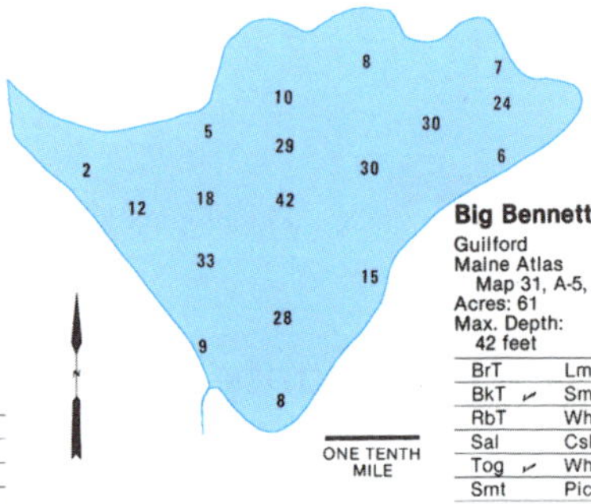

Big Bennett Pond
Guilford
Maine Atlas
Map 31, A-5, B-5
Acres: 61
Max. Depth:
42 feet

BrT	LmB
BkT ✓	SmB
RbT	WhP
Sal	Csk
Tog ✓	WhF
Smt	Pic

Comments: Splake.

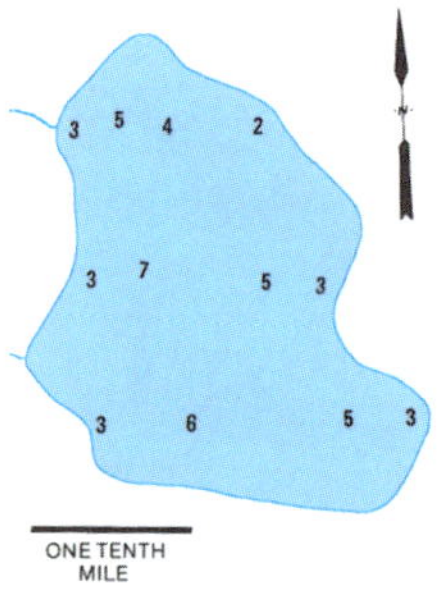

Beaver Pond
Shawtown Twp
Maine Atlas
Map 42, B-2
Acres: 27
Max. Depth:
7 feet

BrT	LmB
BkT ✓	SmB
RbT	WhP
Sal	Csk ✓
Tog	WhF
Smt	Pic

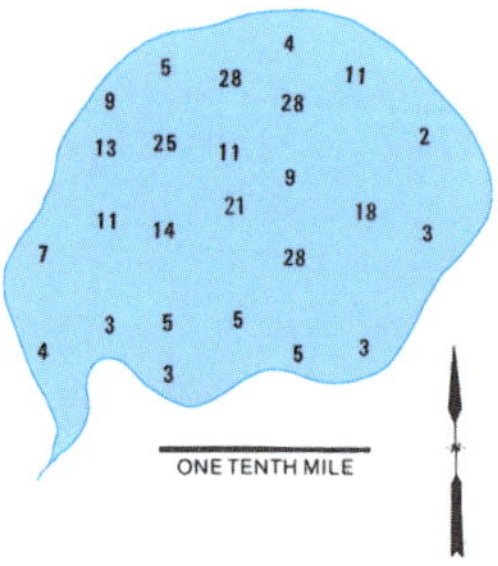

Bell Pond
Monson
Maine Atlas
Map 41, E-3
Acres: 19
Max. Depth:
28 feet

BrT	LmB
BkT ✓	SmB
RbT	WhP
Sal	Csk
Tog	WhF
Smt	Pic

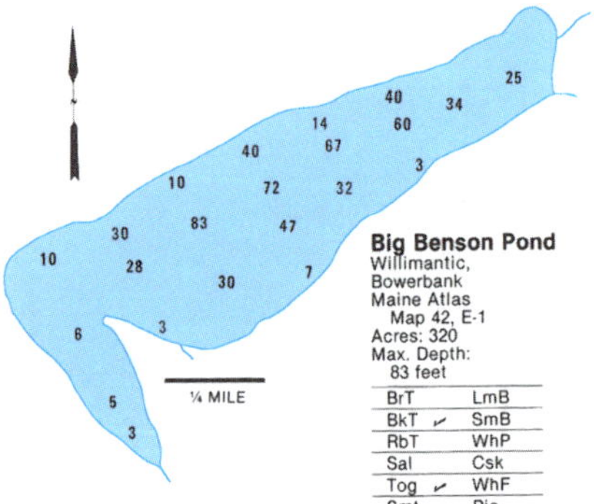

Big Benson Pond
Willimantic,
Bowerbank
Maine Atlas
Map 42, E-1
Acres: 320
Max. Depth:
83 feet

BrT	LmB
BkT ✓	SmB
RbT	WhP
Sal	Csk
Tog ✓	WhF
Smt	Pic

Bennett Pond
Parkman
Maine Atlas
Map 31, C-4
Acres: 36
Max. Depth:
44 feet

BrT	LmB
BkT ✓	SmB
RbT	WhP
Sal	Csk
Tog	WhF
Smt	Pic ✓

Comments:
Splake.

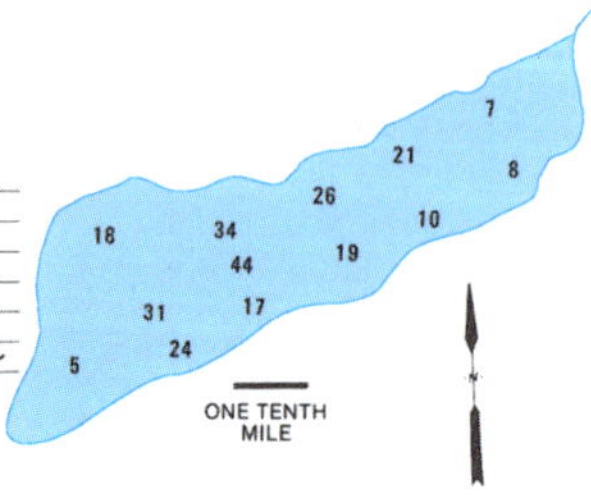

Big Boardway Pond
TA R11 WELS
Maine Atlas
Map 42, B-2
Acres: 15
Max. Depth:
11 feet

BrT	LmB
BkT ✓	SmB
RbT	WhP
Sal	Csk
Tog	WhF
Smt	Pic

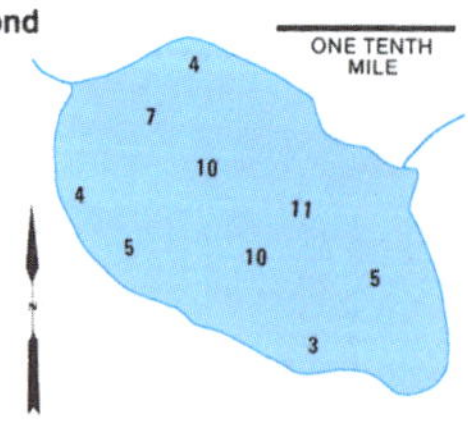

Big Beaver Pond
Rainbow Twp
Maine Atlas
Map 50, E-3, E-4
Acres: 45
Max. Depth:
48 feet

BrT	LmB
BkT ✓	SmB
RbT	WhP
Sal	Csk
Tog	WhF
Smt	Pic

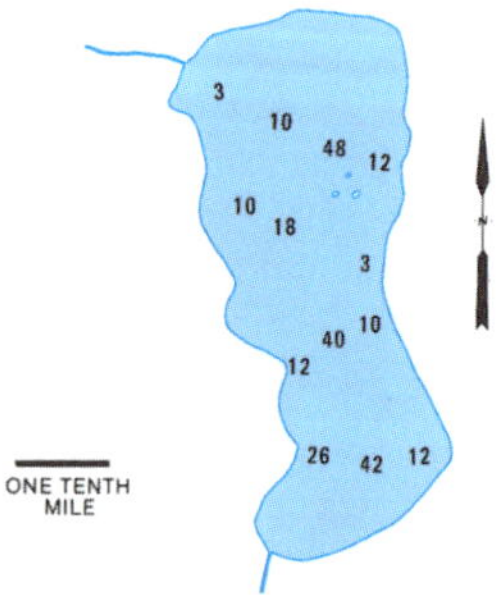

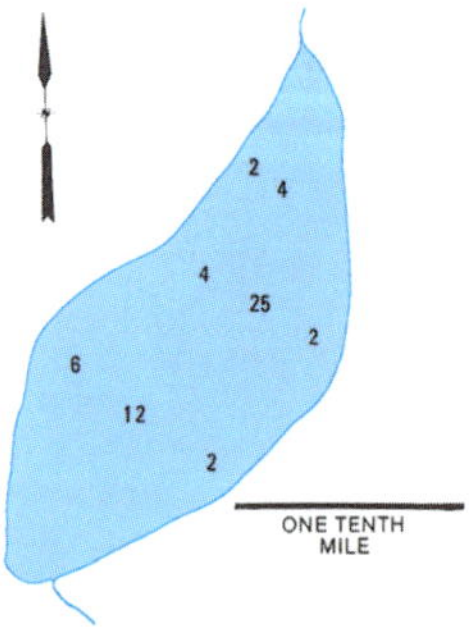

Big Bunker Pond
Shirley, Monson
Maine Atlas
Map 31, A-2, A-3
Acres: 10
Max. Depth:
25 feet

BrT	LmB
BkT ✓	SmB
RbT	WhP
Sal	Csk
Tog	WhF
Smt	Pic

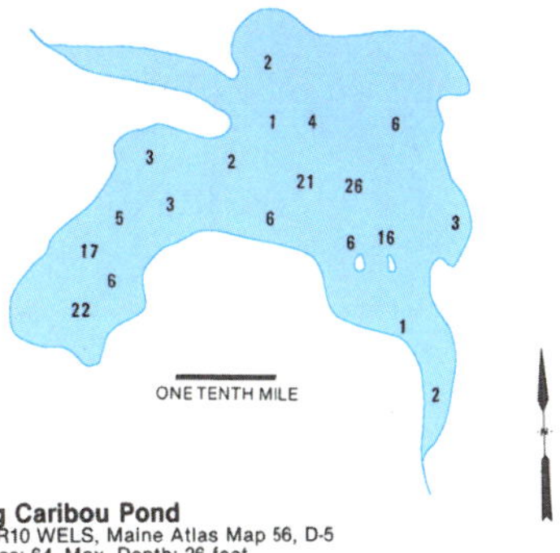

Big Caribou Pond

T7 R10 WELS, Maine Atlas Map 56, D-5
Acres: 64, Max. Depth: 26 feet

BrT	BkT	RbT	Sal	Tog	Smt	LmB	SmB	WhP	Csk	WhF	Pic
	✓										

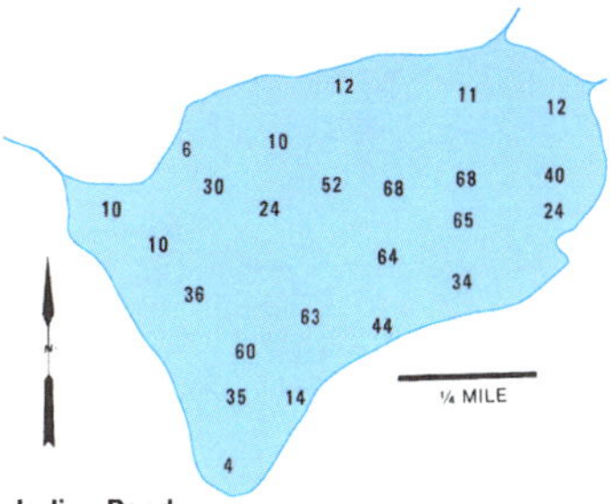

Big Indian Pond

Moosehead Junction Twp, Maine Atlas Map 41, D-1
Acres: 280, Max. Depth: 68 feet

BrT	BkT	RbT	Sal	Tog	Smt	LmB	SmB	WhP	Csk	WhF	Pic
	✓			✓					✓	✓	

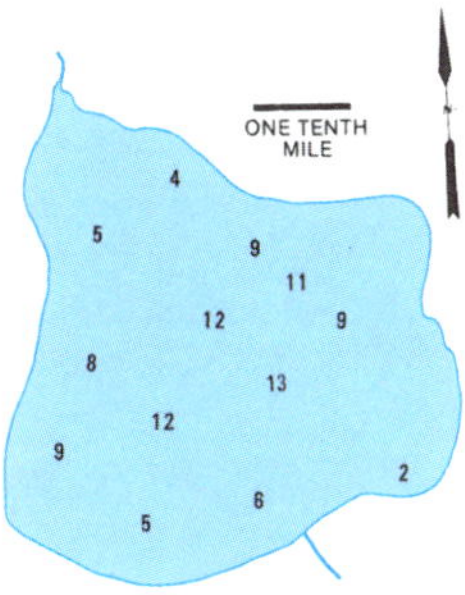

Big Duck Pond

East Middlesex
Canal Grant
Maine Atlas
Map 49, E-2
Acres: 79
Max. Depth:
13 feet

BrT	LmB
BkT ✓	SmB
RbT	WhP
Sal ✓	Csk
Tog	WhF
Smt	Pic

Big Lyford Pond

Shawtown Twp
Maine Atlas
Map 42, B-1
Acres: 152
Max. Depth:
40 feet

BrT	LmB
BkT ✓	SmB
RbT	WhP
Sal	Csk
Tog	WhF
Smt	Pic

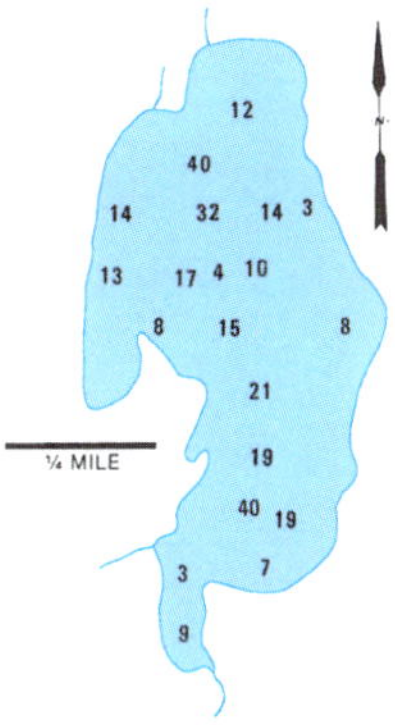

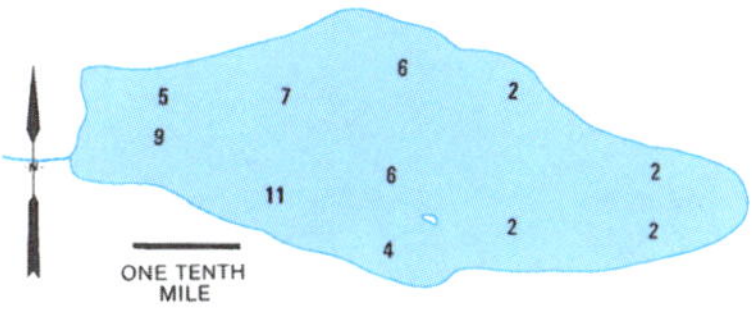

Big Fisher Pond

T2 R12 WELS, Maine Atlas Map 50, E-1
Acres: 56, Max. Depth: 11 feet

BrT	BkT	RbT	Sal	Tog	Smt	LmB	SmB	WhP	Csk	WhF	Pic
	✓										

Big Minister Pond

T2 R10 WELS
Maine Atlas
Map 50, E-4
Acres: 14.5
Max. Depth:
35 feet

BrT	LmB
BkT ✓	SmB
RbT	WhP
Sal	Csk
Tog	WhF
Smt	Pic

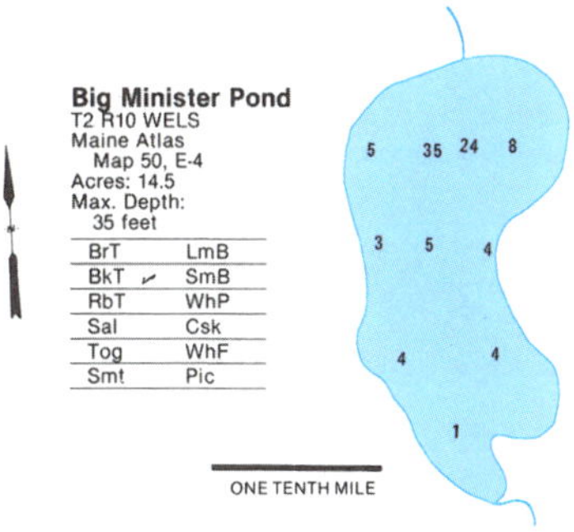

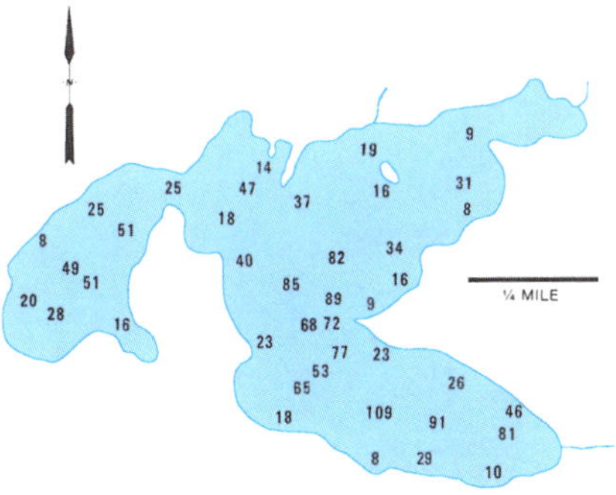

Big Moose Pond

Moosehead Junction Twp
Maine Atlas
Map 41, D-2
Acres: 91
Max. Depth:
96 feet

BrT	LmB
BkT ✓	SmB
RbT	WhP
Sal	Csk
Tog	WhF
Smt ✓	Pic

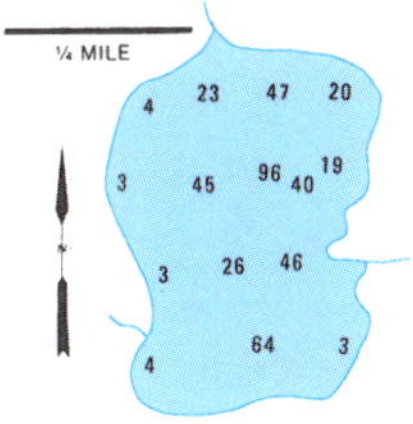

Big Greenwood Pond

Elliotsville Twp, Willimantic, Maine Atlas Map 41, E-5
Acres: 211, Max. Depth: 109 feet, Boat Launch

BrT	BkT	RbT	Sal	Tog	Smt	LmB	SmB	WhP	Csk	WhF	Pic
	✓			✓	✓					✓	

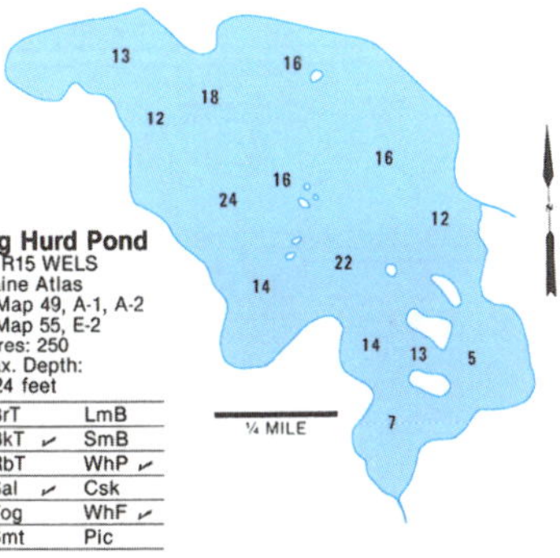

Big Hurd Pond

T6 R15 WELS
Maine Atlas
Map 49, A-1, A-2
Map 55, E-2
Acres: 250
Max. Depth:
24 feet

BrT	LmB
BkT ✓	SmB
RbT	WhP ✓
Sal ✓	Csk
Tog	WhF ✓
Smt	Pic

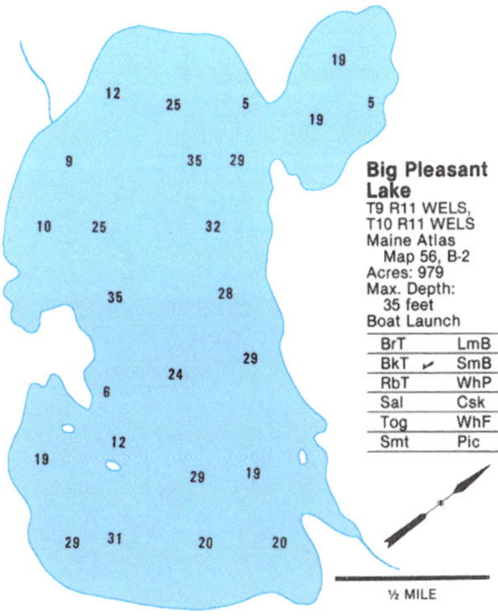

Big Pleasant Lake

T9 R11 WELS,
T10 R11 WELS
Maine Atlas
Map 56, B-2
Acres: 979
Max. Depth:
35 feet
Boat Launch

BrT	LmB
BkT ✓	SmB
RbT	WhP
Sal	Csk
Tog	WhF ✓
Smt	Pic

Big Pine Pond
T3 R13 WELS
Maine Atlas
Map 49, D-4
Acres: 164
Max. Depth:
33 feet

BrT	LmB
BkT ✓	SmB
RbT	WhP
Sal	Csk
Tog	WhF
Smt	Pic

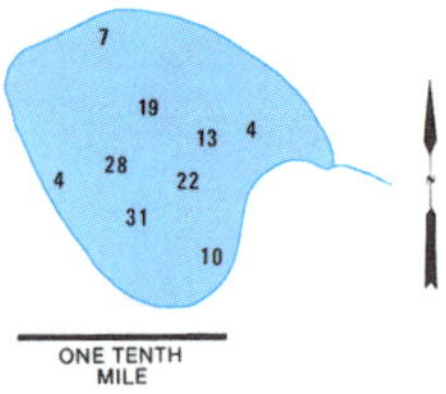

Bluff Pond
Frenchtown Twp
Maine Atlas
Map 41, B-5
Acres: 10
Max. Depth:
31 feet

BrT	LmB
BkT ✓	SmB
RbT	WhP
Sal	Csk
Tog	WhF
Smt	Pic

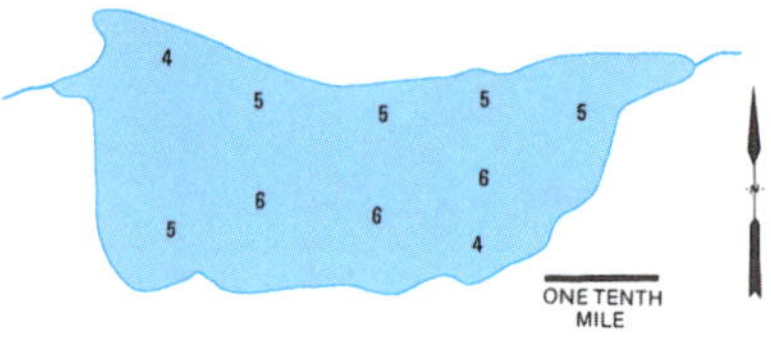

Bluffer Pond
T8 R11 WELS, Maine Atlas Map 56, C-3
Acres: 40, Max. Depth: 6 feet

BrT	BkT	RbT	Sal	Tog	Smt	LmB	SmB	WhP	Csk	WhF	Pic
	✓										

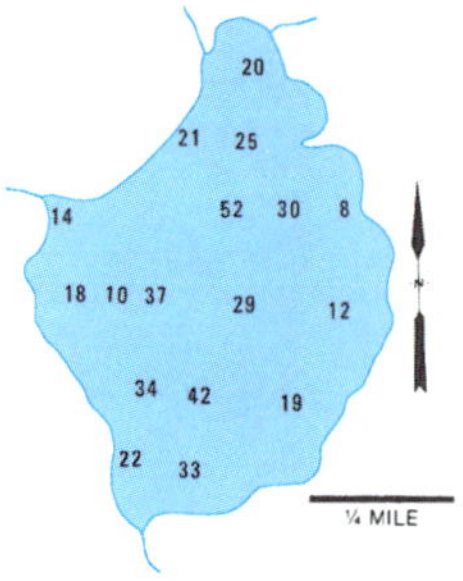

Big Pleasant Pond
TA R11 WELS
Maine Atlas
Map 42, B-2
Acres: 195
Max. Depth:
52 feet

BrT	LmB
BkT ✓	SmB
RbT	WhP
Sal	Csk ✓
Tog ✓	WhF
Smt	Pic

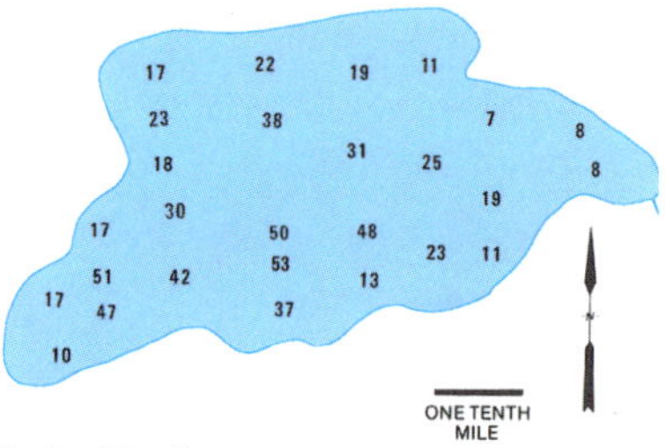

Big Reed Pond
T8 R10 WELS, Maine Atlas Map 56, C-4
Acres: 90, Max. Depth: 53 feet

BrT	BkT	RbT	Sal	Tog	Smt	LmB	SmB	WhP	Csk	WhF	Pic
	✓										

Comments: Blueback trout.

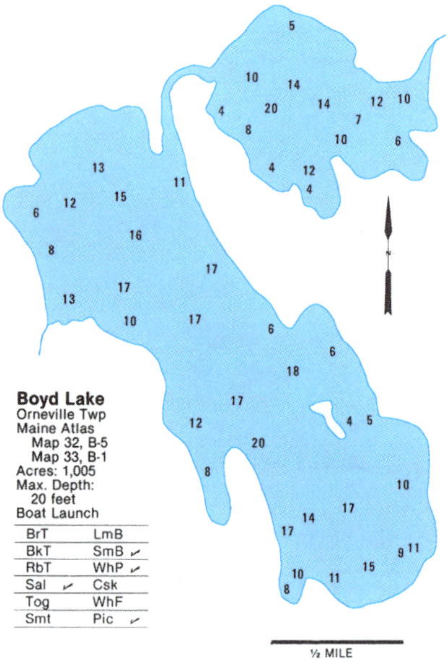

Boyd Lake
Orneville Twp
Maine Atlas
Map 32, B-5
Map 33, B-1
Acres: 1,005
Max. Depth:
20 feet
Boat Launch

BrT	LmB
BkT	SmB ✓
RbT	WhP ✓
Sal ✓	Csk
Tog	WhF
Smt	Pic ✓

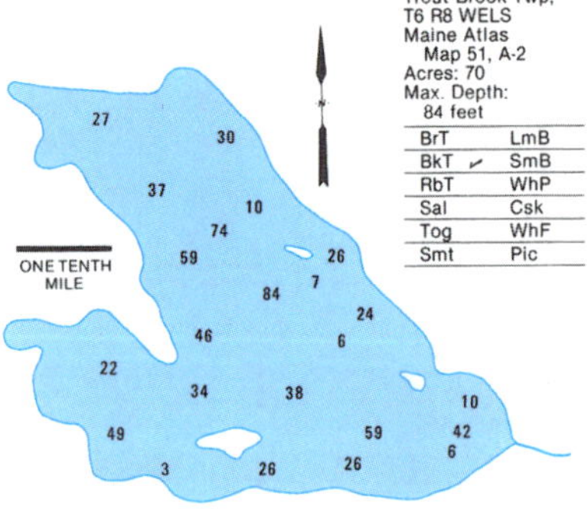

Billfish Pond
Trout Brook Twp,
T6 R8 WELS
Maine Atlas
Map 51, A-2
Acres: 70
Max. Depth:
84 feet

BrT	LmB
BkT ✓	SmB
RbT	WhP
Sal	Csk
Tog	WhF
Smt	Pic

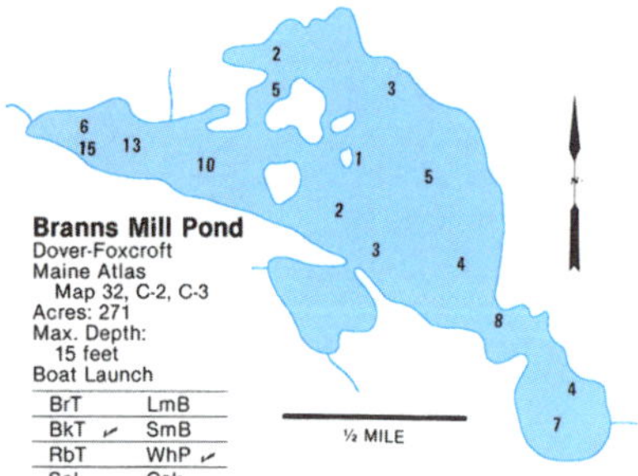

Branns Mill Pond
Dover-Foxcroft
Maine Atlas
Map 32, C-2, C-3
Acres: 271
Max. Depth:
15 feet
Boat Launch

BrT	LmB
BkT ✓	SmB
RbT	WhP ✓
Sal	Csk
Tog	WhF
Smt	Pic ✓

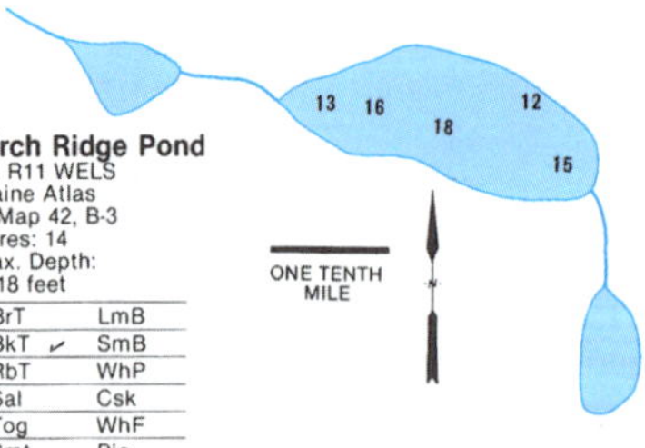

Birch Ridge Pond
TA R11 WELS
Maine Atlas
Map 42, B-3
Acres: 14
Max. Depth:
18 feet

BrT	LmB
BkT ✓	SmB
RbT	WhP
Sal	Csk
Tog	WhF
Smt	Pic

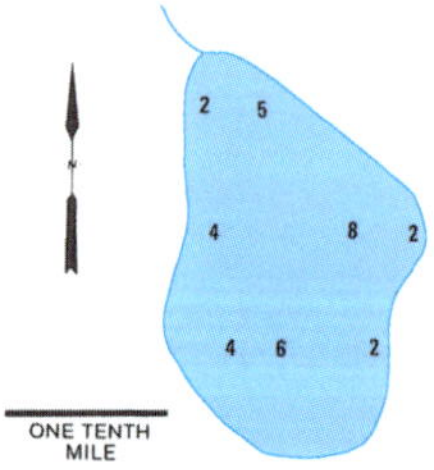

Brown Pond
Bowdoin College
Grant West
Maine Atlas
Map 41, D-4
Acres: 20
Max. Depth:
8 feet

BrT	LmB
BkT ✓	SmB
RbT	WhP
Sal	Csk
Tog	WhF
Smt	Pic

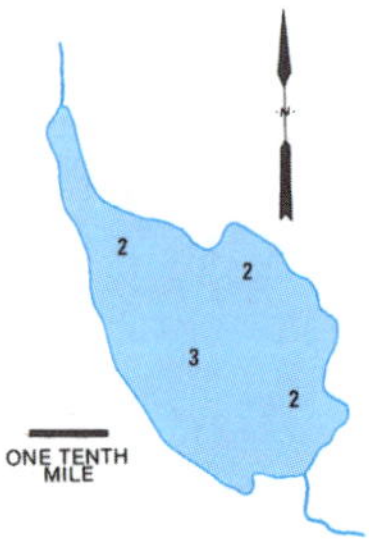

Blood Pond
T2 R13 WELS
Maine Atlas
Map 49, E-4
Acres: 40
Max. Depth:
3 feet

BrT	LmB
BkT ✓	SmB
RbT	WhP
Sal	Csk
Tog	WhF
Smt	Pic

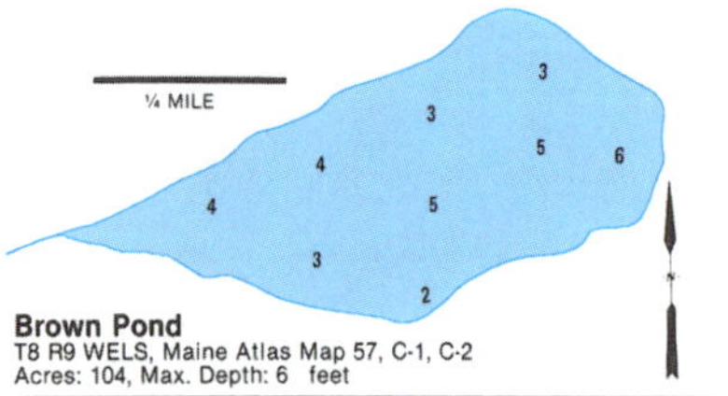

Brown Pond
T8 R9 WELS, Maine Atlas Map 57, C-1, C-2
Acres: 104, Max. Depth: 6 feet

BrT	BkT	RbT	Sal	Tog	Smt	LmB	SmB	WhP	Csk	WhF	Pic
	✓										

Brown Brook Pond
T9 R9 WELS
Maine Atlas
Map 57, B-1, C-1
Acres: 6
Max. Depth:
4 feet
Boat Launch

BrT		LmB
BkT	✓	SmB
RbT		WhP
Sal		Csk
Tog		WhF
Smt		Pic

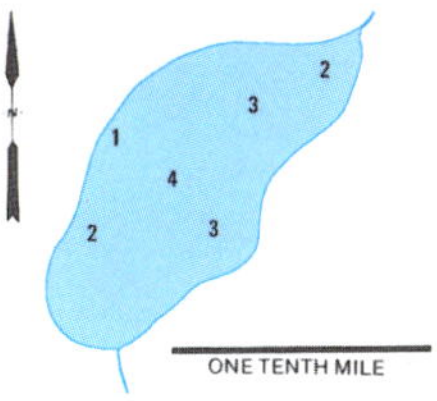

Carry Pond
T3 R11 WELS
Maine Atlas
Map 50, D-2
Acres: 17
Max. Depth:
12 feet

BrT		LmB
BkT	✓	SmB
RbT		WhP
Sal		Csk
Tog		WhF
Smt		Pic

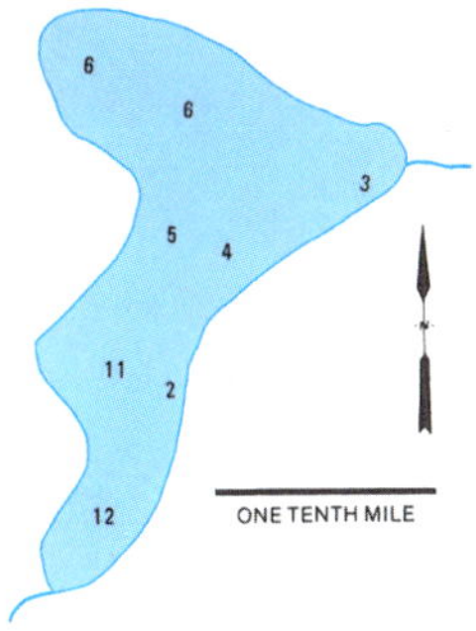

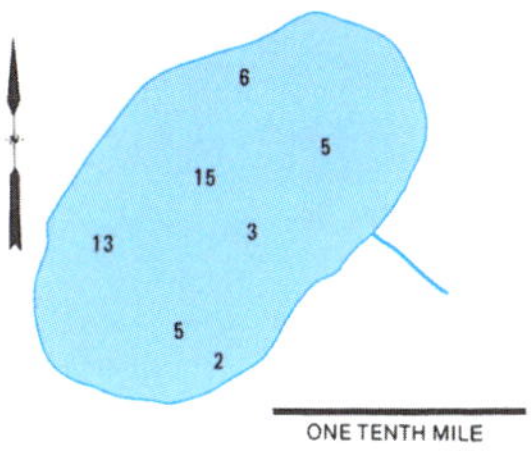

Buck Pond
Rainbow Twp
Maine Atlas
Map 50, E-2
Acres: 6
Max. Depth:
15 feet

BrT		LmB
BkT	✓	SmB
RbT		WhP
Sal		Csk
Tog		WhF
Smt		Pic

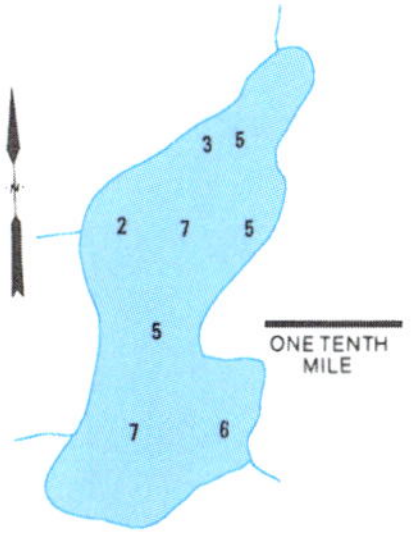

Buckley Pond
T8 R10 WELS
Maine Atlas
Map 56, C-4, D-4
Acres: 18
Max. Depth:
7 feet

BrT		LmB
BkT	✓	SmB
RbT		WhP
Sal		Csk
Tog		WhF
Smt		Pic

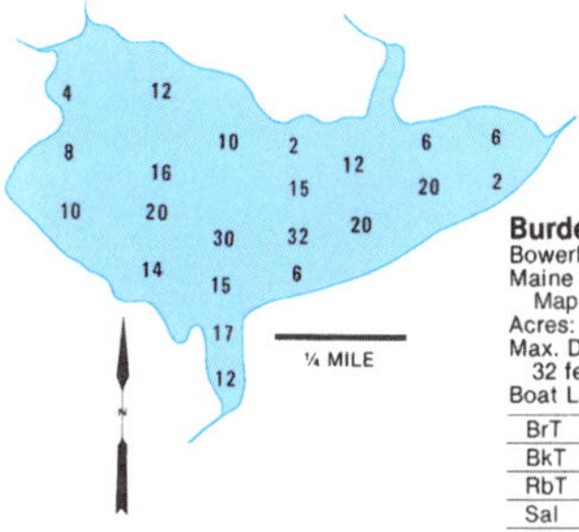

Burden Pond
Bowerbank
Maine Atlas
Map 42, E-2
Acres: 197
Max. Depth:
32 feet
Boat Launch

BrT		LmB
BkT	✓	SmB
RbT		WhP
Sal		Csk
Tog		WhF
Smt		Pic

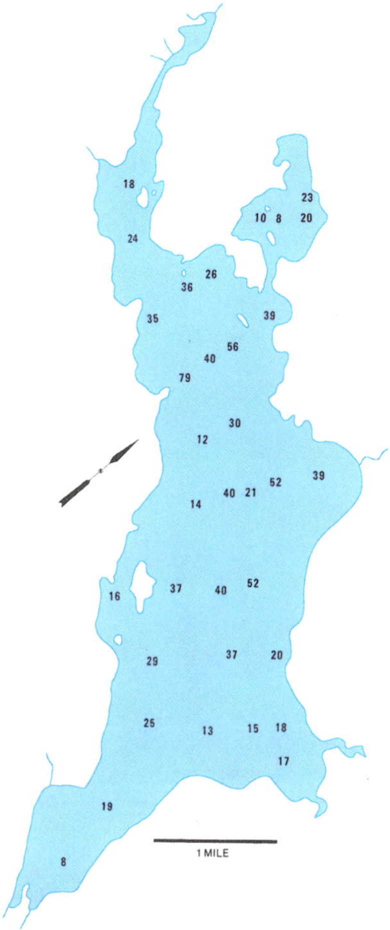

Caucomogomoc Lake
T7 R15 WELS, T7 R14 WELS, T6 R15 WELS, T6 R14 WELS
Maine Atlas Map 55, E-2, E-3
Acres: 5,081, Max. Depth: 79 feet

BrT	BkT	RbT	Sal	Tog	Smt	LmB	SmB	WhP	Csk	WhF	Pic
	✓		✓	✓	✓			✓			

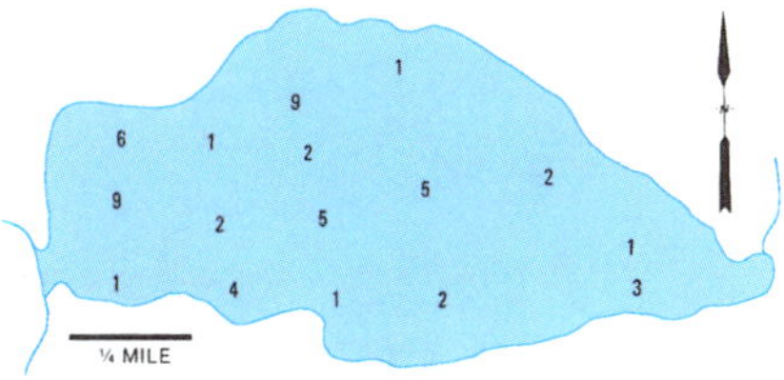

Burnham Pond
Big Moose Twp, Maine Atlas Map 41, C-1
Acres: 426, Max. Depth: 9 feet

BrT	BkT	RbT	Sal	Tog	Smt	LmB	SmB	WhP	Csk	WhF	Pic
	✓										

Cedar Pond
TB R10 WELS
Maine Atlas
Map 42, C-4
Acres: 63
Max. Depth:
50 feet

BrT		LmB
BkT	✓	SmB
RbT		WhP
Sal		Csk
Tog		WhF
Smt		Pic

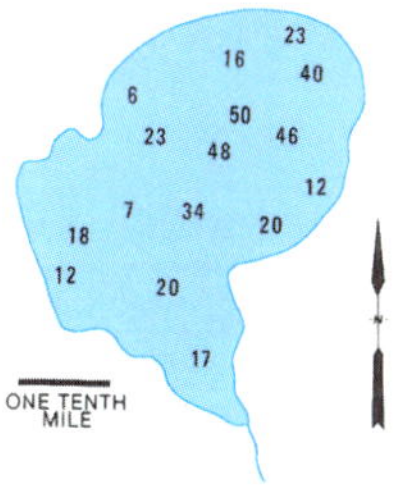

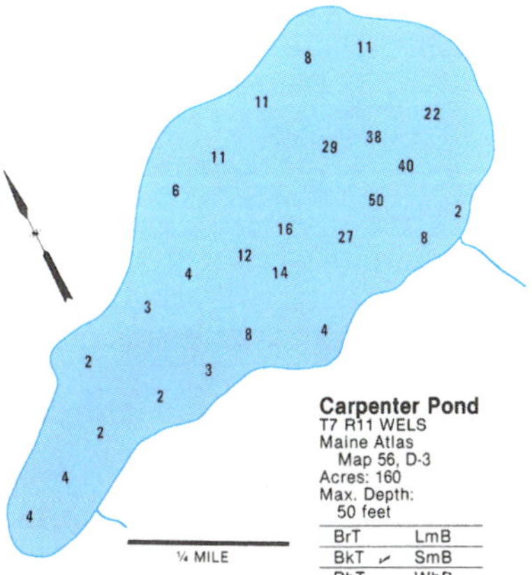

Carpenter Pond
T7 R11 WELS
Maine Atlas
Map 56, D-3
Acres: 160
Max. Depth:
50 feet

BrT		LmB
BkT	✓	SmB
RbT		WhP
Sal		Csk
Tog		WhF
Smt		Pic

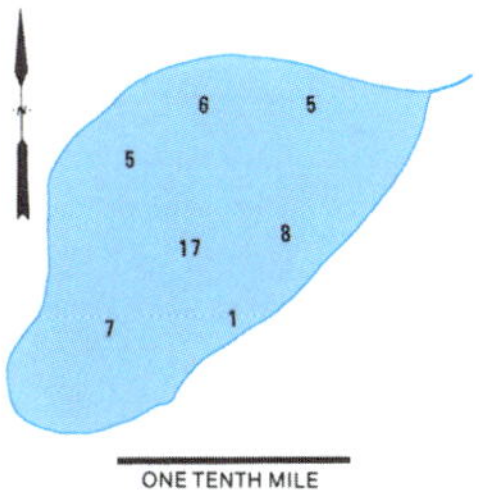

Celia Pond
T3 R10 WELS
Maine Atlas
Map 50, D-4
Acres: 8
Max. Depth:
17 feet

BrT		LmB
BkT	✓	SmB
RbT		WhP
Sal		Csk
Tog		WhF
Smt		Pic

Piscataquis

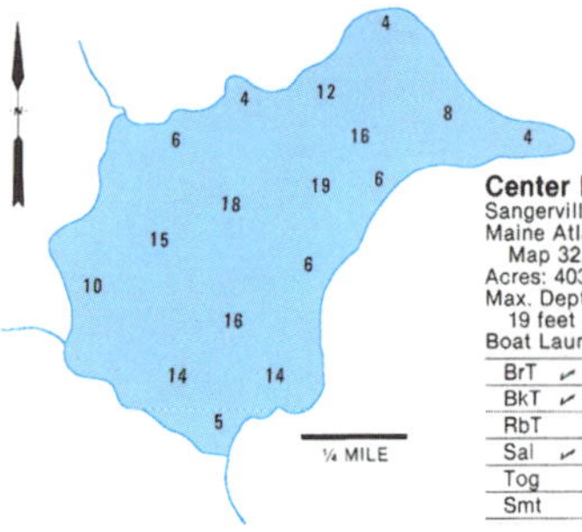

Center Pond
Sangerville
Maine Atlas
Map 32, C-1
Acres: 403
Max. Depth:
19 feet
Boat Launch

BrT	✓	LmB	
BkT	✓	SmB	
RbT		WhP	✓
Sal	✓	Csk	
Tog		WhF	
Smt		Pic	✓

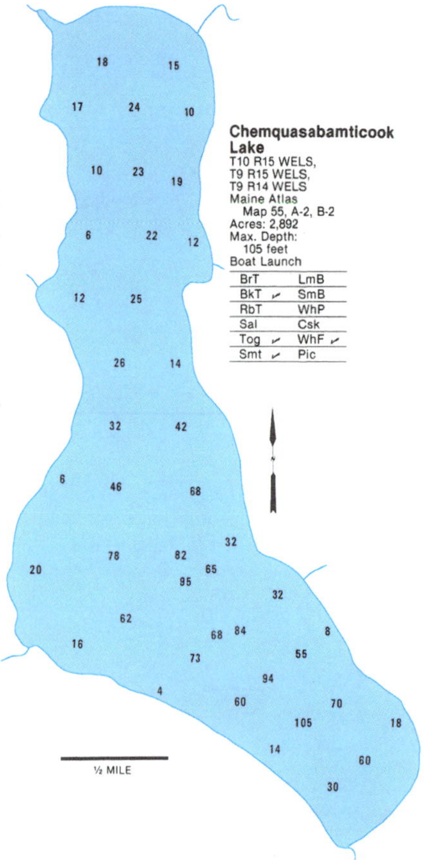

Chemquasabamticook Lake
T10 R15 WELS,
T9 R15 WELS,
T9 R14 WELS
Maine Atlas
Map 55, A-2, B-2
Acres: 2,892
Max. Depth:
105 feet
Boat Launch

BrT		LmB	
BkT	✓	SmB	
RbT		WhP	
Sal		Csk	
Tog	✓	WhF	✓
Smt	✓	Pic	

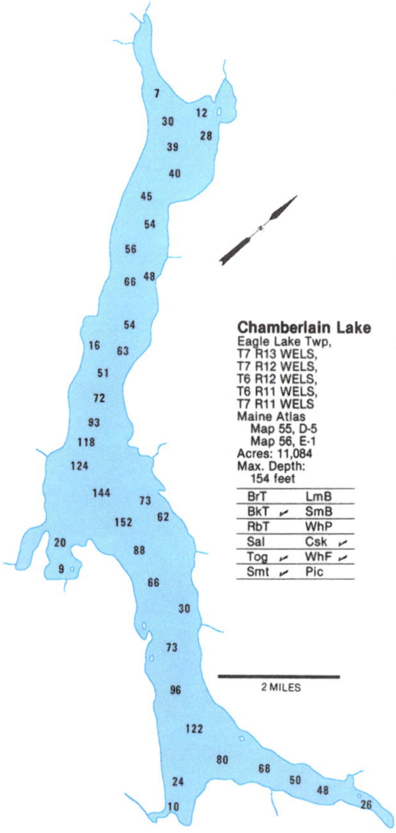

Chamberlain Lake
Eagle Lake Twp,
T7 R13 WELS,
T7 R12 WELS,
T6 R12 WELS,
T6 R11 WELS,
T7 R11 WELS
Maine Atlas
Map 55, D-5
Map 56, E-1
Acres: 11,084
Max. Depth:
154 feet

BrT		LmB	
BkT	✓	SmB	
RbT		WhP	
Sal		Csk	✓
Tog	✓	WhF	✓
Smt	✓	Pic	

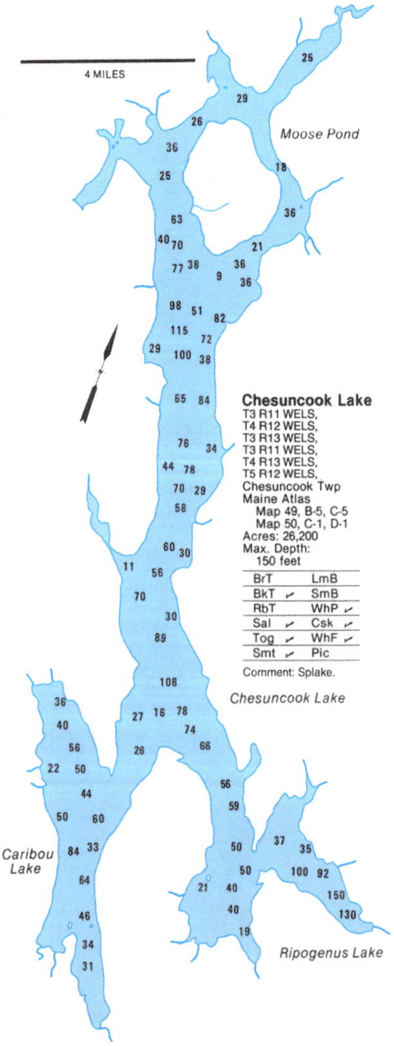

Chesuncook Lake
T3 R11 WELS,
T4 R12 WELS,
T3 R13 WELS,
T3 R11 WELS,
T4 R13 WELS,
T5 R12 WELS,
Chesuncook Twp
Maine Atlas
Map 49, B-5, C-5
Map 50, C-1, D-1
Acres: 26,200
Max. Depth:
150 feet

BrT		LmB	
BkT	✓	SmB	✓
RbT		WhP	✓
Sal	✓	Csk	✓
Tog	✓	WhF	✓
Smt	✓	Pic	

Comment: Splake.

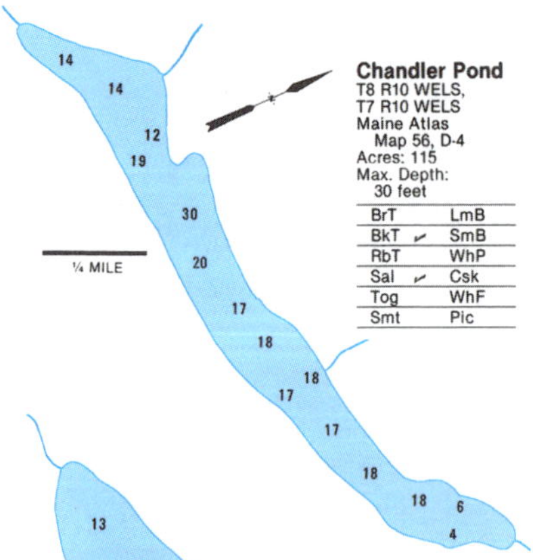

Chandler Pond
T8 R10 WELS,
T7 R10 WELS
Maine Atlas
Map 56, D-4
Acres: 115
Max. Depth:
30 feet

BrT		LmB	
BkT	✓	SmB	
RbT		WhP	
Sal	✓	Csk	
Tog		WhF	
Smt		Pic	

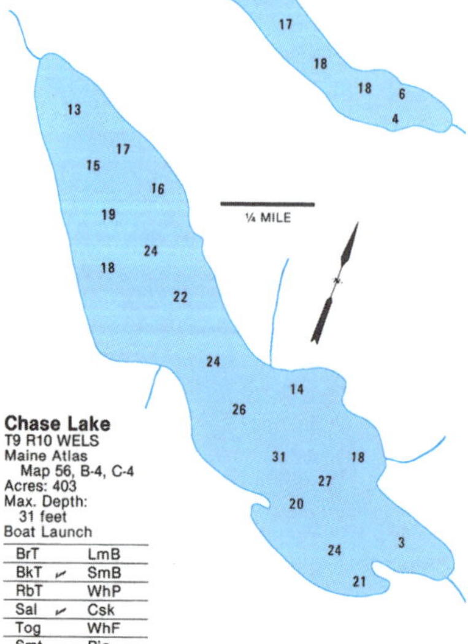

Chase Lake
T9 R10 WELS
Maine Atlas
Map 56, B-4, C-4
Acres: 403
Max. Depth:
31 feet
Boat Launch

BrT		LmB	
BkT	✓	SmB	
RbT		WhP	
Sal	✓	Csk	
Tog		WhF	
Smt		Pic	

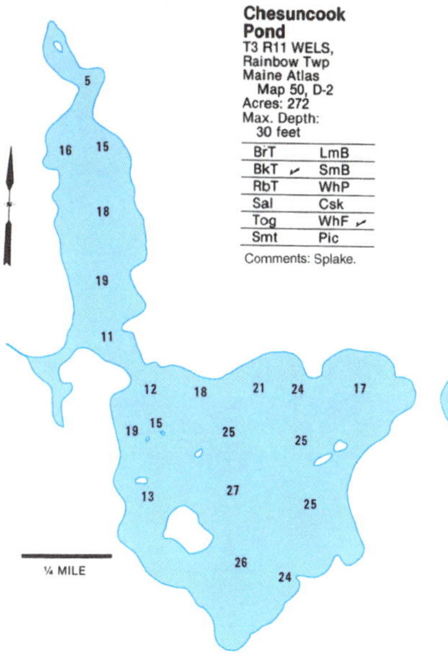

Chesuncook Pond
T3 R11 WELS,
Rainbow Twp
Maine Atlas
Map 50, D-2
Acres: 272
Max. Depth:
30 feet

BrT	LmB
BkT ✓	SmB
RbT	WhP
Sal	Csk
Tog	WhF ✓
Smt	Pic

Comments: Splake.

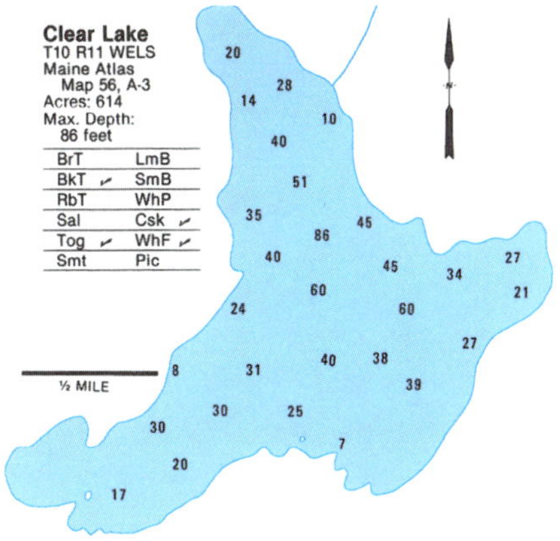

Clear Lake
T10 R11 WELS
Maine Atlas
Map 56, A-3
Acres: 614
Max. Depth:
86 feet

BrT	LmB
BkT ✓	SmB
RbT	WhP
Sal	Csk ✓
Tog ✓	WhF ✓
Smt	Pic

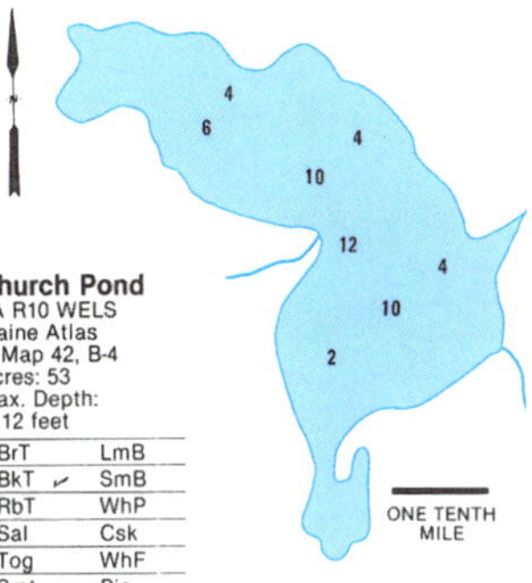

Church Pond
TA R10 WELS
Maine Atlas
Map 42, B-4
Acres: 53
Max. Depth:
12 feet

BrT	LmB
BkT ✓	SmB
RbT	WhP
Sal	Csk
Tog	WhF
Smt	Pic

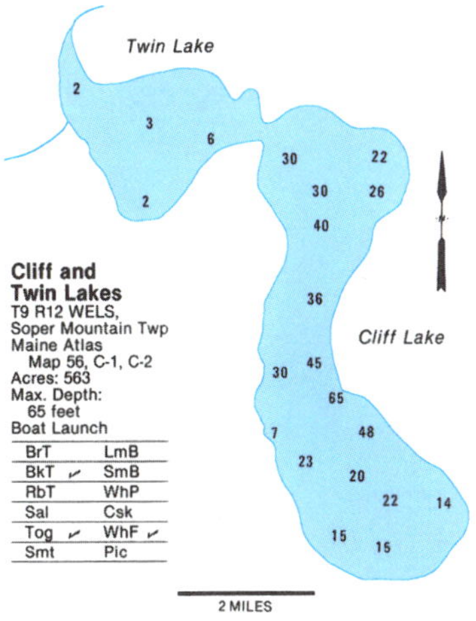

Cliff and Twin Lakes
T9 R12 WELS,
Soper Mountain Twp
Maine Atlas
Map 56, C-1, C-2
Acres: 563
Max. Depth:
65 feet
Boat Launch

BrT	LmB
BkT ✓	SmB
RbT	WhP
Sal	Csk
Tog ✓	WhF ✓
Smt	Pic

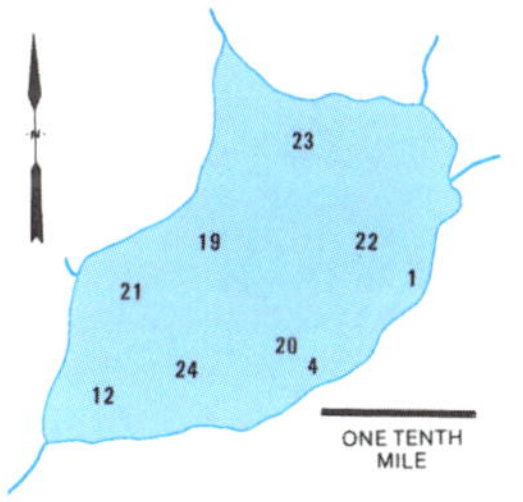

Clifford Pond
Rainbow Twp
Maine Atlas
Map 50, E-3
Acres: 17
Max. Depth:
24 feet

BrT	LmB
BkT ✓	SmB
RbT	WhP
Sal	Csk
Tog	WhF
Smt	Pic

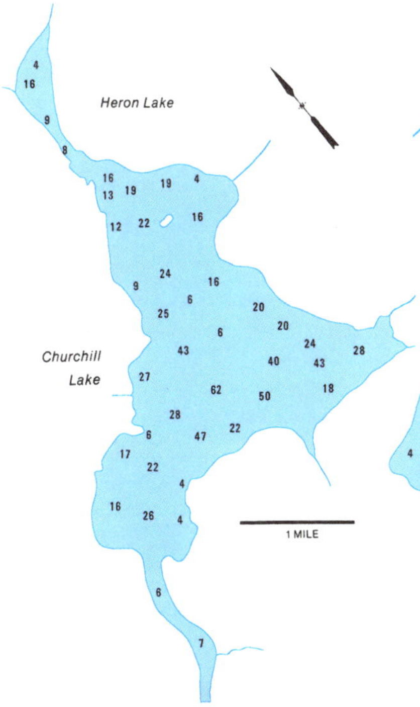

Churchill and Heron Lakes
T9 R12 WELS, T9 R13 WELS, T10 R12 WELS
Maine Atlas Map 56, B-1, Map 55, B-5
Acres: 2,923, Max. Depth: 62 feet, Boat Launch

BrT	BkT	RbT	Sal	Tog	Smt	LmB	SmB	WhP	Csk	WhF	Pic
	✓			✓					✓	✓	

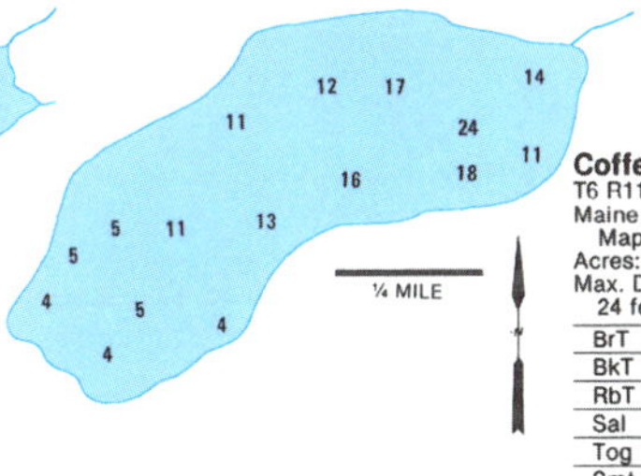

Coffeelos Pond
T6 R11 WELS
Maine Atlas
Map 50, A-3
Acres: 198
Max. Depth:
24 feet

BrT	LmB
BkT ✓	SmB
RbT	WhP
Sal	Csk
Tog	WhF
Smt	Pic

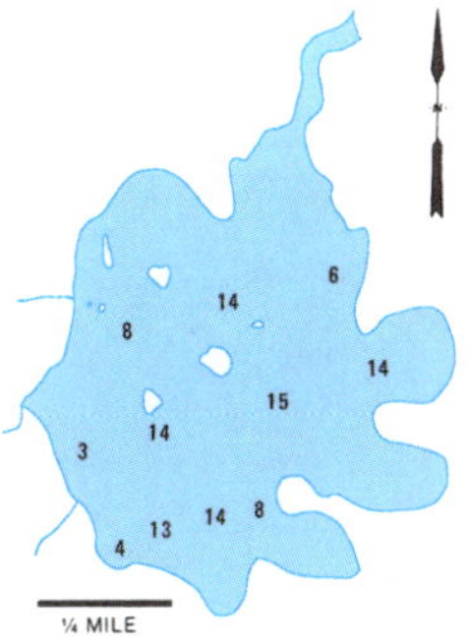

Cooper Pond
TA R10 WELS
Maine Atlas
Map 42, B-4
Acres: 271
Max. Depth:
15 feet

BrT	LmB
BkT ✓	SmB
RbT	WhP ✓
Sal	Csk
Tog	WhF
Smt	Pic

Piscataquis

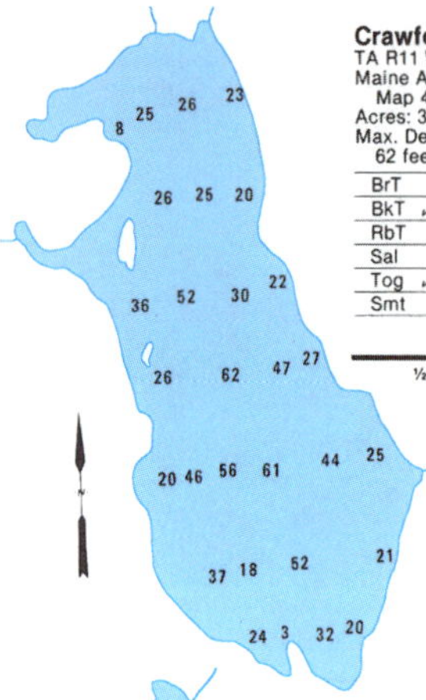

Crawford Pond
TA R11 WELS
Maine Atlas
Map 42, B-3
Acres: 390
Max. Depth:
62 feet

BrT	LmB
BkT ✓	SmB
RbT	WhP
Sal	Csk ✓
Tog ✓	WhF
Smt	Pic

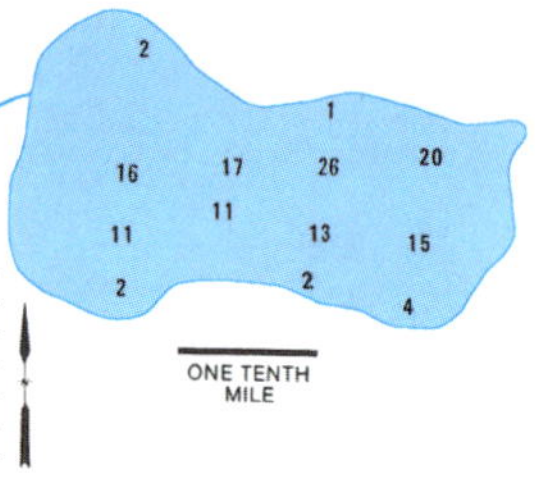

Daicey Pond
T3 R10 WELS
Maine Atlas
Map 50, D-4
Acres: 38
Max. Depth:
26 feet

BrT	LmB
BkT ✓	SmB
RbT	WhP
Sal	Csk
Tog	WhF
Smt	Pic

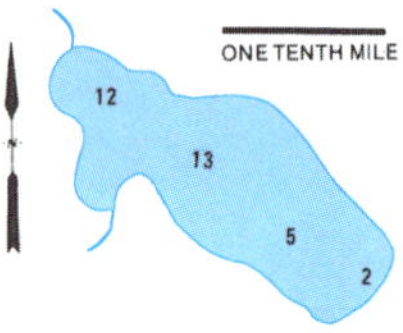

Daisey Pond
T2 R10 WELS
Maine Atlas
Map 50, E-4
Acres: 11
Max. Depth:
13 feet

BrT	LmB
BkT ✓	SmB
RbT	WhP
Sal	Csk
Tog	WhF
Smt	Pic

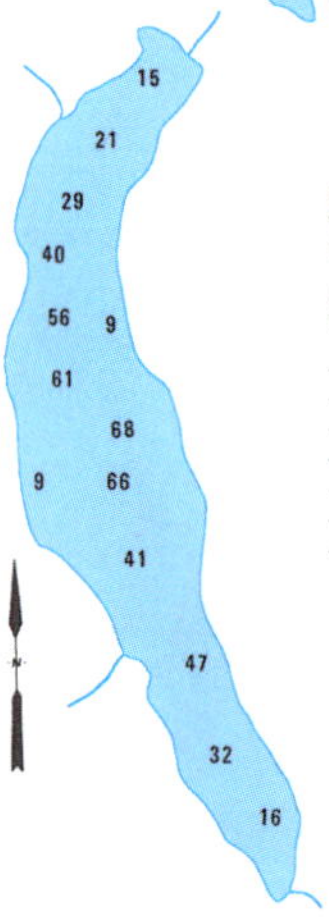

Crescent Pond
T9 R15 WELS
Maine Atlas
Map 55, B-2, C-2
Acres: 320
Max. Depth:
68 feet

BrT	LmB
BkT ✓	SmB
RbT	WhP
Sal	Csk ✓
Tog ✓	WhF ✓
Smt	Pic

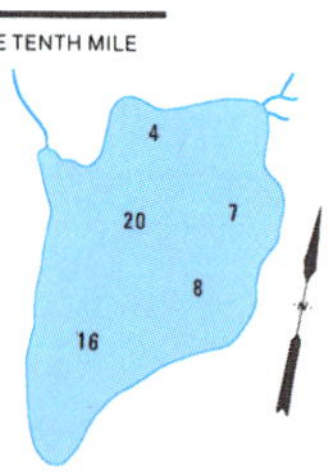

Deep Pond
T4 R9 WELS
Maine Atlas
Map 51, B-1, C-1
Acres: 8
Max. Depth:
20 feet

BrT	LmB
BkT ✓	SmB
RbT	WhP
Sal	Csk
Tog	WhF
Smt	Pic

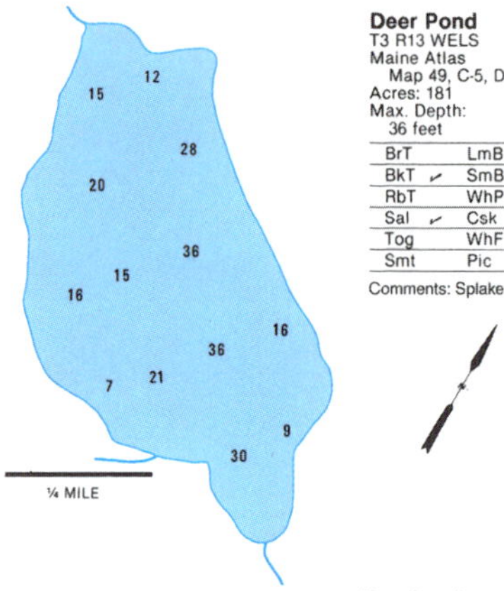

Deer Pond
T3 R13 WELS
Maine Atlas
Map 49, C-5, D-5
Acres: 181
Max. Depth:
36 feet

BrT	LmB
BkT ✓	SmB
RbT	WhP
Sal ✓	Csk
Tog	WhF
Smt	Pic

Comments: Splake.

Crockett Pond
Blanchard Plt
Maine Atlas
Map 31, B-1
Acres: 12
Max. Depth:
6 feet

BrT	LmB
BkT ✓	SmB
RbT	WhP
Sal	Csk
Tog	WhF
Smt	Pic

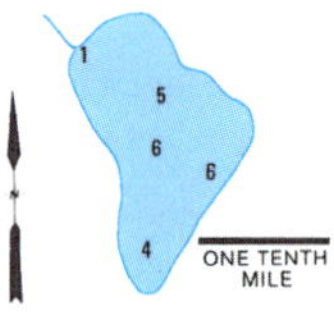

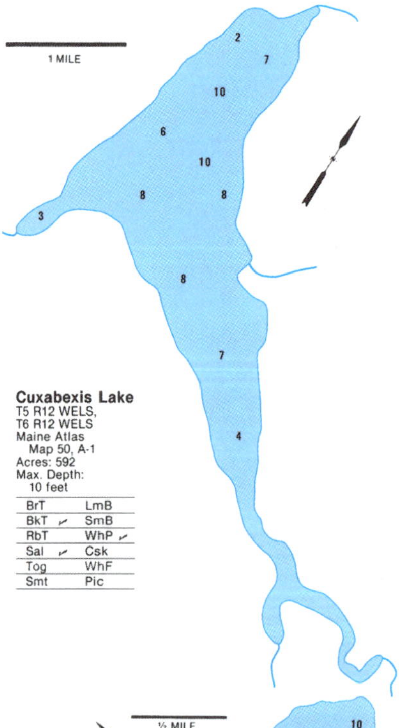

Cuxabexis Lake
T5 R12 WELS,
T6 R12 WELS
Maine Atlas
Map 50, A-1
Acres: 592
Max. Depth:
10 feet

BrT	LmB
BkT ✓	SmB
RbT	WhP ✓
Sal ✓	Csk
Tog	WhF
Smt	Pic

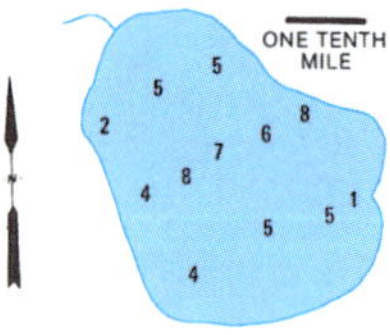

Doe Pond
Monson
Maine Atlas
Map 31, A-3
Acres: 54
Max. Depth:
8 feet
Boat Launch

BrT	LmB
BkT ✓	SmB
RbT	WhP
Sal	Csk
Tog	WhF
Smt	Pic

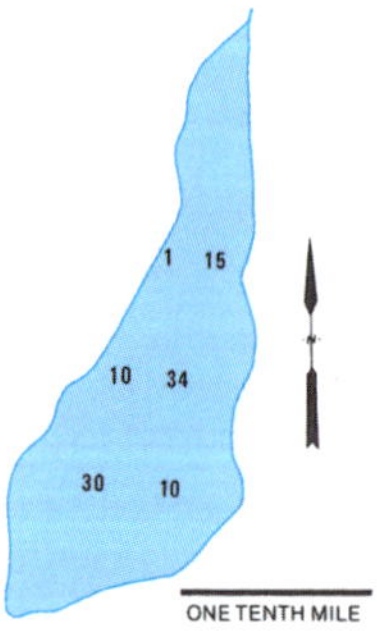

Doughnut Pond
Rainbow Twp
Maine Atlas
Map 50, E-3
Acres: 12
Max. Depth:
34 feet

BrT	LmB
BkT ✓	SmB
RbT	WhP
Sal	Csk
Tog	WhF
Smt	Pic

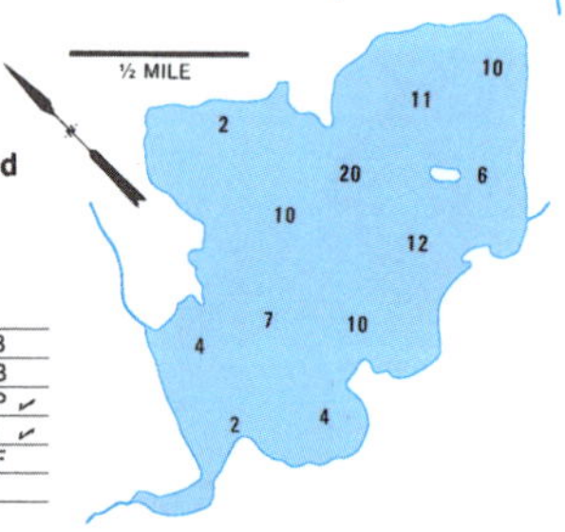

Daggett Pond
T7 R14 WELS
Maine Atlas
Map 55, E-3
Acres: 461
Max. Depth:
20 feet

BrT	LmB
BkT ✓	SmB
RbT	WhP ✓
Sal	Csk ✓
Tog	WhF
Smt	Pic

Doughty Ponds
Monson
Maine Atlas
Map 31, A-3
Acres: Upper-13
Lower-20
Max. Depth:
Upper-40 feet
Lower-25 feet

BrT	LmB
BkT ✓	SmB
RbT	WhP
Sal	Csk
Tog	WhF
Smt	Pic

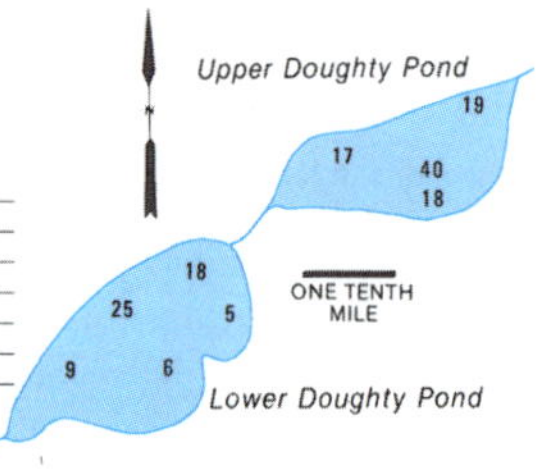

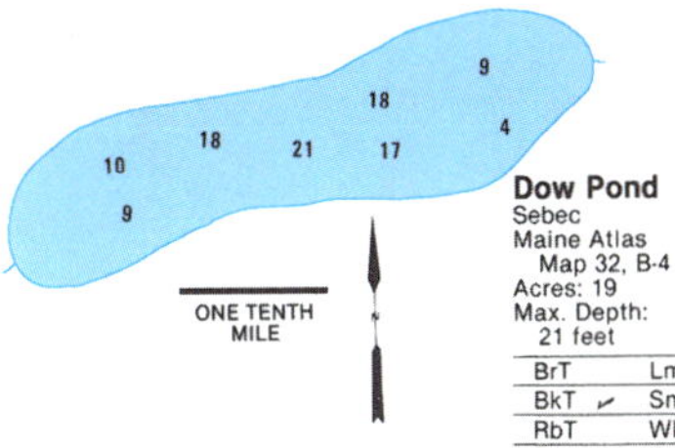

Dow Pond
Sebec
Maine Atlas
Map 32, B-4
Acres: 19
Max. Depth:
21 feet

BrT	LmB
BkT ✓	SmB
RbT	WhP
Sal	Csk
Tog	WhF
Smt	Pic

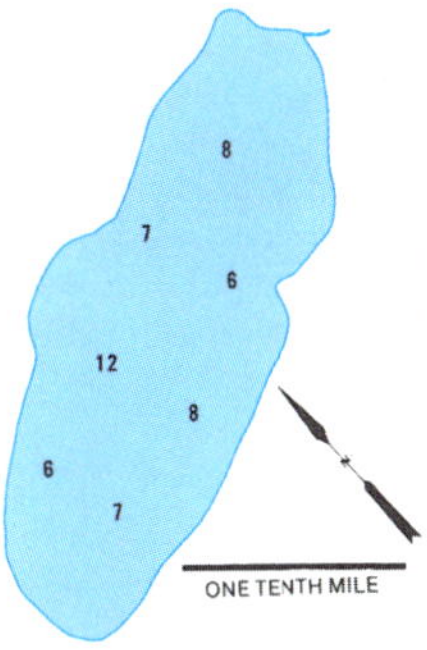

Draper Pond
T3 R10 WELS
Maine Atlas
Map 50, D-4
Acres: 10
Max. Depth:
12 feet

BrT	LmB
BkT ✓	SmB
RbT	WhP
Sal	Csk
Tog	WhF
Smt	Pic

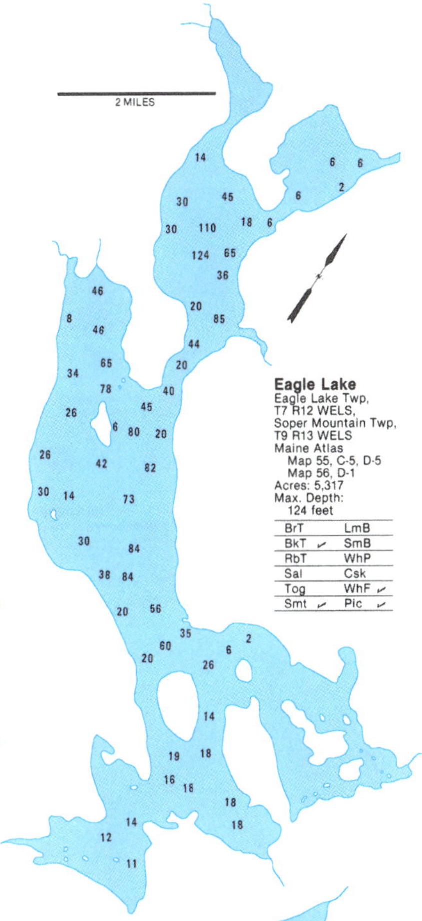

Eagle Lake
Eagle Lake Twp,
T7 R12 WELS,
Soper Mountain Twp,
T9 R13 WELS
Maine Atlas
Map 55, C-5, D-5
Map 56, D-1
Acres: 5,317
Max. Depth:
124 feet

BrT	LmB
BkT ✓	SmB
RbT	WhP
Sal	Csk
Tog	WhF ✓
Smt ✓	Pic ✓

Duck Pond
T4 R11 WELS
Maine Atlas
Map 50, C-2
Acres: 21
Max. Depth:
7 feet

BrT	LmB
BkT ✓	SmB
RbT	WhP
Sal ✓	Csk
Tog	WhF
Smt ✓	Pic

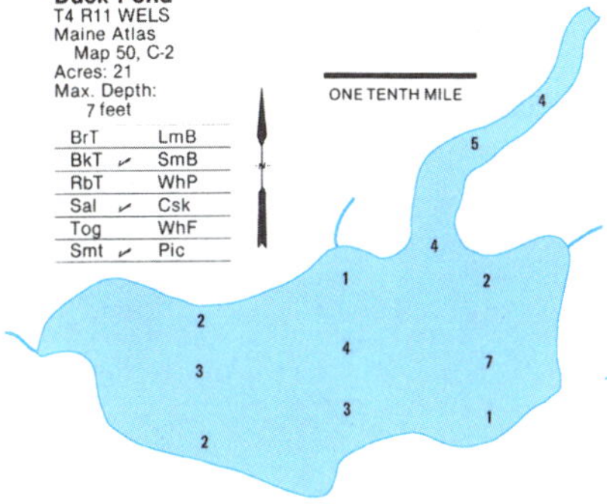

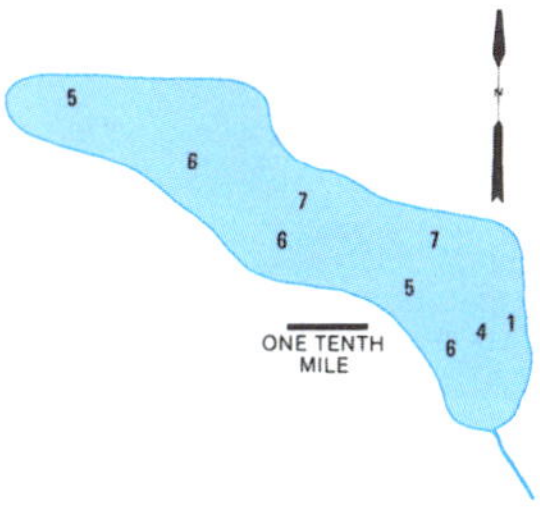

Dunham Pond
Guilford
Maine Atlas
Map 32, B-1
Acres: 48
Max. Depth:
7 feet

BrT	LmB
BkT ✓	SmB
RbT	WhP
Sal	Csk
Tog	WhF
Smt	Pic ✓

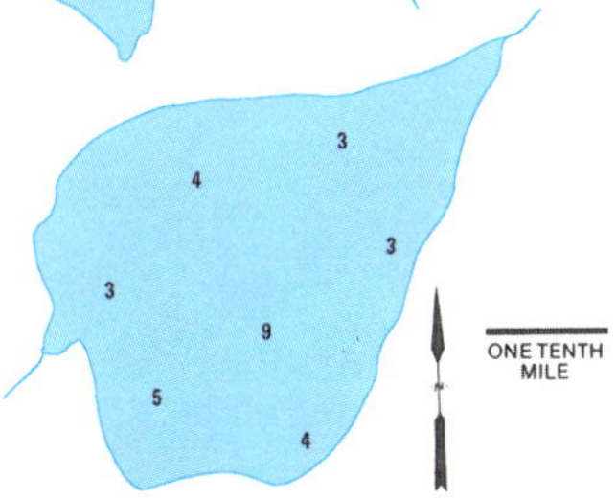

East Branch Pond
T7 R11 WELS, Maine Atlas Map 56, D-3
Acres: 45, Max. Depth: 9 feet

BrT	BkT	RbT	Sal	Tog	Smt	LmB	SmB	WhP	Csk	WhF	Pic
	✓										

Dwelley Pond
Nesourdnahunk Twp
Maine Atlas
Map 50, B-4
Acres: 19
Max. Depth:
4 feet

BrT	LmB
BkT ✓	SmB
RbT	WhP
Sal	Csk
Tog	WhF
Smt	Pic

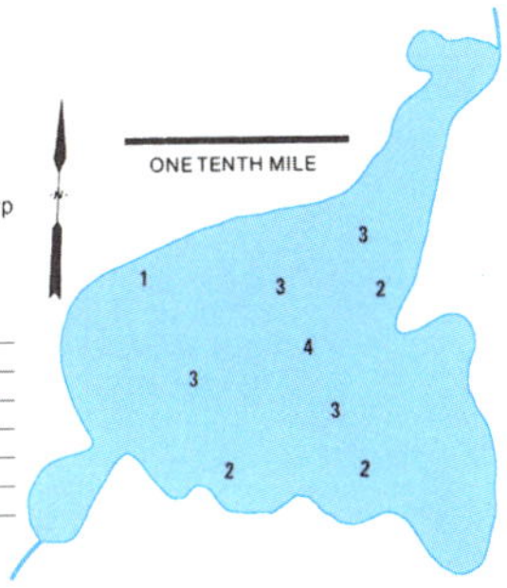

East Chairback Pond
T7 R9 NWP
Maine Atlas
Map 42, D-1
Acres: 40
Max. Depth:
58 feet

BrT	LmB
BkT ✓	SmB
RbT	WhP
Sal	Csk
Tog	WhF
Smt	Pic

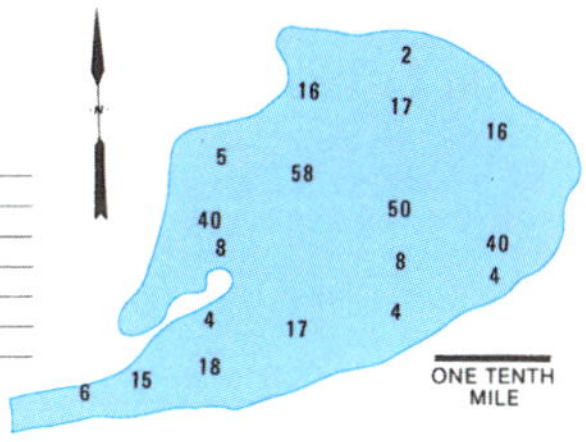

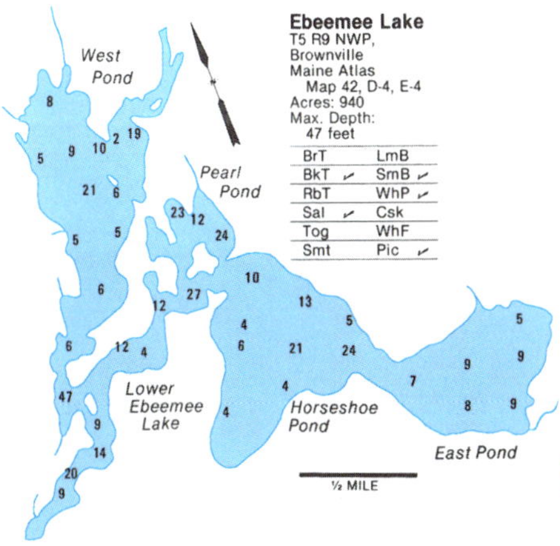

Ebeemee Lake
T5 R9 NWP,
Brownville
Maine Atlas
Map 42, D-4, E-4
Acres: 940
Max. Depth:
47 feet

BrT	LmB
BkT ✓	SmB ✓
RbT	WhP ✓
Sal ✓	Csk
Tog	WhF
Smt	Pic ✓

Echo Lake
T9 R11 WELS
Maine Atlas
Map 56, B-3
Acres: 115
Max. Depth:
45 feet

BrT	LmB
BkT ✓	SmB
RbT	WhP
Sal	Csk
Tog ✓	WhF ✓
Smt	Pic

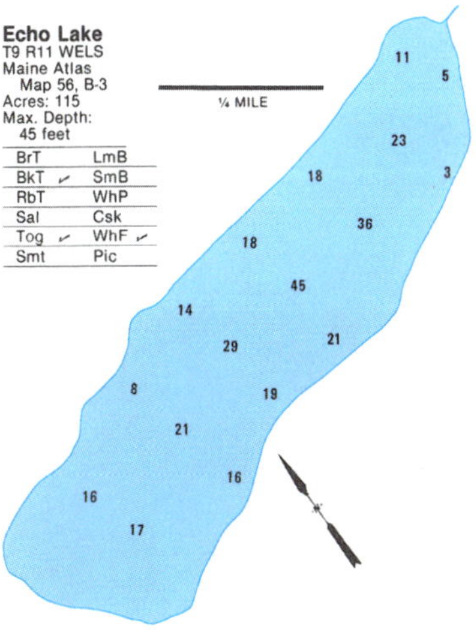

Piscataquis

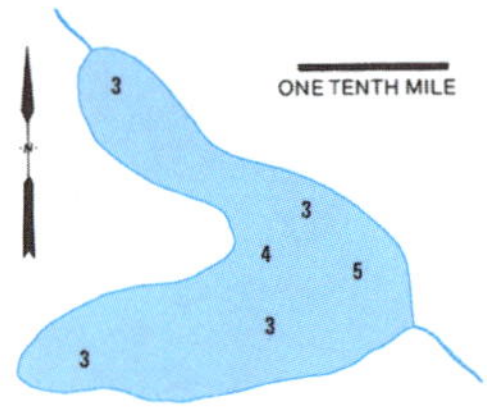

Elbow Pond
T3 R10 WELS
Maine Atlas
Map 50, D-4
Acres: 13
Max. Depth:
5 feet

BrT		LmB	
BkT	✓	SmB	
RbT		WhP	
Sal		Csk	
Tog		WhF	
Smt		Pic	

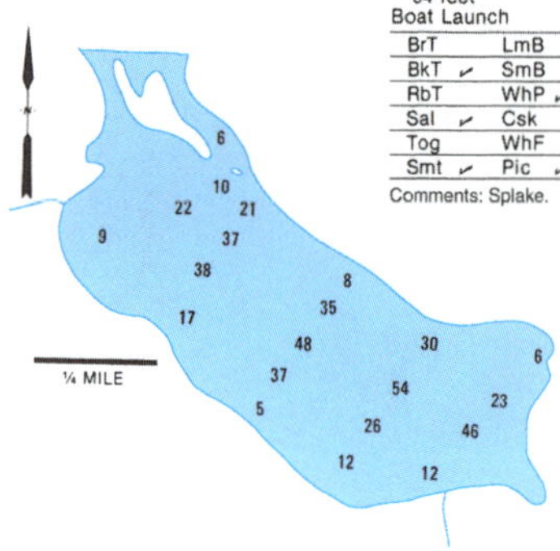

First Davis Pond
Guilford
Maine Atlas
Map 31, B-4
Acres: 128
Max. Depth:
54 feet
Boat Launch

BrT		LmB	
BkT	✓	SmB	
RbT		WhP	✓
Sal	✓	Csk	
Tog		WhF	
Smt	✓	Pic	✓

Comments: Splake.

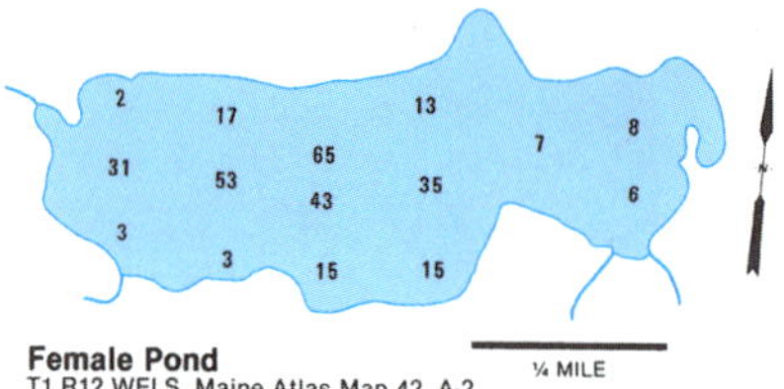

Female Pond
T1 R12 WELS, Maine Atlas Map 42, A-2
Acres: 102, Max. Depth: 65 feet

BrT	BkT	RbT	Sal	Tog	Smt	LmB	SmB	WhP	Csk	WhF	Pic
	✓										

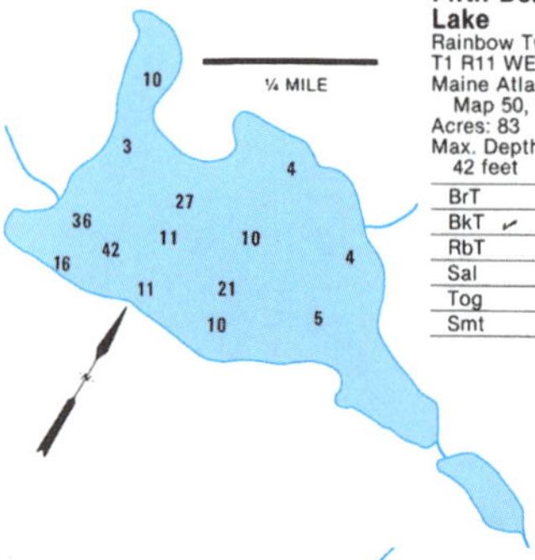

Fifth Debsconeag Lake
Rainbow Twp,
T1 R11 WELS
Maine Atlas
Map 50, E-3
Acres: 83
Max. Depth:
42 feet

BrT		LmB	
BkT	✓	SmB	
RbT		WhP	
Sal		Csk	
Tog		WhF	
Smt		Pic	

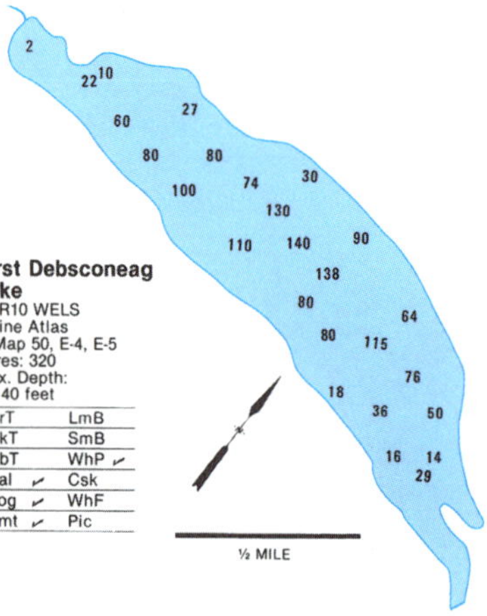

First Debsconeag Lake
T2 R10 WELS
Maine Atlas
Map 50, E-4, E-5
Acres: 320
Max. Depth:
140 feet

BrT		LmB	
BkT		SmB	
RbT		WhP	✓
Sal	✓	Csk	
Tog	✓	WhF	
Smt	✓	Pic	

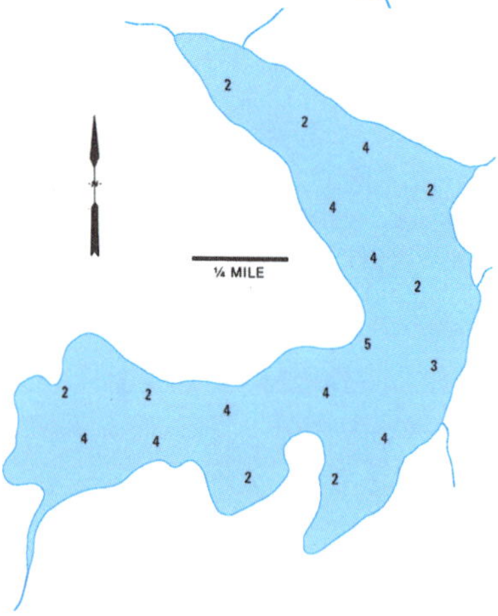

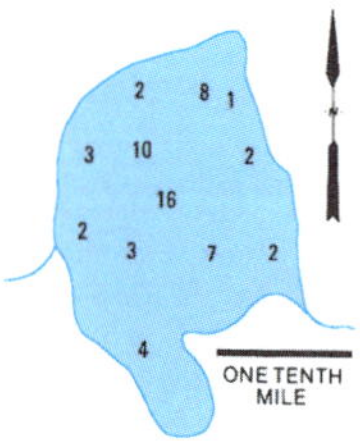

First Little Lyford Pond
Bowdoin College
Grant East
Maine Atlas
Map 41, C-5
Acres: 21
Max. Depth:
16 feet

BrT		LmB	
BkT	✓	SmB	
RbT		WhP	
Sal		Csk	
Tog		WhF	
Smt		Pic	

Fifth Musquacook Lake
T10 R11 WELS, Maine Atlas Map 56, A-3
Acres: 358, Max. Depth: 5 feet

BrT	BkT	RbT	Sal	Tog	Smt	LmB	SmB	WhP	Csk	WhF	Pic
	✓								✓		

First Buttermilk Pond
Bowerbank, Maine Atlas Map 32, A-1
Acres: 384, Max. Depth: 119 feet

BrT	BkT	RbT	Sal	Tog	Smt	LmB	SmB	WhP	Csk	WhF	Pic
	✓		✓	✓	✓		✓				

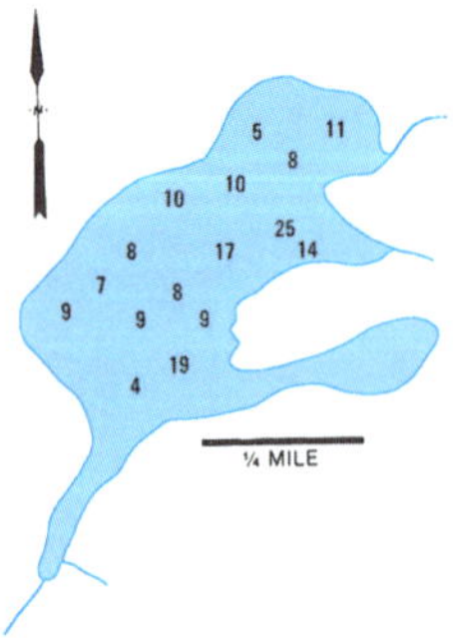

First West Branch Pond
Shawtown Twp
Maine Atlas
Map 42, B-1, C-1
Acres: 119
Max. Depth:
25 feet
Boat Launch

BrT		LmB	
BkT	✓	SmB	
RbT		WhP	
Sal		Csk	
Tog		WhF	
Smt		Pic	

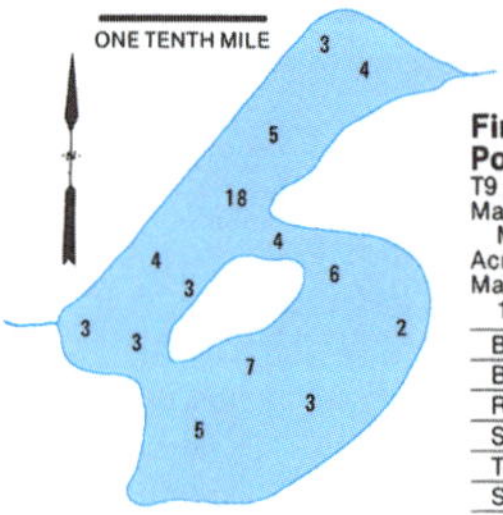

First Currier Pond
T9 R11 WELS
Maine Atlas
Map 56, B-3
Acres: 20
Max. Depth:
18 feet

BrT		LmB	
BkT	✓	SmB	
RbT		WhP	
Sal		Csk	
Tog		WhF	
Smt		Pic	

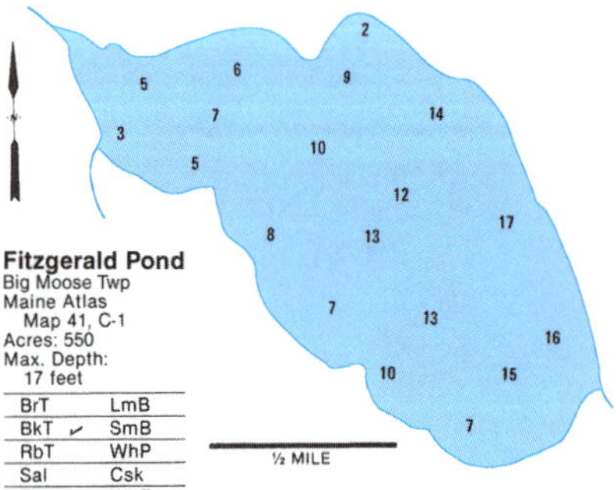

Fitzgerald Pond
Big Moose Twp
Maine Atlas
Map 41, C-1
Acres: 550
Max. Depth:
17 feet

BrT		LmB	
BkT	✓	SmB	
RbT		WhP	
Sal		Csk	
Tog	✓	WhF	
Smt		Pic	

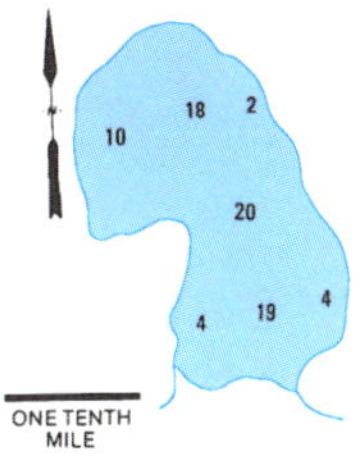

Fogg Pond
Bowdoin College Grant West
Maine Atlas
Map 41, C-4
Acres: 23
Max. Depth:
20 feet

BrT	LmB
BkT ✓	SmB
RbT	WhP
Sal	Csk
Tog	WhF
Smt	Pic

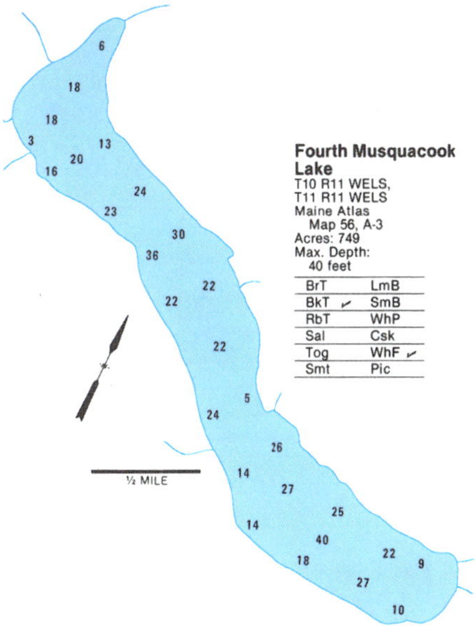

Fourth Musquacook Lake
T10 R11 WELS,
T11 R11 WELS
Maine Atlas
Map 56, A-3
Acres: 749
Max. Depth:
40 feet

BrT	LmB
BkT ✓	SmB
RbT	WhP
Sal	Csk
Tog	WhF ✓
Smt	Pic

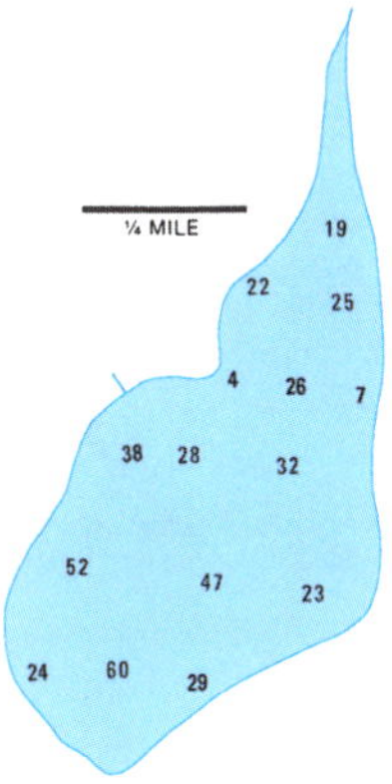

Foss Pond
Kingsbury Plt
Maine Atlas
Map 31, B-2
Acres: 110
Max. Depth:
60 feet

BrT	LmB
BkT ✓	SmB
RbT	WhP
Sal	Csk
Tog ✓	WhF
Smt ✓	Pic

Fowler Pond
T3 R11 WELS
Maine Atlas
Map 50, D-3
Acres: 19
Max. Depth:
12 feet

BrT	LmB
BkT ✓	SmB
RbT	WhP
Sal	Csk
Tog	WhF
Smt	Pic

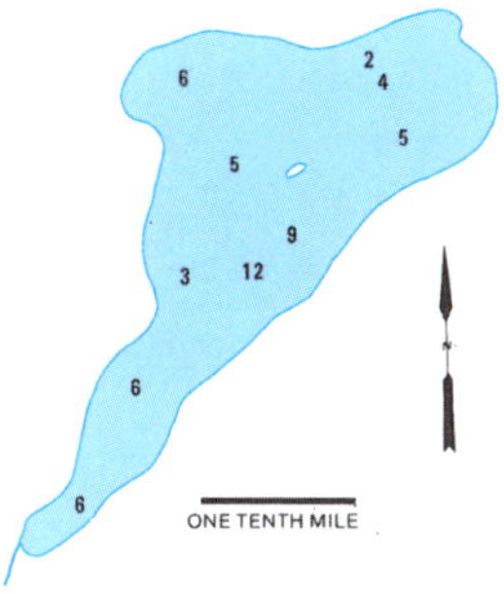

Foss and Knowlton Pond
T3 R10 WELS
Maine Atlas
Map 50, D-4
Acres: 41
Max. Depth:
22 feet

BrT	LmB
BkT ✓	SmB
RbT	WhP
Sal	Csk
Tog	WhF
Smt	Pic

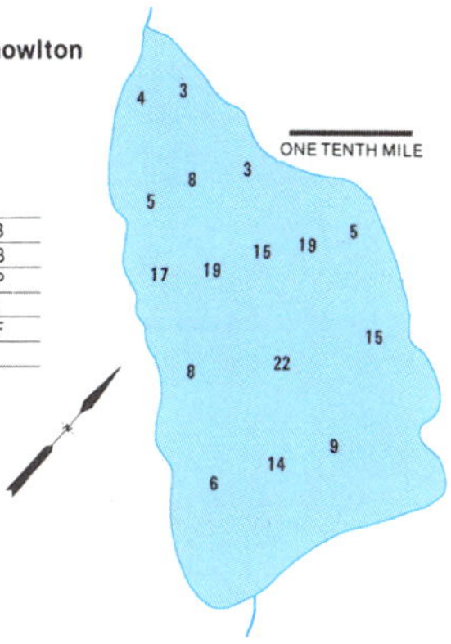

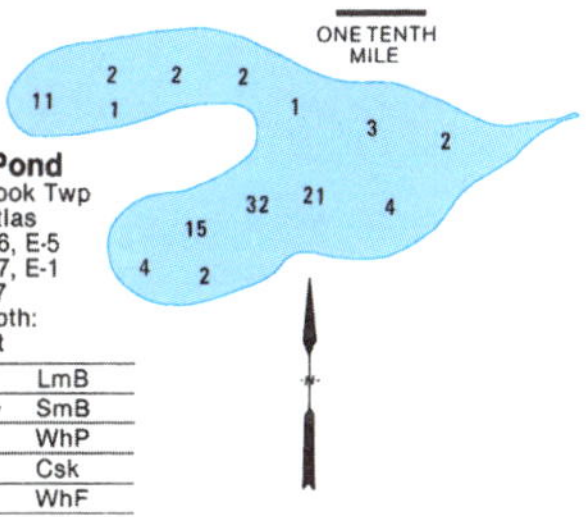

Frost Pond
Trout Brook Twp
Maine Atlas
Map 56, E-5
Map 57, E-1
Acres: 37
Max. Depth:
32 feet

BrT	LmB
BkT ✓	SmB
RbT	WhP
Sal	Csk
Tog	WhF
Smt	Pic

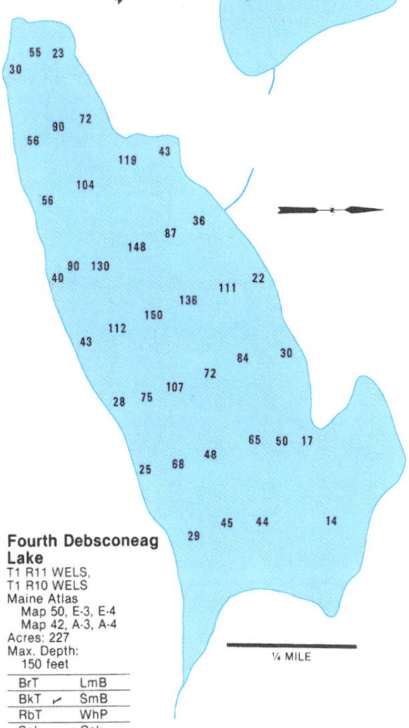

Fourth Debsconeag Lake
T1 R11 WELS,
T1 R10 WELS
Maine Atlas
Map 50, E-3, E-4
Map 42, A-3, A-4
Acres: 227
Max. Depth:
150 feet

BrT	LmB
BkT ✓	SmB
RbT	WhP
Sal	Csk ✓
Tog ✓	WhF
Smt	Pic

Frost Pond
T3 R11 WELS,
T3 R12 WELS
Maine Atlas
Map 50, C-2, D-2
Acres: 198
Max. Depth:
39 feet

BrT	LmB
BkT ✓	SmB
RbT	WhP
Sal	Csk
Tog	WhF
Smt ✓	Pic

Comments: Splake.

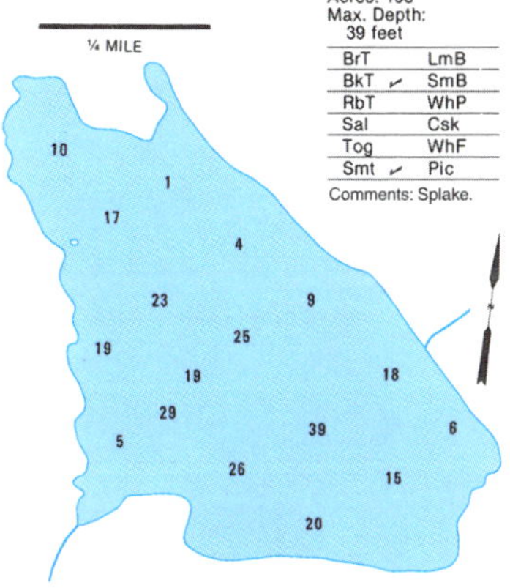

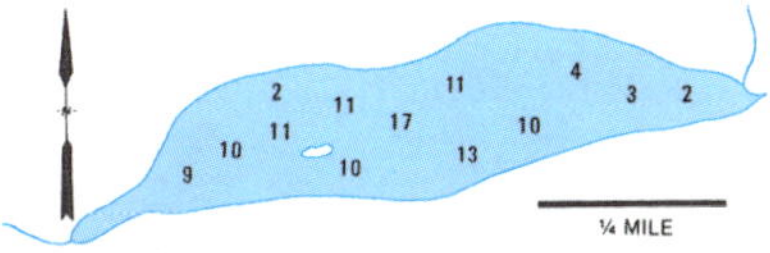

Fourth Lake
T7 R11 WELS, Maine Atlas Map 56, D-2, D-3
Acres: 64, Max. Depth: 17 feet

BrT	BkT	RbT	Sal	Tog	Smt	LmB	SmB	WhP	Csk	WhF	Pic
	✓										

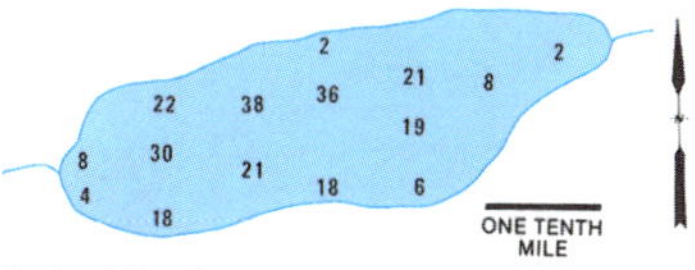

Garland Pond
Sebec, Dover-Foxcroft, Maine Atlas Map 32, B-2
Acres: 28, Max. Depth: 38 feet, Boat Launch

BrT	BkT	RbT	Sal	Tog	Smt	LmB	SmB	WhP	Csk	WhF	Pic
✓											

Comments: Splake.

Piscataquis

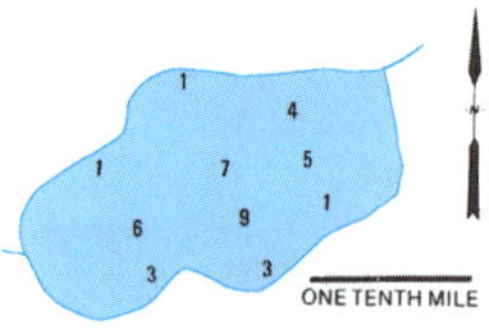

Gauntlet Pond
TB R10 WELS
Maine Atlas
Map 42, C-4
Acres: 11
Max. Depth:
9 feet

BrT	LmB
BkT ✓	SmB
RbT	WhP
Sal	Csk
Tog	WhF
Smt	Pic

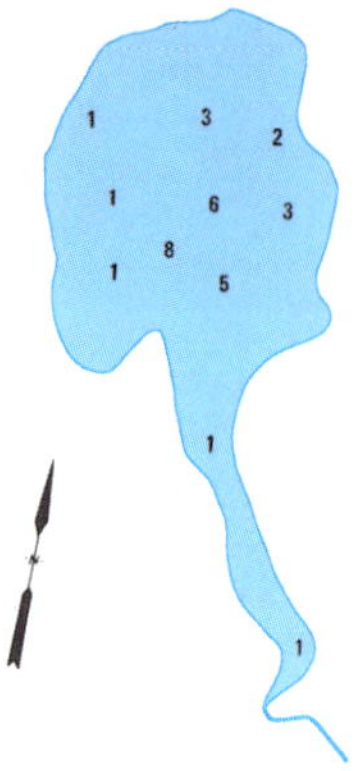

Grassy Pond
T2 R12 WELS
Maine Atlas
Map 50, E-1
Acres: 54
Max. Depth:
8 feet

BrT	LmB
BkT ✓	SmB
RbT	WhP
Sal	Csk
Tog	WhF
Smt	Pic

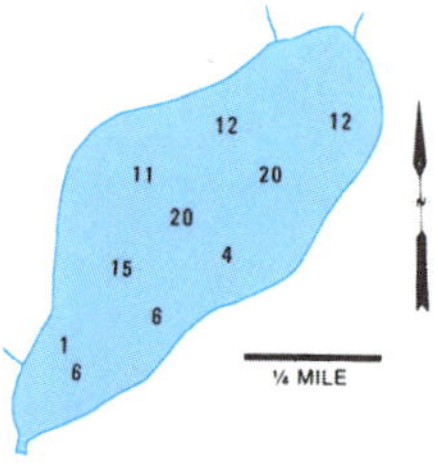

Greenleaf Pond
Abbot
Maine Atlas
Map 31, B-4
Acres: 27
Max. Depth:
20 feet

BrT	LmB
BkT ✓	SmB
RbT	WhP
Sal	Csk
Tog	WhF
Smt	Pic ✓

Greenwood Pond
TB R11 WELS,
Bowdoin College
Grant East
Maine Atlas
Map 42, C-2
Acres: 19
Max. Depth:
42 feet

BrT	LmB
BkT ✓	SmB
RbT	WhP
Sal	Csk
Tog	WhF
Smt	Pic

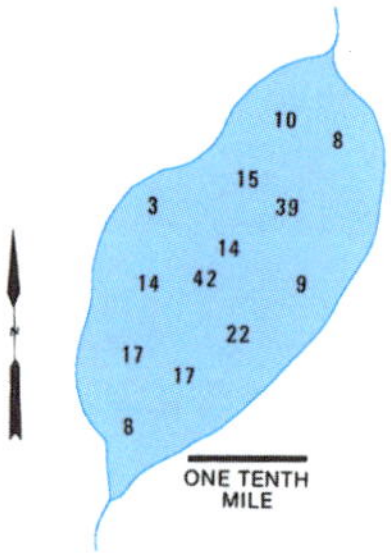

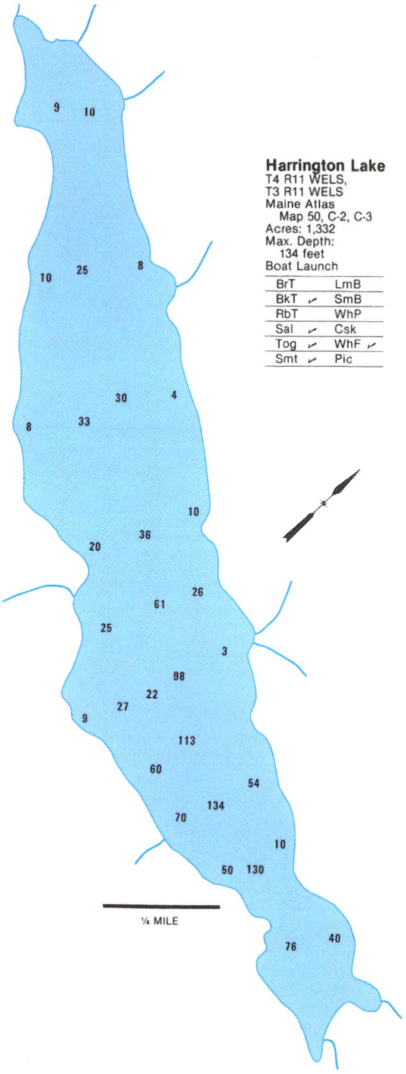

Harrington Lake
T4 R11 WELS,
T3 R11 WELS
Maine Atlas
Map 50, C-2, C-3
Acres: 1,332
Max. Depth:
134 feet
Boat Launch

BrT	LmB
BkT ✓	SmB
RbT	WhP
Sal ✓	Csk
Tog ✓	WhF ✓
Smt ✓	Pic

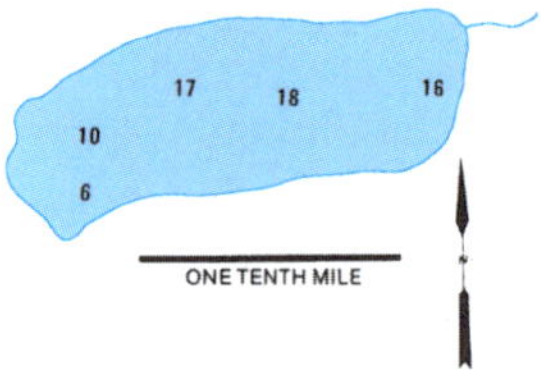

Grenell Pond
Greenville
Maine Atlas
Map 41, D-3
Acres: 6
Max. Depth:
18 feet

BrT	LmB
BkT ✓	SmB
RbT	WhP
Sal	Csk
Tog	WhF
Smt	Pic

Grindstone Pond
Willimantic
Maine Atlas
Map 31, A-5
Acres: 26
Max. Depth:
32 feet

BrT	LmB
BkT ✓	SmB
RbT	WhP
Sal	Csk
Tog	WhF
Smt	Pic

Comments: Splake.

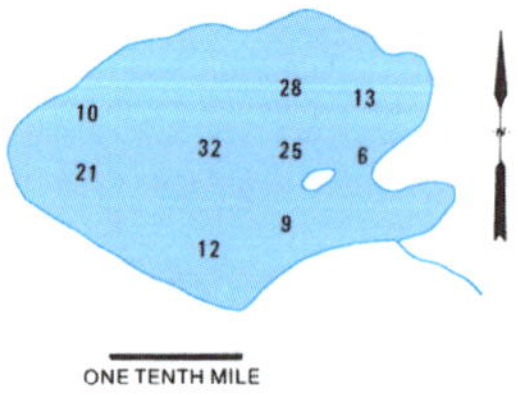

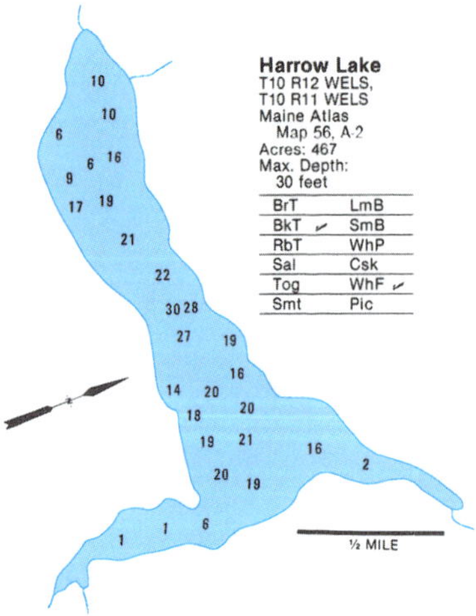

Harrow Lake
T10 R12 WELS,
T10 R11 WELS
Maine Atlas
Map 56, A-2
Acres: 467
Max. Depth:
30 feet

BrT	LmB
BkT ✓	SmB
RbT	WhP
Sal	Csk
Tog	WhF ✓
Smt	Pic

Hale Pond
T2 R10 WELS
Maine Atlas
Map 50, E-5
Acres: 168
Max. Depth:
58 feet

BrT	LmB
BkT ✓	SmB
RbT	WhP
Sal	Csk
Tog	WhF
Smt	Pic

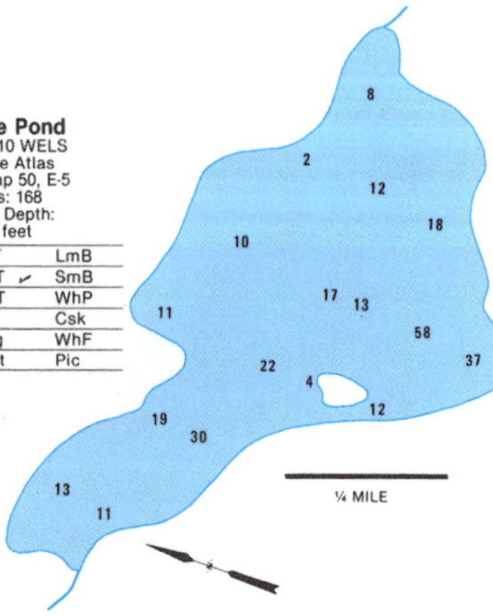

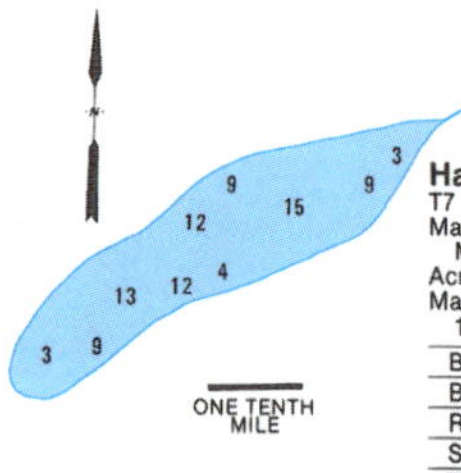

Hay Pond
T7 R11 WELS
Maine Atlas
Map 56, D-3
Acres: 19
Max. Depth:
15 feet

BrT	LmB
BkT ✓	SmB
RbT	WhP
Sal	Csk
Tog	WhF
Smt	Pic

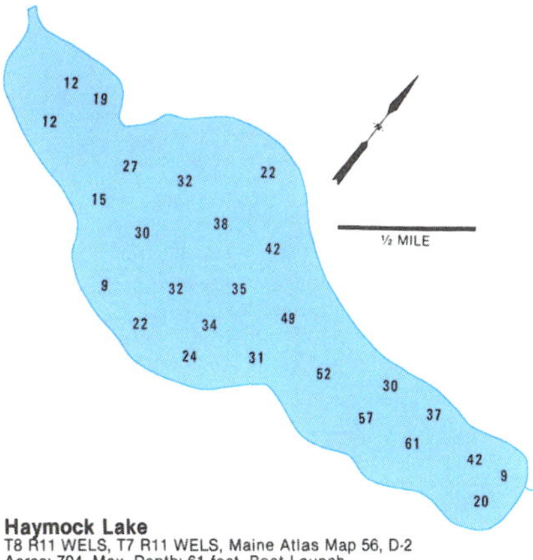

Haymock Lake

T8 R11 WELS, T7 R11 WELS, Maine Atlas Map 56, D-2
Acres: 704, Max. Depth: 61 feet, Boat Launch

BrT	BkT	RbT	Sal	Tog	Smt	LmB	SmB	WhP	Csk	WhF	Pic
	✓			✓							

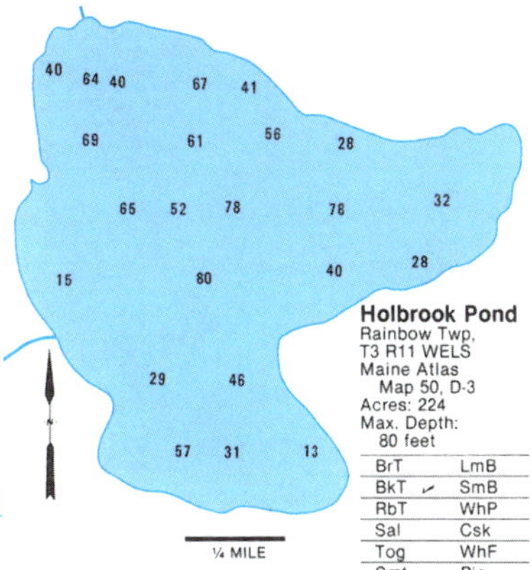

Holbrook Pond

Rainbow Twp,
T3 R11 WELS
Maine Atlas
Map 50, D-3
Acres: 224
Max. Depth:
80 feet

BrT		LmB	
BkT	✓	SmB	
RbT		WhP	
Sal		Csk	
Tog		WhF	
Smt		Pic	

Comments: Splake.

Horserace Ponds

Rainbow Twp,
T3 R11 WELS
Maine Atlas
Map 50, D-3
Acres: 50
Max. Depth:
48 feet

BrT		LmB	
BkT	✓	SmB	
RbT		WhP	
Sal		Csk	
Tog		WhF	
Smt		Pic	

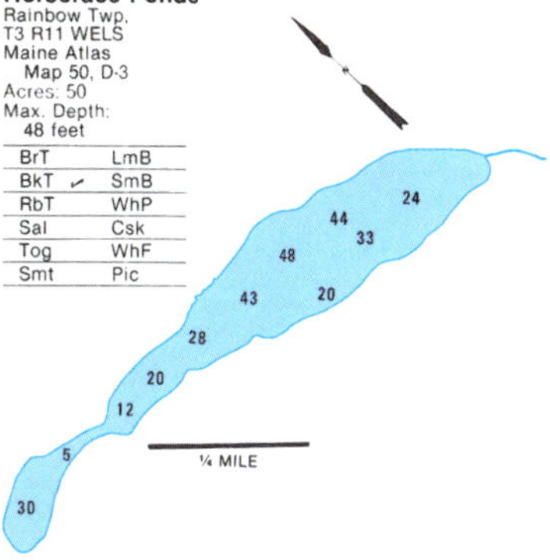

Hebron Lake

Monson
Maine Atlas
Map 31, A-3
Acres: 525
Max. Depth:
102 feet
Boat Launch

BrT		LmB	
BkT	✓	SmB	
RbT		WhP	✓
Sal	✓	Csk	
Tog	✓	WhF	
Smt	✓	Pic	

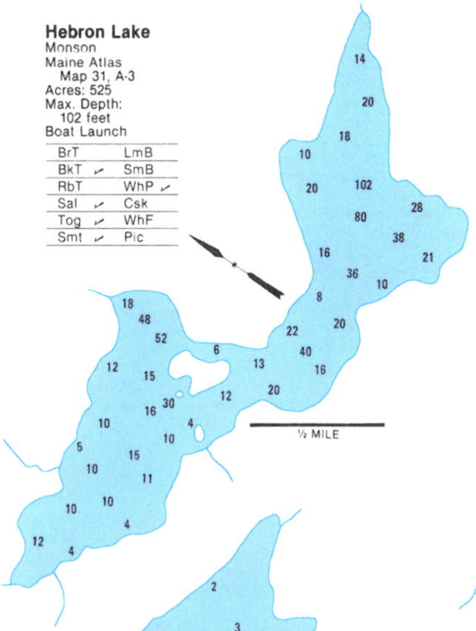

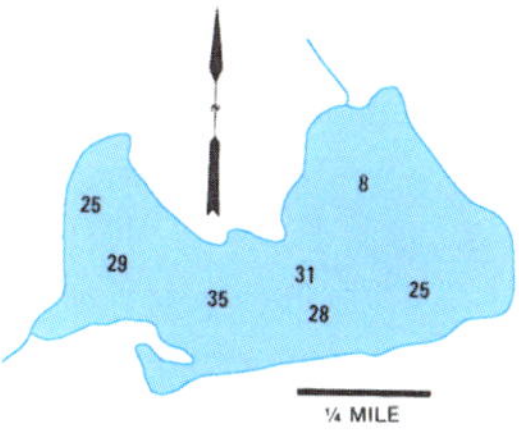

Horseshoe Pond

Bowdoin College
Grant West
Maine Atlas
Map 41, C-5
Acres: 160
Max. Depth:
35 feet

BrT		LmB	
BkT	✓	SmB	
RbT		WhP	
Sal		Csk	
Tog		WhF	
Smt		Pic	

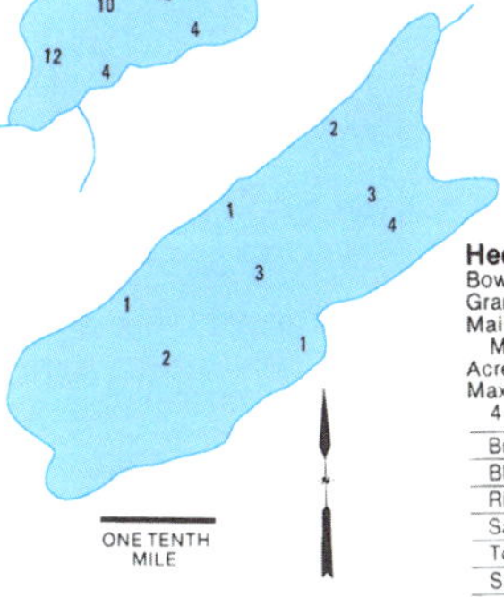

Hedgehog Pond

Bowdoin College
Grant West
Maine Atlas
Map 41, D-4, D-5
Acres: 40
Max. Depth:
4 feet

BrT		LmB	
BkT	✓	SmB	
RbT		WhP	
Sal		Csk	
Tog		WhF	
Smt		Pic	

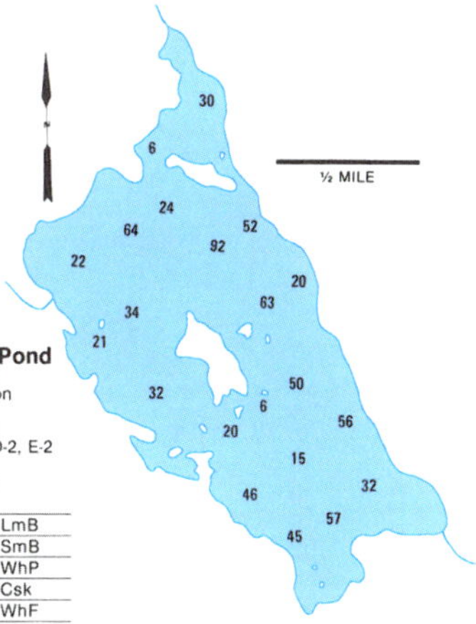

Houston Pond

T7 R9 NWP,
Katahdin Iron
Works Twp
Maine Atlas
Map 42, D-2, E-2
Acres: 694
Max. Depth:
92 feet

BrT		LmB	
BkT	✓	SmB	
RbT		WhP	
Sal	✓	Csk	
Tog	✓	WhF	
Smt	✓	Pic	

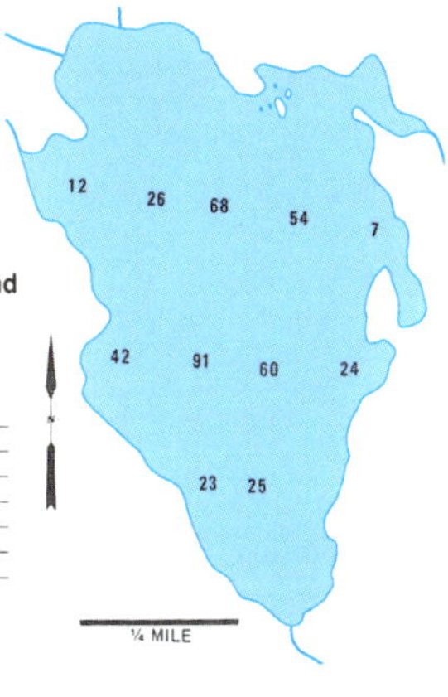

Henderson Pond

TA R11 WELS
Maine Atlas
Map 42, A-3, B-3
Acres: 195
Max. Depth:
91 feet

BrT		LmB	
BkT	✓	SmB	
RbT		WhP	
Sal		Csk	
Tog		WhF	
Smt		Pic	

High Pond

Trout Brook Twp
Maine Atlas
Map 51, A-1
Acres: 17
Max. Depth:
15 feet

BrT		LmB	
BkT	✓	SmB	
RbT		WhP	
Sal		Csk	
Tog		WhF	
Smt		Pic	

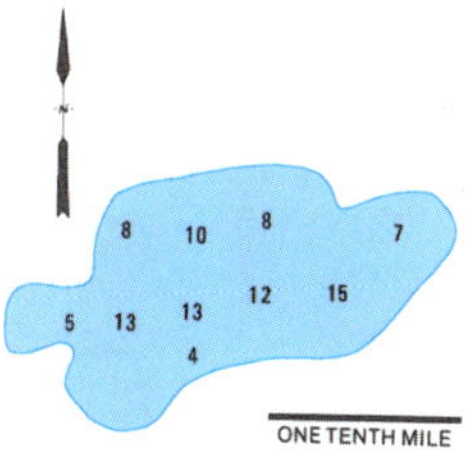

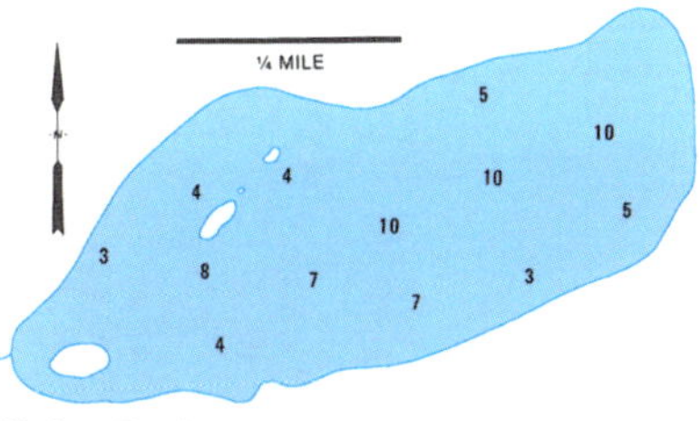

Hudson Pond

T6 R10 WELS, Maine Atlas Map 56, E-4, E-5, Map 50, A-4, A-5
Acres: 128, Max. Depth: 10 feet

BrT	BkT	RbT	Sal	Tog	Smt	LmB	SmB	WhP	Csk	WhF	Pic
	✓		✓								

Piscataquis

Hurd Pond

T2 R10 WELS
Maine Atlas
Map 50, E-4, E-5
Acres: 640
Max. Depth:
92 feet

BrT	LmB
BkT ✓	SmB
RbT	WhP
Sal	Csk
Tog ✓	WhF
Smt	Pic

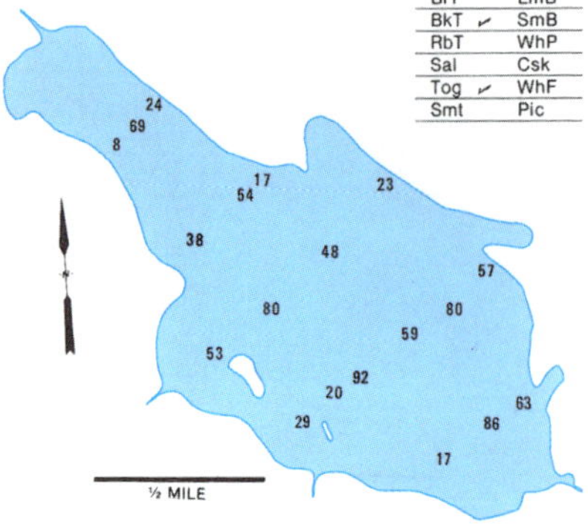

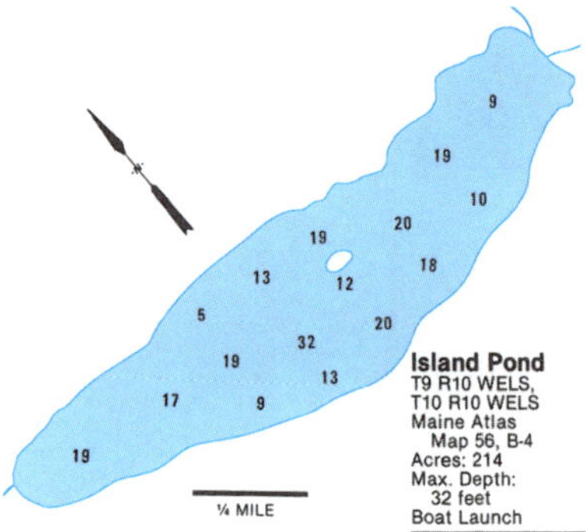

Island Pond

T9 R10 WELS,
T10 R10 WELS
Maine Atlas
Map 56, B-4
Acres: 214
Max. Depth:
32 feet
Boat Launch

BrT	LmB
BkT ✓	SmB
RbT	WhP
Sal ✓	Csk
Tog	WhF
Smt ✓	Pic

Indian Pond

Bowdoin College
Grant West
Maine Atlas
Map 41, D-4
Acres: 70
Max. Depth:
15 feet

BrT	LmB
BkT ✓	SmB
RbT	WhP
Sal	Csk
Tog	WhF
Smt ✓	Pic

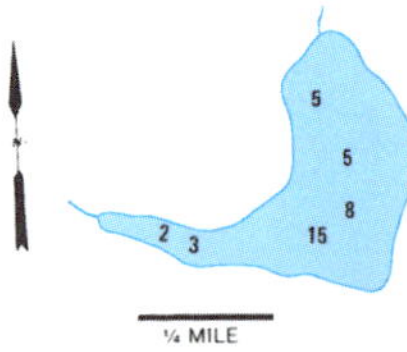

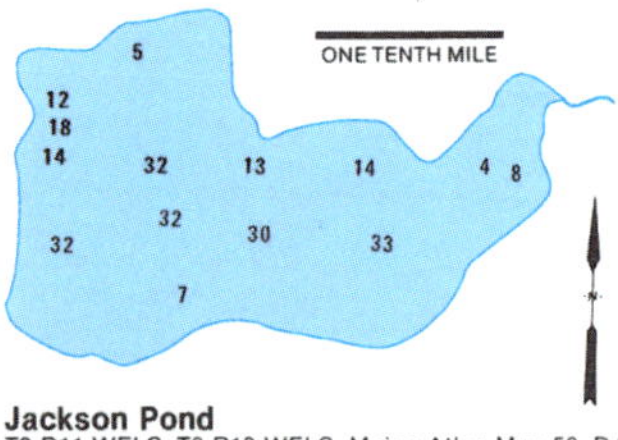

Jackson Pond

T3 R11 WELS, T3 R10 WELS, Maine Atlas Map 50, D-3, D-4
Acres: 23, Max. Depth: 33 feet

BrT	BkT	RbT	Sal	Tog	Smt	LmB	SmB	WhP	Csk	WhF	Pic
	✓										

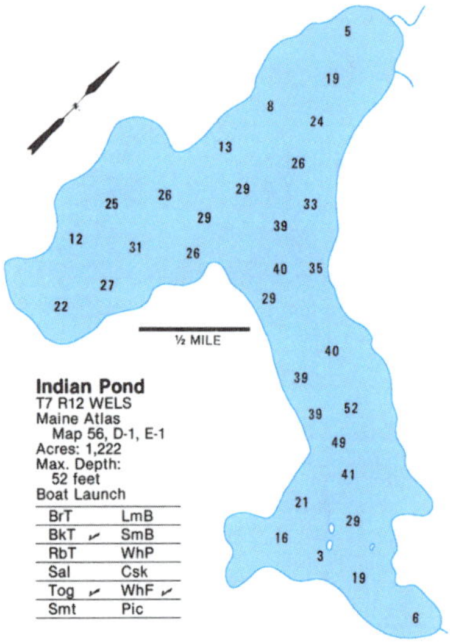

Indian Pond

T7 R12 WELS
Maine Atlas
Map 56, D-1, E-1
Acres: 1,222
Max. Depth:
52 feet
Boat Launch

BrT	LmB
BkT ✓	SmB
RbT	WhP
Sal	Csk
Tog ✓	WhF ✓
Smt	Pic

Jaquith Pond

Brownville
Maine Atlas
Map 42, E-5
Acres: 45
Max. Depth:
20 feet

BrT	LmB
BkT	SmB
RbT	WhP
Sal	Csk
Tog	WhF
Smt	Pic ✓

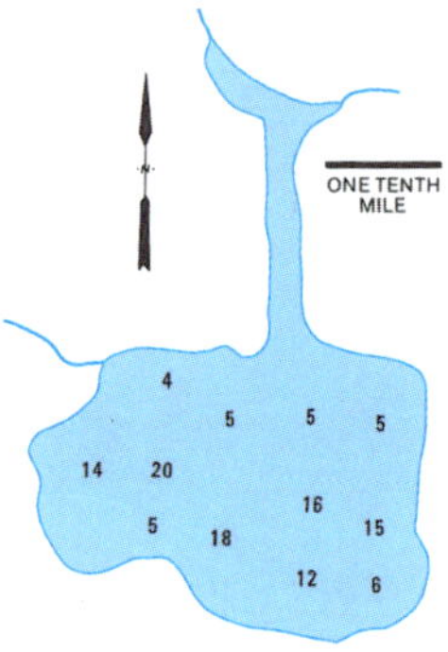

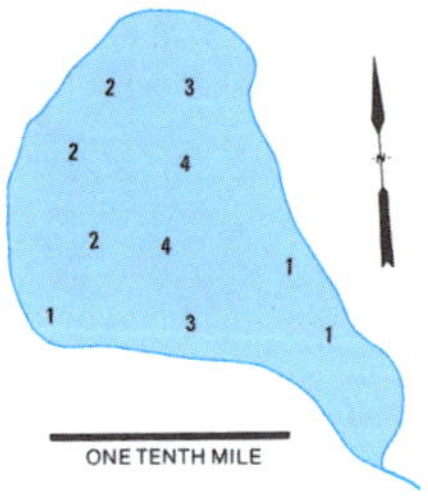

Jewett Pond

Spencer Bay Twp
Maine Atlas
Map 41, A-3, A-4
Acres: 13
Max. Depth:
4 feet

BrT	LmB
BkT ✓	SmB
RbT	WhP
Sal	Csk
Tog	WhF
Smt	Pic

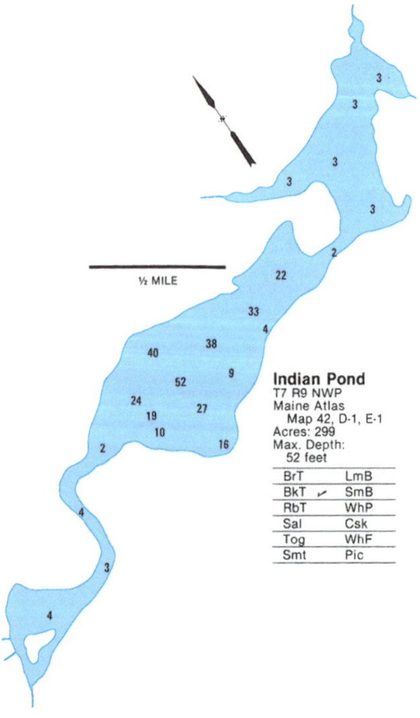

Indian Pond

T7 R9 NWP
Maine Atlas
Map 42, D-1, E-1
Acres: 299
Max. Depth:
52 feet

BrT	LmB
BkT ✓	SmB
RbT	WhP
Sal	Csk
Tog	WhF
Smt	Pic

Johnson Pond

T8 R14 WELS
Maine Atlas
Map 55, D-3
Acres: 197
Max. Depth:
58 feet

BrT	LmB
BkT ✓	SmB
RbT	WhP
Sal	Csk
Tog ✓	WhF ✓
Smt	Pic

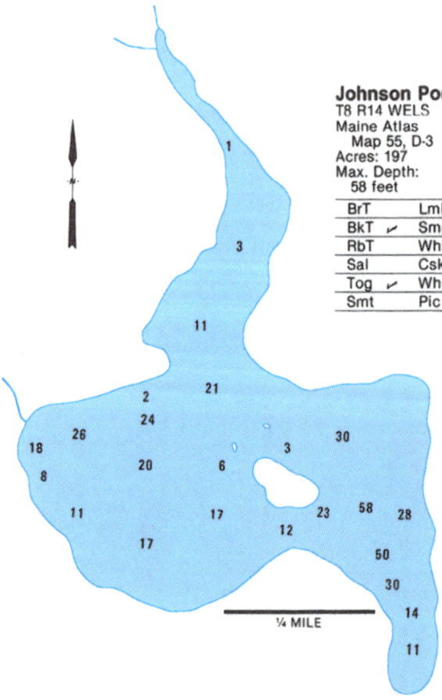

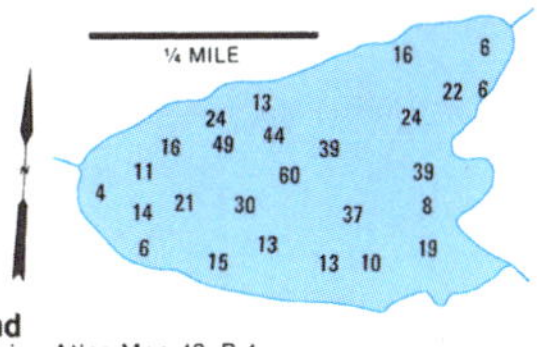

Johnston Pond

TA R10 WELS, Maine Atlas Map 42, B-4
Acres: 59, Max. Depth: 60 feet

BrT	BkT	RbT	Sal	Tog	Smt	LmB	SmB	WhP	Csk	WhF	Pic
	✓										

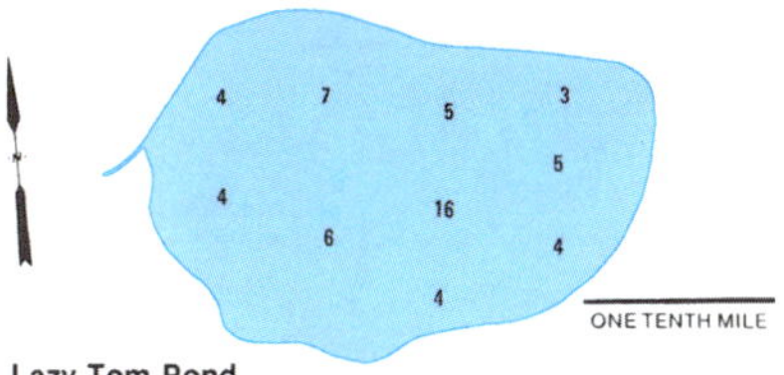

Lazy Tom Pond

T1 R13 WELS, Maine Atlas Map 41, A-4
Acres: 17, Max. Depth: 16 feet

BrT	BkT	RbT	Sal	Tog	Smt	LmB	SmB	WhP	Csk	WhF	Pic
	✓										

Jo-Mary Pond

TB R10 WELS
Maine Atlas
Map 42, C-4
Acres: 38
Max. Depth:
11 feet

BrT		LmB
BkT	✓	SmB
RbT		WhP
Sal		Csk
Tog		WhF
Smt		Pic

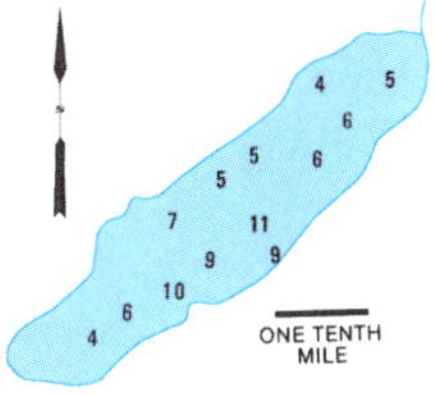

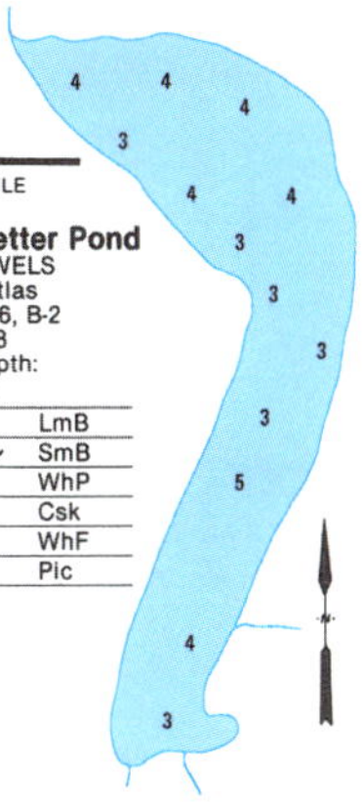

Leadbetter Pond

T9 R11 WELS
Maine Atlas
Map 56, B-2
Acres: 98
Max. Depth:
5 feet

BrT		LmB
BkT	✓	SmB
RbT		WhP
Sal		Csk
Tog		WhF
Smt		Pic

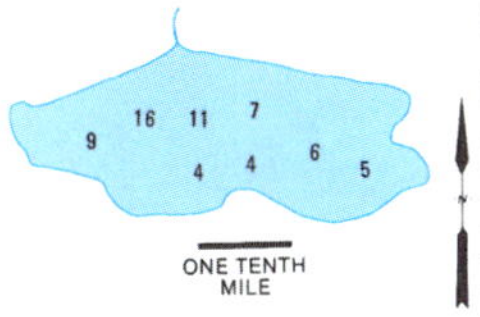

Juniper Knee Pond

Elliotsville Twp
Maine Atlas
Map 41, E-4
Acres: 32
Max. Depth:
16 feet

BrT		LmB
BkT	✓	SmB
RbT		WhP
Sal		Csk
Tog		WhF
Smt		Pic

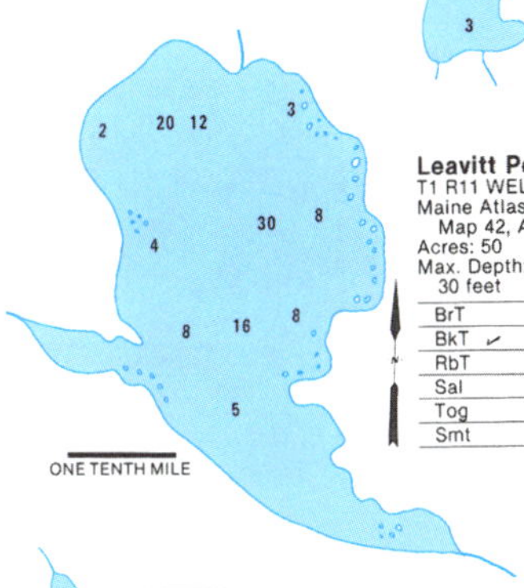

Leavitt Pond

T1 R11 WELS
Maine Atlas
Map 42, A-3
Acres: 50
Max. Depth:
30 feet

BrT		LmB
BkT	✓	SmB
RbT		WhP
Sal		Csk
Tog		WhF
Smt		Pic

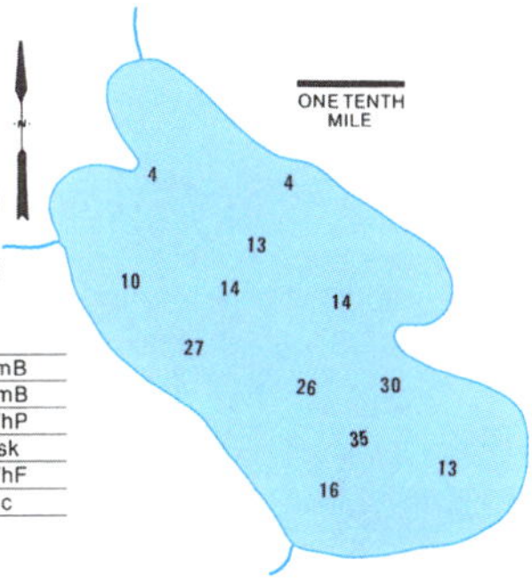

Kelly Pond

T2 R12 WELS
Maine Atlas
Map 50, E-2
Acres: 64
Max. Depth:
35 feet

BrT		LmB
BkT	✓	SmB
RbT		WhP
Sal		Csk
Tog		WhF
Smt		Pic

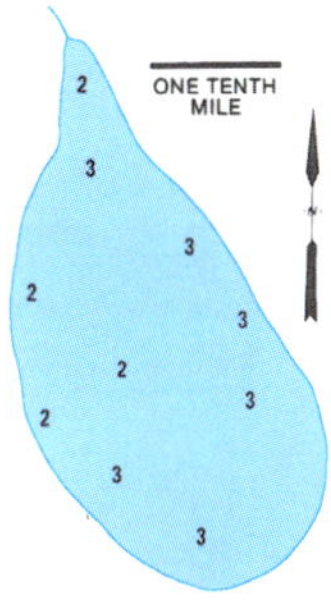

Leonard Pond

T10 R9 WELS
Maine Atlas
Map 57, A-1
Acres: 38
Max. Depth:
3 feet

BrT		LmB
BkT	✓	SmB
RbT		WhP
Sal		Csk
Tog		WhF
Smt		Pic

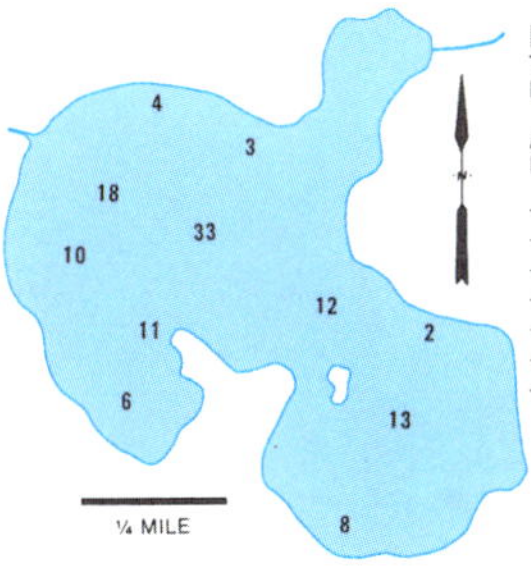

Kidney Pond

T3 R10 WELS
Maine Atlas
Map 50, D-4
Acres: 96
Max. Depth:
33 feet

BrT		LmB
BkT	✓	SmB
RbT		WhP
Sal		Csk
Tog		WhF
Smt		Pic

Lily Pad Pond

T3 R10 WELS
Maine Atlas
Map 50, D-4
Acres: 20
Max. Depth:
15 feet

BrT		LmB
BkT	✓	SmB
RbT		WhP
Sal		Csk
Tog		WhF
Smt		Pic

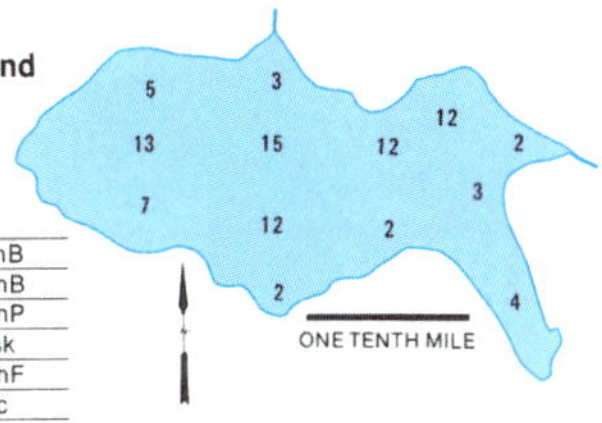

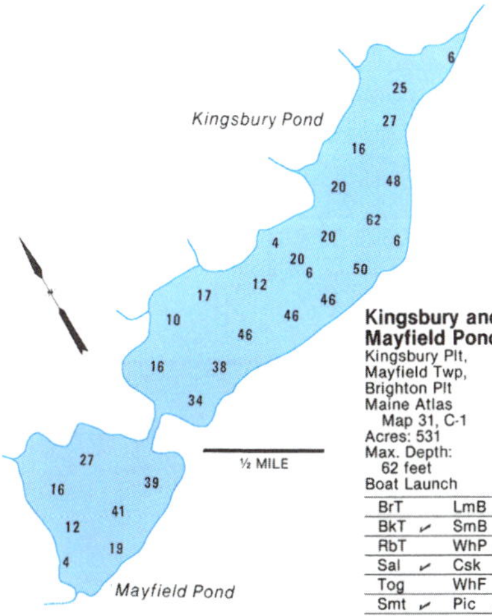

Kingsbury and Mayfield Ponds

Kingsbury Plt,
Mayfield Twp,
Brighton Plt
Maine Atlas
Map 31, C-1
Acres: 531
Max. Depth:
62 feet
Boat Launch

BrT		LmB	
BkT	✓	SmB	
RbT		WhP	✓
Sal	✓	Csk	
Tog		WhF	
Smt	✓	Pic	✓

Comments: Splake.

Little Beaver Pond

T7 R9 WELS
Maine Atlas
Map 57, D-1
Acres: 122
Max. Depth:
25 feet

BrT		LmB
BkT	✓	SmB
RbT		WhP
Sal	✓	Csk
Tog		WhF
Smt		Pic

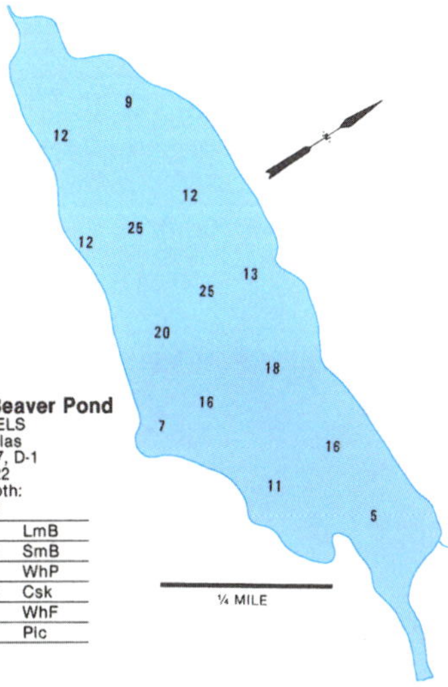

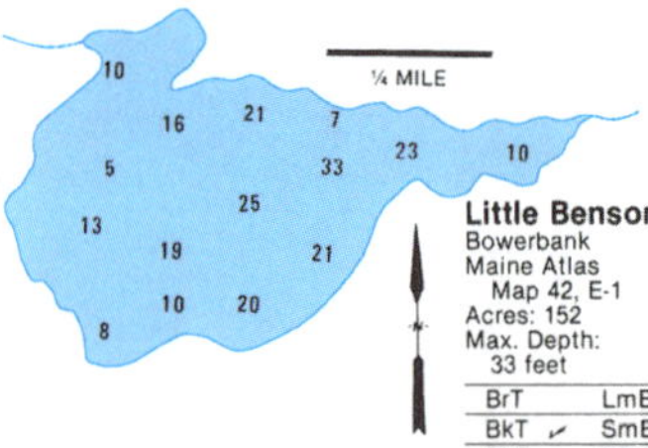

Little Benson Pond

Bowerbank
Maine Atlas
Map 42, E-1
Acres: 152
Max. Depth:
33 feet

BrT		LmB	
BkT	✓	SmB	
RbT		WhP	
Sal		Csk	
Tog		WhF	
Smt		Pic	

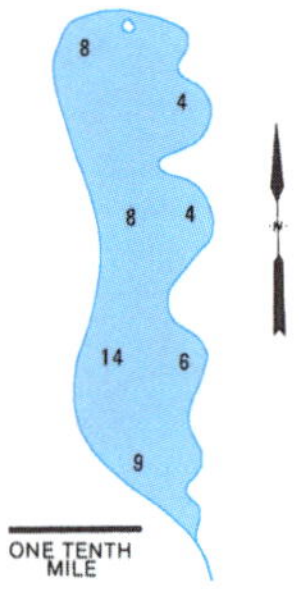

Little Houston Pond

Katahdin Iron Works Twp
Maine Atlas
Map 42, D-2
Acres: 27
Max. Depth:
14 feet

BrT		LmB	
BkT	✓	SmB	
RbT		WhP	
Sal		Csk	
Tog		WhF	
Smt		Pic	

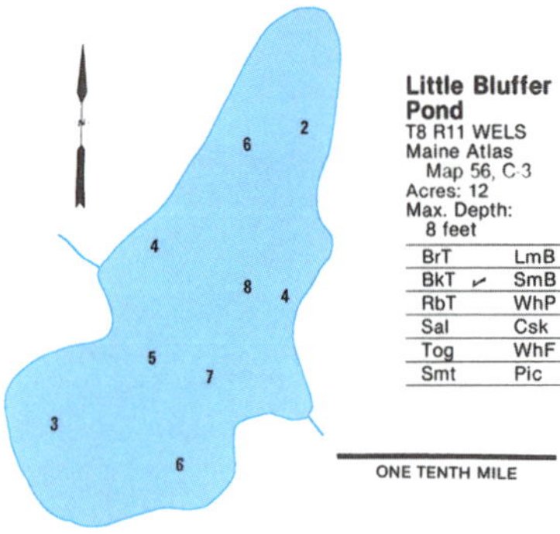

Little Bluffer Pond

T8 R11 WELS
Maine Atlas
Map 56, C-3
Acres: 12
Max. Depth:
8 feet

BrT		LmB	
BkT	✓	SmB	
RbT		WhP	
Sal		Csk	
Tog		WhF	
Smt		Pic	

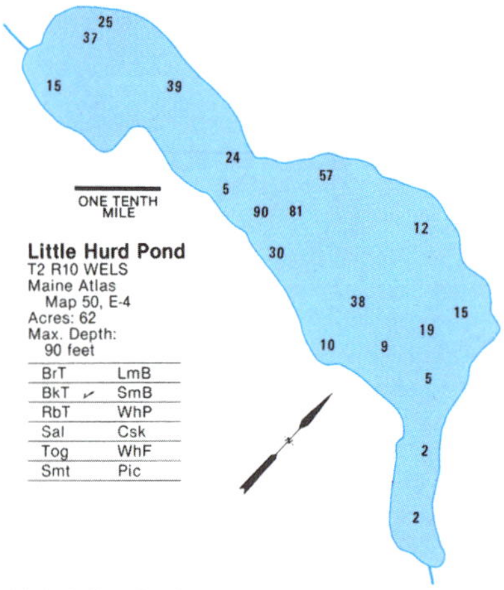

Little Hurd Pond

T2 R10 WELS
Maine Atlas
Map 50, E-4
Acres: 62
Max. Depth:
90 feet

BrT		LmB	
BkT	✓	SmB	
RbT		WhP	
Sal		Csk	
Tog		WhF	
Smt		Pic	

Little Carpenter Pond

T7 R11 WELS
Maine Atlas
Map 56, D-3
Acres: 6
Max. Depth:
12 feet

BrT		LmB	
BkT	✓	SmB	
RbT		WhP	
Sal		Csk	
Tog		WhF	
Smt		Pic	

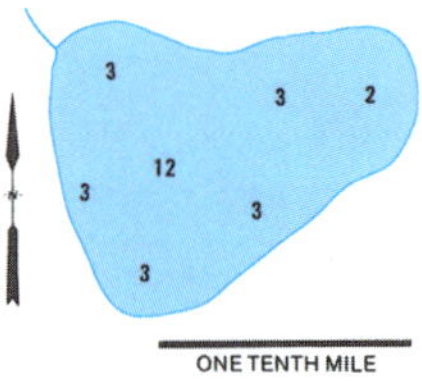

Little Indian Pond

T7 R12 WELS, Maine Atlas Map 56, D-2
Acres: 117, Max. Depth: 7 feet

BrT	BkT	RbT	Sal	Tog	Smt	LmB	SmB	WhP	Csk	WhF	Pic
	✓										

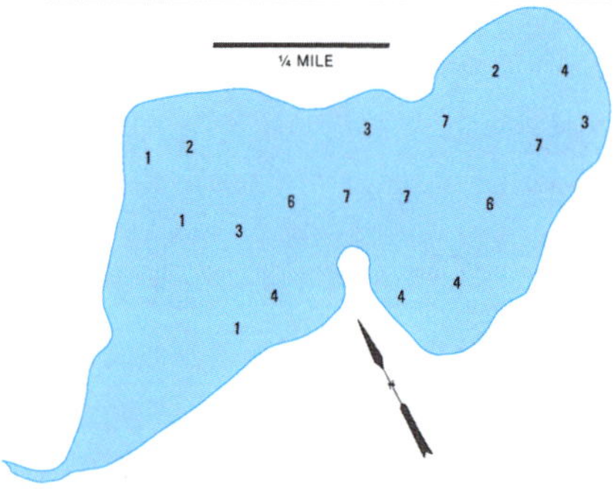

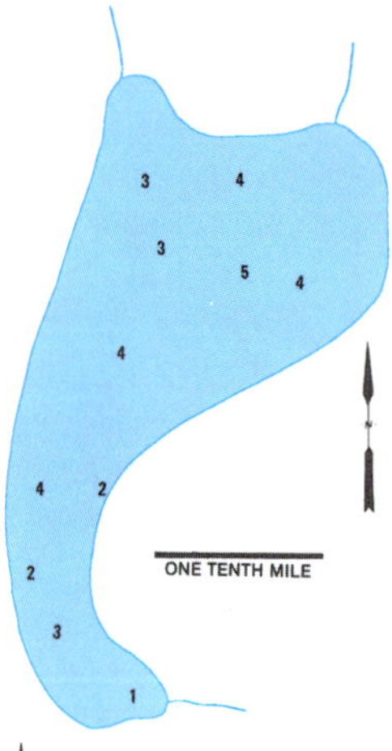

Little Churchill Pond

T10 R13 WELS
Maine Atlas
Map 55, A-5
Acres: 25
Max. Depth:
5 feet

BrT		LmB	
BkT	✓	SmB	
RbT		WhP	
Sal		Csk	
Tog		WhF	
Smt		Pic	

Little Lobster Lake

Lobster Twp
Maine Atlas
Map 49, D-3, D-4
Acres: 230
Max. Depth:
36 feet

BrT		LmB	
BkT	✓	SmB	
RbT		WhP	✓
Sal	✓	Csk	
Tog		WhF	
Smt	✓	Pic	

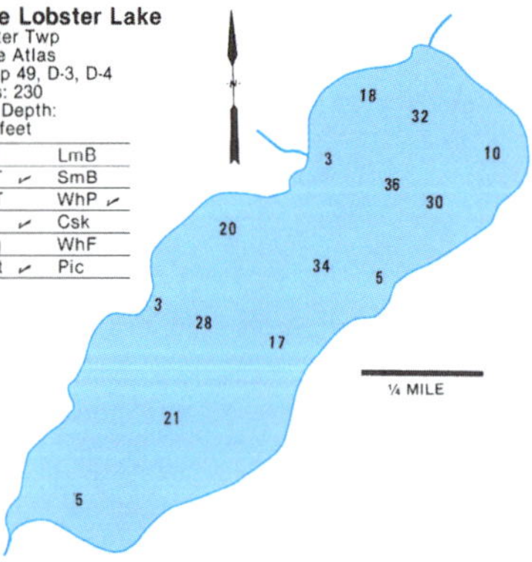

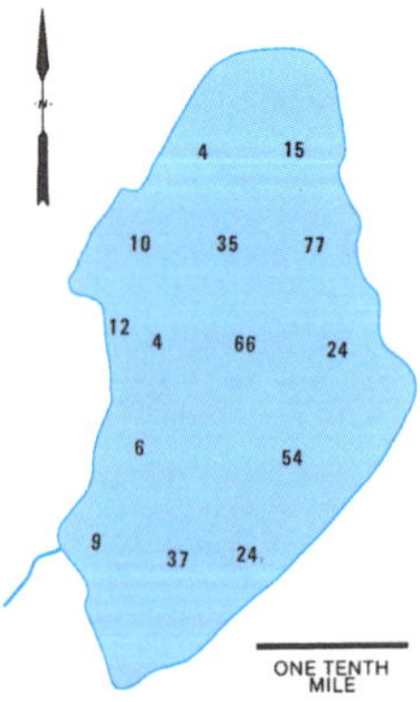

Little Frost Pond

T3 R12 WELS
Maine Atlas
Map 50, C-2, D-2
Acres: 35
Max. Depth:
77 feet

BrT		LmB	
BkT	✓	SmB	
RbT		WhP	
Sal		Csk	
Tog		WhF	
Smt		Pic	

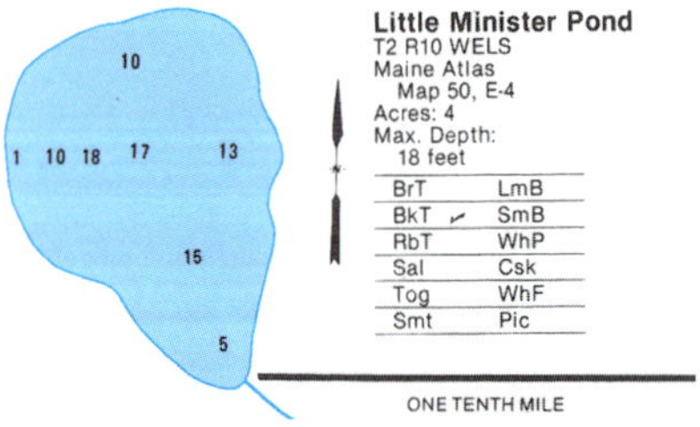

Little Minister Pond

T2 R10 WELS
Maine Atlas
Map 50, E-4
Acres: 4
Max. Depth:
18 feet

BrT		LmB	
BkT	✓	SmB	
RbT		WhP	
Sal		Csk	
Tog		WhF	
Smt		Pic	

Little Greenwood Pond

Elliotsville Twp
Maine Atlas
Map 41, E-4, E-5
Acres: 61
Max. Depth:
38 feet

BrT		LmB	
BkT	✓	SmB	
RbT		WhP	
Sal		Csk	
Tog		WhF	
Smt	✓	Pic	

Comments: Splake.

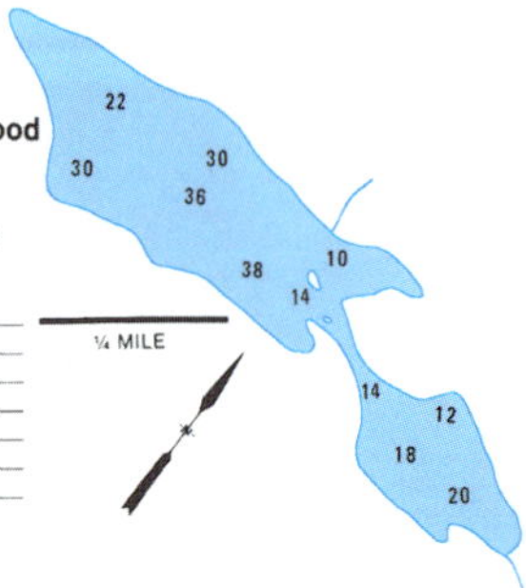

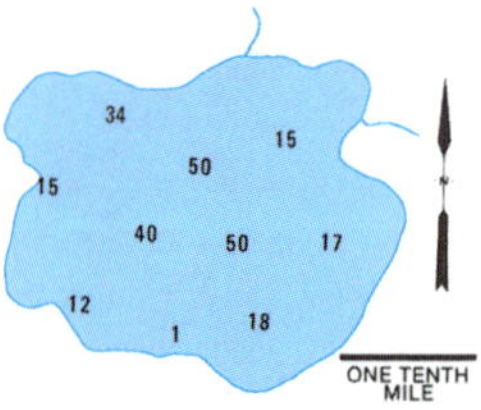

Little Moose Pond

Moosehead Junction Twp
Maine Atlas
Map 41, D-1
Acres: 25
Max. Depth:
50 feet

BrT		LmB	
BkT	✓	SmB	
RbT		WhP	
Sal		Csk	
Tog		WhF	
Smt		Pic	

Little Moxie Pond

East Moxie Twp
Maine Atlas
Map 31, A-1
Acres: 73
Max. Depth:
9 feet

BrT	LmB
BkT ✓	SmB
RbT	WhP
Sal	Csk
Tog	WhF
Smt	Pic

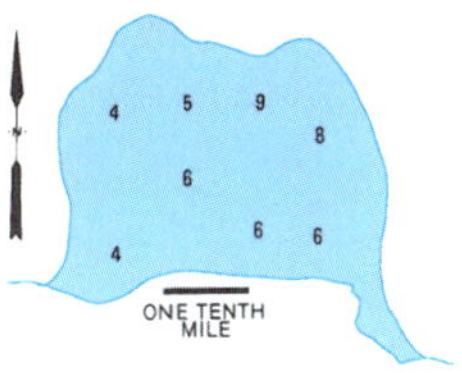

Little Rocky Pond

T3 R10 WELS
Maine Atlas
Map 50, C-4, D-4
Acres: 16
Max. Depth:
22 feet

BrT	LmB
BkT ✓	SmB
RbT	WhP
Sal	Csk
Tog	WhF
Smt	Pic

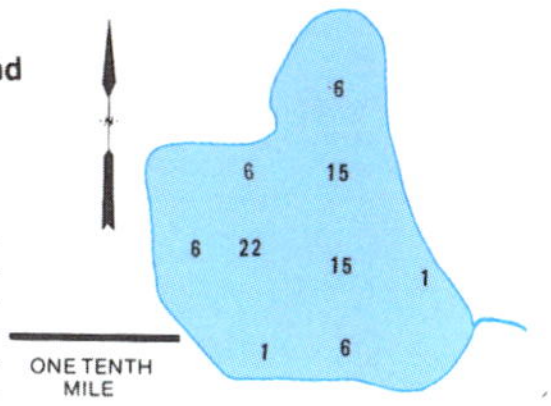

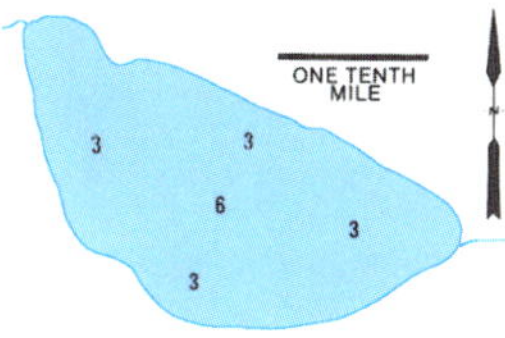

Little Mud Pond

Greenville
Maine Atlas
Map 41, C-3
Acres: 13
Max. Depth:
6 feet

BrT	LmB
BkT ✓	SmB
RbT	WhP
Sal	Csk
Tog	WhF
Smt	Pic

Little Sourdnahunk Lake

T5 R11 WELS
Maine Atlas
Map 50, B-3
Acres: 102
Max. Depth:
15 feet

BrT	LmB
BkT ✓	SmB
RbT	WhP
Sal	Csk
Tog	WhF
Smt	Pic

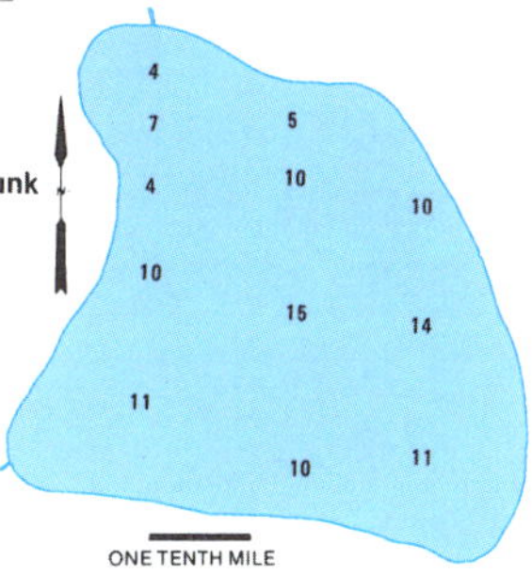

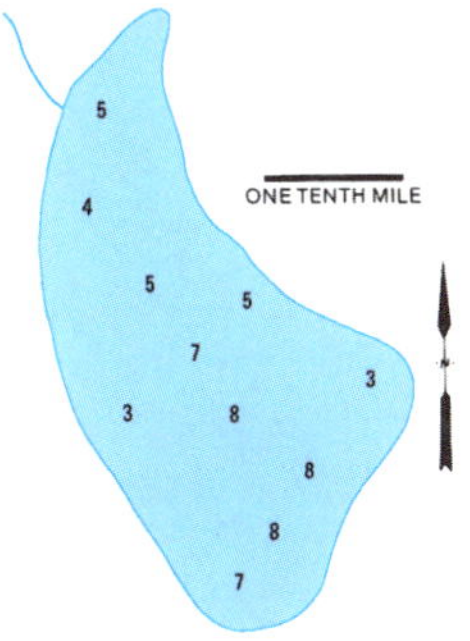

Little Pillsbury Pond

T8 R11 WELS
Maine Atlas
Map 56, C-3, D-3
Acres: 45
Max. Depth:
8 feet
Boat Launch

BrT	LmB
BkT ✓	SmB
RbT	WhP
Sal	Csk
Tog	WhF
Smt	Pic

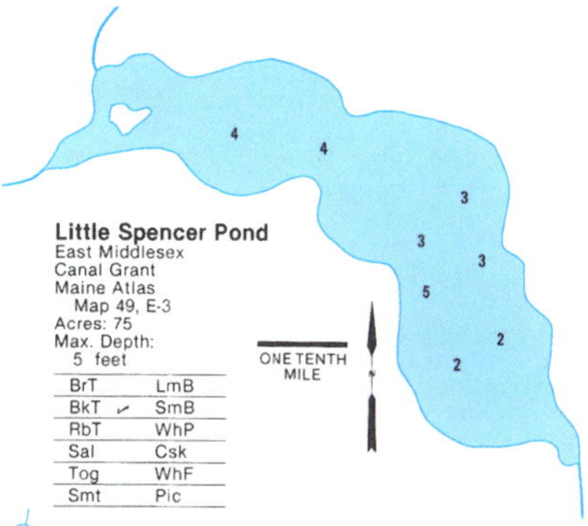

Little Spencer Pond

East Middlesex
Canal Grant
Maine Atlas
Map 49, E-3
Acres: 75
Max. Depth:
5 feet

BrT	LmB
BkT ✓	SmB
RbT	WhP
Sal	Csk
Tog	WhF
Smt	Pic

Little Wassataquoik Lake

T4 R10 WELS
Maine Atlas
Map 50, B-5
Acres: 10
Max. Depth:
10 feet

BrT	LmB
BkT ✓	SmB
RbT	WhP
Sal	Csk
Tog	WhF
Smt	Pic

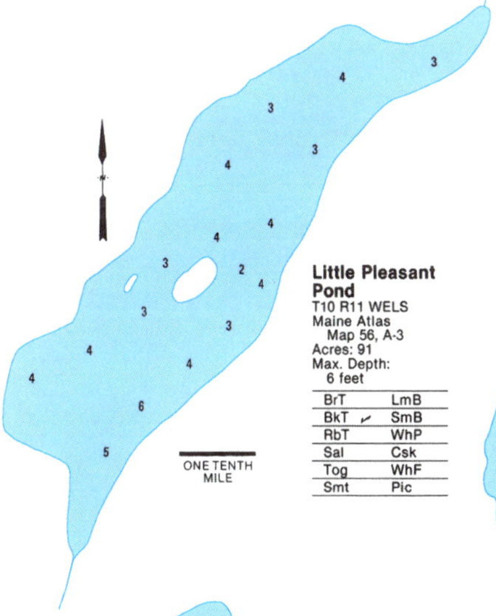

Little Pleasant Pond

T10 R11 WELS
Maine Atlas
Map 56, A-3
Acres: 91
Max. Depth:
6 feet

BrT	LmB
BkT ✓	SmB
RbT	WhP
Sal	Csk
Tog	WhF
Smt	Pic

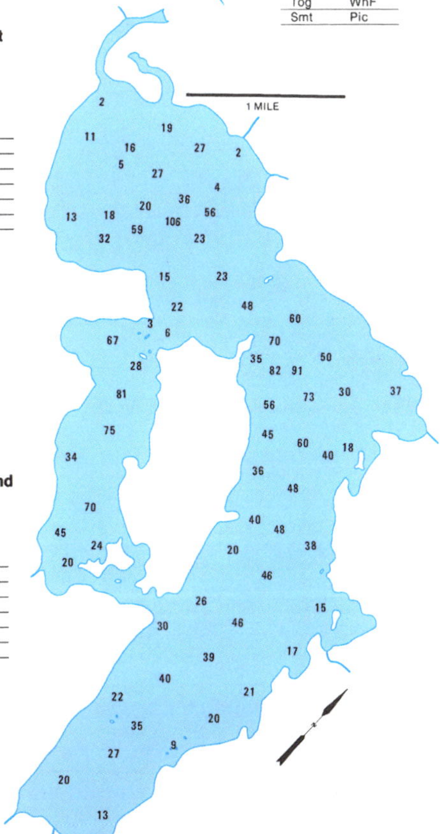

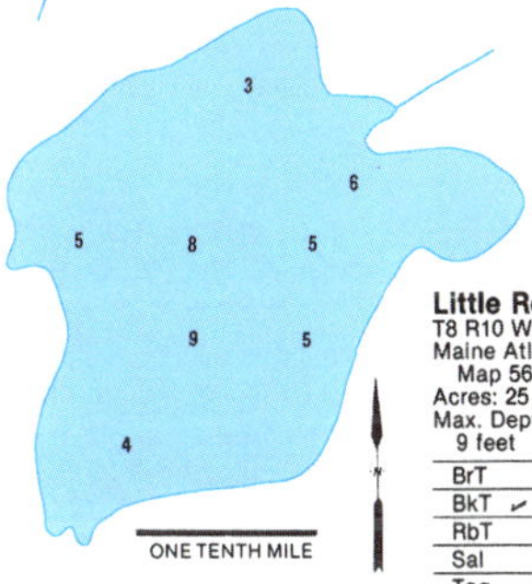

Little Reed Pond

T8 R10 WELS
Maine Atlas
Map 56, C-3 C-4
Acres: 25
Max. Depth:
9 feet

BrT	LmB
BkT ✓	SmB
RbT	WhP
Sal	Csk
Tog	WhF
Smt	Pic

Little Rocky Pond

TA R11 WELS
Maine Atlas
Map 42, B-2
Acres: 14
Max. Depth:
4 feet

BrT	LmB
BkT ✓	SmB
RbT	WhP
Sal	Csk
Tog	WhF
Smt	Pic

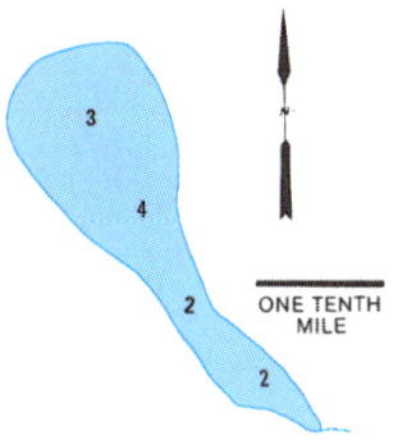

Lobster Lake

Lobster Twp, Northeast Carry Twp, TX R14 WELS,
East Middlesex Canal Grant, Maine Atlas Map 49, D-3, D-4
Acres: 3,475, Max. Depth: 106 feet

BrT	BkT	RbT	Sal	Tog	Smt	LmB	SmB	WhP	Csk	WhF	Pic
	✓		✓	✓	✓			✓	✓	✓	

Piscataquis

Long Bog
Shawtown Twp
Maine Atlas
Map 42, B-1
Acres: 10
Max. Depth:
5 feet

BrT		LmB	
BkT	✓	SmB	
RbT		WhP	
Sal		Csk	
Tog		WhF	
Smt		Pic	

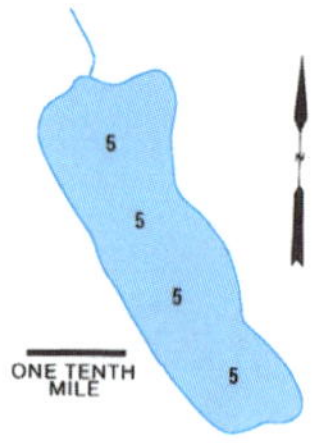

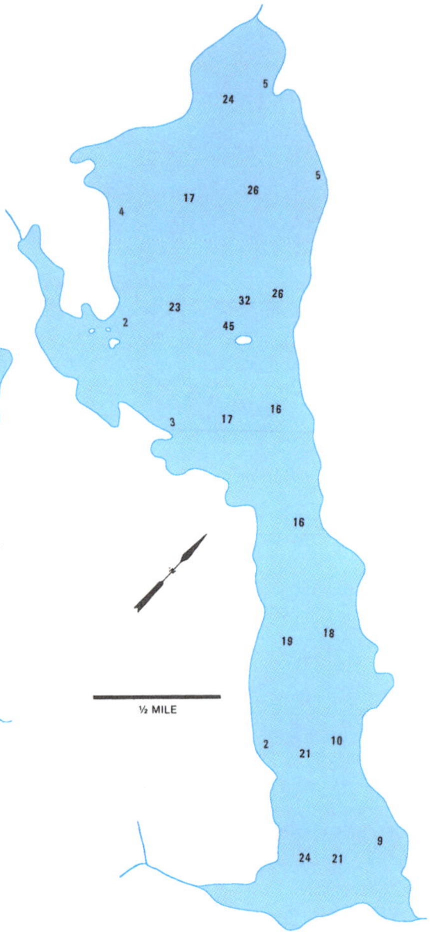

Long Pond
TA R11 WELS,
T1 R11 WELS
Maine Atlas
Map 42, A-3, B-3
Acres: 371
Max. Depth:
50 feet
Boat Launch

BrT		LmB	
BkT	✓	SmB	
RbT		WhP	
Sal		Csk	
Tog	✓	WhF	
Smt		Pic	

Comments: Splake.

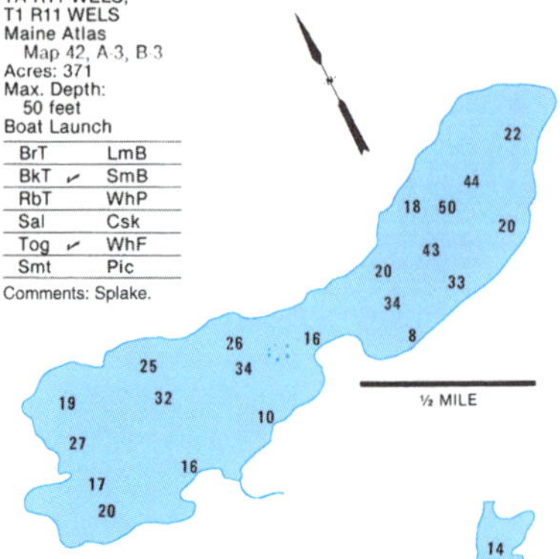

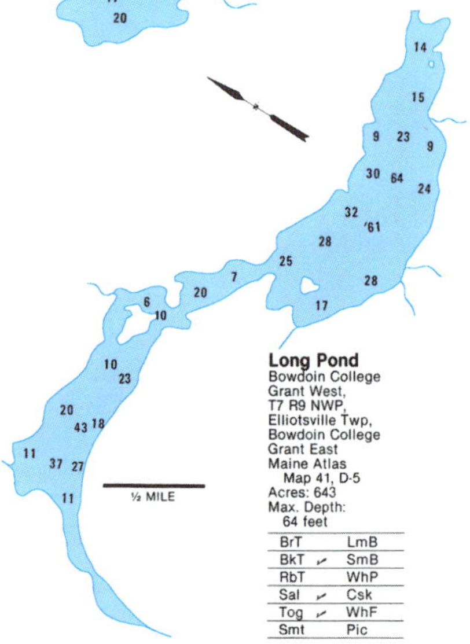

Long Pond
Bowdoin College
Grant West,
T7 R9 NWP,
Elliotsville Twp,
Bowdoin College
Grant East
Maine Atlas
Map 41, D-5
Acres: 643
Max. Depth:
64 feet

BrT		LmB	
BkT	✓	SmB	
RbT		WhP	
Sal	✓	Csk	
Tog	✓	WhF	
Smt		Pic	

Loon Lake
T6 R15 WELS, Maine Atlas Map 49, A-2
Acres: 1,140, Max. Depth: 45 feet

BrT	BkT	RbT	Sal	Tog	Smt	LmB	SmB	WhP	Csk	WhF	Pic
	✓		✓					✓		✓	

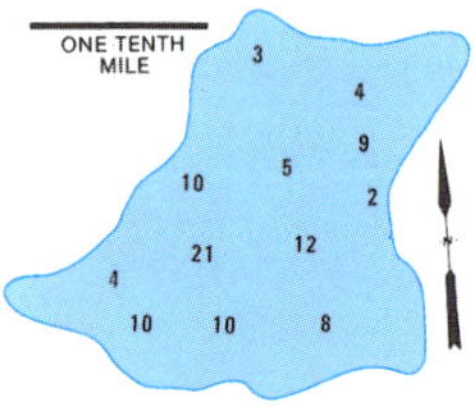

Lost Pond
T3 R10 WELS
Maine Atlas
Map 50, D-4
Acres: 30
Max. Depth:
21 feet

BrT		LmB	
BkT	✓	SmB	
RbT		WhP	
Sal		Csk	
Tog		WhF	
Smt		Pic	

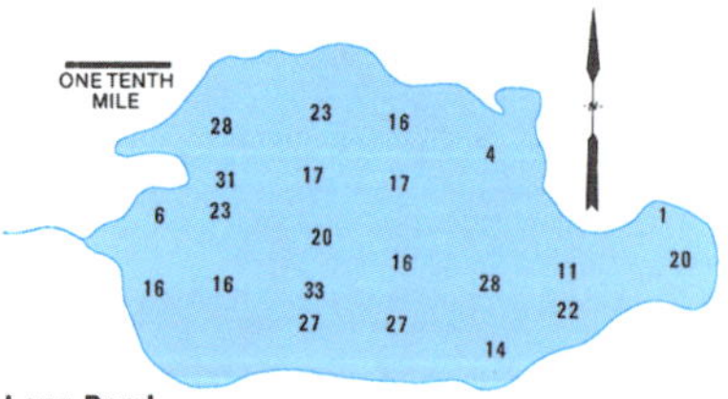

Long Pond
Trout Brook Twp, Maine Atlas Map 51, A-1
Acres: 70, Max. Depth: 33 feet

BrT	BkT	RbT	Sal	Tog	Smt	LmB	SmB	WhP	Csk	WhF	Pic
	✓				✓						

Lower Bean Pond
Rainbow Twp
Maine Atlas
Map 50, E-2
Acres: 37
Max. Depth:
30 feet

BrT		LmB	
BkT	✓	SmB	
RbT		WhP	
Sal		Csk	
Tog		WhF	
Smt		Pic	

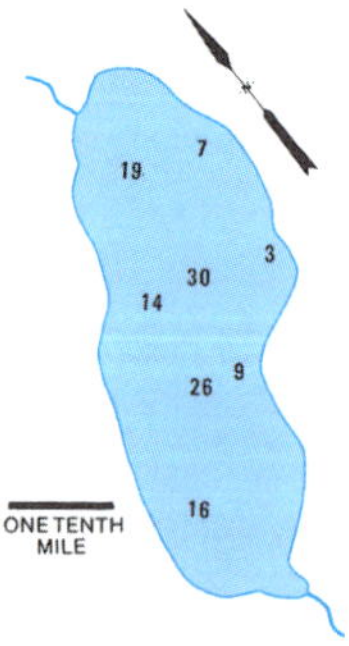

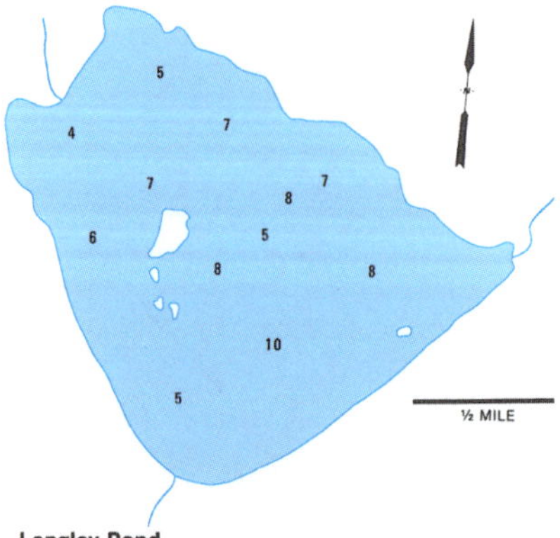

Longley Pond
T6 R13 WELS, Maine Atlas Map 49, A-4
Acres: 749, Max. Depth: 10 feet

BrT	BkT	RbT	Sal	Tog	Smt	LmB	SmB	WhP	Csk	WhF	Pic
	✓							✓			

Lower Ellis Pond
T7 R14 WELS
Maine Atlas
Map 55, D-3, D-4
Acres: 77
Max. Depth:
6 feet

BrT		LmB	
BkT	✓	SmB	
RbT		WhP	
Sal		Csk	
Tog		WhF	
Smt		Pic	

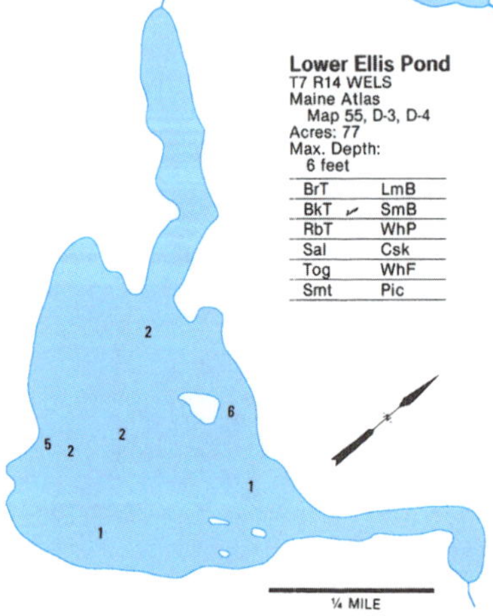

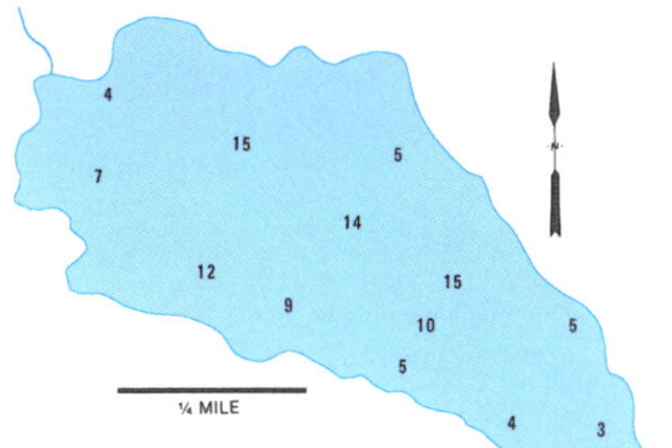

Lower Fowler Pond

Trout Brook Twp, Maine Atlas Map 51, A-1
Acres: 64, Max. Depth: 15 feet

BrT	BkT	RbT	Sal	Tog	Smt	LmB	SmB	WhP	Csk	WhF	Pic
	✓										

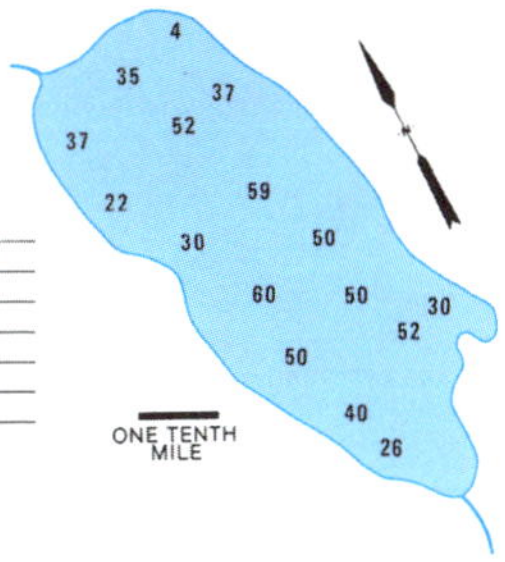

Lower South Branch Pond

T5 R9 WELS
Maine Atlas Map 51, A-1
Acres: 93
Max. Depth: 60 feet

BrT		LmB	
BkT	✓	SmB	
RbT		WhP	
Sal		Csk	
Tog		WhF	
Smt		Pic	

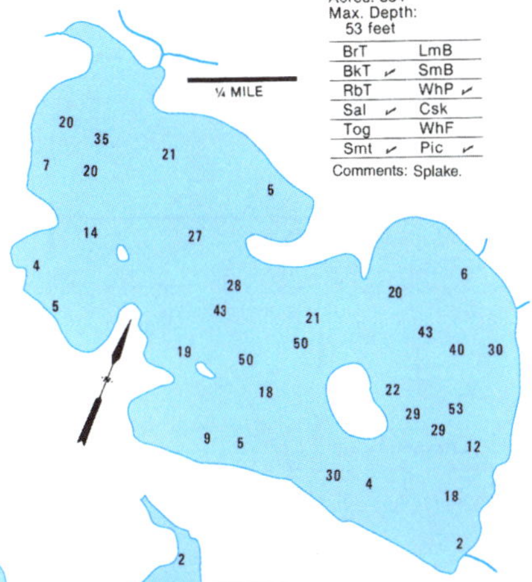

Lower Togue Pond

T2 R9 WELS
Maine Atlas Map 51, E-1
Acres: 384
Max. Depth: 53 feet

BrT		LmB	
BkT	✓	SmB	
RbT		WhP	✓
Sal	✓	Csk	
Tog		WhF	
Smt	✓	Pic	✓

Comments: Splake.

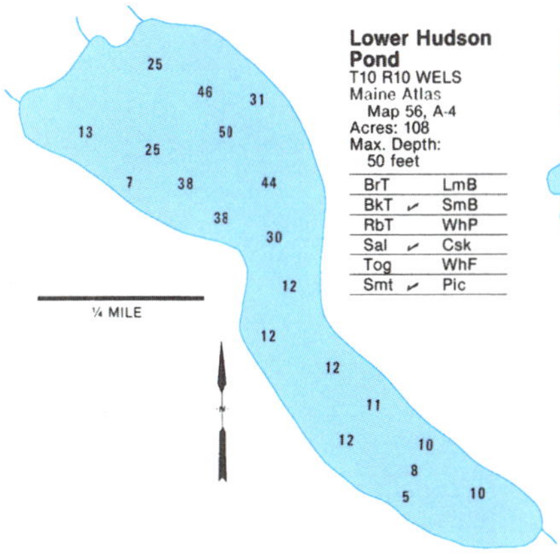

Lower Hudson Pond

T10 R10 WELS
Maine Atlas Map 56, A-4
Acres: 108
Max. Depth: 50 feet

BrT		LmB	
BkT	✓	SmB	
RbT		WhP	
Sal	✓	Csk	
Tog		WhF	
Smt	✓	Pic	

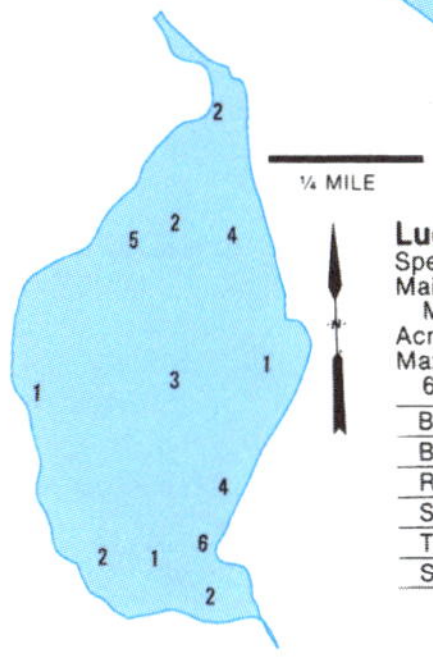

Lucky Pond

Spencer Bay Twp
Maine Atlas Map 41, A-2
Acres: 93
Max. Depth: 6 feet

BrT		LmB	
BkT	✓	SmB	
RbT		WhP	
Sal		Csk	
Tog		WhF	
Smt		Pic	

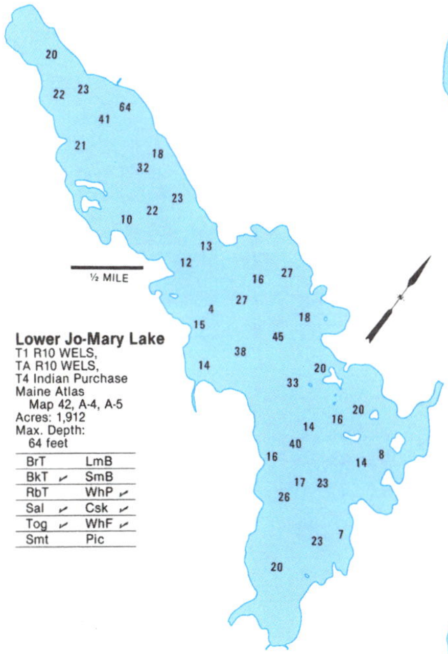

Lower Jo-Mary Lake

T1 R10 WELS, TA R10 WELS, T4 Indian Purchase
Maine Atlas Map 42, A-4, A-5
Acres: 1,912
Max. Depth: 64 feet

BrT		LmB	
BkT	✓	SmB	
RbT		WhP	✓
Sal	✓	Csk	✓
Tog	✓	WhF	✓
Smt		Pic	

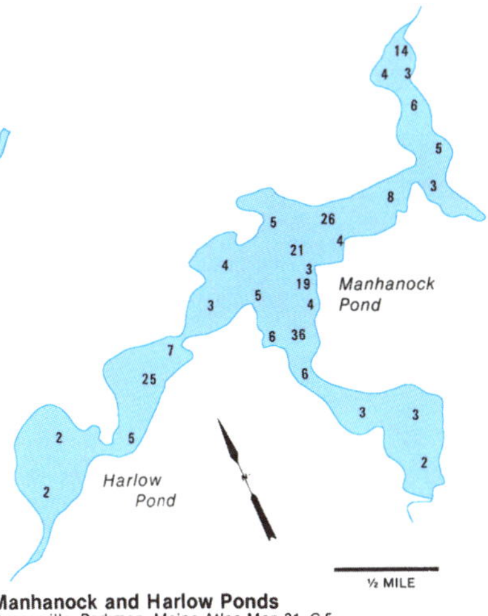

Manhanock and Harlow Ponds

Sangerville, Parkman, Maine Atlas Map 31, C-5
Acres: 595, Max. Depth: 36 feet, Boat Launch

BrT	BkT	RbT	Sal	Tog	Smt	LmB	SmB	WhP	Csk	WhF	Pic
	✓			✓				✓			

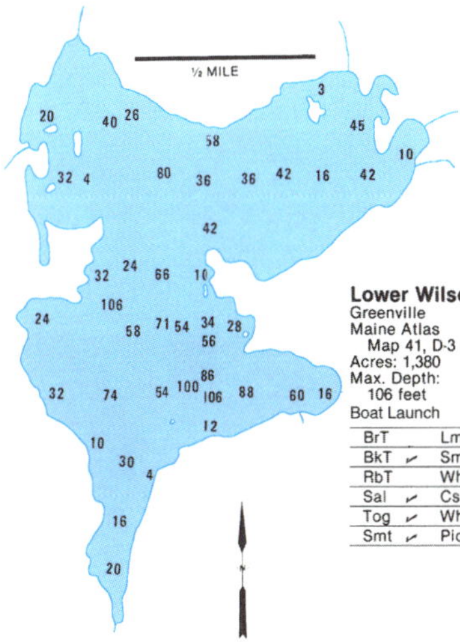

Lower Wilson Pond

Greenville
Maine Atlas Map 41, D-3
Acres: 1,380
Max. Depth: 106 feet
Boat Launch

BrT		LmB	
BkT	✓	SmB	
RbT		WhP	
Sal	✓	Csk	✓
Tog	✓	WhF	
Smt	✓	Pic	

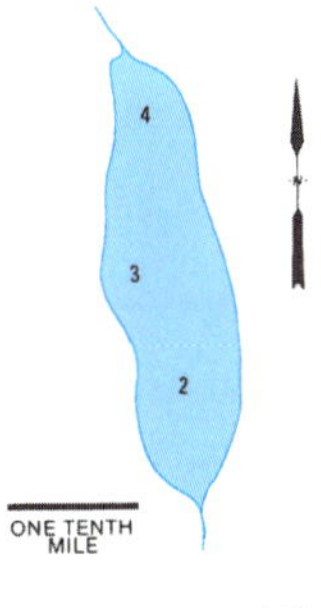

Marble Pond

Blanchard Plt
Maine Atlas Map 31, B-1
Acres: 15
Max. Depth: 4 feet

BrT		LmB	
BkT	✓	SmB	
RbT		WhP	
Sal		Csk	
Tog		WhF	
Smt		Pic	

Piscataquis

Mathews Pond

T8 R10 WELS
Maine Atlas
Map 56, D-4
Acres: 19
Max. Depth:
20 feet

BrT		LmB	
BkT	✓	SmB	
RbT		WhP	
Sal		Csk	
Tog		WhF	
Smt		Pic	

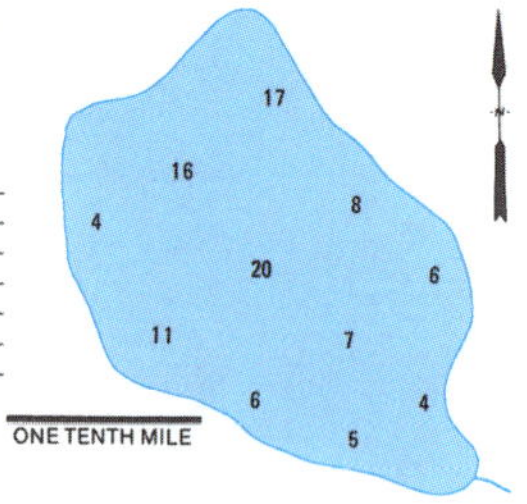

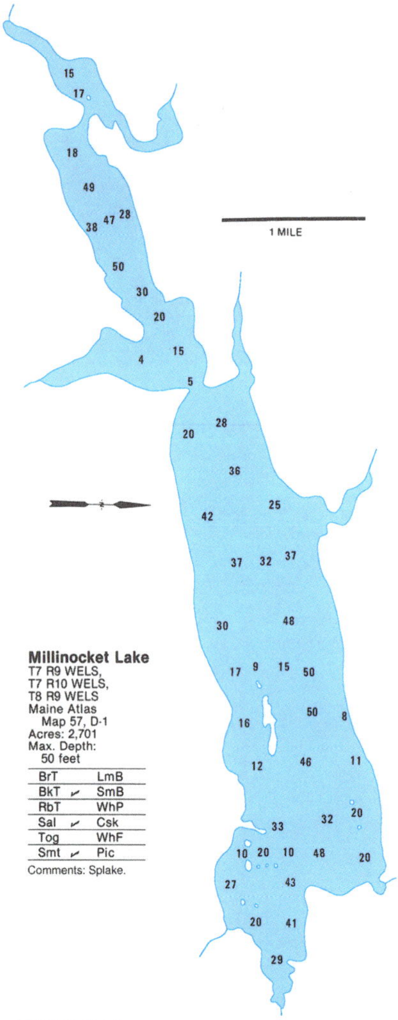

McPherson Pond

T10 R10 WELS, Maine Atlas Map 56, A-5
Acres: 77, Max. Depth: 22 feet

BrT	BkT	RbT	Sal	Tog	Smt	LmB	SmB	WhP	Csk	WhF	Pic
	✓										

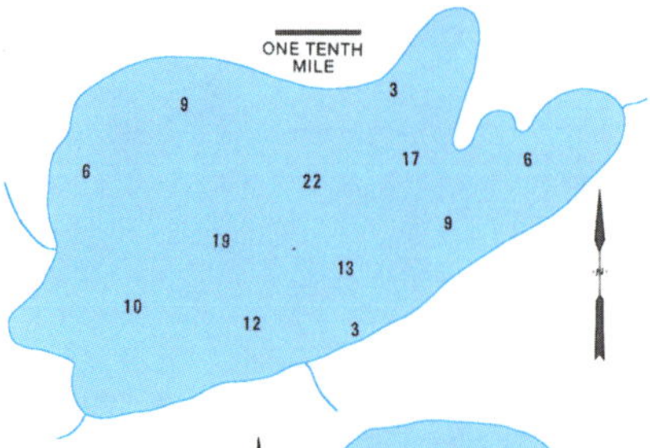

Middle Branch Pond

T5 R9 NWP
Maine Atlas
Map 42, D-3
Acres: 34
Max. Depth:
11 feet

BrT		LmB	
BkT	✓	SmB	
RbT		WhP	
Sal		Csk	
Tog		WhF	
Smt		Pic	

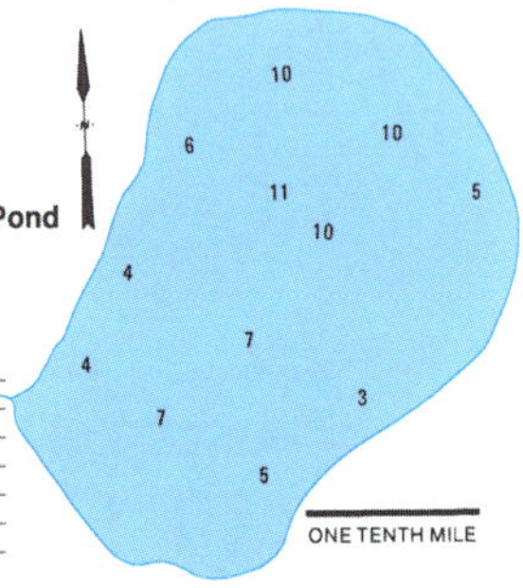

Millinocket Lake

T7 R9 WELS,
T7 R10 WELS,
T8 R9 WELS
Maine Atlas
Map 57, D-1
Acres: 2,701
Max. Depth:
50 feet

BrT		LmB	
BkT	✓	SmB	
RbT		WhP	
Sal	✓	Csk	
Tog		WhF	
Smt	✓	Pic	

Comments: Splake.

Middle Elbow Pond

T10 R10 WELS
Maine Atlas
Map 56, A-4
Acres: 52
Max. Depth:
4 feet

BrT		LmB	
BkT	✓	SmB	
RbT		WhP	
Sal		Csk	
Tog		WhF	
Smt		Pic	

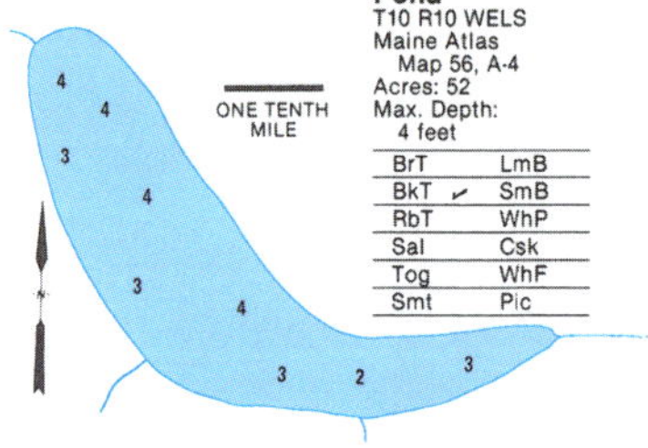

Mitchell Pond

T7 R9 WELS
Maine Atlas
Map 57, E-1
Acres: 30
Max. Depth:
15 feet

BrT		LmB	
BkT	✓	SmB	
RbT		WhP	
Sal		Csk	
Tog		WhF	
Smt		Pic	

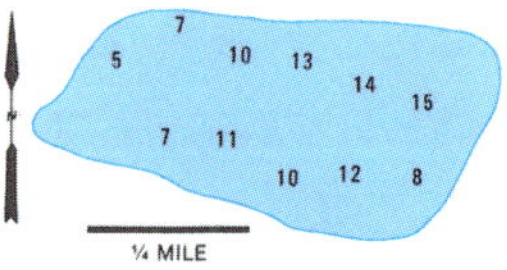

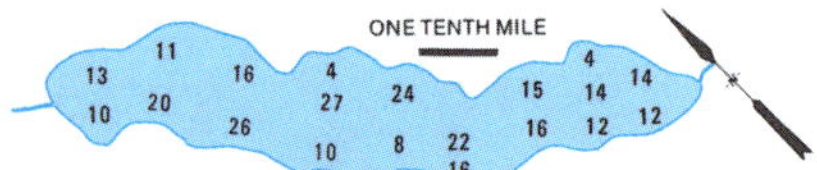

Middle Fowler Pond

T5 R9 WELS, Maine Atlas Map 51, A-1
Acres: 45, Max. Depth: 27 feet

BrT	BkT	RbT	Sal	Tog	Smt	LmB	SmB	WhP	Csk	WhF	Pic
	✓										

Monkey Pond

TA R11 WELS
Maine Atlas
Map 42, B-2
Acres: 30
Max. Depth:
10 feet

BrT		LmB	
BkT	✓	SmB	
RbT		WhP	
Sal		Csk	
Tog		WhF	
Smt		Pic	

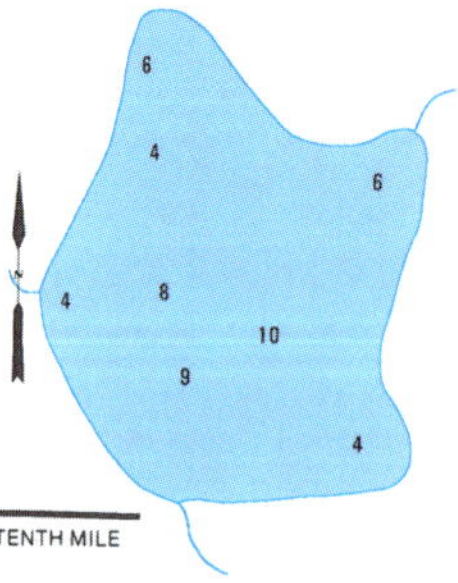

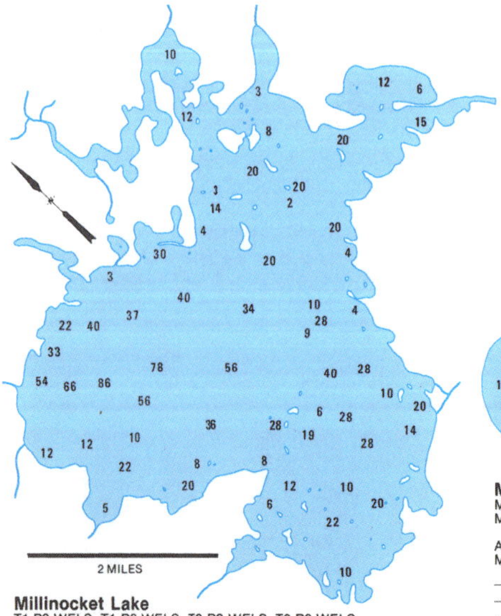

Millinocket Lake

T1 R9 WELS, T1 R8 WELS, T2 R9 WELS, T2 R8 WELS
Maine Atlas Map 51, E-2, Map 43, A-1, A-2
Acres: 8,960, Max. Depth: 86 feet, Boat Launch

BrT	BkT	RbT	Sal	Tog	Smt	LmB	SmB	WhP	Csk	WhF	Pic
	✓		✓	✓	✓			✓	✓	✓	✓

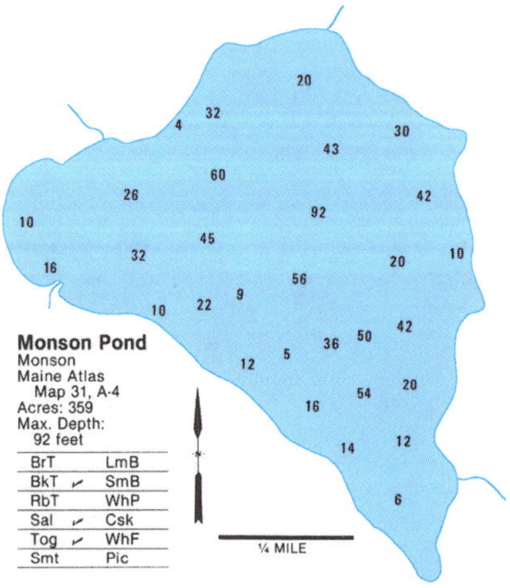

Monson Pond

Monson
Maine Atlas
Map 31, A-4
Acres: 359
Max. Depth:
92 feet

BrT		LmB	
BkT	✓	SmB	
RbT		WhP	
Sal	✓	Csk	
Tog	✓	WhF	
Smt		Pic	

Moosehead Lake

Greenville, Beaver Cove Plt, Lily Bay Twp, Spencer Bay Twp, Days Academy Grant, Kineo Twp, Northeast Carry Twp, Seboomook Twp, Big W Twp, Little W Twp, West Middlesex Canal Grant, Tomhegan Twp, Rockwood Strip, Taunton and Raynham Academy Grant, Sandbar Tract, Misery Gore, Sapling Twp, Big Moose Twp, Moosehead Junction Twp, Harfords Point Twp, Cove Point Twp
Maine Atlas
Map 40, A-5
Map 41, B-1
Map 48, E-5
Map 49, E-1
Acres: 74,890
Max. Depth: 246 feet
Boat Launch

BrT	LmB
BkT ✓	SmB
RbT	WhP
Sal ✓	Csk ✓
Tog ✓	WhF ✓
Smt ✓	Pic

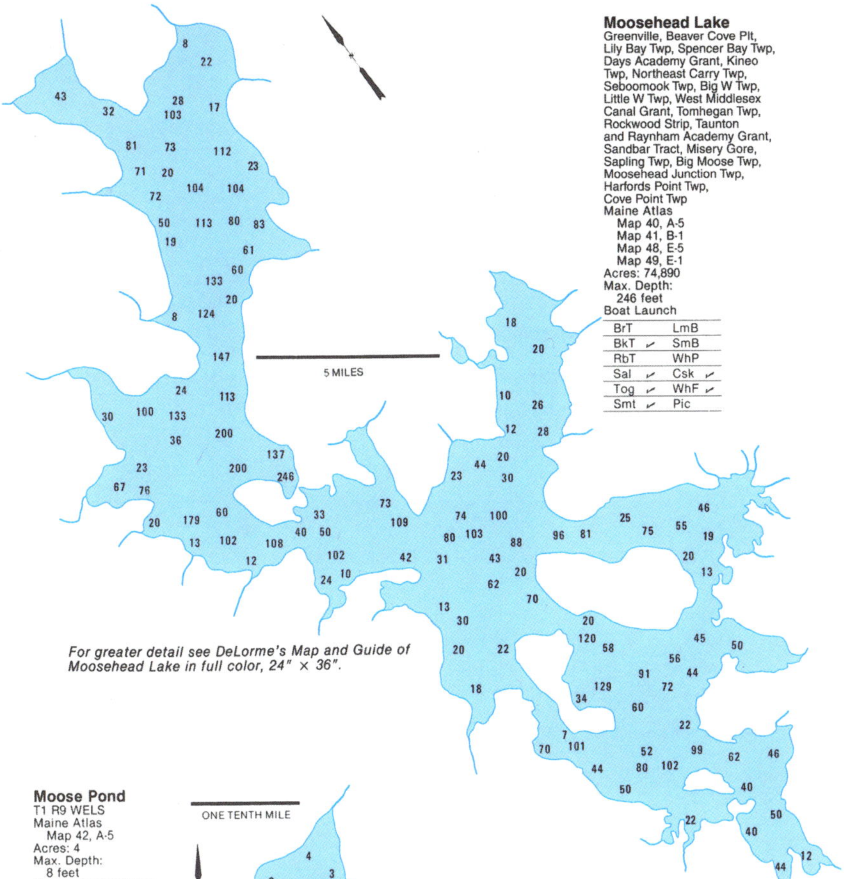

For greater detail see DeLorme's Map and Guide of Moosehead Lake in full color, 24" × 36".

Moose Pond

T1 R9 WELS
Maine Atlas
Map 42, A-5
Acres: 4
Max. Depth: 8 feet

BrT	LmB
BkT ✓	SmB
RbT	WhP
Sal	Csk
Tog	WhF
Smt	Pic

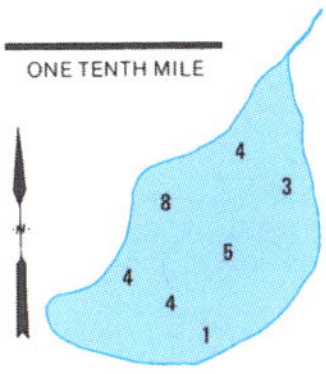

Mountain Pond

T10 R10 WELS
Maine Atlas
Map 56, A-4
Acres: 80
Max. Depth: 9 feet

BrT	LmB
BkT ✓	SmB
RbT	WhP
Sal	Csk
Tog	WhF
Smt	Pic

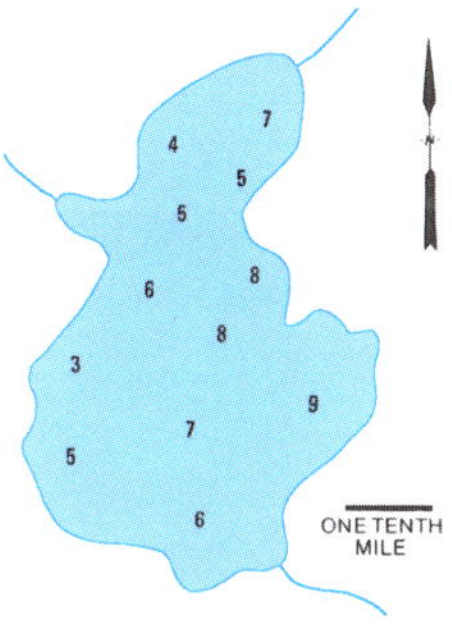

Mooseleuk Lake

T10 R9 WELS
Maine Atlas
Map 57, A-1
Acres: 422
Max. Depth: 6 feet
Boat Launch

BrT	LmB
BkT ✓	SmB
RbT	WhP
Sal ✓	Csk
Tog	WhF
Smt	Pic

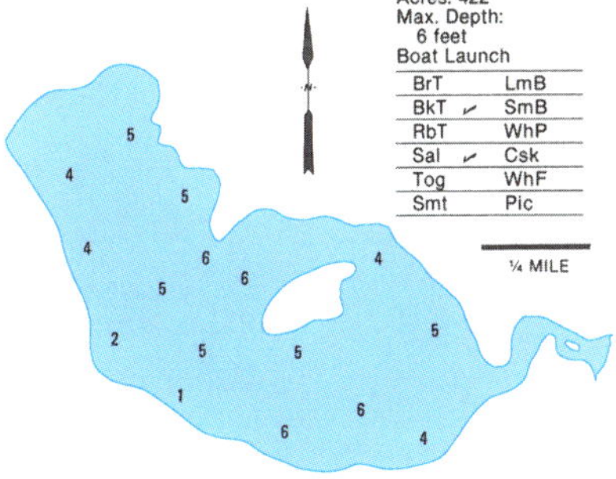

Mountain View Pond

TA R11 WELS
Maine Atlas
Map 42, B-2
Acres: 13
Max. Depth: 12 feet

BrT	LmB
BkT ✓	SmB
RbT	WhP
Sal	Csk
Tog	WhF
Smt	Pic

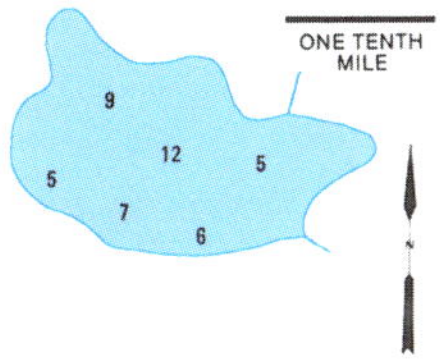

Mountain Brook Pond

Bowdoin College Grant West
Maine Atlas
Map 41, C-5
Acres: 21
Max. Depth: 11 feet

BrT	LmB
BkT ✓	SmB
RbT	WhP
Sal	Csk
Tog	WhF
Smt	Pic

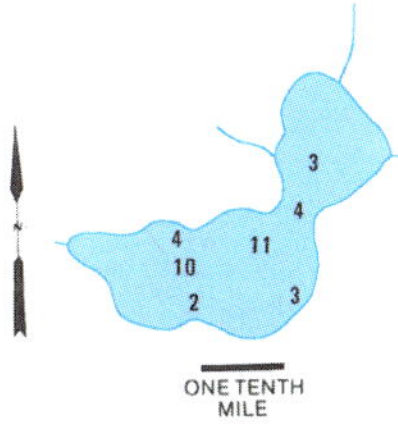

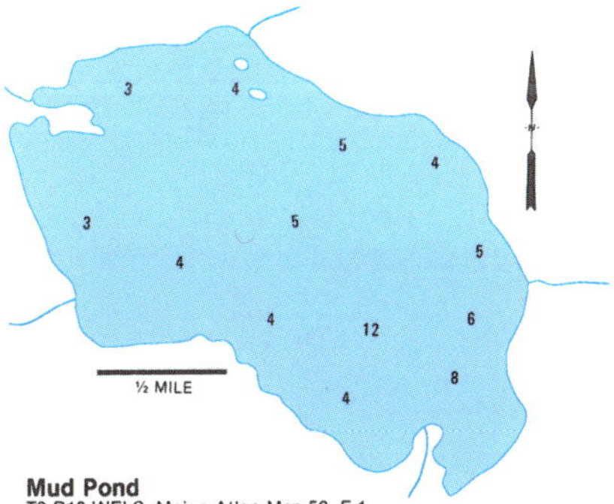

Mud Pond

T6 R12 WELS, Maine Atlas Map 56, E-1
Acres: 1,357, Max. Depth: 12 feet

BrT	BkT	RbT	Sal	Tog	Smt	LmB	SmB	WhP	Csk	WhF	Pic
	✓										

Mountain Pond

Beaver Cove, Bowdoin College Grant West
Maine Atlas
Map 41, C-4
Acres: 56
Max. Depth: 10 feet

BrT	LmB
BkT ✓	SmB
RbT	WhP
Sal	Csk
Tog	WhF
Smt	Pic

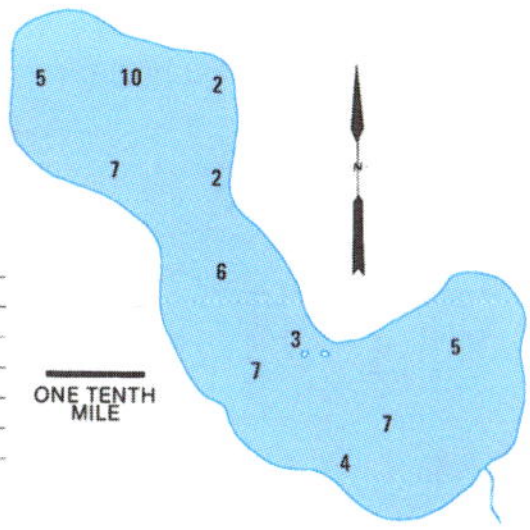

Piscataquis

Mud Greenwood Pond

Willimantic
Maine Atlas
Map 41, E-5
Acres: 23
Max. Depth:
12 feet

BrT	LmB
BkT ✓	SmB
RbT	WhP
Sal	Csk
Tog	WhF
Smt	Pic

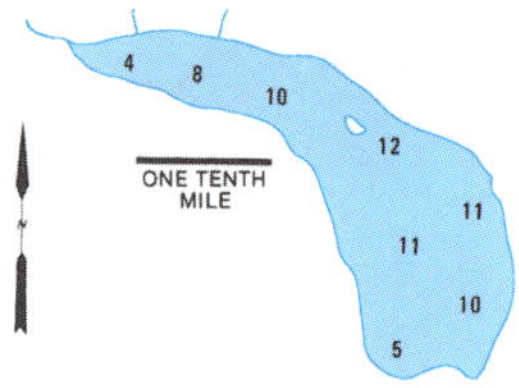

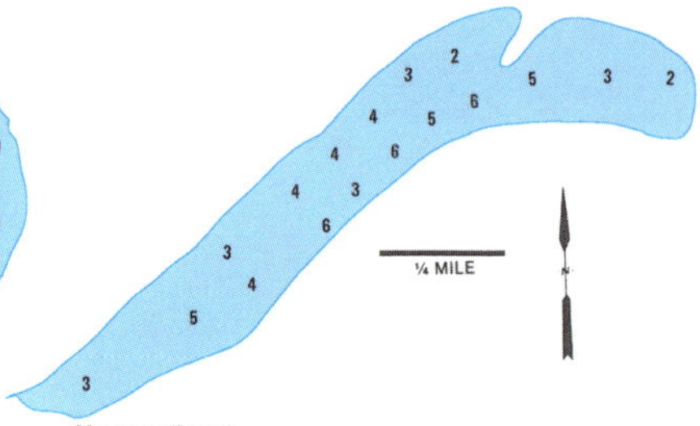

Narrow Pond

T8 R14 WELS, Maine Atlas Map 55, C-3
Acres: 151, Max. Depth: 6 feet

BrT	BkT	RbT	Sal	Tog	Smt	LmB	SmB	WhP	Csk	WhF	Pic
	✓										

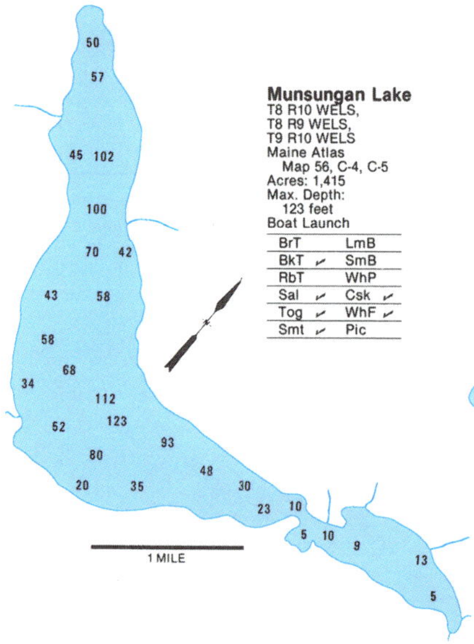

Munsungan Lake

T8 R10 WELS,
T8 R9 WELS,
T9 R10 WELS
Maine Atlas
Map 56, C-4, C-5
Acres: 1,415
Max. Depth:
123 feet
Boat Launch

BrT	LmB
BkT ✓	SmB
RbT	WhP
Sal ✓	Csk ✓
Tog ✓	WhF ✓
Smt ✓	Pic

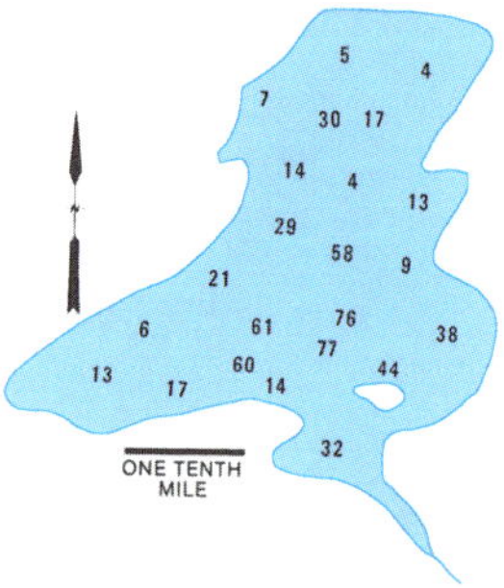

North Pond

Elliotsville Twp
Maine Atlas
Map 41, E-4
Acres: 58
Max. Depth:
77 feet

BrT	LmB
BkT ✓	SmB
RbT	WhP
Sal	Csk
Tog	WhF
Smt	Pic

Norton Pond

Brownville
Maine Atlas
Map 42, E-5
Acres: 24
Max. Depth:
11 feet

BrT	LmB
BkT ✓	SmB
RbT	WhP
Sal	Csk
Tog	WhF
Smt	Pic

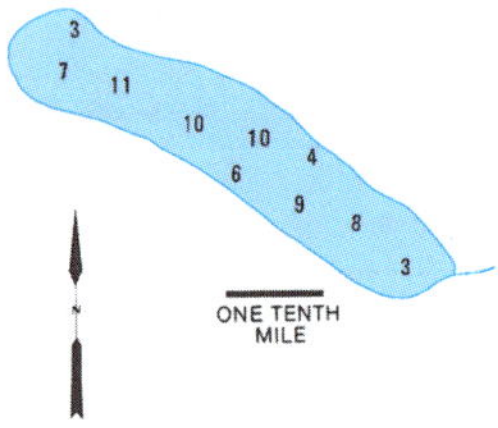

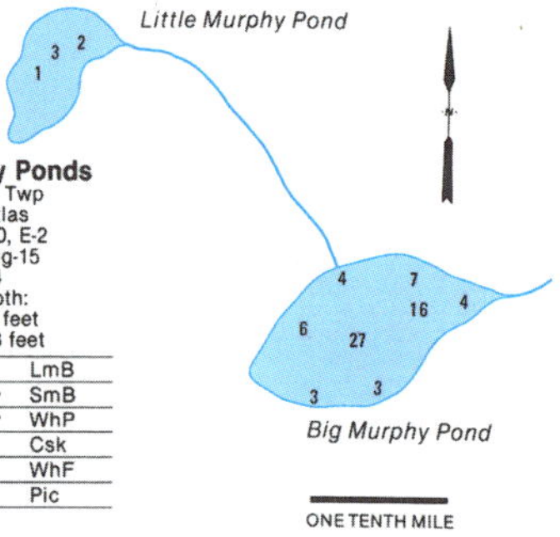

Murphy Ponds

Rainbow Twp
Maine Atlas
Map 50, E-2
Acres: Big-15
Little-4
Max. Depth:
Big-27 feet
Little-3 feet

BrT	LmB
BkT ✓	SmB
RbT ✓	WhP
Sal	Csk
Tog	WhF
Smt	Pic

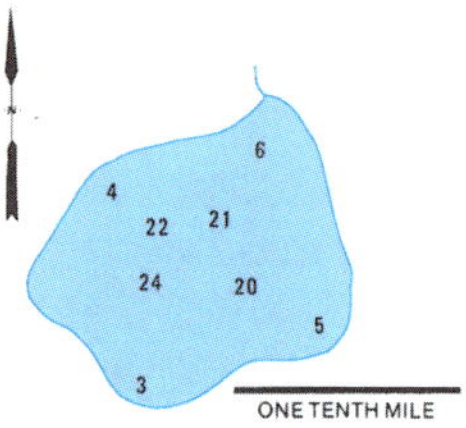

Notch Pond

Bowdoin College
Grant West
Maine Atlas
Map 41, D-4
Acres: 10
Max. Depth:
24 feet

BrT	LmB
BkT ✓	SmB
RbT	WhP
Sal	Csk
Tog	WhF
Smt	Pic

Notch Ponds

Moosehead Junction Twp
Maine Atlas
Map 41, D-1
Acres: Big-15
Little-10
Max. Depth:
Big-40 feet
Little-21 feet

BrT	LmB
BkT ✓	SmB
RbT	WhP
Sal	Csk
Tog	WhF
Smt	Pic

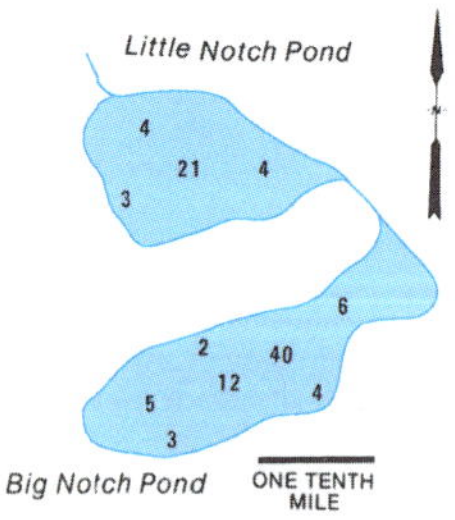

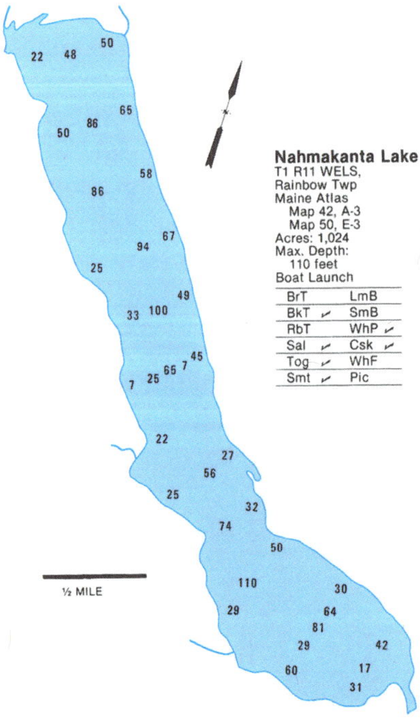

Nahmakanta Lake

T1 R11 WELS,
Rainbow Twp
Maine Atlas
Map 42, A-3
Map 50, E-3
Acres: 1,024
Max. Depth:
110 feet
Boat Launch

BrT	LmB
BkT ✓	SmB
RbT	WhP ✓
Sal ✓	Csk ✓
Tog ✓	WhF
Smt ✓	Pic

Onawa Lake

Elliotsville Twp,
Willimantic
Maine Atlas
Map 41, E-5
Acres: 1,344
Max. Depth:
76 feet
Boat Ramp

BrT	LmB
BkT ✓	SmB ✓
RbT	WhP
Sal ✓	Csk
Tog	WhF
Smt ✓	Pic

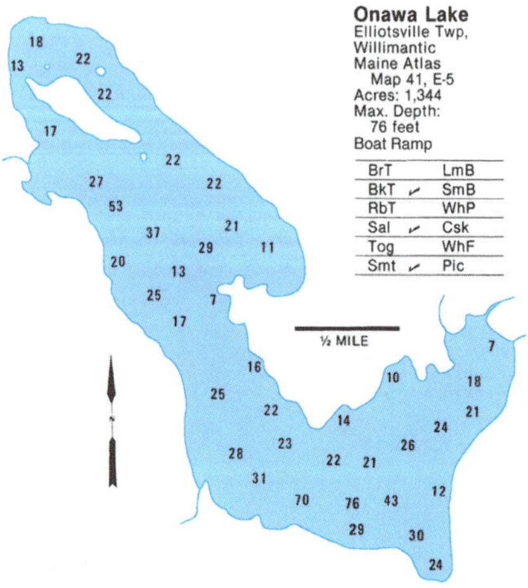

Ordway Pond
Shirley
Maine Atlas
Map 31, A-2
Acres: 75
Max. Depth:
40 feet

BrT	LmB
BkT ✓	SmB
RbT	WhP
Sal	Csk
Tog	WhF
Smt	Pic

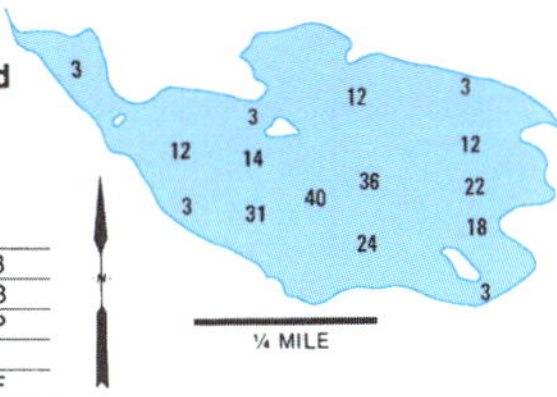

Passamagamet Lake
T1 R9 WELS,
T1 R10 WELS
Maine Atlas
Map 42, A-5
Map 50, E-5
Acres: 461
Max. Depth:
34 feet

BrT	LmB
BkT ✓	SmB
RbT	WhP ✓
Sal ✓	Csk ✓
Tog	WhF
Smt ✓	Pic ✓

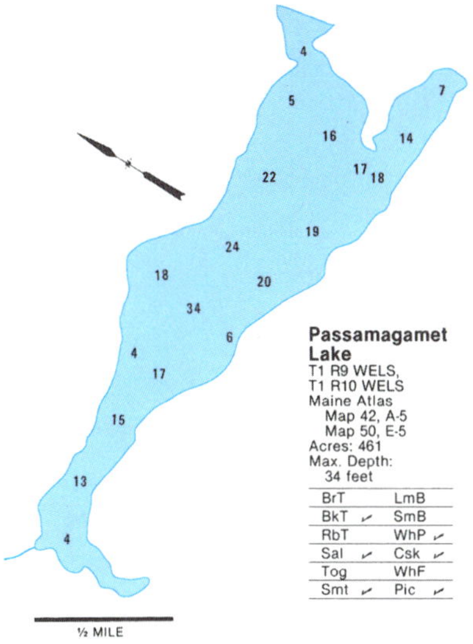

Otter Pond
T8 R14 WELS
Maine Atlas
Map 55, D-4
Acres: 109
Max. Depth:
9 feet

BrT	LmB
BkT ✓	SmB
RbT	WhP
Sal	Csk
Tog	WhF
Smt	Pic

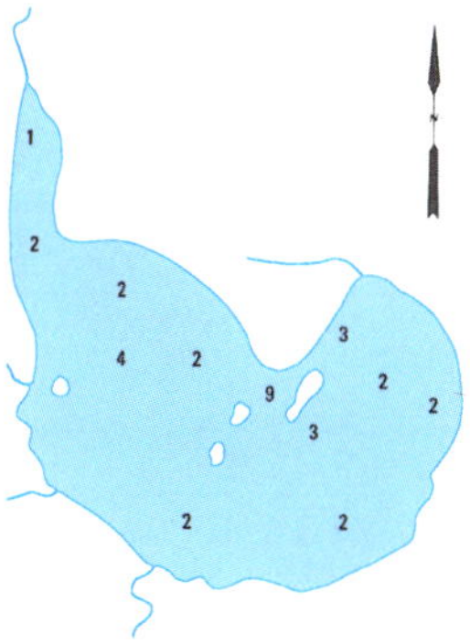

Peaked Mountain Pond
T10 R10 WELS,
T10 R11 WELS
Maine Atlas
Map 56, A-3
Acres: 13
Max. Depth:
7 feet

BrT	LmB
BkT ✓	SmB
RbT	WhP
Sal	Csk
Tog	WhF
Smt	Pic

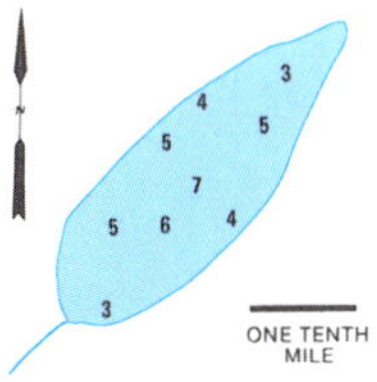

Otter Pond
T3 R13 WELS
Maine Atlas
Map 49, D-5
Acres: 25
Max. Depth:
16 feet

BrT	LmB
BkT ✓	SmB
RbT	WhP
Sal	Csk
Tog	WhF
Smt	Pic

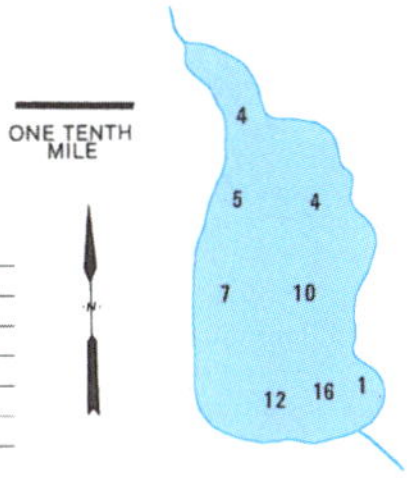

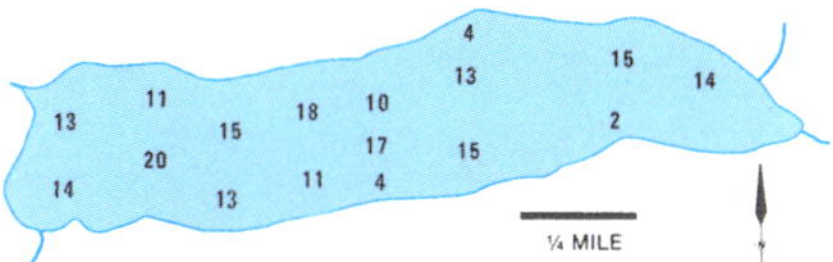

Penobscot Pond
T1 R12 WELS, T1 R11 WELS, Maine Atlas Map 42, A-2
Acres: 279, Max. Depth: 20 feet, Boat Launch

BrT	BkT	RbT	Sal	Tog	Smt	LmB	SmB	WhP	Csk	WhF	Pic
	✓										

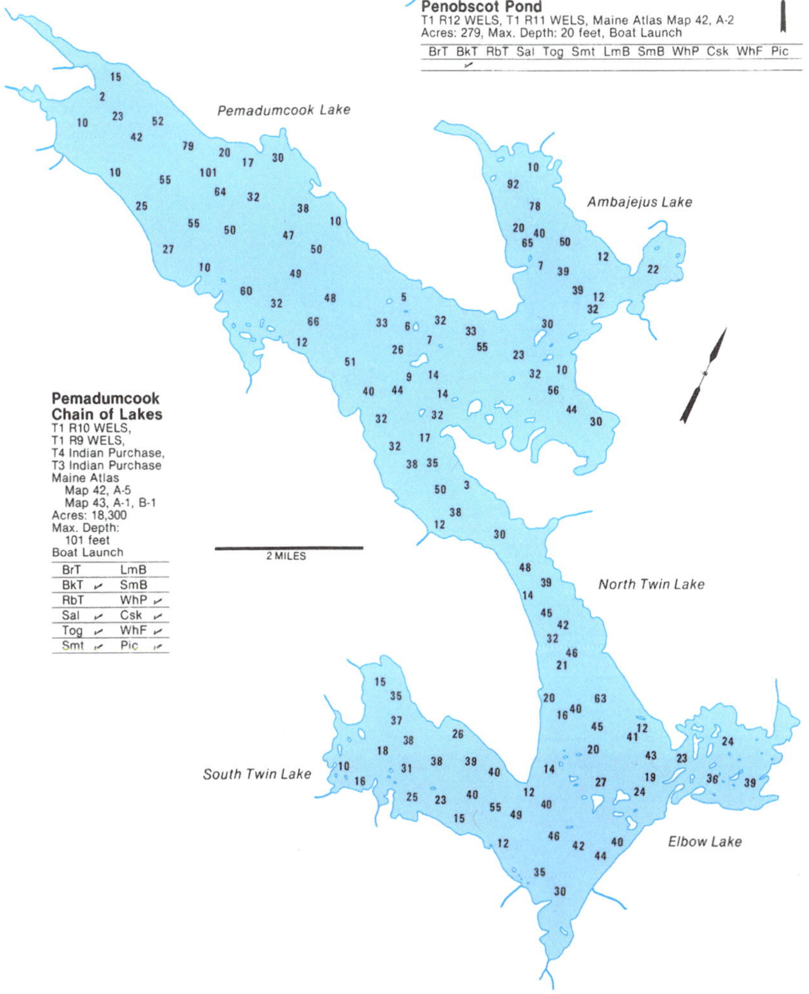

Pemadumcook Chain of Lakes
T1 R10 WELS,
T1 R9 WELS,
T4 Indian Purchase,
T3 Indian Purchase
Maine Atlas
Map 42, A-5
Map 43, A-1, B-1
Acres: 18,300
Max. Depth:
101 feet
Boat Launch

BrT	LmB
BkT ✓	SmB
RbT	WhP ✓
Sal ✓	Csk ✓
Tog ✓	WhF ✓
Smt ✓	Pic ✓

Piscataquis

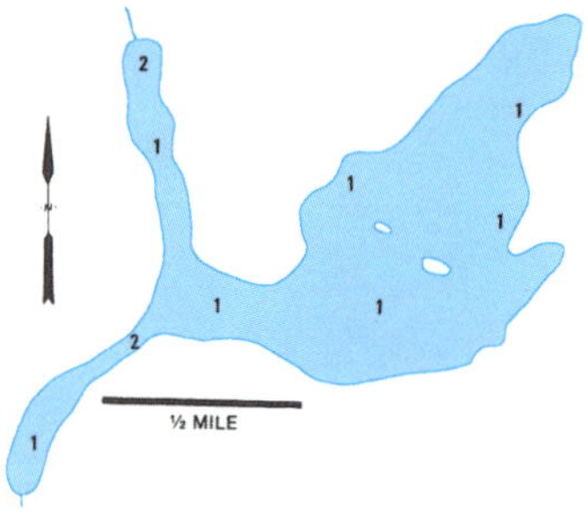

Pillsbury Pond
T8 R11 WELS, Maine Atlas Map 56, C-2, D-2
Acres: 301, Max. Depth: 2 feet

BrT	BkT	RbT	Sal	Tog	Smt	LmB	SmB	WhP	Csk	WhF	Pic
	✓										

Prentiss Pond
T1 R11 WELS
Maine Atlas
Map 42, A-3
Acres: 12
Max. Depth:
9 feet

BrT		LmB	
BkT	✓	SmB	
RbT		WhP	
Sal		Csk	
Tog		WhF	
Smt		Pic	

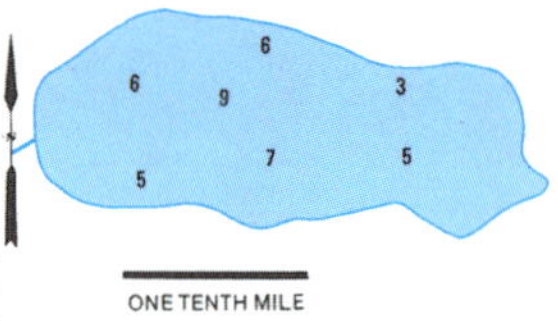

Pretty Pond
T8 R11 WELS
Maine Atlas
Map 56, D-3
Acres: 45
Max. Depth:
5 feet

BrT		LmB	
BkT	✓	SmB	
RbT		WhP	
Sal		Csk	
Tog		WhF	
Smt		Pic	

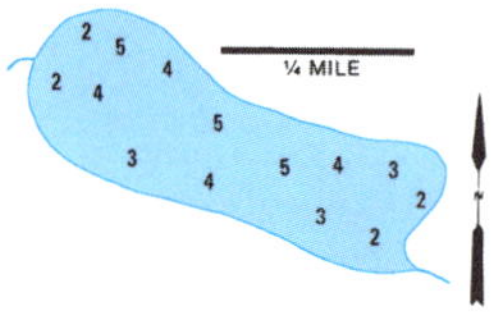

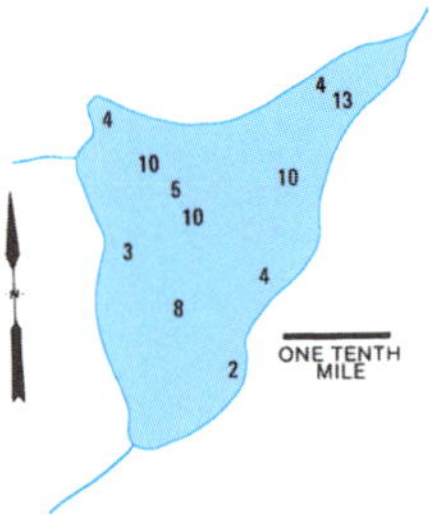

Pingree Pond
Parkman
Maine Atlas
Map 31, C-4
Acres: 34
Max. Depth:
13 feet

BrT		LmB	
BkT	✓	SmB	
RbT		WhP	
Sal		Csk	
Tog		WhF	
Smt		Pic	

Priestly Lake
T10 R13 WELS
Maine Atlas
Map 55, A-5
Acres: 645
Max. Depth:
50 feet

BrT		LmB	
BkT	✓	SmB	
RbT		WhP	
Sal		Csk	
Tog	✓	WhF	✓
Smt		Pic	

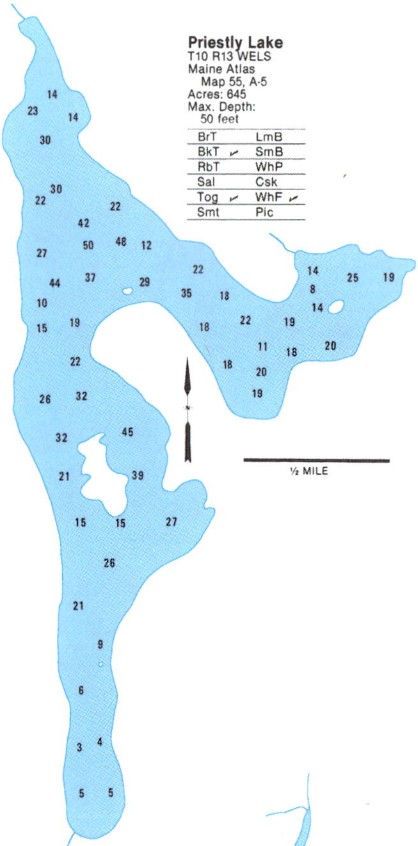

Piper Pond
Abbot
Maine Atlas
Map 31, B-3
Acres: 420
Max. Depth:
56 feet
Boat Launch

BrT		LmB	
BkT	✓	SmB	
RbT		WhP	✓
Sal	✓	Csk	
Tog		WhF	
Smt	✓	Pic	✓

Comments: Splake.

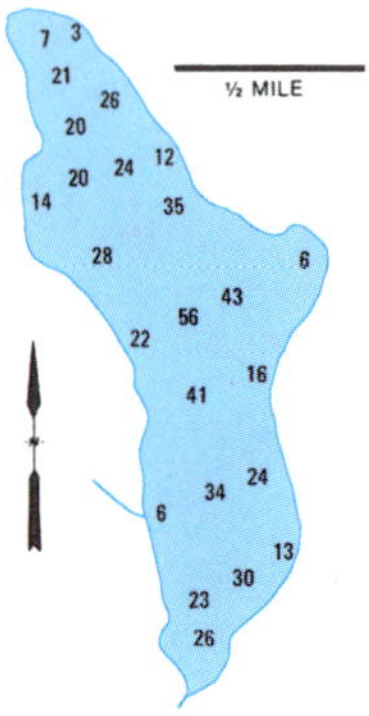

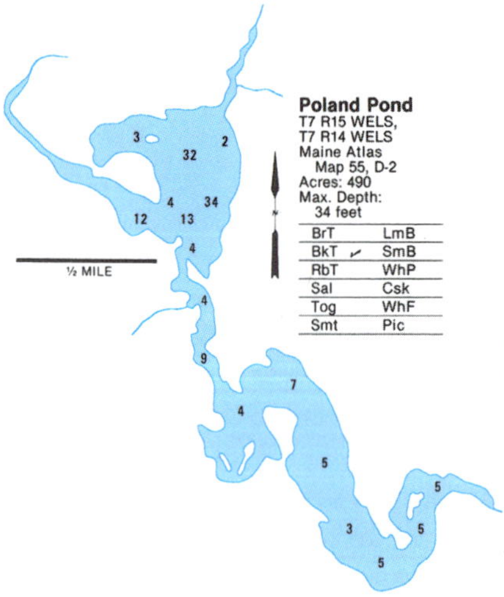

Poland Pond
T7 R15 WELS,
T7 R14 WELS
Maine Atlas
Map 55, D-2
Acres: 490
Max. Depth:
34 feet

BrT		LmB	
BkT	✓	SmB	
RbT		WhP	
Sal		Csk	
Tog		WhF	
Smt		Pic	

Prong Pond
Greenville,
Beaver Cove Plt
Maine Atlas
Map 41, C-3
Acres: 427
Max. Depth:
27 feet
Boat Launch

BrT		LmB	
BkT	✓	SmB	✓
RbT		WhP	
Sal		Csk	
Tog		WhF	
Smt		Pic	

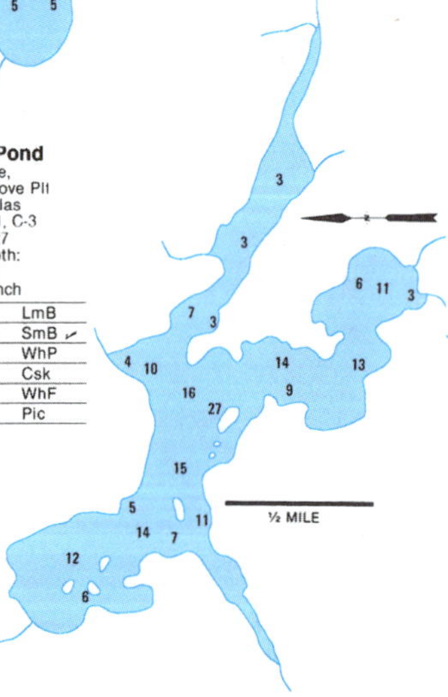

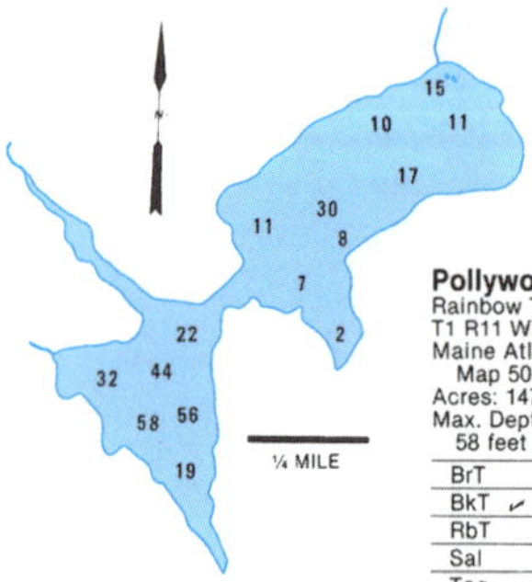

Pollywog Pond
Rainbow Twp,
T1 R11 WELS
Maine Atlas
Map 50, E-2
Acres: 147
Max. Depth:
58 feet

BrT		LmB	
BkT	✓	SmB	
RbT		WhP	
Sal		Csk	
Tog	✓	WhF	
Smt		Pic	

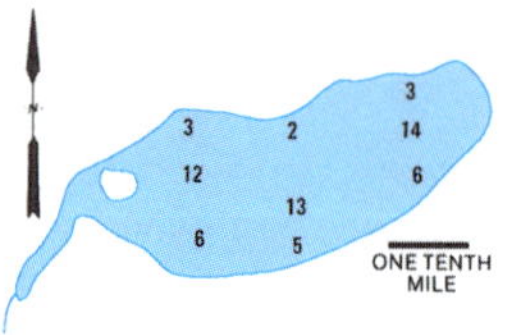

Punchbowl Pond
Blanchard Plt
Maine Atlas
Map 31, B-2
Acres: 40
Max. Depth:
14 feet

BrT		LmB	
BkT	✓	SmB	
RbT		WhP	
Sal		Csk	
Tog		WhF	
Smt		Pic	

Rabbit Pond

Elliotsville Twp
Maine Atlas
Map 41, E-3, E-4
Acres: 9
Max. Depth:
24 feet

BrT	LmB
BkT ✓	SmB
RbT	WhP
Sal	Csk
Tog	WhF
Smt	Pic

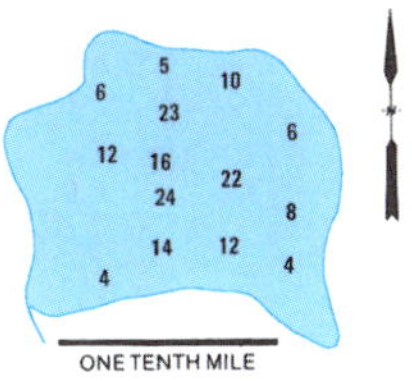

Rainbow Lake

Rainbow Twp
Maine Atlas
Map 50, E-3
Acres: 1,664
Max. Depth:
130 feet

BrT	LmB
BkT ✓	SmB
RbT	WhP
Sal	Csk
Tog	WhF
Smt ✓	Pic

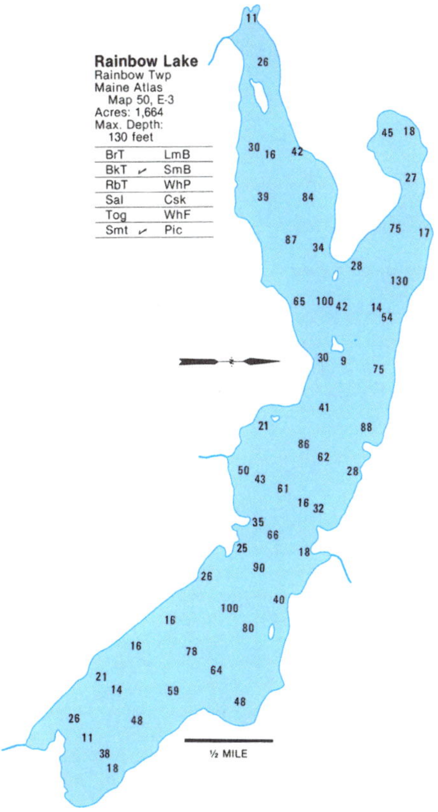

Ragged Lake

T2 R13 WELS,
T3 R13 WELS
Maine Atlas
Map 49, D-5, E-5
Acres: 2,712
Max. Depth:
54 feet

BrT	LmB
BkT ✓	SmB
RbT	WhP
Sal ✓	Csk ✓
Tog ✓	WhF
Smt ✓	Pic

Comments: Splake.

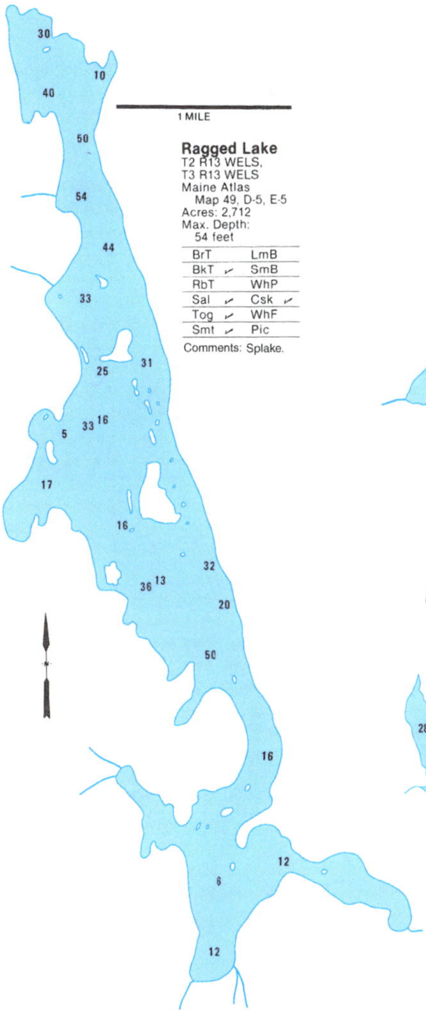

Roach Ponds

First Roach Pond

Frenchtown Twp
Maine Atlas
Map 41, B-5
Acres: 3,270
Max. Depth:
123 feet
Boat Launch

BrT	LmB
BkT ✓	SmB
RbT	WhP
Sal ✓	Csk ✓
Tog ✓	WhF ✓
Smt ✓	Pic

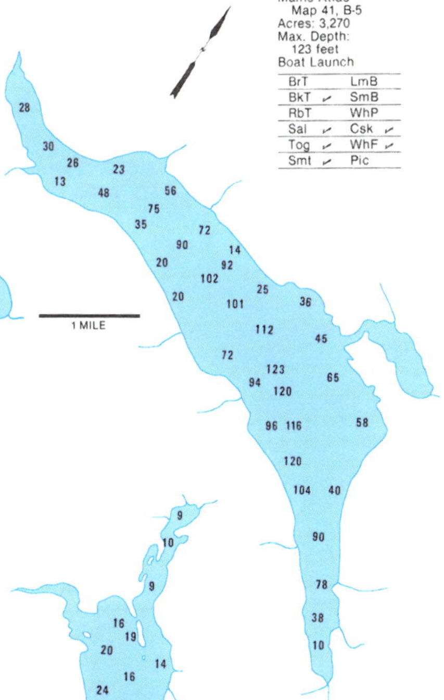

Ragged Pond

T9 R10 WELS
Maine Atlas
Map 56, B-4
Acres: 13
Max. Depth:
8 feet
Boat Launch

BrT	LmB
BkT	SmB
RbT	WhP
Sal	Csk
Tog	WhF
Smt	Pic

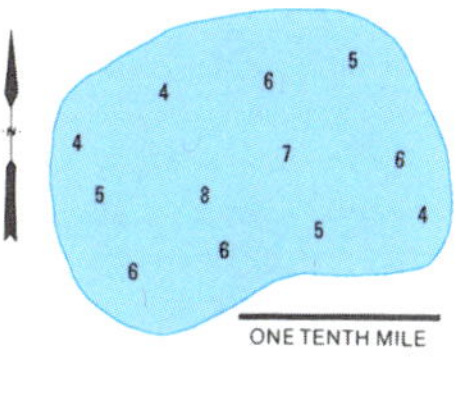

Rainbow Deadwaters

Rainbow Twp
Maine Atlas
Map 50, E-2
Acres: 58
Max. Depth:
22 feet

BrT	LmB
BkT ✓	SmB
RbT	WhP
Sal	Csk
Tog	WhF
Smt	Pic

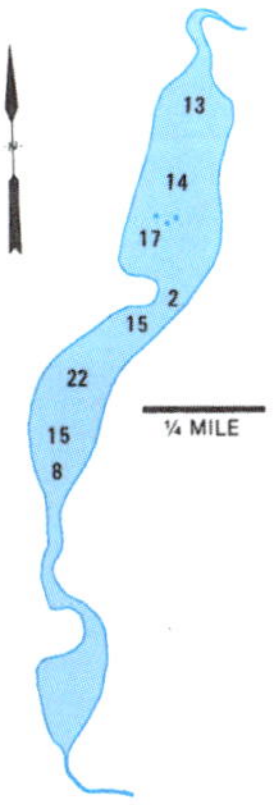

Second Roach Pond

Shawtown Twp,
T1 R12 WELS
Maine Atlas
Map 42, A-1
Acres: 970
Max. Depth:
46 feet

BrT	LmB
BkT ✓	SmB
RbT	WhP
Sal ✓	Csk ✓
Tog	WhF ✓
Smt ✓	Pic

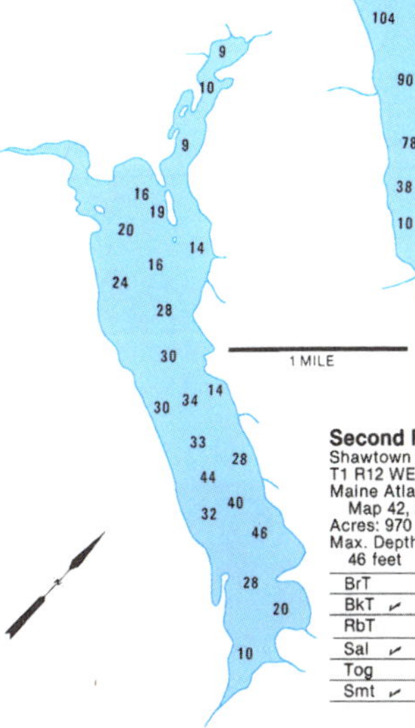

Piscataquis

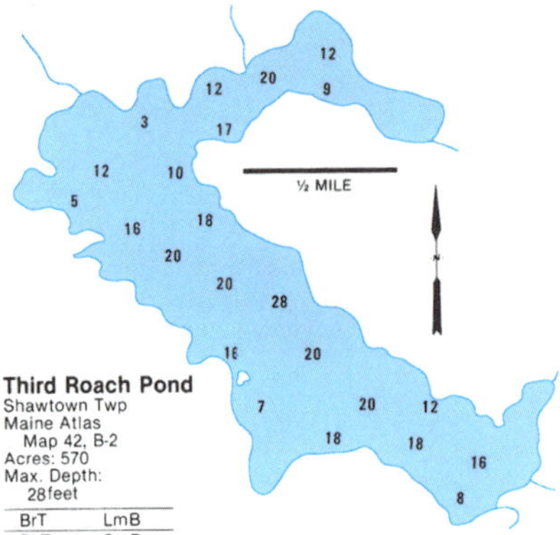

Third Roach Pond
Shawtown Twp
Maine Atlas
Map 42, B-2
Acres: 570
Max. Depth:
28feet

BrT	LmB
BkT ✓	SmB
RbT	WhP
Sal ✓	Csk ✓
Tog	WhF ✓
Smt	Pic

Round Pond
T2 R9 WELS
Maine Atlas
Map 51, D-1
Acres: 8
Max. Depth:
19 feet

BrT	LmB
BkT ✓	SmB
RbT	WhP
Sal	Csk
Tog	WhF
Smt	Pic

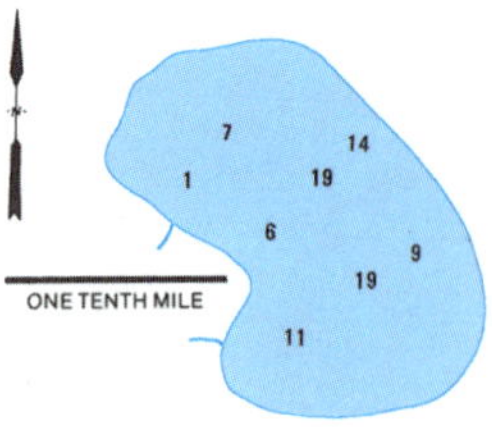

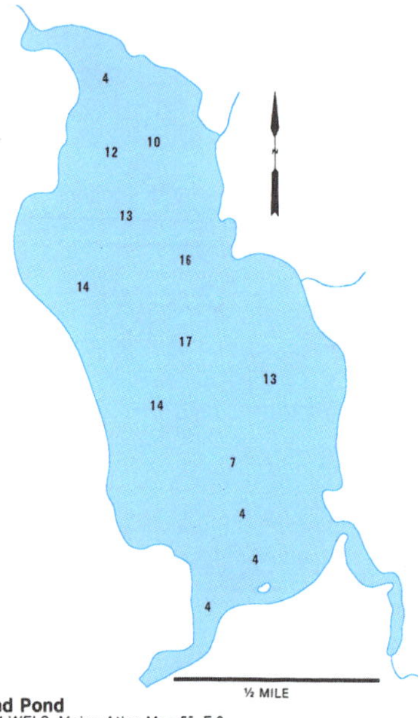

Fourth Roach Pond
Shawtown Twp
Maine Atlas
Map 42, B-2
Acres: 266
Max. Depth:
38 feet

BrT	LmB
BkT ✓	SmB
RbT	WhP
Sal	Csk ✓
Tog	WhF ✓
Smt	Pic

Comments: Splake.

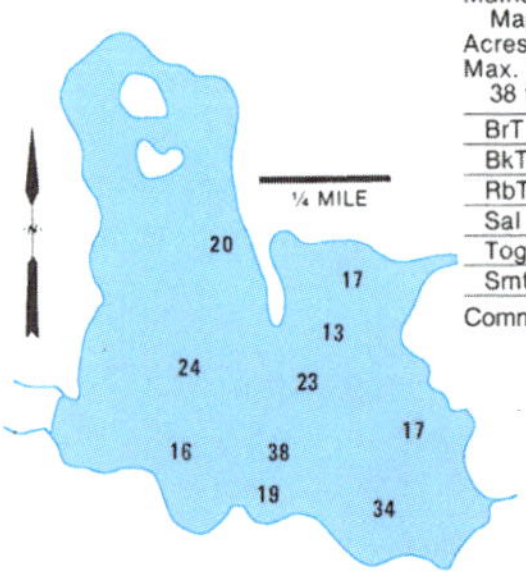

Round Pond
T7 R14 WELS, Maine Atlas Map 55, E-3
Acres: 375, Max. Depth: 17 feet

BrT	BkT	RbT	Sal	Tog	Smt	LmB	SmB	WhP	Csk	WhF	Pic
	✓							✓	✓		

Sixth Roach Pond
Shawtown Twp
Maine Atlas
Map 42, B-2
Acres: 48
Max. Depth:
4 feet

BrT	LmB
BkT ✓	SmB
RbT	WhP
Sal	Csk ✓
Tog	WhF
Smt	Pic

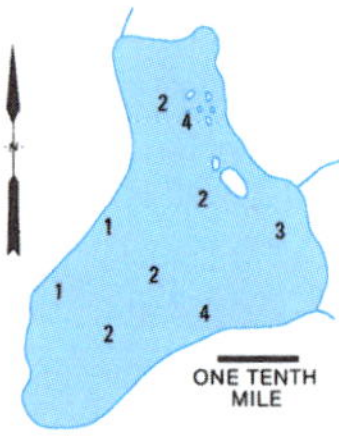

Seventh Roach Pond
TA R11 WELS
Maine Atlas
Map 42, B-2
Acres: 33
Max. Depth:
10 feet

BrT	LmB
BkT ✓	SmB
RbT	WhP
Sal	Csk
Tog	WhF
Smt	Pic

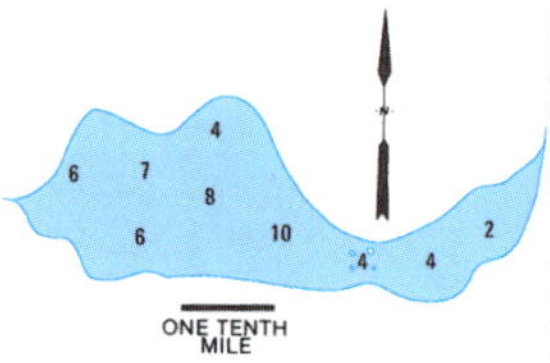

Rum Pond
Greenville,
Bowdoin College
Grant West
Maine Atlas
Map 41, D-3, D-4
Acres: 245
Max. Depth:
77 feet

BrT	LmB
BkT ✓	SmB
RbT	WhP
Sal	Csk
Tog	WhF
Smt ✓	Pic

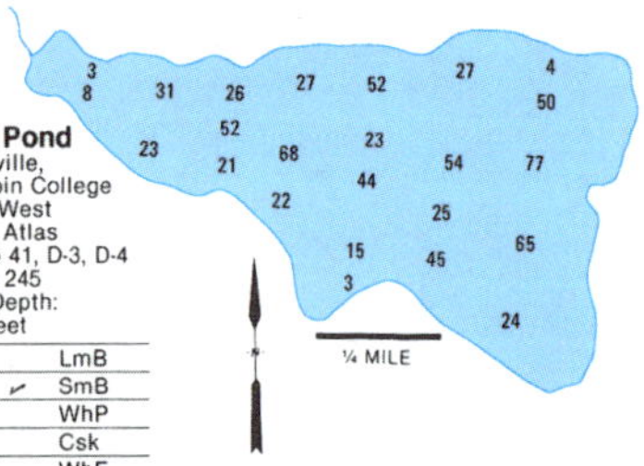

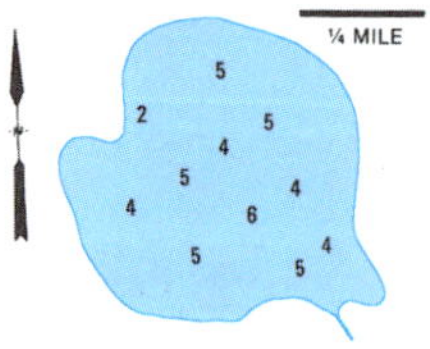

Russell Pond
T4 R9 WELS
Maine Atlas
Map 51, C-1
Acres: 20
Max. Depth:
6 feet

BrT	LmB
BkT ✓	SmB
RbT	WhP
Sal	Csk
Tog	WhF
Smt	Pic

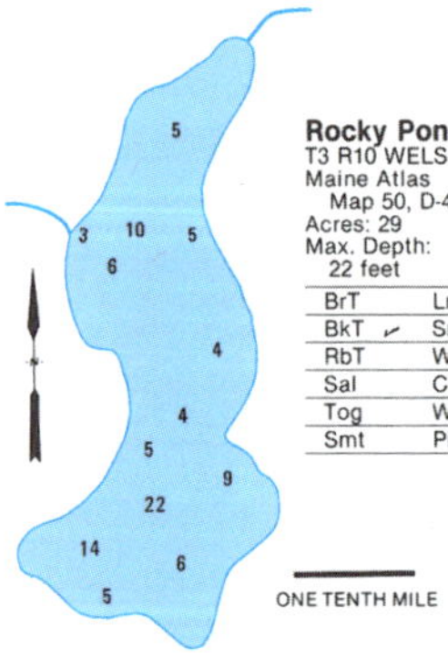

Rocky Pond
T3 R10 WELS
Maine Atlas
Map 50, D-4
Acres: 29
Max. Depth:
22 feet

BrT	LmB
BkT ✓	SmB
RbT	WhP
Sal	Csk
Tog	WhF
Smt	Pic

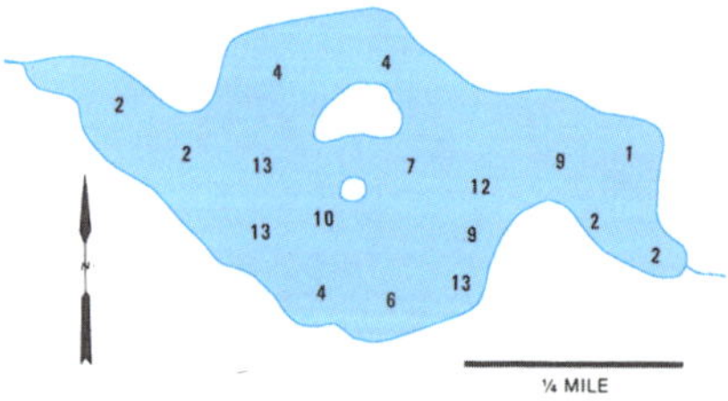

Saddle Pond
T7 R9 WELS, Maine Atlas Map 57, E-1
Acres: 64, Max. Depth: 13 feet

BrT	BkT	RbT	Sal	Tog	Smt	LmB	SmB	WhP	Csk	WhF	Pic
	✓										

Rocky Pond
TA R11 WELS
Maine Atlas
Map 42, B-3
Acres: 115
Max. Depth:
6 feet

BrT	LmB
BkT ✓	SmB
RbT	WhP
Sal	Csk
Tog	WhF
Smt	Pic

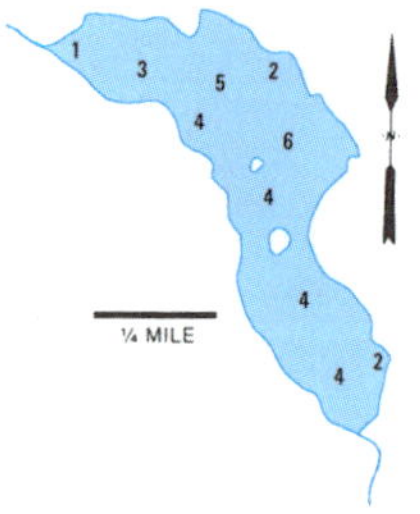

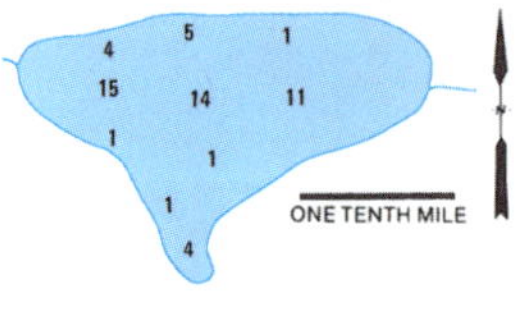

Salmon Pond
Greenville
Maine Atlas
Map 41, D-3
Acres: 19
Max. Depth:
15 feet

BrT	LmB
BkT ✓	SmB
RbT	WhP
Sal	Csk
Tog	WhF
Smt	Pic

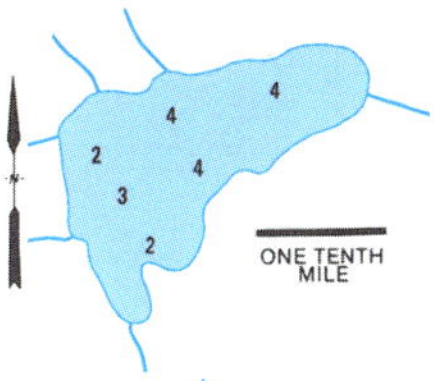

Sandy Stream Pond
Mt. Katahdin Twp
Maine Atlas
Map 51, C-1
Acres: 17
Max. Depth:
4 feet

BrT		LmB	
BkT	✓	SmB	
RbT		WhP	
Sal		Csk	
Tog		WhF	
Smt		Pic	

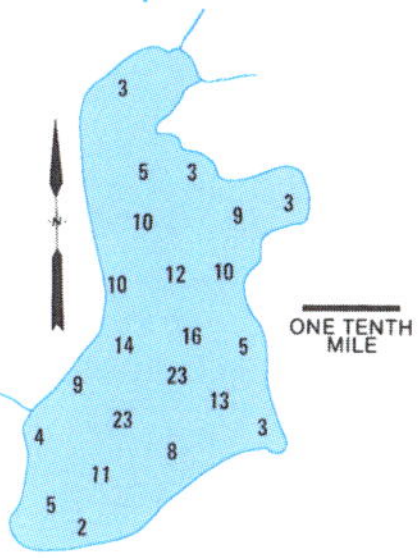

Sawyer Pond
Greenville
Maine Atlas
Map 41, D-3
Acres: 67
Max. Depth:
23 feet
Boat Launch

BrT		LmB	
BkT	✓	SmB	
RbT		WhP	
Sal		Csk	
Tog		WhF	
Smt	✓	Pic	

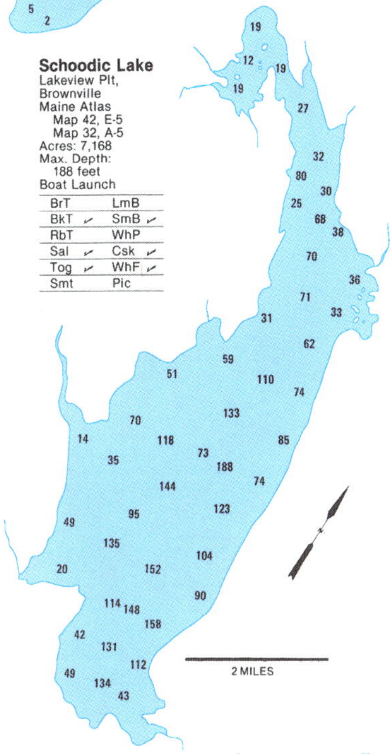

Schoodic Lake
Lakeview Plt,
Brownville
Maine Atlas
Map 42, E-5
Map 32, A-5
Acres: 7,168
Max. Depth:
188 feet
Boat Launch

BrT		LmB	
BkT	✓	SmB	✓
RbT		WhP	
Sal	✓	Csk	✓
Tog	✓	WhF	✓
Smt		Pic	

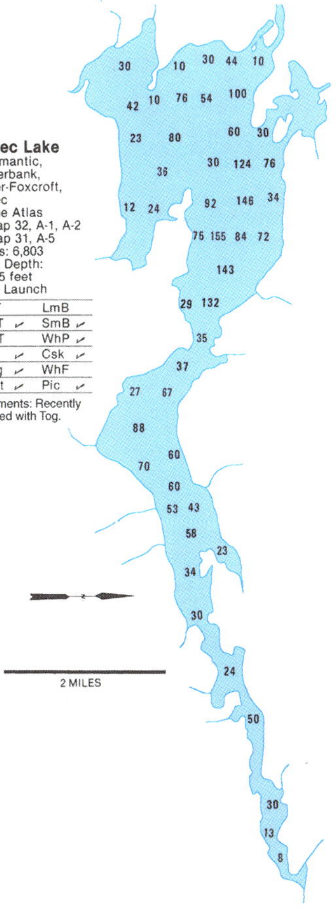

Sebec Lake
Willimantic,
Bowerbank,
Dover-Foxcroft,
Sebec
Maine Atlas
Map 32, A-1, A-2
Map 31, A-5
Acres: 6,803
Max. Depth:
155 feet
Boat Launch

BrT		LmB	
BkT	✓	SmB	✓
RbT		WhP	✓
Sal	✓	Csk	✓
Tog	✓	WhF	
Smt	✓	Pic	✓

Comments: Recently stocked with Tog.

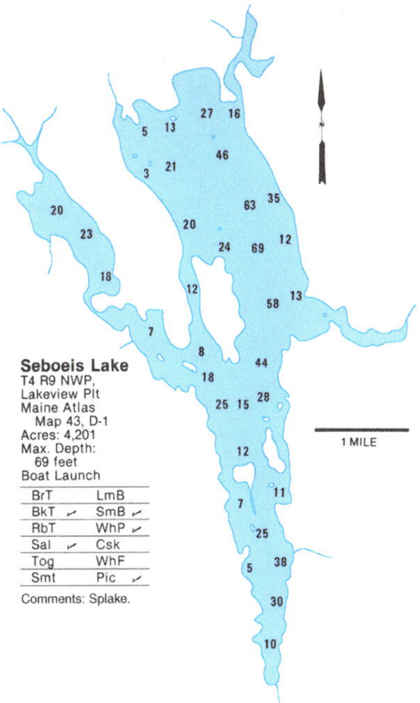

Seboeis Lake
T4 R9 NWP,
Lakeview Plt
Maine Atlas
Map 43, D-1
Acres: 4,201
Max. Depth:
69 feet
Boat Launch

BrT		LmB	
BkT	✓	SmB	✓
RbT		WhP	✓
Sal	✓	Csk	
Tog		WhF	
Smt		Pic	✓

Comments: Splake.

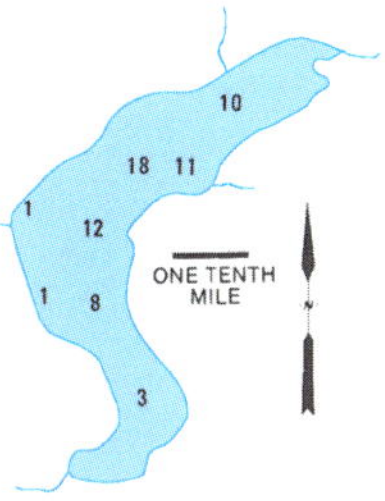

Second Buttermilk Pond
Bowerbank
Maine Atlas
Map 42, E-1
Map 32, A-1
Acres: 62
Max. Depth:
18 feet

BrT		LmB	
BkT	✓	SmB	
RbT		WhP	
Sal		Csk	
Tog		WhF	
Smt		Pic	

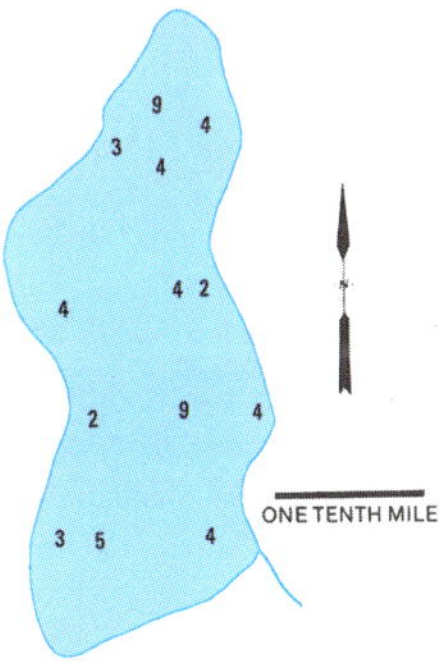

Second Currier Pond
T9 R11 WELS
Maine Atlas
Map 56, B-3, C-3
Acres: 28
Max. Depth:
9 feet

BrT		LmB	
BkT	✓	SmB	
RbT		WhP	
Sal		Csk	
Tog		WhF	
Smt		Pic	

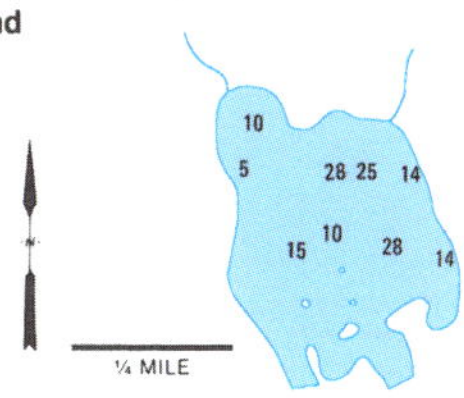

Second Davis Pond
Guilford,
Willimantic
Maine Atlas
Map 31, A-4, B-4
Acres: 58
Max. Depth:
28 feet

BrT		LmB	
BkT	✓	SmB	
RbT		WhP	✓
Sal	✓	Csk	
Tog		WhF	
Smt	✓	Pic	✓

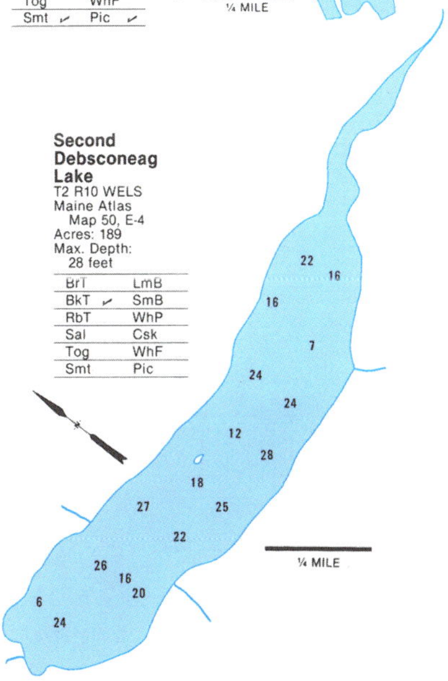

Second Debsconeag Lake
T2 R10 WELS
Maine Atlas
Map 50, E-4
Acres: 189
Max. Depth:
28 feet

BrT		LmB	
BkT	✓	SmB	
RbT		WhP	
Sal		Csk	
Tog		WhF	
Smt		Pic	

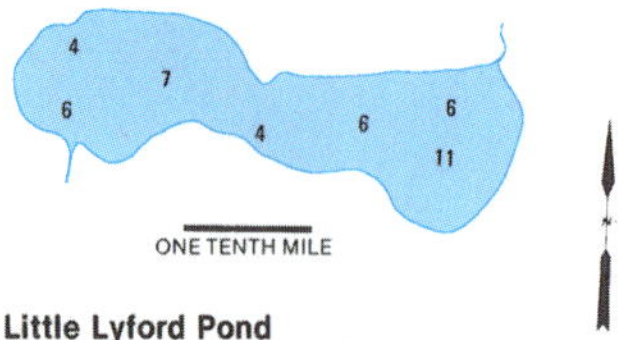

Second Little Lyford Pond
Bowdoin College Grant East, Bowdoin College Grant West
Maine Atlas Map 41, C-5, Acres: 18, Max. Depth: 11 feet

BrT	BkT	RbT	Sal	Tog	Smt	LmB	SmB	WhP	Csk	WhF	Pic
	✓										

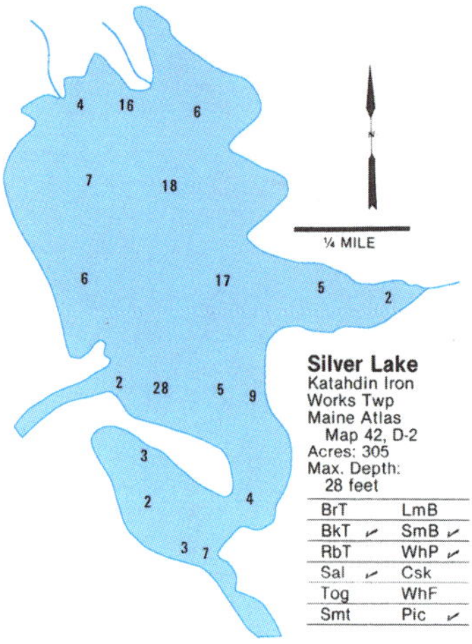

Silver Lake
Katahdin Iron Works Twp
Maine Atlas Map 42, D-2
Acres: 305
Max. Depth: 28 feet

BrT		LmB	
BkT	✓	SmB	✓
RbT		WhP	✓
Sal	✓	Csk	
Tog		WhF	
Smt		Pic	✓

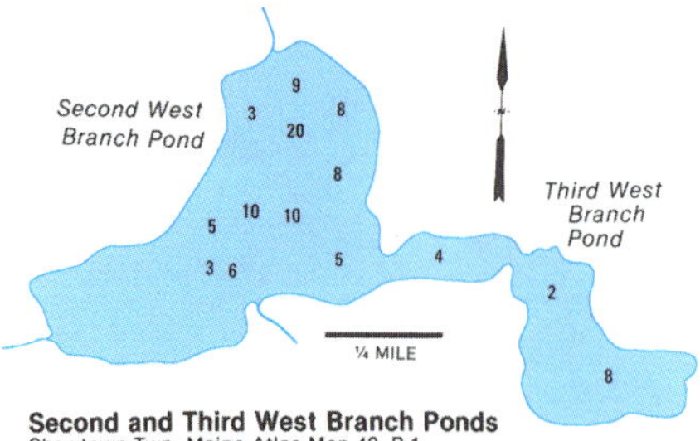

Second and Third West Branch Ponds
Shawtown Twp, Maine Atlas Map 42, B-1
Acres: 214, Max. Depth: 20 feet

BrT	BkT	RbT	Sal	Tog	Smt	LmB	SmB	WhP	Csk	WhF	Pic
	✓										

Sing Sing Pond
T1 R11 WELS
Maine Atlas Map 42, A-3
Acres: 50
Max. Depth: 14 feet

BrT		LmB
BkT	✓	SmB
RbT		WhP
Sal		Csk
Tog		WhF
Smt		Pic

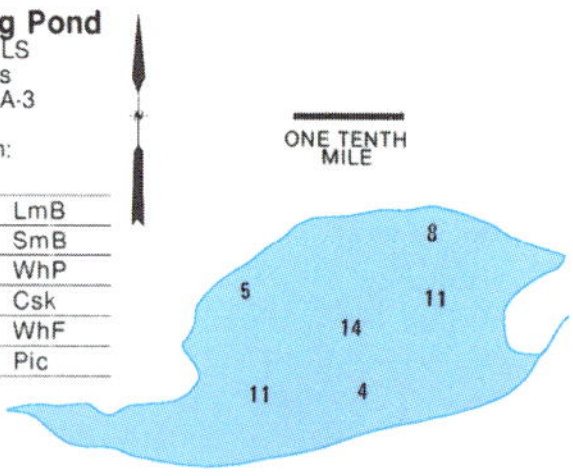

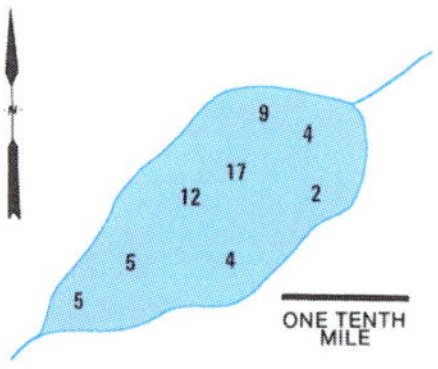

Secret Pond
Elliotsville Twp
Maine Atlas Map 41, D-4
Acres: 12
Max. Depth: 17 feet

BrT		LmB
BkT	✓	SmB
RbT		WhP
Sal		Csk
Tog		WhF
Smt		Pic

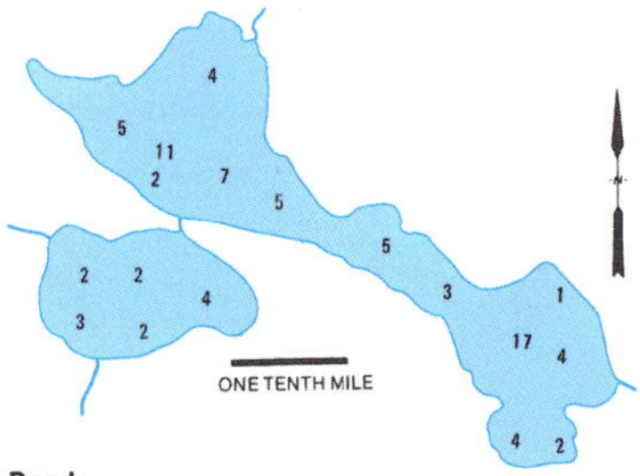

Six Ponds
T4 R9 WELS, Maine Atlas Map 50, B-5
Acres: 35, Max. Depth: 17 feet

BrT	BkT	RbT	Sal	Tog	Smt	LmB	SmB	WhP	Csk	WhF	Pic
	✓										

Secret Pond
Greenville
Maine Atlas Map 41, D-3
Acres: 14
Max. Depth: 34 feet

BrT		LmB
BkT	✓	SmB
RbT		WhP
Sal		Csk
Tog		WhF
Smt		Pic

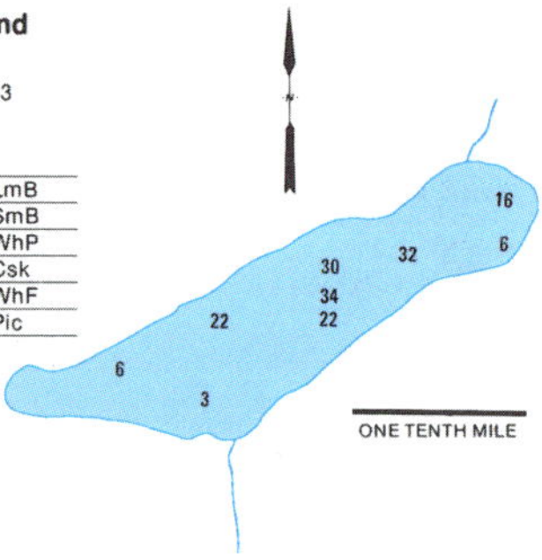

Sixth Debsconeag Pond
Rainbow Twp, T1 R11 WELS
Maine Atlas Map 50, E-3
Acres: 32
Max. Depth: 26 feet

BrT		LmB
BkT	✓	SmB
RbT		WhP
Sal		Csk
Tog		WhF
Smt		Pic

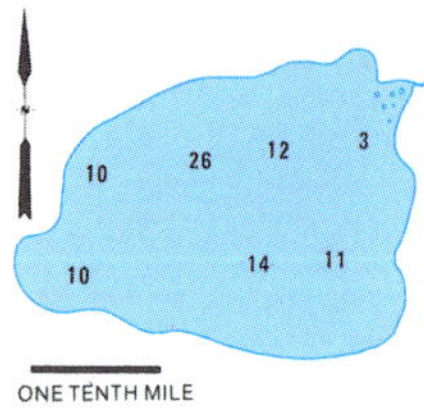

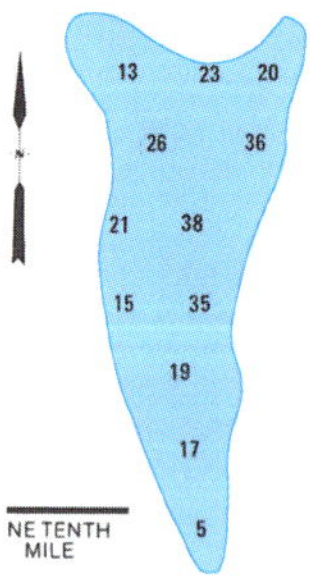

Shadow Pond
Moosehead Junction Twp, Greenville, Cove Point Twp
Maine Atlas Map 41, D-2
Acres: 17.5
Max. Depth: 38 feet

BrT		LmB
BkT	✓	SmB
RbT		WhP
Sal		Csk
Tog		WhF
Smt		Pic

Comments: Splake.

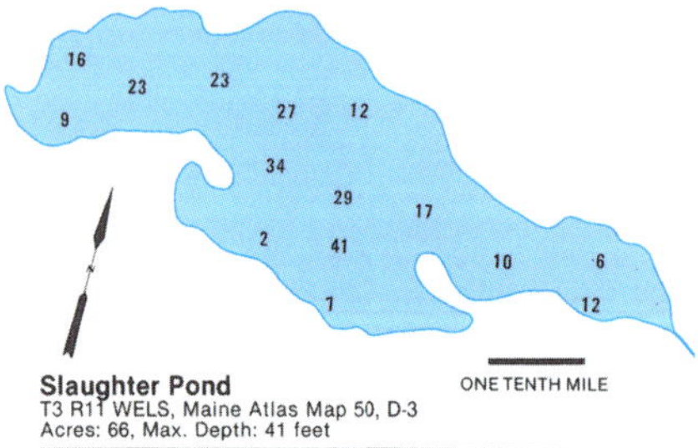

Slaughter Pond
T3 R11 WELS, Maine Atlas Map 50, D-3
Acres: 66, Max. Depth: 41 feet

BrT	BkT	RbT	Sal	Tog	Smt	LmB	SmB	WhP	Csk	WhF	Pic
	✓										

Shirley Pond
Shirley
Maine Atlas Map 41, E-2
Acres: 60
Max. Depth: 15 feet

BrT		LmB
BkT	✓	SmB
RbT		WhP
Sal		Csk
Tog		WhF
Smt		Pic

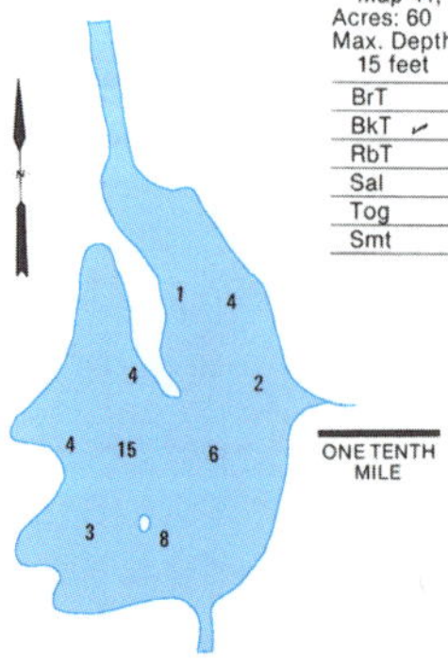

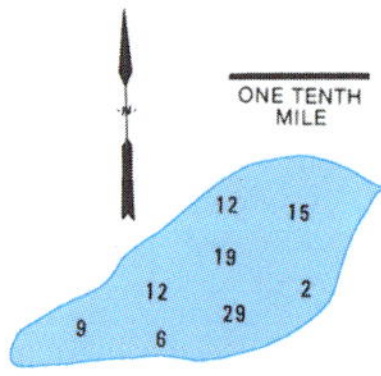

Smith Pond
Elliotsville Twp
Maine Atlas Map 41, E-3, E-4
Acres: 10
Max. Depth: 29 feet

BrT		LmB
BkT	✓	SmB
RbT		WhP
Sal		Csk
Tog		WhF
Smt		Pic

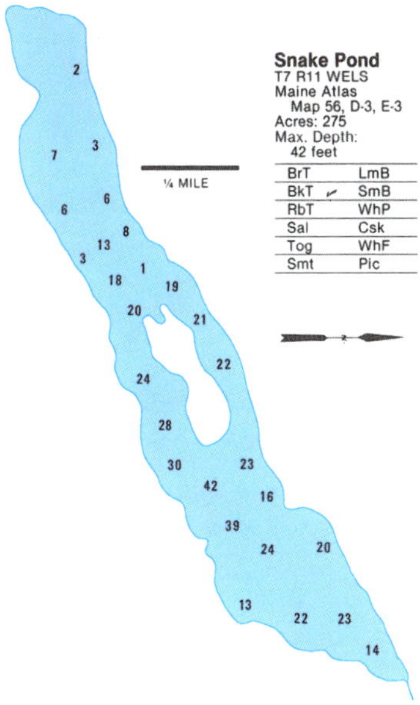

Snake Pond
T7 R11 WELS
Maine Atlas
Map 56, D-3, E-3
Acres: 275
Max. Depth:
42 feet

BrT	LmB
BkT ✓	SmB
RbT	WhP
Sal	Csk
Tog	WhF
Smt	Pic

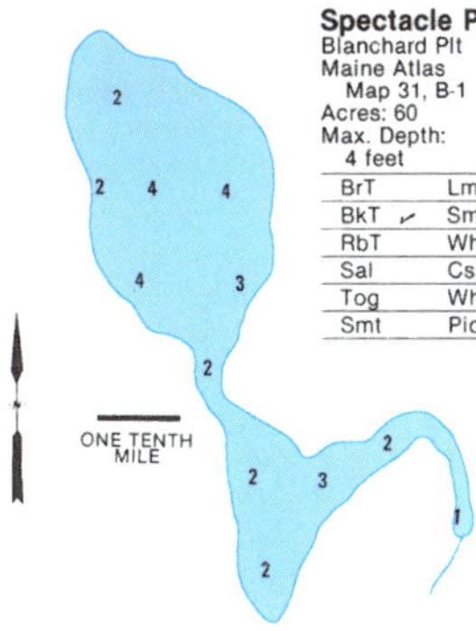

Spectacle Pond
Blanchard Plt
Maine Atlas
Map 31, B-1
Acres: 60
Max. Depth:
4 feet

BrT	LmB
BkT ✓	SmB
RbT	WhP
Sal	Csk
Tog	WhF
Smt	Pic

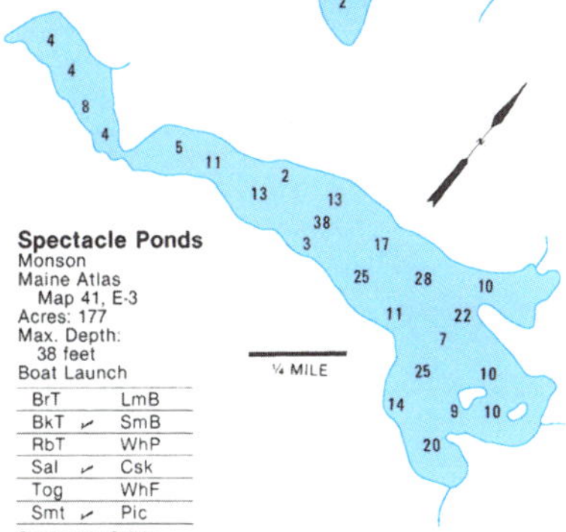

Spectacle Ponds
Monson
Maine Atlas
Map 41, E-3
Acres: 177
Max. Depth:
38 feet
Boat Launch

BrT	LmB
BkT ✓	SmB
RbT	WhP
Sal ✓	Csk
Tog	WhF
Smt ✓	Pic

Comments: Splake.

Snows Pond
Dover-Foxcroft
Maine Atlas
Map 32, B-2
Acres: 21
Max. Depth:
8 feet

BrT	LmB
BkT ✓	SmB
RbT	WhP
Sal	Csk
Tog	WhF
Smt	Pic ✓

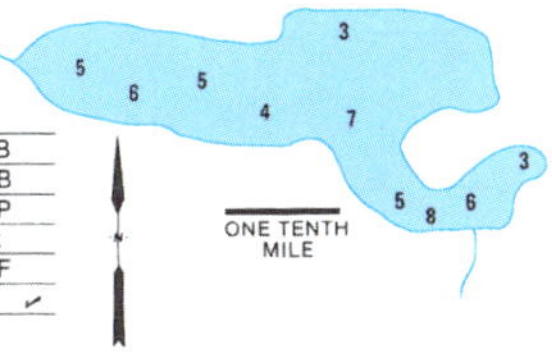

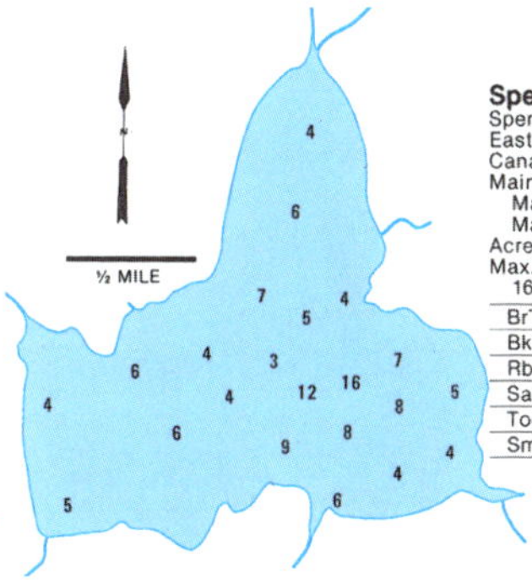

Spencer Pond
Spencer Bay Twp,
East Middlesex
Canal Grant
Maine Atlas
Map 41, A-2, A-3
Map 49, E-3
Acres: 980
Max. Depth:
16 feet

BrT	LmB
BkT ✓	SmB
RbT	WhP
Sal	Csk
Tog	WhF
Smt	Pic

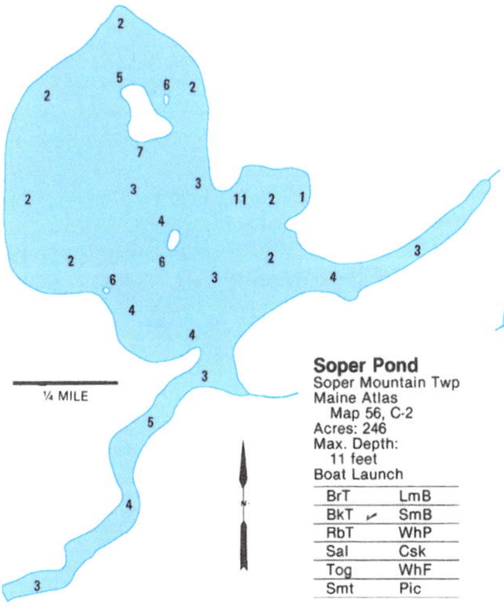

Soper Pond
Soper Mountain Twp
Maine Atlas
Map 56, C-2
Acres: 246
Max. Depth:
11 feet
Boat Launch

BrT	LmB
BkT ✓	SmB
RbT	WhP
Sal	Csk
Tog	WhF
Smt	Pic

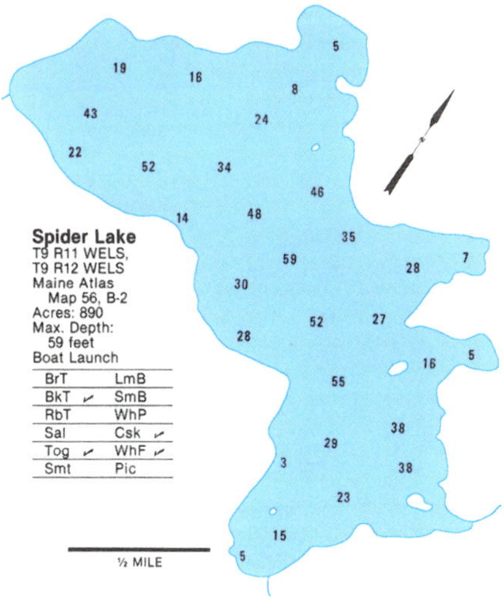

Spider Lake
T9 R11 WELS,
T9 R12 WELS
Maine Atlas
Map 56, B-2
Acres: 890
Max. Depth:
59 feet
Boat Launch

BrT	LmB
BkT ✓	SmB
RbT	WhP
Sal	Csk ✓
Tog ✓	WhF ✓
Smt	Pic

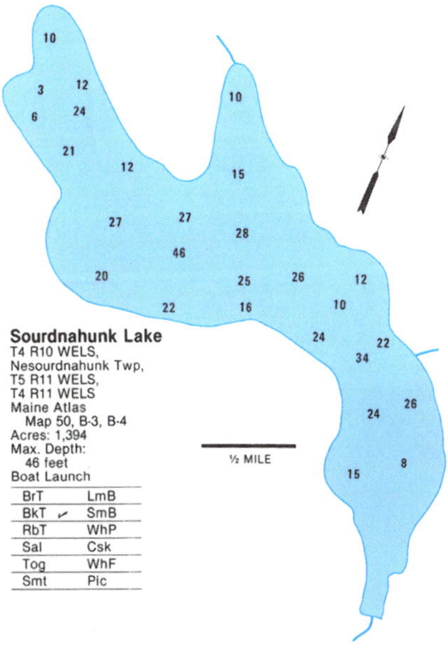

Sourdnahunk Lake
T4 R10 WELS,
Nesourdnahunk Twp,
T5 R11 WELS,
T4 R11 WELS
Maine Atlas
Map 50, B-3, B-4
Acres: 1,394
Max. Depth:
46 feet
Boat Launch

BrT	LmB
BkT ✓	SmB
RbT	WhP
Sal	Csk
Tog	WhF
Smt	Pic

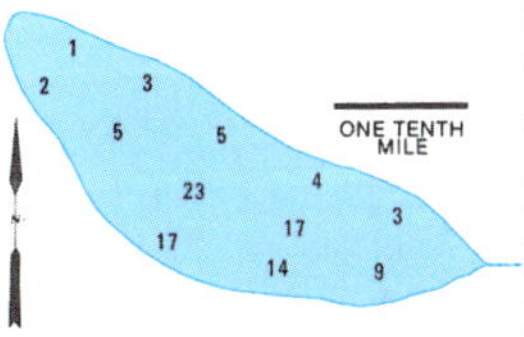

Spring Pond
T7 R10 WELS
Maine Atlas
Map 56, D-4
Acres: 15
Max. Depth:
23 feet

BrT	LmB
BkT ✓	SmB
RbT	WhP
Sal	Csk
Tog	WhF
Smt	Pic

Spruce Mountain Pond
T8 R11 WELS
Maine Atlas
Map 42, C-2
Acres: 20
Max. Depth:
7 feet

BrT	LmB
BkT ✓	SmB
RbT	WhP
Sal	Csk
Tog	WhF
Smt	Pic

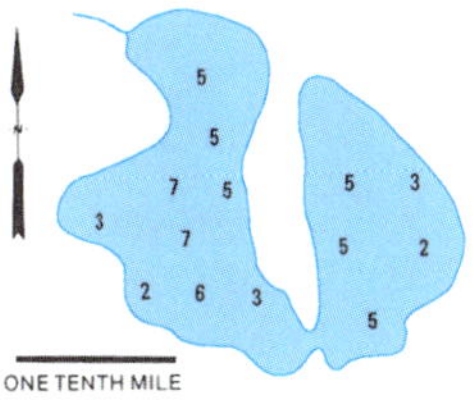

Piscataquis

Stink Pond and Snake Bog
T7 R11 WELS
Maine Atlas
Map 56, D-2, D-3
Acres: 35
Max. Depth:
3 feet

BrT		LmB	
BkT	✓	SmB	
RbT		WhP	
Sal		Csk	
Tog		WhF	
Smt		Pic	

Third Lake
T7 R10 WELS
Maine Atlas
Map 56, D-4, E-4
Acres: 474
Max. Depth:
37 feet

BrT		LmB	
BkT	✓	SmB	
RbT		WhP	
Sal		Csk	✓
Tog		WhF	
Smt		Pic	

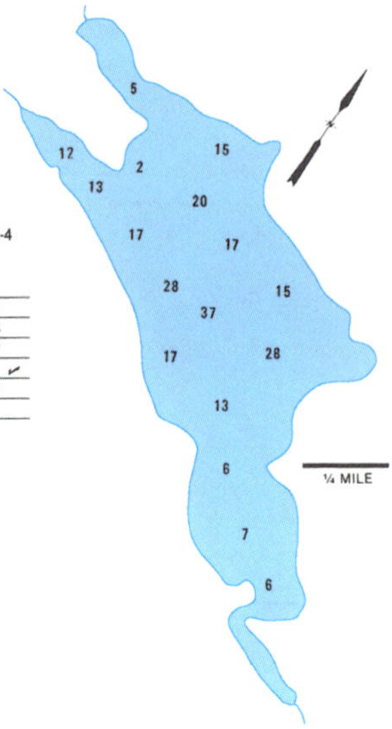

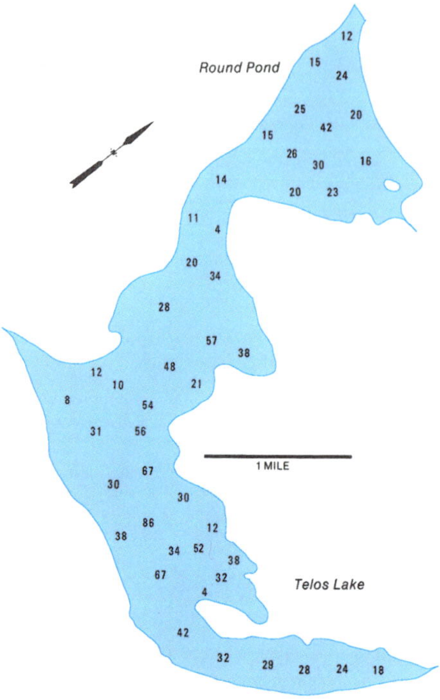

Telos Lake and Round Pond
T6 R11 WELS, Maine Atlas Map 50, A-2, A-3, Map 56, E-2
Acres: 2,276, Max. Depth: 86 feet, Boat Launch

BrT	BkT	RbT	Sal	Tog	Smt	LmB	SmB	WhP	Csk	WhF	Pic
	✓			✓	✓				✓	✓	

Thissell Pond
T5 R11 WELS
Maine Atlas
Map 50, A-3, B-3
Acres: 141
Max. Depth:
42 feet

BrT		LmB	
BkT	✓	SmB	
RbT		WhP	
Sal		Csk	
Tog		WhF	
Smt		Pic	

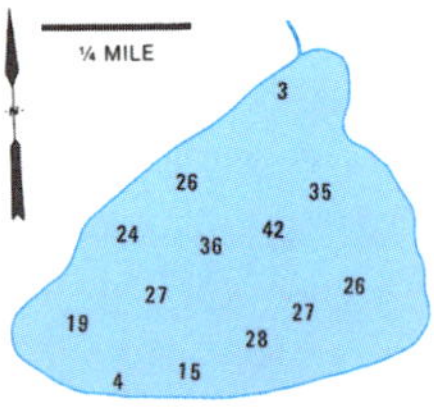

Tom Young Pond
East Middlesex
Canal Grant
Maine Atlas
Map 49, E-2
Acres: 25
Max. Depth:
5 feet

BrT		LmB	
BkT	✓	SmB	
RbT		WhP	
Sal		Csk	
Tog		WhF	
Smt		Pic	

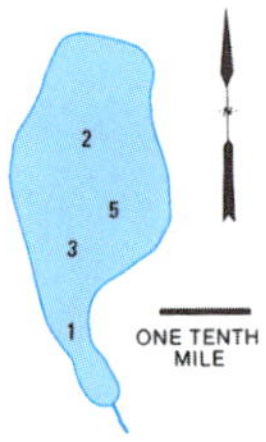

Tracy Pond
T3 R10 WELS
Maine Atlas
Map 50, D-4
Acres: 12
Max. Depth:
4 feet

BrT		LmB	
BkT	✓	SmB	
RbT		WhP	
Sal		Csk	
Tog		WhF	
Smt		Pic	

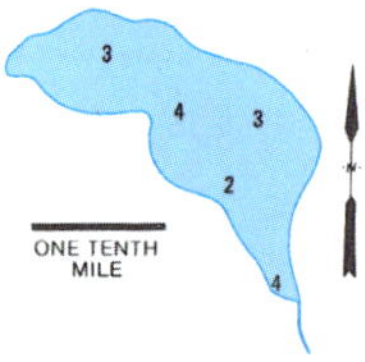

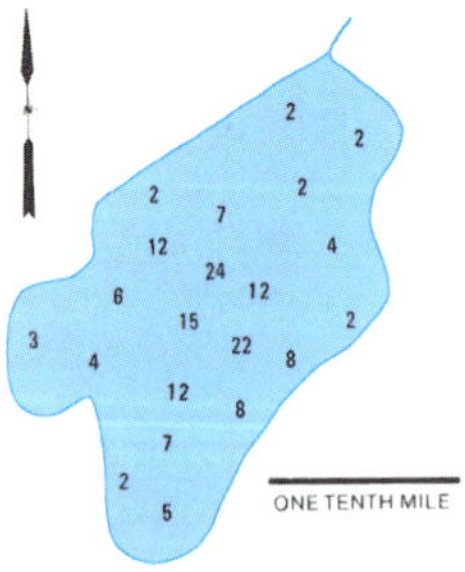

Thanksgiving Pond
Blanchard Plt
Maine Atlas
Map 31, B-2
Acres: 17
Max. Depth:
24 feet

BrT		LmB	
BkT	✓	SmB	
RbT		WhP	
Sal		Csk	
Tog		WhF	
Smt		Pic	

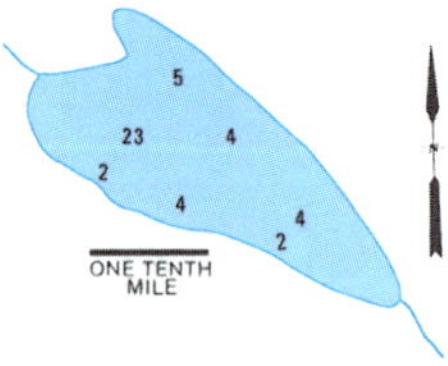

Trout Pond
Bowdoin College
Grant West
Maine Atlas
Map 41, D-5
Acres: 20
Max. Depth:
23 feet

BrT		LmB	
BkT	✓	SmB	
RbT		WhP	
Sal	✓	Csk	
Tog		WhF	
Smt		Pic	

Trout Pond
Moosehead Junction Twp,
Maine Atlas
Map 41, D-1
Acres: 33
Max. Depth:
16 feet

BrT		LmB	
BkT	✓	SmB	
RbT		WhP	
Sal		Csk	
Tog		WhF	
Smt		Pic	

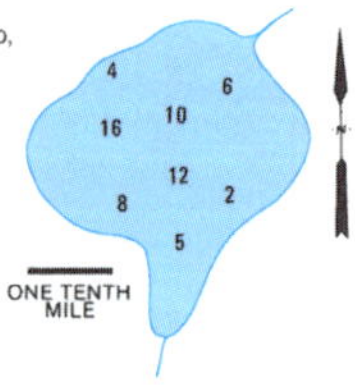

Third Debsconeag Lake
T2 R10 WELS,
T1 R10 WELS
Maine Atlas
Map 50, E-4
Map 42, A-4
Acres: 1,011
Max. Depth:
162 feet

BrT		LmB	
BkT	✓	SmB	
RbT		WhP	
Sal		Csk	✓
Tog	✓	WhF	
Smt		Pic	

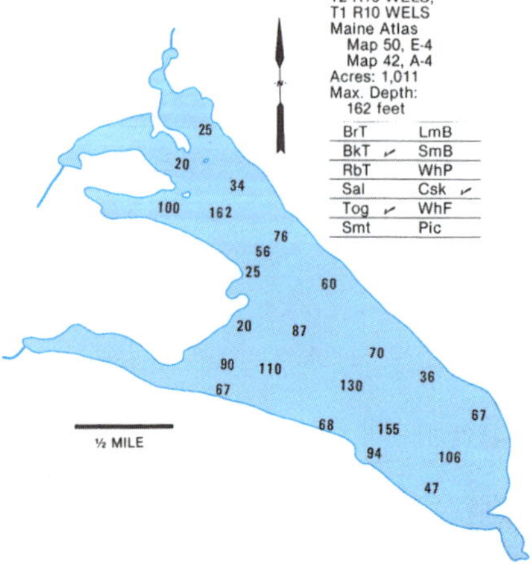

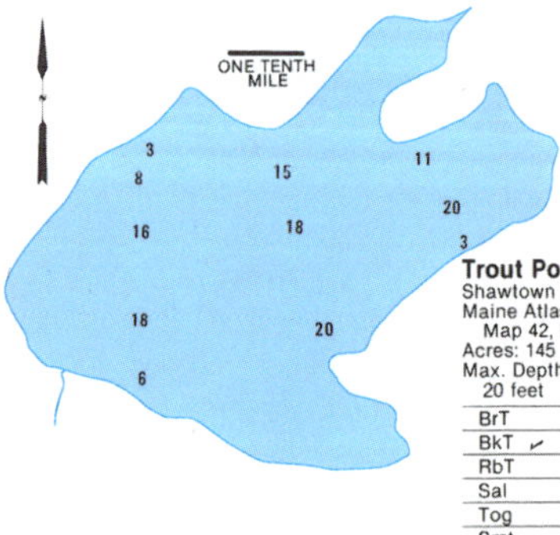

Trout Pond
Shawtown Twp
Maine Atlas
Map 42, B-1
Acres: 145
Max. Depth:
20 feet

BrT		LmB	
BkT	✓	SmB	
RbT		WhP	
Sal		Csk	✓
Tog		WhF	✓
Smt		Pic	

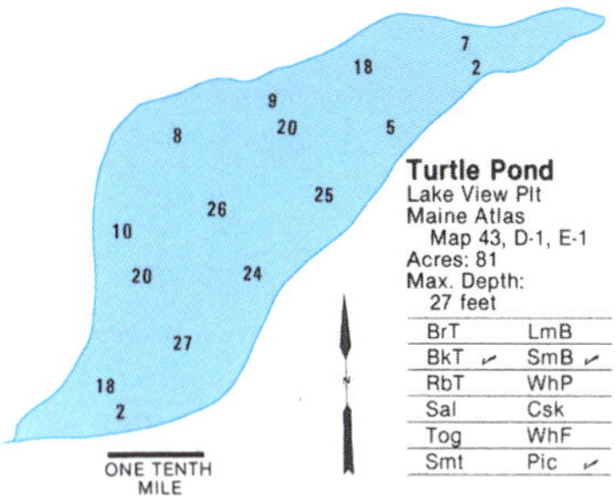

Turtle Pond
Lake View Plt
Maine Atlas
Map 43, D-1, E-1
Acres: 81
Max. Depth:
27 feet

BrT	LmB
BkT ✓	SmB ✓
RbT	WhP
Sal	Csk
Tog	WhF
Smt	Pic ✓

Upper Ebeemee Lake
T4 R9 NWP,
TB R10 WELS
Maine Atlas
Map 42, C-5, D-5
Acres: 196
Max. Depth:
20 feet

BrT	LmB
BkT ✓	SmB ✓
RbT	WhP ✓
Sal	Csk
Tog	WhF
Smt	Pic ✓

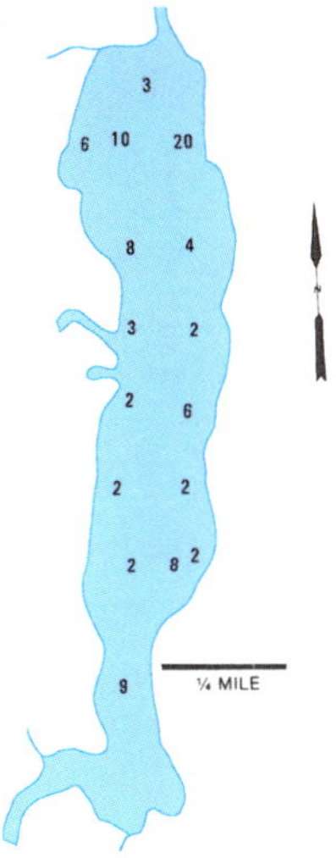

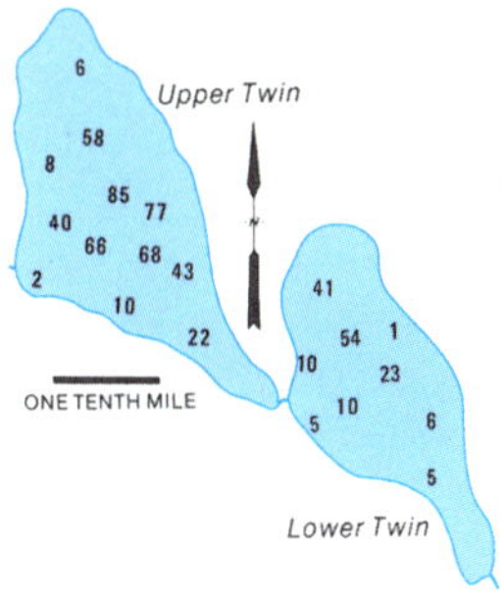

Twin Ponds
T2 R9 WELS
Maine Atlas
Map 51, E-1
Acres: Upper-38
Lower-22
Max. Depth:
Upper-85 feet
Lower-54 feet

BrT	LmB
BkT ✓	SmB
RbT	WhP
Sal	Csk
Tog	WhF
Smt	Pic

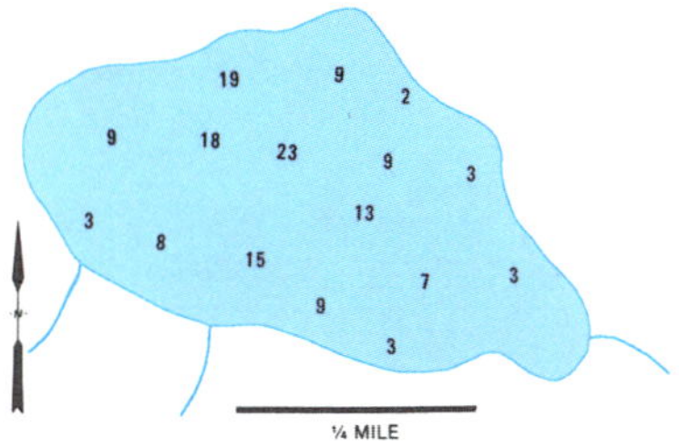

Upper Elbow Pond
T10 R10 WELS, T10 R11 WELS, Maine Atlas Map 56, A-3, A-4
Acres: 88, Max. Depth: 23 feet

BrT	BkT	RbT	Sal	Tog	Smt	LmB	SmB	WhP	Csk	WhF	Pic
	✓		✓								

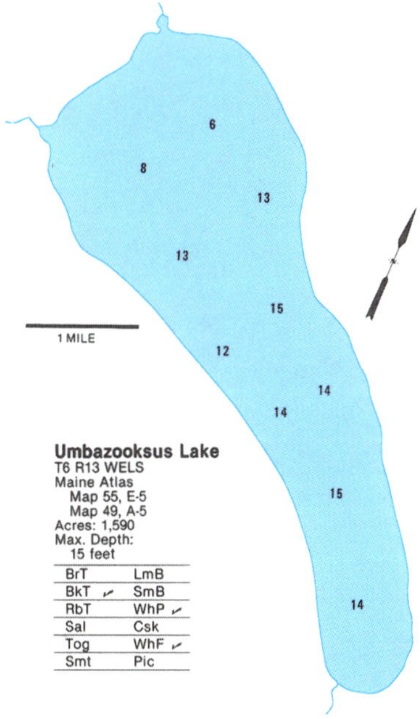

Umbazooksus Lake
T6 R13 WELS
Maine Atlas
Map 55, E-5
Map 49, A-5
Acres: 1,590
Max. Depth:
15 feet

BrT	LmB
BkT ✓	SmB
RbT	WhP ✓
Sal	Csk
Tog	WhF ✓
Smt	Pic

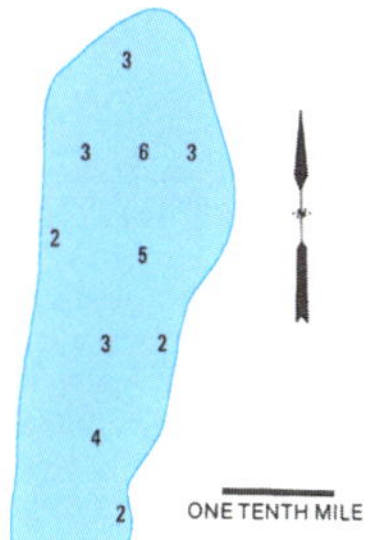

Upper Island Pond
T10 R10 WELS
Maine Atlas
Map 56, A-4
Acres: 45
Max. Depth:
6 feet

BrT	LmB
BkT ✓	SmB
RbT	WhP
Sal	Csk
Tog	WhF
Smt	Pic

Unnamed Pond
T2 R12 WELS
Maine Atlas
Map 50, E-1, E-2
Acres: 30
Max. Depth:
25 feet

BrT	LmB
BkT ✓	SmB
RbT	WhP
Sal	Csk
Tog	WhF
Smt	Pic

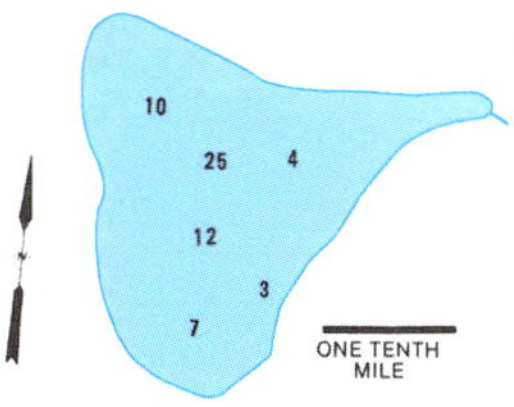

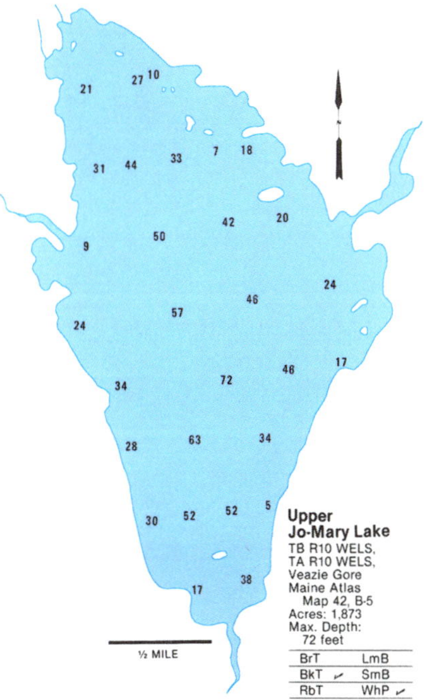

Upper Jo-Mary Lake
TB R10 WELS,
TA R10 WELS,
Veazie Gore
Maine Atlas
Map 42, B-5
Acres: 1,873
Max. Depth:
72 feet

BrT	LmB
BkT ✓	SmB
RbT	WhP ✓
Sal ✓	Csk
Tog ✓	WhF
Smt	Pic ✓

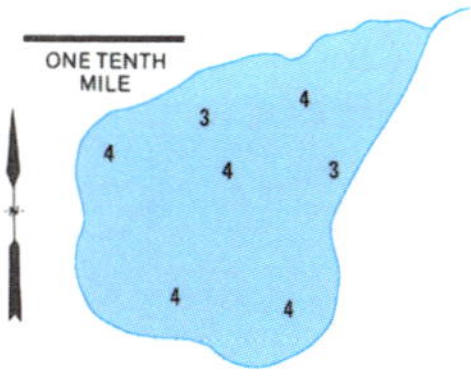

Upper Bluffer Pond
T8 R11 WELS, Maine Atlas Map 56, C-3
Acres: 15, Max. Depth: 4 feet

BrT	BkT	RbT	Sal	Tog	Smt	LmB	SmB	WhP	Csk	WhF	Pic
	✓										

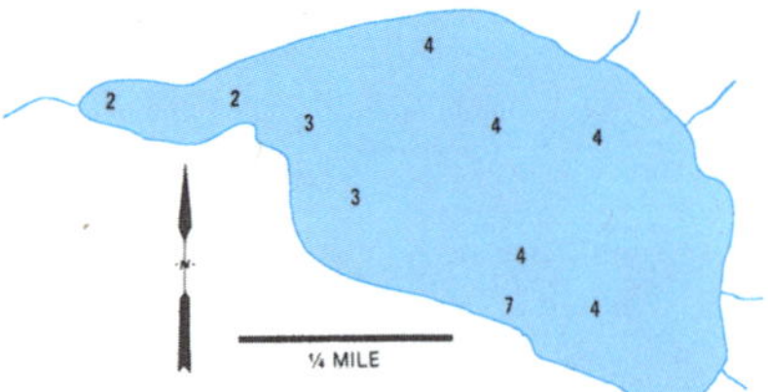

Upper Portage Pond
T9 R11 WELS, Maine Atlas Map 56, B-3
Acres: 96, Max. Depth: 7 feet

BrT	BkT	RbT	Sal	Tog	Smt	LmB	SmB	WhP	Csk	WhF	Pic
	✓										

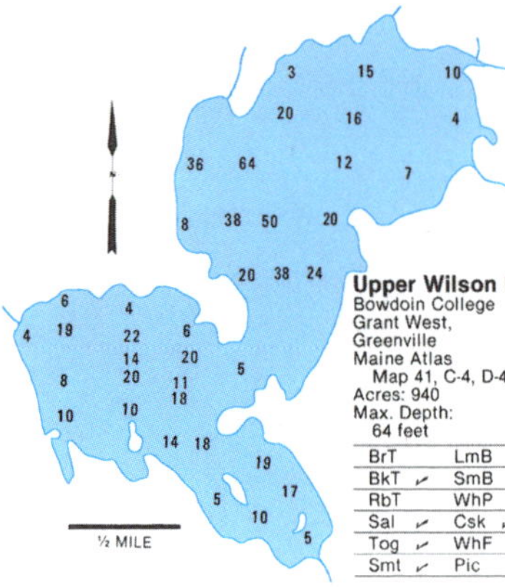

Upper Wilson Pond
Bowdoin College
Grant West,
Greenville
Maine Atlas
Map 41, C-4, D-4
Acres: 940
Max. Depth:
64 feet

BrT		LmB	
BkT	✓	SmB	
RbT		WhP	
Sal	✓	Csk	✓
Tog	✓	WhF	
Smt	✓	Pic	

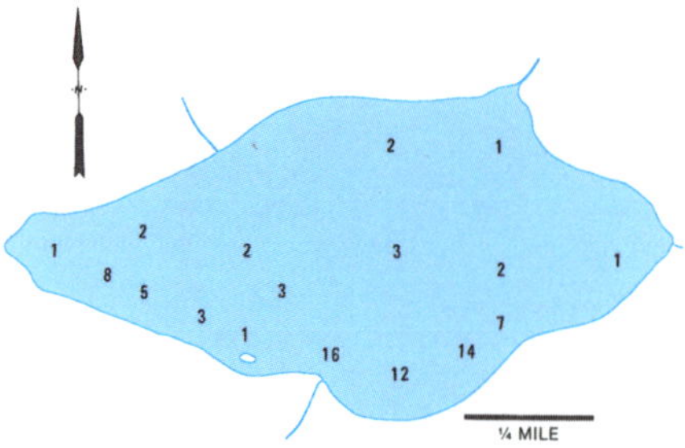

Upper Russell Pond
T9 R14 WELS, Maine Atlas Map 55, B-3, C-3
Acres: 282, Max. Depth: 16 feet

BrT	BkT	RbT	Sal	Tog	Smt	LmB	SmB	WhP	Csk	WhF	Pic
	✓										

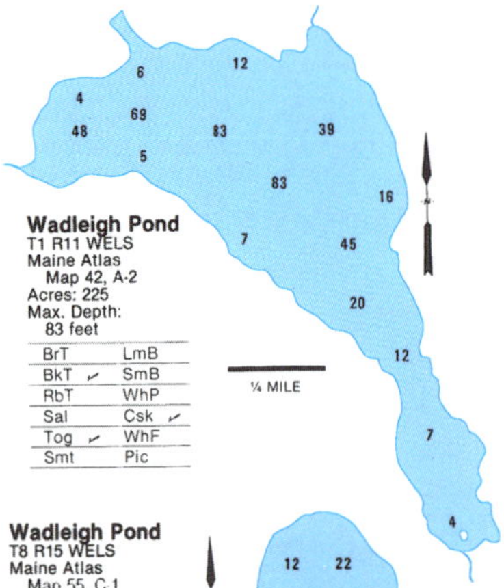

Wadleigh Pond
T1 R11 WELS
Maine Atlas
Map 42, A-2
Acres: 225
Max. Depth:
83 feet

BrT		LmB	
BkT		SmB	
RbT		WhP	
Sal		Csk	✓
Tog	✓	WhF	
Smt		Pic	

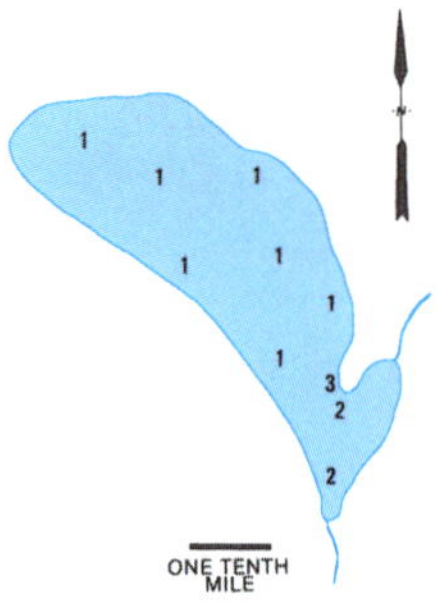

Upper Soper Pond
T8 R11 WELS
Maine Atlas
Map 56, C-2
Acres: 76
Max. Depth:
3 feet

BrT		LmB	
BkT	✓	SmB	
RbT		WhP	
Sal		Csk	
Tog		WhF	
Smt		Pic	

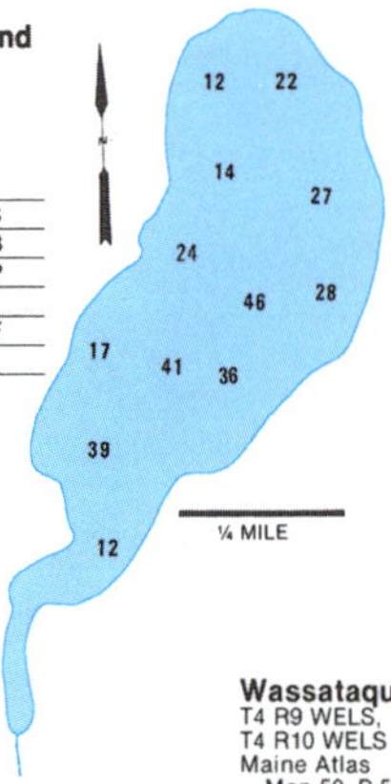

Wadleigh Pond
T8 R15 WELS
Maine Atlas
Map 55, C-1
Acres: 157
Max. Depth:
46 feet

BrT		LmB	
BkT	✓	SmB	
RbT		WhP	
Sal		Csk	
Tog		WhF	
Smt		Pic	

Comments:
Blueback trout.

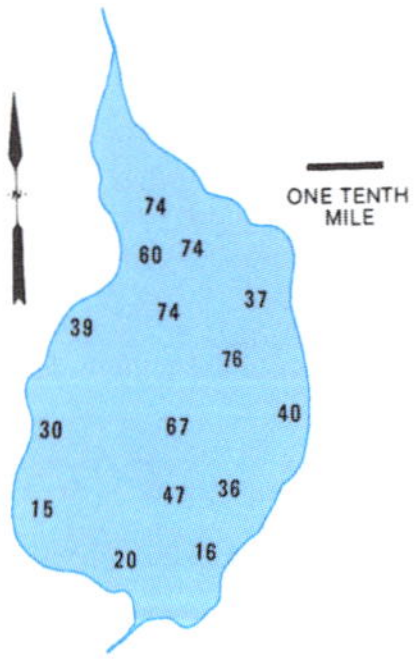

Upper South Branch Pond
T5 R9 WELS
Maine Atlas
Map 51, A-1
Acres: 84
Max. Depth:
76 feet

BrT		LmB	
BkT	✓	SmB	
RbT		WhP	
Sal		Csk	
Tog		WhF	
Smt		Pic	

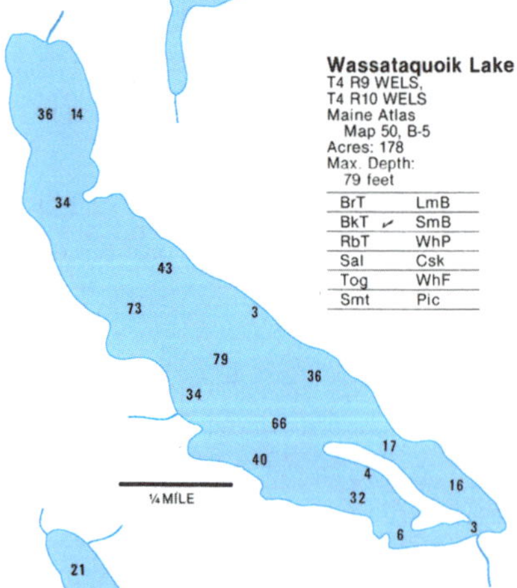

Wassataquoik Lake
T4 R9 WELS,
T4 R10 WELS
Maine Atlas
Map 50, B-5
Acres: 178
Max. Depth:
79 feet

BrT		LmB	
BkT	✓	SmB	
RbT		WhP	
Sal		Csk	
Tog		WhF	
Smt		Pic	

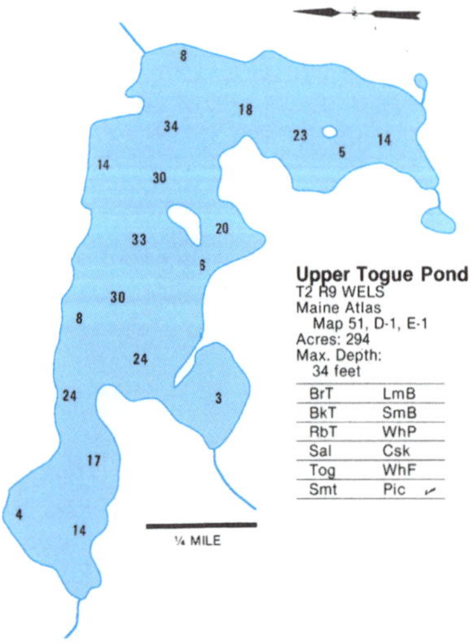

Upper Togue Pond
T2 R9 WELS
Maine Atlas
Map 51, D-1, E-1
Acres: 294
Max. Depth:
34 feet

BrT		LmB	
BkT		SmB	
RbT		WhP	
Sal		Csk	
Tog		WhF	
Smt		Pic	✓

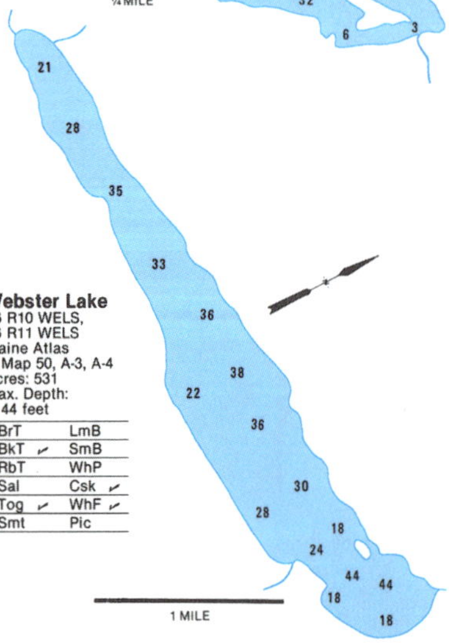

Webster Lake
T6 R10 WELS,
T6 R11 WELS
Maine Atlas
Map 50, A-3, A-4
Acres: 531
Max. Depth:
44 feet

BrT		LmB	
BkT	✓	SmB	
RbT		WhP	
Sal		Csk	✓
Tog	✓	WhF	✓
Smt		Pic	

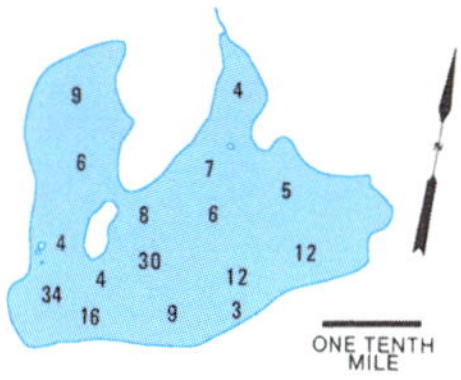

West Chairback Pond

T7 R9 NWP
Maine Atlas
Map 42, D-1
Acres: 60
Max. Depth:
34 feet

BrT		LmB	
BkT	✓	SmB	
RbT		WhP	
Sal		Csk	
Tog		WhF	
Smt		Pic	

Lily Pond

Bath, West Bath
Maine Atlas
Map 6, C-4
Acres: 11
Max. Depth:
10 feet

BrT		LmB	
BkT		SmB	
RbT		WhP	
Sal		Csk	
Tog		WhF	
Smt		Pic	✓

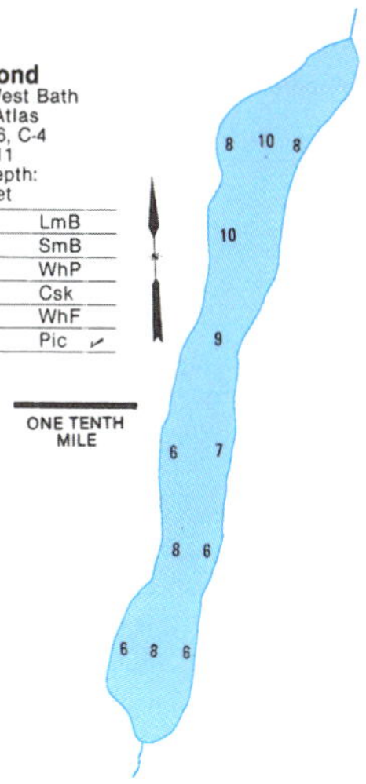

Whetstone Pond

Blanchard Plt,
Kingsbury Plt
Maine Atlas
Map 31, B-3
Acres: 256
Max. Depth:
125 feet
Boat Launch

BrT		LmB	
BkT	✓	SmB	
RbT		WhP	
Sal	✓	Csk	
Tog	✓	WhF	
Smt	✓	Pic	

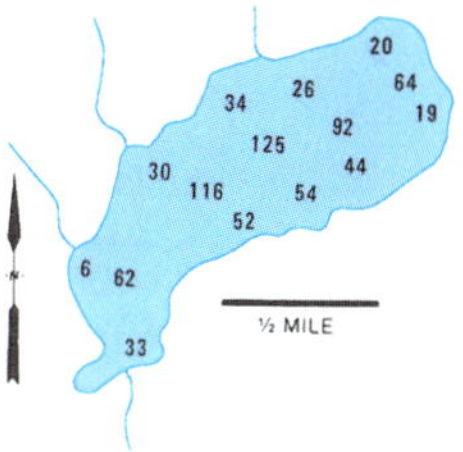

Whidden Ponds

Mt. Katahdin Twp
Maine Atlas
Map 51, C-1
Acres: First-10
Second-7, Third-2
Max. Depth:
First-4 feet
Second-2 feet
Third-3 feet

BrT		LmB	
BkT	✓	SmB	
RbT		WhP	
Sal		Csk	
Tog		WhF	
Smt		Pic	

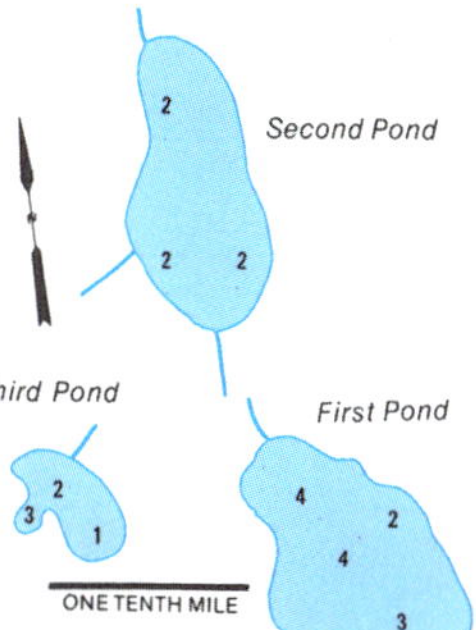

Nequasset Lake

Woolwich
Maine Atlas
Map 6, B-5
Acres: 392
Max. Depth:
63 feet
Boat Launch

BrT	✓	LmB	✓
BkT	✓	SmB	✓
RbT	✓	WhP	✓
Sal	✓	Csk	
Tog		WhF	
Smt	✓	Pic	✓

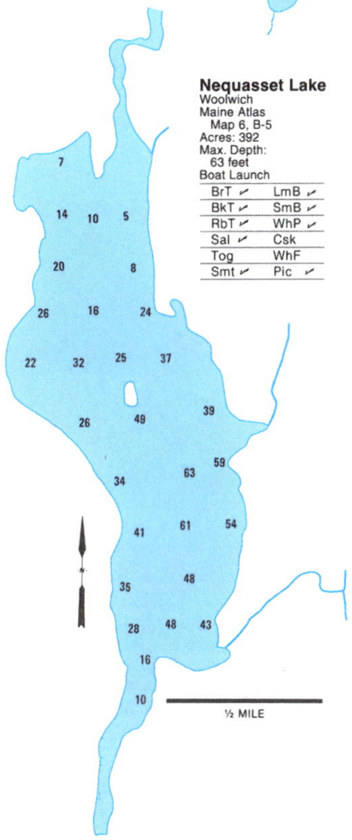

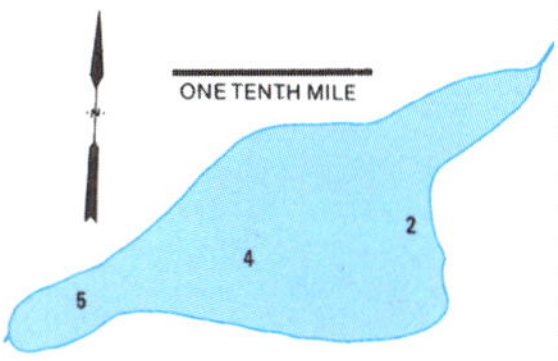

Woodman Pond

Rainbow Twp
Maine Atlas
Map 50, D-3, E-3
Acres: 6
Max. Depth:
5 feet

BrT		LmB	
BkT	✓	SmB	
RbT		WhP	
Sal		Csk	
Tog		WhF	
Smt		Pic	

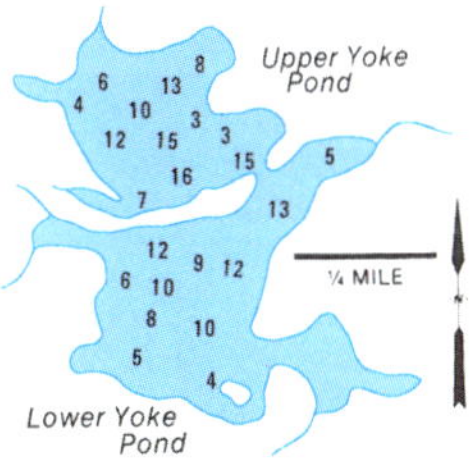

Yoke Ponds

TA R11 WELS
Maine Atlas
Map 42, B-2, B-3
Acres: Upper-53
Lower-81
Max. Depth:
Upper-15 feet
Lower-13 feet

BrT		LmB	
BkT	✓	SmB	
RbT		WhP	
Sal		Csk	
Tog		WhF	
Smt		Pic	

Sagadahoc County

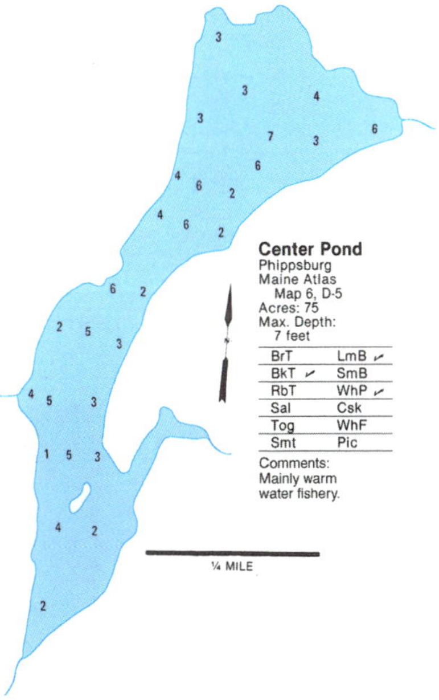

Center Pond

Phippsburg
Maine Atlas
Map 6, D-5
Acres: 75
Max. Depth:
7 feet

BrT		LmB	✓
BkT	✓	SmB	
RbT		WhP	✓
Sal		Csk	
Tog		WhF	
Smt		Pic	

Comments:
Mainly warm water fishery.

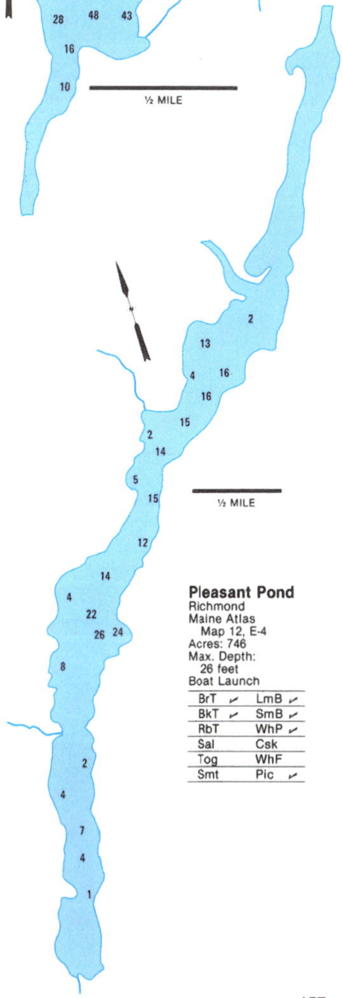

Pleasant Pond

Richmond
Maine Atlas
Map 12, E-4
Acres: 746
Max. Depth:
26 feet
Boat Launch

BrT	✓	LmB	✓
BkT	✓	SmB	✓
RbT		WhP	✓
Sal		Csk	
Tog		WhF	
Smt		Pic	✓

Sagadahoc

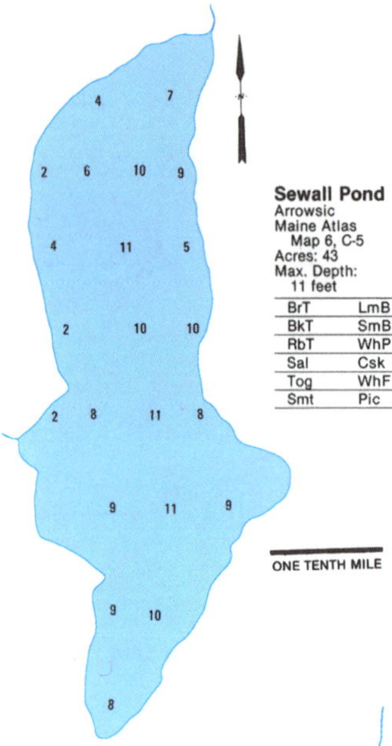

Sewall Pond

Arrowsic
Maine Atlas
Map 6, C-5
Acres: 43
Max. Depth:
11 feet

BrT	LmB ✓
BkT	SmB
RbT	WhP ✓
Sal	Csk
Tog	WhF
Smt	Pic ✓

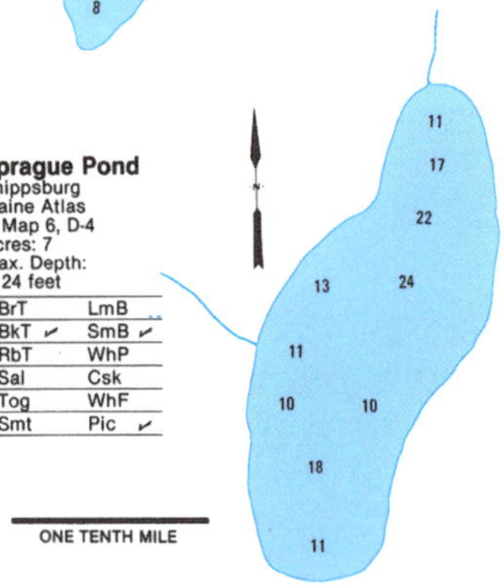

Sprague Pond

Phippsburg
Maine Atlas
Map 6, D-4
Acres: 7
Max. Depth:
24 feet

BrT	LmB
BkT ✓	SmB ✓
RbT	WhP
Sal	Csk
Tog	WhF
Smt	Pic ✓

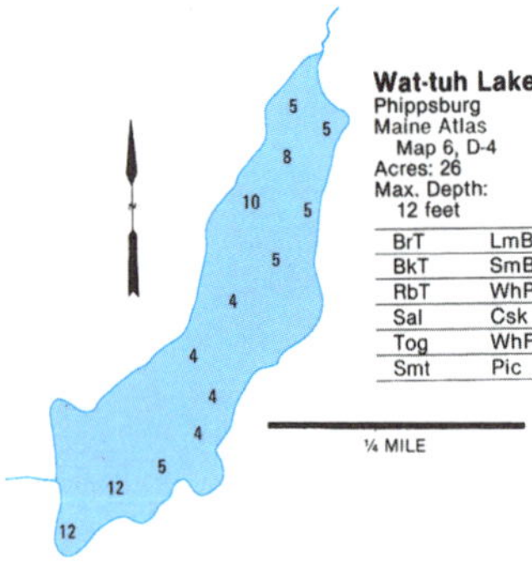

Wat-tuh Lake

Phippsburg
Maine Atlas
Map 6, D-4
Acres: 26
Max. Depth:
12 feet

BrT	LmB ✓
BkT	SmB
RbT	WhP
Sal	Csk
Tog	WhF
Smt	Pic ✓

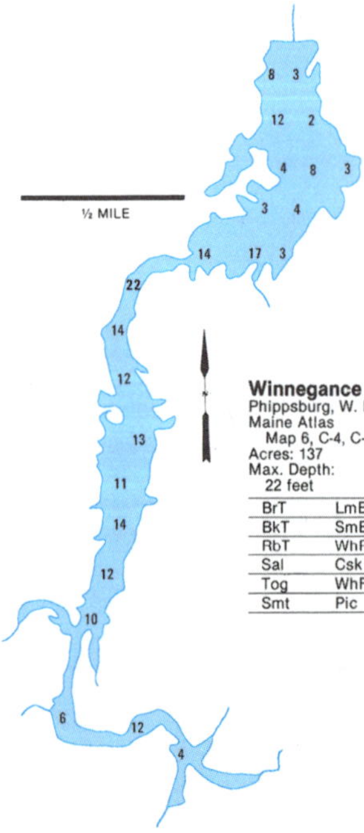

Winnegance Creek

Phippsburg, W. Bath
Maine Atlas
Map 6, C-4, C-5
Acres: 137
Max. Depth:
22 feet

BrT	LmB
BkT	SmB
RbT	WhP
Sal	Csk
Tog	WhF
Smt	Pic ✓

Somerset County

Alder Pond

Alder Brook Twp
Maine Atlas
Map 48, E-1
Acres: 37
Max. Depth:
8 feet

BrT	LmB
BkT ✓	SmB
RbT	WhP
Sal	Csk
Tog	WhF
Smt	Pic

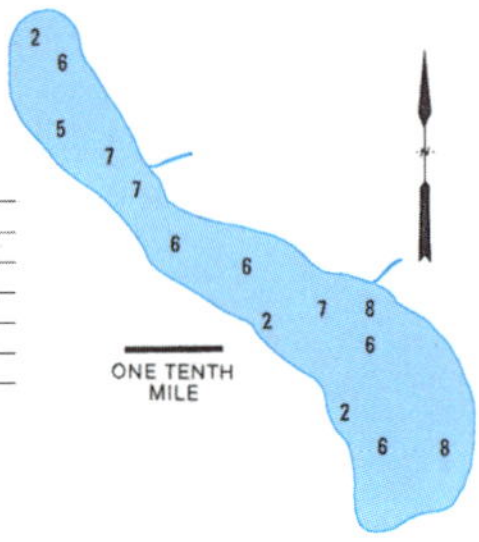

Attean Pond

Attean Twp
Maine Atlas
Map 39, B-4, C-4
Acres: 2,745
Max. Depth:
55 feet
Boat Launch

BrT	LmB
BkT ✓	SmB
RbT	WhP
Sal ✓	Csk ✓
Tog ✓	WhF
Smt ✓	Pic

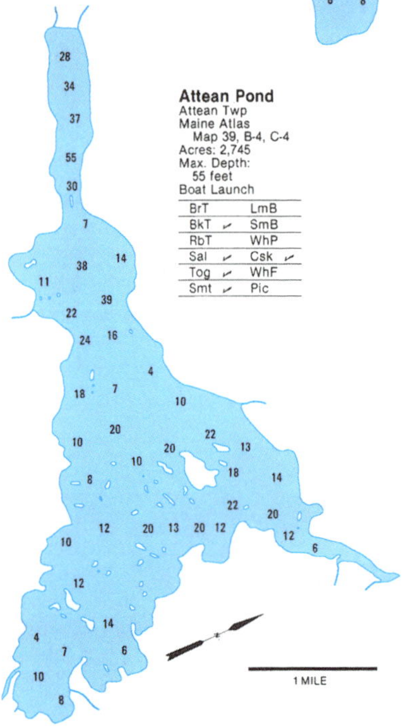

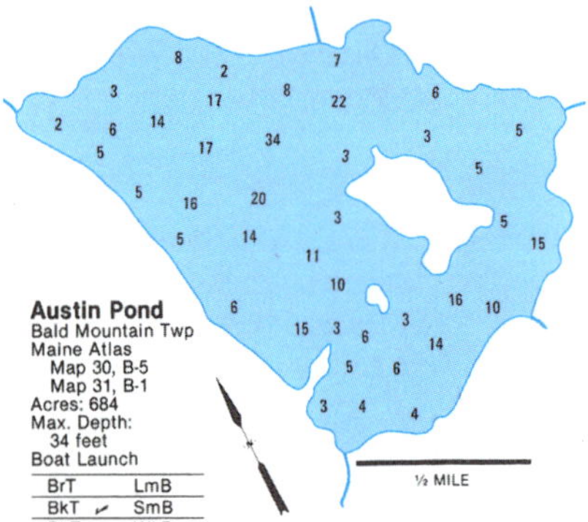

Austin Pond

Bald Mountain Twp
Maine Atlas
Map 30, B-5
Map 31, B-1
Acres: 684
Max. Depth:
34 feet
Boat Launch

BrT	LmB
BkT ✓	SmB
RbT	WhP
Sal ✓	Csk
Tog	WhF
Smt ✓	Pic

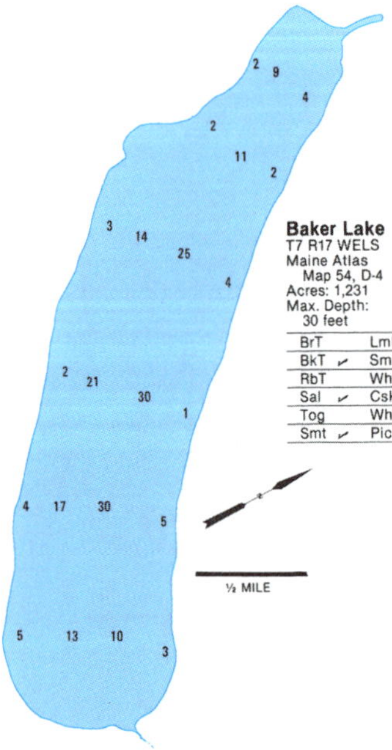

Baker Lake

T7 R17 WELS
Maine Atlas
Map 54, D-4
Acres: 1,231
Max. Depth:
30 feet

BrT	LmB
BkT ✓	SmB
RbT	WhP
Sal ✓	Csk
Tog	WhF
Smt ✓	Pic

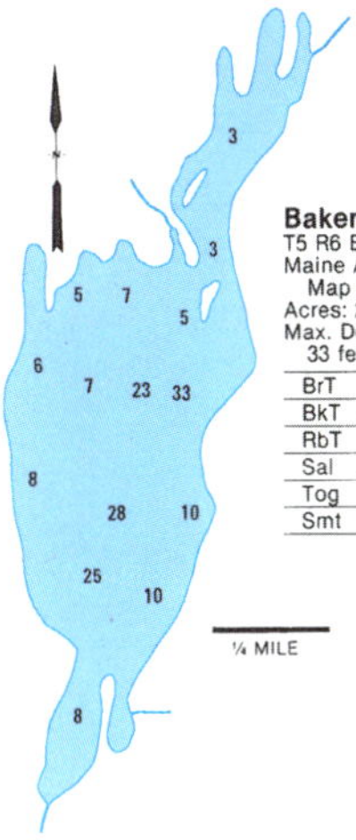

Baker Pond

T5 R6 BKP WKR
Maine Atlas
Map 39, E-3
Acres: 282
Max. Depth:
33 feet

BrT		LmB
BkT	✓	SmB
RbT		WhP
Sal	✓	Csk
Tog		WhF
Smt		Pic

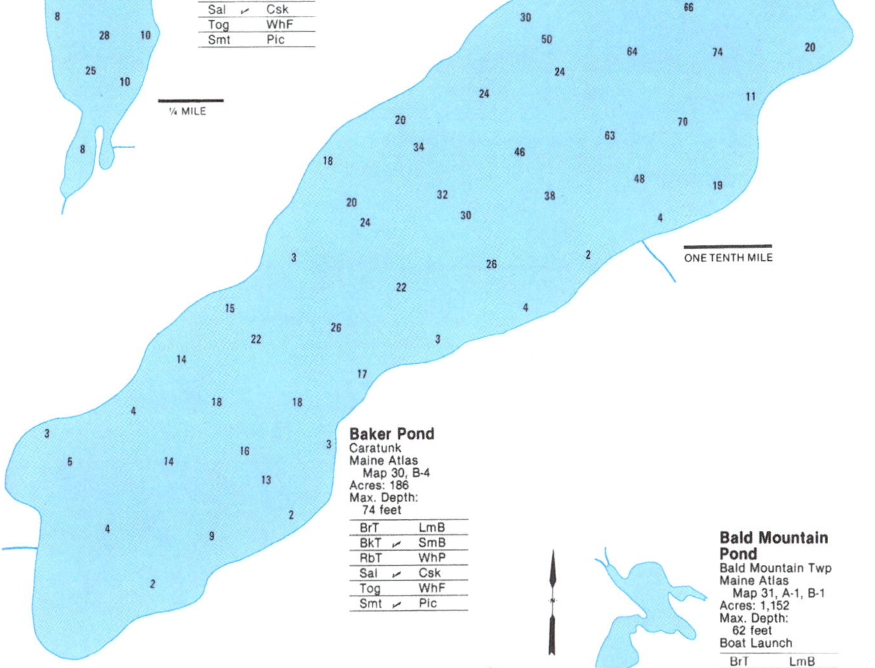

Baker Pond

Caratunk
Maine Atlas
Map 30, B-4
Acres: 186
Max. Depth:
74 feet

BrT		LmB
BkT	✓	SmB
RbT		WhP
Sal	✓	Csk
Tog		WhF
Smt	✓	Pic

Bald Mountain Pond

Bald Mountain Twp
Maine Atlas
Map 31, A-1, B-1
Acres: 1,152
Max. Depth:
62 feet
Boat Launch

BrT		LmB
BkT	✓	SmB
RbT		WhP
Sal		Csk
Tog		WhF
Smt		Pic

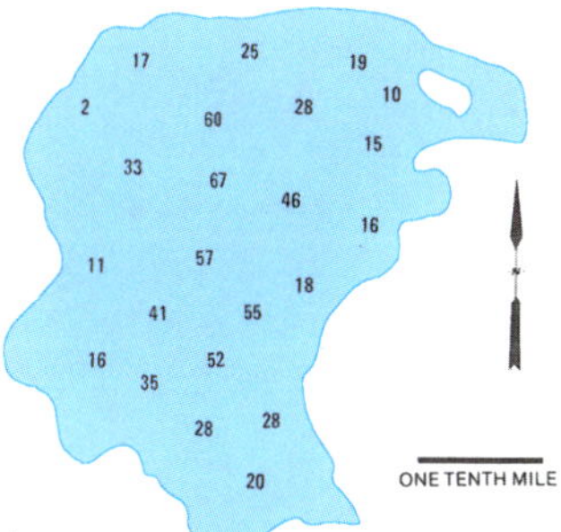

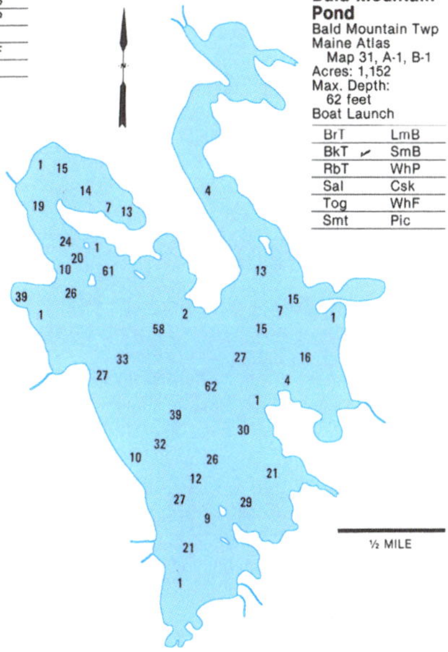

Baker Pond

Solon, Maine Atlas Map 30, E-5
Acres: 50, Max. Depth: 67 feet

BrT	BkT	RbT	Sal	Tog	Smt	LmB	SmB	WhP	Csk	WhF	Pic
✓	✓						✓	✓			

Baker Pond

Tomhegan Twp
Maine Atlas
Map 40, A-4
Acres: 74
Max. Depth:
6 feet

BrT		LmB
BkT	✓	SmB
RbT		WhP
Sal		Csk
Tog		WhF
Smt		Pic

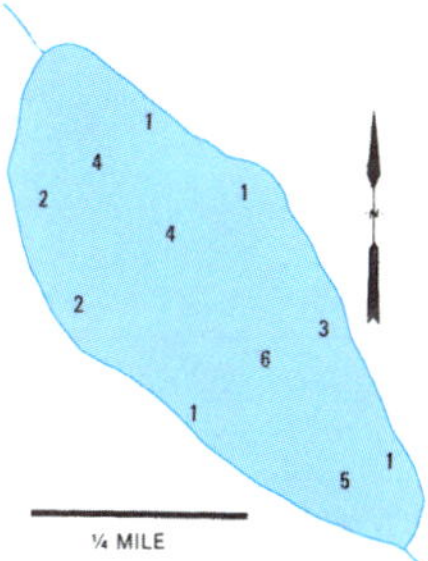

Barrett Pond

Holeb Twp
Maine Atlas
Map 39, C-1, C-2
Acres: 34
Max. Depth:
6 feet

BrT		LmB
BkT	✓	SmB
RbT		WhP
Sal		Csk
Tog		WhF
Smt		Pic

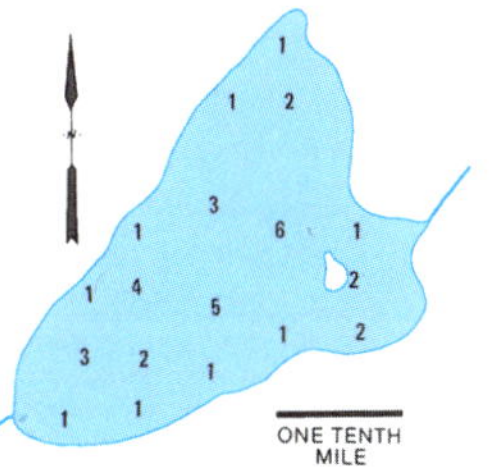

Barker Pond

Cornville
Maine Atlas
Map 21, A-2
Acres: 106
Max. Depth:
42 feet

BrT	LmB	
BkT	SmB	
RbT	WhP	✓
Sal	Csk	
Tog	WhF	
Smt	Pic	✓

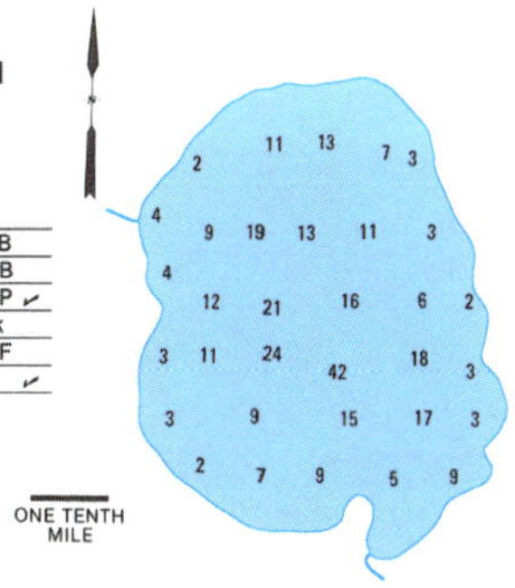

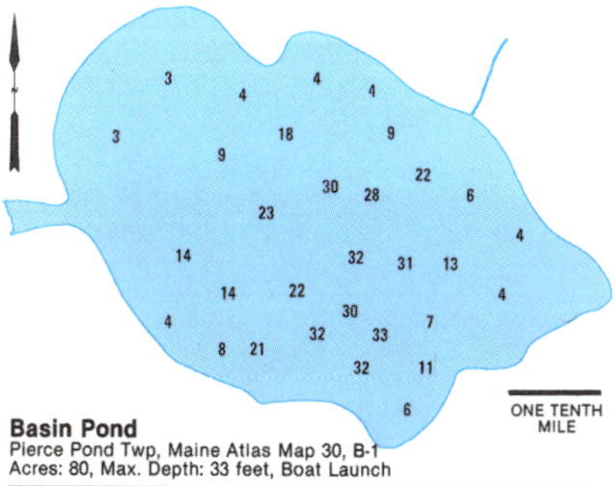

Basin Pond

Pierce Pond Twp, Maine Atlas Map 30, B-1
Acres: 80, Max. Depth: 33 feet, Boat Launch

BrT	BkT	RbT	Sal	Tog	Smt	LmB	SmB	WhP	Csk	WhF	Pic
	✓										

Somerset

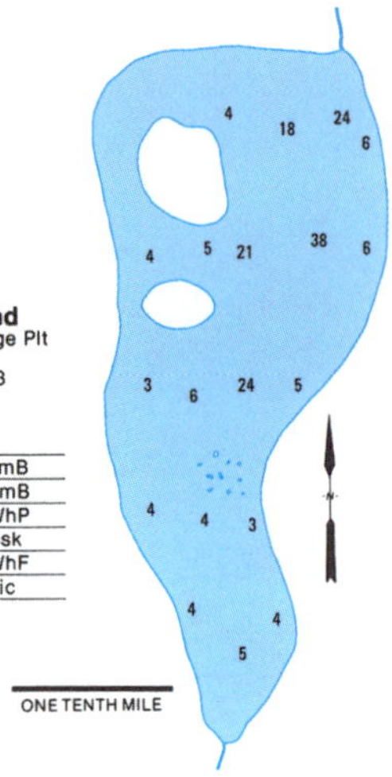

Beans Pond
Pleasant Ridge Plt
Maine Atlas
Map 30, C-3
Acres: 20
Max. Depth:
38 feet

BrT	LmB
BkT ✓	SmB
RbT	WhP
Sal	Csk
Tog	WhF
Smt ✓	Pic

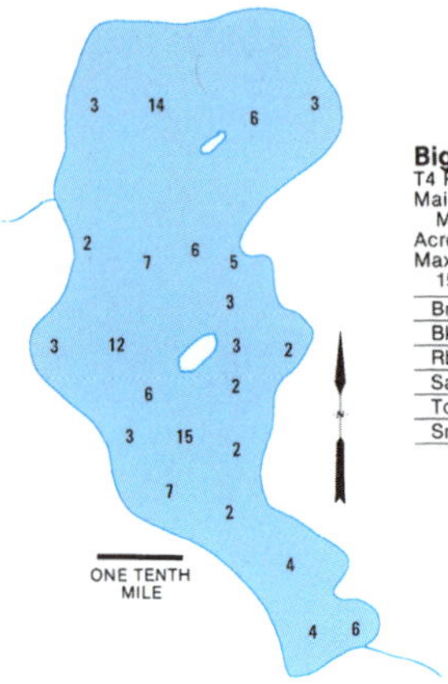

Big Grenier Pond
T4 R5 NBKP
Maine Atlas
Map 47, C-5
Acres: 110
Max. Depth:
15 feet

BrT	LmB
BkT ✓	SmB
RbT	WhP
Sal	Csk
Tog	WhF
Smt	Pic

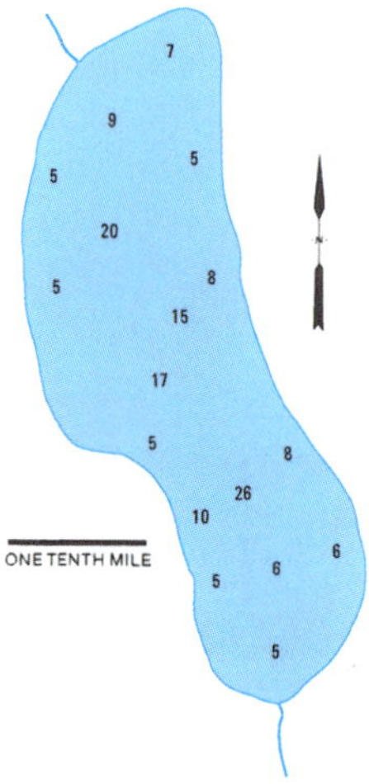

Beck Pond
T3 R5 BKP WKR
Maine Atlas
Map 39, E-3
Acres: 32
Max. Depth:
26 feet

BrT	LmB
BkT ✓	SmB
RbT	WhP
Sal	Csk
Tog	WhF
Smt	Pic

Big Indian Pond
St. Albans
Maine Atlas
Map 31, E-5
Acres: 990
Max. Depth:
28 feet
Boat Launch

BrT ✓	LmB
BkT ✓	SmB ✓
RbT	WhP ✓
Sal	Csk ✓
Tog	WhF
Smt ✓	Pic ✓

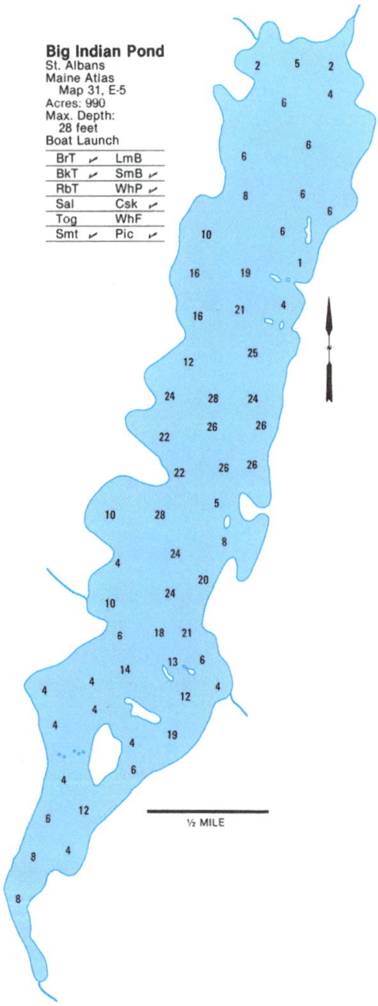

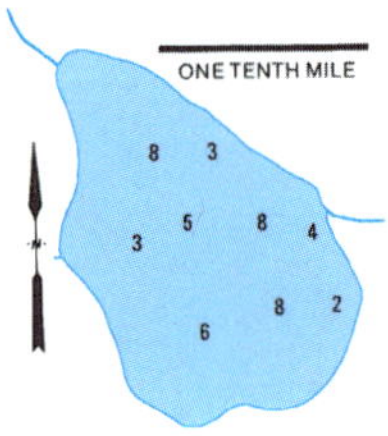

Big Bartley Pond
Holeb Twp
Maine Atlas
Map 39, C-2
Acres: 10
Max. Depth:
8 feet

BrT	LmB
BkT ✓	SmB
RbT	WhP
Sal	Csk
Tog	WhF
Smt	Pic

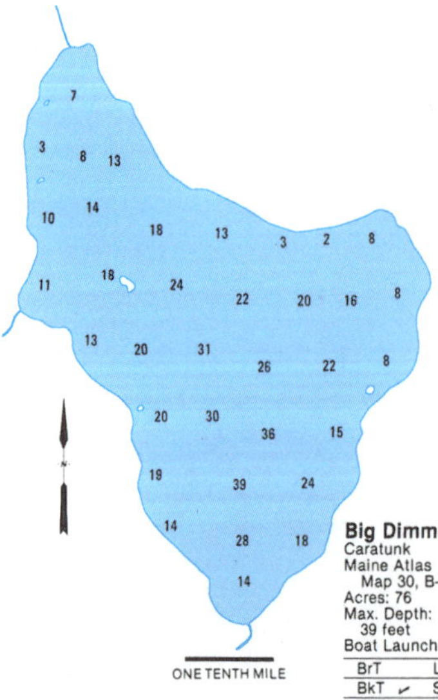

Big Dimmick Pond
Caratunk
Maine Atlas
Map 30, B-4
Acres: 76
Max. Depth:
39 feet
Boat Launch

BrT	LmB
BkT ✓	SmB
RbT	WhP
Sal	Csk
Tog	WhF
Smt	Pic

Bill Morris Pond
T3 R5 BKP WKR
Maine Atlas
Map 39, E-5
Acres: 23
Max. Depth:
23 feet

BrT	LmB
BkT ✓	SmB
RbT	WhP
Sal	Csk
Tog	WhF
Smt	Pic

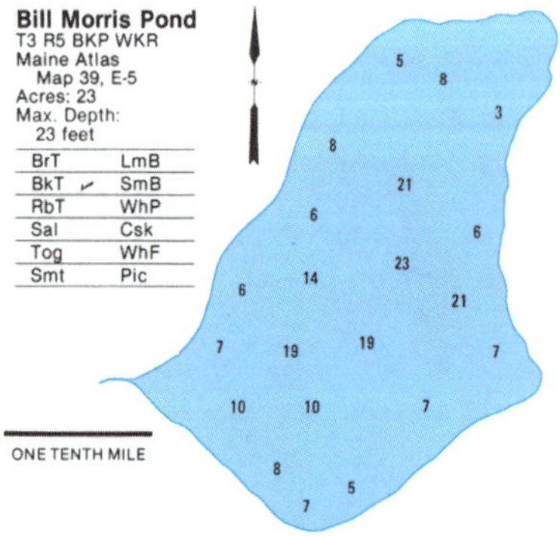

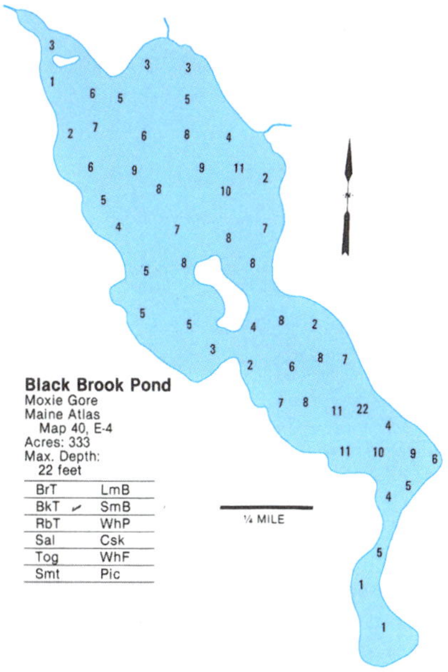

Black Brook Pond
Moxie Gore
Maine Atlas
Map 40, E-4
Acres: 333
Max. Depth:
22 feet

BrT	LmB
BkT ✓	SmB
RbT	WhP
Sal	Csk
Tog	WhF
Smt	Pic

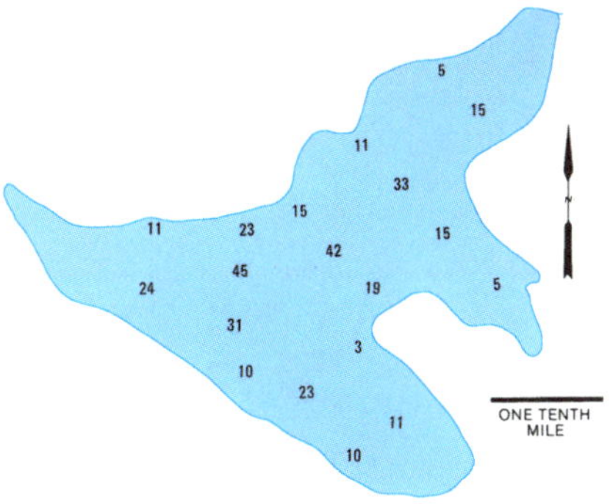

Blakeslee Lake
T5 R6 BKP WKR, Maine Atlas Map 39, E-2, E-3
Acres: 55, Max. Depth: 45 feet

BrT	BkT	RbT	Sal	Tog	Smt	LmB	SmB	WhP	Csk	WhF	Pic
	✓										

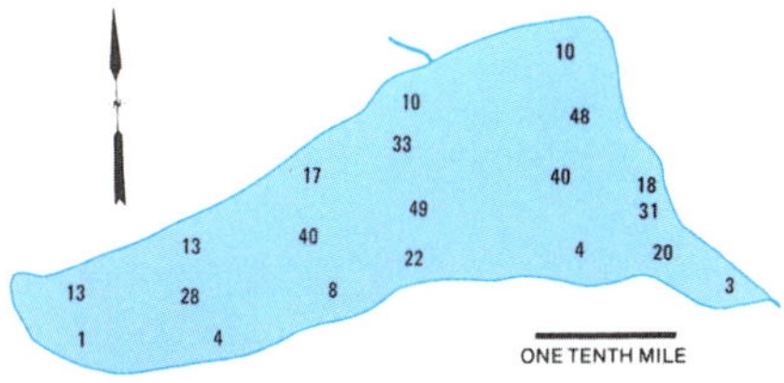

Black Hill Pond
Embden, Maine Atlas Map 20, A-3
Acres: 34, Max. Depth: 49 feet

BrT	BkT	RbT	Sal	Tog	Smt	LmB	SmB	WhP	Csk	WhF	Pic
	✓										

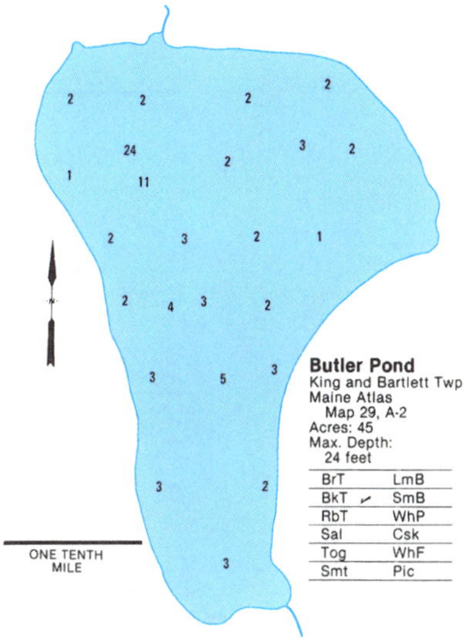

Butler Pond
King and Bartlett Twp
Maine Atlas
Map 29, A-2
Acres: 45
Max. Depth:
24 feet

BrT	LmB
BkT ✓	SmB
RbT	WhP
Sal	Csk
Tog	WhF
Smt	Pic

Brassua Lake
Brassua Twp,
Tomhegan Twp,
Rockwood Strip
T2 R1, Rockwood
Strip T1 R1,
Sandwich Academy
Grant, Taunton
and Raynham
Academy Grant
Maine Atlas
Map 40, B-4
Acres: 8,979
Max. Depth:
65 feet
Boat Launch

BrT	LmB
BkT ✓	SmB
RbT	WhP
Sal ✓	Csk ✓
Tog ✓	WhF
Smt ✓	Pic

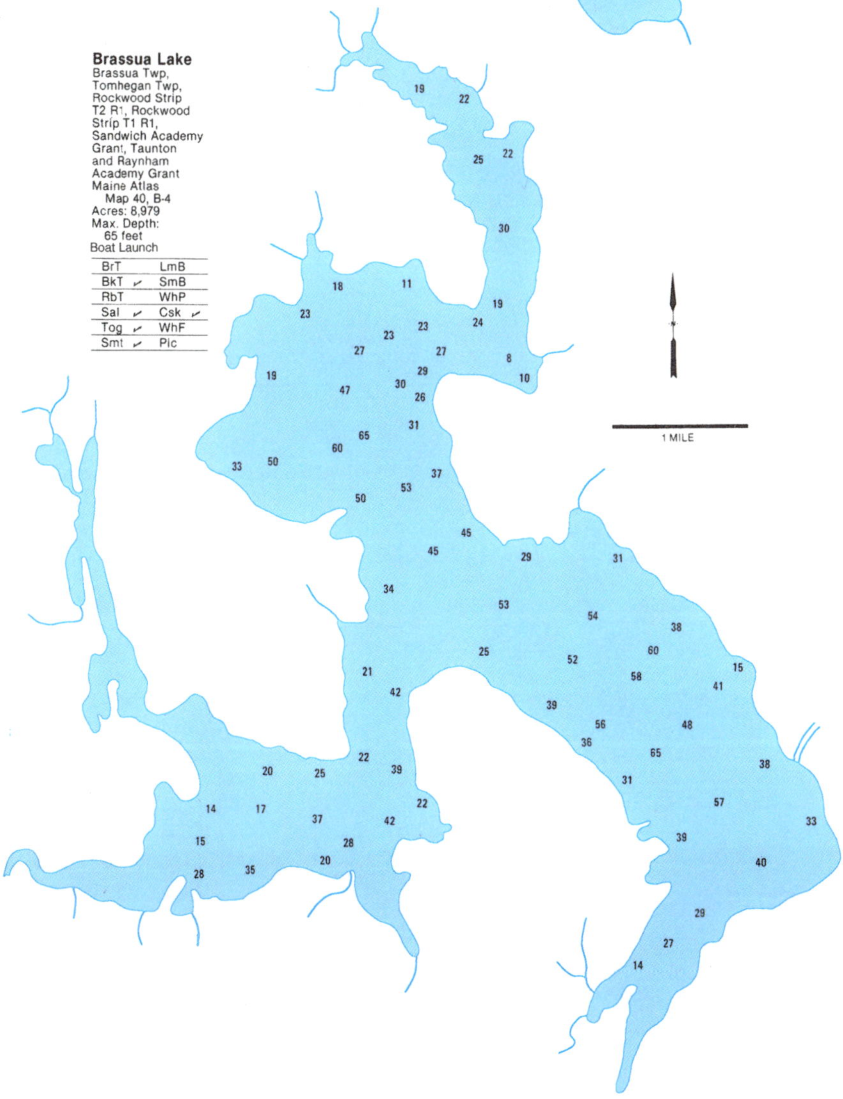

Somerset

Butler Pond
Lexington Twp, Kingfield
Maine Atlas
Map 30, D-1
Acres: 28
Max. Depth: 15 feet

BrT	LmB
BkT ✓	SmB
RbT	WhP
Sal	Csk
Tog	WhF
Smt	Pic

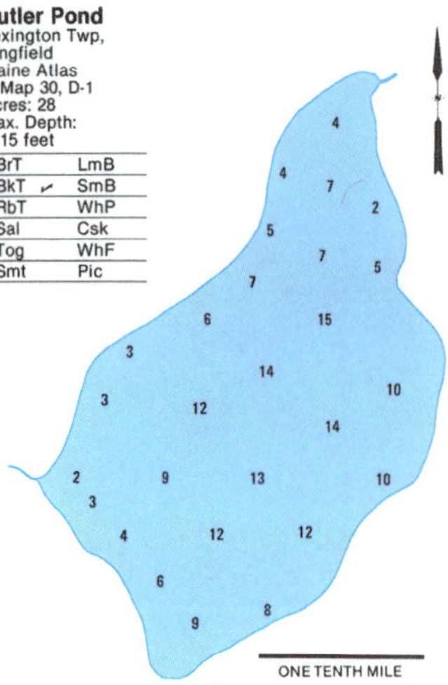

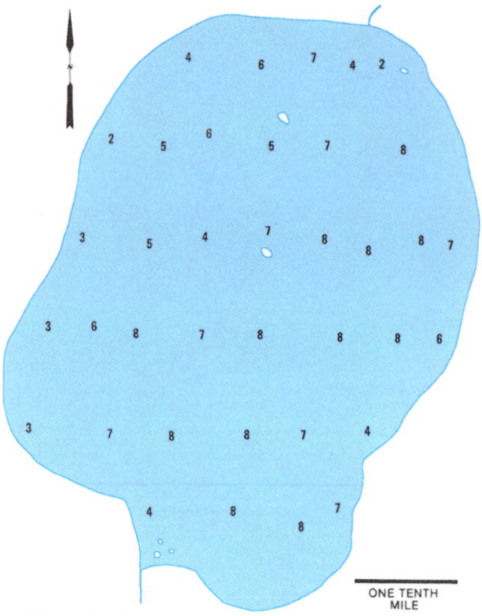

Chase Pond
Moscow, Maine Atlas Map 30, C-4
Acres: 96, Max. Depth: 8 feet

BrT	BkT	RbT	Sal	Tog	Smt	LmB	SmB	WhP	Csk	WhF	Pic
	✓										

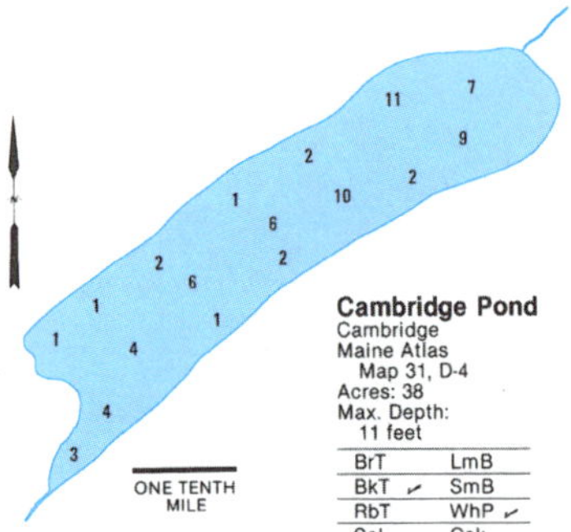

Cambridge Pond
Cambridge
Maine Atlas
Map 31, D-4
Acres: 38
Max. Depth: 11 feet

BrT	LmB
BkT ✓	SmB
RbT	WhP ✓
Sal	Csk
Tog	WhF
Smt	Pic ✓

Chase Pond
Solon
Maine Atlas
Map 30, E-5
Acres: 30
Max. Depth: 5 feet

BrT	LmB
BkT ✓	SmB
RbT	WhP
Sal	Csk
Tog	WhF
Smt	Pic

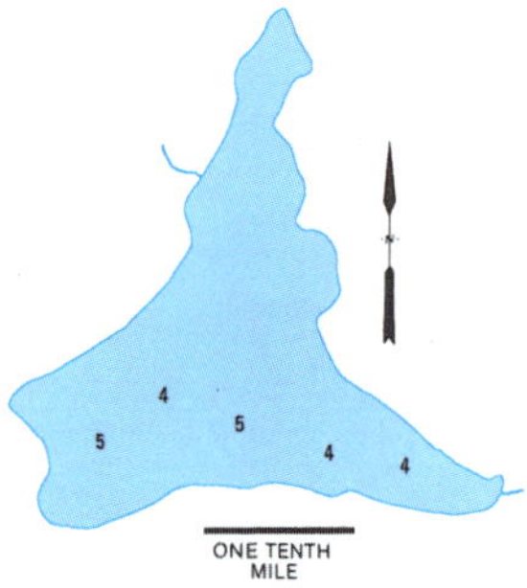

Chase Stream Pond
Misery Twp, Chase Stream Twp
Maine Atlas
Map 40, C-3, D-3
Acres: 31
Max. Depth: 12 feet

BrT ✓	LmB
BkT ✓	SmB
RbT	WhP
Sal	Csk
Tog	WhF
Smt	Pic

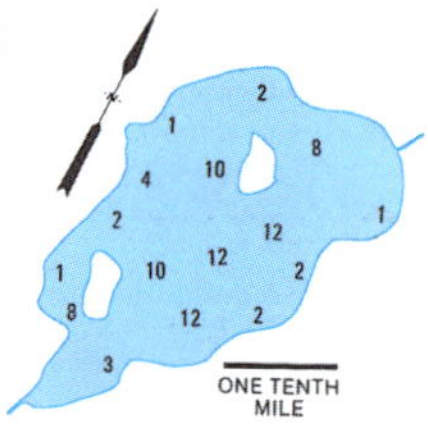

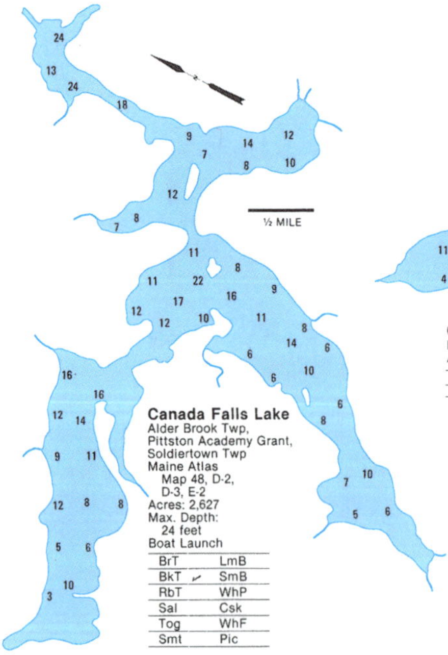

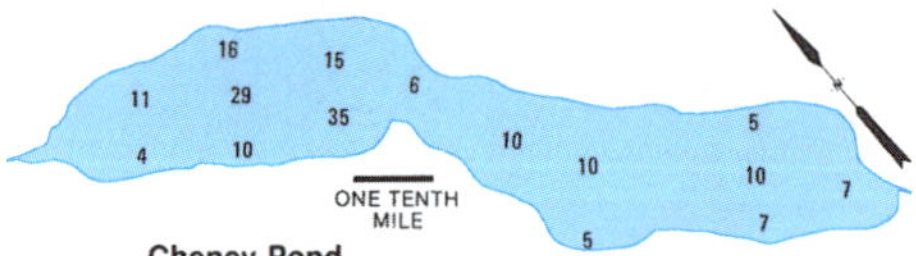

Cheney Pond
Hammond Twp, Prentiss Twp, Maine Atlas Map 47, C-5
Acres: 100, Max. Depth: 35 feet

BrT	BkT	RbT	Sal	Tog	Smt	LmB	SmB	WhP	Csk	WhF	Pic
	✓										

Canada Falls Lake
Alder Brook Twp, Pittston Academy Grant, Soldiertown Twp
Maine Atlas
Map 48, D-2, D-3, E-2
Acres: 2,627
Max. Depth: 24 feet
Boat Launch

BrT	LmB
BkT ✓	SmB
RbT	WhP
Sal	Csk
Tog	WhF
Smt	Pic

Chub Pond
Hobbstown Twp
Maine Atlas
Map 39, D-4
Acres: 24
Max. Depth: 19 feet

BrT	LmB
BkT ✓	SmB
RbT	WhP
Sal	Csk
Tog	WhF
Smt	Pic

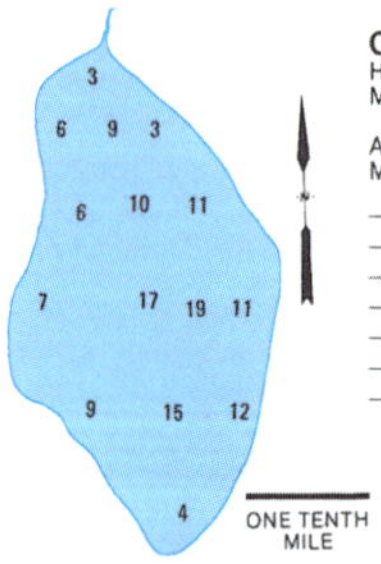

Center Pond
Soldiertown Twp
Maine Atlas
Map 48, E-3
Acres: 51
Max. Depth: 16 feet

BrT	LmB
BkT ✓	SmB
RbT	WhP
Sal	Csk
Tog	WhF
Smt	Pic

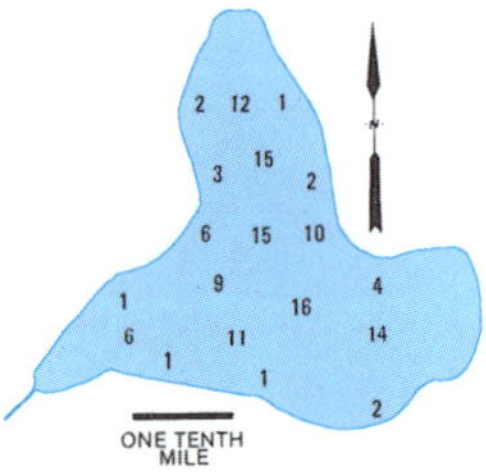

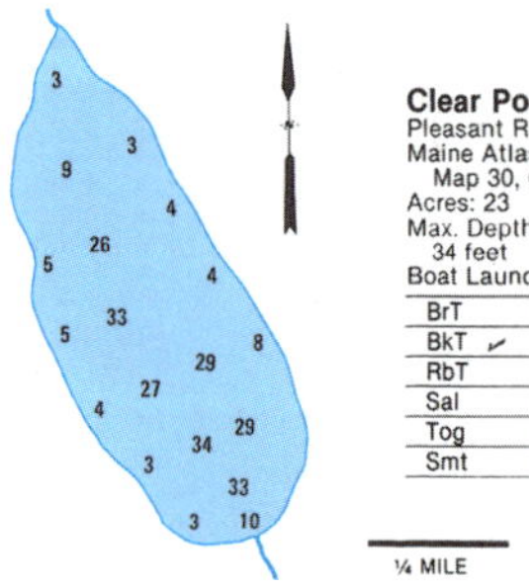

Clear Pond
Pleasant Ridge Plt
Maine Atlas
Map 30, C-3
Acres: 23
Max. Depth: 34 feet
Boat Launch

BrT	LmB
BkT ✓	SmB
RbT	WhP
Sal	Csk
Tog	WhF
Smt	Pic

Clearwater Pond

Attean Twp
Maine Atlas
Map 39, B-3, C-3
Acres: 34
Max. Depth:
35 feet

BrT	LmB
BkT ✓	SmB
RbT	WhP
Sal	Csk ✓
Tog	WhF
Smt	Pic

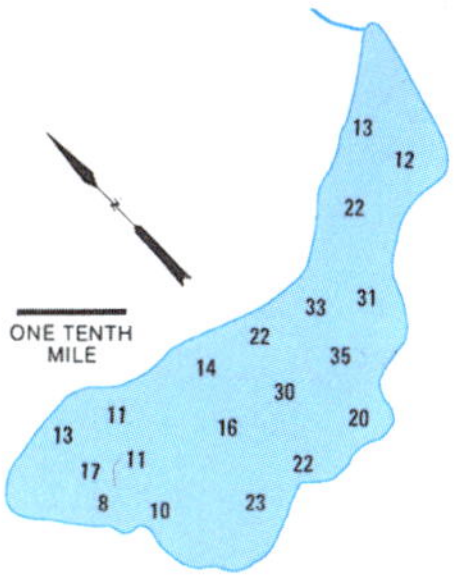

Demo Pond

Rockwood Strip
T2 R1
Maine Atlas
Map 40, B-3
Acres: 192
Max. Depth:
12 feet

BrT	LmB
BkT ✓	SmB
RbT	WhP
Sal	Csk
Tog	WhF
Smt	Pic

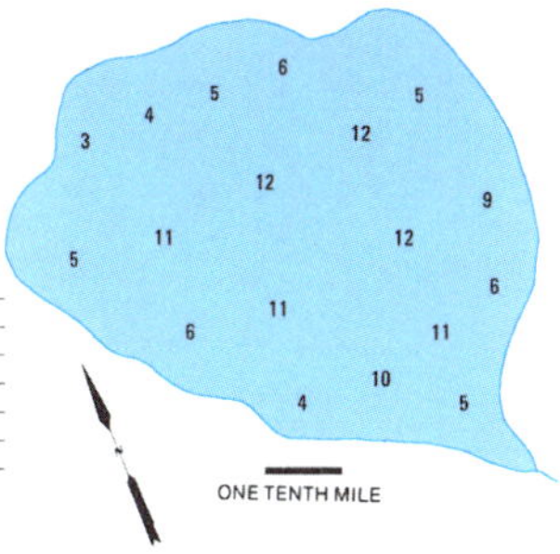

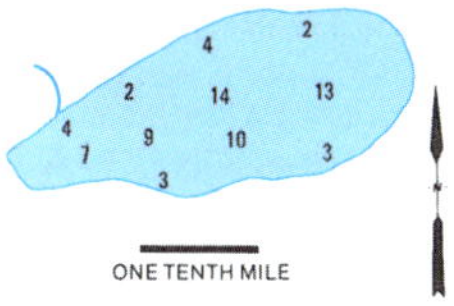

Clish Pond

T5 R20 WELS
Maine Atlas
Map 47, B-4
Acres: 21
Max. Depth:
14 feet

BrT	LmB
BkT ✓	SmB
RbT	WhP
Sal	Csk
Tog	WhF
Smt	Pic

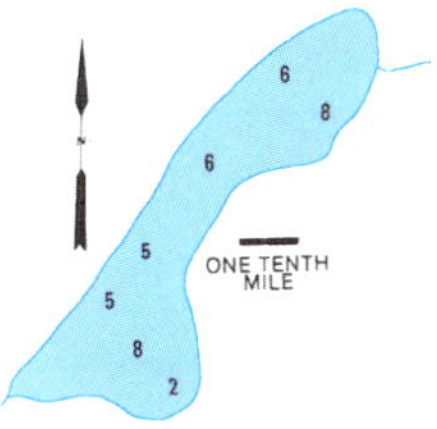

Desolation Pond

T8 R16 WELS
Maine Atlas
Map 55, C-1
Acres: 70
Max. Depth:
8 feet

BrT	LmB
BkT ✓	SmB
RbT	WhP
Sal	Csk
Tog	WhF
Smt	Pic

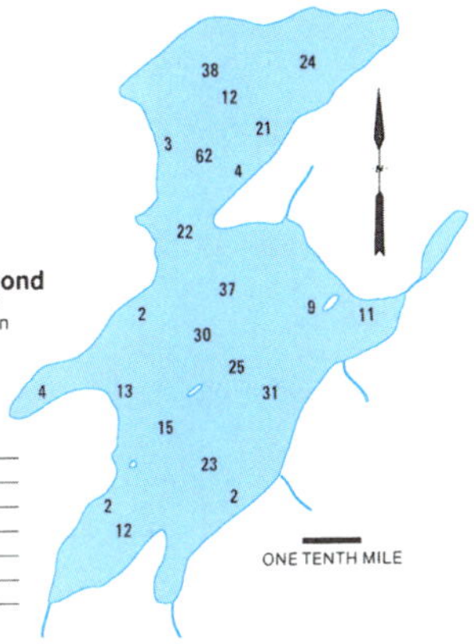

Cold Stream Pond

Misery Twp, Parlin Pond Twp, Johnson Mountain Twp
Maine Atlas
Map 40, C-2
Acres: 205
Max. Depth:
62 feet

BrT	LmB
BkT ✓	SmB
RbT	WhP
Sal	Csk
Tog	WhF
Smt	Pic

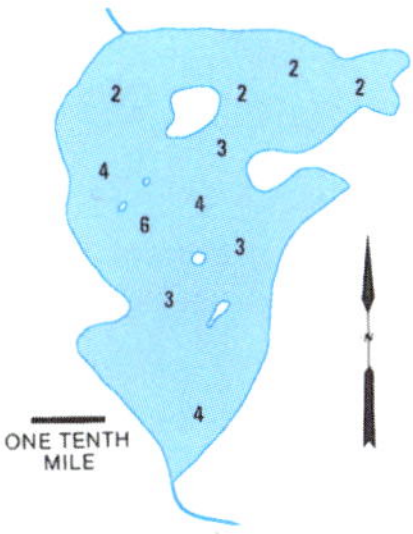

Dingley Pond

T4 R5 NBKP
Maine Atlas
Map 47, C-5
Acres: 71
Max. Depth:
6 feet

BrT	LmB
BkT ✓	SmB
RbT	WhP
Sal	Csk
Tog	WhF
Smt	Pic

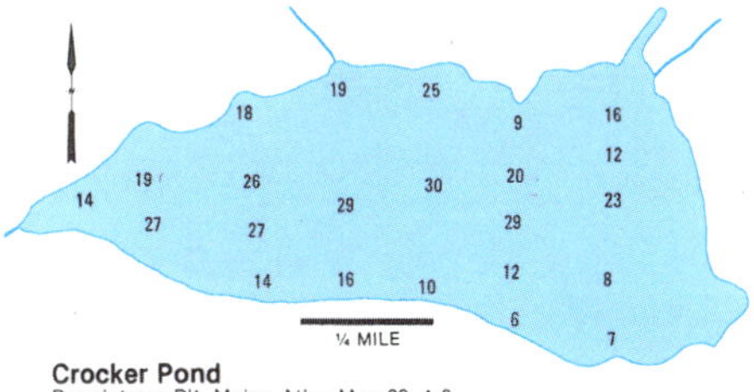

Crocker Pond

Dennistown Plt, Maine Atlas Map 39, A-3
Acres: 227, Max. Depth: 30 feet, Boat Launch

BrT	BkT	RbT	Sal	Tog	Smt	LmB	SmB	WhP	Csk	WhF	Pic
	✓										

ONE TENTH MILE

Dixon Pond

Pierce Pond Twp
Maine Atlas
Map 30, A-1
Acres: 17
Max. Depth:
55 feet

BrT	LmB
BkT ✓	SmB
RbT	WhP
Sal	Csk
Tog	WhF
Smt ✓	Pic

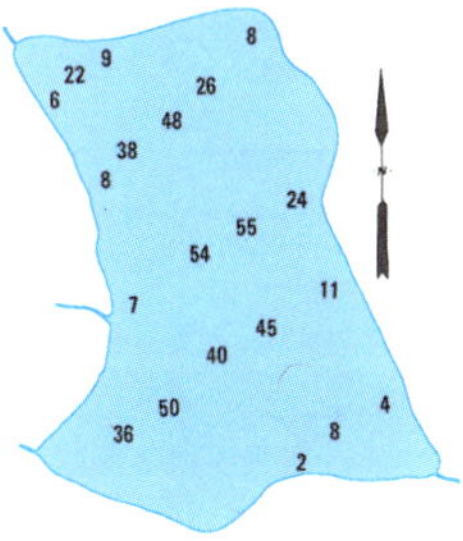

Daymond Pond

Moose River
Maine Atlas
Map 39, A-4
Acres: 11
Max. Depth:
17 feet

BrT	LmB
BkT ✓	SmB
RbT	WhP
Sal	Csk
Tog	WhF
Smt	Pic

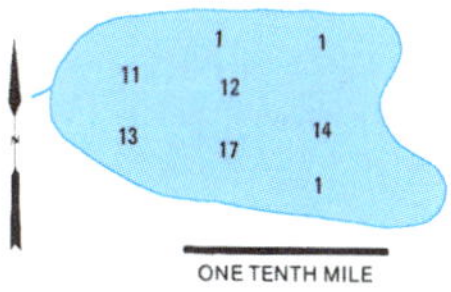

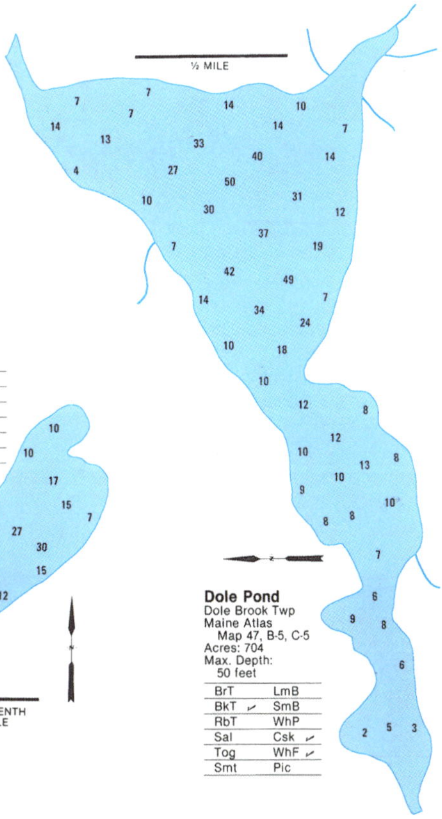

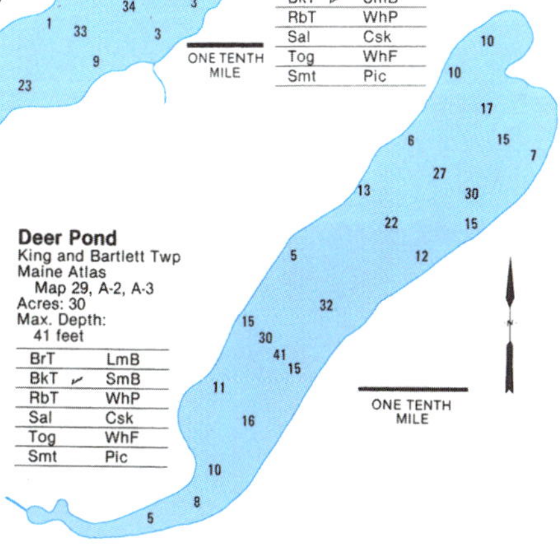

Dead Stream Pond

West Forks Plt, Chase Stream Twp
Maine Atlas
Map 40, D-3
Acres: 67
Max. Depth:
43 feet

BrT	LmB
BkT ✓	SmB
RbT	WhP
Sal	Csk
Tog	WhF
Smt	Pic

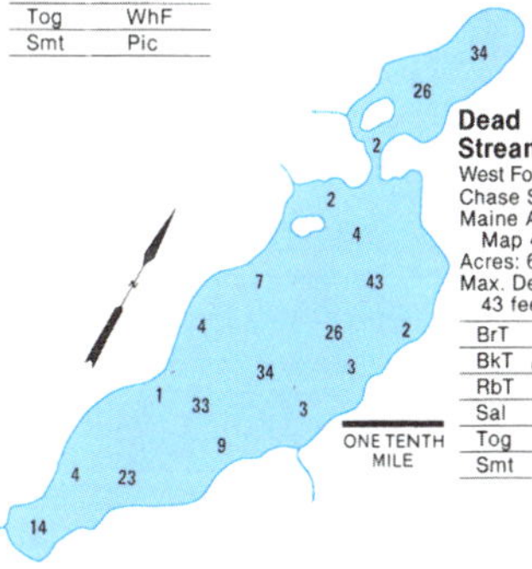

Deer Pond

King and Bartlett Twp
Maine Atlas
Map 29, A-2, A-3
Acres: 30
Max. Depth:
41 feet

BrT	LmB
BkT ✓	SmB
RbT	WhP
Sal	Csk
Tog	WhF
Smt	Pic

Dole Pond

Dole Brook Twp
Maine Atlas
Map 47, B-5, C-5
Acres: 704
Max. Depth:
50 feet

BrT	LmB
BkT ✓	SmB
RbT	WhP
Sal	Csk ✓
Tog	WhF ✓
Smt	Pic

Somerset

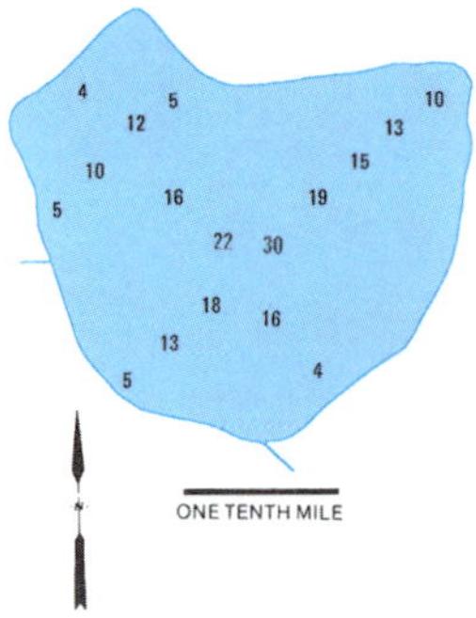

Dority Pond
Hammond Twp,
Prentiss Twp
Maine Atlas
Map 47, D-5
Acres: 30
Max. Depth:
30 feet

BrT	LmB
BkT ✓	SmB
RbT	WhP
Sal	Csk
Tog	WhF
Smt	Pic

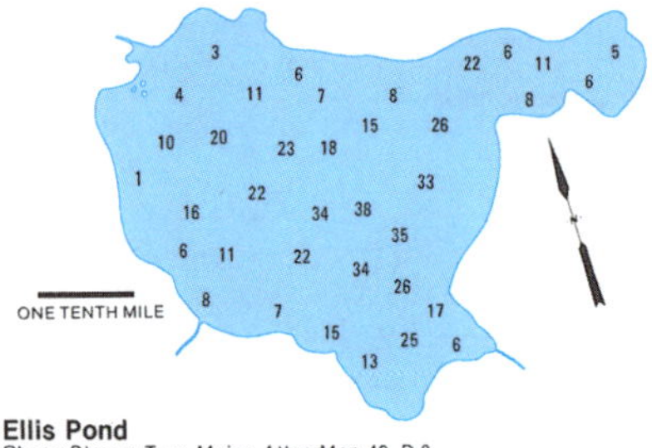

Ellis Pond
Chase Stream Twp, Maine Atlas Map 40, D-3
Acres: 85, Max. Depth: 38 feet

BrT	BkT	RbT	Sal	Tog	Smt	LmB	SmB	WhP	Csk	WhF	Pic
	✓										

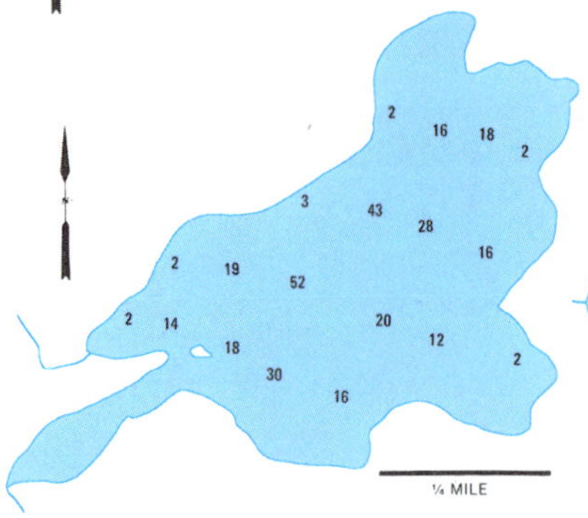

Duncan Pond
Prentiss Twp, Maine Atlas Map 47, D-4
Acres: 143, Max. Depth: 52 feet

BrT	BkT	RbT	Sal	Tog	Smt	LmB	SmB	WhP	Csk	WhF	Pic
	✓		✓	✓							

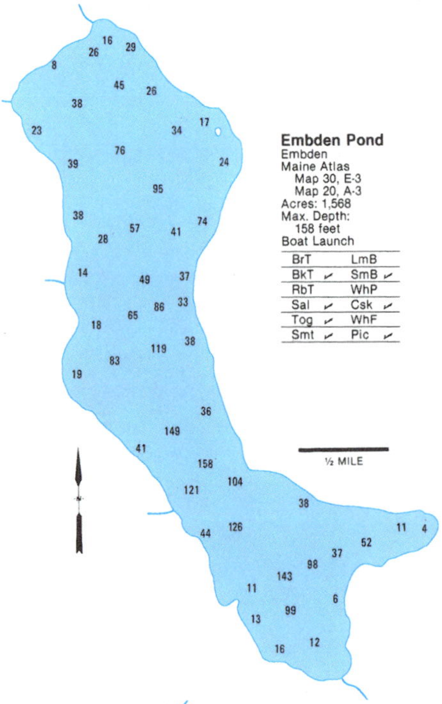

Embden Pond
Embden
Maine Atlas
Map 30, E-3
Map 20, A-3
Acres: 1,568
Max. Depth:
158 feet
Boat Launch

BrT	LmB
BkT ✓	SmB ✓
RbT	WhP
Sal ✓	Csk ✓
Tog ✓	WhF
Smt ✓	Pic ✓

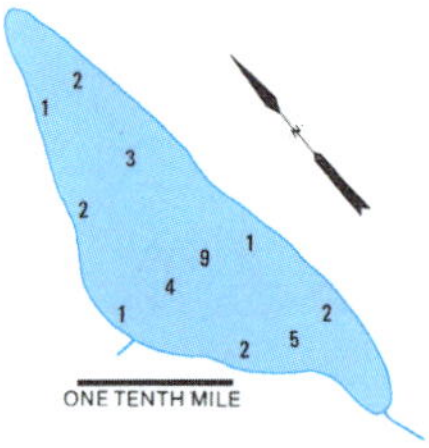

Durgin Pond
Johnson Mountain
Twp
Maine Atlas
Map 40, C-2
Acres: 15
Max. Depth:
9 feet

BrT	LmB
BkT ✓	SmB
RbT	WhP
Sal	Csk
Tog	WhF
Smt	Pic

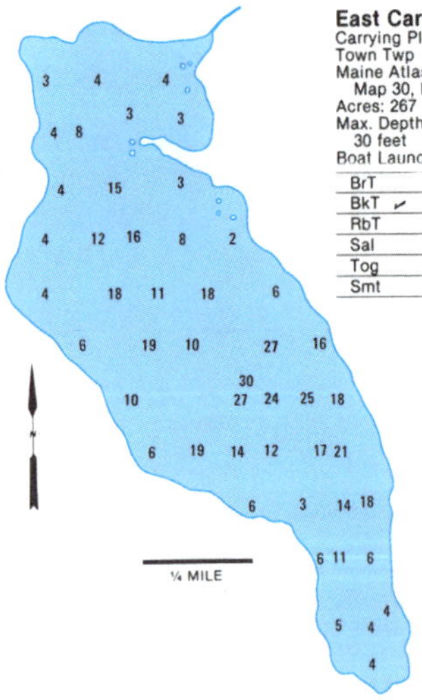

East Carry Pond
Carrying Place
Town Twp
Maine Atlas
Map 30, B-2
Acres: 267
Max. Depth:
30 feet
Boat Launch

BrT	LmB
BkT ✓	SmB
RbT	WhP
Sal	Csk
Tog	WhF
Smt	Pic

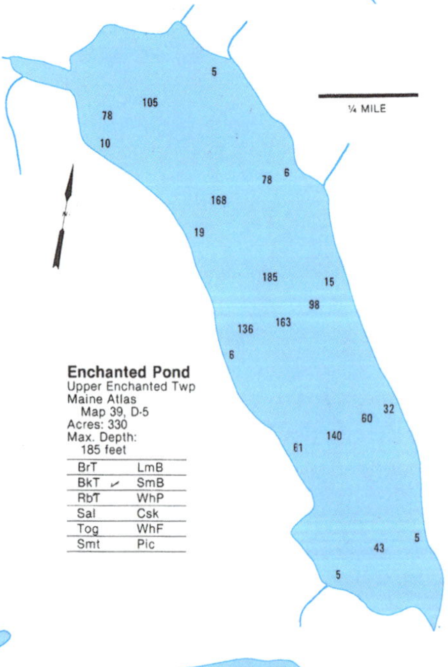

Enchanted Pond
Upper Enchanted Twp
Maine Atlas
Map 39, D-5
Acres: 330
Max. Depth:
185 feet

BrT	LmB
BkT ✓	SmB
RbT	WhP
Sal	Csk
Tog	WhF
Smt	Pic

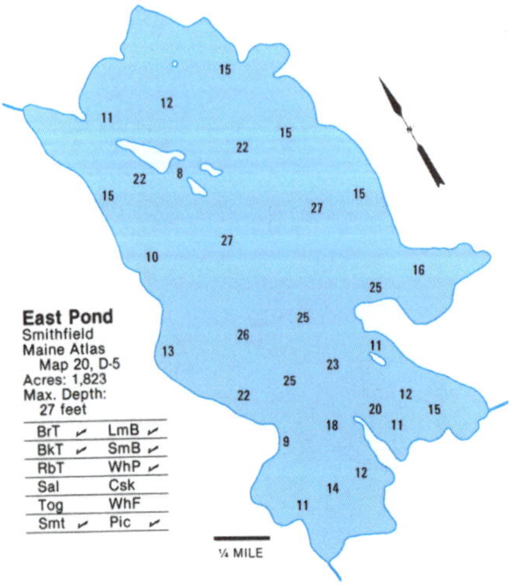

East Pond
Smithfield
Maine Atlas
Map 20, D-5
Acres: 1,823
Max. Depth:
27 feet

BrT ✓	LmB ✓
BkT ✓	SmB ✓
RbT	WhP ✓
Sal	Csk
Tog	WhF
Smt ✓	Pic ✓

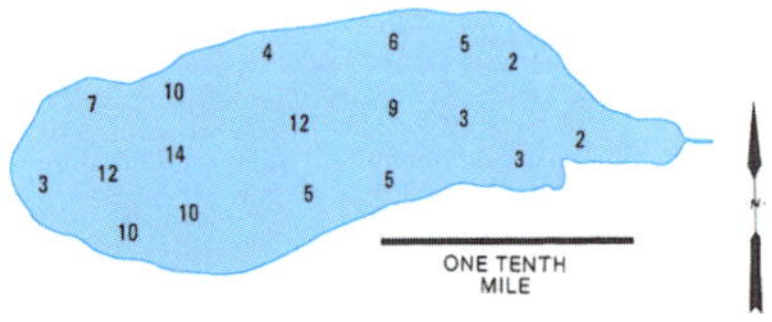

Everett Pond
King and Bartlett Twp, Maine Atlas Map 29, A-2
Acres: 20, Max. Depth: 14 feet

BrT	BkT	RbT	Sal	Tog	Smt	LmB	SmB	WhP	Csk	WhF	Pic
	✓										

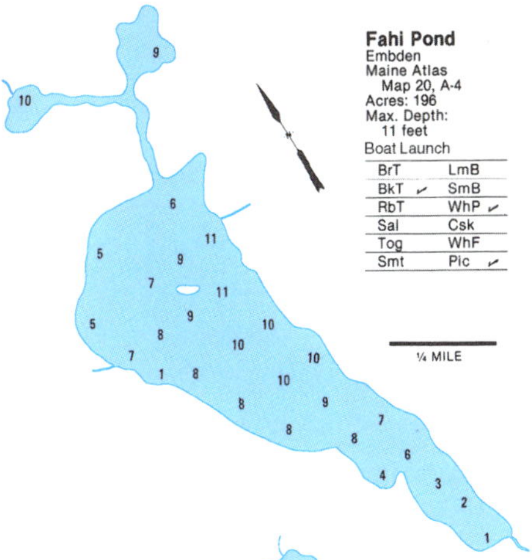

Fahi Pond

Embden
Maine Atlas
Map 20, A-4
Acres: 196
Max. Depth:
11 feet
Boat Launch

BrT		LmB	
BkT	✓	SmB	
RbT		WhP	✓
Sal		Csk	
Tog		WhF	
Smt		Pic	✓

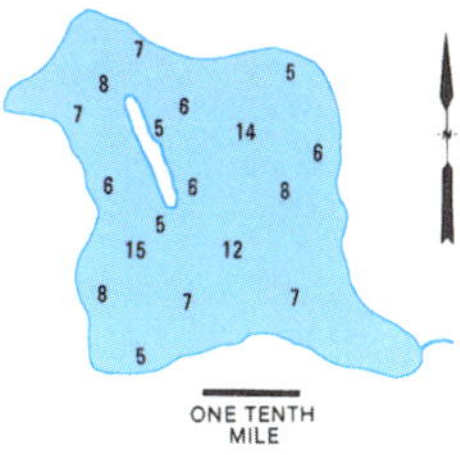

Felker Pond

King and Bartlett Twp
Maine Atlas
Map 39, E-2
Acres: 50
Max. Depth:
14 feet

BrT		LmB	
BkT	✓	SmB	
RbT		WhP	
Sal		Csk	
Tog		WhF	
Smt		Pic	

Fish Pond

Moxie Gore, Maine Atlas Map 40, E-3, E-4
Acres: 15, Max. Depth: 34 feet

BrT	BkT	RbT	Sal	Tog	Smt	LmB	SmB	WhP	Csk	WhF	Pic
	✓										

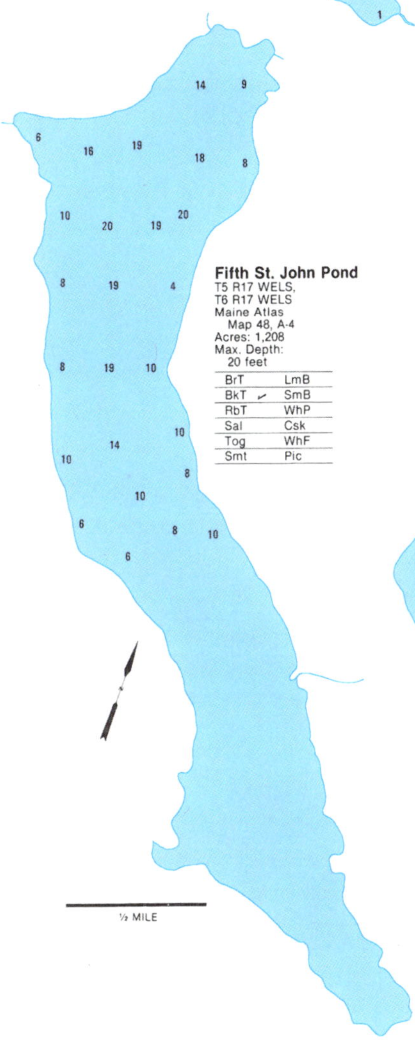

Fifth St. John Pond

T5 R17 WELS,
T6 R17 WELS
Maine Atlas
Map 48, A-4
Acres: 1,208
Max. Depth:
20 feet

BrT		LmB	
BkT	✓	SmB	
RbT		WhP	
Sal		Csk	
Tog		WhF	
Smt		Pic	

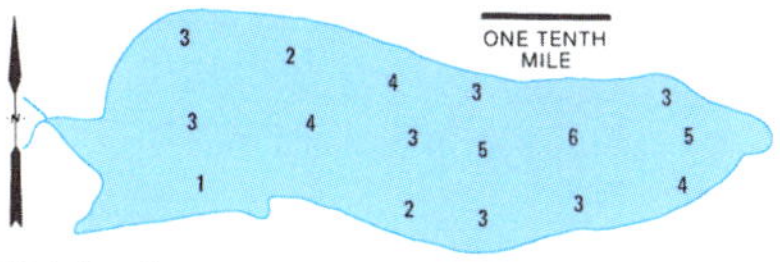

Fish Pond

Holeb Twp, Maine Atlas Map 39, C-2
Acres: 64, Max. Depth: 6 feet

BrT	BkT	RbT	Sal	Tog	Smt	LmB	SmB	WhP	Csk	WhF	Pic
	✓										

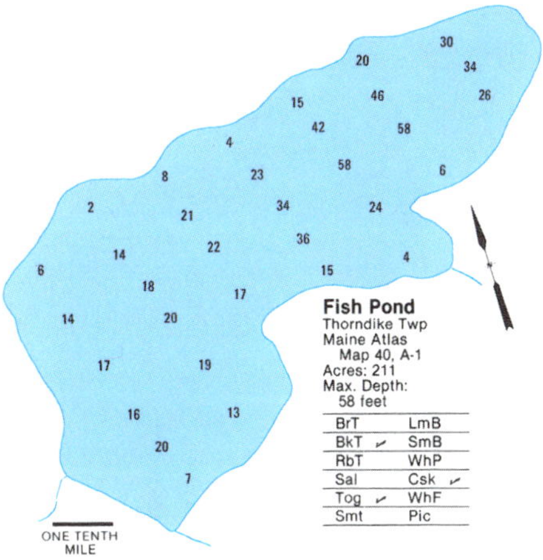

Fish Pond

Thorndike Twp
Maine Atlas
Map 40, A-1
Acres: 211
Max. Depth:
58 feet

BrT		LmB	
BkT	✓	SmB	
RbT		WhP	
Sal		Csk	✓
Tog	✓	WhF	
Smt		Pic	

Fisher Pond

T4 R5 NBKP
Maine Atlas
Map 47, C-4
Acres: 10
Max. Depth:
3 feet

BrT		LmB	
BkT	✓	SmB	
RbT		WhP	
Sal		Csk	
Tog		WhF	
Smt		Pic	

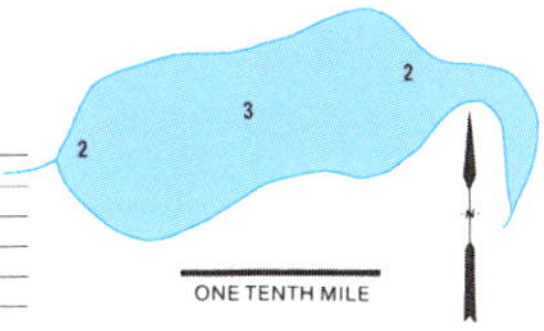

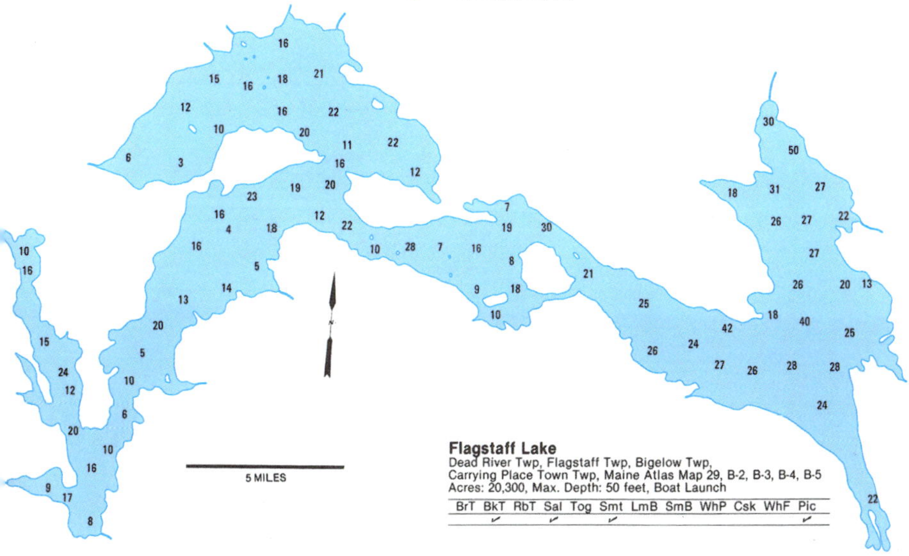

Flagstaff Lake

Dead River Twp, Flagstaff Twp, Bigelow Twp,
Carrying Place Town Twp, Maine Atlas Map 29, B-2, B-3, B-4, B-5
Acres: 20,300, Max. Depth: 50 feet, Boat Launch

BrT	BkT	RbT	Sal	Tog	Smt	LmB	SmB	WhP	Csk	WhF	Pic
	✓		✓		✓						✓

Somerset

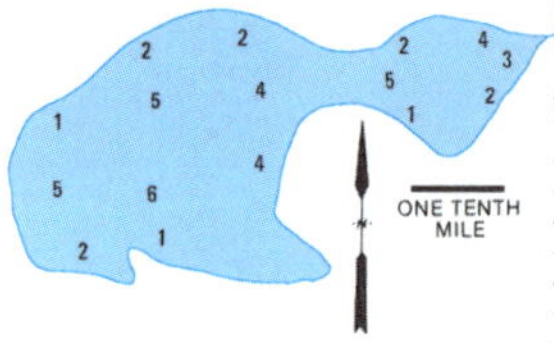

Fogg Pond

Long Pond Twp
Maine Atlas
Map 40, B-2, C-2
Acres: 54
Max. Depth:
6 feet

BrT		LmB	
BkT	✓	SmB	
RbT		WhP	
Sal		Csk	
Tog		WhF	
Smt		Pic	

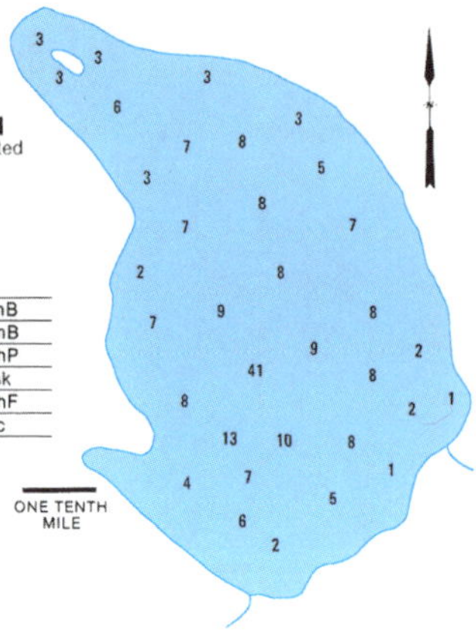

Grace Pond

Upper Enchanted Twp
Maine Atlas
Map 39, D-5
Acres: 150
Max. Depth:
41 feet
Boat Launch

BrT		LmB	
BkT	✓	SmB	
RbT		WhP	
Sal		Csk	
Tog		WhF	
Smt	✓	Pic	

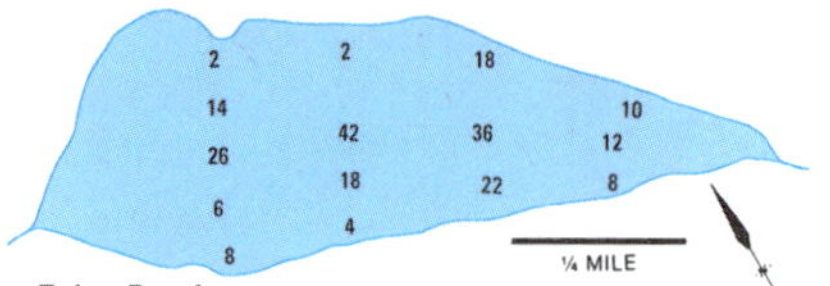

Foley Pond

Comstock Twp, Maine Atlas Map 48, C-2
Acres: 124, Max. Depth: 42 feet

BrT	BkT	RbT	Sal	Tog	Smt	LmB	SmB	WhP	Csk	WhF	Pic
	✓										

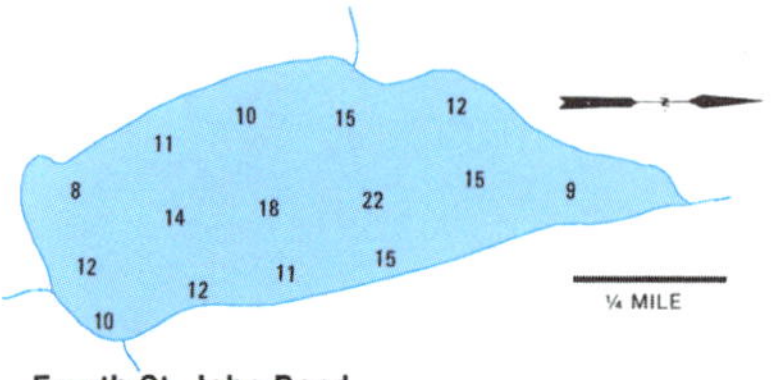

Fourth St. John Pond

T5 R17 WELS, Maine Atlas Map 48, B-4
Acres: 198, Max. Depth: 22 feet

BrT	BkT	RbT	Sal	Tog	Smt	LmB	SmB	WhP	Csk	WhF	Pic
	✓									✓	

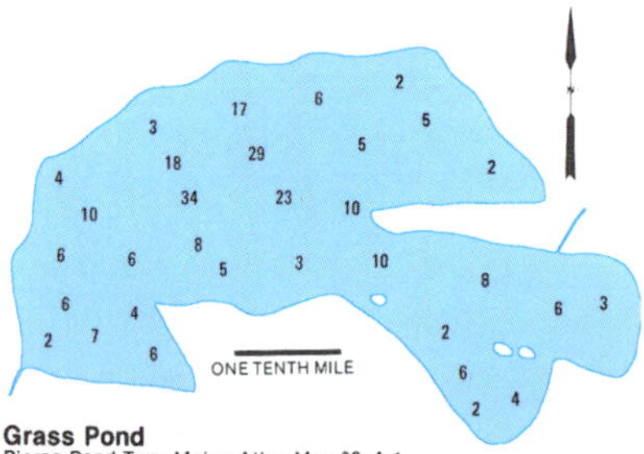

Grass Pond

Pierce Pond Twp, Maine Atlas Map 30, A-1
Acres: 36, Max. Depth: 34 feet, Boat Launch

BrT	BkT	RbT	Sal	Tog	Smt	LmB	SmB	WhP	Csk	WhF	Pic
	✓		✓								✓

Frost Pond

T4 R5 NBKP
Maine Atlas
Map 47, B-4, C-4
Acres: 170
Max. Depth:
10 feet

BrT		LmB	
BkT	✓	SmB	
RbT		WhP	
Sal		Csk	
Tog		WhF	
Smt		Pic	

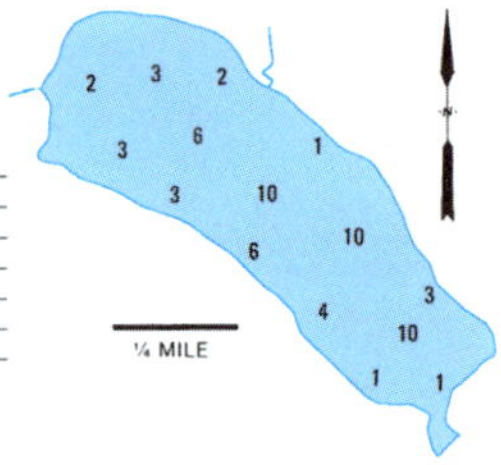

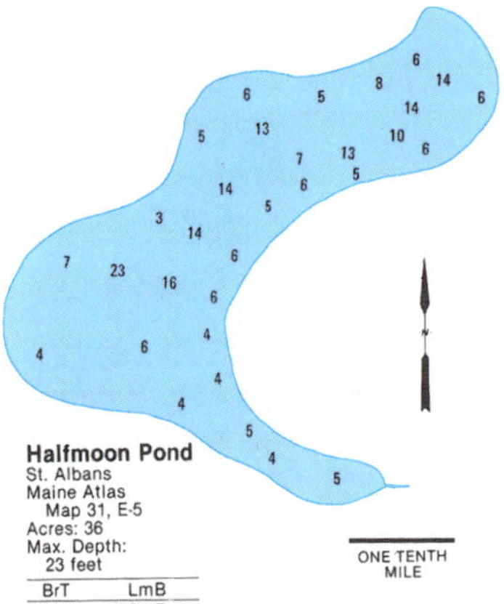

Halfmoon Pond

St. Albans
Maine Atlas
Map 31, E-5
Acres: 36
Max. Depth:
23 feet

BrT		LmB	
BkT		SmB	
RbT		WhP	✓
Sal		Csk	
Tog		WhF	
Smt		Pic	✓

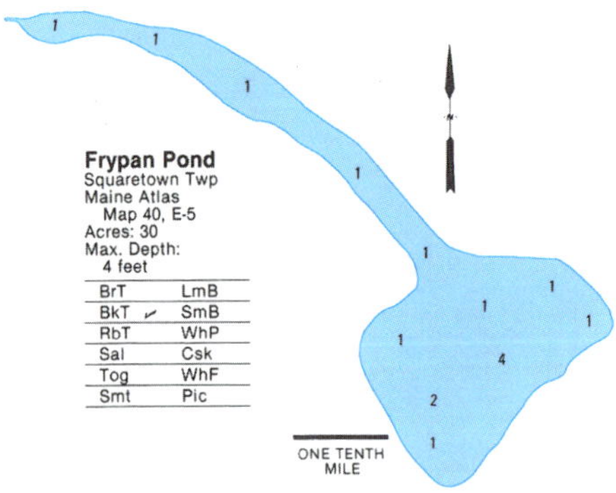

Frypan Pond

Squaretown Twp
Maine Atlas
Map 40, E-5
Acres: 30
Max. Depth:
4 feet

BrT		LmB	
BkT	✓	SmB	
RbT		WhP	
Sal		Csk	
Tog		WhF	
Smt		Pic	

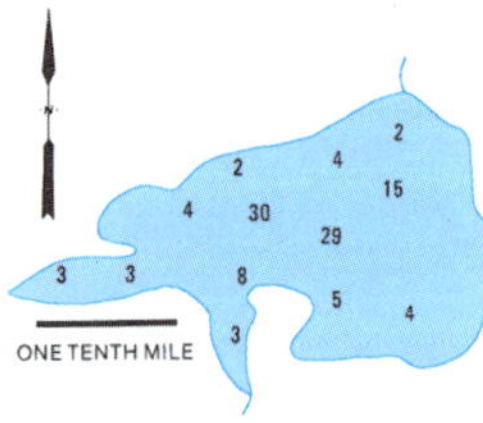

Hall Pond

Prentiss Twp
Maine Atlas
Map 47, D-5
Acres: 19
Max. Depth:
30 feet

BrT		LmB	
BkT	✓	SmB	
RbT		WhP	
Sal		Csk	
Tog		WhF	
Smt		Pic	

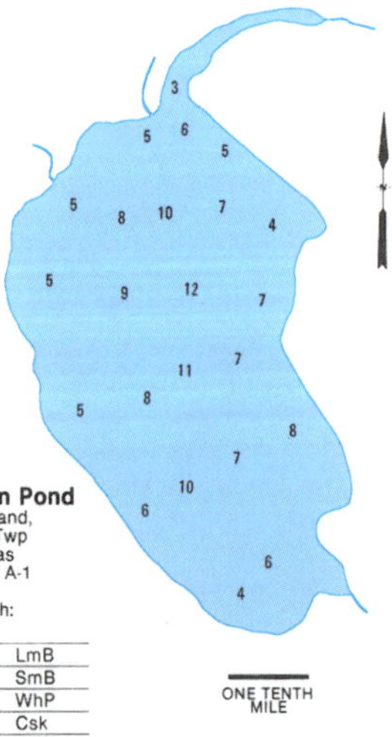

Gammon Pond

New Portland, Freeman Twp
Maine Atlas
Map 20, A-1
Acres: 97
Max. Depth:
12 feet

BrT		LmB	
BkT		SmB	
RbT		WhP	
Sal		Csk	
Tog		WhF	
Smt		Pic	✓

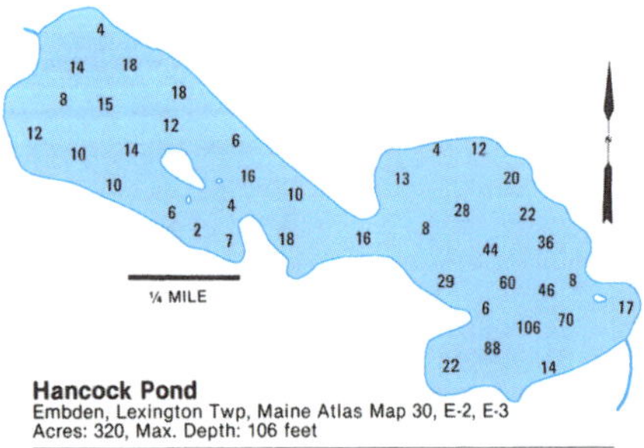

Hancock Pond

Embden, Lexington Twp, Maine Atlas Map 30, E-2, E-3
Acres: 320, Max. Depth: 106 feet

BrT	BkT	RbT	Sal	Tog	Smt	LmB	SmB	WhP	Csk	WhF	Pic
	✓		✓	✓	✓		✓				✓

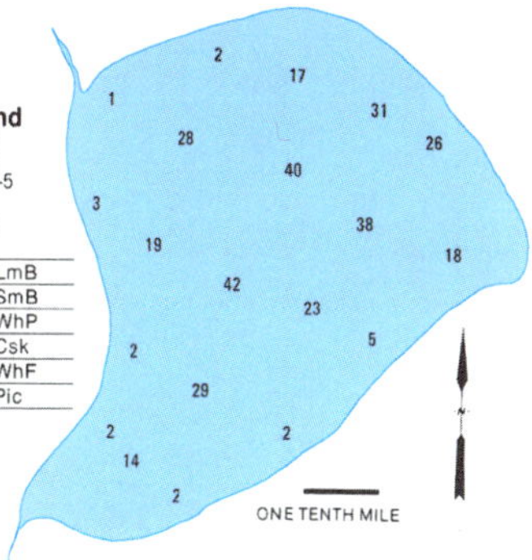

Heald Pond
Moose River
Maine Atlas
Map 39, A-5
Acres: 186
Max. Depth:
42 feet

BrT		LmB	
BkT	✓	SmB	
RbT		WhP	
Sal	✓	Csk	
Tog		WhF	
Smt	✓	Pic	

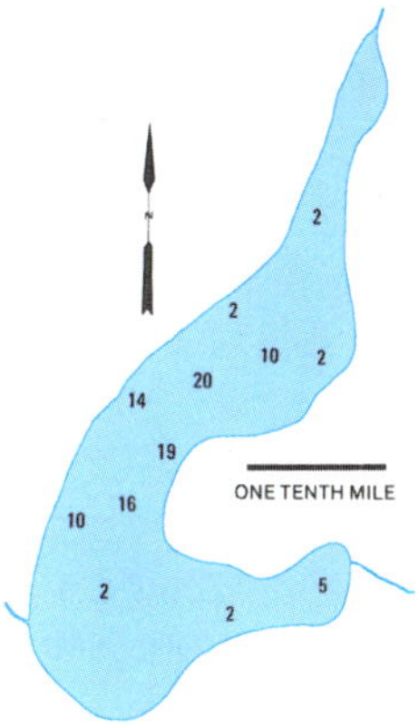

Horseshoe Pond
T3 R5 BKP WKR
Maine Atlas
Map 29, A-4
Acres: 30
Max. Depth:
20 feet

BrT		LmB	
BkT	✓	SmB	
RbT		WhP	
Sal		Csk	
Tog		WhF	
Smt		Pic	

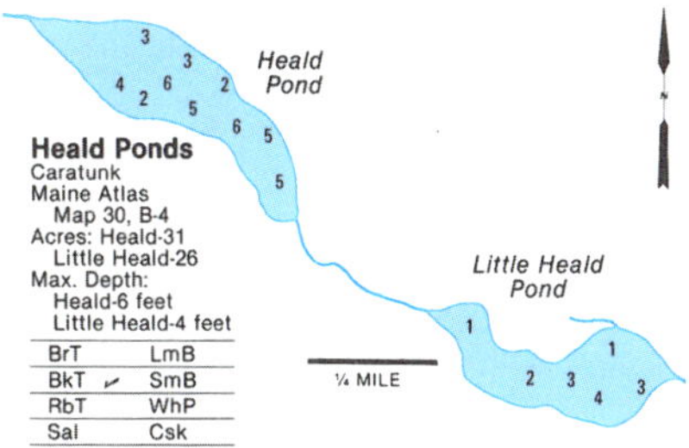

Heald Ponds
Caratunk
Maine Atlas
Map 30, B-4
Acres: Heald-31
Little Heald-26
Max. Depth:
Heald-6 feet
Little Heald-4 feet

BrT		LmB	
BkT	✓	SmB	
RbT		WhP	
Sal		Csk	
Tog		WhF	
Smt		Pic	

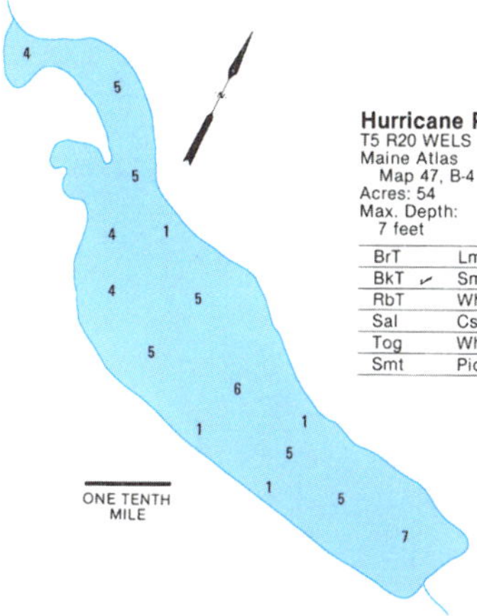

Hurricane Pond
T5 R20 WELS
Maine Atlas
Map 47, B-4
Acres: 54
Max. Depth:
7 feet

BrT		LmB	
BkT	✓	SmB	
RbT		WhP	
Sal		Csk	
Tog		WhF	
Smt		Pic	

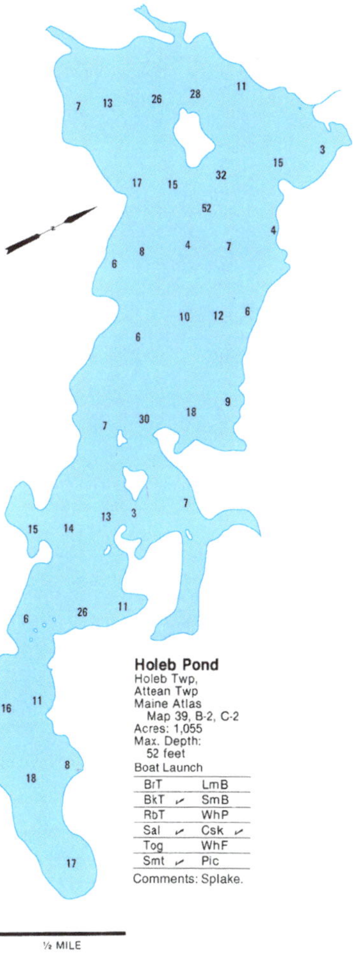

Holeb Pond
Holeb Twp,
Attean Twp
Maine Atlas
Map 39, B-2, C-2
Acres: 1,055
Max. Depth:
52 feet
Boat Launch

BrT		LmB	
BkT	✓	SmB	
RbT		WhP	
Sal	✓	Csk	✓
Tog		WhF	
Smt	✓	Pic	

Comments: Splake.

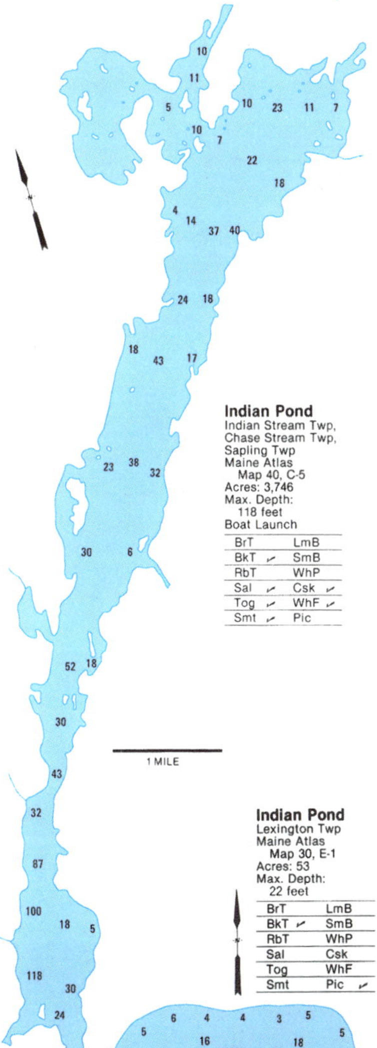

Indian Pond
Indian Stream Twp,
Chase Stream Twp,
Sapling Twp
Maine Atlas
Map 40, C-5
Acres: 3,746
Max. Depth:
118 feet
Boat Launch

BrT		LmB	
BkT	✓	SmB	
RbT		WhP	
Sal	✓	Csk	✓
Tog	✓	WhF	✓
Smt	✓	Pic	

Horseshoe Pond
Chase Stream Twp, Maine Atlas Map 40, D-3
Acres: 27, Max. Depth: 29 feet

BrT	BkT	RbT	Sal	Tog	Smt	LmB	SmB	WhP	Csk	WhF	Pic
	✓										

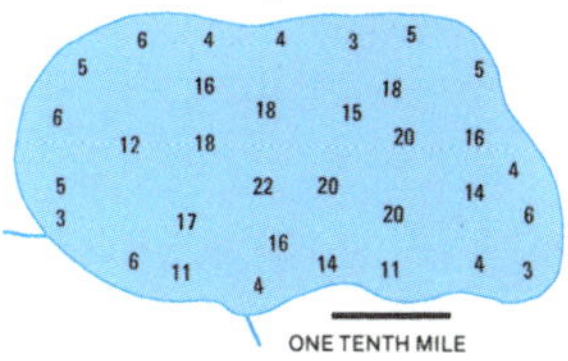

Indian Pond
Lexington Twp
Maine Atlas
Map 30, E-1
Acres: 53
Max. Depth:
22 feet

BrT		LmB	
BkT	✓	SmB	
RbT		WhP	
Sal		Csk	
Tog		WhF	
Smt		Pic	✓

Somerset

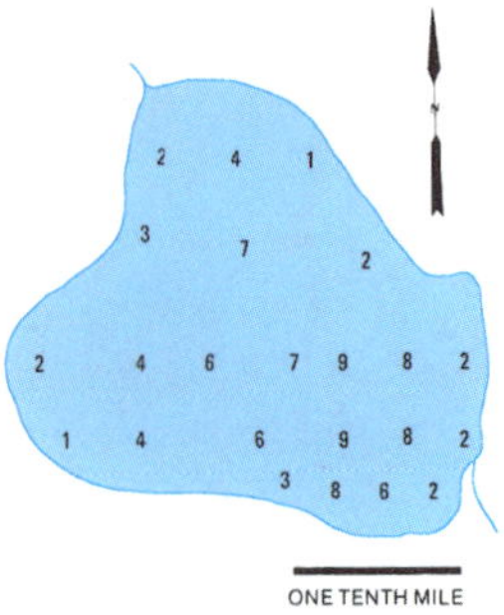

Iron Pond
T5 R6 BKP WKR,
Hobbstown Twp
Maine Atlas
Map 39, D-3
Acres: 32
Max. Depth:
9 feet

BrT		LmB
BkT	✓	SmB
RbT		WhP
Sal		Csk
Tog		WhF
Smt		Pic

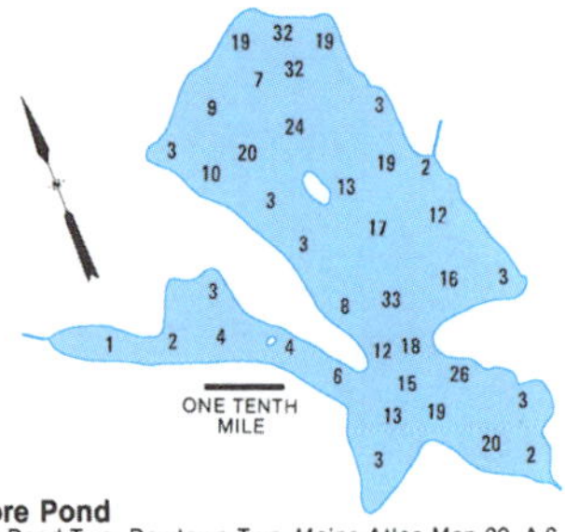

Kilgore Pond
Pierce Pond Twp, Bowtown Twp, Maine Atlas Map 30, A-2
Acres: 96, Max. Depth: 33 feet, Boat Launch

BrT	BkT	RbT	Sal	Tog	Smt	LmB	SmB	WhP	Csk	WhF	Pic
	✓										✓

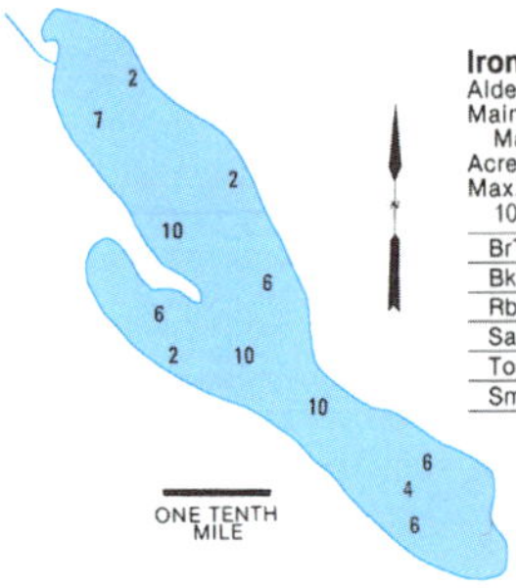

Ironbound Pond
Alder Brook Twp
Maine Atlas
Map 48, E-1
Acres: 40
Max. Depth:
10 feet

BrT		LmB
BkT	✓	SmB
RbT		WhP
Sal		Csk
Tog		WhF
Smt		Pic

King and Bartlett Lake
King and Bartlett Twp
Maine Atlas
Map 39, E-3
Acres: 538
Max. Depth:
159 feet

BrT		LmB
BkT	✓	SmB
RbT		WhP
Sal		Csk
Tog	✓	WhF
Smt	✓	Pic

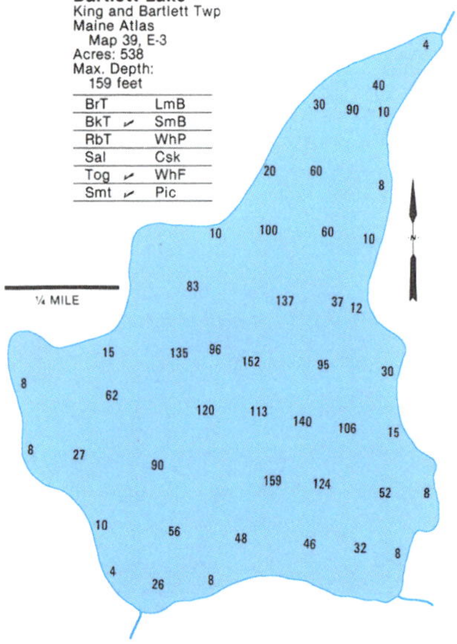

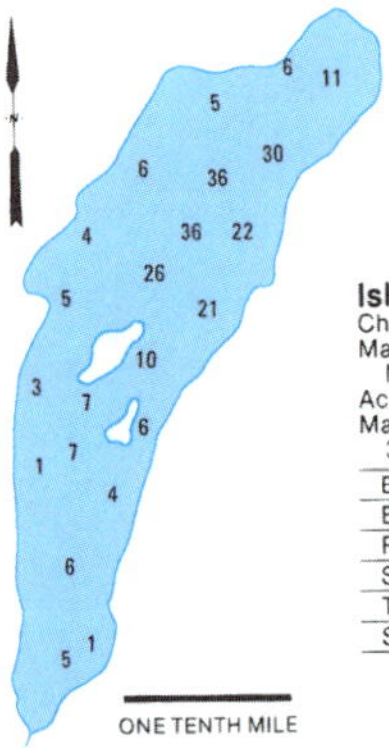

Island Pond
Chase Stream Twp
Maine Atlas
Map 40, D-3
Acres: 24
Max. Depth:
36 feet

BrT		LmB
BkT	✓	SmB
RbT		WhP
Sal		Csk
Tog		WhF
Smt		Pic

Jackson Pond
Concord Twp
Maine Atlas
Map 30, D-4
Acres: 10
Max. Depth:
21 feet

BrT		LmB
BkT	✓	SmB
RbT		WhP
Sal		Csk
Tog		WhF
Smt		Pic

King Pond
Bowtown Twp
Maine Atlas
Map 30, A-2
Acres: 16
Max. Depth:
15 feet

BrT		LmB
BkT	✓	SmB
RbT		WhP
Sal		Csk
Tog		WhF
Smt		Pic

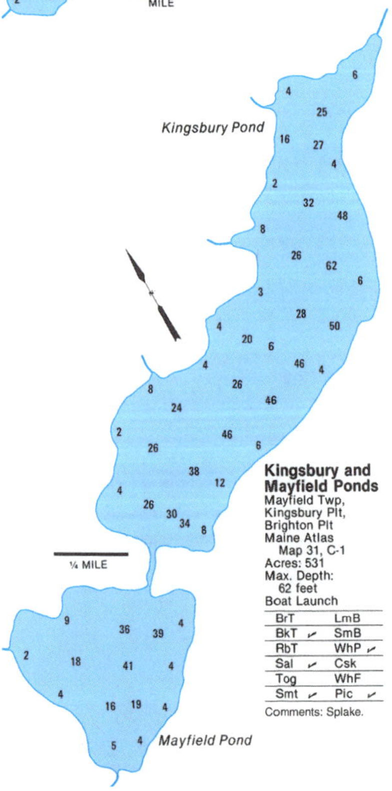

Kingsbury and Mayfield Ponds
Mayfield Twp,
Kingsbury Plt,
Brighton Plt
Maine Atlas
Map 31, C-1
Acres: 531
Max. Depth:
62 feet
Boat Launch

BrT		LmB	
BkT	✓	SmB	
RbT		WhP	✓
Sal	✓	Csk	
Tog		WhF	
Smt	✓	Pic	✓

Comments: Splake.

Jewett Pond
Pleasant Ridge Plt
Maine Atlas
Map 30, C-2, C-3
Acres: 32
Max. Depth:
9 feet

BrT		LmB
BkT	✓	SmB
RbT		WhP
Sal		Csk
Tog		WhF
Smt		Pic

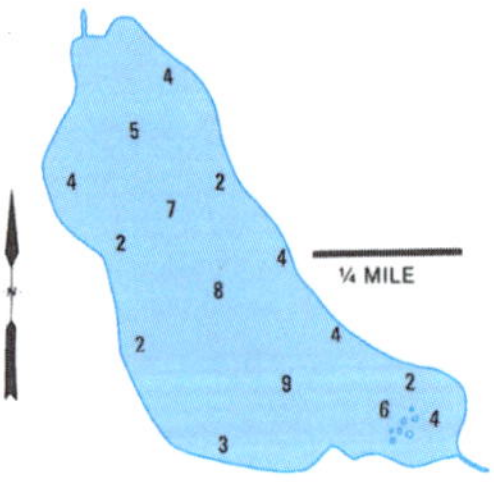

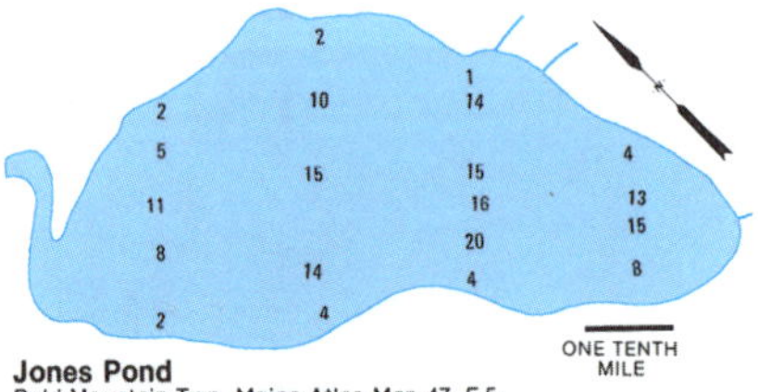

Jones Pond
Bald Mountain Twp, Maine Atlas Map 47, E-5
Acres: 130, Max. Depth: 20 feet

BrT	BkT	RbT	Sal	Tog	Smt	LmB	SmB	WhP	Csk	WhF	Pic
	✓										

Knights Pond

Moxie Gore,
Squaretown Twp
Maine Atlas
Map 40, D-4, E-4
Acres: 128
Max. Depth:
31 feet

BrT		LmB	
BkT	✓	SmB	
RbT		WhP	
Sal		Csk	
Tog		WhF	
Smt		Pic	

Little Austin Pond

Bald Mountain Twp
Maine Atlas
Map 30, B-5
Acres: 110
Max. Depth:
33 feet
Boat Launch

BrT		LmB	
BkT	✓	SmB	
RbT		WhP	
Sal	✓	Csk	
Tog		WhF	
Smt	✓	Pic	

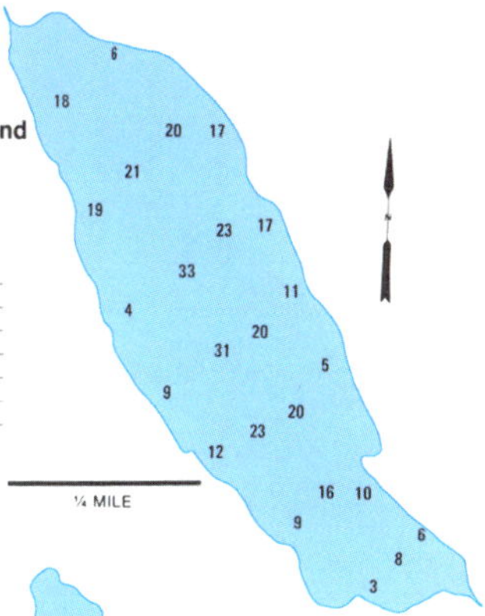

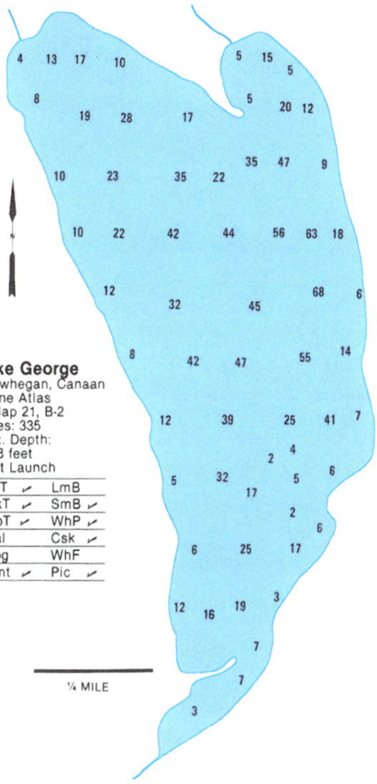

Lake George

Skowhegan, Canaan
Maine Atlas
Map 21, B-2
Acres: 335
Max. Depth:
68 feet
Boat Launch

BrT	✓	LmB	
BkT	✓	SmB	✓
RbT	✓	WhP	✓
Sal		Csk	✓
Tog		WhF	
Smt	✓	Pic	✓

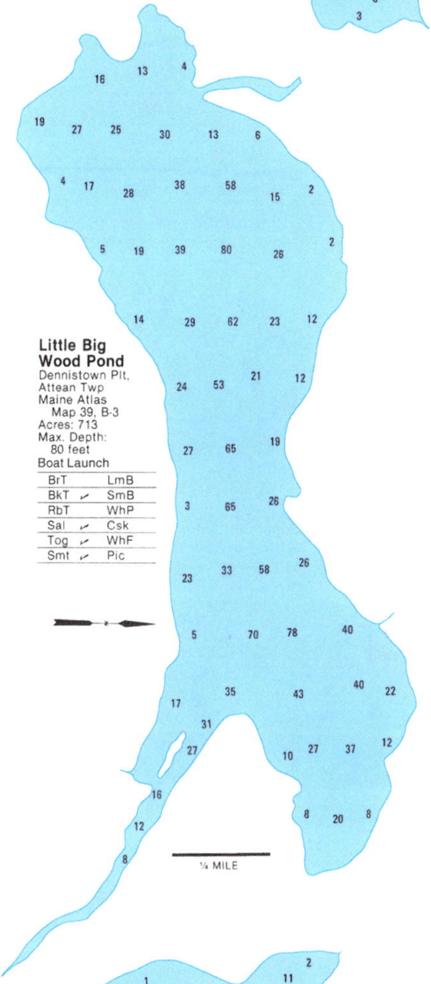

Little Big Wood Pond

Dennistown Plt,
Attean Twp
Maine Atlas
Map 39, B-3
Acres: 713
Max. Depth:
80 feet
Boat Launch

BrT		LmB	
BkT	✓	SmB	
RbT		WhP	
Sal	✓	Csk	
Tog	✓	WhF	
Smt	✓	Pic	

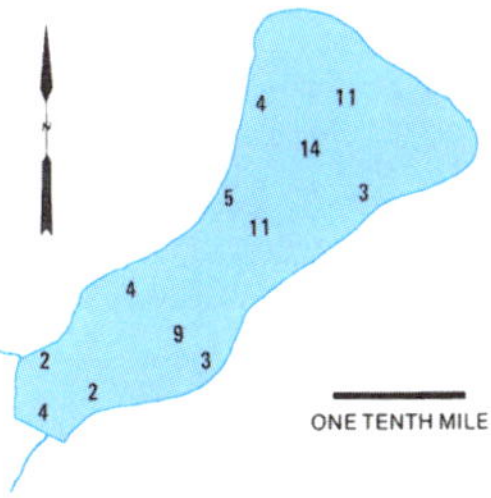

Lane Pond

Comstock Twp
Maine Atlas
Map 48, C-2
Acres: 24
Max. Depth:
14 feet

BrT		LmB	
BkT	✓	SmB	
RbT		WhP	
Sal		Csk	
Tog		WhF	
Smt		Pic	

Lang and Little Lang Ponds

Parlin Pond Twp
Maine Atlas
Map 40, C-2
Acres: Lang-30
Little Lang-13
Max. Depth:
Lang-30 feet
Little Lang-18 feet

BrT		LmB	
BkT	✓	SmB	
RbT		WhP	
Sal		Csk	
Tog		WhF	
Smt		Pic	

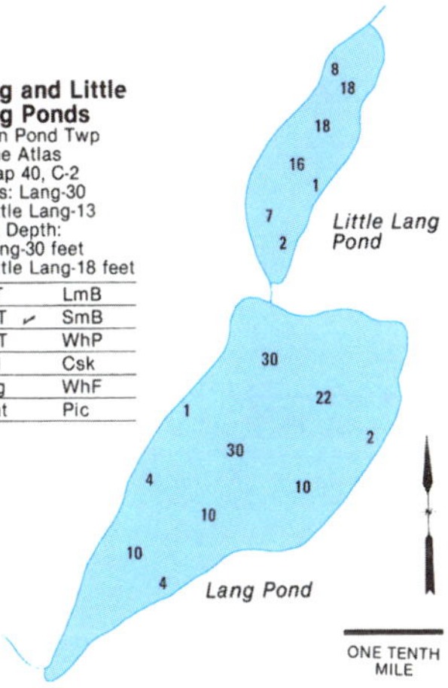

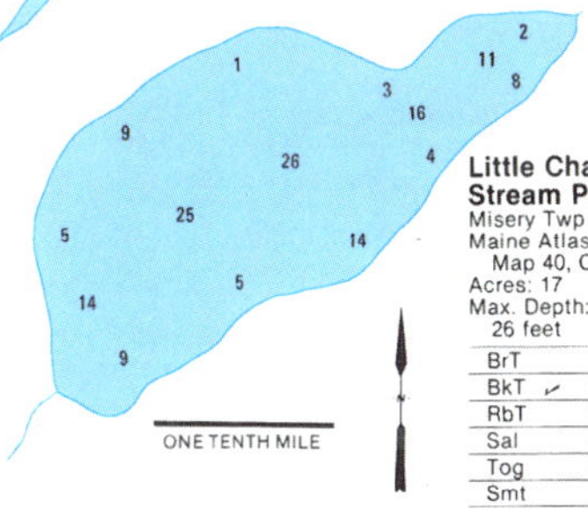

Little Chase Stream Pond

Misery Twp
Maine Atlas
Map 40, C-3
Acres: 17
Max. Depth:
26 feet

BrT		LmB	
BkT	✓	SmB	
RbT		WhP	
Sal		Csk	
Tog		WhF	
Smt		Pic	

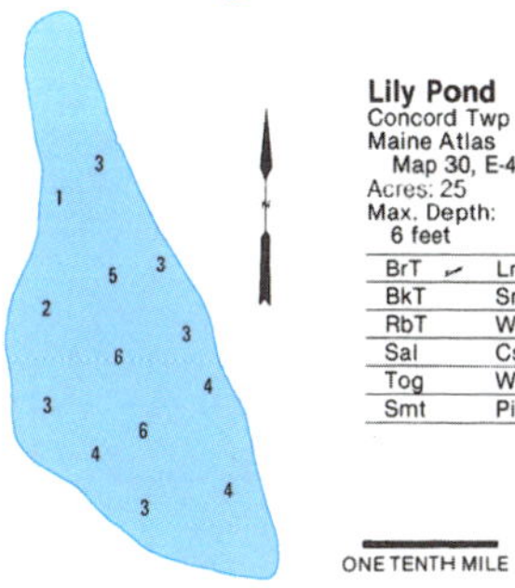

Lily Pond

Concord Twp
Maine Atlas
Map 30, E-4
Acres: 25
Max. Depth:
6 feet

BrT	✓	LmB	
BkT		SmB	
RbT		WhP	
Sal		Csk	
Tog		WhF	
Smt		Pic	✓

Little Dimmick Pond

Caratunk
Maine Atlas
Map 30, B-4
Acres: 41
Max. Depth:
14 feet
Boat Launch

BrT		LmB	
BkT	✓	SmB	
RbT		WhP	
Sal	✓	Csk	
Tog		WhF	
Smt		Pic	

Somerset

Little Dingly Pond
T4 R5 NBKP
Maine Atlas
Map 47, C-5
Acres: 17
Max. Depth:
6 feet

BrT	LmB
BkT ✓	SmB
RbT	WhP
Sal	Csk
Tog	WhF
Smt	Pic

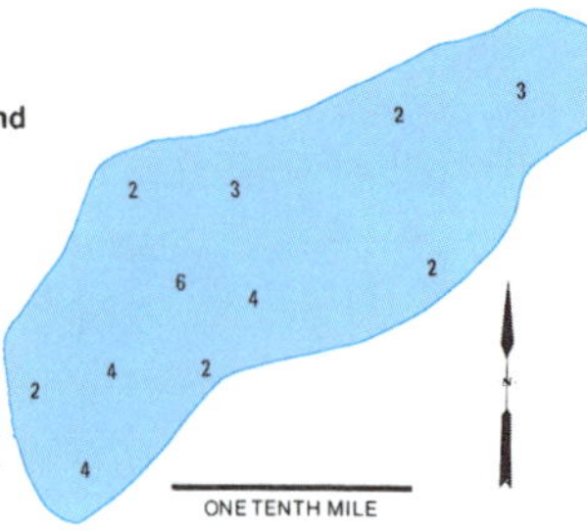

Little Otter Pond
Sandwich Academy
Grant
Maine Atlas
Map 40, B-3
Acres: 9
Max. Depth:
9 feet

BrT	LmB
BkT ✓	SmB
RbT	WhP
Sal	Csk
Tog	WhF
Smt	Pic

Comments:
Recently stocked
with BkT.

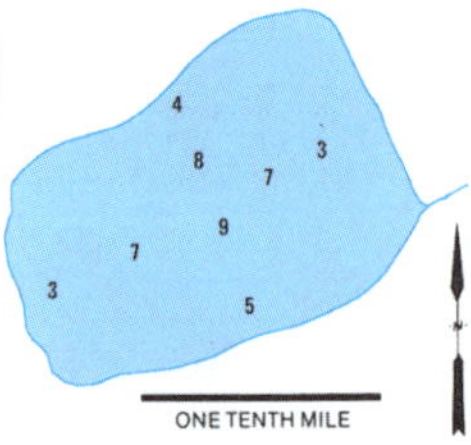

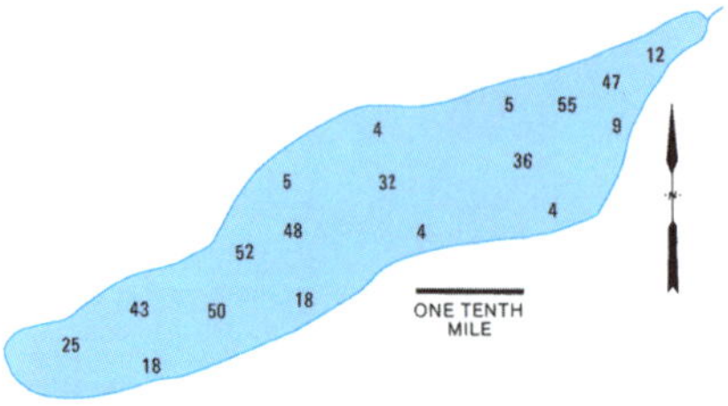

Little Enchanted Pond
Upper Enchanted Twp, Maine Atlas Map 39, D-5
Acres: 35, Max. Depth: 55 feet

BrT	BkT	RbT	Sal	Tog	Smt	LmB	SmB	WhP	Csk	WhF	Pic
	✓										

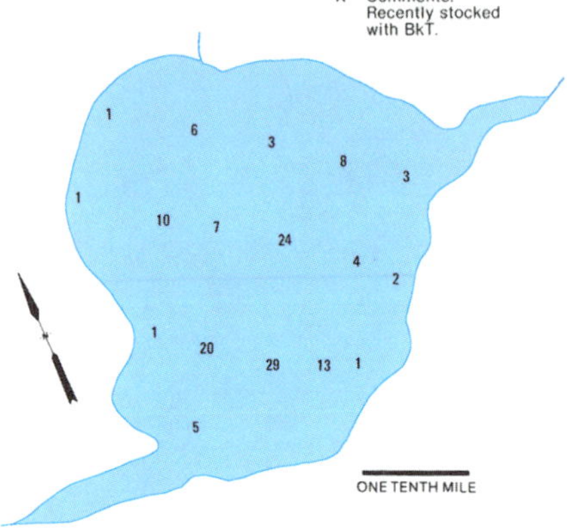

Little Turner Pond
Forsyth Twp, Maine Atlas Map 39, B-2
Acres: 77, Max. Depth: 29 feet

BrT	BkT	RbT	Sal	Tog	Smt	LmB	SmB	WhP	Csk	WhF	Pic
	✓										

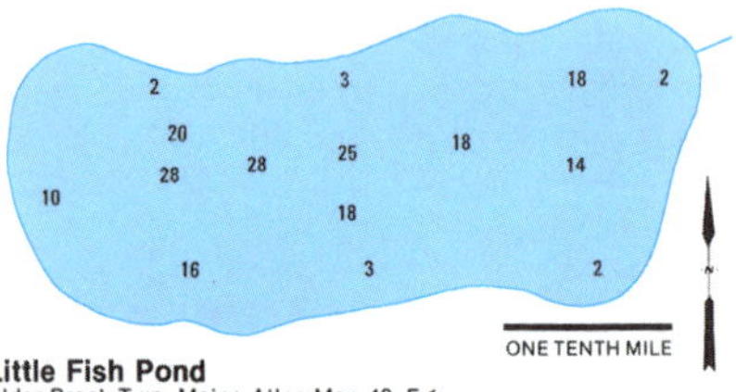

Little Fish Pond
Alder Brook Twp, Maine Atlas Map 48, E-1
Acres: 35, Max. Depth: 28 feet

BrT	BkT	RbT	Sal	Tog	Smt	LmB	SmB	WhP	Csk	WhF	Pic
	✓										

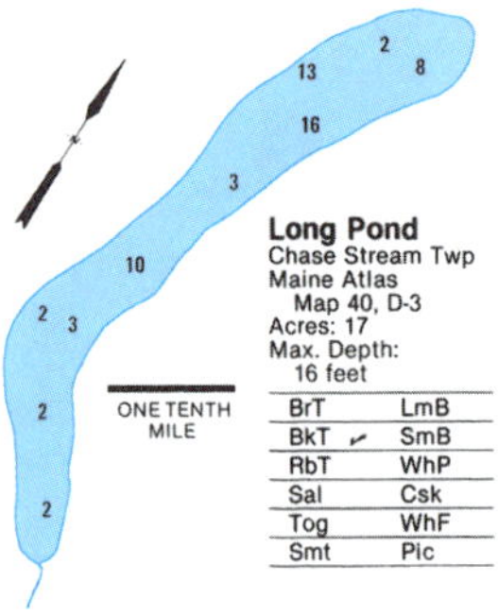

Long Pond
Chase Stream Twp
Maine Atlas
Map 40, D-3
Acres: 17
Max. Depth:
16 feet

BrT	LmB
BkT ✓	SmB
RbT	WhP
Sal	Csk
Tog	WhF
Smt	Pic

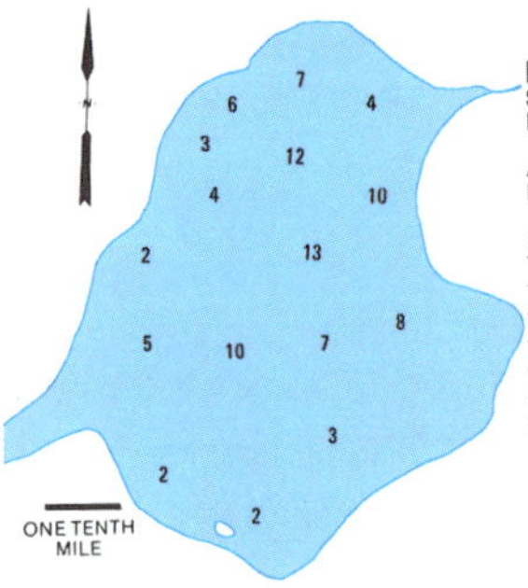

Little Indian Pond
St. Albans
Maine Atlas
Map 31, E-5
Acres: 145
Max. Depth:
13 feet
Boat Launch

BrT	LmB
BkT ✓	SmB ✓
RbT	WhP ✓
Sal	Csk
Tog	WhF
Smt	Pic ✓

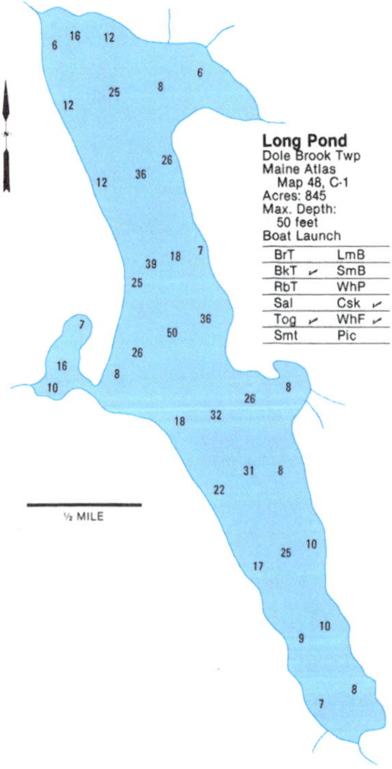

Long Pond
Dole Brook Twp
Maine Atlas
Map 48, C-1
Acres: 845
Max. Depth:
50 feet
Boat Launch

BrT	LmB
BkT ✓	SmB
RbT	WhP
Sal	Csk ✓
Tog ✓	WhF ✓
Smt	Pic

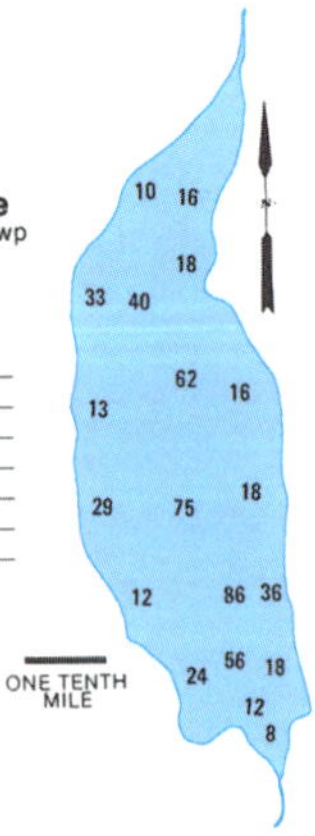

Little King Lake
King and Bartlett Twp
Maine Atlas
Map 39, E-3
Acres: 90
Max. Depth:
86 feet

BrT	LmB
BkT ✓	SmB
RbT	WhP
Sal	Csk
Tog	WhF
Smt	Pic

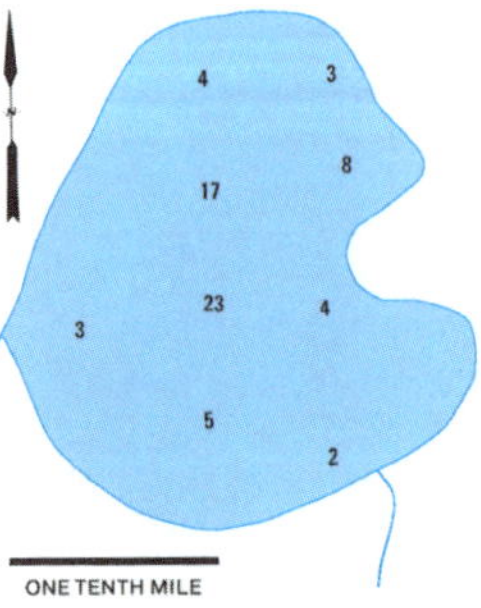

Little Lane Pond
Hammond Twp
Maine Atlas
Map 48, C-1
Acres: 18
Max. Depth:
23 feet

BrT	LmB
BkT ✓	SmB
RbT	WhP
Sal	Csk
Tog	WhF
Smt	Pic

Long Pond
Forsyth Twp, Holeb Twp, Maine Atlas Map 39, B-2
Acres: 98, Max. Depth: 8 feet

BrT	BkT	RbT	Sal	Tog	Smt	LmB	SmB	WhP	Csk	WhF	Pic
	✓										

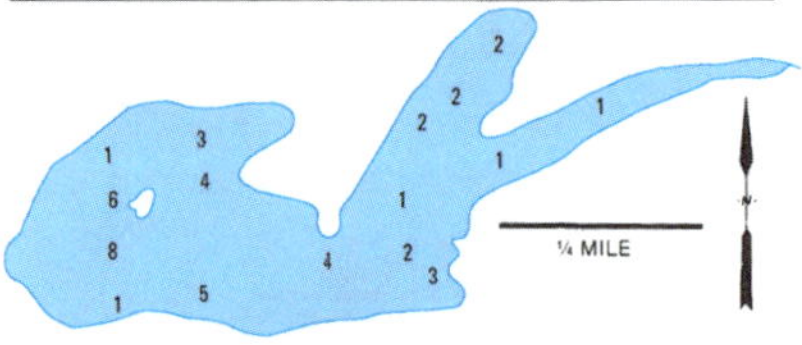

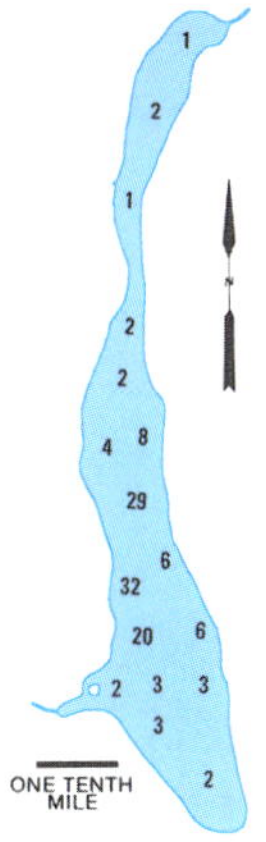

Long Pond
King and Bartlett Twp
Maine Atlas
Map 29, A-2
Acres: 60
Max. Depth:
32 feet

BrT	LmB
BkT ✓	SmB
RbT	WhP
Sal	Csk
Tog	WhF
Smt	Pic

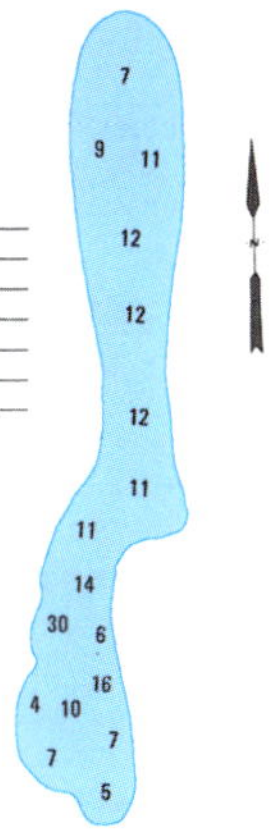

Long Pond
The Forks Plt
Maine Atlas
Map 30, A-3
Acres: 26
Max. Depth:
30 feet

BrT	LmB
BkT ✓	SmB
RbT	WhP
Sal	Csk
Tog	WhF
Smt	Pic

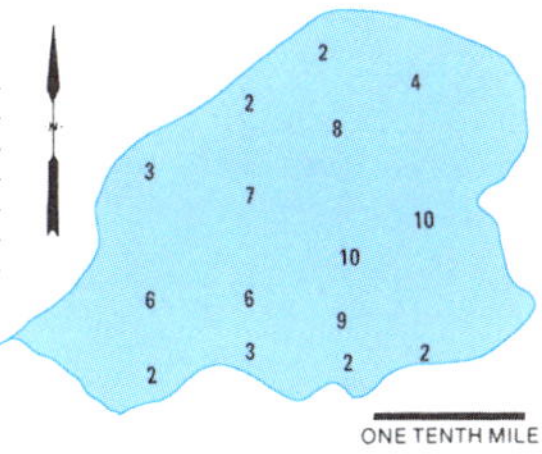

Loon Pond
Attean Twp,
Holeb Twp
Maine Atlas
Map 39, B-3
Acres: 37
Max. Depth:
10 feet

BrT	LmB
BkT ✓	SmB
RbT	WhP
Sal	Csk
Tog	WhF
Smt	Pic

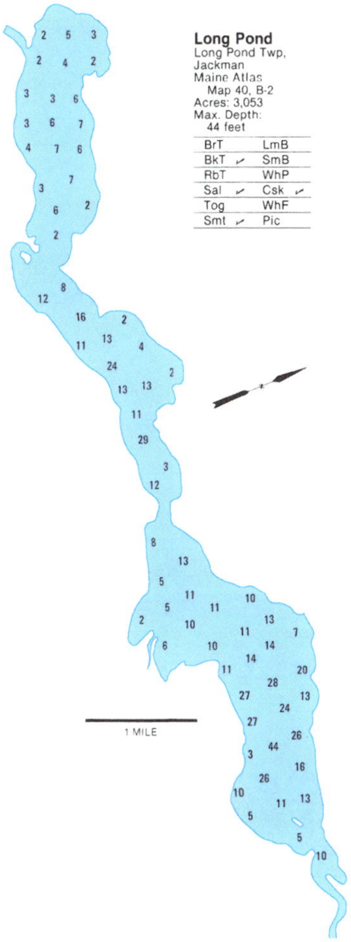

Long Pond
Long Pond Twp,
Jackman
Maine Atlas
Map 40, B-2
Acres: 3,053
Max. Depth:
44 feet

BrT	LmB
BkT ✓	SmB
RbT	WhP
Sal ✓	Csk ✓
Tog	WhF
Smt ✓	Pic

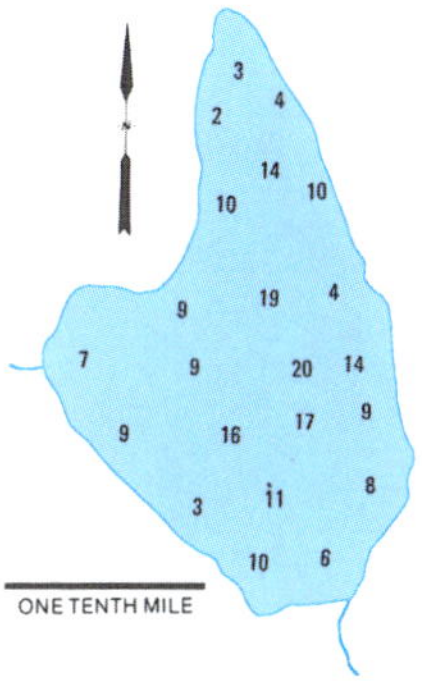

Lost Pond
Pleasant Ridge Twp
Maine Atlas
Map 30, C-3
Acres: 18
Max. Depth:
20 feet

BrT	LmB
BkT ✓	SmB
RbT	WhP
Sal	Csk
Tog	WhF
Smt	Pic

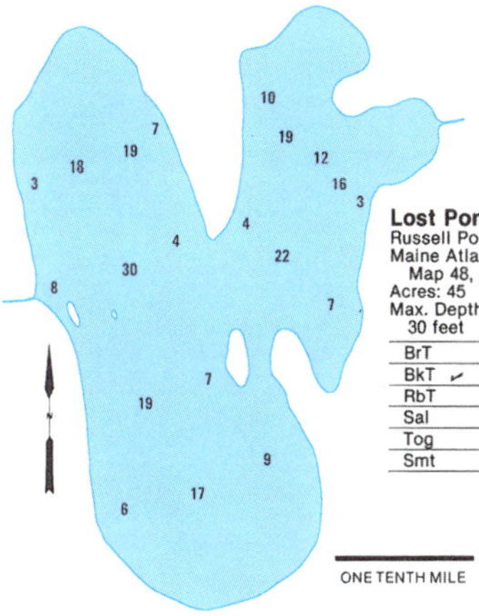

Lost Pond
Russell Pond Twp
Maine Atlas
Map 48, A-5
Acres: 45
Max. Depth:
30 feet

BrT	LmB
BkT ✓	SmB
RbT	WhP
Sal	Csk
Tog	WhF
Smt	Pic

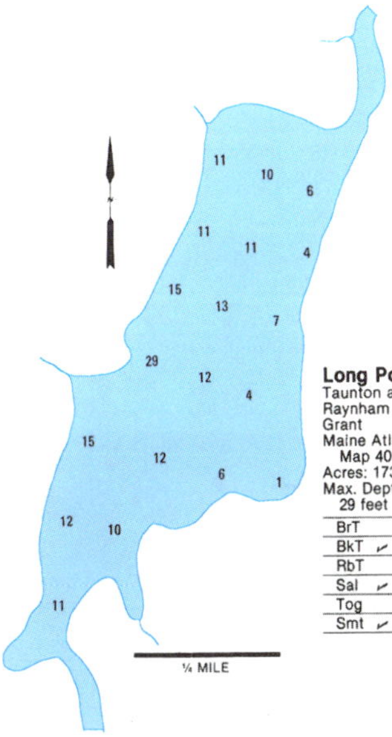

Long Pond
Taunton and
Raynham Academy
Grant
Maine Atlas
Map 40, B-5
Acres: 173
Max. Depth:
29 feet

BrT	LmB
BkT ✓	SmB ✓
RbT	WhP
Sal ✓	Csk
Tog	WhF
Smt ✓	Pic

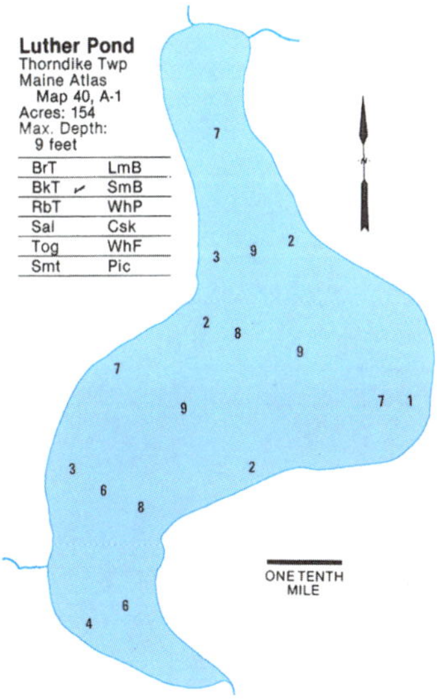

Luther Pond
Thorndike Twp
Maine Atlas
Map 40, A-1
Acres: 154
Max. Depth:
9 feet

BrT	LmB
BkT ✓	SmB
RbT	WhP
Sal	Csk
Tog	WhF
Smt	Pic

Somerset

MacDougall Pond
Caratunk
Maine Atlas
Map 30, B-3
Acres: 7
Max. Depth:
45 feet

BrT		LmB	
BkT	✓	SmB	
RbT		WhP	
Sal		Csk	
Tog		WhF	
Smt		Pic	

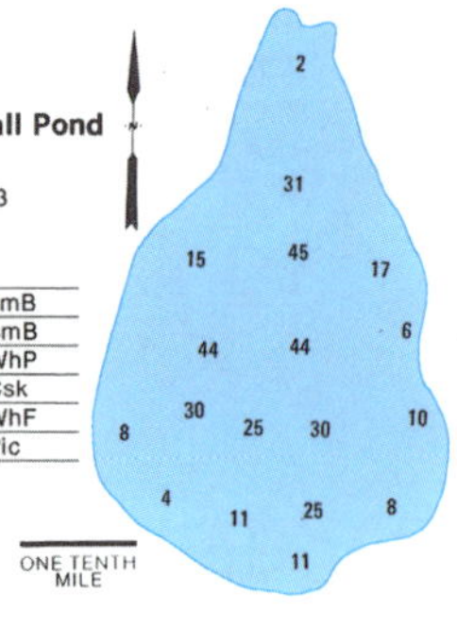

Misery Pond
Misery Twp
Maine Atlas
Map 40, C-3
Acres: 36
Max. Depth:
22 feet

BrT		LmB	
BkT	✓	SmB	
RbT		WhP	
Sal		Csk	
Tog		WhF	
Smt		Pic	

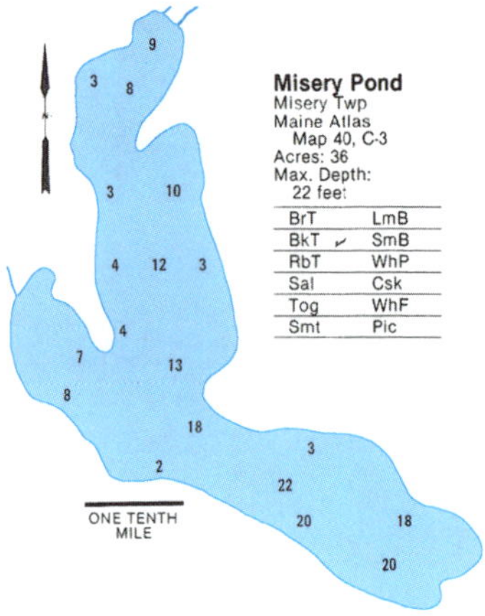

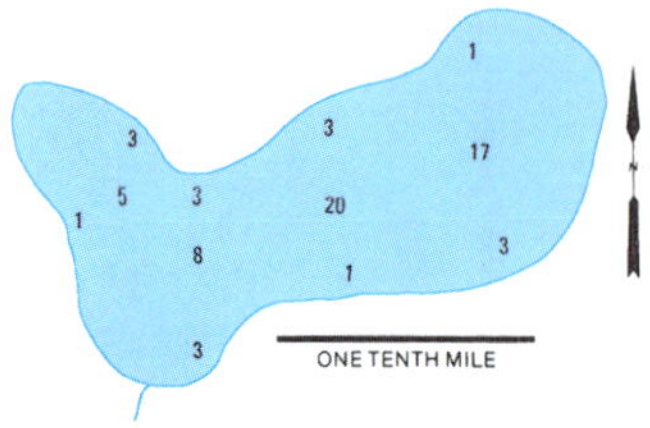

Mary Petuche Pond
Prentiss Twp, Maine Atlas Map 47, D-5
Acres: 10, Max. Depth: 20 feet

BrT	BkT	RbT	Sal	Tog	Smt	LmB	SmB	WhP	Csk	WhF	Pic
	✓										

Moore Pond
Bradstreet Twp
Maine Atlas
Map 39, D-4
Acres: 47
Max. Depth:
29 feet

BrT		LmB	
BkT	✓	SmB	
RbT		WhP	
Sal		Csk	✓
Tog		WhF	
Smt		Pic	

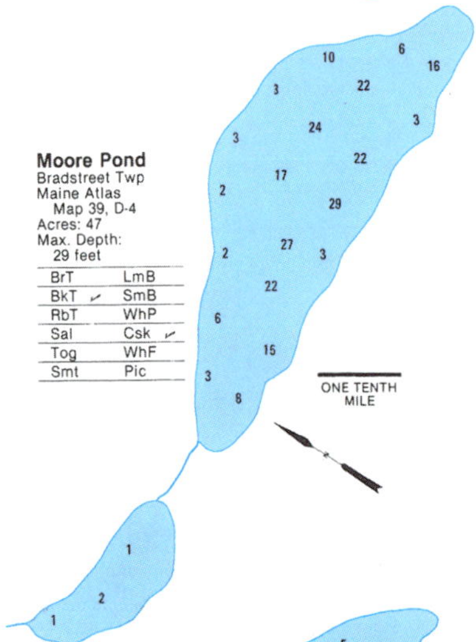

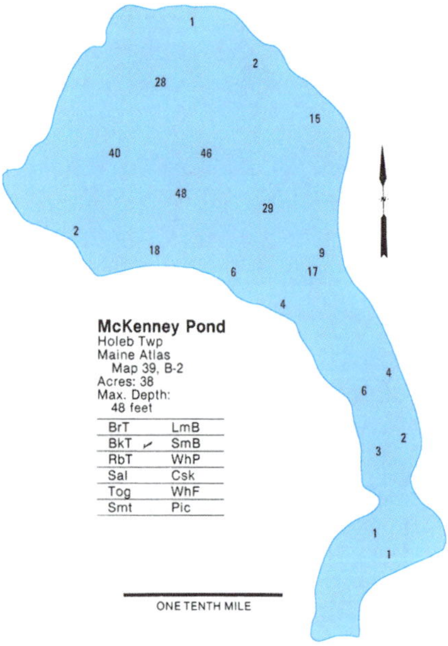

McKenney Pond
Holeb Twp
Maine Atlas
Map 39, B-2
Acres: 38
Max. Depth:
48 feet

BrT		LmB	
BkT	✓	SmB	
RbT		WhP	
Sal		Csk	
Tog		WhF	
Smt		Pic	

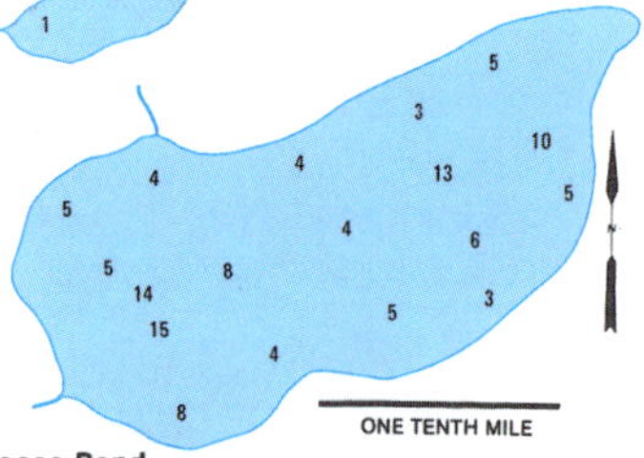

Moose Pond
Bowtown Twp, Maine Atlas Map 30, A-2
Acres: 11, Max. Depth: 15 feet

BrT	BkT	RbT	Sal	Tog	Smt	LmB	SmB	WhP	Csk	WhF	Pic
	✓										

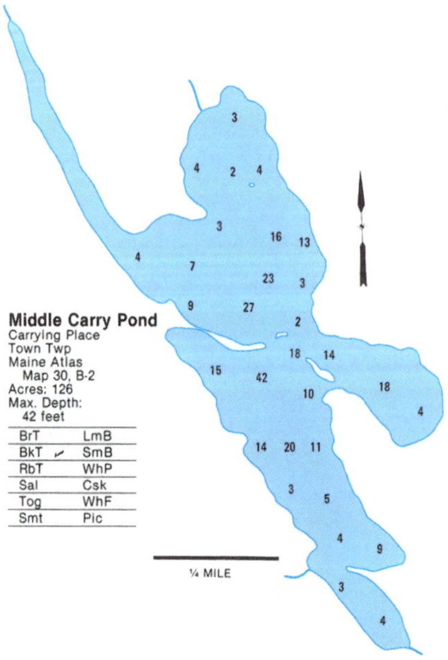

Middle Carry Pond
Carrying Place
Town Twp
Maine Atlas
Map 30, B-2
Acres: 126
Max. Depth:
42 feet

BrT		LmB	
BkT	✓	SmB	
RbT		WhP	
Sal		Csk	
Tog		WhF	
Smt		Pic	

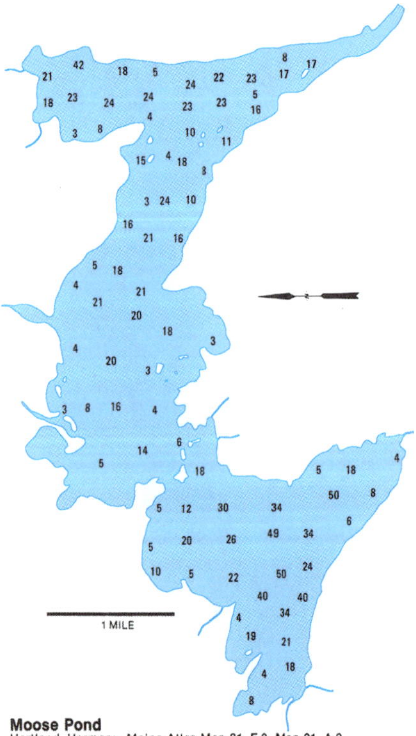

Moose Pond
Hartland, Harmony, Maine Atlas Map 31, E-3, Map 21, A-3
Acres: 3,584, Max. Depth: 50 feet, Boat Launch

BrT	BkT	RbT	Sal	Tog	Smt	LmB	SmB	WhP	Csk	WhF	Pic
✓	✓		✓		✓		✓	✓	✓		✓

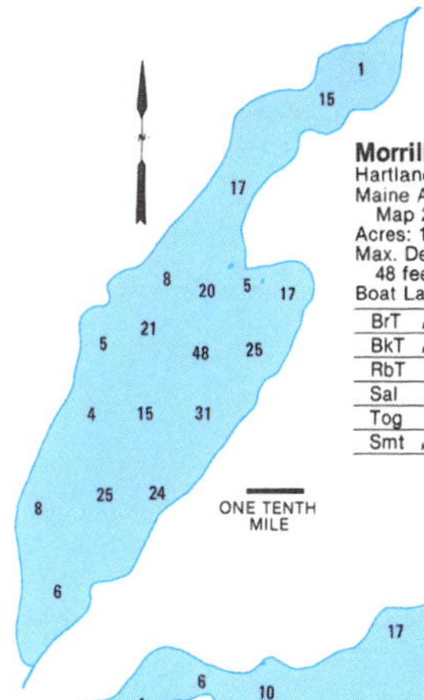

Morrill Pond

Hartland
Maine Atlas
Map 21, A-3, B-3
Acres: 134
Max. Depth:
48 feet
Boat Launch

BrT		LmB	
BkT	✓	SmB	
RbT		WhP	✓
Sal		Csk	
Tog		WhF	
Smt	✓	Pic	✓

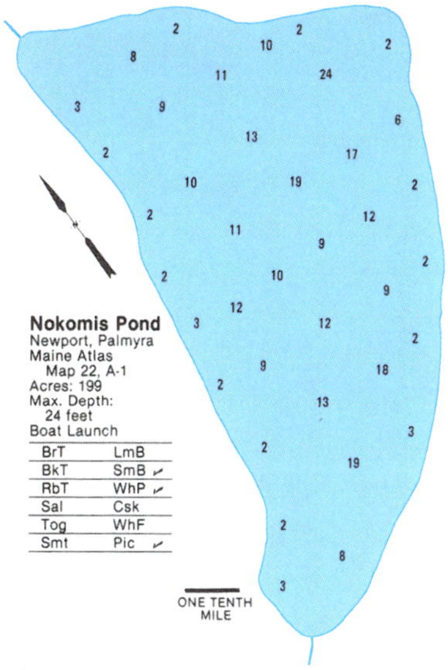

Nokomis Pond

Newport, Palmyra
Maine Atlas
Map 22, A-1
Acres: 199
Max. Depth:
24 feet
Boat Launch

BrT		LmB	
BkT		SmB	✓
RbT		WhP	✓
Sal		Csk	
Tog		WhF	
Smt		Pic	✓

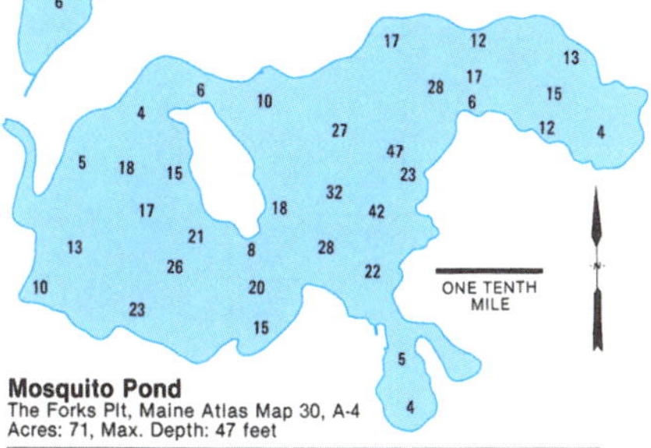

Mosquito Pond

The Forks Plt, Maine Atlas Map 30, A-4
Acres: 71, Max. Depth: 47 feet

BrT	BkT	RbT	Sal	Tog	Smt	LmB	SmB	WhP	Csk	WhF	Pic
	✓		✓								

North and Little Ponds

Smithfield, Mercer, Rome, Maine Atlas Map 20, D-4
Acres: 2,115, Max. Depth: 20 feet, Boat Launch

BrT	BkT	RbT	Sal	Tog	Smt	LmB	SmB	WhP	Csk	WhF	Pic
✓						✓	✓	✓			✓

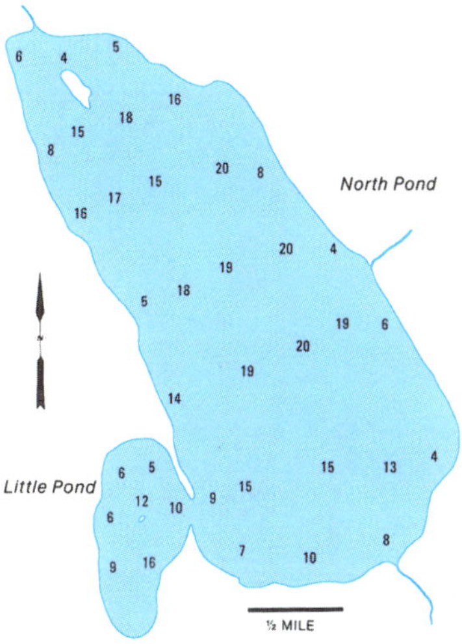

Mountain Dimmick Pond

Caratunk
Maine Atlas
Map 30, B-4
Acres: 30
Max. Depth:
58 feet

BrT		LmB	
BkT	✓	SmB	
RbT		WhP	
Sal		Csk	
Tog		WhF	
Smt		Pic	

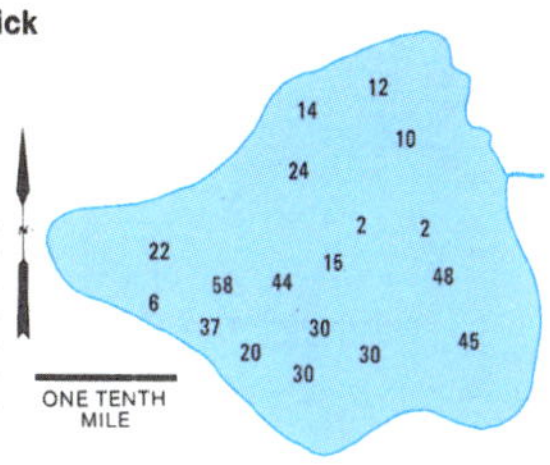

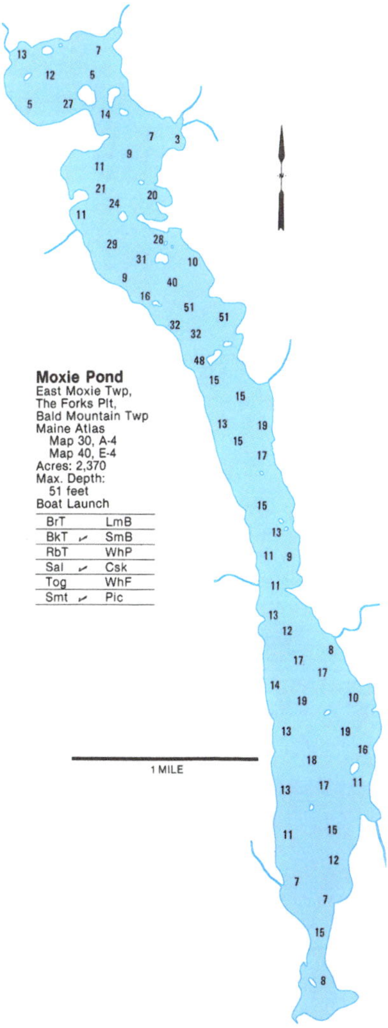

Moxie Pond

East Moxie Twp,
The Forks Plt,
Bald Mountain Twp
Maine Atlas
Map 30, A-4
Map 40, E-4
Acres: 2,370
Max. Depth:
51 feet
Boat Launch

BrT		LmB	
BkT	✓	SmB	
RbT		WhP	
Sal	✓	Csk	
Tog		WhF	
Smt	✓	Pic	

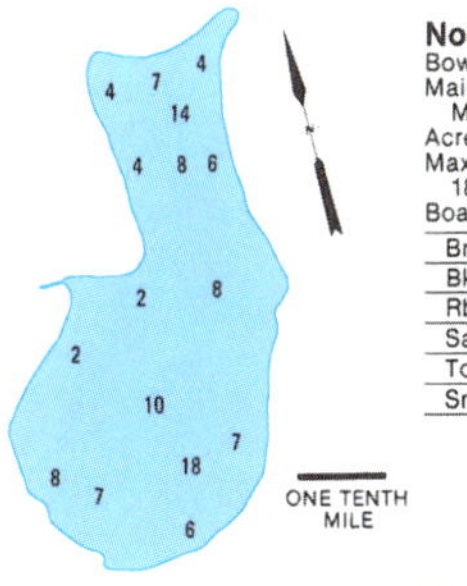

North Otter Pond

Bowtown Twp
Maine Atlas
Map 30, A-2
Acres: 71
Max. Depth:
18 feet
Boat Launch

BrT		LmB	
BkT	✓	SmB	
RbT		WhP	
Sal		Csk	
Tog		WhF	
Smt		Pic	

Oaks Pond

Skowhegan
Maine Atlas
Map 21, B-2
Acres: 102
Max. Depth:
53 feet

BrT	✓	LmB	
BkT	✓	SmB	✓
RbT		WhP	✓
Sal		Csk	
Tog		WhF	
Smt	✓	Pic	✓

Comments: Splake.

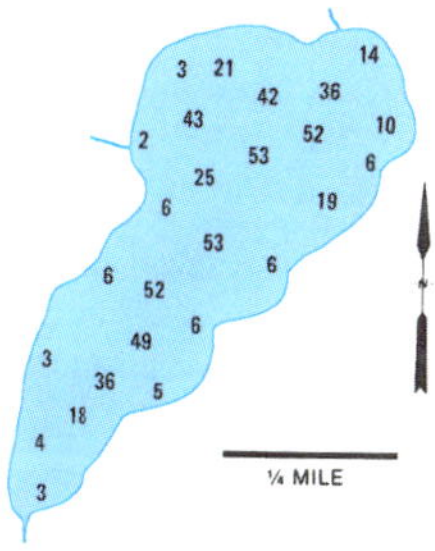

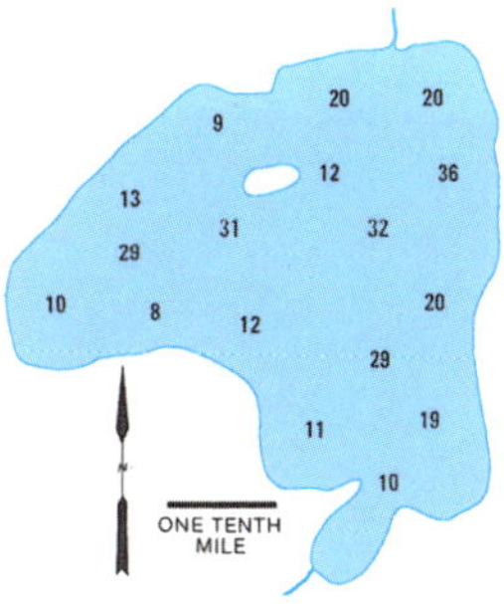

Otter Pond

Bowtown Twp
Maine Atlas
Map 30, A-2
Acres: 77
Max. Depth:
36 feet
Boat Launch

BrT		LmB	
BkT	✓	SmB	
RbT		WhP	
Sal		Csk	
Tog		WhF	
Smt	✓	Pic	

Somerset

Otter Pond
Sandwich Academy Grant
Maine Atlas
Map 40, B-4
Acres: 12
Max. Depth:
15 feet

BrT	LmB
BkT ✓	SmB
RbT	WhP
Sal	Csk
Tog	WhF
Smt	Pic

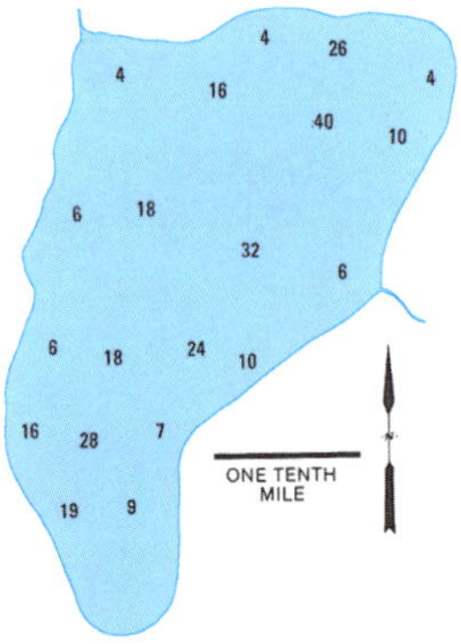

Palmer Pond
Mayfield Twp
Maine Atlas
Map 31, B-1, C-1
Acres: 40
Max. Depth:
40 feet
Boat Launch

BrT	LmB
BkT ✓	SmB
RbT	WhP
Sal	Csk
Tog	WhF
Smt	Pic

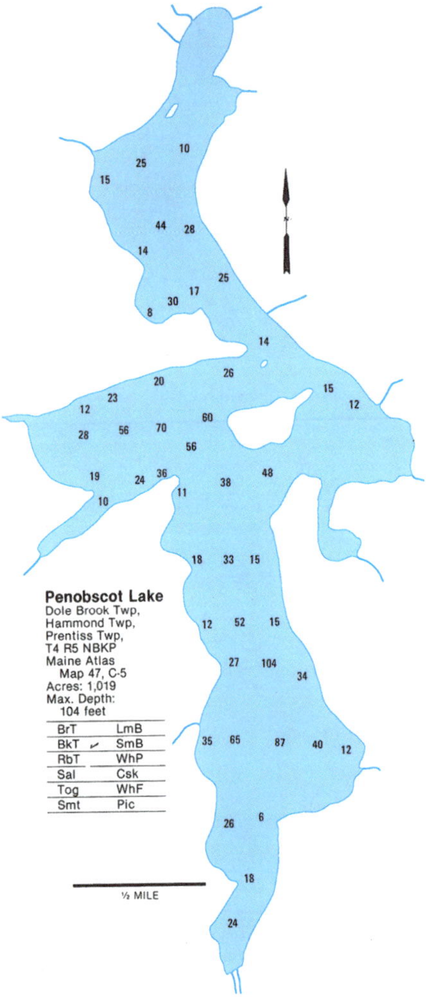

Penobscot Lake
Dole Brook Twp,
Hammond Twp,
Prentiss Twp,
T4 R5 NBKP
Maine Atlas
Map 47, C-5
Acres: 1,019
Max. Depth:
104 feet

BrT	LmB
BkT ✓	SmB
RbT	WhP
Sal	Csk
Tog	WhF
Smt	Pic

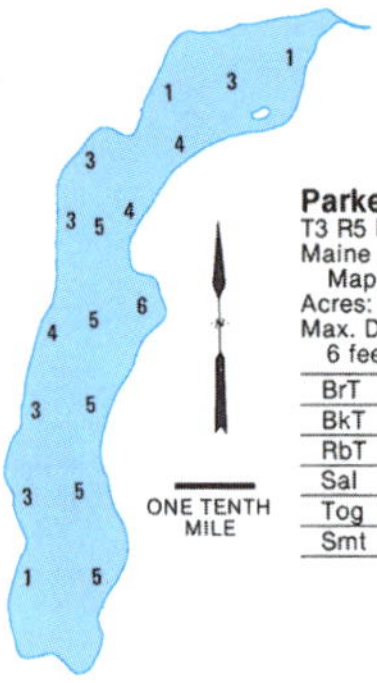

Parker Pond
T3 R5 BKP WKR
Maine Atlas
Map 29, A-4
Acres: 80
Max. Depth:
6 feet

BrT	LmB
BkT ✓	SmB
RbT	WhP
Sal	Csk
Tog	WhF
Smt	Pic

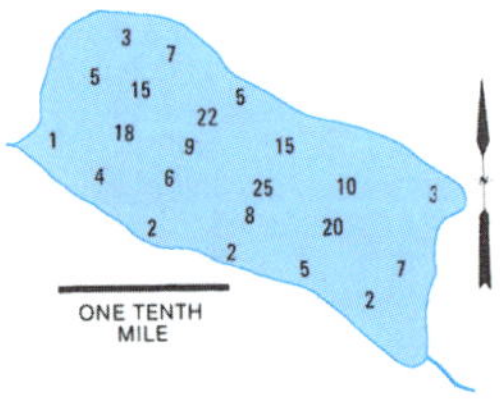

Pickerel Pond
Pierce Pond Twp
Maine Atlas
Map 30, A-1
Acres: 7
Max. Depth:
25 feet

BrT	LmB
BkT ✓	SmB
RbT	WhP
Sal	Csk
Tog	WhF
Smt	Pic ✓

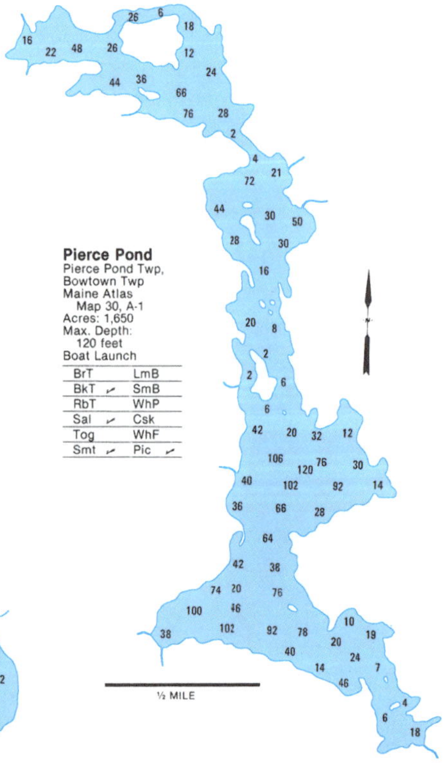

Pierce Pond
Pierce Pond Twp,
Bowtown Twp
Maine Atlas
Map 30, A-1
Acres: 1,650
Max. Depth:
120 feet
Boat Launch

BrT	LmB
BkT ✓	SmB
RbT	WhP
Sal ✓	Csk
Tog	WhF
Smt ✓	Pic ✓

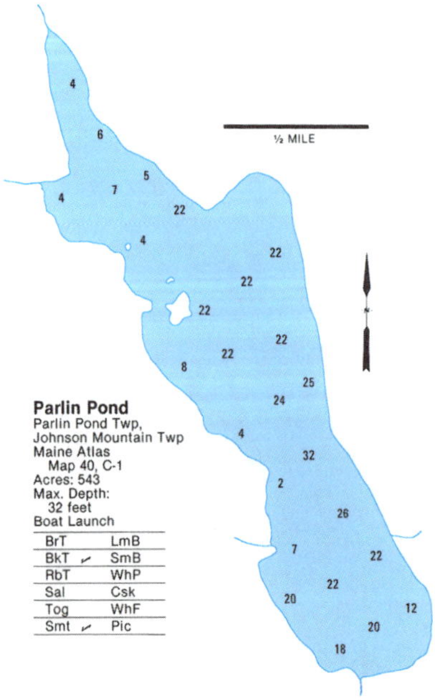

Parlin Pond
Parlin Pond Twp,
Johnson Mountain Twp
Maine Atlas
Map 40, C-1
Acres: 543
Max. Depth:
32 feet
Boat Launch

BrT	LmB
BkT ✓	SmB
RbT	WhP
Sal	Csk
Tog	WhF
Smt ✓	Pic

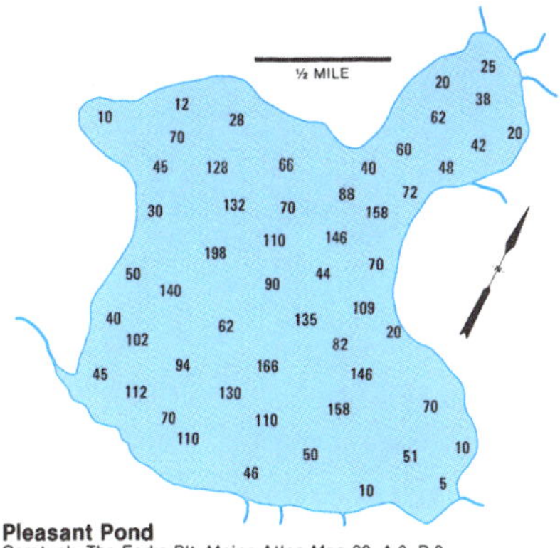

Pleasant Pond
Caratunk, The Forks Plt, Maine Atlas Map 30, A-3, B-3
Acres: 1,120, Max. Depth: 198 feet, Boat Launch

BrT	BkT	RbT	Sal	Tog	Smt	LmB	SmB	WhP	Csk	WhF	Pic
	✓			✓							

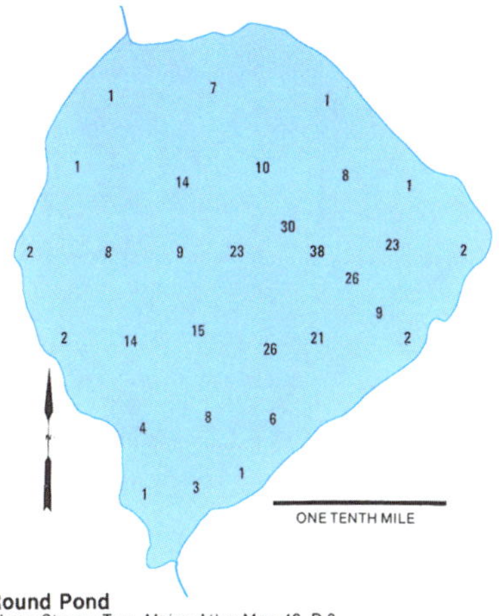

Round Pond
Chase Stream Twp, Maine Atlas Map 40, D-3
Acres: 30, Max. Depth: 38 feet

BrT	BkT	RbT	Sal	Tog	Smt	LmB	SmB	WhP	Csk	WhF	Pic
	✓										

Rancourt Pond
Dennistown Plt
Maine Atlas
Map 39, A-4, B-4
Acres: 23
Max. Depth:
21 feet

BrT	LmB
BkT ✓	SmB
RbT	WhP
Sal	Csk
Tog	WhF
Smt	Pic

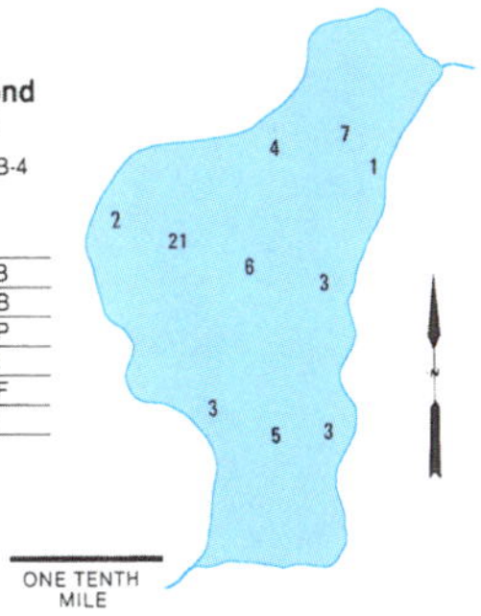

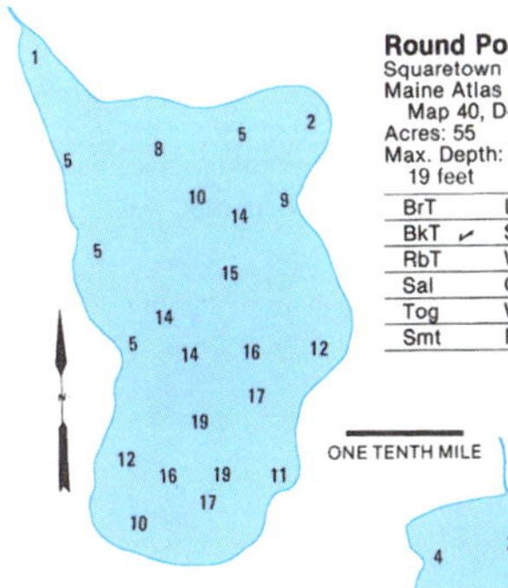

Round Pond
Squaretown Twp
Maine Atlas
Map 40, D-5
Acres: 55
Max. Depth:
19 feet

BrT	LmB
BkT ✓	SmB
RbT	WhP
Sal	Csk
Tog	WhF
Smt	Pic

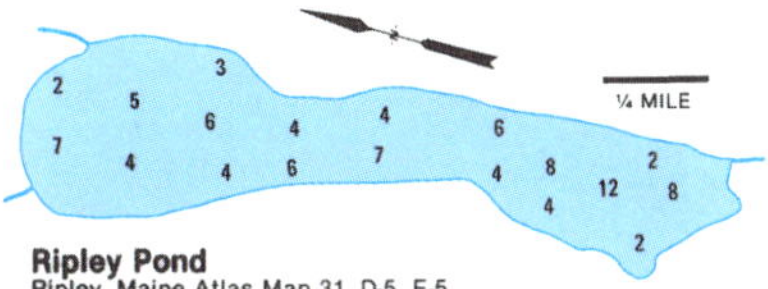

Ripley Pond
Ripley, Maine Atlas Map 31, D-5, E-5
Acres: 220, Max. Depth: 12 feet, Boat Launch

BrT	BkT	RbT	Sal	Tog	Smt	LmB	SmB	WhP	Csk	WhF	Pic
						✓		✓			✓

Rowe Pond
Pleasant Ridge Plt
Maine Atlas
Map 30, C-3
Acres: 205
Max. Depth:
43 feet
Boat Launch

BrT	LmB
BkT ✓	SmB
RbT	WhP
Sal ✓	Csk
Tog	WhF
Smt ✓	Pic

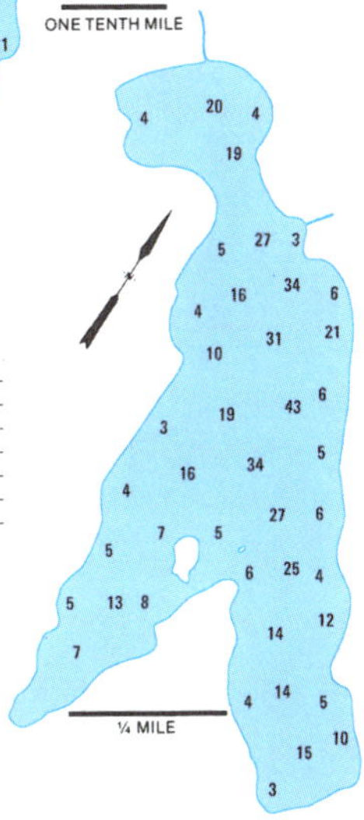

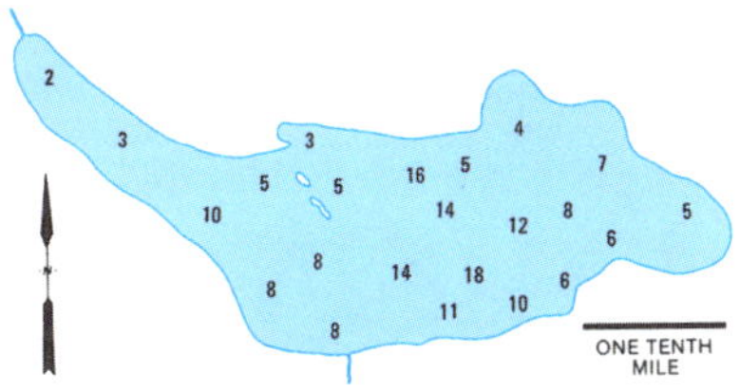

Robinson Pond
Caratunk, Maine Atlas Map 30, B-4
Acres: 40, Max. Depth: 18 feet

BrT	BkT	RbT	Sal	Tog	Smt	LmB	SmB	WhP	Csk	WhF	Pic
	✓										

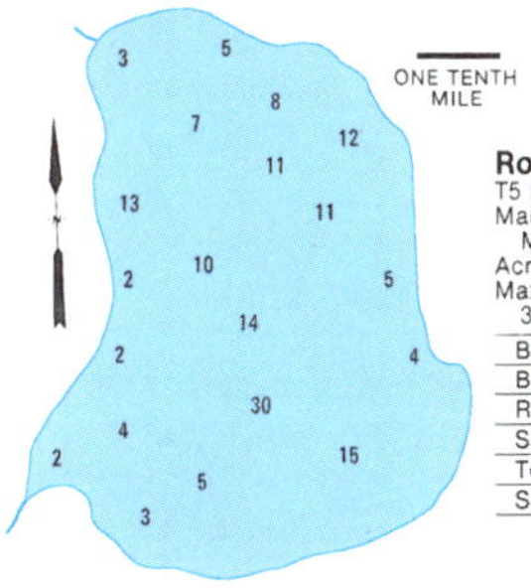

Rock Pond
T5 R6 BKP WKR
Maine Atlas
Map 39, D-3
Acres: 124
Max. Depth:
30 feet

BrT	LmB
BkT ✓	SmB
RbT	WhP
Sal	Csk
Tog	WhF
Smt	Pic

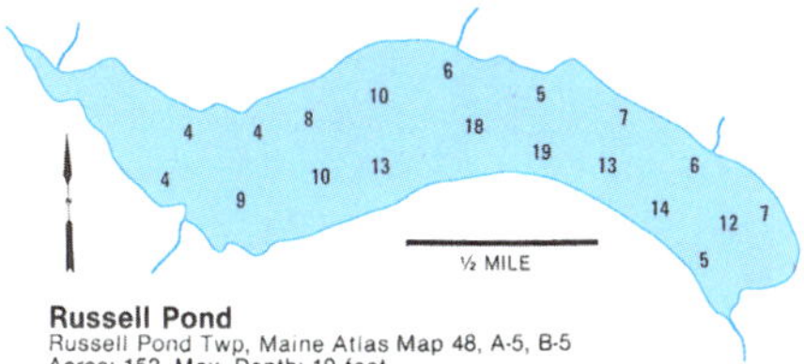

Russell Pond
Russell Pond Twp, Maine Atlas Map 48, A-5, B-5
Acres: 152, Max. Depth: 19 feet

BrT	BkT	RbT	Sal	Tog	Smt	LmB	SmB	WhP	Csk	WhF	Pic
	✓										

Roderique Pond
Rockwood Strip T2 R1
Maine Atlas
Map 40, B-3
Acres: 44
Max. Depth:
16 feet

BrT	LmB
BkT ✓	SmB
RbT	WhP
Sal	Csk
Tog	WhF
Smt	Pic

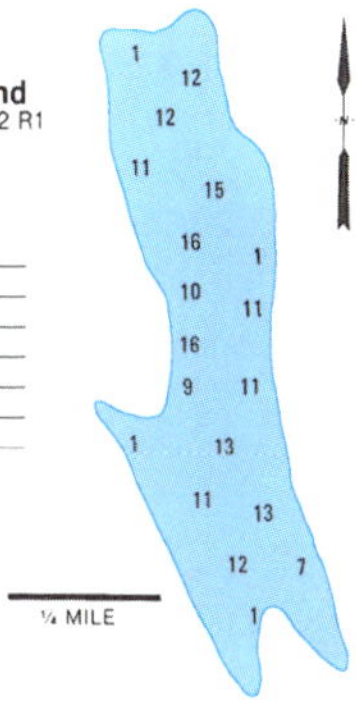

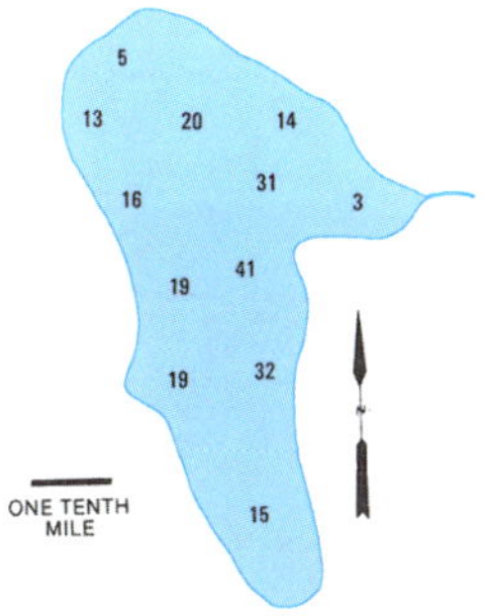

Sandy Pond
Embden
Maine Atlas
Map 20, A-3
Acres: 107
Max. Depth:
41 feet

BrT ✓	LmB
BkT ✓	SmB ✓
RbT	WhP ✓
Sal	Csk
Tog	WhF
Smt	Pic ✓

Somerset

Second St. John Pond

T4 R17 WELS
Maine Atlas
Map 48, B-3
Acres: 105
Max. Depth:
5 feet

BrT	LmB
BkT ✓	SmB
RbT	WhP
Sal	Csk
Tog	WhF
Smt	Pic

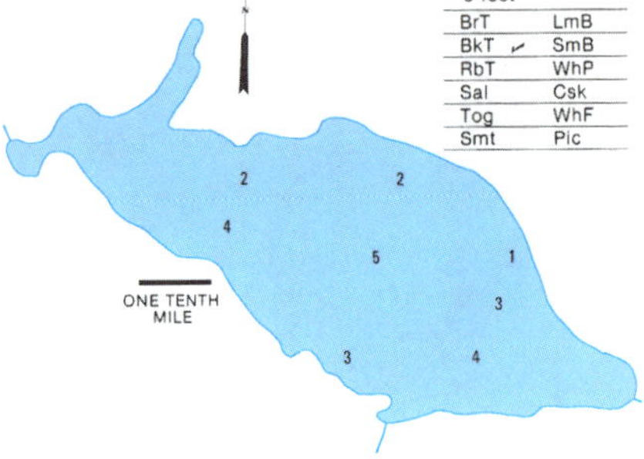

Shaw and Lower Shaw Ponds

T3 R4 BKP WKR
Maine Atlas
Map 29, A-4
Acres: Shaw-45,
Lower Shaw-64
Max. Depth:
Shaw-12 ft
Lower Shaw-14 ft

BrT	LmB
BkT	SmB
RbT	WhP
Sal	Csk
Tog	WhF
Smt	Pic ✓

Comments:
Best fishing in Lower Shaw.

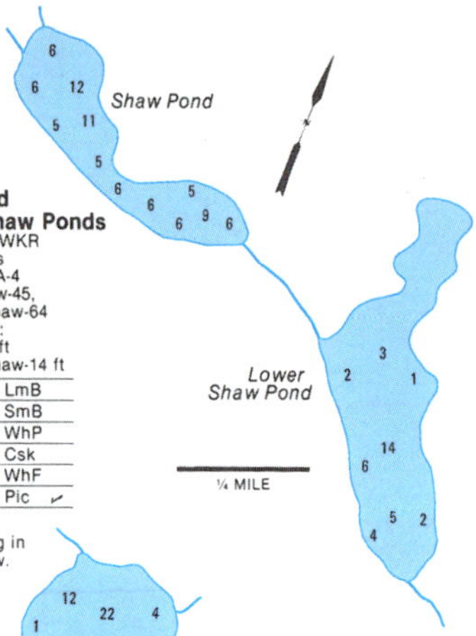

Sibley Pond

Canaan, Pittsfield
Maine Atlas
Map 21, B-3
Acres: 380
Max. Depth:
33 feet
Boat Launch

BrT	LmB ✓
BkT	SmB ✓
RbT	WhP ✓
Sal	Csk
Tog	WhF
Smt	Pic ✓

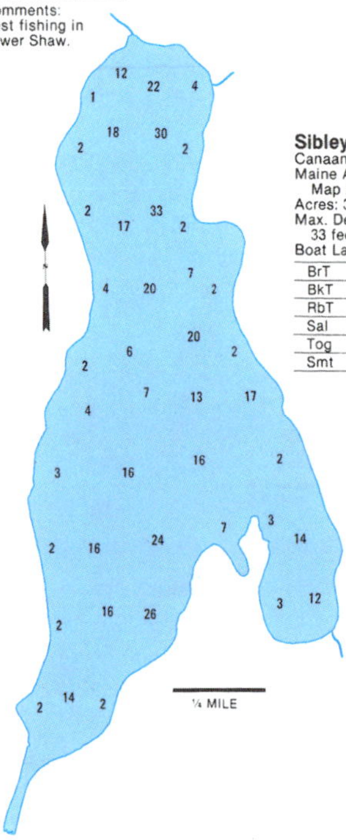

Seeboomook Lake

Pittston Academy
Grant, Plymouth Twp,
Seboomook Twp
Maine Atlas
Map 48, D-4, D-5
Acres: 6,448
Max. Depth:
48 feet

BrT	LmB
BkT ✓	SmB
RbT	WhP
Sal ✓	Csk ✓
Tog	WhF
Smt ✓	Pic

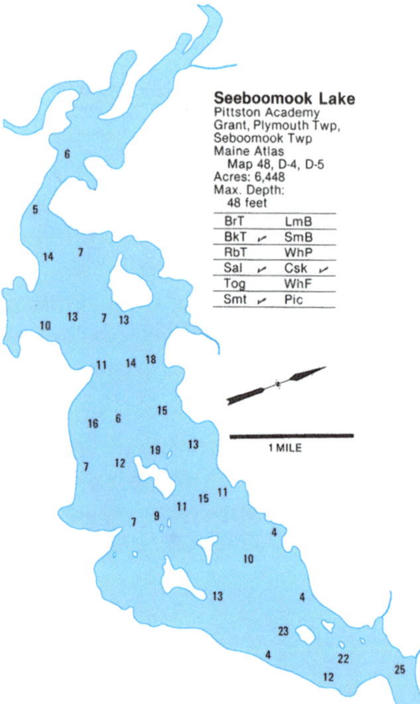

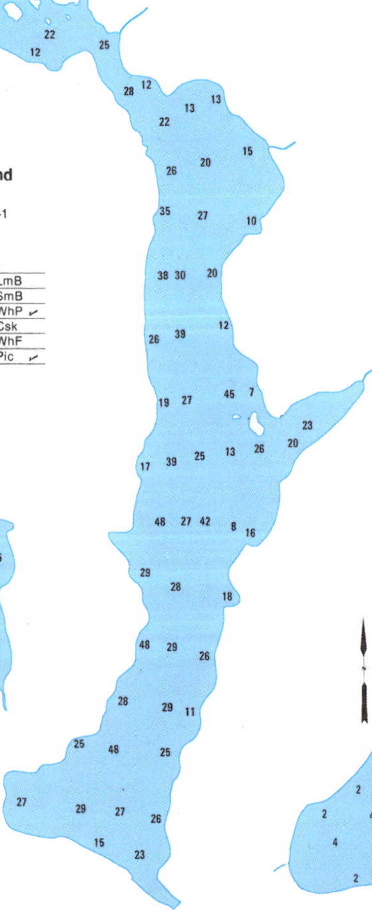

Smith Pond

Brighton Plt
Maine Atlas
Map 31, D-1
Acres: 160
Max. Depth:
32 feet
Boat Launch

BrT ✓	LmB
BkT ✓	SmB
RbT	WhP ✓
Sal	Csk
Tog	WhF
Smt ✓	Pic ✓

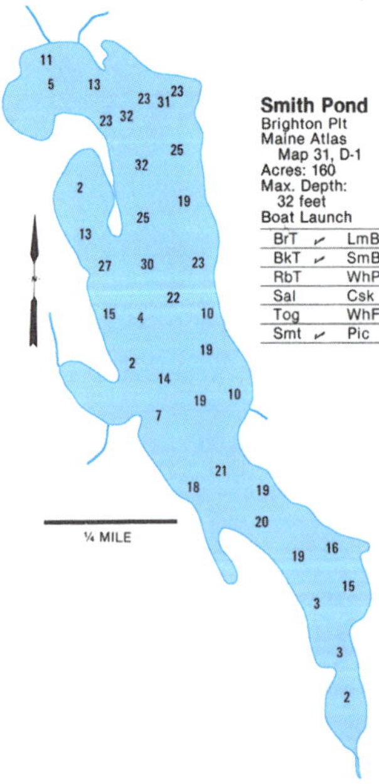

Smith Pond

Parlin Pond Twp,
Misery Twp
Maine Atlas
Map 40, C-2
Acres: 16
Max. Depth:
4 feet

BrT	LmB
BkT ✓	SmB
RbT	WhP
Sal	Csk
Tog	WhF
Smt	Pic

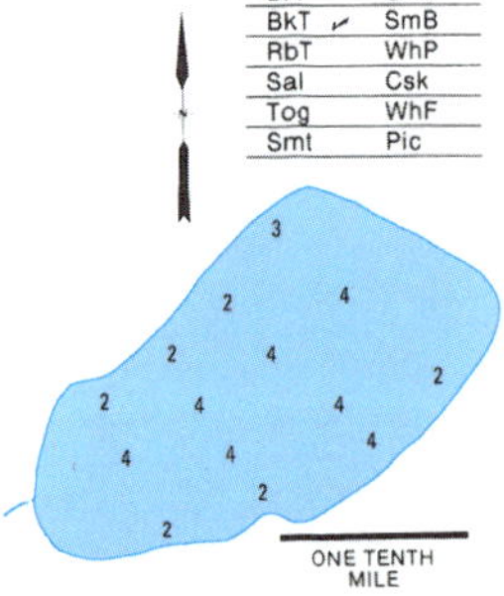

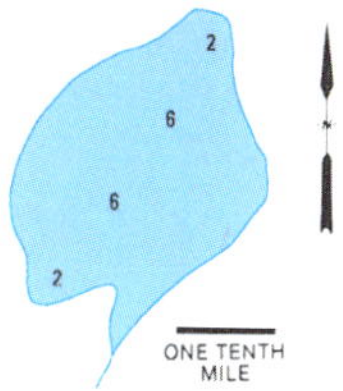

Spaulding Pond
Dole Brook Twp
Maine Atlas
Map 48, C-1
Acres: 28
Max. Depth:
6 feet

BrT	LmB
BkT ✓	SmB
RbT	WhP
Sal	Csk
Tog	WhF
Smt	Pic

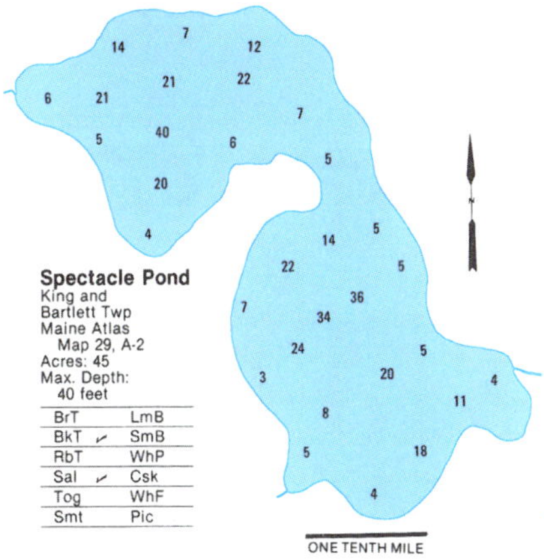

Spectacle Pond
King and
Bartlett Twp
Maine Atlas
Map 29, A-2
Acres: 45
Max. Depth:
40 feet

BrT	LmB
BkT ✓	SmB
RbT	WhP
Sal ✓	Csk
Tog	WhF
Smt	Pic

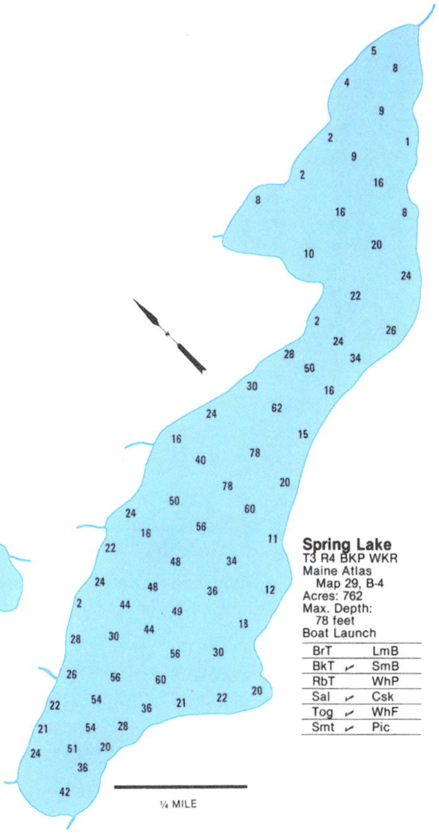

Spring Lake
T3 R4 BKP WKR
Maine Atlas
Map 29, B-4
Acres: 762
Max. Depth:
78 feet
Boat Launch

BrT	LmB
BkT ✓	SmB
RbT	WhP
Sal ✓	Csk
Tog ✓	WhF
Smt ✓	Pic

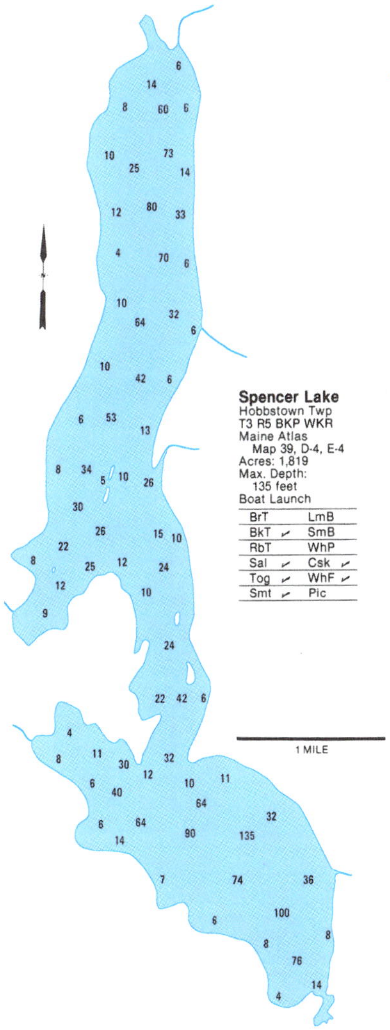

Spencer Lake
Hobbstown Twp
T3 R5 BKP WKR
Maine Atlas
Map 39, D-4, E-4
Acres: 1,819
Max. Depth:
135 feet
Boat Launch

BrT	LmB
BkT ✓	SmB
RbT	WhP
Sal ✓	Csk ✓
Tog ✓	WhF ✓
Smt ✓	Pic

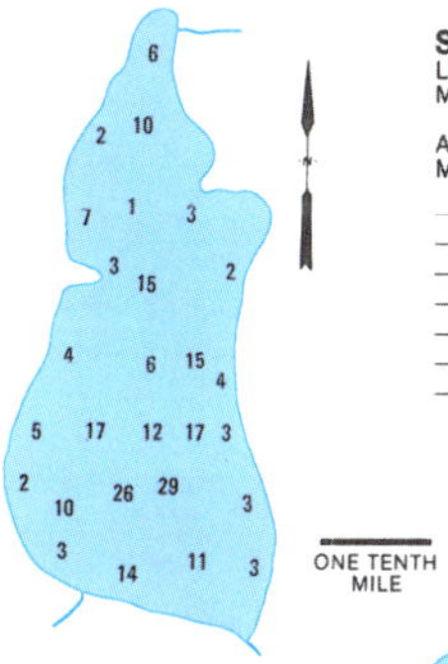

Spruce Pond
Lexington Twp
Maine Atlas
Map 30, D-2, D-3
Acres: 49
Max. Depth:
29 feet

BrT	LmB
BkT ✓	SmB
RbT	WhP
Sal	Csk
Tog	WhF
Smt	Pic

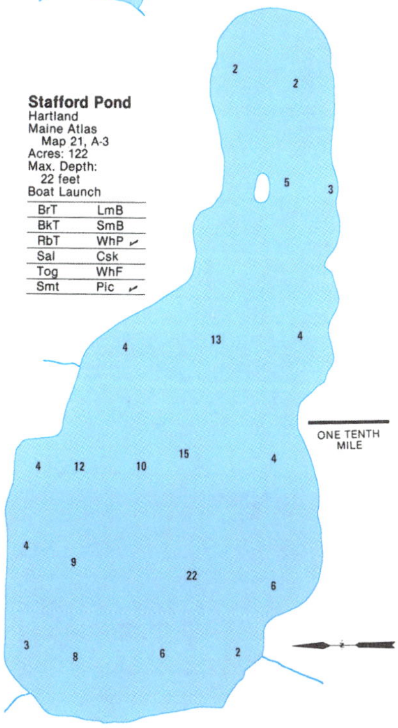

Stafford Pond
Hartland
Maine Atlas
Map 21, A-3
Acres: 122
Max. Depth:
22 feet
Boat Launch

BrT	LmB
BkT	SmB
RbT	WhP ✓
Sal	Csk
Tog	WhF
Smt	Pic ✓

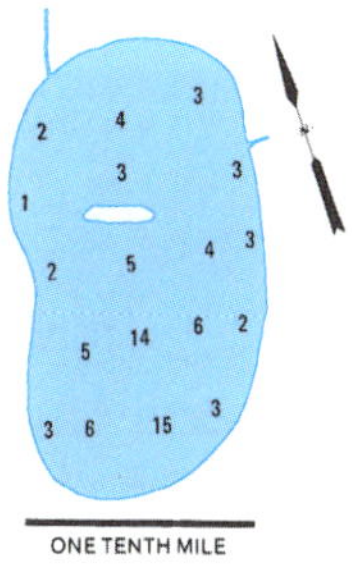

Split Rock Pond
Pierce Pond Twp
Maine Atlas
Map 30, A-2
Acres: 6
Max. Depth:
15 feet

BrT	LmB
BkT ✓	SmB
RbT	WhP
Sal	Csk
Tog	WhF
Smt	Pic

Somerset

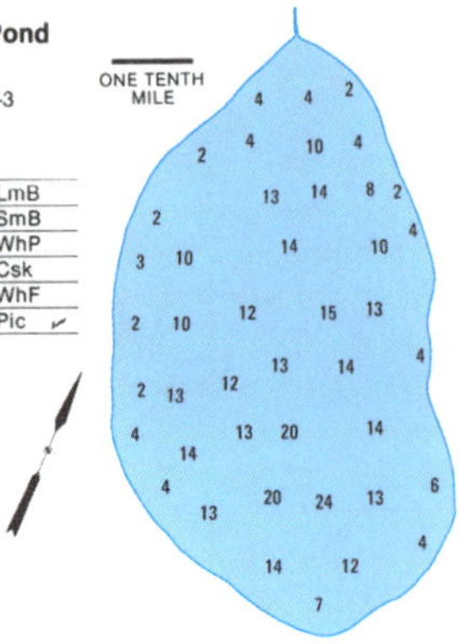

Starbird Pond

Hartland
Maine Atlas
Map 21, A-3
Acres: 32
Max. Depth:
24 feet

BrT		LmB	
BkT		SmB	
RbT		WhP	
Sal		Csk	
Tog		WhF	
Smt		Pic	✓

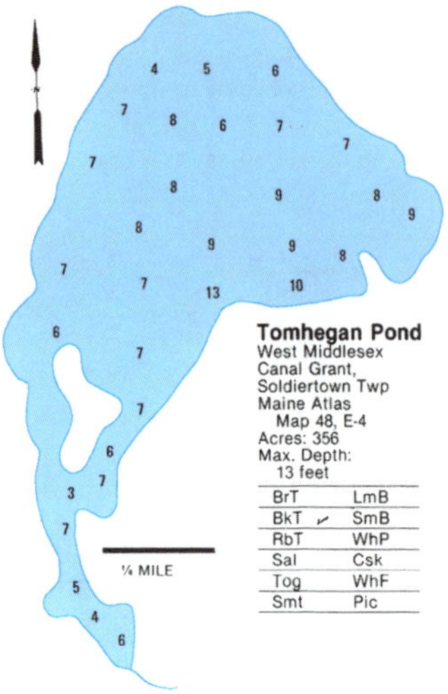

Tomhegan Pond

West Middlesex
Canal Grant,
Soldiertown Twp
Maine Atlas
Map 48, E-4
Acres: 356
Max. Depth:
13 feet

BrT		LmB	
BkT	✓	SmB	
RbT		WhP	
Sal		Csk	
Tog		WhF	
Smt		Pic	

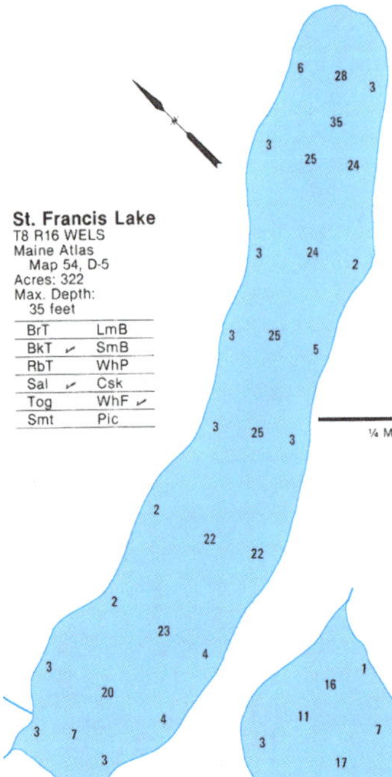

St. Francis Lake

T8 R16 WELS
Maine Atlas
Map 54, D-5
Acres: 322
Max. Depth:
35 feet

BrT		LmB	
BkT	✓	SmB	
RbT		WhP	
Sal	✓	Csk	
Tog		WhF	✓
Smt		Pic	

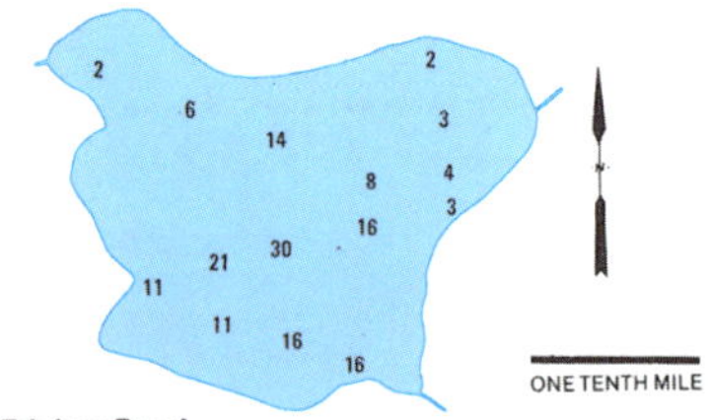

Trickey Pond

Alder Brook Twp, Maine Atlas Map 48, E-1
Acres: 23, Max. Depth: 30 feet

BrT	BkT	RbT	Sal	Tog	Smt	LmB	SmB	WhP	Csk	WhF	Pic
	✓										

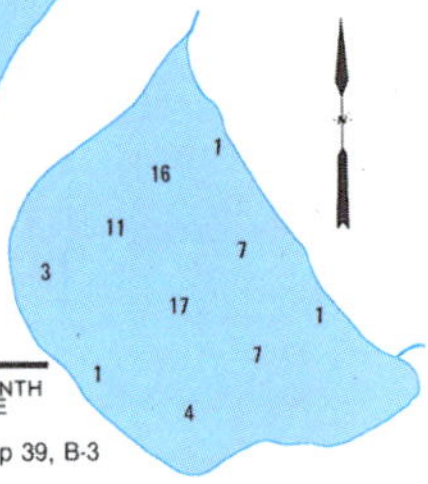

Sugar Berth Pond

Dennistown Plt, Maine Atlas Map 39, B-3
Acres: 23, Max. Depth: 17 feet

BrT	BkT	RbT	Sal	Tog	Smt	LmB	SmB	WhP	Csk	WhF	Pic
	✓										

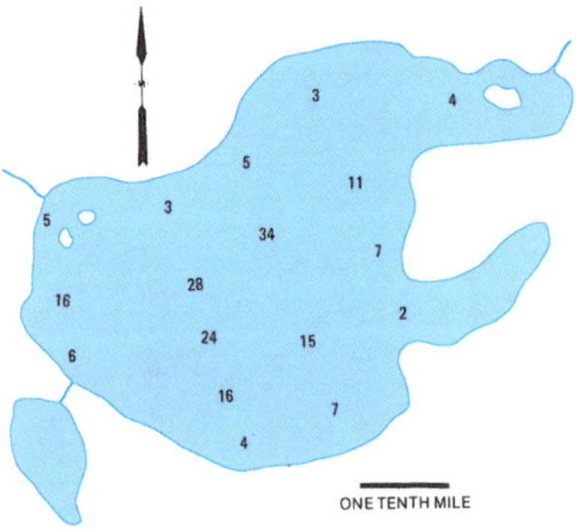

Turner Pond

Forsyth Twp, Maine Atlas Map 39, B-2
Acres: 111, Max. Depth: 34 feet

BrT	BkT	RbT	Sal	Tog	Smt	LmB	SmB	WhP	Csk	WhF	Pic
	✓										

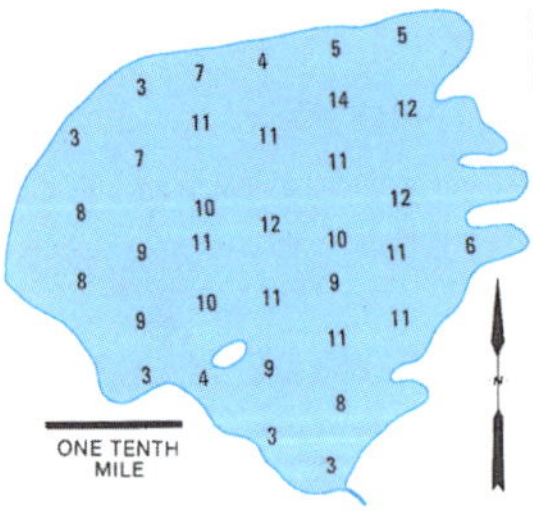

Supply Pond

Jackman,
Moose River
Maine Atlas
Map 39, B-5
Acres: 81
Max. Depth:
14 feet

BrT		LmB	
BkT	✓	SmB	
RbT		WhP	
Sal		Csk	
Tog		WhF	
Smt		Pic	

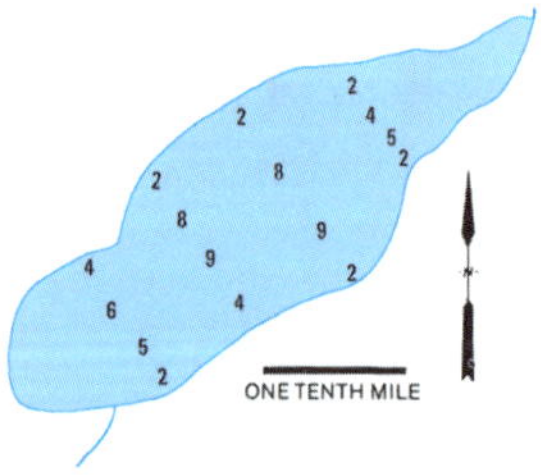

Ten Thousand Acre Pond

Chase Stream Twp
Maine Atlas
Map 40, C-3,
Acres: 37
Max. Depth:
9 feet

BrT		LmB	
BkT	✓	SmB	
RbT		WhP	
Sal		Csk	
Tog		WhF	
Smt		Pic	

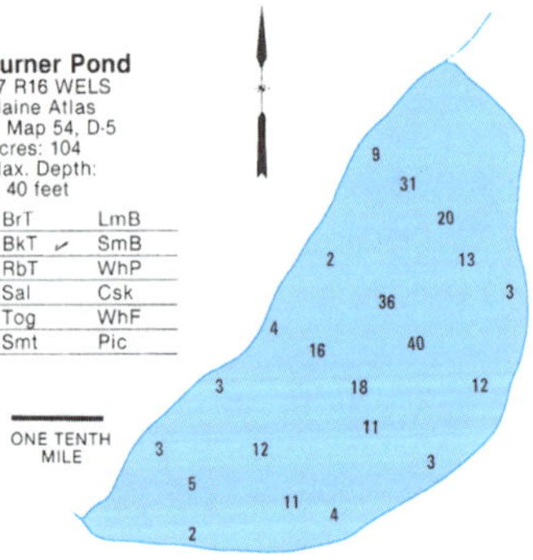

Turner Pond

T7 R16 WELS
Maine Atlas
Map 54, D-5
Acres: 104
Max. Depth:
40 feet

BrT		LmB	
BkT	✓	SmB	
RbT		WhP	
Sal		Csk	
Tog		WhF	
Smt		Pic	

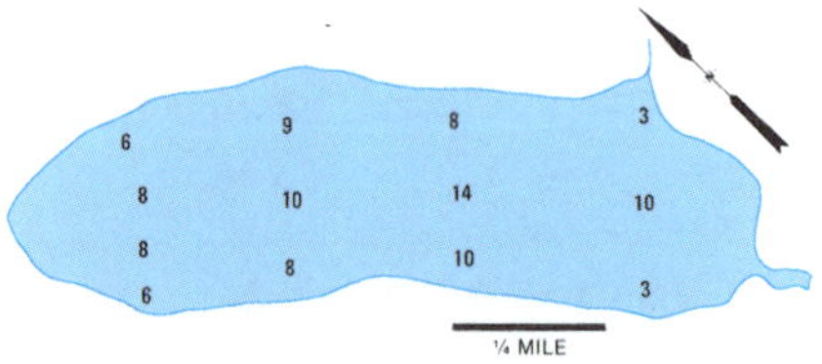

Third St. John Pond

T4 R17 WELS, T5 R17 WELS, Maine Atlas Map 48, B-3
Acres: 190, Max. Depth: 14 feet

BrT	BkT	RbT	Sal	Tog	Smt	LmB	SmB	WhP	Csk	WhF	Pic
	✓										

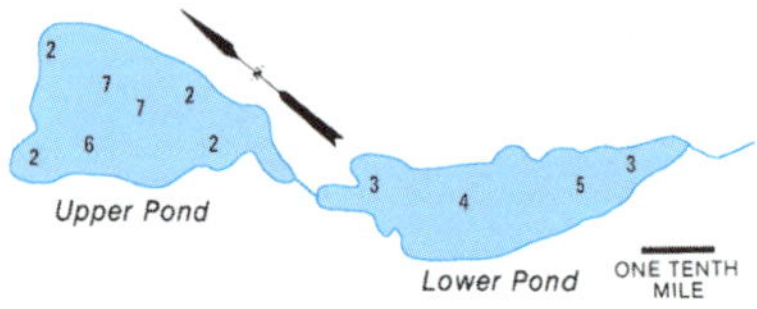

Upper and Lower First St. John Ponds

T4 R17 WELS, Maine Atlas Map 48, B-3
Acres: Upper-30, Lower-29, Max. Depth: Upper-7 feet, Lower-5 feet

BrT	BkT	RbT	Sal	Tog	Smt	LmB	SmB	WhP	Csk	WhF	Pic
	✓										

Somerset

Upper Dingley Pond

T4 R5 NBKP
Maine Atlas
Map 47, C-4, C-5
Acres: 20
Max. Depth:
11 feet

BrT	LmB
BkT ✓	SmB
RbT	WhP
Sal	Csk
Tog	WhF
Smt	Pic

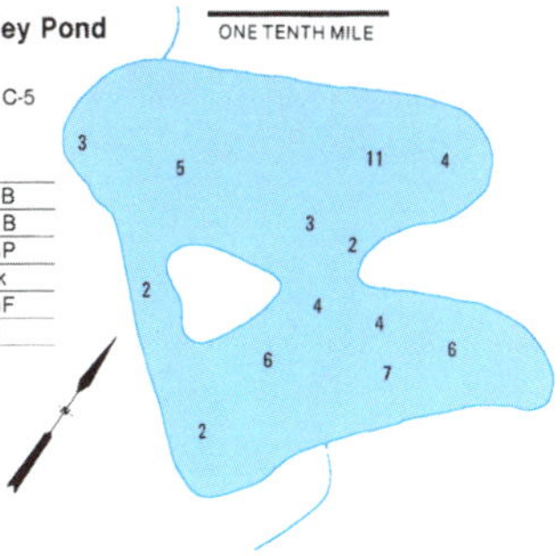

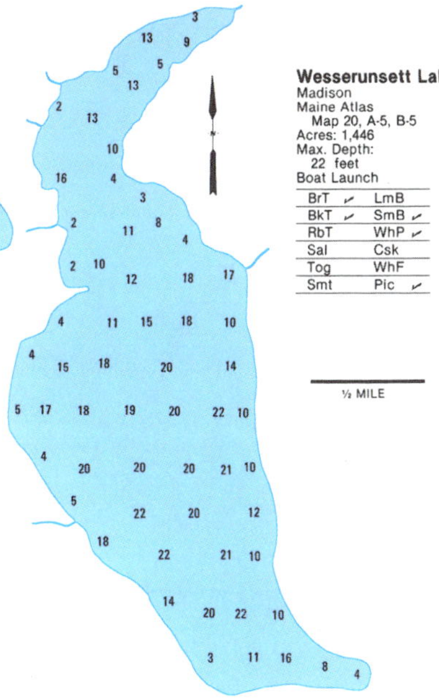

Wesserunsett Lake

Madison
Maine Atlas
Map 20, A-5, B-5
Acres: 1,446
Max. Depth:
22 feet
Boat Launch

BrT ✓	LmB
BkT ✓	SmB ✓
RbT	WhP ✓
Sal	Csk
Tog	WhF
Smt	Pic ✓

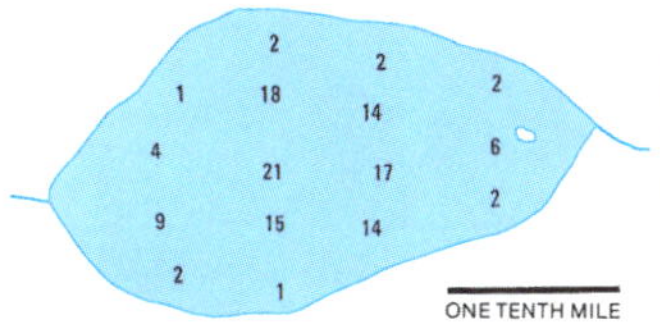

Upper Misery Pond

Misery Twp, Maine Atlas Map 40, C-3
Acres: 18, Max. Depth: 21 feet

BrT	BkT	RbT	Sal	Tog	Smt	LmB	SmB	WhP	Csk	WhF	Pic
	✓										

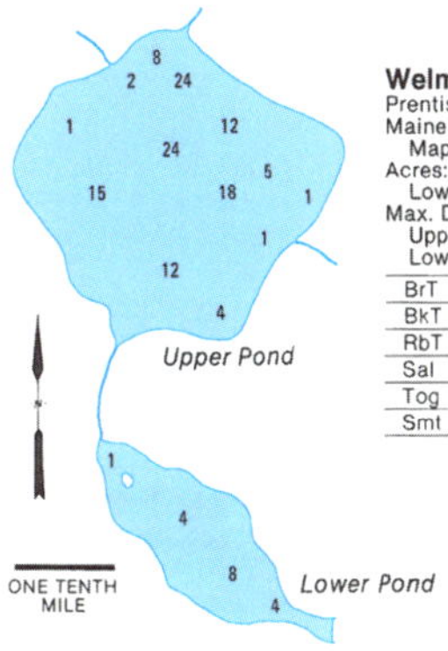

Welman Ponds

Prentiss Twp
Maine Atlas
Map 47, D-5
Acres: Upper-45
Lower-20
Max. Depth:
Upper-24 feet
Lower-8 feet

BrT	LmB
BkT ✓	SmB
RbT	WhP
Sal	Csk
Tog	WhF
Smt	Pic

West Carry Pond

Carrying Place
Town Twp
Maine Atlas
Map 30, B-1, C-1
Acres: 675
Max. Depth:
96 feet

BrT	LmB
BkT ✓	SmB
RbT	WhP
Sal	Csk
Tog ✓	WhF
Smt ✓	Pic

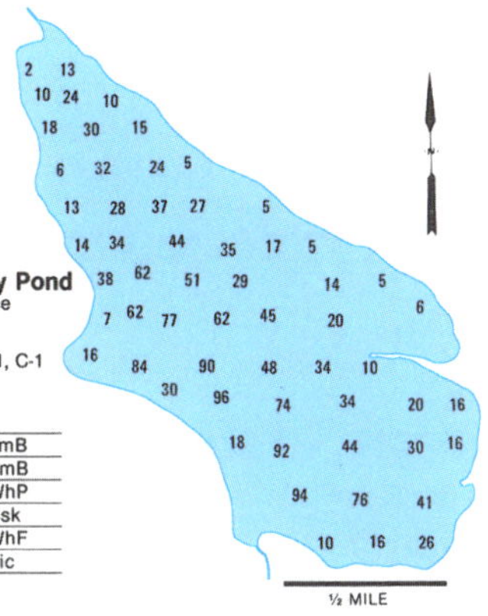

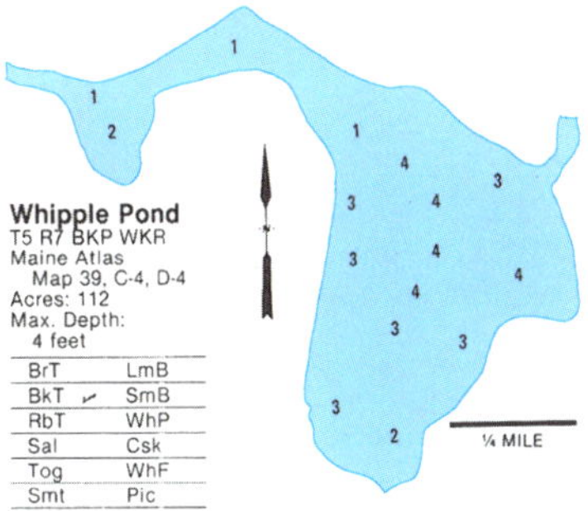

Whipple Pond

T5 R7 BKP WKR
Maine Atlas
Map 39, C-4, D-4
Acres: 112
Max. Depth:
4 feet

BrT	LmB
BkT ✓	SmB
RbT	WhP
Sal	Csk
Tog	WhF
Smt	Pic

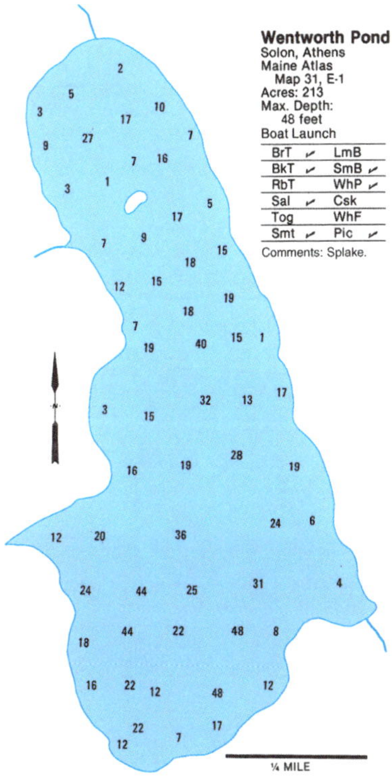

Wentworth Pond

Solon, Athens
Maine Atlas
Map 31, E-1
Acres: 213
Max. Depth:
48 feet
Boat Launch

BrT ✓	LmB
BkT ✓	SmB ✓
RbT	WhP ✓
Sal ✓	Csk
Tog	WhF
Smt ✓	Pic ✓

Comments: Splake.

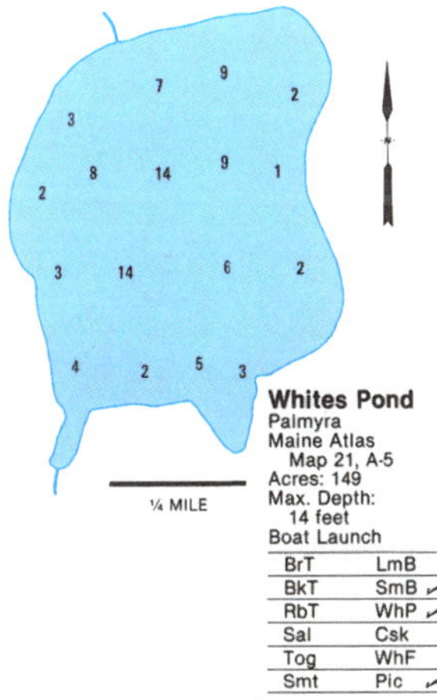

Whites Pond

Palmyra
Maine Atlas
Map 21, A-5
Acres: 149
Max. Depth:
14 feet
Boat Launch

BrT	LmB
BkT	SmB ✓
RbT	WhP ✓
Sal	Csk
Tog	WhF
Smt	Pic ✓

Somerset

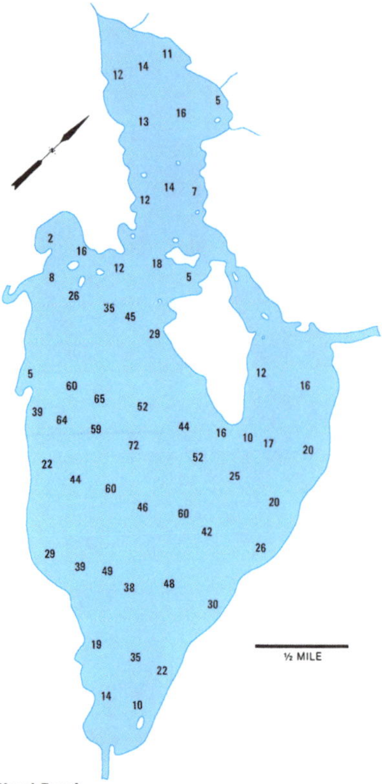

Wood Pond
Attean Twp, Jackman, Dennistown Plt, Maine Atlas Map 39, B-4
Acres: 2,150, Max. Depth: 72 feet, Boat Launch

BrT	BkT	RbT	Sal	Tog	Smt	LmB	SmB	WhP	Csk	WhF	Pic
	✓		✓	✓	✓				✓		

Comments: Splake.

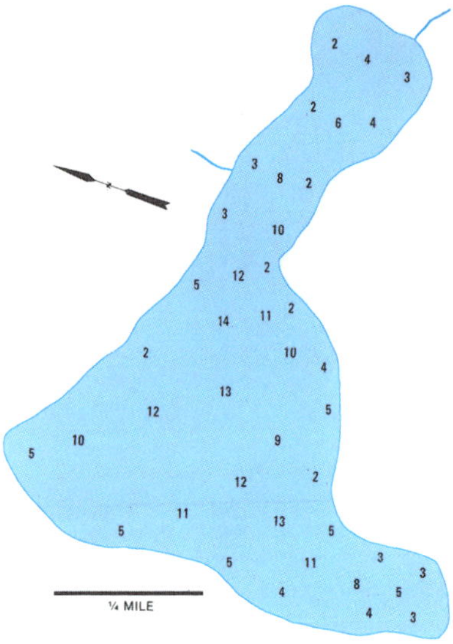

Wyman Pond
Brighton Plt, Maine Atlas Map 31, D-1
Acres: 218, Max. Depth: 14 feet

BrT	BkT	RbT	Sal	Tog	Smt	LmB	SmB	WhP	Csk	WhF	Pic
								✓			✓

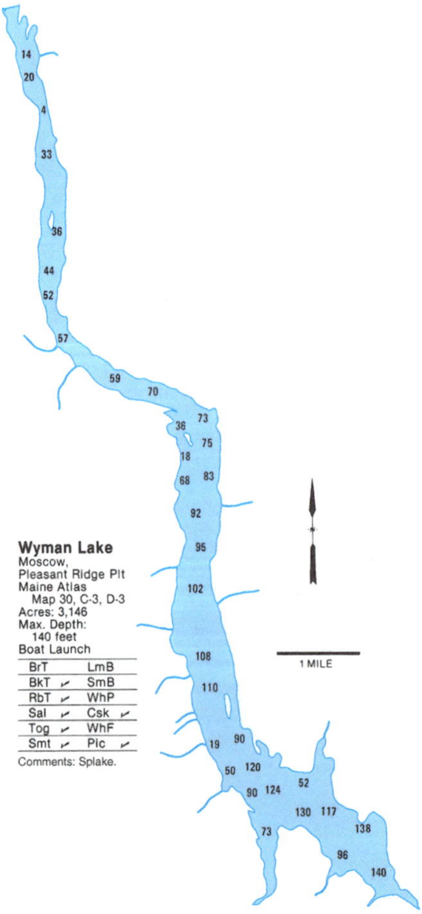

Wyman Lake
Moscow, Pleasant Ridge Plt
Maine Atlas Map 30, C-3, D-3
Acres: 3,146
Max. Depth: 140 feet
Boat Launch

BrT		LmB	
BkT	✓	SmB	
RbT	✓	WhP	
Sal	✓	Csk	✓
Tog	✓	WhF	
Smt	✓	Pic	✓

Comments: Splake.

Waldo County

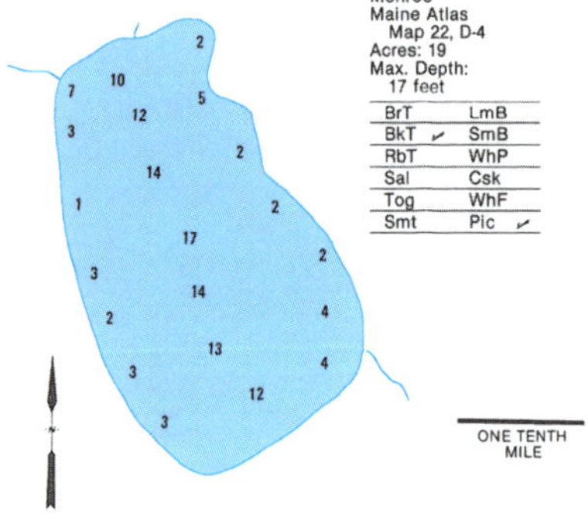

Basin Pond
Monroe
Maine Atlas Map 22, D-4
Acres: 19
Max. Depth: 17 feet

BrT		LmB	
BkT	✓	SmB	
RbT		WhP	
Sal		Csk	
Tog		WhF	
Smt		Pic	✓

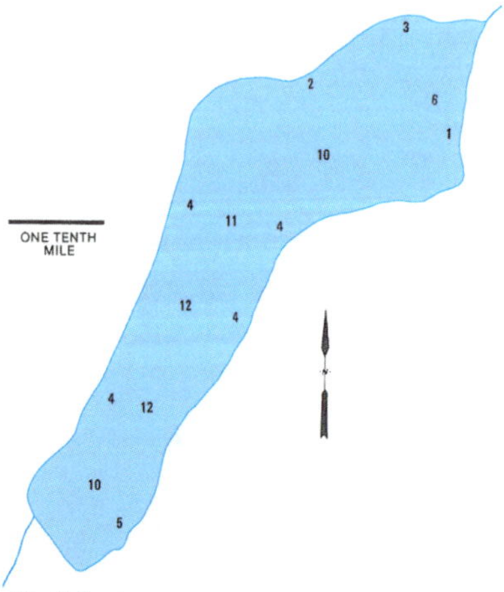

Beech Pond
Palermo, Maine Atlas Map 13, B-4
Acres: 64, Max. Depth: 12 feet

BrT	BkT	RbT	Sal	Tog	Smt	LmB	SmB	WhP	Csk	WhF	Pic
								✓			✓

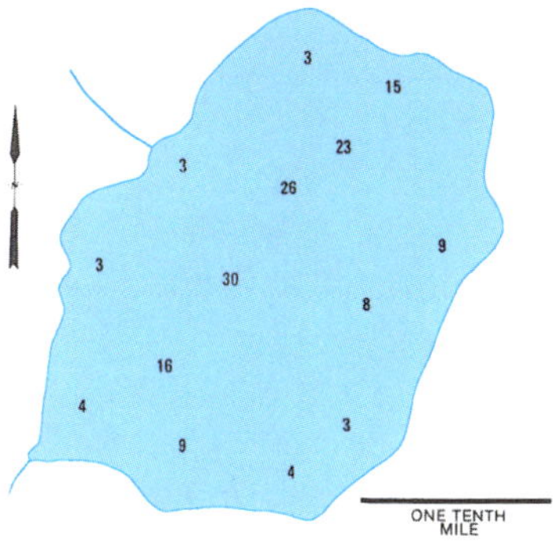

Belden Pond
Palermo, Maine Atlas Map 13, A-5, B-5
Acres: 24, Max. Depth: 30 feet

BrT	BkT	RbT	Sal	Tog	Smt	LmB	SmB	WhP	Csk	WhF	Pic
	✓						✓				✓

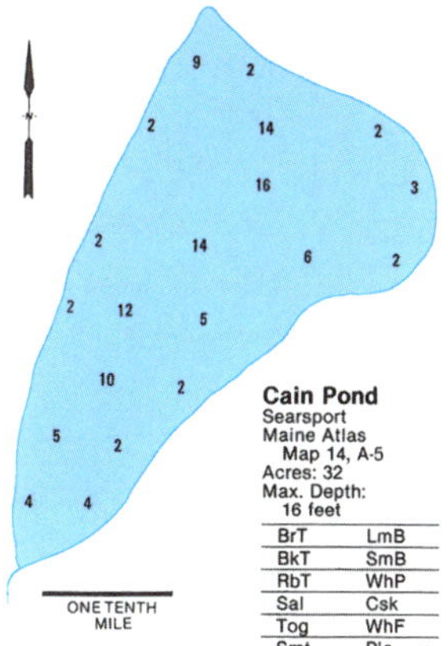

Cain Pond
Searsport
Maine Atlas
Map 14, A-5
Acres: 32
Max. Depth:
16 feet

BrT		LmB	
BkT		SmB	
RbT		WhP	
Sal		Csk	
Tog		WhF	
Smt		Pic	✓

Bowler Pond
Palermo
Maine Atlas
Map 13, A-5, B-5
Acres: 34
Max. Depth:
40 feet

BrT		LmB	
BkT	✓	SmB	✓
RbT		WhP	✓
Sal		Csk	
Tog		WhF	
Smt		Pic	✓

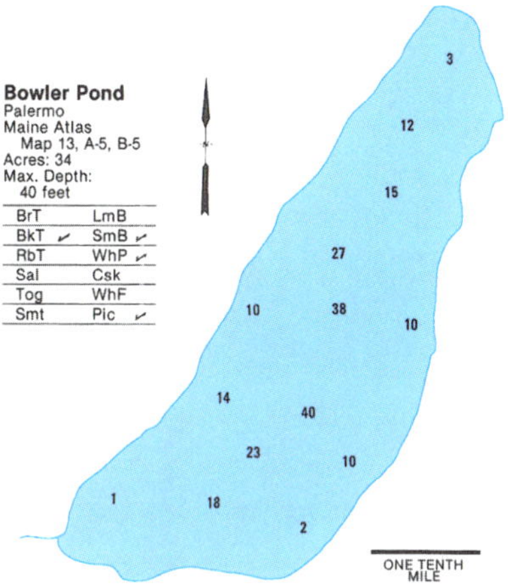

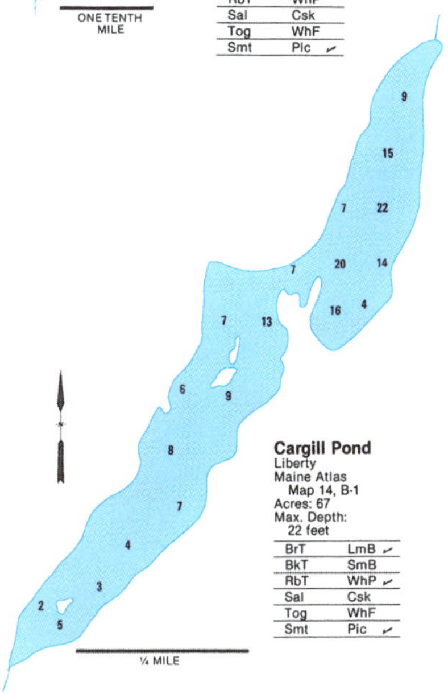

Cargill Pond
Liberty
Maine Atlas
Map 14, B-1
Acres: 67
Max. Depth:
22 feet

BrT		LmB	✓
BkT		SmB	
RbT		WhP	✓
Sal		Csk	
Tog		WhF	
Smt		Pic	✓

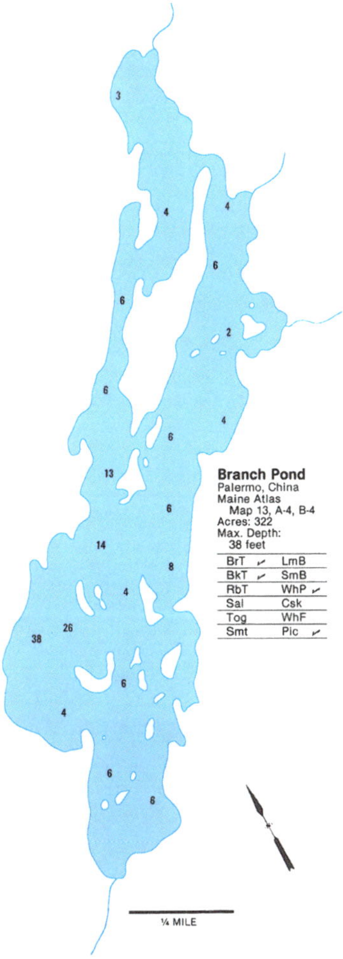

Branch Pond
Palermo, China
Maine Atlas
Map 13, A-4, B-4
Acres: 322
Max. Depth:
38 feet

BrT	✓	LmB	
BkT	✓	SmB	
RbT		WhP	✓
Sal		Csk	
Tog		WhF	
Smt		Pic	✓

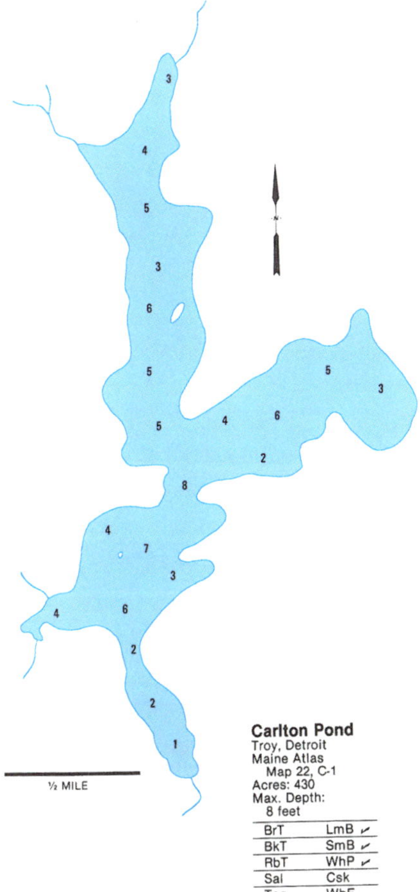

Carlton Pond
Troy, Detroit
Maine Atlas
Map 22, C-1
Acres: 430
Max. Depth:
8 feet

BrT		LmB	✓
BkT		SmB	✓
RbT		WhP	✓
Sal		Csk	
Tog		WhF	
Smt		Pic	✓

Waldo

Chisholm Pond

Palermo
Maine Atlas
Map 13, A-5
Acres: 49
Max. Depth:
24 feet

BrT	LmB
BkT	SmB
RbT	WhP
Sal	Csk
Tog	WhF
Smt	Pic ✓

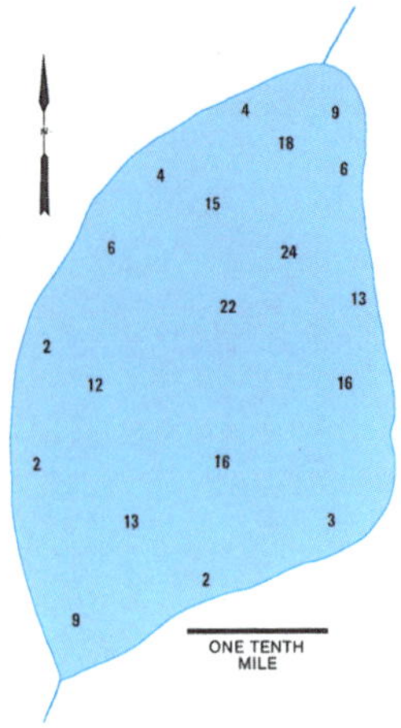

Cross Pond

Morrill
Maine Atlas
Map 14, A-3, B-3
Acres: 162
Max. Depth:
10 feet

BrT	LmB
BkT	SmB
RbT	WhP
Sal	Csk
Tog	WhF
Smt	Pic ✓

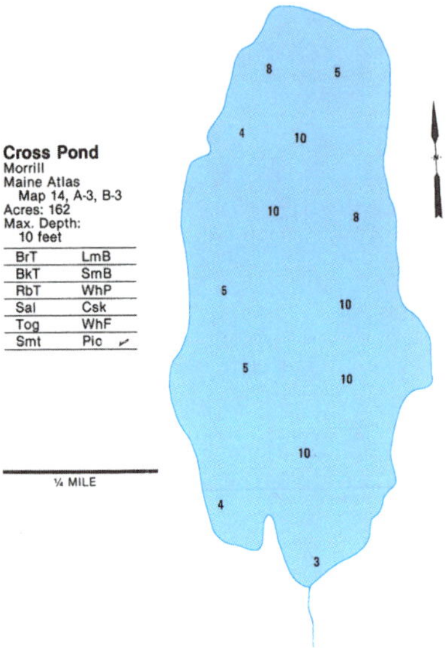

Colby Pond

Liberty, Maine Atlas Map 13, B-5
Acres: 27, Max. Depth: 12 feet

BrT	BkT	RbT	Sal	Tog	Smt	LmB	SmB	WhP	Csk	WhF	Pic
											✓

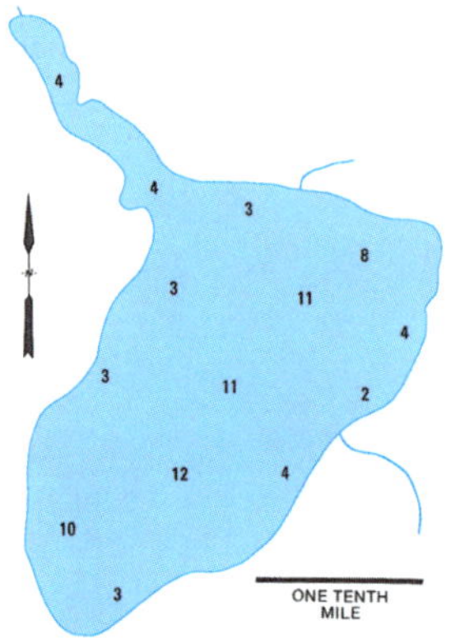

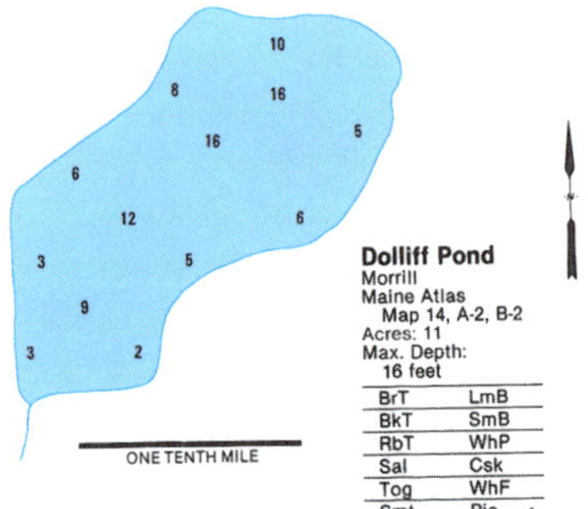

Dolliff Pond

Morrill
Maine Atlas
Map 14, A-2, B-2
Acres: 11
Max. Depth:
16 feet

BrT	LmB
BkT	SmB
RbT	WhP
Sal	Csk
Tog	WhF
Smt	Pic ✓

Coleman Pond

Lincolnville
Maine Atlas
Map 14, C-4
Acres: 198
Max. Depth:
44 feet

BrT	LmB
BkT	SmB ✓
RbT	WhP ✓
Sal	Csk
Tog	WhF
Smt	Pic ✓

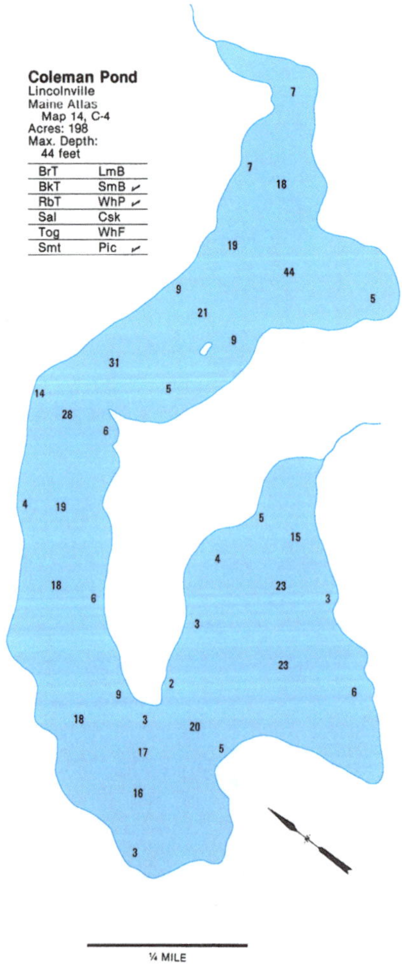

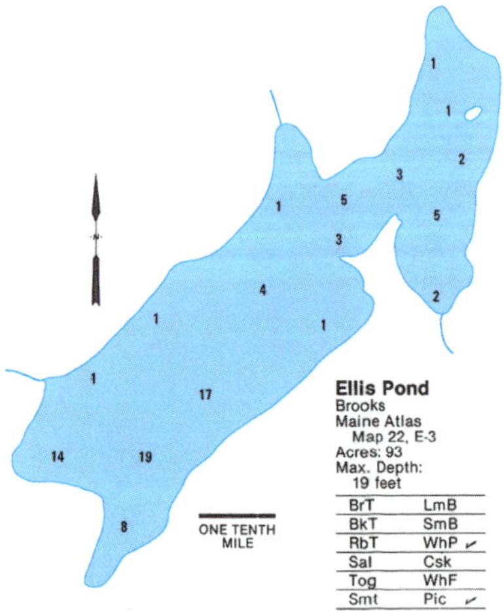

Dutton Pond

Knox, Maine Atlas Map 14, A-3
Acres: 35, Max. Depth: 22 feet

BrT	BkT	RbT	Sal	Tog	Smt	LmB	SmB	WhP	Csk	WhF	Pic
✓	✓						✓	✓			✓

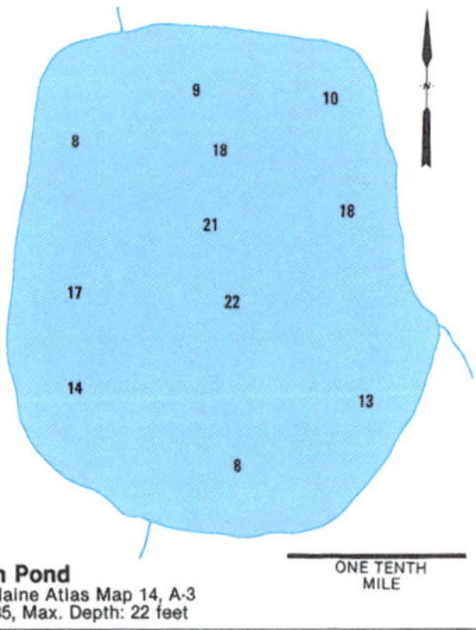

Ellis Pond

Brooks
Maine Atlas
Map 22, E-3
Acres: 93
Max. Depth:
19 feet

BrT	LmB
BkT	SmB
RbT	WhP ✓
Sal	Csk
Tog	WhF
Smt	Pic ✓

Foster Pond

Palermo
Maine Atlas
Map 13, A-5, B-5
Acres: 32
Max. Depth:
68 feet

BrT	LmB
BkT	SmB ✓
RbT	WhP
Sal	Csk
Tog	WhF
Smt ✓	Pic ✓

ONE TENTH MILE

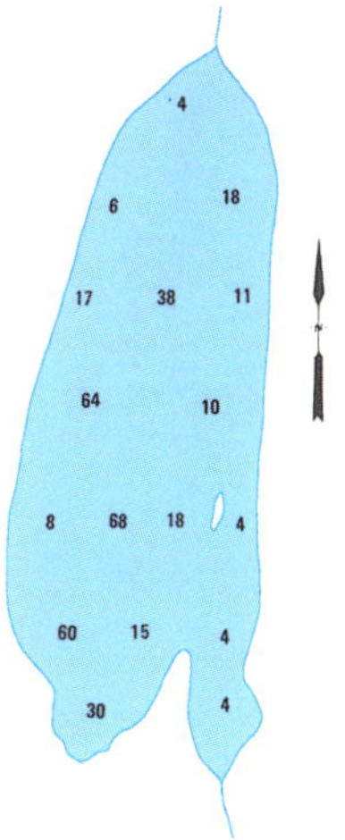

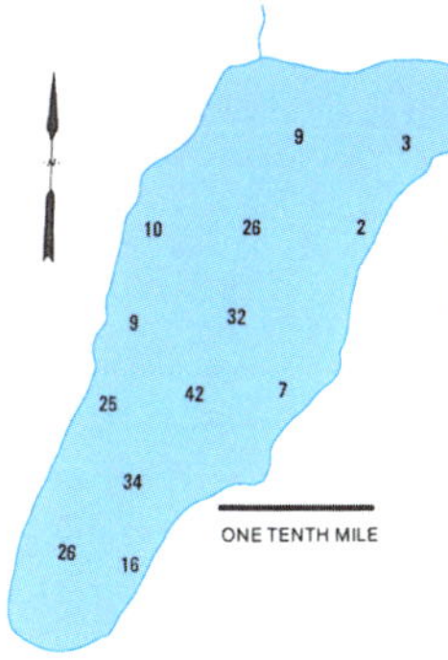

Jump Pond

Palermo
Maine Atlas
Map 13, A-5
Acres: 30
Max. Depth:
42 feet

BrT	LmB
BkT ✓	SmB ✓
RbT	WhP ✓
Sal	Csk
Tog	WhF
Smt	Pic ✓

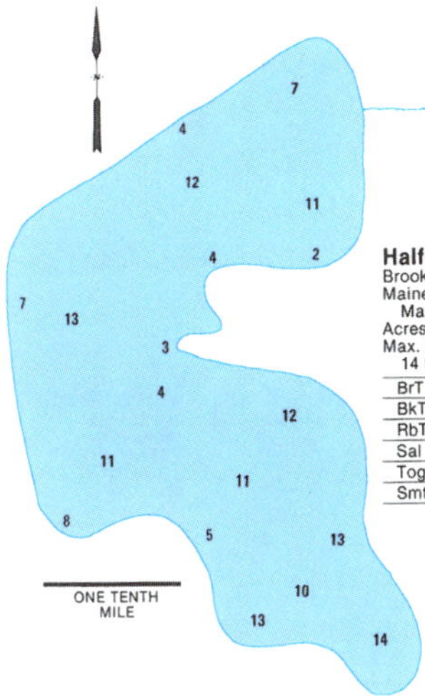

Halfmoon Pond

Brooks
Maine Atlas
Map 22, E-3
Acres: 38
Max. Depth:
14 feet

BrT	LmB
BkT ✓	SmB
RbT	WhP
Sal	Csk
Tog	WhF
Smt	Pic

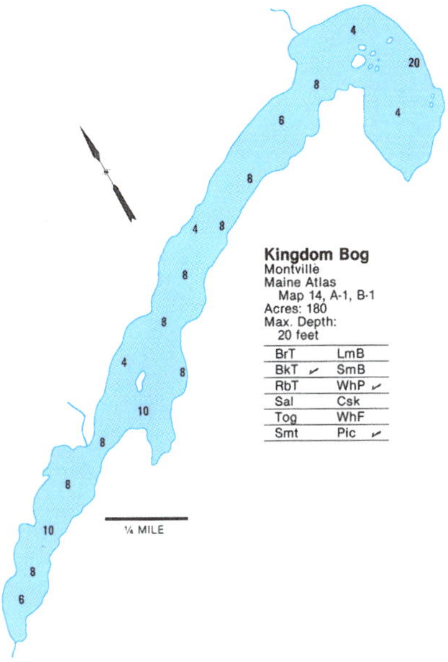

Kingdom Bog

Montville
Maine Atlas
Map 14, A-1, B-1
Acres: 180
Max. Depth:
20 feet

BrT	LmB
BkT ✓	SmB
RbT	WhP ✓
Sal	Csk
Tog	WhF
Smt	Pic ✓

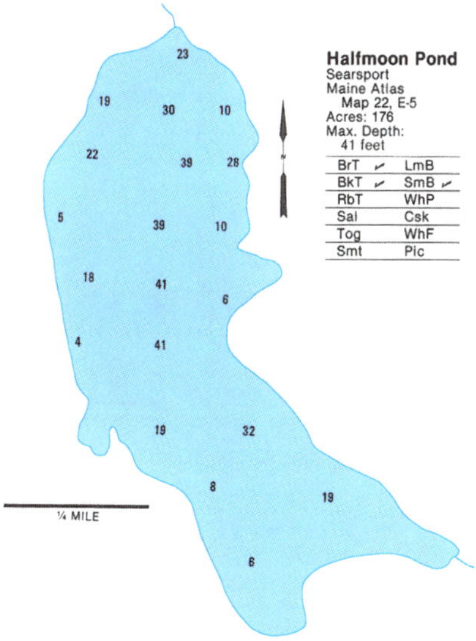

Halfmoon Pond

Searsport
Maine Atlas
Map 22, E-5
Acres: 176
Max. Depth:
41 feet

BrT ✓	LmB
BkT ✓	SmB ✓
RbT	WhP
Sal	Csk
Tog	WhF
Smt	Pic

Knight Pond

Northport
Maine Atlas
Map 14, B-4
Acres: 102
Max. Depth:
13 feet

BrT	LmB ✓
BkT	SmB ✓
RbT	WhP ✓
Sal	Csk
Tog	WhF
Smt	Pic ✓

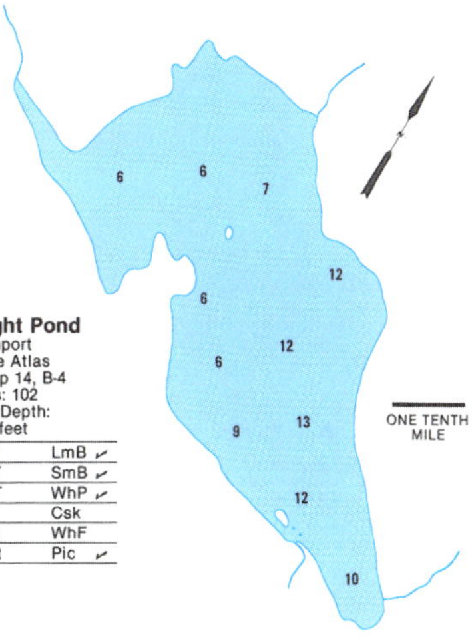

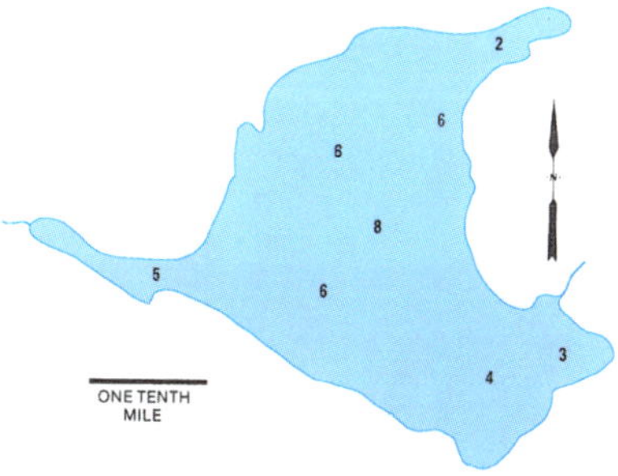

Hurds Pond

Swanville, Maine Atlas Map 14, A-4
Acres: 40, Max. Depth: 8 feet

BrT	BkT	RbT	Sal	Tog	Smt	LmB	SmB	WhP	Csk	WhF	Pic
	✓							✓			✓

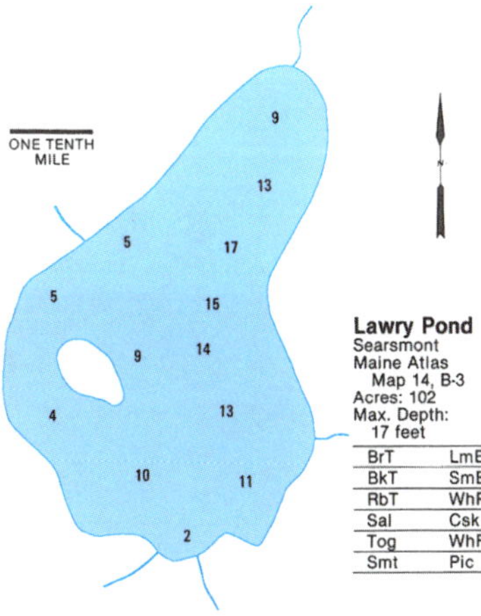

Lawry Pond

Searsmont
Maine Atlas
Map 14, B-3
Acres: 102
Max. Depth:
17 feet

BrT	LmB ✓
BkT	SmB ✓
RbT	WhP ✓
Sal	Csk
Tog	WhF
Smt	Pic ✓

Waldo

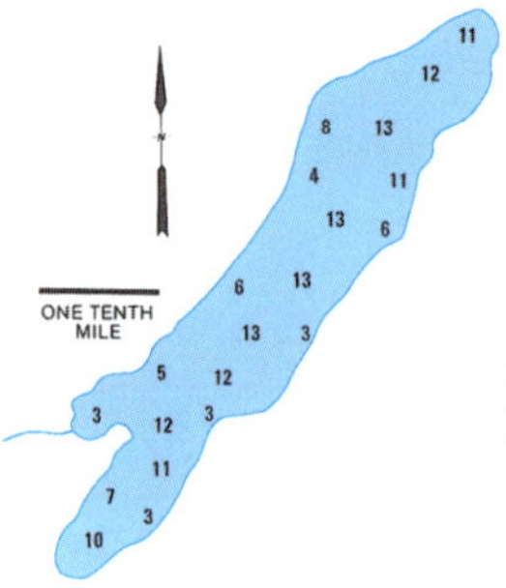

Ledge Pond
Montville
Maine Atlas
Map 14, A-1
Acres: 23
Max. Depth:
13 feet

BrT	LmB ✓
BkT	SmB
RbT	WhP ✓
Sal	Csk
Tog	WhF
Smt	Pic ✓

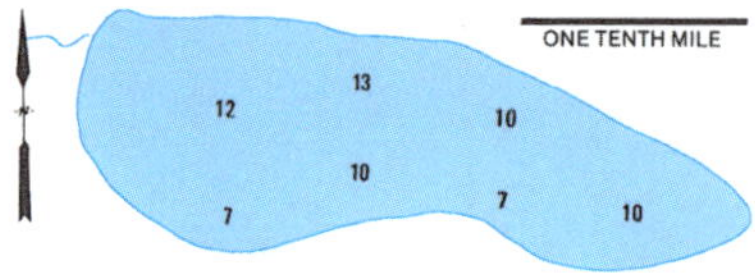

Nichols Pond
Swanville, Maine Atlas Map 14, A-4
Acres: 14, Max. Depth: 13 feet

BrT	BkT	RbT	Sal	Tog	Smt	LmB	SmB	WhP	Csk	WhF	Pic
	✓										

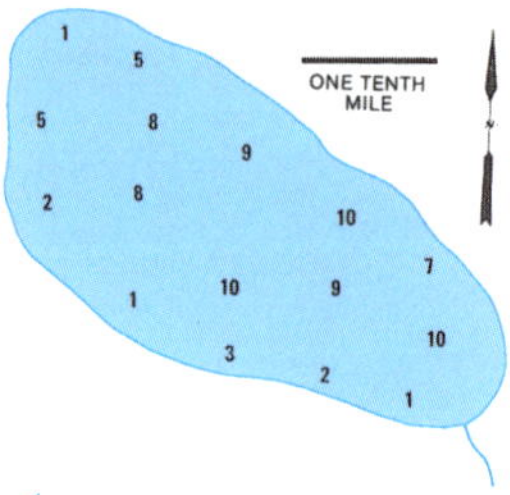

Levenseller Pond
Searsmont,
Lincolnville
Maine Atlas
Map 14, C-3
Acres: 35
Max. Depth:
10 feet

BrT ✓	LmB
BkT ✓	SmB
RbT	WhP ✓
Sal	Csk
Tog	WhF
Smt	Pic ✓

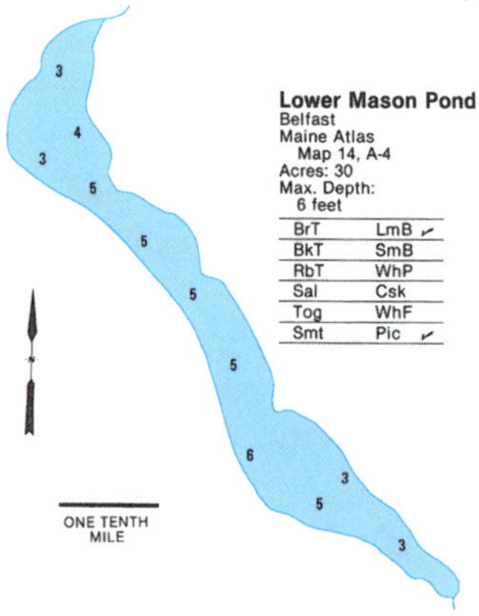

Lower Mason Pond
Belfast
Maine Atlas
Map 14, A-4
Acres: 30
Max. Depth:
6 feet

BrT	LmB ✓
BkT	SmB
RbT	WhP
Sal	Csk
Tog	WhF
Smt	Pic ✓

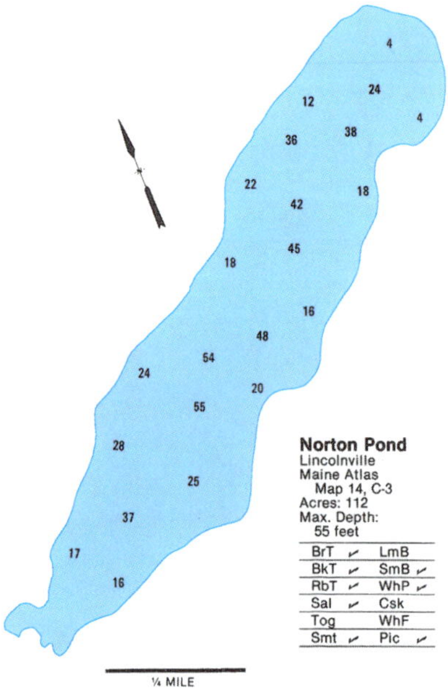

Norton Pond
Lincolnville
Maine Atlas
Map 14, C-3
Acres: 112
Max. Depth:
55 feet

BrT ✓	LmB
BkT ✓	SmB ✓
RbT ✓	WhP ✓
Sal ✓	Csk
Tog	WhF
Smt ✓	Pic ✓

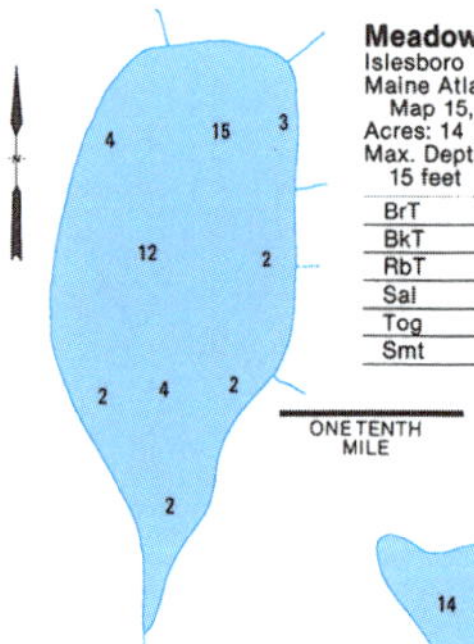

Meadow Pond
Islesboro
Maine Atlas
Map 15, B-1
Acres: 14
Max. Depth:
15 feet

BrT	LmB
BkT	SmB
RbT	WhP ✓
Sal	Csk
Tog	WhF
Smt	Pic ✓

Passagassawaukeag Lake
Brooks
Maine Atlas
Map 22, E-3
Acres: 118
Max. Depth:
40 feet

BrT	LmB
BkT	SmB ✓
RbT	WhP ✓
Sal	Csk
Tog	WhF
Smt ✓	Pic ✓

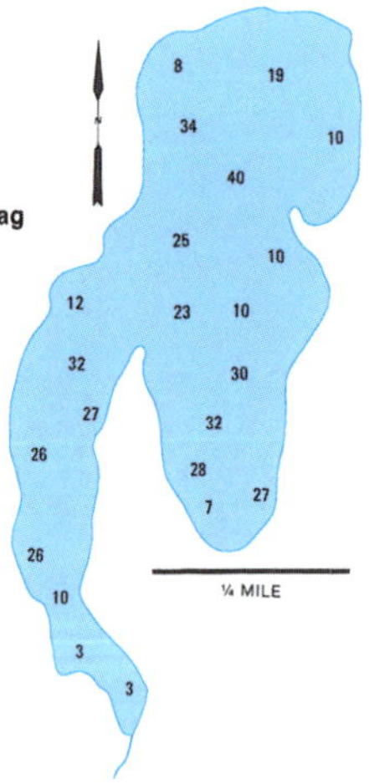

Mixer Pond
Knox, Morrill
Maine Atlas
Map 14, A-2, A-3
Acres: 35
Max. Depth:
29 feet

BrT	LmB
BkT ✓	SmB
RbT	WhP
Sal	Csk
Tog	WhF
Smt ✓	Pic

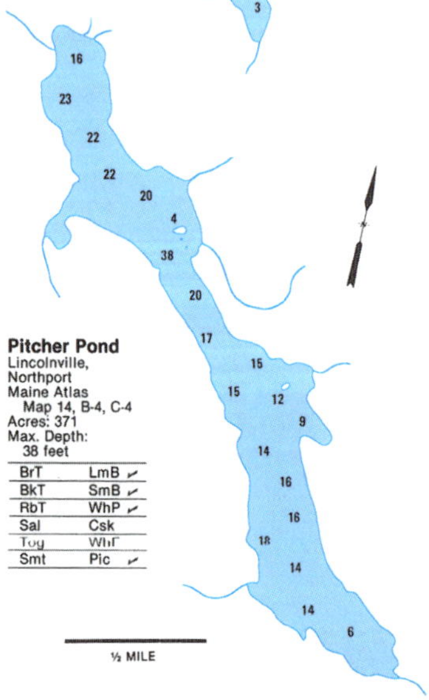

Pitcher Pond
Lincolnville,
Northport
Maine Atlas
Map 14, B-4, C-4
Acres: 371
Max. Depth:
38 feet

BrT	LmB ✓
BkT	SmB ✓
RbT	WhP ✓
Sal	Csk
Tog	WhF
Smt	Pic ✓

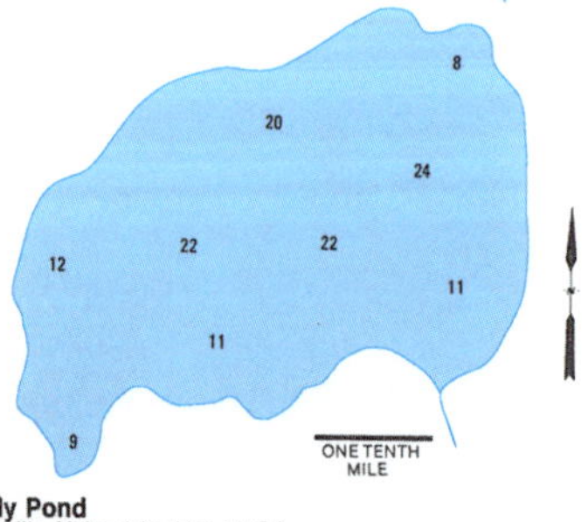

Moody Pond
Lincolnville, Maine Atlas Map 14, C-3
Acres: 90, Max. Depth: 26 feet

BrT	BkT	RbT	Sal	Tog	Smt	LmB	SmB	WhP	Csk	WhF	Pic
	✓						✓				✓

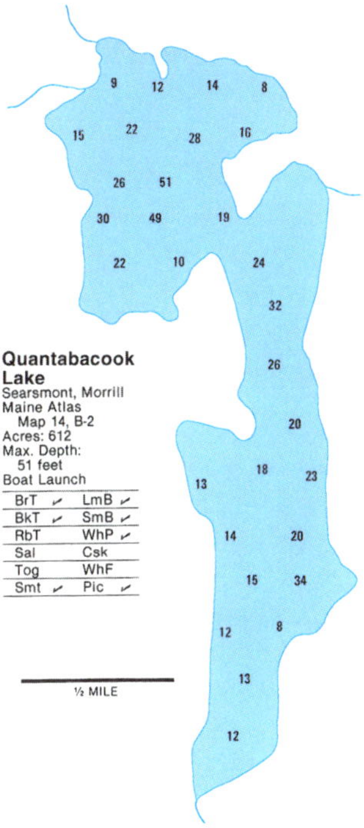

Quantabacook Lake
Searsmont, Morrill
Maine Atlas
Map 14, B-2
Acres: 612
Max. Depth:
51 feet
Boat Launch

BrT	✓	LmB	✓
BkT	✓	SmB	✓
RbT		WhP	✓
Sal		Csk	
Tog		WhF	
Smt	✓	Pic	✓

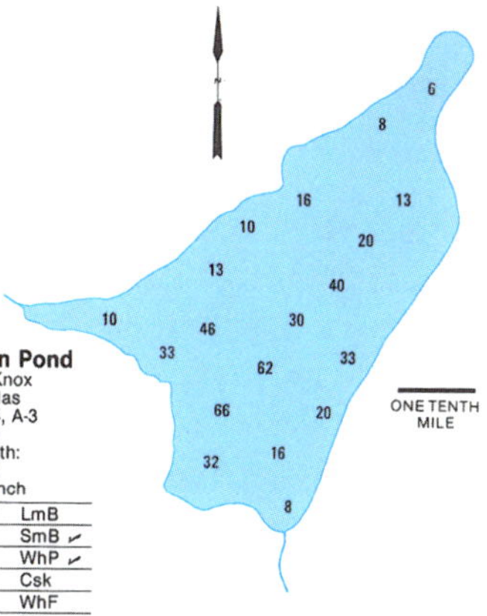

Sanborn Pond
Brooks, Knox
Maine Atlas
Map 14, A-3
Acres: 87
Max. Depth:
66 feet
Boat Launch

BrT	✓	LmB	
BkT	✓	SmB	✓
RbT		WhP	✓
Sal		Csk	
Tog		WhF	
Smt	✓	Pic	✓

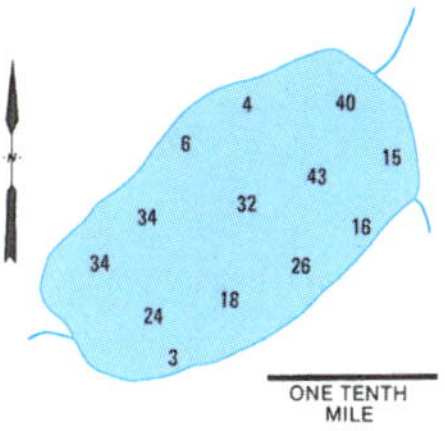

Saban Pond
Palermo
Maine Atlas
Map 13, B-4, B-5
Acres: 11
Max. Depth:
43 feet

BrT		LmB	
BkT	✓	SmB	✓
RbT		WhP	
Sal		Csk	
Tog		WhF	
Smt		Pic	

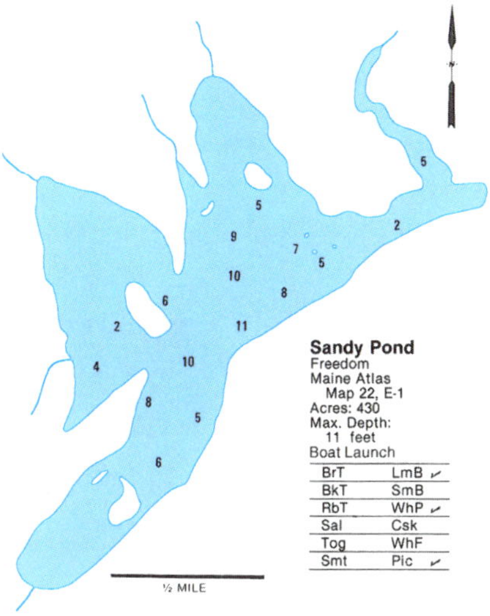

Sandy Pond
Freedom
Maine Atlas
Map 22, E-1
Acres: 430
Max. Depth:
11 feet
Boat Launch

BrT		LmB	✓
BkT		SmB	
RbT		WhP	✓
Sal		Csk	
Tog		WhF	
Smt		Pic	✓

St. George Lake
Liberty, Maine Atlas Map 14, B-1, Map 13, B-5
Acres: 1,017, Max. Depth: 65 feet, Boat Launch

BrT	BkT	RbT	Sal	Tog	Smt	LmB	SmB	WhP	Csk	WhF	Pic
✓	✓		✓		✓	✓	✓	✓			✓

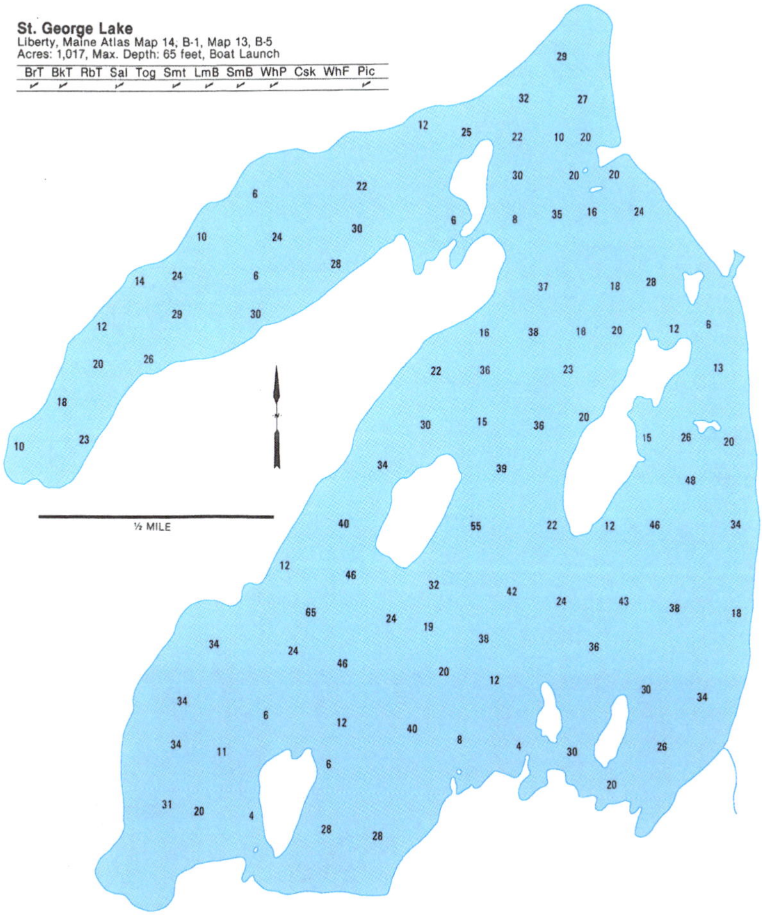

Waldo

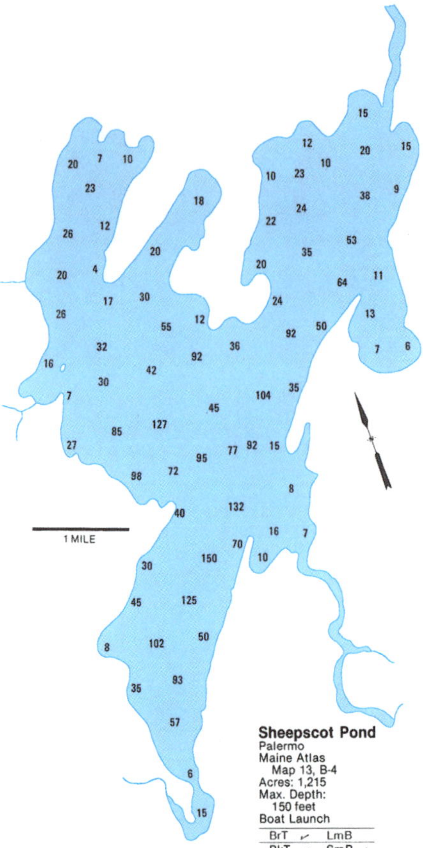

Sheepscot Pond

Palermo
Maine Atlas
Map 13, B-4
Acres: 1,215
Max. Depth:
150 feet
Boat Launch

BrT	✓	LmB	
BkT	✓	SmB	✓
RbT		WhP	✓
Sal	✓	Csk	
Tog	✓	WhF	
Smt	✓	Pic	✓

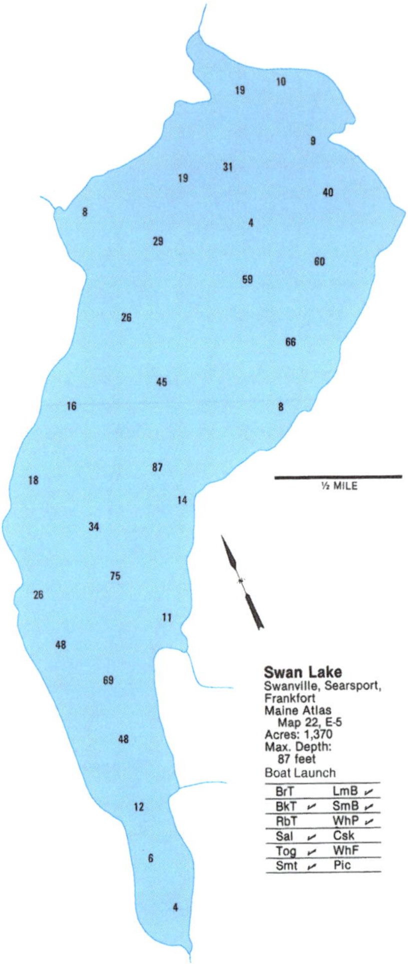

Swan Lake

Swanville, Searsport, Frankfort
Maine Atlas
Map 22, E-5
Acres: 1,370
Max. Depth:
87 feet
Boat Launch

BrT		LmB	✓
BkT	✓	SmB	✓
RbT		WhP	✓
Sal	✓	Csk	
Tog	✓	WhF	
Smt	✓	Pic	

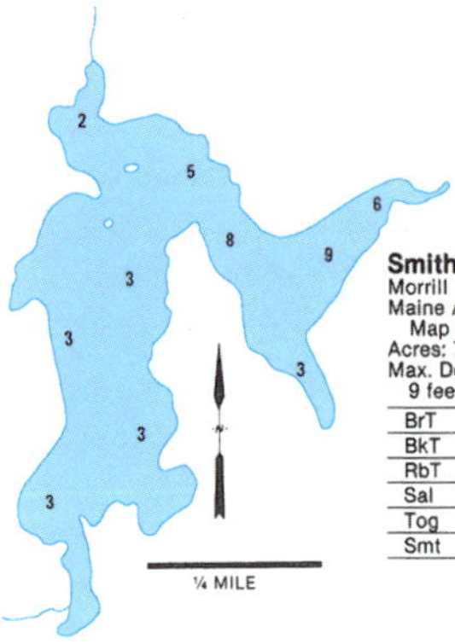

Smiths Mill Pond

Morrill
Maine Atlas
Map 14, A-3
Acres: 77
Max. Depth:
9 feet

BrT		LmB	
BkT		SmB	
RbT		WhP	✓
Sal		Csk	
Tog		WhF	
Smt		Pic	✓

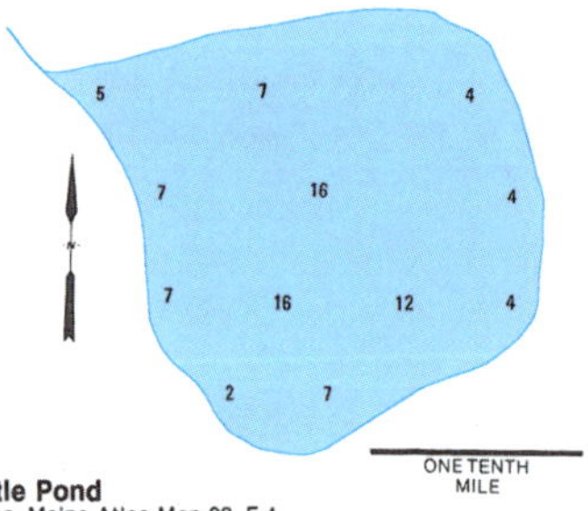

Thistle Pond

Monroe, Maine Atlas Map 22, E-4
Acres: 12, Max. Depth: 16 feet

BrT	BkT	RbT	Sal	Tog	Smt	LmB	SmB	WhP	Csk	WhF	Pic
											✓

Stevens Pond

Liberty
Maine Atlas
Map 14, B-1
Acres: 396
Max. Depth:
43 feet
Boat Launch

BrT		LmB	✓
BkT		SmB	✓
RbT		WhP	✓
Sal		Csk	
Tog		WhF	
Smt		Pic	✓

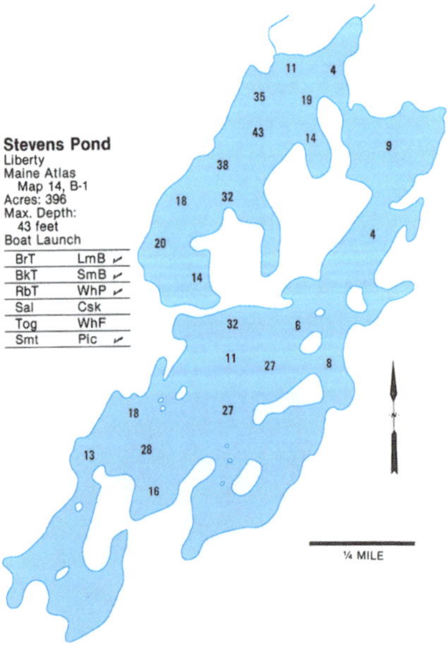

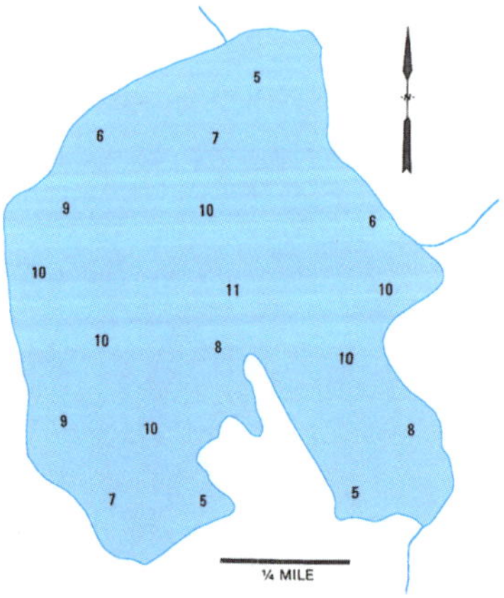

Tilden Pond

Belmont, Maine Atlas Map 14, B-3
Acres: 343, Max. Depth: 11 feet

BrT	BkT	RbT	Sal	Tog	Smt	LmB	SmB	WhP	Csk	WhF	Pic
						✓	✓	✓			✓

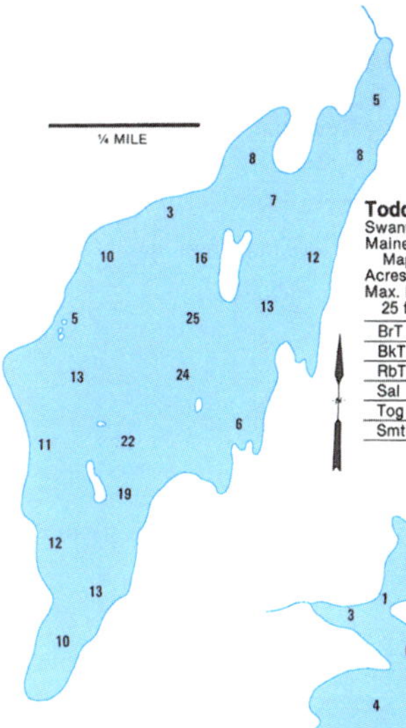

Toddy Pond
Swanville, Brooks
Maine Atlas
Map 22, E-4
Acres: 156
Max. Depth:
25 feet

BrT		LmB	
BkT		SmB	✓
RbT		WhP	✓
Sal		Csk	
Tog		WhF	
Smt		Pic	✓

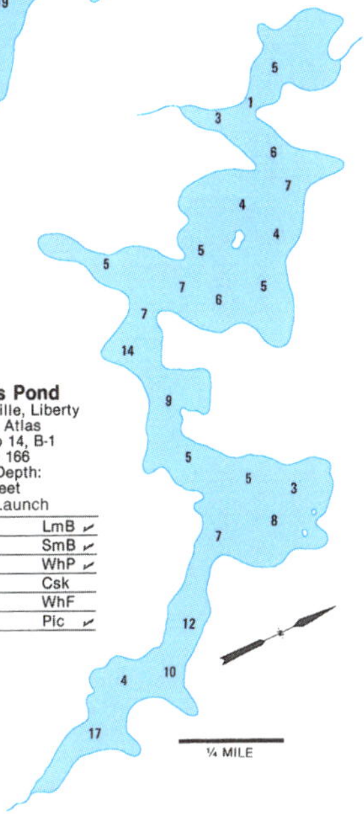

Trues Pond
Montville, Liberty
Maine Atlas
Map 14, B-1
Acres: 166
Max. Depth:
17 feet
Boat Launch

BrT		LmB	✓
BkT		SmB	✓
RbT		WhP	✓
Sal		Csk	
Tog		WhF	
Smt		Pic	✓

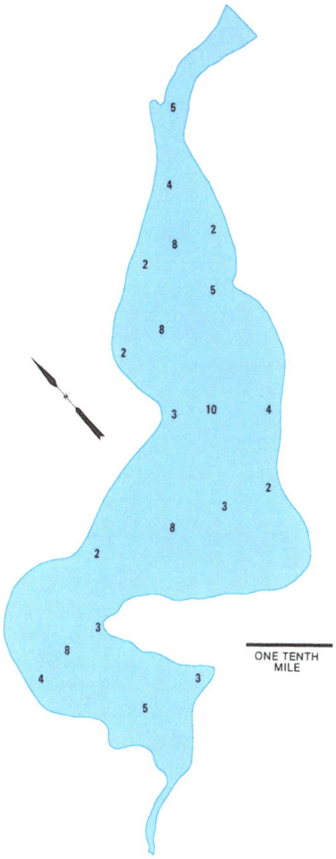

Upper Mason Pond
Belfast, Maine Atlas Map 14, A-4, A-5
Acres: 75, Max. Depth: 10 feet

BrT	BkT	RbT	Sal	Tog	Smt	LmB	SmB	WhP	Csk	WhF	Pic
						✓	✓	✓			✓

Unity Pond
Unity, Burnham, Troy, Maine Atlas Map 22, D-1, Map 21, D-5
Acres: 2,528, Max. Depth: 41 feet, Boat Launch

BrT	BkT	RbT	Sal	Tog	Smt	LmB	SmB	WhP	Csk	WhF	Pic
✓	✓					✓	✓	✓	✓	✓	✓

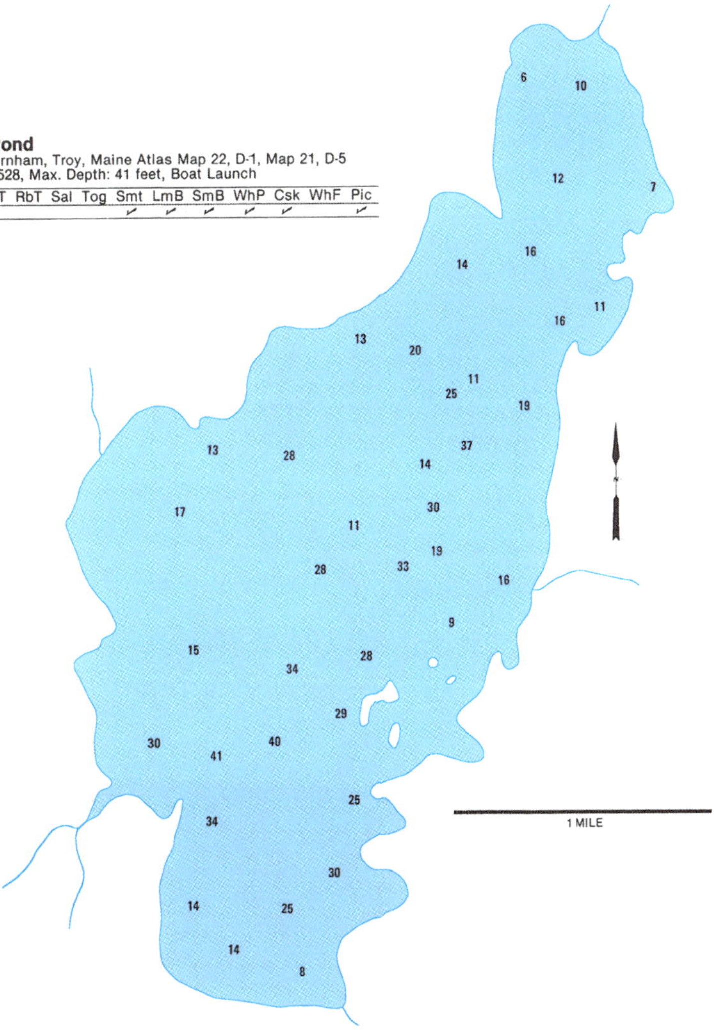

Washington County

Barren Pond

T24 MD BPP
Maine Atlas
Map 25, A-3
Acres: 11
Max. Depth:
5 feet

BrT		LmB	
BkT		SmB	
RbT		WhP	
Sal		Csk	
Tog		WhF	
Smt		Pic	✓

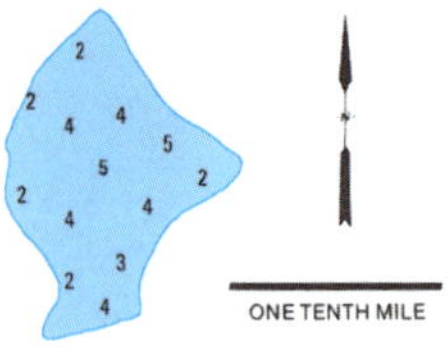

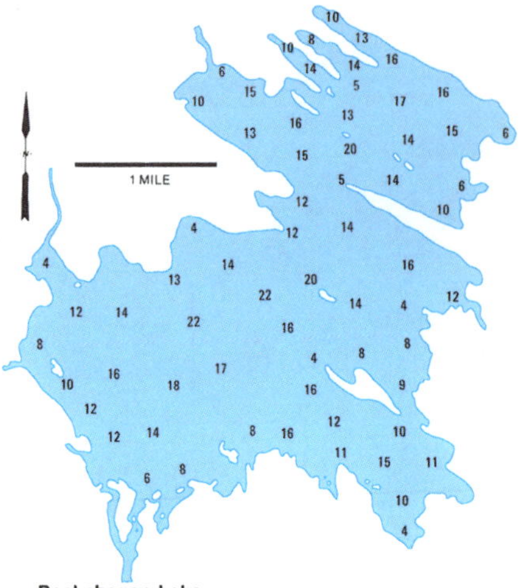

Baskahegan Lake

Brookton Twp, Topsfield, Maine Atlas Map 45, C-3, C-4
Acres: 6,944, Max. Depth: 22 feet, Boat Launch

BrT	BkT	RbT	Sal	Tog	Smt	LmB	SmB	WhP	Csk	WhF	Pic
	✓						✓	✓			✓

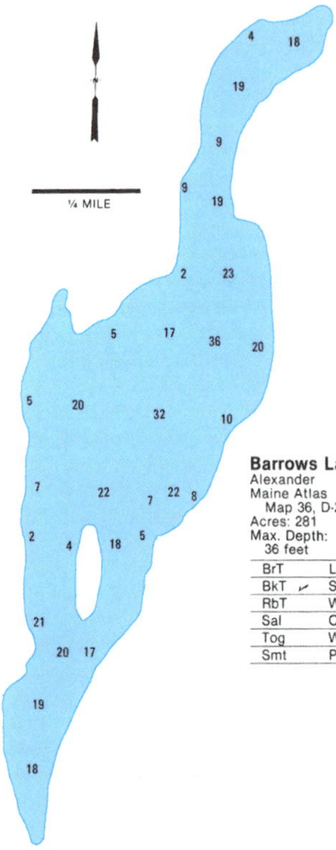

Barrows Lake

Alexander
Maine Atlas
Map 36, D-2, D-3
Acres: 281
Max. Depth:
36 feet

BrT		LmB	
BkT	✓	SmB	
RbT		WhP	✓
Sal		Csk	
Tog		WhF	
Smt		Pic	✓

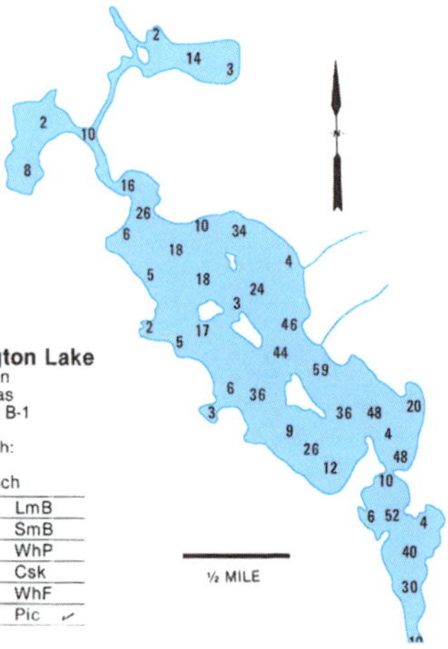

Beddington Lake

Beddington
Maine Atlas
Map 25, B-1
Acres: 404
Max. Depth:
59 feet
Boat Launch

BrT		LmB	
BkT	✓	SmB	
RbT		WhP	
Sal	✓	Csk	
Tog		WhF	
Smt	✓	Pic	✓

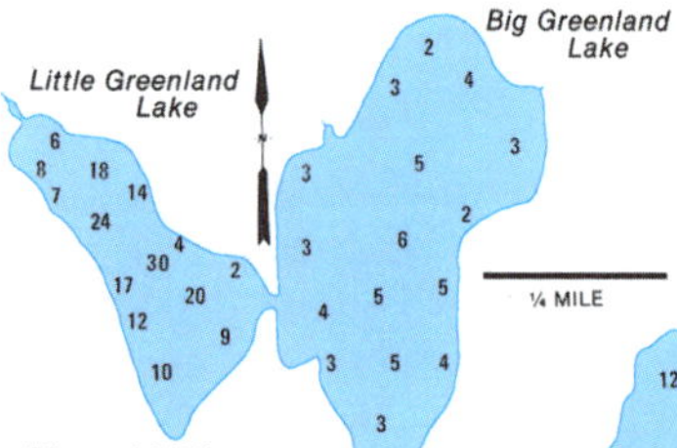

Big and Little Greenland Lakes

Danforth
Maine Atlas
Map 45, B-4
Acres: Big-86
Little-44
Max. Depth:
Big-6 feet
Little-30 feet

BrT		LmB	
BkT	✓	SmB	
RbT		WhP	
Sal		Csk	
Tog		WhF	
Smt		Pic	✓

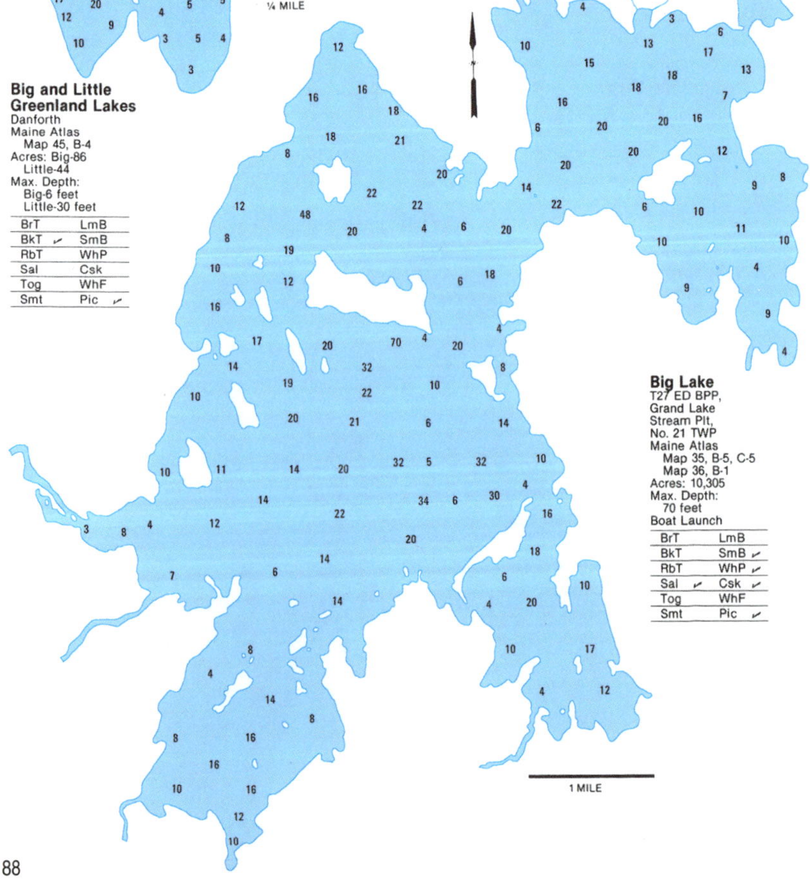

Big Lake

T27 ED BPP,
Grand Lake
Stream Plt,
No. 21 TWP
Maine Atlas
Map 35, B-5, C-5
Map 36, B-1
Acres: 10,305
Max. Depth:
70 feet
Boat Launch

BrT		LmB	
BkT		SmB	✓
RbT		WhP	✓
Sal	✓	Csk	✓
Tog		WhF	
Smt		Pic	✓

Bog Lake

Northfield
Maine Atlas
Map 26, A-1, A-2
Acres: 826
Max. Depth:
46 feet
Boat Launch

BrT		LmB	
BkT		SmB	
RbT		WhP	✓
Sal	✓	Csk	
Tog		WhF	
Smt	✓	Pic	✓

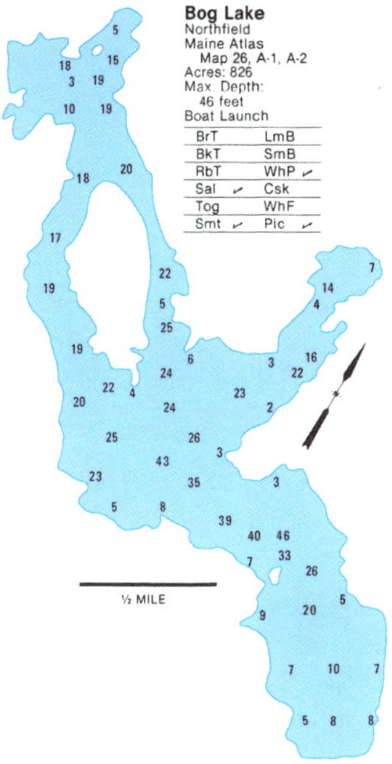

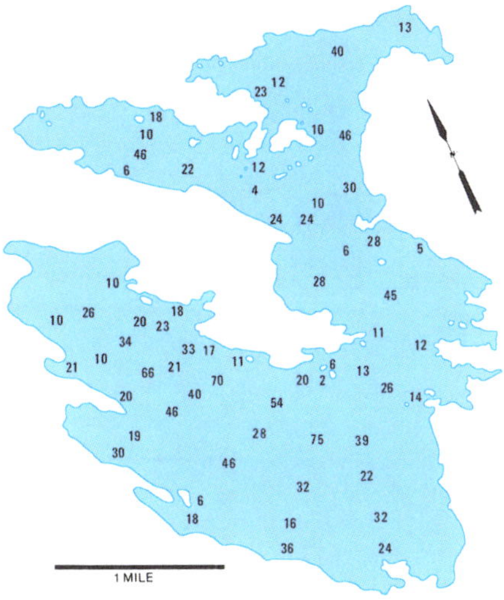

Cathance Lake

No. 14 Plt, Cooper, Maine Atlas Map 36, E-3, E-4
Acres: 2,905, Max. Depth: 75 feet, Boat Launch

BrT	BkT	RbT	Sal	Tog	Smt	LmB	SmB	WhP	Csk	WhF	Pic
	✓		✓		✓		✓				

Comments: Excellent Sal and SmB fishing.

Bonney Brook Lake

Grand Lake
Stream Plt
Maine Atlas
Map 35, B-4
Acres: 6
Max. Depth:
4 feet

BrT		LmB	
BkT	✓	SmB	
RbT		WhP	
Sal		Csk	
Tog		WhF	
Smt		Pic	✓

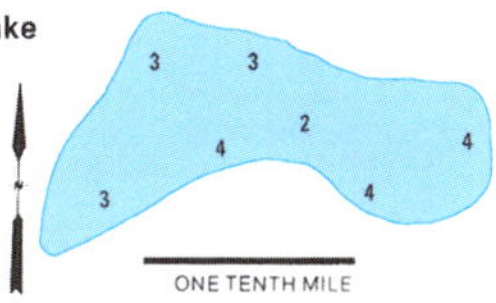

Clifford Lake

T26 ED BPP, T27 ED BPP, Maine Atlas Map 35, D-5
Acres: 954, Max. Depth: 50 feet

BrT	BkT	RbT	Sal	Tog	Smt	LmB	SmB	WhP	Csk	WhF	Pic
							✓	✓	✓		✓

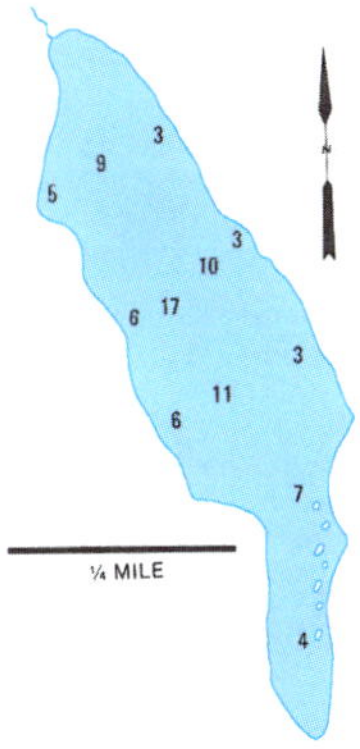

Bowles Lake

T31 MD BPP
Maine Atlas
Map 35, E-4
Acres: 64
Max. Depth:
17 feet

BrT		LmB	
BkT	✓	SmB	
RbT		WhP	
Sal		Csk	
Tog		WhF	
Smt		Pic	✓

Comments: Fairly good BkT fishing in early spring.

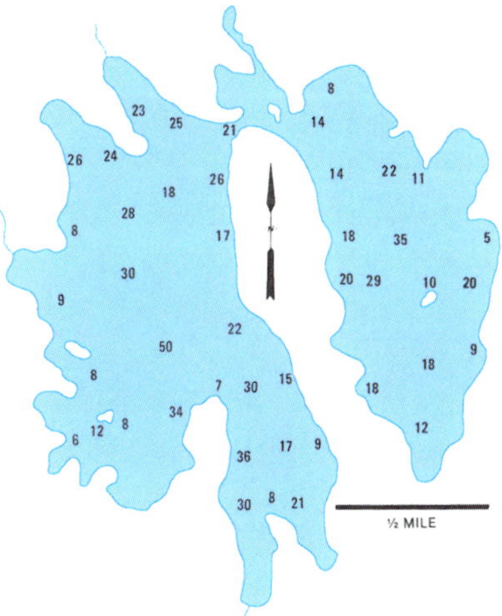

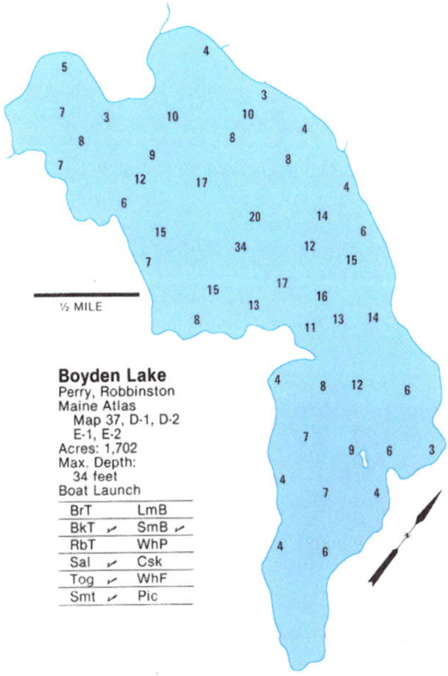

Boyden Lake

Perry, Robbinston
Maine Atlas
Map 37, D-1, D-2
E-1, E-2
Acres: 1,702
Max. Depth:
34 feet
Boat Launch

BrT		LmB	
BkT	✓	SmB	✓
RbT		WhP	
Sal	✓	Csk	
Tog	✓	WhF	
Smt	✓	Pic	

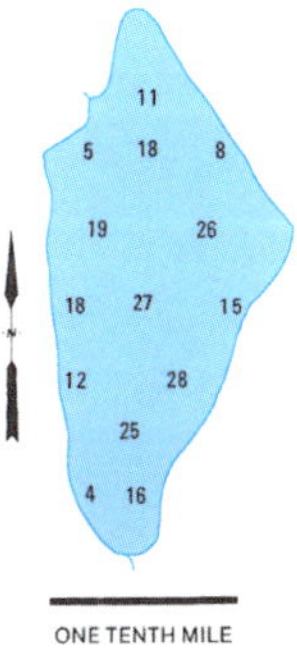

Coleback Lake

Charlotte
Maine Atlas
Map 37, D-1
Acres: 25
Max. Depth:
28 feet
Boat Launch

BrT		LmB	
BkT	✓	SmB	
RbT		WhP	
Sal		Csk	
Tog		WhF	
Smt	✓	Pic	

Comments: Splake.

Washington

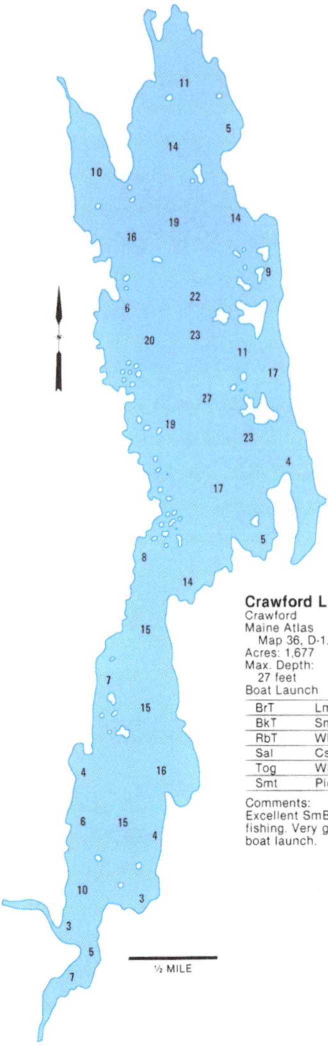

Crawford Lake

Crawford
Maine Atlas
Map 36, D-1, D-2
Acres: 1,677
Max. Depth:
27 feet
Boat Launch

BrT	LmB
BkT	SmB ✓
RbT	WhP ✓
Sal	Csk
Tog	WhF
Smt	Pic ✓

Comments:
Excellent SmB fishing. Very good boat launch.

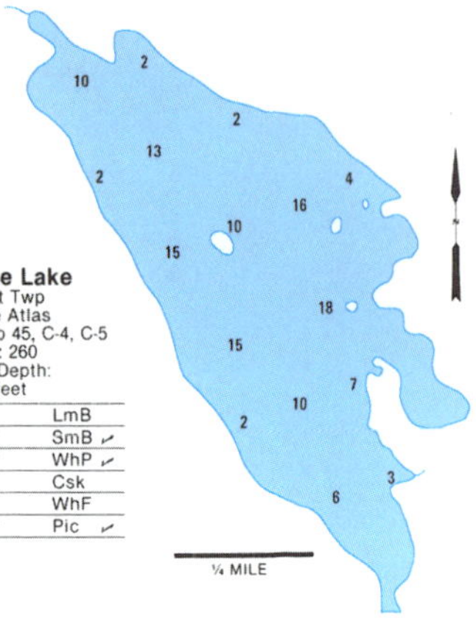

Drake Lake

Forest Twp
Maine Atlas
Map 45, C-4, C-5
Acres: 260
Max. Depth:
18 feet

BrT	LmB
BkT	SmB ✓
RbT	WhP ✓
Sal	Csk
Tog	WhF
Smt	Pic ✓

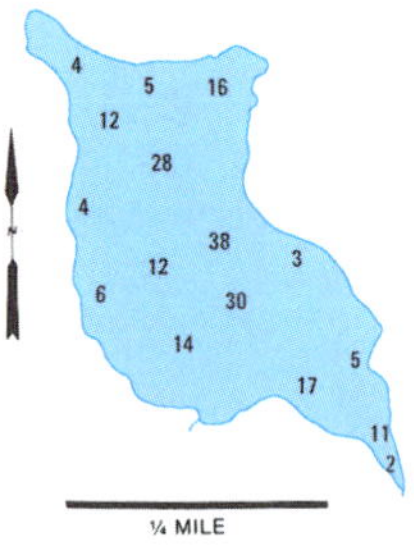

Eastern Lake

Robbinston
Maine Atlas
Map 37, C-2, D-2
Acres: 38
Max. Depth:
38 feet

BrT	LmB
BkT ✓	SmB
RbT	WhP
Sal	Csk
Tog	WhF
Smt	Pic

East Monroe Pond

T43 MD BPP
Maine Atlas
Map 35, C-4, D-4
Acres: 10
Max. Depth:
26 feet

BrT	LmB
BkT ✓	SmB
RbT	WhP
Sal	Csk
Tog	WhF
Smt	Pic

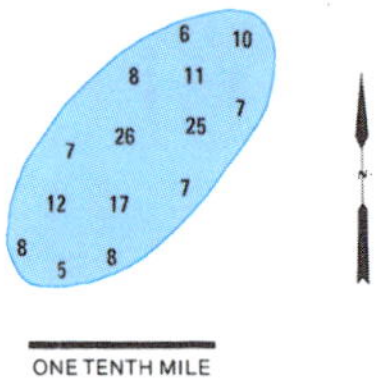

Crooked Brook Flowage

Danforth
Maine Atlas
Map 45, B-3
Acres: 1,645
Max. Depth:
20 feet
Boat Launch

BrT	LmB
BkT	SmB ✓
RbT	WhP ✓
Sal	Csk
Tog	WhF
Smt	Pic ✓

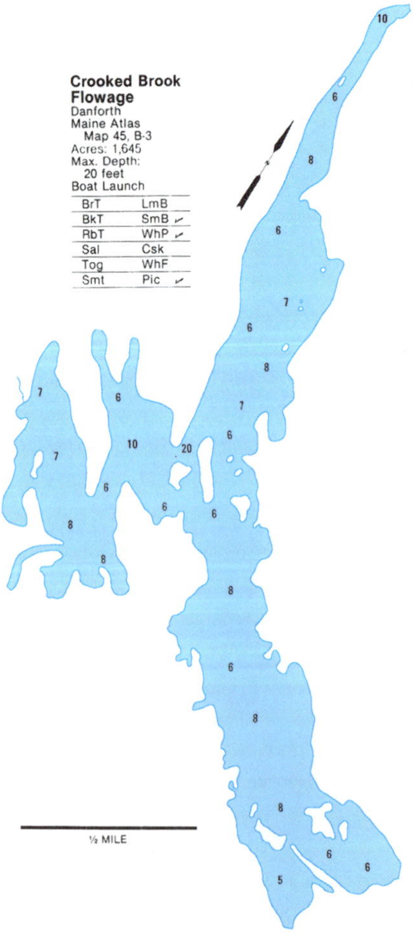

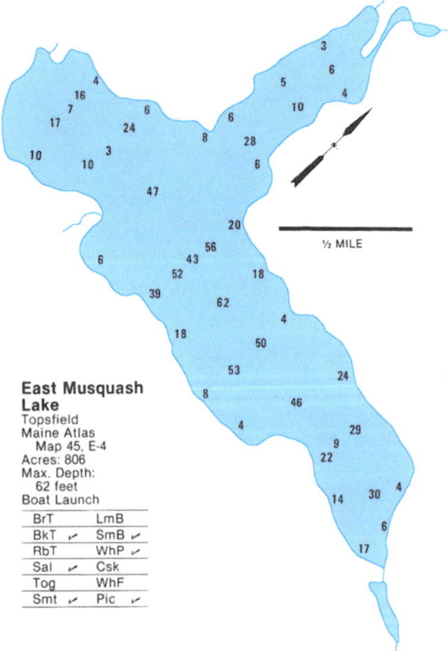

East Musquash Lake

Topsfield
Maine Atlas
Map 45, E-4
Acres: 806
Max. Depth:
62 feet
Boat Launch

BrT	LmB
BkT ✓	SmB ✓
RbT	WhP ✓
Sal ✓	Csk
Tog	WhF
Smt ✓	Pic ✓

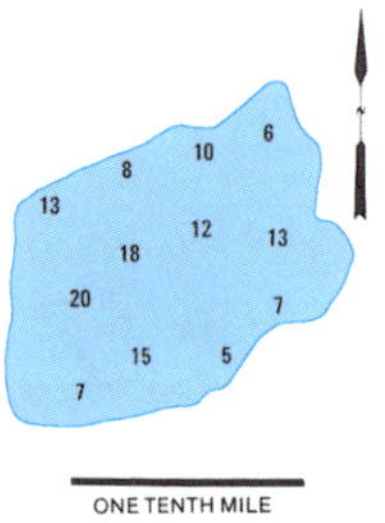

East Pike Brook Pond

T18 MD BPP
Maine Atlas
Map 25, C-3
Acres: 12
Max. Depth:
20 feet

BrT	LmB
BkT ✓	SmB
RbT	WhP
Sal	Csk
Tog	WhF
Smt	Pic

Farrow Lake
Topsfield
Maine Atlas
Map 45, D-4
Acres: 224
Max. Depth:
76 feet

BrT		LmB	
BkT	✓	SmB	
RbT		WhP	
Sal	✓	Csk	✓
Tog	✓	WhF	
Smt	✓	Pic	

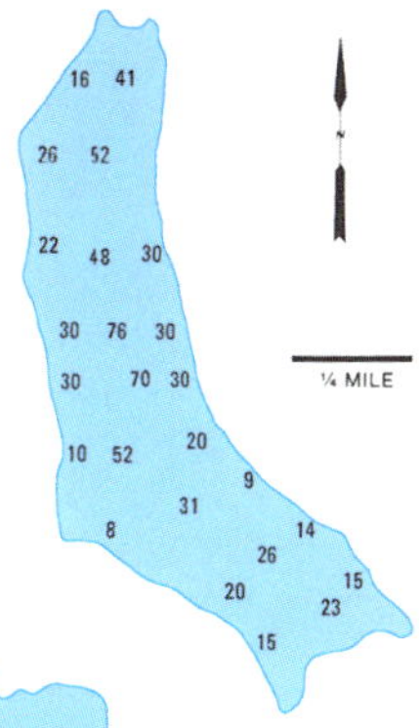

Fourth Machias Lake
T5 ND BPP,
T42 MD BPP
Maine Atlas
Map 35, C-1, C-2
Acres: 1,539
Max. Depth:
26 feet
Boat Launch

BrT		LmB	
BkT		SmB	✓
RbT		WhP	✓
Sal		Csk	
Tog		WhF	
Smt		Pic	✓

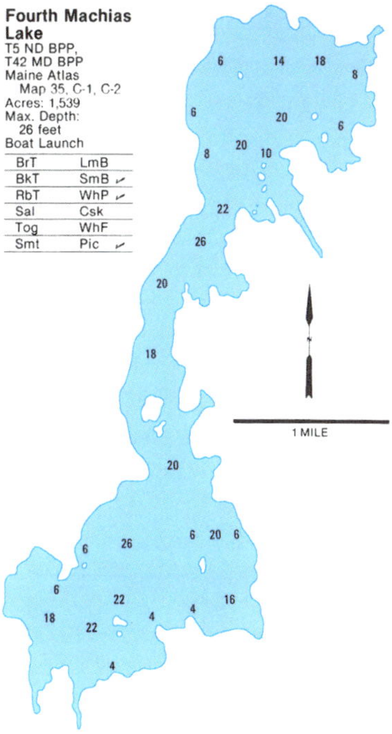

Fifth Machias Lake
T36 MD BPP
Maine Atlas
Map 35, D-2
Acres: 1,069
Max. Depth:
27 feet

BrT		LmB	
BkT	✓	SmB	
RbT		WhP	✓
Sal		Csk	
Tog		WhF	
Smt		Pic	✓

Comments:
Excellent BkT fishing after ice out.

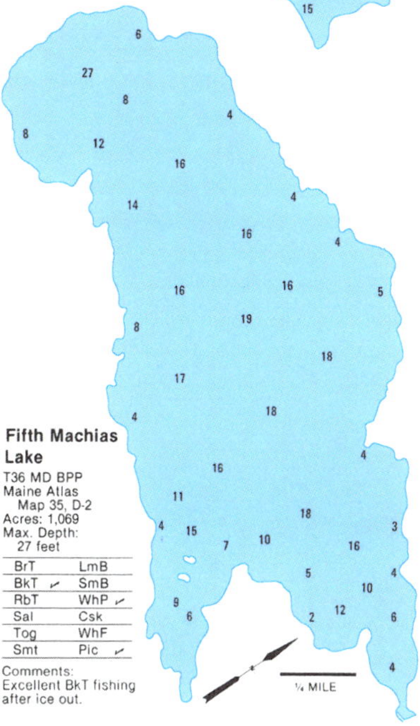

Fulton Lake
Northfield
Maine Atlas
Map 26, A-2
Acres: 96
Max. Depth:
16 feet

BrT		LmB	
BkT		SmB	
RbT		WhP	✓
Sal		Csk	
Tog		WhF	
Smt		Pic	✓

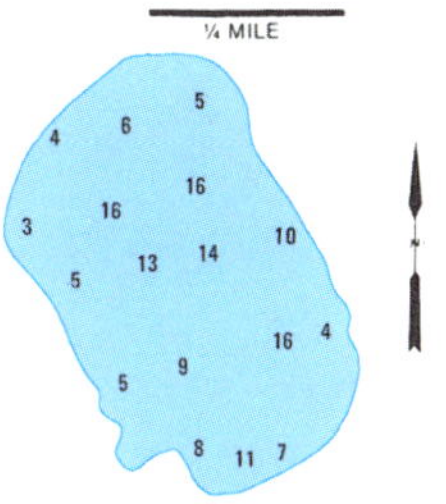

First Chain Lake
T26 ED BPP
Maine Atlas
Map 35, E-5
Acres: 336
Max. Depth:
35 feet
Boat Launch

BrT		LmB	
BkT	✓	SmB	
RbT		WhP	✓
Sal		Csk	
Tog		WhF	
Smt	✓	Pic	✓

Comments: Good Pic and WhP fishery.

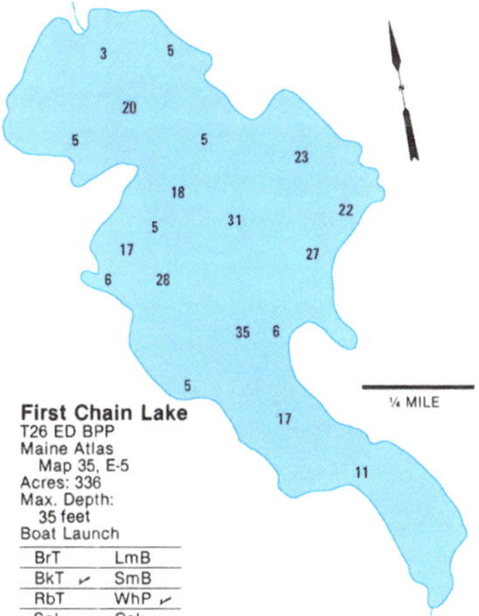

First Machias Lake
T37 MD BPP, Maine Atlas Map 35, D-3
Acres: 109, Max. Depth: 27 feet

BrT	BkT	RbT	Sal	Tog	Smt	LmB	SmB	WhP	Csk	WhF	Pic
	✓						✓	✓			✓

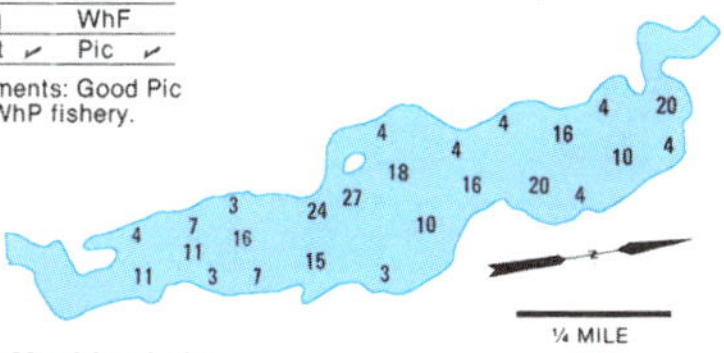

Gardner Lake
East Machias,
Marion Twp,
Whiting
Maine Atlas
Map 26, B-4, C-4
Acres: 3,886
Max. Depth:
56 feet
Boat Launch

BrT		LmB	
BkT		SmB	✓
RbT		WhP	✓
Sal	✓	Csk	
Tog		WhF	
Smt	✓	Pic	✓

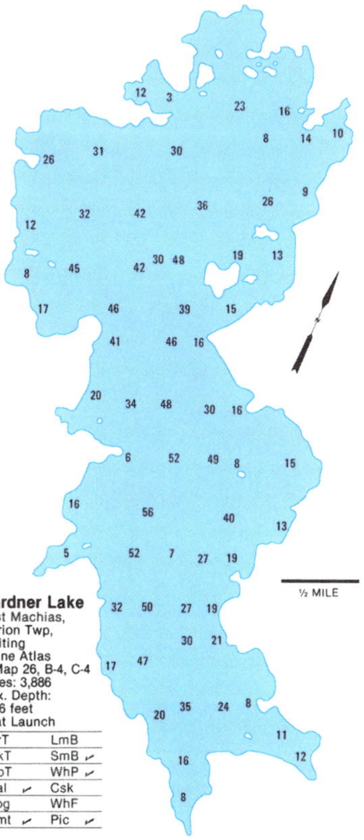

First Mopang Lake
T30 MD BPP
Maine Atlas
Map 25, A-2
Acres: 83
Max. Depth:
12 feet

BrT		LmB	
BkT	✓	SmB	
RbT		WhP	✓
Sal	✓	Csk	
Tog		WhF	
Smt		Pic	✓

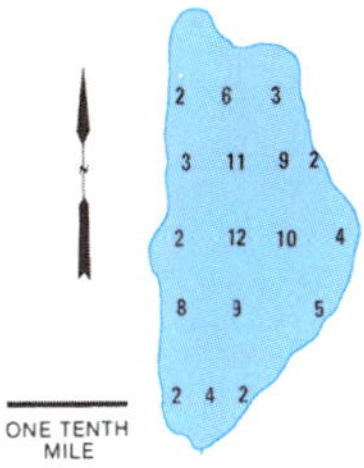

Goulding Lake
Robbinston
Maine Atlas
Map 37, D-1
Acres: 17
Max. Depth:
26 feet
Boat Launch

BrT		LmB	
BkT	✓	SmB	
RbT		WhP	
Sal		Csk	
Tog		WhF	
Smt		Pic	

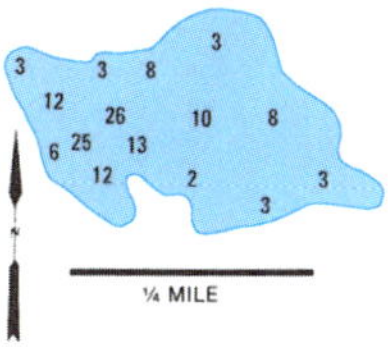

Washington

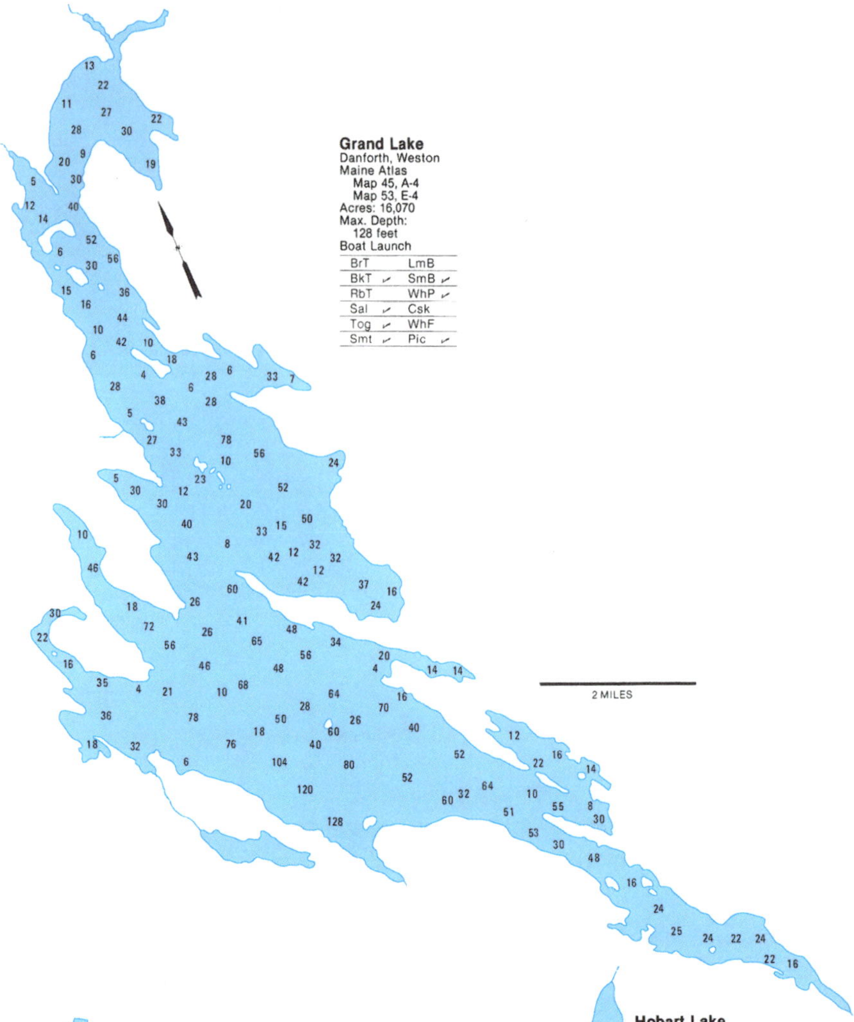

Grand Lake

Danforth, Weston
Maine Atlas
Map 45, A-4
Map 53, E-4
Acres: 16,070
Max. Depth:
128 feet
Boat Launch

BrT		LmB	
BkT	✓	SmB	✓
RbT		WhP	✓
Sal	✓	Csk	
Tog	✓	WhF	
Smt	✓	Pic	✓

Hadley Lake

East Machias
Maine Atlas
Map 26, B-3
Acres: 1,776
Max. Depth:
31 feet
Boat Launch

BrT		LmB	
BkT	✓	SmB	✓
RbT		WhP	✓
Sal		Csk	
Tog		WhF	
Smt	✓	Pic	✓

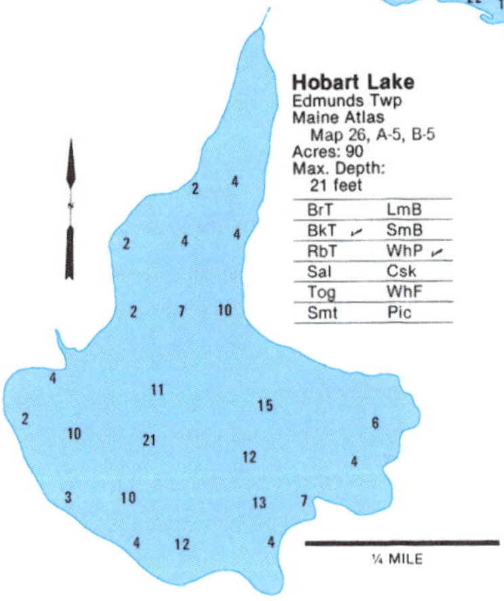

Hobart Lake

Edmunds Twp
Maine Atlas
Map 26, A-5, B-5
Acres: 90
Max. Depth:
21 feet

BrT		LmB	
BkT	✓	SmB	
RbT		WhP	✓
Sal		Csk	
Tog		WhF	
Smt		Pic	

Horseshoe Pond

T18 MD BPP
Maine Atlas
Map 25, C-2, C-3
Acres: 12
Max. Depth:
36 feet

BrT		LmB	
BkT	✓	SmB	
RbT		WhP	
Sal		Csk	
Tog		WhF	
Smt		Pic	

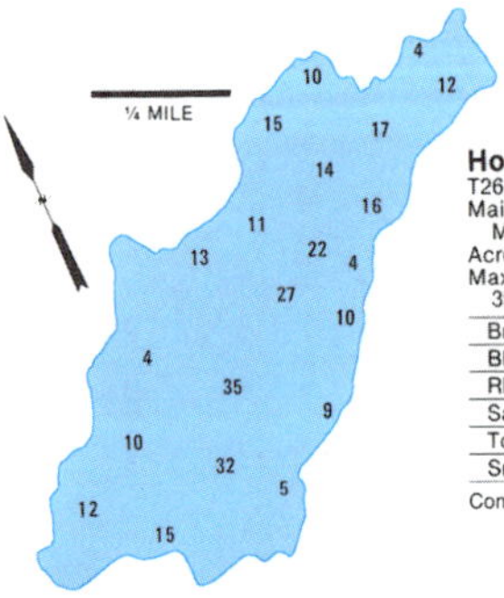

Hosea Pug Lake

T26 ED BPP
Maine Atlas
Map 35, D-5
Acres: 58
Max. Depth:
35 feet

BrT		LmB	
BkT	✓	SmB	✓
RbT		WhP	
Sal		Csk	
Tog		WhF	
Smt		Pic	✓

Comments: Splake.

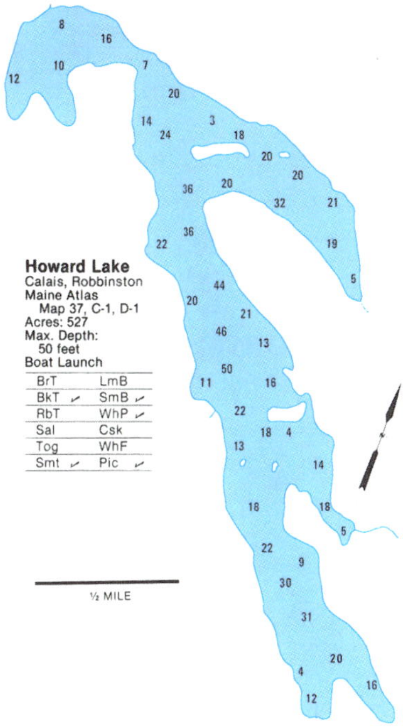

Howard Lake
Calais, Robbinston
Maine Atlas
Map 37, C-1, D-1
Acres: 527
Max. Depth:
50 feet
Boat Launch

BrT	LmB
BkT ✓	SmB ✓
RbT	WhP ✓
Sal	Csk
Tog	WhF
Smt ✓	Pic ✓

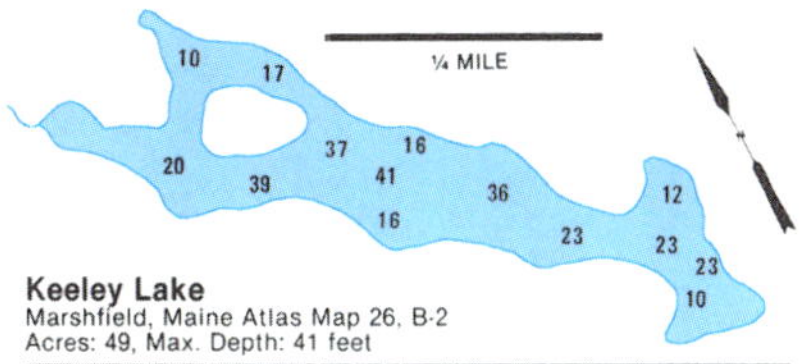

Keeley Lake
Marshfield, Maine Atlas Map 26, B-2
Acres: 49, Max. Depth: 41 feet

BrT	BkT	RbT	Sal	Tog	Smt	LmB	SmB	WhP	Csk	WhF	Pic
	✓				✓						

Comments: Splake.

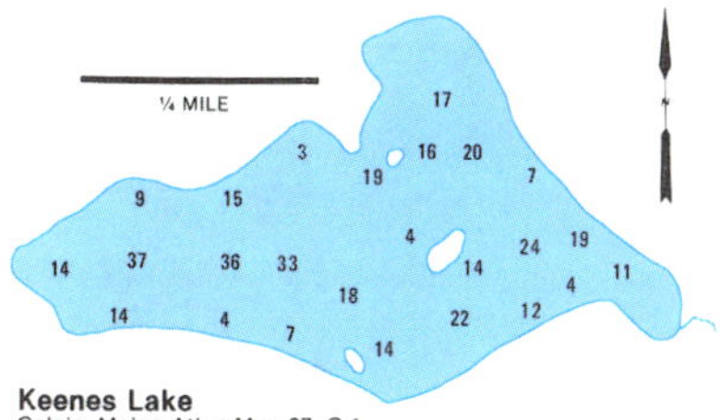

Keenes Lake
Calais, Maine Atlas Map 37, C-1
Acres: 115, Max. Depth: 37 feet

BrT	BkT	RbT	Sal	Tog	Smt	LmB	SmB	WhP	Csk	WhF	Pic
	✓		✓		✓						

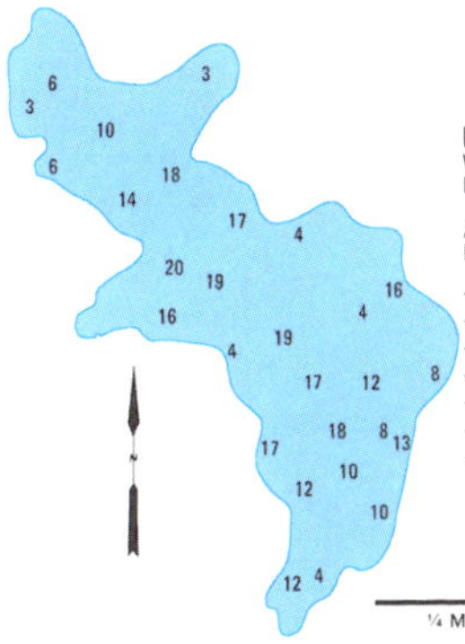

Indian Lake
Whiting
Maine Atlas
Map 26, B-5
Acres: 120
Max. Depth:
20 feet

BrT	LmB
BkT ✓	SmB
RbT	WhP
Sal	Csk
Tog	WhF
Smt	Pic

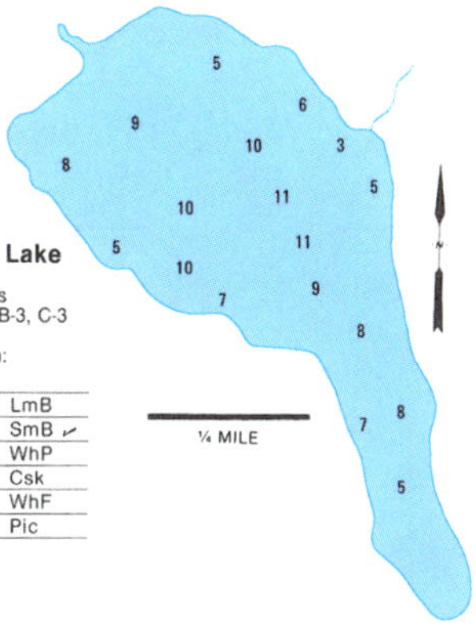

LaCoute Lake
Vanceboro
Maine Atlas
Map 46, B-3, C-3
Acres: 137
Max. Depth:
11 feet

BrT	LmB
BkT	SmB ✓
RbT	WhP
Sal	Csk
Tog	WhF
Smt	Pic

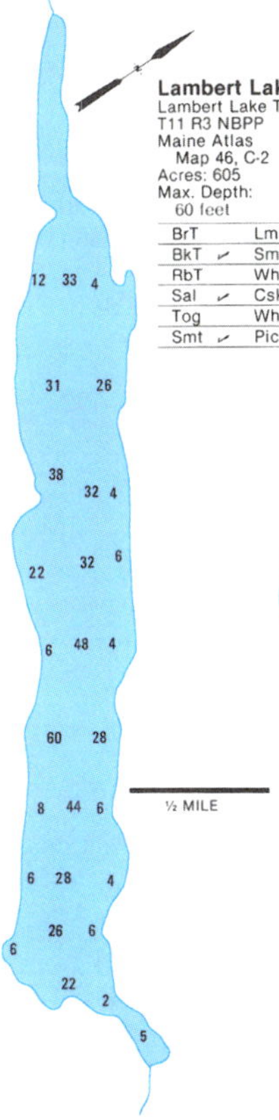

Lambert Lake
Lambert Lake Twp,
T11 R3 NBPP
Maine Atlas
Map 46, C-2
Acres: 605
Max. Depth:
60 feet

BrT	LmB
BkT ✓	SmB ✓
RbT	WhP
Sal ✓	Csk
Tog	WhF
Smt ✓	Pic ✓

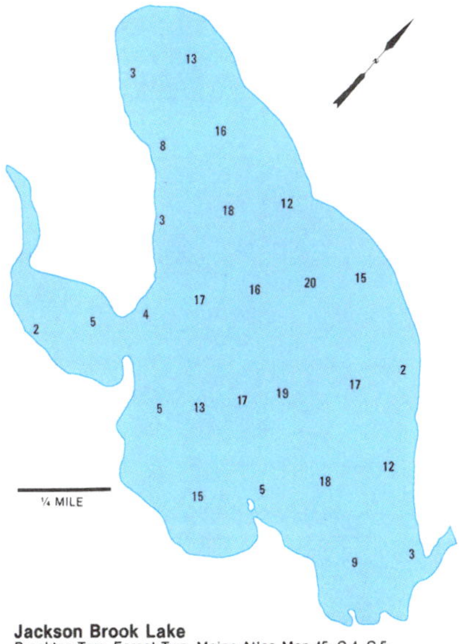

Jackson Brook Lake
Brookton Twp, Forest Twp, Maine Atlas Map 45, C-4, C-5
Acres: 731, Max. Depth: 20 feet, Boat Launch

BrT	BkT	RbT	Sal	Tog	Smt	LmB	SmB	WhP	Csk	WhF	Pic
							✓	✓			✓

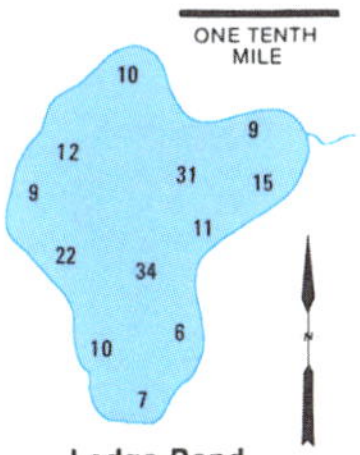

Ledge Pond
Charlotte
Maine Atlas
Map 36, D-5
Acres: 17
Max. Depth:
34 feet

BrT	LmB
BkT ✓	SmB
RbT	WhP
Sal	Csk
Tog	WhF
Smt	Pic ✓

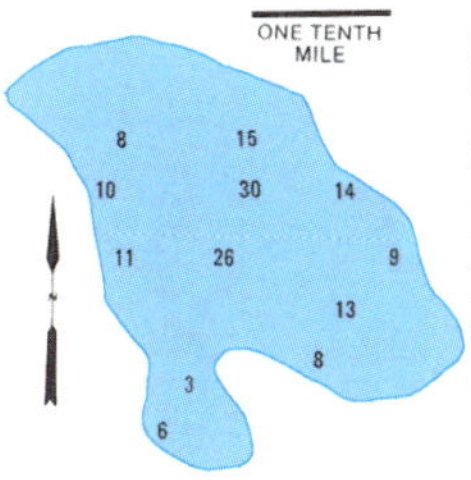

James Pond
Charlotte
Maine Atlas
Map 36, D-5
Acres: 31
Max. Depth:
30 feet

BrT	LmB
BkT ✓	SmB
RbT	WhP
Sal	Csk
Tog	WhF
Smt	Pic

Lily Lake
Trescott Twp, Maine Atlas Map 27, A-2, B-2
Acres: 31, Max. Depth: 7 feet

BrT	BkT	RbT	Sal	Tog	Smt	LmB	SmB	WhP	Csk	WhF	Pic
	✓										

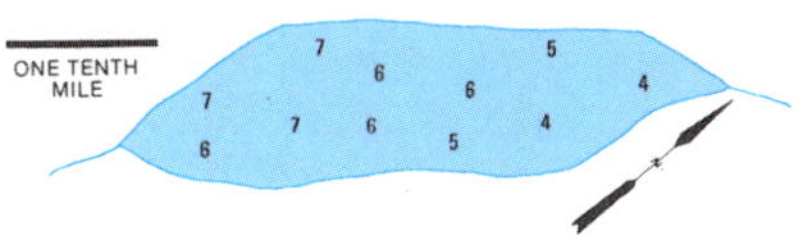

Washington

Lily Lake
T30 MD BPP
Maine Atlas
Map 25, A-3
Acres: 32
Max. Depth:
24 feet

BrT	LmB
BkT ✓	SmB ✓
RbT	WhP
Sal	Csk
Tog	WhF
Smt	Pic ✓

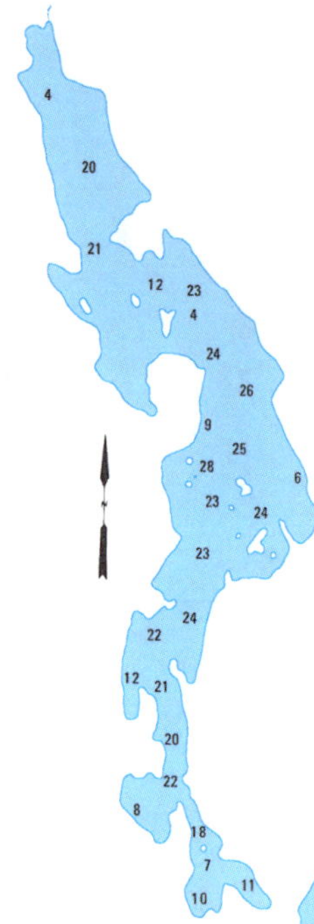

Long Lake
T18 ED BPP,
T19 ED BPP,
Wesley, Northfield
Maine Atlas
Map 26, A-2
Acres: 698
Max. Depth:
28 feet
Boat Launch

BrT	LmB
BkT	SmB ✓
RbT	WhP ✓
Sal	Csk
Tog	WhF
Smt	Pic ✓

Comments:
Good Pic fishing.
Occasional SmB.

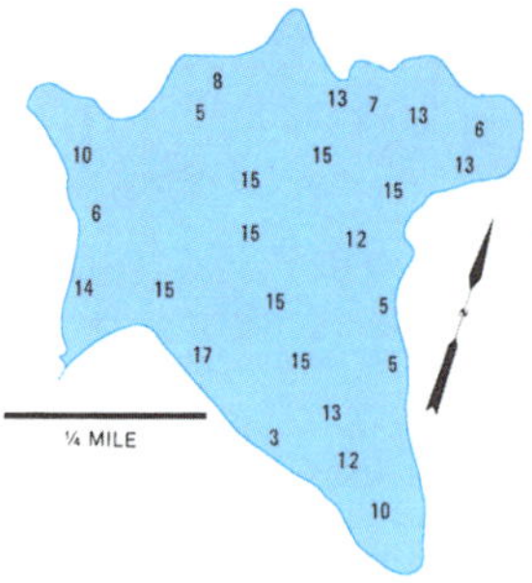

Little Cathance Lake
No. 14 Plt
Maine Atlas
Map 36, E-4
Acres: 140
Max. Depth:
17 feet

BrT	LmB
BkT ✓	SmB ✓
RbT	WhP
Sal	Csk
Tog	WhF
Smt	Pic

Little Lily Lake
Marshfield,
East Machias
Maine Atlas
Map 26, B-3
Acres: 6
Max. Depth:
22 feet

BrT	LmB
BkT ✓	SmB
RbT	WhP
Sal	Csk
Tog	WhF
Smt	Pic

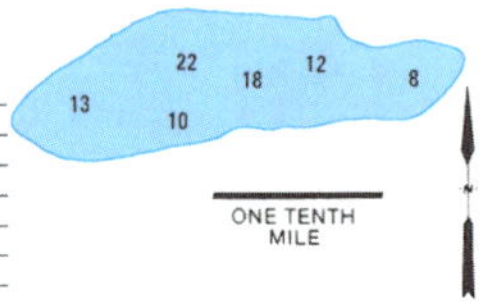

Love Lake
T19 ED BPP,
Crawford
Maine Atlas
Map 36, D-2, E-2
Acres: 672
Max. Depth:
40 feet
Boat Launch

BrT	LmB
BkT ✓	SmB ✓
RbT	WhP ✓
Sal ✓	Csk
Tog	WhF
Smt ✓	Pic ✓

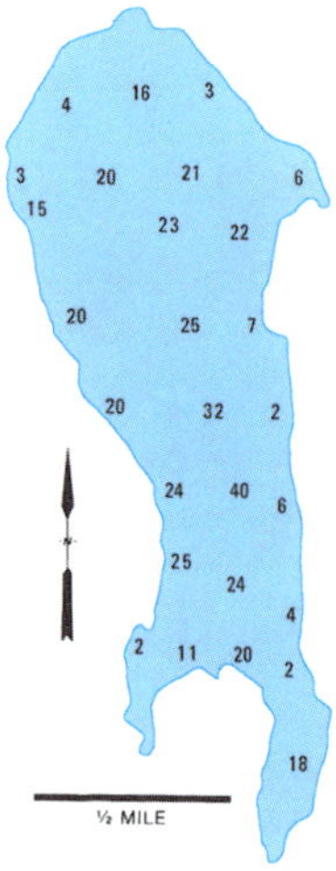

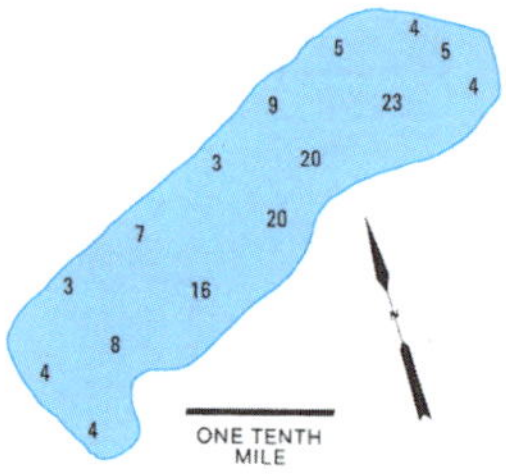

Little Pickerel Pond
Brookton Twp
Maine Atlas
Map 45, C-4, C-5
Acres: 27
Max. Depth:
23 feet

BrT	LmB
BkT	SmB ✓
RbT	WhF
Sal	Csk
Tog	WhF
Smt	Pic ✓

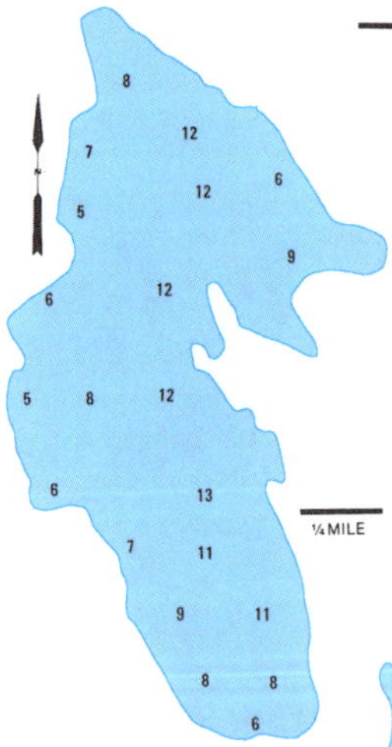

Lower Hot Brook Lake
Danforth,
T8 R4 NBPP
Maine Atlas
Map 45, B-2
Acres: 713
Max. Depth:
13 feet

BrT	LmB
BkT ✓	SmB ✓
RbT	WhP ✓
Sal ✓	Csk
Tog	WhF
Smt	Pic ✓

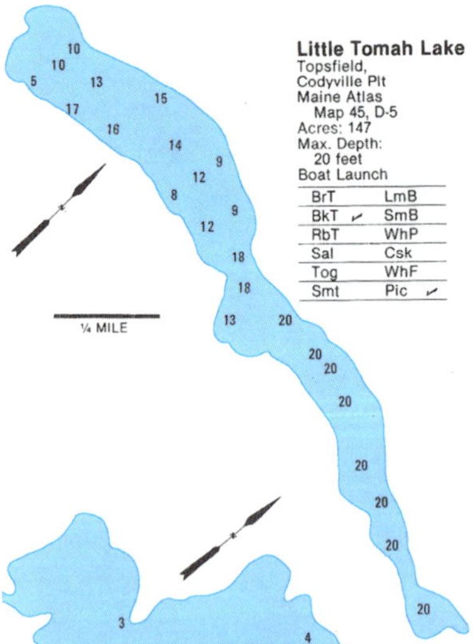

Little Tomah Lake
Topsfield,
Codyville Plt
Maine Atlas
Map 45, D-5
Acres: 147
Max. Depth:
20 feet
Boat Launch

BrT	LmB
BkT ✓	SmB
RbT	WhP
Sal	Csk
Tog	WhF
Smt	Pic ✓

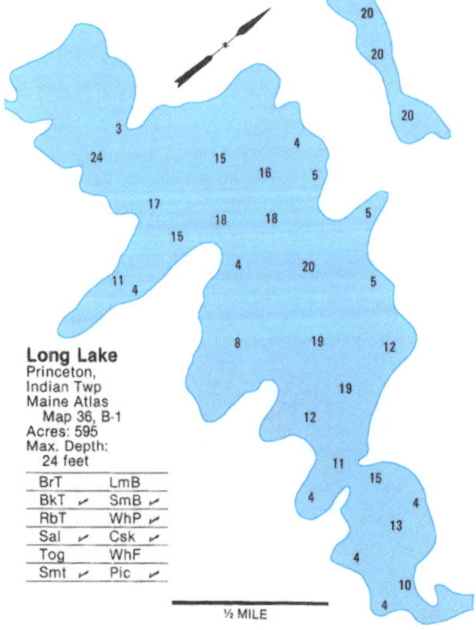

Long Lake
Princeton,
Indian Twp
Maine Atlas
Map 36, B-1
Acres: 595
Max. Depth:
24 feet

BrT	LmB
BkT ✓	SmB ✓
RbT	WhP ✓
Sal ✓	Csk ✓
Tog	WhF
Smt ✓	Pic ✓

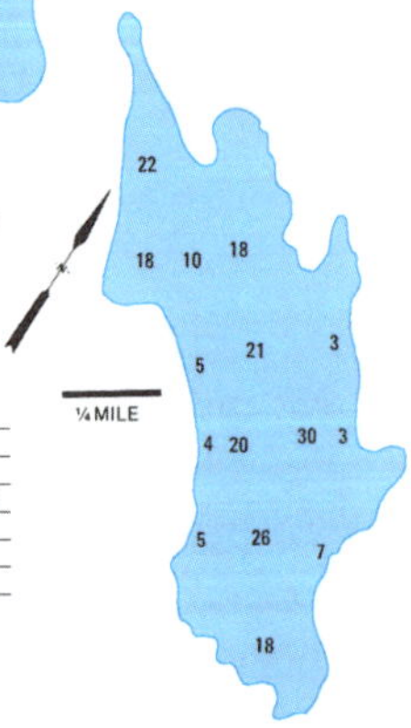

Lower Oxbrook Lake
T6 ND BPP
T6 R1 NBPP
Maine Atlas
Map 35, A-3
Acres: 365
Max. Depth:
30 feet

BrT	LmB
BkT ✓	SmB
RbT	WhP ✓
Sal ✓	Csk
Tog	WhF
Smt ✓	Pic

Marks Lake
Marshfield
Maine Atlas
Map 26, B-2, B-3
Acres: 240
Max. Depth:
27 feet

BrT	LmB
BkT ✓	SmB ✓
RbT	WhP
Sal	Csk
Tog	WhF
Smt	Pic

Meddybemps Lake

Meddybemps, Alexander, Baileyville, Baring Plt
Maine Atlas Map 36, D-4
Acres: 6,765, Max. Depth: 38 feet, Boat Launch

BrT	BkT	RbT	Sal	Tog	Smt	LmB	SmB	WhP	Csk	WhF	Pic
			✓		✓		✓	✓			✓

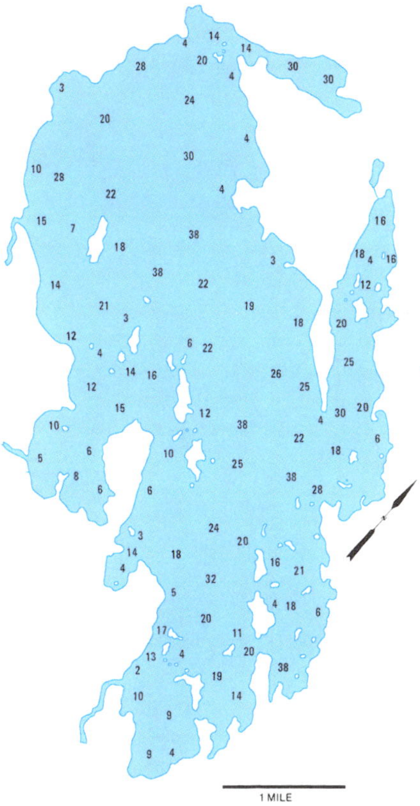

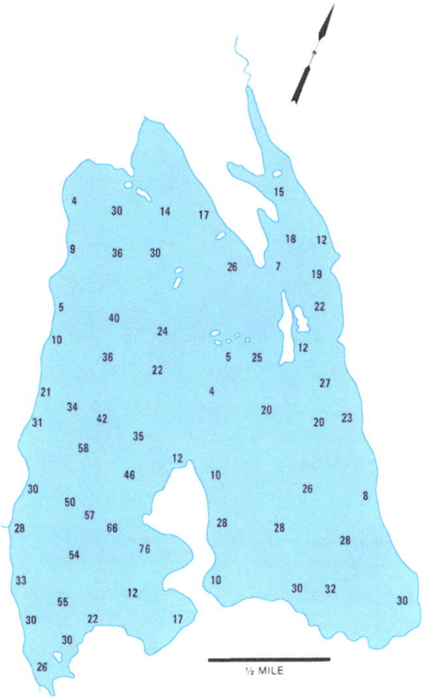

Mopang Lake

Devereaux Twp, Maine Atlas Map 35, E-1, Map 25, A-1, A-2
Acres: 1,487, Max. Depth: 76 feet, Boat Launch

BrT	BkT	RbT	Sal	Tog	Smt	LmB	SmB	WhP	Csk	WhF	Pic
	✓		✓		✓			✓			✓

Comments: Splake.

Moneymaker Lake

Robbinston
Maine Atlas Map 37, C-1
Acres: 32
Max. Depth: 39 feet

BrT		LmB	
BkT	✓	SmB	
RbT		WhP	
Sal		Csk	
Tog		WhF	
Smt	✓	Pic	

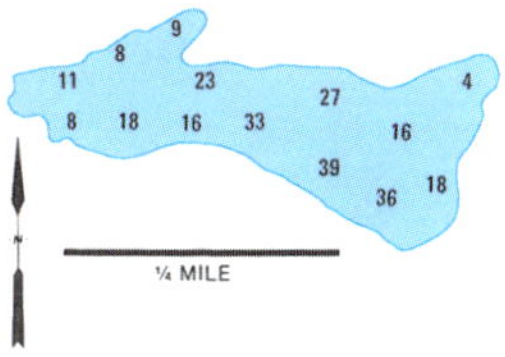

Monroe Lake

T43 MD BPP
Maine Atlas Map 35, C-4
Acres: 45
Max. Depth: 28 feet
Boat Launch

BrT		LmB	
BkT	✓	SmB	
RbT		WhP	
Sal		Csk	
Tog		WhF	
Smt		Pic	

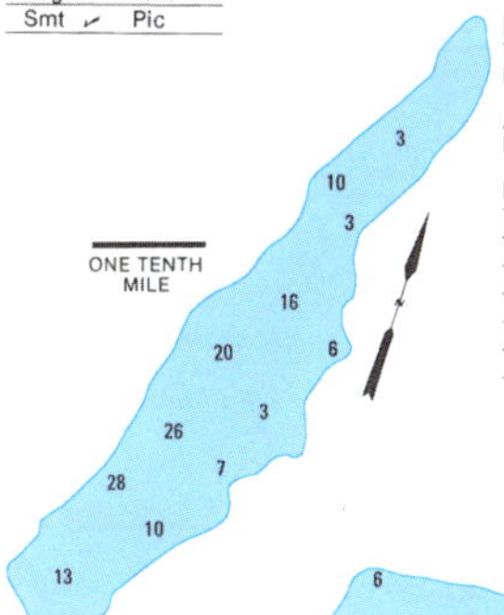

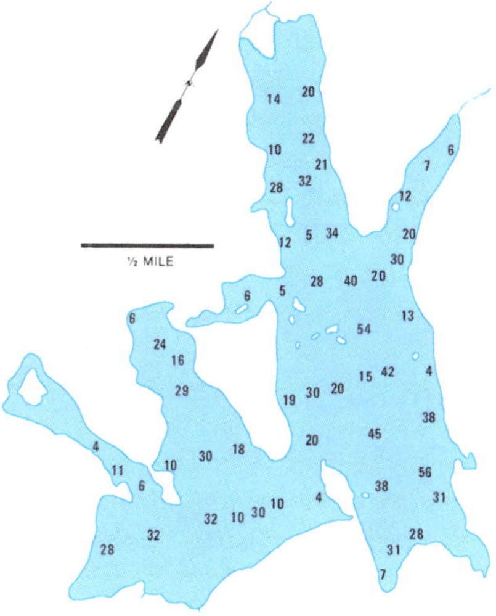

Nash's Lake

Calais, Maine Atlas Map 37, C-1
Acres: 627, Max. Depth: 56 feet

BrT	BkT	RbT	Sal	Tog	Smt	LmB	SmB	WhP	Csk	WhF	Pic
	✓		✓		✓		✓				✓

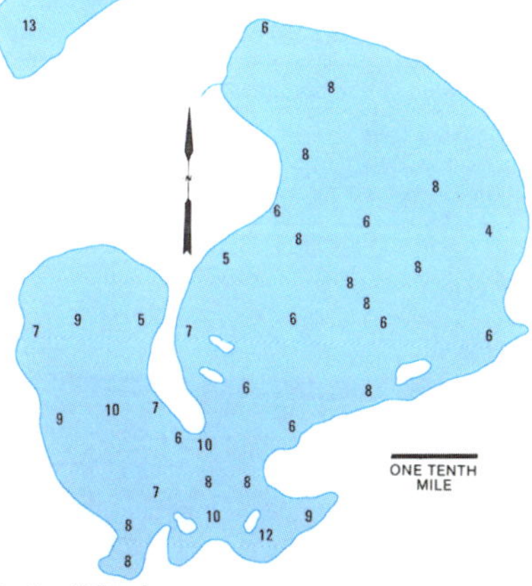

Montegail Pond

T19 MD BPP, Maine Atlas Map 25, B-4
Acres: 170, Max. Depth: 12 feet, Boat Launch

BrT	BkT	RbT	Sal	Tog	Smt	LmB	SmB	WhP	Csk	WhF	Pic
	✓				✓						

North Beaverdam Lake

T26 ED BPP
Maine Atlas Map 35, D-5
Acres: 147
Max. Depth: 21 feet

BrT		LmB	
BkT		SmB	✓
RbT		WhP	
Sal		Csk	
Tog		WhF	
Smt		Pic	✓

Washington

North Myers Pond
Columbia
Maine Atlas
Map 25, C-3
Acres: 6
Max. Depth:
29 feet

BrT	LmB
BkT ✓	SmB
RbT	WhP
Sal	Csk
Tog	WhF
Smt	Pic

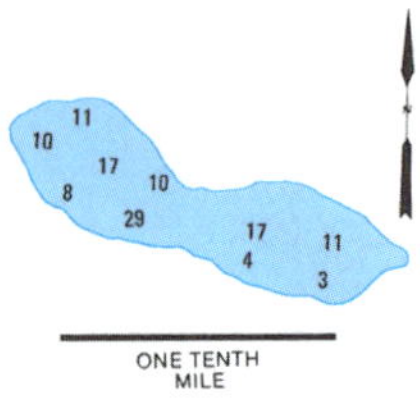

Peep Lake
T30 MD BPP
Maine Atlas
Map 25, A-3
Acres: 32
Max. Depth:
20 feet

BrT	LmB
BkT ✓	SmB
RbT	WhP
Sal	Csk
Tog	WhF
Smt	Pic

Comments: Clear water offers good visibility.

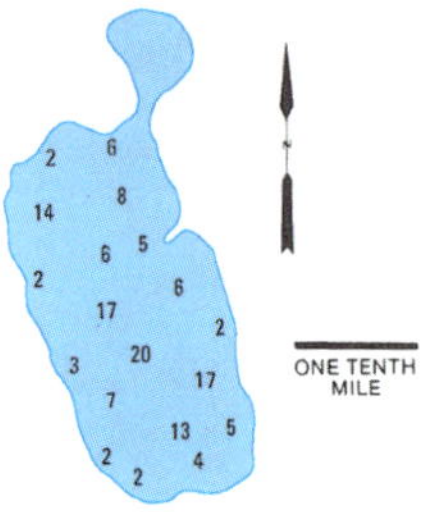

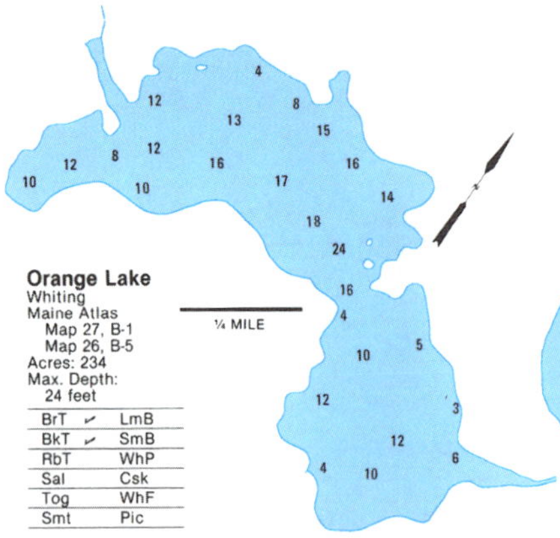

Orange Lake
Whiting
Maine Atlas
Map 27, B-1
Map 26, B-5
Acres: 234
Max. Depth:
24 feet

BrT ✓	LmB
BkT ✓	SmB
RbT	WhP
Sal	Csk
Tog	WhF
Smt	Pic

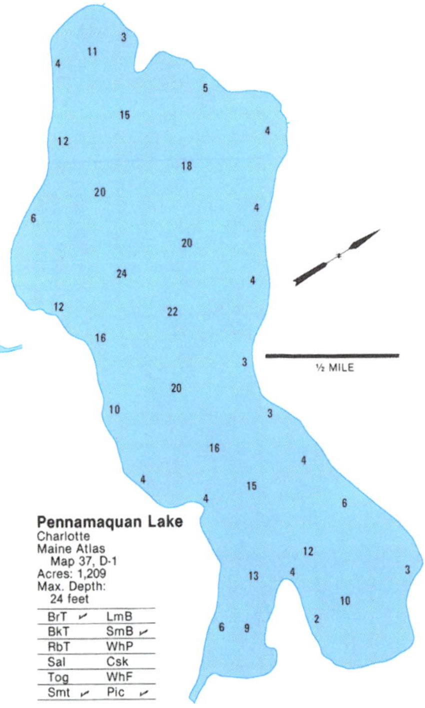

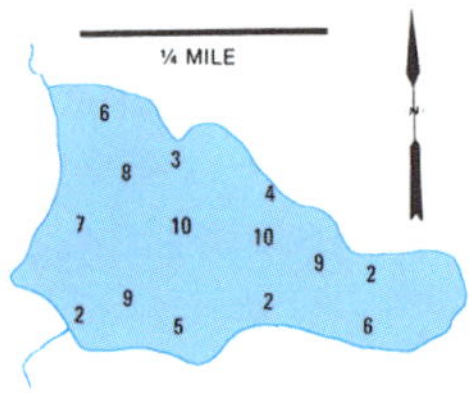

Orie Lake
T6 R1 NBPP,
Kossuth Twp
Maine Atlas
Map 45, E-3
Acres: 42
Max. Depth:
10 feet
Boat Launch

BrT	LmB
BkT ✓	SmB
RbT	WhP
Sal	Csk
Tog	WhF
Smt	Pic

Pennamaquan Lake
Charlotte
Maine Atlas
Map 37, D-1
Acres: 1,209
Max. Depth:
24 feet

BrT ✓	LmB
BkT	SmB ✓
RbT	WhP
Sal	Csk
Tog	WhF
Smt ✓	Pic ✓

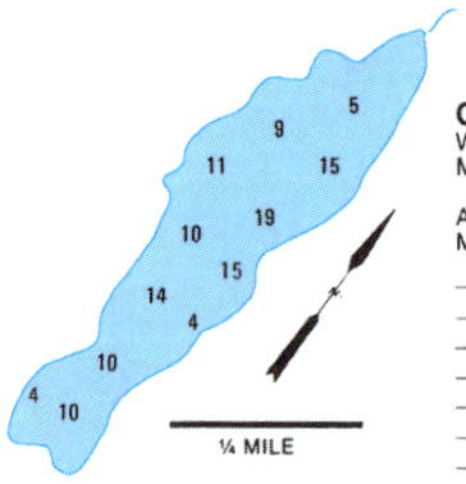

Otter Lake
Wesley
Maine Atlas
Map 26, A-1
Acres: 44
Max. Depth:
19 feet

BrT	LmB
BkT	SmB
RbT	WhP ✓
Sal	Csk
Tog	WhF
Smt	Pic ✓

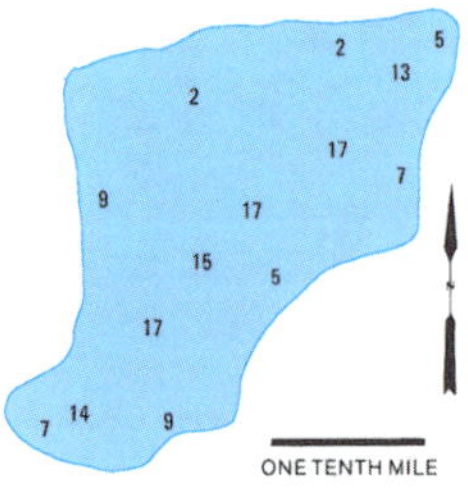

Pickerel Pond
Topsfield
Maine Atlas
Map 45, D-4
Acres: 39
Max. Depth:
17 feet

BrT	LmB
BkT	SmB
RbT	WhP
Sal	Csk
Tog	WhF
Smt	Pic ✓

Patrick Lake
Marion Twp,
No. 14 Plt
Maine Atlas
Map 26, A-4
Acres: 275
Max. Depth:
32 feet
Boat Launch

BrT ✓	LmB
BkT	SmB
RbT	WhP ✓
Sal	Csk
Tog	WhF
Smt ✓	Pic ✓

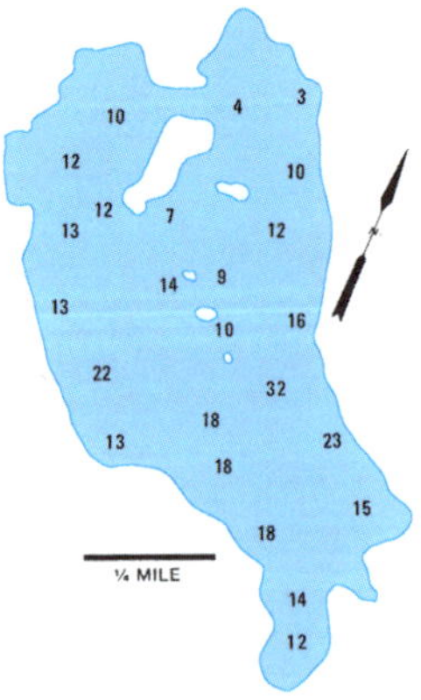

Pineo Pond
Deblois
Maine Atlas
Map 25, C-2
Acres: 7
Max. Depth:
52 feet

BrT	LmB
BkT ✓	SmB
RbT	WhP
Sal	Csk
Tog	WhF
Smt	Pic

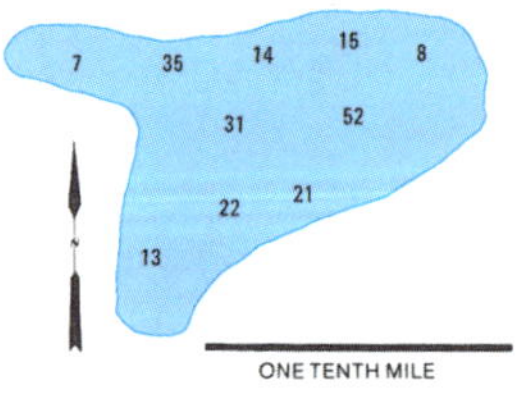

Pleasant Lake
Alexander, Maine Atlas Map 36, D-3
Acres: 339, Max. Depth: 36 feet

BrT	BkT	RbT	Sal	Tog	Smt	LmB	SmB	WhP	Csk	WhF	Pic
	✓		✓		✓			✓			✓

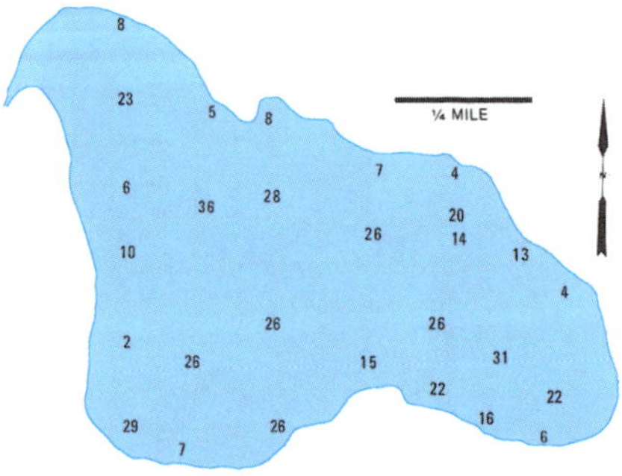

Peaked Mountain Pond
T19 MD BPP,
Northfield,
Centerville
Maine Atlas
Map 25, B-5
Acres: 227
Max. Depth:
48 feet

BrT	LmB
BkT ✓	SmB
RbT	WhP
Sal	Csk
Tog	WhF
Smt ✓	Pic ✓

Comments: Splake.

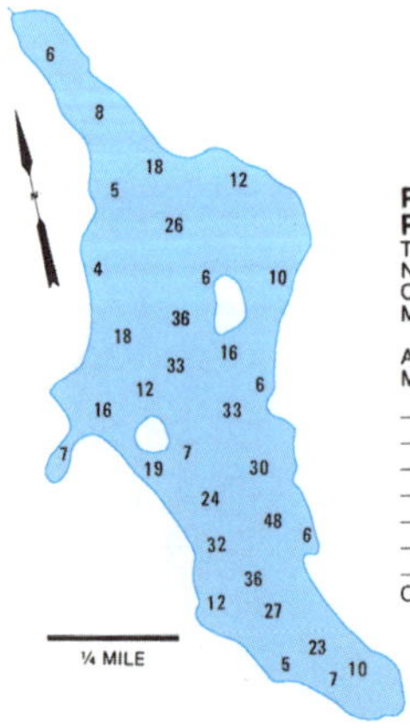

Pleasant Lake
Kossuth Twp, T6 R1 NBPP, Maine Atlas Map 45, E-2, E-3
Acres: 1,574, Max. Depth: 92 feet, Boat Launch

BrT	BkT	RbT	Sal	Tog	Smt	LmB	SmB	WhP	Csk	WhF	Pic
	✓		✓	✓	✓		✓	✓		✓	

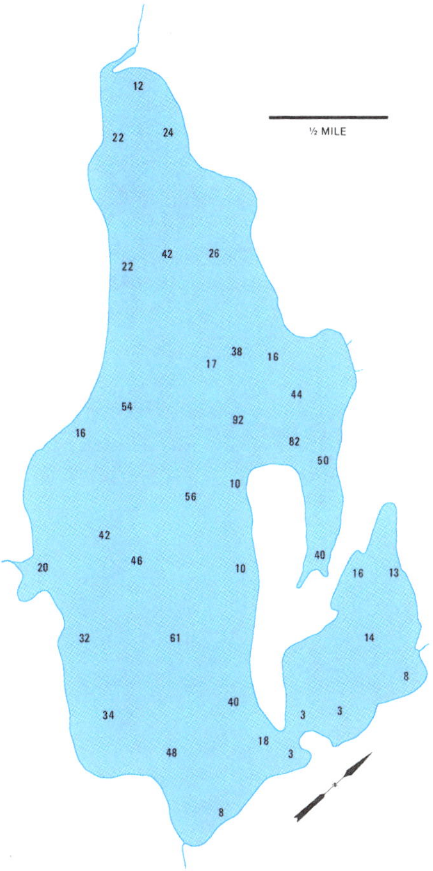

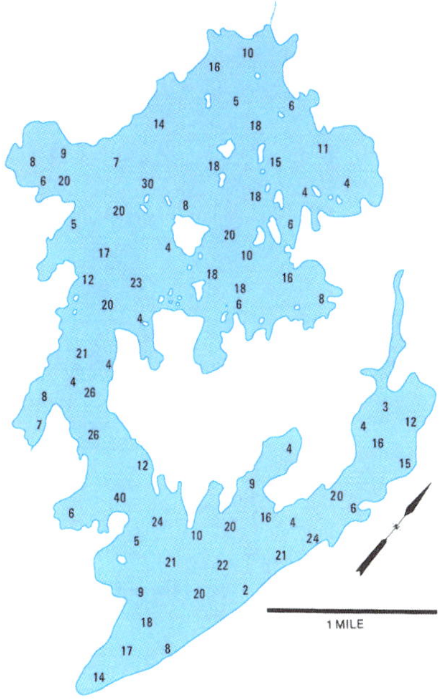

Pocomoonshine Lake
Princeton, Alexander, Maine Atlas Map 36, C-2
Acres: 2,464, Max. Depth: 40 feet, Boat Launch

BrT	BkT	RbT	Sal	Tog	Smt	LmB	SmB	WhP	Csk	WhF	Pic
							✓	✓			✓

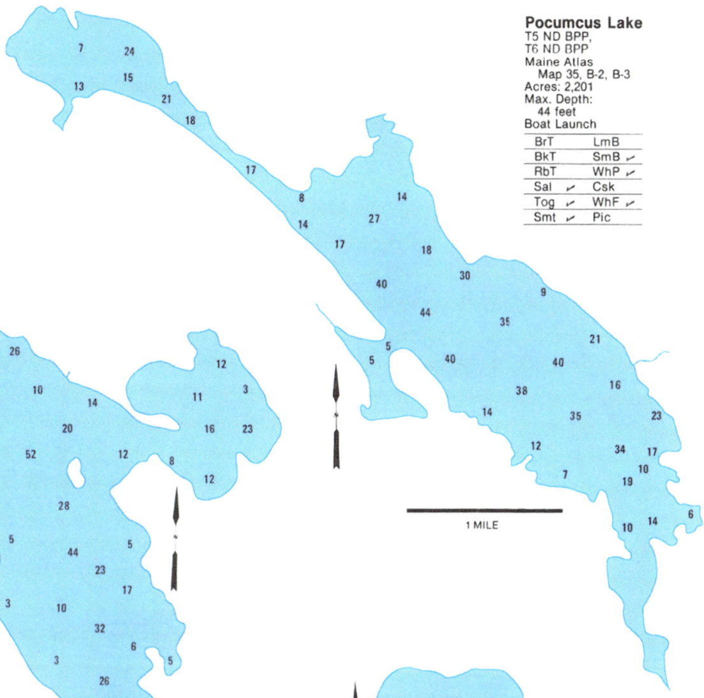

Pocumcus Lake
T5 ND BPP,
T6 ND BPP
Maine Atlas
Map 35, B-2, B-3
Acres: 2,201
Max. Depth:
44 feet
Boat Launch

BrT	LmB
BkT	SmB ✓
RbT	WhP ✓
Sal ✓	Csk
Tog ✓	WhF ✓
Smt ✓	Pic

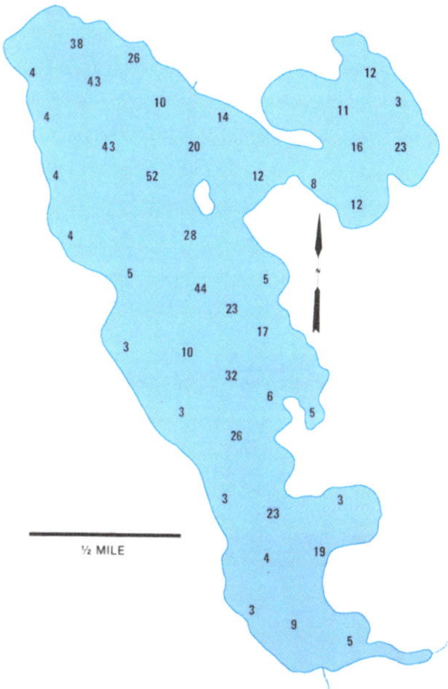

Pleasant River Lake
Beddington, Devereaux Twp, Maine Atlas Map 25, A-2
Acres: 949, Max. Depth: 52 feet, Boat Launch

BrT	BkT	RbT	Sal	Tog	Smt	LmB	SmB	WhP	Csk	WhF	Pic
	✓		✓		✓		✓	✓			

Comments: Splake.

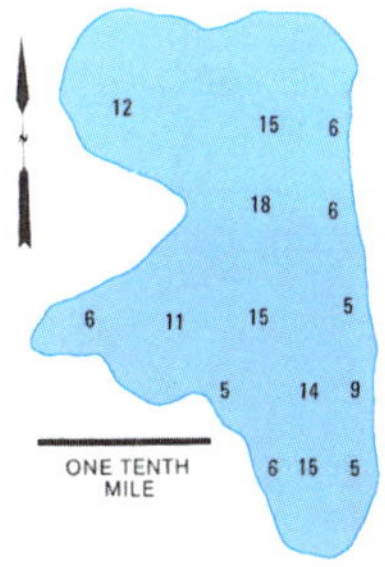

Possum Lake
T26 ED BPP
Maine Atlas
Map 35, D-5
Acres: 30
Max. Depth:
18 feet

BrT	LmB
BkT	SmB
RbT	WhP
Sal	Csk
Tog	WhF
Smt	Pic ✓

Washington

Pug Lake
T26 ED BPP
Maine Atlas
Map 35, D-5
Acres: 198
Max. Depth:
39 feet

BrT		LmB	
BkT		SmB	✓
RbT		WhP	✓
Sal		Csk	
Tog		WhF	
Smt	✓	Pic	✓

Comments: Splake.

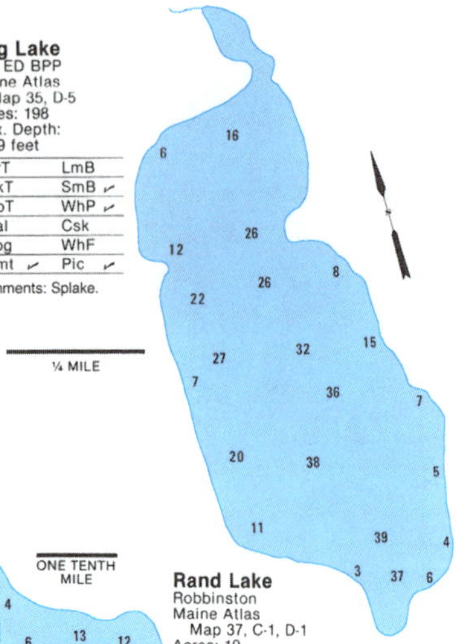

Rand Lake
Robbinston
Maine Atlas
Map 37, C-1, D-1
Acres: 19
Max. Depth:
16 feet

BrT		LmB	
BkT		SmB	
RbT		WhP	
Sal		Csk	
Tog		WhF	
Smt		Pic	✓

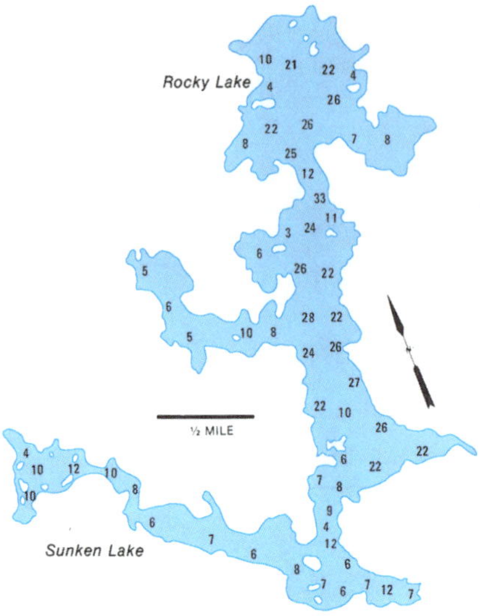

Rocky and Sunken Lakes
Whiting, Marion Twp, Edmunds Twp, Maine Atlas Map 26, B-5
Acres: 1,126, Max. Depth: 33 feet

BrT	BkT	RbT	Sal	Tog	Smt	LmB	SmB	WhP	Csk	WhF	Pic
✓	✓				✓						

Roaring Lake
Whiting
Maine Atlas
Map 27, B-1
Acres: 51
Max. Depth:
10 feet

BrT		LmB	
BkT	✓	SmB	
RbT		WhP	
Sal		Csk	
Tog		WhF	
Smt		Pic	

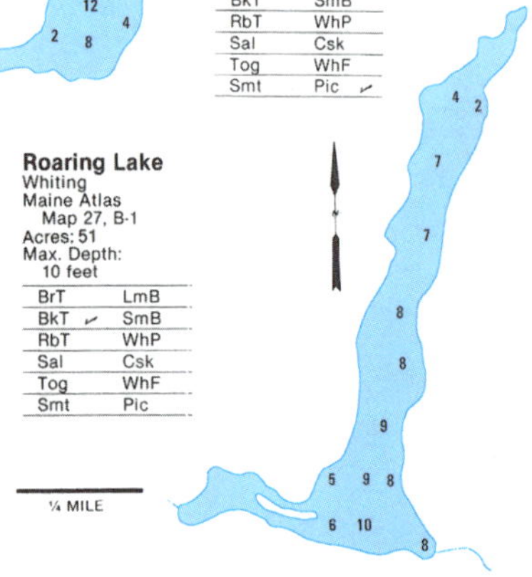

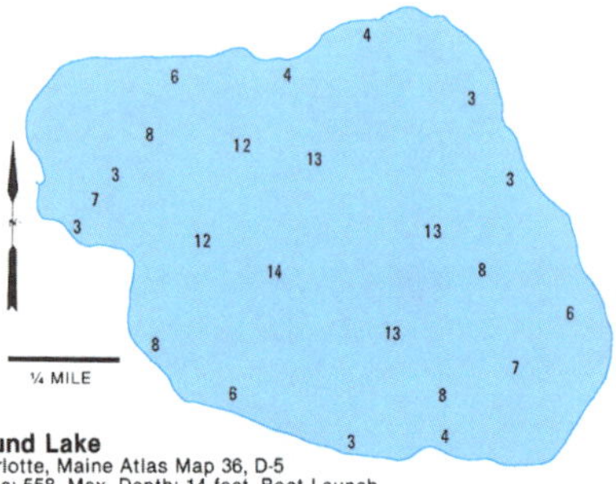

Round Lake
Charlotte, Maine Atlas Map 36, D-5
Acres: 558, Max. Depth: 14 feet, Boat Launch

BrT	BkT	RbT	Sal	Tog	Smt	LmB	SmB	WhP	Csk	WhF	Pic
✓	✓				✓		✓				✓

Rocky Lake
T18 ED BPP
Maine Atlas
Map 26, A-3
Acres: 1,555
Max. Depth:
37 feet
Boat Launch

BrT		LmB	
BkT	✓	SmB	✓
RbT		WhP	✓
Sal		Csk	
Tog		WhF	
Smt		Pic	✓

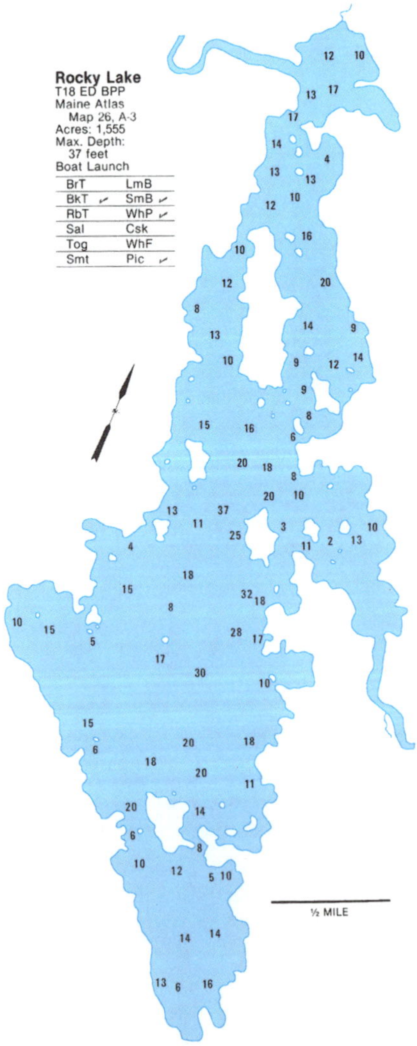

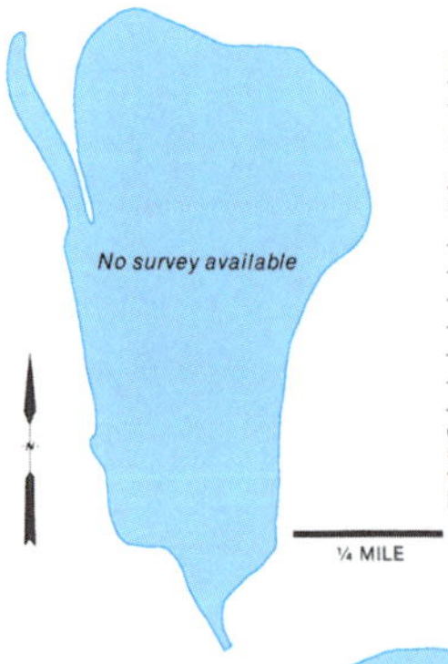

Round Lake
T18 ED BPP
T19 ED BPP
Maine Atlas
Map 26, A-2
Acres: 352
Max. Depth:
25 feet

BrT		LmB	
BkT	✓	SmB	✓
RbT		WhP	✓
Sal		Csk	
Tog		WhF	
Smt		Pic	✓

Comments: Easiest access is to go up the East Machias River.

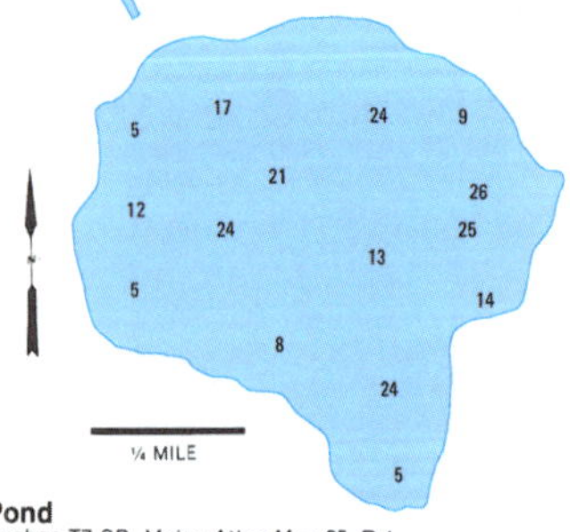

Round Pond
T10 SD, Stueben,T7 SD, Maine Atlas Map 25, D-1
Acres: 205, Max. Depth: 26 feet

BrT	BkT	RbT	Sal	Tog	Smt	LmB	SmB	WhP	Csk	WhF	Pic
	✓	✓	✓		✓						

Salmon Pond
T30 MD BPP
Maine Atlas
Map 35, E-3
Acres: 11
Max. Depth:
22 feet
Boat Launch

BrT		LmB	
BkT	✓	SmB	
RbT		WhP	
Sal		Csk	
Tog		WhF	
Smt		Pic	

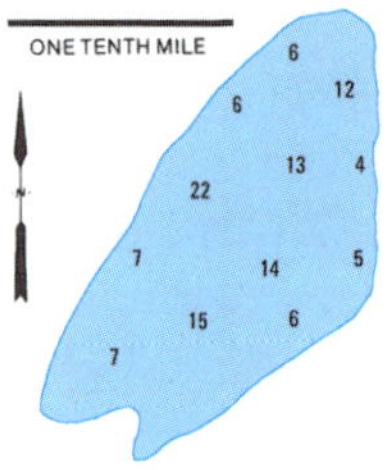

Sam Hill Lake

T31 MD BPP
Maine Atlas
Map 25, A-4, A-5
Acres: 46
Max. Depth:
35 feet

BrT	LmB
BkT ✓	SmB
RbT	WhP
Sal	Csk
Tog	WhF
Smt	Pic ✓

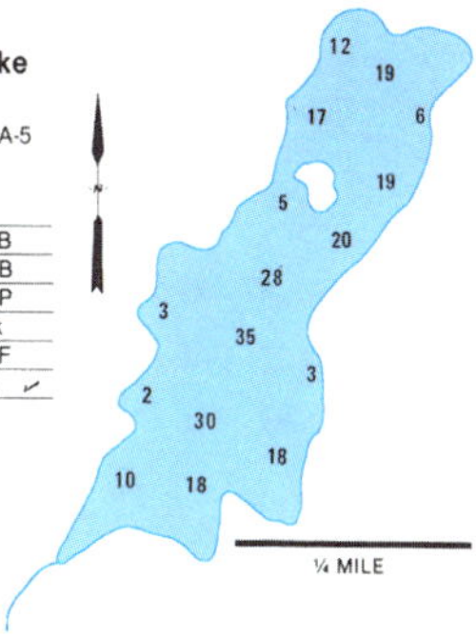

Second and Third Lakes

T37 MD BPP
Maine Atlas
Map 35, D-4
Acres: 243
Max. Depth:
56 feet

BrT	LmB
BkT ✓	SmB
RbT	WhP ✓
Sal	Csk
Tog	WhF
Smt	Pic ✓

Comments: Splake.

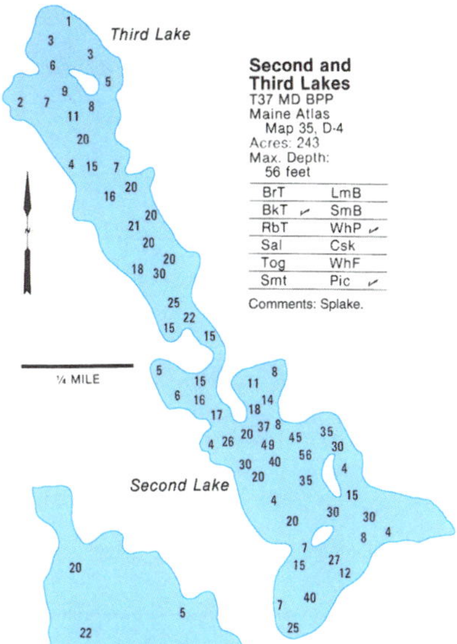

Schoodic Lake

T18 MD BPP,
Cherryfield,
Columbia
Maine Atlas
Map 25, C-3
Acres: 389
Max. Depth:
37 feet
Boat Launch

BrT	LmB
BkT ✓	SmB ✓
RbT	WhP
Sal ✓	Csk
Tog	WhF
Smt ✓	Pic ✓

Comments: Very good boat launch.

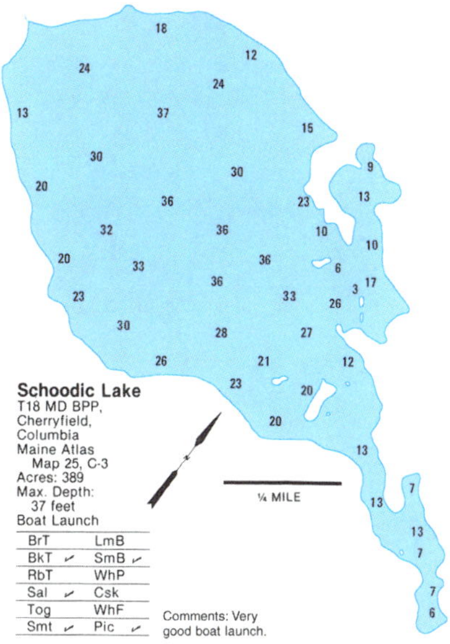

Second Chain Lake

T31 MD BPP,
T37 MD BPP,
T26 ED BPP
Maine Atlas
Map 35, D-5, E-5
Acres: 589
Max. Depth:
30 feet

BrT	LmB
BkT	SmB
RbT	WhP ✓
Sal	Csk
Tog	WhF
Smt ✓	Pic ✓

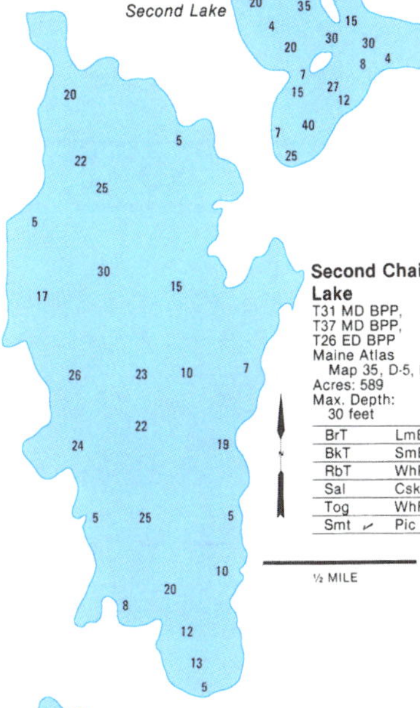

Second Lake

Marion Twp
Maine Atlas
Map 26, B-4
Acres: 1,650
Max. Depth:
25 feet

BrT	LmB
BkT ✓	SmB ✓
RbT	WhP ✓
Sal ✓	Csk
Tog	WhF
Smt ✓	Pic ✓

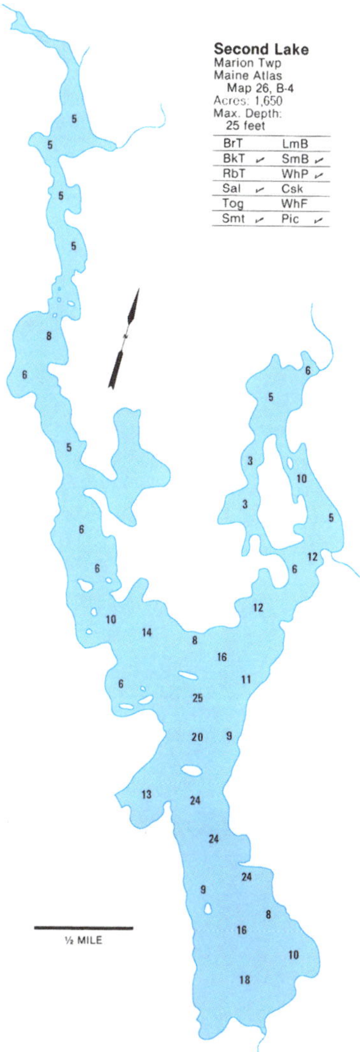

Second Machias Lake

T37 MD BPP
Maine Atlas
Map 35, D-3
Acres: 192
Max. Depth:
14 feet
Boat Launch

BrT	LmB
BkT	SmB ✓
RbT	WhP ✓
Sal	Csk
Tog	WhF
Smt	Pic ✓

Second Marks Lake

Marshfield
Maine Atlas
Map 26, B-2
Acres: 51
Max. Depth:
22 feet

BrT	LmB
BkT ✓	SmB
RbT	WhP
Sal	Csk
Tog	WhF
Smt	Pic

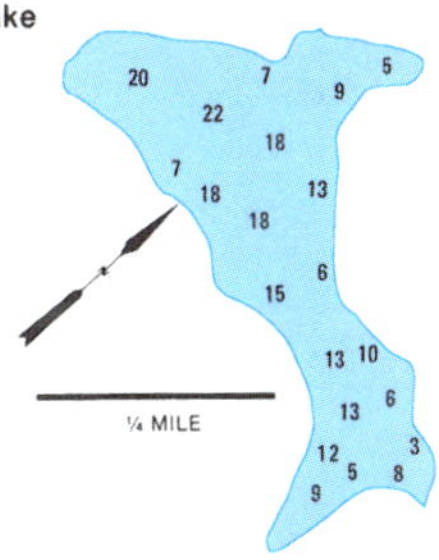

Second Mopang Lake

Devereaux Twp,
T30 MD BPP
Maine Atlas
Map 25, A-2
Acres: 145
Max. Depth:
20 feet
Boat Launch

BrT	LmB
BkT	SmB
RbT	WhP ✓
Sal ✓	Csk
Tog	WhF
Smt	Pic ✓

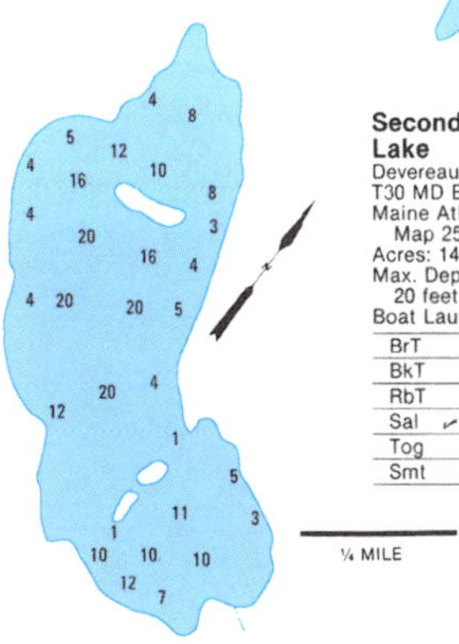

Washington

Shattuck Lake
Robbinston, Calais
Maine Atlas
Map 37, C-1
Acres: 25
Max. Depth:
17 feet

BrT	LmB
BkT ✓	SmB
RbT	WhP
Sal	Csk
Tog	WhF
Smt	Pic ✓

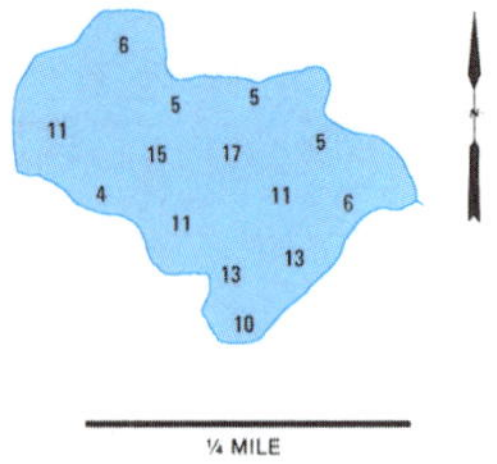

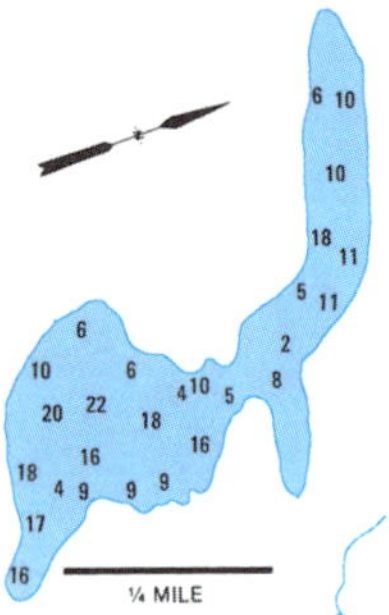

Six Mile Lake
Marshfield
Maine Atlas
Map 26, B-2
Acres: 55
Max. Depth:
22 feet
Boat Launch

BrT ✓	LmB
BkT ✓	SmB
RbT	WhP
Sal	Csk
Tog	WhF
Smt ✓	Pic

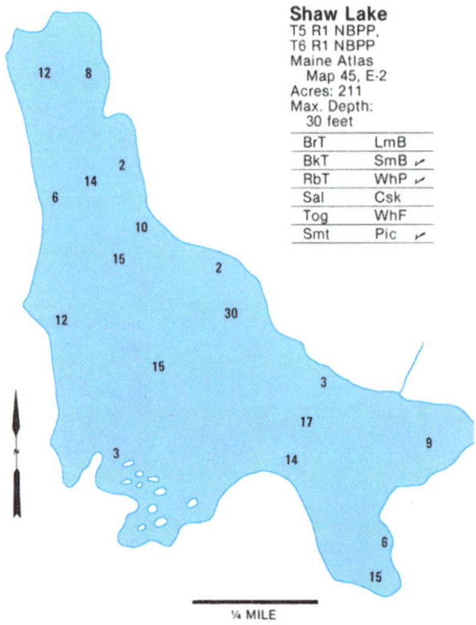

Shaw Lake
T5 R1 NBPP,
T6 R1 NBPP
Maine Atlas
Map 45, E-2
Acres: 211
Max. Depth:
30 feet

BrT	LmB
BkT	SmB ✓
RbT	WhP ✓
Sal	Csk
Tog	WhF
Smt	Pic ✓

South Beaverdam Lake
T26 ED BPP
Maine Atlas
Map 35, D-5, E-5
Acres: 160
Max. Depth:
40 feet

BrT	LmB
BkT ✓	SmB ✓
RbT	WhP ✓
Sal	Csk
Tog	WhF
Smt	Pic

¼ MILE

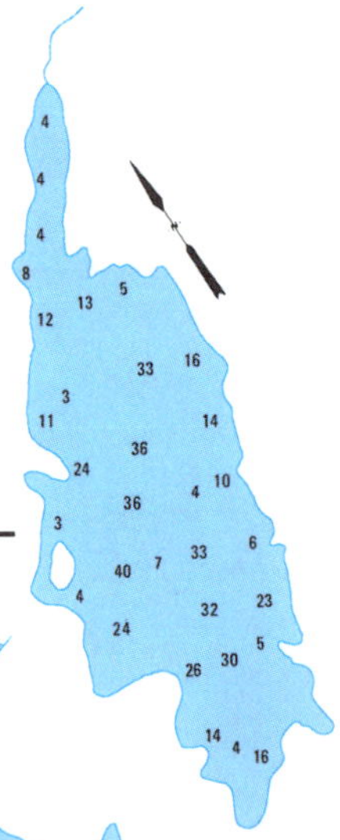

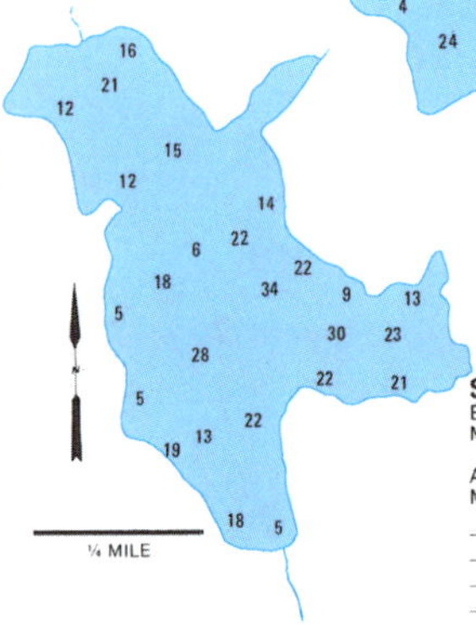

Southwest Pond
Beddington
Maine Atlas
Map 25, B-2
Acres: 138
Max. Depth:
34 feet

BrT	LmB
BkT ✓	SmB
RbT	WhP ✓
Sal	Csk
Tog	WhF
Smt	Pic

Comments: Splake

Spednik Lake
Forest Twp,
T11 R3 NBPP,
Vanceboro
Maine Atlas
Map 45, B-5,
Map 46, B-1, B-2
Acres: 17,219
Max. Depth:
54 feet
Boat Launch

BrT	LmB
BkT	SmB ✓
RbT	WhP ✓
Sal ✓	Csk ✓
Tog	WhF
Smt ✓	Pic ✓

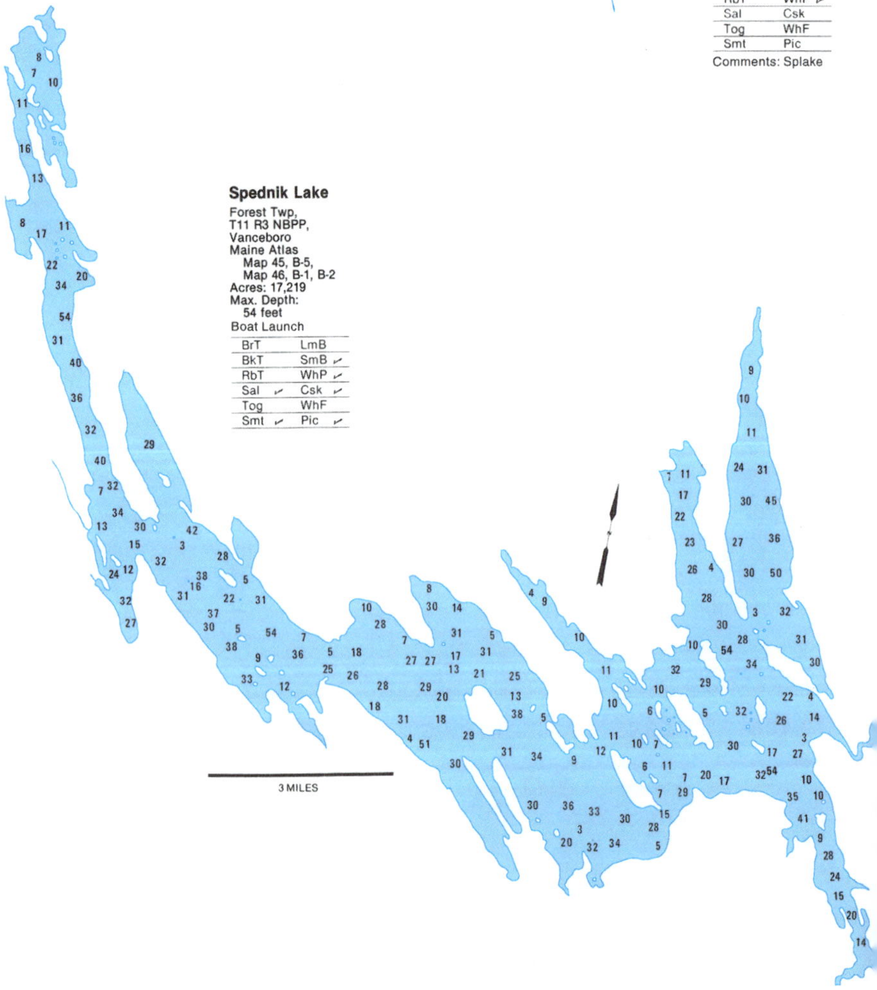

Spruce Mountain Lake

Beddington
Maine Atlas
Map 25, B-1
Acres: 448
Max. Depth:
43 feet

BrT		LmB	
BkT	✓	SmB	
RbT		WhP	
Sal	✓	Csk	
Tog		WhF	
Smt	✓	Pic	✓

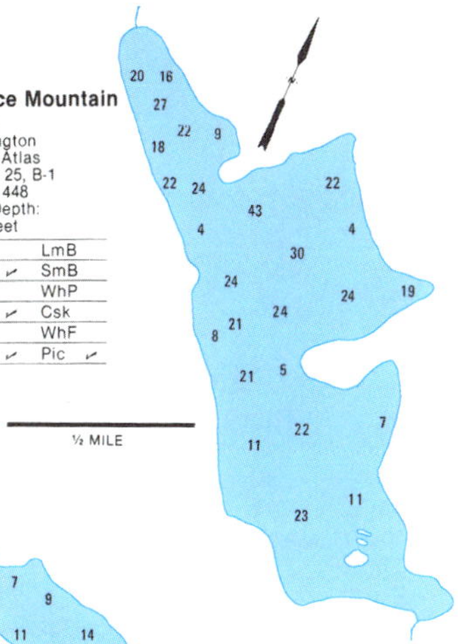

Trout Lake

Kossuth Twp
Maine Atlas
Map 45, E-3
Acres: 5
Max. Depth:
11 feet

BrT		LmB	
BkT	✓	SmB	
RbT		WhP	
Sal		Csk	
Tog		WhF	
Smt		Pic	

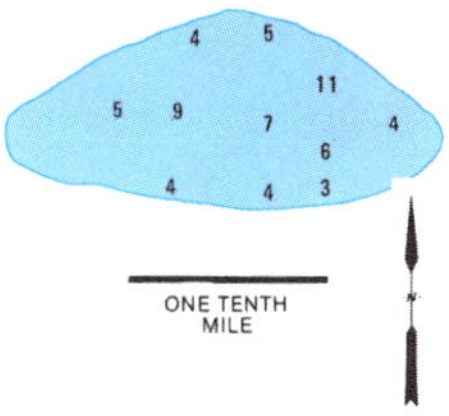

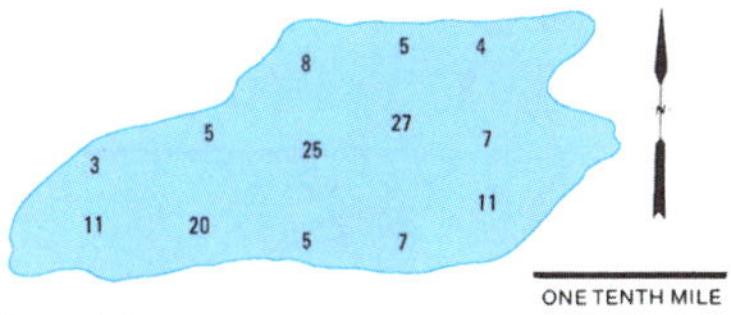

Trout Lake

T31 MD BPP, Maine Atlas Map 35, E-5
Acres: 21, Max. Depth: 27 feet

BrT	BkT	RbT	Sal	Tog	Smt	LmB	SmB	WhP	Csk	WhF	Pic
											✓

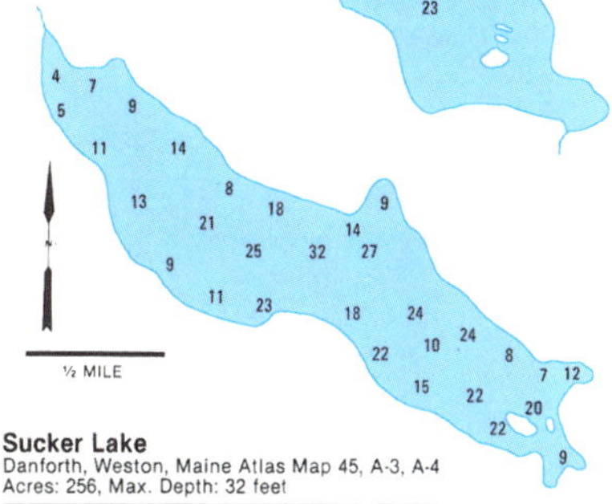

Sucker Lake

Danforth, Weston, Maine Atlas Map 45, A-3, A-4
Acres: 256, Max. Depth: 32 feet

BrT	BkT	RbT	Sal	Tog	Smt	LmB	SmB	WhP	Csk	WhF	Pic
					✓			✓			✓

Third Chain Lake

T26 ED BPP
Maine Atlas
Map 35, D-5
Acres: 157
Max. Depth:
36 feet

BrT		LmB	
BkT		SmB	
RbT		WhP	✓
Sal		Csk	
Tog		WhF	
Smt	✓	Pic	✓

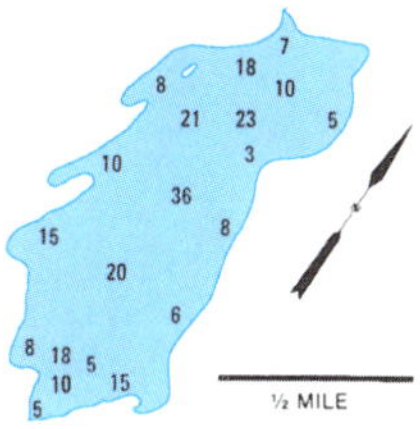

Unnamed Pond

T31 MD BPP
Maine Atlas
Map 25, A-5
Acres: 5
Max. Depth:
15 feet

BrT		LmB	
BkT	✓	SmB	
RbT		WhP	
Sal		Csk	
Tog		WhF	
Smt		Pic	

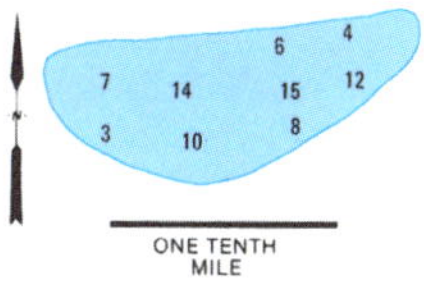

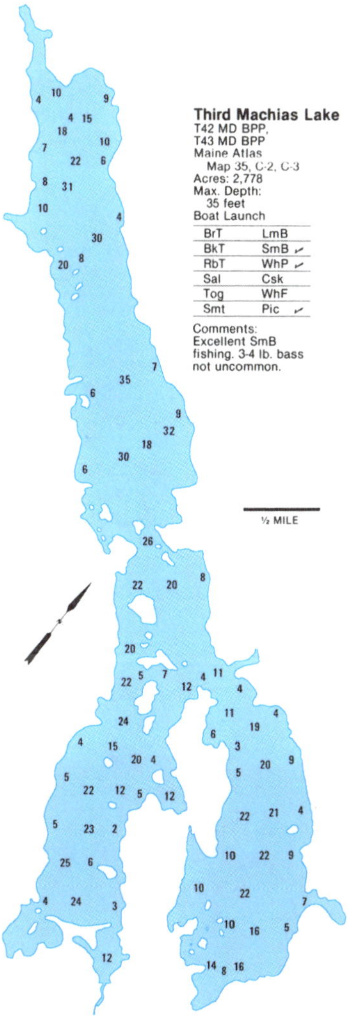

Third Machias Lake

T42 MD BPP,
T43 MD BPP
Maine Atlas
Map 35, C-2, C-3
Acres: 2,778
Max. Depth:
35 feet
Boat Launch

BrT		LmB	
BkT		SmB	✓
RbT		WhP	✓
Sal		Csk	
Tog		WhF	
Smt		Pic	✓

Comments:
Excellent SmB fishing. 3-4 lb. bass not uncommon.

Upper Hot Brook Lake

T8 R4 NBPP, Danforth, Maine Atlas Map 45, B-2
Acres: 912, Max. Depth: 18 feet, Boat Launch

BrT	BkT	RbT	Sal	Tog	Smt	LmB	SmB	WhP	Csk	WhF	Pic
	✓		✓				✓	✓			✓

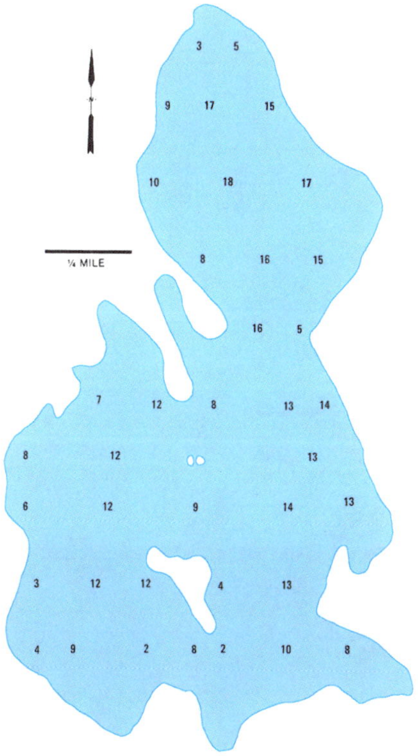

Washington

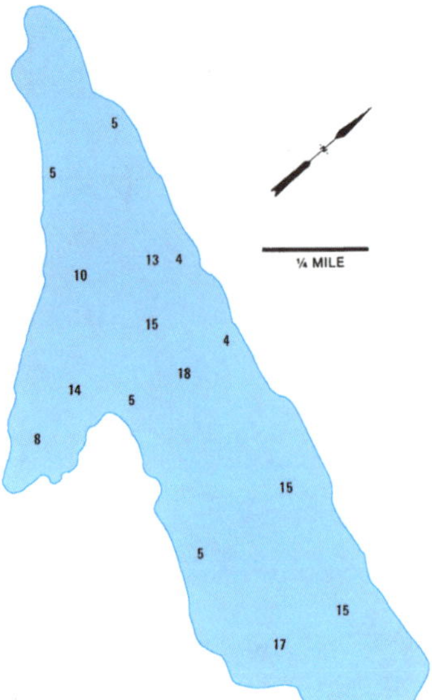

Upper Oxbrook Lake
T6 R1 NBPP, Talmadge, Maine Atlas Map 35, A-3, A-4
Acres: 422, Max. Depth: 18 feet, Boat Launch

BrT	BkT	RbT	Sal	Tog	Smt	LmB	SmB	WhP	Csk	WhF	Pic
	✓		✓		✓			✓			

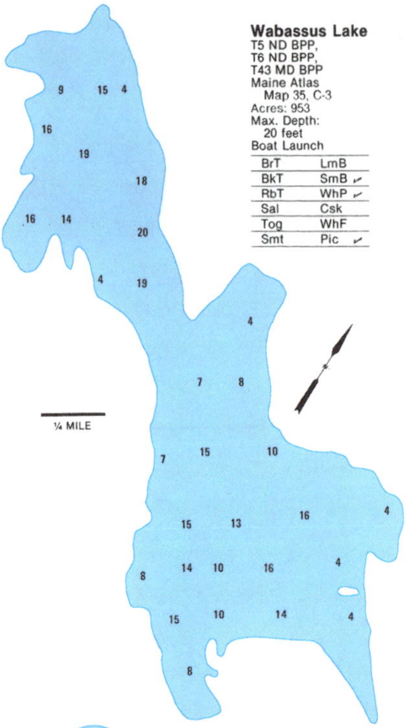

Wabassus Lake
T5 ND BPP,
T6 ND BPP,
T43 MD BPP
Maine Atlas
Map 35, C-3
Acres: 953
Max. Depth:
20 feet
Boat Launch

BrT		LmB	
BkT		SmB	✓
RbT		WhP	✓
Sal		Csk	
Tog		WhF	
Smt		Pic	✓

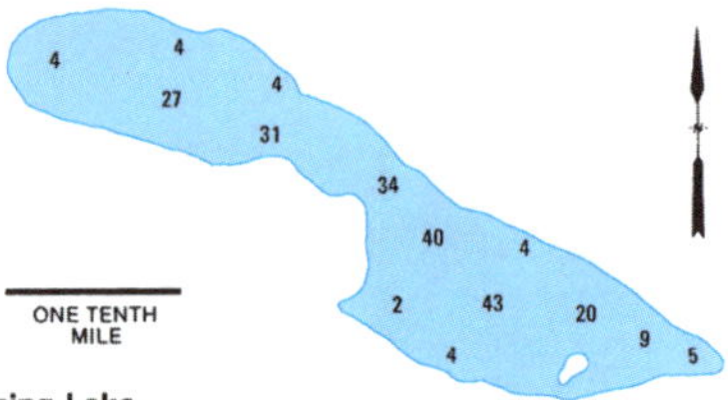

Vining Lake
Cooper, No. 14 Plt, Maine Atlas Map 36, E-3
Acres: 19, Max. Depth: 43 feet

BrT	BkT	RbT	Sal	Tog	Smt	LmB	SmB	WhP	Csk	WhF	Pic
	✓										

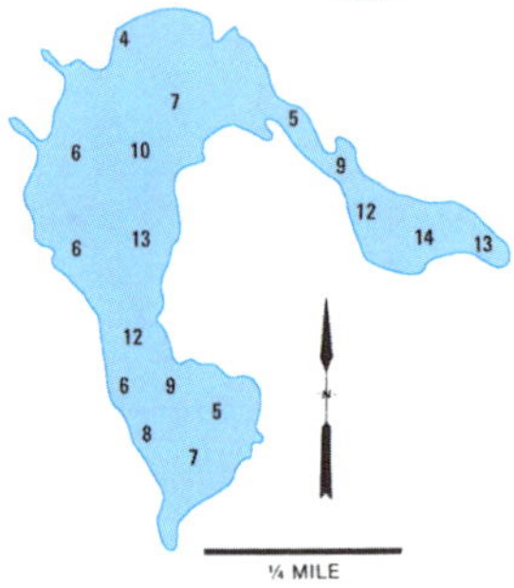

Western Lake
Robbinston
Maine Atlas
Map 37, D-1, D-2
Acres: 65
Max. Depth:
14 feet
Boat Launch

BrT		LmB	
BkT	✓	SmB	
RbT		WhP	
Sal		Csk	
Tog		WhF	
Smt		Pic	

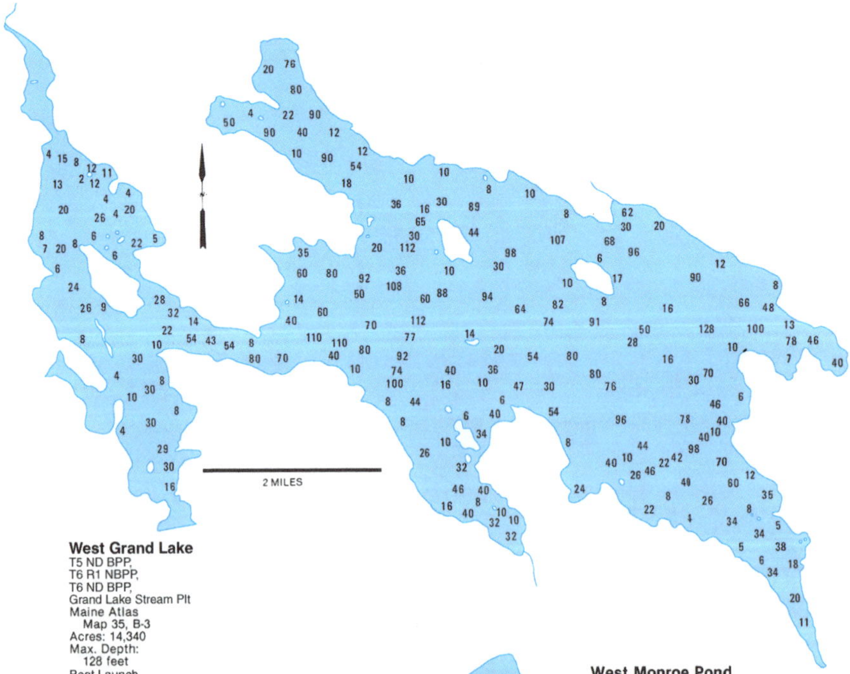

West Grand Lake
T5 ND BPP,
T6 R1 NBPP,
T6 ND BPP,
Grand Lake Stream Plt
Maine Atlas
Map 35, B-3
Acres: 14,340
Max. Depth:
128 feet
Boat Launch

BrT		LmB	
BkT		SmB	✓
RbT		WhP	✓
Sal	✓	Csk	
Tog	✓	WhF	✓
Smt	✓	Pic	✓

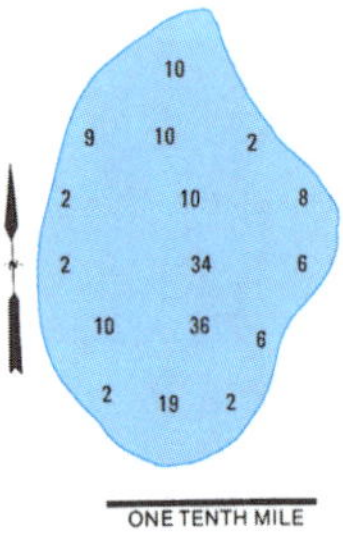

West Monroe Pond
T43 MD BPP
Maine Atlas
Map 35, C-4, D-4
Acres: 13
Max. Depth:
36 feet

BrT		LmB	
BkT	✓	SmB	
RbT		WhP	
Sal		Csk	
Tog		WhF	
Smt		Pic	

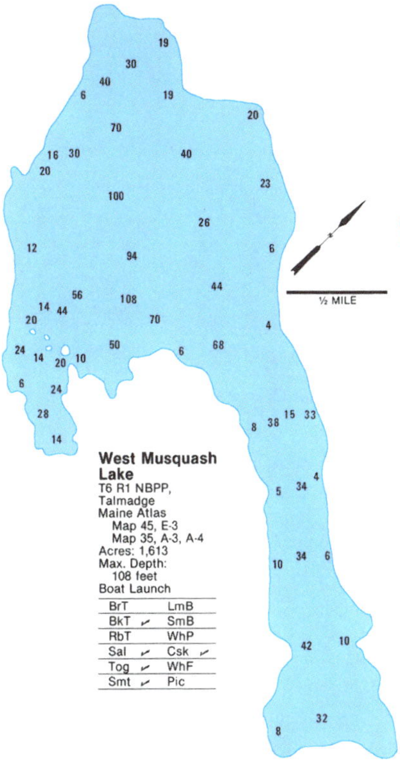

West Musquash Lake
T6 R1 NBPP,
Talmadge
Maine Atlas
Map 45, E-3
Map 35, A-3, A-4
Acres: 1,613
Max. Depth:
108 feet
Boat Launch

BrT		LmB	
BkT	✓	SmB	
RbT		WhP	
Sal	✓	Csk	✓
Tog	✓	WhF	
Smt	✓	Pic	

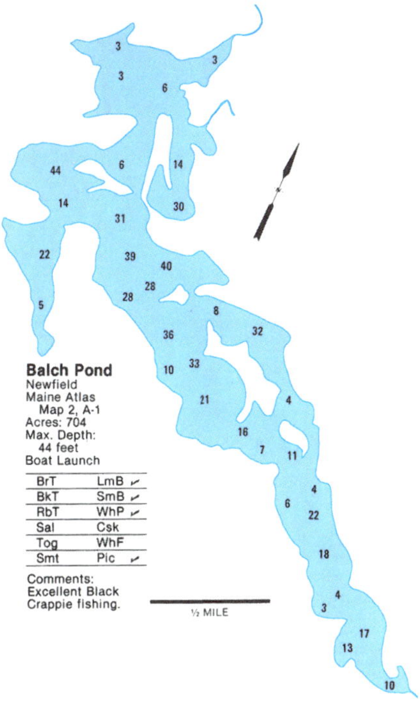

Balch Pond
Newfield
Maine Atlas
Map 2, A-1
Acres: 704
Max. Depth:
44 feet
Boat Launch

BrT		LmB	✓
BkT		SmB	✓
RbT		WhP	✓
Sal		Csk	
Tog		WhF	
Smt		Pic	✓

Comments:
Excellent Black
Crappie fishing.

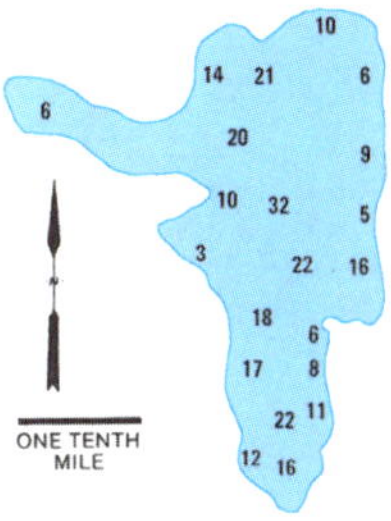

West Pike Brook Pond
T18 MD BPP
Maine Atlas
Map 25, C-2, C-3
Acres: 32
Max. Depth:
32 feet

BrT		LmB	
BkT	✓	SmB	
RbT		WhP	
Sal		Csk	
Tog		WhF	
Smt		Pic	

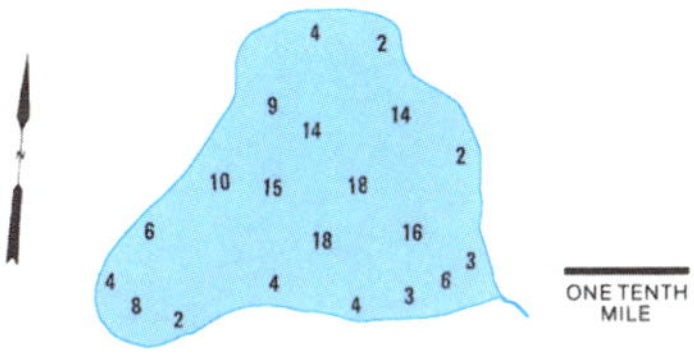

Bartlett Pond
Waterboro, Lyman, Maine Atlas Map 2, B-5
Acres: 30, Max. Depth: 18 feet, Boat Launch

BrT	BkT	RbT	Sal	Tog	Smt	LmB	SmB	WhP	Csk	WhF	Pic
						✓		✓			✓

York County

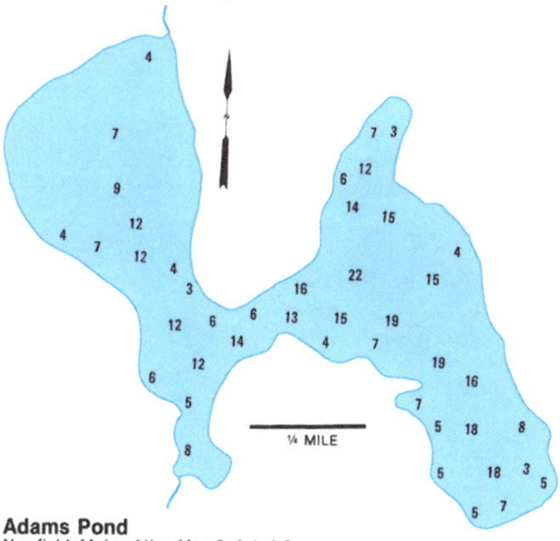

Adams Pond
Newfield, Maine Atlas Map 2, A-1, A-2
Acres: 210, Max. Depth: 22 feet, Boat Launch

BrT	BkT	RbT	Sal	Tog	Smt	LmB	SmB	WhP	Csk	WhF	Pic
	✓					✓	✓				✓

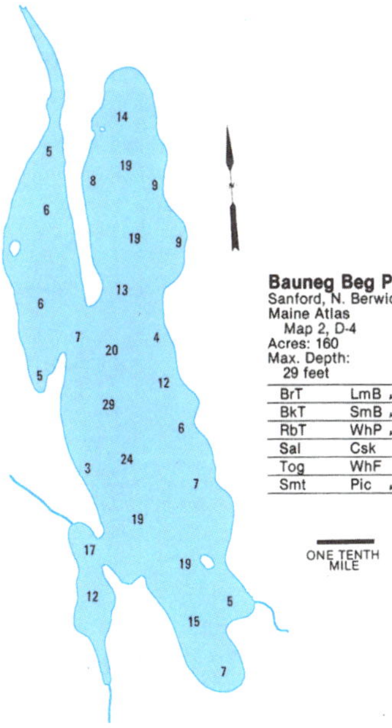

Bauneg Beg Pond
Sanford, N. Berwick
Maine Atlas
Map 2, D-4
Acres: 160
Max. Depth:
29 feet

BrT		LmB	✓
BkT		SmB	✓
RbT		WhP	✓
Sal		Csk	
Tog		WhF	
Smt		Pic	✓

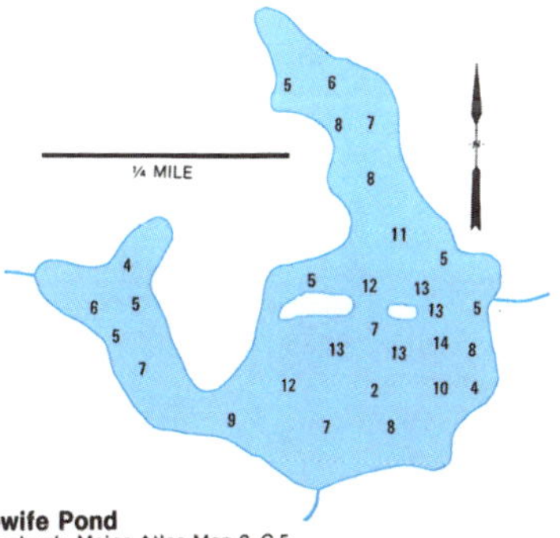

Alewife Pond
Kennebunk, Maine Atlas Map 2, C-5
Acres: 37, Max. Depth: 14 feet, Boat Launch

BrT	BkT	RbT	Sal	Tog	Smt	LmB	SmB	WhP	Csk	WhF	Pic
	✓					✓					✓

Beaver Dam Pond
Berwick
Maine Atlas
Map 2, E-3
Acres: 19
Max. Depth:
5 feet

BrT		LmB	
BkT		SmB	
RbT		WhP	
Sal		Csk	
Tog		WhF	
Smt		Pic	✓

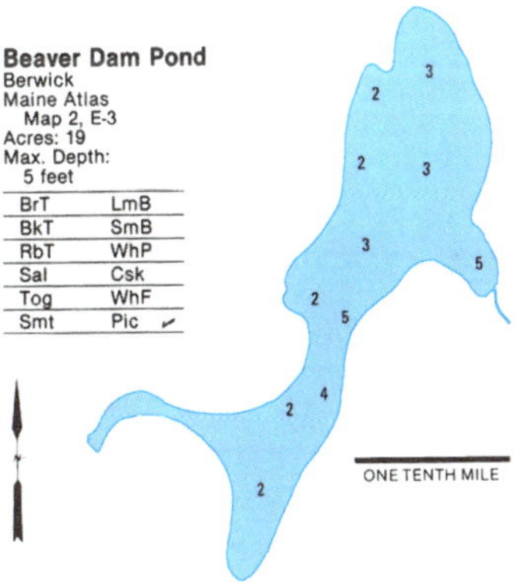

York

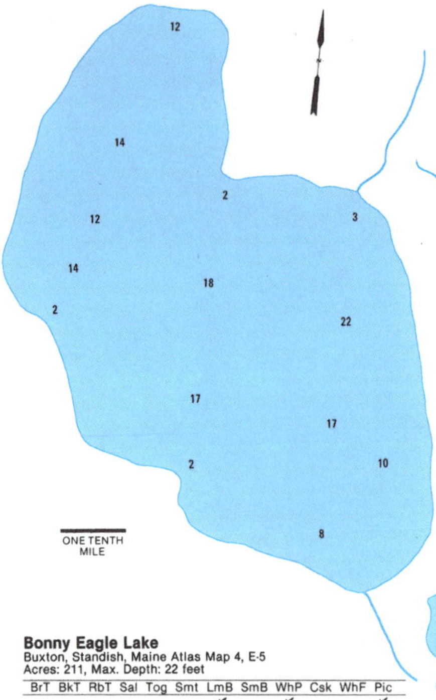

Bonny Eagle Lake
Buxton, Standish, Maine Atlas Map 4, E-5
Acres: 211, Max. Depth: 22 feet

BrT	BkT	RbT	Sal	Tog	Smt	LmB	SmB	WhP	Csk	WhF	Pic
						✓		✓			✓

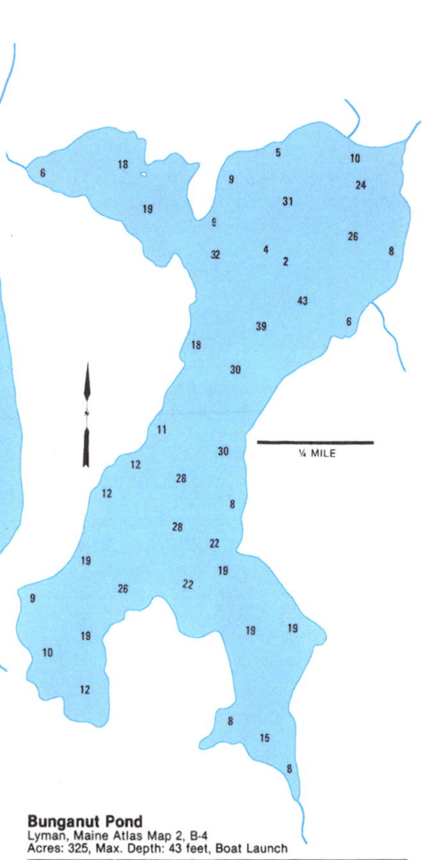

Bunganut Pond
Lyman, Maine Atlas Map 2, B-4
Acres: 325, Max. Depth: 43 feet, Boat Launch

BrT	BkT	RbT	Sal	Tog	Smt	LmB	SmB	WhP	Csk	WhF	Pic
✓						✓	✓	✓			✓

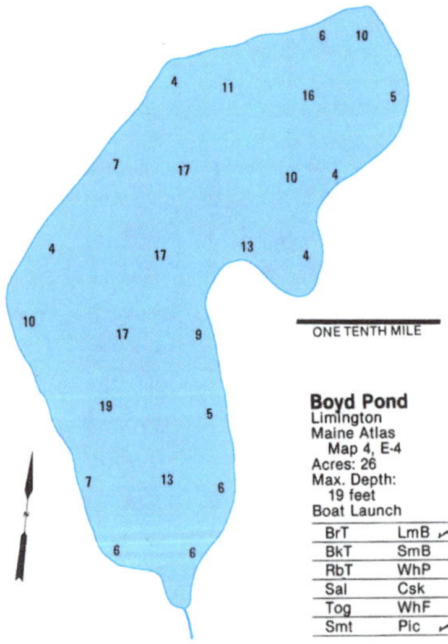

Boyd Pond
Limington
Maine Atlas Map 4, E-4
Acres: 26
Max. Depth: 19 feet
Boat Launch

BrT	LmB ✓
BkT	SmB
RbT	WhP
Sal	Csk
Tog	WhF
Smt	Pic ✓

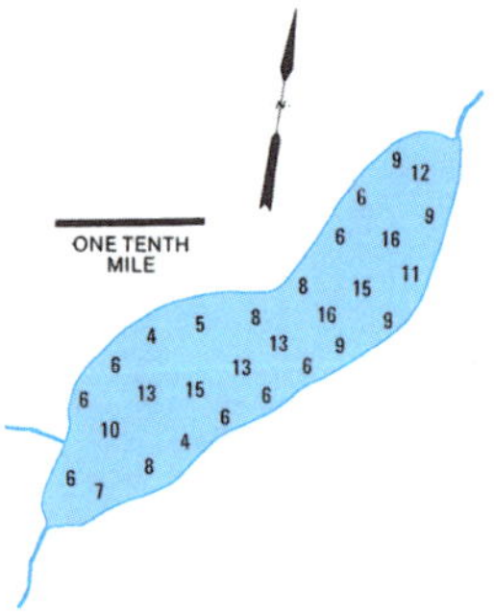

Cox Pond
South Berwick, Maine Atlas Map 1, A-3
Acres: 7, Max. Depth: 16 feet

BrT	BkT	RbT	Sal	Tog	Smt	LmB	SmB	WhP	Csk	WhF	Pic
											✓

Brimstone Pond
Arundel, Maine Atlas Map 3, C-1
Acres: 12, Max. Depth: 7 feet

BrT	BkT	RbT	Sal	Tog	Smt	LmB	SmB	WhP	Csk	WhF	Pic
											✓

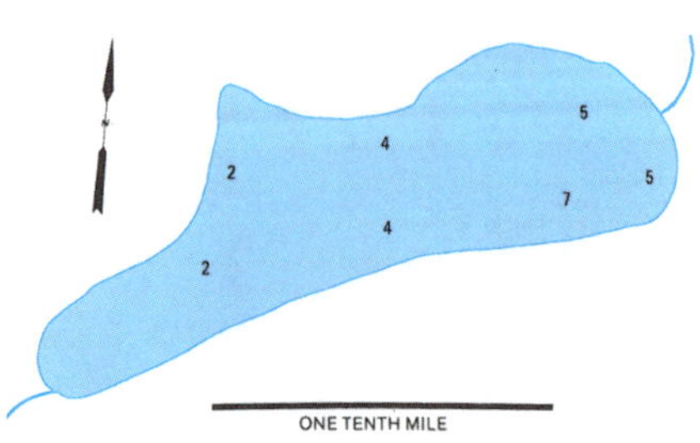

Deer Pond
Hollis
Maine Atlas Map 2, A-5
Acres: 32
Max. Depth: 65 feet

BrT ✓	LmB
BkT ✓	SmB
RbT ✓	WhP
Sal	Csk
Tog	WhF
Smt	Pic ✓

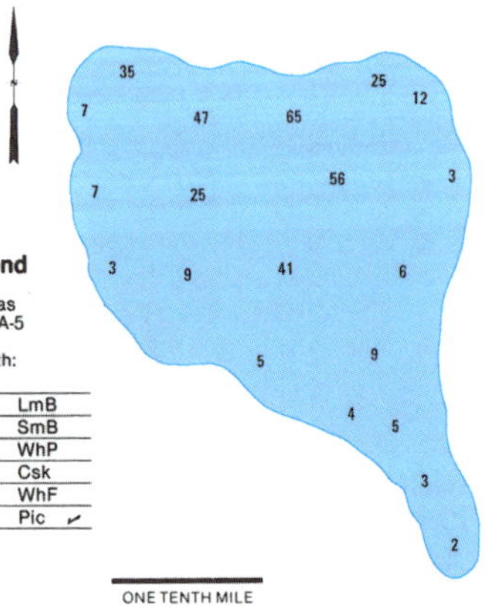

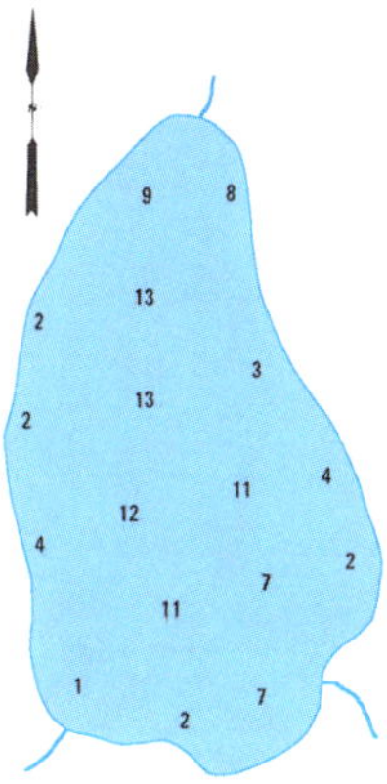

Deering Pond

Sanford
Maine Atlas
Map 2, C-2, C-3
Acres: 26
Max. Depth:
13 feet

BrT	LmB
BkT	SmB
RbT	WhP
Sal	Csk
Tog	WhF
Smt	Pic ✓

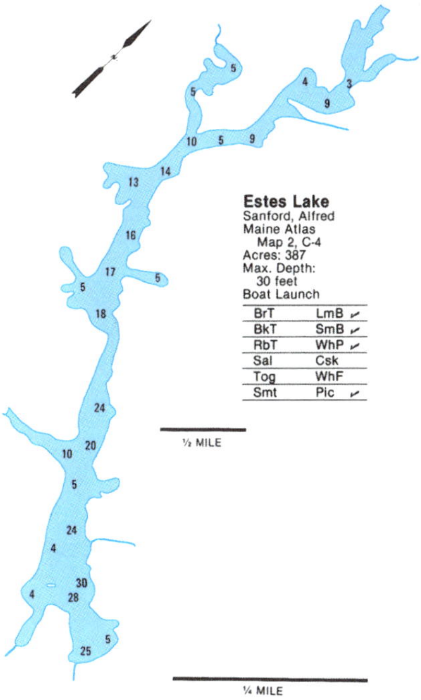

Estes Lake

Sanford, Alfred
Maine Atlas
Map 2, C-4
Acres: 387
Max. Depth:
30 feet
Boat Launch

BrT	LmB ✓
BkT	SmB ✓
RbT	WhP ✓
Sal	Csk
Tog	WhF
Smt	Pic ✓

Doles Pond

Limington
Maine Atlas
Map 4, E-4
Acres: 25
Max. Depth:
8 feet

BrT	LmB
BkT	SmB
RbT	WhP
Sal	Csk
Tog	WhF
Smt	Pic ✓

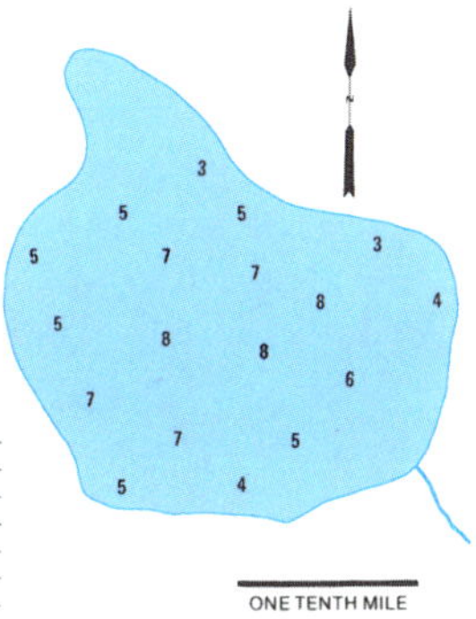

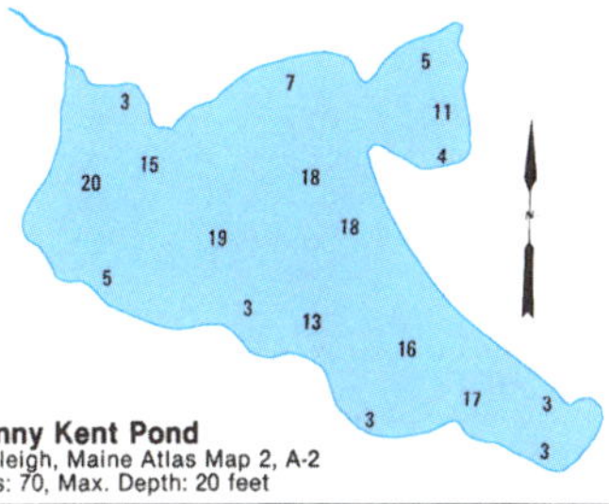

Granny Kent Pond

Shapleigh, Maine Atlas Map 2, A-2
Acres: 70, Max. Depth: 20 feet

BrT	BkT	RbT	Sal	Tog	Smt	LmB	SmB	WhP	Csk	WhF	Pic
						✓	✓	✓			✓

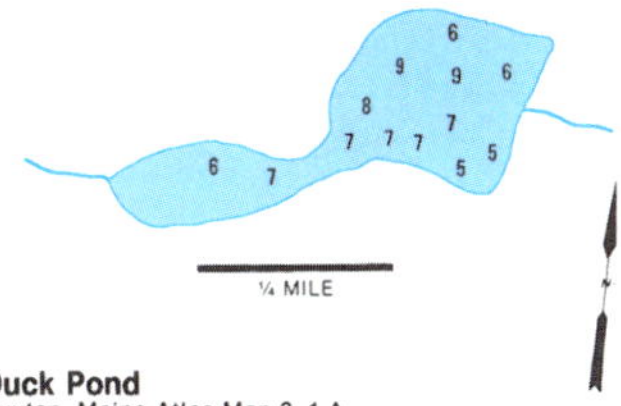

Duck Pond

Buxton, Maine Atlas Map 3, 1-A
Acres: 7, Max. Depth: 9 feet

BrT	BkT	RbT	Sal	Tog	Smt	LmB	SmB	WhP	Csk	WhF	Pic
											✓

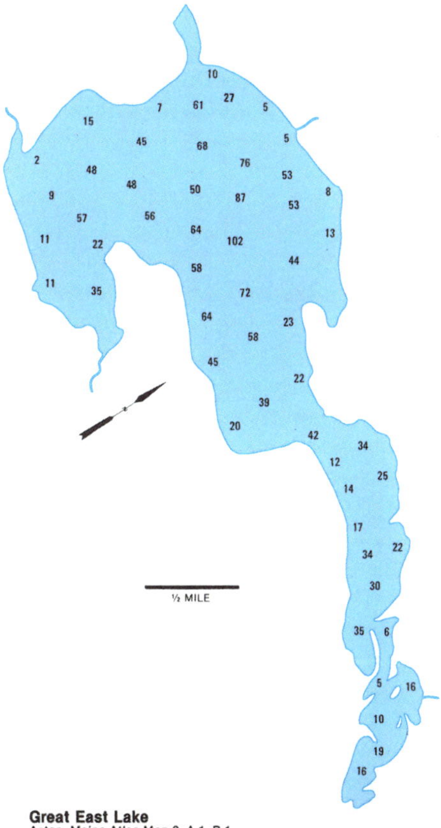

Ell Pond

Sanford
Maine Atlas
Map 2, D-4
Acres: 32
Max. Depth:
51 feet

BrT ✓	LmB
BkT ✓	SmB
RbT ✓	WhP
Sal	Csk
Tog	WhF
Smt	Pic

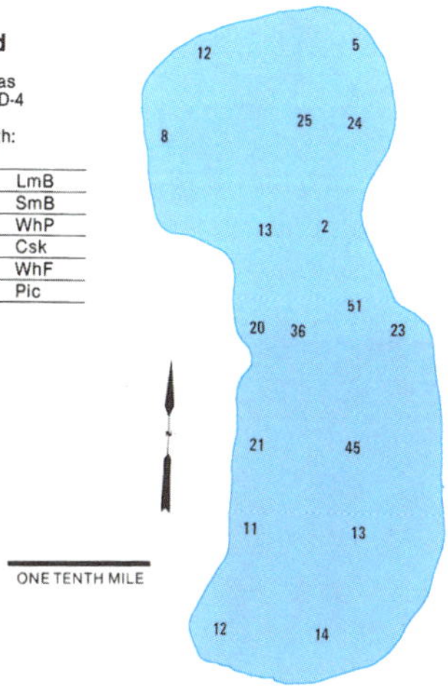

Great East Lake

Acton, Maine Atlas Map 2, A-1, B-1
Acres: 1,768, Max. Depth: 102 feet, Boat Launch

BrT	BkT	RbT	Sal	Tog	Smt	LmB	SmB	WhP	Csk	WhF	Pic
✓		✓	✓	✓		✓	✓	✓			✓

York

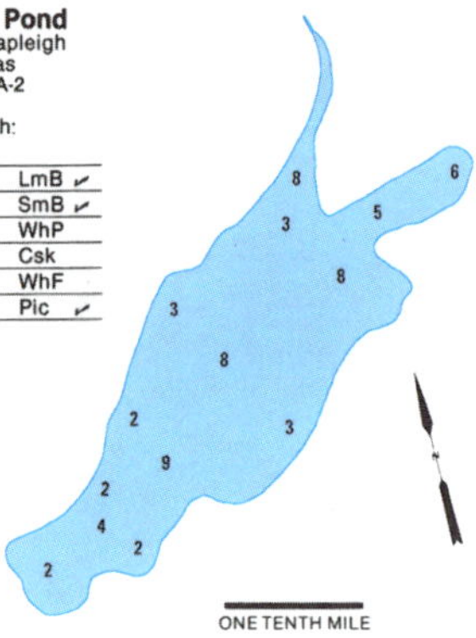

Hansen Pond

Acton, Shapleigh
Maine Atlas
Map 2, A-2
Acres: 30
Max. Depth:
8 feet

BrT		LmB	✓
BkT		SmB	✓
RbT		WhP	
Sal		Csk	
Tog		WhF	
Smt		Pic	✓

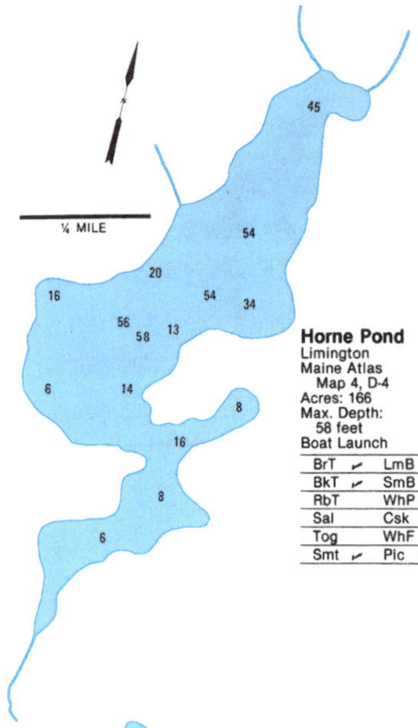

Horne Pond

Limington
Maine Atlas
Map 4, D-4
Acres: 166
Max. Depth:
58 feet
Boat Launch

BrT	✓	LmB	
BkT	✓	SmB	✓
RbT		WhP	✓
Sal		Csk	
Tog		WhF	
Smt	✓	Pic	✓

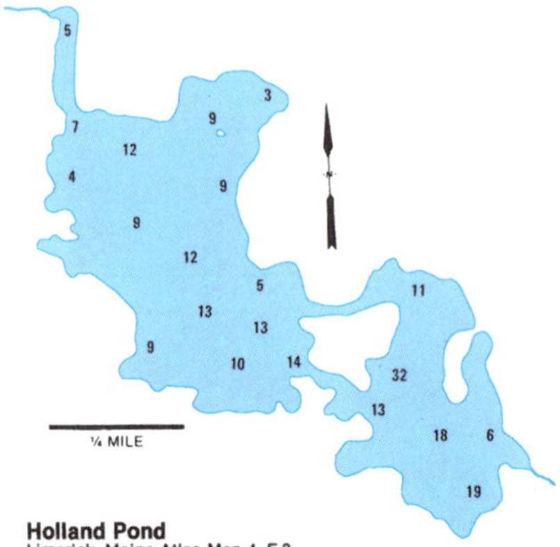

Holland Pond

Limerick, Maine Atlas Map 4, E-3
Acres: 192, Max. Depth: 32 feet

BrT	BkT	RbT	Sal	Tog	Smt	LmB	SmB	WhP	Csk	WhF	Pic
						✓	✓				✓

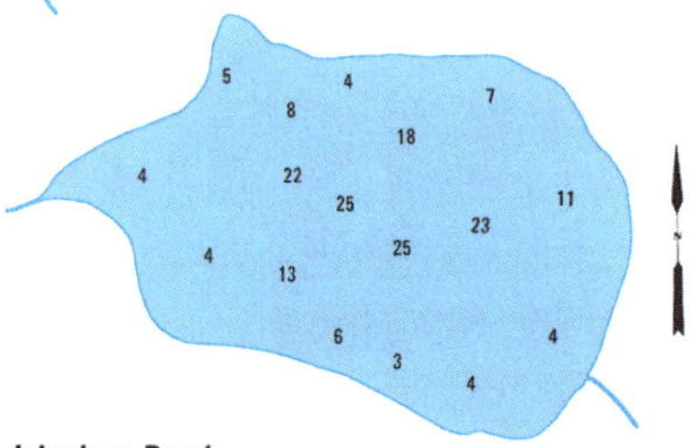

Isinglass Pond

Limington, Waterboro, Maine Atlas Map 4, E-4
Acres: 30, Max. Depth: 25 feet, Boat Launch

BrT	BkT	RbT	Sal	Tog	Smt	LmB	SmB	WhP	Csk	WhF	Pic
	✓										✓

ONE TENTH MILE

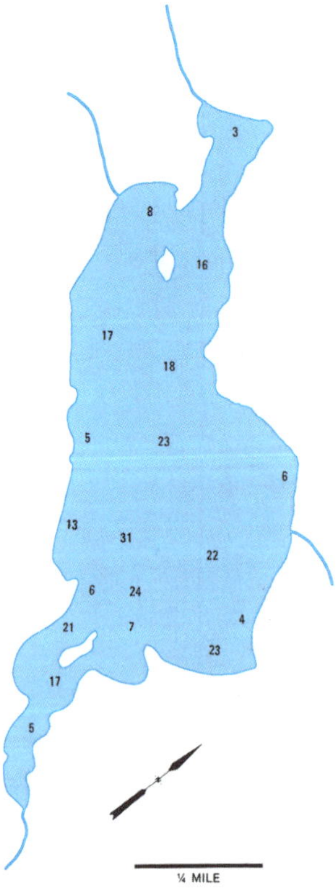

Horn Pond

Acton, Maine Atlas Map 2, B-1
Acres: 205, Max. Depth: 31 feet, Boat Launch

BrT	BkT	RbT	Sal	Tog	Smt	LmB	SmB	WhP	Csk	WhF	Pic
✓			✓			✓	✓	✓			✓

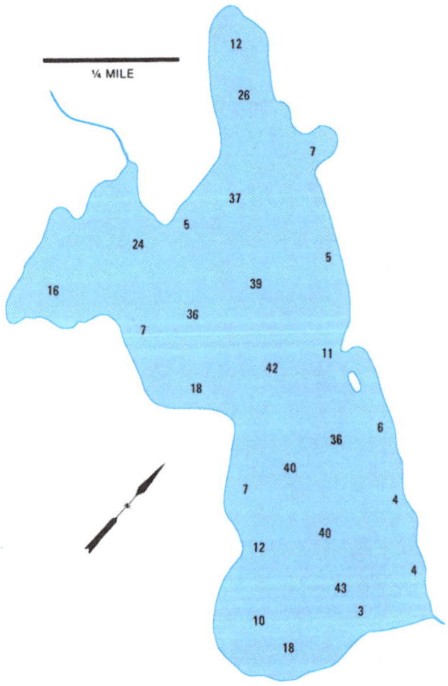

Kennebunk Pond

Lyman, Maine Atlas Map 2, B-5
Acres: 224, Max. Depth: 43 feet, Boat Launch

BrT	BkT	RbT	Sal	Tog	Smt	LmB	SmB	WhP	Csk	WhF	Pic
✓	✓	✓				✓	✓	✓			✓

Killick Pond

Hollis
Maine Atlas
Map 4, E-5
Acres: 45
Max. Depth:
12 feet

BrT		LmB	✓
BkT	✓	SmB	
RbT		WhP	
Sal		Csk	
Tog		WhF	
Smt		Pic	✓

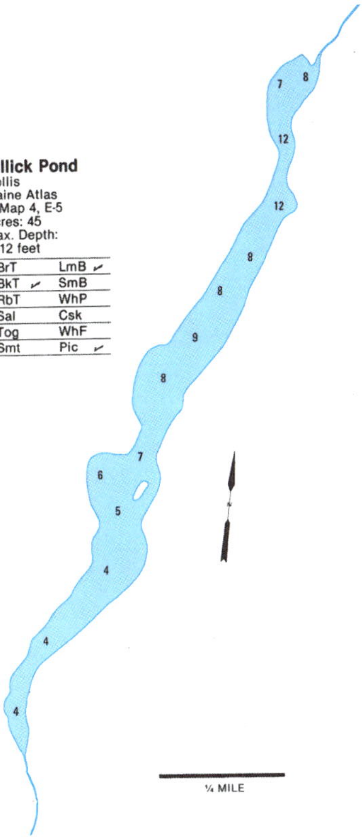

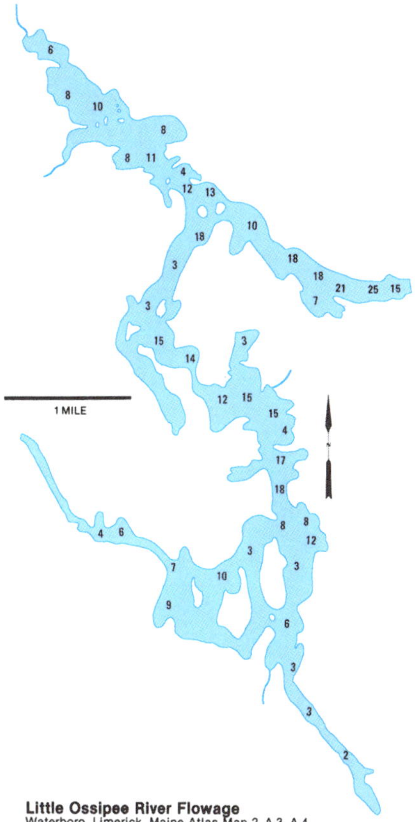

Little Ossipee River Flowage

Waterboro, Limerick, Maine Atlas Map 2, A-3, A-4
Acres: 1,005, Max. Depth: 25 feet, Boat Launch

BrT	BkT	RbT	Sal	Tog	Smt	LmB	SmB	WhP	Csk	WhF	Pic
✓	✓	✓		✓		✓	✓	✓			✓

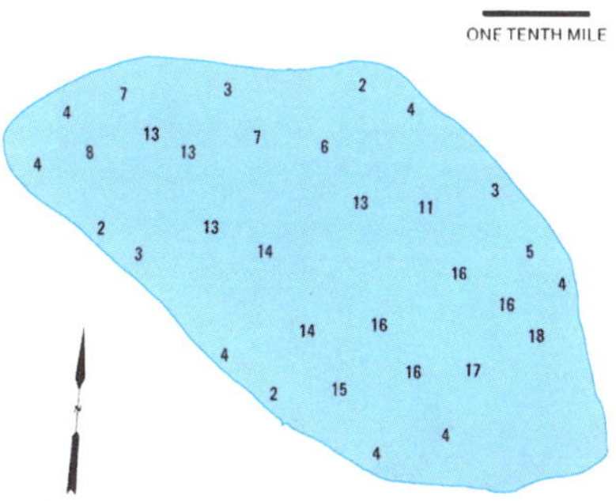

Knights Pond

South Berwick, Maine Atlas Map 2, E-3
Acres: 49, Max. Depth: 18 feet

BrT	BkT	RbT	Sal	Tog	Smt	LmB	SmB	WhP	Csk	WhF	Pic
	✓							✓			✓

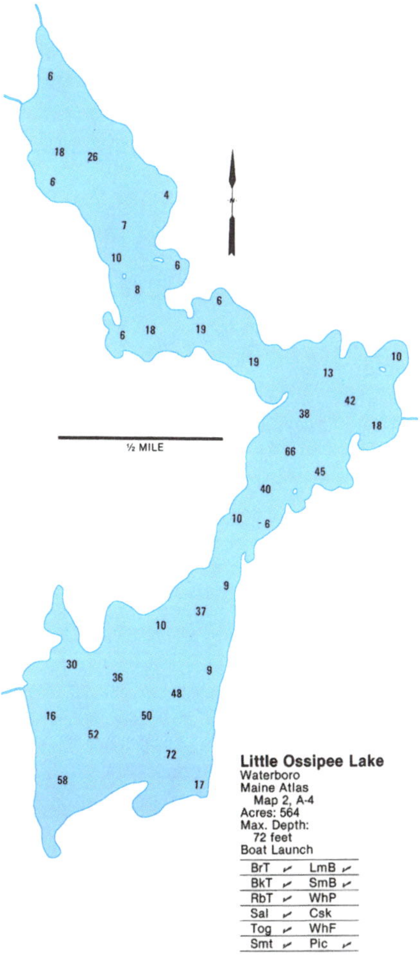

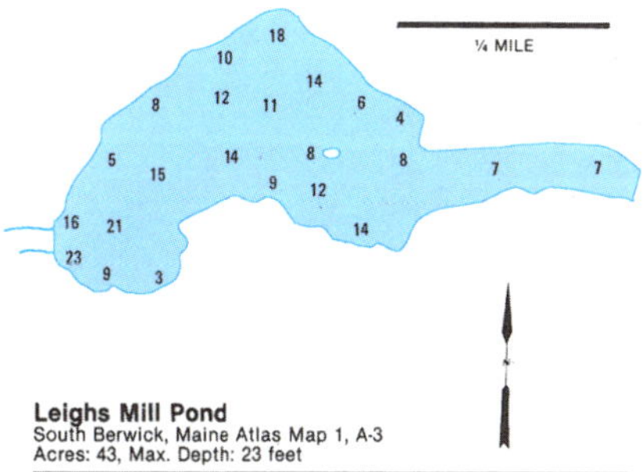

Leighs Mill Pond

South Berwick, Maine Atlas Map 1, A-3
Acres: 43, Max. Depth: 23 feet

BrT	BkT	RbT	Sal	Tog	Smt	LmB	SmB	WhP	Csk	WhF	Pic
✓	✓							✓			✓

Little Ossipee Lake

Waterboro
Maine Atlas
Map 2, A-4
Acres: 564
Max. Depth:
72 feet
Boat Launch

BrT	✓	LmB	✓
BkT	✓	SmB	✓
RbT	✓	WhP	
Sal	✓	Csk	
Tog	✓	WhF	
Smt	✓	Pic	✓

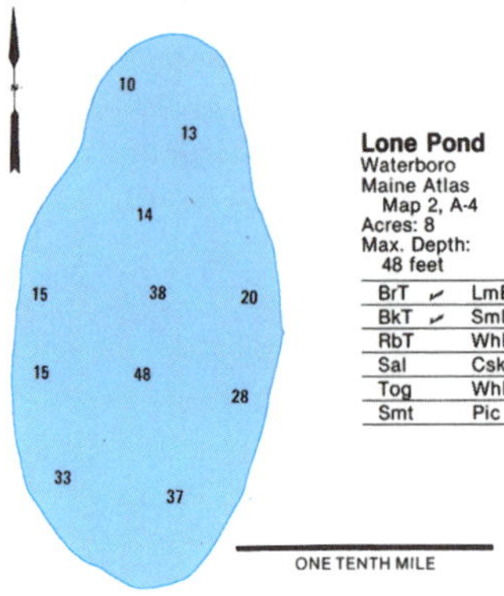

Lone Pond
Waterboro
Maine Atlas
Map 2, A-4
Acres: 8
Max. Depth:
48 feet

BrT	✓	LmB	
BkT	✓	SmB	
RbT		WhP	
Sal		Csk	
Tog		WhF	
Smt		Pic	

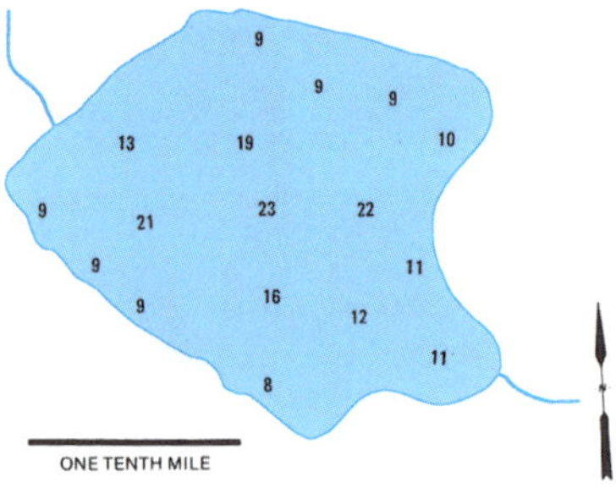

Moody Pond
Waterboro, Maine Atlas Map 2, B-4
Acres: 18, Max. Depth: 23 feet

BrT	BkT	RbT	Sal	Tog	Smt	LmB	SmB	WhP	Csk	WhF	Pic
	✓										

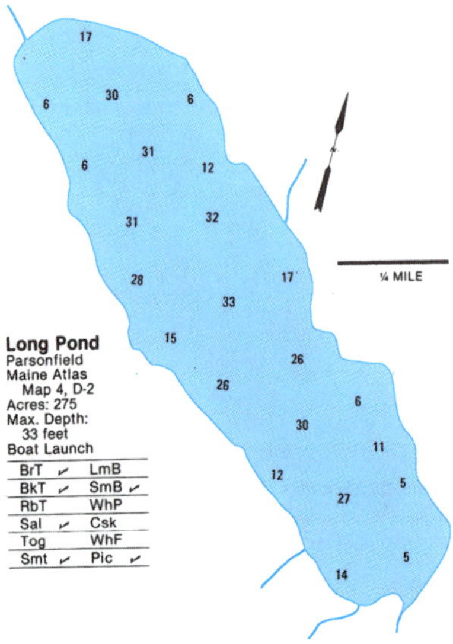

Long Pond
Parsonfield
Maine Atlas
Map 4, D-2
Acres: 275
Max. Depth:
33 feet
Boat Launch

BrT	✓	LmB	
BkT	✓	SmB	✓
RbT		WhP	
Sal	✓	Csk	
Tog		WhF	
Smt	✓	Pic	✓

Moose Pond
Acton
Maine Atlas
Map 2, A-1
Acres: 27
Max. Depth:
20 feet

BrT		LmB	
BkT	✓	SmB	✓
RbT		WhP	
Sal		Csk	
Tog		WhF	
Smt		Pic	✓

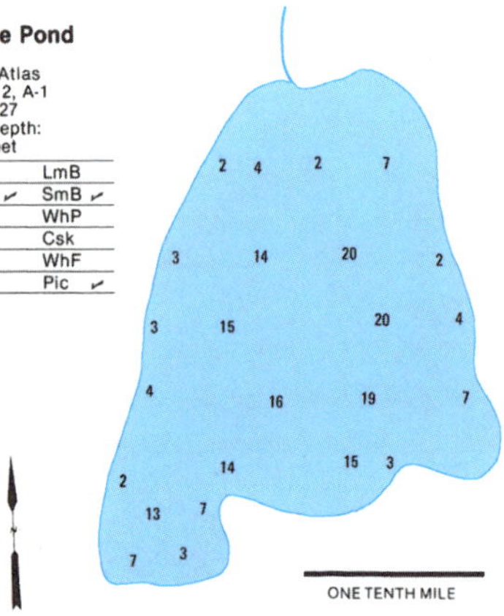

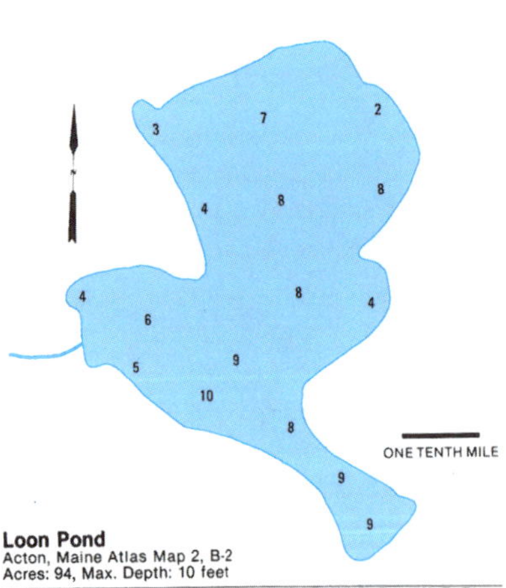

Loon Pond
Acton, Maine Atlas Map 2, B-2
Acres: 94, Max. Depth: 10 feet

BrT	BkT	RbT	Sal	Tog	Smt	LmB	SmB	WhP	Csk	WhF	Pic
						✓	✓	✓			✓

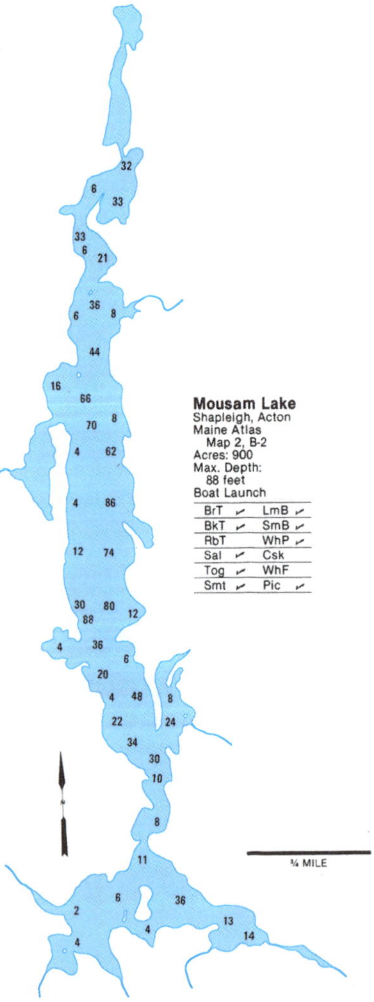

Mousam Lake
Shapleigh, Acton
Maine Atlas
Map 2, B-2
Acres: 900
Max. Depth:
88 feet
Boat Launch

BrT	✓	LmB	✓
BkT	✓	SmB	✓
RbT		WhP	✓
Sal	✓	Csk	
Tog	✓	WhF	
Smt	✓	Pic	✓

Middle Branch Pond
Waterboro, Alfred, Maine Atlas Map 2, B-3
Acres: 38, Max. Depth: 26 feet

BrT	BkT	RbT	Sal	Tog	Smt	LmB	SmB	WhP	Csk	WhF	Pic
						✓					✓

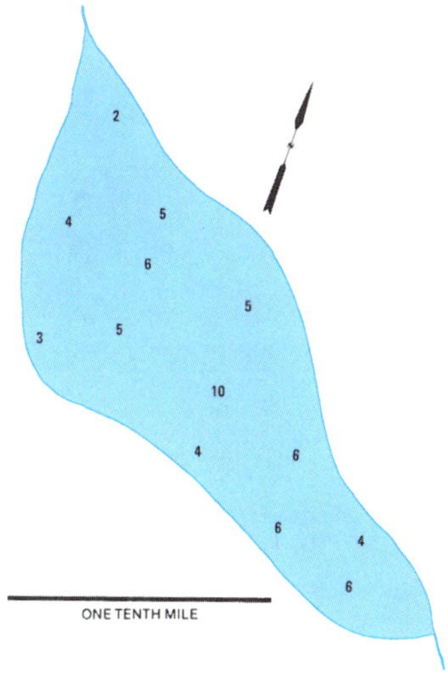

Mud Pond

Newfield, Maine Atlas Map 2, A-2
Acres: 9, Max. Depth: 10 feet

BrT	BkT	RbT	Sal	Tog	Smt	LmB	SmB	WhP	Csk	WhF	Pic
											✓

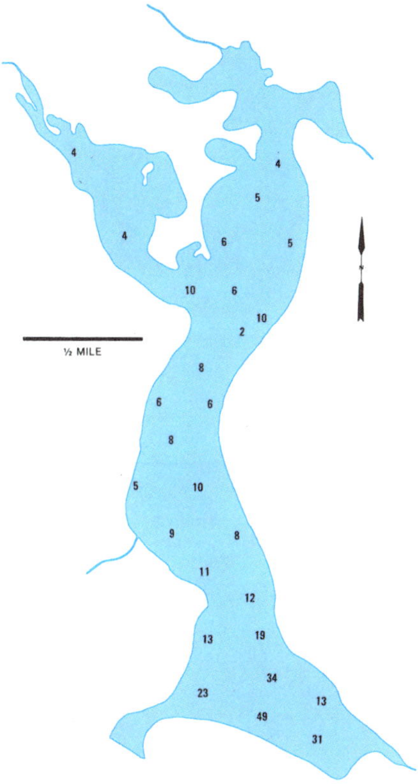

Northeast Pond

Lebanon, Maine Atlas Map 2, C-1
Acres: 778, Max. Depth: 49 feet, Boat Launch

BrT	BkT	RbT	Sal	Tog	Smt	LmB	SmB	WhP	Csk	WhF	Pic
✓						✓	✓	✓			✓

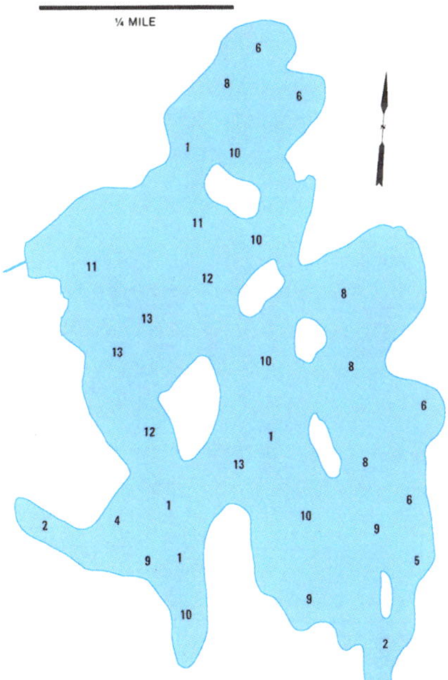

Murdock Lake

Berwick, Maine Atlas Map 2, E-2
Acres: 300, Max. Depth: 13 feet, Boat Launch

BrT	BkT	RbT	Sal	Tog	Smt	LmB	SmB	WhP	Csk	WhF	Pic
						✓					✓

North Shapleigh Pond

Shapleigh, Newfield
Maine Atlas
Map 2, A-2
Acres: 80
Max. Depth:
11 feet

BrT		LmB	✓
BkT		SmB	✓
RbT		WhP	
Sal		Csk	
Tog	✓	WhF	
Smt		Pic	✓

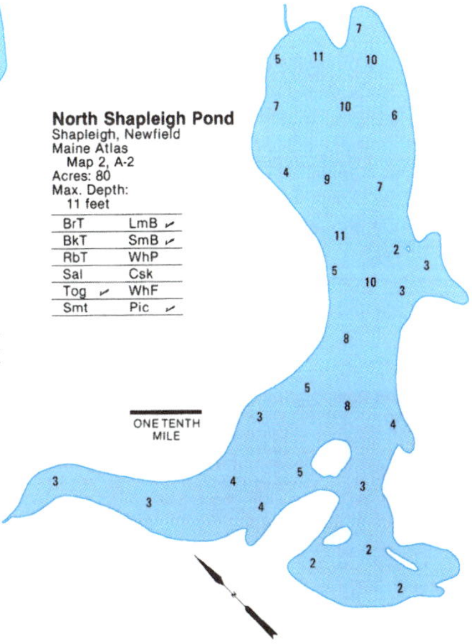

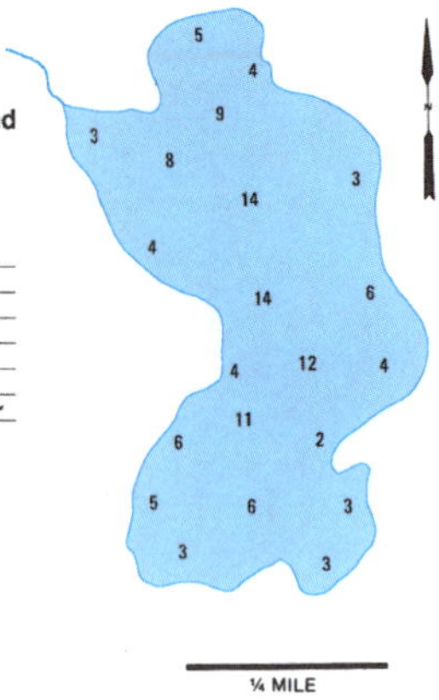

Northwest Pond

Waterboro
Maine Atlas
Map 2, B-3
Acres: 38
Max. Depth:
14 feet

BrT		LmB	
BkT		SmB	
RbT		WhP	
Sal		Csk	
Tog		WhF	
Smt		Pic	✓

Pinkham Pond

Newfield
Maine Atlas
Map 2, A-1
Acres: 49
Max. Depth:
24 feet

BrT		LmB	✓
BkT		SmB	
RbT		WhP	✓
Sal		Csk	
Tog		WhF	
Smt		Pic	✓

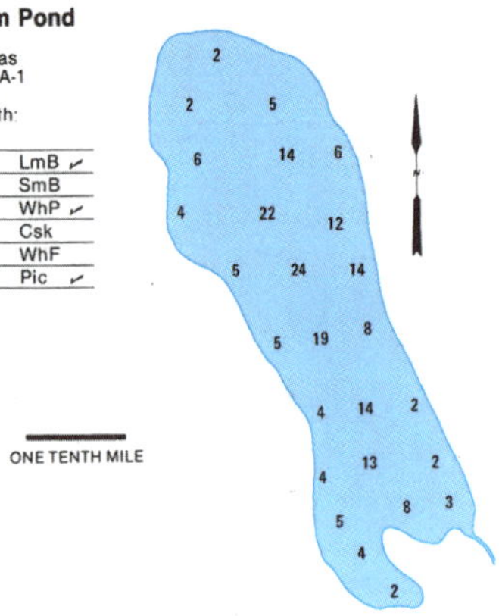

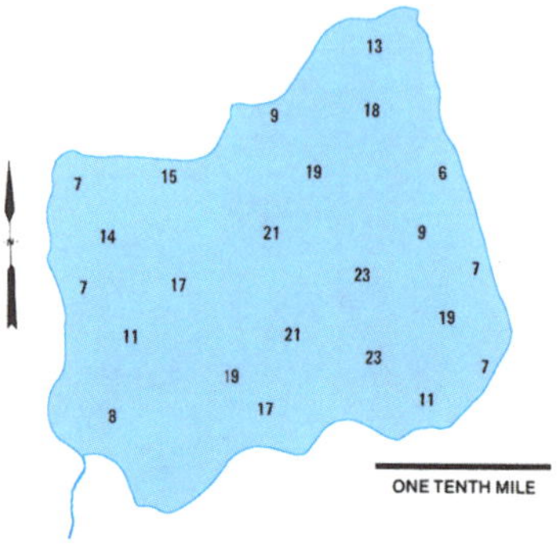

Parker Pond

Lyman, Maine Atlas Map 2, B-5
Acres: 26, Max. Depth: 23 feet

BrT	BkT	RbT	Sal	Tog	Smt	LmB	SmB	WhP	Csk	WhF	Pic
	✓										✓

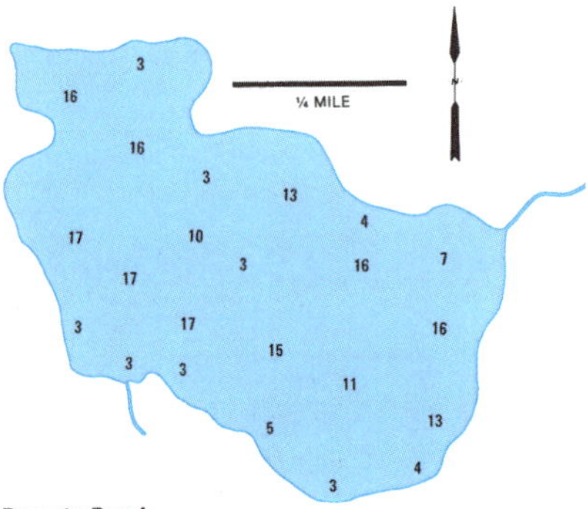

Poverty Pond

Newfield, Maine Atlas Map 2, A-2, A-3
Acres: 166, Max. Depth: 17 feet, Boat Launch

BrT	BkT	RbT	Sal	Tog	Smt	LmB	SmB	WhP	Csk	WhF	Pic
✓	✓					✓					✓

Comments: Alternate name Silver Lake.

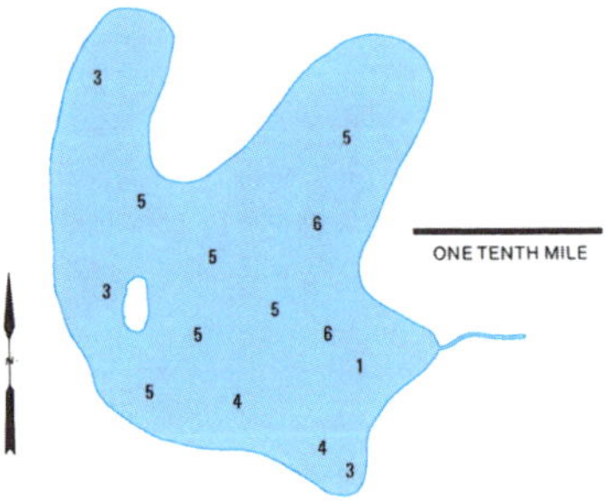

Passaconway Pond

York, Maine Atlas Map 1, A-5
Acres: 26, Max. Depth: 6 feet

BrT	BkT	RbT	Sal	Tog	Smt	LmB	SmB	WhP	Csk	WhF	Pic
											✓

Province Lake

Parsonfield
Maine Atlas
Map 4, E-1
Acres: 90
Max. Depth:
15 feet

BrT		LmB	
BkT		SmB	✓
RbT		WhP	
Sal		Csk	
Tog		WhF	
Smt		Pic	✓

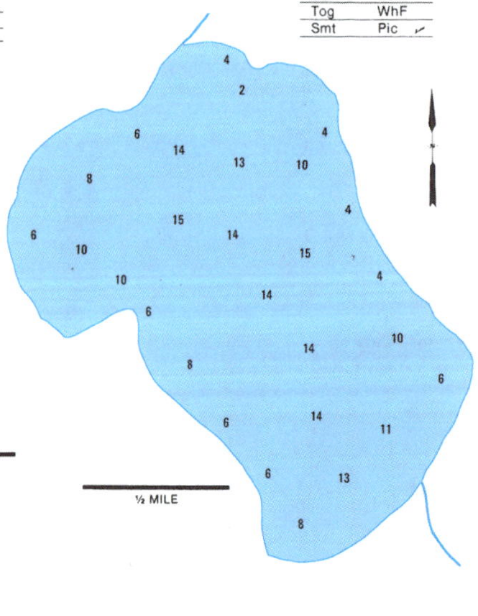

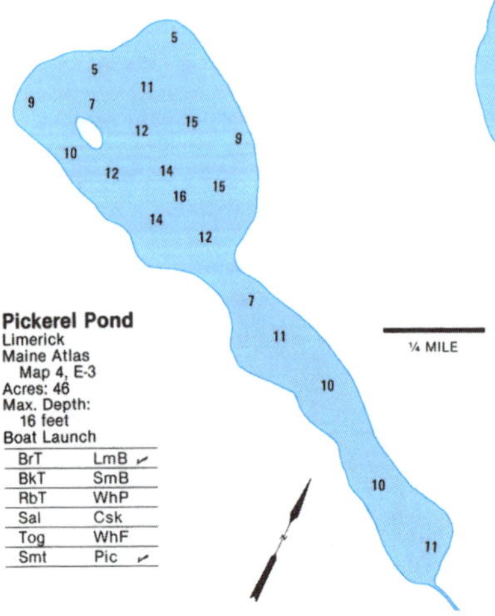

Pickerel Pond

Limerick
Maine Atlas
Map 4, E-3
Acres: 46
Max. Depth:
16 feet
Boat Launch

BrT		LmB	✓
BkT		SmB	
RbT		WhP	
Sal		Csk	
Tog		WhF	
Smt		Pic	✓

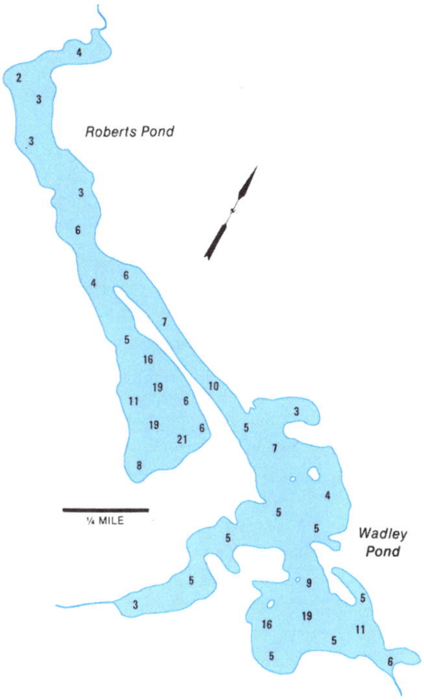

Roberts and Wadley Ponds

Lyman, Maine Atlas Map 2, B-5
Acres: Roberts-83, Wadley-120
Max. Depth: Roberts-21 feet, Wadley-19 feet

BrT	BkT	RbT	Sal	Tog	Smt	LmB	SmB	WhP	Csk	WhF	Pic
						✓	✓				✓

Sand Pond

Limington
Maine Atlas
Map 4, E-5
Acres: 26
Max. Depth:
61 feet

BrT		LmB	
BkT	✓	SmB	
RbT		WhP	
Sal		Csk	
Tog		WhF	
Smt		Pic	

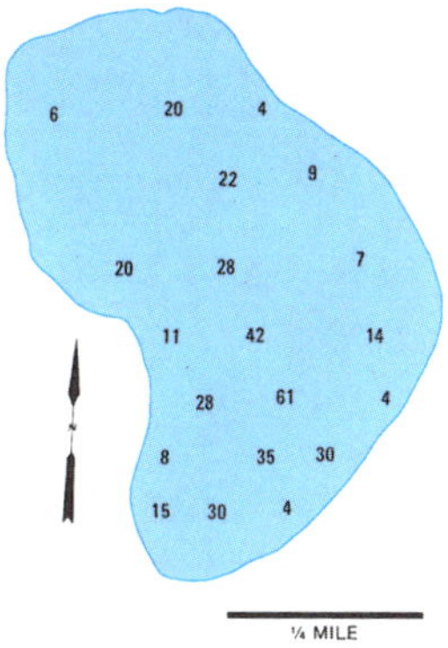

Scituate Pond

York
Maine Atlas
Map 1, A-4
Acres: 42
Max. Depth:
7 feet

BrT		LmB	✓
BkT		SmB	
RbT		WhP	
Sal		Csk	
Tog		WhF	
Smt		Pic	✓

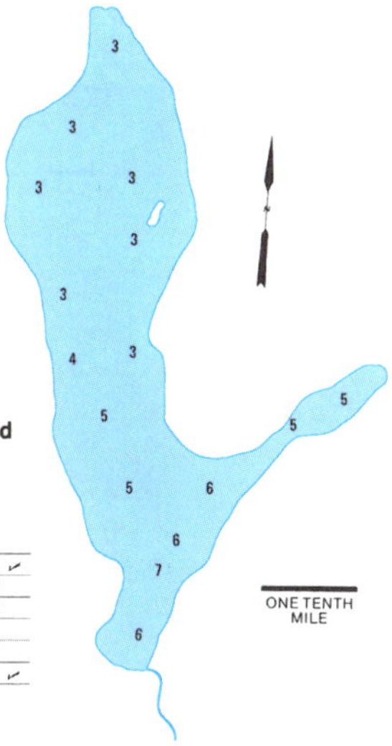

Round Pond

Lyman, Dayton
Maine Atlas
Map 2, B-5
Acres: 6
Max. Depth:
36 feet

BrT		LmB	
BkT	✓	SmB	
RbT		WhP	
Sal		Csk	
Tog		WhF	
Smt		Pic	

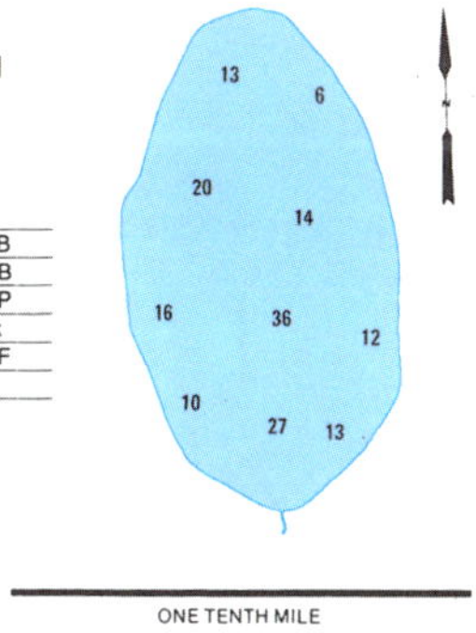

Shaker Pond

Alfred, Maine Atlas Map 2, B-4
Acres: 78, Max. Depth: 22 feet

BrT	BkT	RbT	Sal	Tog	Smt	LmB	SmB	WhP	Csk	WhF	Pic
						✓	✓	✓			✓

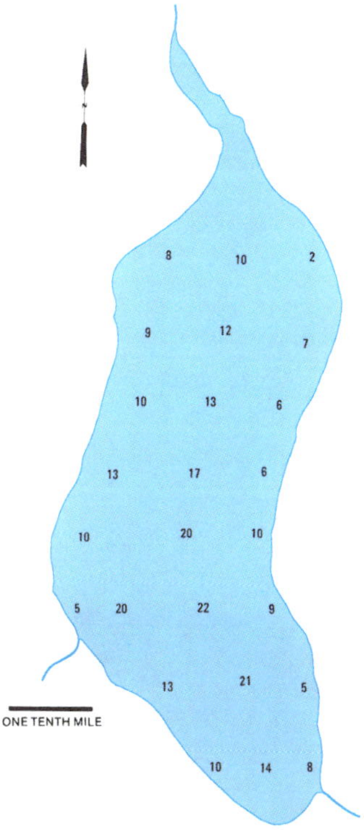

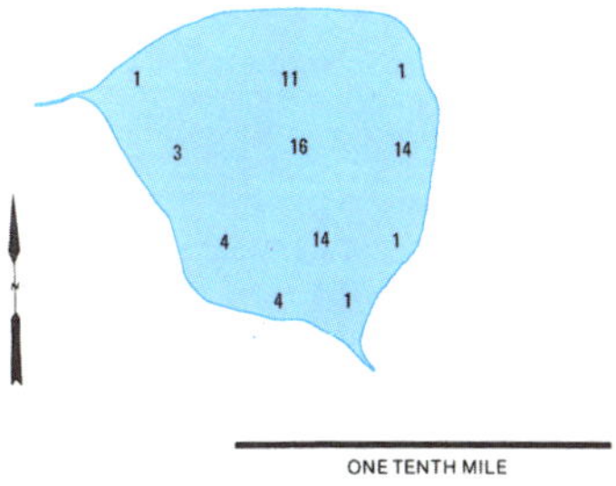

Round Pond

Newfield, Maine Atlas Map 2, A-2
Acres: 3, Max. Depth: 16 feet, Boat Launch

BrT	BkT	RbT	Sal	Tog	Smt	LmB	SmB	WhP	Csk	WhF	Pic
											✓

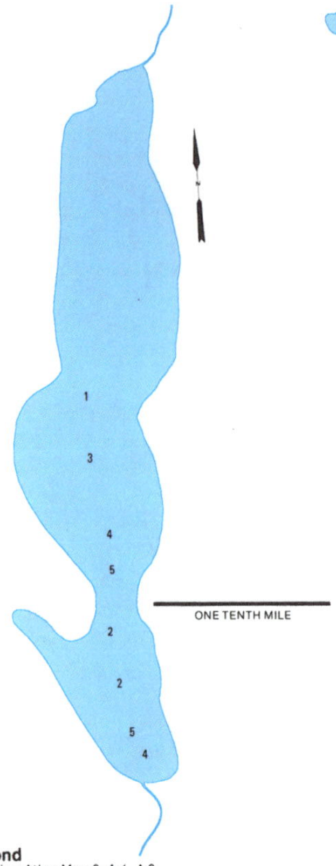

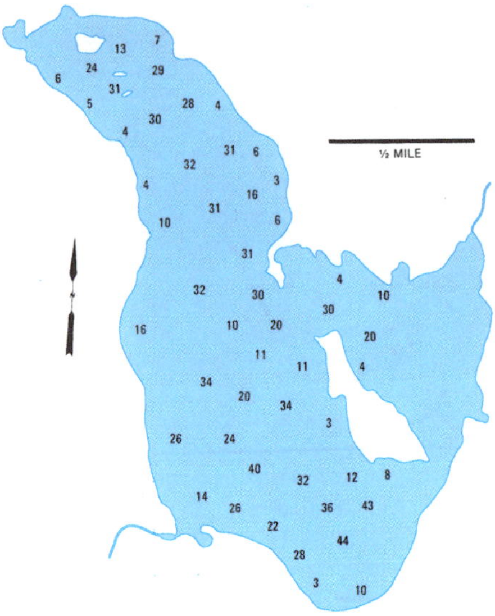

Square Pond
Acton, Shapleigh, Maine Atlas Map 2, B-2
Acres: 910, Max. Depth: 44 feet, Boat Launch

BrT	BkT	RbT	Sal	Tog	Smt	LmB	SmB	WhP	Csk	WhF	Pic
✓						✓	✓	✓			✓

Smarts Pond
Newfield, Maine Atlas Map 2, A-1, A-2
Acres: 20, Max. Depth: 5 feet

BrT	BkT	RbT	Sal	Tog	Smt	LmB	SmB	WhP	Csk	WhF	Pic
											✓

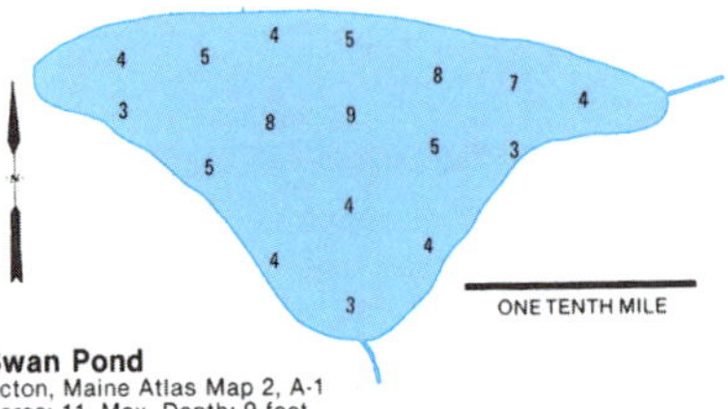

Swan Pond
Acton, Maine Atlas Map 2, A-1
Acres: 11, Max. Depth: 9 feet

BrT	BkT	RbT	Sal	Tog	Smt	LmB	SmB	WhP	Csk	WhF	Pic
						✓					✓

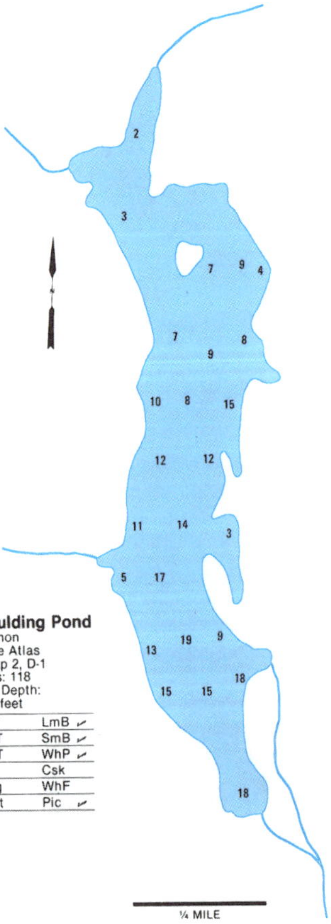

Spaulding Pond
Lebanon
Maine Atlas
Map 2, D-1
Acres: 118
Max. Depth:
19 feet

BrT		LmB	✓
BkT		SmB	✓
RbT		WhP	✓
Sal		Csk	
Tog		WhF	
Smt		Pic	✓

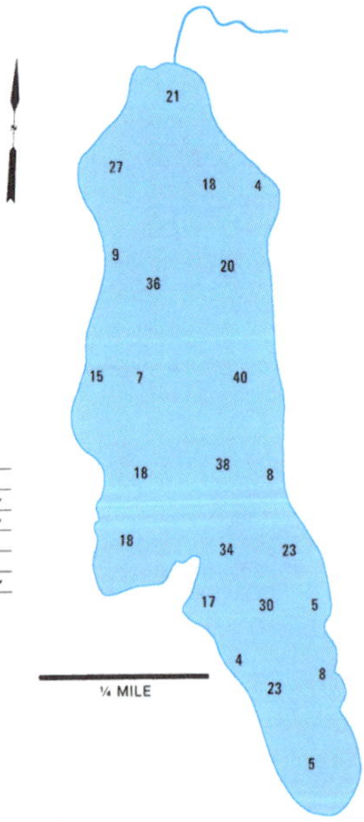

Swan Pond
Lyman
Maine Atlas
Map 2, B-5
Acres: 147
Max. Depth:
40 feet

BrT	✓	LmB	
BkT	✓	SmB	✓
RbT		WhP	✓
Sal		Csk	
Tog		WhF	
Smt		Pic	✓

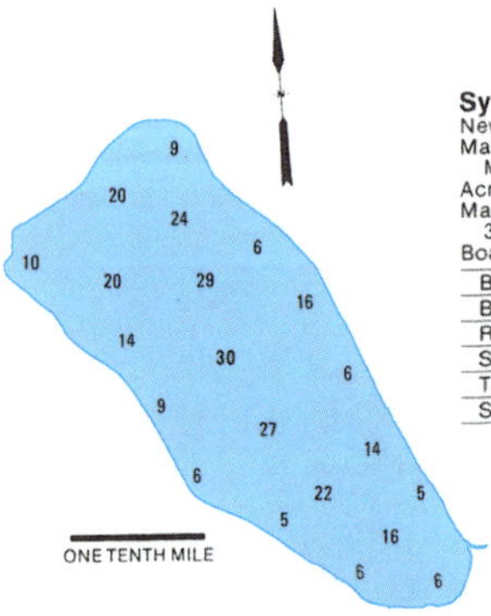

Symmes Pond
Newfield
Maine Atlas
Map 2, A-2
Acres: 36
Max. Depth:
30 feet
Boat Launch

BrT		LmB	
BkT	✓	SmB	
RbT		WhP	
Sal		Csk	
Tog		WhF	
Smt		Pic	✓

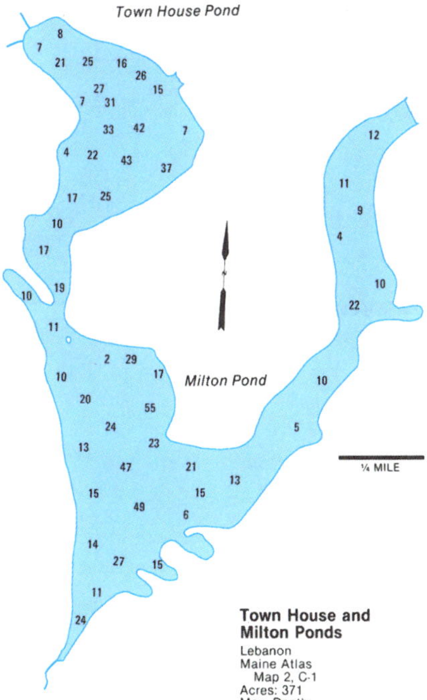

Town House and Milton Ponds

Lebanon
Maine Atlas
Map 2, C-1
Acres: 371
Max. Depth:
55 feet

BrT	✓	LmB	✓
BkT		SmB	✓
RbT		WhP	✓
Sal		Csk	
Tog		WhF	
Smt		Pic	✓

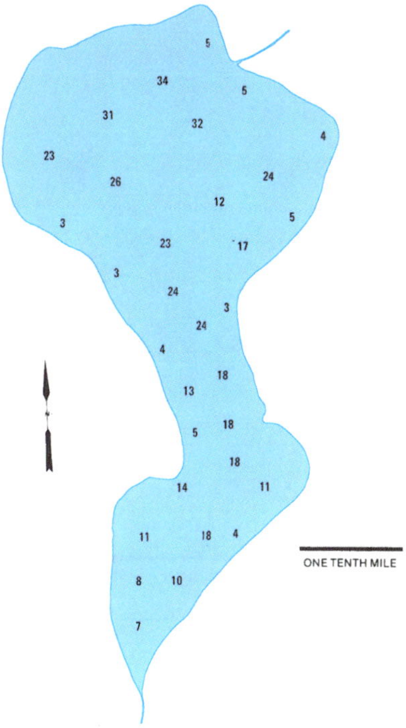

Wards Pond

Limington, Maine Atlas Map 4, D-4, D-5
Acres: 44, Max. Depth: 34 feet

BrT	BkT	RbT	Sal	Tog	Smt	LmB	SmB	WhP	Csk	WhF	Pic
						✓	✓	✓			✓

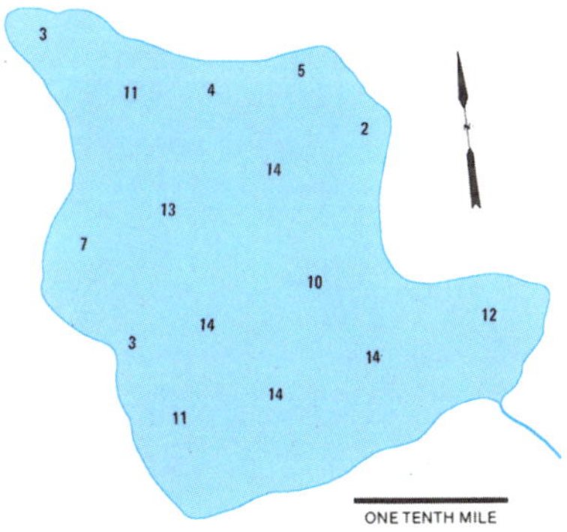

Turner Pond

Newfield, Maine Atlas Map 2, A-2
Acres: 32, Max. Depth: 14 feet

BrT	BkT	RbT	Sal	Tog	Smt	LmB	SmB	WhP	Csk	WhF	Pic
							✓				✓

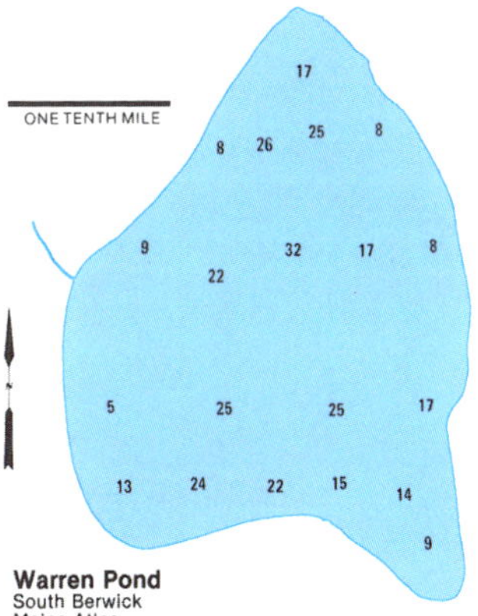

Warren Pond

South Berwick
Maine Atlas
Map 1, A-4
Acres: 45
Max. Depth:
32 feet

BrT		LmB	
BkT	✓	SmB	
RbT	✓	WhP	
Sal		Csk	
Tog		WhF	
Smt		Pic	

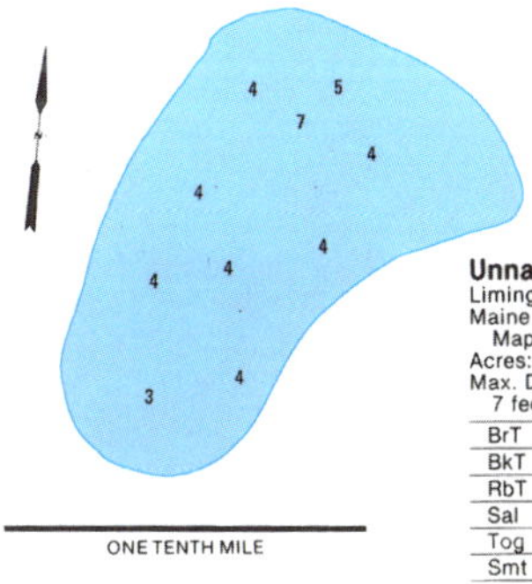

Unnamed Pond

Limington
Maine Atlas
Map 4, E-4
Acres: 10
Max. Depth:
7 feet

BrT		LmB	✓
BkT		SmB	
RbT		WhP	
Sal		Csk	
Tog		WhF	
Smt		Pic	✓

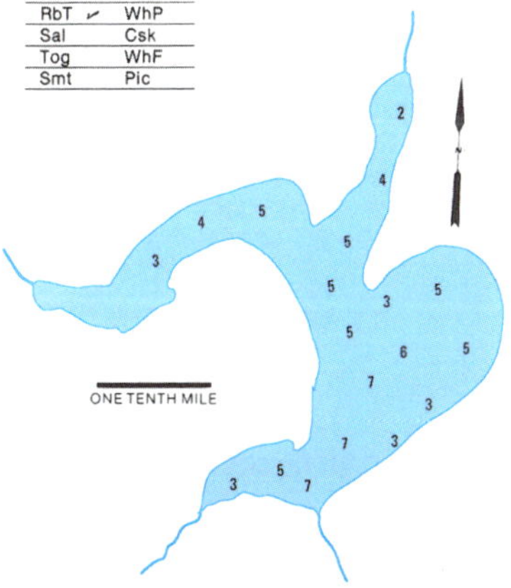

Webster's Mill Pond

Limington, Maine Atlas Map 4, D-4
Acres: 40, Max. Depth: 7 feet, Boat Launch

BrT	BkT	RbT	Sal	Tog	Smt	LmB	SmB	WhP	Csk	WhF	Pic
							✓	✓			✓

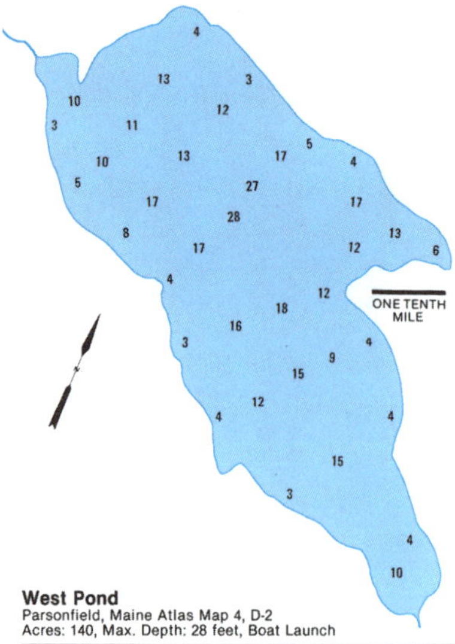

West Pond

Parsonfield, Maine Atlas Map 4, D-2
Acres: 140, Max. Depth: 28 feet, Boat Launch

BrT	BkT	RbT	Sal	Tog	Smt	LmB	SmB	WhP	Csk	WhF	Pic
						✓	✓				✓

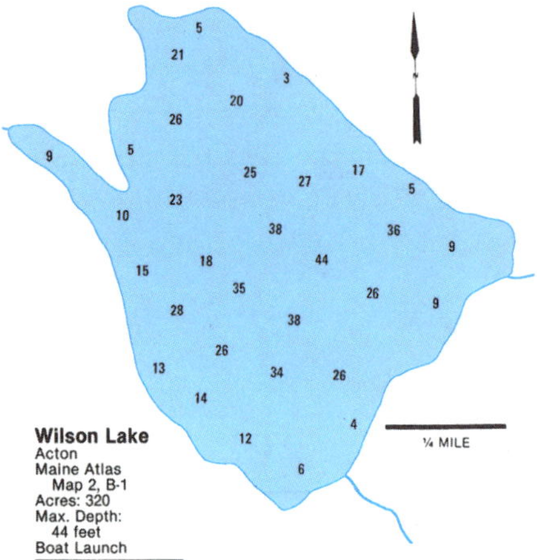

Wilson Lake

Acton
Maine Atlas
Map 2, B-1
Acres: 320
Max. Depth:
44 feet
Boat Launch

BrT	✓	LmB	✓
BkT	✓	SmB	✓
RbT	✓	WhP	✓
Sal		Csk	
Tog		WhF	
Smt	✓	Pic	✓

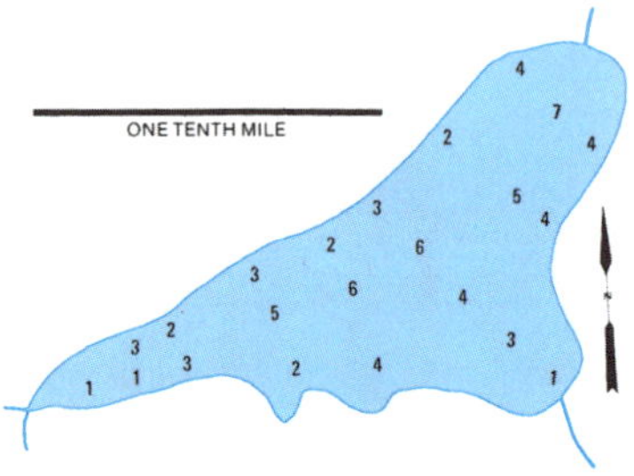

Wilcox Pond

Biddeford, Maine Atlas Map 3, C-2
Acres: 3, Max. Depth: 7 feet

BrT	BkT	RbT	Sal	Tog	Smt	LmB	SmB	WhP	Csk	WhF	Pic
	✓										

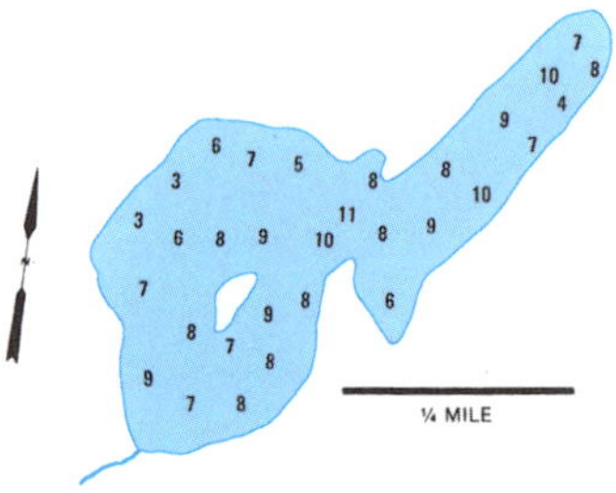

York Pond

Eliot, Maine Atlas Map 1, A-3
Acres: 45, Max. Depth: 11 feet

BrT	BkT	RbT	Sal	Tog	Smt	LmB	SmB	WhP	Csk	WhF	Pic
	✓					✓					✓

Notes:

Notes:

IT ALL BEGAN WITH THE MAINE ATLAS AND GAZETTEER™

In 1975, David DeLorme saw the need for a detailed collection of large-scale maps showing Maine's back roads and backcountry features. So, he created *The Maine Atlas and Gazetteer*. It was an immediate success, and over the years, it has consistently been the best-selling book in the entire state!

The full-color topographic maps found in the Atlas are updated on a regular basis and feature the kind of detail Mainers need—logging roads, the smallest ponds and streams, boat ramps, hiking trails, campgrounds and campsites, and much more. There are also street maps for 30 cities and towns. And, the Gazetteer section is packed with information on places to go and things to do throughout the state. As many Mainers say, "You can't get there from here without the Atlas and Gazetteer!"

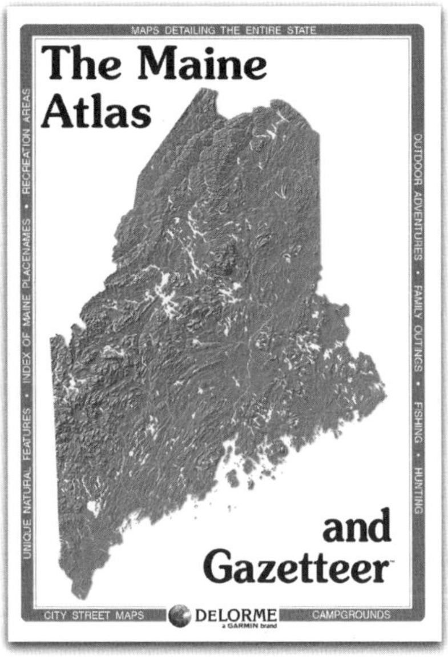

Quality paperback, 11″ × 15½″,
88 map pages, 96 pages in all.

Similar atlases are now available for all 50 states.
For more information visit
www.garmin.com/DeLormeAtlas